MW01097468

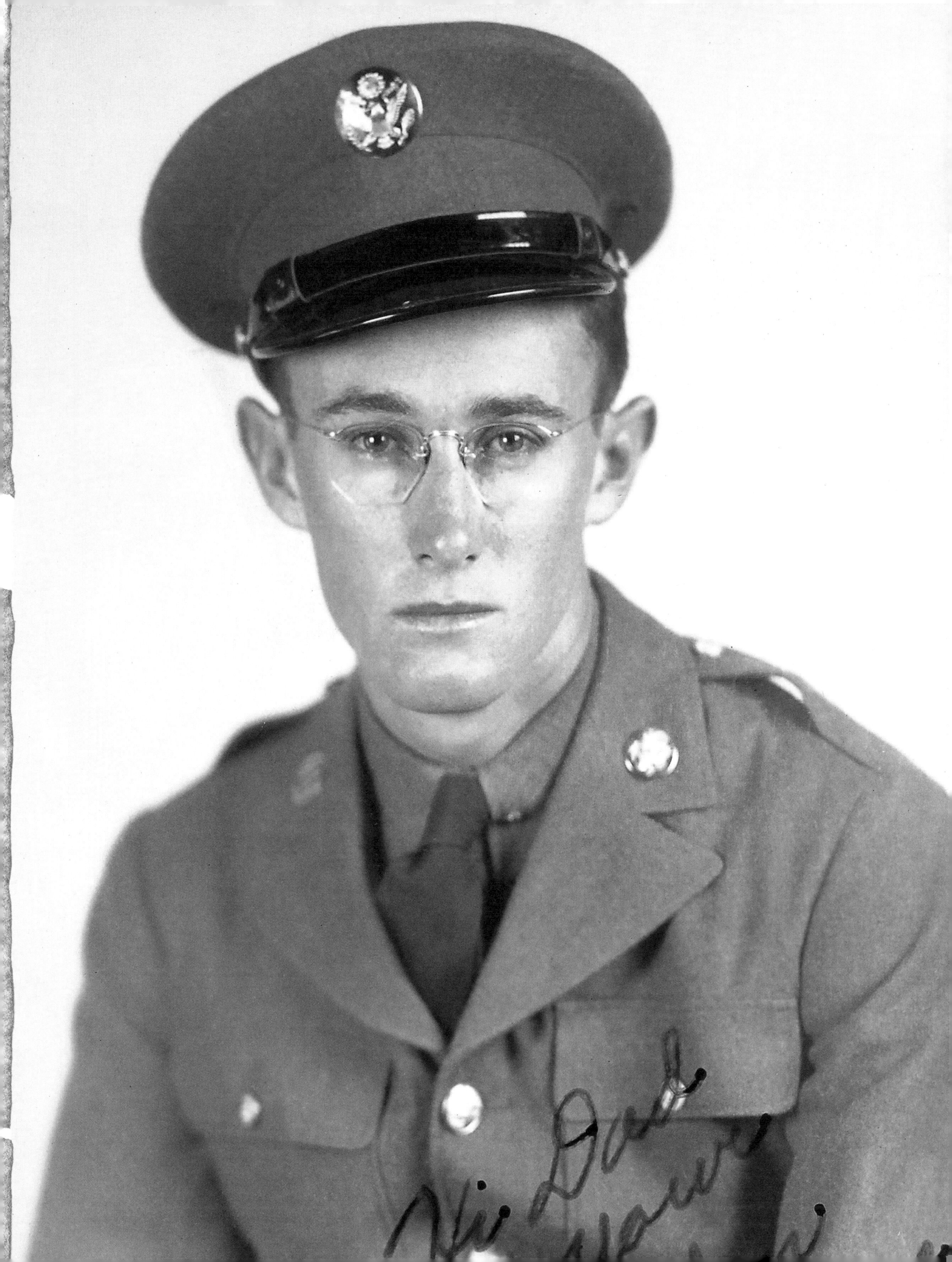
Hi Dad

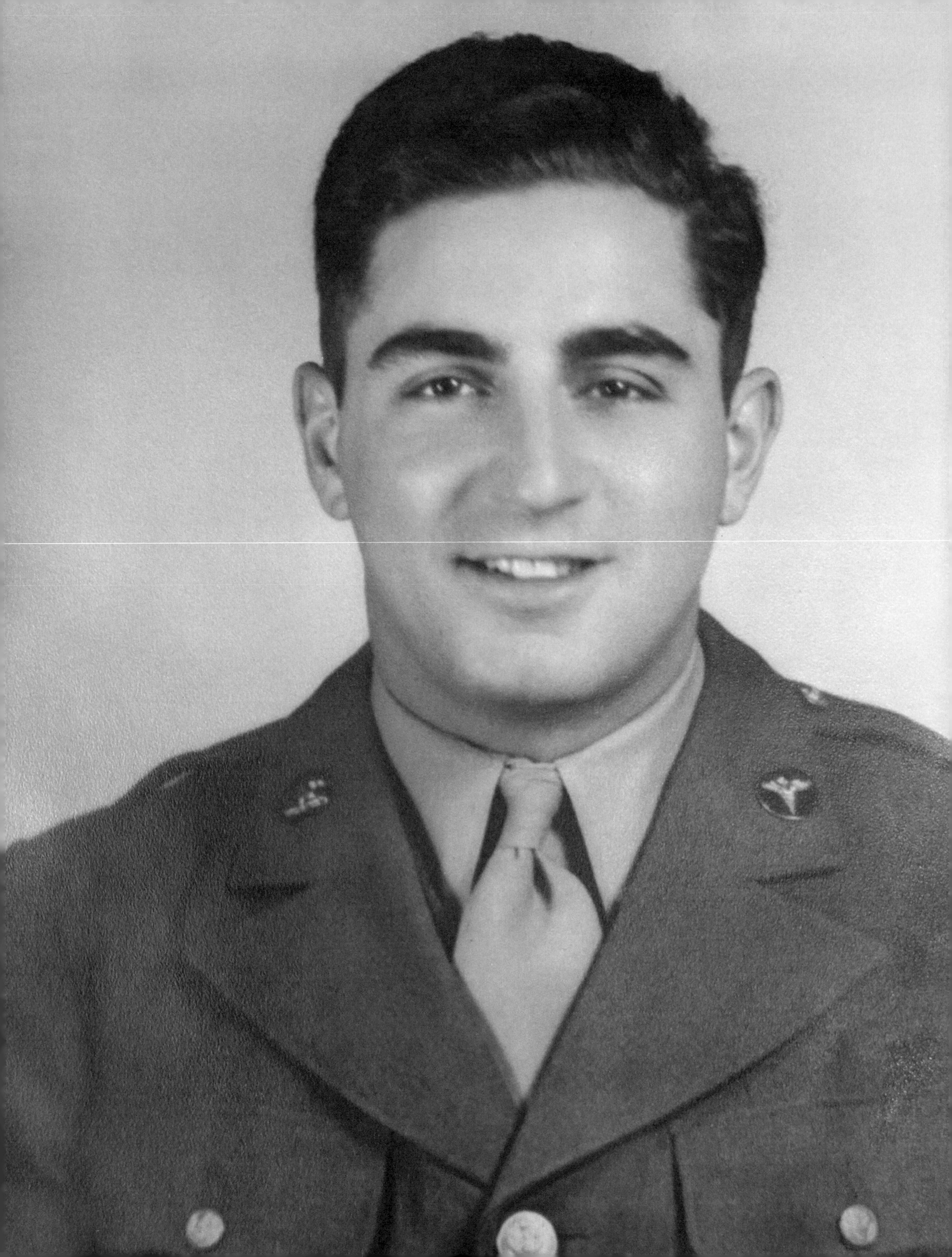

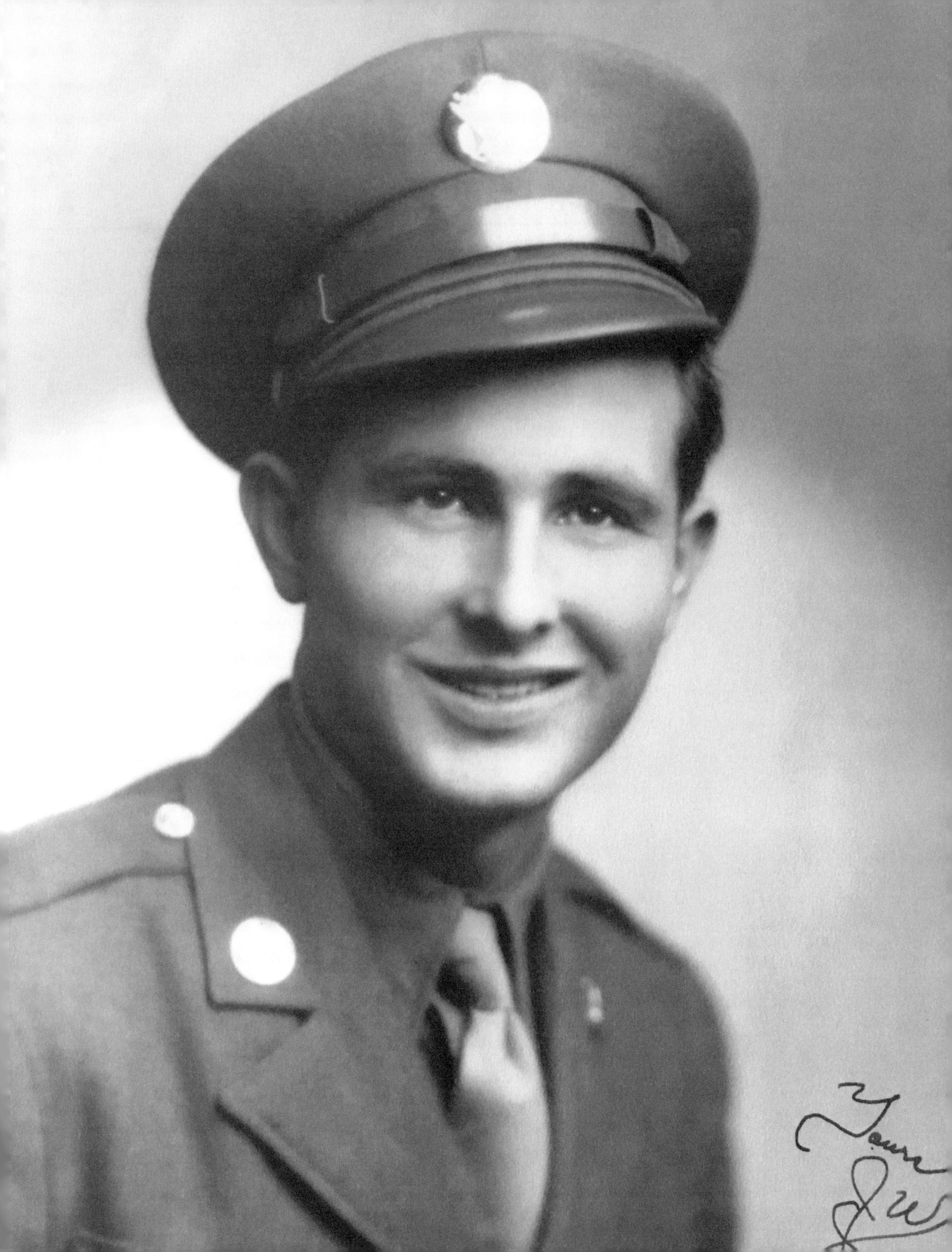
Yours

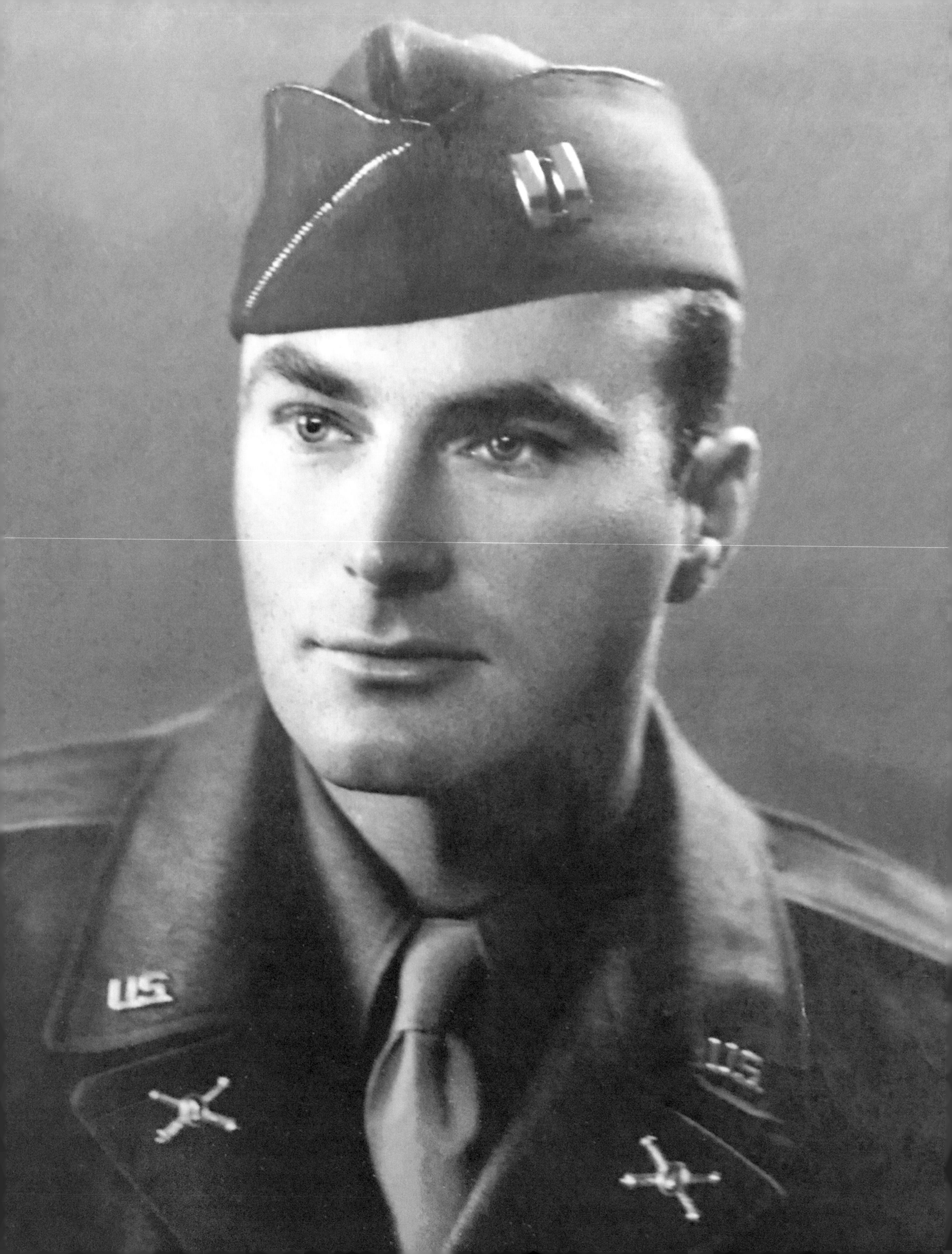
US
US

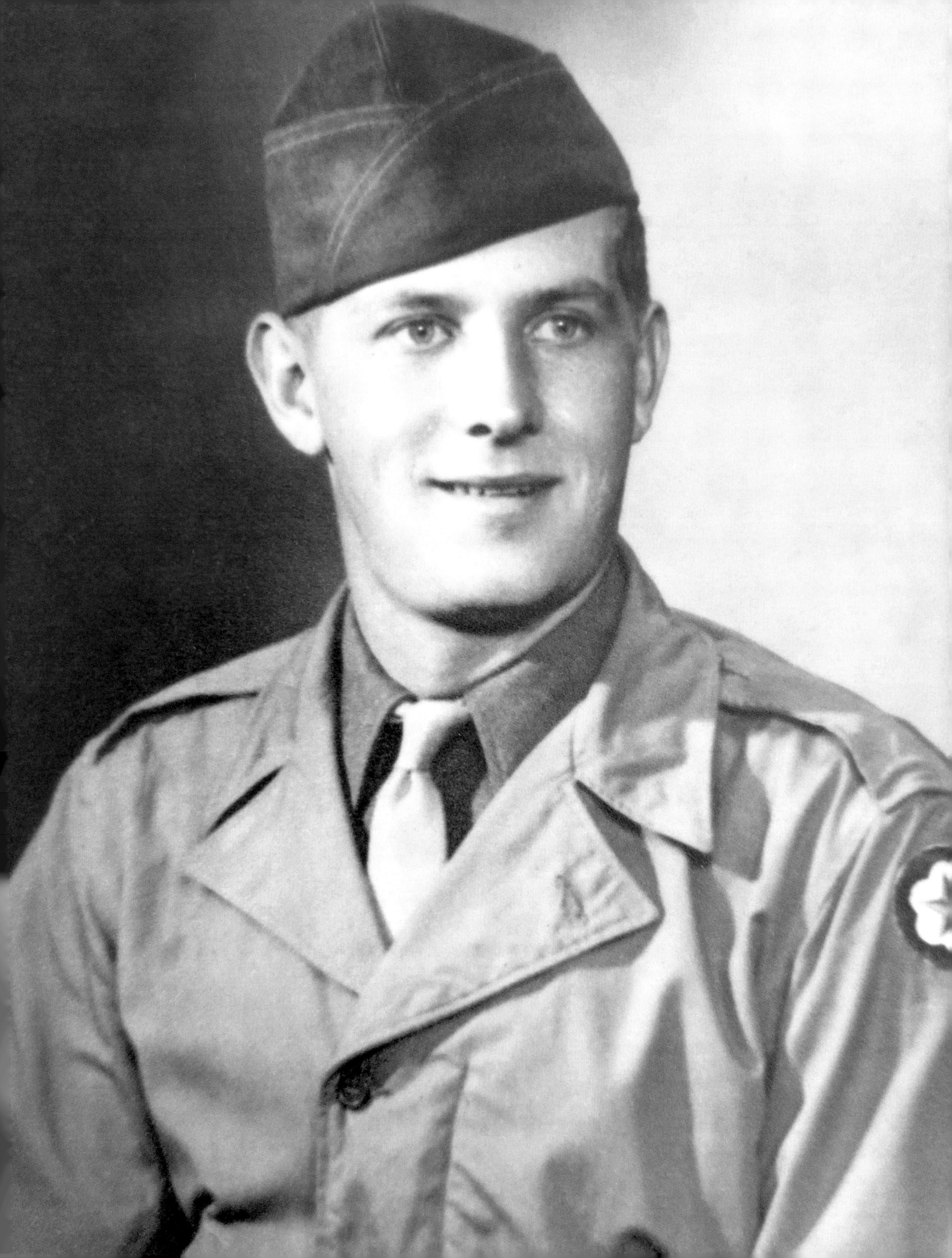

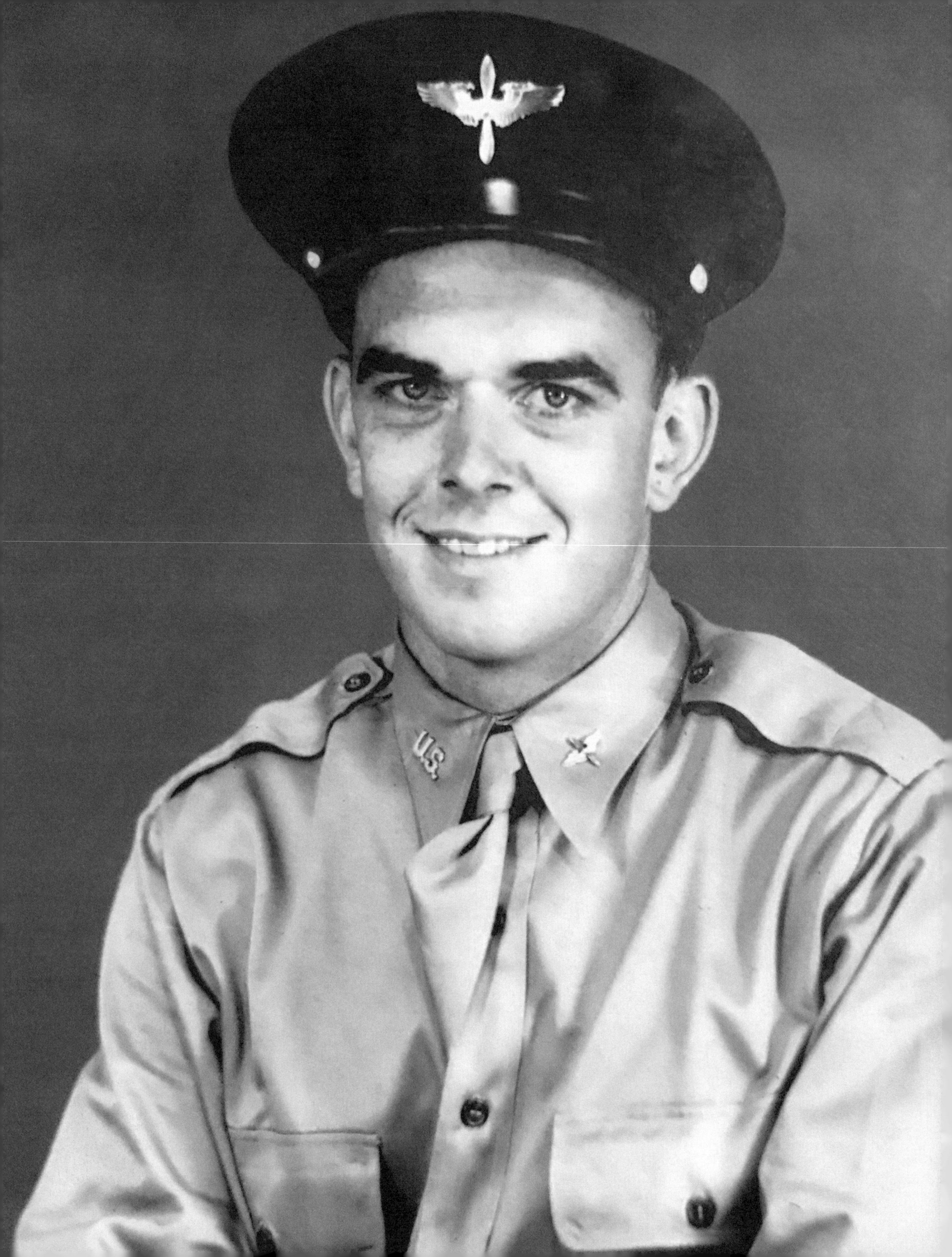

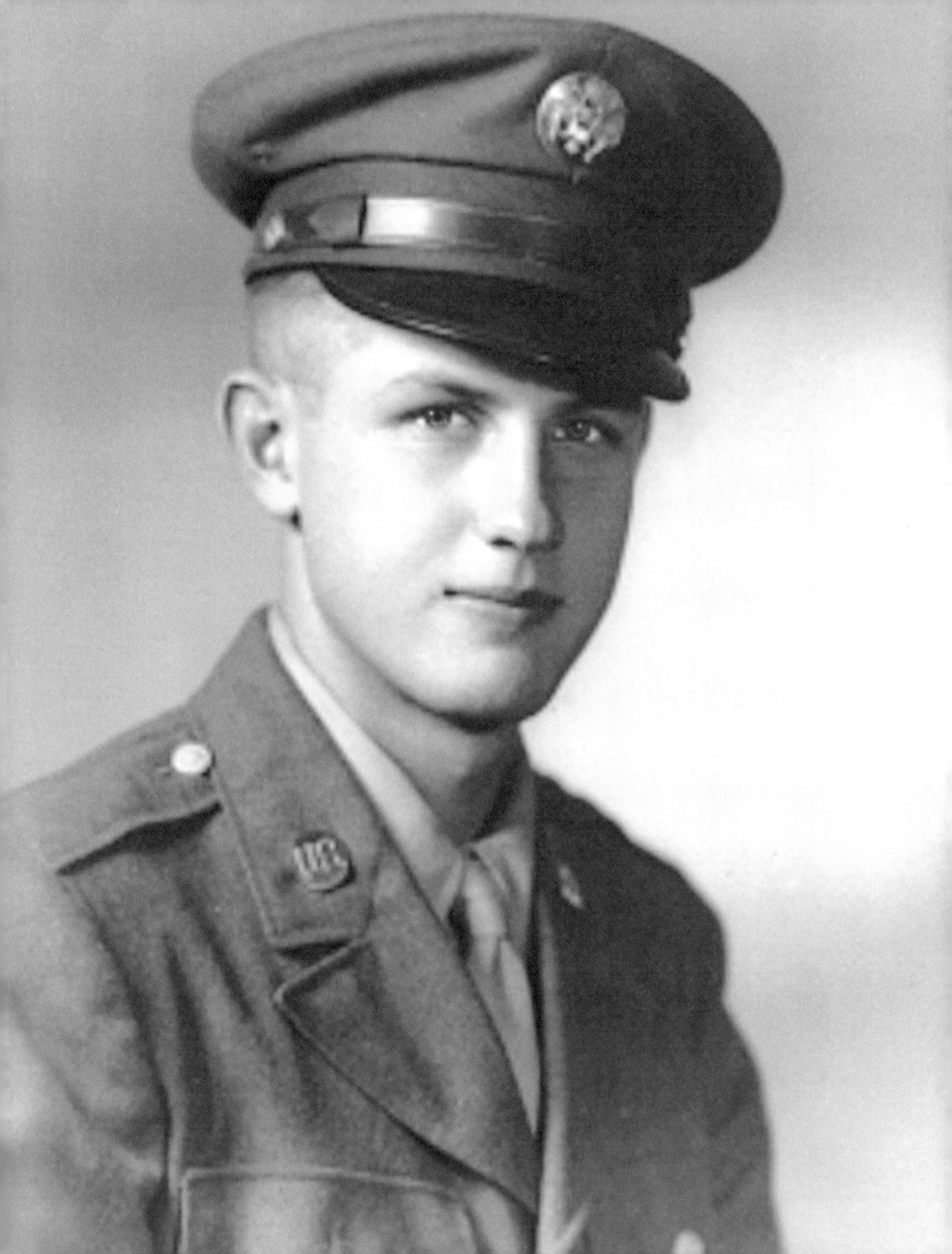

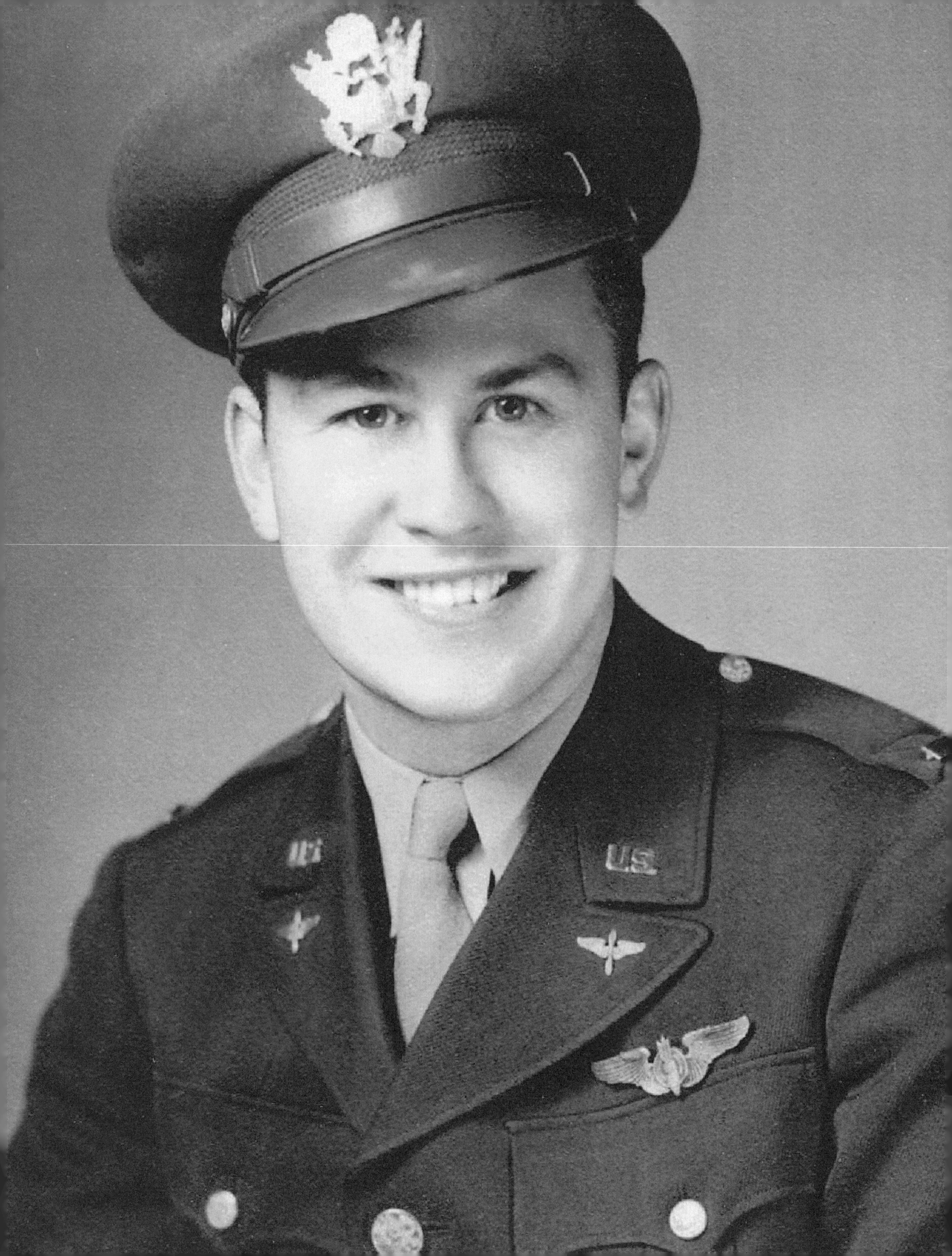

THE FACES OF MARGRATEN

THEY WILL REMAIN FOREVER YOUNG

Fields of Honor Foundation
Authored and edited by Jori Videc, Sebastiaan Vonk, and Arie-Jan van Hees

Amsterdam
University
Press

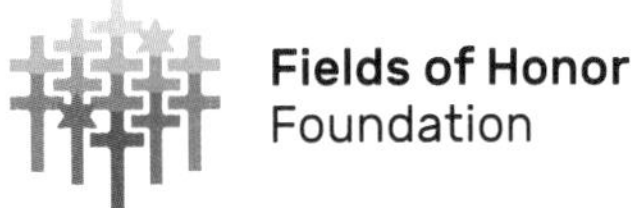

I HAVE ALWAYS HAD DIFFICULTIES, AND STILL DO, WITH READING IN THE NEWSPAPER THAT SOLDIERS 'GIVE THEIR LIVES.' I REALLY DO NOT KNOW IF THERE IS ANY SOLDIER WHO REALLY 'GIVES' HIS LIFE. ALL THOSE THOUSANDS OF BOYS IN MARGRATEN HAD THEIR LIVES TAKEN FROM THEM.

Jefferson Wiggins, gravedigger at the American Cemetery in Margraten, 1944–1945

www.aup.nl
www.fieldsofhonorfoundation.com

1st printing, Dutch, April 2020
2nd printing, Dutch, May 2020
3rd printing (revised), Dutch, August 2020
1st printing, English, November 2022

Cover photo
Staff Sergeant Maurice E. Gosney, 71st Infantry Division. Buried in Margraten in Plot I, Row 2, Grave 11

Cover design
Erwin Bomans[BNO] Leucq!, Hof van Twente

Interior design
studio frederik de wal (www.frederikdewal.nl)

Lithography
BFC, Bert van der Horst, Amersfoort

ISBN 978 94 6372 957 4
e-ISBN 978 90 4855 611 3
NUR 689

CONTENT

Portraits P 1 – 8
The numbers refer to
the Honor Roll on P 270 - 343

P 1. JOHNSON, Vince P [165]
P 2. LE CURSI, Nicholas A [216]
P 3. WHITE, James W [349]
P 4. CHISHOLM, John A Jr [80]
P 5. LINDER, Gerard P [224]
P 6. GARVEY, James A [124]
P 7. ADAMS, William H [6]
P 8. UTLEY, Walter A [340]

▶ P 12. American soldiers celebrate the surrender of Nazi-Germany on Victory in Europe Day (VE Day), May 8, 1945. SOURCE: Michael Gabriel/Wikipedia

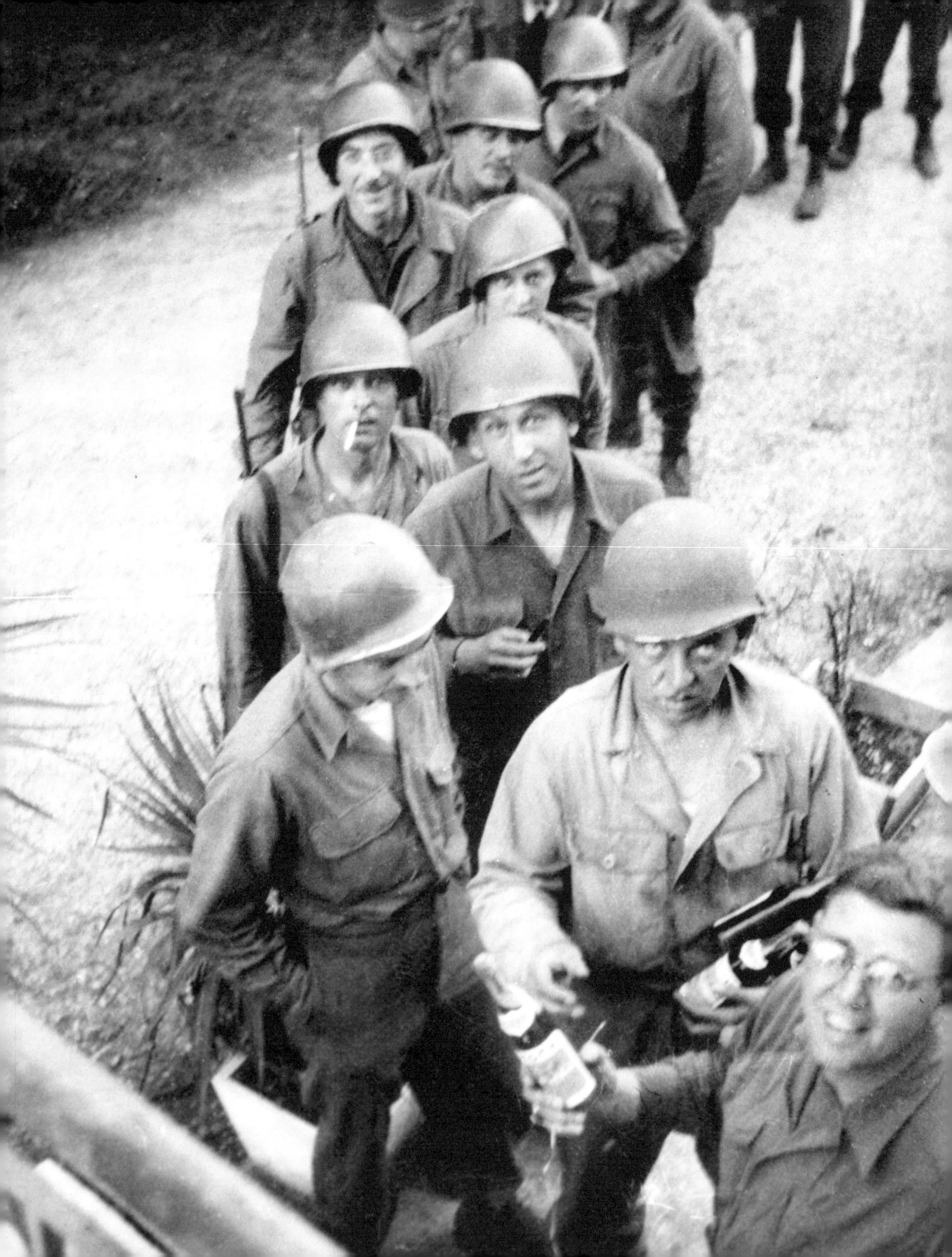

A LASTING MONUMENT IN PRINT

FOREWORD

Maurice Gosney closed his last letter with a promise that he, as it would turn out, sadly was not able to keep: 'That's about all for now. So, I will close for now and write soon. Love, Maurice.' He put these words to paper five days before his death. There would never be another letter. Maurice would never come home again.

During World War II, about 400,000, mostly young, Americans lost their lives. Far from their homes, they became victims of a war that would ultimately cost the lives of tens of millions of people. American soldiers predominantly served and died in North Africa, Italy, (North)western Europe, and the Pacific. Of those who were killed in Europe, about forty percent is buried in or memorialized as missing at thirteen different American military cemeteries across the continent, all administered by the American Battle Monuments Commission.

The Dutch town of Margraten, close to the city of Maastricht and the Belgian-Dutch border, is the site of one of these cemeteries. About 10,000 Americans are either buried at the Netherlands American Cemetery and Memorial, or memorialized on the cemetery's two so-called Walls of the Missing. Among them is Maurice. He is buried underneath one of the about 8,300 white marble crosses and Stars of David that have been arranged in wide arches on the green fields.

Before climbing the stairs leading to the graves, visitors will pass through the Court of Honor. Central to the court, right in front of the Memorial tower, is the reflection pond that is headed by the statue of the Mourning Woman. The woman is surrounded by three doves and a new branch growing from a destroyed tree, symbolizing peace and new life. To the average visitor, the female figure will represent the grieving mothers, including those of the 1,722 soldiers memorialized on the two Walls of the Missing that flank the court. The map room highlighting the Allied advance and the cemetery's visitor building are situated along the court as well.

When arriving at the last few steps of the stairs, any visitor is likely to be impressed by the looming sight of all the graves. The seemingly endless rows of headstones serve as a powerful and impressive reminder of the scale of the war. In particular, they highlight the war's toll on mankind.

After that first impression one can easily spend hours walking among the graves. First and foremost, to read the names inscribed on the headstones. However, reading these names will inevitably raise questions. Who were these people? How old were they? What were their stories? These are questions to which the crosses and the Stars of David do not provide answers.

The search for these answers began in 2008. It was then that the first soldier was entered into what is now known as the *Fields of Honor – Database*. Over the years, thanks to many volunteers, it has grown into a virtual memorial that has personal tribute pages for tens of thousands of American soldiers who are buried in or memorialized at American war cemeteries in Belgium, France, Luxembourg, and the Netherlands. The pages offer a first glimpse into the soldiers' personal lives and their time in the service.

Particularly poignant are the pictures from a time long gone, showing the soldiers posing in their uniforms in a local portrait studio, being surrounded by their family at home, going out with their friends in town, or behind the front lines. As the saying goes: 'a picture is worth a thousand words.' While this obviously is a cliché, it does not mean that it holds less truth. That is why, in 2015, *The Faces of Margraten* were on display at the cemetery for the first time. The 3,300 photographs accompanying the headstones and the Walls of the Missing allowed visitors to emotionally connect to the soldiers on a much more personal level. They were able to look them in the eyes. To some of those who visited the tribute, the soldiers even came, in a way, back to life.

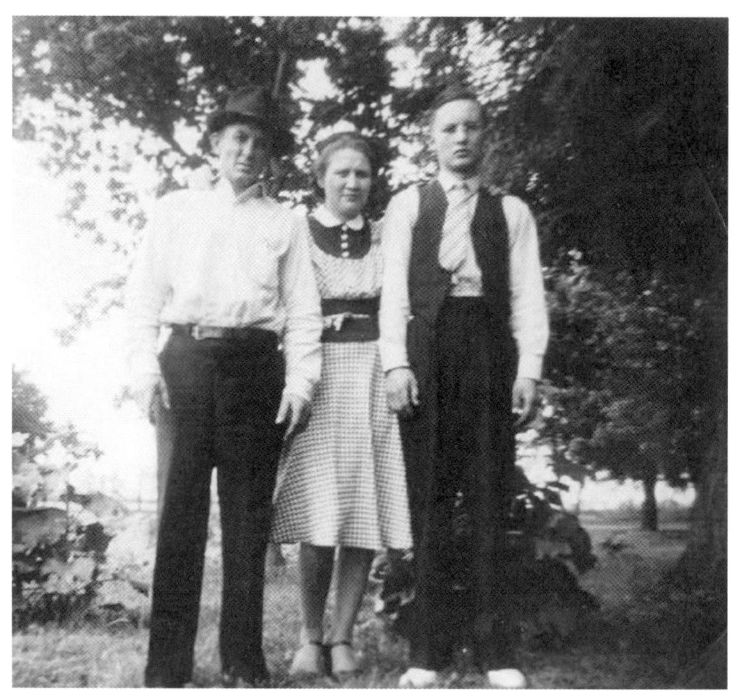

Maurice Gosney together with his father and stepmother.
SOURCE: Gosney family

Since the first time that the faces were on display, the number of photos has continued to increase. Volunteers in the Netherlands, Belgium, and the United States have devoted countless hours of their time to find the faces that are still missing. The ultimate goal: to put a face to every name. We are not there yet. However, at the time of writing this book, there is a photo available for almost 8,500 soldiers. The photos of less than 1,500 soldiers are still missing.

It is in this biennial tribute at the cemetery that this book has its roots. While a picture might be worth a thousand words, it never paints the full picture. Moreover, the photos are only on display at the cemetery for a few days every two years. That is why we have turned to paper to tell the stories behind the pictures. The result is this lasting monument in print to all 10,000 Americans who are either buried or memorialized in Margraten. In our vision, it is a book that is not to be put away on the bookshelf. Rather, the book is deserving of a prominent spot on one's coffee table or in the classroom as a respectful, subtle daily reminder of people who are no longer among us, but to whom we owe our freedom and whose memory still lives on in the hearts and minds of many.

Maurice Gosney is one of the people that this book honors. Thousands of people will now come to know his name. Firstly, because his story is one of the about 250 stories that we tell in this book. These stories shine a light on these soldiers' lives before the war, how their deaths impacted their loved ones, how they are still remembered today, but above all, their time in the service and the moments leading up to their deaths. However, this is not the only way people, including you as a reader, will get to know Maurice. In fact, you have already met him. Maurice covers the front of this book.

Yet, the reality is that for each story we tell, we fail to tell forty others. It is not because those other stories are not as deserving and important, but because they were often simply unknown to us as authors. Even if all 10,000 of them had been known, they would not all have fit into just one single book. The stories in here are therefore at best a randomly chosen reflection of all the stories that could and deserve to be told.

Nevertheless, that does not stop us from continuing to speak the names of each and every soldier who has been either buried or memorialized in Margraten. You will find all 10,000 of them in an impressive, 73-page honor roll that follows after the selection of stories that we have included in the book; hundreds of faces accompany the names. As long as we speak their names, they all will not be forgotten.

The book starts off with a little history lesson. Those who are remembered in Margraten primarily died in Northwestern Europe between 1942 and the months following the German capitulation in 1945. We wish to revisit some of the key battles in this part of Europe at the beginning of this book to provide useful context to the stories of the soldiers that follow. Included in chronological order, the stories reflect the footsteps of the Allies during the final chapter of the war in Europe.

The cemetery itself has a rich history of its own that starts in October 1944, when the current site of the cemetery was still in use as farming land. Over the years, several books and documentaries have captured the history of the site that became the final resting place of close to 8,300 soldiers. So rather than providing a full overview, this book will just briefly recount the hard labor that went into the construction of the cemetery and highlight the special relationship the site has with the local community up and until this day. It will be enough to understand why Margraten is unique.

What also is unique about memorial sites like Margraten is the power they hold to make us reflect about our own lives and the meaning of concepts like war and freedom. That is why, to us, the stories are not just a tribute to their main protagonists. We hope they will also inspire to do good and, by doing so, uphold the legacy of these American men and women.

But first and foremost, this book is a lasting tribute to them. There is no better way to honor them than to make sure they are not forgotten. As the words on the memorial tower at the cemetery remind us:

> ***Each for his own memorial earned praise that will never die and with it the grandest of all sepulchers. Not that in which his mortal bones are laid, but a home in the minds of men.***

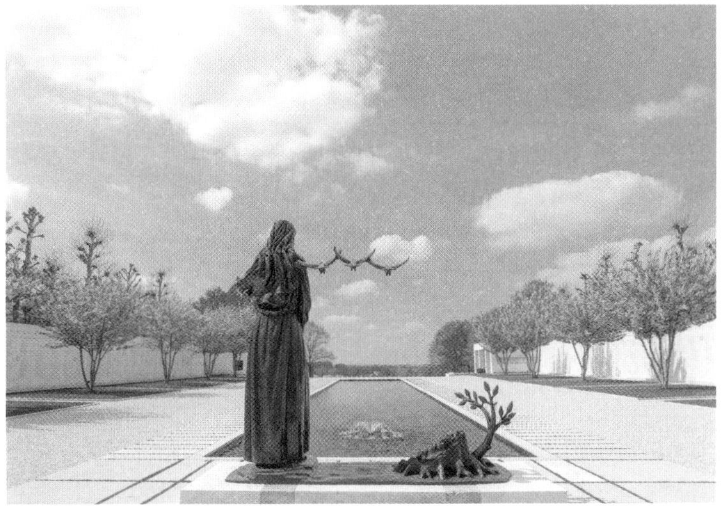

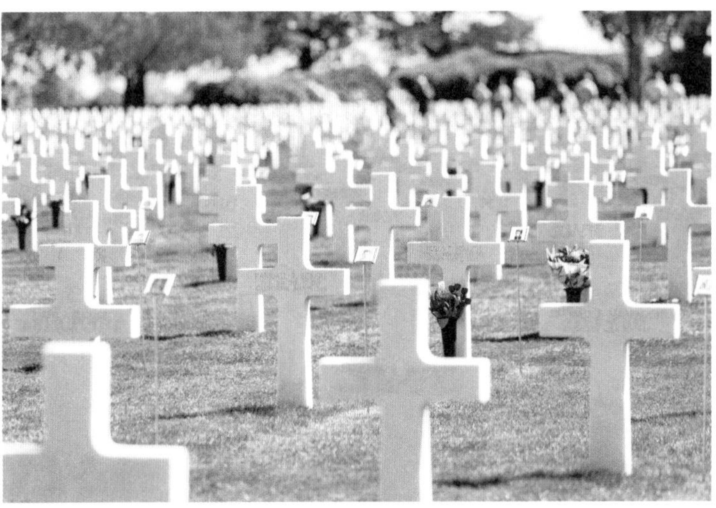

The 'Court of Honor' with the statue of the Mourning Woman, the pool of reflection, and the Walls of the Missing.
SOURCE: Kees Verburg/Wikipedia

The Faces of Margraten in May 2018

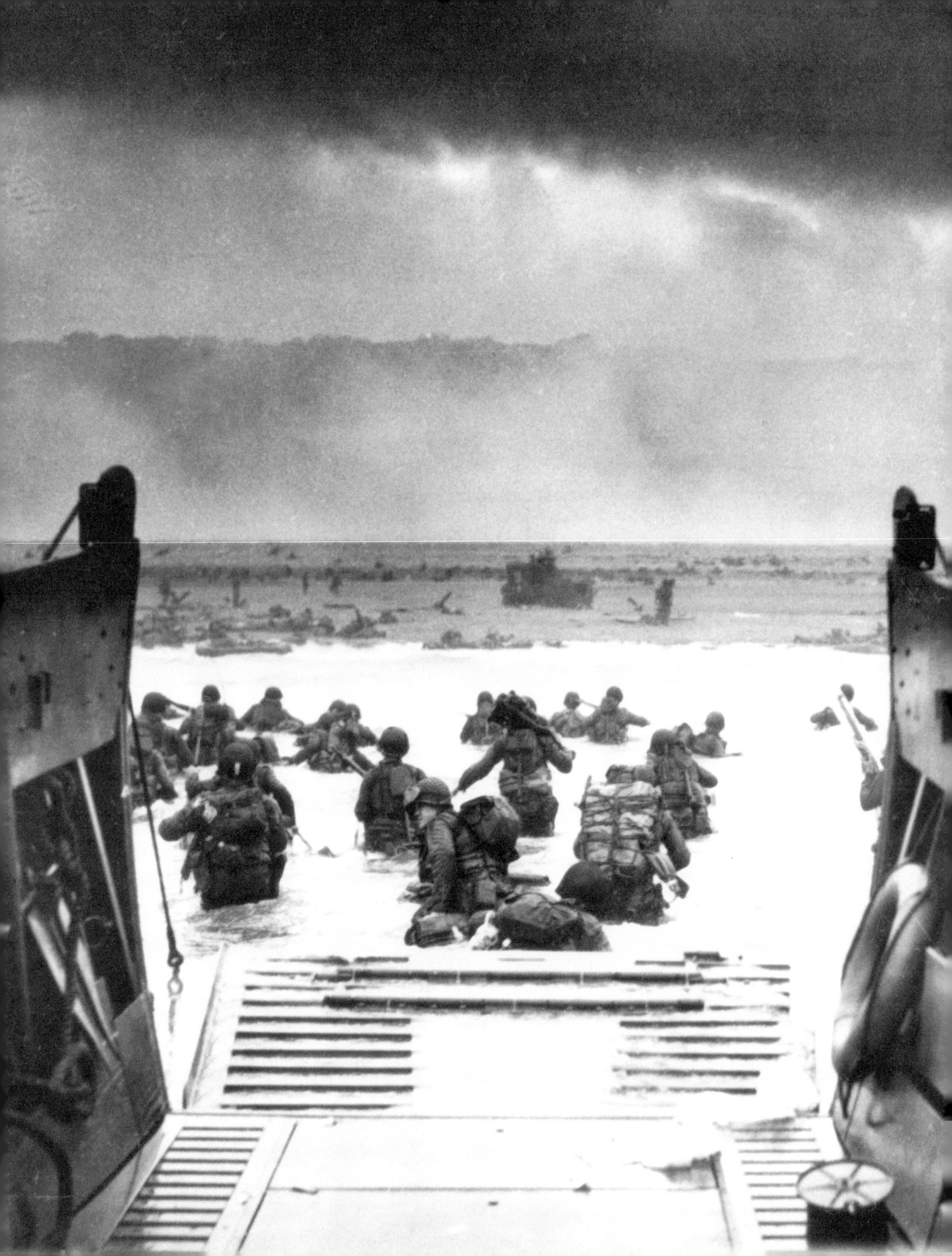

THE AMERICAN WAR EFFORT IN NORTHWESTERN EUROPE: UNCLE SAM COMES TO THE RESCUE

When the German army invaded Poland in September 1939, which would turn out to be the beginning of World War II, the war was still a distant notion for Americans. The vast majority of the American people felt that the United States should stay out of this European conflict. However, due to the German and Japanese aggression, President Roosevelt was convinced that his country would sooner or later become involved in the war. Therefore, he felt that the U.S. should start preparing for the inevitable.

Roosevelt was right, because on December 7, 1941, Japanese fighter planes attacked the American naval ships that were anchored in Pearl Harbor on Hawaii. The Japanese pilots had taken off from aircraft carriers on the ocean. It was a Sunday morning and many sailors were still asleep; the Americans were taken by surprise. The Japanese bombs and torpedoes sunk nine ships and damaged twelve others. Coincidence or not, the aircraft carriers *Lexington* and *Enterprise* fortunately happened to be out at sea that day. They would prove invaluable for the further course of the war in the Pacific. Of the American fighter planes stationed at Pearl Harbor's airfields, 188 were destroyed and 159 damaged. Two thousand four hundred Americans lost their lives on this 'Day of Infamy,' as Roosevelt called it in his speech to the Congress the following day.

EYEWITNESS ACCOUNT OF THE ATTACK ON PEARL HARBOR

'The first airplane that came in my direction was olive drab. I thought it was an Army plane. Then he came in flying low and slow. He had machine guns, so when the machine guns opened up, the bullets went right over my head! That's when war became very personal. We were tied up with the *Oklahoma* in front of us and the *Arizona* behind. The *Oklahoma* capsized and turned over, so here we were with the *Oklahoma* upside down in front of us and the *Arizona* burning like a volcano behind.'

Jim Downing
***Serving on the battleship* USS West Virginia.**

This dramatic event completely changed the mood of the American people. The U.S. declared war on Japan, and a few days later Japan's ally Germany declared war on the U.S. in return. In retrospect, this overconfident decision by Hitler turned out to be one of his most fatal; Great Britain and the Soviet Union gained a powerful ally and the American war industry was soon operating at full capacity. As a result, the U.S. managed to build an enormous military force in a relatively short period of time. Moreover, Congress, pushed by Roosevelt, had already introduced the draft in 1940 by passing the Selective Training and Service Act. However, after the attack on Pearl Harbor, there were also many Americans who simply volunteered to serve their country and fight for freedom and democracy.

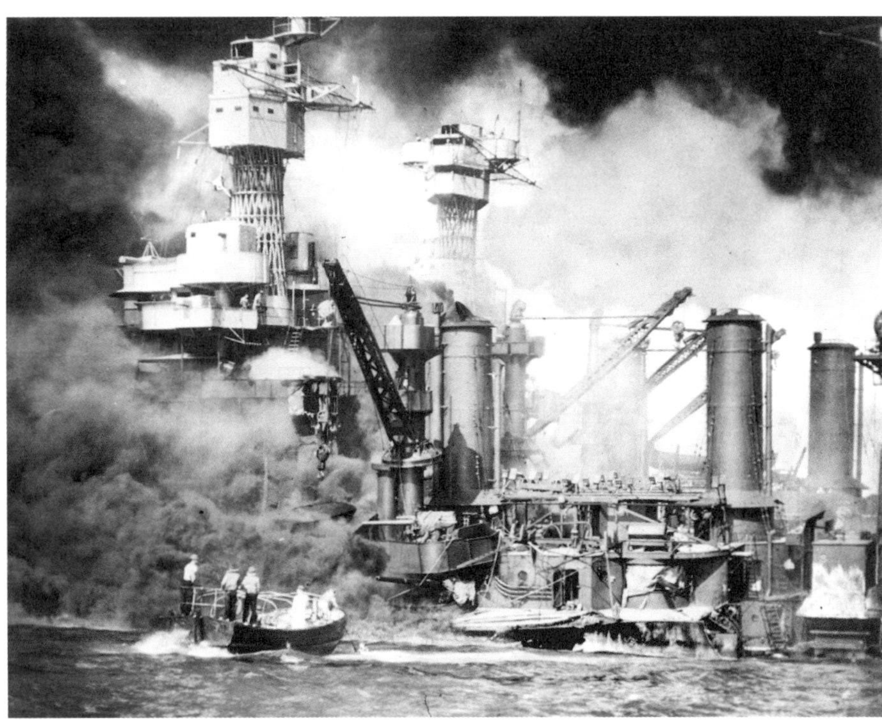

Thick smoke rolls out of a burning ship during the attack on Pearl Harbor by the Japanese on December 7, 1941. SOURCE: National Archives and Records Administration

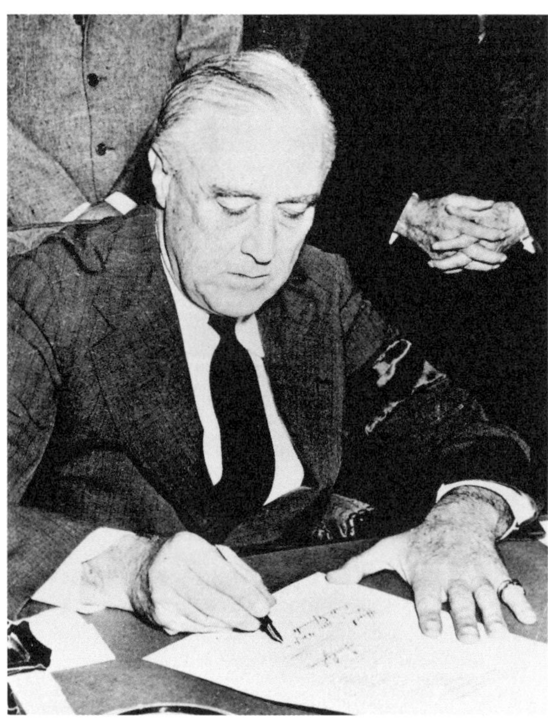

President Franklin D. Roosevelt signs the declaration of war a day after the Japanese attack on Pearl Harbor. SOURCE: National Archives and Records Administration

Despite the Japanese attack, the political and military leaders of the United States, in consultation with their British allies, decided to make the defeat of Hitler's Nazi Germany their top priority: 'Germany First.' Hitler had thought that he would have nothing to fear from the Americans for the time being, because he presumed that they would first deploy all their military resources against Japan. Furthermore, Hitler assumed that Japan's armed forces were capable of defeating the Americans. Both assumptions proved to be wrong. Firstly, the United States had so much industrial capacity and manpower that the American armed forces could fight on two fronts simultaneously. Secondly, as the battle in the Pacific raged on, the tables would slowly turn, and the Americans eventually succeeded in gaining the upper hand. So, in the end, Japan proved not to be an invincible ally for Hitler.

The Lend-Lease Act

The U.S. war industry not only produced for the nation's own armed forces, but also supplied large quantities of arms, ammunition, tanks, army trucks, and other war equipment to Great Britain, the Soviet Union, and other countries fighting against Nazi Germany. This was done under the so-called Lend-Lease Act, which had been approved by Congress in March 1941 at the initiative of President Roosevelt's administration. At the time of the law's passing, the U.S. was not yet at war with either Japan or Germany, but the act allowed military equipment to be supplied to all countries whose defense the American president deemed to be vital to the security of the U.S.

The shiploads of American war equipment that were shipped to the country's allies had a total value of 50 billion dollars. About eighty percent of all aid went to Britain. The British government could not pay this amount during the war years. For this reason, the settlement stipulated that the war goods supplied would not have to be paid until after Nazi Germany had been defeated.

The bombing of Germany

Well before the U.S. were able to deploy their ground forces against the Nazis, the U.S. Army Air Forces (USAAF) started to conduct bombing raids against Germany. The British Royal Air Force (RAF) had already begun doing so in 1940 – initially in retaliation for the German bombing raids on London and other cities in Great Britain.

While the British mainly targeted German cities, the Americans concentrated from June 1942 onwards on bombing airfields, infrastructure, and factories that sustained the German war effort. Not only in Germany itself, but also in the Nazi-occupied countries like the Netherlands. The goal of the Allied bombing campaign was to damage the German war industry and to disrupt the logistics of the German army. Unlike the British bomber groups, the American bombers conducted their missions during the hours of daylight, so that the specific targets were more visible from the air; the British conducted their bombings at night because the German cities were heavily defended by Flak (anti-aircraft guns) and their bombers were less visible then.

The Allied bombing raids eventually resulted in great destruction and many German casualties, but U.S. bomber crews suffered a high number of losses as well. During the bombing raids, enemy anti-aircraft guns and German fighter planes downed many bombers. As a result, thousands of American airmen were killed or taken prisoner by the Germans.

The price that the men of the USAAF paid for disrupting the German war effort was high. In 1943, the chances of the American 'bomber boys' to survive the 25 missions they were required to fulfill were only twenty percent. Losses to the crews of bombers only started to decrease when new long-range fighters such as the P-51 Mustang became operational in 1943. These fighters could escort the heavy bombers to the farthest corners of Germany thanks to their drop tanks (containing extra fuel). Not only did they protect the bombers against Luftwaffe fighters, the newly developed fighters were also used for strafing and bombing runs on ground targets, such as German anti-aircraft positions.

> **EYEWITNESS ACCOUNT OF A BOMB RAID**
> **'My first raid was on December 31, 1943, over Ludwigshafen. Naturally, not knowing what it was going to be like, I didn't feel scared. A little sick, maybe, but not scared. That comes later, when you begin to understand what your chances of survival are. (...) We made our run over the target, got our bombs away, and apparently did a good job. Maybe it was the auto-pilot and bomb sight that saw to that, but I'm sure I was cool enough on that first raid to do my job without thinking too much about it. Then, on the way home, some Focke-Wulfs showed up, armed with rockets, and I saw three B-17s in the different groups around us suddenly blow up and drop through the sky. Just simply blow up and drop through the sky. Nowadays, if you come across something awful happening, you always think, "My God, it's just like a movie," and that's what I thought. I had a feeling that the planes weren't really falling and burning, the men inside them weren't really dying, and everything would turn out happily in the end. Then, very quietly through the interphone, our tail gunner said, "I'm sorry, sir, I've been hit."'**
>
> ***Joseph Hallock***
> ***Bombardier in a B-17 of the 306th Bombardment Group.***

Until the end of the war, the USAAF continued to conduct bombing raids on the German industry and infrastructure. In doing so, the bombardment groups of the USAAF significantly contributed to the eventual Allied victory. In addition, the superiority of the American and British fighter-bombers was often a decisive factor in the Allied ground offensives that took place after the invasion of Normandy. The fighter-bombers were an effective and very important weapon. The almost constant bombing and strafing of German troops by Allied fighters and fighter-bombers weakened their ability to hold off the advance of Allied tanks and infantry.

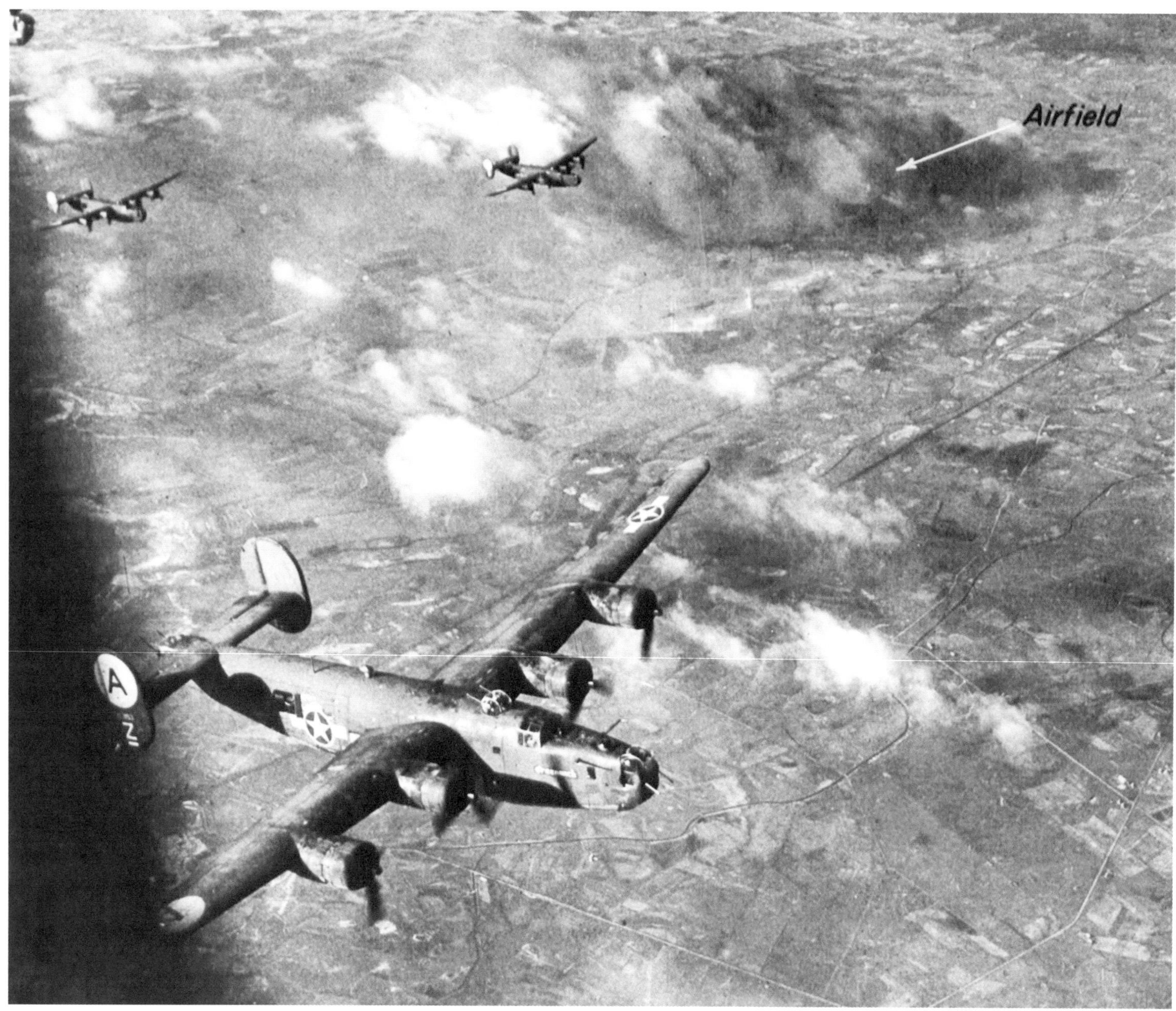

American bombers over Germany.
SOURCE: National Archives and Records Administration

Bombers in the Battle of the Atlantic

The four-engine B-24 'Liberators' of the USAAF also played an important role in the Battle of the Atlantic. From the beginning of the war, German U-boats (submarines) torpedoed Allied ships on the Atlantic to cut off the supply of food, raw materials, and military goods to Great Britain. The B-24s could fly such a long range that they could be deployed to destroy German submarines in the middle of the Atlantic. The U-boat packs mainly hunted for Allied transport convoys there because this part of the ocean was previously out of reach of the Allied aircraft. To turn the tide in the Atlantic in favor of the Allies, the B-24s were equipped with sonar and radar equipment to search the ocean for U-boats.

Whenever the Liberators located enemy submarines, they immediately reported their position to British and American naval destroyers, which in turn attacked the submerged U-boats with special depth charges. These depth charges usually damaged the U-boats to such an extent that the submarines perished with their entire crew. The few that could still surface were usually no match for the guns of the destroyers.

D-Day in Normandy

On June 6, 1944, the liberation of Northwestern Europe began with Operation Overlord, the major Allied invasion in Normandy. Preceded by airborne landings of paratroopers and gliders, and by aerial and naval bombardments, tens of thousands of American, British, Canadian, and French soldiers stormed ashore on five beaches. American troops landed on Utah and Omaha Beach, the British attacked Gold and Sword Beach, and the Canadians headed for Juno Beach.

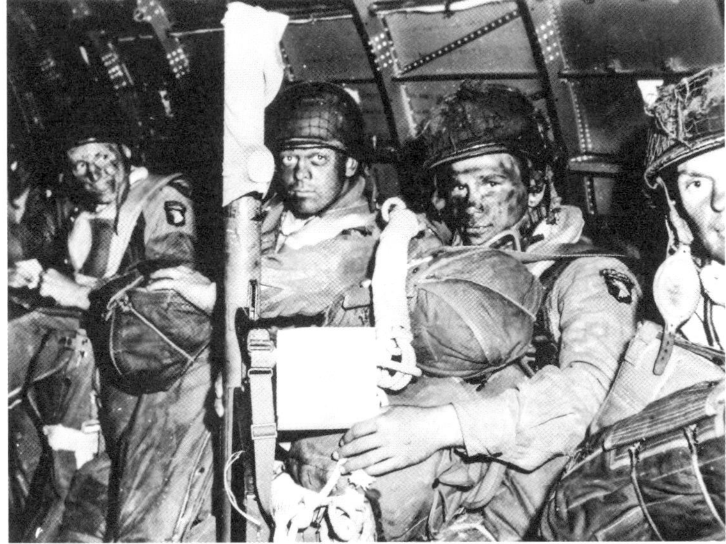

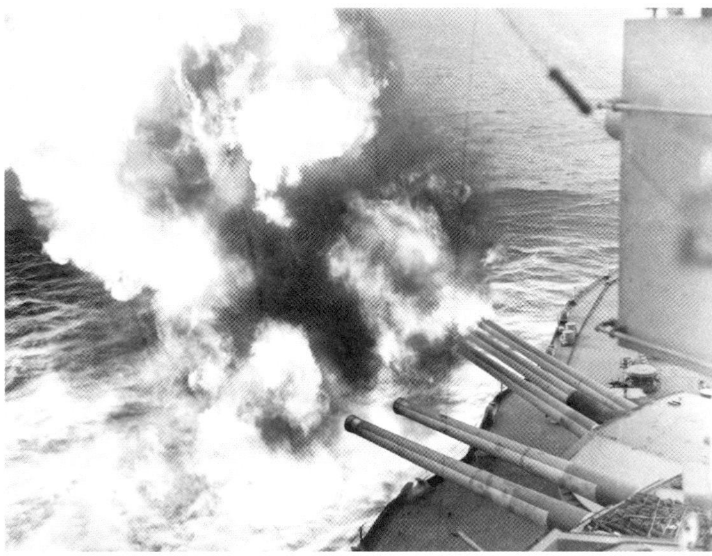

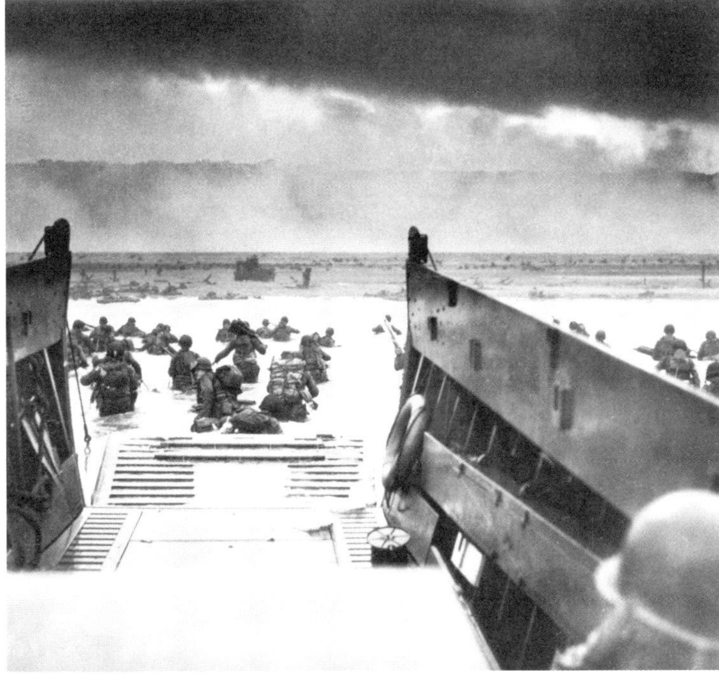

The D-Day landings in Normandy were undeniably a success. Nevertheless, that day's victory came at a high price, especially on Omaha Beach. There, the German defenses were significantly stronger compared to the other beaches. Moreover, the German resistance nests on Omaha Beach were mostly built on a steep slope that rose to a height of 30 to 40 meters directly behind the beach. This geographical advantage gave the Germans an excellent view of the beach and enabled them to rake every stretch of sand with their deadly crossfire.

In order to neutralize the formidable German defenses and firepower on Omaha Beach before the first waves of infantry would come ashore, heavy bombers dropped their bombs on the coast and the Allied naval ships shelled the German positions for 40 minutes. However, due to the low clouds, the fog, and the morning dusk, the coastal defenses could not be seen clearly. As a result, the naval fire was mostly ineffective, and the bombers did not hit the enemy defenses at all. Not a single one of the German fortifications along Omaha Beach was neutralized, and the German troops were ready to open fire. So, when the first assault wave of infantry closed in on the beach, disaster awaited them: as soon as the landing craft dropped their ramps, the American soldiers were mowed down by a murderous combination of machine gun fire and exploding mortar and artillery shells.

To make matters even worse, almost all of the 'swimming' Duplex Drive tanks (DD tanks) destined for Omaha Beach sank off the coast almost immediately after their disembarkation from the LCTs (Landing Craft Tank). These modified Sherman tanks should have been able to sail to the coast and then drive onto the beach to eliminate the German machine gun nests and to provide cover for the infantrymen coming ashore. But most were lost as the rough sea caused cracks in the canvas screens that were supposed to keep the tanks afloat, or because the waves simply washed over them. The DD tanks that did reach the beach – most of them were brought all the way to the beach by the LCTs after it was noticed that 27 of the 29 tanks that had already been launched had sunk – were in most cases an easy prey for the German guns.

Because the assault plan for Omaha Beach thus largely failed, the German defenders could cause a bloody carnage among the Americans. Many of them were killed even before they reached the sand; they were struck by machine gun bullets or shrapnel while wading through the water. As a result, the water slowly turned red with blood...

Paratroopers of the 101st Airborne Division shortly before departing for Normandy. SOURCE: National Archives and Records Administration

Soldiers wading through the water, making their way to Omaha Beach while being subjected to heavy machine gun fire. SOURCE: National Archives and Records Administration

The *USS Nevada* fires its 14" guns at the German fortifications along Utah Beach prior to the landing of infantry forces and tanks. SOURCE: National Archives and Records Administration

EYEWITNESS ACCOUNT OF D-DAY
'About 500 yards offshore I began to realize we were in trouble. The nearer we got to the beachline, the more certain I was that the landing was a disaster. Dead and wounded from the first waves were everywhere. There was little or no firing from our troops. On the other hand, German machine guns, mortars, and 88s were laying down some of the heaviest fire I'd ever experienced.'

Al Smith
1st Infantry Division.

Many of the soldiers who managed to reach the beach were soaked and exhausted. The constant rattling of the German MG-42s, the explosion of shells, and the sight of so many of their countrymen being killed was so overwhelming that many went into a state of shock. They were in the middle of a slaughter and desperately sought cover behind the many obstacles, the dunes, or the beach wall.

The situation on 'Bloody Omaha' seemed hopeless. However, in some sectors of the beach, groups of soldiers led by brave officers and NCOs managed to overcome their fear of death and got moving. They blew openings in the barbed wire with Bangalore torpedoes and began to climb the slope in places where the German fire was less concentrated: not near the five heavily defended draws, but in between them. On the way up and near the edge of the slope, these soldiers then knocked out several hostile machine gun nests. This reduced the intensity of the enemy fire and as a result, the tide slowly began to turn.

In the end, the battle on Omaha Beach was definitively decided in favor of the Americans when, from about two hours after the landing had begun, Navy destroyers began to get involved in the battle again. These destroyers sailed along the coast just a few hundred yards off the beach. This allowed the commanders to use binoculars and optical targeting equipment to see how the situation on the beach was unfolding. In doing so, the destroyers were moving dangerously close to shore, within range of German fire and at the risk of getting stuck on the ground. Nevertheless, the guns of the destroyers started shelling the German fortifications from a relatively short distance. This resulted in the elimination of several German positions, or it forced the German soldiers to take cover or run away.

The contribution of the destroyers to the ultimate success on Omaha Beach can hardly be underestimated. Because these naval ships eliminated important German resistance nests, more groups of Americans were able to get off the beach and fight their way to the top of the slope. As a result, the Omaha Beach landing ultimately succeeded despite its disastrous beginning and the loss of approximately 2,000 to 2,500 American dead, wounded, and missing.

After most German fortifications had been neutralized and captured, the five draws that led from the beach to the plateau could be cleared by engineers. Subsequently, the tanks and infantry reinforcements that had been brought ashore could begin to advance inland. A couple of days later, the troops that had landed on Omaha linked up with the American troops who had landed on Utah Beach, closing the gap between the two American bridgeheads.

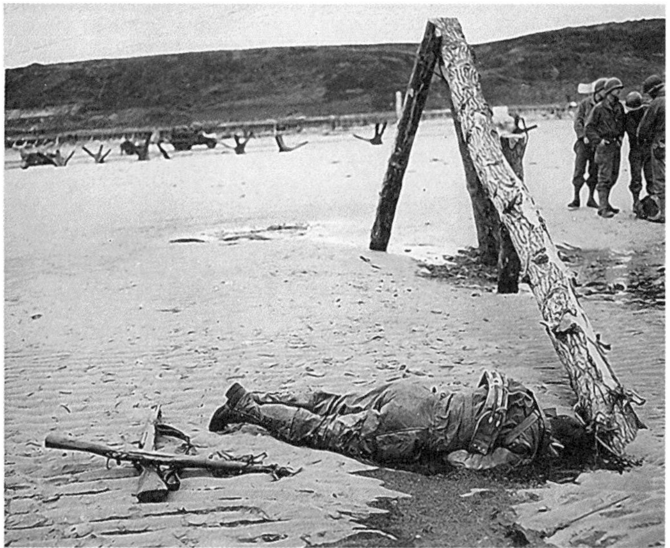

An American soldier who lost his life on Omaha Beach on June 6, 1944. Another soldier improvised a memorial by making a cross out of two rifles. SOURCE: National Archives and Records Administration

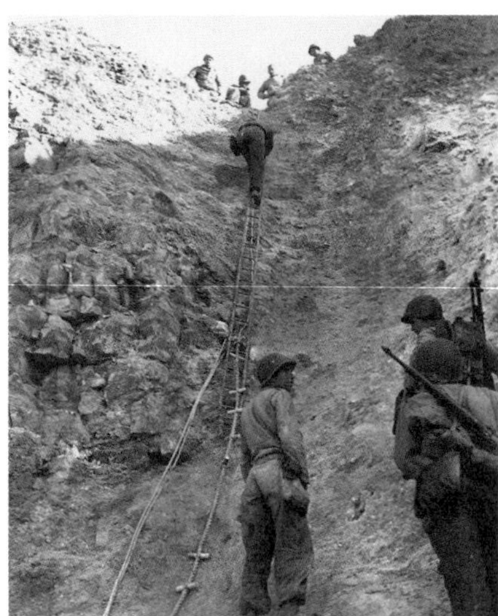

Rangers of the 2nd Ranger Battalion on Pointe du Hoc on June 6, 1944. SOURCE: National Archives and Records Administration

EYEWITNESS ACCOUNT OF D-DAY
'"Fire, Wegner, fire!" Corporal Lang yelled to me. I was paralyzed; I had seen all those men in khaki uniforms wading their way through the water towards the sand. They looked defenseless in the midst of the beach. Lang took the stock of his pistol and violently hit my helmet with it. The metallic sound roused me and I pressed the trigger. The machine gun rumbled, sending bullets into the men who were running across the beach. I saw some of them fall; I knew I had hit them. The bullets raked the sand from top to bottom. A young man from Hannover had just killed several men. My mind rationalized it all, this was war. But even so, it left a bitter taste. The time had come to stop talking, and simply to survive.'

Karl Wegner
German soldier of the 352. Infantry Division on Omaha Beach.

Pointe du Hoc

Simultaneously with the landings of American troops on Utah and Omaha Beach, an elite force of about 200 American Rangers scaled the cliffs near Pointe du Hoc, between the two beaches, using ropes and rope ladders. The Germans had deployed an artillery battery there and were still constructing several of the artillery casemates that were supposed to protect the six 155mm guns on the site. Heavy Allied bombing raids had only destroyed one of these guns in the run-up to D-Day.

At the top of the plateau, the Rangers were pinned down by heavy German small arms and machine gun fire in a lunar-like landscape that had been torn to pieces by bombs and heavy naval shells. Only when the most threatening machine gun bunker on the east side of the plateau was literally blown off the cliff by well-targeted naval fire, the Rangers could advance in groups toward the casemates and open platforms where the guns reportedly were.

When they arrived at the gun emplacements, the Rangers discovered that they had been misled; the Germans had removed the five remaining guns a few days before the invasion and had replaced them with telegraph poles. But the Rangers did not leave it at that and started to look for them. They found the five guns in an orchard, ready to direct fire at Utah Beach, but unmanned. The two Ranger sergeants who found the guns then neutralized them one by one with special thermite grenades. As a result, the guns were no longer a threat to the invasion fleet or the troops on the beaches. The Rangers had done their job, but when the fighting at Pointe du Hoc was over, they had lost half of their men.

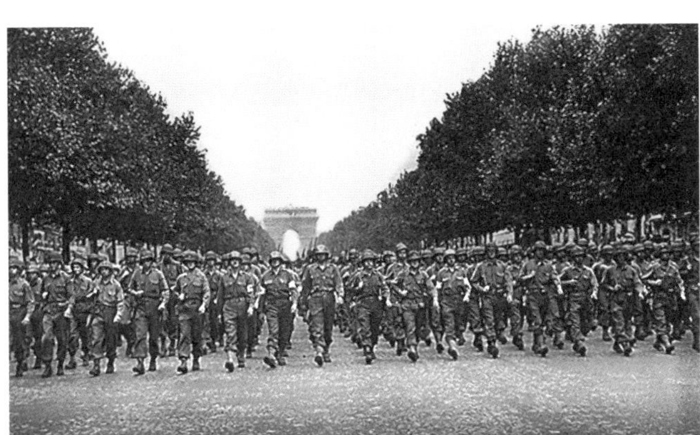

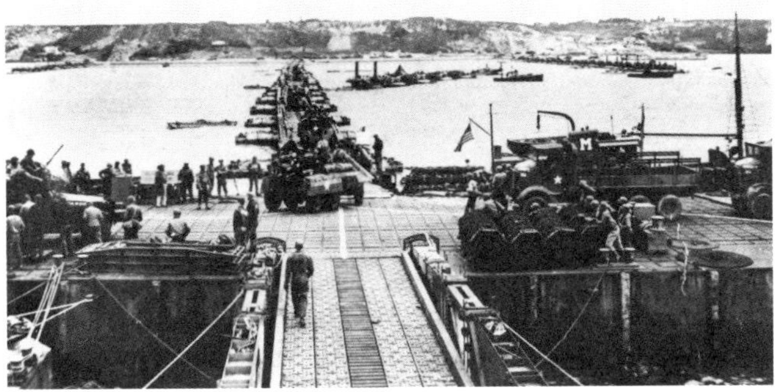

Advancing through the Bocage

Thanks to the successful invasion, the Allies were able to liberate a small piece of France on D-Day. They built up a huge army there and the Allied divisions soon began to fight their way towards Paris, the Low Countries, and the western border of Germany.

However, in the first weeks following the invasion, the advance was more difficult and resulted in higher losses than the Allied commanders had expected. This was particularly caused by the fact that the Normandy countryside was a labyrinth of small farming fields surrounded by hedgerows. These hedgerows were excellent defensive positions for the Germans, who turned every field surrounded by hedges into a small battlefield. Fighting between the hedgerows in Normandy was, therefore, a hellish experience for the Allies. The advance of their infantry divisions and armored units was constantly hampered by cunningly hidden machine gun nests, snipers, anti-tank guns, and tanks. The Allies had to fight bloody battles to drive the Germans out of Normandy. They literally had to do this hedge by hedge.

> **EYEWITNESS ACCOUNT OF THE HEDGEROW FIGHTING**
> **'The Germans would dig into the back of a hedgerow, put a machine gun nest in there, and then cut a very small slit looking forward, providing them with a field of fire with what was for practical purposes absolute protection. You couldn't see them as they fired.'**
>
> ***John Raaen***
> ***5th Ranger Battalion.***

Most of the time, there was only one opening in the hedgerows that gave access to a farming field. Logically, the Germans had their weapons zeroed-in at these openings. Therefore, the Americans started to use TNT and so-called 'Rhino'-tanks. TNT was used to blow gaps in the hedges; the Rhino was a tank with a hedgerow cutter welded to the front. With the help of these 'tusks' they could break through the earthen walls and the hedgerows to force alternate openings. Regular Sherman tanks could drive through the forced openings into the field, firing their machine guns and cannons at the hidden German positions and providing some cover for the vulnerable infantrymen.

The breakthrough towards Paris

Once the Allies had managed to chase the Germans out of the Bocage of Normandy, they could finally unleash their tanks into open terrain, whereupon the battered German divisions were quickly driven back towards Belgium and Germany. Thanks in part to the rapid breakout of General George Patton's armored divisions after 'Operation Cobra,' some

American soldiers of the 28th Infantry Division march on the Champs-Elysées during a military parade days after the liberation of Paris, August 29, 1944. SOURCE: National Archives and Records Administration

Allied trucks and other vehicles transporting supplies from the Mulberry harbor at Omaha Beach. SOURCE: Nederlands Instituut voor Militaire Historie/Beeldbank WO2

60,000 German soldiers were surrounded in the so-called 'Falaise Pocket' in August 1944. On August 25, 1944, Paris was liberated. The liberation of the French capital and the withdrawal of the German forces across the Seine River concluded Operation Overlord.

Mulberry harbors and the 'Red Ball Express'

After D-Day, two artificial 'Mulberry'-harbors (Mulberry A for the Americans and Mulberry B for the British) were built near Omaha and Gold Beach to supply the Allied armies with everything they needed. Later on, several pipelines were laid on the bottom of the English Channel to help ensure the supply of fuel from England.

Both harbors consisted of floating docks where ships could moor with supplies, equipment and troops, and of floating piers over which supplies could be brought ashore. Written-off warships and concrete caissons were sunk off the coast to serve as breakwaters and to make the harbors stormproof. Nevertheless, Mulberry A at Omaha Beach was so badly damaged during a severe storm that raged across the English Channel from June 19–21 that this harbor could no longer be used. Elements of this harbor were used to repair Mulberry B at Arromanches, the remains of which can still be seen today. But since two artificial harbors, let alone one, did not have sufficient capacity to meet the demand for supplies, it was of vital importance that later that month, after heavy fighting, the Americans captured the port city of Cherbourg.

Thousands of trucks of the so-called 'Red Ball Express' transported the supplies and fuel that arrived in the Mulberry harbors and Cherbourg to the advancing divisions in the front line. Without the continuous supply of fuel and other necessities, the tanks and infantry troops at the front could not sustain the Allied offensive. Therefore, the motto of the personnel of the Red Ball Express was 'Keep them rolling.' Most of the trucks were driven by African American soldiers.

EYEWITNESS ACCOUNT OF THE RED BALL EXPRESS

'We took supplies all the way to the front line, back and forth, back and forth. (...) When General Patton said for you to be there, you were there if you had to drive all day and all night. Those trucks just kept running. They'd break down, we'd fix them and they'd run again. We had to drive slowly at night because we had to use "cat eyes" [slitted headlight covers that reduced light to a dim beam on the highway] and you could hardly see. If you turned on your headlights, the Germans could bomb the whole convoy. So, we had to feel our way down the road. (...) My worst memories of being in the Red Ball Express were seeing trucks get blown up and being afraid that I might get killed. There were dead bodies and dead horses on the highways after bombs dropped. I was scared, but I did my job, hoping for the best. Being young and about 4,000 miles away from home, anybody would be scared.'

James D. Rookard
African American driver in the 'Red Ball Express,' 514th Quartermaster Truck Regiment.

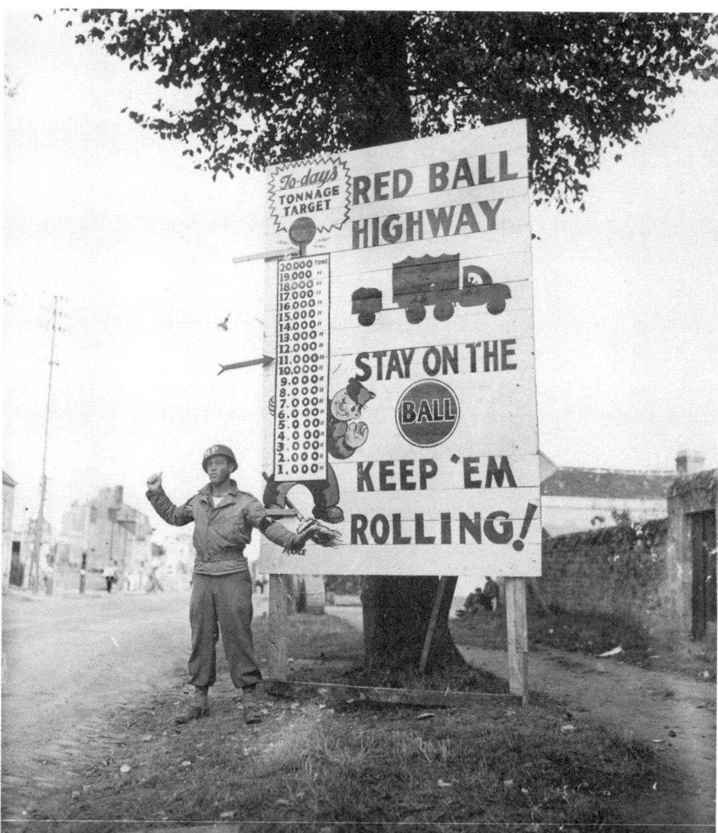

A member of the Military Police directs the traffic of the Red Ball Express. SOURCE: National Archives and Records Administration

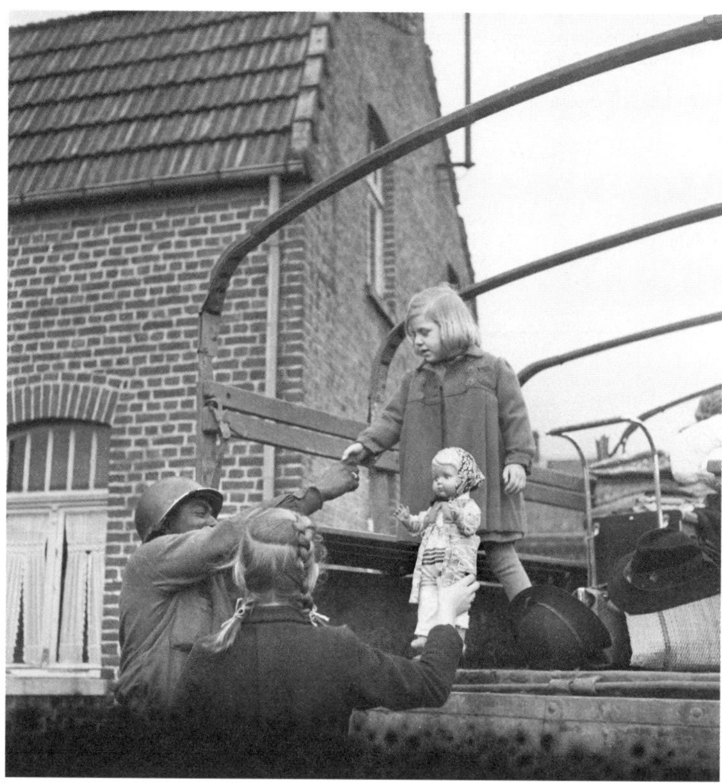

An African American soldier shakes the hand of a girl from Roermond, the Netherlands. The city had been evacuated by the Germans. SOURCE: Nationaal Archief, collectie Anefo

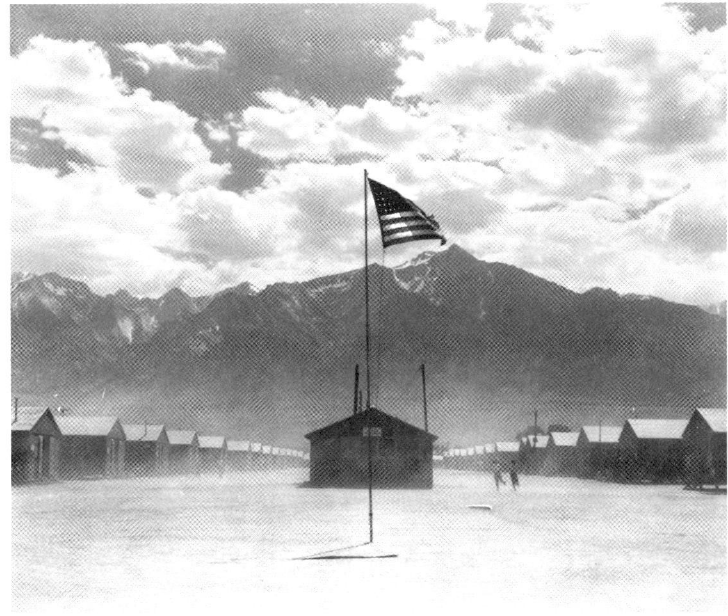

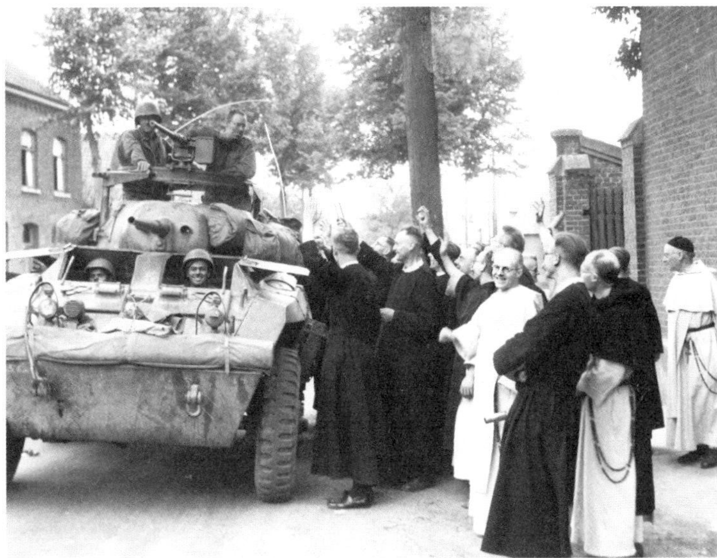

It was no coincidence that African American soldiers spearheaded the Red Ball Express. At the time of World War II, U.S. society, and thus the military, was still segregated. Looked down upon, African Americans were not allowed to serve alongside white Americans. Moreover, many of their white countrymen believed that African Americans were not capable to be good soldiers. Therefore, African Americans were primarily assigned to the supporting elements of the military, such as the Quartermaster Corps, Ordnance Corps, and Engineer Corps. There they made a vital contribution to the war effort. After all, every soldier at the front line was supported by a large number, estimates range from ten to twenty, of soldiers behind the line who enabled him to do his job.

Manzanar was one of the camps where Japanese Americans were incarcerated during the war. SOURCE: National Archives and Records Administration

Dominicans in the Dutch town of Rijckholt welcome their liberators. SOURCE: NIOD/Beeldbank WO2

Exceptionally, there were some African American combat units that were generally led by white officers. Soldiers like the 'Tuskegee Airmen' of the 332nd Fighter Group, the 'Black Panthers' of the 761st Tank Battalion, and the 'Buffalo Soldiers' of the 92nd Infantry Division proved themselves in combat. Consequently, they gained fame both during and after the war.

African Americans were not the only ones to face discrimination. Out of fear of espionage, and due to racism, about 120,000 Americans of Japanese descent living along the U.S. West Coast were interned in camps in 1942, until in December 1944 the Supreme Court ruled that the incarceration was unconstitutional. It forced the Roosevelt administration to allow Japanese Americans to return to the West Coast, starting January 2.

Initially, it was neither possible for them to join the army. That changed in 1943. Eventually some 30,000 Americans of Japanese descent served in the U.S. armed forces, most of them in the 442nd Regimental Combat Team. This Japanese American unit became the most-decorated American unit of the war.

The liberation of Southern Limburg

After the liberation of Paris, the Allies rapidly pushed the battered German divisions even further back. Allied forces entered Belgium on September 2. They liberated the country in a relatively short time. So just ten days later, the men of the 30th 'Old Hickory' Infantry Division and the 2nd Armored Division 'Hell on Wheels' were ready to cross the Belgian-Dutch border. Both divisions were part of General Hodges' First Army, which fell under the command of Omar Bradley's 12th Army Group.

On September 12, 1944, the first American units crossed the Dutch border. They liberated the villages of Mesch, Noorbeek, and Mheer in the province of Limburg that day. The following day, Eijsden and Margraten were liberated, and one day later the 'Yanks' and their tanks had driven the enemy out of Maastricht, the first major Dutch city to be liberated. The Germans had blown up the bridges across the river Meuse, requiring the help of the engineers to construct pontoon bridges. When these were ready, the long columns of tanks, halftracks, and jeeps could cross the river on September 15. The Allied advance towards the so-called 'Mijnstreek,' the coal mining area around the city of Heerlen, and the Siegfried Line could continue.

Following the liberation of Maastricht, the front line moved to the nearby town of Valkenburg. German forces offered fierce resistance there, which made it difficult for the Americans to cross the river Geul. While the locals hid in the caves in and around Valkenburg, the Germans fired their machine guns, anti-tank guns, and artillery at the Americans who attempted to move up through the streets. Only after the American artillery had almost depleted their ammunition stock to shell the German artillery positions, the troops of the 30th Infantry Division and the supporting tank units were able to cross the river Geul on September 16. Although the Germans on the higher grounds tried to stop the Americans with mortar fire, the Yanks could continue their advance. A day later, the American tanks rolled into the Mijnstreek and liberated Heerlen.

On September 19, 1944, the front line halted beyond Sittard and Brunssum. Almost all of southern Limburg had been liberated by then. The Germans only still controlled Kerkrade and Vaals. The inhabitants of these two towns expected to be liberated imminently. However, both Kerkrade and Vaals are located along the border with Germany and the Siegfried Line. So, the Germans wanted to defend their positions there at any cost. The 30,000 inhabitants of Kerkrade initially stayed in the cellars of their homes, until the German commander ordered their evacuation on September 25. The German troops sent the town's residents in a long procession to liberated territory, right through the line of fire. After eleven days of fighting, the city finally fell into American hands on October 5, 1944. The inhabitants of Vaals had to wait another two weeks, until October 20.

EYEWITNESS ACCOUNT OF THE LIBERATION

'The day of liberation. Deo Gratias! From the direction of Spekholz, the liberators are coming closer and closer under heavy fire. It is a continuous rumble of machine gun fire and tank guns. The tension among the people has risen to the top. People are already standing with their flags ready, yearning to hold them out. Finally, at 4.30 p.m., the tanks of the liberators drive into Heerlen. Here on the Monseigneur Savelbergplein [a square in Heerlen] there was still resistance from machine gun nests, so the guns [probably from the American tanks] came into action again and some houses were hit hard. Immediately after the last resistance on the Monseigneur Savelbergplein was broken, people began celebrating the liberation – so spontaneous and so sudden that it is incomprehensible where everything came from so quickly. Everywhere flags, orange, party caps, sashes, and music. Dancing and hopping in crowded streets. Like bees around their queen, the people stood by or on the American tanks, so that the tanks could hardly be seen.'

Herman Klören
Excerpt from his diary written on September 17, 1944, the day his hometown Heerlen was liberated by the Americans.

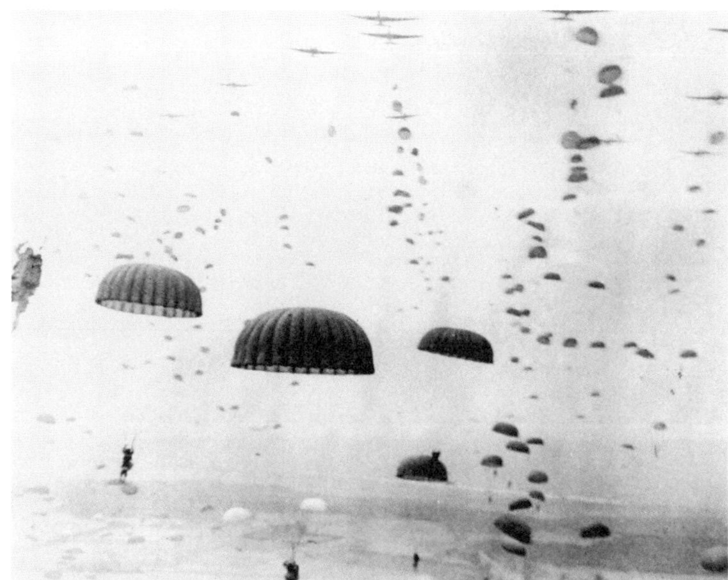

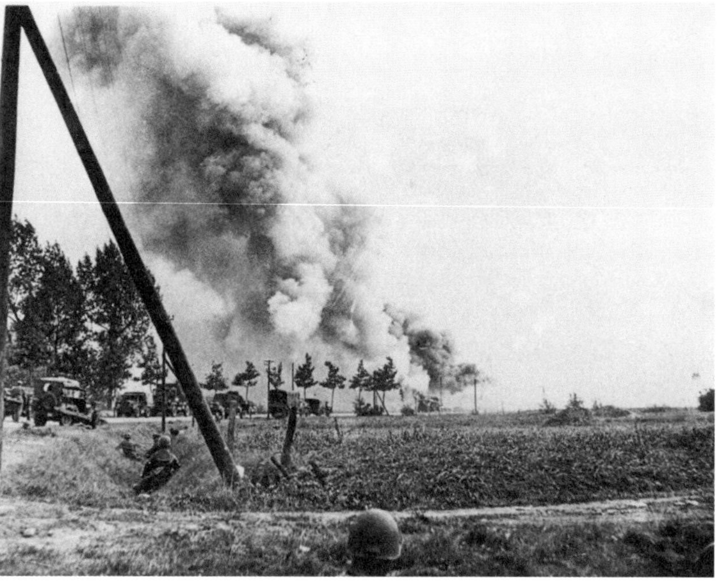

Operation Market Garden

While the liberation of South Limburg was still in full swing, Operation Market Garden began on September 17, 1944. Thousands of American and British paratroopers landed with parachutes and gliders near Eindhoven, Grave, Nijmegen, and Arnhem that day. These airborne troops had to conquer several vital bridges to ensure that tanks of the British army could quickly advance to the bridge over the Rhine in Arnhem. The plan was that the Allies, after crossing the river in Arnhem, would move into western Germany, circumventing the Siegfried Line, to firstly conquer the industrial Ruhr area and then launch a rapid assault towards Berlin. According to Field Marshal Montgomery, who devised the plan, Nazi Germany would be defeated before the end of 1944 – if the plan would succeed.

However, things did not go as planned and Operation Market Garden ended in failure. This was mainly because just 740 lightly armed British paratroopers were able to reach the northern part of the Arnhem bridge. They were able to hold the terrain around the northern ramp, but were isolated and under constant attack by well-armed Waffen SS troops supported by tanks and self-propelled guns. This forced the paratroopers to surrender after a few days of fierce fighting. Thanks to information passed on by the Dutch resistance and the decryption of German code messages, Allied intelligence knew that there were German armored units stationed in the vicinity of Arnhem, but the quality of these units had been underestimated or even downplayed by the generals involved.

Allied paratroopers descend over the Netherlands during Operation Market Garden, September 1944. SOURCE: National Archives and Records Administration

Heavy fighting along Hell's Highway between Son and Eindhoven delayed the advance of the ground forces. SOURCE: NIOD/Beeldbank WO2

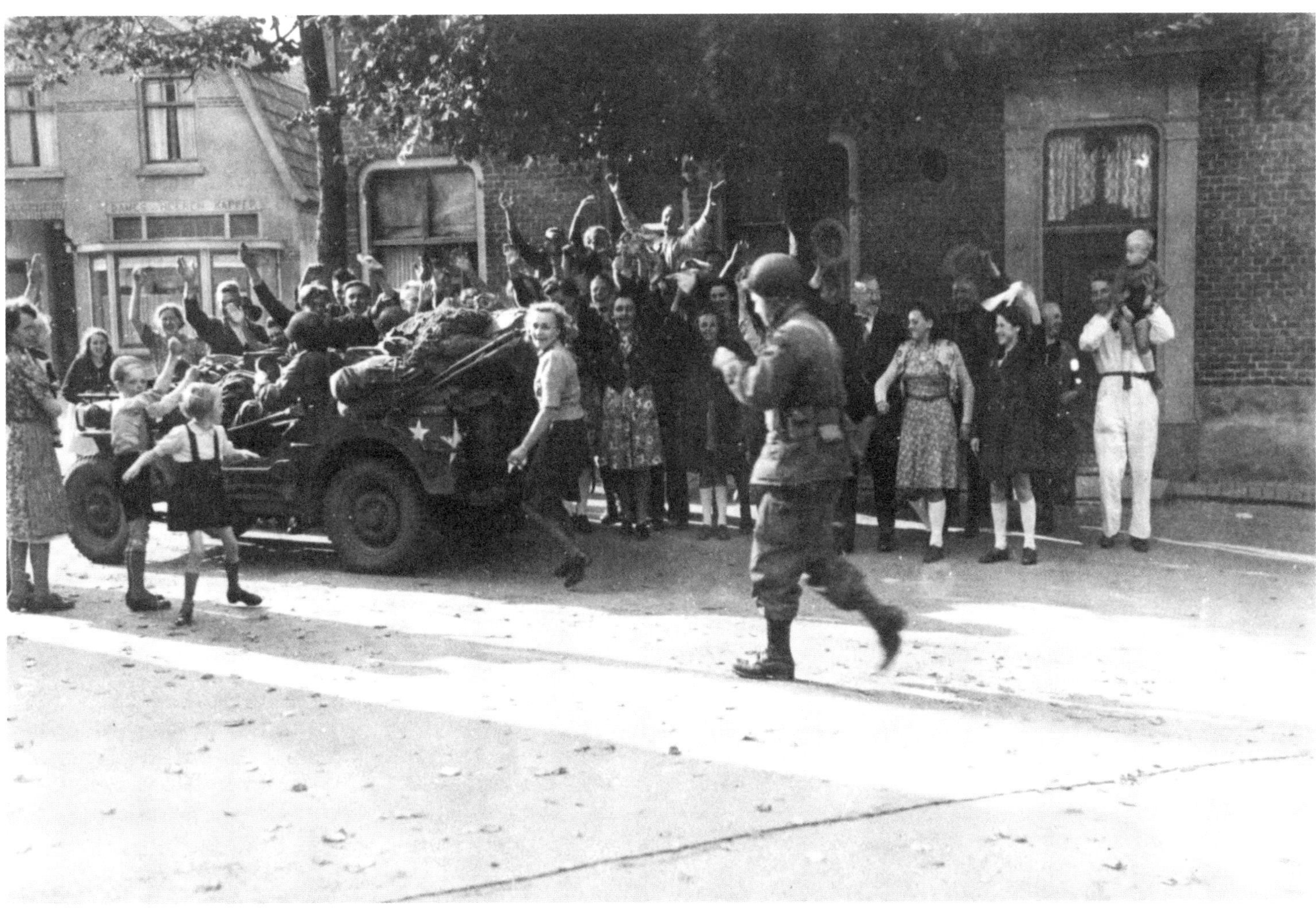

> **EYEWITNESS ACCOUNT OF OPERATION MARKET GARDEN**
> **'A beautiful day. Amazing sight – planes could be seen forward and backward as far as the eye could see. The front of the air column was over Holland while the rear was over England.'**
>
> ***Robert E. Jones***
> ***101st Airborne Division.***

Simultaneously, the advance on the ground did not go according to plan either. Fierce German opposition repeatedly delayed and stopped the British tanks and ground troops that were given the task to relieve the British airborne troops at the bridge in Arnhem, whose mission it was to capture that crucial bridge and then hold it for three days. Over and over again, German units blocked the route the British column had to take or fired their anti-tank weapons from the woods on either side of the road. As the British tanks continued to run into German ambushes time and again, the narrow two-lane road towards Eindhoven, Grave, and Nijmegen was soon called 'Hell's Highway' by the American paratroopers who had to clear and defend the route. The advance on this doomed road could only be continued when the paratroopers and British infantrymen, supported by fighter-bombers, had eliminated the German soldiers and when the destroyed tanks, as well as other vehicles, no longer blocked the road.

American airborne troops in Groesbeek just after landing. Locals welcome their liberators. SOURCE: Vrijheidsmuseum/Beeldbank WO2

These, however, were not the only setbacks. Near the village of Son everything went differently than planned as well. Here paratroopers of the 101st Airborne Division had to capture the bridge across the Wilhelmina Canal, which was the first major bridge the British tanks had to cross during their advance towards Nijmegen and Arnhem. Following their landing, some paratroopers closed in on the bridge, but just as they approached it, the Germans blew it up. As a result, a Bailey bridge had to be built across the canal by engineer troops. The British column could not continue until this construction was completed. The new bridge became operational in the early morning of September 19.

In addition to the troublesome advance on 'Hell's Highway' and the setback in Son, the Allies did not succeed in capturing the two important bridges across the river Waal in Nijmegen until September 20, due to fierce German opposition. This further delayed the advance of the British XXX Corps. The capture of the vital Waal bridges finally succeeded after American paratroopers of the 82nd Airborne Division had crossed the Waal under German fire in rickety canvas boats west of the bridges, after which both bridges could be attacked from two sides simultaneously with support of other paratrooper companies and British tanks.

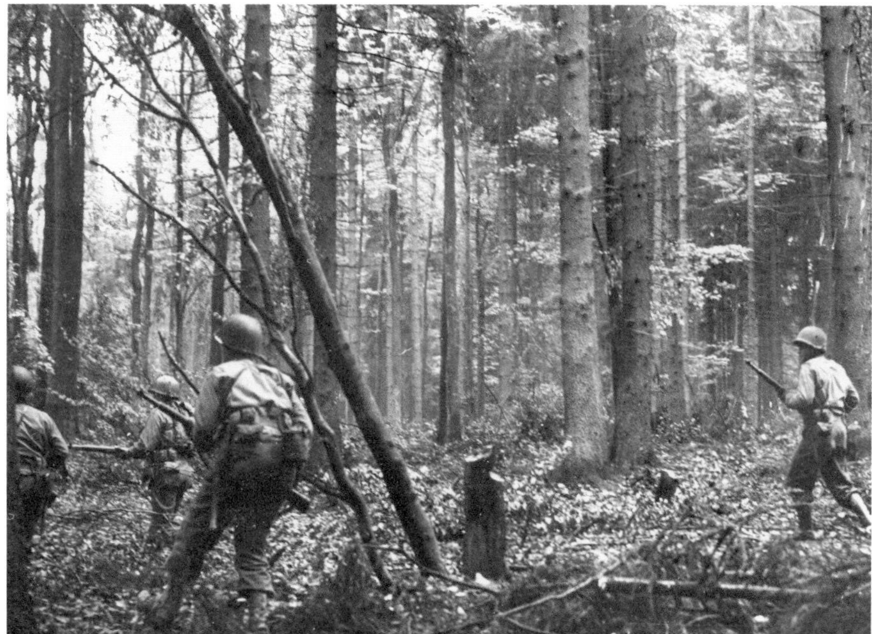

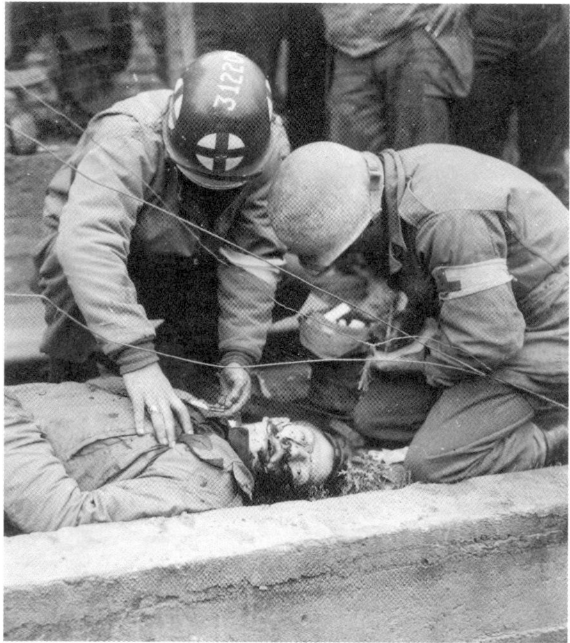

American soldiers advance in the Hürtgen Forest. SOURCE: National Archives and Records Administration

Medics document the identity of a soldier killed by German gunfire.
SOURCE: National Archives and Records Administration

In the early evening, four British tanks drove across the road bridge. On the north side, two of them were knocked out, but the other two were able to continue until they were stopped by German fire in the darkness near Lent. This gave the Germans time to organize a strong line of defense between Arnhem and Nijmegen. Here the advance of the British tanks was finally halted by heavy German fire the next day. Therefore, the isolated British paratroopers near the northern ramp of the bridge in Arnhem could not be relieved. This resulted in their surrender, because due to lack of ammunition, water and food, and too many dead and wounded, they could not resist the continuous German pressure any longer. When the British airborne troops in Arnhem marched into German captivity, the decisive Battle of Arnhem was definitively lost.

Because Operation Market Garden had failed and Arnhem had proven to be 'a bridge too far,' the Allied advance came to a standstill between the Waal and the Rhine. Therefore, only the south of the Netherlands could be largely liberated in the fall of 1944.

EYEWITNESS ACCOUNT OF THE FAMOUS WAAL CROSSING IN NIJMEGEN

'When we were a third of the way across the Waal, the river suddenly exploded. As the Krauts [German soldiers] unleashed their full firepower, the surface of the water looked like it was in the middle of a sudden rainstorm, the sky actually hailing bullets. They kicked up little spouts of water everywhere. Men began to slump forward in their boats. Some screamed, but most went silently. Paddles and rifles fell overboard and spun away in the dark water. One, two, and then three boats sustained direct hits from mortar shells and disintegrated in a burst of flame, with bodies cast in all directions. The men began to paddle desperately and zig-zagged the boats across the water, not to avoid enemy fire but because their strokes were no longer coordinated. (...) As we approached the north bank of the river, I looked across the 900-yard plain between us and the dike. The grass was bristling with machine guns, and the only way to reach our objective was to charge straight into them. Not a happy prospect, but we had no other choice.'

T. Moffatt Burriss
82nd Airborne Division.

Meanwhile, General Dwight D. Eisenhower, Supreme Commander of the Allied Expeditionary Force in Europe, decided that the American and British troops should advance eastward along a broad front into Germany in order to cross both the Roer and the Rhine. However, the Allies first had to fight their way through the Siegfried Line (Westwall). This was a 390-mile-long defensive line consisting of bunkers, numerous machine gun nests, minefields, and concrete 'dragon's teeth.' Hitler had ordered the construction of this line in the 1930s to protect the western border of the Third Reich.

Battle of Overloon

As a part of the eastward offensive, the Allied commanders planned an attack on the bridges across the river Meuse near Venlo, the Netherlands. From there, they believed they could invade the German Ruhr area. However, the Germans were determined to prevent an Allied breakthrough to their most important industrial region at all costs. Therefore, they had already begun establishing a strong line of defenses on the west bank of the Meuse River near Venlo in September 1944. Moreover, only one single road led to these vital bridges. This road went through the villages of Overloon and Venray. The terrain on both sides of the road was not very suitable for tanks, because of the forests, the swampy meadows, and the many streams. Nevertheless, the U.S. 7th Armored Division launched its attack on September 30, 1944.

The advance towards Overloon proved to be very difficult, not in the last place because of the muddy terrain and German mines. The Americans suffered considerable losses. The Germans had built strong positions in the woods around Overloon. From these woods, the German soldiers raked the slowly advancing American tanks and infantry with heavy fire from machine guns, Panzerfausts, 88mm guns, Nebelwerfers, and a few well-camouflaged tanks. The Americans kept trying, but they did not succeed in driving the Germans out of the woods near Overloon. In the process, they lost dozens of tanks and many infantrymen.

Two British divisions relieved the battered 7th Armored Division in the night of October 7 to 8. After overwhelming artillery barrages, air strikes and bloody fighting, these troops were finally able to liberate Overloon on October 14. Four days later, they could also liberate Venray. The Germans, however, entrenched themselves on the western bank of the Meuse and held control over the bridges. Therefore, the Allies could not penetrate into the vital German Ruhr area until the spring of 1945.

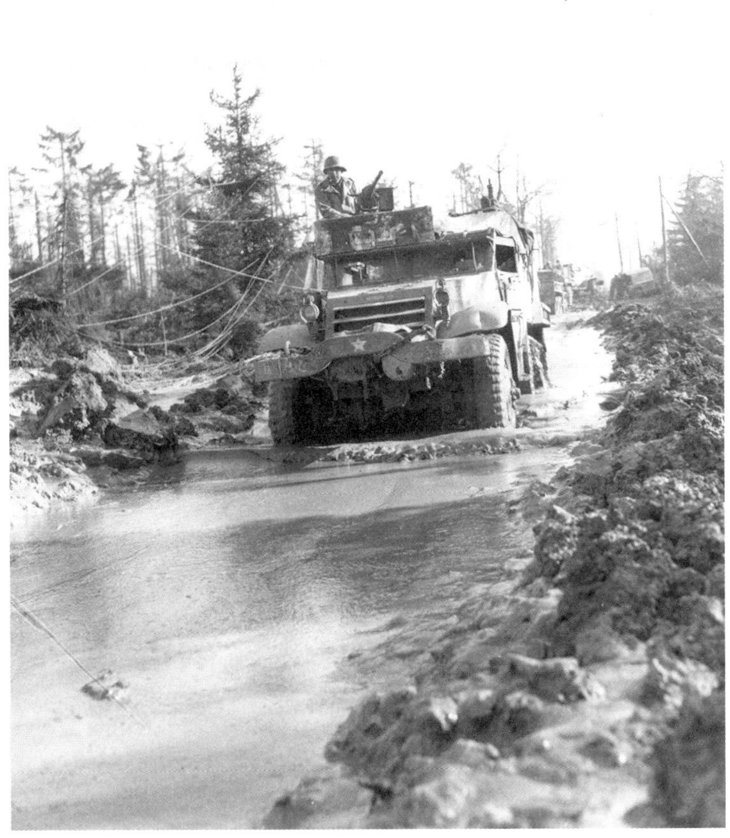

The roads in the Hürtgen Forest were difficult to navigate, which strongly affected the fighting in the area. SOURCE: National Archives and Records Administration

Hell of the Hürtgen Forest

Further south, American troops had crossed Germany's western border near Trier and Aachen in mid-September 1944 to attack the Siegfried Line in this sector as well. To this end, American troops entered the Hürtgen Forest, a hilly and dense forest at the northern edge of the Eifel, southeast of Aachen. The Americans had to fight their way through this forest to be able to reach the Roer. They had to cross this river in order to advance towards the Rhine and the heart of Hitler's Third Reich. Allied generals felt that circumventing the Hürtgen Forest was not an option, because the Germans might otherwise use it as a base from which to launch flanking attacks.

The battle of the Hürtgen Forest became the longest battle the U.S. Army has ever fought, and at the beginning of it, the American troops had no idea of the horrors that awaited them in this forest. The Germans had constructed many trenches and machine gun bunkers in the dense woods. These served as outposts of the Siegfried Line. Additionally, the Germans had zeroed-in their artillery at the forest. To make matters even worse, they had laid millions of mines and the dense woods were a natural obstacle in themselves. The Germans were thus able to defend their fortified positions for a long time, which was also important to them because many units would be assembling in the Eifel region for their upcoming winter offensive in the Ardennes. These units would otherwise have been vulnerable to a flank attack.

During the previous months, tanks had been the spearhead of the American advance, but this would prove to be impossible in the Hürtgen Forest as tanks could hardly move because of the mud, and the Germans had mined the narrow paths that led through the woods. Moreover, the tanks on the so-called 'Kall Trail' – the most important path – were like sitting ducks that were constantly fired upon by the German artillery and German soldiers armed with Panzerfausts and anti-tank guns, who could hide anywhere in the woods. It forced the American soldiers to storm the many German trenches and pillboxes with bayonets fixed on their rifles, often without tank support. While doing so, German machine gun fire mercilessly mowed down many Americans. When the American infantrymen did manage to penetrate the German trenches, they had to engage in ruthless hand-to-hand combat with the German troops.

In addition, German mortar and artillery fire turned the trees in the forest themselves into lethal weapons. The detonators of German rounds had been set extremely sensitive, often causing them to explode in the treetops, rather than when hitting the ground. Many Americans were killed or seriously wounded by shrapnel and razor-sharp wooden splinters from the trees that rained down on them. The foxholes that the soldiers dug offered little protection against this. Especially because of the lethal tree bursts, the risk to lose your life was always imminent in the Hürtgen Forest.

Meanwhile, the Americans tried several times to capture Schmidt. South of this small town is the Roer reservoir. The Schwammenauel dam regulates the water level in both the reservoir and the river. The Americans feared that the Germans would blow up the dam, which would lead to the Roer River flooding most of the valley and thus causing delay to any operations there. The first two attacks, in October and November 1944, were repelled by the Germans with a murderous hail of machine gun fire, artillery shells, and mortars, forcing the American soldiers to withdraw into the woods. Then, in mid-December, the Battle of the Bulge temporarily put a halt to the fighting in the Hürtgen Forest.

After the Battle of the Bulge had resulted in a German retreat, the fighting in the Hürtgen Forest once more intensified. Again, the Germans offered fierce resistance, but after engineers had cleared alternative paths through the forest, and a significant number of tanks, tank destroyers, and self-propelled guns were able to support the attacks, the Americans finally succeeded in chasing the Germans out of Schmidt in February 1945.

Nevertheless, because the Germans had sabotaged and opened the sluices of the Schwammenauel dam, a tidal wave flooded large parts of the Roer valley. This delayed the Allied advance for another two weeks. Then, with air and artillery support, the Americans were able to cross the Roer during Operation Grenade and continue their advance towards the Rhine. The victory in the relatively unknown but bloody battle of the Hürtgen Forest had cost the American armed forces an estimated 33,000 dead and wounded.

> **EYEWITNESS ACCOUNT OF THE BATTLE OF THE HÜRTGEN FOREST**
> **'The forest was a helluva eerie place to fight. You can't get protection. You can't see. You can't get fields of fire. Artillery slashes the trees like a scythe. Everything is tangled. You can scarcely walk. Everybody is cold and wet, and the mixture of cold rain and sleet keeps falling. They jump off again, and soon there is only a handful of the old men left.'**
>
> ***George Morgan***
> ***4th Infantry Division.***

Breaking through the Siegfried Line

Simultaneously with the bloody battle in the Hürtgen Forest, the Allies also attacked the Siegfried Line in other places during the autumn of 1944. Heavy bombardments and devastating artillery fire wore out the Germans defending the line in many places to such an extent that American infantry troops, with the help of flamethrowers and support from tanks, tank destroyers, and self-propelled guns, were able to neutralize the German bunkers and other positions in the line. Having broken through the Siegfried Line, they could now advance towards the Roer and Rhine rivers.

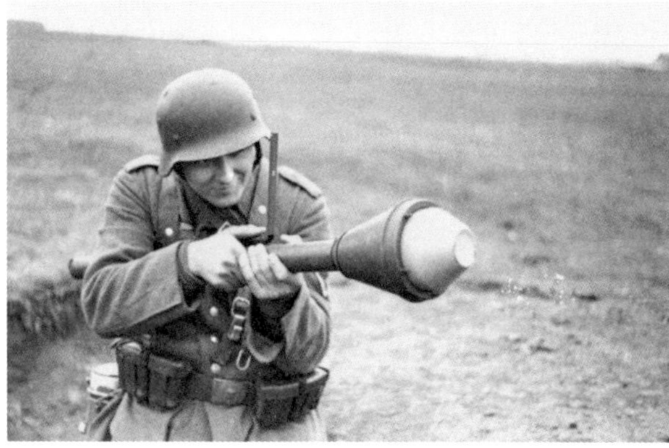

A German soldier with a Panzerfaust, which was very effective against enemy tanks from a short distance. SOURCE: Bundesarchiv, Bild 101I-710-0371-20 / Gronefeld, Gerhard / CC-BY-SA 3.0

Operation Clipper

While several parts of the Siegfried Line had already been penetrated by the Allies, a dangerous salient arose around the city of Geilenkirchen that posed a threat to the boundaries of both the British Second and the Ninth U.S. Armies. The reduction of this salient – a cornerstone stronghold in one of the strongest sections of the Siegfried Line – was necessary in order to gain control of the Roer valley. To this end, the Allies launched a joint British-American offensive called 'Operation Clipper.' Despite the miserable weather, American infantry, supported by Sherman tanks, flamethrower tanks, and flail tanks of the British, began their joint attack towards Geilenkirchen on November 18.

Geilenkirchen was taken the following day, but the capture of this city did not mean that German resistance in this part of the Roer valley collapsed. Beyond Geilenkirchen, the German defenders occupied a line of concrete pillboxes supported by artillery situated on a strategic ridge along the river Wurm, a tributary of the Roer, near the villages of Prummern, Süggerath, Beeck, and Müllendorf. So, when the American GIs attempted to advance towards these lines of defenses, the Germans started to rake them with machine gun fire, mortar rounds, and artillery shells, inflicting many casualties among the Americans. From within their pillboxes on the ridge, the German machine gunners and artillery observers had an excellent view on their exposed enemies in the open fields, whose attacks were badly hampered by the persistent rain and mud. To make matters worse, the British tanks could hardly support the attacks at first because their efforts were also hampered by the mud and because the Germans had mined all the roads. Only when engineers had cleared the mines and the British flamethrower tanks had slogged through the mud to be able to target the pillboxes, the German machine guns were silenced and the advance towards the Roer could be continued.

> **EYEWITNESS ACCOUNT ABOUT OPERATION CLIPPER**
> **'The concentration of German firepower was absolutely overwhelming with its violence, surprise, and intensity. Artillery fire, 88s and 75s from hidden tanks, and 120[mm] mortars with apparently limitless supplies of ammunition hit us. Machine gun fire whipping in from pillboxes seemed almost an afterthought. The noise, the shock, the sensation of total helplessness and bewilderment, the loss of control, the sudden loss of every familiar assumption – nothing in civilian life or training offered an experience remotely comparable... Our new-boy illusions of the past two days dissolved in a moment.'**
>
> ***Harold Leinbaugh and John Campbell***
> ***84th Infantry Division.***

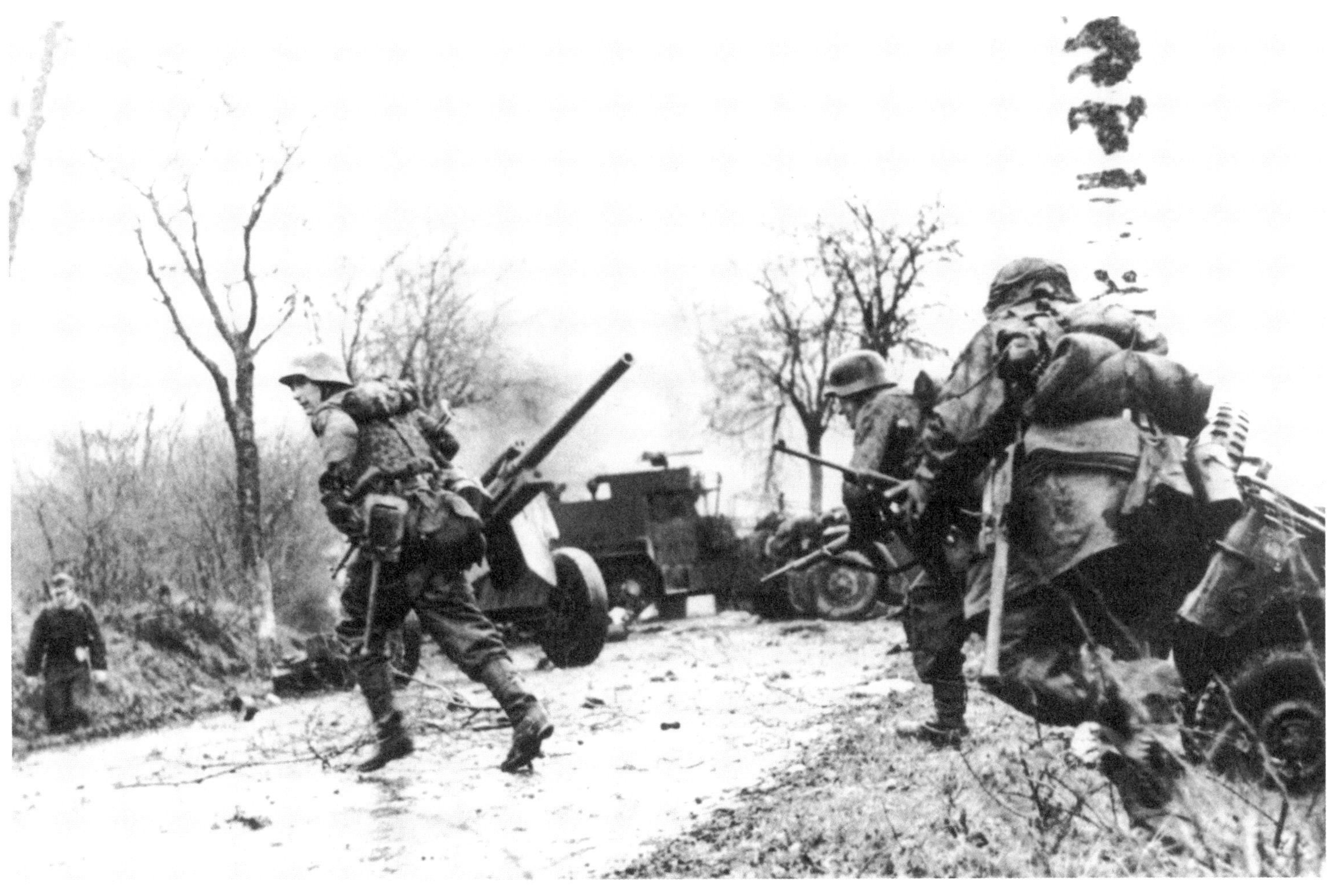

Not going down without a fight

With Allied troops having crossed Germany's western border and the Red Army of the Soviet Union rapidly approaching from the east, it became increasingly clear that the German defeat was only a matter of time. Nevertheless, Hitler ordered that every German who could handle a weapon should help defend the fatherland. Older men of the so-called Volkssturm and young Hitlerjugend-boys were sent to the front lines, often equipped with outdated rifles and Panzerfausts. Both these combatants and the regular German soldiers were ordered to resist until the last man, but they often realized that Germany's situation was getting only more dire every day.

However, the American troops of the First, Third, Seventh and Ninth Armies that had entered Germany soon experienced that their German opponents would not surrender without putting up a fight. The German defenders hid in houses with rifles, machine guns, and Panzerfausts and surprised their American counterparts with well-concealed anti-tank guns and tanks. The Americans, on the other hand, used tanks, tank destroyers, self-propelled guns, and Bazookas to knock out these threats to both their tank crews and the infantrymen. The soldiers often had to engage in house-to-house combat to clear the buildings, throwing in hand grenades and firing their rifles and sub-machine guns to eliminate those who were resisting until the bitter end. Out on the streets of the German towns and cities, or what was left thereof, the soldiers were vulnerable to sniper fire, which would cause many casualties until the very end of the war.

The refusal of the Germans to surrender was clearly demonstrated in the city of Aachen and near Geilenkirchen. The battle of Aachen exemplified the German determination. Only after three weeks of fighting, the German forces defending the city surrendered. Likewise, German armored units counterattacked south of Geilenkirchen, near Puffendorf, in mid-November 1944. The Sherman tanks of the 2nd Armored Division were no match for the German Tiger and Panther tanks during this tank battle, and many were lost.

EYEWITNESS ACCOUNT ABOUT COMBATTING GERMAN TANKS
'The higher muzzle velocity of the German tanks enables them to far outrange our Sherman tanks. I have seen them knock our tanks out at ranges up to 1,000 yards and know of no incident where a Sherman tank has knocked out a Mark V [Panther] or Mark VI [Tiger] at more than 300 yards.'

Captain Henry W. Johnson
2nd Armored Division.
Killed in action on April 17, 1945 and buried at Margraten.

German soldiers advancing during the Battle of the Bulge. SOURCE: National Archives and Records Administration

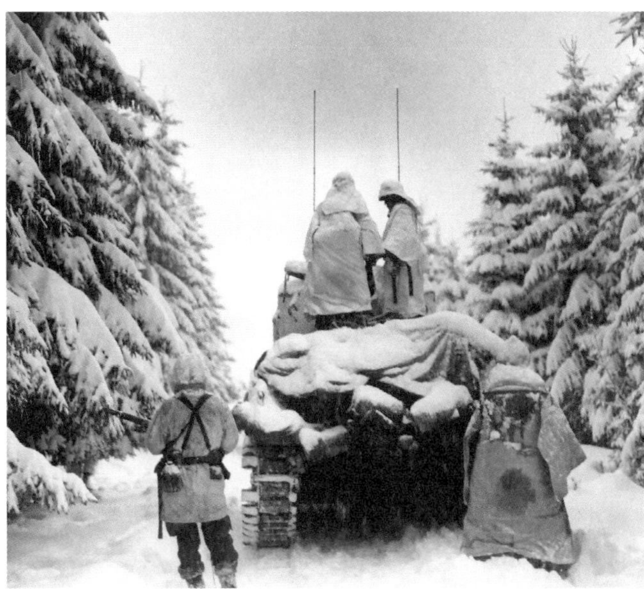

Weather conditions were severe during the Battle of the Bulge. SOURCE: U.S. Army/Wikipedia

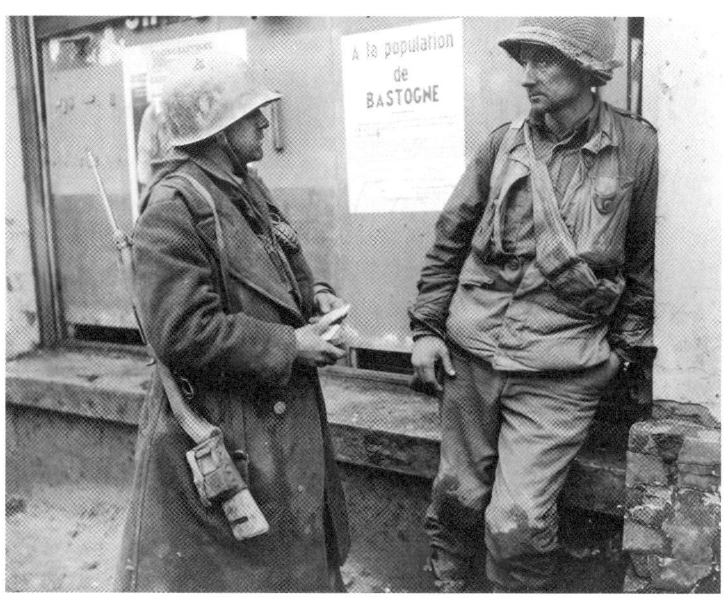

Two American soldiers in the encircled city of Bastogne. SOURCE: National Archives and Records Administration

The Battle of the Bulge

At the dawn of winter in December 1944, when the Allied advance had come to a halt near the Roer and the Saar rivers, many Allied commanders thought that the victory over Germany was only a matter of time. The German army had been considerably weakened since D-Day. The German forces, the senior Allied commanders believed, would only be capable of desperately trying to postpone the obvious outcome of the war.

However, whereas some had hoped that the war would be over by Christmas 1944, the American troops in the Ardennes were taken by surprise by a large-scale German counteroffensive: Unternehmen Wacht am Rhein, which was launched on December 16. The purpose of this counteroffensive, devised by Hitler himself, was to cut off Allied supply lines and separate the British and American armies from each other by means of an armored assault towards the port of Antwerp. Hitler thought that he could still turn the tide in Western Europe if his troops were able to recapture this major port. In fact, he even believed that the German troops could ultimately destroy the Allied armies one by one.

Initially, the German counterattack in the woods of the Ardennes was successful. They benefitted from the bad weather, which prevented the Allies from exploiting their superiority in the air against the German armored columns. The Americans in the Ardennes were overwhelmed and simply did not have enough men, artillery and tanks to stop the German armored forces. The Americans considered the Ardennes as being rather unsuitable for military operations and the deployment of Germany's heavy tanks. Therefore, they used the Ardennes as a rest area for units that had just come out of the Hürtgen Forest and which were in urgent need of recuperation and replenishment. Additionally, several units that had only just arrived in Europe were stationed here to gain some front line experience. As a result, the German forces fairly quickly broke through the American lines, taking many American soldiers prisoner along the way. The German tanks and infantry created a deep bulge in the Allied lines, which is why the Americans soon would call the offensive the 'Battle of the Bulge.'

During the first days of the German offensive, the situation looked extremely dire for the Americans. Yet the German offensive in the Ardennes ultimately failed. This was partly due to the fact that there was not enough fuel available for the heavy German tanks from the very beginning. Therefore, the German troops had to capture Allied fuel depots, but because American units set fire to some of these, the advancing German columns, with a few exceptions, did not succeed.

The main reason for the failure of Hitler's offensive, however, was the fact that the Germans were unable to capture the crucially important town of Bastogne, where all seven main roads through the woods of the Ardennes came together. The paratroopers of the 101st Airborne Division, who had been rushed to the town in trucks, found themselves surrounded, but managed to repel the attacks of the German infantry and tanks time and again. With their anti-tank guns, Bazookas, and machine guns – and thanks to the support of artillery units, tanks, and tank destroyers – the paratroopers held their ground. On December 26 (Boxing Day), after several days of bitter fighting, General Patton's tanks managed to penetrate the bulge and break through to Bastogne. Now the encirclement had been broken, a corridor was established to get much-needed supplies to the defenders of Bastogne. With the help of reinforcements and a growing number of tanks, the exhausted paratroopers ultimately managed to push back the German troops.

Bastogne was not the only place where the German armored forces experienced setbacks. Fierce American opposition in crucial towns like St. Vith had repeatedly slowed down the German advance. Moreover, several bridges were blown up in time. As a result, the advancing German forces had to make detours in order to reach the Meuse River (which they had to cross to be able to continue their advance towards Antwerp). However, they would never make it to this river. About a week after the start of the offensive, the advance of the German tanks came to a halt just east of the Meuse River because of a lack of fuel. American and British troops also started to attack the bulge from all sides.

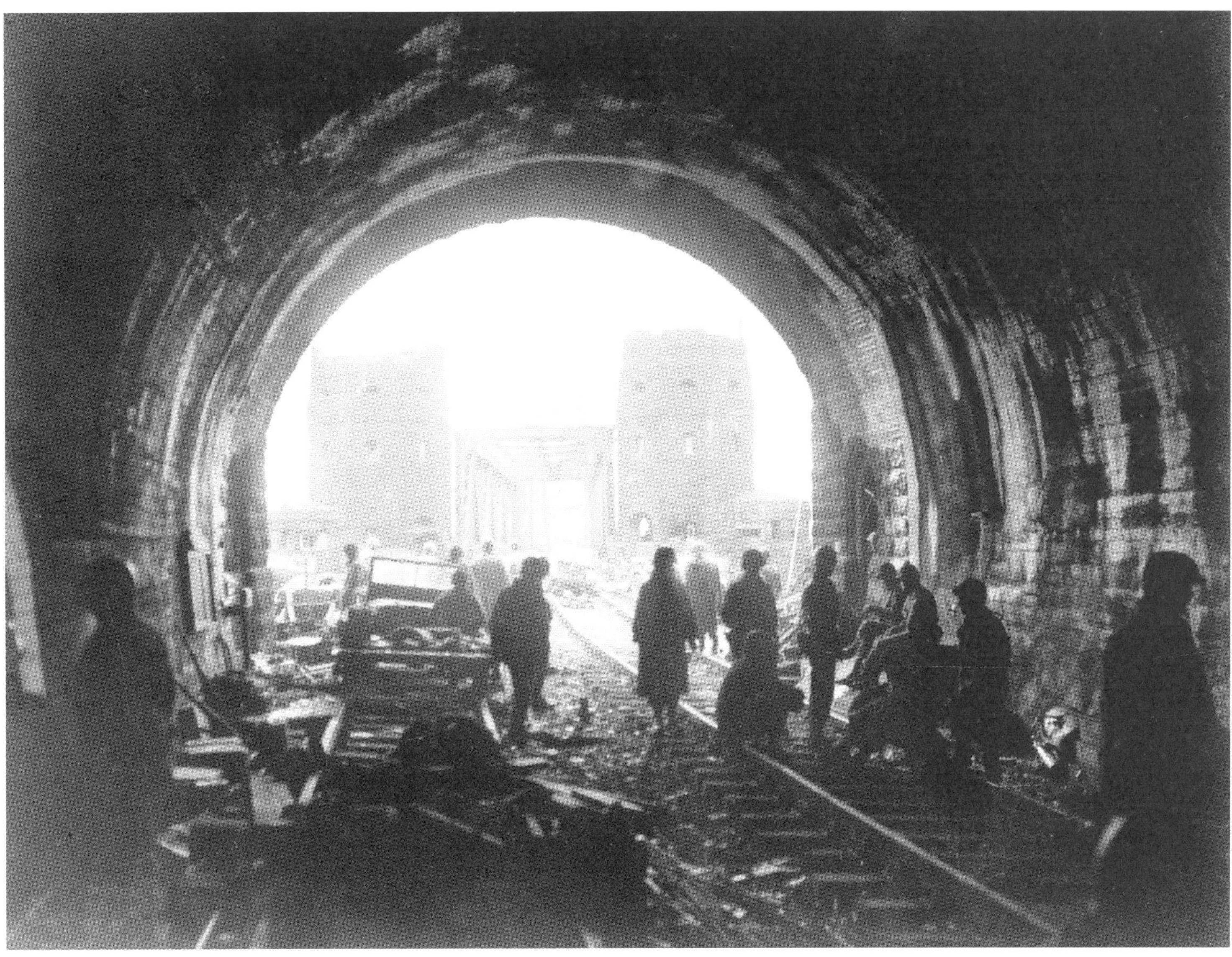

To make matters worse for the Germans, the weather had cleared on December 23. As the fog and low-hanging clouds dissipated, Allied transport planes were able to drop crucial supplies near Bastogne, and the USAAF could finally deploy its dreaded fighter-bombers against the German troops and armor in the snowy Ardennes. As a result, about a month after Hitler had launched the offensive, the retreating Germans had been forced back to the lines from which they had begun their attacks. The Americans had suffered about 80,000 casualties, of whom more than 19,000 had been killed. About 25,000 were missing or had been captured. On the German side the number of dead and wounded was even somewhat higher.

The bridge at Remagen. SOURCE: National Archives and Records Administration

EYEWITNESS ACCOUNT OF THE SIEGE OF BASTOGNE

'Machine gun bullets crackled past my head. Then I heard the roar of a big engine. I glanced over my shoulder and caught a glimpse of a Tiger tank lurching forward like some prehistoric monster intent on catching me. I made it to the road and ran straight down its center with every ounce of strength and speed I could muster. The Tiger was only a couple of hundred yards or so behind and gaining. I didn't try to zigzag; I just wanted to put as much distance as I could between that metal monster and myself and make it to the safety of one of the houses in town [Noville, north of Bastogne]. Bursts of machine gun bullets lanced past me, splattering the pavement around and ahead of me before whining off in different directions. I could see sparks fly where the bullets struck the pavement to my front. Glancing over my shoulder and seeing the muzzle of the big 88mm gun pointed straight at me sent a feeling churning through the pit of my stomach that is impossible to describe. Goose bumps rose on my arms, and I could feel the hair crawling on the nape of my neck.'

Donald R. Burgett
Paratrooper of the 101st Airborne Division.

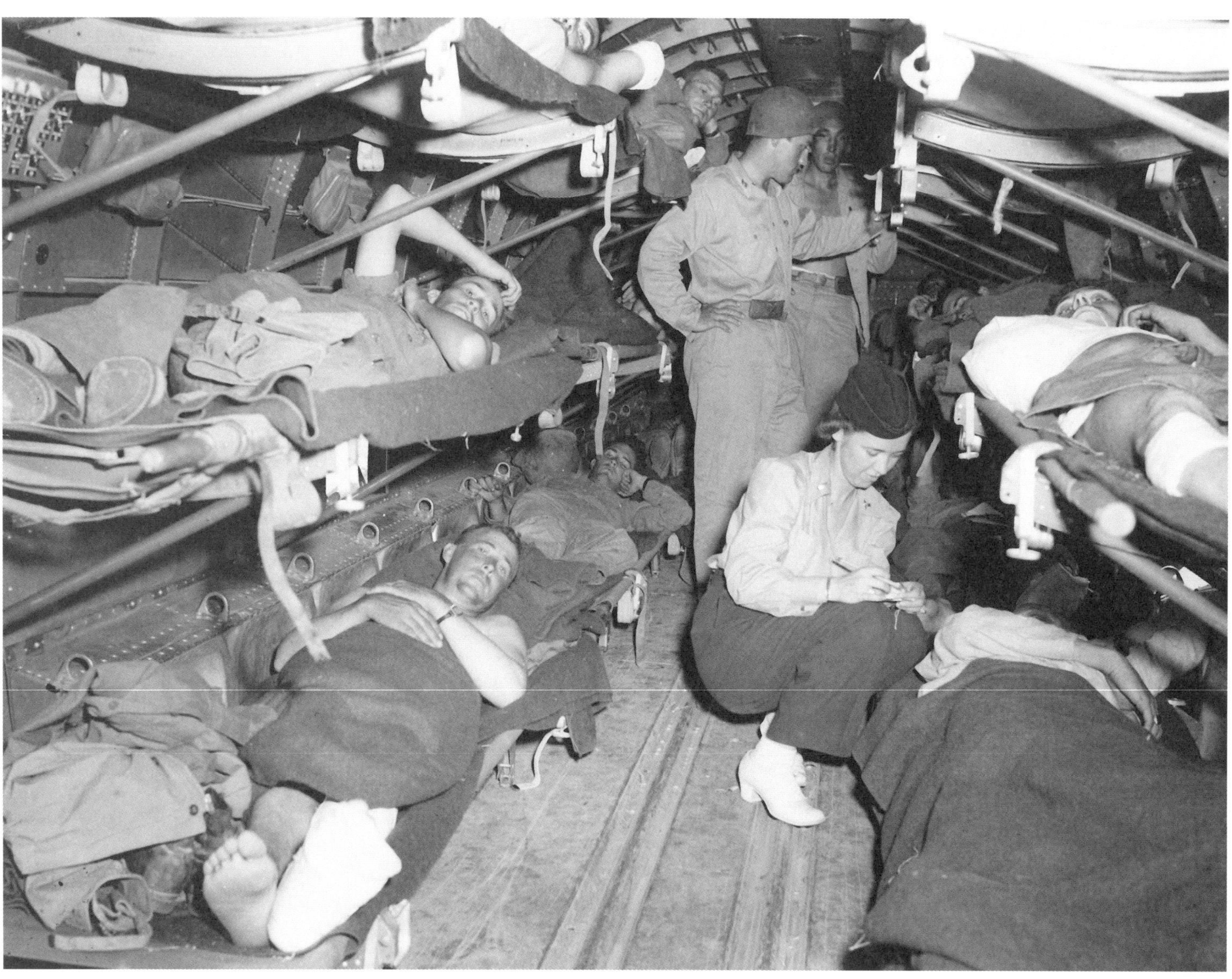

Crossing the Rhine

In the early spring of 1945, the Allied advance in western Germany finally reached the crucial Rhine River. On March 7, 1945, a group of soldiers and tanks from the First U.S. Army found the Ludendorff bridge near the town of Remagen still intact. This was the only bridge over the Rhine in Germany that had not been blown up, despite the fact that Hitler had ordered the destruction of all bridges.

While American tanks fired at the German soldiers in the bridge towers from the riverbank, American infantry soldiers fought their way across the bridge while being subjected to heavy enemy fire. When they succeeded in reaching the other side, the soldiers eliminated the German machine gunners and snipers in the bridge towers with their rifles, submachine guns and hand grenades. Moments later, the Americans were in full control of the Ludendorff bridge. Shortly after midnight, the first American tanks crossed the Rhine. Soon thereafter, more troops and tanks of the U.S. Army crossed the Rhine at Remagen and a strong bridgehead was established.

EYEWITNESS ACCOUNT OF THE CAPTURE OF THE LUDENDORFF BRIDGE

'While we were running across the bridge – and, man, it may have been only 250 yards but it seemed like 250 miles to us – I spotted this lieutenant [John W. Mitchell], standing out there completely exposed to the machine gun fire that was pretty heavy by this time. He was cutting wires and kicking the German demolition charges off the bridge with his feet! Boy that took plenty of guts. He's the one who saved the bridge and made the whole thing possible – the kinda guy I'd like to know.'

Alexander A. Drabik
9th Armored Division. He was the first one to reach the other side of the Ludendorff bridge.

American wounded are being evacuated by plane.

SOURCE: U.S. Army Air Force/National Museum of the United States Air Force

Two weeks later, in the night of March 22 to 23, 1945, the troops of General Patton's Third Army also crossed the Rhine at Oppenheim. Infantry troops in landing craft, assault boats, and amphibious vehicles crossed first, then the 'swimming' DD tanks (which had also been used on D-Day), followed by regular tanks on rafts. Then the engineers built several pontoon bridges.

Patton's crossing was followed by a crossing of Montgomery's British 21st Army Group, which included the Ninth U.S. Army. His operation to cross the Rhine near Wesel and Rees began late on March 23. To support this crossing, the British 6th Airborne Division and the U.S. 17th Airborne Division were dropped behind the German lines east of the Rhine near Hamminkeln and Wesel. This large-scale airborne operation was conducted on March 24 and has become known as Operation Varsity. The airborne troops had to occupy the higher grounds overlooking the river. Additionally, they had the task to eliminate the German artillery that could pose a threat to the troops crossing the Rhine and the bridgehead that would be established. While the operation was successful, both divisions lost about fifteen percent of their strength on just one single day.

The U.S. Army Nurse Corps

While the U.S. armed forces were mainly made up of men during World War II, thousands of American women also served their country, both in Europe and the Pacific. Many of them were working as nurses. By the end of the war the U.S. armed forces alone employed no less than 59,000 nurses. They took care of the enormous numbers of wounded that were brought into field hospitals, military hospitals, and hospital ships.

In order to be able to transfer seriously injured soldiers with life-threatening injuries to specialized military hospitals more quickly, so-called 'flight nurses' were trained from 1942 onwards. These nurses had been trained to carry out evacuation flights. Most of the aircraft used for such flights were C-47s. Because these planes were also used to transport military supplies and to drop paratroopers, international war regulations did not allow red crosses to be painted on them. The flight nurses, therefore, were always at risk of being shot down by enemy anti-aircraft fire or fighter planes.

> **EYEWITNESS ACCOUNT OF A FLIGHT NURSE**
> **'Was sleeping quite soundly in the back of our hospital plane until suddenly awakened by terrific sounds of guns and cracklings of the plane as if it had gone into bits. For a few moments I hardly knew what to think. Can assure anyone a more than startled expression and sensation. Suddenly looked at my Surgical Tech opposite me with blood flowing from his left leg. The noise by this time seemed to be much worse. But to see the left engine blazing away is simply more than I can express. But never thought I would land on the ground in one piece. My prayers were used and quick.'**
>
> *Reba Z. Whittle*
> ***Flight nurse whose C-47 was shot down during an air evacuation flight on September 27, 1944. She survived the hard landing and was captured by the Germans.***

The approximately 500 brave flight nurses of the U.S. Army Air Forces evacuated more than 1,176,000 wounded and sick soldiers worldwide during the war. Thanks to the excellent care provided by the flight nurses, only 46 of the wounded succumbed to their injuries during the evacuation flights. Seventeen of these dedicated nurses did not survive the war.

Besides the women who served as nurses, there were the so-called 'Rosie the Riveters', the hundreds of thousands of American women who were recruited for the industrial labor force to replace the male workers who had joined the military. These female workers were employed in U.S. factories to manufacture, for example, bombers, arms, and ammunition. Therefore, they were crucial to the U.S. war effort.

Longing for home

As the Allies advanced further and further into Germany, they knew that the war would not go on for much longer – the final victory was within reach. For the soldiers, this intensified their longing for home and for the end of the hostilities. Most soldiers had been away from home for months or even years and missed their loved ones. Great was the comfort and joy when they received a heart-warming letter or package from home. The letter below exemplifies a soldier's feelings of both joy and homesickness:

> **SOMEWHERE IN GERMANY**
>
> **'My darling beloved wife,**
>
> **I am very happy to say that I received five letters from you and I was so very happy to hear from you. I feel so bad dear that you are not receiving my mail. I sure hope you have received some by now. I received the letter you wrote on Donna's birthday. I sure was thinking of her on her birthday.**
>
> **I love you both and miss you so very much. I sure hope this all ends soon. I will be so glad when I can come home to you. See dear won't it be well when we can live a normal life again. I won't mind working for you and my Donna.**
>
> **Well dearest I must sign off for now. Kiss Donna for me darling. Good bye for now little girl of my dreams. I love you my darling wife. All my love. Your Bill.'**
>
> *William G. Aubut*
> ***Sergeant in the 30th Infantry Division.***
> ***Excerpts from his last letter, written to his wife Doris and his daughter Donna, who had just turned three years old. William wrote this letter on February 22, 1945, the day before he was to be killed in action. He rests in peace in Margraten.***

Despite the fact that most American soldiers longed for a return to a normal life on the other side of the ocean, duty called. They knew that before they could actually go home, they had to finish what they had come for. Aware that there was a chance that they would never see their loved ones again, they braved the danger again and again.

On leave

While their lack of combat experience got 'replacements' killed often fairly quickly, growing numbers of battle-hardened veterans had been through so much that they began to experience combat fatigue at some point. The veterans, many of whom had been involved in the fighting since Normandy (and some even since the campaigns in North Africa and Italy), had seen so much suffering, had already lost so many comrades, and had looked death in the eye so often that they hit the limit of what a human can emotionally handle. Therefore, soldiers were given passes to go on a short leave far behind the lines to unwind. The French capital of Paris was a popular destination for relaxation and entertainment. The troops enjoyed the monumental ambiance and the famous nightlife to the fullest. Near Margraten, cities like Maastricht and Heerlen became so-called 'Rest and Recreation Centers' as well. Troops could go to the movies, shows, and dance halls here. Moreover, celebrities like Vera Lynn and Josephine Baker regularly performed in these centers to boost the troops' morale.

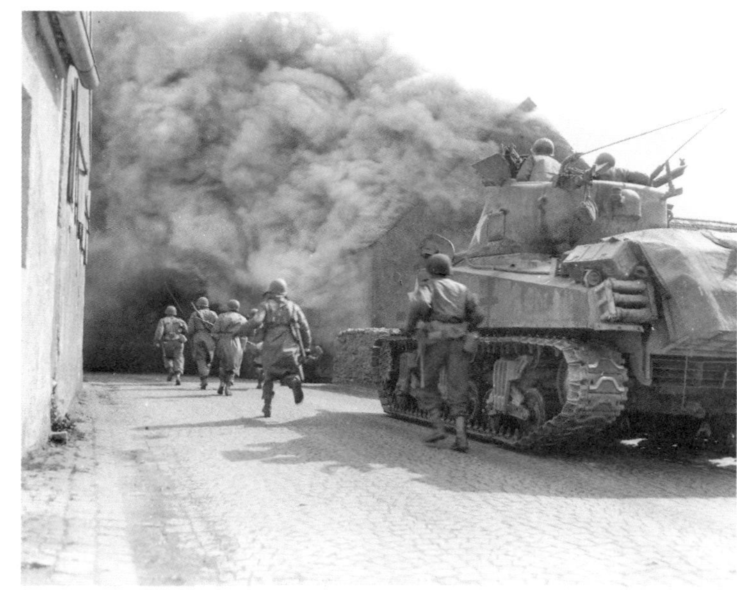

Germany defeated

After the crucial crossing of the Rhine, the western Allies continued their advance from the west. The Americans surrounded the Ruhr area – therefore now called the 'Ruhr Pocket' – and rushed eastwards towards the Elbe. The British troops began to advance northeast towards Hamburg. The Canadians, meanwhile, continued northwest to liberate the still-occupied parts of the Netherlands. Troops of the Soviet army were rapidly approaching from the east.

Over time, more and more soldiers would see the atrocities that had been committed by the Nazis in the camps all over Europe with their own eyes. The confrontation with the emaciated and worn-out camp prisoners, the many dead, the miserable barracks, the stench, the crematoria, and in some camps even the gas chambers, left deep mental scars. The chilling, traumatic memories of what they witnessed in the camps have haunted many soldiers ever since.

EYEWITNESS ACCOUNT OF THE LIBERATION OF A CONCENTRATION CAMP

'The memory of starved, dazed men who dropped their eyes and heads when we looked at them through the chain-link fence, in the same manner that a beaten, mistreated dog would cringe, leaves feelings that cannot be described and will never be forgotten. The impact of seeing those people behind that fence left me saying, only to myself, "Now I know why I am here!"'

Richard Winters

Major in the 101st Airborne Division, known from the book and the series **Band of Brothers*****, recalling the liberation of a sub-camp of Dachau.***

On April 25, 1945, troops of the First U.S. Army broke through to the town of Torgau on the banks of the Elbe River. It was there that American and Soviet troops met each other for the first time. The total collapse of Nazi Germany was imminent. Hitler's days were numbered. He committed suicide on April 30.

Days before, the first Soviet troops had reached the outskirts of Berlin. On May 2, the Soviet troops defeated the last German defenders in the German capital. One week later, Nazi Germany surrendered unconditionally. The German capitulation was signed in Reims and Berlin on respectively May 7 and 8, 1945. In Europe the war had come to an end. However, the war would rage on for another three months in the Pacific until two atomic bombs forced Japan to surrender as well.

The liberation of Europe had cost approximately 200,000 American lives. More than 70,000 of these soldiers have found their final resting place in thirteen different American war cemeteries in Western and Southern Europe. The Netherlands American Cemetery and Memorial in Margraten is one of these hallowed burial sites for the fallen.

American soldiers advance in a smoke-filled street in the German town of Wernberg. SOURCE: National Archives and Records Administration

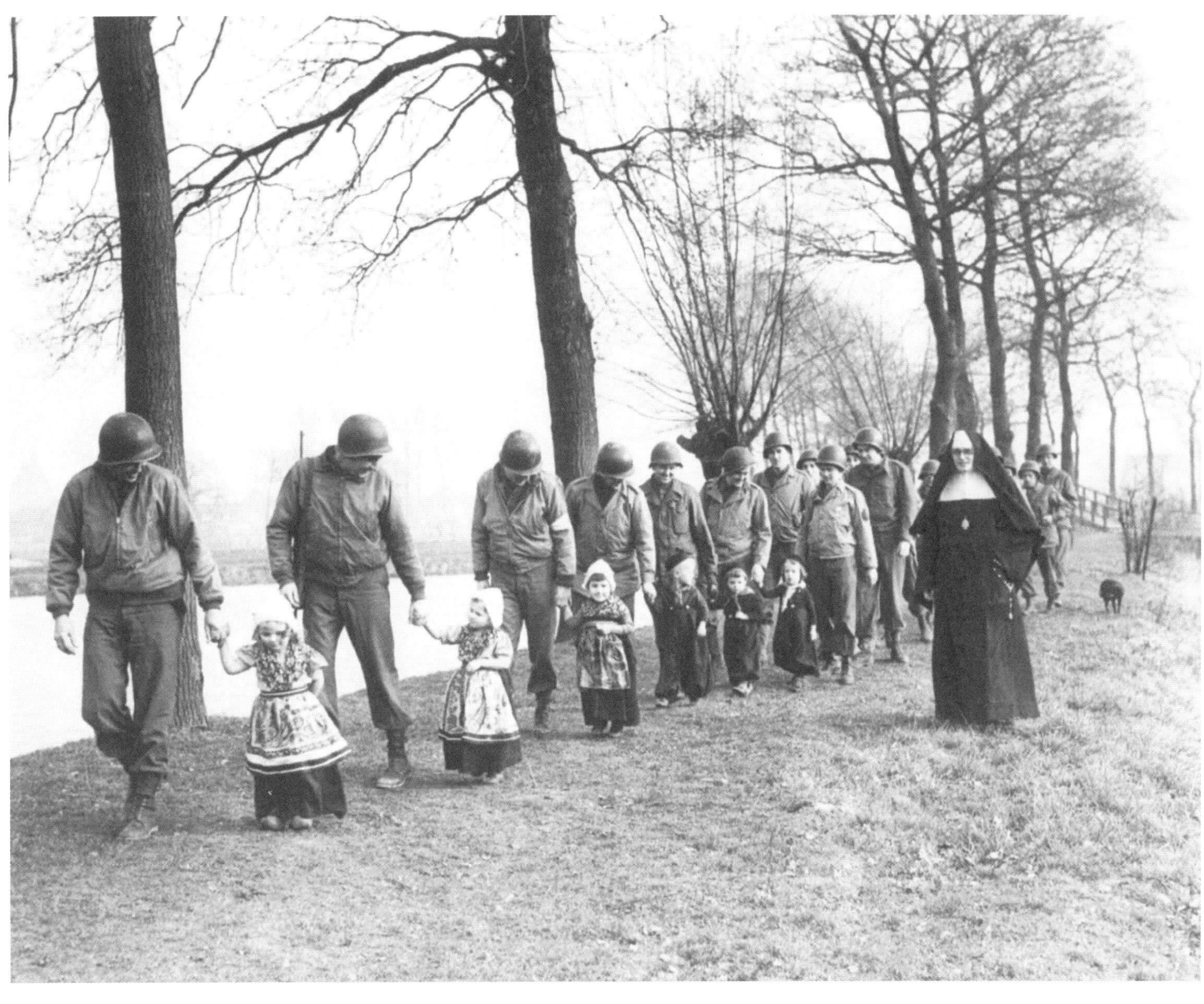

Dutch children entertain American soldiers on a walk around Hoensbroek Castle. SOURCE: Beeldbank WO2/NIOD

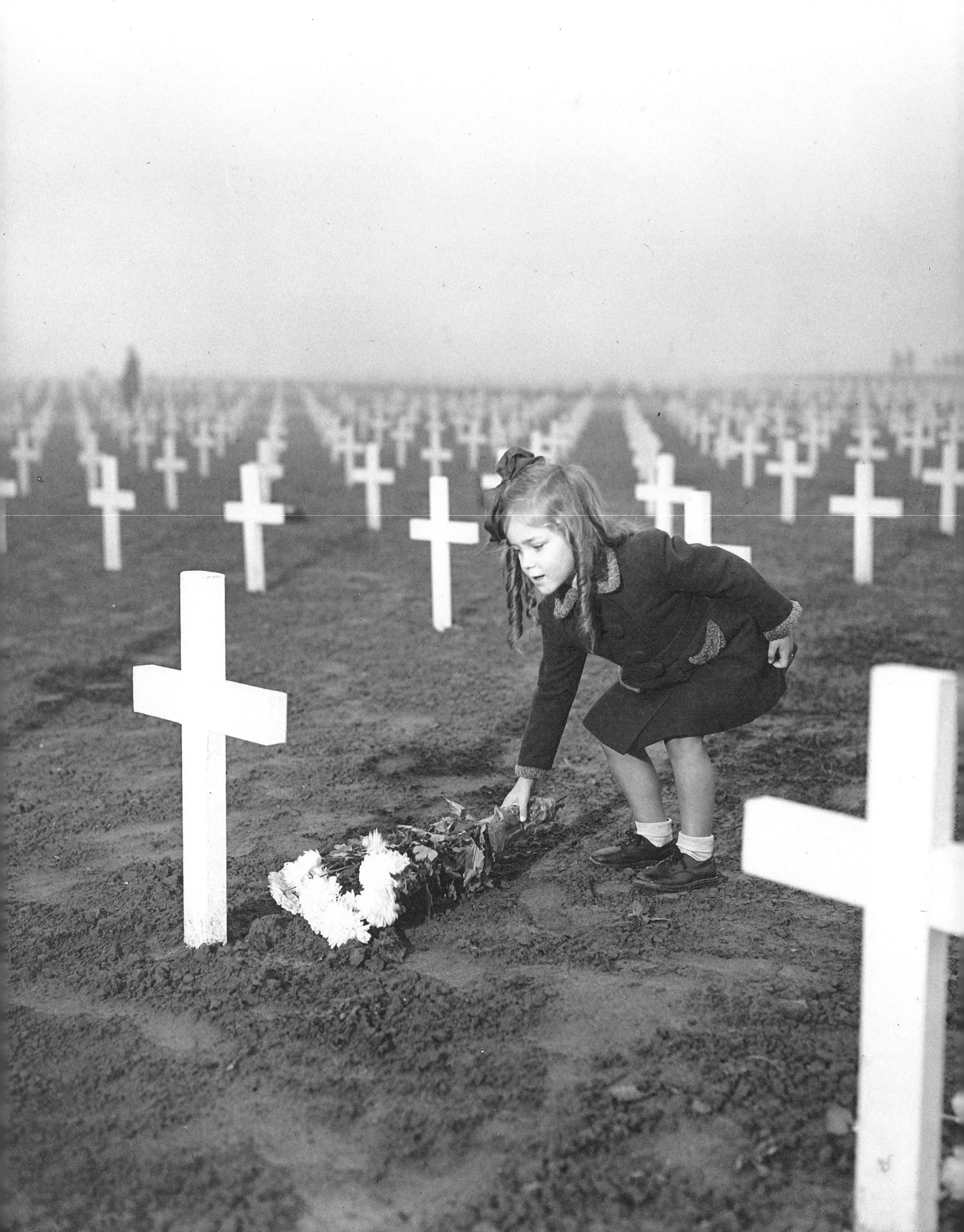

THE ONLY AMERICAN CEMETERY IN THE NETHERLANDS

It all began in October 1944. The Ninth U.S. Army was looking for a suitable site in South Limburg to establish a cemetery for its soldiers who were to die during the upcoming march to Berlin. The Americans approached the town hall of Margraten to ask whether they could use a beautiful, high-lying location in Margraten along the Maastricht-Aachen motorway for this purpose. When a civil servant of Margraten told the officer on duty, Captain Joseph Shomon, that it was their best agricultural land, he answered: 'Even the best soil is not good enough for our dead.' The civil servant and the local farmers quickly accepted the loss of their land and the Americans took possession of the 30 acres. The farmland became a military cemetery that would change the Limburg village forever.

On a soaking wet November 10, 1944, the men of the 611th Quartermaster Graves Registration Company, under the command of Shomon, assembled around an open grave for the first burial in the new cemetery. In Plot A, Row 1, Grave 1 the body of Corporal John David Singer was buried. Many thousands more would follow. By the time the last body was buried on March 30, 1946, the cemetery had become one of the largest military cemeteries on the European continent. In addition to 17,742 Americans and 1,026 other Allied personnel, 3,075 Germans were buried here. The latter would soon be transferred to Ysselsteyn. The fallen from the British Commonwealth were eventually moved to separate Commonwealth cemeteries and the bodies of the soldiers from the Soviet Union were ultimately buried in a special field of honor in Leusden.

Slogging in mud and icy cold

Digging the graves and burying the dead soldiers was hard and depressing work. The rain turned the cemetery into one big pool of mud and the bodies brought in were often badly mutilated and already in a state of decomposition. Moreover, in the winter it became so freezing cold on the plain near Margraten that the ground froze solid. The shovels broke off and therefore the graves had to be hacked out inch by inch with pickaxes in the freezing weather.

The emptying of the trucks and the digging of the graves at the time employed primarily African American soldiers from the 960th and 3136th Quartermaster Service Companies. One of them, Jefferson Wiggins, described the days there: 'In all the eight, nine, sometimes ten hours a day we were digging there, there was fear in the air. Or maybe it was sadness. Every day was the same. Yet you didn't get used to it.' Although African Americans were formally disadvantaged in the segregated U.S. Army, they were usually treated with respect at the cemetery by the white officers in charge. Nevertheless, the African American gravediggers were housed separately from the white army personnel in Gronsveld and Margraten. When they later returned to American society, the black gravediggers again suffered discrimination and did not have to count on appreciation for their work.

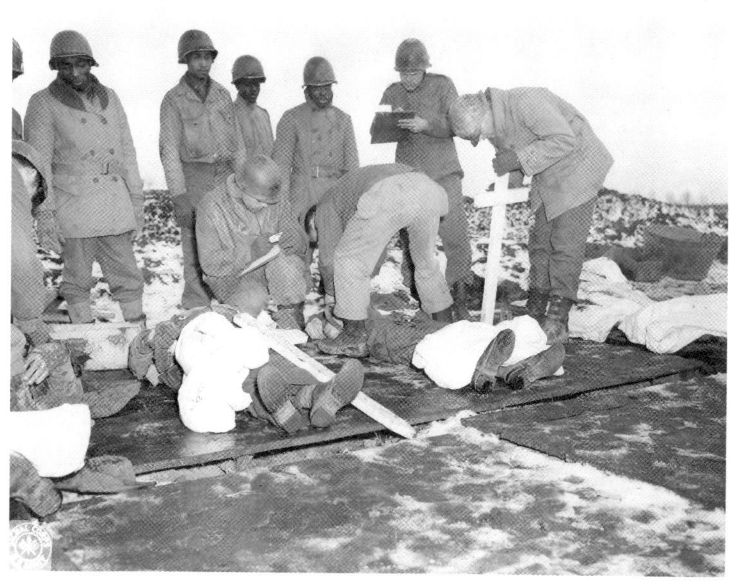

PROCESSING THE BODIES

All remains of dead soldiers that were brought in by the trucks were first brought to the so-called 'Stripping Line.' Here the bodies were stripped of ammunition and personal belongings. Then they were identified and registered by white hospital soldiers if possible. After this procedure the remains were placed in white body bags and buried. Each time a fallen soldier was laid in his grave, there was a small ceremony. A U.S. Army chaplain blessed the grave and then said a prayer. Also, every working day ended with a short military ceremony: the American Stars and Stripes flag was lowered, 'Taps' was played, and an Honor Guard fired three rifle volleys.

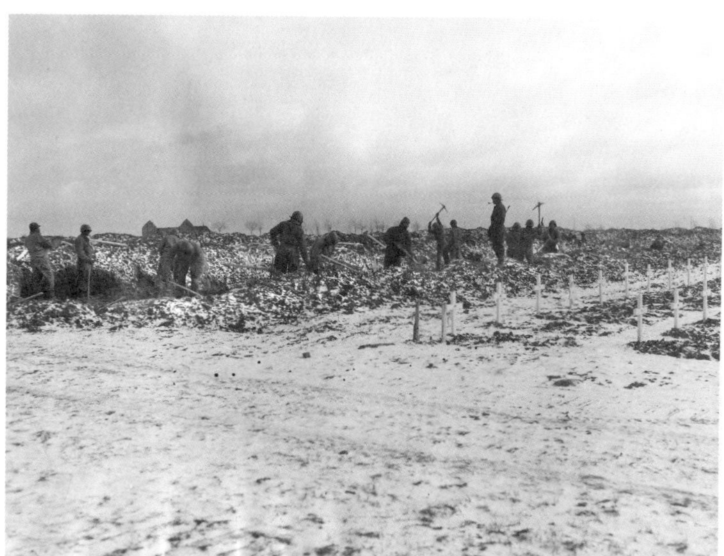

Members of the Graves Registration Company carefully record the details of the dead that are about to be buried. SOURCE: U.S. Army Signal Corps via Kimo Mc Cormick and Arie-Jan van Hees

African American soldiers are digging graves at the cemetery in Margraten. SOURCE: U.S. Army Signal Corps via Kimo Mc Cormick and Arie-Jan van Hees

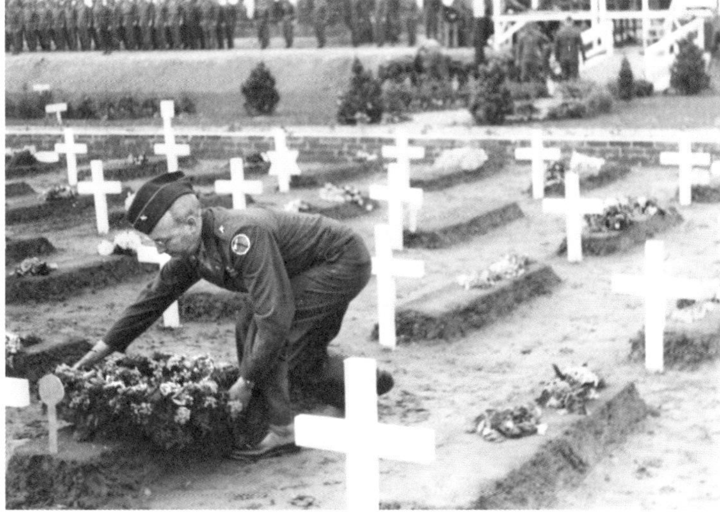

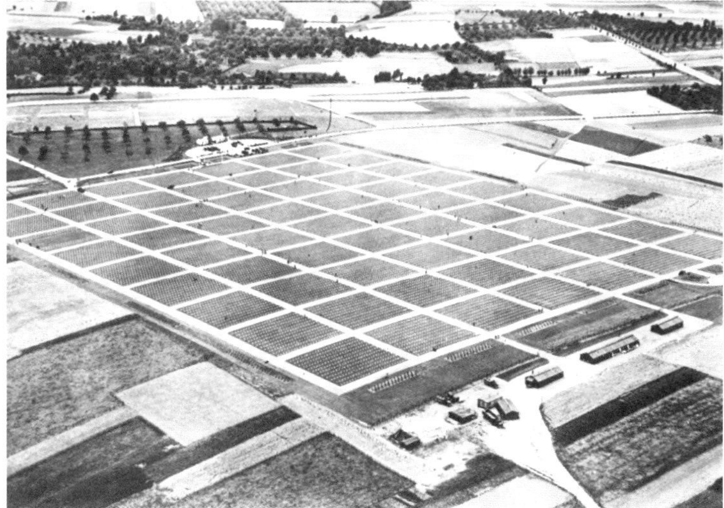

Locals help out

From November 1944, the people of Margraten were confronted daily with the many trucks which drove from Germany to the cemetery loaded with corpses, often leaving a trail of blood in the streets. The smell of decomposing corpses could be smelled in the far surroundings of the cemetery.

In 1945, a local initiative in Margraten led to the formation of a Civilian Committee with the aim of supporting the Americans. In the spring of 1945, many citizens from the surrounding communities helped to dig the graves in the cemetery. Math Robroek was one of them and remembered: 'If you didn't have a handkerchief with you, you would faint from the stench. That was a smell, it was just awful.'

Memorial Day 1945

On May 30, 1945, three weeks after the German capitulation, the first Memorial Day commemoration took place at the cemetery in Margraten. General William H. Simpson, commander of the Ninth U.S. Army, attended the ceremony. He laid wreaths and expressed his appreciation for the hard work that had been put into creating the cemetery.

On this special day the Americans also realized for the first time how great the gratitude and sympathy was among the people of Limburg. Many citizens and school classes came to the cemetery to pay their respects to the fallen. Thanks to the Civilian Committee of Margraten, the cemetery was beautifully decorated with an impressive sea of flowers. The day before, twenty trucks had driven through more than 60 Limburg villages to collect the bouquets and wreaths. The night before the ceremony over 200 people had been busy placing the flowers at the graves.

More crosses and Stars of David

Even when the war was over, bodies continued to arrive in Margraten. These were mainly the remains of soldiers who had been buried in cemeteries that the American War Department wanted to close. In the Netherlands, these were the temporary cemeteries in Son and Molenhoek, where the casualties of Operation Market Garden had initially been buried. Because the Americans did not want their dead to rest in enemy soil, they closed the temporary cemeteries in Germany as well. In addition, the American grave registration units traveled to villages, towns, and battlefields looking for the field graves of fallen American soldiers and airmen. When these were found, the remains were exhumed and brought to a cemetery such as the one in Margraten. The Americans chose to create a few large cemeteries for their fallen soldiers and not to bury their dead in countless local cemeteries as was done with the fallen soldiers from the British Commonwealth.

Only in very rare cases an exception was made. In these cases, one speaks of 'isolated burials.' Such graves can be found at the local cemetery in Opijnen, the Netherlands, where eight crew members of an American bomber that crashed there are still buried. These bodies should have been exhumed, but because the local community had taken care of the graves in an extraordinary way, the families requested that their loved ones be left permanently in Opijnen. The American authorities honored this request.

General William H. Simpson, commander of the Ninth U.S. Army, lays a wreath during the Memorial Day ceremony at the cemetery in Margraten on May 30, 1945. SOURCE: Nationaal Oorlogs- en Verzetsmuseum Overloon/Beeldbank WO2

The temporary cemetery in Margraten seen from above. SOURCE: NIOD/Beeldbank WO2

THE EIGHT OF OPIJNEN

On July 30, 1943, 186 bombers took off from England to bomb various targets in Germany. Twenty aircraft of the 91st Bombardment Group took off from Bassingbourn airfield, which was located west of Cambridge. The B-17 'Flying Fortress' with serial number 41-24399 and the nickname 'Man O' War' (named after a world-famous thoroughbred racehorse) was flown by a crew of ten under the command of pilot Keene C. McCammon.

The target of the group of bombers was the aircraft factory of Fieseler near Bettenhausen, east of Kassel in Germany. After the target was bombed, the B-17 fell behind the formation because it was damaged by anti-aircraft fire. Stragglers were often easy targets for German fighters, and it wasn't long before '399' was attacked by two German fighters. Over the Land of Maas and Waal region, the attacking fighter killed two crewmembers and damaged the aircraft in such a way that the bomber pilot was forced to give the order to bail out. Eight men left the plane with their parachutes. The parachute of the bomb aimer, Lieutenant Ohman, apparently did not open properly; he fell through the thatched roof of a farm and died shortly afterwards from his injuries. Pilot McCammon landed in the river Waal and his co-pilot John Bruce landed near the village of Varik. They were lucky to survive their parachute jump. The other five crew members were not so fortunate. Hanging under their parachutes, they were shot at several times by the German fighters during their descent. None of them survived these attacks.

Two days later, on August 1, at 9 o'clock in the morning, the eight Americans who had died were buried in the cemetery near the Reformed Church of Opijnen. The Germans allowed only mayor Formijne to attend the funeral. Nevertheless, the village came out to attend the funeral and to hear the mayor speak. After the speech, the cemetery filled up with people who wanted to show their respect to the eight Americans who had died. The gravediggers were assisted with closing the graves and soon there was a large sea of flowers.

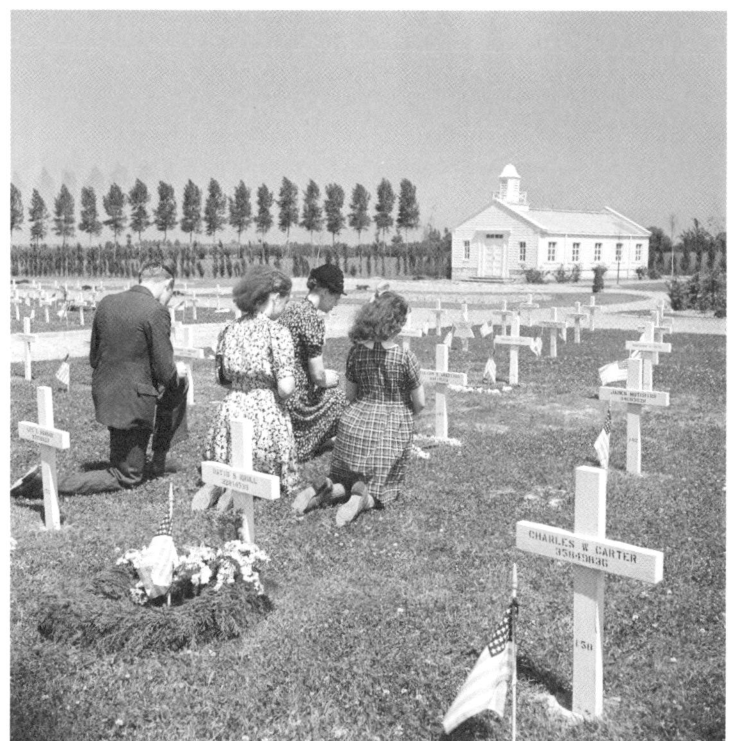

From early on, locals came to the cemetery in Margraten to lay flowers on the graves. The photo also shows the initial chapel that was built at the cemetery. SOURCE: Nationaal Archief, collectie Anefo

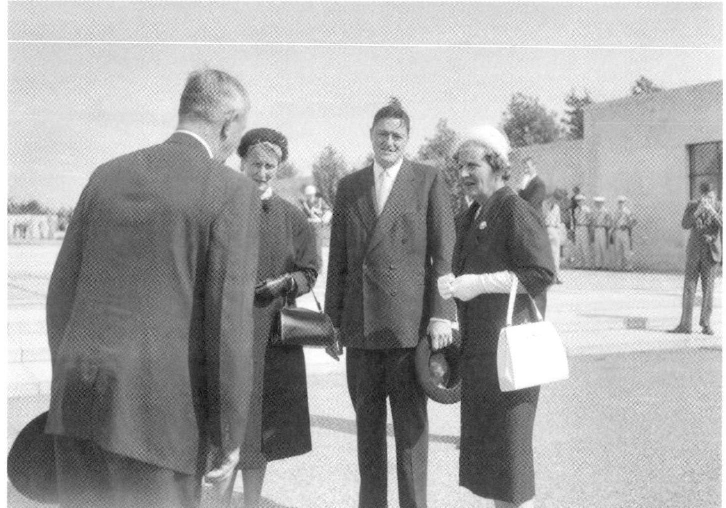

Dutch queen Juliana attends the official inauguration of the cemetery in 1960. SOURCE: Nationaal Archief, collectie Anefo

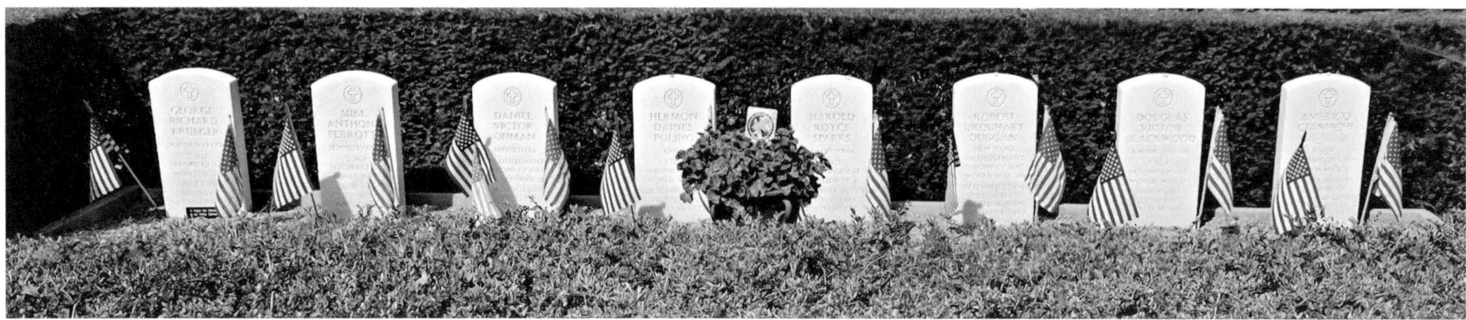

The eight American war graves in Opijnen. SOURCE: Richard van de Velde

Margraten becomes a permanent cemetery

In 1947, Margraten was designated to become the only permanent American cemetery in the Netherlands. The American government also decided that relatives could choose whether to have their fallen repatriated to America or to have them laid to rest permanently overseas, where they had made the ultimate sacrifice. This meant that all bodies had to be exhumed. Again, many local citizens were put to work. One of them was Jules van Laar. He could remember the following about this work: 'Of course the bag in which they were buried was gone. We dug to where we thought we were getting close to the body and then handed over the final exhumation to the Americans.'

After the exhumations, the bodies were prepared for transport or for reburial. In a large shed the remains were cleaned of clothing and other debris. Then they were first placed in zinc coffins and then in a wooden box. About ten thousand remains were then repatriated from Margraten. The about 8,300 American soldiers who remained in Margraten were given their eternal resting place in the Limburg loess. Their coffins were placed in fan-shaped rows, after which soil was poured over them. Until shortly before the final burial an American flag was draped over each coffin.

After the repatriation and reburial of the thousands of dead, the cemetery was embellished in the 1950s. The wooden crosses were replaced with crosses of marble, and during this period the Court of Honor with its memorial tower and reflecting pool were also constructed. A bronze sculpture group consisting of the Mourning Woman, three doves and a new shoot on the war-damaged tree was placed by this pond. Also, on either side of the Court of Honor, the two Memorial Walls of the Missing were erected, bearing the names of 1,722 American servicemen whose remains have not been found or could not be identified. When all these works were completed, the cemetery in its present form was officially inaugurated by the Dutch queen Juliana on July 7, 1960.

PERPETUAL LOAN

As a token of gratitude, the Dutch government has given the land on which the cemetery is located on perpetual loan to the United States. In addition, the government has stipulated in a treaty that no further buildings may be built in the vicinity of the cemetery so that its rustic and rural location is preserved.
The management of the cemetery in Margraten and 25 other overseas American cemeteries is in the hands of the American Battle Monuments Commission (ABMC). This American government organization was established after the First World War, in 1923.

The grave adoption program

Already during the first phase of the cemetery's construction, American relatives in their despair and grief sent letters to Margraten because they had received word that their son or husband was buried there. This is how the Civilian Committee of Margraten came to the idea of adopting graves and maintaining contact with the families in America. The adopters embraced the fallen liberators whose graves they adopted into their hearts, treating them as if they had been family of their own. On Memorial Day in 1946, all the nearly 19,000 Allied graves had been adopted.

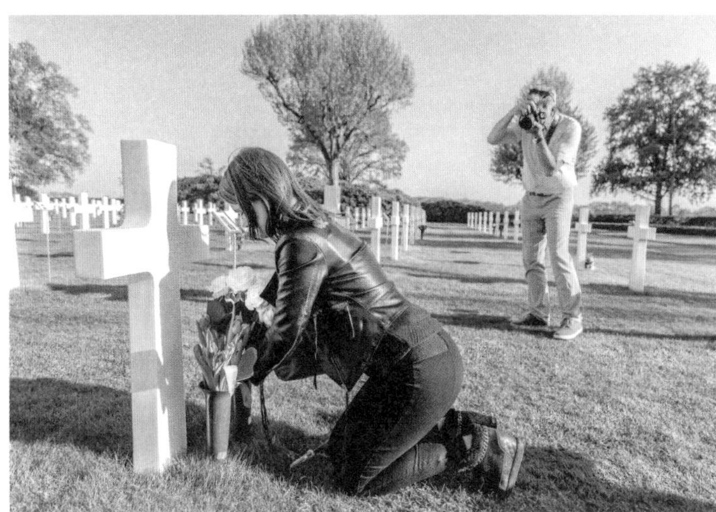

Today, all of the nearly 8,300 graves and 1,722 names on the Walls of the Missing are still being adopted. The Foundation for Adopting Graves at the American Cemetery in Margraten, which manages the adoption program, works with a waiting list that has over a thousand people on it in 2022. The fact that citizens in Limburg and elsewhere have adopted the graves and the names of American soldiers and consider them members of their own family is greatly appreciated by American relatives. Many American relatives do not have the opportunity to make the expensive trip to visit their brother, father, or uncle. Knowing that there are adoptive families in Limburg is a great comfort to them. Partly for this reason, and at the request of UNESCO, adopting the American war graves in Margraten has been on the national inventory of intangible cultural heritage since 2017.

For Ton Hermes, chairman of the Foundation for Adopting Graves at the American Cemetery in Margraten, this official recognition confirms that adopting the graves of soldiers has truly become a tradition that is passed on within families from generation to generation. Making the new generations aware that all these soldiers gave their lives for our freedom is, according to Hermes, one of the fundamental objectives of the adoption program:

'It is of great importance that the story of World War II is passed on to younger generations, so that they learn to appreciate the freedom in our society and that they realize that freedom is a verb. We must not forget the sacrifices that these American soldiers made. They gave their lives for us. Telling the stories of a number of these soldiers is an important contribution to this awareness.'

During his visit to the cemetery on May 8, 2005, then-U.S. President George W. Bush thanked the adopters for their years of dedication. 'Your kindness has brought comfort to thousands of American families separated from their loved ones here by an ocean. And on behalf of a grateful America, I thank you for treating our men and women as your sons and daughters.'

A grave adopter puts flowers on the grave that she has adopted

The memory lives on

As long as new stories are found, the memory of the soldiers in Margraten remains alive. This is partly due to new generations of adopters who have signed up to adopt a grave, even though they did not experience the war in which the soldiers died. The many projects set up by the local remembrance community have further contributed to this. In 2009 and 2010, for example, the book *From Farmland to Soldiers Cemetery* and the documentary *Bitter Harvest* were published and released, based on the Oral History project *Akkers of Margraten*. The project recorded the stories of eyewitnesses of the construction of the cemetery. One of the authors, Mieke Kirkels, has since been working to highlight the African American contribution to the construction of the cemetery and the war in general. Also important in the historiography of the cemetery was the book *The Margraten Boys* by Peter Schrijvers, which described the special adoption program. This program was depicted by documentary filmmaker Jotja Bessems in 2015 in *Onze Soldaat* ('Our Soldier'). Then, of course, there is the annual Liberation Concert that has been organized since 2006, in addition to the official Memorial Day ceremony at the end of May. Furthermore, there are the countless smaller initiatives by grateful citizens. Sometimes it is a tribute to soldiers of a particular unit or from a particular state. In other cases, it is a tribute to their own adopted soldiers, which has only been made easier by the advent of digital technology. Many websites about these soldiers can be found on the Internet.

World War II is not yet a closed book for the U.S. government either. The Defense POW/MIA Accounting Agency (DPAA) is still trying to identify the more than 70,000 missing American soldiers from World War II. In recent years, the organization has intensified its efforts to identify the 'Unknown Soldiers' buried in Margraten. These still ongoing efforts have already paid off several times and the relatives of the soldiers who have been identified can finally close this chapter.

A LEGACY EFFORT

'Solving the cases of missing servicemen is unlike the historical research most historians do. Our work is to solve decades-old mysteries and provide conclusions. More importantly, doing our job well helps people in a way most historical research does not. Even though World War II was more than 70 years ago, the pain and trauma of a death from that period can carry across generations. Most of the family members we meet with were born after their missing relative died. Yet they are connected to that loss – not because they knew the soldier, but because they grew up seeing their parents or grandparents grieving. Therefore, this is a legacy effort, and the recovery is a sort of conclusion to that family's search. Each soldier we identify means a family has an answer and their relative home, and a historical mystery has been solved. Ultimately, this mission is more fulfilling than any other historian job I can think of.'

Dr. Ian Spurgeon
Military historian with the Defense POW/MIA Accounting Agency in Washington, D.C

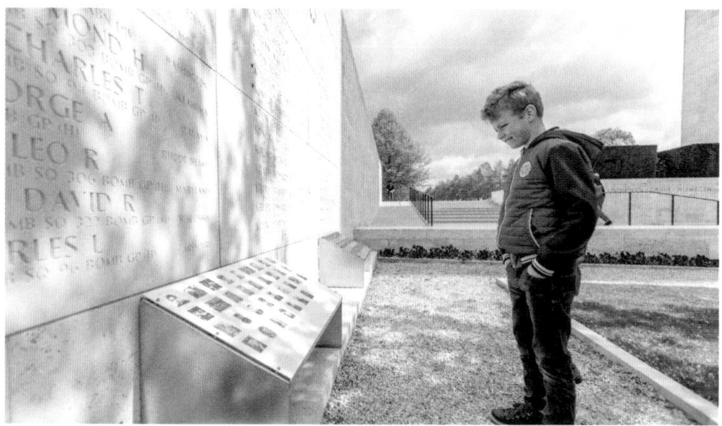

The search for stories

As time passes, it becomes harder to piece together the stories of the men and women in Margraten. Eyewitnesses, whether family members, veterans, or local citizens, pass away. Often letters, photographs, newspaper clippings, and other documents that could have told us at least a part of the story are discarded after their deaths. On the other hand, digital technologies offer us new possibilities. More and more, archives are being digitized and can therefore be consulted via the Internet from anywhere in the world. The search for stories of the soldiers commemorated at Margraten is far from over.

The large-scale gathering and sharing of these stories began in 2008. Some adopters who had done extensive research themselves decided to help others and to make the information that was found available for everyone. Moreover, after years of contact between soldiers' families and adopters, many grave adopters had already found a lot of information, but it just was not publicly available yet. Today, the *Fields of Honor – Database* has over 38,000 tribute pages. Volunteers of all ages, mainly from the Netherlands, Belgium, and the United States have maintained this database for over ten years now. They are part of the *Fields of Honor Foundation*, which also organizes *The Faces of Margraten* tribute.

Each volunteer does this from his or her own motivation. Justine Camps, then still an eighteen-year-old volunteer, aptly described her motivation in a letter she wrote to one of the unknown soldiers buried in Margraten:

'What I know about you is that you died to give my country back its freedom and that you and many others from the United States and other allied countries know what I just wrote about. You had a tough training, came to Holland, and did what you were asked to do. You probably didn't know the people who lived here. You sacrificed yourself in a tremendous mission that cost many others their lives as well. And now you're buried here in Margraten. It occurs to me that you do have a story. It's about peace and remembrance, and being thankful. You are part of a very big story, the story of the liberation of occupied Europe.'

The names of 1,722 soldiers are inscribed on the Walls of the Missing. The names of those who have been recovered and identified are marked with a rosette

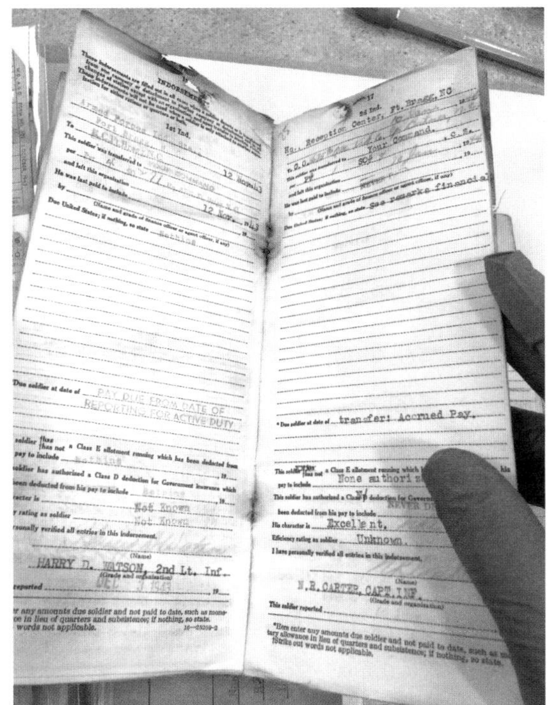

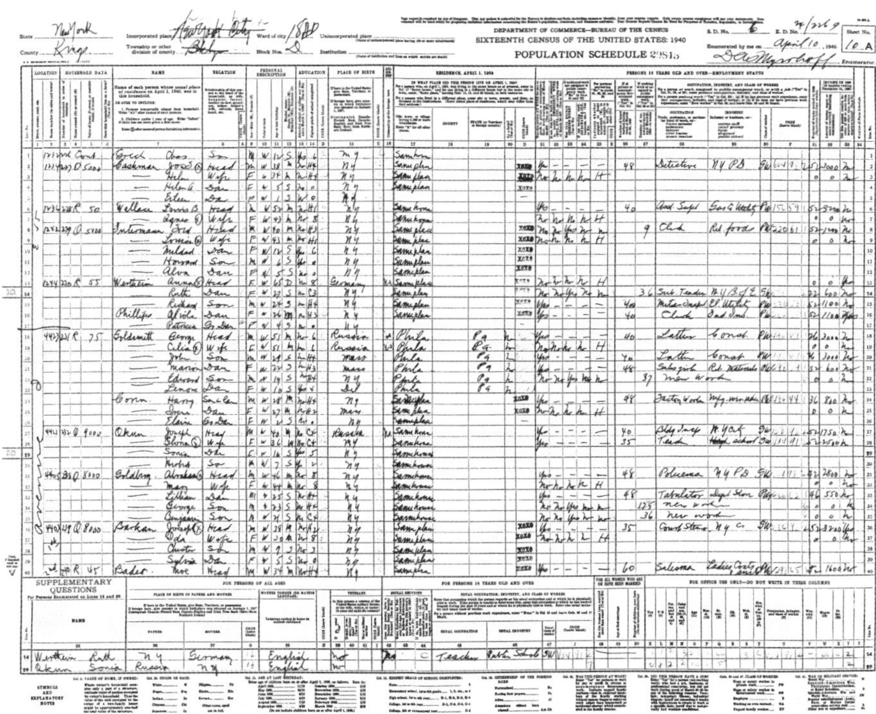
DEPARTMENT OF COMMERCE—BUREAU OF THE CENSUS
SIXTEENTH CENSUS OF THE UNITED STATES: 1940
POPULATION SCHEDULE

USMC. Margraten
Plot A. Row 1. Grave 31
Date of Burial: 16 Dec 48
Verified by
GRS OFFICER
Buried on:
Right: Jesse F. Swick 36313444
Left: Harold F. Krauss. J 0-2057648

DISINTERMENT DIRECTIVE ... TED BY M, MA...

SECTION A — NAME AND BURIAL LOCATION OF DECEASED

DIRECTIVE NUMBER	DATE DAY	MONTH	YEAR
4650 01226	15	10	48

NAME	SERIAL NUMBER	GRADE	ARM	RACE	RELIGION
AUSTIN EUGENE	34648050	PVT	1	2	5

CEMETERY	PLOT	ROW	GRAVE	DISPOSITION OF REMAINS CODE	DIST. CTR.
MARGRATEN HOLLAND	PP	9	213	4601	80

FLAG SENT 21 Dec. 48

SECTION B — CONSIGNEE AND NEXT OF KIN

NAME AND ADDRESS OF CONSIGNEE	NAME AND ADDRESS OF NEXT OF KIN
MARGRATEN, HOLLAND	MR. GETTIES AUSTIN (FATHER) GENERAL DELIVERY GREER, SOUTH CAROLINA

SECTION C — DISINTERMENT AND IDENTIFICATION

NAME | SERIAL NUMBER | GRADE | DATE OF DEATH | DATE DISINTERRED

IDENTIFICATION TAG ON: REMAINS / MARKER | ORGANIZATION: USAGF | RELIGION | IDENTIFICATION VERIFIED BY | NAME AND TITLE

SECTION D — PREPARATION OF REMAINS FOR SHIPMENT

NATURE OF BURIAL | CONDITION OF REMAINS

OTHER MEANS OF IDENTIFICATION

MINOR DISCREPANCIES (*Prepare Discrepancy Report QMC Form 1194a for major discrepancies.*)

REMAINS PREPARED AND PLACED IN CASKET

DATE | BY

CASKET SEALED BY | EMBALMER (*Signature*)

CASKET BOXED AND MARKED | SHIPPING ADDRESS VERIFIED BY

DATE | BY

I hereby certify that all the foregoing operations were conducted and accomplished under my immediate supervision and that the report above is correct.

SIGNATURE OF AGRS INSPECTOR

REMARKS AND SPECIAL INSTRUCTIONS

NAT FILE RECORDS ANNOTATED DATE FEB 24 1949

Lawrence Shea, Casualty in Reich

MAY 2 1945

Corp. Lawrence Shea of 749 President St. was killed in action in Germany on April 2, according to word received by his family. He was 21.

Born in Brooklyn, Corporal Shea attended Visitation School and was employed by Oakite Products, Inc., at Bush Terminal, when he entered the army air forces in January, 1942. He was stationed at Avon Park, Fla., until November, 1944, when he was transferred to the infantry, and went overseas last March. While with Oakite, he pitched on the company baseball team.

Surviving are his father, Walter J. Shea; two brothers, Corp. Walter J. Jr., in the air forces in Europe, and James, recently discharged from the army for medical reasons, and three sisters, Mrs. Mary Loughlin, Mrs. Joseph Moore and Genevieve Shea.

The research done by the many volunteers and others is no easy task. In 1973, there was a major fire in the National Archives in St. Louis. The military files of millions of soldiers were lost in this fire. Only twenty percent of all American soldiers' documents have survived. These files, especially the Official Military Personnel File (OMPF), help us to track a soldier's footsteps. They paint a picture of where they trained, the units they served in, and even small details such as when they paid money for washing their laundry. In the papers we also find traces of the soldiers

Archival research in St. Louis has helped to reconstruct the stories of the soldiers

Page taken from the 'Individual Deceased Personnel File' about the reburial of Eugene Austin

Documents such as U.S. Census records and obituaries are valuable sources of information when doing research

themselves, such as a signature and a fingerprint. These yellowed papers bring us close to the soldiers.

But even if the files have been lost, there are other documents that can help in researching the service of a fallen soldier. For example, units kept records. Morning Reports reported on personnel matters each day. In the After-Action Reports, army units looked back on the past month. In the case of larger units, such as the 69th Infantry Division, one can even find the minutes of the deliberations of the senior officers, allowing us to exactly track which decisions they took, and when. In reports of smaller units, however, references to the circumstances of a specific soldier's death are more likely to be found. In the search for information on fallen soldiers, the Individual Deceased Personnel File (IDPF) is also of value. This file was created for each soldier who died. It contains information about a person's death, identification, and burial. It also contains correspondence from the government to the next of kin or vice versa. Obtaining these documents, however, requires either great patience or a trip to the American archives.

Although finding out information about a fallen soldier is usually a difficult and time-consuming process, digitization has made research a lot easier in the past decade. Many valuable archives can now be viewed online on websites such as Ancestry, Fold3, and Newspapers.com. This applies, for example, to the Missing Air Crew Reports, which were drawn up if an aircraft was lost over enemy territory. These reports often contain eyewitness reports and sometimes even correspondence from the German army about captured or killed American airmen. In addition to military archives, it also concerns, for example, the U.S. Census, of which the records up to and including the year 1950 can now be consulted digitally. The census records help to determine where a soldier lived and with whom. These names, often those of family members, are a starting point for further searches in other documents that are sometimes available, such as birth certificates and marriage certificates. Scanned newspapers, containing obituaries, and class books are other sources of information and photographs. In the search for stories, volunteers systematically search through such historical sources.

Of course, even in the digital age, traditional fieldwork remains very important. So, although more and more material is becoming available digitally, that does not apply to the boxes of information that are lying around in someone's attic. Nor is it true for the photo of a soldier who is commemorated at his former high school in a special memorial corner for all former students who once died in the service of the armed forces. American volunteers know how to find these by making a call to or visiting the local library, historical society, or veterans' organization.

Relatives of the soldiers can be traced in a similar way. Even when close relatives are no longer alive, surviving family members can often still tell the stories they heard in their youth. The inheritance of the old generations still includes family photos, letters from the front, and the official papers which, for example, describe the reason why a soldier received a particular award. Correspondence with these families have played an important role in reconstructing the stories that now follow in this book.

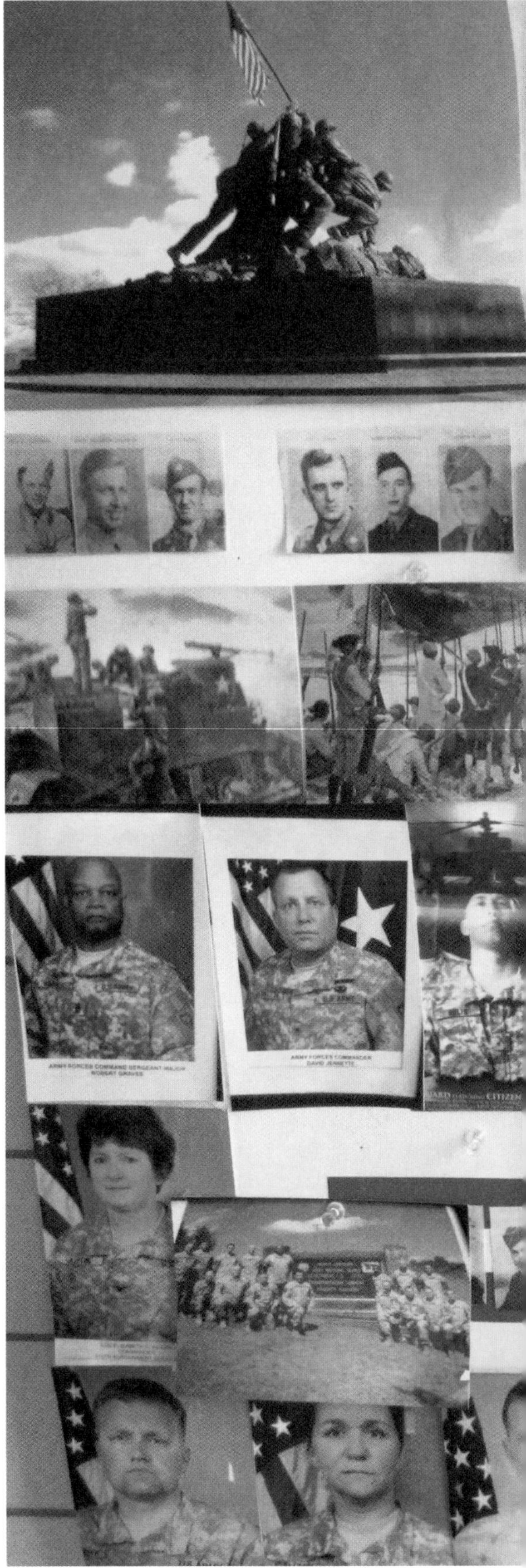

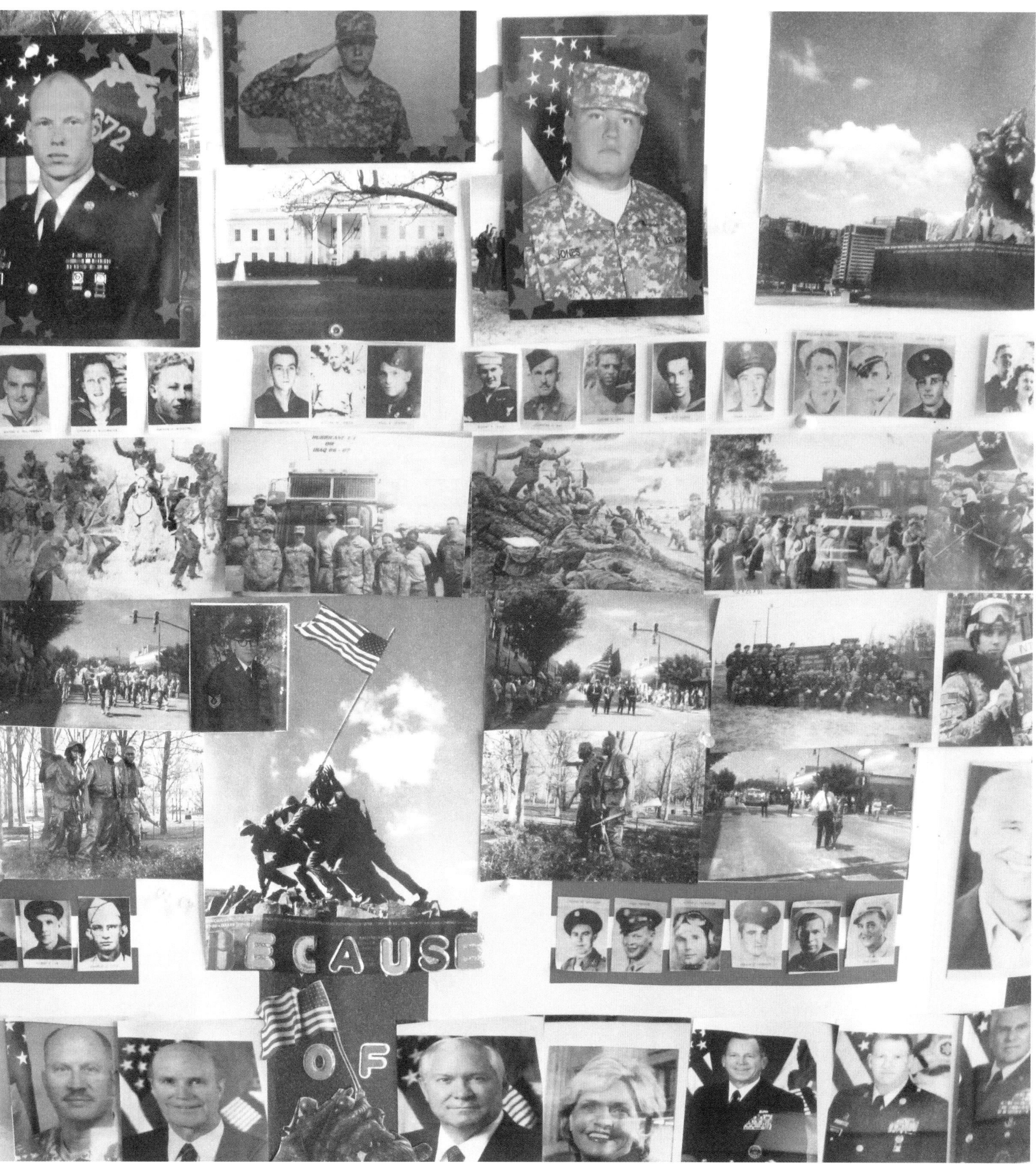

A Waffle House in South Carolina honors service members from the local community at the entrance of its restaurant

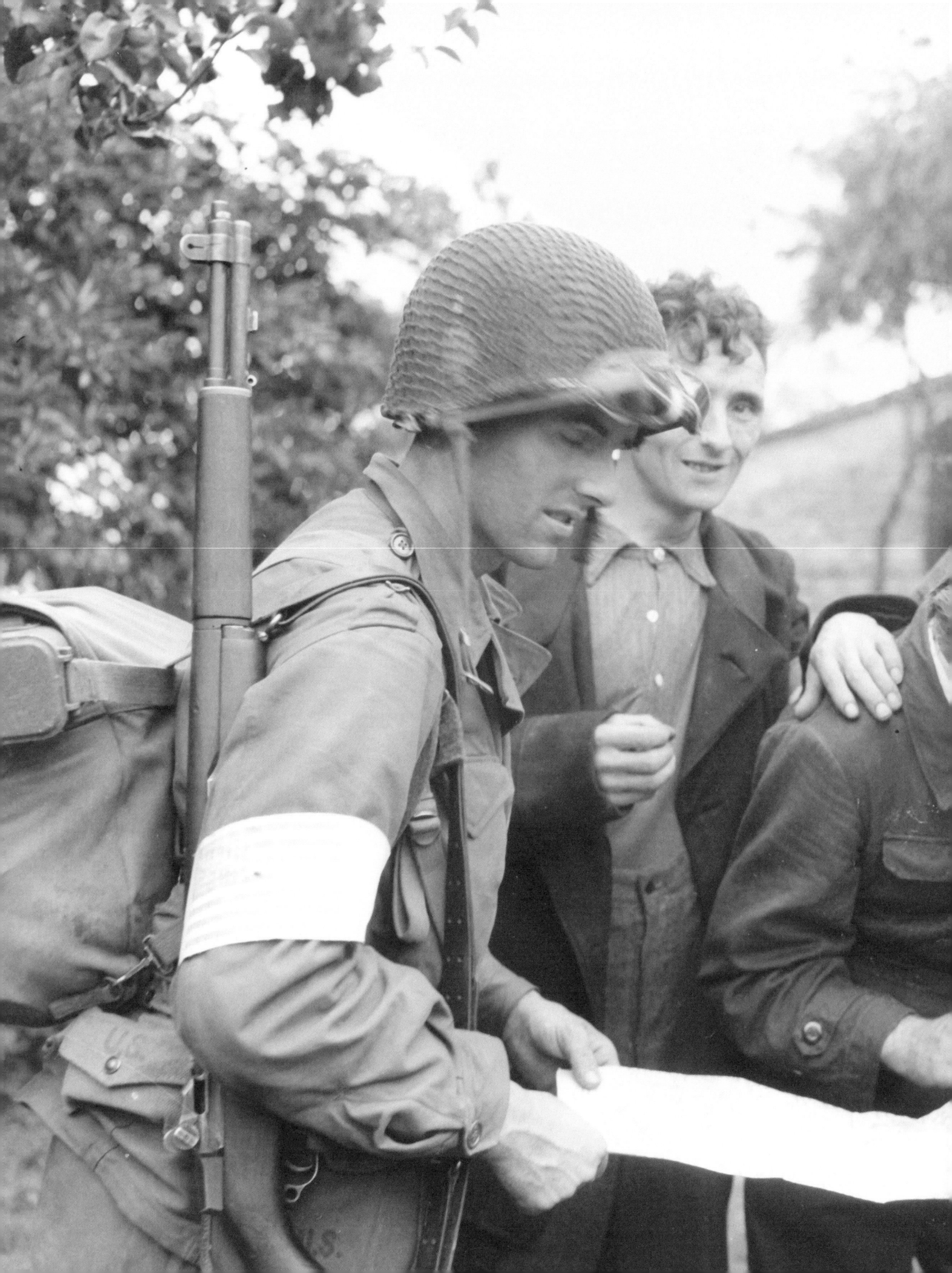

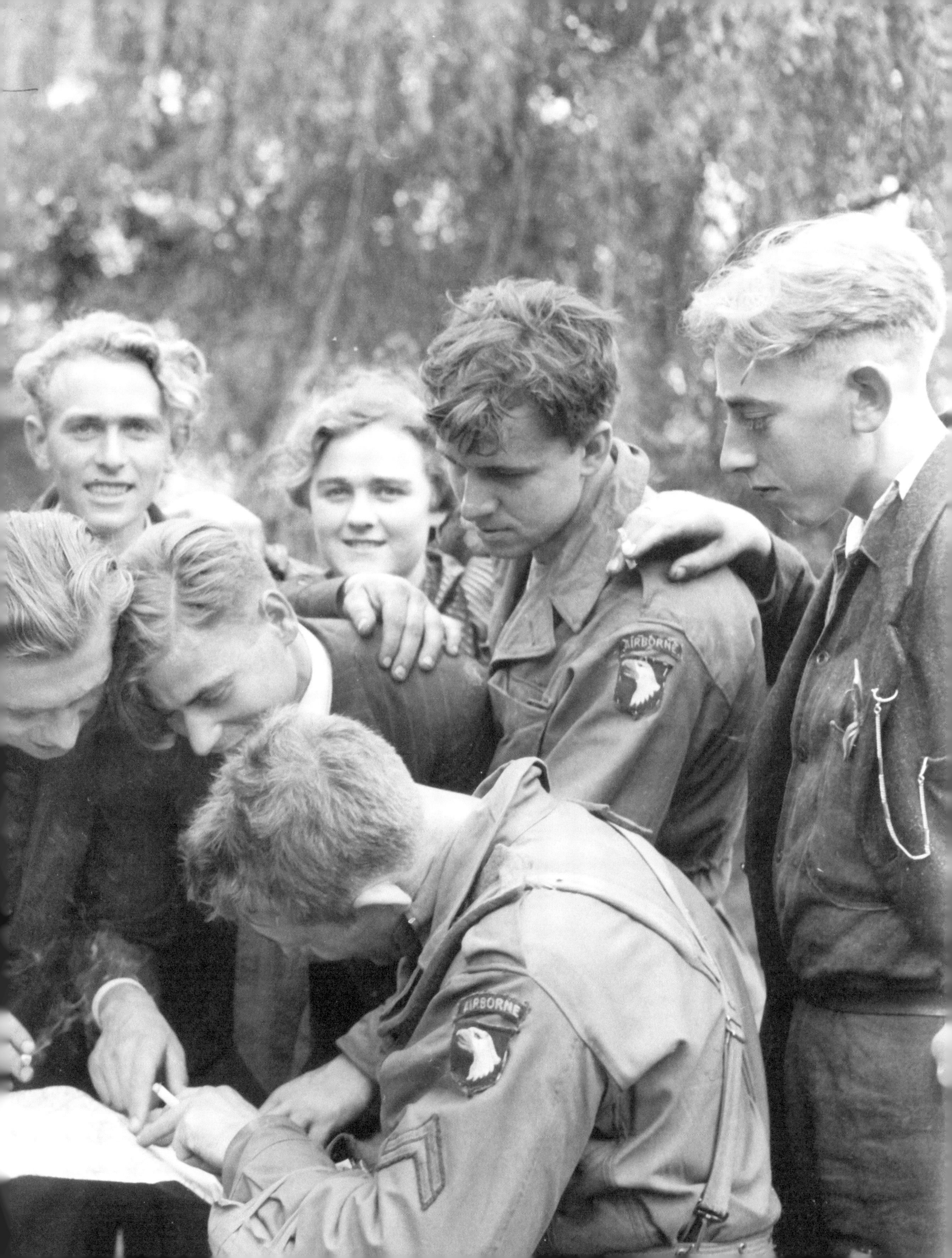
AIRBORNE
AIRBORNE

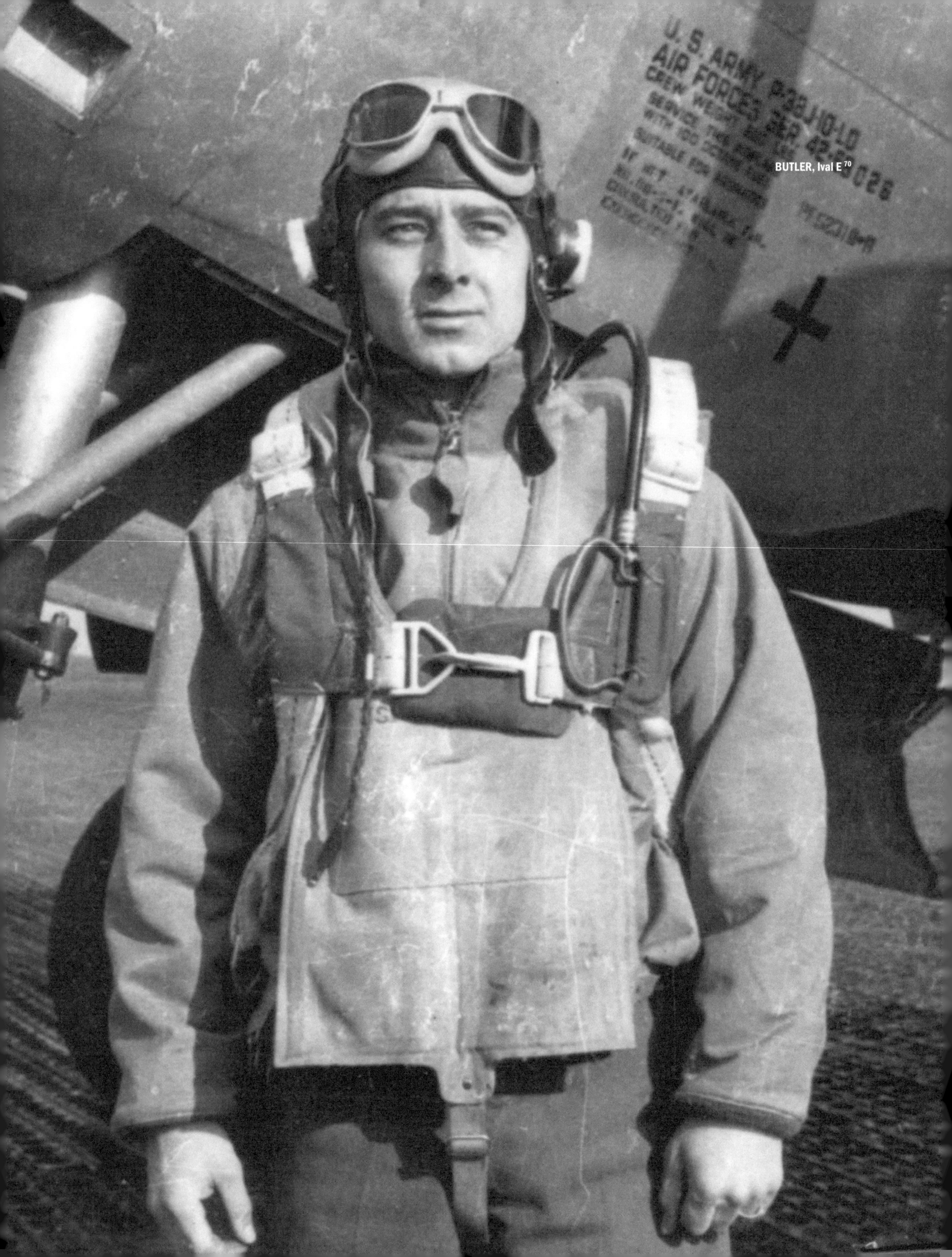

BUTLER, Ival E [70]

THE STORIES BEHIND THE NAMES

CHARLES L. SUMMERS

Second Lieutenant

No. 53 Squadron RAF

The first American killed

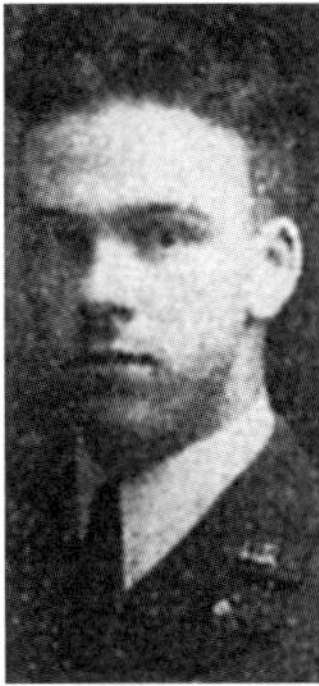

Charles Luther Summers was born in Cedar Rapids, Iowa, in 1918. He attended various technical schools and graduated from the University of Berkeley in California in 1940. On August 1, 1941, before the United States entered World War II, Charles enlisted as a reserve officer in the Signal Corps of the U.S. Army Reserve.

At the end of 1941, Charles was sent to England and assigned as a Liaison Officer to the British Naval Air Service, Coastal Command, of the Royal Air Force. The intention was that he would gain experience with a new British secret weapon, a radar that could detect submarines: the ASV (Air to Surface Vessel) radar. Off the American east coast, German submarines regularly torpedoed oil tankers that were heading in a convoy for the United Kingdom. It was therefore of the utmost importance that the Americans quickly acquired knowledge of this radar system to combat these submarines.

After undergoing specialist training at Prestwick, Scotland, Charles was posted to No. 53 Squadron of RAF Coastal Command on April 1, 1942. On May 4, 1942, he flew as crew member in a RAF Lockheed Hudson which was equipped with specialized radar equipment. His task was to monitor and intercept German ships off the coast of Holland and to carry out an armed attack where possible. While attacking a German convoy, the plane of Charles and his four British colleagues was hit by anti-aircraft fire. With a burning right wing, the pilot was forced to make an emergency landing in the North Sea. He did this successfully; other planes saw the five crew members standing on the left wing before the plane sank.

In such situations, both sides alerted their respective rescue units, but unfortunately for the crew, all help came too late. The five men died of hypothermia followed by drowning. Eventually, the five bodies washed up on beaches near Bergen and Egmond aan Zee. Charles was temporarily buried at the Protestant cemetery of Egmond aan Zee.

After the war, the four British air crew members were buried at the Nieuwe Ooster cemetery in Amsterdam. Charles Luther Summers was the first American who died during an operational action over the Netherlands in World War II. His final resting place in Margraten is in Plot B, Row 2, Grave 16.

WILLIAM G. LYNN JR.

Second Lieutenant

15th Bomb Squadron

The Independence Day Raid

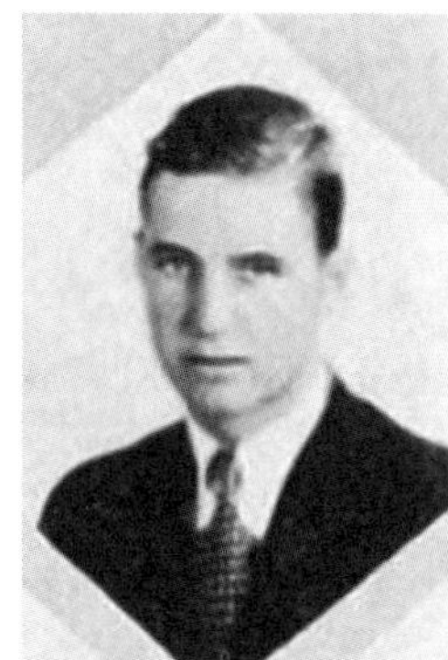

Second Lieutenant William G. Lynn Jr. from Los Angeles, California, was born in 1915. A graduate of Hollywood High School and Santa Monica Junior College, he attended the University of California at Los Angeles one semester before he entered the U.S. Army Air Corps in 1941.

Five days after the Japanese attack on Pearl Harbor, William received his pilot wings at Mather Field near Sacramento. On the same day he married his girlfriend Rae. Several weeks later, William left for England, where he was then further prepared to be deployed in the air war against Nazi Germany.

On July 4, 1942 – Independence Day – William participated in the first coordinated American bombing mission on German targets in Nazi-occupied Holland. Twelve two-engine A-20 'Havoc' bombers took off in England that day to attack German airfields along the Dutch coast. Six aircraft were flown by American crews, the other six by British crews from the RAF. The airfield to be bombed by William's crew was the Bergen/Alkmaar Airfield.

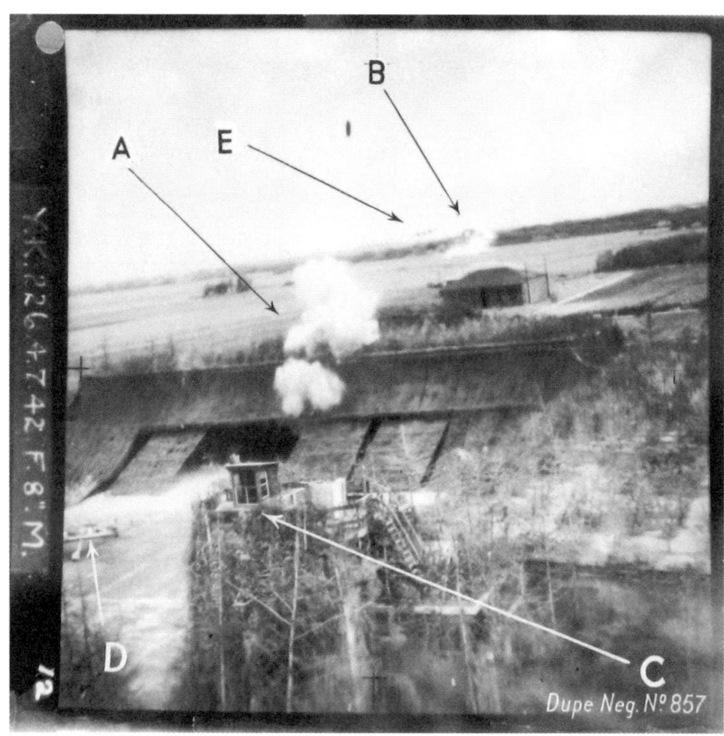

The A-20s reached their target. But just before William could drop his bombs, his plane was struck by enemy Flak (anti-aircraft fire). The bomber crashed on the airfield. William was killed at the age of 27. His three fellow crew members also lost their lives in the crash. Together with the fallen crew members of the other downed A-20s, they were the first American servicemen who died on Dutch soil during the war.

Several weeks after William was shot down over Holland, his wife Rae gave birth to their daughter Nancy. When she was born, William was officially listed as missing, and Rae still cherished the hope that one day he would return home. At the time, a local newspaper interviewed her as a brand-new mother. She was asked to describe how it felt to bring a child into the world knowing that the fate of her husband was still unknown.

'Gee, I wish Bill could be here,' Rae answered as she cuddled her new-born baby daughter, 'but I'll never give up hope.' A few weeks later, the War Department notified her and William's parents with the tragic news that would dash her hopes: William was dead, killed in action as one of the first American pilots to be downed in World War II...

William is buried beneath a white marble cross at the Netherlands American Cemetery in Margraten. His final resting place there can be found in Plot B, Row 5, Grave 10.

◄ Attack on the airfield of Bergen/Alkmaar on July 4, 1942. The smoke coming from William Lynn's plane can be seen at point B. SOURCE: National Archives and Records Administration via Hans Nauta and Arie-Jan van Hees

JOHN T. SLATER JR.

Second Lieutenant

4th Fighter Group

American killed in British service

John T. Slater Jr. enlisted as an Aviation Cadet on November 22, 1940, in Elmira, New York. He received his initial training with the U.S. Army Air Corps (in June 1942 this name was changed to U.S. Army Air Forces) in Alabama. During his training, the United States was still neutral; the Japanese had not yet attacked Pearl Harbor. Yet there were many young American men who wanted to go to England to fight to preserve Western democracy and against Nazism. John was one of them, and so he enlisted in the British Royal Air Force (RAF). After going through all the procedures, he received further training as a RAF cadet in California. Christmas 1941 was spent with his parents in New York. Although the U.S. was recently drawn into World War II due to the Japanese attack on Pearl Harbor on December 7, 1941, John left for the United Kingdom in January 1942.

After additional training John was assigned to a so-called 'Eagle Squadron' in June 1942. Such Squadrons consisted almost entirely of American volunteers, and all members of the Squadron wore on the shoulder of their British RAF uniform a stylized American eagle with the letters 'E.S.' ('Eagle Squadron') with pride. At RAF No.121 Squadron Pilot Officer John Slater flew the famous Supermarine Spitfire.

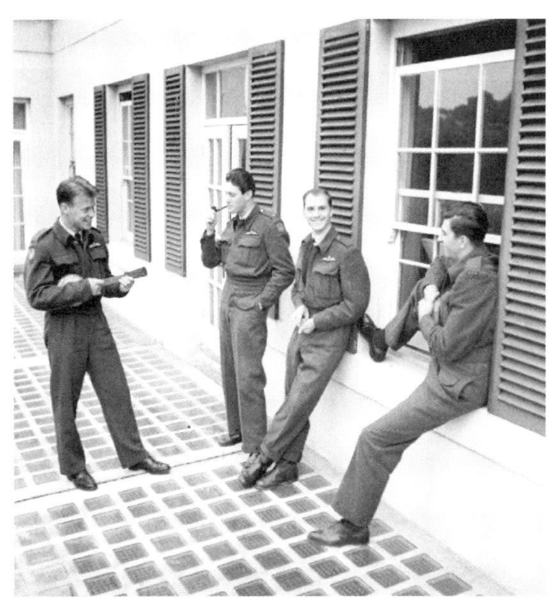

John Slater, second from the right, in a British uniform. SOURCE: Unknown

In the period shortly before his fatal last flight on September 21, 1942, there was talk that all 'Eagle Squadron' pilots would be transferred to the U.S. Army Air Forces (USAAF). Now that the United States was involved in the world war and had sent an air force to the United Kingdom, they wanted the 'Eagle Squadron' pilots, who had a wealth of experience in the Royal Air Force, back. These pilots would then be placed in the 4th Fighter Group, which was administratively activated on September 12, 1942.

On September 21, 1942, John and his colleague William Kelly took off from Southend Airfield in Essex on a reconnaissance mission to Haamstede Airfield in the Dutch province of Zeeland. Flying in Spitfires Mk. V they attacked an anti-aircraft ship that was lying off the coast of Holland. John's aircraft (with Serial Number 'P8339') was hit by a German 20mm anti-aircraft shell in the coolant system, after which the engine soon failed. His Spitfire crashed into the North Sea near Hoek van Holland. His body was never found.

On September 23, 121 Squadron moved to USAAF station Debden and on September 29, the three 'Eagle Squadrons' were officially incorporated into the 4th Fighter Group of the USAAF. John T. Slater Jr. was the last American pilot of an 'Eagle Squadron' who died in service with the Royal Air Force. On the Walls of the Missing in Margraten his rank is chiseled as Second Lieutenant. As a reward for his services the British authorities and the Royal Air Force had posthumously promoted him to Flying Officer. This was equal to the rank of First Lieutenant within the U.S. Army Air Forces.

JAMES A. NORTON JR.
Second Lieutenant
322nd Bombardment Group

Inseparable twin brothers died together

James A. Norton Jr. and his twin brother Edward from Conway, South Carolina, were born on August 18, 1920. From an early age onwards, they were infatuated with flying. They loved anything to do with aviation. As teenagers, they even bought a second-hand plane with which they flew around Conway.

The adventurous Norton twins were inseparable. During their senior year at Conway High School, they were named, jointly, 'most popular boy,' and at age eighteen, they both attended Clemson University to study civil engineering. While studying there, they ran track and played football – they both wore the No. 4 jersey.

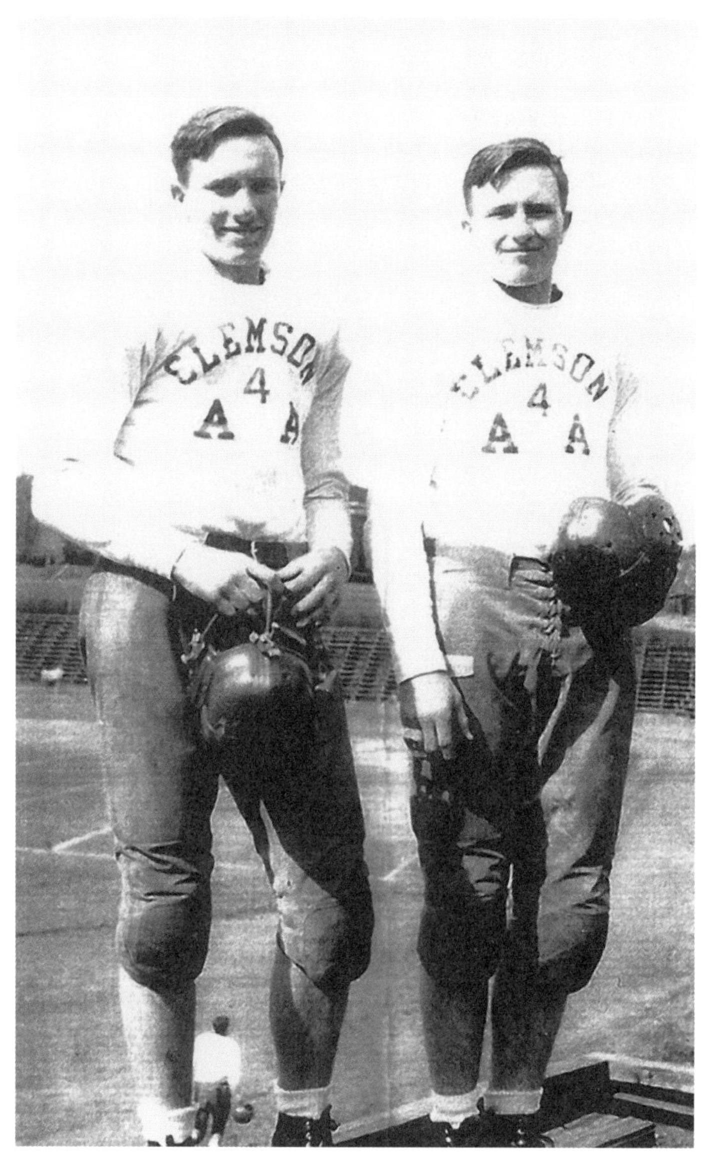

After two years at Clemson, James and Edward decided to enter the Army Air Corps. Together, they were accepted for pilot training in November 1941. In September 1942, the twins got their 'wings', whereupon they were deployed to England with the 322nd Bombardment Group. There they were each other's co-pilots in the cockpit of a B-26 Marauder bomber.

On May 17, 1943, James and Edward took off for their first bombing flight over enemy territory. The goal of the mission was to bomb a power plant in Velsen, the Netherlands, which supplied electricity to a German submarine bunker, the railroad network between Amsterdam and Rotterdam, and to the blast-furnaces in IJmuiden. All these were very important for the Germans.

The attack formation of which James and Edward were a part consisted of eleven B-26s, each carrying four 500-pound bombs. The planes flew at about 50 feet above the sea to avoid being spotted by the radars of the German coast guard. However, one of the bombers experienced technical problems and decided to turn back. The pilots of this plane made the fatal mistake to climb to a higher altitude for the return flight. This caused the Germans to see an aircraft on their radar and the German coast guard was alerted. As a result, the other B-26s were hit hard by German anti-aircraft fire a short time later.

The bomber of James and Edward was shot down by German Flak above IJmuiden and crashed into the North Sea shortly after. Both were killed in the crash. They were 22 years old. James' body washed ashore near Den Helder two months later and is buried at the Netherlands American Cemetery in Margraten (Plot P, Row 16, Grave 5). Edward's body was never found. That is why his name is listed on the Walls of the Missing in Margraten. Of the rest of the crew, only one survived the crash.

When their father, Dr. James 'Jamie' Norton, was asked if he wanted James' remains transported home, he replied that this was not his wish. He wrote to officials: 'As I have so often said before, this boy is one of twins, the other now lying at the bottom of the North Sea not far off the coast of Holland...and never having been separated in life, they are as close as they can ever be, just where they are, and so I wish this boy to stay exactly where he is, not only at the moment, but for evermore.'

Conway mourned but never forgot the flying twins. In memory of the brothers a new terminal at the Myrtle Beach Airport, just east of Conway, was named after them in 2010: Norton General Aviation Terminal.

◀ The twin brothers James and Edward

ROY E. RIGHTMIRE JR.

Technical Sergeant

95th Bombardment Group

A lack of oxygen in the air

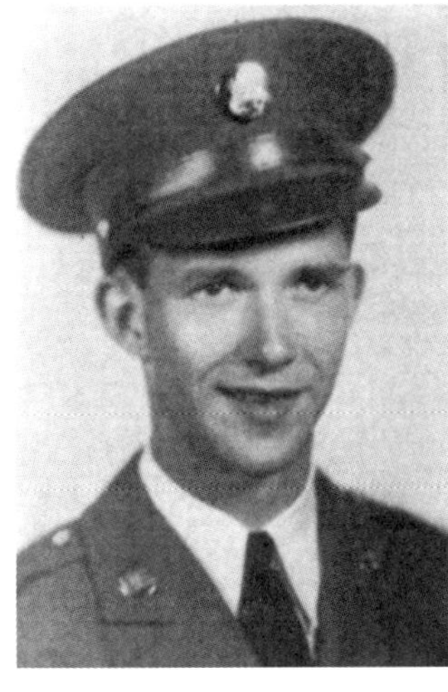

Technical Sergeant Roy E. Rightmire Jr. from Pennsylvania was born in 1920 and joined the U.S. Army Air Forces in July 1941. In 1943, he was the engineer and top turret gunner in the four-engine B-17 nicknamed 'Fritz Blitz.' This heavy bomber was part of the 335th Bomb Squadron of the 95th Bombardment Group.

On October 10, 1943, Roy's bomber took off to bomb targets near the German city of Münster. However, shortly after the bomb run was made, the B-17 was crippled by Flak. According to a statement of Technical Sergeant Frank D. Dean, one of the aircraft's waist gunners, the bomber was shot down by an enemy fighter about fifteen minutes later.

Prior to the crash, Roy was found unconscious (and possibly already dead) on the platform of the top turret. Some of his fellow crew members who saw him lying there later reported that they assumed he was unconscious due to a lack of oxygen. One of them stated that he had heard him saying: 'my guns have frozen in upper position. I need oxygen.' Shortly after Roy had passed out, and before bailing out themselves, other crew members first readied Roy's parachute harness. They pulled Roy's rip cord to release his chute and pushed him out of the damaged aircraft.

Surviving crew members who were taken prisoner later reported that a German interrogation team had told them that Roy was dead and buried. Most likely, he had already died in the air due to a lack of oxygen. Roy was 23 years old at the time and was initially buried at Haaksbergen, the Netherlands. Later his body was transferred to Margraten, where he was given his final resting place in Plot J, Row 17, Grave 14.

ISRAEL LEVINE
Second Lieutenant
100th Bombardment Group

The refusal to speak his name

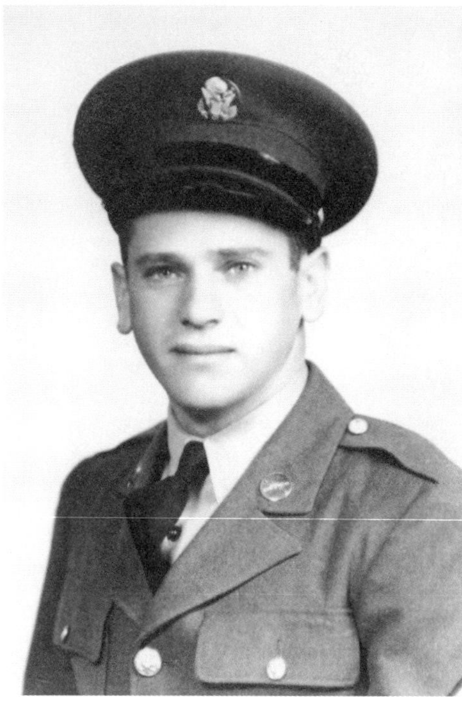

Israel Levine was born in Boston, Suffolk County, Massachusetts, on February 11, 1917. He had three brothers and three sisters. When he was seven years old, the family moved to Los Angeles, California. After graduating from Washington High School in 1935, Israel worked as a foreman with the Civilian Conservation Corps during the Great Depression.

Israel enlisted on June 4, 1941. Due to an accident suffered in his youth, one of his legs was shorter than the other, shattering his dreams to become a pilot. Instead, he was trained as a navigator at Santa Ana airfield, California. After graduating and finalizing his training in August 1943, he was assigned to the 100th Bombardment Group at Thorpe Abbotts in the United Kingdom.

Second Lieutenant Israel Levine was the navigator in the ten-men crew of Second Lieutenant William M. Beddow, 351st Bomb Squadron. Their aircraft with Serial Number #42-30723 was nicknamed 'Holy Terror.' On October 10, 1943, a massive attack of 307 B-17s was planned on the railroad facilities and waterway/ canals at Münster, Germany. The 100th Bombardment Group participated with fourteen aircraft. The formation was attacked by hundreds of German fighters which caused the formations to break-up.

After bombing the target, the 'Holy Terror' was involved in a mid-air collision with an attacking Messerschmitt Me-109. Subsequently the bomber struck another B-17 in the 'box formation' (#42-30047 nicknamed 'Sweater Girl'). Several crew members managed to bail out before the aircraft went into a vertical dive and crashed and exploded in the Vinneberger Forest near Ostbevern, Germany. Levine's crew suffered six killed in action and four prisoners of war. For the crew of the other aircraft the tally was four KIA and six POW. The 'Bloody 100th' lost twelve out of fourteen aircraft (36 KIA, 84 POW / 1 Evaded).

The co-pilot of 'Holy Terror' witnessed Israel Levine helping the wounded tail gunner to attach his parachute to his harness and helping him to bail out of the emergency exit. Both Levine and the tail gunner successfully opened their parachutes.

What happened next was witnessed by shocked German civilians. While descending under his parachute, a German fighter pilot shot the helpless Second Lieutenant Israel Levine. When German civilians reached his body, he was found dead. Staff Sergeant Samuel Hicks, the right waist gunner, was also found dead. On basis of their Jewish names both men were denied a proper burial by the Nazi town mayor and were deliberately buried as 'unknowns.' Post-war, the local civilians – who had seen the names on the dog tags prior to their burials – informed the American Graves Registration Units on their findings, and both men were identified so that they could be properly buried in a marked grave.

Staff Sergeant Hicks is buried in the U.S., and the final resting place of Second Lieutenant Israel Levine is at Margraten, in Plot E, Row 17, Grave 11.

LEONARD R. HENLIN
Sergeant
305th Bombardment Group

Killed by a German fighter plane

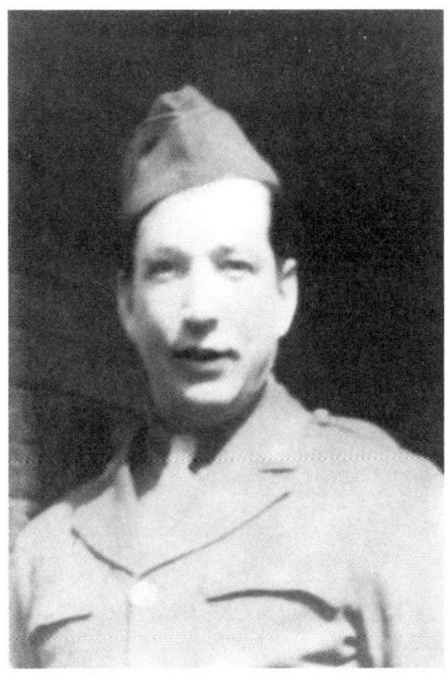

Sergeant Leonard Roy Henlin from Rhode Island was born in 1911. He enlisted in the USAAF in 1942 and was assigned as a left waist gunner in a B-17 bomber of the 305th Bombardment Group. The heavy bombers of this type were called 'Flying Fortresses,' because they were armed with as many as twelve machine guns to defend themselves against attacks by German fighters. Because of this, the Air Force commanders initially believed – erroneously – the B-17s did not need protection from their own fighter squadrons.

On October 14, 1943, Roy and nine other crew members flew their B-17 from England to Germany to bomb ball bearing factories in the German city of Schweinfurt. These factories were very important to the German war industry, as ball bearings are indispensable parts for aircraft, trucks, armored vehicles, and tanks.

During the flight over Germany, Roy's bomber was attacked by German fighter planes armed with machine guns, cannons, and rockets. With their heavy machine guns, Roy and his fellow gunners managed to bring down one of the German Messerschmitt Bf 109s. However, one of their engines was then badly damaged by another enemy fighter plane, which caused the bomber to crash. The debris of the B-17 came down near the Dutch village of Eygelshoven and the German town of Finkenrath.

According to a crew member who survived, ball turret gunner Ben Roberts, Roy had already been killed in mid-air at his waist gunner position by a 20mm shell from a German fighter. Therefore, he remained forever 32. His remains were found near the tail section in Eygelshoven. In Margraten, Roy is buried in Plot B, Row 21, Grave 26.

HARLAN D. BURTON
Staff Sergeant
351st Bombardment Group

Killed in a fierce air battle

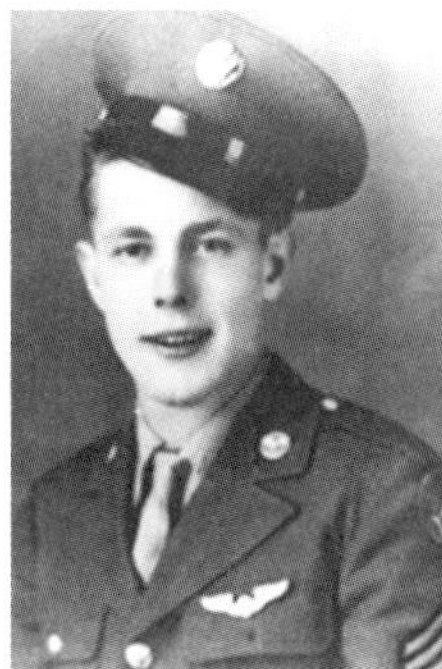

Staff Sergeant Harlan D. Burton from Missouri was born in 1921. After attending high school, he was employed as a truck driver until he joined the USAAF in August 1942. Harlan eventually served as a ball turret gunner in a four-engine B-17 of the 511th Bomb Squadron. This squadron was part of the 351st Bombardment Group.

In December 1941, Harlan had married Verna L. Newton. While Harlan was in the service, she gave birth to their daughter Verna Charlene Burton on March 27, 1943. Sadly, the baby girl died two days later...

Shortly after the tragic loss of his baby daughter, Harlan was stationed in England to be deployed in the Allied bombing campaign against Nazi Germany. On November 3, 1943, Harlan and his fellow crew members took off to join a large formation which had been assigned to bomb submarine pens and facilities near Wilhelmshaven. There were no significant problems during the flight toward Germany, but as the B-17s approached their targets, they came under intense fire from German anti-aircraft guns and enemy fighter planes. One of the other B-17s was hit and then collided with the bomber Harlan was in. The mid-air collision caused so much damage to Harlan's plane that it was no longer possible to maintain its position.

Almost immediately after dropping out of formation, Harlan's damaged bomber was attacked and fired upon by two or three enemy aircraft. From his position, Harlan fired with the two machine guns that he was operating and reportedly managed to bring down one of the German fighters. However, shortly thereafter his B-17 exploded and crashed near Wilhelmshaven. Six of his fellow crew members were able to bail out with their parachutes, but Harlan had no opportunity to escape. Therefore, he perished in the crash. Harlan was only 22 years old at the time. Because his body was never found, his name is inscribed on the Walls of the Missing in Margraten.

One of the surviving crew members, Bradley E. Squires Jr., the bombardier, wrote a letter to Harlan's mother. 'In an aerial collision near Bremen, Germany, the ship was badly damaged and, in an attempt to return to our base, the plane crashed near Wilhelmshaven, Germany. To the best of my knowledge, your son was unable to get out of the ship. The other three men who were killed were drowned in the North Sea, I believe. (...) Your son was an excellent soldier and gunner and his work against the enemy was very important to us. Harlan was very well liked by all the officers and men of his crew and squadron. He had many enemy aircraft to his credit and destroyed one the day that he lost his life in the service of his country.'

FRANK D. GALLION
Flight Officer
4th Fighter Group

Recovered from the IJsselmeer

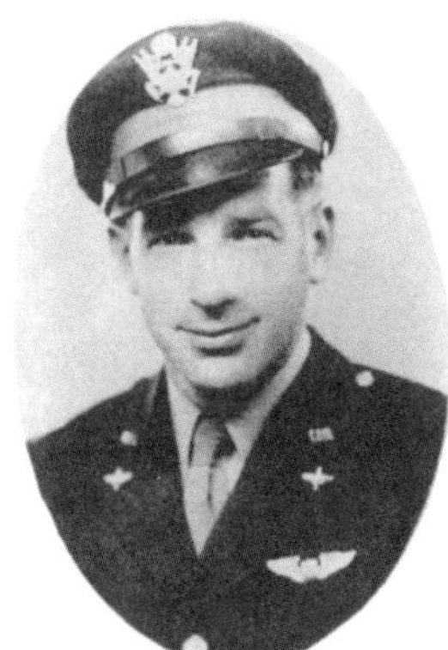

Flight Officer Frank D. Gallion from Ohio didn't want to wait for America to declare war – if they ever would. Therefore, he left home in 1941 to join the Royal Canadian Air Force. In 1942, after the U.S. entry into the war following the attack on Pearl Harbor, Frank was transferred to the United States Army Air Forces' 4th Fighter Group and assigned to its 334th Fighter Squadron.

On November 3, 1943, Frank piloted a P-47 Thunderbolt to escort a formation of B-17 bombers that were part of a 500-plane attack force that passed over the Netherlands on its way to their primary target in Wilhelmshaven, Germany. He took off from the forward air base at Halesworth, England. However, soon after, when the P-47s flew over the Dutch coast, Frank and the other fighter pilots involved in this mission were attacked by German fighters. The Messerschmitt Bf-109s raked the Thunderbolts with machine gun fire and Frank's P-47 was hit. The plane spiraled out of control and then disappeared into the IJsselmeer near Hyppolytushoef and Den Oever. Frank lost his life, and while still seated in the plane's cockpit, he sank to the bottom with the wreckage. Two weeks later, Frank's wife Phyllis received a message saying that her 29-year-old husband was recorded as missing in action. She never remarried and passed away in 1990.

In 1993, a Dutch dredging ship in the lake hit something about ten feet below the surface, which turned out to be Frank's long-lost P-47; his skeleton, almost intact, was still seated in the cockpit, Dutch Navy divers later discovered.

The incident was reported to officials, but the plane's salvage was delayed until 1995. On Wednesday February 8, Dutch salvagers retrieved Frank's pilot jacket, his dog-tags, his boots and part of his skeleton from the wreckage of his plane. Two days later, the rest of his remains and the plane's wreckage itself were salvaged. The wreckage, consisting of a muddied tail section, the left wing and the heavily damaged cockpit, was raised from the water by cranes. For all those involved it was a special operation, because it was the most complete airplane wreckage recovered in the IJsselmeer since the war.

A few weeks later, six members of the Gallion family traveled from Ohio to the Netherlands to visit the site where Frank's plane had crashed into the IJsselmeer and where his remains had been recovered. One of them was Ottmar Gallion, Frank's brother. Especially for the occasion, he bought red, white and blue flowers at the Amsterdam flower market. 'That seemed to us a fitting combination,' his son Gary said to a Dutch journalist. 'Because we don't just want to remember our brother and uncle here. We also want to pay tribute to the Dutch authorities, who have done so much to recover him and other American airmen.'

Rijkswaterstaat, the executive agency of the Dutch Ministry of Infrastructure and Water Management, provided the service's finest vessel to sail the Gallion family to the crash site. There, Ottmar and his accompanying family members threw the bouquets into the water. The following day, Ottmar went to the city of Lelystad. There he was able to see and touch the wreckage of his brother's plane. It was part of a large exhibition on the air war over the IJsselmeer that was officially opened the same day.

Meanwhile, Frank's remains had been flown to the army's central identification laboratory in Hawaii. After the final identification was completed there, Frank returned home more than 52 years after he was shot down over the IJsselmeer. He received a hero's welcome and was laid to rest in Ohio.

Frank is also listed on the Walls of the Missing in Margraten. A small rosette was placed next to his name there to indicate that he was found.

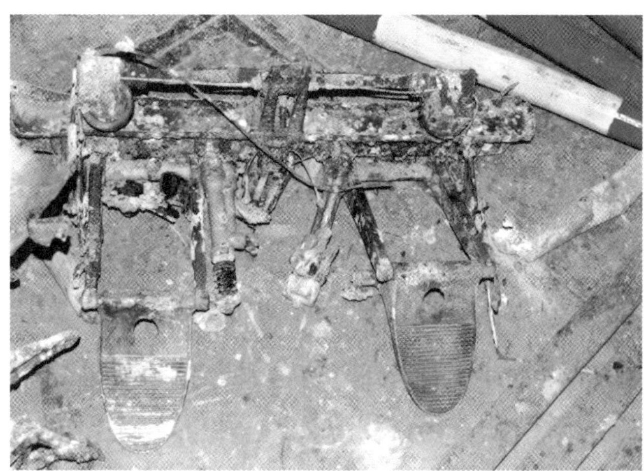

The foot pedals of the wreckage of Frank D. Gallion's Republic P-47 Thunderbolt recovered from the IJsselmeer. SOURCE: Nederlands Instituut voor Militaire Historie/ Koninklijke Luchtmacht

RICHARD E. WOODYATT

Staff Sergeant

381st Bombardment Group

Crashed in the Hollands Diep

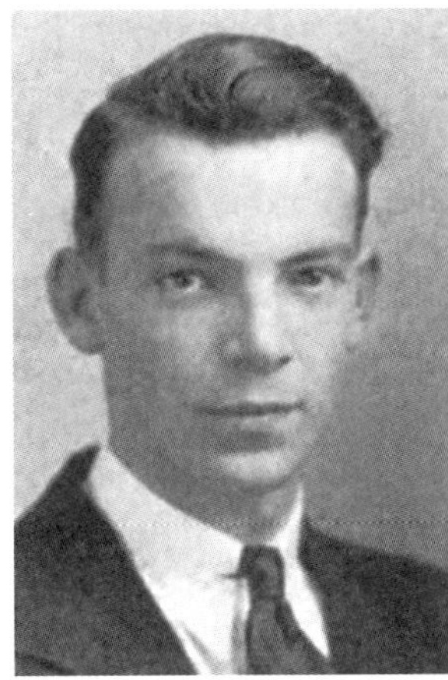

Staff Sergeant Richard E. Woodyatt from Illinois was born in 1916 and enlisted in October 1942. He served in the 535th Bomb Squadron of the 381st Bombardment Group and was the tail gunner in the B-17 bomber that was nicknamed 'Blowin' Bessie.' Richard took part in thirteen missions over enemy territory. He was posthumously awarded the Air Medal with Oak Leaf Cluster for this in 1945.

On November 5, 1943, the 'Blowin' Bessie' left the runway in England with Richard and nine other crew members on board to bomb targets at the German city of Gelsenkirchen. The objective of the mission was to destroy synthetic oil production facilities that were important to the German war effort.

Over the target, Richard's B-17 was hit by German Flak. The pilots managed to keep the plane in the formation for a few minutes, but then they began to lose altitude. Because of this the 'Blowin' Bessie' became isolated, whereupon it was attacked by German fighters. The B-17 was shot down and crashed near Klundert in the Hollands Diep. Six of the ten crew members were still in the plane at the time and sank to the bottom of this Dutch river with its wreckage. One of them was Richard. According to a statement included in the Missing Air Crew Report, he was presumably struck and killed at his tail position by the machine gun or cannon fire from the German fighters. As a result, he remained forever 27.

Richard's mortal remains were not found afterwards. Therefore, his name is inscribed on the Walls of the Missing in Margraten. This also applies to some other members of the 'Blowin' Bessie' crew.

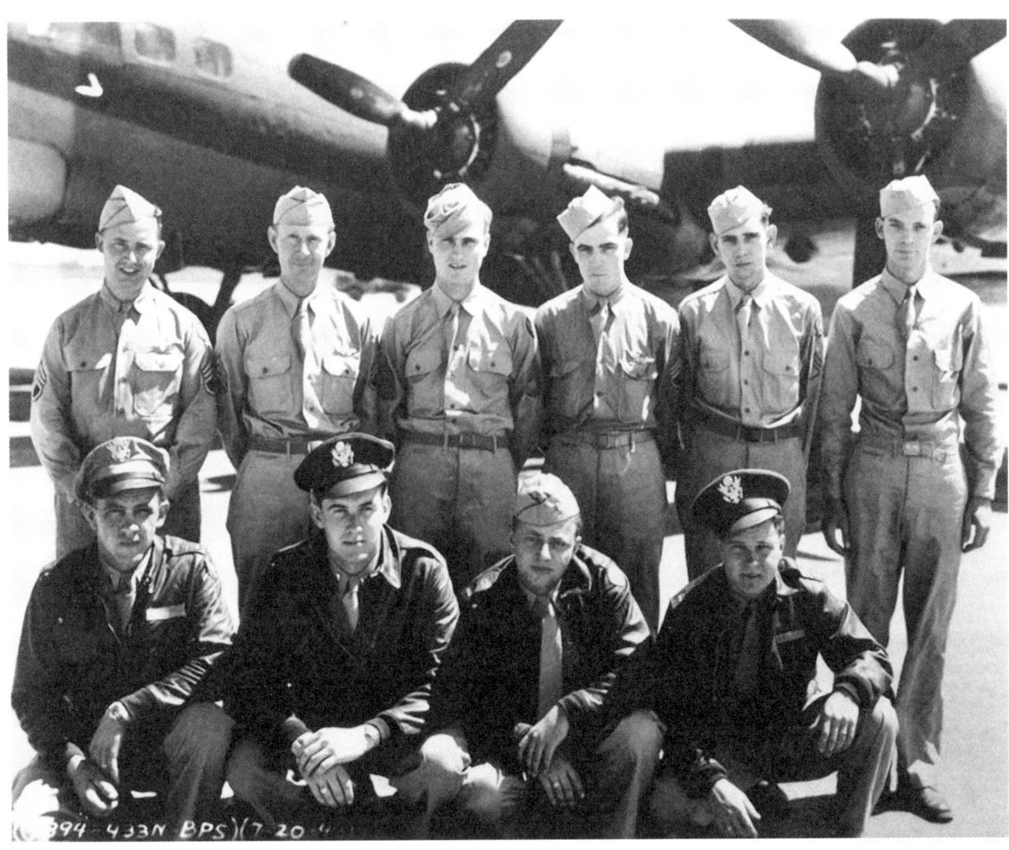

The crew of the 'Blowin' Bessie.'
Richard Woodyatt stands far right in the back row.
SOURCE: U.S. Army Air Forces via Arie-Jan van Hees

ROBERT B. O'HARA
Second Lieutenant
94th Bombardment Group

Killed in riddled cockpit

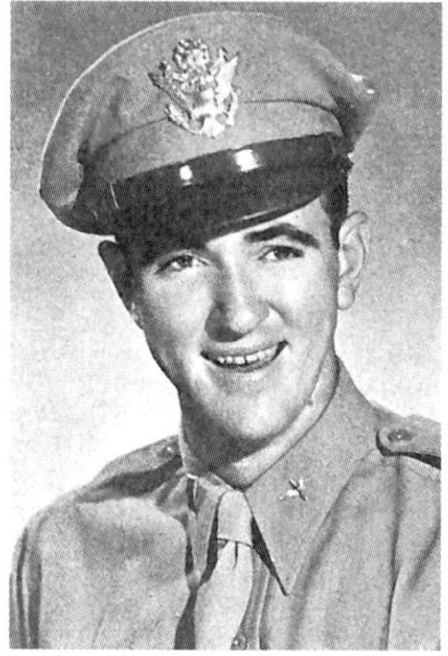

Second Lieutenant Robert B. O'Hara from Pennsylvania was born in 1920. Later he lived in Texas. Robert joined the U.S. Army Air Forces, whereupon he began training as a pilot. The unit in which he served was the 331st Bomb Squadron of the 94th Bombardment Group, which had been stationed in the United Kingdom since the spring of 1943. The aircraft in which Robert flew was a four-engine B-17 'Flying Fortress.'

In the morning of November 11, 1943, there were thick clouds over the English Channel. Nevertheless, the aircraft of the 331st Bomb Squadron took off for a bombing flight to the German city of Münster. The bombs that the B-17s were carrying had to be dropped over a railroad junction that was of great importance to German logistics.

After takeoff, Robert flew his bomber toward the designated target. Münster was reached without significant problems and the bombs were dropped. However, while flying back over Holland, the B-17 was suddenly attacked by the Luftwaffe. Three Focke-Wulf 190 fighters began strafing them, knocking out one of the bomber's engines and also hitting its left wing. The wing caught fire and the plane went into a spin, whereupon it exploded in mid-air. The wreckage came down in the Molenpolder near Numansdorp. Three crew members miraculously survived because they were blown out of the aircraft by the explosion and managed to save themselves with their parachutes. They became prisoners of war a short time later when the Dutch fishermen who had pulled them out of the water were spotted by a German patrol boat.

Robert was not among the survivors. He died at the age of 23. According to the Missing Air Crew Report, Robert was already dead before the explosion and the plane's crash – he is believed to have been killed when the German fighters raked his cockpit with their machine guns. After his body was found, he was initially buried near Rotterdam. Later, Robert was transferred to the U.S. Military Cemetery in Margraten, where he is permanently interred in Plot B, Row 14, Grave 23.

DOYLE C. MC CUTCHEN
Sergeant
381st Bombardment Group

Crash landing on the Lek River

Sergeant Doyle C. Mc Cutchen was born in Western Grove, Arkansas on September 7, 1921. Later he was a resident of Rupert, Idaho. Doyle was proud of being a boy from the countryside.

In November 1942, Doyle enlisted in the U.S. Army Air Forces. He was the ball turret gunner of the B-17 nicknamed 'Mission Belle.' This bomber was part of the 535th Bomb Squadron of the 381st Bombardment Group. Shortly before leaving for England, Doyle married his beloved Lola, and while still in basic training, he sent the following letter to his sister Ardella and brother-in-law Jerry on January 23, 1943:

> ***'Dear Sis and Jerry,***
> ***Well here goes for a few lines. It won't be very much because nothing happens here except, I work, study, eat, work, study and sleep though it's darn little sleep I get.***
>
> ***I just finished my 3rd week test. All my academic work is over now except for a final test 2 weeks from now. I've got 95% average in academics so now if I can only qualify in my air firing.***
>
> ***I'll graduate 2 weeks from today with a Sgts. rating and also draw flying pay... All next week will be spent firing on the ground and next Saturday will find me soaring thru the clouds with a machine gun in my hands. I've just got to pass. If I do, I can be an instructor if I care to but think I'll pass it up for combat duty unless I'm forced to be an instructor... Please don't tell Mom I'm passing up a teaching job to go overseas. I'm afraid she wouldn't understand...'***

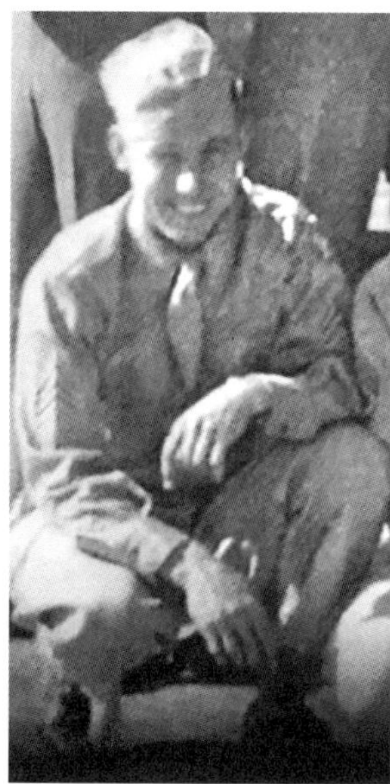

On December 1, 1943, ten months after writing this letter, Doyle and his fellow crew members took off in England to bomb chemical plants of IG Farben in the German city of Leverkusen. It was Doyle's second mission. Being the ball turret gunner, Doyle knew he was in a very vulnerable position.

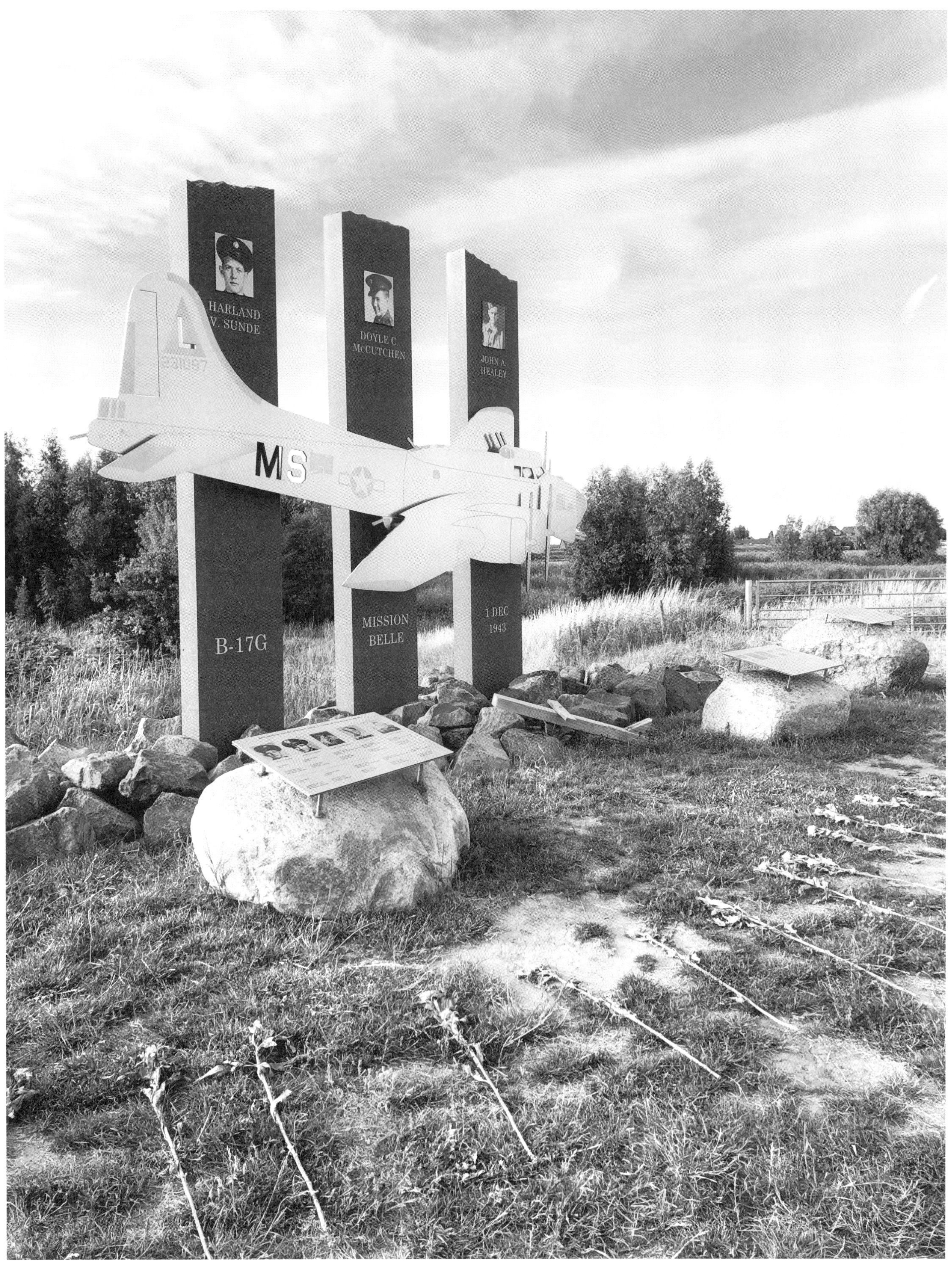
HARLAND
V. SUNDE
DOYLE C.
McCUTCHEN
JOHN A.
HEALEY
231097
MS
B-17G
MISSION
BELLE
1 DEC
1943

After bombing the factories, while on the way back to England, the Mission Belle was both heavily fired upon by enemy Flak and riddled by German fighters. Several engines were knocked out and the control cables were shot away. The seriously injured pilot realized that they wouldn't make it to England and therefore finally took the decision to make a crash landing on the river Lek in Holland.

Moments later, the heavily damaged B-17 made a landing on the water, about halfway between the villages of Nieuw-Lekkerland and Streefkerk. The bomber came to a stop against a crib and then began to sink rapidly. Seven crew members survived the landing, but Doyle and two others did not. Doyle had been badly injured by Flak fragments and machine gun fire from the German fighters, but with some help was still able to escape from the wreckage. Almost immediately afterwards he was killed, as the sinking wreck broke in two with the tail section settling atop him. Doyle disappeared underwater, could not be rescued, and did not resurface. He was only 22 years old at the time and his wife Lola was just a few months pregnant with their daughter Patricia.

About six months after his death, Doyle's remains washed ashore near Rotterdam and were found on May 30, 1944. Local people buried his body at Crooswijk, but in 1946 the remains were transferred to Margraten. Here Doyle got his final resting place in Plot J, Row 3, Grave 20.

In 2018, amidst great interest, a monument was unveiled to honor the crew. It stands near the spot where the Mission Belle crashed. With this monument, the foundation that made it possible aims to keep the memory of Doyle and the two other fallen crew members alive. One of those two, pilot Harland V. Sunde, is also buried in Margraten (Plot O, Row 9, Grave 12).

WALTER E. CHANCE
Sergeant
323rd Bombadment Group

Did not return from an attack on Schiphol

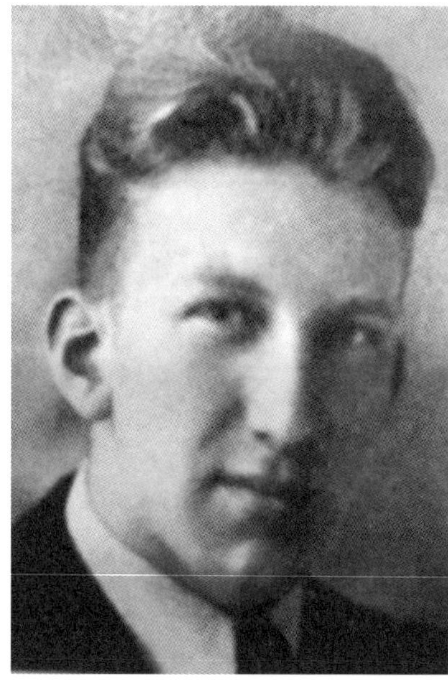

Walter E. Chance from New Jersey was born on June 17, 1919. Before joining the American Smelting and Refining Company, he attended high school for four years. In 1940, his mother Edith passed away. She was only 63 years old at the time. In January 1942, Walter also lost his father Edward in a traffic accident at the age of 51.

A few months after his father's death, Walter entered the USAAF in June 1942. A year later he was stationed in England. During his active service, Walter was the tail gunner in the twin-engine B-26 Marauder 'Raunchy Rascal' of the 455th Bomb Squadron. This squadron was part of the 323rd Bombardment Group.

On December 13, 1943, Walter was deployed in an attack by a large number of American bombers on Schiphol Airport near Amsterdam. At the time, the German Luftwaffe used Schiphol as an air base for its fighter planes and bombers. The German fighters that took off from there were dangerous opponents for the heavy Allied bombers that were bombing targets in Germany and other occupied countries. Therefore, the B-26s had to damage Schiphol so heavily that the Luftwaffe could no longer use this airfield.

When the formation of B-26s flew over Schiphol to drop their bombs, they were heavily and accurately shot at by the German anti-aircraft guns (Flak). The B-26 in which Walter manned the tail position was shot down. Not much later, the aircraft crashed into the North Sea. All six crew members were killed in the crash. Walter was only 24 years old at the time and his body was never found afterwards. Therefore, his name is listed on the Walls of the Missing in Margraten.

DONALD D. PIPPITT

Staff Sergeant

392nd Bombardment Group

Tail gunner fell out of the plane

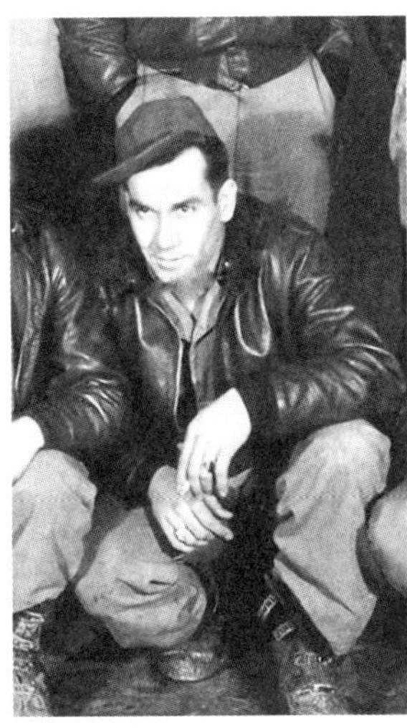

Donald Dale Pippitt from Kansas was a tail gunner with the 579th Bomb Squadron of the 392nd Bombardment Group, stationed at USAAF Station 118 'Wendling' in the British county of Norfolk. On December 20, 1943, this group flew its seventeenth operational mission with 22 aircraft. The target was the port of Bremen in Germany.

At 11:30 British time, flying over the North Sea and only 45 minutes away from the target, fate struck. Donald Pippitt's plane, a B-24 with the painted nickname 'El Lobo,' suddenly lost the tail turret containing the unfortunate Staff Sergeant. He crashed with his turret on the Dutch island of Texel. Opinions differ about the exact cause. There are two different reports about this incident. One report states that the propeller of a B-24 flying next to 'El Lobo' was hit by anti-aircraft fire and parted from the engine. This runaway propeller then spun through the air towards Donald's tail turret and knocked it off the plane like a hot knife through butter.

The plane returned to the base, even though its tail turret with the unfortunate Donald had been cut off the plane. SOURCE: U.S. Army Air Forces via Arie-Jan van Hees

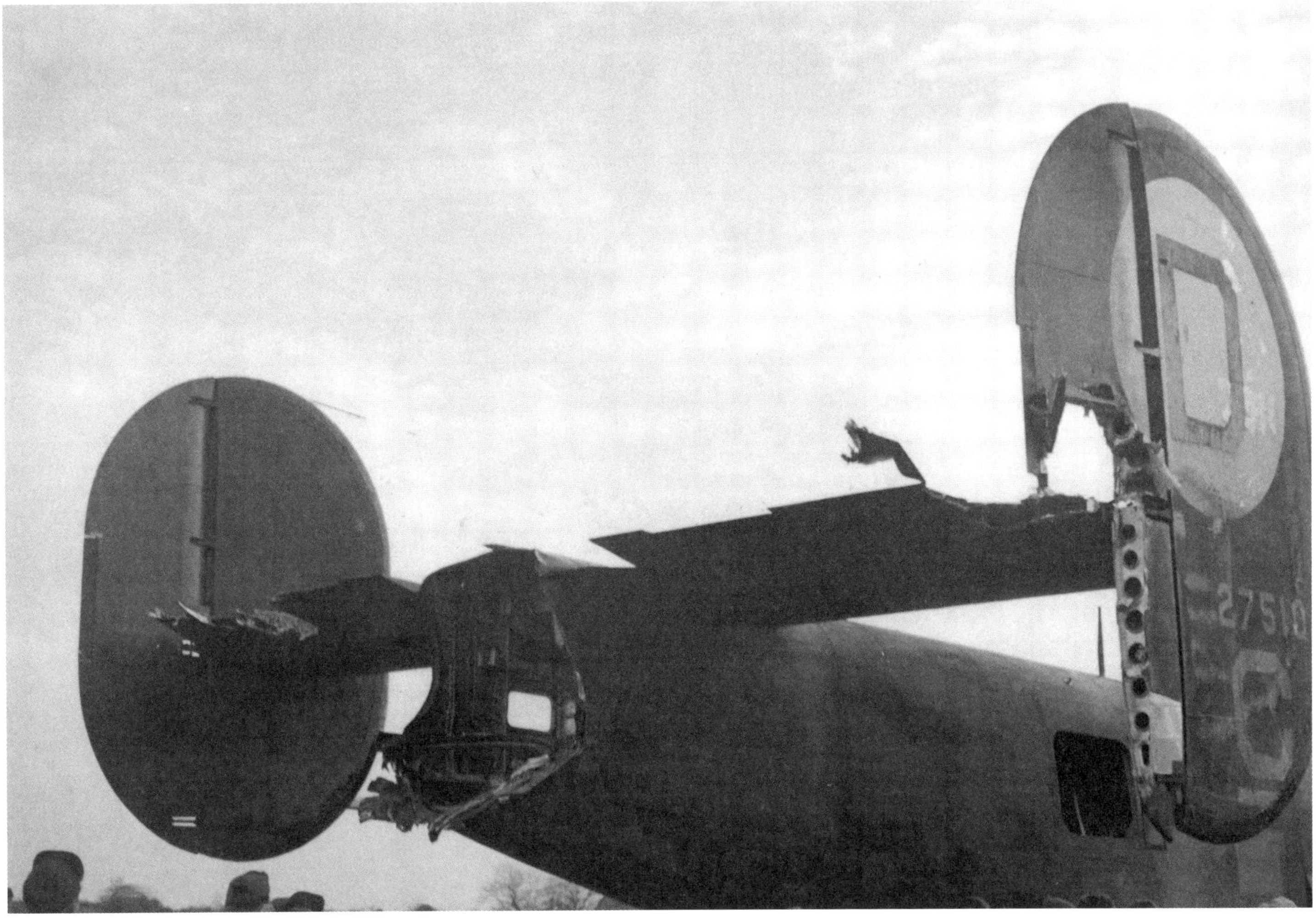

Another version reports the following: 'El Lobo' would have flown in the slipstream of an aircraft in front of him. The speed would have suddenly decreased due to the sudden appearance of the 'prop wash' (wind wake effect). As a result of this loss of speed, an aircraft that was coming up behind suddenly overtook 'El Lobo' and the left outer propeller of that aircraft hit the turret, Donald's position, cutting it off completely from the aircraft.

Despite the fact that one of the two tail rudders of the B-24 bomber was badly damaged, the plane remained controllable, and the pilot therefore decided not to abort the mission (and fly back to England on his own), but to continue the mission. On the way to the target another aircraft was shot down. Eventually 21 aircraft with 1,134 bombs bombed the harbor of Bremen, and despite heavy anti-aircraft fire and attacks by single and twin-engine German fighters, the bombers reached their home base in Norfolk safely. During this mission the 392nd Bombardment Group lost twelve men. Eleven of them were in the lost aircraft, the twelfth was Donald D. Pippitt.

His tail turret crashed into a small dune valley, locally known as 'Moesvlakje' near Paal ('marker') 14 in the dunes near Westerslag, on the west side of the island of Texel. The body of Donald Dale Pippitt was found and identified the same day. He was buried on December 21 in the cemetery of the village of Den Burg. His last resting place in Margraten is Plot H, Row 4, Grave 3.

KENT F. MILLER
Flight Officer
44th Bombardment Group

Found on the bottom of the IJsselmeer

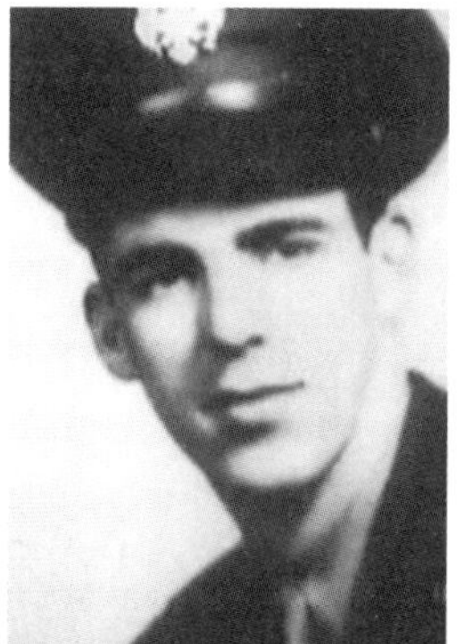

Flight Officer Kent F. Miller from West Virginia was born in 1922. He entered the U.S. Army Air Forces in 1941 and eventually piloted the B-24 Liberator bomber 'Big Banner' of the 66th Bomb Squadron. This squadron was part of the 44th Bombardment Group.

On December 22, 1943, the 'Big Banner' participated in a bombing mission over Germany. It would be Kent's last flight because while they were bombing the city of Münster, the plane was hit by Flak. A short time later, when they had begun the return flight to England, Kent noticed that several of the bomber's engines had been damaged. As a result, they began to lose altitude rapidly.

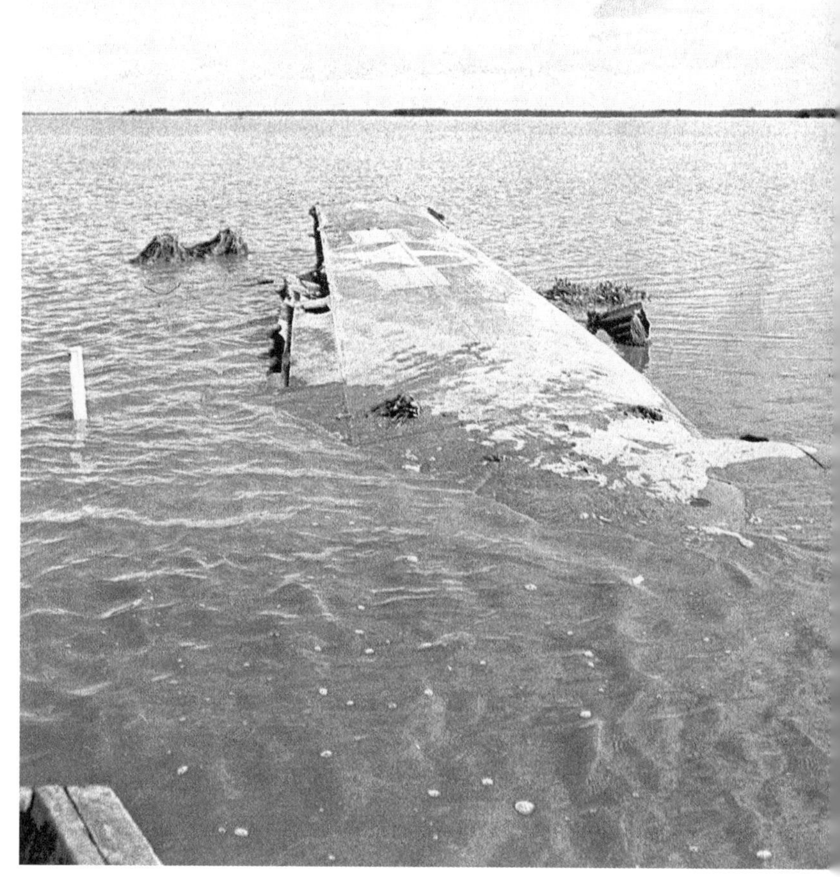

As Kent concluded that the aircraft was going to crash, he ordered his fellow crew members to bail out. Shortly thereafter, however, he became aware that they were now flying over the IJsselmeer, the largest lake in the Netherlands. Therefore, Kent quickly ordered the others to remain in the plane and to prepare themselves for a crash landing on the water. Four crew members had already made a parachute jump.

Shortly after Kent's order to stay in the plane, the 'Big Banner' crashed into the cold waters of the IJsselmeer. The emergency landing failed and with Kent and the other crew members still on board, the B-24 sank straight to the bottom. Kent and four of his crew members lost their lives. As a result, Kent remained forever 21.

The co-pilot was the only one to survive. He was picked up by a German patrol boat and captured. The four crew members who had jumped out of the plane just before the crash had landed in the cold water with their parachutes and drowned...

Because the sunken B-24 was untraceable at the time, Kent was reported as missing in action. The wreckage of the bomber was not salvaged until 32 years later, in 1975. This happened when parts of the IJsselmeer were drained step by step to create polder land (now the Dutch province of Flevoland). Kent and his golden pilot ring were found inside the cockpit. As a result, he could then be buried in the United States. In Margraten, a rosette was placed next to his name on the Walls of the Missing. This indicates that his remains have been found.

◄ Recovery of the wreckage in the IJsselmeer in 1975.
Source: *De Legerkoerier* via Arie-Jan van Hees

WELTON P. TESTON
Staff Sergeant
306th Bombardment Group

A fatal collision in the air

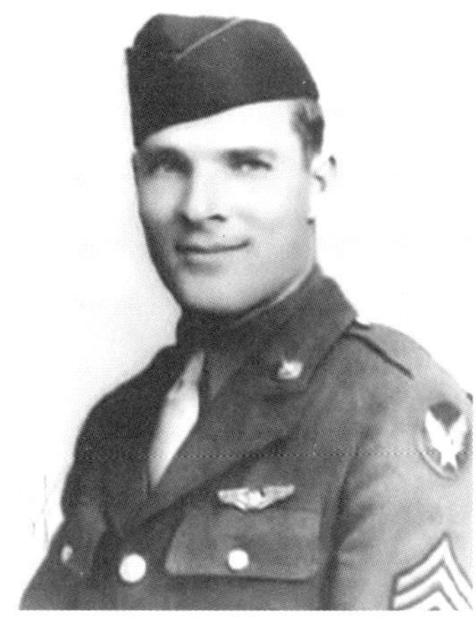

Welton P. Teston from California was born in 1920. He enlisted in the USAAF in September 1942, whereupon Welton served as a right waist gunner in a heavy four-engine B-17. The unit he served in was the 367th Bomb Squadron of the 306th Bombardment Group.

The bombers of this formation, like other bomber groups of the U.S. Eighth Air Force, carried out bombing raids on enemy targets from England. Usually these were factories, railroad junctions or other industrial and infrastructural targets that were important to the German war effort. The purpose of this bombing campaign was to cripple the weapon production and logistics of the German armed forces.

To hit the enemy war industries as hard as possible, the American bombers usually flew their missions in broad daylight. This allowed the pilots and bomb aimers to see the targets better, but it made the bombers also more vulnerable to German Flak and interceptions by the Luftwaffe.

On January 11, 1944, Welton's B-17 was deployed on a mission to Halberstadt. During the flight over the Netherlands, his squadron was suddenly attacked by German fighters, probably Focke-Wulf 190s. The German fighter pilots raked the American bombers with their machine guns, inflicting damage to several of the B-17s.

In the chaos that ensued, Welton's plane collided in mid-air with another B-17 from the same squadron. Both the bomber Welton was in and the aircraft they had collided with subsequently crashed. The debris from both bombers came down near Raalte, a town in the Dutch province of Overijssel. There, the remains of the killed crew members were found.

Because he had not survived the mid-air collision and the subsequent crash, Welton's life ended at the age of 24. His final resting place in Margraten is in Plot E, Row 15, Grave 21.

LEROY E. LEIST

Staff Sergeant

100th Bombardment Group

A daughter's desire to bring her father home

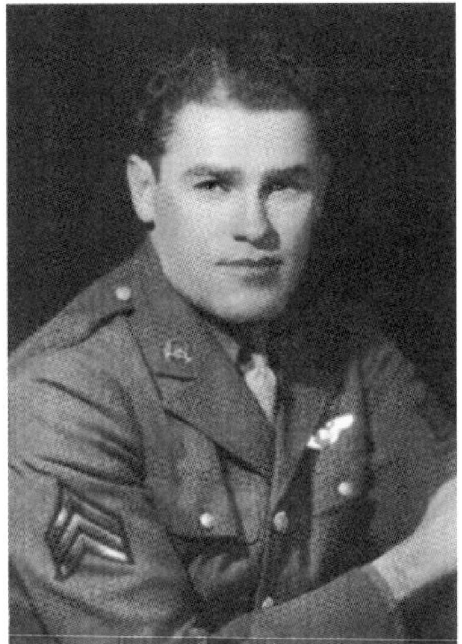

It was a moment of hope for Adrian Caldwell. In March 2009, a boat dredged up a Browning .50 caliber machine gun in the port of Rotterdam. The serial number on the gun revealed that it had belonged to the bomber plane in which her father, Staff Sergeant Leroy E. Leist, had served. He and five other crew members had been missing ever since their B-17 had disappeared on February 4, 1944. It seemed only a matter of time before the wreckage and the remains of its crew would be discovered.

Leroy was born in Delphios, Ohio, on October 18, 1915, as the son of Earnest and Eva. His brother Vernon was born two years later. The two boys were mostly raised by their father. Leroy was only eight years old when his mother passed away.

His military career started in the Ohio Army National Guard. The unit was activated in 1940 and sent for training to Camp Shelby, Mississippi. It was during that time that he met his soon-to-be wife Avis, who studied in the nearby town of Hattiesburg. They got married in March 1941. Their daughter Adrian would be born in July 1942.

By then, Leroy had already been released from the national guard as he had fulfilled his time. However, with a war raging in both Europe and the Pacific, he was drafted a couple of months later. He received a postponement as his daughter was about to be born, but ultimately enlisted into the U.S. Army Air Forces at Camp Shelby at the end of August 1942.

Leroy received his training at different bases in the U.S. So, Adrian said, her mother would take her on the train to go see him. In October 1943, Leroy was about to be sent overseas and called home at night. My mother 'drove the 60 miles frantically. She got to the gate and the guard wouldn't let her in and at that time he came running up! She did not think to bring me along, but he wanted to see me. So, they drove back to our house. They woke me up as it was the middle of the night. Then he had to go back to the base,' Adrian recalls. 'I can picture her standing at the gate watching the plane take off as it was the last time she saw him.'

On February 4, 1944, Leroy flew his fifteenth mission as a B-17 tail gunner with the 100th Bombardment Group. They were sent to Frankfurt, where their bomber was hit by German Flak. However, it was only near Brussels that the plane got in serious trouble, when German fighter pilot Erich Scheyda attacked the bomber. Nevertheless, while he seriously damaged the plane, he was unable to down it. German Flak positions near the Dutch city of Vlissingen gave the final blow. The plane was last seen turning north and descending, but there were no witnesses of the actual crash.

The bodies of four crew members washed ashore in the days and weeks after the crash. Based on where bodies were found, researchers in Europe and the U.S. who have been helping Adrian to find her father ever since 1999, first believed that the plane had crashed near the coast of the island of Goeree-Overflakkee. The recovery of the machine gun not only showed that this could not be true, it also was a breakthrough that led the government to announce a recovery mission in 2011. But then it was canceled due to cost constraints. 'I felt like the air had gone out of my body as I was totally devastated with the news,' Adrian said. No attempt has been made since.

And so in 2022, Leroy is still memorialized on the Walls of the Missing in Margraten, together with the other five members of his crew that went down with the plane. All that remains for Adrian, who was sixteen months old at the time of her father's death, are the stories told about him, and the photos and the scrapbook that her mother gave to her.

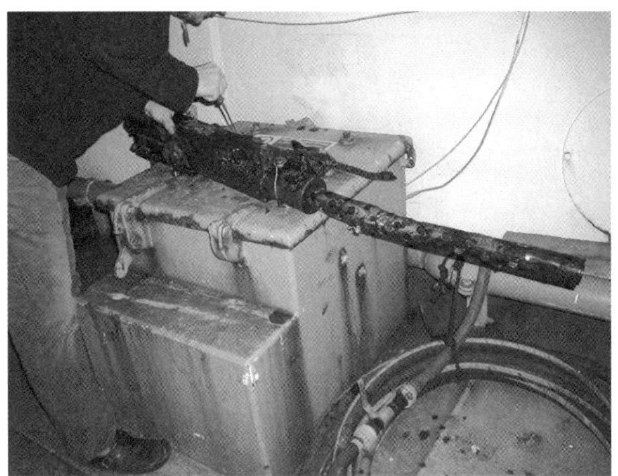

The dredged-up machine gun from the plane of Leroy Leist. SOURCE: WO2GO

WILLIAM P. JOHNSTON
Second Lieutenant
44th Bombardment Group

Navigator fell from the sky

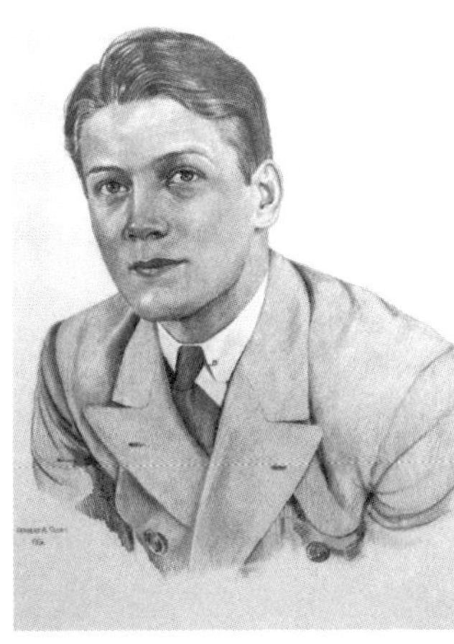

Second Lieutenant William P. Johnston from Missouri was born in 1914. In March 1942, he enlisted in the United States Army Air Forces. Then, after training as a navigator, William was assigned to the 506th Bomb Squadron of the 'Flying Eightballs,' which was the nickname of the 44th Bombardment Group.

As a navigator, William's job was to give instructions to the pilots of his bomber regarding the plotted flight route and the exact locations of the designated targets to be bombed. Therefore, William's seat was close to the cockpit of the two pilots.

On February 20, 1944, William and the nine other crew members aboard his bomber participated in a mission to Germany. The target of the attack was the German town of Oschersleben, where production facilities of the German aircraft industry were to be destroyed. For this purpose, William's B-24 carried a heavy bomb load.

Over the target, William's B-24 sustained heavy damage when one of the engines was hit by German Flak. As a result, the aircraft became a straggler and was then attacked at least four times by an enemy Messerschmitt Bf 109. Completing the return flight to England became impossible. The pilot in charge therefore ordered the crew to bail out with their parachutes.

Soon thereafter, William jumped out of the plane with his parachute harness on. In the Missing Air Crew Report, it was later stated by members of the crew who survived that his parachute failed to open. As a result, William fell from the sky... He was only 29 years old.

William's body was found near Treisbach. He is buried at the Netherlands American Cemetery in Margraten. There he is permanently laid to rest in Plot H, Row 12, Grave 9.

Crew of the plane of William P. Johnston, who is second from left on the front row

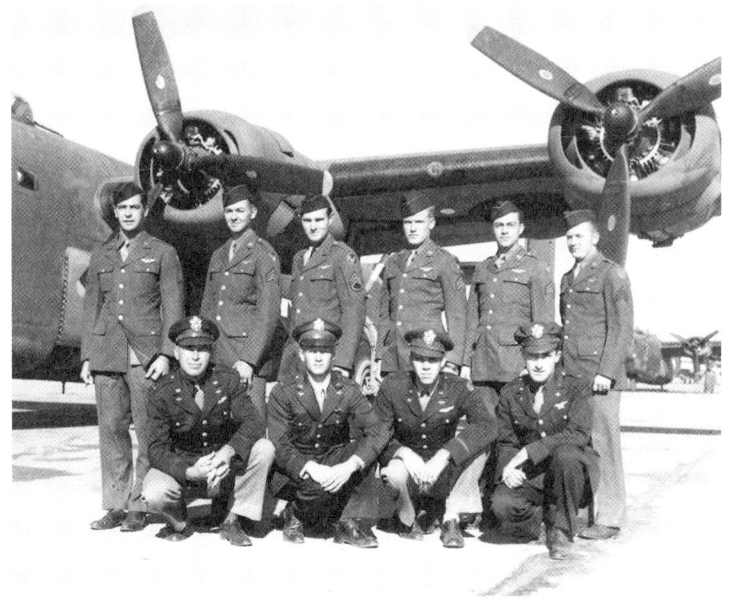

RUSSELL E. MASTERS
Second Lieutenant
359th Fighter Group

Engine trouble over the North Sea

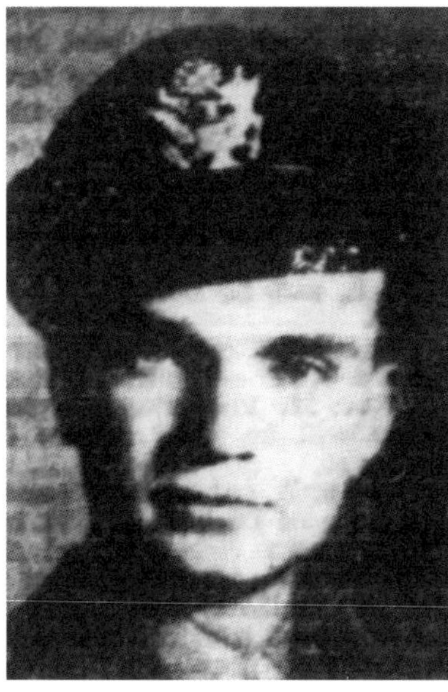

Second Lieutenant Russell E. Masters from Indiana was born in 1921. He graduated from high school in 1940 and then attended Indiana University until he enlisted in the USAAF. Russell was trained as a fighter pilot and left for Europe in January 1944.

Russell was assigned to the 369th Fighter Squadron of the 359th Fighter Group. He flew P-51 Mustangs and was mainly deployed to escort heavy bombers to protect them from attacks by German fighters.

On February 22, 1944, Russell boarded the cockpit of his P-51 to be deployed in another escort mission. He took off in England and began his flight toward the European mainland and Germany. However, soon after takeoff, he reported to the other pilots of his squadron that his plane suffered engine trouble over the North Sea. Using the on-board radio, he said that the oil pressure was gone and his engine was quitting. When the engine caught fire moments later, Russell had no choice but to abandon his Mustang and bail out.

One of the other pilots, First Lieutenant Ivan B. Hollomon, saw Russell bail out from his burning Mustang just before the plane crashed. He then observed Russell's parachute landing in the North Sea, a few miles from the Dutch coast near the city of Alkmaar. In the Missing Air Crew Report Hollomon stated that he saw Russell disappear underwater immediately after his landing. Hollomon had patrolled the area for over an hour, but he never saw him again.

Two alerted P-47's of the Air-Sea Rescue Service did not spot him either. It was therefore concluded that Russell had drowned in the North Sea after hitting the water beneath his parachute. He was only 24 years old. Because his body has never been found, he is still listed as missing. Therefore, his name is inscribed on the Walls of the Missing in Margraten.

JAMES F. FALLON
Sergeant
379th Bombardment Group

An exploded bomber

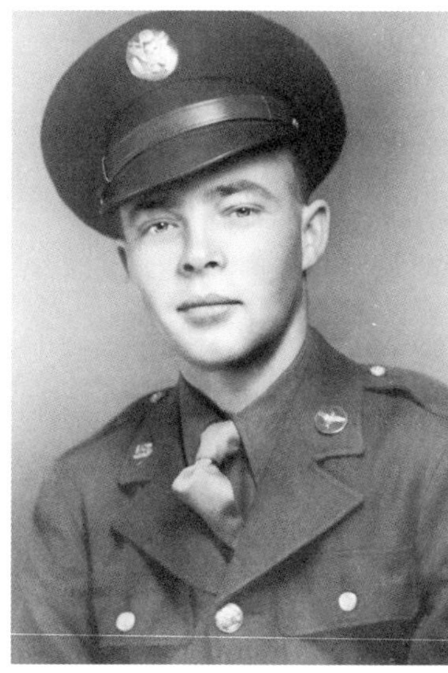

James F. Fallon from Pennsylvania was born in Philadelphia in 1916. He attended high school for four years and graduated in 1935. James' hometown was Yeadon, and before entering the USAAF in October 1942, he was employed by the United Shoe Machinery Company.

During his military service, James served as a sergeant in the 524th Bomb Squadron of the 379th Bombardment Group. He was the engineer and top turret gunner in the heavy B-17 bomber nicknamed 'Mojo.' With this dual role, James was primarily responsible for the proper operation of the engines during the flight, but when danger approached, he manned the plane's machine gun turret immediately behind the cockpit. From this position he could see 360 degrees around above the aircraft.

The 379th Bombardment Group to which James was assigned was activated in Idaho in November 1942. In 1943, the group was stationed in England to be deployed in bombing raids on Germany. The unit's home base in England was American Air Force Station 117 in Kimbolton.

On February 22, 1944, the ten-man crew of the 'Mojo' took off to bomb targets located in Wernigerode, Germany. At some point during the flight, disaster struck when the aircraft's bomb bay was hit by German Flak and caught fire. The B-17 exploded and some of the crew members were blown out of the plane. Three of them managed to survive thanks to their parachutes. James, however, did not and died at the age of 27. His remains were found after the crash and buried in Dülmen. James' body was later exhumed and reburied in Margraten, where his final resting place can be found in Plot E, Row 20, Grave 24.

CHARLES G. CASSADAY
Captain
7th Reconnaissance Group
Shot down during a reconnaissance flight

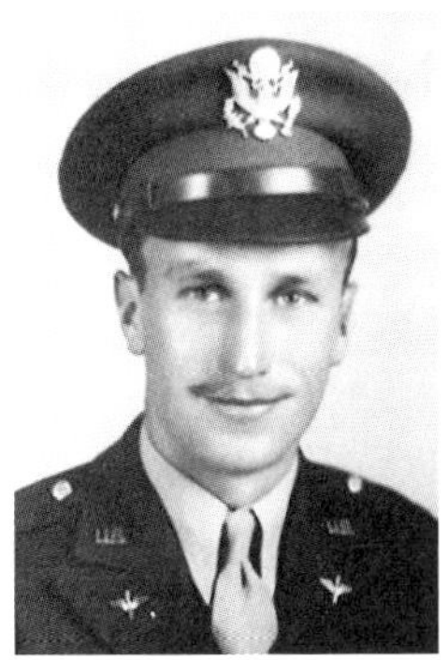

Captain Charles G. Cassaday from Iowa was born in 1917. Shortly after the United States became involved in World War II, he enlisted in the USAAF in January 1942. After enlisting, Charles started pilot training. He was assigned to the 27th Photographic Squadron of the 7th Reconnaissance Group. This squadron photographed enemy airfields, industrial complexes, railroad junctions, and harbors. This enabled the operation planners of the Eighth Air Force to determine targets for the heavy bombers.

In 1943, Charles and his unit were stationed in England. On D-Day, Charles flew an unarmed P-38 Lightning with special film equipment on board. With this plane he flew over the coastal area of Normandy to capture the Allied invasion from the air. After returning to England, Charles reported what he had seen:

> ***'Boats of every description crowded the Channel and ran in steady streams from one coast to another. Huge warships were broadside to the coast hurling fire at enemy defense installations. I could see the flash from their guns and that from enemy guns returning the fire. Several boats had been hit and were burning. A few of the tanks and vehicles our troops were unloading on the beach were burning too. Soldiers were pouring from invasion craft and were splashing through the choppy Channel to worm their way through obstructions on the sandy beach. (...) In some places the ground was dotted with various colored parachutes and I could see gliders here and there where our airborne troops had landed. Although the enemy resistance was tough and his fire heavy, our boys appeared to be pushing him back and streams of tanks and trucks were moving towards the front.'***

On June 8, 1944, two days after his adventure over Normandy, Charles took off in England in a F-5B-1LO Lightning. This was a special aircraft equipped with photographic equipment. The purpose of his mission was to take aerial reconnaissance photographs of potential bomber targets in Nazi-occupied Belgium. During the flight to Belgium, Charles flew over the Dutch city of Eindhoven. Here his aircraft was hit by German Flak, which caused it to crash near Veldhoven a short time later. Because of the low altitude he was flying at, Charles had no chance to use his parachute. Therefore, he was killed on the spot when his burning plane crashed onto the ground. Initially Charles was buried in Woensel, but his remains were later moved to Margraten. Here he was given his final resting place in Plot P, Row 11, Grave 5.

DOYLE C. MILLER
Staff Sergeant
492nd Bombardment Group
Shot down by German fighters

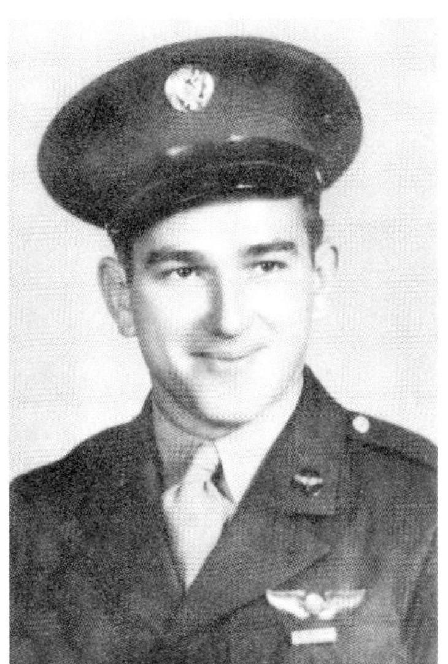

Doyle C. Miller from Illinois was born on December 17, 1919, and attended high school for four years. He entered the USAAF in October 1941 and served as a right waist gunner in a B-24 Liberator of the 856th Bomb Squadron. This squadron flew its missions under the operational command of the 492nd Bombardment Group.

The 492nd Bombardment Group was activated in the fall of 1943. In April 1944, the group was sent overseas to England to participate in the air war against Nazi Germany. Several weeks later, their first mission followed. Subsequently, the B-24s of the 492nd Bombardment Group were deployed on D-Day to bomb enemy targets in Normandy.

One month after D-Day, on July 7, 1944, Doyle and his fellow crew members took off for a dangerous mission to Bernburg, Germany. Over the target, the American bombers were attacked by a swarm of German fighters (according to the Missing Air Crew Report). Doyle and the other gunners defended their bomber fiercely with their machine guns, but this could not prevent their B-24 from being shot down by the German fighters. The bomber then crashed in the vicinity of the German towns of Gröningen and Halberstadt.

Doyle and three other crew members did not survive the crash. The remaining crew members had been able to leave the aircraft by parachute and were captured by the enemy on the ground. According to several testimonies from the Missing Air Crew Report, Doyle was already killed in the air by the fire of the German fighters. One of the surviving crew members stated that Doyle was killed in the upper turret by a 20mm shell, fired by one of the enemy fighters. Just before he was killed, Doyle is said to have shouted that he had shot down one of the German fighter aircraft. At the time of his death, Doyle was only 24 years old. In Margraten he rests in Plot O, Row 13, Grave 11.

WILLIAM R. MC GINNIS

Staff Sergeant

379th Bombardment Group

Unfortunate timing of a sad message

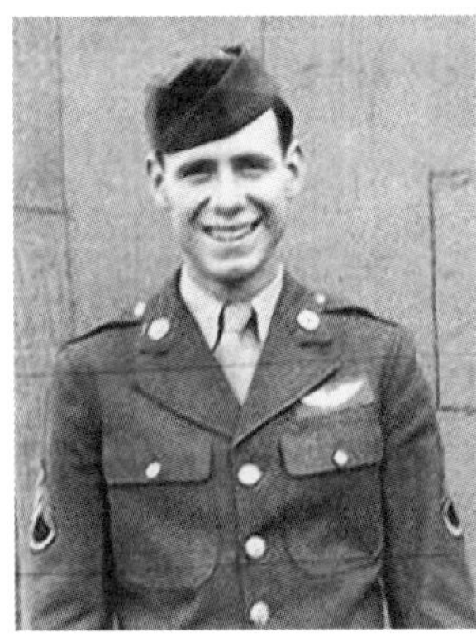

Staff Sergeant William R. Mc Ginnis was born in Johnson County, Iowa, on August 14, 1923. He grew up with a brother and two sisters. In 1941, William graduated from Iowa City High School. He enlisted in the U.S. Army Air Forces the following year.

In November 1943, William was sent overseas to England. There he was assigned to the 524th Bomb Squadron of the 379th Bombardment Group. This bomber unit had already arrived in England a few months earlier.

On August 9, 1944, William manned the machine gun position in the nose of the four-engine B-17 nicknamed 'Big Barn Smell.'

The original crew of the 'Big Barn Smell'. They flew their thirtieth and final mission on June 20, 1944. The crew was sent home after that mission. SOURCE: U.S. Army Air Forces via Arie-Jan van Hees

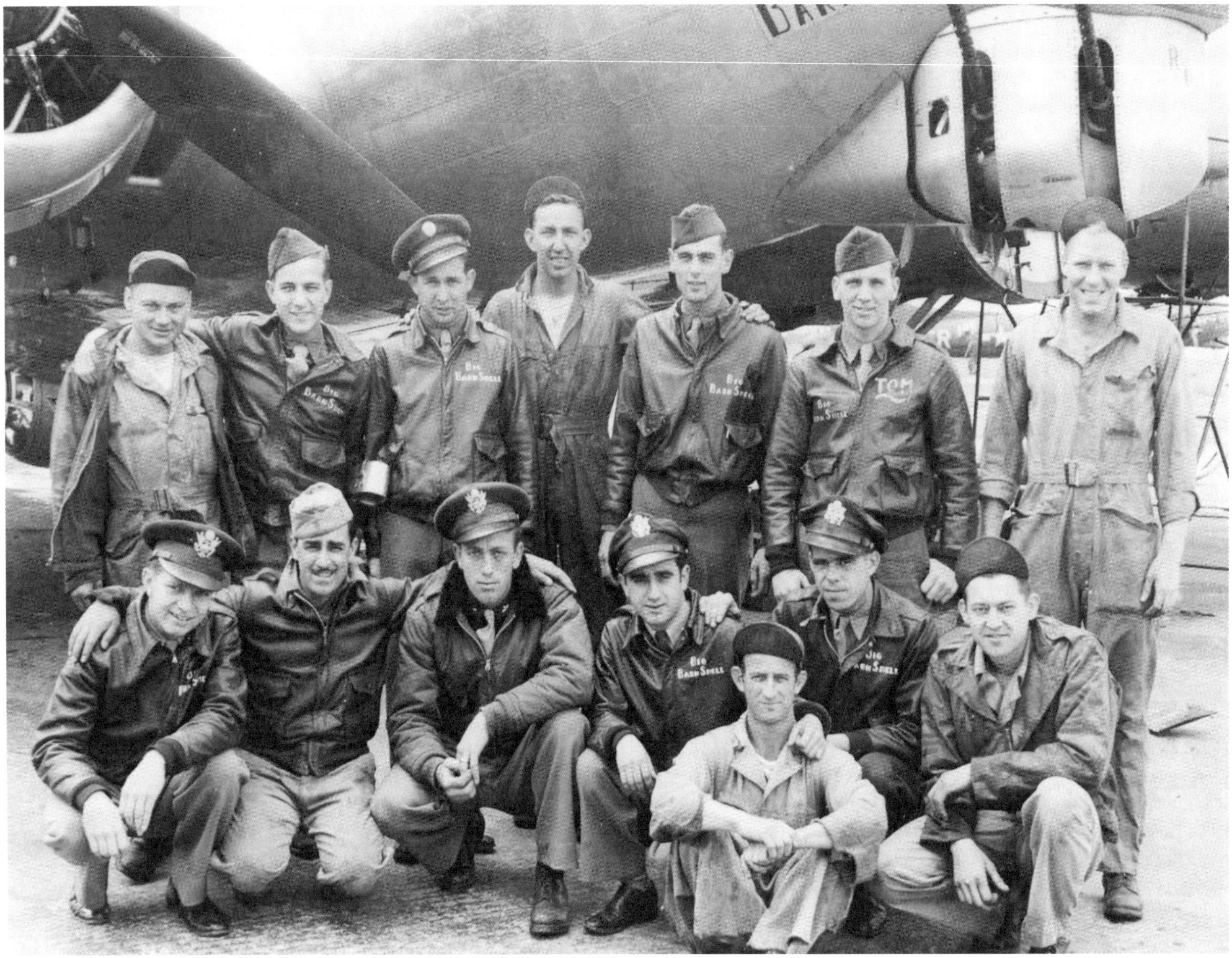

The bomber took off from USAAF Station 117 at Kimbolton to participate in a bombing mission to Germany. The target of the mission was a Luftwaffe factory or airfield near the city of Munich.

At some point during the flight, disaster struck for William when the bomber's nose was hit by German anti-aircraft fire (Flak). Other crew members who survived believed that this part of the bomber, containing William and the bombardier, was blown off the ship. The bomber then crashed near Walheim, about seven kilometers southeast of the city of Aachen. William's mortal remains were not found near the plane's wreckage. Therefore, he was reported as 'missing in action.'

More than a year after his disappearance, William's family was notified that he had been declared dead. The timing of the message was extremely painful, as his parents received it on the day their son would have celebrated his 22nd birthday...

William's body was later found near the Belgian town of Eupen and is now buried at the U.S. Military Cemetery in Margraten. He rests in Plot D, Row 10, Grave 18.

WILLIAM M. HEATON
First Lieutenant
56th Fighter Group

Helped close friend to escape death

William M. Heaton from North Carolina was born in 1920. He joined the U.S. Army Air Forces in March 1942 and eventually became the pilot of a P-47 Thunderbolt.

After arriving in England, William served in the 61st Fighter Squadron. This squadron was part of the 56th Fighter Group. With their P-47s, William and the other pilots of this fighter group regularly escorted heavy bombers. They were also deployed to attack enemy ground targets. During escort missions, their job was to protect the bombers from attacks by German fighters.

During his service in the 61st Fighter Squadron, William became good friends with Colonel Francis S. Gabreski, who gained fame as one of the top pilots in the USAAF. In the end, Gabreski had shot down a total of 28 German Luftwaffe fighters.

On June 12, 1944, William and Gabreski both participated in a combat mission over France. During this mission, Gabreski was attacked and chased by a German Messerschmitt Bf 109. This put him in serious danger of being shot down himself. From his cockpit William saw that Gabreski was in trouble and so he came to his rescue. William's Thunderbolt headed down on the Messerschmitt, which rolled over and dove away. Thanks to William, Gabreski narrowly escaped death.

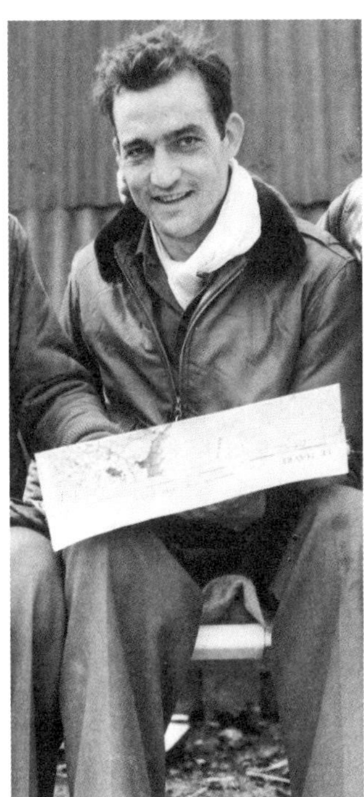

About three months later, the Thunderbolts of the 56th Fighter Group attacked several German airfields on September 5, 1944. In the process, they damaged and destroyed dozens of Luftwaffe aircraft.

This mission over Germany was William's last flight. Shortly after he had strafed a German train at Niederneisen, his P-47 was shot down by enemy Flak. Sitting in the cockpit of his Thunderbolt, William then made a fatal crash there. He was only 24 years old. His final resting place in Margraten is in Plot B, Row 4, Grave 23

RICHARD F. WELLS

Corporal

82nd Engineer Combat Battalion

A deadly ambush

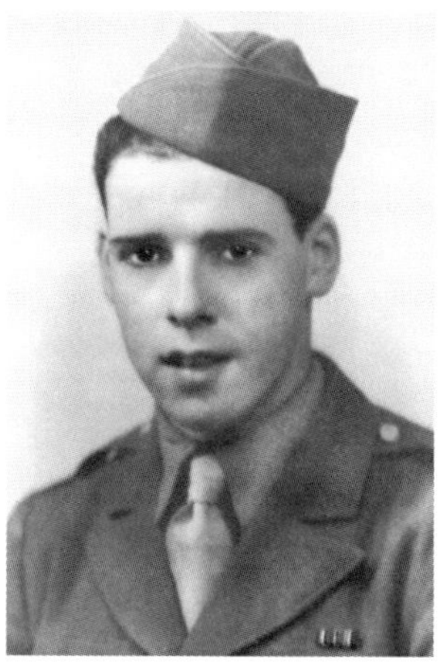

Corporal Richard F. Wells from New York was born in 1924. During the war, he served in the 82nd Engineer Combat Battalion. This battalion was deployed to, for example, build pontoon bridges and Bailey bridges, clear barbed wire obstacles, and demolish enemy bunkers.

On September 9, 1944, Richard was in the front line near the Belgian-Dutch border, where he was sent on a patrol mission together with three other combat engineers. Their assignment was to find a suitable place to build a pontoon or Bailey bridge over the Albert Canal so that the infantry troops of the 30th Infantry Division and the tanks of the 2nd Armored Division could advance into the Dutch province of Limburg. The German troops had already retreated across the canal and had also blown up all the bridges to halt the Allied advance.

During the patrol, Richard drove the jeep in which the four of them were making their way from Kesselt to Veldwezelt. Somewhere on the route between these two Belgian towns, the jeep was suddenly ambushed: a group of German soldiers who had stayed behind, hidden in small bushes on two sides of the road, opened fire. When the shooting started, Richard was hit by several German bullets, which struck him in his legs and stomach. As a result, he suffered fatal injuries. His three fellow soldiers surrendered. They were taken prisoner by the Germans and eventually were to be imprisoned in German POW camps. When they captured the others, the German soldiers saw that Richard was dying and therefore did not capture him as well. Instead, they laid him on the pavement in front of the house of the Vanham family. There, at the age of twenty, Richard died a few moments later.

When other soldiers from the unit later arrived at the village, they too were subjected to heavy fire from the German soldiers. Only when an American tank intervened, the enemy soldiers withdrew. After this, other engineers of Richard's battalion could start building a new bridge across the canal. Richard's final resting place in Margraten is in Plot J, Row 6, Grave 6.

HARVEY G. HOGANSON

Staff Sergeant

392nd Bombardment Group

Downed three German Messerschmitts before he died

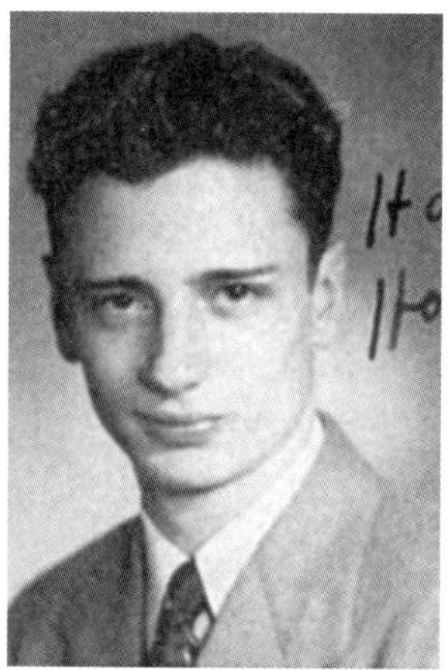

Staff Sergeant Harvey G. Hoganson was born on June 18, 1924. His hometown was Glen Ellyn, Illinois, where he attended Glenbard High School. While attending this school, he played on the basketball team.

In June 1942, Harvey enlisted in the USAAF, eventually becoming the right waist gunner in the B-24 bomber 'Ford's Folly' of the 578th Bomb Squadron. This squadron was part of the 392nd Bombardment Group. As a waist gunner, he operated a .50 caliber Browning machine gun.

The 392nd Bombardment Group had been stationed in England since August 1943. The airfield where the formation's bombers took off for their missions was located in the county of Norfolk. This remained the base of the 392nd Bombardment Group until April 1945.

On September 11, 1944, the Ford's Folly's crew took off there to bomb a German factory in Hannover. However, before they reached the target, the Luftwaffe attacked them with several Messerschmitt Bf 109s. The German fighter pilots started firing their machine guns as they closed in. The Ford's Folly's number three engine was hit and set afire, and fire broke out in the bomb bay. At some point, only Harvey's waist gun was still firing. According to Staff Sergeant Odell F. Dobson, the other waist gunner who survived, Harvey accounted for at least three enemy fighter planes. Dobson later wrote: 'Two of these ME 109s were seen to explode by myself and one was seen by myself and T/Sgt. Roger Clapp – the radio operator – to dive by the right wing completely enveloped in flames after it was hit by S/Sgt. Hoganson's machine gun fire.'

While Harvey was firing his machine gun, he was repeatedly wounded himself. Despite bleeding profusely, he struggled back up both times and retook the position behind his machine gun to resume firing. In a moment he was hit again, struck in the head by a 20mm shell (according to Dobson's memories). Again, Harvey fell down, bleeding heavily. 'The third time he was shot away, he was not able to return,' Dobson recalled. 'He was last seen by myself lying on the floor bleeding about the face and head. He made the supreme sacrifice willingly and with utter disregard for his own safety.' Harvey was only twenty years old.

Shortly after, the heavily damaged bomber went into a spin and crashed near the German village of Winnen. Harvey's remains were found near the wreckage and were subsequently buried in the local cemetery. After the war, his body was exhumed and transferred to the U.S. Military Cemetery in Margraten. There he was given his final resting place in Plot P, Row 9, Grave 11.

The 'Ford's Folly.' SOURCE: U.S. Army Air Forces via Arie-Jan van Hees

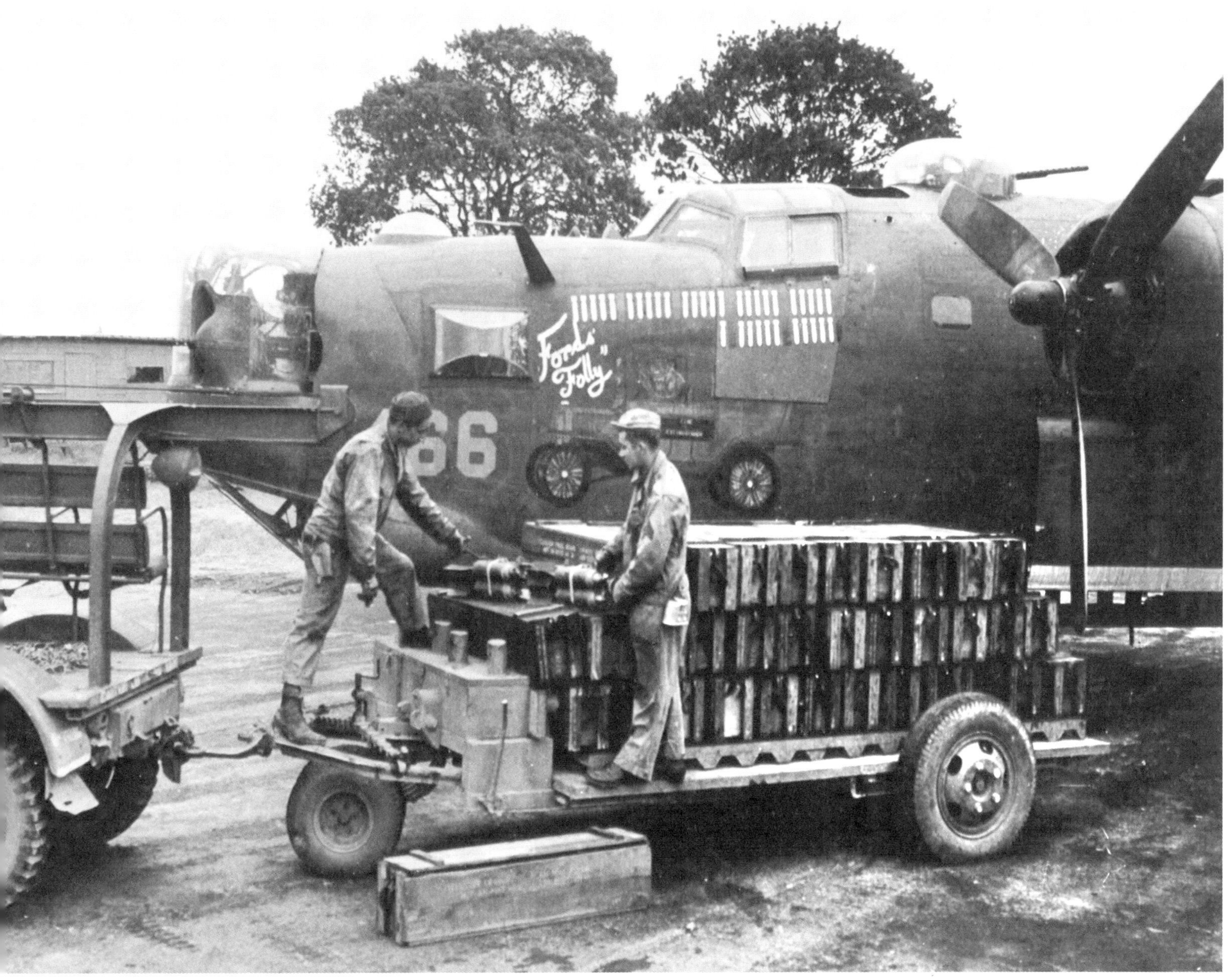

PAUL R. CARTER
Private
101st Airborne Division

Killed by a German '88'

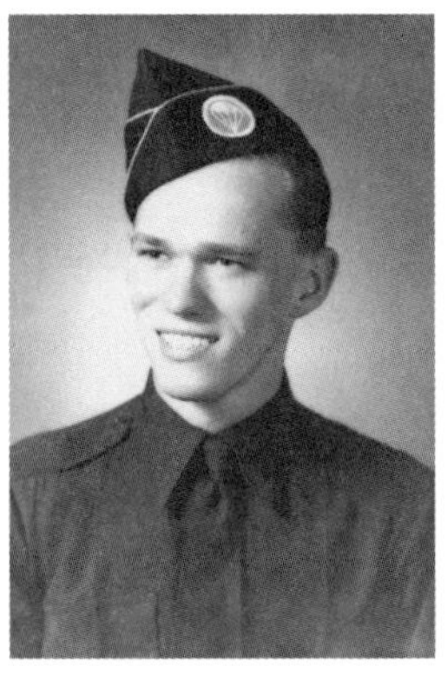

Private Paul R. Carter from Minnesota was born in 1921. He grew up with seven brothers and two sisters and the family lived on a farm. His mother died in the 1930s when Paul was still a boy. Paul's family members remembered him as a kind and hardworking young man who always smiled.

In July 1942, Paul volunteered for military service. He was then trained as a paratrooper at Camp Toccoa, Georgia, and assigned to the 506th Parachute Infantry Regiment. This was one of the regiments of the 101st Airborne Division. After completing infantry and parachute training, the 506th Parachute Infantry Regiment was sent to England to prepare for Operation Overlord.

On D-Day, Paul was involved in the American airborne landings in German-occupied Normandy. Within Company A, Paul was his platoon's machine gunner.

More than three months later, Paul was deployed in Operation Market Garden. At the start of this major Allied operation on September 17, 1944, Paul parachuted into Holland and landed near the village of Son. There the paratroopers of the 506th PIR had to capture the bridge over the Wilhelmina Canal.

After their parachute landings, Paul's Company A advanced to Son and the bridge on the right flank of their regiment. They marched through the so-called Sonsche Forest. When Paul and the other paratroopers of the company reached the edge of the forest, they were pinned down by enemy fire from German 88mm guns. German shells exploded everywhere and a bloody carnage lurked. Paul saw one of the guns and started firing at it with his machine gun. However, the German gunners caught sight of him and then returned his fire with their big gun. As a result, Paul and his assistant machine gunner, Private First Class Prentice Hundley, were struck by a German 88mm shell. Both men were killed on the spot.

Paul, who was 23 years old when he lost his life, was initially buried at the temporary American cemetery near Son. His remains were transferred to the permanent U.S. Military Cemetery in Margraten in 1948. Here he rests in Plot J, Row 18, Grave 6.

HALE L. WATSON
First Lieutenant
435th Troop Carrier Group

Emergency landing caused terrible explosion

First Lieutenant Hale L. Watson from New Hampshire enlisted in the USAAF in 1942. Before enlisting, Hale graduated from Gorham High School. While in his senior year there, he was the vice president of his class and also the captain of the football team.

After completing pilot training, Hale served as co-pilot in a Douglas C-47 'Skytrain' of the 78th Troop Carrier Squadron. This squadron was part of the 435th Troop Carrier Group.

On D-Day, Hale flew his first mission over enemy-held territory when he was to drop American paratroopers in Normandy at night. Despite intense fire from German Flak, he and his plane returned to England unscathed.

On September 17, 1944, Hale participated in Operation Market Garden. He flew his C-47 towards the Dutch city of Eindhoven, where he had to drop paratroopers of the 101st Airborne Division. However, after they had flown over the front line along the Belgian-Dutch border, the plane was badly damaged by German anti-aircraft fire. The left engine of Hale's aircraft caught fire, but despite this, the first pilot and co-pilot Hale managed to keep the aircraft under control until all the paratroopers had left it above the planned drop zone. After that, however, the heavily damaged C-47 lost altitude so rapidly that the crew members were unable to bail out with their parachutes themselves.

Moments later, the C-47 made a belly-landing north of Eindhoven. Upon landing it skidded about 100 yards over the ground. The fuselage of the aircraft passed close to two trees, causing both wings to break off. Moments later, the plane exploded. Three crew members were killed, including co-pilot Hale. He was only 22 years old. In Margraten, Hale is permanently laid to rest in Plot A, Row 4, Grave 7.

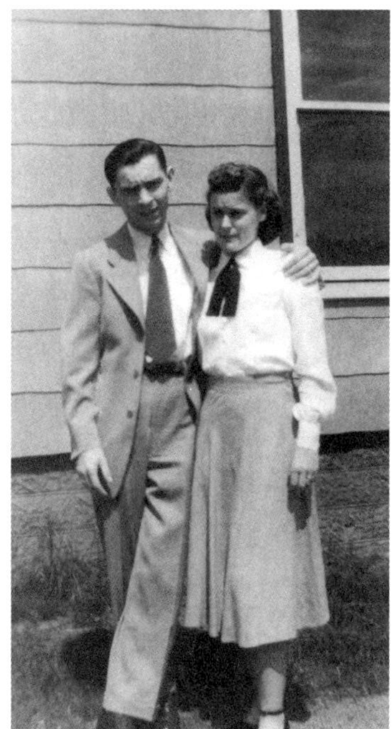

ROY B. LEWIS

Corporal

82nd Airborne Division

Unfortunate paratrooper jumped on a bayonet

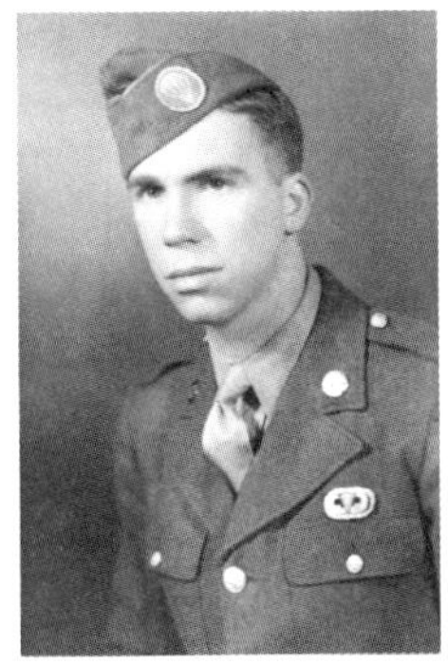

Corporal Roy B. Lewis was born in Denver, Colorado, on January 26, 1920. There he lived with his father, mother, sister, and three brothers. He attended East High School and then studied at the University of Colorado. According to the university's 1941 yearbook, Roy was a member of what is known as the Acacia Fraternity.

In 1942, Roy entered the army. He attended the challenging training for the paratroopers and was then assigned to Company A of the 508th Parachute Infantry Regiment. This regiment was part of the 82nd 'All American' Airborne Division.

The 82nd Airborne Division was created in August 1942 as a transformation of the 82nd Infantry Division and became the first airborne division in the history of the U.S. Army. The recruits were all volunteers.

In July 1943, the paratroopers of the 82nd Airborne Division took part in the American airborne landings in Sicily. Two months later, the division was deployed again, this time for the airborne operation near Salerno on the Italian mainland. After this, the troops were transferred to England. There the division prepared to participate in Operation Overlord. When D-Day arrived, the paratroopers of the 'All American' Division landed in Normandy.

Following Normandy, the division returned to England to participate in the most ambitious and risky airborne operation of the war, Operation Market Garden. On September 17, 1944, the day this operation began, Roy landed with his regiment at Drop Zone T near Groesbeek, after which he and his platoon cautiously advanced to Nijmegen.

As the platoon reached the intersection of Groesbeekseweg and Fransestraat, a German machine gun suddenly opened fire on them. As the men took cover, Roy jumped into a foxhole that another trooper had already occupied. This trooper had a fixed bayonet and Roy struck his leg, cutting the artery. Roy subsequently bled to death before he could receive proper medical aid. He was only 24 years old...

Roy was initially buried at the temporary American cemetery in Molenhoek, but when this burial site was closed after the war, his remains were transferred to the U.S. Military Cemetery in Margraten. There he is permanently buried in Plot F, Row 3, Grave 3.

WALTER DIKOON

Private

82nd Airborne Division

Killed at the Keizer Karelplein in Nijmegen

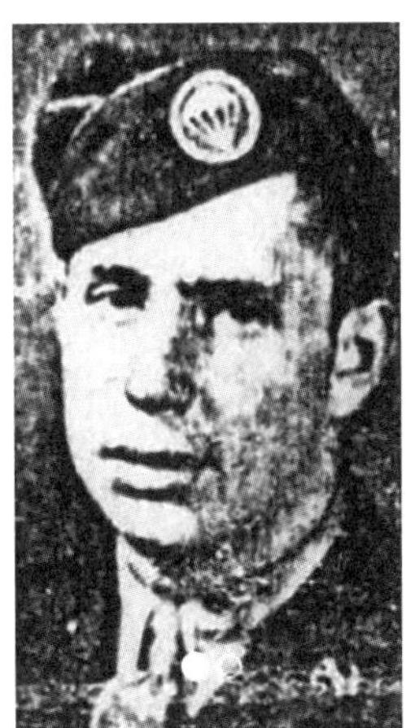

Private Walter Dikoon was born in 1924 and lived in Providence, Rhode Island. In October 1942, he entered the army and volunteered for the paratroopers. Walter managed to pass the demanding training and was assigned to the 508th Parachute Infantry Regiment of the 82nd Airborne Division.

On September 17, 1944, Walter served as a scout in his battalion's Company A during Operation Market Garden. The drop zone where he landed was near Groesbeek, southeast of Nijmegen and the crucial Waal River. The big road bridge over this river had to be captured by Walter's division to enable British tanks and ground troops to advance toward the British paratroopers who had landed near Arnhem.

After darkness fell, Walter led a patrol through the streets of Nijmegen to reconnoiter the route to the Waal bridge. At one point during this reconnaissance, his platoon came under fire from a German machine gun. Tracer bullets flashed past him and ricocheted off the cobblestone street. Fortunately, Walter could see where the bullets were coming from. With his Browning Automatic Rifle, he managed to kill the German soldiers manning the machine gun. After this, the platoon continued their way towards the Sint Annastraat.

Not much later the paratroopers approached the Keizer Karelplein, the large traffic circle southwest of the bridge. Here again a German machine gun opened fire on them. This time Walter had no chance to take out the German soldiers because a burst of machine gun fire took his life. He was twenty years old. His remains were initially buried at Molenhoek. After the war, this temporary U.S. Military Cemetery was closed, whereupon Walter's remains were transferred to Margraten. There he is permanently interred in Plot F, Row 4, Grave 10.

RAY M. JOHNSON

Private First Class

82nd Airborne Division

Fell dead on his comrade

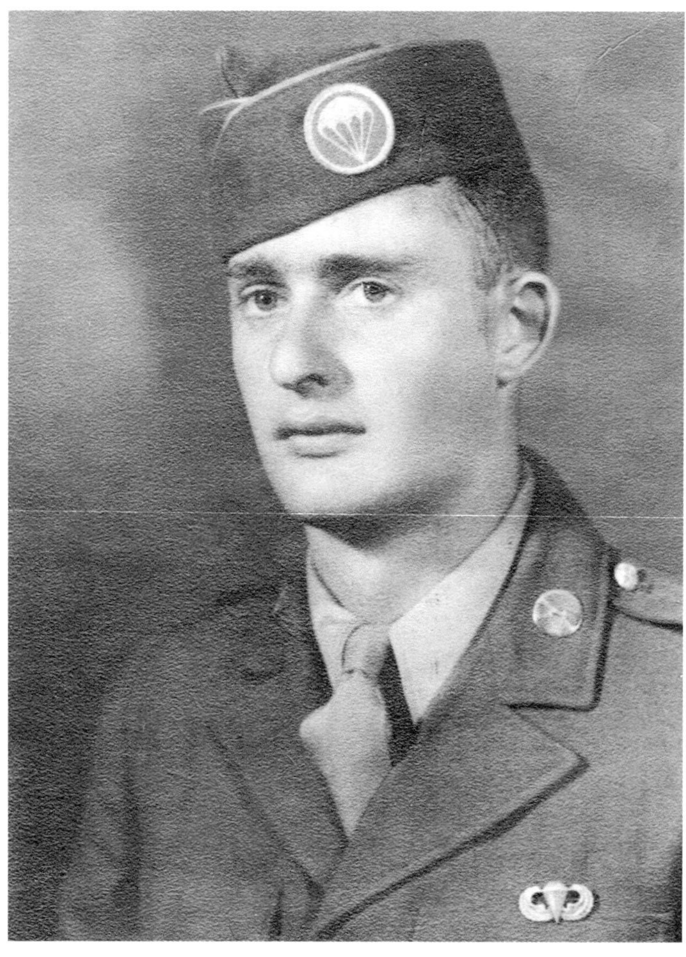

Private First Class Ray M. Johnson from Alabama was born on September 11, 1920. In 1944, Ray was a member of Company A, 508th Parachute Infantry Regiment. This was one of the regiments of the 82nd Airborne Division, the first airborne division in the history of the U.S. Army.

On September 17, 1944, the first day of Operation Market Garden, Ray parachuted onto Drop Zone T near Groesbeek. From there he and his company headed for Nijmegen. There his division had to capture the big road bridge over the Waal.

After dark, Ray was one of the first American paratroopers in the heart of Nijmegen to reach the Keizer Karelplein, the large traffic circle southwest of the bridge. There, the group of paratroopers with whom he had advanced encountered German machine guns and a halftrack with SS soldiers.

The halftrack was disabled with Bazooka rockets, after which the German SS men jumped off and ran in all directions. Ray and another soldier, Corporal James Blue, were between two houses. He had a M1 rifle with fixed bayonet in his hands and was ready to use it. A few moments later, when Ray and Blue saw a fleeing SS officer coming in their direction, Blue said to Ray, 'Get him with your bayonet.' The SS officer approached unsuspectingly and just as he came between them, Ray gave him a thrust but completely missed him. The rifle dislodged from his hands, whereupon his companion Blue decided to use his Tommy gun. Blue pulled the trigger and quickly killed the German officer.

After this hair-raising moment, the company was ordered to attack the dug-in Germans on the Keizer Karelplein. During this attack, Ray was killed by German machine gun fire. Corporal Blue dove for a foxhole and witnessed how his buddy was struck. 'As I landed in the hole and looked up, I saw Ray Johnson falling toward the hole,' he later said. 'The tracers from the German machine gun provided enough light for me to know they were striking him. Johnson fell on me, mortally wounded.' Ray died within a moment and was only 24 years old. His remains were buried at the temporary U.S. Military Cemetery in Molenhoek. After the war, they were moved to Margraten, where Ray is permanently interred in Plot F, Row 3, Grave 15.

JAMES E. WICKLINE

Private First Class

82nd Airborne Division

The parachute that didn't open

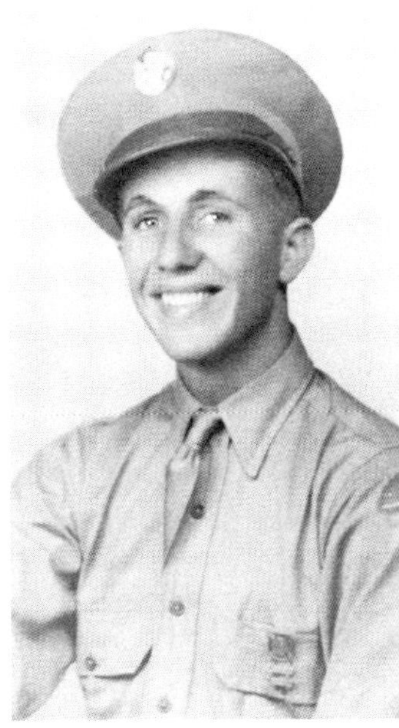

Private First Class James E. Wickline was born on January 10, 1923. His place of birth was Crellin, a small village in Maryland, but he spent most of his childhood amidst the coal mining industry in West Virginia. Here he lived as an only child with his parents in Morgantown, where he also attended high school. His father was employed in the mines there and his mother was a nurse.

During his school years, James played on the basketball team. He was also a member of the drama club. In addition, James was involved in the school's newspaper. After graduation, James was drafted into the army in 1943. He then volunteered to be trained as a paratrooper and was assigned to the 508th Parachute Infantry Regiment, 82nd Airborne Division.

On September 17, 1944, James boarded a C-47 aircraft to be deployed in Operation Market Garden. In the afternoon, as the green light in the plane's cabin was turned on, he jumped out of the C-47 to make a parachute jump near Groesbeek, Holland. Unfortunately, James lost his life shortly afterwards. It is assumed that his parachute didn't open, causing him to fall out of the sky; considering his wounds, this would be correct. He was only 21 years old.

James is permanently interred at the Netherlands American Cemetery in Margraten, where his final resting place can be found in Plot I, Row 17, Grave 21. His grave is adopted by Maarten Vossen from Heerlen. When he became the adopter of James' grave, he was only thirteen years old. Maarten did extensive research to uncover the story of James Wickline. On this subject, Dutch filmmaker Marijn Poels made a documentary, titled 'Ageless Friends.' This has received several awards in the United States.

In Morgantown, James' hometown, a bridge was named after him in 2015. It was unveiled in the presence of, among others, a childhood friend and a former basketball teammate. On January 28, 2017, a memorial plaque dedicated to him was unveiled in Groesbeek, close to the spot where James had lost his life.

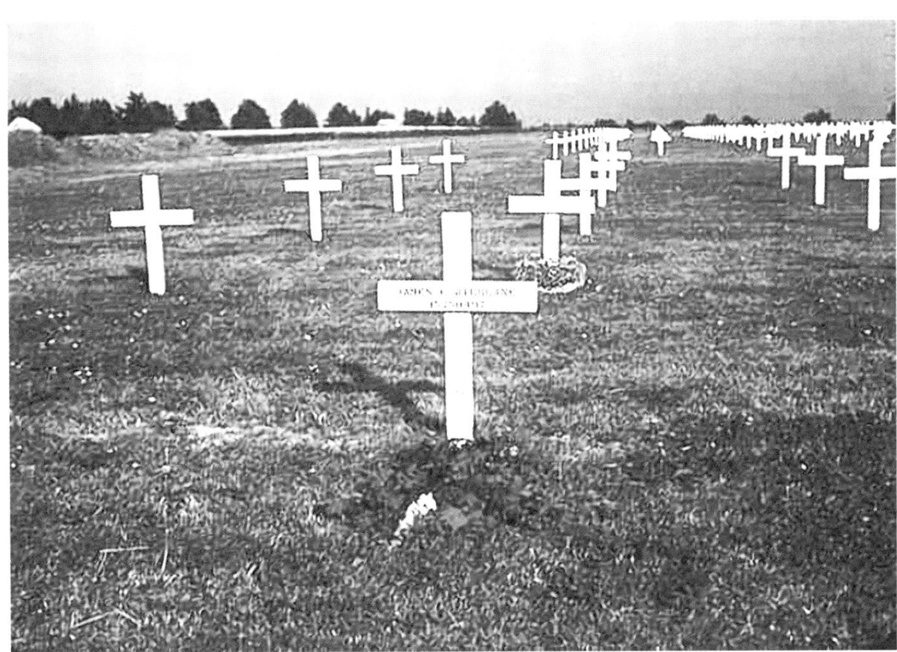

The temporary grave of James Wickline.
SOURCE: Maarten Vossen

DONALD A. PAHLOW

First Lieutenant

434th Troop Carrier Group

Pilot didn't choose for himself

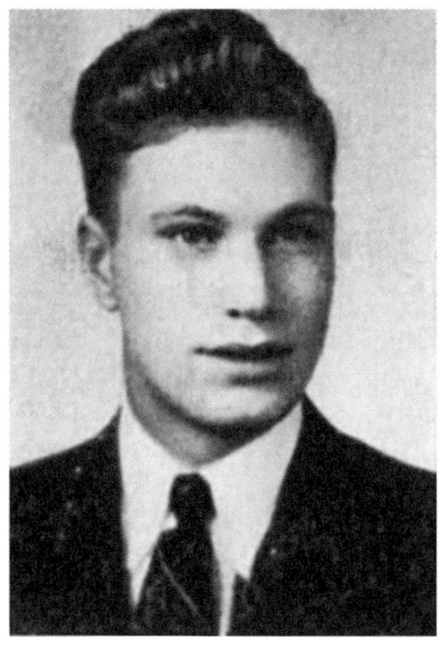

First Lieutenant Donald A. Pahlow from Wisconsin was born in 1922. After completing high school and subsequent college education, he joined the U.S. Army Air Forces in April 1942. Donald was trained as a pilot and assigned to the 434th Troop Carrier Group. With this unit he was stationed in England in the fall of 1943.

When the long period of practice flights in England was finally completed, Donald took part in Operation Overlord. On June 6, 1944 – D-Day – he piloted his Douglas C-47 transport aircraft to enemy-occupied Normandy. His task was to tow a glider towards one of the planned landing zones there.

When the formation of aircraft of which Donald's plane was a part flew over the French coastline, the German anti-aircraft weapons opened up. The night sky around his plane lit up everywhere due to the explosions of Flak shells and the flashes of tracer bullets. Despite being subjected to heavy enemy fire, Donald's plane suffered just one bullet hole. The glider was disconnected successfully, and Donald made it back to England unhurt.

After D-Day, Donald made several more supply flights to Normandy. Then, on September 17, 1944, Donald's 434th Troop Carrier Group was deployed in Operation Market Garden. Donald and his crew took off from Aldermaston and flew to Holland to drop sixteen American paratroopers behind German lines. 'Captain William Wade, Intelligence Officer, and Tom A. Hoge, War Correspondent, were going along with us to take pictures and report on the mission,' the plane's co-pilot, Second Lieutenant William F. Baker, later reported. He also recalled that 'everything went along as planned until we had dropped our troopers on the Drop Zone and began to come back. We were fired upon on the way in but were not hit. We could see bullets and tracers coming from our left. However, just after we made our 180° turn and started out over the same area where we had received fire, hell broke loose. We were just over Boxtel, Holland. Just about this time I felt the jar of a direct hit on our plane. The Crew Chief told us we were on fire but it was not until I felt the jar of a second burst that we heard them calling us on the radio telling us we were on fire and to jump. Lt. Pahlow immediately yelled to the others to get ready to jump. By the time he and I got out of our seats, removed our Flak suits and snapped on our chutes, I figured it was time to get out. Ellis, Hoge, Dimitrovich and I jumped and I remember Pahlow was fiddling with Wade's chute when I left. He told me to go ahead and I thought they were ready to go.'

Staff Sergeant Rollin D. Ellis, the radio operator, also reported what happened. 'Our plane, which was number 316033, caught light machine gun fire, on course, about four minutes from the "DZ" but we were able to continue on to the "DZ" where we dropped our troopers. All paratroopers left the plane uninjured. We proceeded to the turning point, which was Boxtel, Holland. At this point we heard MG bullets hitting the tail. (...) About 1304 hours on 17 September 1944, we were hit by Flak, approximately 40mm. The bursts hit our right rear gas tanks and we noticed smoke coming in from the right side of the plane. We received radio indication from other ships in our element telling us we were on fire and to bail out.' S/Sgt. Ellis then readied himself to jump and when he left the plane, he saw Donald had his chute on and was ready to leave the plane too. 'Lt. Pahlow was last seen by me, helping Captain Wade, a passenger, adjust his leg strap to his chute. I was the first to leave the plane, and was unarmed. I observed three more chutes leave my plane. The plane was burning on the bottom side and it disappeared from vision,' Ellis continued.

Despite the fact that Donald was ready to jump, he did not follow Ellis, Dimitrovich, Hoge, and Baker when they left the plane. He went back to help Captain Wade put on his parachute. However, his help came too late as the plane crashed in Oostelbeers, near Oirschot. Both Donald and Wade were killed. Donald was only 22 years old. Their severely burned remains were first buried at the Roman Catholic cemetery in Oostelbeers and were reburied at the U.S. Military Cemetery in Margraten in 1946. A final reburial took place there in 1949: Wade now lies in grave P-9-17, Pahlow in grave B-2-5.

HANFORD A. FILES

First Lieutenant

82nd Airborne Division

Killed by tank fire

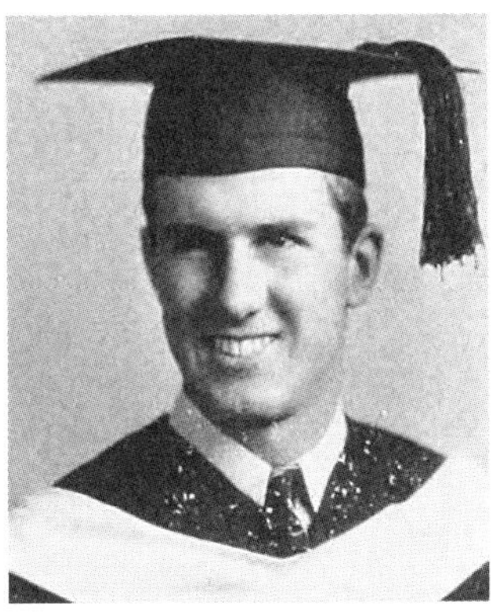

First Lieutenant Hanford A. Files was born in 1920. According to a newspaper article, he won a local American history contest at the age of fifteen in 1937, and went to Washington, D.C. to see the presidential inauguration. Hanford graduated from Hollywood High School, whereupon he attended the University of California, Los Angeles. While studying there, he was a member of the university's rowing team. Hanford graduated in 1942. He then entered the army, whereafter he was trained as a paratrooper at Fort Benning, Georgia.

Hanford was assigned to Company E, 504th Parachute Infantry Regiment, 82nd Airborne Division, with which he fought in both North Africa and the Italian Campaign. The regiment was then transferred to England, arriving there in April 1944. Because the near-continuous fighting in Italy had cost the 504th dearly, the regiment did not participate in the Normandy Invasion.

The 504th returned to combat when the Allies launched Operation Market Garden. Hanford took part in this major operation and parachuted into German-occupied Holland on September 17, 1944. He landed near the town of Grave, where his company captured the bridge across the river Meuse. After capturing the bridge, Hanford's platoon was ordered to set up a roadblock at the junction of the Bosschebaan and the Generaal De Bonsweg, south of Grave near De Elft. To halt any German counterattacks, the men placed mines on the road and put machine guns and Bazooka teams into position.

Soon after the mines had been placed and all the outposts had been manned, Hanford and the others heard the sound of approaching tanks. He probably assumed that the British were already approaching, jumped up, and went to take a look. It turned out to be two German tanks, presumably StuG III's. They opened fire and killed Hanford, who was hit in the throat. He was 23 years old. Hanford was initially buried at the temporary U.S. Military Cemetery at Molenhoek. When this cemetery was closed after the war, his remains were transferred to Margraten. He was given his final resting place here in Plot K, Row 9, Grave 20.

Two of Hanford's brothers – Gordon and Roger – were also serving in the military at the time he was killed. Gordon was an officer in the U.S. Navy and Roger served as a Captain in the Ninth Air Force.

ROBERT G. COLE

Lieutenant Colonel

101st Airborne Division

Earned the Medal of Honor in Normandy

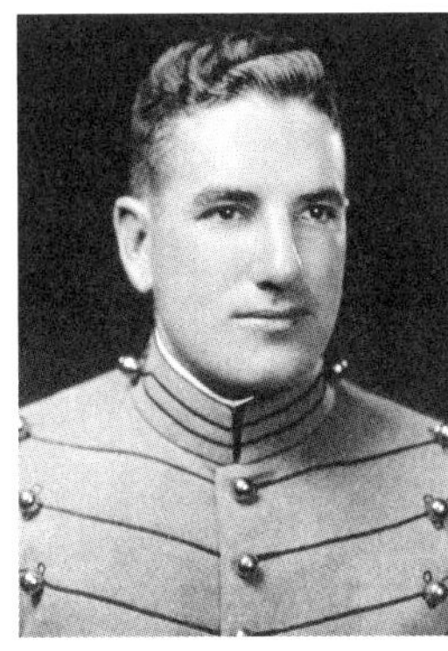

Robert G. Cole from Texas was born in 1915. From 1935 to 1939, he attended the famous United States Military Academy at West Point, New York. Shortly after his graduation, he married Allie Mae Wilson.

Robert received his 'jump wings' at Fort Benning, Georgia, in 1941 and was assigned to the 502nd Parachute Infantry Regiment in 1942. In 1943, Robert was given command of the regiment's 3rd Battalion. Soon thereafter, he was promoted to Lieutenant Colonel.

On D-Day, Robert parachuted into Normandy. A few days later, he earned the Medal of Honor 'for gallantry and intrepidity at the risk of his own life, above and beyond the call of duty on 11 June 1944.' His citation continues as follows:

> ***'Lt. Col. Cole was personally leading his battalion in forcing the last four bridges on the road to Carentan when his entire unit was suddenly pinned down to the ground by intense and withering enemy rifle, machine gun, mortar, and artillery fire placed upon them from well-prepared and heavily fortified positions [in farmhouses and behind hedgerows] within 150 yards of the foremost elements. After the devastating and unceasing enemy fire had for over one hour prevented any move and inflicted numerous casualties, Lt. Col. Cole, observing this almost hopeless situation, courageously issued orders to assault the enemy positions with fixed bayonets. With utter disregard for his own safety and completely ignoring the enemy fire, he rose to his feet in front of his battalion and with drawn pistol shouted to his men to follow him in the assault. Catching up a fallen man's rifle and bayonet [and quickly moving behind a smokescreen laid by American artillery], he charged on and led the remnants of his battalion across the bullet-swept open ground and into the enemy position. His heroic and valiant action in so inspiring his men resulted in the complete establishment of our bridgehead across the Douve River. The cool fearlessness, personal bravery, and outstanding leadership displayed by Lt. Col. Cole reflect great credit upon himself and are worthy of the highest praise in the military service.'***

Over three months later, Robert took part in Operation Market Garden. Together with his regiment he landed near the Dutch village of Son on September 17, 1944. To the west of this village, he and his men had to capture the bridge over the Wilhelmina Canal at Best. The American paratroopers did not succeed in capturing this bridge. The Germans offered stubborn resistance and held them off at the edge of a forest. Enemy artillery, mortar, and small arms fire prevented Robert's men from assaulting their objective.

The next day, on September 18, the men witnessed the arrival of much needed air support in the form of P-47s. However, their first strafing attack caught Robert's battalion in its positions on the edge of the wood. Robert was furious and ordered his men to place Air Recognition Panels – orange identification markers – in front of their positions, so that the fighter pilots knew they were firing on their own troops. Shortly thereafter, the P-47s made another strafing run. This one was more effective and enemy fire noticeably slackened. Taking advantage of the respite, Robert walked beyond the woods into an open field to make sure the panels were firmly in place for another effective run. He stopped and watched a plane for a few moments. As he did so, a German sniper fired a shot. The bullet tore through the rim of Robert's helmet and struck him in the head, instantly killing him. Robert was 29 years old.

Six months after Robert's death, his widow Allie received a personal letter of condolence from General Eisenhower. It reads as follows:

> ***'Dear Mrs. Cole,***
> ***Only recently I learned that your husband lost his life during our airborne operations last fall. Although I do not wish to bring afresh to your mind memories of your tragic loss, I admired and liked him so much that I feel impelled to send you some expression of my sympathy and regret.***
> ***He was one of our ablest and certainly one of our most gallant officers. He had earned among his associates a universal respect and liking and, of course, I had an additional interest in him because of our old association in the 15th Infantry.***
> ***I do hope that the knowledge of his superb gallantry and of his invaluable services to his country will bring to you some comfort, even though it cannot diminish your grief.***
>
> ***Most sincerely,***
> ***Dwight D. Eisenhower.'***

On September 18, 2009, a monument dedicated to Robert was unveiled in Best near the spot where he died. This took place in the presence of his son (who was two years old when his father was killed), dozens of veterans, and a few hundred other interested spectators.

Robert is permanently laid to rest in Margraten, where he lies in grave B-15-27.

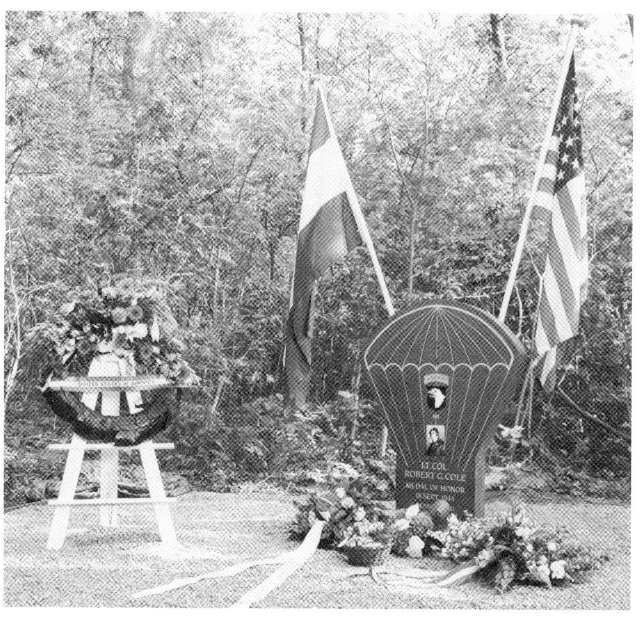

A monument in Best marks the location where Robert Cole died.
SOURCE: Wammes Waggel/Wikipedia

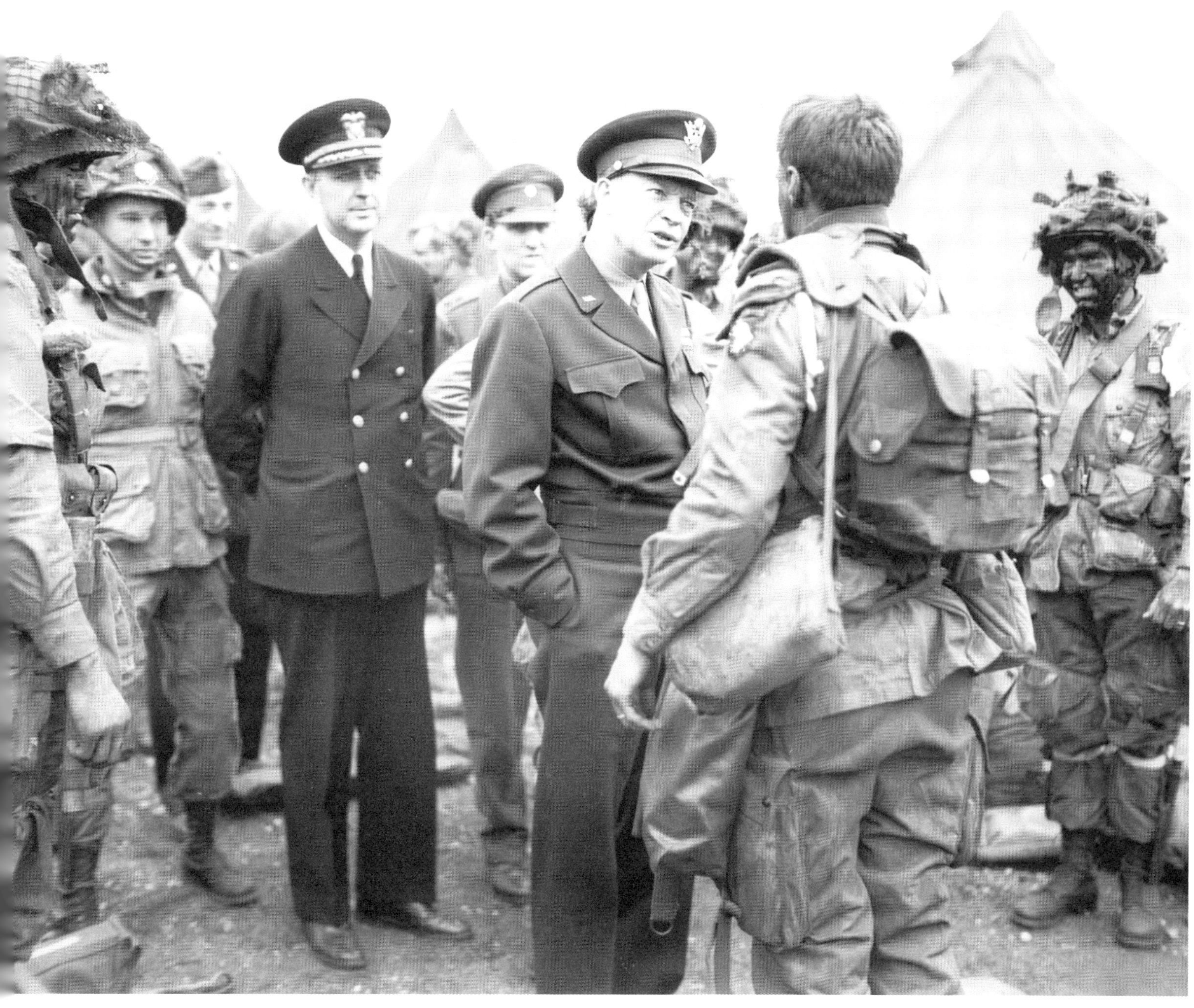

Robert G. Cole speaks with supreme commander Dwight D. Eisenhower just before boarding the plane to Normandy. SOURCE: U.S. Army

JAMES H. PERRY

First Lieutenant

356th Fighter Group

Pilot crashed into a row of trees

First Lieutenant James H. Perry from Kentucky was the pilot of a P-47 Thunderbolt of the 356th Fighter Group. On September 18, 1944, the second day of Operation Market Garden, he flew a mission to Arnhem and the surrounding area to take out German Flak positions. Allied transport planes and gliders carrying supplies and reinforcements for the British paratroopers would then be in less danger of being shot down.

James did not return from this mission and was reported missing in action. First Lieutenant Rolfe L. Chickering, a fellow pilot of James' 359th Fighter Squadron, witnessed what happened. His statement concerning James' death was included in the Missing Air Crew Report and reads as follows:

> ***'I was flying White Three and Lt. Perry was flying my wing. We were circling the area at 2500 feet looking for Flak positions. Lt. Perry called on the R/T [radio] and said that he had been hit by Flak and was going to have to belly land. I could see oil and black smoke coming from his engine. He headed for some small fields but apparently, they were too small and he made a left turn. By this time, he had lost his altitude and speed and the plane hit in a grove of trees. As it hit the trees, the plane cartwheeled and blew up.'***

James instantly lost his life when his plane hit the trees. Therefore, he remained forever 26. He is permanently interred at the Netherlands American Cemetery in Margraten. Visitors can pay tribute to him here by going to Plot G, Row 3, Grave 17.

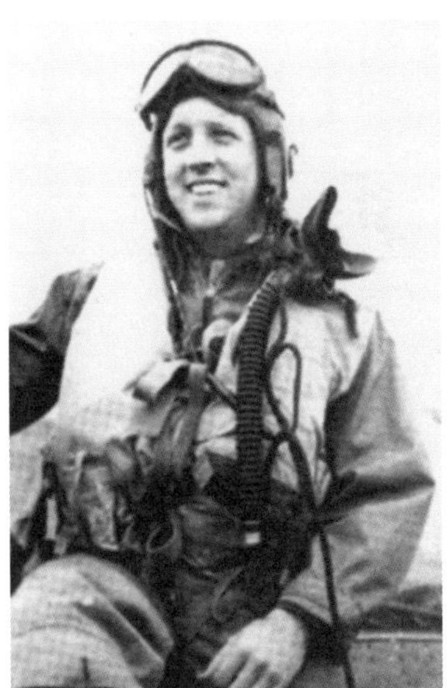

During a previous mission, James was forced to bail out from his plane above the North Sea. He had landed in the ice-cold water and had then floated around fourteen hours before the British Air-Sea Rescue Service rescued him.

JACOB H. WINGARD

Sergeant

101st Airborne Division

Died before the eyes of his best friend

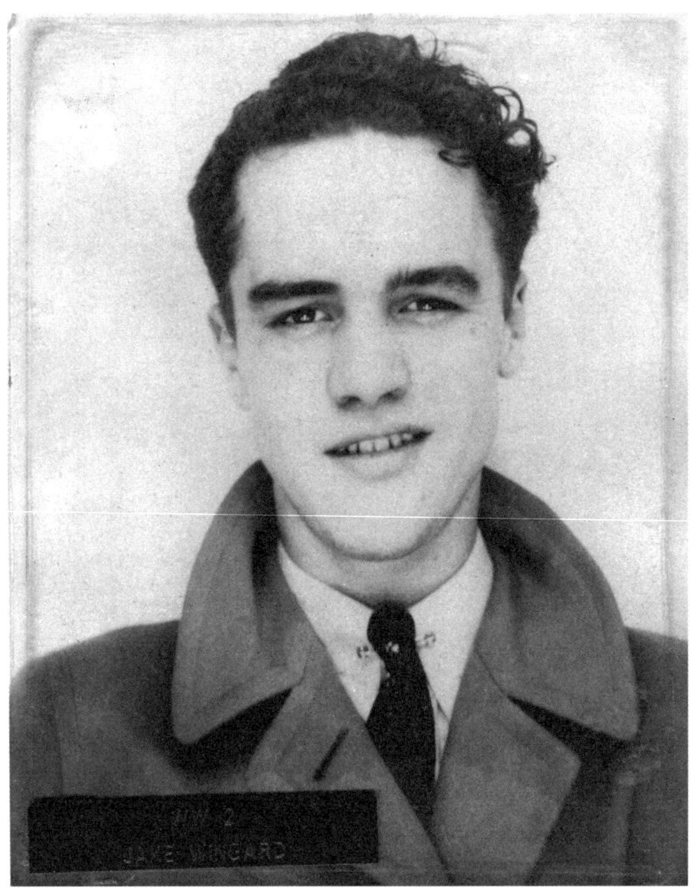

Sergeant Jacob H. Wingard from Pennsylvania was born in 1922. In 1942, he volunteered for the army, after which he was trained as a paratrooper and assigned to the 501st Parachute Infantry Regiment of the 101st Airborne Division. During his service, he soon became very close friends with Corporal Dick Klein from Ohio.

Dick and Jacob entered combat in Normandy when they parachuted into the darkness on D-Day. After returning to England in mid-July, Dick, Jacob, and the other men of the 501st were prepared for the next major airborne operation: Operation Market Garden.

On September 17, 1944, the first day of this operation, Jacob and Dick were both dropped near the Dutch village of Veghel. As paratroopers of the 101st Airborne Division they had to defend 'Hell's Highway,' the road to Nijmegen and Arnhem which the German troops repeatedly attacked to frustrate the advance of the British tanks toward the Rhine.

The next day, September 18, Jacob set up an observation post inside a windmill in Eerde, a small village near Veghel. From this spot he had a good view of the nearby sand dunes where the Germans had dug themselves in.

The Germans attacked the American positions in Eerde several times, but the Americans subjected them to mortar fire which Jacob was directing from inside the windmill. However, as he was looking through the window to observe the situation, Jacob was suddenly shot by a German sniper. His buddy Dick was standing only a few feet away and watched him fall down and die. Dick later wrote: 'Jake, who was my best buddy, took a rifle round into his chest and matter of factly said, "I'm dead – I'm dead!" He was.'

Jacob was 22 years old when he died. Initially, he was buried at the temporary U.S. Military Cemetery near Son. Shortly after the war this cemetery was closed. The disinterred bodies were transferred to Margraten, where Jacob was given his final resting place in Plot A, Row 4, Grave 29.

WILLIAM H. KIRLIN
Technical Sergeant
93rd Bombardment Group

Radio operator rescued seriously injured pilot

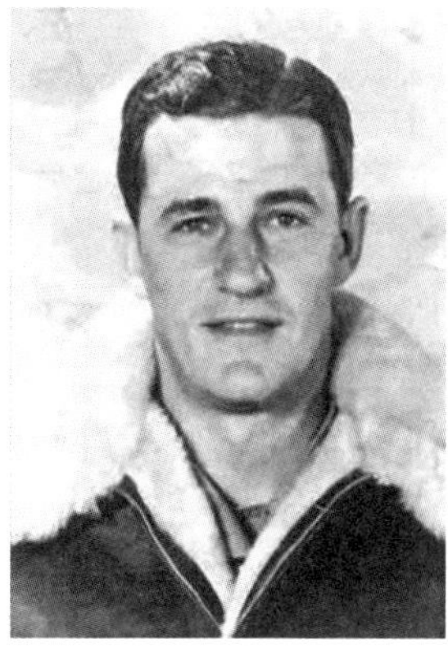

Technical Sergeant William H. Kirlin from Pennsylvania was the radio operator of the B-24 bomber 'Baggy Maggy' of the 409th Bomb Squadron. This squadron was part of the 93rd Bombardment Group.

On September 18, 1944, the second day of Operation Market Garden, William and nine fellow crew members flew to Groesbeek to resupply the paratroopers of the 82nd Airborne Division. According to the Missing Air Crew Report the bomber was hit and damaged by German machine gun fire (Flak) from the ground, injuring several crewmembers, including the nineteen-year-old pilot Larry Hewin. William saw Hewin was bleeding profusely and went to his aid, whereupon he applied tourniquets to stop the severe bleeding in Hewin's neck and legs.

Meanwhile, co-pilot Richard Scott, aided by flight engineer Donald Dukeman, was frantically trying to keep the plane in the air to reach a part of Belgium that was already liberated. But after having passed Baarle-Nassau they began to lose so much altitude that they had to make an emergency landing as soon as possible. The crew was ordered to take up their crash positions and fasten the safety belts, but William chose to stay on the flight deck to hold the bandages he had applied to Hewin.

Soon thereafter, the 'Baggy Maggy' made a crash landing near the village of Castelré. When the bomber hit the ground, Hewin was thrown to the front while William was crushed and killed under the upper machine gun turret (top turret), which broke loose from the fuselage because of the impact. He was the only crew member of the 'Baggy Maggy' who did not survive. All the others were able to leave the wreckage and were then taken prisoner by the Germans. The wounded pilot Hewin eventually recovered and was grateful to William for saving his life.

William was 24 years old when he lost his life beneath the 'Baggy Maggy's top turret. After the war, his body was transferred to Margraten, where he was given his final resting place in Plot M, Row 2, Grave 8.

JOHN W. ELL
First Lieutenant
101st Airborne Division

The vanguard of the invasion

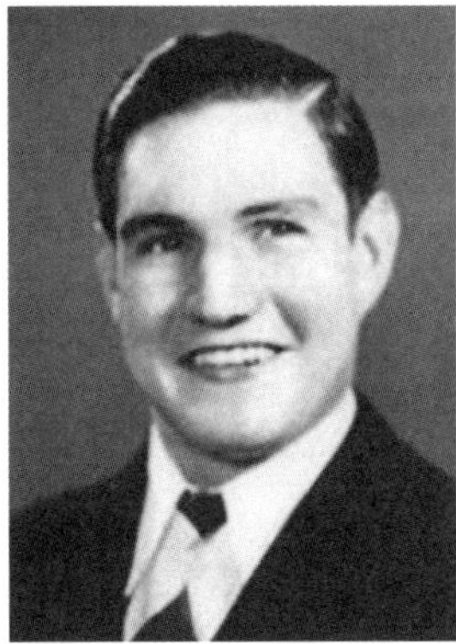

First Lieutenant John W. Ell from Pennsylvania was born in 1918. After graduating from Nanticoke High School, he attended Dickinson College for four years. While studying there, John worked on the 'Dickinsonian,' the student newspaper. He also served as president of the Catholic Student Club and the Belles Lettres Society. John graduated in 1940 and was then employed by the Library of Congress in Washington, D.C.

In August 1941, John entered the army and soon after volunteered for the newly formed parachute infantry units. He was commissioned at Fort Benning, Georgia in January 1943 and went overseas to England a year later.

In England, John volunteered to become a 'pathfinder' for the American airborne landings on D-Day. This made him one of the first American soldiers to land in Normandy on the night of June 6, 1944. Pathfinders like John had to mark the landing zones for the main force with special holophane lights and so-called 'Eureka' radar beacons. Therefore, they were the vanguard of the invasion.

John was a deeply religious Catholic and struggled with personal concerns about death. In his letters home, he wrote that he had escaped death several times and that this was thanks to his mother's prayers. When John thought about the possibility that he might not survive the war, he was especially concerned about how his death would affect his parents. In one of his letters, he wrote:

> ***'Now then, Mother and Father, understanding this, can you receive news of my death with composure and resignation? Naturally, my death would be much harder on you than it would be on me. But it should not be a catastrophe to you and that is what I am trying so desperately to explain to you with clarity and certainty. So, just read over what I have written until you feel you see the picture the same way I do.'***

On September 17, 1944, John participated in Operation Market Garden. His regiment, the 501st Parachute Infantry Regiment of the 101st Airborne Division, landed near the Dutch village of Eerde. John lost his life during a German counterattack on this village the following day; he was killed by enemy mortar fire or a German tank shell. Therefore, he remained forever 26.

With the consent of his parents, John's remains were permanently interred at the Netherlands American Cemetery in Margraten, where he lies in grave D-16-31.

My dear Mother, Father, and Brother:

Greetings and salutations at long last! I suppose that the sight of the envelope bearing this epistle gave you a great feeling of relief. I'd have written much sooner had time permitted. I've been right up front, however, ever since D Day, and consequently have not had the chance to do anything but tend to immediate necessities, which have been many and pressing. I have wanted very much to write this letter, for I have been wishing to tell you a few things, which, once told, will relieve my mind and make my peace perfect.

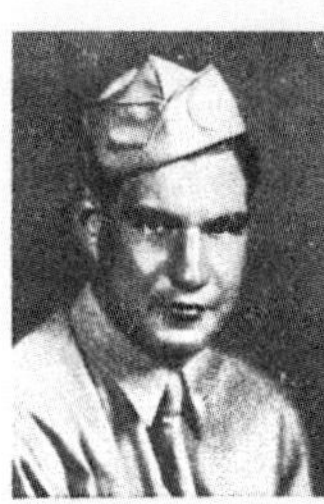

Lieutenant Ell

It will be pretty hard to say what I wish to, but try hard to understand, and perhaps my thoughts will be appreciated in the sense that I intend.

To begin with, my dear Parents, I am now a veteran soldier, having gone through some of the toughest fighting of the war. You can gain some idea of it from the newspaper reports for the present, and, God willing, I'll tell you more some day. It has been a terrible yet wonderful and unique experience, just what I wanted to get. So, I am richer in spirit than I was before. And, I'm proud, too, of being one who took an actual part in the invasion of France. For, I believe, that military operation has brought the end of the war clearly into view. And, bringing this infernal thing to a conclusion is, to my mind, the greatest work a man at present can devote himself to.

The only thing that is—unpleasant—about this occupation is that in pursuing it, more or less people get killed, and one is never out from under the shadow of the old Reaper. He has struck men down all around me, and once or twice he has come within a hair of cutting my own stalk. Somehow, however, I have been spared. The best reason for that, which I can adduce, is your constant prayer, Mother. In any event, I have viewed the visage of death at close quarters.

And that brings us to the important matter which I want to have you understand.

All the time I have been in the battle, only one thing has disturbed my mind. I wanted to write you this letter before anything happened to me, for I have been afraid of the effect which news of my death might have on you, dearest Parents. Through this letter I hope to make you understand a couple of things which, once understood, would take most of the sting out of that news, should it come some day in the future.

First of all, my dearest Parents—let me put it this way—as long as this war is the major event of the time, I would not be happy or satisfied in mind anywhere except in the middle of it. Why that should be I shall not go into. It's just a fact beyond argument or discussion and I, your son, would not be happy in a war plant or Washington office, or any secure place like that.

Naturally, this being the case, I am resigned to the possibility of a sudden and early death. And I want you to realize that I am prepared to die should I have to. Let that sink into your mind now and think it over. I, myself, am ready and willing to meet my Maker at any time that He should call. I've seen how it is to be killed on a battlefield, and believe me, my good Parents,

it is a much better way to go than
ing with sickness, or pining with w
The face of every dead man I've
was serene and composed; excep
the absence of respiration, they
merely peacefully sleeping. I hav
fear of death. (That is no boast, m
a statement of fact.) And, after
letter is finished, there will be no
more to worry me or disturb
serenity of mind.

Now then, Mother and Fa
understanding this, can you re
news of my death with composur
resignation? Naturally, my
would be much harder on you th
would be on me. But, it should n
a catastrophe to you, and that is
I am trying so desperately to expl
you with clarity and certainty. So
read over and over what I have wr
until you feel you see the pictur
same way I do.

As a matter of fact, my dearest
I am in a much better shape, h
survived thus far, to see this
through to a successful conclusion
I was before D Day. I'm battle
now, know the tricks and exer
constant vigilance. All that rema
the element of chance, or, in
words, the Will of God. God w
I'll be home one day, otherwise I
That is the stark fact that mu
squarely faced. As far as seeking
job somewhere far in the rear, th
out. To me, life spent in seeking
security is worthless. Just under
that, and everything else I've sai
be easy to apprehend.

Now, I've said what I wanted t
and I'm much relieved. I'll
speak on this subject again, and I
want you to mention it. Just u
stand and that is all.

Yours as eve
Jo

One of the letters that John sent home was later published. SOURCE: Unknown

JAMES A. CHILDS

Private First Class

82nd Airborne Division

An old man by paratrooper standards

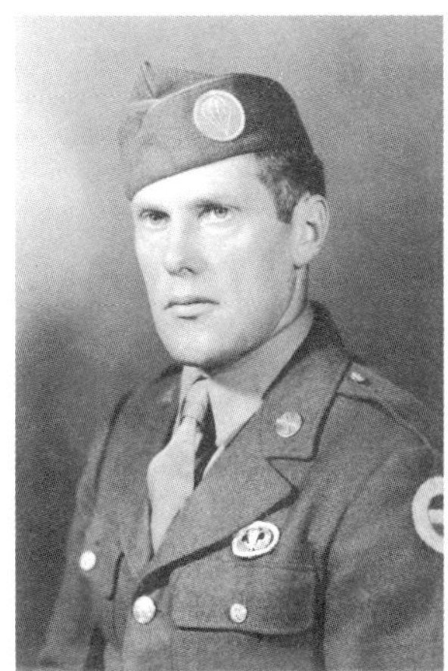

Private First Class James A. Childs from Deerfield, Massachusetts was born on July 12, 1913. He was part of the eighth generation of the Childs family in Deerfield and worked on various family farmlands until he entered the army on September 21, 1942. 'Jimmy,' as he was called by his family and friends, volunteered for the paratroopers and was an original member of Company C, 508th Parachute Infantry Regiment of the 82nd Airborne Division.

On D-Day, Jimmy was one of the first American paratroopers whose boots hit French soil in Normandy after parachuting behind enemy lines overnight. Two months later, he was awarded the Bronze Star Medal for the courage he displayed during the invasion. His citation reads:

> ***'For heroic conduct in action on 6 June 1944, about one mile from Picauville, France. In enemy territory, and not yet having contacted friendly troops, Private Childs, acting as lead scout for his squad, encountered about a company of German infantry. With one companion, Childs fired on the enemy until his squad could withdraw. During this action, Private Childs continued to face the enemy and by his disregard for personal safety, prevented the enemy's advance. In a later action, he was captured, but he and a companion escaped, bringing their German guard with them to our lines.'***

After the 508th returned to England in mid-July, Jimmy penned his last letter to his mother on July 29, 1944. 'I was behind enemy lines for thirteen days,' he wrote. 'I was also captured by the Germans and was held prisoner for three days. Then we got away. I will sure be glad when this war is over. I hope all the folks and you are well and don't worry about me. I'll get back there someday, I'm sure. Lots of Love, Jim.'

Unfortunately, Jimmy's prediction that he for sure would return home someday did not come true. On September 18, 1944 – one day after parachuting into eastern Holland during the launch of Operation Market Garden – he was killed by German sniper fire.

Jimmy was shot in his shoulder and head when he and his Company C comrades charged across the Wylerbaan to courageously clear Drop Zone T outside Groesbeek, allowing incoming gliders from England to land safely with more troops and supplies. As a result, Jimmy remained forever 31. At this age, he was an old man by paratrooper standards, as most of the men in his regiment were just eighteen to twenty years old. It was fitting that his comrades called their old-man paratrooper 'Bones.'

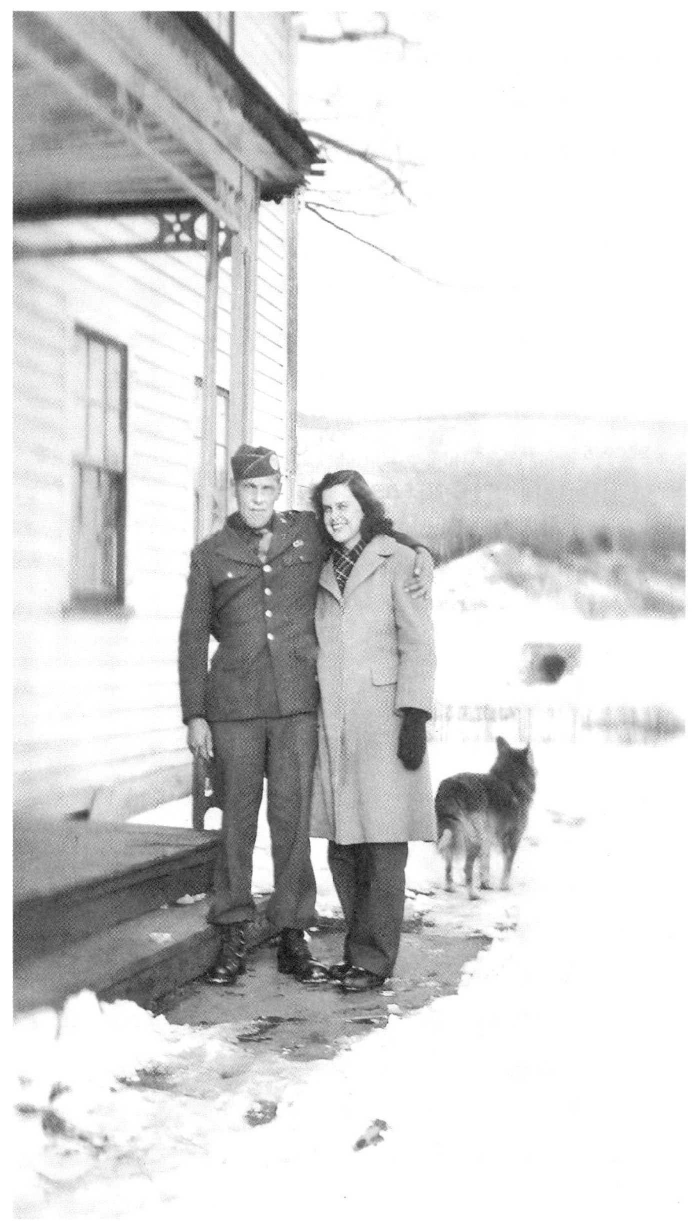

Jimmy and his sister Alice in March 1943. SOURCE: Chris Harris

Jimmy was not the only paratrooper in the Childs family. His younger brother Lewis, who served with the 517th Parachute Infantry Regiment and fought in Italy, parachuted into Southern France in August 1944, and then fought in the Battle of the Bulge in December 1944–January 1945, ironically alongside the 508th PIR of the 82nd Airborne Division, Jimmy's comrades. Letters early-on between the brothers reveal their plans to both volunteer for the airborne without consulting their family.

Alice Childs Harris, Jimmy's younger sister by ten years, would recall memories of her favorite brother, Jimmy, at age 93. 'Jimmy was the strongest kid in the neighborhood, but he was a kind brother. One summer when I suffered from tonsillitis, he would spend the small amount of money he made at odd jobs buying me ice cream every day to sooth my throat pain. I'll never forget that.' Alice and Jimmy last saw each other in March 1943 when Jimmy was on leave after training in Camp Mackall, North Carolina. The telegram announcing his death arrived the same day as her wedding shower in October 1944, when Alice was twenty years old. Alice remembered that day, saying, 'My sister and I went to the wedding shower and did not tell anyone. We did not want to ruin the party.' While raising six children, Alice would knit and crotchet sweaters, hats and mittens and sell them locally to raise extra money to one day visit Europe and her brother's gravesite in Holland. In April 1970, she chaperoned local high school students on a trip to Paris, and via train and taxi was able to visit Jimmy's gravesite in Margraten (Plot F, Row 3, Grave 1). She would return many times over the ensuing decades, the last time laying flowers at age 81 on September 18, 2004, the 60th anniversary of Jimmy's death.

In 2019, on the 75th anniversary of Jimmy's death, a historical marker honoring him was unveiled in his historical hometown of Deerfield, Massachusetts.

JAMES L. DIEL
Second Lieutenant
101st Airborne Division

Charging a German tank

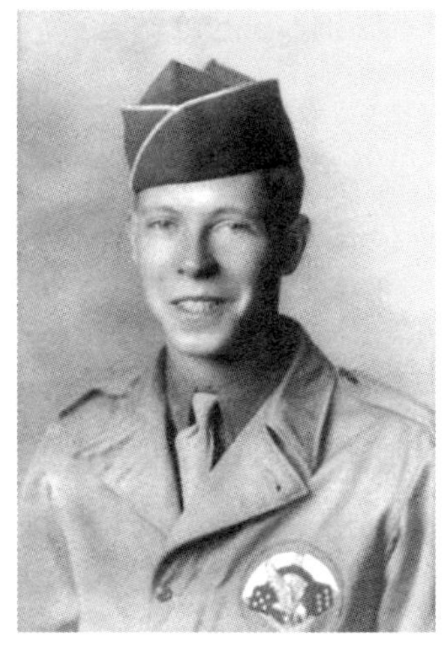

Second Lieutenant James L. Diel from Illinois was born in 1922. In August 1942, he entered the army, whereupon he volunteered for the airborne troops. James was trained as a paratrooper and joined the 506th Parachute Infantry Regiment of the 101st Airborne Division. With this unit, James participated successively in the airborne landings on D-Day and Operation Market Garden in 1944.

Initially, James was the First Sergeant of Easy Company, known from the book and television series 'Band of Brothers.' His immediate superior was Richard 'Dick' Winters, the famous commander of Easy Company, with whom James became good friends. Winters was very satisfied with how James performed his duties. In his memoirs, he later wrote of him:

> ***'Diel was by no means the biggest, strongest, toughest guy in the outfit. He was not an athlete, but he possessed a command voice, a command attitude, and he took no backtalk or guff from any soldier. He was what I called a "can-do" man. Give him an order and you could forget about it; he got the job done. He was the kind of soldier who made any outfit look good, and he made a platoon leader's job easy. Diel was also a self-starter, highly motivated, entirely dependable, and he had a no-nonsense, low-key leadership style that commanded the respect of the men. Diel performed commendably in Normandy and I was confident that he was ready for the next step. While I knew that Easy Company would be losing a first-class leader and that I would be losing a good friend, recommending 1st Sergeant Diel for a battlefield commission was the highest honor I could bestow on him for a job well done.'***

Because Winters admired James' personality and qualities, he nominated him for a battlefield commission after the company had returned to England from Normandy. James was promoted to Second Lieutenant and transferred to Company A to assume command of its first platoon.

On September 17, 1944 – the first day of Operation Market Garden – James landed in Holland near the village of Son, where his regiment's main objective was capturing the bridge over the Wilhelmina Canal. However, as the Americans approached the bridge, it was blown up by the Germans. Therefore, Allied engineers had to build a so-called Bailey bridge across the canal. This new bridge was constructed during the night of September 18–19, whereupon the first British tanks crossed it to resume their advance to Grave and Nijmegen.

James' platoon was ordered to protect the Bailey bridge at Son against a possible enemy counterattack. In the late afternoon of September 19, a number of German Panther tanks supported by infantry launched an attack along the south side of the canal to destroy the bridge. On seeing the first enemy tank approaching with its machine guns blazing, James began packing Composition C-2 together in his hands and started running toward it, intending to blow it up. As he ran toward it, the tank's big 75mm gun fired several shells. The fifth round struck James and 'took his head off at the shoulders,' Sergeant Donald Burgett recalled. James was killed on the spot and therefore he remained forever young. He is buried at the U.S. Military Cemetery in Margraten, where visitors can find his final resting place in Plot L, Row 15, Grave 8.

ALFRED H. CONRAD
Second Lieutenant
82nd Airborne Division

Took responsibility under murderous fire

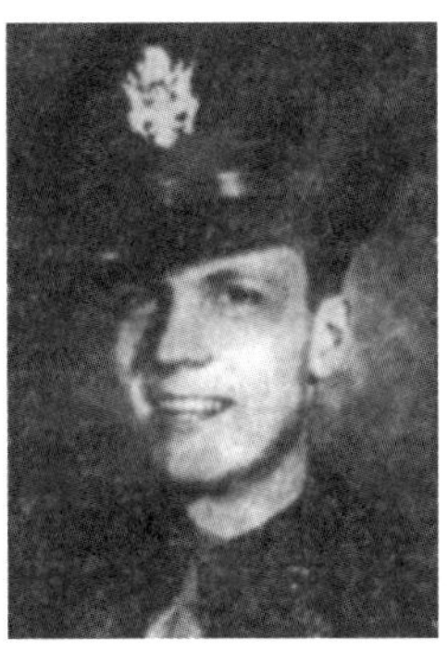

Second Lieutenant Alfred H. Conrad from Indiana was born on November 13, 1921. In June 1942, he enlisted at Fort Benjamin Harrison. Alfred was trained as an engineer and was assigned to the 307th Airborne Engineer Battalion. This battalion was attached to the 82nd Airborne Division.

In September 1944, Alfred's airborne division played an important role in Operation Market Garden. His unit landed near Nijmegen to capture the major road bridge over the river Waal. This bridge had to be captured as quickly as possible to facilitate the further advance of the British tanks toward Arnhem. However, the Germans offered fiercer resistance here than the Allies had expected in advance. Therefore, during the first three days of fighting, they did not succeed in capturing the bridge.

On September 19, 1944, the day before the Waal bridge at Nijmegen was to fall into Allied hands, Alfred and his company attacked a German machine gun position east of Nijmegen near the village of Berg en Dal. This was located on a hill that the locals called 'Devil's Hill'. Alfred made the ultimate sacrifice during this action and was posthumously awarded the Silver Star. His citation reads:

> ***'Second Lieutenant Conrad, Platoon Commander, was leading his platoon in an attack on a hill occupied by strong enemy forces in dug in positions. The platoon was forward of the main line of resistance. A machine gun from a dug in position pinned the platoon down by fire. Second Lieutenant Conrad, noting the machine gun position and that it pinned down the troops on the flanks and effectively held up their forward movement, set out to eliminate it as quickly as possible. He proceeded with one man to wipe it out by use of a hand grenade. While attempting to get within throwing distance, Second Lieutenant Conrad was killed by fire from the machine gun. His gallant actions and dedicated devotion to duty, without regard for his own life, were in keeping with the highest traditions of military service and reflect great credit upon himself and the United States Army.'***

Alfred gave his life at the age of 22. He is permanently interred in Margraten, where his final resting place can be found in Plot K, Row 1, Grave 7.

EDWIN W. HIRO
Major
357th Fighter Group

Shot down during his last scheduled mission

Major Edwin W. Hiro from Minnesota was born on August 13, 1916. He had enlisted in the USAAF in 1942 and was a fighter pilot in the 363rd Fighter Squadron. This squadron was part of the 357th Fighter Group, the first P-51 Mustang Group in the U.S. Eighth Air Force.

On September 19, 1944, Edwin piloted his P-51 'Horse's Itch' to provide air support near Arnhem during Operation Market Garden. The base from which he took off was AAF Station F-373 at Leiston, located in the county of Suffolk, England. For Edwin, who had already shot down four enemy aircraft, this mission would be the last scheduled flight of his 'tour of combat' before he was due to return home.

While Edwin's squadron was flying above the Arnhem area, the Mustang force encountered about ten to twelve German Me 109s. The aerial combat quickly developed into a wild dog fight between the P-51s and the Messerschmitts. At some point, Edwin dove on the tail of a Me 109. Edwin strafed his prey with his machine guns and shot it down. Flight Officer Johnnie Carter, who piloted another Mustang, saw the Messerschmitt crash and burn. It was Edwin's fifth aerial victory, making him an 'ace.'

Minutes later, however, Edwin's Mustang itself became the prey of another Messerschmitt Bf 109. This one was flown by Leutnant Richard Franz, whose machine gun and cannon fire hit the P-51 in its cockpit and engine, after which Edwin's Mustang slammed into the ground, killing him at the age of 28. Edwin's remains have never been recovered afterwards. Therefore, his name is recorded on the Walls of the Missing in Margraten.

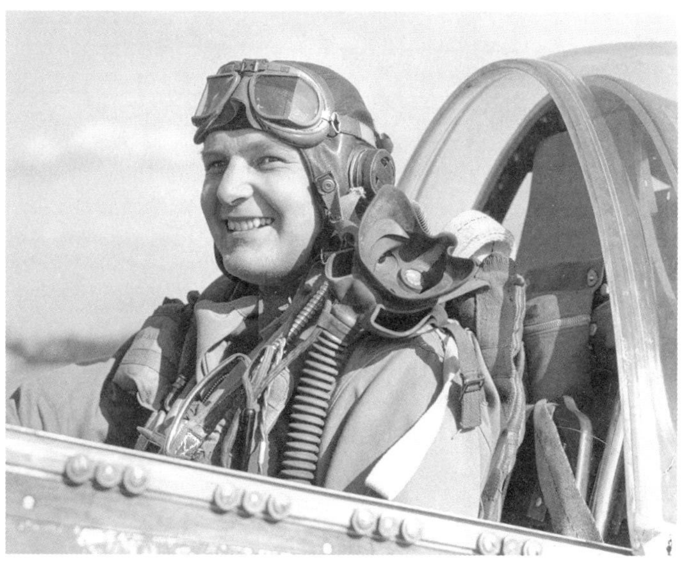

ROBERT VAN KLINKEN
Private First Class
101st Airborne Division

Paratrooper had a Dutch grandfather

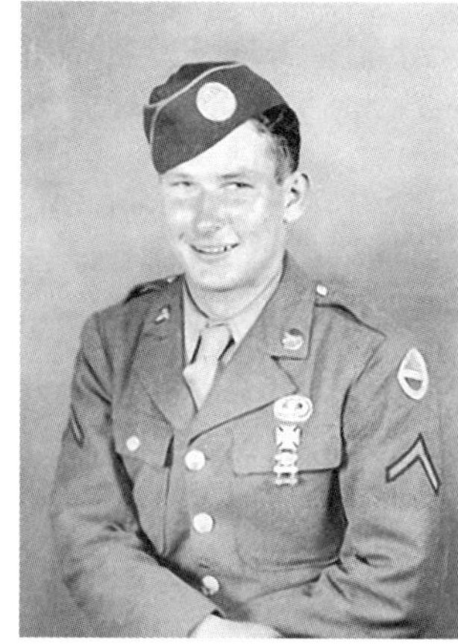

Private First Class Robert van Klinken from Washington state was born on October 31, 1919. His grandfather was originally from the Dutch province of Groningen and had emigrated to the United States in the 1890s. Robert attended high school for three years and then went to work in the mines. In 1937, he decided to change professions and continue as an auto mechanic.

After the Japanese attack on Pearl Harbor, many young American men, whether through conscription or not, entered the military. So did Robert. He volunteered for service in August 1942 and, after arduous training, became a paratrooper in a new army unit: the 506th Parachute Infantry Regiment of the 101st Airborne Division. Along with his comrades, he went to fight in Easy Company, known from the book and television series 'Band of Brothers.' In late 1943, Robert and the other paratroopers of the 506th were sent overseas to England. There they were further prepared for their role in the invasion.

When the big day of the invasion finally arrived on June 6, 1944, Robert landed in Normandy. There he was wounded a few days later. As a result, he was taken to a hospital in England. While recovering there, Robert sent a letter to his sister and brother-in-law. In it he wrote:

> ***'Well Johnny, I got a piece of shrapnel in my arm so they sent me back to England. My arm is O.K. as it is just a flesh wound. You know Johnny, it's worse back here in the hospital than it is at the front. You get thinking about your buddies you lost over there and you can't do anything about it. Hope they can send me back soon so I can get another crack at them.'***

Several weeks after sending this letter, Robert was sufficiently recovered. He then participated in Operation Market Garden. When this major Allied operation began, Robert landed on one of the drop zones near the Dutch city of Eindhoven on September 17, 1944.

Three days later, on September 20, Easy Company and some British tanks headed for the village of Nuenen. There they encountered stubborn resistance from a German armored unit that had been ordered to cut the Eindhoven-Nijmegen road – 'Hell's Highway' – to block the advance of the Allied ground troops. During the fighting that broke out, Robert was killed at the age of 24. This happened at the moment he stormed forward through a hedgerow.

Sergeant Darrell 'Shifty' Powers, a veteran of Easy Company, had witnessed Robert's death and later described it in his biography. He wrote:

> ***'As I pushed through a hedgerow, I heard a German machine gun burst a few rows over. Robert van Klinken was pelted in the chest with three bullets and went down. Those closest to him pulled him to safety, but his face was ashen; he'd soon be dead. I hardly had time to notice when it happened, but later I remembered how I'd talked to him lots of times, and that he was a young mechanic from Washington state. All he wanted to do was go home, get married, and have a bunch of kids. Robert van Klinken was kindhearted, always laughing, and then he was gone.'***

Robert's final resting place in Margraten can be found in Plot C, Row 8, Grave 32.

WALTER J. MUSZYNSKI
Private
82nd Airborne Division

The famous Waal Crossing

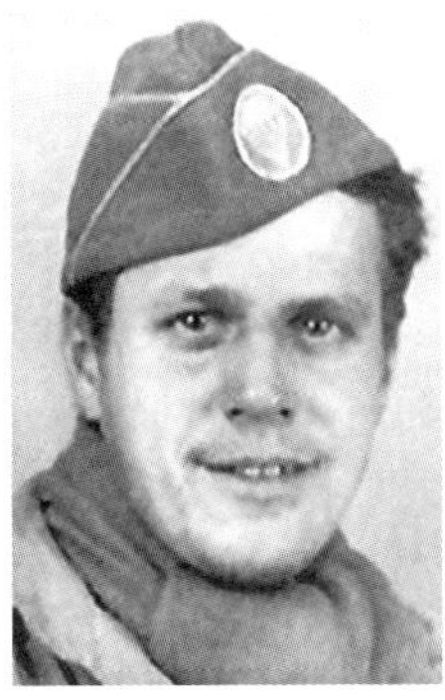

Private Walter J. Muszynski from Wisconsin was born in 1921. He entered the army in March 1942 and joined the paratroopers. At the start of Operation Market Garden, he landed near Nijmegen on September 17, 1944. Walter was assigned to the 82nd Airborne Division and served as light machine gunner in Company I, 504th Parachute Infantry Regiment.

The main objective at Nijmegen was the capture of the road bridge over the river Waal. This bridge had to fall into American hands quickly so that the tanks of the British army could advance to the British paratroopers at Arnhem without delay. However, the attacks of the American paratroopers were repeatedly halted near the southern ramp. Therefore, on September 20, 1944, brave paratroopers from the 504th Parachute Infantry Regiment crossed the Waal River in canvas boats, about one and a half miles west of the road bridge. Private Walter Muszynski was one of them. He was in one of the lead boats.

The daring Waal Crossing in which Walter participated was supported by artillery and British tanks. However, the smoke screen and shellfire could not prevent that Walter and the other paratroopers in the boats encountered heavy fire from German positions dug in on the north bank of the river.

As heavy machine gun and 20mm Flak fire greeted the forward elements, Walter quickly mounted his machine gun in the bow of his boat and directed heavy fire on the enemy dug in on the riverbank. Upon reaching the opposite bank, Walter maintained a continuous cover of protective fire for the movement of his squad to the main dike and from the dike to the railroad embankment, accounting for at least twenty enemy dead and wounded. At times he fired his machine gun from the hip, while moving forward as to keep pace with his squad.

At the railroad embankment, Walter and his platoon encountered strong opposition from self-propelled Flak guns. One of the nearby flanking guns knocked Walter's machine gun out of his hands, destroying it. Unhesitatingly, and without orders from anyone, Walter crept to within fifteen yards of the gun position directing devastating flanking fire on his platoon, and knocked it out with hand grenades, killing four of the enemy. Not long after, he was mortally wounded by German rifle fire.

Walter was only 23 years when he gave his life. Because his brave determination and valorous execution of his duties was an inspiring example for all his comrades and contributed directly to the successful establishment of the vital Waal bridgehead, he was posthumously awarded the Distinguished Service Cross – the U.S. Army's second highest military decoration.

Walter's remains were initially buried at the temporary U.S. Military Cemetery at Molenhoek. After the war, he was transferred to Margraten, where he is permanently interred in Plot F, Row 19, Grave 26.

WILLARD JENKINS
Private First Class
307th Airborne Engineer Battalion

DNA from elderly sister led to his identification

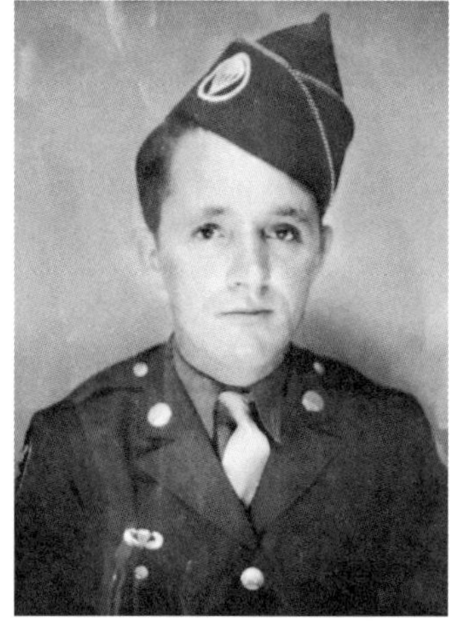

Willard Jenkins from Scranton, Pennsylvania was born in 1917. After high school, he was employed as a truck driver for some time. In June 1942, Willard entered the army, eventually becoming an engineer in the 307th Airborne Engineer Battalion. This battalion was part of the 82nd Airborne Division.

During Operation Market Garden, Willard went missing near Nijmegen on September 20, 1944, as he was participating in the crossing of the Waal River. He was steering one of rickety canvas boats used to carry paratroopers from the 504th Parachute Infantry Regiment across the river.

The purpose of this attack was to finally capture the main road bridge at Nijmegen so that British tanks could continue advancing toward the British paratroopers in Arnhem. The previous attempts to capture the Waal bridge had been repelled by the Germans with machine gun fire, mortar fire, and 88mm guns.

The Waal Crossing on September 20, 1944, began after an artillery bombardment and was supported by British tanks. However, the smoke screen and shellfire could not neutralize the Germans on the north bank of the river. As a result, the American paratroopers in the boats crossed the river under heavy fire from enemy machine guns, mortars, and 20mm Flak guns. This killed or wounded many men. One of the Americans who was killed was Willard. How he met his death and why he went missing was later recalled by Captain T. Moffatt Burriss, the commander of Company I, 504th PIR who was sitting next to him:

> ***'I was sitting on the stern of our boat next to the engineer [who later turned out to be PFC Willard Jenkins]. Suddenly, I noticed his wrist turn red. "Captain," he said, "take the rudder. I've been hit." Just as I reached for the rudder, he leaned forward and caught a 20mm high explosive shell through the head, a round that was meant for me. As the shell exploded, I felt a stinging sensation in my side. I had caught some of the shrapnel, though I felt no real pain. I grabbed the rudder and tried to steer. At that moment, the upper part of the engineer's body fell overboard; when the current hit his head and torso, the drag swung the boat upstream. "Straighten out! Straighten out!" the men at the front of the boat shouted. I couldn't. His***

feet were caught under the seat and his body was acting as a second rudder. I was finally able to reach down, disengage his feet, and push him overboard. As I watched his body float downstream, I could see the red blood streaming from what was left from his head. We resumed our frantic paddling toward the opposite shore.'

According to historical records, on September 29, 1944, two residents of Werkendam, Holland, were in a rowboat on the Waal River when they saw a body in the river. German soldiers stationed nearby took possession of the remains and buried them on the riverbank.

In late August 1948, an investigator from the American Graves Registration Command visited the Werkendam area and inquired about the remains. The AGRC learned that a person of the Information Bureau for missing English flyers had been to Werkendam to examine the remains and determined them to be of American nationality, and had them moved to Werkendam General Cemetery. The remains were disinterred on September 17, 1948, and sent to the Identification Section at the U.S. Military Cemetery at Neuville-en-Condroz, Belgium, for further analysis. The remains could not be identified and were buried as Unknown X-7838 Neuville on October 1, 1948. Nearly two years later, in 1950, Willard's remains were declared non-recoverable.

In 2018, after thorough research and historical analysis, historians from the Defense POW/MIA Accounting Agency (DPAA) determined that Willard Jenkins was a strong candidate for association to the remains. Therefore, X-7838 Neuville was disinterred on April 18, 2018, and sent to DPAA.

Several months later, on July 3, 2018, the remains were positively identified by comparing DNA samples to the DNA of Willard's 83-year-old sister Edna, whereupon Willard was reburied in his hometown of Scranton in September 2018. In Margraten, where Willard is listed on the Walls of the Missing, a rosette was then placed next to his name to indicate that he had been found.

JOHN RIGAPOULOS

Private First Class

82nd Airborne Division

'Here's another Purple Heart'

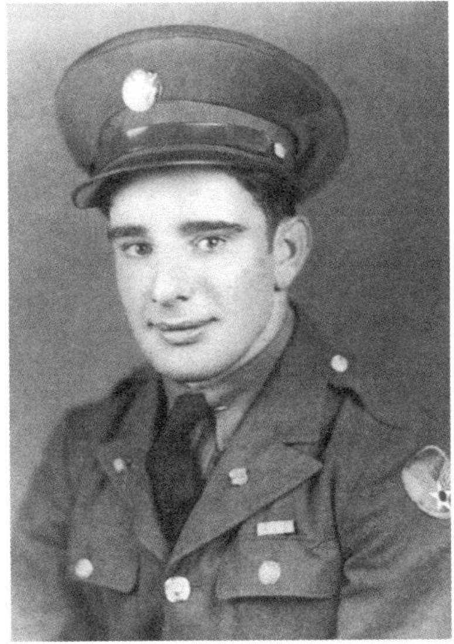

Private First Class John Rigapoulos from Massachusetts volunteered for the paratroopers. In 1944, he joined the 3rd Battalion of the 504th Parachute Infantry Regiment as a replacement at Anzio, Italy. After the regiment returned to England, it was decided that it would not be deployed in the Normandy invasion due to the high casualty rate and a lack of replacements. But John was one of the men from the 504th who volunteered for the pathfinders after a call from Brigadier General James Gavin, the assistant division commander of the 82nd Airborne Division. So, on June 6, 1944, John was one of the first American paratroopers to jump into Normandy.

After landing, John's objective was to mark one of the drop zones for the planes carrying the main force of paratroopers or towing gliders that were to follow up a short time later. For this purpose, the pathfinder sticks were equipped with Holophane lamps, so-called 'Eureka' radar beacons, yellow-colored panels, and colored smoke.

A few months later, John participated in Operation Market Garden. He jumped into Holland from a C-47 and three days later, on September 20, 1944, he was among the men who conducted the famous Waal Crossing near Nijmegen to capture the crucial bridges across this river. Despite the fact that the American paratroopers in the flimsy boats were subjected to a withering combination of enemy small arms, machine gun and mortar fire, John and dozens of others made it to the other side. Then, after charging through a hail of 20mm and machine gun fire, the men finally reached the relative shelter of the dike. When John was subsequently making his way up the road leading to the railroad bridge, he met Sergeant Albert Tarbell, with whom he had gone through jump school. John showed Tarbell the nub of his thumb, which had been shot off by an enemy bullet, and said airily, 'Well, here's another Purple Heart.' Instead of going back to the riverbank for medical aid, John stayed with a group that was moving on the railroad bridge.

Shortly after, as the group moved along the railroad embankment leading to the bridge, John was struck and killed by either a sniper or a burst of German machine gun fire – the sources are not entirely unambiguous on this. The Dutch historian Frank van Lunteren, for example, suggested it was a sniper who shot him while another renowned historian, Phil Nordyke, wrote that 'suddenly a German machine gun opened up on them' and 'Lieutenant Richard La Riviere ("Rivers") and Private First Class John Rigapoulos were kneeling beside one another trying to locate the machine gun when Rigapoulos was hit in the chest with a burst, knocking him over backward, killing him.' Perhaps the alleged sniper was armed with a machine gun. This might possibly explain why both are mentioned.

John was 23 years old when he was killed. He is permanently interred in Margraten, where he rests in Plot K, Row 1, Grave 9. His name is also listed on the Waal Crossing memorial which has been erected near the riverbank where the daring assault was conducted.

ROBERT WASHKO
Private
82nd Airborne Division

'A sniper shot him quick'

Private Robert Washko, born on September 8, 1922, was a native of Scalp Level, Pennsylvania. He enlisted into the army in 1943 and volunteered for jump school to become a paratrooper.

At some point after enlisting, Robert was assigned to Company A of the 504th Parachute Infantry Regiment. This regiment was an element of the 82nd 'All American' Airborne Division which entered combat during the airborne assault on Sicily – Operation Husky – in July 1943. Thereafter, the division was deployed in the Allied campaign on the Italian mainland.

While fighting in Italy on January 30, 1944, Robert came to the rescue of Second Lieutenant Reneau Breard's squad. Breard and his men had just taken up a defensive position near a blown bridge across the Mussolini Canal and was leading his squad up a deep ditch as Germans were coming toward them. Breard's carbine was hitting them, but they kept coming and threatened to overrun his position, when Robert, the platoon's BAR man, pushed him aside and opened fire. He fired a clip of ammo upon the approaching

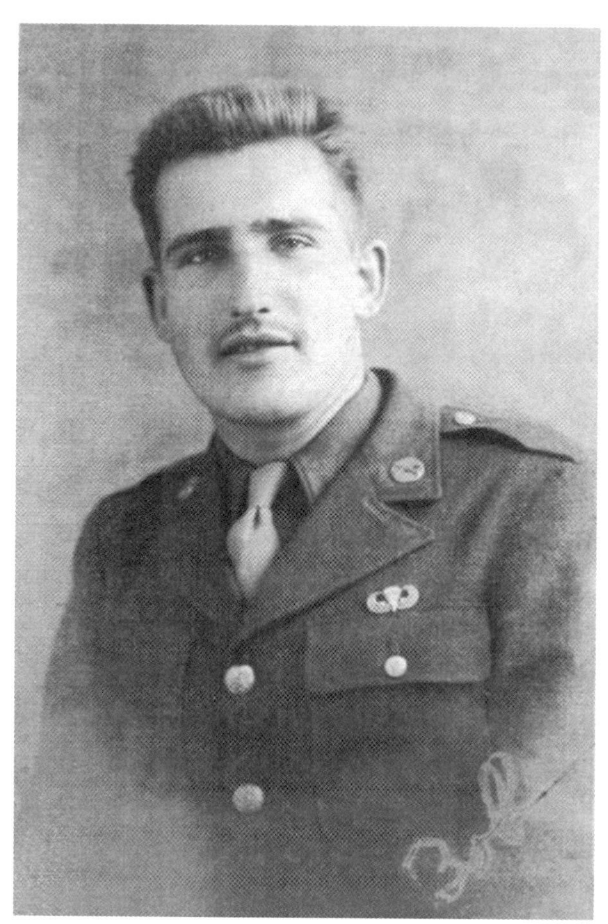

Germans and cleared the ditch. It was a close call, but thanks to Robert and his bullet-spitting light machine gun, Breard and his men could hold out.

Nearly eight months later, Robert took part in Operation Market Garden. On September 17, 1944, he jumped into German-occupied Holland from a C-47. Three days later, on September 20, he was among the men who conducted the daring Waal Crossing near Nijmegen in order to capture the crucial bridges across this wide river. Robert's Company A crossed the Waal with the fourth wave in the afternoon. Once they had made it to the northern bank, Robert's platoon went to Fort Hof van Holland. As in Italy, Robert was in the same platoon as Lieutenant Breard, who, although he did not witness Robert's death himself, was informed of it by a sergeant and learned how it had happened: Robert got up on the north side and was shooting his BAR from the hip. He had just reached the top of the fort when 'a sniper shot him quick.'

Shortly thereafter, Sergeant Mitchell E. Rech took position on the top edge. 'I looked to my left and saw Private Washko face down with his arm on his BAR. There was a perfectly round hole in his temple with a trickle of blood coming from it. He was close enough for me to touch him. I cried out for a medic even though I knew it was useless. He was gone.'

Robert made the ultimate sacrifice at the age of 22. He was initially buried at Molenhoek, but after the war his remains were moved to Margraten. He was given his final resting place there in Plot F, Row 4, Grave 3. Robert is also mentioned on the Waal Crossing memorial which is erected near the riverbank and close to the fort where he lost his life.

BENJAMIN S. UPTON
Private
82nd Airborne Division

Comrades met death together

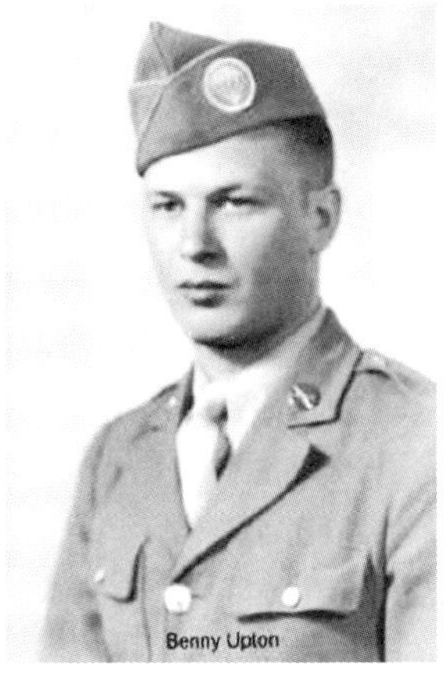
Benny Upton

Private Benjamin S. Upton from Arizona was born in 1925. He had just completed four years of high school when he volunteered for military service in 1943. 'Bennie' then went through the arduous training to become a paratrooper and was assigned to Company D of the 508th Parachute Infantry Regiment. This regiment was part of the 82nd 'All American' Airborne Division.

On September 17, 1944, Benjamin boarded a C-47 that would fly him to Holland to participate in the airborne landings of Operation Market Garden. In the afternoon, he landed near Nijmegen. A few days later, he was in a foxhole near the Wylerbaan, north of Groesbeek, with his comrade Charles Tuttle and a Bazooka. In front of them was the German Reichswald. According to the information their commanders had at the time, the Germans were assembling strong units and a large number of tanks here for a counterattack towards Nijmegen.

Together with Charles, Benjamin kept an eye on the Reichswald on September 20, 1944, and was ready to go into action with their Bazooka as soon as the Germans would unleash tanks on them. What happened next was later recalled by an eyewitness, Private Norbert Studelska:

> ***'It was while the platoon was dug in on this small road that Bennie was killed with his buddy Tuttle. There was a farm site in front of their position. I don't know what their target was (probably some enemy movement at the farm site), but they fired a couple of rounds from the Bazooka. A little more than half a mile to our front was the German Reichswald forest, which was crawling with German soldiers, tanks, and field guns. Apparently, a German tank or field gun observed the flash from the Bazooka. An 88mm [shell] zeroed-in on Bennie's position, which received a direct hit. This is very sad to say, but as the rest of us surmised, that also set off the Bazooka ammunition that was stored near or in the hole. Needless to say, neither of those two brave boys suffered.'***

Benjamin was only nineteen years old when the German shell scored a direct hit on his position. He is buried in Margraten in Plot L, Row 10, Grave 2. There one can read on his cross that Benjamin's date of death was September 22. This must have been a clerical mistake, or Pvt. Studelska has misremembered the date he mentioned in his account.

JACOB T. HERMAN JR.
Private
82nd Airborne Division

The Oglala Lakota Paratrooper

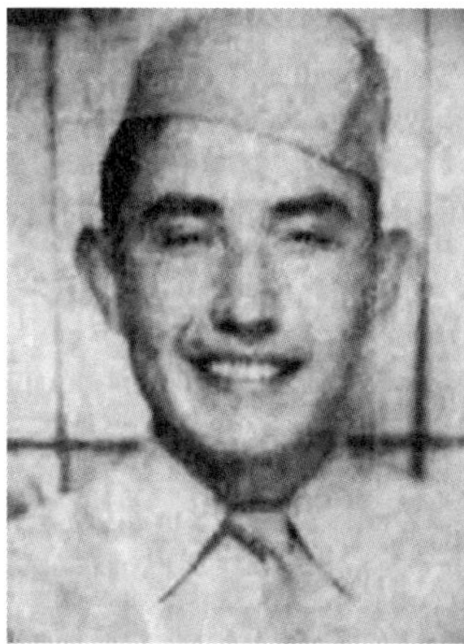

Paratrooper Jacob T. Herman Jr. was a member of the Oglala Lakota tribe on the Pine Ridge Indian Reservation in South Dakota. Jab, as his family called him, was born there on September 5, 1925. The oldest of five children, he grew up in the Badlands, a dry region which is characterized by steep slopes, minimal vegetation, ravines, and gullies in the north of the reservation. Jab's father was a famous Indian cowboy and rodeo clown.

In the summer of 1942, when hundreds of young men from the tribe were already in military service, the ritual Sun Dance was re-enacted for the first time in many years. During the fast, one of the old shamans had a vision: 'two hands, with the palm facing the sky, rise up from a pit of bison skulls.' It was a supernatural sign from Wakan Tanka that their pleas for victory on the warpath would be heard.

In the summer of that same year, the War Department seized 140,000 acres in the Badlands so fighter pilots and bomber crews could be trained there. About 125 Oglala families, including Jab's family, were forced to leave the soil on which they had lived for generations. Among them were tribal elders who had witnessed the massacre at Wounded Knee in 1890. They could remember how U.S. Army soldiers had killed many unsuspecting Lakota men, women, and children there. Following their enforced departure, Jab and his family spent the bitterly cold winter that followed in a tipi, as no log cabin was available.

Soon after graduating from Red Cloud Indian School, Jab turned eighteen and was drafted. Just before leaving for a large army post in Texas, he probably, like many other departing Oglala soldiers, underwent a ritual purification of body and mind in a traditional Inipi (sweat lodge) ceremony.

After his sixteen weeks of basic infantry training, Jab volunteered for the paratroopers. Following his airborne training at Fort Benning, he was sent to England along with hundreds of other replacements. There he was assigned to Company D, 505th Parachute Infantry Regiment, 82nd Airborne Division. This unit had already suffered heavy losses in Normandy.

On September 17, 1944, Jab landed in a field just east of Groesbeek. Three other members of his tribe were also dropped around this Dutch town. With only a small number of casualties, the regiment reached its objectives for the first day. However, the division failed to capture the crucial railroad and road bridges across the Waal River in Nijmegen, and had to defend itself against fierce German counterattacks over the next few days.

During the fighting in Nijmegen, Jab made the ultimate sacrifice just two weeks after his nineteenth birthday. There are conflicting reports about how and when he was killed. According to military files, he went missing on the 19th, but did not die until the 22nd. This date is also inscribed on his cross. However, according to his commander, Lt. James L. Meyers, Jacob was killed on the 19th near the Nijmegen railroad bridge. 'After advancing about fifty yards, we met a hail of automatic weapons fire [machine gun or submachine gun fire] coming straight down the tracks from the bridge,' Meyers later wrote. 'I glanced to my rear to check on the squad and saw Private Jacob T. Herman Jr., kneeling directly behind me. I shouted an order for him to get down, but he did not move. I took a second look and saw a bullet hole in his forehead. He was dead.'

In any case, the Oglala paratrooper was initially buried at the temporary military cemetery in Molenhoek on September 22. Three weeks later his parents received the tragic news. His grieving mother then said, 'our son sacrificed his life for the country that robbed us of our own property.' For her, the Sun Dance shamanic vision was not fulfilled, but rituals remained essential in processing the grief. Rough Feather, an elderly neighbor who had survived the massacre at Wounded Knee, sang to the stricken family the traditional akicita song, a fitting tribute to warriors.

Jacob T. Herman Jr. was the first of many North American Indians to die in the Netherlands. He is the only Lakota still buried there. His final resting place in Margraten is in Plot F, Row 4, Grave 22.

ARTHUR L. GREGORY
Private
82nd Airborne Division

Rushed into a bullet-swept street

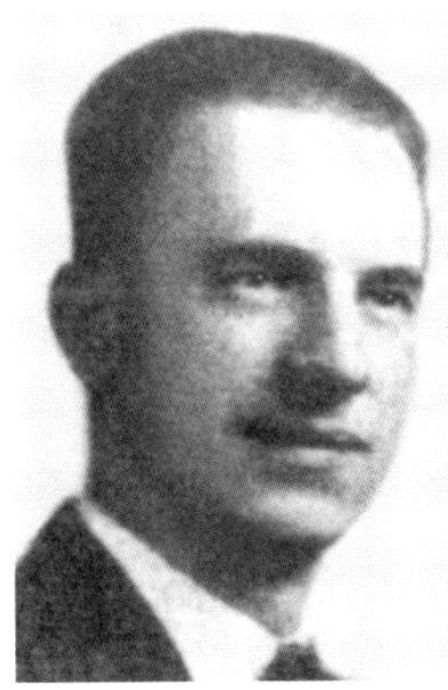

Private Arthur L. Gregory, who was born in Indiana in 1911, joined the military in 1942 and served in Company F, 2nd Battalion, 505th Parachute Infantry Regiment. This regiment was an element of the 82nd Airborne Division.

On October 6, 1943, while fighting near Arnone and the Volturno River in Italy, Arthur was wounded by shrapnel from an exploding German mortar or artillery shell. That same month, Arthur had recovered sufficiently and was discharged from the hospital.

Eleven months later, Arthur took part in Operation Market Garden. On September 17, 1944, he parachuted into Holland from a C-47 and landed on or in the vicinity of Drop Zone N, just south of Groesbeek. Three days later, on September 20, Arthur and his Company F attacked the strong German defenses guarding the southern end of the crucial road bridge across the river Waal in Nijmegen. As the paratroopers fought their way to the bridge and the enemy-occupied Hunnerpark, the Germans raked them with machine gun, mortar, and artillery fire.

At some point during the attack, Arthur rushed into a bullet-swept street in full view of the enemy in an attempt to rescue his platoon leader who was wounded. With total disregard for his own personal safety, he attempted to carry him to safety, only to be wounded himself by sniper fire – or by a machine gun bullet, as his digitalized Hospital Admission Card suggests. Due to his injury and loss of blood, Arthur was unable to continue and later died of wounds received in this action; his death was recorded on September 22, 1944.

Several months after Arthur died of his wounds, he was posthumously awarded the Silver Star for his gallantry in action in Nijmegen. 'As a result of his exemplary performance the men of his company were inspired to high feats of action, enabling the seizure of the Waal River bridges,' his citation states. 'Private Gregory's gallant action and evaluation of his platoon leader's life above that of his own upheld the highest traditions of the parachute forces of the United States Army.'

Arthur is permanently interred at the Netherlands American Cemetery and Memorial in Margraten. His final resting place there can be found in Plot J, Row 10, Grave 4.

JAMES A. COLON
Sergeant
101st Airborne Division

Mother's health suffered from her son's death

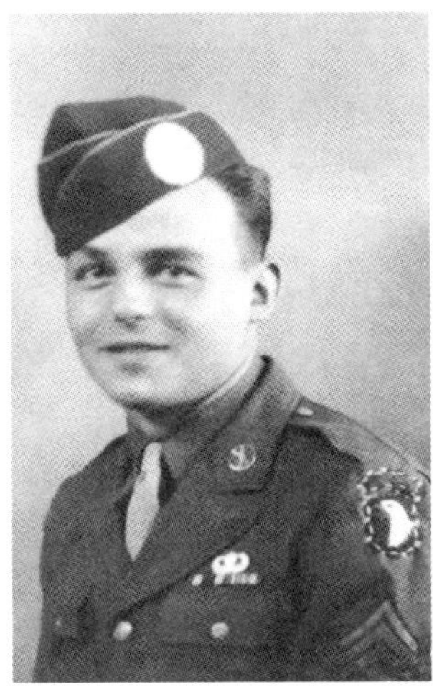

Sergeant James A. Colon from The Bronx, New York was born on August 7, 1922. He enlisted in the army on July 25, 1942, volunteered for the paratroopers and became a member of Company C, 1st Battalion, 502nd Parachute Infantry Regiment. This regiment was a part of the 101st Airborne Division.

James participated in the D-Day invasion and parachuted into Normandy. Over three months later, he was also deployed in Operation Market Garden, the largest airborne assault ever conducted. James' regiment jumped on Drop Zone B northwest of Son and south of St. Oedenrode. In the latter village, James was killed in action on September 22, 1944. His death is briefly described in the records of the First Allied Airborne Army (FAAA) of which the 101st Airborne Division was a part, stating he was shot and killed by a German sniper. The particular excerpt of the FAAA's records is also quoted in the book *Arnhem: The Battle for the Bridges, 1944*, written by the well-known British military historian Antony Beevor. Incidentally, the location of the quote in this book suggests that James would have been killed one day earlier, on September 21.

Initially, James' body was buried in the temporary U.S. Military Cemetery in Molenhoek. His remains were disinterred in 1948 and then brought over to Margraten. Soon after this was done, the U.S. Department of State received a letter from a twenty-year-old Dutch young man from Hengelo named J. Wevers. In his letter Wevers wrote he was corresponding with James' father Manuel since he had found James' grave in Molenhoek. He also described he had learned that James was now resting at the U.S Military Cemetery in Margraten and that James' father had asked him to send him some pictures of his son's grave. The young Wevers traveled to Margraten to fulfill this grieving father's wish, but wasn't allowed to enter the cemetery. In his letter to the U.S. Department of State, he wrote:

> ***'I am a Dutchman by birth and so I am very thankful to those American soldiers who brought us our freedom. Therefore, I felt that it's my highest duty to meet my liabilities to somebody whose dear son sacrificed his young life for our freedom. However, the American Information Service at Margraten, Holland couldn't afford me the consent for entering the burial place on account of closing the Cemetery for 2 years. All my work was in vain till now.***

> ***So, I am asking Your Excellency if you are willing to give me your esteemed permission for entering the cemetery to fulfill this human duty. The name of the paratrooper is James A. Colon. (...) His father's name is Mr. M. Colon.'***

Wever's request was provisionally denied by the U.S. authorities. The reason was explained in a letter to James' father: 'The United States Military Cemetery at Margraten, Holland, was closed for exhumation operations in May of this year and will remain closed to all visitors until such time as all disinterments have been completed, and all permanent burials have been made. This policy has been established in order to prevent families and other visitors subjecting themselves to an unnecessary ordeal and because visitors at such time would delay and interfere with essential operations.'

Meanwhile, in 1947, James' parents had also been asked by the U.S. War Department whether they wanted James' remains repatriated to the U.S. or permanently reburied at Margraten. They decided to have him permanently interred in Margraten. James' mother Angela wrote a letter to the War Department explaining why they chose to leave him in Holland:

> ***'Since the notice that my son James was dead my health suffered great break down. With a thought that his remains would be removed and brought here to its resting place disturb me greatly and I am afraid that it would break down my health completely by return of living memory of my dear son.'***

In accordance with the request of his parents, James' remains were permanently interred in Margraten, where he rests in peace in Plot G, Row 3, Grave 7.

NORMAN F. BETTIN
First Lieutenant
364th Fighter Group

Shot down near Deelen Air Base

Norman F. Bettin from Wisconsin was born in 1920. After attending high school for four years, he had gone to work as a farmer, but in May 1942, he enlisted in the United States Army Air Forces. Norman was then trained as a fighter pilot. After receiving his 'pilot wings,' he was assigned to the 383rd Fighter Squadron of the 364th Fighter Group.

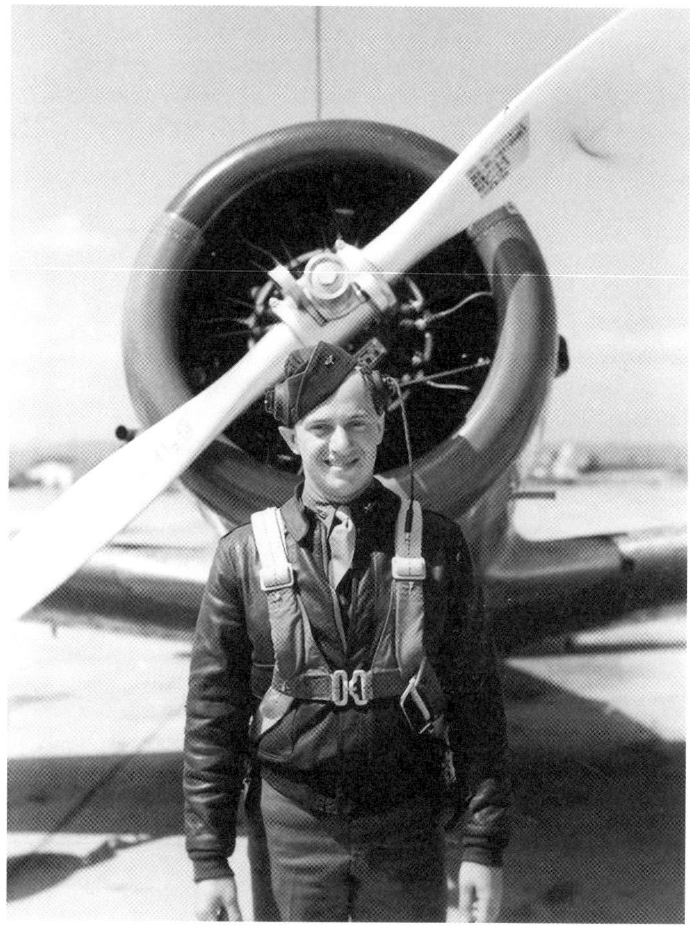

In early 1944, Norman's Fighter Group was stationed in England. Norman's squadron initially operated primarily as an escort for heavy B-17 and B-24 bombers over territory held by the Germans. The bomber groups attacked enemy weapon factories, marshalling yards, and oil refineries, and fighter pilots like Norman had to make sure that Luftwaffe fighters had no chance of shooting down the bombers.

On September 23, 1944, Norman flew a P-51 Mustang to take aerial photographs of Deelen Air Base near Arnhem, the Netherlands. The Luftwaffe used this airfield as a base for fighter planes that were primarily deployed as night fighters. These enemy fighters regularly attacked British bombers tasked with bombing German cities and industry at night.

Norman was unable to complete this mission. The crash database of the Dutch Air War Study Group 1939–1945 mentions that his P-51 was shot down that day near Arnhem by German Flak. As a result, he crashed near Otterlo and Hoenderloo a short time later. His aircraft exploded, and Norman was almost certainly killed immediately. He was only 24 years old.

Norman's body was reportedly not found in the woods until October 7, 1944. This might explain why this date is inscribed on his cross in Margraten and not September 23. The crash database states that October 7, 1944, is not the correct date of Norman's death. Norman's final resting place in Margraten can be found in Plot C, Row 19, Grave 30.

GEORGE A. KOS

Private

101st Airborne Division

'We are going to get it'

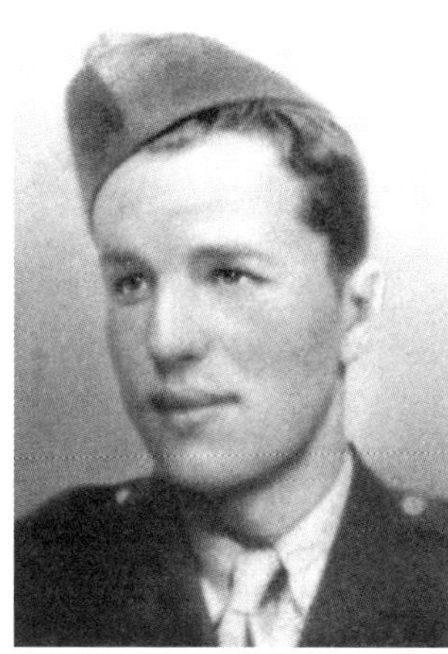

Private George A. Kos from Pennsylvania was born on July 8, 1924. His hometown was Gallitzin, a small town in the heart of the state. He enlisted in September 1943 and volunteered for the paratroopers.

George was assigned to the 501st Parachute Infantry Regiment of the 101st Airborne Division – the 'Screaming Eagles.' This unit was created in August 1942 to provide the U.S. Army with airborne troops. The successful German deployment of paratroopers in the early years of the war had impressed the Allies.

On September 17, 1944, the first day of Operation Market Garden, George landed with Company D on the drop zone near the small Dutch village of Eerde. There the paratroopers of his regiment had to secure the advance route towards Grave and Nijmegen for the British ground troops. That turned out to be no easy task, because the Germans wanted to block the route at all costs to thwart the plans of the Allies.

Five days later, George, along with Private William J. Houston, was ordered to man an outpost near the neighboring village of Veghel. About daylight the next morning, George said, 'Houston, if we get attacked today, we are going to get it.'

George turned out to have a foresight: their position was indeed attacked that day by a unit of German soldiers. George and Private Houston saw the Germans coming across a field and, while standing behind two separate trees, started firing on them. They also saw a Bazooka shell bounce off an approaching German tank. This tank was swinging its gun around them, but at that moment a couple of British tanks effectively fired on the tank.

In the meantime, a German 88mm gun had opened fire on George's and Houston's position. 'We saw the 88 that got us,' Houston later wrote. 'I shot at the 88 – it was a trailer gun. About that time, it hit Kos. Nothing was left but from the waist down.' George was killed instantly and, as a result, remained forever twenty years old. Initially, he was buried at the temporary U.S. Military Cemetery in Son, but after the war his remains were moved to Margraten. Here, visitors can find his final resting place in Plot B, Row 7, Grave 32.

CARMAN S. LADNER

Corporal

101st Airborne Division

'Here my phoenix rose from its ashes'

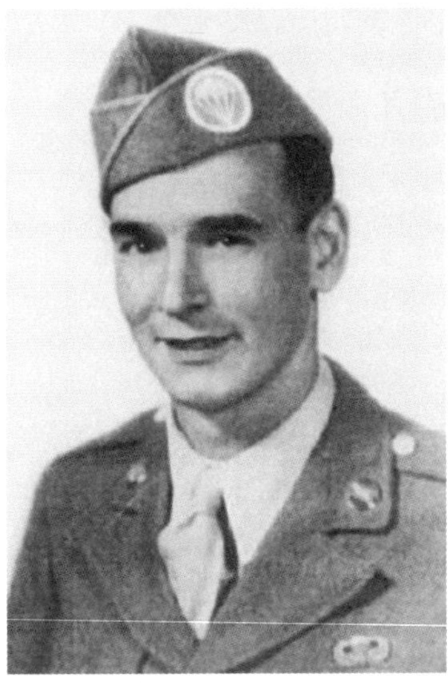

Corporal Carman S. Ladner, who was born in Canada in 1922, entered the U.S. Army on December 11, 1942, and volunteered for the paratroopers. In 1944, before Carman went to New York to be deployed to Europe, he and his fiancée Elaine got into an argument. Elaine thought it was far too dangerous and wanted to stop him. Carman had previously told her how small a paratrooper's chances were to come back home alive and she was afraid he would be killed. She sobbed and then got angry. Yet Carman left for New York to embark.

After Carman had left, Elaine regretted the quarrel. She traveled from Maine to New York to look for him because she did not want the love of her life to go to war without saying goodbye properly. Against all odds she found him. They promised each other to write as much as possible, and before Carman embarked for England, they resolved the argument and embraced – not knowing that this would be the last time they saw each other.

Once Carman arrived in England, he was attached to the 501st Parachute Infantry Regiment of the 101st Airborne Division. Then, on September 17, 1944, he jumped into Holland to be deployed in Operation Market Garden. He was dropped near the little village of Eerde, which became the scene of bitter fighting.

Seven days after his jump boots had touched Dutch soil for the first time, Carman lost his life, close to the fields where he had landed. On that fateful day, September 24, 1944, when his company was committed in fierce fighting in Eerde, he and some others were ordered to get some hard-needed ammunition. They found a British ammunition truck and parked it near a farm on the outskirts of the village, thinking this was a safe spot to unload and not knowing that a Jagdpanther (a German tank destroyer) was closing in on them. Carman had just climbed on top of the truck, and was passing ammunition down to the men, when the Jagdpanther fired a round. The shell hit the truck and caused the ammunition to explode. The terrible explosion could be heard far beyond Eerde. Carman died instantly and nothing has ever been found of him since. He was just 22 years old and because his remains are unrecoverable, his name is recorded on the Walls of the Missing in Margraten.

Carman's fiancée Elaine, meanwhile, unsuspectingly did what she always did: write letters to him from the United States. Carman had written a letter back almost every day, but suddenly no new letters were delivered to Elaine's home. Elaine became more and more worried, but for a long time she did not know what had happened to Carman. She only learned of his death when one day she received back one of her letters to Carman unopened with the word 'Deceased' stamped on it...

It wasn't until she traveled to the Netherlands in 2006 that Elaine learned the full facts surrounding Carman's death. She visited the farm site where Carman was killed. Erwin Janssen, a member of the local Airborne Committee and an expert on what happened in Eerde during the war, parked an army truck especially for her at the farm and then told her the story of Carman's tragic death. When Elaine saw children playing near the truck, her sorrow gave way to gratitude. 'He did this for you. I'm so happy about that,' she said. 'Here my phoenix rose from its ashes.' Elaine passed away in 2011.

VERL E. MILLER

Private

82nd Airborne Division

His war lasted one day

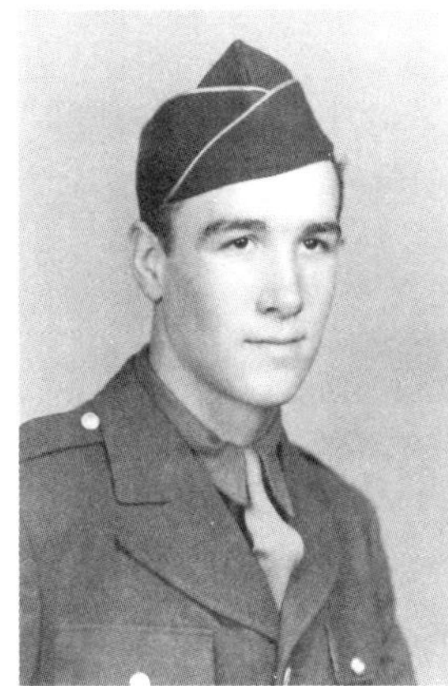

Verl Miller was born in Grover Hill, Washington Township, Paulding County, Ohio, on May 16, 1925. Son of Elonzo L. Miller and Effie M. Ashbaugh, he had three brothers (John, Samuel and Cloyd) and three sisters (Cleota Ruth, Bessie and Marilyn). Verl is remembered by his siblings as a sweet, humorous, kind, fun-loving brother who enjoyed joking around and making up silly rhymes. He played on the high school basketball team, enjoyed wood-working, and was skilled at making furniture.

Verl volunteered to serve in place of his oldest brother John, who had been drafted. Their father Elonzo had suddenly died in July 1941 and John had recently married. Family members have said that Verl felt he should serve in John's place so that John could look after their mother, his bride Rita and take care of the family farm. Thus, Verl enlisted in the U.S. Army in November 1943 in Toledo, Ohio. He received his basic training at Camp Croft in South Carolina, followed by additional training at Fort George Meade, Maryland.

Verl departed for overseas duty in late June 1944. He was attached to the 82nd Airborne Division and was a member of a mortar-squad in 2nd Platoon, Easy Company, 325th Glider Infantry Regiment. During Operation Market Garden his unit landed on Glider Landing Zone O at Overasselt, west of Groesbeek, the Netherlands, on September 23, 1944. Soon after landing, his regiment was ordered to march to the Plasmolen area, south of Groesbeek, where his mortar squad dug in on top of the hill between the Rijksweg (main road) and the Zevendalseweg.

His comrade Frank A. Plebanck, who was his assistant mortar gunner, recalled what happened:

> ***'The road at the base of the hill on our side ran between Riethorst and another little larger town named Mook about two miles away to the right of us. This ridge was probably only about two miles from the German border. We positioned our mortar between the farmhouse and the embankment, so we could fire in any direction. We spent the afternoon digging the hole and sat down next to the mortar for a badly needed break. Verl and I each opened a K-ration and had dinner. About 4:00 p.m. Verl stood up, stretched and walked to the right around the corner of the farmhouse. I was still sitting next to the mortar watching him.***
>
> ***He couldn't have taken more than three steps past the corner of the house, where I couldn't see him, when I heard a shot, then a long-drawn-out moan and groan. I stood up and walked to the corner of the house and looked around it. I had my carabine in my hands, if needed. There lay Verl Miller, flat on his back, with his head nearest to me, his right arm from the elbow up was more or less pointing upward, with his right palm facing upward. His left arm was flat upon the ground, alongside his body. His legs were crossed at the ankles. He still had his helmet on, his face was looking straight into the sky and he wasn't moving. He must have been killed instantly. He probably never knew what hit him.***
>
> ***It must have been a sniper's bullet, as the shot didn't seem to be that far away when I heard it. Our troops had been going around the corner of the farmhouse all day long and not one of them had been shot at. Of course, there had always been more than one person going by in groups of three or more. The sniper took a chance and fired at one man when he knew he wouldn't reveal his location. Verl was one of my best buddies and it made me sick to think of him being killed that way. He didn't have a fighting chance. I think Miller was probably the first one killed in our company that day.'***

In fact, he was. Verl Miller's war lasted just one day as he was killed on September 24, 1944.

Verl's family was first notified that Verl was missing in action. In October 1945, it was confirmed that he had been killed in action. Verl was buried at Margraten Cemetery on November 28, 1945, in Plot PPP, Row 10, Grave 247. His final resting place is in Plot H, Row 6, Grave 4.

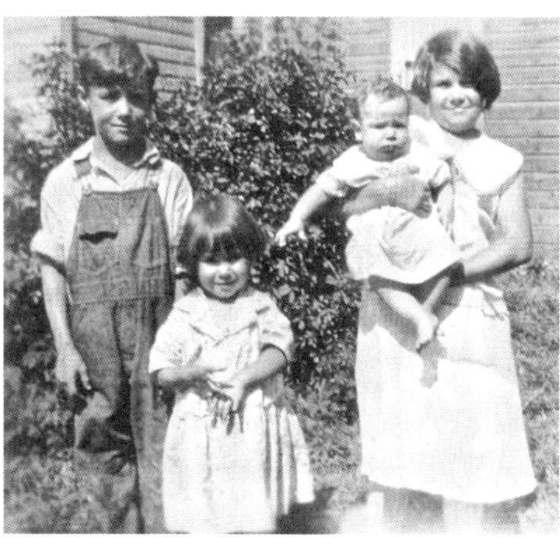

Verl and his siblings.
SOURCE: Miller family

In November 2005, his grave was adopted by the Van Hees family and contact with Verl's family was established in 2008. Further research into the circumstances surrounding his death ultimately led to the Dutch Ministry of Defense posthumously honoring Verl E. Miller with the Orange Lanyard in July 2020. The lanyard was ultimately presented to his family at the Margraten Cemetery in September 2022.

> ***Netherlands Orange Lanyard***
> ***Headquarters, 82nd Airborne Division***
> ***Cited in Department of Army General Orders 43, 19 December 1950***
>
> ***Considering that the outstanding performance of duty of the 82nd Airborne Division, United States Army, during the airborne operations and the ensuing fighting actions in the central parts of the Netherlands in the period from 17 September to 4 October has induced HER MAJESTY, THE QUEEN, to decorate its divisional color with the Military Order of William, degree of the knight of the fourth class, considering also, that is desirable for each member of the personnel of the 82nd Airborne Division, United States Army, who took part in the aforesaid operations, to possess a lasting memento of this glorious struggle; decrees: that each member of the personnel of the 82nd Airborne Division, United States Army, who took part in the operations in the area of Nijmegen in the period from 17 September to 4 October 1944 is allowed to wear the Orange Lanyard of the Royal Netherlands Army.***

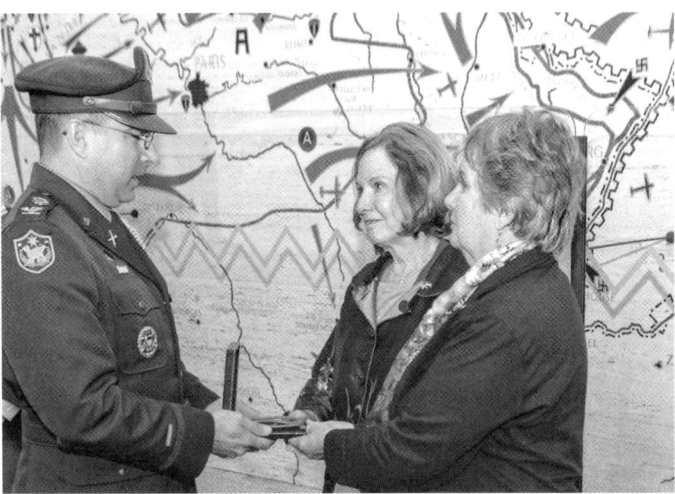

Colonel Sadler handed the Orange Lanyard to Verl's family in the cemetery's map room during a small ceremony, September 2022. SOURCE: Henk Korzelius

JOHN B. PURDIE

Private First Class

101st Airborne Division

Killed by a British Sherman tank

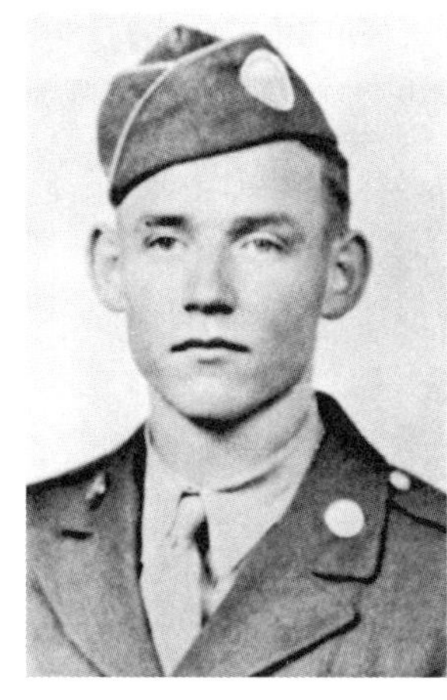

Private First Class John B. Purdie from Mississippi was born in 1921. In August 1942, he went to Camp Shelby to enlist for service in the U.S. Army. He volunteered for the paratroopers and after he obtained his 'jump wings,' John went to Europe with Company H of the 506th Parachute Infantry Regiment. This regiment was part of the 101st Airborne Division.

On September 17, 1944, John participated in Operation Market Garden. At the start of this operation, John made a parachute landing near the Dutch village of Son. A week later, his regiment was involved in heavy fighting near Eerde, Koevering, and Sint Oedenrode. Here the paratroopers had to fend off German counterattacks to keep the corridor – the road to Grave and Nijmegen – open for the ground forces of the British army.

A week after John parachuted into Holland, the corridor was blocked by German troops supported by some Jagdpanthers (tank destroyers) near Koevering. The 502nd Parachute Infantry regiment and British Sherman tanks tried to reopen the road, but their attacks were repulsed.

The next day, September 25, 1944, John and a number of comrades were sent on a combat patrol near Koevering. The purpose of this mission was to surround a farm that was occupied by well-armed German soldiers and from where heavy bursts of machine gun fire were coming. Eliminating the Germans at this farm site would contribute to the reopening of the corridor. As John and the other paratroopers approached the farm in the afternoon, they became subjected to a rain of bullets, but moments later they also saw a British Sherman tank approaching. This Sherman, however, was captured by the Germans. John and his comrades could not know there were German soldiers inside the British tank. They were advancing through a ditch and assumed that the crew of the tank was British. Therefore, they displayed orange flags to make it clear to them that they were friendly troops. In response, the German soldiers in the Sherman tank opened fire. The tank's machine guns rattled, and the main gun began firing high explosive shells into the tree trunks shortly behind the paratroopers in the ditch. As a result, John was struck by shrapnel and died at the age of 23.

John was initially buried at the temporary U.S. Military Cemetery near Son, but was reburied in Margraten after the war. One can find his final resting place there in Plot E, Row 7, Grave 27.

KENNETH F. SHAMBURG

Private

9th Infantry Division

His mother was never the same

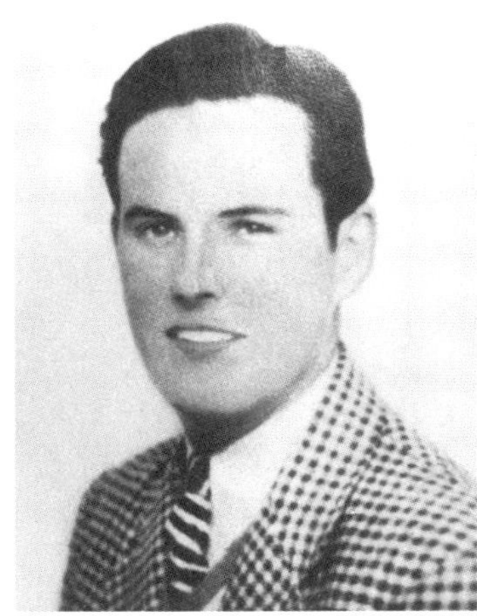

Private Kenneth F. Shamburg from Charlotte, North Carolina, was born in 1922. His family lovingly refers to him as 'Kink' for his curly hair. Kink was a much-beloved member of the family and he was very keen on his mother Lois, of whom he affectionally said she was his girlfriend and his sweetheart.

Kink entered the army in 1943, and after training at Camp Van Dorn, Mississippi, and Fort Meade, Maryland, he went overseas in July 1944. Upon his arrival in the European Theater of Operations, Kink was attached to Company K, 3rd Battalion, 47th Infantry Regiment. This regiment formed a part of the 9th Infantry Division, which by then had already been involved in the war against the Axis armies since the Allied campaign in the Mediterranean. Within his company, Kink was assigned to a rifle platoon, with which he saw action in France, Belgium and Germany.

In September 1944, Kink and his regiment entered the dense and hilly Hürtgen Forest, south of Aachen. Like the other American GIs who saw action there, Kink and his buddies soon learned that this treacherous forest was a grim nightmare of minefields, ambushes, tree bursts, and well-camouflages pillboxes. For ordinary infantrymen like Kink, death lurked literally everywhere here, for at any moment one could be blown up by the blast of a mine or horribly ripped open by shrapnel or wood splinters. Another grave danger was that advancing U.S. infantrymen, no matter how cautious, always ran the risk of being shot by an invisible enemy sniper or by a sudden burst of machine gun fire from equally well-concealed German positions.

On September 26, 1944, Kink was sent out with a combat patrol near Schevenhütte, a village in the northern part of the forest. According to a letter his mother later received from the company's First Lieutenant, the patrol was surrounded by a superior force of German troops when it reached enemy lines. Nine of the original sixteen members of the patrol returned to the company, but Kink was among the ones who did not. Initially, he was reported as missing in action, but his remains were recovered later, and his status was then changed to KIA.

What exactly happened to Kink that fateful day is not entirely clear. Most likely, the German soldiers who surrounded the patrol opened fire and shot him. Kink was only 22 years old and is permanently laid to rest in Margraten. There, visitors can pay tribute to him by going to Plot E, Row 7, Grave 26.

Kink's death had a big impact on his next of kin, especially on his mother Lois. Kink's niece, Lisa Abernethy Edwards, said Kink's mother (her grandmother) was never the same after losing Kink. 'She died in her early 40s when my mother Margaret was 21, leaving my mother with no immediate family. My mom did not talk a lot about her brother. It was just too painful...'

WADE J. VERWEIRE JR.

Technical Sergeant

30th Infantry Division

Disappeared during a patrol

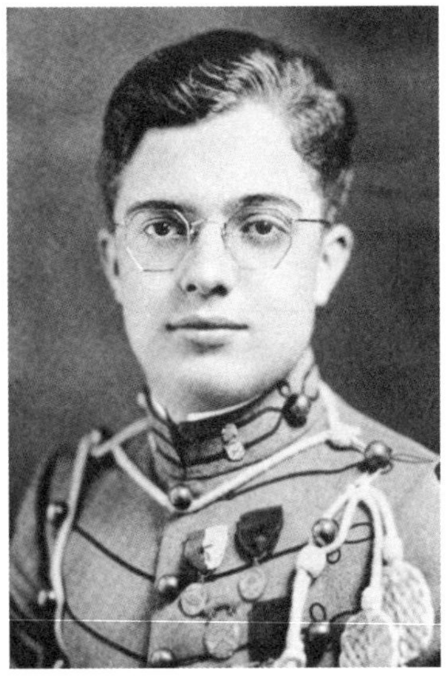

Technical Sergeant Wade J. Verweire Jr. was born on November 21, 1918, and was a native of Fort Wayne, Indiana. He was a graduate from the Culver Military Academy and was married to his girlfriend Mildred.

Wade entered the army in November 1942. Eventually, he was assigned to Company C of the 119th Infantry Regiment. This regiment formed a part of the 30th 'Old Hickory' Infantry Division, which entered combat in France in the summer of 1944 and subsequently marched through Belgium. In September 1944, the Old Hickory men liberated a large part of south Limburg, Holland.

On September 27, 1944, after his division had liberated most of southern Limburg, Wade was sent out to lead a seven-man patrol across the Wurm River, east of Rimburg, to blow up a pillbox. This pillbox was part of the Siegfried Line and it was believed to be not occupied by enemy soldiers.

The patrol went out into enemy territory, but Wade did not return back to the company afterwards. He disappeared and was reported missing. Wade could not be recovered, and it proved to be impossible to determine exactly what had happened to him (and several other men of his patrol) that day. Based on various military investigation reports and eyewitness statements, it is known that the patrol was pinned down by German machine gun fire in a railroad cut, approximately between 1,000 to 1,500 yards in front of Charlie Company's positions, and then some German soldiers approached them on their flank. According to Staff Sergeant Truman W. Manes, a member of the patrol who did make it back to the company, these German soldiers fired down the railroad track, wounding three of the men (whose names are not mentioned in his statement).

From then on, nothing had been seen or heard of Wade and two other soldiers who had accompanied him, PFC Anthony T. Drabecki and PFC John W. Kreigh. A search was made after darkness, but the patrol was not located. Later captured German records contained no information on them, so it is unlikely that they were captured and taken away as prisoners of war. On September 28, 1945 – one year and one day after his disappearance – the army therefore officially changed Wade's status from MIA to 'Finding of Death,' meaning he was presumed dead.

Meanwhile, Wade's wife Mildred had received a letter from Lieutenant U.B. Ortega, whom she identified as the platoon leader of Wade's platoon. Ortega also could not give a definitive answer on what exactly had happened to her husband. He wrote:

> ***'Wade took out this patrol – daylight – and it was about 1,500 yards or so from our lines. No, he wasn't the only one that didn't return – some did come back; the information was secured. We don't know whether Wade or any of the rest of the men were hit. It's possible that they were because the patrol was in enemy territory and bullets were flying around. We tried that afternoon to get to the spot where this happened and up to 3 o'clock next morning, but we couldn't locate or find them.'***

Investigation conducted by the American Graves Registration Command in the area after the war also failed to locate Wade's remains. Possibly the German soldiers buried him and the other missing men in unknown and unmarked field graves shortly after they died, but this too is far from certain.

More than three-quarters of a century later, Wade's case is still unsolved. The chance that it ever will be solved is unfortunately very small as the Defense POW/MIA Accounting Agency has listed him as non-recoverable. What remains is to continue to remember him for his sacrifice, for example by taking a moment to think of him during a walk at the U.S. Military Cemetery in Margraten, where his name is recorded on the Walls of the Missing.

LEON E. BALDWIN

Staff Sergeant

82nd Airborne Division

Cut off by an enemy tank

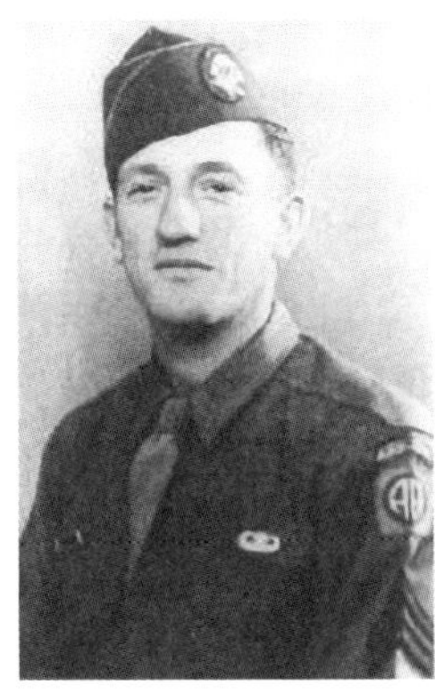

Leon E. Baldwin, born on October 30, 1916, and a native of Oregon, was a Staff Sergeant in Company I of the 504th Parachute Infantry Regiment. This regiment was part of the 82nd Airborne Division. During Operation Market Garden, Leon landed on the drop zone near Grave on September 17, 1944. About a week and a half later, Leon's company occupied positions at the Den Heuvel Farm near the Wylerbaan and Groesbeek. There, during the night of September 27–28, 1944, Leon directed the fire of his BAR men from an advanced position upon small groups of enemy infantry who were trying to infiltrate his company's lines. At dawn, German infantry supported by tanks made a determined attack on Item Company's positions. Leon's Silver Star citation tells us what happened next:

> ***'Staff Sergeant Baldwin saw an enemy infantryman kill one of his machine gunners about twenty yards to his left flank and crawl into the foxhole behind the gun. Without hesitation and completely unmindful of his own safety, Staff Sergeant Baldwin leaped from his own foxhole, charged across the open ground in full view of the advancing enemy, and bayoneted the German. He then threw the dead German aside and turned the gun on the enemy. Remaining exposed to the full concentration of enemy fire, he caused innumerable casualties in the enemy ranks by his fearless and skillful operation of the gun. Seeing the untenable situation the company was in, the company commander gave the order to move to the main line of resistance. Staff Sergeant Baldwin took charge of 45 enemy prisoners and started to evacuate them. Suddenly, an enemy tank bore down on them and drove between Staff Sergeant Baldwin and his prisoners, thus cutting him off from all possibility of withdrawing. As a result of this action Staff Sergeant Baldwin has been missing in action.'***

Corporal Ralph N. Tison was probably the last one alive who witnessed Leon's final action, as he said in his memoirs. 'I saw Staff Sergeant Baldwin firing from behind a tree with an M-1 rifle,' he also recalled. 'He would then fall back to another tree to unload and reload his gun. This happened several times. I do not know how many Krauts went down, as I wasn't counting. Soon a tank came up and got him with its machine gun.'

Leon's body was never found afterwards. Therefore, his name is recorded on the Walls of the Missing in Margraten. At the time of his disappearance, Leon was 27 years old.

ROBERT G. DEW

Sergeant

82nd Airborne Division

Killed as he lay wounded on a stretcher

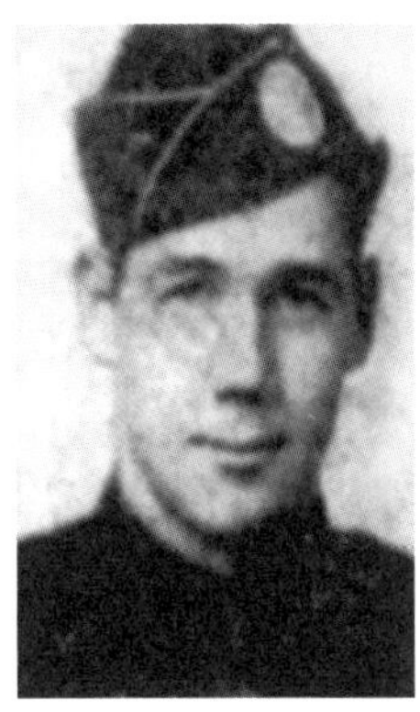

Robert G. Dew from Iowa was born on January 17, 1921. He attended Grundy Center High School and also played on the football team there. In 1939, Robert graduated and in April 1942, he entered the army. Robert volunteered for the paratroopers, completed the arduous training and eventually became a sergeant in the 504th Parachute Infantry Regiment of the 82nd Airborne Division.

With this division, Robert participated in the U.S. airborne operation in Sicily in July 1943. Subsequently, he also fought on the Italian mainland. In Italy, Robert sustained injuries to his right arm due to shrapnel from an enemy hand grenade, after which he was taken to a hospital in North Africa to recover.

Following the fighting in Italy, the 504th Parachute Infantry Regiment was transferred to England. Because of the considerable number of casualties suffered in the Italian campaign and a shortage of replacements, this regiment was not deployed in the invasion of Normandy. It was not until September 17, 1944, that Robert and the other men of the 504th PIR were back in action. On this day the Allies launched Operation Market Garden. Robert made a parachute landing on the drop zone between Grave and Nijmegen. He was 23 years old at the time.

On September 20, 1944, Robert and his Company I participated in the famous Waal Crossing near Nijmegen. The paratroopers crossed the river in rickety canvas boats to capture the north side of the crucial Waal Bridge. Despite German machine guns, 20mm Flak-guns and mortars opening fire on them in the boats, the attack was a success.

A few days later, Robert's Company I had taken positions southeast of Nijmegen near Groesbeek, close to the so-called Den Heuvel farm. During the night of September 27–28, 1944, Robert and the other paratroopers there were heavily shelled by German artillery and attacked by German troops and at least three light tanks. Captain Thomas Moffatt Burriss, the commander of Robert's company, later described what happened to Robert at the time:

> ***'The three tanks continued to spit machine gun and 20mm fire into our position. During the artillery barrage, Sgt. Robert Dew, who was in the trench with me, received a shrapnel wound to the chest. Dew, a huge, quiet man, lay gasping beside me. He was in a bad way. Two medics, one carrying a stretcher, came running toward us. "Put the sergeant on your stretcher and get***

him out of here!" I yelled, knowing he couldn't last much longer without medical care. They nodded, slid into the trench, and expertly rolled him onto the stretcher. Just as they lifted him out and started to move between the trees, a burst of 20mm fire from one of the tanks ripped through the middle of the stretcher and killed Sergeant Dew instantly.'

Staff Sergeant Louis Orvin also witnessed Robert's death, remembering that 'the guys had to drop that stretcher with him on it, because that tank just riddled him with machine gun fire.'

Because the German troops and tanks were overrunning Item Company's positions, Captain Burriss and his remaining men had to withdraw. They couldn't take Robert's body with them, with the result that his remains went missing. They were not found after the war either. That is why his name is inscribed on the Walls of the Missing in Margraten.

HENRY BROADWAY JR.
Sergeant
445th Bombardment Group

'Do you know Margraten?'

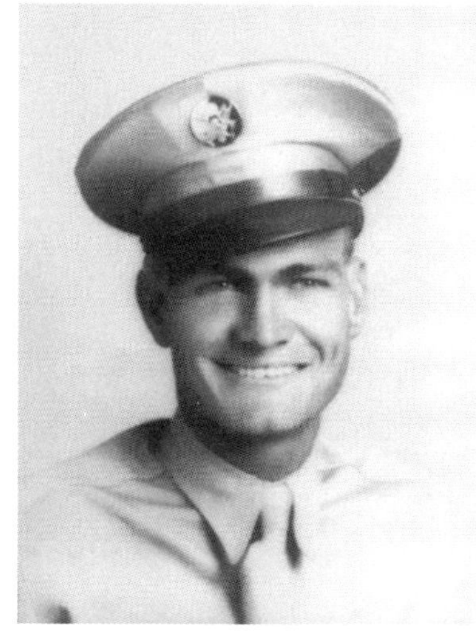

While visiting the British Virgin Islands in 1996, Jaap and Elly de Vries signed up for some lessons at a diving school owned by Butch and Kathleen Belanger. They could tell that Kathleen got emotional when she read on the forms that Jaap and Elly were from the Netherlands. They asked her later why that was. 'Do you know Margraten?' she said. 'My father has been buried there. He died in Europe during World War II.'

Henry Broadway Jr. was born in Clinton, Louisiana on April 14, 1920. The family moved to Port Neches in Texas, where Henry attended Port Neches-Groves High School, from which he graduated in 1938. Beatrice Hall was a year below him. They got married on March 23, 1940. Almost three years later, on March 9, their first daughter was born: Kathleen.

However, on April 12, Henry had to report for duty in Houston. After receiving his training, he was assigned to the 702nd Bomb Squadron, 445th Bombardment Group. He was the engineer and the top turret gunner of a B-24 piloted by Second Lieutenant Herbert Potts. On September 27, 1944, he flew his second and yet last mission. Today, that mission is infamously known as the 'Kassel Mission.' No other bomber group has suffered as many losses on one single day as the 445th Bomber Group did on that fateful day.

The bombers had taken off from Tibenham, England, for a raid over Kassel that morning. A navigational error resulted not only in missing their initial target, they also lost their fighter escort. It proved to be disastrous. After dropping their bombs over an alternative target, they were attacked by 100 to 150 fighter planes of the German Luftwaffe. In a matter of just six minutes, 25 B-24 Liberators of the 445th were shot down. Six more crashed later. Only four planes made it back to Tibenham.

Henry had last been seen in the waist of his plane and seemed to have been hit in the stomach by bullets. He and four others died as a result of the attack and the ensuing crash; four members of the crew bailed out of the burning plane and were taken prisoner. In total, 118 Americans had been killed and a similar number of men had been taken prisoner. The 445th Bombardment Group had lost two-thirds of its personnel.

After an incredible time on the British Virgin Islands, Jaap and Elly promised Kathleen that they would visit her father's grave in Plot A, Row 11, Grave 18 and send her pictures. She insisted on giving them money so they could buy, on her behalf, flowers for her father. They picked her favorite flowers and in her favorite colors. Jaap and Elly took as many photos as they could of both Henry's grave and the cemetery, and sent it to both a grateful Kathleen and his widow Beatrice. They all continued to correspond, but Kathleen and Beatrice have now passed. Their little family has been reunited in heaven.

FRED M. COGSWELL JR.
Sergeant
457th Bombardment Group

Shot down by the Luftwaffe

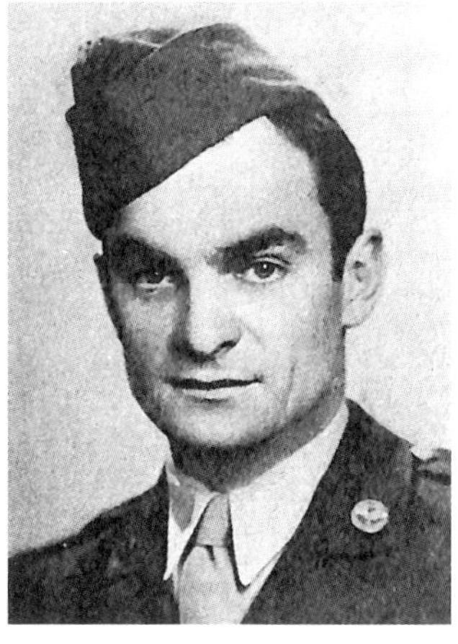

Sergeant Fred M. Cogswell Jr. was born on May 23, 1916. His place of birth was Holbrook, a town in Massachusetts. In September 1942, Fred enlisted in the United States Army Air Forces in Boston, eventually becoming tail gunner in the B-17 bomber 'Gini' of the 751st Bomb Squadron. This squadron fell under the command of the 457th Bombardment Group.

The 457th Bombardment Group was created in July 1943 and was part of the U.S. Eighth Air Force. In January 1944, the bombers flew from Nebraska to England to participate in the combined Allied bombing campaign against Nazi Germany. USAAF Station 130 in Glatton, Cambridgeshire, then became the base of operations for the B-17s of this unit.

On September 28, 1944, Fred's bomber took off from this base to bomb Krupp's arms factories in the German city of Magdeburg. After flying for quite a while, when the bombers had their targets in sight, the B-17s were attacked by 25 to 50 Messerschmitt Bf 109s and Focke-Wulf 190 fighters of the Luftwaffe. According to a description in the Missing Air Crew Report, Fred's aircraft 'apparently burst into flames between #3 engine and the fuselage on the right side. Black smoke was pouring from the aircraft when last seen a few seconds after it was hit. The aircraft slid off to the left when hit, then salvoed [sic] its bombs, and then immediately went into a spin.'

The 'Gini' crashed near Dorstadt and Wolfenbüttel. None of the nine crew members survived. Fred died at the age of 28. His final resting place in Margraten is in Plot F, Row 17, Grave 24.

DAVID ROSENKRANTZ

Staff Sergeant

82nd Airborne Division

'Known but to God,' until 2018

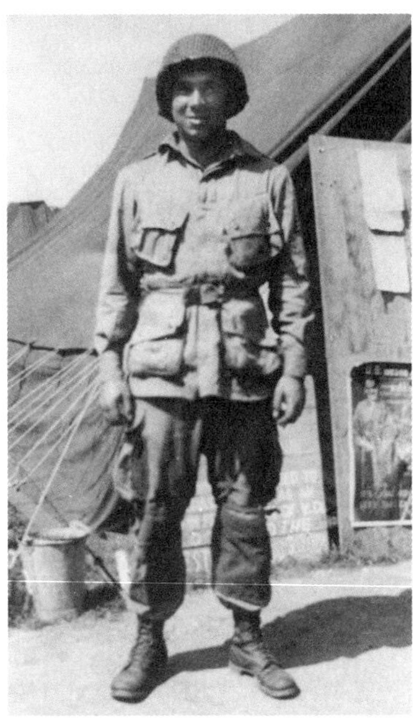

Staff Sergeant David Rosenkrantz from California was born in 1915. His parents were both Russian Jewish immigrants from what is Poland today. In 1942, David entered the army and volunteered for the paratroopers. He was then assigned to Company H, 504th Parachute Infantry Regiment. This regiment was part of the 82nd 'All American' Airborne Division.

In July 1943, David was involved in the American airborne landings in Sicily. He was mis-dropped and landed well outside the intended drop zone, after which he and another paratrooper – Corporal Lee Black – were captured by about 200 Italian soldiers. What happened next may sound rather unimaginable, but the group of Italians surrendered to David and Corporal Black. David was interviewed about this the same month by a reporter from the Los Angeles Times:

> ***'They captured us, but then strange things began to happen. They held a conference and decided to turn themselves over to us for they heard that the Americans were only eight kilometers away. They presented us to the Chief of Police of the nearby town and he fed us, wined us, gave us good beds and declared on his honor that he was glad to see us. In fact, everyone was happy, including our prisoners. Around 4 o'clock that afternoon the Italians marched into Scicli, where they surrendered. They gave us their guns an hour before, so we let them go in alone. They were singing and just about raising hell, and a couple of them remarked that they hoped they would be sent to a prison camp in the United States.'***

After fighting in Sicily, David also participated in the fighting on the Italian mainland. Then, the 504th PIR was transferred to England by ship. There, David's regiment was given a rest and therefore he was not deployed in the invasion of Normandy.

David made his next parachute jump on September 17, 1944, the first day of Operation Market Garden. He landed on the drop zone near the Dutch town of Grave. Three days later, he participated in the famous Waal Crossing near Nijmegen on September 20, 1944.

More than a week later, on September 28, 1944, David's platoon had occupied positions at Heuvelhof Farm near the Wylerbaan and Groesbeek. The Germans counterattacked and David's squad was overrun. What happened to David next was later described by various eyewitnesses, such as PFC Larry Dunlop and Sergeant Ted Finkbeiner. Dunlop said that he had tried to warn David that they were already surrounded: 'Rosie didn't hear me. I heard the burp of

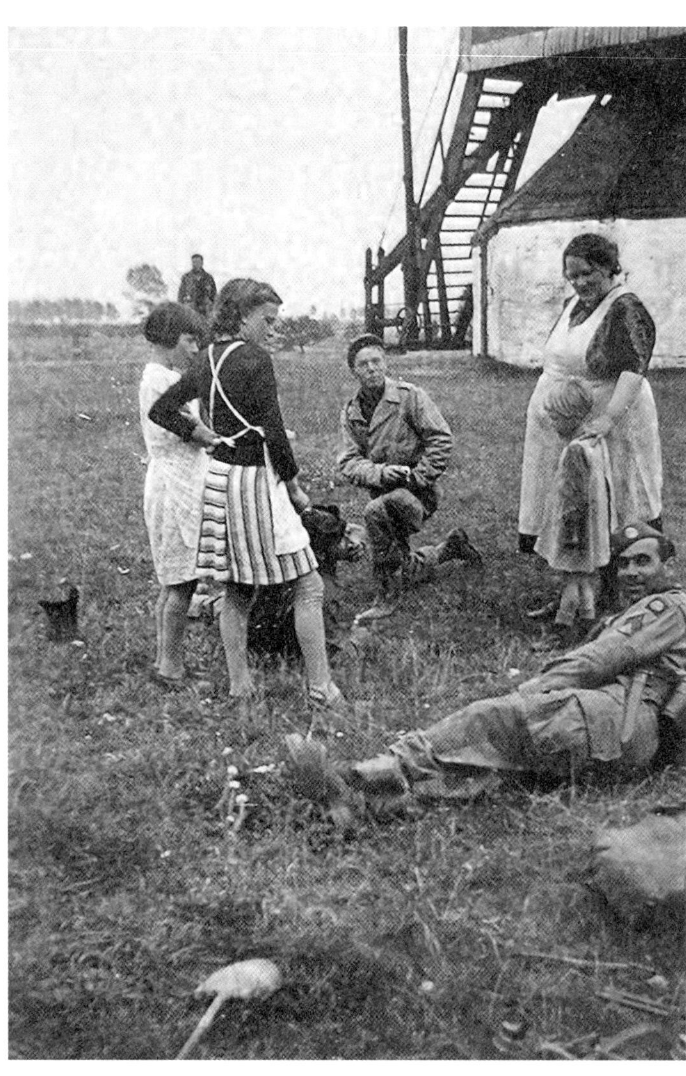

a German Schmeisser machine pistol that got Rosie 50 feet in front of me. I could see him when he went down and I was pretty sure he was killed. If I tried to get anywhere near him, I would be a goner too.'

Finkbeiner said that he too had tried to warn David: 'At one point we were being attacked from one side and platoon Sgt. David Rosenkrantz stood up behind a tree to fire when he was killed by enemy fire from another direction. I was calling for him to get down when machine gun fire killed him.' When he was killed, David was 28 years old.

Due to heavy enemy fire and the proximity of German troops, the Americans had to give up their positions near the farmhouse, so David's comrades were unable to take his body with them. His remains could not be recovered and therefore he was recorded as Missing in Action.

The mystery of David's missing remains was not solved until many decades later, after thorough research by David's nephew Phil Rosenkrantz and the Dutch researchers Ben Overhand and Frank van Lunteren. In 2017, the remains of unknown soldier X-1234, buried in Plot O, Row 22, Grave 16 at the Netherlands American Cemetery in Margraten, were exhumed for DNA-investigation. The following year, these remains were identified as belonging to Staff Sergeant David Rosenkrantz. So, 73 years after his death, David had finally been found.

On July 20, 2018, David's funeral took place at Riverside National Cemetery in his home state of California. He was given his final resting place there, and in September 2019, his nephew Phil placed a rosette next to David's name on the Walls of the Missing in Margraten. The solemn rosette ceremony in Margraten marked the conclusion of the search that had ultimately lasted more than 35 years.

David Rosenkrantz, far right, in the Netherlands during Operation Market Garden

LESLIE H. HANSEN

Corporal

82nd Airborne Division

Acted courageously against German tanks

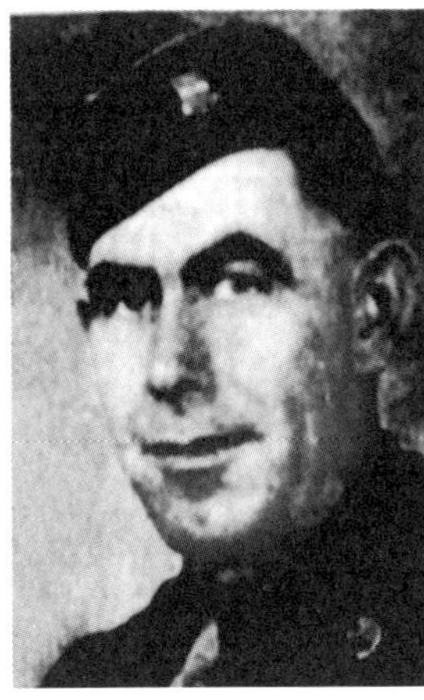

Leslie H. Hansen from Illinois was born in 1912, about two years before World War I broke out in Europe. In March 1942, he went to Camp Grant and entered the U.S. Army.

Leslie eventually served as a corporal in the 80th Airborne Anti-Aircraft Battalion. This unit's main duty was to provide protection for the paratroopers of the 82nd Airborne Division. To be able to do so, the battalion was equipped with guns effective against enemy tanks in addition to anti-aircraft weapons.

The 80th Airborne Anti-Aircraft Battalion was created in September 1942 and arrived in North Africa in May 1943. In September of that same year, the battalion participated in Allied operations on the Italian mainland. Subsequently, the men of the unit prepared themselves in Northern Ireland and England for participation in Operation Overlord. On D-Day, Batteries A, B, and C landed by glider in Normandy near Sainte-Mère-Église. Batteries D, E, and F were brought to Normandy by two Liberty Ships and arrived at Utah Beach two days later.

In September 1944, the battalion was involved in Operation Market Garden. By then, Leslie was a squad leader in Battery E. Due to bad weather conditions, his battery could only be flown in by gliders on September 23, 1944. They landed near Nijmegen, where paratroopers of the 82nd Airborne Division had already captured the crucial bridge over the river Waal. The Germans, however, tried to turn the tide with counterattacks.

On September 28, 1944, Leslie's battery had taken position near Molenhoek, a village near Nijmegen, where they were attacked by German infantry supported by tanks. Leslie was in charge of the crew of a 57mm gun and coolly directed fire on the approaching tanks. Two rounds of his gun destroyed one of the German tanks, but fire from another tank knocked out his gun and killed him. For his personal bravery and destruction of one enemy tank, Leslie was posthumously awarded the Silver Star in November 1944.

Leslie is permanently interred at the Netherlands American Cemetery in Margraten. His final resting place there can be found in Plot P, Row 1, Grave 8.

ASA T. HANCOCK
First Lieutenant
82nd Airborne Division

'How else will I become a combat officer?'

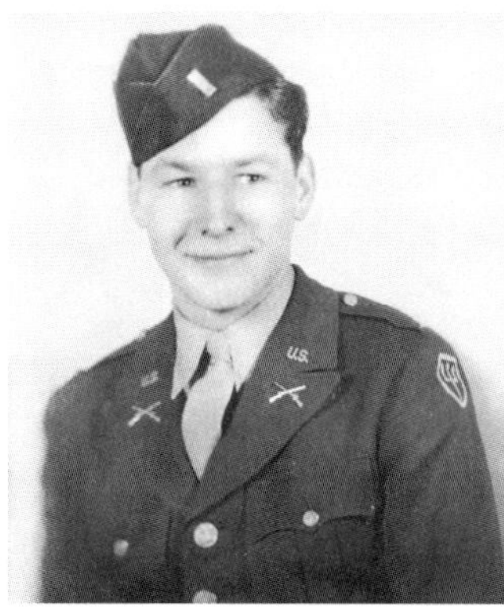

First Lieutenant Asa T. Hancock was a member of Company G, 3rd Battalion, 505th Parachute Infantry Regiment. This regiment was activated in 1942 and assigned to the 82nd 'All American' Airborne Division. It was first deployed in combat during the Allied assault on Sicily in July 1943, and then also participated in the Allied campaign on the Italian mainland near Salerno in September 1943.

On D-Day, the 505th parachuted into Normandy to participate in Operation Overlord. One of the regiment's first objectives gained there was the capture of Sainte-Mère-Église. This is the well-known French village where Pvt. John Steele's parachute was caught in one of the pinnacles of the local church tower, leaving him hanging on the side of the church while the Germans beneath him fired on other descending American paratroopers.

Following the Normandy campaign, the 505th Parachute Infantry Regiment participated in Operation Market Garden. The men were dropped near Groesbeek on September 17, 1944, and elements of the regiment then got involved in fierce fighting to secure the crucial Waal Bridges in Nijmegen. Once these bridges were captured and secured, the regiment was moved back to the Groesbeek area. There, on September 29, 1944, Asa approached Lieutenant William Mastrangelo. Asa was recently assigned as a replacement to Mastrangelo's platoon and asked Mastrangelo to let him lead a patrol. According to Mastrangelo's memories, Asa insisted 'on gaining experience, saying "How else will I become a combat officer, and besides, I want a German Luger [pistol]."'

Mastrangelo decided not to dampen Asa's eagerness and reluctantly let him lead a patrol going out that night. 'On patrol,' Mastrangelo later said, 'he and ten men were ambushed by German machine guns. Nine or ten men [were] killed or wounded. He was himself killed.'

Asa, the young replacement officer who was perhaps too eager to prove himself and to get a war souvenir, is permanently interred at the Netherlands American Cemetery and Memorial in Margraten. There he rests in peace in Plot M, Row 12, Grave 12.

JAMES H. WALTERS
Private First Class
82nd Airborne Division

Voluntarily led a patrol

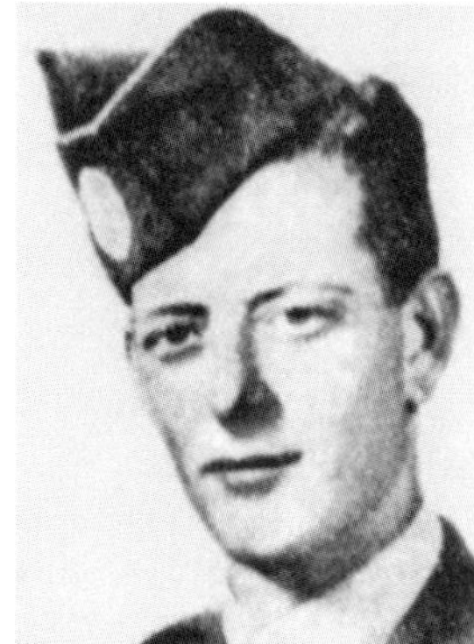

Private First Class James H. Walters from Akron, Ohio, was born in Maryland in 1918. On March 10, 1942, he reported to Fort Benjamin Harrison, Indiana to enter the army. He volunteered for the paratroopers and completed his final qualifying jumps at Fort Benning, Georgia in 1943.

While serving with the paratroopers, James was a member of Company G, 3rd Battalion, 504th Parachute Infantry Regiment. This regiment was an element of the 82nd Airborne Division.

On September 17, 1944, James jumped into Holland from a C-47 during Operation Market Garden. His regiment, minus Company E, was dropped onto Drop Zone O near the village of Overasselt, north of the river Meuse.

Two weeks later, James' regiment was holding the front line southeast of Nijmegen, close to the German border in the vicinity of the Wylerbaan. There, on October 1, 1944, James courageously made a survey of enemy-held ground and located a strong enemy position. He reported its location to his platoon leader and then voluntarily led a patrol to the enemy position. For this action he received the Silver Star, which was posthumously awarded to him in May 1945. The final part of his citation mentions that the patrol made contact with the enemy and James was seriously wounded by machine gun fire. It also states that he later died in a hospital.

Remarkably, his digitalized Hospital Admission Card offers other information; it states that he died of injuries sustained from artillery fire. So, this would mean that either the citation contains errors or that after he was wounded during the patrol he must have been injured again. The latter could well have been the case because it is known that during the night of October 2 – the date James' death was reported – the 3rd Battalion sector was struck by German artillery.

When James lost his life, he was 25 years old. He was given his final resting place at the U.S. Military Cemetery in Margraten, where he lies in Plot G, Row 4, Grave 20.

FREDERICK D. MELTON
Second Lieutenant
113th Cavalry Reconnaissance Squadron

Born leader rescued wounded men

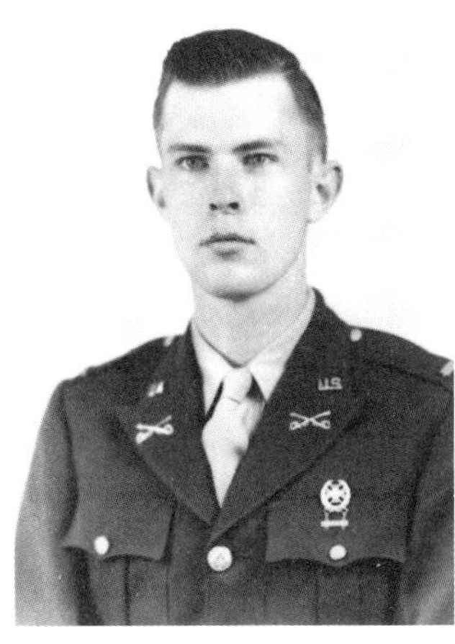

Frederick D. Melton was born in Georgia on August 15, 1924. He grew up in Griffin and was a boy scout during his youth. Frederick also was an excellent athlete, as he lettered in both football and basketball. Furthermore, he had a lot of friends. 'A more popular boy never grew up in Griffin,' his brother Quimby Melton Jr. later wrote of him.

After graduating from high school in 1941, Frederick entered The Citadel, the military academy in Charleston, South Carolina. He completed his freshman year there, but then decided to attend advanced classes in the Horse Cavalry regiment of the Reserve Officers' Training Corps at the University of Georgia.

Immediately after his 18th birthday, Frederick enlisted. He completed his basic training at Fort Riley, where officers had quickly noticed his leadership qualities. Therefore, despite his young age, they gave him a recommendation for the Officer Candidate School. Frederick graduated several months later and was sent to Europe in August 1944. During the journey on the transport ship, he turned twenty years old and wrote prophetic words in his diary:

> ***'Today is my birthday and I am an old man of 20. Ha...ha. I wonder if I'll ever see 21, not that it makes a hell of a lot of difference to me but I want to so Mother will be happy. I am not afraid to die, except that it would hurt Mother and Pop and Quimby and Kitty [Fred's fiancée] and May. If I live to be 21, I will live to be 70. And I am going to live to be 70 and then some.'***

After his arrival in England, Frederick was transferred to France. From there he was sent to the south of the Netherlands, and assigned to B Troop of the 113th Cavalry Reconnaissance Squadron.

On October 3, 1944, as one of the youngest officers in the U.S. Army, Second Lieutenant Frederick Melton and his B Troop headed toward the German village of Havert. What happened next is described by both his platoon sergeant and Corporal Robert E. Griffin, a member of Frederick's platoon. His sergeant wrote:

> ***'We had advanced on a small German town. The platoon to our right failed to come up and we were ordered back into our original position. Checking up on the platoon when we got back, Lt. Melton found five of the men missing and told us "Give me what protection you can with rifle fire" (we were fighting as infantry that day). The lieutenant went into the city and one by one brought back men who were wounded, carrying them over his shoulder. Time and again one of us asked him to let us rescue the next man. But his reply always was "they're my men and I'll bring them back." He was successful in rescuing four men and was bringing back the fifth, and had almost reached our lines, when a German sniper killed both the lieutenant and the man he was carrying. No wonder everyone in our outfit loves the memory of such a brave man.'***

Robert Griffin confirmed Frederick's heroism in a letter to Mr. Oliver Quimby Melton, Frederick's father. 'We jumped off at daylight Oct. 3rd. Everything started grand until the Krauts started throwing everything in the book at us. O Boy did they pin the old 3rd down with small arms fire. The last I saw of Georgia [Frederick's nickname] alive I mean he was running to the aid of a wounded man who was pretty well shot up. He was crying for someone to help him and Georgia was heading for him on the run,' Griffin recalled. He subsequently wrote that at the same time a German machine gun cut loose, and Frederick didn't even have a chance. 'In spite of the covering fire we were trying to give him. He fell in the attempt to help one of his fellow platoon members.'

After this description, Griffin also emphasized how much he and the others admired Frederick:

> ***'Georgia (Lt. Melton) was a great leader, and a firm leader. Well-liked by the men under him and respected. And during the short time he was with us he became a good friend of mine. (...) I am proud to have served under him. And I know all the boys did too. He was a grand guy ("Old Georgia!") and it grieved us deeply to lose him. He died a hero's death.'***

For rescuing four of his wounded men and his brave attempt to rescue the fifth wounded man too, Frederick was posthumously awarded the Silver Star. The remains of this young hero are permanently interred at the Netherlands American Cemetery and Memorial in Margraten. There he rests in peace in Plot D, Row 10, Grave 6.

JAMES J. BARRAS
Corporal
17th Tank Battalion

Missing in Action since tank was destroyed

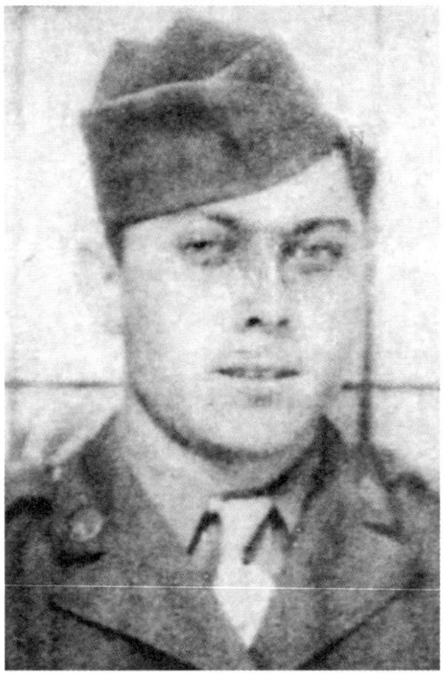

Corporal James J. Barras was born in Krotz Springs, Louisiana on February 26, 1922. In 1942, he enlisted in the army in Lafayette. James eventually served as a gunner in a Sherman tank of the 17th Tank Battalion. This was one of the tank battalions of the 7th Armored Division, nicknamed the 'Lucky Seventh.'

In late September and early October 1944, James' Company C was involved in the Battle of Overloon in Holland. This battle took place on the border between the Dutch provinces of Limburg and Noord-Brabant. At Overloon and the surrounding countryside, the Americans had to march through wooded areas. This proved dangerous, because the woods were full of Germans whose machine gun fire, Panzerfausts, mortars, and anti-tank guns inflicted heavy losses on the American tank units and infantry.

On October 4, 1944, during the fighting north of Overloon, James' Sherman tank was hit three times by enemy anti-tank fire near the village of St. Anthonis. The tank immediately caught fire and, according to a survivor, T/4 Albert H. Litchfort, James was unable to escape the tank after it was hit. As a result, he died at the age of 22. According to one of the reports included in his IDPF, the fatal shots that destroyed James' tank were presumably fired by an 88mm gun.

Another report, written by the 7887 Graves Registration Detachment after a field investigation, concludes that it is logical to assume that James' remains were cremated inside the tank by the fire and explosions. This may be the explanation for the fact that his remains have never been found to this day. Because he is still missing, and his remains were declared 'Non-Recoverable,' James is listed on the Walls of the Missing in Margraten.

HOWARD T. BONDS
Private
17th Tank Battalion

Still missing after the Battle of Overloon

Private Howard T. Bonds from Mississippi was born in 1917 and attended high school for four years. In March 1942, he went to Camp Shelby to enter the army, eventually being assigned to the 17th Tank Battalion of the 7th Armored Division. Over two years later, Howard entered combat in Europe as a machine gunner in a Sherman tank.

On October 4, 1944, Howard's Company A took part in an attack on German troops near the Dutch village of Overloon. As the American tanks approached the German positions there, the Germans opened fire: from the woods and positions near castle De Hattert, they began firing at the tanks with numerous anti-tank guns. The German soldiers had camouflaged their guns so well that the Americans could not see them. Therefore, when the Shermans started firing at the woods, their fire was not very accurate and effective. For this reason, the attack was not a success.

During the fighting on this day, Howard went missing at the age of 27. Nothing has ever been found of him to this day. Also, no details are known about what happened to Howard at the time. However, thanks to the After-Action Report of the 17th Tank Battalion we do know that five tanks of Company A were knocked out by German anti-tank guns that day. It is therefore logical to assume that this was probably also the fate of Howard's tank and that he was killed as a result.

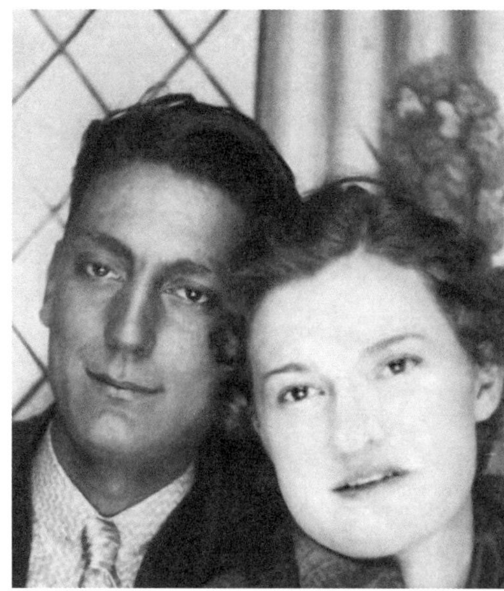

Because of the fact that Howard's remains are still missing today, he is listed on the Walls of the Missing in Margraten.

WILLIAM H. DUKEMAN JR.
Corporal
101st Airborne Division

Easy Company soldier killed on Dutch soil

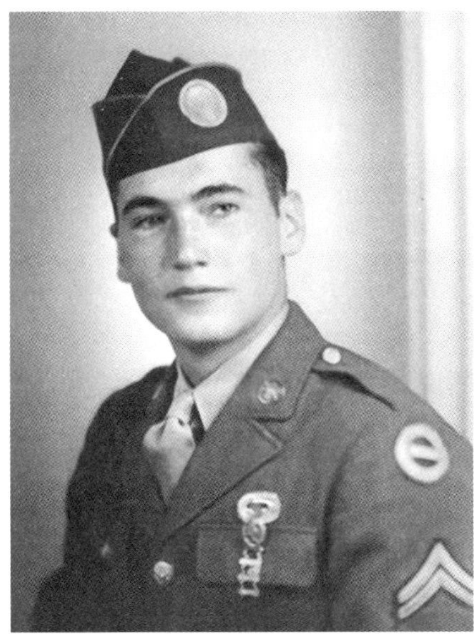

William H. 'Buddy' Dukeman Jr. from Colorado was born in 1921. He entered military service in August 1942 and served as a paratrooper in Easy Company, 506th Parachute Infantry Regiment, 101st Airborne Division.

On D-Day, William was dropped into Normandy, where he was struck in the chin by German fire. Over three months later, William participated in Operation Market Garden. On September 17, 1944, he landed on the drop zone near the Dutch village of Son.

In early October 1944, after the failure of Market Garden, William's division was moved to 'The Island.' This was the American name for the Betuwe, the area between the rivers Waal and Rhine. There, on October 5, 1944, William took part in Easy Company's night attack on a group of German soldiers around a machine gun on the dike near the village of Heteren that had been discovered earlier that night by a patrol. William, not keen on going, said: 'Can I not even get one day of rest?'

Led by Captain 'Dick' Winters, fifteen paratroopers including William ambushed the German machine gun post at the crossroads on the dike. Silently, they approached in the darkness through a drainage ditch until they were within about 40 yards of the German position. Winters then gave his instructions: he ordered William and Corporal Burt Christenson to set up the .30 caliber machine gun and to fire at the MG-42 on his signal. Winters then assigned each of his riflemen a particular target among the Germans, instructing them to hold their fire until he gave the command. Then he said softly, 'On my command. Ready. Aim. Fire!'

The paratroopers opened fire. The machine gun fire was aimed a little too high, but the riflemen's shots eliminated the seven German soldiers around the machine gun. Just an instant later, Sergeant Muck and PFC Penkala dropped a mortar round on the machine gun, whereafter Winters shouted, 'Fall Back!' The men withdrew through the ditch. From the east side of the road that led from the dike to the river unseen Germans opened fire on them, their tracer bullets streaking by overhead.

When the men withdrew, William was killed. Some Germans hiding in a culvert that ran under the road fired a rifle grenade. A piece of shrapnel struck William's shoulder and then pierced his heart. He died on the spot at the age of 23 and was the only one who did not survive the surprise attack on the enemy machine gun position. William's final resting place in Margraten can be found in Plot G, Row 2, Grave 11.

THOMAS W. CALL
Technician Fifth Grade
101st Airborne Division

Courageous medic

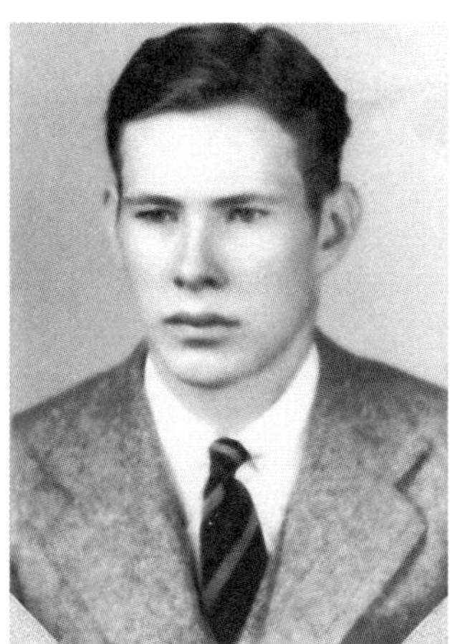

Thomas W. Call was born in Maryland in 1924. He lived in Ohio when he entered the army after graduating from high school in 1942.

In 1944, Thomas served as a medic in the 3rd Battalion of the 506th Parachute Infantry Regiment. This regiment was part of the 101st Airborne Division, whose men called themselves the 'Screaming Eagles.'

On D-Day, Thomas participated in the Allied invasion of Normandy, Operation Overlord. Like the other medics in his battalion, he jumped from a plane at night. Despite the fire of German machine guns and anti-aircraft guns, Thomas landed somewhere northeast of the town of Carentan without being hit.

As a medic, it was Thomas' job to provide medical aid to the wounded paratroopers of his battalion. Therefore, according to the history of the medical section of his battalion, at some point after the airborne landing, he braved enemy machine gun and mortar fire to reach the objective near the Douve River and set up an aid station in a French house. Together with another medic and a medical officer, Thomas treated wounded paratroopers here for about two or three days.

After the division had returned to England, Thomas participated in Operation Market Garden in September 1944. Then, in October 1944, he and his division were sent to 'The Island' between the rivers Waal and Rhine.

On October 5, 1944, while Thomas was driving in a jeep to convey wounded men to the Dutch village of Zetten, he was killed during an enemy artillery barrage. On further examination it turned out that a small sliver of shrapnel from a German shell had penetrated deep into his brain near his eyeball. There was no blood, but he was instantly killed. He was only twenty years old.

Thomas' remains were initially buried at the temporary American cemetery in Molenhoek, but after the war he was reburied in Margraten. Visitors can find his final resting place there in Plot M, Row 14, Grave 3.

OLIVER M. HORTON
Major
101st Airborne Division

Killed by mortar fire

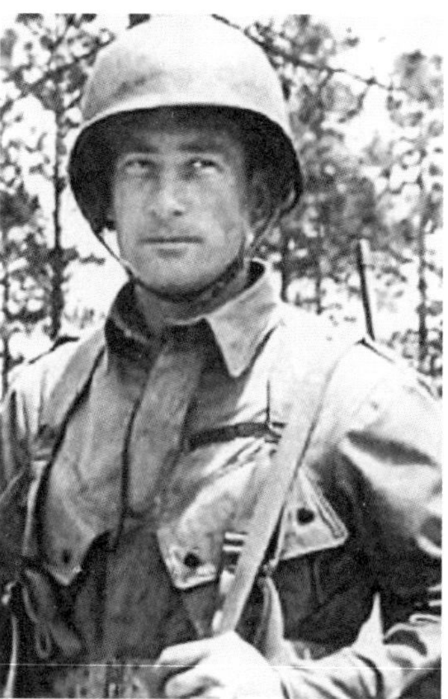

Major Oliver M. Horton from North Carolina was born in 1912. In 1944, he served in the 101st Airborne Division. Within this division, he commanded the 3rd Battalion of the 506th Parachute Infantry Regiment. On June 6, 1944 – D-Day – Oliver parachuted into Normandy at night, and in September 1944 he subsequently participated in the American airborne landings of Operation Market Garden.

In early October, after the tough battle for 'Hell's Highway,' the paratroopers of the 506th PIR were transferred to the front line in the Betuwe, called 'The Island.' There, the paratroopers of Oliver's battalion took over the positions of the British 43rd Wessex Division in the village of Opheusden.

The battalion's positions in Opheusden were frequently shelled by German mortars and artillery. Oliver's men were also repeatedly attacked by German troops, who had crossed the Rhine at the Grebbeberg and who were sometimes supported by tanks. This resulted in fierce fighting and many casualties on both sides.

On October 5, 1944, the battalion was again heavily shelled and attacked by the Germans. Fierce firefights broke out near the railroad and the small train station of Opheusden. At Oliver's command post, the rattling of the machine guns and the explosions of mortar and artillery shells could be heard clearly. At some point, Oliver decided he wanted to see how his men were doing. However, as he was walking along the railroad, he was fatally wounded by German mortar fire. Oliver died at the age of 32 and is buried in Margraten. His final resting place there can be found in Plot G, Row 1, Grave 11.

To honor Oliver and the other paratroopers of the 101st Airborne Division who fell during the battle for Opheusden, a small bridge is named after him there. A commemorative plaque has been attached to this bridge.

GARLAND W. COLLIER

Sergeant

101st Airborne Division

Identified after being missing for 78 years

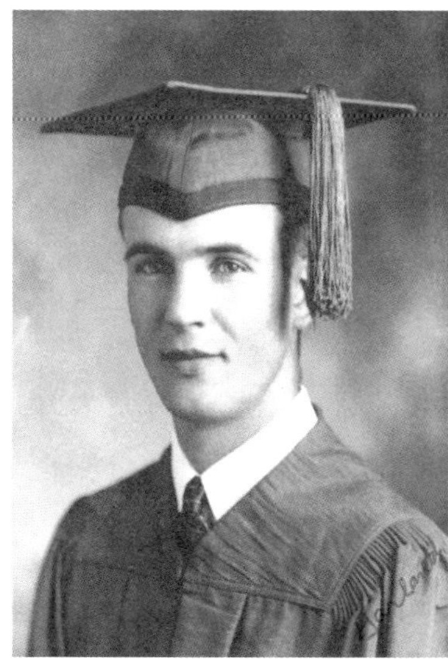

Garland W. Collier was born in Texas in 1918 and grew up with six siblings. He was the youngest child in the family. Garland liked sports and therefore he played both football and basketball while attending high school. During his military service, Garland also regularly played football with his buddies.

After his enlistment in Phoenix, Arizona, Garland trained to be a paratrooper in the 101st Airborne Division. He was assigned to the 3rd Battalion of the 506th Parachute Infantry Regiment, which was commanded by Major Oliver M. Horton. As a sergeant, Collier served in a light machine gun platoon consisting of four squads with machine guns.

On D-Day, Garland parachuted into Normandy. The C-47 that dropped his paratrooper 'stick' was hit several times by enemy anti-aircraft fire while approaching the drop zone, eventually crashing into the English Channel during its return flight, killing all the crew aboard.

Garland had no knowledge of this and, after his landing, was involved in fierce fighting. After D-Day, he was wounded. However, the injuries sustained were not serious enough for evacuation to England.

Over a month after D-Day, Garland and the other paratroopers of the 101st Airborne Division returned to England for much-needed rest. Then, on September 17, 1944, he took part in the U.S. airborne landings of Operation Market Garden. He landed on the drop zone near Son. Until the end of that month, his platoon was involved in the defense of 'Hell's Highway.' After this route was secured, the 101st Airborne Division was transferred to the Betuwe. There, near the village of Opheusden, Garland was killed by mortar fire during a German counterattack on October 5, 1944. He was 25 years old.

Two of Garland's buddies – Pvt. Darvin Lee and Cpl. Andrew T. Bryan Jr. – were next to him when he was hit. They witnessed his death and also helped to prepare his body for Graves Registration officers who were to follow behind them. While doing this, Lee and Bryan found a German Luger pistol which Garland had carried with him as a war souvenir. Before leaving him, they took the pistol with them with the intention to turn it over to a member of Garland's family. Amazingly, Garland's older brother, Grady A. Collier, who served in the 834th Aviation Engineer Battalion of the Ninth Air Force, met up with Lee when the 506th PIR had returned from Holland to Mourmelon, France. Lee was able to hand the Luger over to Grady and told him the story of Garland's death in Opheusden.

Despite the fact that Lee and Bryan had prepared Garland's body for the Graves Registration officers, Garland nevertheless went missing after they had left him. However, in the summer of 2022 – 78 years after his death – it was announced that Garland's remains have been recovered and identified through DNA matching. To indicate this, a rosette is placed next to his name on the Walls of the Missing in Margraten.

WILLIAM H. ARLEDGE

Private First Class

101st Airborne Division

'Another friend lost'

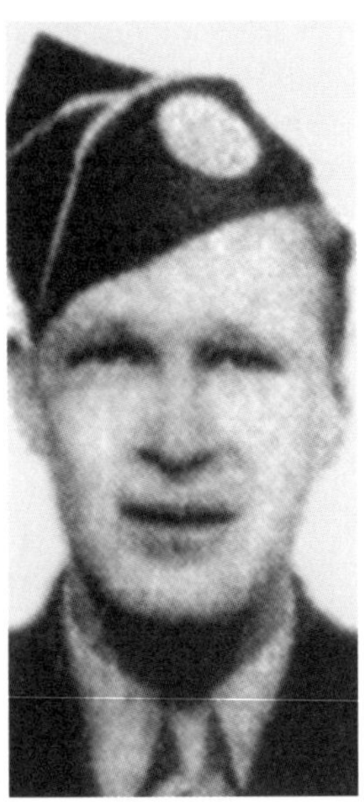

Private First Class William H. Arledge was born in Jefferson, Alabama, on January 21, 1921. He graduated from Phillips High School and prior to entering the army he was employed by the Birmingham Printing Company.

William enlisted at Fort McClellan on August 5, 1942. He was trained to be a paratrooper and was assigned to Company B of the 506th Parachute Infantry Regiment, which was an element of the 101st Airborne Division. In 1944, William took part in the Allied airborne landings of Operation Market Garden. His regiment landed on the drop zone near Son on September 17, after which it was deployed in the bitter fighting for 'Hell's Highway.'

After the Allied advance was halted south of the Rhine and it had become clear that Market Garden had failed, William and his regiment were moved to the Dutch village of Opheusden to take up front positions there. Near this village, German infantry and tanks attacked the positions of the 506th on October 6, 1944. The well camouflaged enemy tanks came out of the morning mist and sprayed the Americans with machine gun fire and their main guns.

During the attack, William and a good friend, Corporal Henry Gogola, were hugging the ground as machine gun bullets from the German tanks buzzed overhead. One of the tanks then swiveled its turret in their direction and fired an artillery round. The shell tore much of William's torso away, mortally wounding him. Gogola crawled to him and gave William a shot of morphine to make his final moments as comfortable as possible. 'There was not much more I could do for him. He was gone within a very short time,' Gogola remembered. 'Another friend lost.' William was 23 years old.

Because the fierce fighting continued and the surviving men had to withdraw, William's body went missing. To this day, his remains have not been recovered. Therefore, his name is recorded on the Walls of the Missing in Margraten.

GLENN E. HAMLIN

Private First Class

101st Airborne Division

A name in a helmet

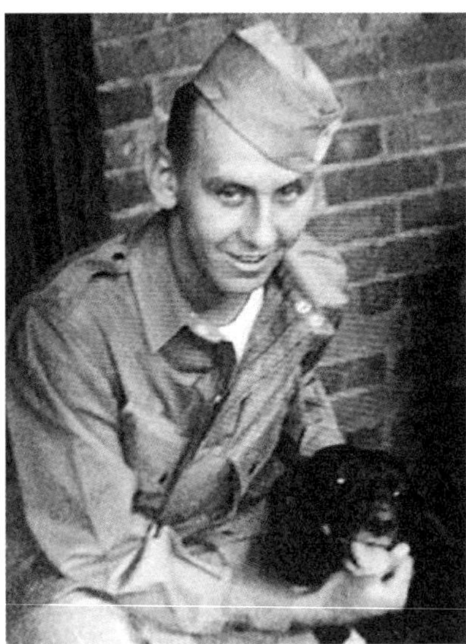

Tim Sloots' interest in World War II began at a young age. Like so many others, he started collecting military objects. When he was sixteen, he bought an American army helmet at a militaria dump store. It was not just a helmet. It was a helmet that had a name in it. From that point on, he was set on learning more about the life story of the helmet's previous owner. 'I talked about it all the time. My friends and my family, they knew I was always looking. Who was Glenn E. Hamlin?' After ten years, he had found the answer.

That the paratrooper had found his final resting place in Margraten was not the hardest thing to find out. Tim returned the helmet to its former owner and placed it on his grave, along with an American flag. Glenn ultimately found his final resting place in Margraten after he had previously been buried in the temporary U.S. cemetery in Molenhoek, the Netherlands.

Molenhoek is a 30-minute drive from the village of Opheusden. Glenn's unit was on the outskirts of the village. He was probably badly wounded by enemy mortar fire and had to be hospitalized with a skull base fracture. He died on October 7, 1944.

It was harder for Tim to find out more about Glenn himself. That changed when, at 26, Tim came into contact with Gerald Goolkasian, a World War II veteran. Gerald had trained with Glenn in their early army days. The two became good friends during that time. After basic training, however, their paths separated. Gerald was seriously injured as a tank driver during Battle of the Bulge in December 1944. But he remained level-headed about it. 'What can I say? I survived. I came back. I've had a good life. A lot of guys didn't live long enough to get their driver's license. They are the heroes.'

Through Gerald's recollections, Tim finally got a sense of the person behind the name in the helmet. 'He told me Glenn was a very nice, a warm person. A good friend when a man needs to be a good friend.' Gerald also happened to have a picture of Glenn that he sent to Tim. It gave 'me goosebumps to hear the stories, and to see the picture that he sent.' Simultaneously, Tim was able to provide some answers to Gerald, who only knew that Glenn had died in the Netherlands. After the training, he had received one letter from him, never to hear from him again. 'It made him come alive for me again, and it gave me closure.'

Tim felt an incredibly strong bond with Glenn. That is why he named his son, who was born in November 2009, after Glenn. Tim took a picture of little Glenn in the helmet of the soldier he was named after. It was that helmet that had started all of this more than ten years ago. Glenn is buried in Plot G, Row 2, Grave 9.

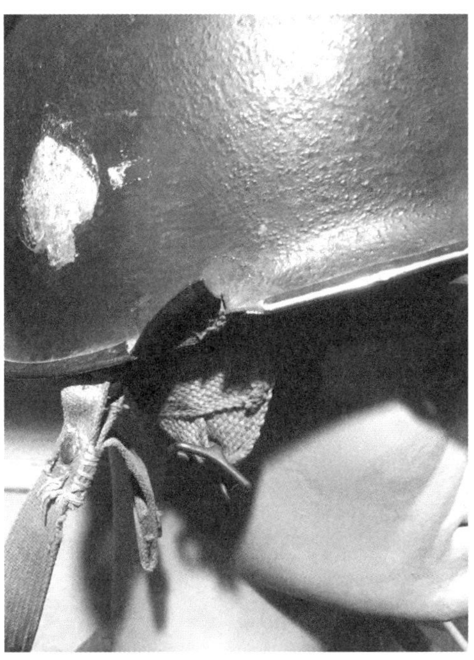

The damage that Glenn's helmet sustained indicates he suffered a head wound. SOURCE: Tim Sloots

STANLEY V. CLARK
Private First Class
101st Airborne Division

Veteran of the Utah Beach landing

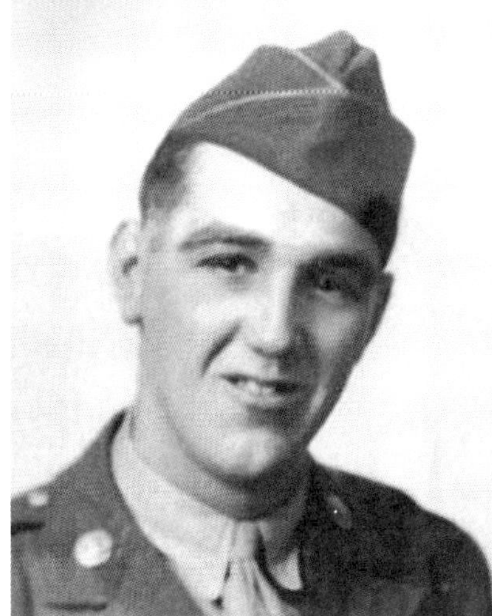

Private First Class Stanley V. Clark from Maine was born in 1924. He joined the army in March 1943, and served in Company C of the 401st Glider Infantry Regiment. This regiment was part of the 101st Airborne Division.

On June 6, 1944, Stanley participated in the Allied invasion of Normandy. Because the U.S. military needed more infantrymen on the beaches than in gliders for this particular mission, Stanley and the other members of his company did not arrive in Normandy by air. Instead, they arrived by boat with the 4th Infantry Division on Utah Beach. After overcoming weak German resistance there, they linked up with the paratroopers who had landed further inland shortly after midnight.

After D-Day, Stanley fought among the hedgerows in Normandy for over a month, after which the 401st GIR was brought back to England. On September 17, 1944, Stanley then participated in Operation Market Garden. This time he entered the area of combat aboard a glider. He landed somewhere between Eindhoven and Nijmegen. Stanley and his comrades then fought for two weeks between Son and Veghel, where the important advance route to Nijmegen was repeatedly attacked by the Germans.

In early October 1944, after the failure of Market Garden, the 401st GIR was transferred to Zetten, a small Dutch village in the Betuwe. There, at 3:00 a.m. on the morning of October 9, 1944, Company C awoke to a barrage of enemy mortar and artillery fire. They were also attacked by two German tanks that broke through their outpost line. Sometime between the start of the shelling and the attack of the two tanks, Stanley was killed by German artillery fire. He was fatally hit in the chest and died at the age of twenty. He was given his final resting place in Margraten in Plot G, Row 2, Grave 15.

BERNARD B. TOM
Private First Class
101st Airborne Division

Killed by a mortar shell

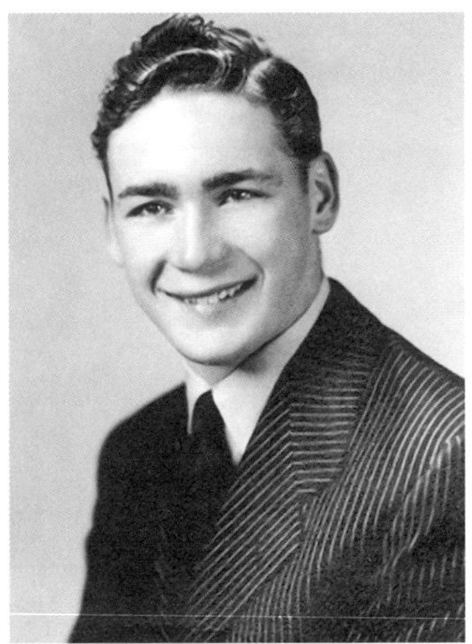

Private First Class Bernard B. Tom, born in Ohio in 1924, served as a paratrooper in Company F, 506th Parachute Infantry Regiment, 101st Airborne Division. On D-Day, he was deployed in the invasion of Normandy and subsequently he was also involved in Operation Market Garden over three months later.

On September 17, 1944, Bernard made a parachute landing on the drop zone near Son, Holland. The Americans were immediately involved in heavy fighting with the Germans, and the paratroopers did not succeed in capturing the bridge over the Wilhelmina Canal that was their objective. Just as the Americans approached the bridge, it was blown up by the Germans.

The next day, Bernard and the other paratroopers of the 506th entered Eindhoven from the north. There too they encountered German resistance. The Germans opened fire with 88mm guns. However, the Americans managed to neutralize and capture the guns, after which they liberated Eindhoven the same day.

After the failure of Operation Market Garden, Bernard's division was transferred to the Betuwe in early October 1944. There, a new front line had been formed after the advance of the British tanks towards Arnhem had finally been halted by the Germans.

Bernard and the other members of his company took up front line positions near the village of Heteren. Just west of this village, on October 9, 1944, he and two other paratroopers (Kenneth Hull and Orel Lev) brought a machine gun into position on the dike at Randwijk. At this spot a German counterattack was expected. Shortly after it got dark, all hell broke loose as the Germans indeed attacked the American positions. During the firefights that broke out here, Bernard was killed when enemy mortar fire hit his machine gun position. He was only twenty years old. His final resting place in Margraten is in Plot G, Row 1, Grave 15.

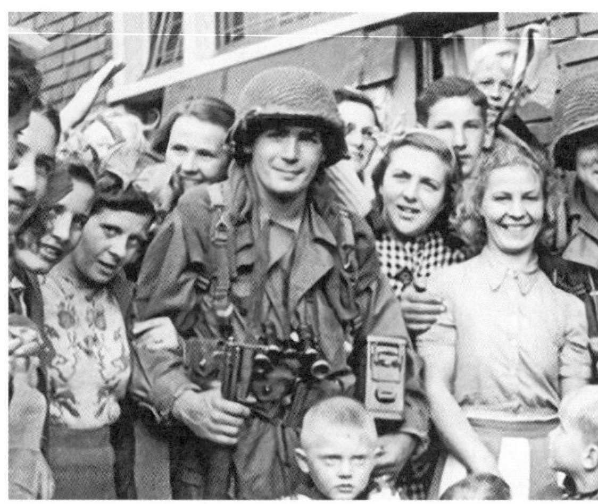

Bernard Tom poses together with liberated Dutch citizens in Eindhoven

JOHN S. HEMSTREET

Private

111th Field Artillery Battalion

Landed on Omaha Beach on D-Day

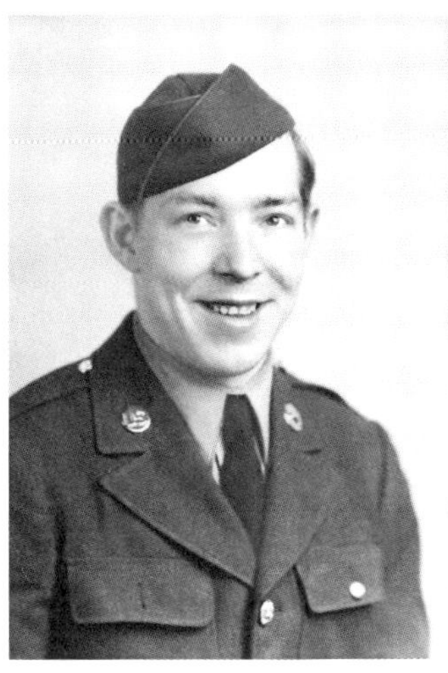

John S. Hemstreet from Scotia, New York, was born in 1920 and his family had Dutch roots. He entered the army in 1941 and served as a Field Lineman in the 111th Field Artillery Battalion of the 29th Infantry Division.

On D-Day, John went ashore on Omaha Beach, where the murderous German machine gun and shellfire caused a bloody carnage among the American soldiers. John was not part of the decimated first wave. That was his fortune.

The landing on Omaha Beach did not go according to plan for John's battalion. Due to rough seas and heavy German fire, it went completely wrong: of the thirteen DUKWs (amphibious trucks) with 105mm howitzers on board, ten sank after launching. Another DUKW got as far as a few hundred yards from the beach, but then suffered engine problems and was subsequently sunk by machine gun fire. The last two other DUKWs approached the beach, but due to obstacles and wrecks of destroyed landing craft, found nowhere to go ashore. One of them was then sunk by machine gun fire and a hit of artillery fire. The last 105mm howitzer could only just be transferred from a sinking DUKW to a so-called 'Rhino Ferry' and was then handed over to an artillery unit of the 1st Infantry Division in the afternoon. With all but one of the howitzers lost, John and the other members of the battalion fought on as infantrymen with their rifles.

After D-Day, the 111th Field Artillery Battalion was equipped with new howitzers, after which it supported the advance of the American armored units and infantry. Because he was responsible for the communication with the troops in the front line, John often drove a jeep back and forth between his battalion's batteries and the infantry and tank units.

On October 17, 1944, John lost his life near Breberen, north of Aachen. On that day, his jeep detonated a mine. He was killed by the explosion and was only 24 years old. John was given his final resting place in Margraten, which can be found in Plot G, Row 17, Grave 21.

WILLIAM C. MC CULLY

First Lieutenant

2nd Armored Division

Tank commander knew his tank would be hit

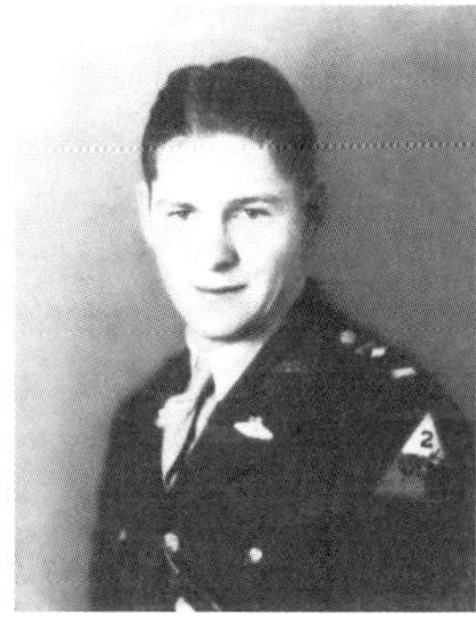

First Lieutenant William C. Mc Cully from Vero Beach, Florida, was a tank commander in the 66th Armored Regiment of the 2nd Armored Division. He went overseas in 1942, whereupon he was first involved in both the North African and Sicily campaigns. According to a local newspaper, his wife Violet and young son were making their new home in Rome, Georgia, while William served overseas.

In the same article, published on September 8, 1944, it was described that William was recently wounded by shrapnel in France and was hospitalized in England, where he received the Purple Heart. From there, William sent a letter to his wife in which he wrote the shrapnel had been removed and he expected to return to duty soon.

On October 20, 1944, William met his death in the vicinity of Baesweiler, Germany while he was courageously leading his tank platoon. He ignored his own personal safety and exposed himself to hostile fire in order to direct artillery fire upon the enemy. For this action he was posthumously awarded the Distinguished Service Cross. His citation provides more details and was published in the *Miami Herald* on July 8, 1945. It reads as follows:

> ***'For extraordinary heroism in connection with military operations against the enemy. On Oct. 20, 1944, in Europe, Lt. Mc Cully led his tank platoon to a position well in advance of his infantry mounting an attack on an enemy-held town. For more than three hours, he acted as forward observer for artillery fire which prevented enemy elements from counterattacking in force. He remained in this position, exposed to a hail of fire from enemy artillery and anti-tank guns, well knowing his vehicle must sooner or later be hit and destroyed. He would not withdraw until ordered to do so, and while this order was being given, his tank was hit and Lt. Mc Cully was killed.'***

During a formal ceremony, William's Distinguished Service Cross was presented to his widow Violet and his two-year-old son William C. Mc Cully Jr., whose husband and father would be permanently buried in Margraten. William's final resting place there can be found in Plot P, Row 2, Grave 9.

MARSHALL CORNELIUS JR.

Private First Class

82nd Airborne Division

'Now I lay me down to sleep, I pray...'

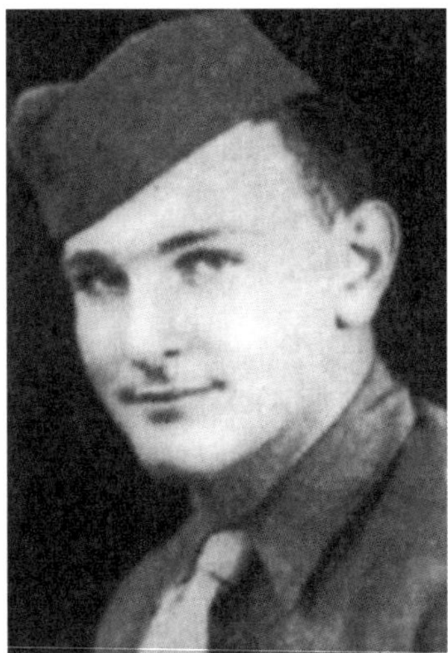

Marshall Cornelius Jr. from Pennsylvania was born in 1924. In high school, he excelled as a football player. At the time Marshall entered the army, he was a student at Lebanon Valley College. Following his enlistment, he joined the paratroopers and was assigned to the 504th Parachute Infantry Regiment. This was one of the regiments of the 82nd Airborne Division. Marshall's first combat experience with this division was in Italy. There, in January 1944, he was bayoneted in the stomach while capturing German prisoners.

After his injuries healed well enough, Marshall left the military hospital and was transferred to a convalescent camp. From this camp, Marshall sent a letter home to tell how he was doing. In it he wrote:

> ***'I am looking over a big harbor from where I sit. It is really a beautiful spot. I have seen the war and I know it is hell. I hope it will soon be over. I am O.K. now and please don't worry. I cannot tell you where I am or where I was but I am getting along O.K. Send me cigarettes, candy, socks. I received a box from Uncle Jim.'***

When Marshall had fully recovered, he was sent to England. He was then deployed in Operation Market Garden in the Netherlands. He served as a Bazooka man in the Headquarters Company of the 2nd Battalion. His regiment took the Meuse Bridge at Grave and then had to advance to Nijmegen to help capture the even larger bridge over the river Waal.

After it became clear that Market Garden was a failure, Marshall's regiment was deployed to defend the front line near Groesbeek. This village was not far from the German border. On the night of October 24–25, 1944, Marshall joined a combat patrol in enemy territory there. For about 200 yards the patrol encountered no enemy resistance. But then, according to eyewitness PFC Leo Hart, 'suddenly a burst of enemy machine gun fire cut waist high from my right to the left.' After this first burst 'everything went dead quiet,' Hart later told. 'Then out of the quiet I heard Cornelius, who must have taken the burst right in the middle, cry very softly, "Mamma... Mamma." He then began reciting, "Now I lay me down to sleep, I pray ...", and that was all. I can't express how I felt, but the enemy artillery came barreling in, and cover was of the utmost importance from then out.'

Because the enemy machine gun burst killed him, Marshall's life ended abruptly at the age of nineteen. His body was first buried in the temporary U.S. Military Cemetery in Molenhoek. After the war, this cemetery was closed, and his remains were transferred to what became the Netherlands American Cemetery and Memorial in Margraten. Marshall was given his final resting place there in Plot G, Row 3, Grave 2.

LEO W. GOERS

Technician Fourth Grade

17th Tank Battalion

Tank driver still missing

Leo W. Goers of Mendota, Minnesota, was born in 1917. In 1944, he was the driver of a Sherman tank. His unit, the 17th Tank Battalion, was part of the 'Lucky Seventh.' This was the nickname of the 7th Armored Division. This division arrived in Normandy in mid-August 1944 and participated in the Battle of Overloon.

Before Leo was sent to the Netherlands, he was allowed to go on leave and briefly returned home. During his leave, Leo married his fiancée, Loretta. When Leo returned to his unit and left her again, this would prove to be the last time they saw each other.

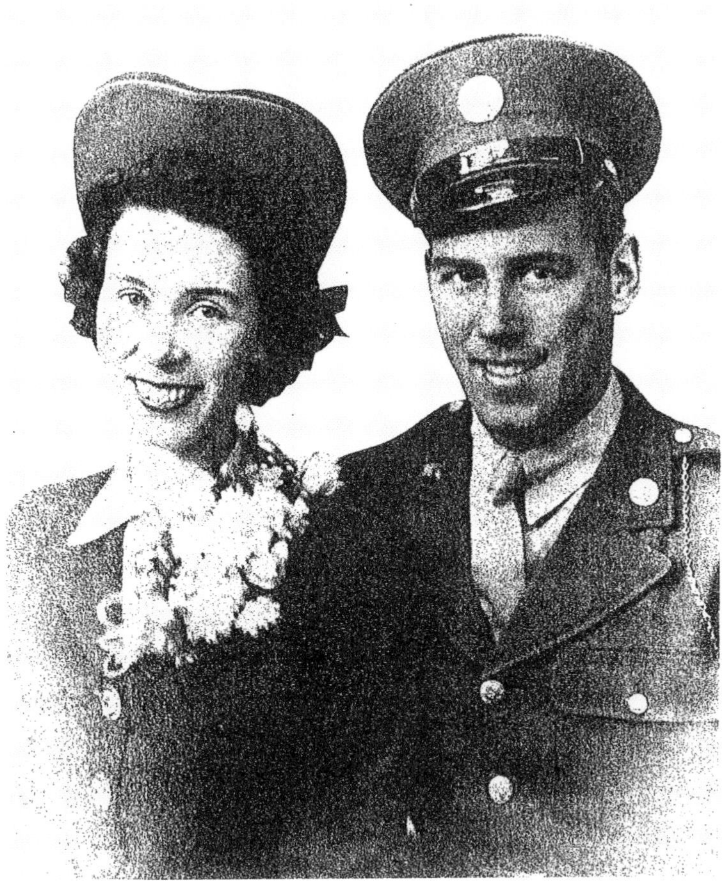

On October 29, 1944, the Sherman tanks of the 17th Tank Battalion were deployed near the road from Asten to Meijel to repulse a German counterattack. German troops armed with machine guns, submachine guns and Panzerfausts repeatedly attacked the Allied 'Corridor' and were supported by a number of tanks and their own artillery. The Shermans had to push back the German units, but the advance of the American tanks was met with heavy enemy fire.

During the fighting and the heavy artillery shelling that took place here on this day, Leo went missing in action at the age of 27. He was killed when his Sherman tank was hit by enemy fire and started to burn. Later, military reports stated that the tank lay under direct enemy artillery fire at the time and that Leo's remains were most likely burned inside the wreckage of his tank.

Because of the ongoing fighting, the tank was not recovered until later. The remains of the three other casualties – 2nd Lt. Robert W. Denny, Cpl. Elwyn Holdiman, Pvt. Michael Ferris – were then found and buried. The charred torso of the fourth casualty – almost certainly Leo's – remained in the tank because it was too fragile to remove. Subsequently, British ordnance troops who did not know that there were still remains in the tank transported it to Paris for salvage by the U.S. Army in December 1944. At the railyard north of Paris, the remains were discovered in the tank, but since all documentation remained in the Netherlands, there was no way to identify the burnt man. Therefore, he was buried as Unknown X-43 at the temporary U.S. Military Cemetery in Solers, France. Later, he was reburied as an unknown soldier in the permanent American Cemetery in Epinal, France.

In 2020, the Defense POW/MIA Accounting Agency (DPAA) approved the disinterment of 'Solers X-43.' DNA of several family members should reveal whether these remains are indeed Leo's. However, because of the COVID-19 pandemic, all disinterments were suspended. But there is still a chance that in the near future Leo's status as 'Missing in Action' may finally come to an end. How wonderful it would be if, as a result, a rosette could then be placed next to his name on the Walls of the Missing in Margraten.

NICHOLAS D. PUGLIA
Sergeant
486th Bombardment Group

Former baker was shot down

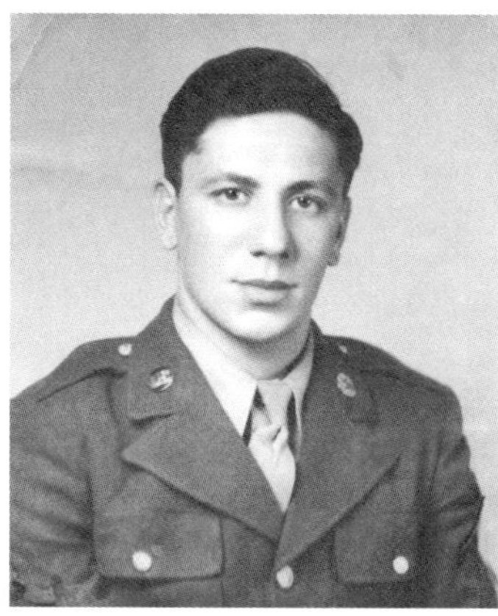

Sergeant Nicholas D. Puglia was born in New York in 1920. After attending high school for three years, he had gone to work as a baker. He enlisted in the United States Army Air Forces in March 1943.

Nicholas served as a radio operator in a four-engine B-17 'Flying Fortress.' The bomber in which he flew was nicknamed 'Blue Streak' by the crew and was part of the 834th Bomb Squadron. This squadron was part of the 486th Bombardment Group.

The 486th Bombardment Group was activated in September 1943. Six months later, the aircraft flew to England and the group was stationed at Sudbury airfield, one of the many airfields of the British RAF that were used by the Americans. There, the 486th Bombardment Group was placed under the command of the U.S. Eighth Air Force and began to participate in the Allied bombing campaign against Nazi Germany. At first the crews flew their missions in B-24 'Liberators,' but in July 1944 the transition to B-17s began.

On November 2, 1944, the 'Blue Streak' participated in a bombing raid on a synthetic oil refinery near the German town of Merseburg. It was to be Nicholas' last mission, because shortly after dropping the bombs, the B-17 was hit by Flak (German anti-aircraft fire). An explosion followed, after which the 'Blue Streak' broke into several burning pieces and crashed near the German town of Wallendorf. No parachutes were seen. Nicholas and all the other crew members did not survive. As a result, Nicholas remained forever 24. Like the other fallen crew members, he was initially buried at a local German cemetery in Kreypau, near Merseburg. His remains were later transferred to Margraten, where he was given his final resting place in Plot E, Row 8, Grave 4.

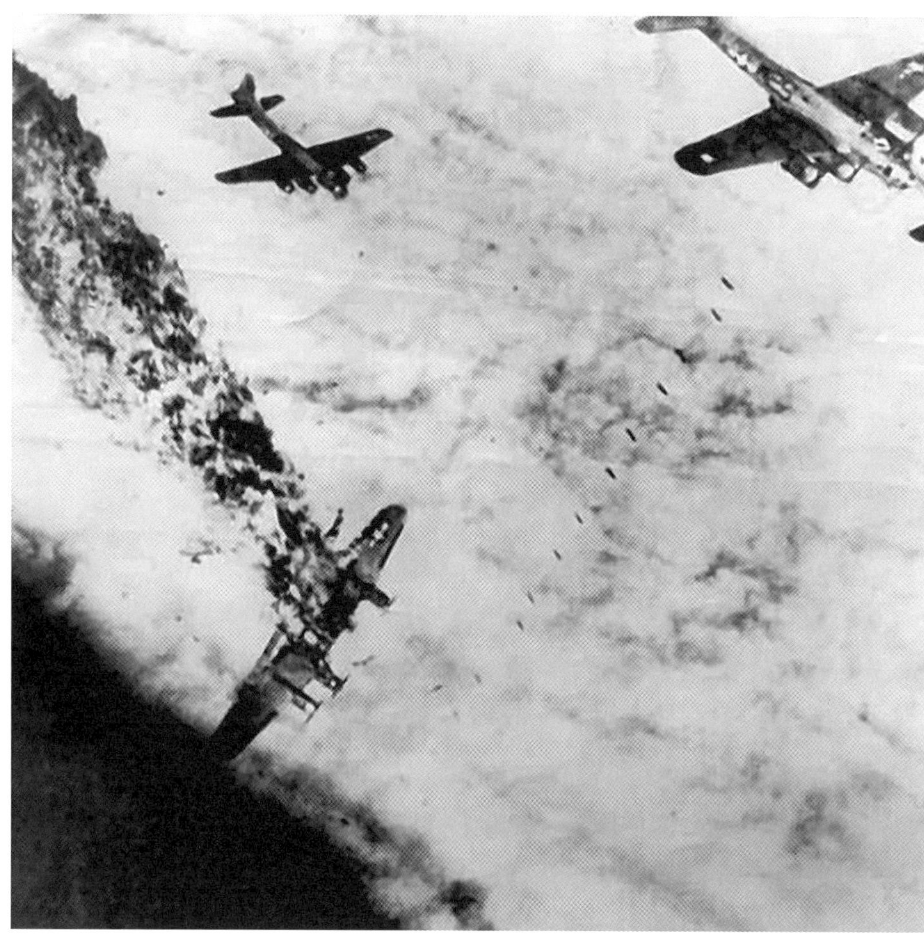

The burning and crashing 'Blue Streak' with Nicholas Puglia on board was captured in a photograph. SOURCE: U.S. Army Air Forces/ Staff Sergeant Bill Stewart via Arie-Jan van Hees

HENRY E. MARQUEZ
Private
28th Infantry Division

Young replacement died in the Hürtgen Forest

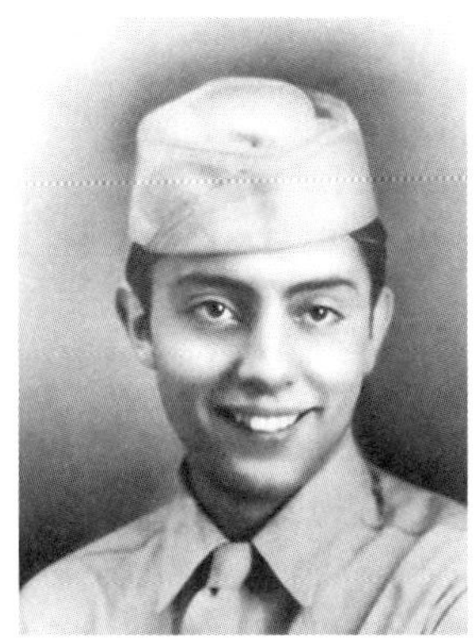

Private Henry E. 'Rickey' Marquez was born on January 13, 1926. He grew up in the Armourdale district of Kansas City, played basketball, and loved to sing and play the piano. Rickey had also learned to shoot and hunt on his grandparents' farm in southern Missouri. To make money, he polished shoes and later on raised show pigeons and sold their squabs to local restaurants. Further, he made ashtrays from cow horns and sold them. Rickey washed dishes at the West Height Coffee Shop and also worked at the Gustin-Bacon Insulation Co.

Rickey was a sprightly young man when he was drafted. After a brief basic training as an infantryman, he was sent to the front lines in Germany as a replacement. There he was attached to Company G of the 2nd Battalion, 112th Infantry Regiment, which was part of the 28th Infantry Division.

On November 2, 1944, Rickey's regiment launched a major assault in the Hürtgen Forest to capture the German towns of Vossenack, Kommerscheidt, and Schmidt. Rickey's battalion secured Vossenack and then dug in to defensive positions on the eastern end of the village. For the next few days, Rickey and his comrades faced unrelenting German machine gun, mortar, and artillery fire. The American troops could only stay low in their foxholes and try to survive the barrage. On November 4, during this fierce combat, Rickey was reported Missing in Action. A historical document included in his IDPF states that a Missing Report claims he was killed by enemy machine gun fire in his foxhole in the company defense area. Therefore, he remained forever eighteen...

Because Rickey's battalion faced continuous enemy mortar and artillery fire at the time, it was very difficult for medical personnel to evacuate wounded soldiers. Recovering remains of the fallen was often too dangerous as well, and they had to be left in place. Then, on November 6, 1944, the battered 2nd Battalion fell back. German troops recaptured the eastern half of Vossenack and held it for several days. By the time American troops secured the area again, many of the remains previously left behind could not be found – either they had been covered by earth incidentally during combat operations, or by German forces who conducted hasty field burials.

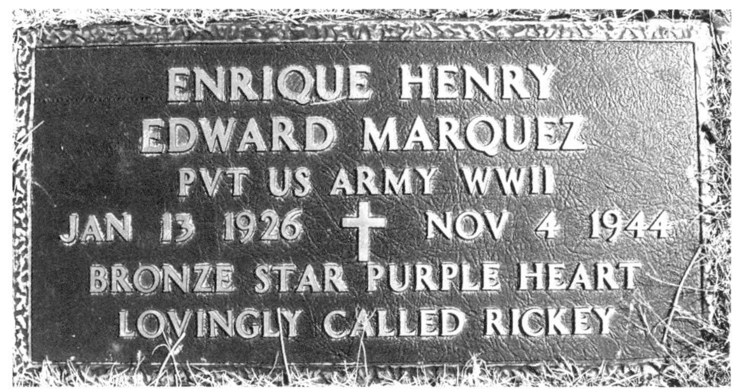

Henry Marquez' gravesite in the United States

The circumstances described here could explain why Rickey's remains could not be recovered during the battle nor were they found after the area was definitively secured by U.S. troops. Because of the above-mentioned statement that he was killed by machine gun fire and the fact that his remains were still missing at the time, Rickey's status was changed to 'Finding of Death' on November 5, 1945 – one year and one day after his disappearance was reported.

Over six decades later, in 2007, a German citizen searching for wartime relics in the Hürtgen Forest uncovered human remains and Rickey's dog tag. He notified U.S. officials and a Joint POW/MIA Accounting Command (JPAC) team excavated the site later that year. Using dental records, other forensic identification tools, circumstantial evidence, and mitochondrial DNA, scientists from JPAC and the Armed Forces DNA Identification Laboratory managed to identify the remains. In January 2009, it was announced that 64 years after his death, Rickey was no longer missing. He was then permanently buried at Highland Park Cemetery in Kansas City. To indicate that Rickey is no longer missing, a rosette was placed next to his name on the Walls of the Missing in Margraten.

RAYMOND J. BAUER
Corporal
893rd Tank Destroyer Battalion

Ambushed in the Hürtgen Forest

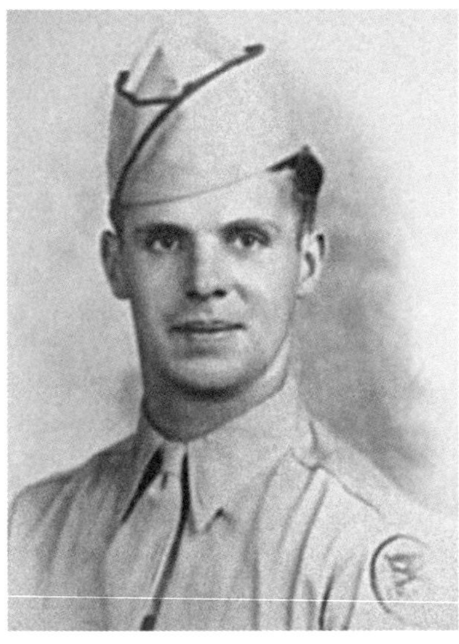

Corporal Raymond J. Bauer was born in 1922 and was a native of Ohio. He entered the army in Columbus on December 18, 1942. Prior to his enlistment, Raymond had attended high school for four years and was employed as a stock clerk, according to his enlistment record.

After joining the military, Raymond was assigned to a reconnaissance platoon of the 893rd Tank Destroyer Battalion. This battalion arrived in England in January 1944 and entered combat several months later in July. After advancing through France and toward the Siegfried Line, the battalion entered the German Hürtgen Forest in November. There, a veritable hell awaited the men.

In this hilly and treacherous forest, Raymond was killed in a German ambush near the village of Vossenack on November 6, 1944. This happened when he was on his way to the hill at Kommerscheidt in a jeep or another vehicle loaded with ammunition. Raymond suffered fatal wounds to his thorax and abdomen and died. According to his digitalized Hospital Admission Card his injuries were caused by enemy machine gun fire.

Judging from a document titled 'Operations of the 893rd TD Battalion in support of the 28th Infantry Division in the vicinity of Vossenack, Germany,' written by Major John J. Lavin (S-3 Officer), Raymond was almost certainly in the jeep of his reconnaissance platoon leader, Lt. Jack W. Fuller. Despite the fact that Raymond's name is not mentioned in this document, the following excerpt from it must also refer to him:

'About 0530 6 November C Company commander, a replacement officer, and the Reconnaissance Platoon Leader, with their jeeps loaded with ammunition followed the Reconnaissance platoon leader for another try at the Kall valley. They had not gone more than 300 yards south of Vossenack when the Reconnaissance Officer spotted an ambush of about 40 Germans. Both sides opened fire at the same time, a Panzerfaust hit the Reconnaissance Officers' jeep and a burst from a German machine gun hit his machine gunner and a man in the back seat. C Company commander's machine gun jammed and he was forced to bail out as a German lunged at him with a bayonet. This he slapped aside and with those who had not been hit [he] returned to Vossenack. (...) The Reconnaissance Platoon Leader asked for two destroyers to help him get his two men who had been wounded. It was still dark and foggy and as they neared the ambush, he gave the order to fire. The destroyers opened up with machine guns they had installed on the top of the turrets, killing and wounding some of the Germans, the rest fled. They found the two men, one dead, the other seriously wounded.'

The above-mentioned man who died must be Raymond for the fact that he was the only one of his battalion to be killed on November 6, 1944. At the time of his death, he was only 22 years old. Raymond is permanently laid to rest at the Netherlands American Cemetery and Memorial in Margraten. More than three-quarters of a century after he was killed, visitors can pay tribute to him there in Plot F, Row 6, Grave 18.

CHARLES A. DIMMOCK

Second Lieutenant

36th Fighter Group

Friendly fire caused fatal crash

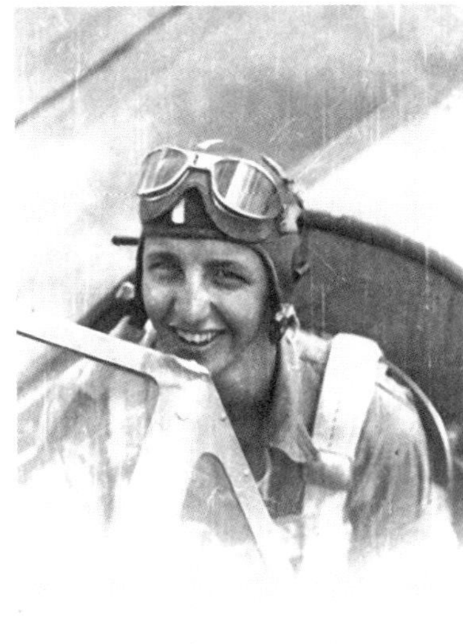

Second Lieutenant Charles A. Dimmock from Pennsylvania was born in 1923. After attending high school, he enlisted in the United States Army Air Forces in October 1942. Then, after completing his pilot training, Charles went to Europe, where he served as a fighter pilot in the 53rd Fighter Squadron. This squadron was part of the 36th Fighter Group. When Charles flew his last mission, he was in the cockpit of a P-47 Thunderbolt.

During his service in Europe, Charles regularly escorted formations of heavy bombers or was involved in tactical attacks on specific German ground targets. For this purpose, the P-47s were armed with several machine guns, some bombs and rockets.

On November 7, 1944, Charles was returning from a combat mission over enemy territory when he became the victim of a tragic mistake. As he flew over the Dutch town of Kerkrade, he was accidentally shot down by mobile American anti-aircraft guns on trucks that were stationed in the Haghenstraat. Apparently, the Americans on the ground mistook his plane for a German one...

Because his P-47 was heavily damaged by the anti-aircraft fire, Charles did not return to his base in Belgium. He did not survive the friendly fire incident as the plane crashed into two houses in the Bockstraat (numbers 29 and 31). The P-47 exploded immediately and the devastation was enormous. Unfortunately, a five-year-old local girl called Maria Meys also died. She was in the garden at the time of the crash and died as the heavy engine of Charles' exploded Thunderbolt fell on her...

Charles was only twenty years old when he was accidentally shot down. Presumably he was already killed in his cockpit before the crash. A few days later, Charles was one of the first fallen Americans to be buried in Margraten, where he still lies today. His final resting place can be found in Plot F, Row 8, Grave 20.

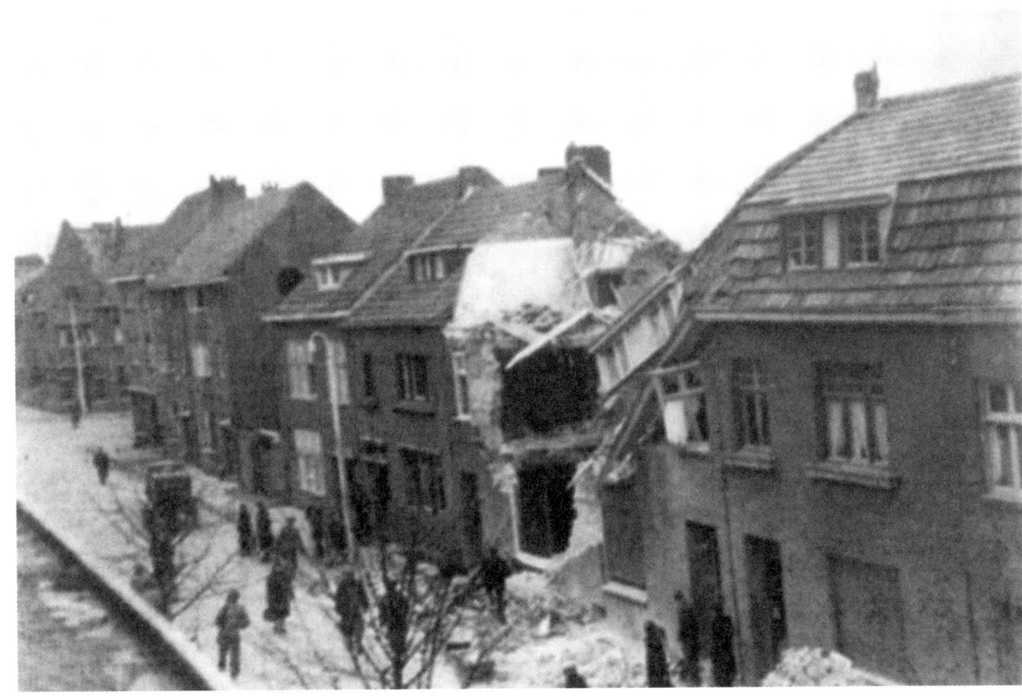

Charles Dimmock's plane crashed into a neighborhood of Kerkrade. SOURCE: Collection Ron Pütz via Arie-Jan van Hees

GEORGE T. VAN GIESEN
First Lieutenant
104th Infantry Division

Fearless devotion for his comrades

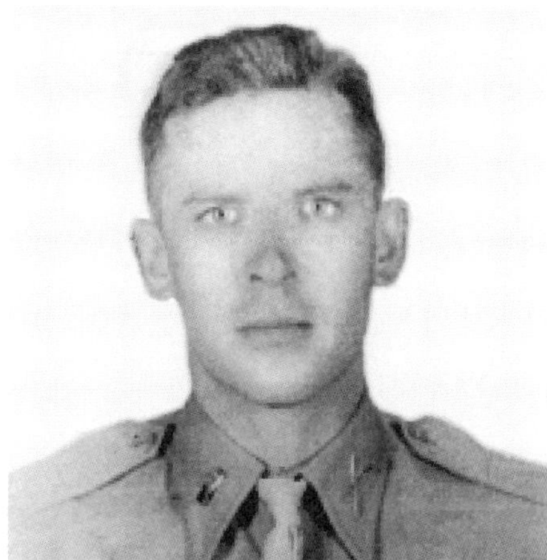

First Lieutenant George T. Van Giesen from San Francisco, California, was an officer in Company F, 2nd Battalion, 414th Infantry Regiment. This regiment was part of the 104th Infantry Division, also known as the 'Timberwolf' Division.

The Timberwolves arrived in France in September 1944, and moved into a defensive position in the vicinity of Wuustwezel, Belgium, on October 23. There it relieved the British 49th Division and joined the I British Corps, First Canadian Army. A few days later, the men crossed the Dutch border and soon they liberated Zundert, Etten, Leur, and Oudenbosch.

North of Oudenbosch, the Timberwolves encountered stubborn German resistance while advancing toward the Mark River near Standdaarbuiten. A coordinated attack on November 2 resulted in the establishment of a bridgehead across the river. The division then liberated Zevenbergen, after which the Divisional Headquarters received orders from the First U.S. Army to relieve the 1st Infantry Division near the German city of Aachen. Only elements of the 414th Infantry Regiment remained in Holland to secure Moerdijk, the last German stronghold on the south bank of the Hollands Diep.

While the bulk of the division was moving toward Aachen, George's 2nd Battalion attempted to liberate Moerdijk on November 7, 1944. According to the records of the ABMC, George lost his life that same day. Several months later, in 1945, it was announced that George was posthumously awarded the Distinguished Service Cross for his extraordinary courage on the day he was killed. An interesting fact is that his citation suggests that George would have been killed not on November 7 but one day later:

'The President of the United States of America takes pride in presenting the Distinguished Service Cross (Posthumously) to First Lieutenant (Infantry) George T. Van Giesen, United States Army, for extraordinary heroism in connection with military operations (...) against enemy forces on 8 November 1944. Lieutenant Van Giesen, a Platoon Leader, volunteered to lead a combat patrol against enemy positions which he had located the previous night while on a reconnaissance patrol. While skillfully leading his men over the same route he had passed the night before, he and his men were suddenly subjected to intense machine gun fire which caused many casualties. Realizing that maneuvering was impossible, he ordered his men to withdraw while he, completely disregarding his own personal safety, moved among his wounded men, rendering first aid and moving them to safer positions. This courageous act was done without thought for himself and amid intense machine gun fire which took his life. Lieutenant Van Giesen demonstrated a spirit of unselfishness and fearless devotion for his comrades that is an inspiring example for all. The extraordinary heroism and courageous actions of Lieutenant Van Giesen exemplify the highest traditions of the military forces of the United States and reflect great credit upon himself, the 104th Infantry Division, and the United States Army.'

George was 27 years old when he made the ultimate sacrifice. He is buried at the Netherlands American Cemetery and Memorial in Margraten, where he was given his final resting place in Plot A, Row 9, Grave 28. George is also honored at Fort Carson, Colorado, where his division was stationed for a time in 1944. One of the streets there was named after him – 'Van Giesen Street.'

HOWARD G. KRAPF

Private First Class

4th Infantry Division

A three-time decorated replacement

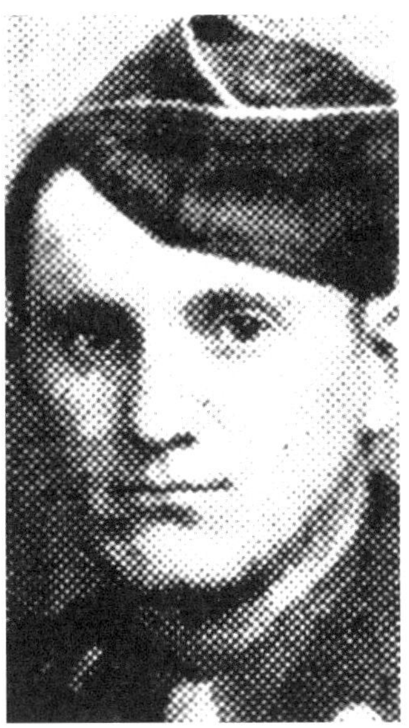

Private First Class Howard G. Krapf was born on October 3, 1918. His hometown was West Catasauqua, Pennsylvania, and he grew up with a brother and a sister. Before entering the army in November 1942, Howard was employed at Brown's Shoe Factory.

After his induction, Howard was sent to Camp Beale in California for basic training. Later, he was transferred to Camp Bowie, Texas, where he was awarded the expert infantryman medal in the spring of 1944. This award was already his third medal. Previously, he was awarded marksmanship badges for being an expert rifleman and an expert machine gunner. So, when Howard went overseas in July 1944, he had a lot to prove as he was then assigned to the 12th Infantry Regiment of the already combat-hardened 4th Infantry Division. This division had landed on Utah Beach on D-Day, and by the time Howard entered combat, it had already seen much heavy fighting.

Exactly five months after some of his experienced fellow soldiers had stormed the Normandy coast, the division entered the Hürtgen Forest on November 6, 1944. In this German forest, Howard lost his life two days later on November 8, 1944. According to two newspaper articles in *The Morning Call* he was killed by German machine gun bullets while attacking with his company. He was 26 years old.

Because of the ongoing fighting in the woods, Howard's remains went missing. That is why his name is inscribed on the Walls of the Missing in Margraten. Sadly, still nothing is known about his mortal remains...

RAYMOND P. KELLY

Private

2nd Armored Division

The aspirant priest in Limburg

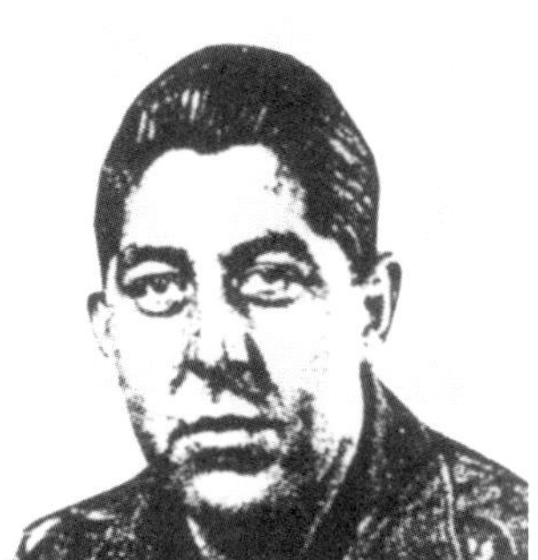

Private Raymond P. Kelly from Michigan was born in 1925. When the United States entered World War II, Raymond was a seminarian to become a priest. Therefore, he did not actually have to serve in the military. However, Raymond himself believed that he too had to fulfill his duty for his country. Therefore, he voluntarily joined the U.S. Army, after which he served as assistant gunner in a Sherman tank of the 67th Armored Regiment. This regiment was part of the 2nd Armored Division 'Hell on Wheels.' In September 1944, while serving in this division, Raymond was involved in the liberation of the southern part of Limburg in Holland.

After the liberation of southern Limburg, Raymond's division crossed the German border to break through the Siegfried Line (Westwall). In October 1944, he was granted a leave and briefly returned to Limburg. Raymond had a good time there. In the letters he sent home he wrote for example that he enjoyed being able to take a nice hot shower again after a long time. Raymond also described the friendliness of the local people. Furthermore, Raymond wrote in one of his letters to his parents:

> ***'In the streets I saw kids coming home from school with books under their arms and smiles on their faces. It's a great feeling to know that you helped to make these children happy once again. I guess you'd call it: what we're fighting for...'***

Raymond's pleasant stay in Limburg was short-lived. He had to return to the front line and on November 17, 1944, he was killed near the German village of Puffendorf. Enemy Panther and Tiger tanks suddenly attacked his regiment while the Shermans were drawn up on a slope outside the village, ready to attack toward Gereonsweiler. During the tank-on-tank engagement near Puffendorf, Raymond's Sherman tank was destroyed by a direct hit. He was only nineteen years old. Nothing has ever been found of his remains. That is why his name is listed on the Walls of the Missing in Margraten.

Six weeks after his death, Raymond's family in the United States received a Christmas card he had sent. He had written 'Merry Christmas' on it in several languages, including Dutch: 'Vroolijk Kerstfeest.' It was the last sign of life his family received from him...

CLIFFE H. WOLFE

Technical Sergeant

28th Infantry Division

Search for missing sergeant is still ongoing

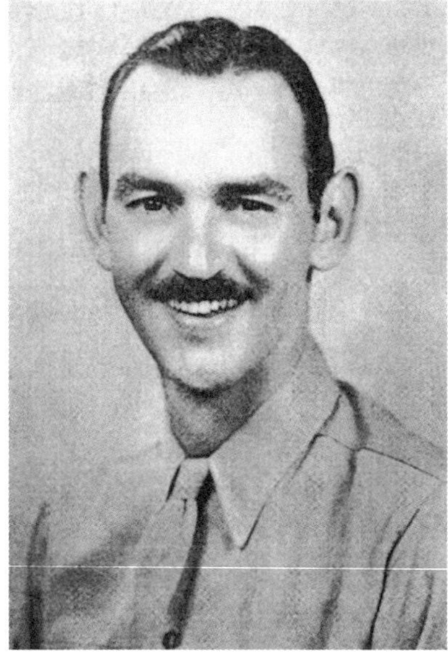

In 2008, Dutchman Bart van der Sterren adopted twelve engraved letters on the impressive Walls of the Missing in Margraten. Together these letters form the name of Cliffe H. Wolfe, a sergeant from Michigan who was reported missing in action on November 17, 1944. Because Wolfe was still not accounted for, Van der Sterren began a search that has been going on for fourteen years now.

During the process, Van der Sterren partnered with 'Stichting Missing in Action,' a Dutch non-profit foundation whose goal it is to search and find missing World War II soldiers. With the cooperation of this foundation, he searched through numerous archival records to find more information about 'his' soldier. Wolfe served in Company A, 109th Infantry Regiment, 28th Infantry Division and disappeared during the bloody battle that was fought in the Hürtgen Forest, Van der Sterren learned. While studying Wolfe's IDPF, he also found out how his adopted soldier was killed: 'Sgt. Wolfe received a direct hit from a mortar and was buried in his foxhole,' a record in his IDPF states. As a result, Wolfe remained forever 31 (he was born on February 23, 1913).

Because the 109th Infantry Regiment was under constant fire by counterattacking Germans, members of the unit could not evacuate Wolfe's remains. Instead, he was reportedly buried in his own foxhole by Technical Sergeant L. Ballegeer (KIA on December 21, 1944). When Van der Sterren received the IDPF, he found in it a map on which Capt. M. Whitetree had marked the possible location of Wolfe's grave. Thanks to this map, Van der Sterren and Stichting MIA discovered that Wolfe's probable field grave was located along a road near the village of Hürtgen, southeast of Aachen. 'Of course, we continued our search with this information and through Google Maps we found out that this road still exists,' Van der Sterren said. 'At some point, the captain's widow sent some pictures (found in the attic) to Stichting MIA, which were taken by the captain himself in 1948. However, the problem was that in the meantime apparently another road had been built by the military. The exact location of the probable grave therefore was still not clear. This road no longer exists so we went looking for aerial photographs.' However, when they received some, these particular photographs did not prove to be very useful. 'Together with others from the foundation, I then went to investigate the site with metal detectors,' Van der Sterren recalled. 'But we could not find anything useful (afterwards it proved to be not the right location).'

Later, after receiving another letter from the United States which contained aerial photographs that did show the now disappeared road, Van der Sterren and members of the foundation returned to the Hürtgen Forest to conduct another search. This time they received free cooperation of two employees of a Dutch engineering company, who brought with them an expensive ground-radar. They scanned the area with it and found a few soil disturbances, deeper into the ground than could be detected with a normal metal detector.

Because these soil disturbances may indicate possible field graves, Van der Sterren and the foundation tried to get in touch with the Joint POW/MIA Accounting Command (JPAC). However, they received no response to their e-mails until JPAC was reorganized and became the Defense POW/MIA Accounting Agency (DPAA). 'DPAA became so interested in our case that they decided to join us in searching for Cliffe H. Wolfe,' Van der Sterren said. 'So, in 2018, we spent a week with DPAA staff searching for Cliffe H. Wolfe. After this week of digging in Hürtgen and finding several hidden foxholes containing ammunition (bullets, mortars, hand grenades) and personal military items, we were unfortunately unable to find Cliffe H. Wolfe.'

Still, Van der Sterren, the foundation, and the DPAA team, including Dr. Ian Spurgeon, did not give up the search. One of the reasons for this is that a declassified file has shown that shortly after the war American Graves Registration personnel had also searched the same area for remains of missing soldiers. During this search, remnants of human bones were recovered. These were, as it turned out, buried as an Unknown American soldier in a U.S. military Cemetery in France. DPAA requested the disinterment of these remains, which was done in 2019. The bones were sent to Hawaii, where DNA research is being done. So, the search for Cliffe H. Wolfe is still ongoing. Hopefully, the combined efforts of his dedicated adopter, Stichting MIA, and DPAA will result in Wolfe's case finally being solved in the near future.

WINTHROPE N. HASTINGS

Second Lieutenant

743rd Tank Battalion

Killed in the turret of his tank

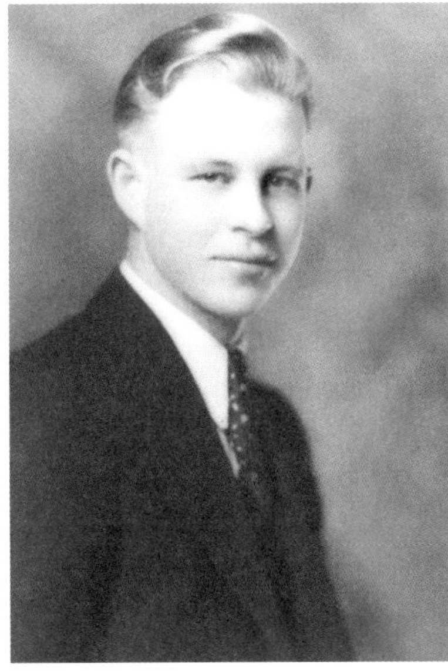

Second Lieutenant Winthrope N. Hastings was born in 1909. He lived in North Mankato, Minnesota, and was employed by the Standard Oil Company there. In 1934, Winthrope married his girlfriend Mildred.

In the fall of 1944, Winthrope was the commander of a Sherman tank in Company B of the 743rd Tank Battalion, which supported the 30th Infantry Division. In September 1944, the battalion was involved in the liberation of southern Limburg in Holland. During the advance through this part of Limburg, the tanks moved through Maastricht, Valkenburg, and Heerlen to the Dutch border with Germany.

The 743rd Tank Battalion broke through the Siegfried Line north of Aachen and penetrated further into German territory. The tanks then advanced in the direction of the Roer. During this difficult and slow advance, Winthrope's company attacked the German towns of Euchen and Linden on November 17, 1944. There they encountered seven German tanks that delivered direct fire on them, supplementing artillery and mortar fire.

According to the After-Action Report and the Combat History, none of Baker Company's Sherman tanks were destroyed by the enemy fire, but the battalion did lose one of its officers. That was Second Lieutenant Winthrope Hastings, who commanded one of the tank platoons. During the fighting, he was killed in the turret of his tank, struck in the head by shell fragments. Winthrope was 35 years old at the time, making him one of the older fallen buried at the Netherlands American Cemetery in Margraten. His final resting place there can be found in Plot G, Row 20, Grave 14.

HUBERT L. HUGHES

Private First Class

30th Infantry Division

Buried alongside his brother

Private First Class Hubert L. Hughes from Tennessee was born in 1915 and spent his childhood on his parents' farm. He helped out in the fields and with the care of the cows and chickens. In his spare time, he enjoyed playing baseball with his friends and often went fishing or hunting. Hubert also liked working on cars, together with his older brother Carl.

In March 1944, Hubert, who by now was married and had a daughter named Phyllis, was drafted into the army. After training as an infantryman, Hubert went overseas to Europe, where he was assigned to Company C of the 117th Infantry Regiment in October. This regiment was part of the 30th 'Old Hickory' Infantry Division, which had been involved in the liberation of southern Limburg in the Netherlands several weeks earlier.

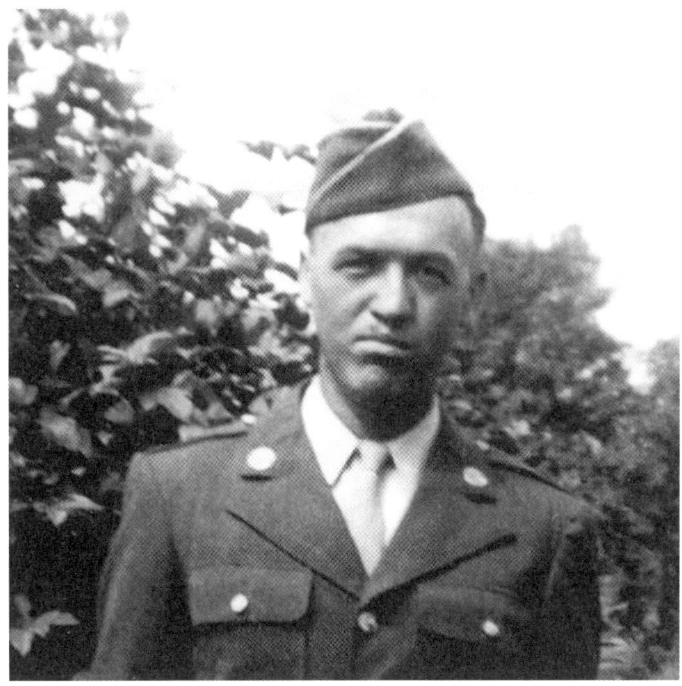

On November 17, 1944, Hubert and his unit went on a patrol through the streets of the German town of Mariadorf. The purpose of this patrol was to eliminate German snipers still hiding in the houses. At some point, when Hubert was looking into one of the houses, a German mortar or artillery shell struck this building. It caught him by surprise and Hubert was buried under the falling debris. As a result, he died at the age of 30, never to see his beloved wife Graham and daughter Phyllis again.

Hubert is buried in Margraten, where his final resting place can be found in Plot F, Row 19, Grave 14. Directly beside him lies his brother Carl. He was killed in action on June 16, 1944, north of Rome. This occurred under almost similar circumstances: Carl was standing next to a tree when it was hit by a bomb or shell and he was fatally wounded by the splinters. Their parents thus received a telegram twice in a short time informing them that their son had given his life for his country and the liberation of Europe...

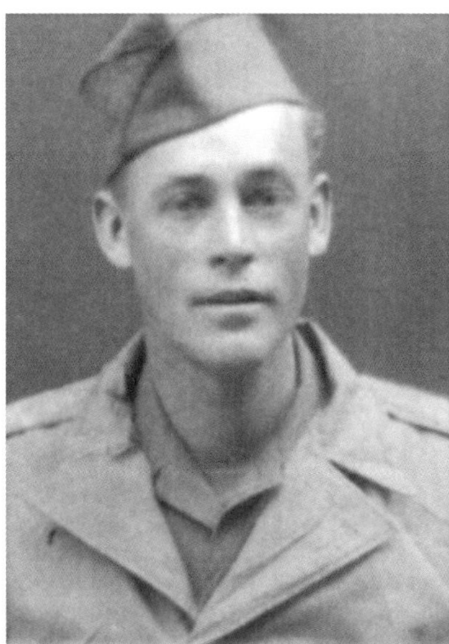

Hubert's brother Carl

PETER BACLE

Sergeant

17th Armored Engineer Battalion

Mortally wounded by a mine while rescuing wounded men

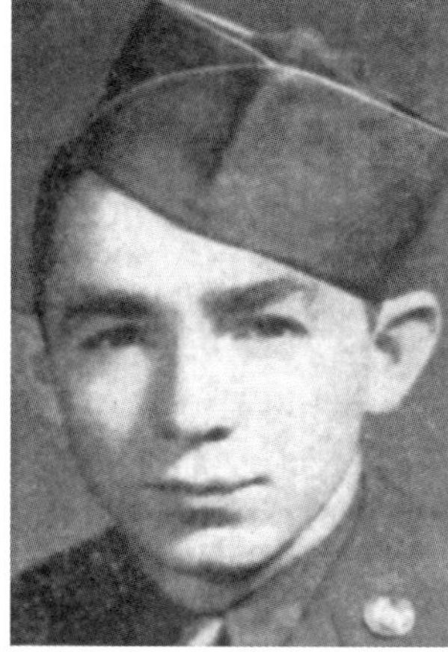

Sergeant Peter Bacle from Louisiana was born in 1922. In 1940, he entered the army. He eventually served as a halftrack driver in the 17th Armored Engineer Battalion. This unit was specialized in, for example, clearing mines and building pontoon and Bailey bridges over streams and rivers. By performing these tasks, the battalion supported the advance of the armored infantry and tanks of the 2nd Armored Division 'Hell on Wheels.'

On November 16, 1944, Peter's engineer platoon was assigned a mission of clearing a large and dense minefield near the German town of Baesweiler. Upon his arrival at the area, he found approximately twenty seriously wounded infantrymen lying in the field. Others who had made previous attempts to reach the helpless men also had become casualties.

Peter decided to ignore his own safety and entered the minefield to rescue the wounded. For this act of extraordinary valor, he was later honored with the Distinguished Service Cross. The citation tells us:

> ***'Sergeant Bacle, with utter disregard for his own safety, courageously probed for mines, cleared a path to two wounded soldiers and evacuated them to safety. Although the area was subjected to intermittent artillery and mortar fire, Sergeant Bacle unflinchingly resumed his hazardous task and successfully reached a third comrade who was so severely wounded that he could not be lifted. In turning the wounded man over to roll him upon a stretcher, a mine was set off which resulted in the death of both men.'***

Peter did not die immediately. The explosion of the German mine mortally wounded him. He was evacuated to a field hospital that was set up in the Dutch town of Heerlen. There he succumbed to his injuries on November 19, 1944. He was only 22 years old. Peter is buried in Margraten, where visitors can pay tribute to him by going to Plot P, Row 17, Grave 1.

WILLIAM M. ROYALL
First Lieutenant
29th Infantry Division

Company commander for only five hours

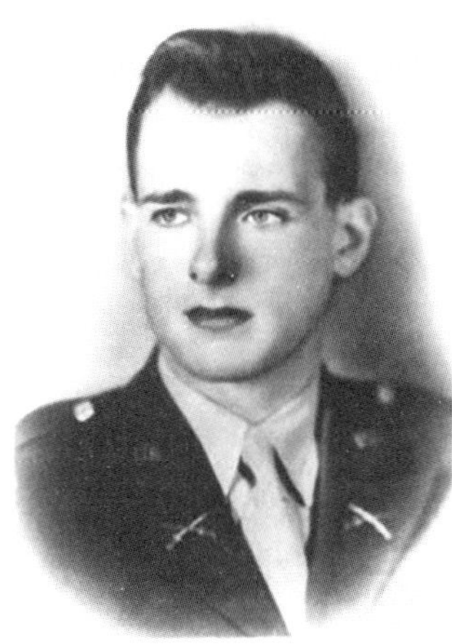

First Lieutenant William M. Royall was born on May 20, 1921. His hometown was Florence, South Carolina. His father was a veteran of World War I and a successful lawyer. After high school, William went to study at The Citadel, South Carolina's military college in Charleston. He graduated in 1942 and then entered active military service.

After enlisting into the army, William was initially stationed in several army posts in the United States. First at Camp Breckinridge in Kentucky, then at Fort Huachua in Arizona, and afterwards at Camp Van Dorn in Mississippi. For further training, he also spent some time at Fort Benning, Georgia. William went overseas to Europe in September 1944. Upon his arrival on the European battlefield, he was attached to the 115th Infantry Regiment of the 29th Infantry Division. This division had entered combat on D-Day when it landed on Omaha Beach.

As a newly arrived replacement-officer, William was immediately given command of Company K on November 19, 1944. His predecessor, Captain Sidney Young, had been killed by a shell fragment during an enemy artillery barrage shortly before. William took the lead and with his men he attacked the German village of Siersdorf. The attack was supported by some tanks, but there was still scattered resistance from German soldiers who sniped at the company's men from houses inside the town.

During the attack on Siersdorf, William was shot and killed by a German sniper, barely five hours after he had assumed command of the company. William died at the age of 23. He is buried at the Netherlands American Cemetery and Memorial in Margraten. Today, visitors can find his final resting place there in Plot D, Row 15, Grave 3.

LEO LICHTEN
Private First Class
84th Infantry Division

Highly intelligent soldier didn't stand a chance

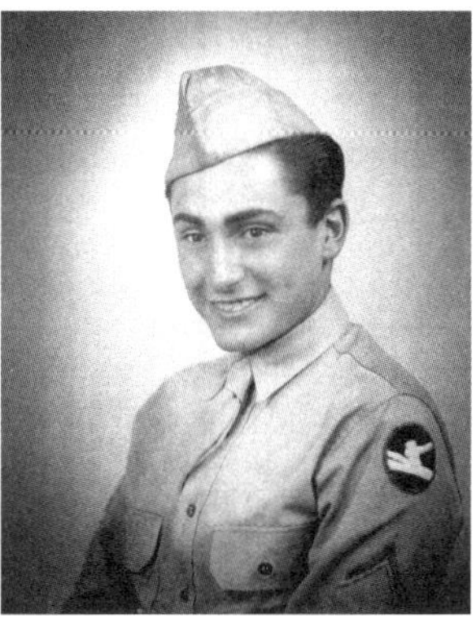

Private First Class Leo Lichten was born in New York in 1925 and was the son of two Jewish immigrants from Europe. His father Max was originally from Galicia, which was a province of the Austrian-Hungarian Empire at the time but today is part of Poland. Leo's mother Mollie was born in the east of Galicia, an area that now is in Ukraine. Max and Mollie did not have a happy marriage and divorced during Leo's childhood. A childhood friend of Leo's, Paul Slater, called him a 'dear friend to all.' According to Paul, Leo was a 'gifted intellectual, an athlete and a comrade.'

After a year of college, Leo enlisted in the army in 1943. Because he was a highly intelligent boy, he was selected for the prestigious Army Specialized Training Program (ASTP). The ASTP offered the most intelligent young men the chance to be educated as doctors, engineers, or interpreters in exchange for several years of service in the armed forces.

The ASTP that Leo attended was prematurely and abruptly terminated in February 1944. Because a shortage of soldiers was looming, he was then transferred to the infantry to become a rifleman. After a brief training, he was assigned to the 334th Infantry Regiment of the 84th Infantry Division and in September 1944, Leo went overseas.

Leo and the other men of the 334th arrived in Normandy on November 1, 1944, whereupon the troops were transferred to a bivouac area near Laon, France. The regiment spent two days there but on November 7, the men mounted trucks for a cold drive to the village of Wittem, Holland, where they arrived on the 8th. As the soldiers stepped from the trucks, they could hear friendly artillery firing against the Siegfried Line to the east.

The regiment entered combat ten days later, on November 18, 1944, during Operation Clipper. The objective of this joint British-American operation was to drive the Germans out of Geilenkirchen and the surrounding area and to break through the Siegfried Line there.

On November 20, 1944, the third day of the operation, Leo's Company A was ordered to take out enemy pillboxes on a hill near the German village of Prummern. Despite deteriorating weather conditions, the attack was launched in the early morning. The Germans on the hill expected the attack and responded with deadly machine gun fire.

Leo was one of the first soldiers of his company to lose his life during this attack: while storming an enemy pillbox, he was struck and killed by German machine gun bullets. He died at the age of nineteen and is permanently laid to rest on the Netherlands American Cemetery and Memorial in Margraten. Because he was a Jewish soldier, there is a Star of David on his grave. Leo is buried in Plot E, Row 7, Grave 13.

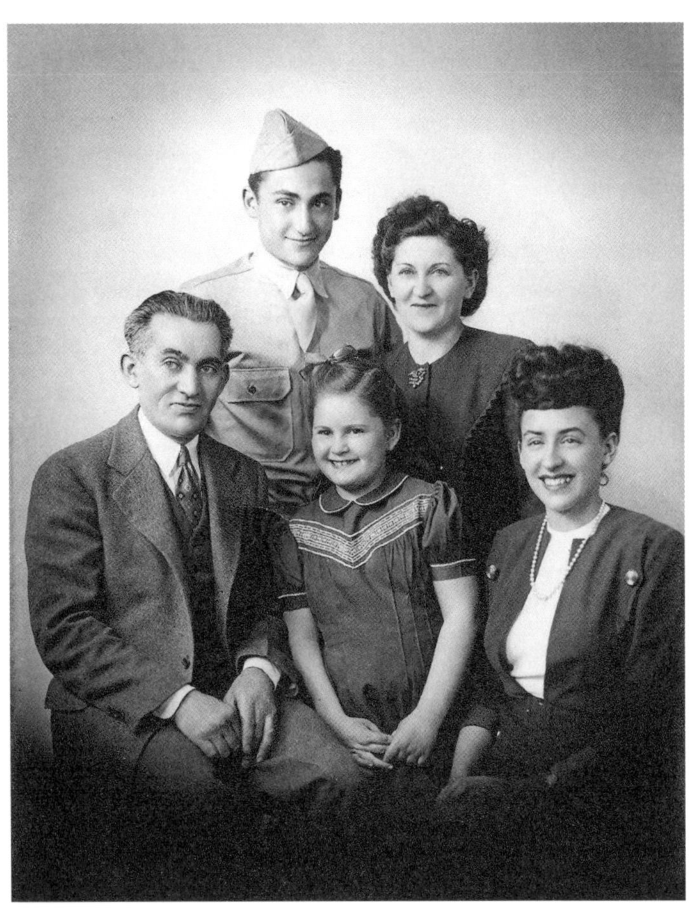

Leo Lichten and his family

JAMES J. CALLERY
Private
84th Infantry Division

Granddaughter visited his grave in 2018

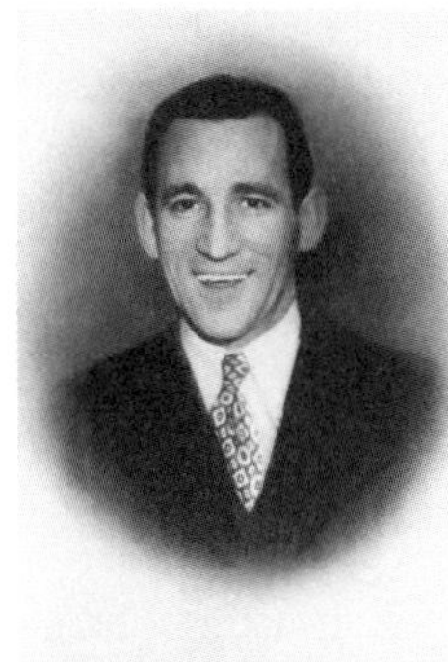

Private James J. Callery was born on July 29, 1913, about a year before World War I broke out. He married his girlfriend Dorothy with whom he lived in Lowell, Massachusetts. Before he was drafted into the army on January 21, 1944, James was employed by the Diamond Taxi Co.

After entering the service, James was assigned to Company I of the 333rd Infantry Regiment. This regiment was part of the 84th Infantry Division, which was also known as the 'Railsplitters' Division. James' regiment was first deployed in combat near the German city of Geilenkirchen during Operation Clipper. The city was taken on November 19, and the following day, Company I and the 333rd Infantry Regiment continued the attack toward the town of Süggerath. James took part in this attack, for which he was attached to the Regimental Anti-Tank Company in a special Mine Clearing Platoon.

During the attack on Süggerath, James was killed in action at the age of 31. A letter from Captain John C. Bowen, a company commander in the 333rd Infantry Regiment, sent to one of James' brothers, revealed more details surrounding his death:

> ***'It was in the early phase of this attack on Süggerath on the 20th of November that your brother was shot and killed by a German sniper. With him at the time of his death were PFC Thomas W. Campbell, now of Company I, this Regiment, and PFC William R. Bedford, now of HQ. & HQ. Company, this Regiment. It is my belief that your brother was killed instantly and did not suffer at all.'***

Shortly after James gave his life, Dorothy received a letter of condolence from the Office of Brigadier General Alexander R. Bolling, commander of the 84th Infantry Division in the ETO. He wrote to her that 'the entire division has suffered a personal loss in the death of your husband, for we knew him to be a conscientious and energetic soldier whose military duties were always performed well and faithfully. All who knew Private Callery join with me in extending to you our heartfelt sympathy and condolence.'

In the same letter, Dorothy could read that James was buried at the temporary U.S. Military Cemetery in Margraten. 'A United States Army chaplain administered the last rites in accordance with his Catholic faith,' Bolling's Office wrote. Later she received her husband's personal efforts including James' dog tags, rosaries, and his small military missal prayer books.

After the war, when it was decided that the temporary cemetery in Margraten would become a permanent burial site, Dorothy chose not to repatriate her husband's remains home but to have them permanently interred there among others who had made the ultimate sacrifice. In 1949, the U.S. War Department informed her that James was permanently laid to rest in Plot G, Row 6, Grave 12.

Dorothy later remarried and out of respect for her new husband, James wasn't talked about much. For that reason, Laurie McAnespie, James' granddaughter, didn't know a lot about her late paternal grandfather until 2018, when a research volunteer of *The Faces of Margraten* sent her a letter in hopes that she may receive a photograph of him and perhaps even an obituary. Soon she also got in touch with Pierre Erens, the current Dutch adopter of James' grave. Laurie learned her grandfather's grave has been adopted since 1945, and when she told her then 78-year-old father James T. Callery about this, his eyes teared up and he was at a loss for words. He was surprised to learn there have been people taking care of his father's grave this whole time.

The same year, Laurie traveled to the Netherlands, where she visited her grandfather's grave for the first time. She then also met Pierre Erens. Visiting her grandfather's grave was the highlight of her trip.

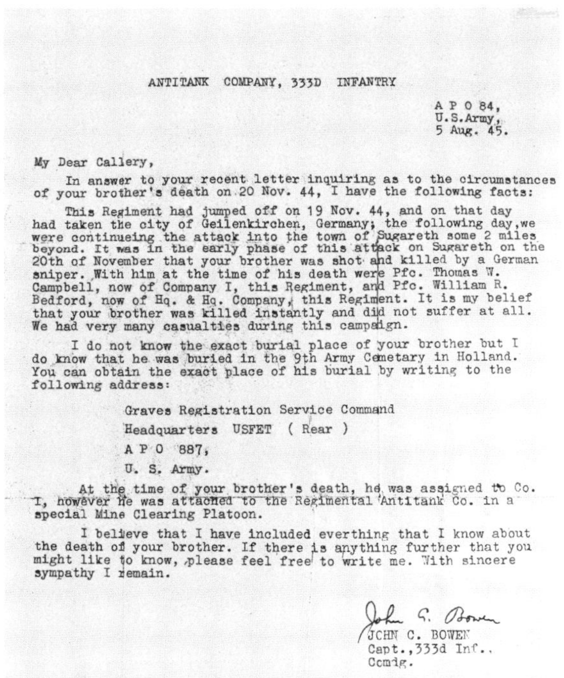

ANTITANK COMPANY, 333D INFANTRY

A P O 84,
U.S.Army,
5 Aug. 45.

My Dear Callery,

In answer to your recent letter inquiring as to the circumstances of your brother's death on 20 Nov. 44, I have the following facts:

This Regiment had jumped off on 19 Nov. 44, and on that day had taken the city of Geilenkirchen, Germany; the following day,we were continueing the attack into the town of Sugareth some 2 miles beyond. It was in the early phase of this attack on Sugareth on the 20th of November that your brother was shot and killed by a German sniper. With him at the time of his death were Pfc. Thomas W. Campbell, now of Company I, this Regiment, and Pfc. William R. Bedford, now of Hq. & Hq. Company, this Regiment. It is my belief that your brother was killed instantly and did not suffer at all. We had very many casualties during this campaign.

I do not know the exact burial place of your brother but I do know that he was buried in the 9th Army Cemetary in Holland. You can obtain the exact place of his burial by writing to the following address:

Graves Registration Service Command
Headquarters USFET (Rear)
A P O 887,
U. S. Army.

At the time of your brother's death, he was assigned to Co. I, however he was attached to the Regimental Antitank Co. in a special Mine Clearing Platoon.

I believe that I have included everthing that I know about the death of your brother. If there is anything further that you might like to know, please feel free to write me. With sincere sympathy I remain.

John C. Bowen
JOHN C. BOWEN
Capt.,333d Inf..
Comdg.

The letter describing the death of James Callery. SOURCE: Pierre Erens

ADOLPH J. NEGRI

Private First Class

84th Infantry Division

A hail of bullets

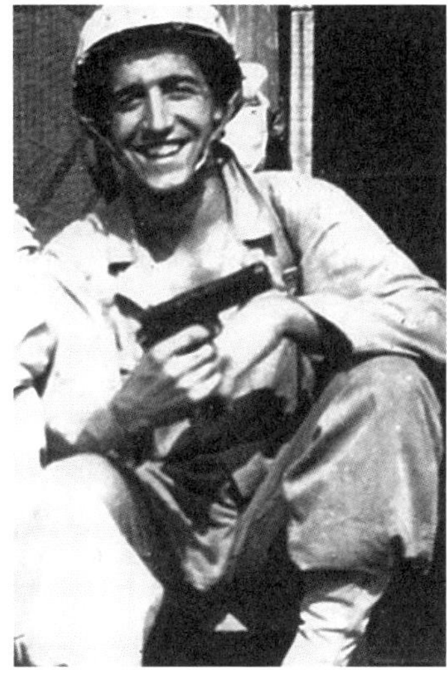

Private First Class Adolph J. Negri was born in Santa Cruz, California in 1922. Both his parents were immigrants from Italy. Adolph attended Santa Cruz High School. After his graduation in 1940, he moved to San Francisco and entered the building trades as an apprentice.

In December 1942, Adolph was inducted into the army. He was sent to Camp Howze in Texas for basic training and was then stationed at Camp Claiborne in Louisiana. After completing his advanced training there, Adolph briefly returned home and married his fiancée. She would later give birth to a son.

In May 1944, Adolph visited Santa Cruz for the last time. He then left for Europe. Adolph was assigned to Company G of the 334th Infantry Regiment, which was part of the 84th Infantry Division. The troops of this division called themselves the 'Railsplitters.'

On November 20, 1944, during Operation Clipper, Adolph and his company attacked strong German positions in the vicinity of the German village of Prummern, east of Geilenkirchen. Adolph lost his life during this attack and was posthumously awarded the Silver Star. The citation reads:

> ***'For gallantry in action against the enemy in Germany, November 20, 1944. When enemy machine gun fire delayed the advance of his company on a German town, PFC Adolph Negri, moving forward aggressively with his light machine gun, assaulted the enemy position alone in an effort to enable the advance to continue. He lost his life in this section when fire from several enemy positions was directed upon him.'***

Adolph was only 22 years old when he was killed. The final resting place of this brave young soldier in Margraten can be found in Plot P, Row 7, Grave 8.

ARTHUR W. COUNTRYMAN

Technical Sergeant

4th Infantry Division

They had already reserved a spot for him

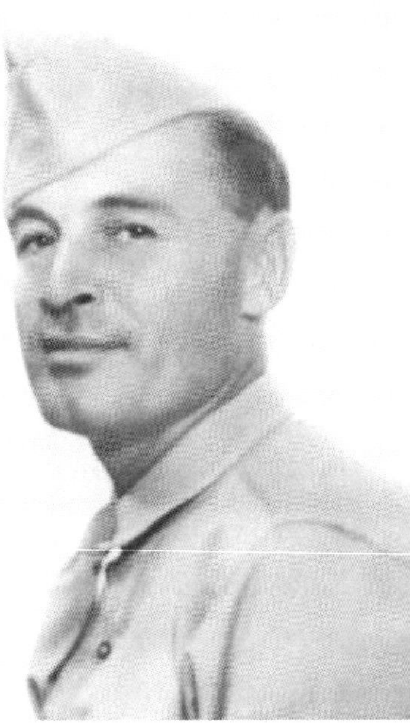

It had not just been her name that had been on the headstone on the grave of Lorretta Countryman in Plainfield, Illinois. It had also read the name of her husband Arthur W. Countryman, even though he was not actually buried there. The Technical Sergeant had been reported missing on November 20, 1944. When Lorretta passed away in 2000, it had still not become clear what had happened to him. Nevertheless, the family decided to put Arthur's name on the headstone as well, as an expression of their hopes that he would be found one day. And he was.

Arthur was the son of Charles and Emma. He was born in Plainfield on September 19, 1907. From an early age on, Arthur had had an interest in the military. He liked playing soldier and hoped to become one himself one day. As a matter of fact, when he was just fourteen years old, he ran away from home to get into the navy. He succeeded. When the navy called home, Arthur's father said: 'Fine. You can have him. At least I'll know where he's at for the next four years.' Arthur actually stayed in the navy even longer. He got out of the service in 1928.

After getting out, he got married to Lorretta Hamilton, with whom he started a family. Their first child, Eleanor, was born in 1930. Georgia was the last one of four and was born in 1936. The family continued to live in Plainfield in a house that Arthur had built himself.

But not long after he had finished the work on the house, Arthur enlisted into the National Guard in March 1941. He was ultimately sent overseas with Company F, 12th Infantry Regiment, 4th Infantry Division in 1944. The last his family saw of him was when he got on the train in Joliet to leave for training. 'He kissed us all and then got on the train and left,' Georgia remembered. Loretta, in the meantime, worked at the Elwood Ordinance Plant.

It was there that the army broke her the news that her husband had been killed. The telegram had been delivered to the house, but only Eleanor, fourteen at the time, was home. She went straight to Charles and Emma, who lived next door. They directed people to get Lorretta at the plant, while Eleanor phoned her siblings for them to come home. When Georgia did, she saw a uniformed man escorting her mum out of the car into the house. 'Well, I guess I don't have a dad anymore,' she thought. Lorretta had to raise the four children on her own.

In April 1947, German woodcutter Peter Rippegather came across unburied remains in the Hürtgen Forest near Germeter. Based on the circumstances in which the remains were found, the recovery team believed that this soldier had likely been killed by shrapnel. However, apart from Technical Sergeant stripes, they found nothing that could help identify the remains. They were sent to Margraten, but the dental records of soldiers who had gone missing in the area did not match with the remains that had been recovered. Therefore, the remains were buried as unknown in the Ardennes American Cemetery and Memorial. In 2021, DNA-analysis revealed that it was Arthur who had been found.

So, on August 6, 2021, his two surviving, grateful daughters, Mary and Georgia, were moved to tears when they could finally lay their father to rest. While they had also been given the option to bury him in either Margraten or Ardennes, they decided to bury Arthur in the place where there had already been reserved a spot for him: next to his wife. In Margraten, a rosette next to his name on the Walls of the Missing indicates that he is no longer missing.

FRANK X. MC WILLIAMS

First Lieutenant

743rd Tank Battalion

Died a few weeks after the death of his infant son

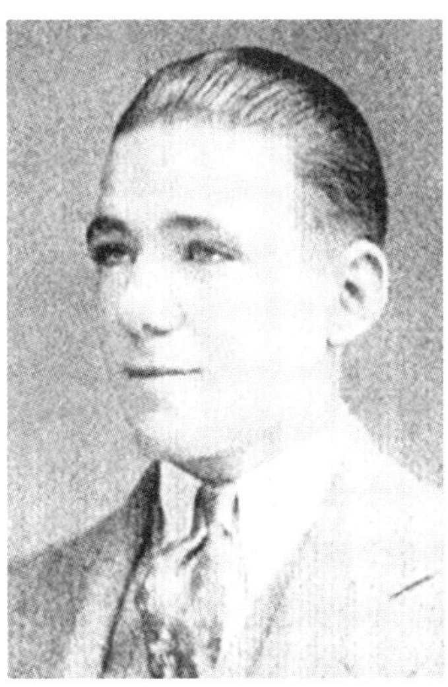

First Lieutenant Frank Xavier Mc Williams from New Jersey graduated from high school in 1934. He then attended John Marshall Law School. Prior to entering the army, Frank was employed as a lawyer.

Having already entered military service, Frank married Miss Jane Wiersching in January 1942. The couple settled in Campbell, Kentucky, and had an infant son, who sadly died on October 16, 1944, while Frank was already serving overseas.

Frank had left for Europe in August 1944. Upon his arrival in the ETO, he was attached to the 743rd Tank Battalion. This tank unit had been involved in combat since D-Day and crossed the Dutch border into the province of Limburg in September 1944. While the unit was advancing to the Dutch border with Germany, inhabitants of Maastricht, Valkenburg, and Heerlen saw tanks of the 743rd Tank Battalion rolling through their streets. The tanks then crossed the German border to break through the Siegfried Line.

Several weeks after he had lost his infant son, Frank himself lost his life when he suffered fatal injuries as a tank commander near the German village of Erberich on November 22, 1944. According to the combat history of his battalion, he was killed when three light tanks in a muddy orchard outside the village were caught by fire from what is thought to have been a self-propelled 75mm gun. Despite the fact that both the combat history and the After-Action Report of Frank's battalion stated that he was killed on November 22, the U.S. military recorded his date of death as November 21.

Frank was 28 years old when he was killed in action. He is permanently interred at the Netherlands American Cemetery and Memorial in Margraten. Anyone who wants to pay tribute to him there, should look for grave M-1-7.

FRANCIS P. PAGE

First Lieutenant

747th Tank Battalion

Killed inside the turret of his tank

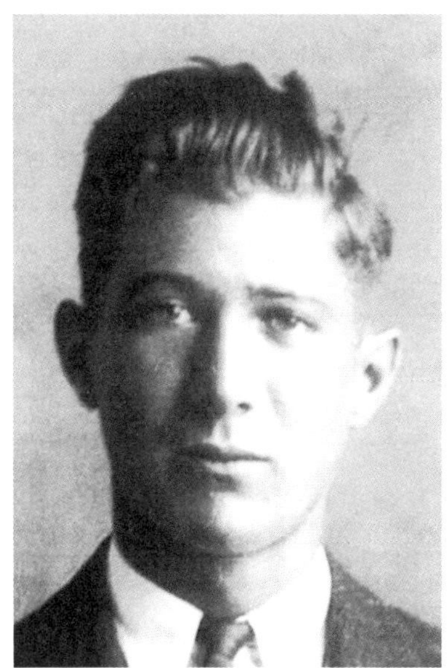

First Lieutenant Francis P. Page from Newark, New York, was born in 1914. In 1933, Francis graduated from Fairport High School. He married his beloved Mary and entered the U.S. Army in 1942.

After joining the army, Francis completed officer training at Fort Knox, Kentucky. In March 1944, he went overseas to Europe. There he fought in the 747th Tank Battalion. This independent tank unit disembarked in Normandy on Omaha Beach on D+1 (June 7, 1944) and then, like the other Allied units, fought its way through northern France and Belgium toward the German border. There, the tank battalion was then deployed in the assault against the Siegfried Line.

Within the battalion's Company B, Francis commanded a platoon of Sherman tanks. On November 21, 1944, the tanks of his platoon assisted the troops of the 29th Infantry Division in the attack on the German towns of Engelsdorf and Koslar. The Shermans slowly advanced behind the infantry troops who encountered heavy German machine gun and mortar fire. Three of the Sherman tanks of another platoon were demobilized by German Teller mines and were unable to keep up with the vulnerable infantrymen.

Francis' tank platoon continued the advance, but near the town of Koslar three of his tanks were knocked out by enemy anti-tank guns. One of these tanks was Francis' own tank. An 88mm shell fired by one of the German anti-tank guns penetrated the turret of his tank and killed him instantly. He was 30 years old.

Francis is permanently laid to rest at the Netherlands American Cemetery in Margraten. Visitors can pay tribute to him there by going to Plot C, Row 1, Grave 6.

LYLE A. WILLIAMS
Private First Class
84th Infantry Division

An improvised stretcher

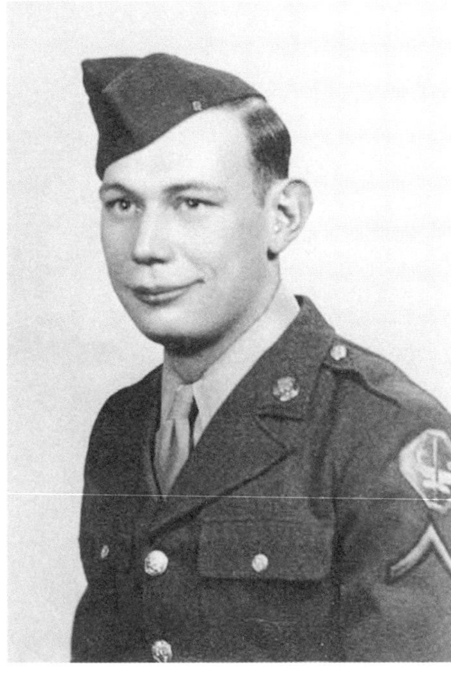

Private First Class Lyle A. Williams from Dubuque, Iowa, was a member of Company K, 333rd Infantry Regiment, 84th Infantry Division. He was born on December 22, 1921, and entered the army in 1943. In 1944, Lyle left for overseas duty in Europe.

Lyle and his buddies of Company K entered combat in November 1944, when they were to take part in Operation Clipper, a joint British-American attack in the vicinity of Geilenkirchen to eliminate a worrisome salient on the boundary between the British Second Army and the Ninth U.S. Army.

After the city of Geilenkirchen was taken, the 84th Infantry Division attempted to push the lines further forward. On November 21, Company K was ordered to attack along the Wurm River toward the villages of Kogenbroich and Würm, over a mile away. Lyle and the other men jumped off from Süggerath and attacked in full view of the six pillboxes on the forward slope in front of Müllendorf, which immediately began to strafe them. Nonetheless, driving the Germans before them, the riflemen advanced 400 yards and reached Schloss Leerodt, a castle located about halfway between Süggerath and Müllendorf. The Americans took the deserted castle without a struggle, but when they ventured out into the fields beyond all hell broke loose. The Germans raked them with an overwhelming concentration of machine gun, mortar and artillery fire. Company K was pinned down and had no choice but to pull back to positions around the castle.

At around 4:00 p.m. – after Battalion Headquarters had ordered to do so – Company K renewed the attack. Again, they were met by a murderous hail of machine gun bullets, artillery shells, and mortar rounds. The men sought cover in the heavy muck, but Lyle was one of the unlucky ones who was hit. 'Williams took a full burst of German machine gun fire in the stomach' and was mortally wounded, one of the company's veterans recalled. Four men carried him back on a stretcher 'crudely fashioned from rifles and raincoats,' but by the time they arrived at the castle he was dead.

Lyle lost his life one month short of his 23rd birthday. In the last week of November, he was buried at the temporary U.S. Military Cemetery at Margraten. After it was decided in 1947 that this would become a permanent cemetery, Lyle eventually received his final resting place there in Plot C, Row 4, Grave 16.

Several weeks after Lyle was killed, his mother Harriet had received a letter of condolence sent to her by Brigadier General Alexander R. Bolling, commander of the 84th Infantry Division in the ETO. In it he told her, 'The entire division has suffered a personal loss in the death of your son. He met his death while engaged in action against the enemy. During the stress of combat he remained cheerful and cool-headed, and was an inspiration to his fellow soldiers. All who knew Private Williams join with me in extending to you our heartfelt sympathy and condolence.'

ARTHUR B. HUNT JR.

Second Lieutenant

84th Infantry Division

Killed in the midst of overwhelming German fire

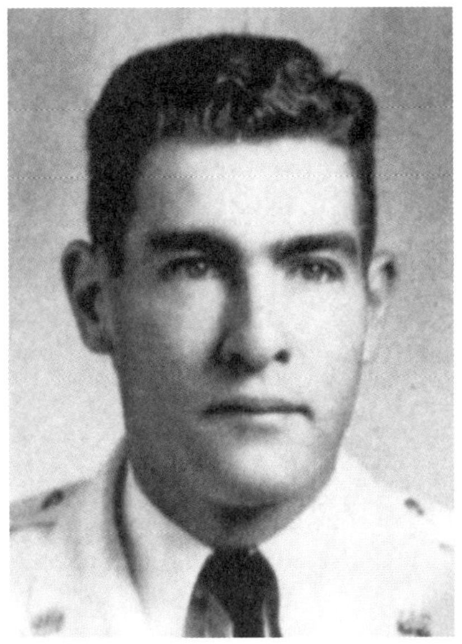

Second Lieutenant Arthur B. Hunt Jr., whose hometown was Ocean Springs in Mississippi, was born in 1920. He studied at Tulane University in New Orleans, but after the first year he switched to The Citadel, the military academy of South Carolina in Charleston. Arthur was never able to graduate there, as his entire class was inducted into active military service.

After completing officer training at Fort Benning, Arthur was assigned to Company I of the 333rd Infantry Regiment. This regiment was part of the 84th Infantry Division. With this division, Arthur entered combat in the vicinity of the German city of Geilenkirchen in November 1944.

After Geilenkirchen had been taken on November 19, 1944, Arthur's regiment had to continue advancing along the Wurm River. This was an extremely difficult task. The British tanks that had to support the American infantrymen hardly made any progress due to the heavy rainfall, the muddy ground, and German mines. Nevertheless, Arthur's regiment managed to capture the village of Süggerath by nightfall on the 19th.

On November 21, the attack was resumed toward Müllendorf and Würm. The 3rd Battalion, of which Arthur's Company I was a part, tried to advance, but was heavily fired upon by German machine guns and artillery. Arthur was killed during the attack. He therefore remained forever 24. He is permanently interred in Margraten, where his final resting place can be found in Plot E, Row 6, Grave 18.

JOHN W. CAHILL

Technical Sergeant

446th Bombardment Group

Drowned in the IJsselmeer

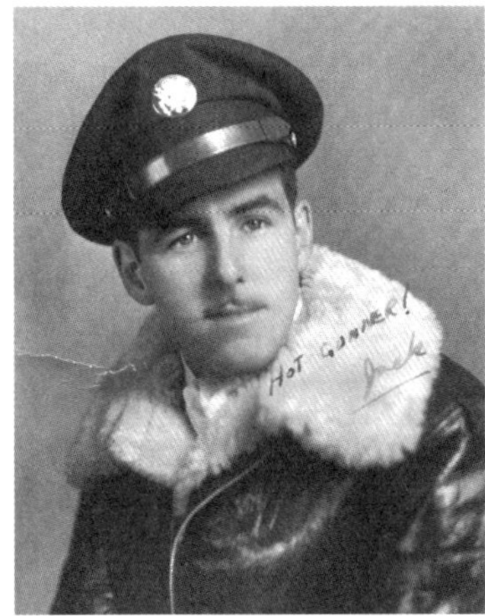

Technical Sergeant John W. Cahill from New Hampshire was born in 1923. When John joined the U.S. Army Air Forces in 1942, he lived in California. His father had already died of diabetes by then. Financially, the family was struggling since their cigar factory went bankrupt in 1929. While in military service, John therefore sent as much of his pay to his mother and sister at home.

In 1944, John served as radio operator in a B-24 'Liberator' of the 706th Bomb Squadron. This squadron was part of the 446th Bombardment Group. The bomber in which he flew had been nicknamed 'Satan's Little Sister' by him and the other members of the crew.

Four of John's brothers were also in the military. They wrote letters to each other and their mother regularly from the time they entered the army. Many of the letters can be found in the book *Dear Mom: A Family Finds Its Past in World War II Letters Home.*

On November 21, 1944, John's B-24 took off in England to participate in a bombing attack on the German city of Hamburg. However, over the target, after making the bomb run, the plane was hit by German anti-aircraft fire (Flak). The bomber was severely damaged as a result and one of the engines was feathered. Despite this, the pilot managed to keep the plane in the air for quite a while during the return flight. But when they almost flew over the Dutch island of Texel, it became clear that they would not reach England. Therefore, the pilot gave the order to bail out.

John bailed out of the aircraft. Because they were flying over the Dutch coastline at the time, this seemed to be the right moment. However, due to a sudden change in wind direction, John landed in the IJsselmeer – a large Dutch lake. The sad result was that John subsequently drowned in the icy water. He was only 21 years old.

A fishing boat found John's body on February 3, 1945. Three days later, he and several others were buried at Rusthof cemetery in Amersfoort. A cemetery employee described the scene in letters to John's mother: 'The coffins were in the central hall, covered with flowers and a flag. The organist played a few songs and then they were brought out by employees. They were buried next to other airmen.'

On February 28, 1946, U.S. Army personnel exhumed the bodies and brought them to Margraten. The employee of Rusthof cemetery promised John's mother to go there to take a picture of the grave. In Margraten, John was given his final resting place in Plot J, Row 1, Grave 8. His brother Tom, who lost his life when his B-25 crashed in Italy two days after John's body was found, is buried in Kansas.

John and the rest of his crew. John stands far right.
SOURCE: Michelle Cahill

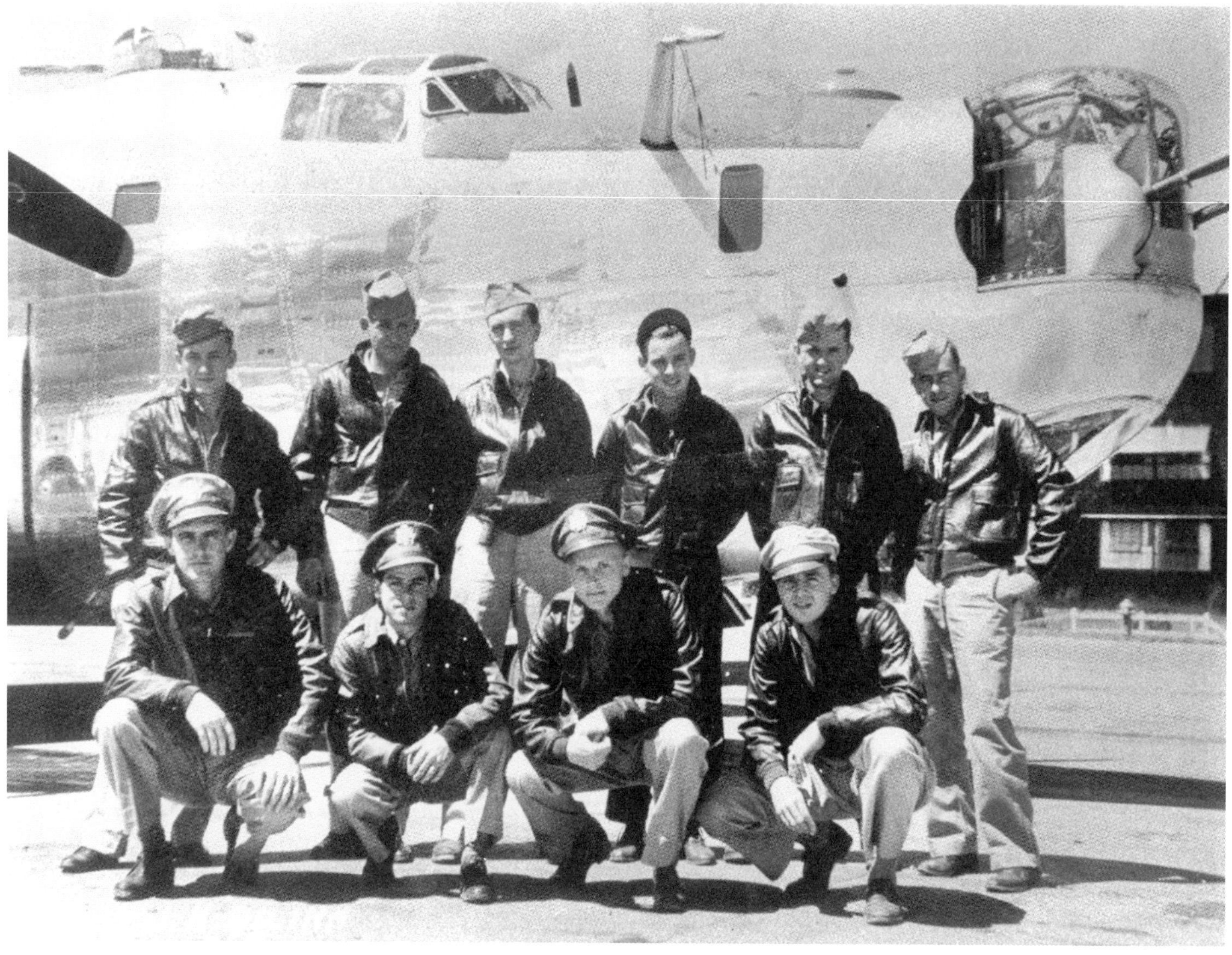

JOHN W. HORTON

First Lieutenant

771st Tank Destroyer Battalion

Hit by an enemy gun

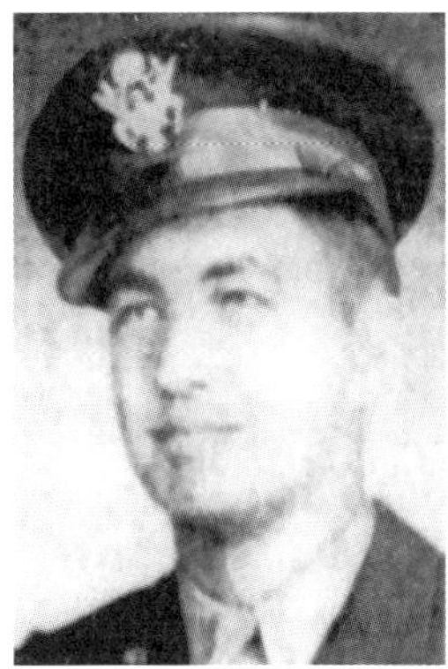

John W. Horton from North Carolina was born in 1917 and served as First Lieutenant in the 771st Tank Destroyer Battalion. This unit was activated at Fort Ethan Allen in Vermont in December 1941. In October 1943, the battalion left New York Harbor to set sail for England, arriving in Liverpool on November 2, 1943. From England, the various companies were transferred to France in August and September 1944. From there, the 771st Tank Destroyer Battalion was sent to the front lines in Germany to assist in the breakthrough offensives against the Siegfried Line.

During his service with the 771st Tank Destroyer Battalion, John served as a platoon leader in Company A and was the commander of an M10 tank destroyer. Tank destroyers of this type were commonly called 'Wolverine' and featured an open turret with a 76mm gun and a heavy machine gun. While the open turret provided the crew with a good view, it simultaneously made the men in the M10s vulnerable to artillery fire and enemy air strikes.

On November 22, 1944, John's platoon left its assembly area in Gereonsweiler to support an attack of the 102nd Division's 405th Infantry Regiment in the vicinity of the German villages of Lindern and Beeck. During this attack, John was killed at the age of 27 when his tank destroyer was hit by a German gun. According to his battalion's After-Action Report, the fatal round must have been fired by what appeared to be an 88mm gun or the gun of a dug-in German tank.

John's remains are buried at the U.S. Military Cemetery in Margraten. His final resting place there can be found in Plot P, Row 9, Grave 2. John's death is reported on November 22, 1944, but the information in the After-Action Report suggests that he was killed a day earlier.

WILLIAM F. DELANEY

Private First Class

4th Infantry Division

Killed in his foxhole

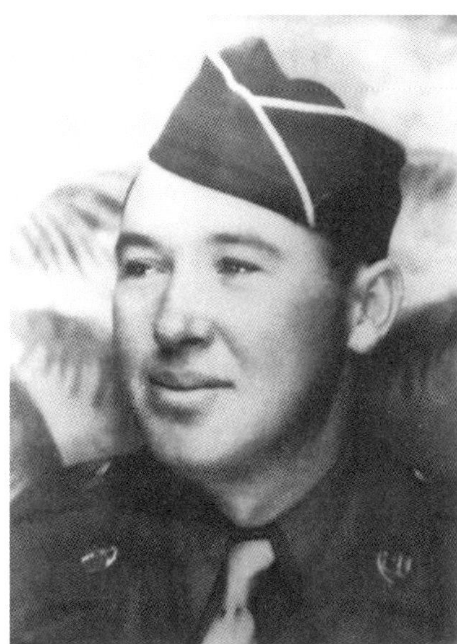

Private First Class William F. Delaney from Kingston, Tennessee, entered the army at Fort Oglethorpe, Georgia, on November 14, 1942. He was a member of Company A, 1st Battalion, 22nd Infantry Regiment, 4th Infantry Division. This division entered combat in Normandy where it assaulted Utah Beach on D-Day, and then took part in the capture of Cherbourg and its crucial harbor facilities.

While the 'Ivy Division' – which was the 4th Division's nickname – was still fighting in Normandy, William was wounded. His digitalized Hospital Admission Card states that he was hospitalized in June 1944 and that fragments of an artillery shell were removed from his lower extremity. In August, William was discharged from the hospital to rejoin his unit.

In November 1944, the men of the 4th Infantry Division entered the Hürtgen Forest. During the brutal battle that took place there William lost his life at the age of 24. On November 22, 1944, an enemy artillery shell struck his foxhole near the town of Grosshau, and he died before he could be medically evacuated. Due to ongoing fighting, William's remains could not be recovered at that time. Therefore, he was listed as Missing in Action.

Following the end of the war, American Graves Registration Command (AGRC) teams traveled to Grosshau to search for William's remains, but all efforts proved unsuccessful.
In December 1950, the War Department therefore declared him non-recoverable.

In 1947, during the period of field investigation, AGRC had recovered a set of unknown remains from a section of the forest west of Grosshau. The remains were first discovered by a local citizen, Siegfried Glassen, who concluded they were of an American soldier who had been killed by artillery fire. The remains were sent to the AGRC central identification point in Neuville, Belgium, but all efforts to identify them were unsuccessful. Therefore, the remains, by then designated as X-5425 Neuville, were declared unidentifiable and interred at the temporary

American cemetery that was situated there (today's Ardennes American Cemetery).

Following thorough analysis of military records and AGRC documentation, historians and scientists from the Defense POW/MIA Accounting Agency (DPAA) determined that PFC Delaney was a strong candidate for association with remains X-5425 Neuville. The remains were disinterred in June 2017 and were then sent to the DPAA for analysis. Using dental, anthropological and DNA analysis, DPAA scientists were able to determine that X-5425 Neuville was indeed PFC Delaney. He was accounted for on December 17, 2018, and his remains were permanently laid to rest in Lawnville, Tennessee on May 27, 2019. In Margraten, where William's name is recorded on the Walls of the Missing, a small rosette is placed next to his name to indicate he has been accounted for.

LAWRENCE B. CARTER
Second Lieutenant
17th Tank Battalion

A direct hit

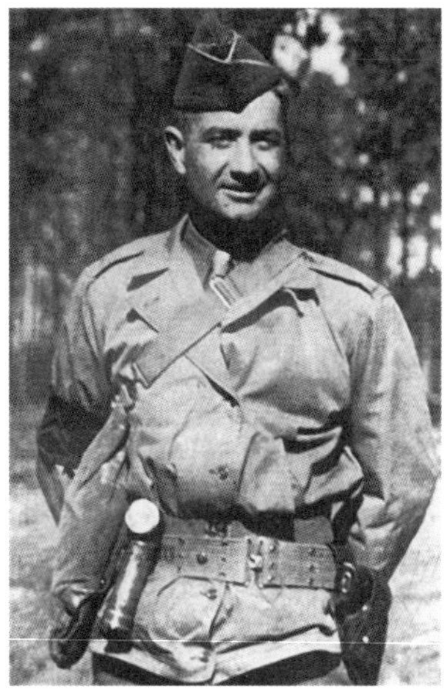

Second Lieutenant Lawrence B. Carter from New York was born on May 12, 1914. After graduating from Olean High School in 1932, Lawrence had enlisted in the Regular Army in 1933. In 1936, he was discharged at the expiration of his term of enlistment. The following year, Lawrence married Miss Genevieve Archibald. They resided in Portville.

In 1940, Lawrence enlisted in the Regular Army Reserve. He was again honorably discharged in 1941. In July 1942, he again volunteered for service in the army and went to the Officer Candidate School at Fort Knox. He was commissioned as a Second Lieutenant in November and was assigned to the 7th Armored Division. Lawrence then went overseas to Europe, where he acted as Company A commander in the 17th Tank Battalion, which was equipped with Sherman tanks. He was given command of the company in October 1944.

On November 23, 1944, the 17th Tank Battalion supported the 405th Infantry Regiment's attack on Beeck, northeast of the German city of Geilenkirchen. Lawrence directed the movements of his company's tanks, but according to the After-Action Report 'they started receiving heavy anti-tank fire, artillery fire and small arms fire from the town of Beeck to their front and from the high ground to the northeast of Beeck. The enemy positions were smoked by the tanks and supporting elements but Lt. Carter's tank received a direct hit on the turret at about 1500.' A little further on in the report, it is described that Lt. Nizenski, whose tank was knocked out a few minutes after Carter's tank, 'had very little hope for Lt. Carter having gotten out of his tank for he was sure that he was hit in the turret and that the tank had burned.'

The direct hit in the tank's turret took Lawrence's life. He died at the age of 30. Lawrence is permanently interred at the U.S. Military Cemetery in Margraten. Visitors can pay tribute to him there by going to Plot H, Row 3, Grave 1.

WILLIAM V. LUNDY JR.
Private
41st Armored Infantry Regiment

In the footsteps of his father

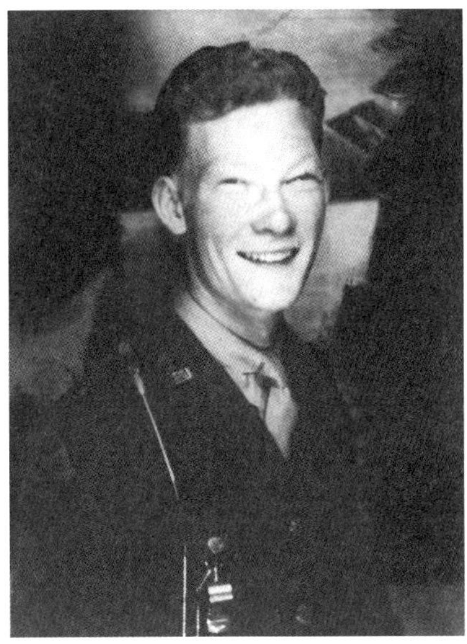

Charles Lundy grew up without thinking too much about his late father. His mother had remarried just after the war. His stepfather was the only 'Dad' he knew. Besides, he knew that it was too painful for his mother to bring up old memories. His grandparents did tell him about their son, his father, though. They also had an old army footlocker full of his toys, photos, and other documents. Charles loved playing with his father's old toys. He forgot most of the stories his grandparents had told him as he grew older, but there came a time in his life when his interest in his dad began to grow. It ultimately led to a trip to his father's grave and site of death.

William Vernon Lundy Jr. grew up in the Deep South, in the state of Mississippi. Only just an adult, he decided to join the army in October 1940, even though the U.S. was not yet engaged in the war that was raging in the rest of the world. His training took him a number of states, including Kentucky, Georgia, and North Carolina. However, he met his wife in the place where he had spent most of his life: Lexington. Mary Sue Morgan and William got married in August 1941.

He had trained for nearly two years before his unit was sent overseas. In November 1942, the unit experienced its baptism of fire in North Africa. Serving in the 41st Armored Infantry Regiment, 2nd Armored Division, William would then see action in Italy, Normandy, and Germany, among other places.

While William saw much of the world, he would never get to see his son. Charles was born in March 1943; William was far from home by then. All he ever would hold were photos of his son, who only was one year old at the time of his death.

In 2008, Charles began searching the Internet for more information about his father. Slowly but surely, the pieces of the puzzle fell into place. He managed to trace most of his father's journey through the war.

Moreover, he got in touch with the adopters of his father's grave, the Fijten family. William had been billeted in their house on the Oudestraat in Amstenrade. The family's children loved the presence of American soldiers in the town as the soldiers gave them candy and chewing gum. That is why William, just before his unit moved out, left behind a surprise for them: he filled one of the house's drawers completely with candy, gum, cigarettes, and others treats. After the war, the family adopted his grave. It has been passed on from generation to generation since.

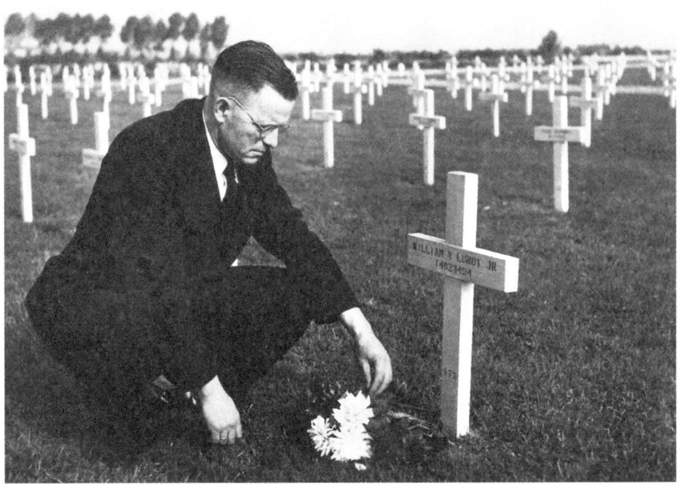

Fijten senior at the grave of William Lundy. SOURCE: Charles Lundy

Charles often talked with the Fijten family about his desire to visit his father's grave. In 2014, he finally decided to go. He knew that there would come a time when he would no longer be able to make the long trip from Hawaii, where he still lives. And so, in September of that year he stood, with a lump in his throat, at his father's gravesite in Plot C, Row 19, Grave 3 for the first time. When he rubbed in his father's name on the grave marker with sand from Omaha Beach, he realized that had finally made the journey he had long been wanting to make.

But this was not the end of Charles' journey. After the visit to the cemetery, he followed his father's footsteps in Germany. He made it to the town of Merzenhaus, where his father had lost his life on November 23, 1944. Where his father's life had ended, Charles' journey came to an end 70 years later.

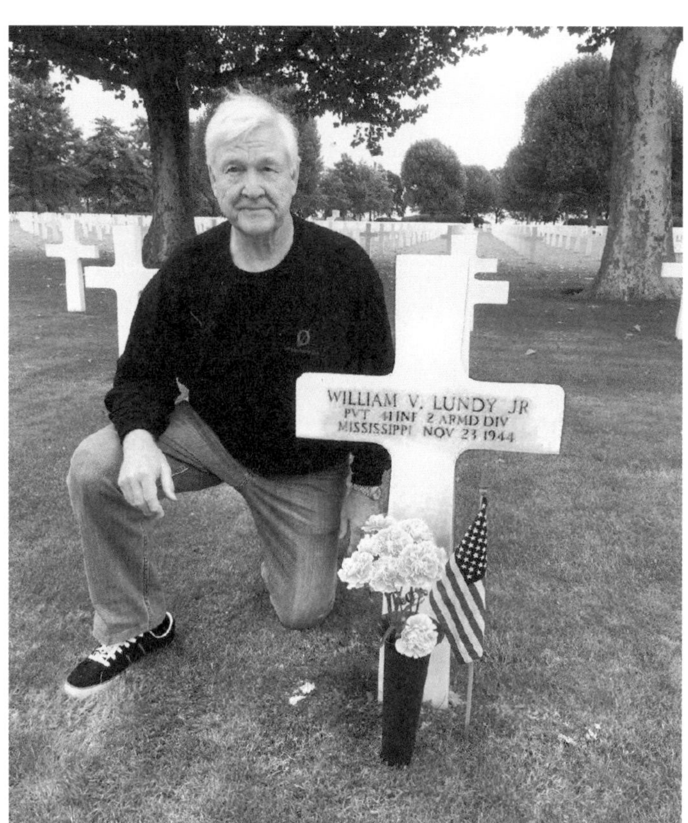

After all those years, Charles is finally able to visit his father's grave.
SOURCE: Charles Lundy

RAYMOND J. BELANGER
Private First Class
102nd Infantry Division

'A fine boy in school'

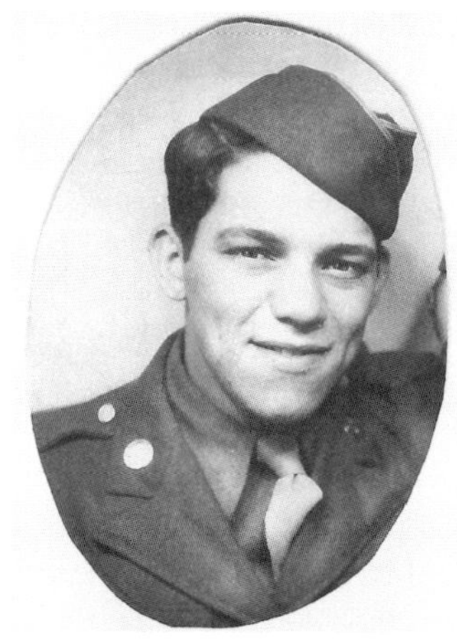

Private First Class Raymond J. Belanger was born in Quebec, Canada in 1925. He moved to Massena, New York, when he was two years old and attended local schools there. On June 28, 1943, Raymond joined the U.S. Army at Utica, New York.

Raymond served as a combat medic with the 405th Infantry Regiment, which was part of the 102nd Infantry Division. This division arrived in France in September 1944, and entered the front line several weeks later. During the final weeks of 1944, it then took part in the Allied attack to the river Roer.

On November 23, 1944, when the 405th Infantry was fighting just across the Netherlands-German border near the German towns of Beeck and Prummern, Raymond displayed extraordinary courage for which he was later awarded the Silver Star. 'Although his company was pinned down by intense machine gun fire, Private First Class Belanger moved freely over open ground to administer first aid and evacuate the wounded from the battlefield,' the citation reads in part. While 'constantly fired upon by enemy snipers, he unhesitatingly continued on his mission until he was mortally wounded.' The book *With the 102nd Infantry Division Through Germany* says that Raymond's fatal wounds were caused by machine gun fire.

Raymond was only nineteen years old when he lost his life. He is buried at the Netherlands American Cemetery and Memorial in Margraten, where his final resting place can be visited in Plot A, Row 19, Grave 19.

Massena veteran Roy Mittiga, who had attended school together with Raymond and who had also served as a medic during the war, cherishes his memories of his childhood friend. Every time he goes by 104 East Orvis Street, the house in which Raymond had grown up, his memories flash back, Mittiga told a journalist of the Watertown Daily Times in 2021. 'He was a fine boy in school,' he recalled. 'We were friends in school.' Mittiga also told that Raymond 'deserved some sort of tribute.' Therefore, he arranged a small ceremony in front of 104 East Orvis Street, during which members of the Amvets Post 4 Rifle Squad fired off several volleys to honor Raymond.

JOSEPH AKERS

Corporal

803rd Tank Destroyer Battalion

Identified after almost 74 years

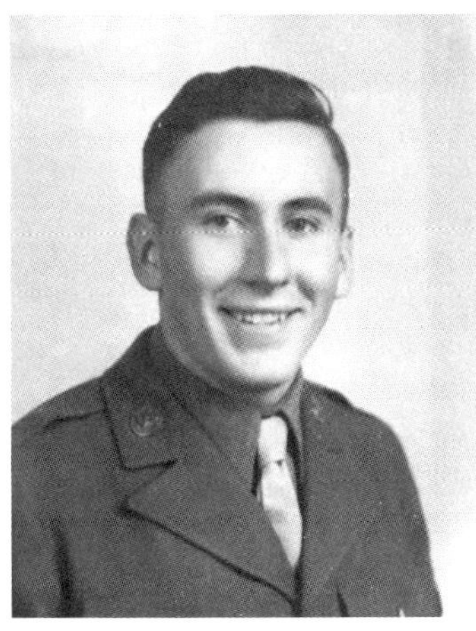

Corporal Joseph Akers from West Virginia was born in 1921. He attended high school for three years, lived in Kenova and worked on his father's farm. In 1942, Joseph entered the army and after an intensive period of training he went overseas to Europe.

During his service, Joseph fought in an M10 tank destroyer of the 803rd Tank Destroyer Battalion. The M10 was the first type of tank destroyer to be put into service by the U.S. Army. As armament, the M10s had a powerful long-barreled 76mm cannon and a heavy machine gun. The major disadvantage of the M10 was its open turret. This made the crew vulnerable to artillery fire and enemy air strikes.

On November 25, 1944, Joseph's Company C was deployed in the German Hürtgen Forest to support an infantry attack on the village of Grosshau. During this attack, Joseph was killed at the age of 23 when his tank destroyer was knocked out by enemy fire. The After-Action Report of his battalion states that Company C was subjected to fire from dug-in German anti-tank guns and artillery at the time his tank destroyer was hit.

After the battle, Joseph was listed as missing in action. Despite the fact that nothing of his remains had been recovered at the time, his status was changed to 'killed in action' on December 21, 1944.

Almost 74 years after Joseph went missing, the Defense POW/MIA Accounting Agency (DPAA) announced that he was accounted for on April 30, 2018. It turned out that his remains had been found in 1947, inside a destroyed American tank destroyer near Grosshau. Due to their condition, the remains could not be identified at the time. The advent of mitochondrial DNA analysis later offered new possibilities for the investigation of remains that were buried as unknown soldiers in U.S. military cemeteries. The identification of Joseph's remains is a result of this.

After Joseph was officially accounted for, his remains were handed over to his family, whereupon he was permanently interred in the United States. At Margraten, a rosette was placed next to his name on the Walls of the Missing. This indicates to visitors that he has been found.

RICHARD A. KNOTT

Private First Class

7th Armored Division

A fatal joke

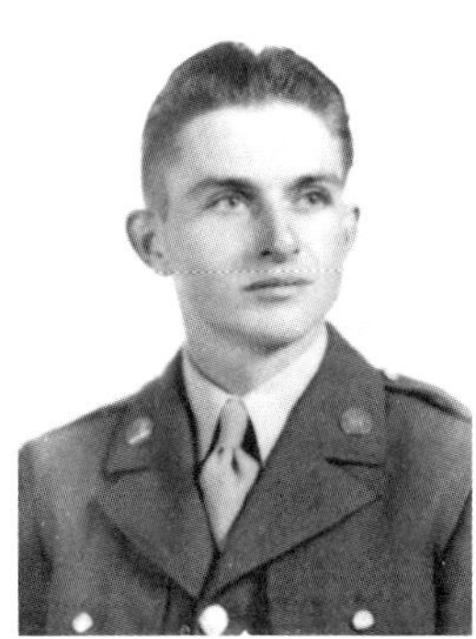

Richard A. Knott, born in Winchester, Tennessee, on December 18, 1920, was a jeep driver in the 38th Infantry Battalion of the 7th Armored Division. On November 26, 1944, he and his buddies were offered lodging for the night in the home of the Brull family in Ransdaal, the Netherlands. Mrs. Brull did not like it that the American soldiers otherwise had to sleep outside in the cold.

The next morning, after sleeping in a nice bed, Richard went outside to get some food. He took a can of peaches from the mess truck and started eating them on his way back to the house of the Brull family. Richard shared a few peaches with some of his buddies inside the house, but jokingly told his squad leader, Cpl. Walter Gapinski, that he couldn't have any. Cpl. Gapinski continued the joke by replying that if Richard didn't give him some peaches, he would shoot him. He grabbed what he thought was his rifle, which he had just cleaned and knew was not loaded, and pointed it at Richard. The bantering suddenly came to an abrupt end with the explosive report of a gunshot. Cpl. Gapinski had mistakenly grabbed another rifle that had been leaning next to his, one which was loaded and didn't have the safety on, and accidentally bumped the trigger when he pointed it at Richard. To his and everyone's horror, the bullet struck the 23-year-old Richard in the chest-neck area, fatally wounding him. Richard bled to death almost immediately...

The Brull family and the soldiers who witnessed the incident inside the house were deeply shocked, especially Gapinski. He did not understand how this could have happened, but then found out that he had accidentally grabbed Sam Carrubba's rifle. Carrubba, an inexperienced replacement who had recently joined the squad, had forgotten to put his rifle's safety on when he had set it with the others by the fireplace. The consequence of that mistake would haunt him for years.

The deadly incident at the Brull family home was investigated by the U.S. Army Military Police, but because the eyewitnesses could prove that the shooting was accidental, not intentional, Gapinski was not charged. Nevertheless, he was transferred to the division's 48th Armored Infantry Battalion the following day.

In December 1944, Richard was buried at the U.S. Military Cemetery in Margraten. At his family's request he got his final resting place there too. Visitors can find it in Plot F, Row 20, Grave 13. On the 64-year anniversary of PFC Richard A. Knott's death in 2008, a memorial plaque in his honor was unveiled near the house where he had died.

HUBERT T. BAUMAN II

First Lieutenant

29th Infantry Division

He elected to fight

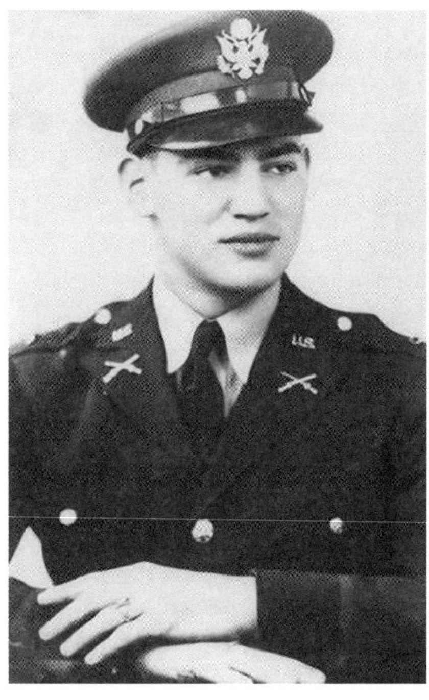

First Lieutenant Hubert T. Bauman II from Michigan was born in 1921. He studied at the Michigan State College of Agriculture and Applied Science and after graduation entered military service at some point. Then, after arriving in Europe, Hubert served in Company E, 115th Infantry Regiment, 29th Infantry Division. He joined this unit in Brest, France, on August 31, 1944.

On November 27, 1944, Hubert was in charge of his company during fierce fighting near the German town of Kirchberg. Just north of the village, Company E was pinned down by enemy fire near a paper mill. Hubert reported back to the 2nd Battalion commander, Major Warfield, that their advance was halted by approximately 100 German troops and four self-propelled guns.

Nevertheless, an eleven-man squad from Company E led by Staff Sergeant John Kwekel managed to work its way into one of the mill buildings, but according to the action report, the Germans reacted by 'infiltrating between this group and the remainder of the company from trenches and woods south of the mill,' resulting in the surrounding of the group. Kwekel's men used their rifles, rifle grenades, and hand grenades to flush out the infiltrating Germans, but the enemy countered with machine gun fire. Kwekel's squad was completely isolated and their situation was very worrisome.

Meanwhile, Hubert drew the conclusion that his company was too weakened to be able to relieve Kwekel's squad. Therefore, he sent a message to the battalion command post asking for reinforcements. A platoon of Company G, supported by some M5 Stuart tanks, tried to reach Kwekel's besieged squad, but failed to break through along the main road to the mill. The road was filled with mines and the Germans forced the infantrymen and the supporting tanks to withdraw with intense small arms, mortar, and self-propelled gun fire. Therefore, Kwekel and his men could not be relieved.

A little later, Hubert saw a rifle platoon of Company I approaching. By now darkness had fallen, but he decided to pick up the soldiers to give them instructions and lead them to the mill. When he had picked up the men, Hubert walked back in the direction of the mill along a path parallel to a stone fence. Then, with the rifle platoon strung out behind him, suddenly several German soldiers popped up from the other side of the fence. They ordered him to put his hands up, but Hubert made a motion as if to reach for his carbine. The German soldiers immediately shot him. As a result, Hubert died at the age of 23. He is buried in Margraten, where he was given his final resting place in Plot C, Row 6, Grave 24. Hubert was also posthumously awarded the Silver Star. His citation reads:

> ***'On November 27, 1944, during the attack on the strongly-held town of Kirchberg, Germany, Company 'E' sustained heavy casualties including all officers with the exception of First Lieutenant Bauman, company commander. In desperate need of reinforcements, he was leading a platoon of Company 'I' into position when they were ambushed by a strong enemy force. In the face of overwhelming odds, he elected to fight rather than surrender his command and was killed in an effort to cover the withdrawal of his men. The courage and leadership displayed by Lieutenant Bauman in this action were of the highest order and reflect great credit upon himself and the military service.'***

SHIRLEY E. BAILEY
Private
4th Infantry Division

Saved many lives

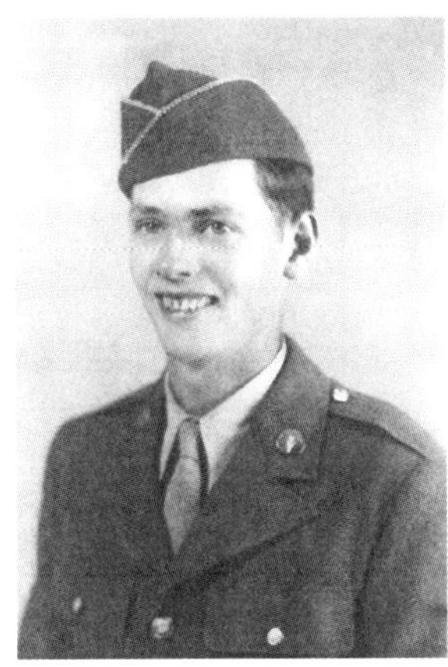

Private Shirley E. Bailey from Charleston, West Virginia, was born in 1925 and entered the army in 1943. In the fall of 1944, he was a medic with Company G, 8th Infantry Regiment, 4th Infantry Division, which at the time was attempting the capture the northern parts of the Hürtgen Forest in Germany. For his extraordinary efforts to administer aid to wounded men of his unit, Shirley was awarded the Silver Star. His citation reveals the dangerous conditions in which he bravely performed his tasks:

> ***'Pvt. Bailey went forward through heavy enemy machine gun, mortar and artillery fires during an attack against a strong German position in the Hürtgen Forest to direct and assist in the removal of several hundred casualties. Pvt. Bailey worked continually for over fourteen hours under recurrent hostile artillery barrages to administer aid to the wounded and direct litter bearers in the evacuation of the seriously wounded. He unhesitatingly went back and forth through mine fields from one point to another until all wounded were evacuated. Pvt. Bailey's medical skill and daring in constantly exposing himself to the most hazardous conditions of combat were responsible for saving many lives.'***

The fact that Shirley was not wounded during this action seems almost a miracle. However, he too had to pay the ultimate price for his courage when he went missing on November 29, 1944. A sworn statement from a fellow medic, T/5 James S. Sweatt, which is included in Shirley's IDPF, provides details of what has happened to him:

> ***'I was a medical aid man with Company G, 8th Infantry on the 29th of November 1944 in the Hürtgen Forest, Germany. We jumped off at about 1000 that morning across a trail and met small arms and mortar fire. During the attack two or three men were wounded by small arms fire. PFC [sic] Shirley E. Bailey, 35772887, an aid man also attached to Company G, 8th Inf., went to the aid of PFC Castulo Camarillo, 38367351, Company G, who was wounded. As he was running to assist Camarillo he was shot through the head by small arms fire. When I went over to him and looked him over, he was already dead, laying face down. (...) His body was approximately 40 yards from German dugouts built of logs with dirt roofs.'***

T/5 Sweatt thus stated that Shirley had been killed by 'small arms fire.' This primarily referred to rifles and (sub-)machine guns. Due to his regiment's After-Action Report, it is known that his unit was subjected to German machine gun fire throughout the day, but it is not clear whether Shirley was killed by a bullet from a machine gun or a rifle; this cannot be determined. What we do know with certainty, is that Shirley was just nineteen years old when he lost his life...

Due to the ongoing fighting in the wooded area where he was shot, Shirley's remains were not recovered by members of his unit during the battle. After the war, the American Graves Registration Command collected hundreds of unknown sets of remains from battlefields in Germany, and labeled each set with an X-number. One set of remains, designated X-4734 Neuville, had been recovered from an isolated grave near Schlich, Germany, in December 1946. Medical technicians were unable to identify them in the 1940s and the remains were buried in the Ardennes American Cemetery at Neuville-en-Condroz, Belgium, as an unknown soldier.

In October 2016, DPAA researchers, including Dr. Ian M. Spurgeon, made a historical association between X-4734 Neuville and Pvt. Shirley E. Bailey, based on the recovery site of the remains and his location of loss. Spurgeon, who began working on cases of soldiers missing from combat in the Hürtgen Forest in 2015, provided the authors of this book more details about the investigation of X-4734 Neuville. He wrote:

> ***'The American graves registration team which had found the remains in 1946 in a field grave along the northern edge of the Hürtgen Forest had learned that the remains had originally been found deeper within the forest by a German civilian shortly after the war. He had discovered them lying on the ground. They had a U.S. uniform and equipment, but no dog tags or obvious means of identification. The civilian had taken the remains a couple of miles away and buried them closer to a town. Fortunately, he told the graves registration team in 1946 where he had originally found them. The graves registration officials at the time did not have a comprehensive understanding of everyone missing in the Hürtgen Forest, or in that part of the forest. They were unable to associate the remains to Pvt. Bailey and eventually buried the remains as an unknown soldier.'***

By the time Spurgeon reviewed the case in 2016, the investigators did have a comprehensive view of who was still missing from the Hürtgen Forest campaign and where each soldier was likely killed:

'When I looked at the area where the German civilian had found the X-4734 remains, it overlapped the coordinates recorded as Pvt. Bailey's likely loss location. With this information, I wrote a comprehensive historical report explaining the known details of X-4734 Neuville and the combat history in the area. I listed Pvt. Bailey as the top historical candidate. (...) Fortunately, this case proved to be relatively straightforward. The DPAA scientists reviewing the documentation (such as dental charts and medical forms) confirmed that X-4734 Neuville could be Pvt. Bailey, and we received permission to exhume the remains. Very importantly, we received a DNA family reference sample from Pvt. Bailey's family. So, once the remains were exhumed from the Ardennes American Cemetery in Belgium and sent to the DPAA laboratory in Nebraska, our scientists collected the necessary anthropological data and DNA samples for comparison. The results came back that X-4734 Neuville was indeed Pvt. Bailey.'

Thanks to the efforts of Dr. Spurgeon and a many other researchers, both American and German, Pvt. Shirley E. Bailey was finally accounted for in 2017. His remains were subsequently buried with full military honors in Dunbar, West Virginia. In Margraten, where Shirley is listed on the Walls of the Missing, a rosette was placed next to his name to indicate he has been found.

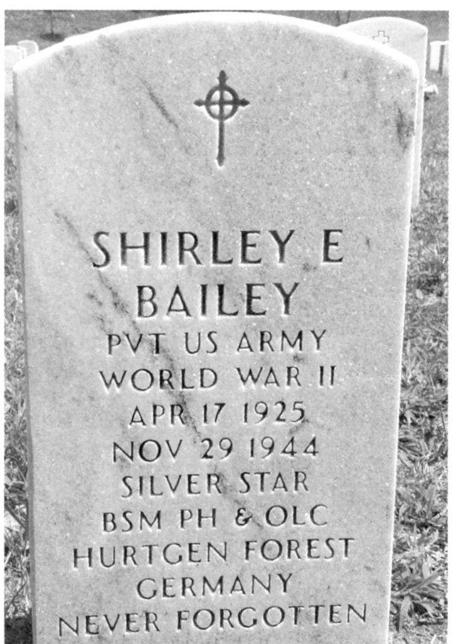

Pvt. Shirley E. Bailey's grave at the Donel C. Kinnard Memorial State Veterans Cemetery in Dunbar, West Virginia. SOURCE: FindAGrave.com

SYLVAN VAN AALTEN

Private First Class

8th Infantry Division

Jewish soldier with Dutch roots

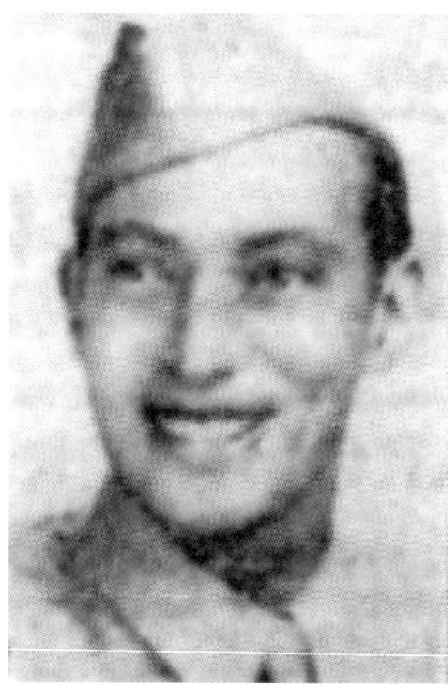

Sylvan van Aalten was born in the Belgian city of Antwerp on May 17, 1913. His father was born in London and his mother was from Amsterdam. She died in 1935. Sylvan was 21 years old at the time.

The Van Aalten family had emigrated to the United States in 1916, where they had settled in New York. Sylvan attended high school for four years and then worked in the jewelry business. Before he entered the U.S. Army in January 1944, he was a sergeant in the New York State Guard. After he arrived in Europe, Sylvan was assigned to Company E of the 28th Infantry Regiment. This was one of the regiments of the 8th Infantry Division.

In November 1944, Sylvan and his division were involved in the bloody fighting in the Hürtgen Forest. This vast and hilly German forest was a veritable hell of mines, mud, machine gun nests and exploding enemy shells. It took many thousands of American lives to push back the Germans and break through to the Roer.

At the end of the bloody November month in the Hürtgen Forest, Sylvan's regiment was fighting in the vicinity of Vossenack. According to a newspaper article, Sylvan was killed near this village on November 30, 1944, after he had volunteered to wipe out a German machine gun nest. Whether the machine gun nest was responsible for Sylvan's death is not known, and could not be determined.

When he was killed, Sylvan was 31 years old. In Margraten, he is buried beneath a marble Star of David in Plot K, Row 20, Grave 18.

BILL F. MOORE
First Lieutenant
467th Bombardment Group

Victim of a war crime

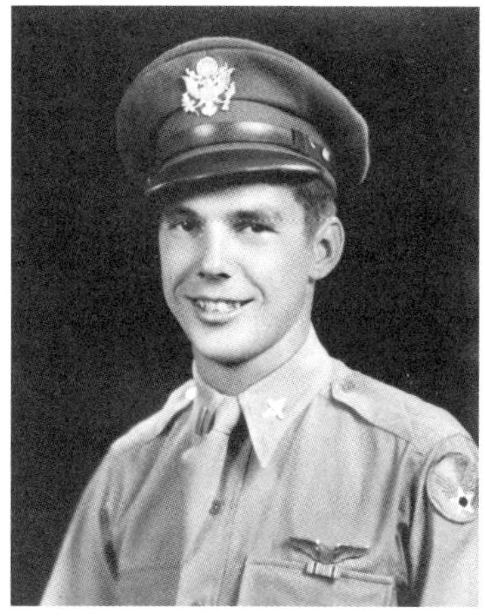

First Lieutenant Bill F. Moore from Atlanta, Georgia, was born in 1921 and grew up in the days when aviation was still emerging and very much captured the imagination. Therefore, from an early age, he dreamed of becoming a pilot.

After the Japanese attack on Pearl Harbor, Bill seized his chance. He joined the USAAF, became a pilot and went to England. There he went to fly in B-24s of the 788th Bomb Squadron. This was one of the squadrons of the 467th Bombardment Group.

On April 29, 1944, Bill participated in a bombing raid on the German capital of Berlin. The attack was successful, but during the return flight his bomber was badly damaged by German Flak. Despite this, Bill managed to keep the aircraft under control for quite some time. However, while flying over the Veluwe, a large nature park in the Netherlands, it became clear that they would not make it back to England. Therefore, Bill ordered the crew to bail out. He then jumped out of the bomber with a parachute after the other crew members had done the same. All of them landed safely on the ground. The damaged B-24 then crashed on a farm in the village of Uddel. Unfortunately, this caused the death of the local farmer's daughter, who was only nineteen years old at the time...

Once they landed with their parachutes, most of the crew were captured by the Germans. Bill, however, who was the last one to jump from the B-24, had managed to hide in the woods. He received help from a Dutch game warden who was affiliated with the local resistance. The resistance arranged a hiding place for Bill with the Kliest family in Apeldoorn. He was taken there by bicycle.

For fear of betrayal, Bill and four other airmen staying with the Kliest family were taken to another hiding address on October 1. The next evening, German military policemen saw Bill walking through the house with a burning candle and rang the doorbell. Bill discussed with the others what would be best. He offered to surrender, hoping to give them a chance to escape. Bill opened the door and while the Germans came in, they arrested him. However, upon entering the room, the Germans saw a portrait of a German officer in uniform hanging on the wall (the man on the picture was a relative of the houseowner, who wasn't at home when the Germans entered her house). After seeing this picture, the Germans became a bit uncertain. Without further searching the house, they left with Bill to ask for orders. As a result, the four other airmen managed to escape.

Bill was taken to the Willem III barracks in Apeldoorn. There he was interrogated by the Sicherheitsdienst (SD), the intelligence agency of the SS, for about two months. Bill refused to betray his helpers and the other people in hiding. When the Germans subsequently discovered that members of the resistance were preparing an action to free the prisoners, they executed Bill near the barracks on December 2, 1944. According to eyewitnesses, he is said to have shouted shortly before 'You can't shoot me because I am an American officer.' He tried to appeal to the international law of war, but to no avail. Bill was shot and therefore died at the young age of 23.

Initially, Bill was buried at Heidehof cemetery in Ugchelen, a village near Apeldoorn. His mother visited the grave in 1949. She bought the rights to the land and had a headstone placed there. She did not want her son's rest to be disturbed. In 1952, she changed her mind, and Bill was transferred to Margraten. There visitors can find his final resting place in Plot G, Row 9, Grave 27. In memory of Bill and the other executed prisoners, a memorial stone has been placed at the Willem III Barracks in Apeldoorn, reminding passers-by of the events of December 2, 1944.

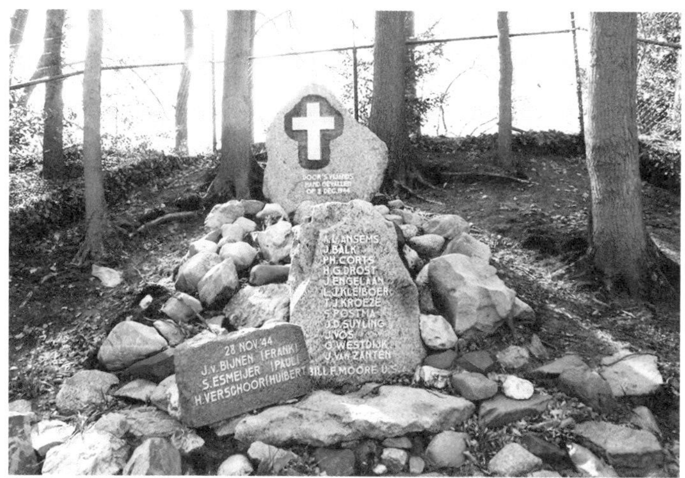

A monument next to the entrance of the Willem III barracks in Apeldoorn memorializes Bill F. Moore and members of the resistance who were shot. SOURCE: Koninklijke Marechaussee

CRESWELL GARLINGTON JR.

Second Lieutenant

84th Infantry Division

Blood transfusion was to no avail

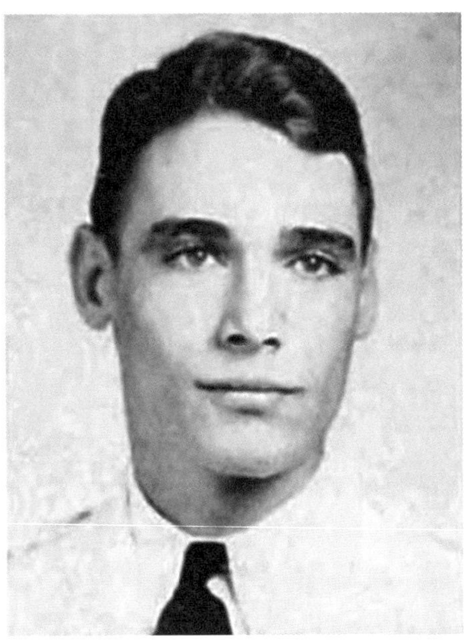

Second Lieutenant Creswell Garlington Jr. was born in Paris in 1922, but grew up in Georgia. He entered Saint Paul's School in Concord, New Hampshire, in 1936, where he played on the 2nd Delphian football team and rowed on the 3rd Halcyon crew.

After graduating in 1940, Creswell went to The Citadel, the military academy of South Carolina in Charleston. Creswell was unable to complete his studies there, because after the third year, his entire class was inducted into active military service. He was sent to the Officer Training School at Fort Benning, from which he graduated first in his class, and was commissioned as Second Lieutenant on May 2, 1944. He was assigned to Company I, 335th Infantry Regiment, 84th Infantry Division at Camp Claiborne, Louisiana. Creswell went overseas in September 1944.

On November 29, 1944, Creswell led his platoon in an attack on the Siegfried Line near the German town of Lindern. During this attack, his platoon was temporarily stopped by heavy fire from four German machine guns approximately 300 yards away. Creswell crawled forward and with hand grenades eliminated two of the German machine gun nests while a member of his platoon eliminated the other two. Later the same day, he and one of his men broke up enemy patrols that tried to infiltrate through their lines. The next day, during a German counterattack, Creswell and four of his men crawled to an advantageous point and killed or wounded 60 of the enemy, allowing his platoon to hold the line.

On December 1, 1944, German troops again counterattacked his platoon's positions. Creswell went back to check up on a group of four men who had been left to protect his rear under heavy artillery fire. He returned to his platoon command post and the artillery fire increased in intensity. Again, he returned to the four men and ordered them back to a safer position. In getting back, one of the four men was wounded. Creswell carried the wounded man through intense enemy artillery fire to a place of safety (reportedly his own foxhole). While getting the other three men into position, an artillery shell hit approximately ten yards away. Creswell received a penetrating wound in the right ankle, but refused to be evacuated. He insisted that the enlisted men be treated and evacuated first. Despite being in great pain, Creswell then continued to lead his men and tried to show them the position of a concealed enemy machine gun. Only when the others were evacuated, Creswell was taken to an evacuation hospital. There he died two days later on December 3, 1944, while undergoing a blood transfusion. Creswell was only 22 years old.

Creswell was posthumously awarded the Distinguished Service Cross for his leadership and courageous actions at Lindern. It is also noteworthy that General Eisenhower, Supreme Commander of the Allied Expeditionary Force in Europe, wrote a report on Creswell's bravery and how he was fatally injured. 'The men of his platoon, both officers and enlisted men, say that he was the best lieutenant in the division. The sergeant who accompanied him is convinced he can never be replaced. Because of his consistent courage, he had been cautioned many times about over-bravery. All who know him praised him for his courage and for the confidence which he inspired in his men,' Eisenhower wrote of him.

Creswell was buried at the temporary U.S. Military Cemetery in Margraten. After it was decided that this site would become a permanent American cemetery, he was given his final resting place in Plot A, Row 12, Grave 7.

THOMAS H. ROWLAND JR.

First Lieutenant

2nd Ranger Battalion

Replacement officer proved to be courageous

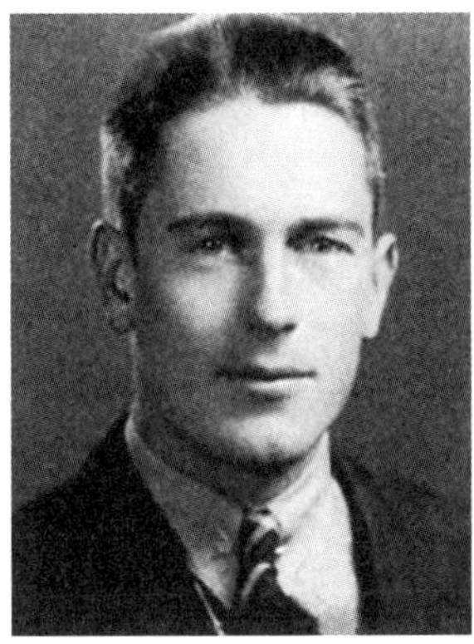

Thomas H. Rowland Jr. from New Jersey was born in 1916. He entered the army in 1942 and in the fall of 1944, he was assigned to Company F of the 2nd Ranger Battalion as a replacement officer. Thomas then had to lead troops of whom some were elite soldiers who had climbed the cliffs of Pointe du Hoc on D-Day and by now were battle hardened.

On December 7, 1944, Thomas was one of the Rangers who attacked 'Hill 400' ('Castle Hill') in the German Hürtgen Forest. The Germans used this strategic hill near the village of Bergstein as an observation point for their artillery. During the assault, Thomas and the other Rangers encountered enemy fire, but thanks to fire support from American artillery and some tanks, they were able to eliminate the Germans in the trenches and bunkers. This enabled the Rangers to take control of the hill after a terrible fight. Leonard Lomell, who fought in Company D, later gave an account of it in 1998:

> ***'Dec. 7, 1944, was the worst day of my life. People say D-Day was the longest day, but I was there, too, and it was much easier on me than Hill 400 in the Hürtgen Forest. Five thousand men had already tried to capture the hill and the town below. We passed their bodies and burnt-out tanks on the way in. At 7:30 a.m., 130 men in D and F companies assaulted across flat table land as German machine gunners sprayed fire at us. It was icy cold, artillery was raining down and we couldn't even dig in. But we took the 400-meter-high hill.'***

Almost immediately after Lomell's Company D and Thomas' Company F took Hill 400, the Germans started shelling the hilltop. It rained mortar and artillery shells on the Rangers' positions. Not much later, German troops launched a counterattack. The Germans who rushed the hill, were supported by machine gun fire and used their bayonet-fixed rifles, machine pistols and hand grenades against the Americans.

During the counterattack, Thomas was seen among his men, encouraging them. He reportedly yelled, 'If you gotta go you gotta go!' and then charged forward. While doing so, Thomas was shot in the chest. He fell down and Private First Class Paul Barscenski ran to him. He hoisted Thomas on his shoulder and began carrying him back up the hill. While carried back by Barscenski, Thomas was struck by another German bullet, killing him. Thomas' final resting place in Margraten is in Plot F, Row 10, Grave 19.

EDWARD P. TUMAS

Sergeant

629th Tank Destroyer Battalion

Struck by a mortar round while aiding wounded

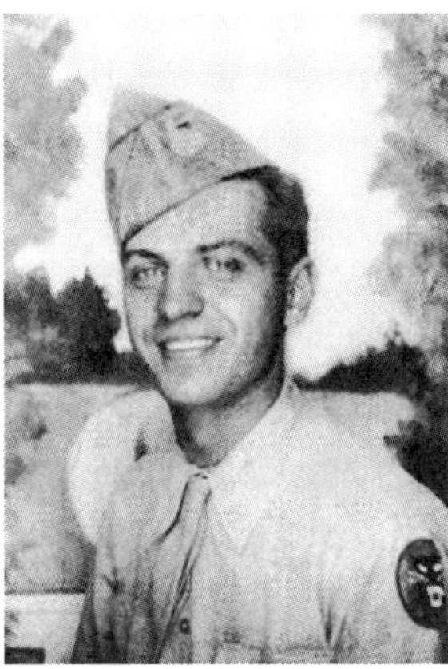

Edward P. Tumas was born in Vandergrift, Pennsylvania on December 5, 1922. Both his parents were immigrants from Lithuania. In 1941, he graduated from the local high school, after which he got an office job with U.S. Steel.

In January 1943, Edward entered the army at Greensburg, Pennsylvania. He was assigned to the 629th Tank Destroyer Battalion. This unit was shipped to England a year later and on July 2, 1944, the tank destroyers landed on Omaha Beach in Normandy. The battalion then moved with the Allied advance through northern France and on August 29, the men participated in the American military parade in Paris. Then the advance continued through Luxembourg. The battalion also participated in the attacks on the Siegfried Line.

On December 10, 1944, Edward fought in one of three M10 tank destroyers that repulsed a German counterattack near the German village of Strauss in the Hürtgen Forest. He was later awarded the Silver Star for his actions during the fighting that took place there. Part of his citation reads:

> ***'Sergeant Tumas was a member of one of three tank destroyer crews supporting an infantry battalion attack on a German town [Strauss]. On the night of 10 December 1944, the enemy succeeded in infiltrating to the rear of the town. After a heavy pre-dawn barrage of artillery, mortar and machine gun fire, three enemy Royal Tiger tanks entered the town. One of the destroyers knocked out two of the tanks at ranges of less than 100 yards and forced the third to withdraw. Shortly thereafter the enemy again attacked with a large number of self-propelled guns. Although hopelessly outnumbered, the three destroyer crews remained at their posts and fearlessly returned the enemy fire until all of the destroyers were knocked out. In the course of this gallant action six members of the destroyer crews were killed and five were injured.'***

Edward volunteered to stay the rest of the night in an old building where the wounded men of his platoon had been brought in. He spent the night aiding the wounded until the following morning, when suddenly a mortar shell smashed through the roof and struck him. Edward was killed on the spot and was only 22 years old at the time. In Margraten, Edward is buried in Plot B, Row 9, Grave 16.

BENJAMIN T. POTTS
First Lieutenant
81st Tank Battalion

His tank detonated a mine

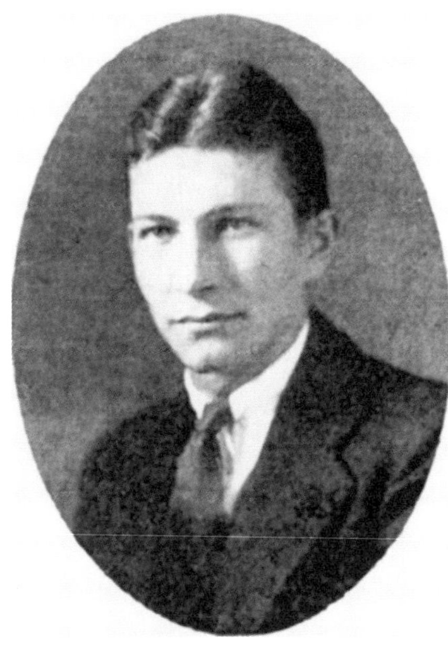

First Lieutenant Benjamin T. Potts from Virginia was born in 1912. He graduated at John Handley High School in 1934 and entered the army in May 1941, several months before the United States became involved in World War II.

Over three years later, Benjamin was the commander of a platoon of light tanks of Company D, 81st Tank Battalion. This tank battalion was part of the 5th Armored Division. This division was also called the 'Victory' Division by its men.

In August 1944, Benjamin narrowly escaped death in France. While driving in a jeep through the village of Maigné, a German sniper suddenly fired at him from the doorway of a burned-out house. His bullet just missed Benjamin. Before the German could pull the trigger a second time, he was quickly shot by a member of the French resistance.

On December 12, 1944, during the fierce Battle of the Hürtgen Forest, Benjamin received the order to bring supplies to the front troops with the light tanks he commanded. In this forest, however, there were few paths suitable for tanks. Moreover, these narrow paths were often muddy and full of German mines. But because intense artillery and mortar fire made it impossible for trucks, jeeps, or other thin-skinned vehicles to haul badly needed supplies up to the front, Benjamin's platoon of light tanks was nevertheless called on to do the job. Benjamin ordered his men to load rations, water, and clothing on the rear decks of their tanks and then gave the order to drive up to the front.

In the darkness, Benjamin's platoon missed the guide who was to show them where to unload the supplies. Going beyond the outposts, they went into territory still held by the enemy. Fired on by small arms and mortars, Benjamin concluded it was better to retreat. They turned around the tanks and started back up the road. Going back, they found their route around two knocked-out Shermans was now blocked by a light tank from their platoon which had hit a mine. Climbing out of the turret, Benjamin got in front of his tank and started to lead it between the two Shermans when it, too, struck an anti-tank mine. The explosion killed him and seriously wounded his driver, T/4 Peter J. Thauwald. As a result, Benjamin's life abruptly ended at age 31. His remains went missing and still are. Therefore, his name is listed on the Walls of the Missing in Margraten.

A few weeks after his death, 5th Armored Division Headquarters announced that Benjamin was posthumously awarded the Silver Star for his gallantry in action on the day he was killed. His citation gives a brief summary of what had happened to him and reads as follows:

> ***'First Lieutenant Potts was given the mission of carrying supplies to forward troops on the tanks which he commanded. Unable to locate the guide who was to direct them to the forward unit, he attempted to locate them by making dismounted reconnaissance in spite of the fact that the area was known to be heavily mined. During this action First Lieutenant Potts was killed when the forward tank struck an anti-tank mine. The devotion to duty and disregard for his own safety displayed by First Lieutenant Potts is worthy of the highest traditions of the military service.'***

ROBERT T. CAHOW

Corporal

78th Infantry Division

An accidentally discovered field grave

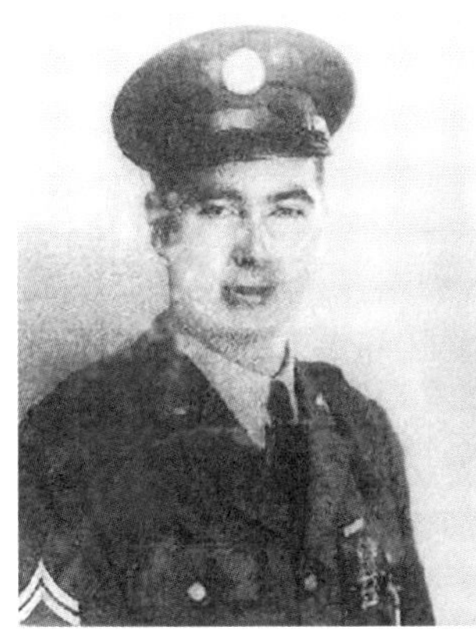

Robert T. Cahow from Wisconsin was born on October 10, 1916. He was the oldest of eight sons and grew up in a farming family. He entered military service in April 1941 and initially served as a Military Policeman (MP) back home in the United States. Later, Robert decided to volunteer for service on the front line and was transferred to Europe. He was assigned to the 311th Infantry Regiment of the 78th Infantry Division as a BAR gunner. In the autumn of 1944, this division was involved in the heavy fighting in the German Hürtgen Forest.

On December 13, 1944, Robert's company had to take out German pillboxes (concrete bunkers) that were built on a strategic hill called Ochsenkopf. During the attacks several of Robert's comrades were wounded by mines and the deadly crossfire of German machine guns and rifles. Robert volunteered to save them, but while he was trying to do so, he stepped on a German mine. The explosion seriously injured him. Because the blast also alerted the German soldiers in the nearby bunkers and trenches, other soldiers of his company could not come to his aid due to the German crossfire. As a result, Robert succumbed to his injuries a short time later at the age of 28.

After the fighting was over, Robert's body was buried in the woods, most likely by German soldiers. As a result, his remains were not recovered after the war by the American Graves Registration Command. Therefore, Robert was listed as missing in action.

Eventually, Robert's remains were found 56 years later in April 2000 by German engineers who were doing a mine clearing operation in the area around the Ochsenkopf. They were using metal detectors and accidentally discovered Robert's unmarked field grave. The remains could then be successfully identified, whereupon Robert was given his final resting place in Clear Lake, Wisconsin. In Margraten, a rosette was placed next to his name on the Walls of the Missing to indicate that he is no longer missing. In the Hürtgen Forest, near the spot where Robert's field grave was found, now stands a small memorial to honor him.

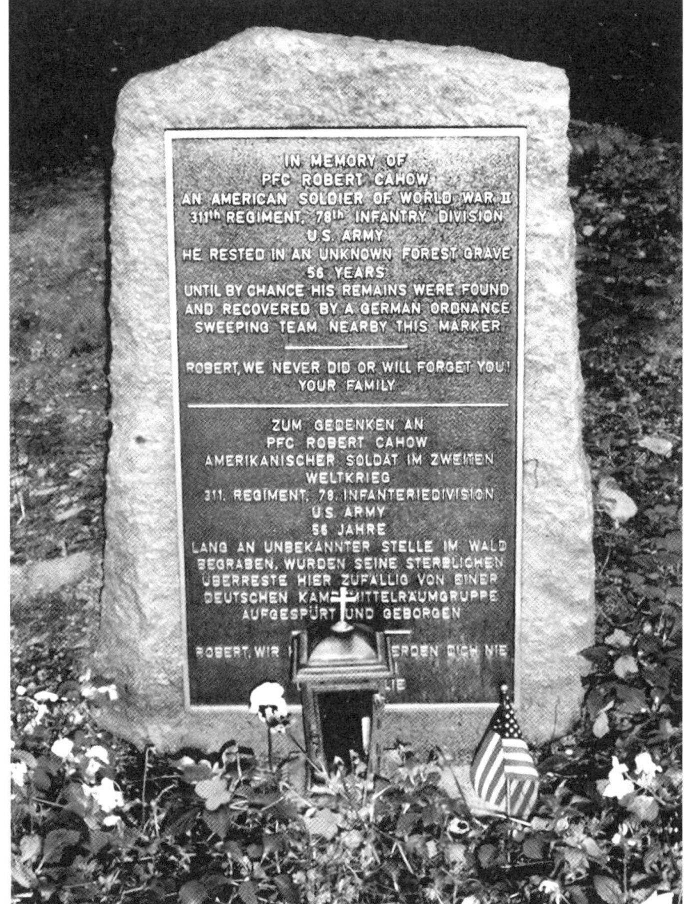

Robert Cahow's memorial marker in the Hürtgen Forest. SOURCE: Ray/FindAGrave.com

ALPHONSE FLEURY

Private First Class

5th Armored Division

A very strong man

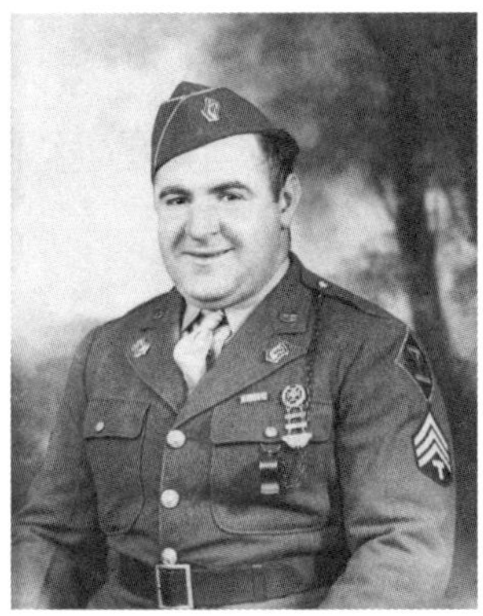

Alphonse Fleury was one of fourteen children born to Oliva and Victoria Fleury from Holyoke, Massachusetts, which was predominantly a city of hard-working Irish and French-Canadian immigrants. His father was born in Quebec, Canada, and primarily spoke French. Alphonse and his siblings spoke both French and English. Two of his siblings died in infancy and one died in his teens.

Like his parents, brothers, and sisters, Alphonse was a devote Catholic. Every Sunday the whole family went to church to attend mass. During their spare time they loved to play cards. Canasta was the family's favorite, but they also enjoyed cribbage and pitch.

According to the memories of Marcel Fleury, one of his brothers, Alphonse loved to laugh and have fun. He was not very tall, but he was a very strong man who could lift up a car. Just for a joke, he was known for lifting up cars and putting them on the sidewalk, Marcel remembered.

On March 7, 1940, Alphonse joined the National Guard. In January 1941, he was inducted into the army, whereupon he was trained at Camp Edwards and participated in maneuvers down South. In 1943, he married Ruth Turner, a nurse whom Alphonse had met when he was injured and sent to a hospital near Boston, Massachusetts. The following year, Alphonse was sent overseas to the European Theater of Operations, where he served with the 15th Armored Infantry Battalion of the 5th Armored Division.

Both Alphonse's military service and life abruptly ended on December 20, 1944, when he was killed in Winden, Germany. His wife Ruth learned the details surrounding his death through a letter she received from one of her husband's Army buddies: during the First Army drive for the Roer, Alphonse was killed by a German sniper's bullet. The shot passed directly through his heart and when medics reached him two or three minutes later, he was dead. As a result, Alphonse remained forever 28.

Alphonse is buried at the Netherlands American Cemetery and Memorial in Margraten, where he was interred in his permanent grave on January 7, 1949. Amidst the graves of over 8,000 fellow servicemen and -women, he rests in peace beneath a white marble cross in Plot D, Row 10, Grave 28.

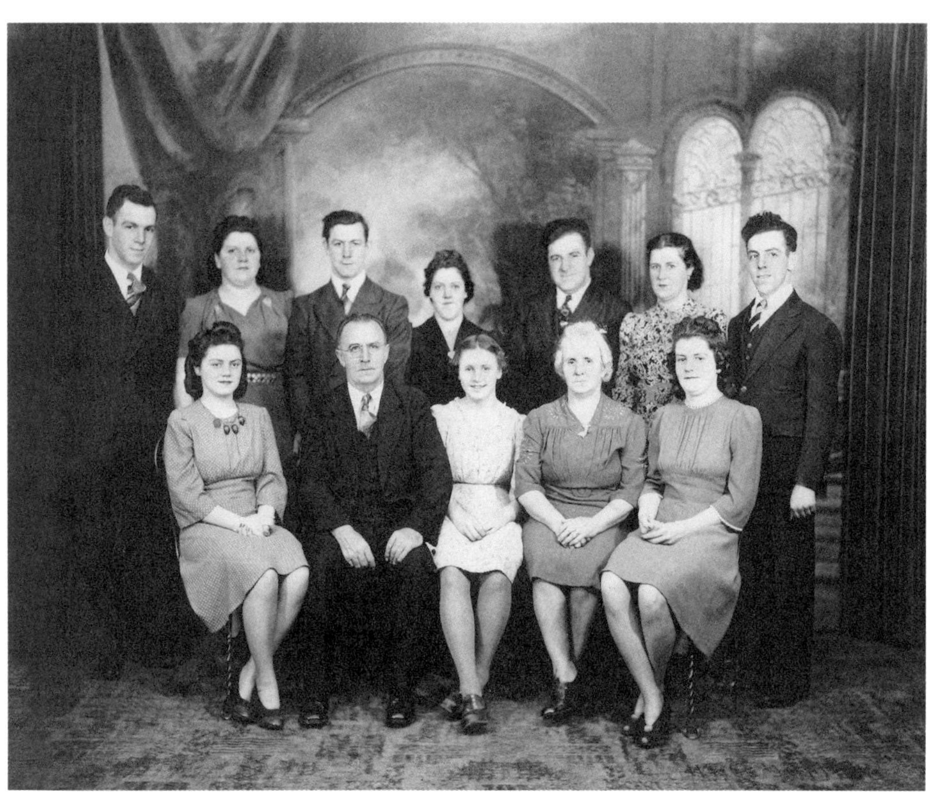

Pfc. Fleury, Long Missing, Was Killed In Action

Pfc. Alphonse Fleury, previously listed as missing in action on Dec. 20, was killed on that date at Winden, Germany, a War Department communique informed his parents, Mr. and Mrs. Oliva Fleury of 560 Summer St. His wife is the former Ruth Turner, formerly of Holyoke, now of Boston.

It was during the First Army drive for the Roer that Pfc. Fleury was killed by a German sniper's bullet. The shot passed directly thru his heart and when medics reached him two or three minutes later he was dead. Circumstances of his death were told to his wife in a letter from a buddy from Fleury's division.

Pfc. Fleury was overseas 10 months when he was killed.

Besides his parents he leaves six sisters, Mrs. Deliha Anderson, Springfield; Mrs. Germaine Lavigne, Granby; Mrs. Doris Nadeau of this city, the Misses Rita and Therese Fleury, at home; three brothers, Pfc. Cleo Fleury, stationed in China with the Army; Rene Fleury and Marcel Fleury, both of Holyoke.

Pfc. Fleury joined the National Guard on March 7, 1940 and was called to the Army in January, 1941. After training at Camp Edwards and southern camps he was sent overseas on Jan. 29, 1944.

JUL 7 1945

2 of 2

Alphonse Fleury

A group portrait of the Fleury family. Alphonse is standing third from right. SOURCE: Susan Fleury Fortin

Newspaper article describing details of Alphonse's death in Germany. SOURCE: Susan Fleury Fortin

DONALD L. BERRY

Second Lieutenant

8th Infantry Division

A courageous leader

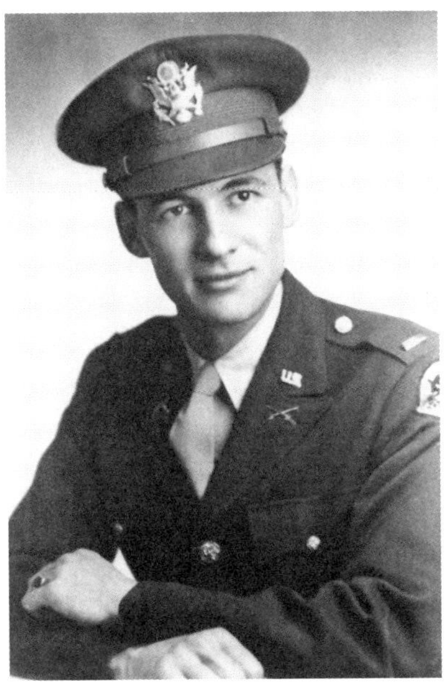

Second Lieutenant Donald L. Berry from New York was born in 1918. He graduated from Hornell High School and the Pratt Institute for Technology. Before entering the army in 1941, Donald worked as an illustrator for an advertising agency in New York.

After enlisting in the army, Donald was initially assigned to a tank destroyer battalion. However, he later requested a transfer to the infantry, and this was honored by the army. He was then assigned to the 28th Infantry Regiment of the 8th Infantry Division.

Donald went overseas in the fall of 1944 and was killed the same year on December 23 in Germany during the 'Battle of the Bulge.' For his courageous leadership he displayed at the time of his death, he was posthumously awarded the Silver Star in September 1945. His citation reads:

> ***'Lieutenant Berry led his platoon in a coordinated attack against a strong pocket of German resistance. During the early stages of the advance his men were pinned down by enemy machine gun cross fire. Aware that the majority of his men were experiencing their initial engagement, Lieutenant Berry shouted encouragements to them and personally led them forward. Halfway to his objective, he was caught by a burst of machine gun fire and killed. His gallant courage and outstanding leadership gave confidence to his men and proved a great source of inspiration to them.'***

Donald was 26 years old when the German machine gun fire killed him. Like more than 8,000 fellow soldiers who died about just as young, he is buried at the Netherlands American Cemetery and Memorial in Margraten. Visitors can pay tribute to him there by visiting Plot B, Row 9, Grave 1.

LARRY S. WASSIL

Sergeant

8th Infantry Division

'I'd never thought that they'd find anything'

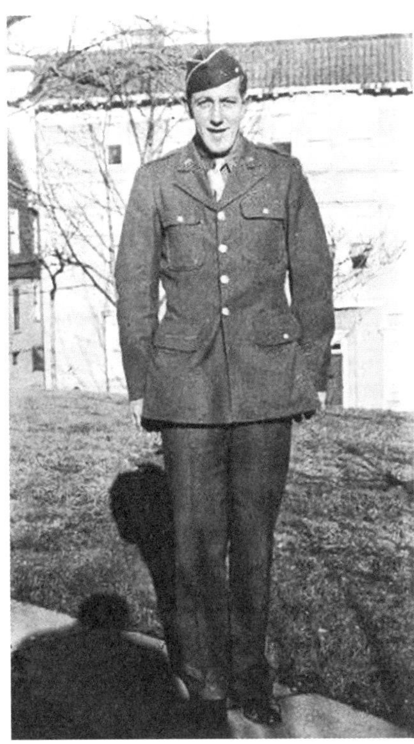

Sergeant Larry S. Wassil from Bloomfield, New Jersey, was born in 1911. He was divorced from his first wife, with whom he had two children, Barbara and Larry. Larry would often visit them until he entered the army in March 1942.

Once in the service, Larry was assigned to Company K, 13th Infantry Regiment, 8th Infantry Division. In late 1944, this division was deployed in the Battle of the Hürtgen Forest in Germany, where Larry was reported missing in action on December 28. According to the Defense POW/MIA Accounting Agency (DPAA), he was leading a three-man reconnaissance team scouting enemy positions near the village of Bergstein when they started taking enemy machine gun fire, forcing them to scatter and find cover. When the gunfire ceased, the other two men found each other, but were unable to find Larry. He was not listed as a prisoner of war by the Germans after going missing, and the War Department therefore issued a presumptive finding of death on December 29, 1945. In December 1951, Larry was declared non-recoverable.

Decades later, while studying unresolved American losses in the Hürtgen Forest area, a DPAA historian determined that one set of unidentified remains, designated X-9118 Griesheim Mausoleum, originally discovered by German wood cutters near Bergstein and recovered by the AGRC in 1952, possibly belonged to Larry. The remains, which had been buried at the Ardennes American Cemetery, were disinterred in April 2019 and sent to the DPAA laboratory at Offutt Air Force Base, Nebraska, for examination and identification.

Using dental and anthropological analysis, as well as DNA analysis, DPAA was able to identify remains X-9118 as being Larry's. He was officially accounted for on July 27, 2021, more than three-quarters of a century after he went missing. Larry's daughter, Barbara Loock, who was twelve years old when her father died, couldn't believe that the remains were found after all this time. 'I'd never thought that they'd find anything,' she said. Her younger brother Larry had died in 2019, a couple of weeks after they had gotten the news that their father's remains might have been located.

Larry Wassil's name is recorded on the Walls of the Missing in Margraten, where a rosette is placed next to his name to indicate he has been accounted for. In May 2022, Larry's funeral took place at Arlington National Cemetery, Virginia.

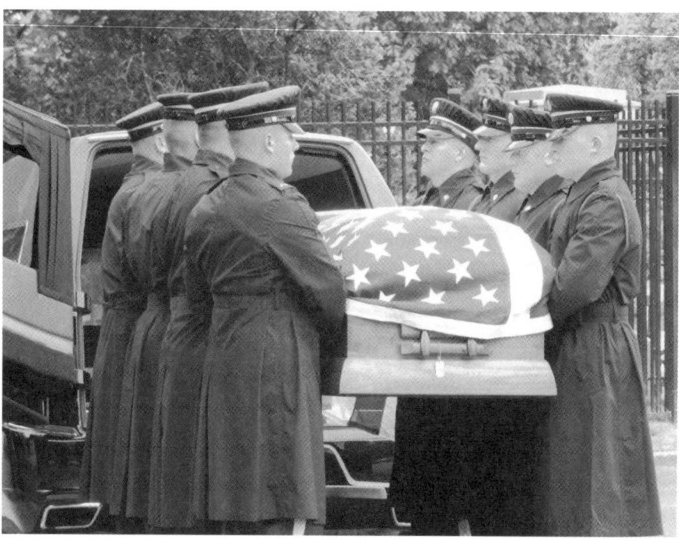

The coffin containing the recently identified remains of Sgt. Larry S. Wassil shortly after its arrival at Arlington National Cemetery, where his funeral took place on May 13, 2022.
SOURCE: DPAA

DONALD R. EMERSON
Captain
4th Fighter Group

Luck ran out

Captain Donald R. Emerson from North Dakota was born on May 17, 1923. He grew up in the farmlands of North Dakota and Minnesota, and graduated from high school in 1941. With the advent of the Pearl Harbor attack he felt that he or his brother would be drafted. Donald, not interested in running the farm, decided to enlist so his older brother would be deferred to attend that duty.

Donald enlisted in July 1942 and was accepted as an aviation cadet. He finished pilot training and was assigned to the 336th Fighter Squadron of the 4th Fighter Group, stationed in Debden, England. He flew in P-51 Mustangs. The P-51 was one of the most successful long-range fighters developed during World War II.

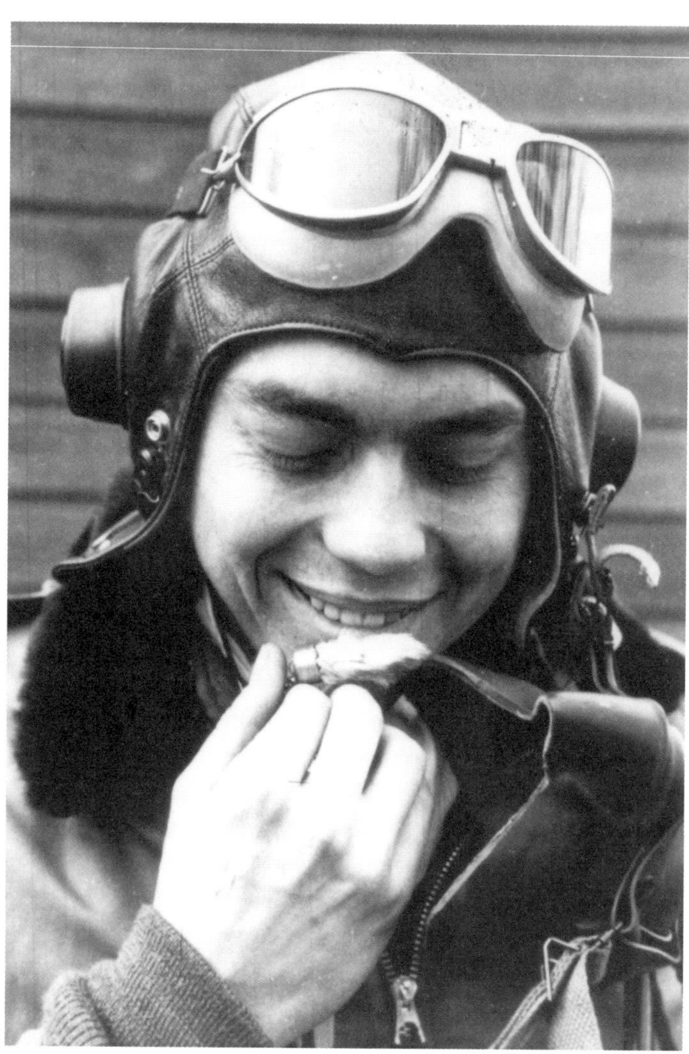

As a fighter pilot, Donald flew around 80 missions over enemy territory during his service in Europe. Mostly to protect bombers from attacks by German Luftwaffe fighters. During these flights he destroyed numerous enemy ground targets and destroyed seven German aircraft (4.5 in the air and 2.5 destroyed on the ground). Donald carried a small rabbit's foot talisman with him, which he wore on a chain around his neck. It was a gift from his girlfriend.

Donald was well aware of the dangers he faced. In a letter dated October 31, 1942, he wrote:

> ***'I admit I'm sticking my neck out but I'd rather take my chances in the air than in the infantry, armored division, tank corps or the navy. Of course, it's dangerous but name me a war job that isn't. Anyway, I'm one of those that believe that if a guy is supposed to lose his life in this war it will happen no matter what or where and vice versa.'***

In July 1944, Donald wrote a combat report on the downing of a German Messerschmitt Bf-109:

> ***'I was leading a Section of six 336 Fighter Squadron pilots. We were flying north from the target after a group of Me 109s that had been reported at the base of the clouds. I sighted an Me 109 flying with some Mustangs as if he were part of their Section. I pulled in line astern of him and gave chase, but closed very slowly as my engine would not pull more than 40" of Mercury (without my knowledge, the air intake was set in unrammed filtered air). When I finally got within reasonable range, Lt. Higgins was also in position to fire. I got numerous strikes on the fuselage and cockpit of the 109, which then pulled up in a steep climb. I stalled out and started to spin. When I recovered, the Me 109 was spiraling down. I followed him down because I was not sure if he was out of control or not. At this time, I saw pieces of the wing come off, and the 109 continued to spiral into the deck. I saw no one bail out of the e/a [enemy aircraft]. I claim one Me 109 Destroyed, shared with Lt. Higgins.'***

On December 25, 1944 – Christmas Day – Donald was engaged in combat with six Messerschmitt Bf-109s and/or Focke-Wulf 190s of the Luftwaffe. He had become separated from the other pilots of his group, but managed to shoot down two of the German fighters before exhausting his ammunition. To escape the other enemy fighters, he then ducked in some nearby clouds. Shortly thereafter, while crossing into Allied territory, his Mustang was hit and accidentally shot down by Allied anti-aircraft fire, whereupon he crashed on the Kollenberg near the Dutch town of Sittard.

Donald was only 21 years old when he died. His body was found in the wreckage of his aircraft and was buried in Margraten. Today visitors can find his final resting place there in Plot B, Row 15, Grave 21.

Donald Emerson and the rabbit's foot talisman that he always carried with him. SOURCE: Collection Ron Pütz via Arie-Jan van Hees

EDWARD ETZEL JR.
Sergeant
92nd Bombardment Group

Bomber exploded in mid-air

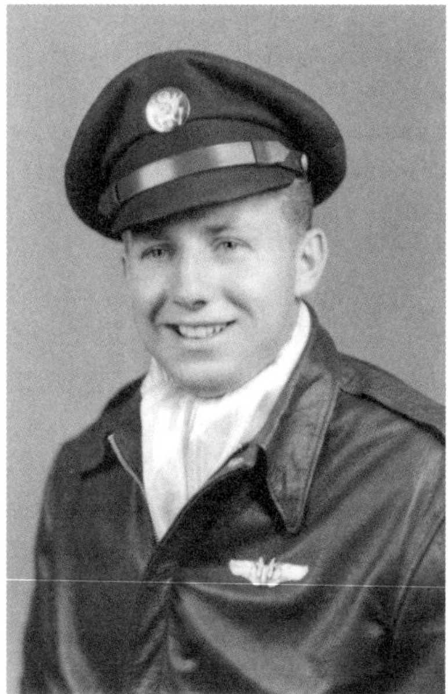

Sergeant Edward Etzel Jr. from Wisconsin was born on August 21, 1924. In January 1944, he joined the United States Army Air Forces and was assigned to the 407th Bomb Squadron of the 92nd Bombardment Group. He served as a ball turret gunner on a four-engine B-17.

On December 11, 1944, Edward's bomber was deployed to bomb the German city of Frankfurt. However, after dropping their bombs, three of the bomber's engines began to falter, presumably due to the usage of a different blend of fuel that was used to figure out if this could improve the power and efficiency of the bomber's engines. Because of this the pilot had to feather the propellers, until only one of four was still working. 'Eddie came out of the ball-turret and we all started to throw things over board, guns etc. in order to lighten the ship,' wrote Carl Green, one of Edward's fellow crew members on this plane, in a letter to Edward's mother in 1946.

Despite that he had to shut down three of the plane's engines, the pilot managed to keep the aircraft in the air until they flew over liberated territory. Edward and the other crew members then bailed out with their parachutes and landed unscathed near the French city of Metz. The whole crew proceeded to Paris, where they recovered for a week in a nice hotel.

A few days after returning to their base in England, the new bomber of Edward and his comrades was badly hit by Flak during another mission on Christmas Eve. Two of Edward's buddies were injured as a result, but this time the pilots did manage to fly all the way back to AAF Station 109 in England. One of the injured men was Carl Green, who was brought to a hospital. In his letter to Edward's mother, he wrote:

'Eddie as usual attended early mass before take-off time. The target was an airfield in the Ardennes Sector and it was a visual target. The weather in England was terrible to say the least with the fog clear down on the ground, but the mission was very necessary, so after taking off on instruments and getting clear of the ground fog we proceeded to the target, only to find that the weather over there was perfect, with no clouds at all. The Flak was intense and very accurate, with the result that our ship was badly damaged and two of us got hurt. On returning back to our base I remember well how sorry Eddie and the boys were for the two of us who had to be hospitalized, on Christmas Eve, little realizing that we were really the fortunate ones. This is the last time I saw Eddie and the boys.'

Carl Green was indeed fortunate in retrospect, because on January 1, 1945, Edward and his fellow crew members were assigned to a mission that turned out to be their last. This mission was a special one: instead of bombs, Edward's B-17 carried a large load of tin foil strips called 'Chaff' toward the German city of Kassel. The tin foil strips had to be dropped to disrupt German radars, after which other bombers would bomb their assigned targets. During this mission, however, Edward's bomber was strafed and badly hit by German fighters. According to eyewitnesses, the B-17 exploded in the air not long after. No chutes were seen. Edward and all other crew members were killed. Edward was only twenty years old at the time. The Germans found his body and buried him and the other found crew members at the POW Cemetery at Stendal. Later he was permanently interred in Margraten. His final resting place there can be found in Plot P, Row 19, Grave 12.

JACK TOMLIN

First Lieutenant

102nd Infantry Division

Overwhelmed by a machine gun

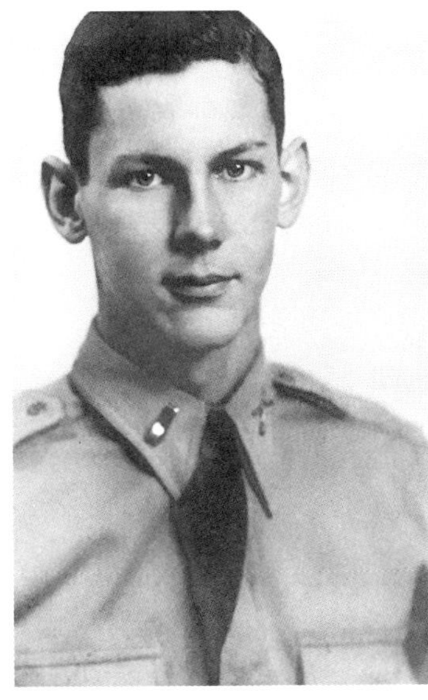

First Lieutenant Jack Tomlin was born in 1924 and grew up in Georgia. He served in the Headquarters Company of the 406th Infantry Regiment, which was part of the 102nd Infantry Division. This division, nicknamed 'Ozark,' entered combat in October 1944.

While fighting in Europe, Jack served in the Intelligence and Reconnaissance platoon. This platoon functioned as the Headquarters Company's 'eyes and ears.'

By the end of January 1945, shortly after his division had driven the Germans out of the village of Brachelen, Jack was sent on a patrol with a small group of other soldiers from his platoon. His mission was to take his men into the town of Hilfarth and reconnoiter. At that point, Hilfarth was the only town on the west bank of the Roer River that the Germans still held in the 406th Regiment's sector.

As the patrol approached Hilfarth, the town looked deserted. But according to a letter of Ken Tobin, a member of the patrol, the Germans suddenly opened fire on them with a machine gun: 'Lt. Tomlin was hit several times by a MG 42 and badly wounded,' he wrote. 'Everyone dived for the side of the road. We fought for fifteen minutes, hoping to hold off until dark and get away, but the MG 42 and mortars kept our heads down as the Jerry infantry closed in from all sides. We finally saw it was no use. Cpl. Al Hansel raised a white flag on his carbine. It was all over. We held out as long as possible because we thought they would shoot us anyway.'

Tobin, Jack, and the others were captured by the Germans. Jack was then taken to a German field hospital, bleeding profusely. In his letter, Tobin also wrote that 'the day after we were captured, the Jerries told us that Jack had died in a German field hospital.' According to the records of the ABMC, Jack died on January 27, 1945.

Jack was only twenty years old when he was mortally wounded and lost his life. His body somehow disappeared without a trace. That is why he is listed on the Walls of the Missing in Margraten.

Jack's mother Corrie could never fully process the loss of her son. She tried to find out as much as possible about what might have happened to him. She even went to Germany herself twice to find Jack's body. Sadly, it was to no avail...

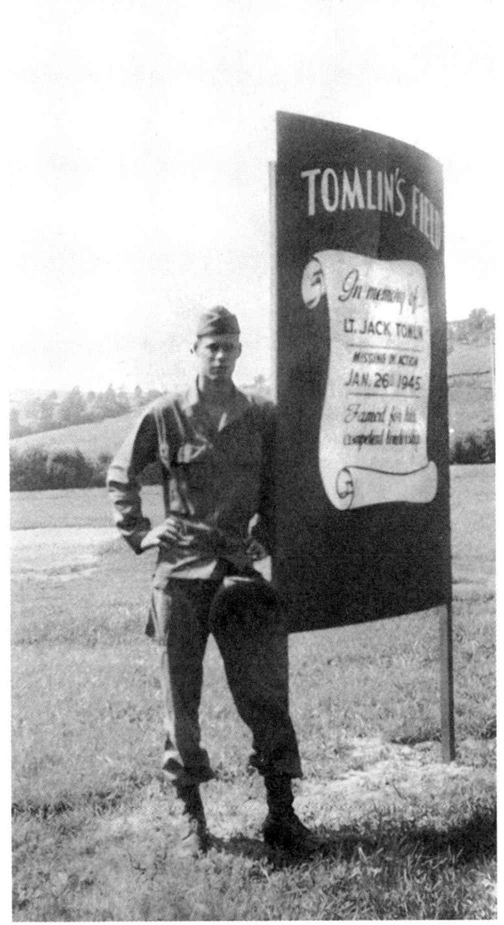

A veteran poses next to a sign of a sports field that was named after Jack Tomlin

ITSUMU SASAOKA

Staff Sergeant

442nd Regimental Combat Team

Most-decorated unit

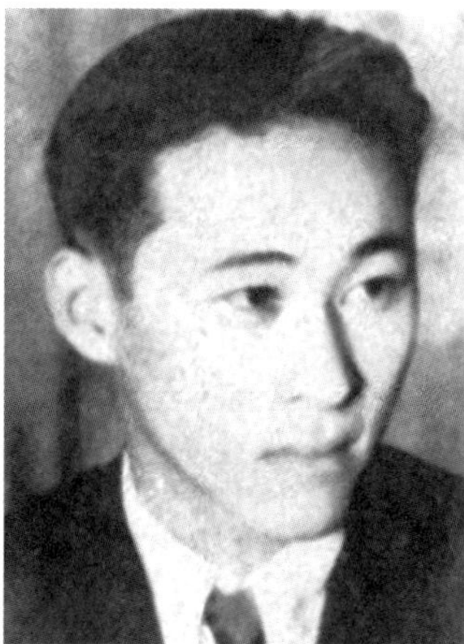

Staff Sergeant Itsumu Sasaoka was born in Honolulu, the capital of Hawaii. His parents were of Japanese descent and he lived in the town of Aiea, near Pearl Harbor. In 1944, Itsumu served as a machine gunner in the U.S. Army's 100th Battalion of the 442nd Regimental Combat Team. This was a Japanese American unit that was attached to the 36th Infantry Division.

For fear of espionage and suspicion of collaboration with the Japanese government, nearly 120,000 Japanese Americans were incarcerated in special internment camps in 1942. They were allowed to serve in the military on only a limited basis and within racially segregated units.

The Japanese American troops proved themselves on the battlefields. Itsumu's unit would even become one of the most highly decorated units in U.S. military history. Itsumu contributed to this in person by being awarded the Distinguished Service Cross for gallantry in action on October 22, 1944. The citation reads:

> ***'Staff Sergeant Sasaoka was assigned as a machine gunner on the last tank of a task force during the execution of a daring thrust through enemy-held terrain in an effort to relieve a friendly unit which had been surrounded and cut off by the enemy [near Belmont, France]. As the task force advanced over a mountain trail, the enemy opened fire from well dug-in positions on both sides of the trail. Although seriously wounded by the first burst of hostile fire, Sergeant Sasaoka, displaying a disdain for personal safety seldom surpassed, clung to his machine gun and directed a hail of bullets into the enemy positions in a last desperate attempt to prevent the other members of his platoon from being subjected to the lethal enemy crossfire. Finally, unable to hang on any longer due to his weakened condition, Sergeant Sasaoka fell from the lurching tank. His magnificent courage and devotion to duty were in large measure responsible for the successful accomplishment of his platoon's mission and for saving the lives of many of his comrades.'***

After Itsumu fell from the tank, he was taken prisoner by the Germans. They transferred him to POW Camp Stalag III-C near Alt Drewitz, Poland. When troops and tanks of the Soviet army approached this camp on January 31, 1945, the German guards sent Itsumu and many other prisoners of war on foot to another camp. That same day, Itsumu went missing. The American Graves Registration Command later investigated what happened to Itsumu and the other missing American prisoners. Interrogations of several returned prisoners disclosed that 'shortly after the prisoners were forced to evacuate the camp, they were fired upon by Russian tanks at a distance of 600–800 yards. Several men were killed or wounded at that time, while other prisoners were forced to find protection from the Russian and German cross fire.'

The same report included a statement of Staff Sergeant Michael M. Tokunaga:

> ***'Staff Sergeant Sasaoka lived with me in the same barracks and on the morning of Jan 31st, moved out together under German orders. Approximately 2 ½ to 3 miles out of the camp, we were suddenly fired upon by Russians who had mistaken the identity of the marching column. Sgt. Sasaoka was alive at this moment. I crossed the road and lay down behind a tree. After that I did not see Sgt. Sasaoka. I made my way back to the camp with the aid of two friends. I was separated from another Japanese American boy, Sgt. Harry Kamikawa, the only one in this camp besides Sgt. Sasaoka and myself. This boy went with a group of approximately 300 to be immediately rescued by the Russians. We each thought that Sgt. Sasaoka was with the other. About two weeks later, I met Sgt. Kamikawa in a small Polish town near the German border and was surprised to find that Sgt. Sasaoka was not with him. I inquired but could not locate Sgt. Sasaoka or learn of his fate. I do know that some bodies became unidentifiable due to shell fire and the result of Russian tanks crushing bodies. I believe the Russians could have identified him by means of his dog tags or a German prisoner identification tag, both of which I definitely know he had on his person. I cannot say that I saw the body of Sgt. Sasaoka or saw him wounded but I believe that he is now dead.'***

In 1949, the American Graves Registration Command concluded that Itsumu's remains were non-recoverable. In another of their investigation reports it is stated that Itsumu and at least nine other prisoners are believed to have been killed by fire from the Russian tanks during the evacuation of Stalag III-C.

Because he was killed, Itsumu's life abruptly ended at the age of 28. His remains have still not been recovered. Therefore, he is commemorated on the Walls of the Missing in Margraten.

MARION L. BELL
Sergeant
95th Bombardment Group

War crime after emergency landing

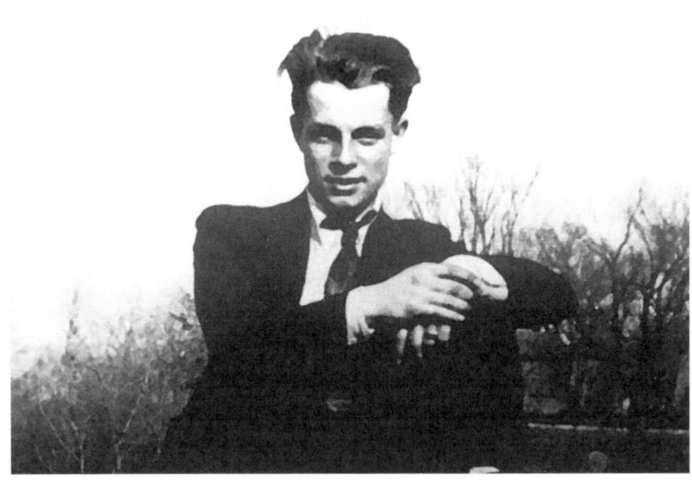

Sergeant Marion L. Bell, born on April 23, 1918, was raised in Lyle, Mower County, Minnesota. Following high school, he went to work for Hormel Corporation in Austin, Minnesota, then one of the main suppliers of food for the U.S. Army, known for the cans of Spam. He married Mary Jane and together they had a daughter, named Lynda.

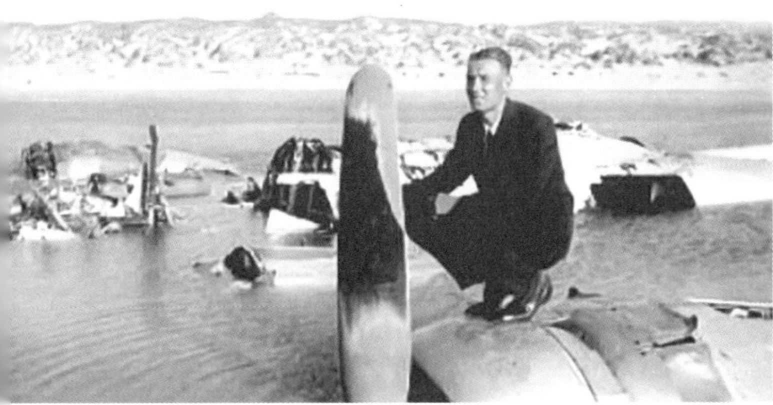

Wreckage of the plane on Texel.
SOURCE: American Air Museum Britain

In September 1943, Marion was called up for military service. He joined the USAAF and was trained to become a ball turret gunner. In December 1944, Marion was assigned to the 334th Bomb Squadron of the 95th Bombardment Group, which was stationed at USAAF Station 119 in Horham, England.

On February 3, 1945, an armada of American bombers took off from several British airfields for a heavy bombing attack on Berlin. One of these aircraft was the four-engine Boeing B-17 'Flying Fortress' piloted and commanded by Second Lieutenant Richard P. Morris. In addition to Morris, there were eight other crew members on board. One of them was Marion. He was the ball turret gunner and had to protect the bottom of the plane from attacks by German fighters. It was his third mission, and would be his last...

After dropping the bombs, the aircraft was hit by Flak. One of the wings caught fire. Nevertheless, pilot Morris managed to keep the plane under control for a considerable time during the return flight. But when they flew over the Dutch province of Friesland in the afternoon, the plane lost altitude and had to leave the formation to make an emergency landing.

Not much later, German troops targeted the heavily damaged bomber with anti-aircraft weapons from the island of Texel. Flak shells exploded next to the plane, producing black clouds. The B-17 turned north and as a sign of surrender the crew fired a few red flares. Nevertheless, the German Flak guns continued to fire. Moreover, the aircraft was now also being fired upon with rifles and machine guns from German positions in the dunes.

Shortly afterwards, the B-17 made a belly landing in the sea about 400 meters from the beach. The crew members survived and climbed onto the wings, but then – according to eyewitnesses – German soldiers on the beach shot them. It was later assumed that this was out of pure revenge. The Germans on Texel had little to worry about and felt useless. Perhaps they had heard of the bombing of their homeland and thus were out for retribution.

Marion was only 26 years old when the German soldiers killed him. He left behind a wife and a two-year-old daughter. His remains were buried a few days later near Den Burg, but his family only received confirmation of his death on July 7, 1945. In December 1945, he was taken to Margraten. There he was given his final resting place in Plot H, Row 6, Grave 2.

NANDO A. CAVALIERI
Captain
91st Bombardment Group

Airman accounted for in 2021

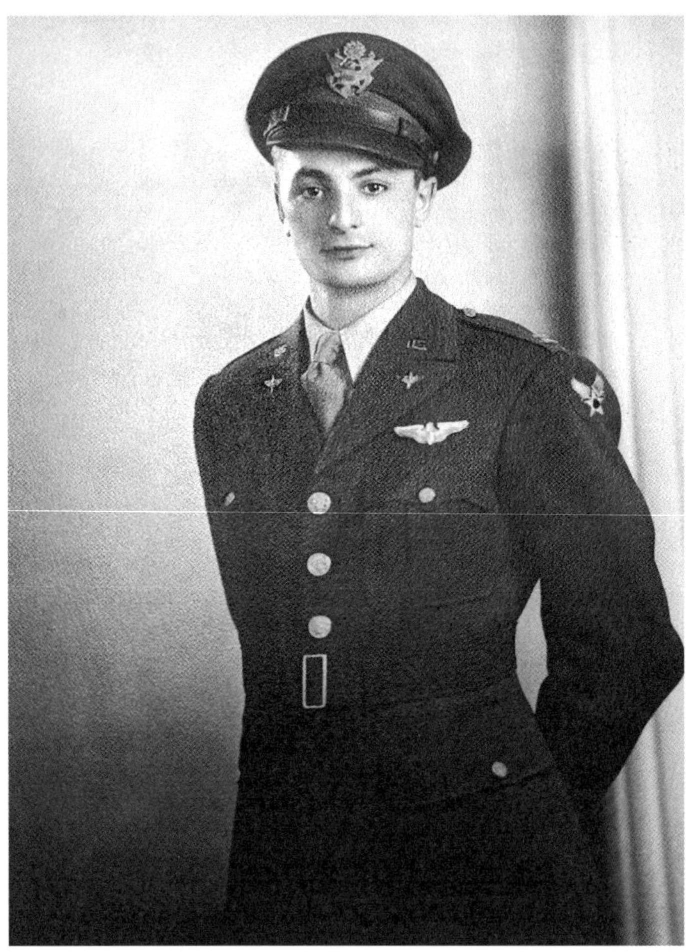

Captain Nando A. Cavalieri from Eveleth, Minnesota, was born on January 26, 1921. He graduated from Lane Technical High School and was employed as a photographer before he joined the Air Corps. Upon entering the service, Nando was trained to become a bombardier and was assigned to the 324th Bomb Squadron, 91st Bombardment Group, U.S. Eighth Air Force.

On February 3, 1945, the B-17 'Flying Fortress' bomber on which Nando was serving as a bombardier took part in a bombing raid to Berlin. Shortly after bombs away, the plane was struck by Flak (anti-aircraft fire). The bomber broke into two pieces and crashed. The plane's disintegration was witnessed by several crew members aboard other bombers, including Second Lieutenant Marvin M. Goldberg, also assigned to the 324th Bomb Squadron. He reported:

> ***'I was flying as Pilot in No. 2 position of the 4th element, and at about ten (10) seconds after bombs away I observed an explosion of a direct Flak hit in the waist section of Aircraft B-17-G, 42-97632. At this time, I also saw what appeared to be a secondary explosion in the interior of the aircraft as fire shot out of the nose. The aircraft disintegrated from about the horizontal stabilizer to the trailing edge of the wing. The tail section floated back through the formation and the forward section nosed downward. No flames or smoke were visible. I saw no crew members leave the aircraft or parachutes open.'***

Nando did not survive the downing of his bomber and died at the age of 24. German forces reportedly recovered his body and identification tags after the crash and buried him in Döberitz, Germany, on February 7.

Following the end of the war, the American Graves Registration Command (AGRC) recovered all of the American remains buried in Döberitz, but were unable to identify Nando Cavalieri. He was declared non-recoverable in 1951.

Between 2016 and 2018, historians of the Defense POW/MIA Accounting Agency (DPAA) completed a comprehensive research project focused on the eight sets of unknown remains recovered from Döberitz. As a result, one set of remains, designated X-4983 Neuville, was determined to be a strong candidate for association with Cavalieri. The remains, which had been buried in the Ardennes American Cemetery in Belgium, were disinterred in June 2018 and sent to the DPAA laboratory at Offutt Air Force Base, Nebraska, for examination and identification.

With the usage of anthropological analysis, circumstantial evidence, and DNA analysis, DPAA was able to identify the remains as being Nando's. He was officially accounted for on July 27, 2021. His remains were handed over to his relatives for final burial at Arlington National Cemetery in Arlington, Virginia. In Margraten, where Nando is recorded on the Walls of the Missing, a rosette next to his name indicates he has been accounted for.

CARMELO J. AMOROSO

Private First Class

78th Infantry Division

The memory that lives on

'It has not been in vain as long as anyone remembers your name.' Anthony Amoroso often spoke these words to his own children when he talked about his brother Carmelo. He visited his brother's grave in Margraten in 1979. Today, Mariska and Thijs Schijns-Sipers, who have adopted Carmelo's grave, make sure that Carmelo is not forgotten. His memory literally lives on.

When Mariska and Thijs were assigned Carmelo's grave in February 2017, little was known about him. Neither was there a photo of him. However, the records showed that he served as a Private First Class in the 78th Infantry Division and died in Kesternich, Germany, on February 4, 1945, from wounds sustained earlier that day. A week after receiving the adoption certificate, Mariska and her boyfriend visited the village in the German Eifel. They left a flower at the unit's monument in memory of Carmelo.

A year later, they were in contact with the Amoroso family. From them, they learned that Anthony and Carmelo were children of Italian immigrants who had settled in the state Massachusetts. Within the family, Carmelo simply went by 'Melo.' One of the photos that the family still had showed a six-year-old Carmelo saluting in a navy uniform. Also, the photo that the family had used for his obituary survived. It is a photo of a twenty-year-old Carmelo together with his fiancée Sally, taken minutes after he proposed to her. It is the last photo the family has of him. However, Sally never got to call Carmelo her husband. He died before they were able to get married.

The year Mariska and Thijs adopted Carmelo's grave, Mariska also became pregnant with her first child. She soon thought of naming the child after the soldier. 'I wanted to do something for a family that had lost a son. Moreover, this would be a good way to teach my son about history and to make him realize how precious it is that we can live in freedom.'

Little Carmelo, only six years old at that time.
SOURCE: Amoroso family via Mariska Schijns-Sipers

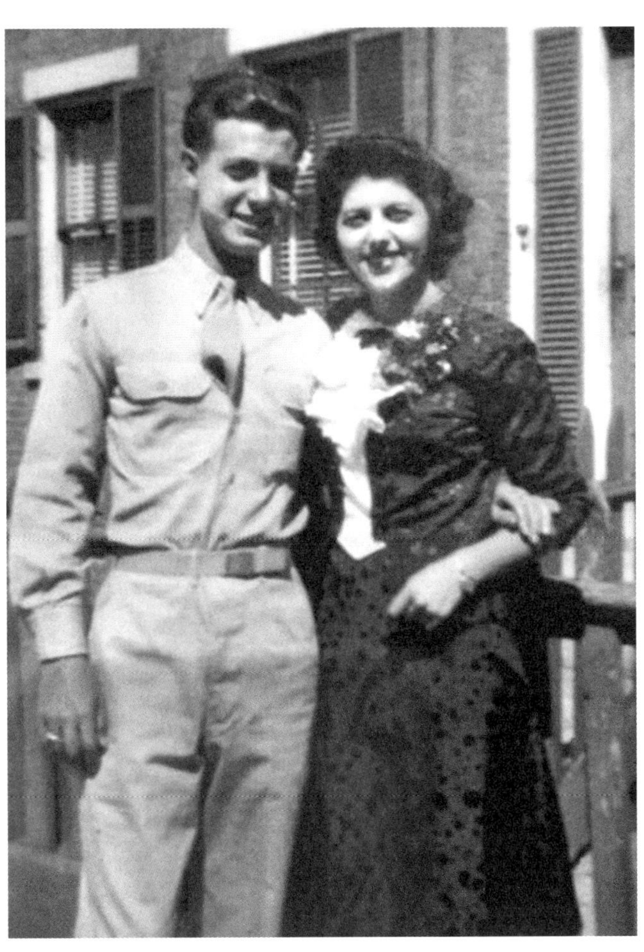

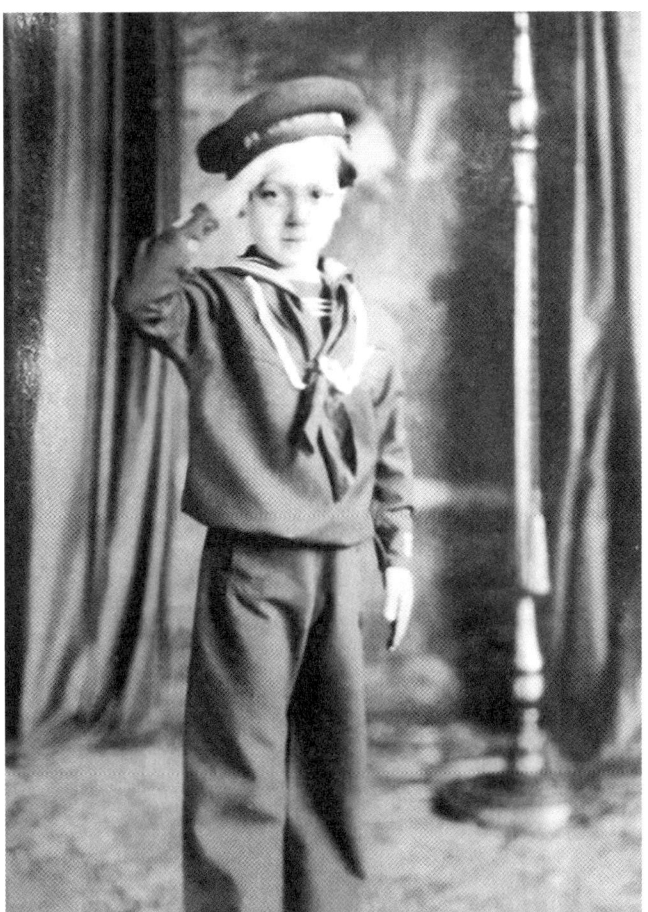

When she got to know Carmelo better, she was sure of her plan. 'We saw similarities. He was the first grandchild in the Amoroso family, our child the first in our family. He played flugelhorn and I play that too. And we heard about his beautiful personality.'

After the death of the previous grave adopter, the family was afraid that 'Melo' would be forgotten. So, when they learned of the idea of naming the child after their loved one, they were deeply moved. And so it happened. On May 7, 2018, Mariska gave birth to Floris Carmelo Amoroso. A few weeks later, flowers with a card announcing the birth of the newborn marked the grave of the child's namesake in Plot G, Row 8, Grave 5. From then on, the memory of Private First Class Carmelo Amoroso has lived on in new life.

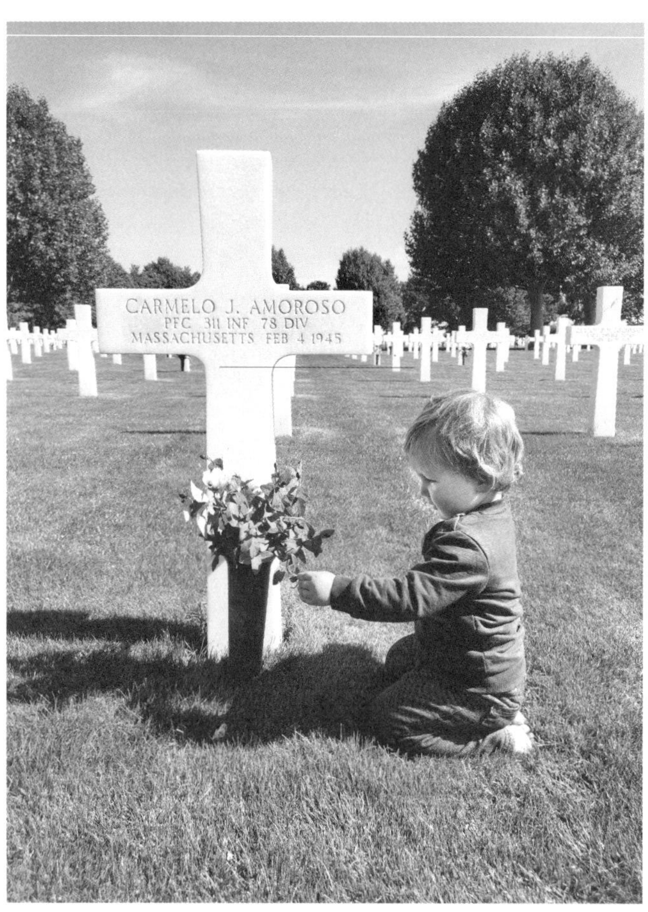

The two Carmelos together. SOURCE: Mariska Schijns-Sipers

ROBERT P. WOODHULL
Captain
460th Parachute Field Artillery Battalion

Forward artillery observer killed in the Hürtgen Forest

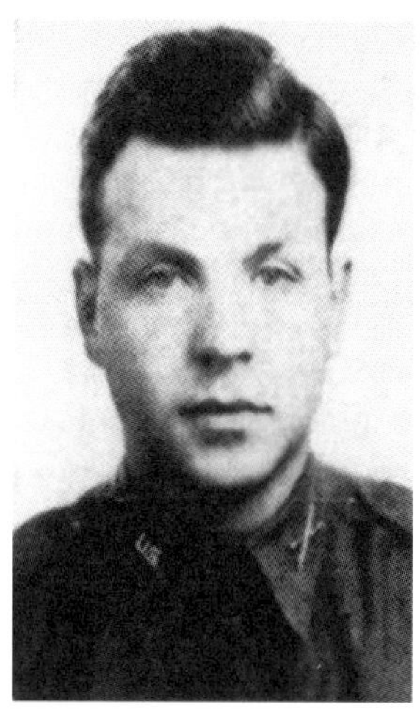

Captain Robert P. Woodhull from Ohio was born in Toledo on July 6, 1917. In 1940, he graduated from Princeton University, New Jersey, and went to work for a mining company, the Pocahontas Coal Company in West Virginia.

The following year, Robert entered the army and volunteered for the paratroopers. During his training for the airborne troops, Robert had to make several practice jumps. First, he made both day and night jumps from a nearly 80-meter-high tower to train his landing technique, followed by real jumps from airplanes. Although he was afraid of heights, Robert enjoyed the paratrooper training, as he reveals in one of his letters:

> ***'I will admit that I've never been so scared as I've been in the past week and a half...but on the other hand I like it.'***

After completing training, Robert was sent overseas to Italy in May 1944. He served as a forward observer in the 460th Parachute Field Artillery Battalion, which was attached to the 517th Parachute Regimental Combat Team. His job was to go forward as far as possible to direct artillery fire on enemy positions.

While fighting in Italy, Robert described his first combat experiences in a letter dated June 28, 1944, in which he said:

> ***'Can now say I've been in combat. Needless to say, you have so many 'impressions' that you can't put them down. It's quite a shock suddenly to hear the lead fly by, watch some of the lads brought in, hit the dirt as Jerry opens up with his artillery and see the dead etc.... we all get scared – really scared – plenty. (...) I used to think that after waiting around so damn long it would take a close shell or a few close bullets to make me realize I was in combat.'***

On August 15, 1944, Robert parachuted into southern France during Operation Dragoon. There he patrolled together many times with Lt. Howard Hensleigh, HQ Company, 3rd Battalion, 517th PIR. Hensleigh wrote:

'"Woody" of the 460th was a buddy. He had been assigned to the 3rd Bn. as our artillery liaison officer for a long time. He and his radio operator, Herbert Jeff, were virtually part of the 3rd Battalion. From the jump in Southern France on August 15, 1944, I was the Battalion S-2 responsible for obtaining information about the enemy. We did this mainly by patrolling. Woody and Herb went on almost all of our patrols (...) If we got in too deep and were being pursued by the Germans, Woody would call in artillery to give us time to make it back to our lines. (...) After a successful combat patrol, Woody would call in artillery to finish the job and keep the enemy troops from deciding to follow us as we withdrew.'

During one of their combat patrols, they took some German prisoners, of which Hensleigh later wrote:

'Once on a combat patrol in Southern France we had a platoon of Germans partially surrounded. When I yelled at them to surrender and several times the Germans stood up with their hands up, their noncom [non-commissioned officer] fired his machine gun to thwart the surrender. Woody crawled forward with me to within a few feet of the gun position where we silenced him. I put an M-1 clip [filled with rifle bullets] into the bush I thought his fire came from. Luckily, I guessed right, because I don't think there would have been a second chance. (...) We captured the platoon, all their weapons, ammo and equipment.'

While they were fighting in southern France, Robert was awarded the Bronze Star and promoted from First Lieutenant to Captain. About six months later, Robert and the 517th PIR found themselves in the front line in the German Hürtgen Forest. There he joined an attack on well-organized German positions near Bergstein on February 7, 1945. Hensleigh went with Robert and later recalled what happened:

'What Woody and I were attempting to do was to give G, H and I Companies artillery support in their attacks. We got too close that morning. Woodhull was killed by a burst of machine gun fire not more than three feet from me... We were doing our "damnedest" to assist the attack with artillery, probably a little too far forward...which was usual with Woody.'

Robert was only 27 years old when the German bullets fatally struck him. A few days later, he was laid to rest in Margraten. Then, on February 14, a thorough itemized inventory of his personal effects was sent to his sister. The list included all items of his clothing, his military insignias, a tattered Bronze Star, four books, cash, and the sunglasses that he had received only a few weeks before. Five months later, a letter was received from the army in which was described that among his personal effects the army had also found a Bronze Star ribbon which was damaged by bullet marks. The army did not want to remove it from his effects but neither did they want to send it if it would be too shocking a confrontation with the fact that Robert had been killed.

Two years after the war, in November 1947, Robert's father received another letter concerning the disinterment and final burial of those who died in the U.S. military during World War II. His father chose to leave Robert's remains in Margraten, where he was then permanently laid to rest among his fellow soldiers. Robert's final resting place there can be found in Plot F, Row 8, Grave 1.

RALPH H. WHEELER

Technical Sergeant

306th Bombardment Group

Shot down by German fighters

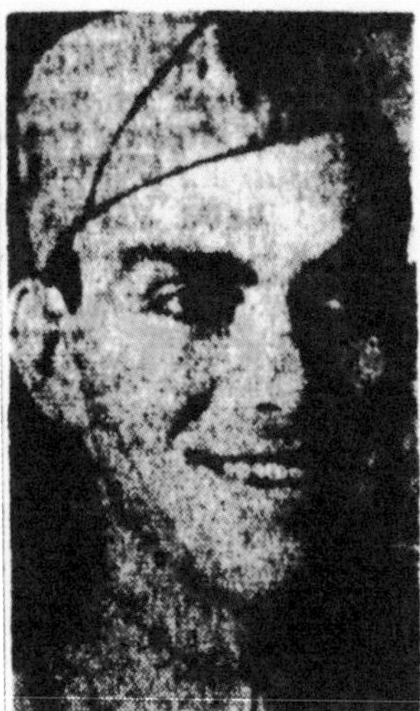

Sgt. Ralph H. Wheeler

Sgt. R. H. Wheeler, Bomber Engineer

Tech. Sgt. Ralph H. Wheeler of Brooklyn, previously reported missing after his B-17 bomber was shot down over Germany during his 15th mission, was killed in action, his mother, Mrs. Margaret M. Wheeler, has been informed by the War Department.

Confirmation of his death, which occurred Feb. 22, 1944, came through the nternational Red Cross which received its information from the German government.

Sergeant Wheeler, who was an aerial engineer, would have been 24 on Jan. 8. He was born in Bay Ridge and was graduated from Manual Training High School. He was a member of the Roosevelt Chapter of the Order of De Molay and was active in the South Reformed Church.

Besides his mother, he is survived by a sister, Mrs. David Love of 523 Senator St., and a brother, Robert, of 7002 Ridge Boulevard.

Technical Sergeant Ralph H. Wheeler was born in Bay Ridge, New York in 1921. He graduated from Manuel Training High School and enlisted in September 1942. Ralph joined the USAAF and served as an engineer and top turret gunner in the four-engine B-17 'Holy Hellcat' of the 423rd Bomb Squadron. This squadron was part of the 306th Bombardment Group.

Ralph's unit, the 306th Bombardment Group, was formed in 1942 and was nicknamed 'The Reich Wreckers.' That same year, the group was stationed in England at USAAF Station 111 in Thurleigh, located in the county of Bedfordshire.

On February 22, 1945, Ralph took off for the fifteenth time to participate in a bombing mission to Germany. His bomber group was assigned to destroy production facilities of the German aircraft industry at Bernburg. During this mission, Ralph operated the two machine guns in the turret above the plane's fuselage.

During the return flight to England, Ralph's B-17 was attacked by German fighters. As a result, the 'Holy Hellcat' did not return from this mission, as the German fighters shot the aircraft out of the sky over Germany. The 'Holy Hellcat' subsequently crashed near Herfen-Waldbröl. Ralph and six other crew members were killed in the crash. Ralph was only 23 years old when he lost his life. In Margraten, visitors can find his final resting place in Plot D, Row 8, Grave 5.

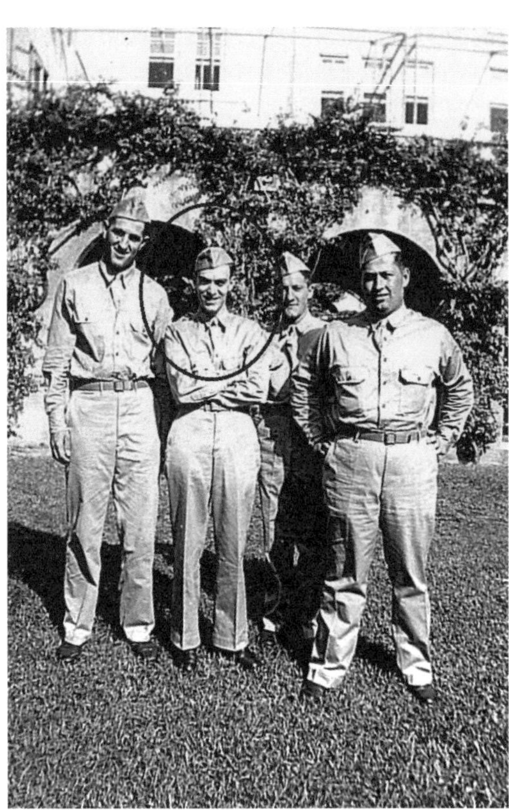

JOSEPH J. DI FAZIO

Sergeant

104th Infantry Division

A friendship between two families

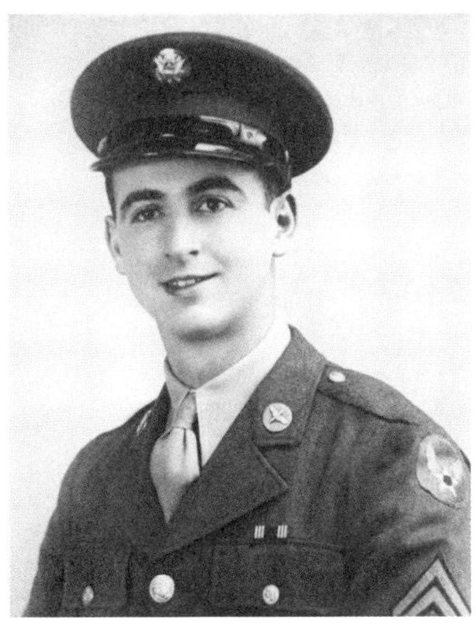

One day in 2015, Gail Phelps was reading the newspaper when she learned about *The Faces of Margraten* tribute and its mission to put a face to every name. She knew that one of her uncles had been killed in the war, but she was not sure where he had been buried. Could it be Margraten? She took the question to the Internet and yes indeed: her uncle Joseph Di Fazio had been laid to rest in Margraten. Among the photos her mother had given to her was a photo of a guy in uniform. Her cousins confirmed it was Joseph. And so, she submitted the photo to the tribute, not knowing that it would mark the beginning of a friendship between two families on two different continents.

Joseph James Di Fazio was the son of Italian immigrants. His father Giuseppe, born in the town of Alvito, was only seven years old when he arrived in New York in 1898. But he became an American citizen only after he had married Concetta Nero and their two children had been born, almost twenty years later. The family lived in Pennsylvania. It was there, in Wilson, that Joseph was born on October 31, 1919.

By the 1930s, the family had moved to Detroit. At the outbreak of the war, Giuseppe worked in the auto industry there, while Joseph worked in his brother Anthony's store in the city. But Joseph was drafted. A photo shows him in an U.S. Army Air Forces uniform. However, at the time of his death, he served as a sergeant with the 415th Infantry Regiment, 104th Infantry Division. He was killed on February 23, 1945, the day on which the division crossed the Roer River in Germany.

Joseph, only 25 years old when he died, rests in Plot B, Row 13, Grave 29. Dymphie Weusten has adopted his grave. 'It was first adopted by my grandfather. Then by my father, who has passed away. So then I adopted his grave,' Dymphie said. 'I hope my children will look after his grave after I am gone.' However, she had never seen a picture of him, until the photo that Gail had submitted was put next to his grave. 'He was such a young guy, and handsome.'

Nobody in Joseph's family had ever been to the grave, or had even seen it. So, when Dutch TV channel RTL Nieuws came to see the family and showed the video of Dymphie visiting the grave of 'uncle Joe,' everyone was 'in tears,' Gail recalled. According to Joseph's youngest and then only surviving brother Ben, the family thought it was better to 'leave him with the boys' because bringing him back home was too much to bear, especially for their mother. But he said while holding back tears, 'we miss him, all the time.' Ben passed away a year after seeing his brother's grave for the first time.

In 2017, Gail was the first one of the family to visit Joseph's grave. In return, Dymphie visited Gail in Michigan in 2019. To this day, they frequently exchange messages. It is a friendship that would not have existed without Joseph's sacrifice.

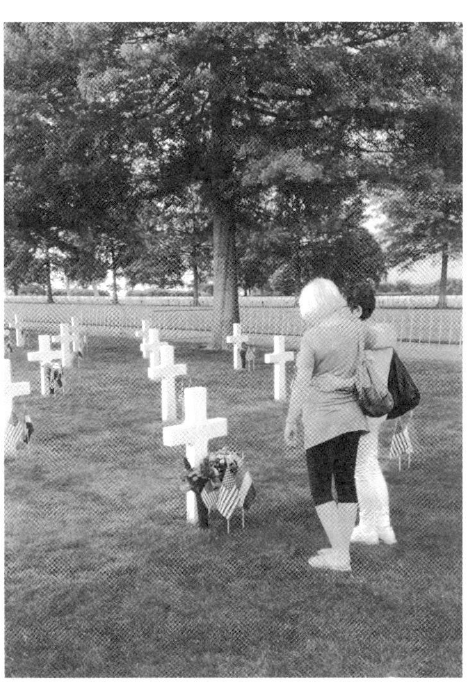

Dymphie and Gail stand at the grave of Joseph, Memorial Day 2017. SOURCE: Dymphie Weusten

WILLIAM G. AUBUT
Sergeant
30th Infantry Division

Wrote 225 letters to his wife

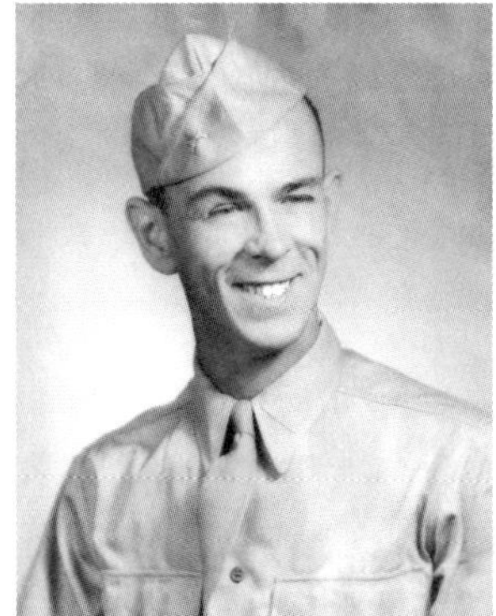

Sergeant William G. Aubut from Massachusetts was born on September 29, 1917. He was married to his beloved Doris and together they were the proud parents of a daughter named Donna. In March 1944, William was drafted into the military. He reported to Fort Devens to enter the army and was then sent to Camp Wheeler, Georgia, for basic training.

After completing his training, William was sent overseas to Europe as an infantryman. He was assigned to Company F of the 119th Infantry Regiment. This regiment was part of the 30th 'Old Hickory' Infantry Division, which had entered combat in Normandy a few days after D-Day.

During his eleven months of military service, William wrote a total of 225 letters to his wife. In his last letter home, dated February 22, 1945, he wrote to her that he was 'somewhere in Germany.' Further on he wrote:

> ***'Well darling please try not to worry about getting a telegram. (...) I love you both and miss you so very much. I hope this all ends soon. I will be so glad when I can come home to you. See dear won't it be well when we can live a normal life again. I won't mind working for you and my Donna. Well dearest I must sign off for now. Kiss Donna for me darling. Goodbye for now little girl of my dreams. I love you my darling wife. All my love, Your Bill'***

The next day, February 23, 1945, William and his company crossed the Roer River near the village of Selgersdorf. Company F then advanced toward Daubenrath. During this advance, William and another soldier, PFC Arlon L. Adams, were suddenly fired upon and killed side by side. According to William's grandson Mark LaPointe, their deaths were caused by German machine gun fire from a sniper's nest concealed within a haystack. Mark obtained this information in 2000, when he visited Sgt. Charles Miner. Miner had also served in Company F and told Mark that he saw William and Arlon fall after the concealed sniper's nest had opened fire on them. Sgt. Miner's memories correspond to a description in the Combat History of the 119th Infantry Regiment, which was published in 1946. On page 104 one can read: 'Company F advanced across the open fields to within 800 yards of Daubenrath. Suddenly the leading platoon was hit by machine gun fire, losing two men. The enemy [four German soldiers] had skillfully concealed the gun under a haystack 300 yards away.' It is very plausible that this fragment refers to the fate of William and Arlon.

William was only 27 years old when he made the ultimate sacrifice in the open fields near Daubenrath. His daughter Donna had just celebrated her third birthday shortly before. She was thus too young to realize that her father would never come home again. Meanwhile, William was laid to rest in Margraten. He was also given his final resting place there, which visitors can find in Plot D, Row 7, Grave 8.

William's story does not end with his death and burial in Margraten. For example, what happened to all his letters? The answer to this question is a gripping story in itself: 'My grandmother remarried when my mother Donna was 9 years old,' Mark LaPointe wrote in 2019 in response to an e-mail from one of the authors of this book. 'The man that she married said that he did not want to compete with William's ghost. He was gone and she had a new life now with him. My mother told me that they were not allowed to talk about William in the house, so, growing up, all she ever knew about her father was that he was killed in the war by a German.'

Mark continued his anecdote by writing that his grandmother 'hid the letters in a small shoe box underneath a floorboard in the attic of the home.' This remained her well-guarded secret for 30 years.

> ***'My grandmother kept the location of the letters a secret until 1980. She was living out the final days of her life in the home (she died of cancer) and told my mother that she had some letters that were written by her father, and where they could be found. She instructed my mother to retrieve them, which she did. They sat together on my grandmother's bed and together they read every letter. My grandmother said, "I will tell you everything about your father now."'***

So, after all these years, Donna got to know her father a little through his letters.

ARLON L. ADAMS

Private First Class

30th Infantry Division

Bravely battled German tanks

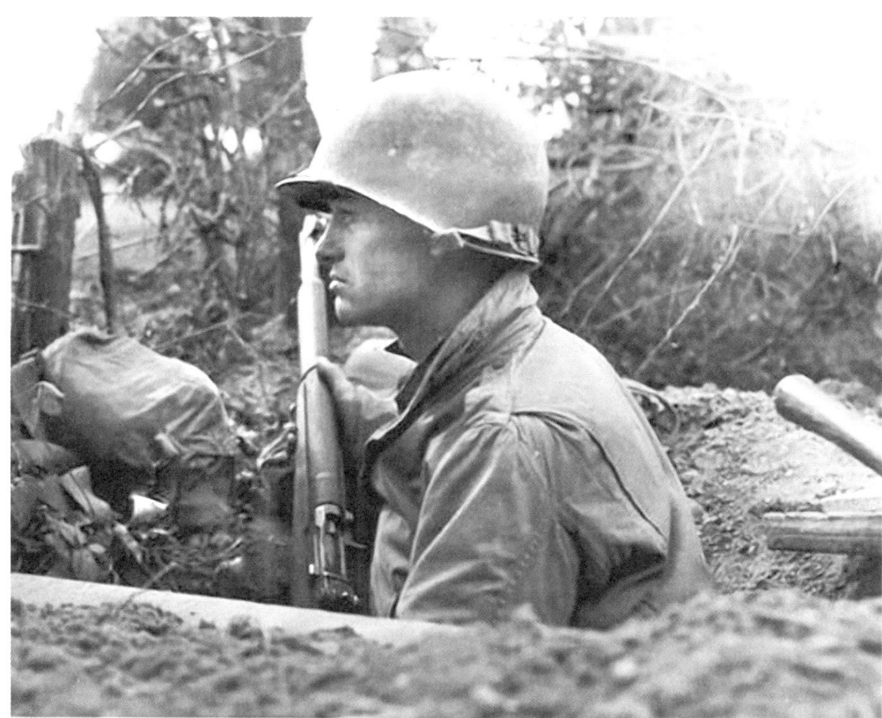

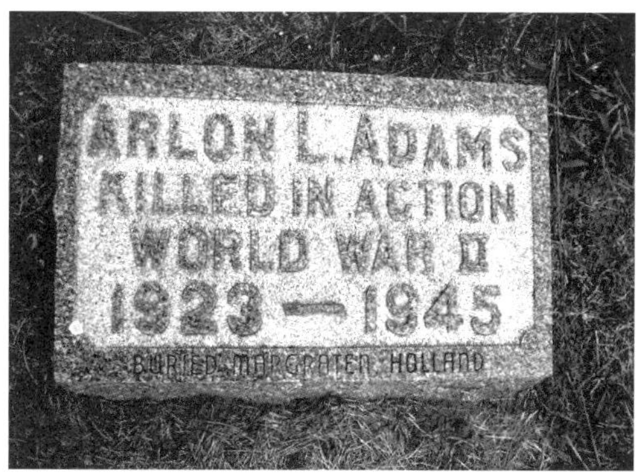

Many families erected markers in memory of their loved ones in local cemeteries. This marker in the Whiteford Union Cemetery memorializes Arlon Adams. SOURCE: Laura Phillips

Private First Class Arlon L. Adams from Michigan was born on January 11, 1923. He entered the army in 1942 and served in Company F, 119th Infantry Regiment, 30th Infantry Division. As described in the previous story, Arlon, along with Sgt. William G. Aubut, was killed on February 23, 1945, by German machine gun fire from a sniper's nest concealed in a haystack. As a result, his life ended abruptly at the age of 22.

During a 30th Division action in Germany a few months earlier on November 26, 1944, Arlon and another Fox Company soldier, Pvt. Russell R. Teague, had managed to halt an attack of six German tanks and a company of enemy infantry. According to the Combat History of the 119th Infantry Regiment, Arlon and his companion hit two of the tanks with their Bazooka, after which the tanks stopped and turned back. However, their Bazooka flashes had given away their position and the enemy infantry, with grenades and small arms, forced them to abandon their foxholes and take cover in a creek. They remained in the ice-cold water for 40 minutes, bringing fire on the enemy infantry until artillery fire caused the enemy to withdraw. Arlon was awarded the Silver Star for this gallant action.

After Arlon died in February 1945, his remains were laid to rest at the U.S. Military Cemetery in Margraten. He was also given his final resting place there, which can be found in Plot J, Row 21, Grave 22.

Anyone who visits his grave in Margraten will possibly notice that on his cross February 24, 1945 is listed as the date of his death. The memories of Sgt. Charles Miner described in William G. Aubut's story suggest that a clerical error may therefore have been made in the registration of Arlon's death. After all, according to Sgt. Miner, Arlon, like Sgt. Aubut, was killed on the previous day and not on the 24th.

RAYMOND F. THERIOT SR.
Private
84th Infantry Division

Almost certainly drowned in the Roer River

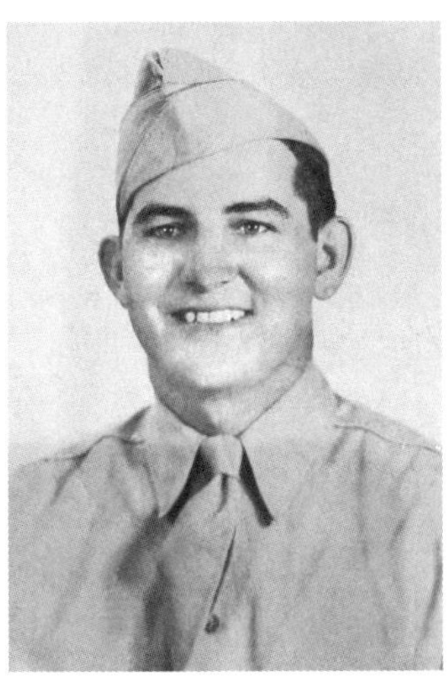

Private Raymond F. Theriot Sr. was born on November 20, 1921, and was a native of Terrebonne Parish, Louisiana. He was married to Mrs. Mae D. Theriot and had become the father of two children, a daughter and a son.

On August 21, 1944, Raymond entered the U.S. Army at the age of 22. He was assigned to Company C of the 334th Infantry Regiment. This regiment was part of the 84th Infantry Division, which was ordered into active military service in 1942 and shipped to Europe during the autumn of 1944. After arriving on Omaha Beach on November 1, the subsequent motor march through northern France and Belgium, and a short stay in Wittem, the Netherlands, Raymond's regiment entered combat across the German border near Geilenkirchen on November 18, 1944.

More than three months after the division's arrival on the front lines, Raymond lost his life and was reported missing in action on February 23, 1945. A report of the 7887 Graves Registration Detachment, signed by Captain C.W. Steinsiek on October 20, 1950, states that reports indicated that Raymond was part of a group of twelve men of Company C, 334th Infantry Regiment who were in an assault boat, crossing the Roer River near Linnich, Germany. The report further states that the boat was subjected to enemy machine gun fire, which caused it to sink. Also because of the fact that it was known that Raymond and the other casualties were heavily clothed and carried heavy equipment, the researchers at the time determined that 'it can only be concluded that they were wounded and drowned in the Roer River.'

Even more than three-quarters of a century later, nothing is known about Raymond's remains – he is still missing. Therefore, his name is listed on the Walls of the Missing in Margraten. Back home in Louisiana, a memorial stone bearing his name has been placed at the Saint Eloi Cemetery.

LYNN H. MEAD JR.
First Lieutenant
30th Infantry Division

Medals for courageous leadership

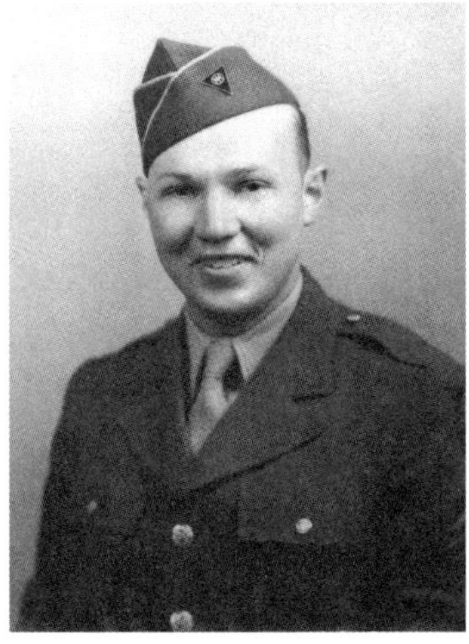

Lynn H. Mead Jr. was born in 1916. In 1941, he graduated from The Agricultural and Mechanical College of Texas. Lynn then entered the army in October 1942. Before Lynn left for Europe, he first married Marie De Nerge.

After arriving on the front lines, Lynn served as a platoon commander in Company E of the 117th Infantry Regiment, which formed part of the 30th 'Old Hickory' Infantry Division. This division played a major role in the liberation of South Limburg, the Dutch region in which the American cemetery in Margraten is now located.

On January 2, 1945, Lynn led a dangerous combat patrol into enemy territory in Belgium. He had volunteered for this task and crossed a river with a group of soldiers, using rubber rafts. Across the river, they had to obtain information about German troop dispositions. For this purpose, they were tasked with capturing a German prisoner for interrogation.

During this mission, Lynn and his men were discovered by the Germans. Nevertheless, Lynn successfully accomplished the mission under enemy fire, after which he and his men returned to the company area without a single casualty. For the courageous leadership he displayed during this patrol, Lynn was awarded the Bronze Star.

Exactly twenty days later, on January 22, 1945, Lynn earned an even higher medal: the Silver Star. On this day, the tanks on which his platoon was attacking in Belgium got stuck in deep snow. Lynn and his platoon were forced to dismount. Then Lynn and his men continued the attack through the snowy terrain and intense enemy fire from a tank and a self-propelled gun. Again, Lynn's leadership was outstanding. He exposed himself to the enemy fire to maneuver his platoon, with the result that he and his men reached the objective and managed to put the self-propelled gun out of action. Lynn then directed friendly fire that knocked out the enemy tank, allowing his platoon to advance.

Over a month later, Lynn was killed near Hambach-Niederzier in Germany on February 24, 1945. This happened when the company's command post was hit by shellfire. Lynn was 28 years old at the time. In Margraten, he is buried in Plot G, Row 8, Grave 21.

A 'citation' motivates why a soldier received a particular award, in this case the Silver Star

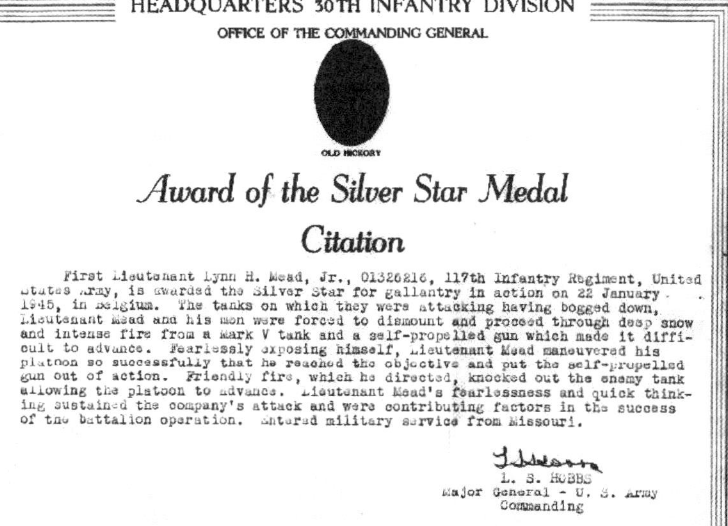

HEADQUARTERS 30TH INFANTRY DIVISION

OFFICE OF THE COMMANDING GENERAL

OLD HICKORY

Award of the Silver Star Medal

Citation

First Lieutenant Lynn H. Mead, Jr., 01326216, 117th Infantry Regiment, United States Army, is awarded the Silver Star for gallantry in action on 22 January 1945, in Belgium. The tanks on which they were attacking having bogged down, Lieutenant Mead and his men were forced to dismount and proceed through deep snow and intense fire from a Mark V tank and a self-propelled gun which made it difficult to advance. Fearlessly exposing himself, Lieutenant Mead maneuvered his platoon so successfully that he reached the objective and put the self-propelled gun out of action. Friendly fire, which he directed, knocked out the enemy tank allowing the platoon to advance. Lieutenant Mead's fearlessness and quick thinking sustained the company's attack and were contributing factors in the success of the battalion operation. Entered military service from Missouri.

L. S. HOBBS
Major General - U. S. Army
Commanding

DAVID OGLENSKY

First Lieutenant

740th Tank Battalion

A roadblock in the Ardennes

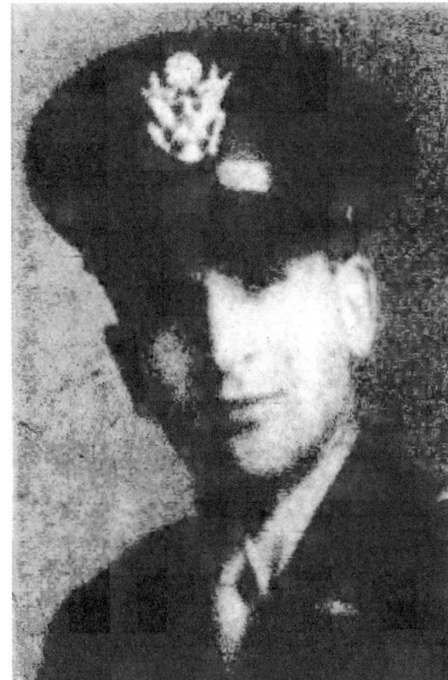

The Jewish officer David Oglensky was born in Connecticut in 1914, but by the time he entered the army he and his wife Helen resided in Freehold, New Jersey. Before enlisting, David was employed as the manager of the Lincoln Auto Store in his hometown.

In March 1945, the local newspaper of David's hometown, *The Freehold Transcript and The Monmouth Inquirer,* published an article announcing that David was awarded the Silver Star for gallantry in action a few months earlier during the Battle of the Bulge. His citation reads:

> ***'Lt. David Oglensky, with the 740th Tank Battalion, distinguished himself by leading a platoon of tanks in an attack against the enemy on December 20, 1944 in Belgium [near the village of Stoumont]. His tank was hit to such an extent that his gun was put out of action. After evacuating the crew, he re-entered the tank and placed it across the road as a block. Taking over command of the tank immediately behind this roadblock, he continued to fire at the enemy until the second tank was also knocked out of action by enemy fire.'***

David's actions near Stoumont were also reported by Captain Franklin Ferriss, Historical Officer of the 30th Infantry Division, who wrote:

> ***'The leading tank, commanded by Lt. Oglensky, was hit by a well-camouflaged direct-fire weapon, emplaced at the crossroads on the north side of town. The tank's gun was disabled, but the motor was alright. As it was almost dark, and too late to attack the town, Capt. Berry ordered Lt. Oglensky to turn his tank sideways across the road to form a roadblock. Lt. Oglensky did so.'***

This report corresponds to a narrative written by Lieutenant-colonel George Rubel, the commanding officer of the 740th Tank Battalion. His report, which dates the actions in question to December 21 and not 20, provides more details:

> ***'The attack was resumed at 4:00 hrs. It moved forward about 100 yards when an anti-tank gun knocked out the lead tank. Lieutenant Oglensky, who was riding the tank, found that his gun had been rendered useless and fearing that Jerry was about to begin a tank attack he placed his own tank crosswise in the road to form a roadblock. As he was doing this another shot hit his tank. He ordered his crew to get out and go to the rear, while he took over the tank immediately to the rear. He hardly got aboard when an enemy Panzerfaust hit the tank and the machine started to burn. He and his crew dismounted and almost at the same instant two more tanks were hit by Panzerfausts.'***

David survived the fierce fighting in the Ardennes and on February 25, 1945, his tank platoon of Company C was ordered to advance towards Girbelsrath in Germany. During their advance, three of the platoon's tanks were hit and destroyed by enemy 88mm fire. David, who commanded one of these knocked out tanks, was killed as a result. He was 30 years old at the time and was listed as missing in action. Because nothing of his body has ever been found since, his name is mentioned on the Walls of the Missing in Margraten.

ROBERT C. ROLPH

Staff Sergeant

102nd Infantry Division

Killed by shrapnel

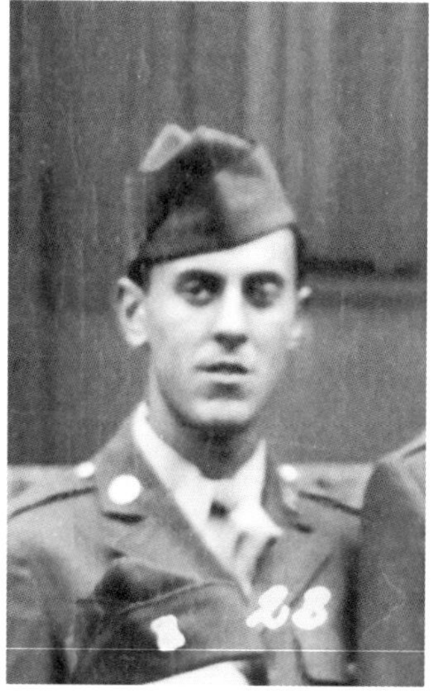

Staff Sergeant Robert C. Rolph was born on February 8, 1922. His place of birth was Whittier in California, but by the time he entered the military he was living in Philadelphia, Pennsylvania. In the summer of 1942, Robert entered The Citadel, the military academy of South Carolina. He was supposed to graduate in 1946, but after just one year he was drafted into the army.

In October 1943, Robert was selected for the Army Specialized Training Program, abbreviated as the ASTP. This special training program of the U.S. Army trained intelligent young men to become medical or technical officers within the armed forces. To attend this program, Robert was placed at the Catholic University of America in Washington, D.C. Here he would be trained as an army engineer.

Although the army was also in need of highly trained engineers, the ASTP was suspended in 1944 because the army had an even more urgent need for new infantrymen. Robert was assigned to the 406th Infantry Regiment of the 102nd Infantry Division and sent overseas to Europe.

In February 1945, Robert's division spearheaded the Ninth U.S. Army's advance across the Roer River toward the Rhine. Two days after crossing the Roer, Robert was killed near Hottorf on February 25, 1945. He was struck down by shrapnel from a German artillery or tank shell while he was erecting communication lines.

Robert was only 23 years old when he died. His remains were buried at the Netherlands American Cemetery and Memorial in Margraten. Today, visitors can find his final resting place there in Plot D, Row 9, Grave 8.

ANTHONY L. LO CARRO

Corporal

701st Tank Battalion

One last cigarette

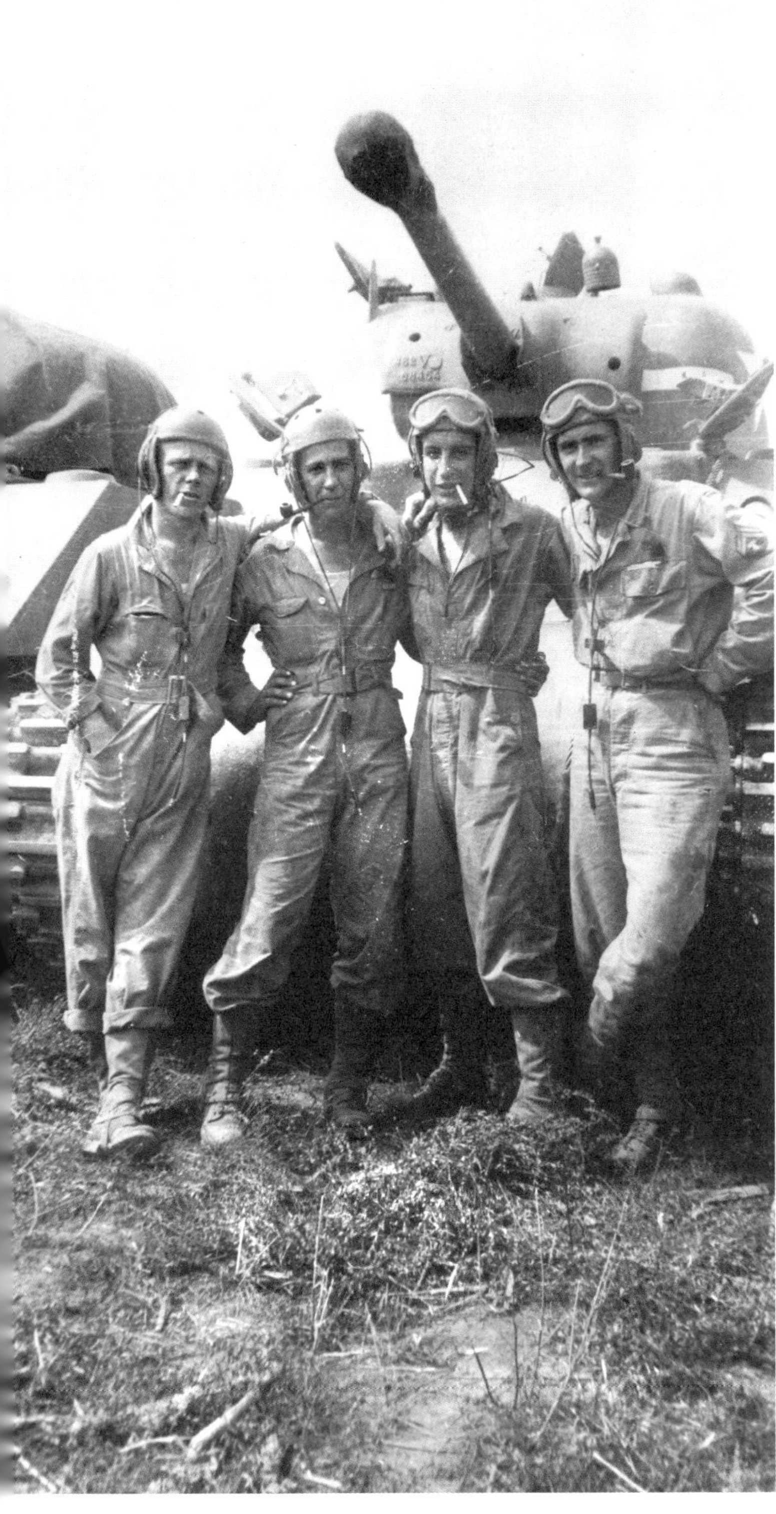

The tank crew with Anthony Lo Carro being second from left

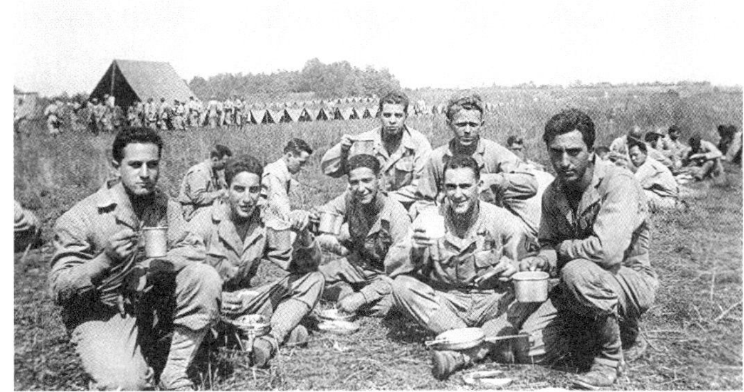

Taking a break. Anthony Lo Carro is third from left

Corporal Anthony L. Lo Carro from New York was born in 1924, and together with his father, mother, and brother he lived in The Bronx. He was studying at Manhattan College, but was called into service in February 1943. This prevented him from fulfilling his dream of becoming an engineer.

After enlisting in the army, Anthony was assigned to the 701st Tank Battalion. This tank unit had been formed in March 1943 and was shipped to England over a year later in April 1944. In this battalion, Anthony served as a crew member of a Sherman tank.

At the end of February 1945, after crossing the Roer River, the tanks of Anthony's battalion supported the advance of the 102nd Infantry Division toward the Rhine. Near the village of Hottorf they met strong resistance. The German defenders appeared to have a considerable number of 88mm guns at their disposal in this area and took the Americans heavily under fire. These enemy guns were so well camouflaged that the American tank crews and infantry soldiers could hardly see them until it was too late.

During the fighting at Hottorf, the German firepower inflicted considerable losses on the Americans. On February 25, 1945, Anthony's tank was also hit and disabled by enemy fire. As a result, he suffered severe injuries to his legs. A close friend, Sergeant Clement Patriarca, found him outside the tank not much later. Anthony then asked Clement if he had a cigarette for him. Shortly thereafter, Anthony went into shock and died from his injuries.

Anthony is permanently interred at the U.S. Military Cemetery in Margraten. Visitors can pay tribute to him there by going to Plot D, Row 8, Grave 28.

CHARLES B. PICKARD

Private First Class

58th Armored Infantry Battalion

First soldier killed

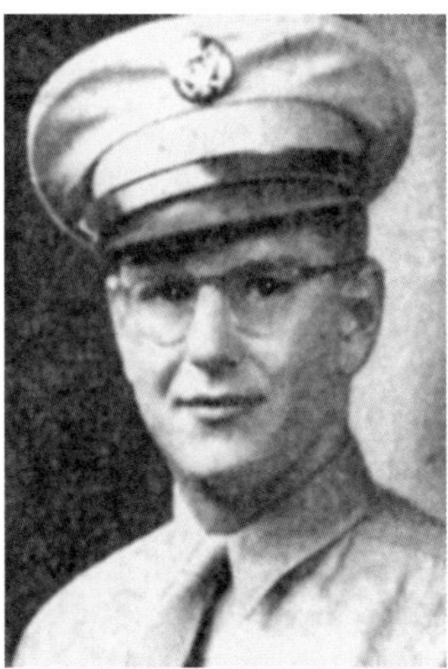

Private First Class Charles B. Pickard was born in North Carolina in 1925. He later moved to Dubuque, Iowa. In March 1944, when Charles was in his senior year of high school, he was drafted into the military. Charles reported to Camp Dodge Herrold to enter the army.

In November 1944, Charles went overseas to England as an infantryman. He served in Company C of the 58th Armored Infantry Battalion. This battalion was part of the 8th Armored Division.

After the 58th Armored Infantry Battalion had arrived in France in January 1945, the troops traveled through northern France and Belgium to the Dutch province of Limburg. The unit then moved further north toward the town of Roermond in February.

South of Roermond, however, formidable German opposition halted the Allied advance near Linne. The Germans held strong positions here and could inflict a significant number of casualties on the Americans.

One of the Americans who made the ultimate sacrifice in this area was the then nineteen-year-old Charles, who was killed in action on February 25, 1945. According to his best friend and fellow soldier PFC Leonard Justofin, Charles was shot by a German sniper in the doorway of the local Graven Farm while he was carrying ammo to the machine gunners upstairs. Charles was the first soldier of Company C who lost his life due to direct enemy action. He was buried at the temporary American cemetery in Margraten and later received his final resting place here as well. It can be found today in Plot B, Row 14, Grave 18.

EDWIN K. NEWMAN

First Lieutenant

7th Armored Infantry Battalion

Prankish fellow always became serious when necessary

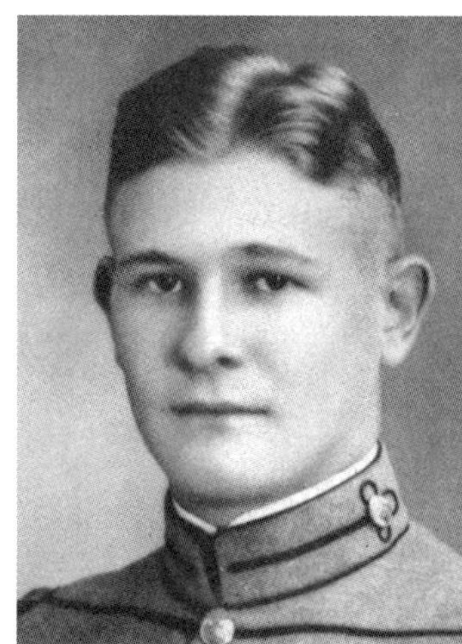

First Lieutenant Edwin Karl Newman from Winston-Salem, North Carolina, was born on July 13, 1917. Edwin, whose nickname was 'Benny,' graduated from Richard J. Reynolds High School and subsequently entered The Citadel. In 1939, he graduated from this famous military college with a degree in Business Administration.

According to the 1939 edition of *The Sphinx*, the official yearbook of The Citadel, Benny was a 'jolly, good-natured fellow.' He was playful and prankish, 'but he has always succeeded in becoming serious when necessary.' The yearbook also tells that Benny possessed an unsurpassed ability for telling tales. But the cadet staff wrote with a humorous tone, 'we sometimes wonder about their veracity.'

Following his graduation, Benny was employed by the Duke Power company in Winston-Salem. In 1941, he married Ms. Daisy Faircloth Groner. Several months later, on January 3, 1942, Benny entered the military. Initially, he was assigned as an instructor at the Infantry School at Fort Benning, Georgia, but at some point, he left for Europe to serve as a combat officer in the 8th Armored Division. Benny was assigned to the division's 7th Armored Infantry Battalion and assumed command of its Charlie Company on January 26, 1945.

Exactly one month later, on February 26, 1945, Benny was killed in action in the vicinity of Aandenberg near the village of Montfort, Holland, located a few miles east of the river Meuse and southwest of the Roer. According to information obtained by The Citadel Memorial Europe, a foundation founded by '89 Citadel graduate Roger Long, Benny was killed during a mortar attack. As a result, he remained forever 27. His final resting place in Margraten can be found in Plot D, Row 7, Grave 14.

EARL MORGAN
Corporal
784th Tank Battalion

African American soldier was killed inside his tank

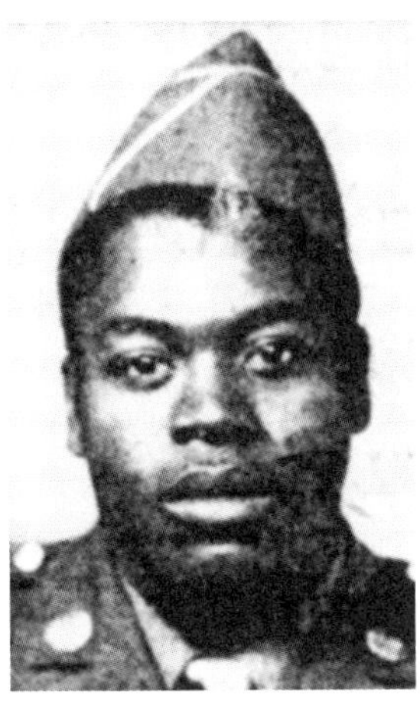

Corporal Earl Morgan from New Jersey was born in 1922. He lived in Plainfield and grew up with four brothers and one sister. Earl was educated at the local Plainfield High School and entered the army in 1943. Two of his brothers, Daniel and Frederick, also served in the military during the war.

After his enlistment, Earl was stationed and trained in army camps in Mississippi and Texas. Because he was an African American, he probably did not feel too comfortable in these two southern states. After all, racial segregation and discrimination against black Americans was most prevalent in the southern United States at the time. After this training period, Earl was sent to New York to embark for England.

Earl arrived in Europe in November 1944. He served in Company A of the 784th Tank Battalion, a segregated tank unit that consisted entirely of African Americans. Only the senior officers in charge were white. Along with four comrades, Earl went to fight in a Sherman tank.

On February 27, 1945, Earl was killed in action at Wassenberg, Germany. His body was taken to the 110th Clearing Station, but unfortunately his Hospital Admission Card File does not tell us anything about the nature of his injuries or cause of death. However, a book on his battalion describes that Earl's unit 'encountered three deadly anti-tank guns that destroyed one 784th tank.' Furthermore, it claims that 'Corporal Earl Morgan perished inside the blazing tank.'

The fact that on February 27 one Able Company tank was lost during an encounter with enemy anti-tank guns is also briefly described in the battalion's After-Action Report. Although no names of Enlisted Men are mentioned in this description, it is likely that this excerpt from the report refers to Earl and the tank he was in. However, the report says nothing about the number of German anti-tank guns encountered and whether or not the lost tank had caught fire.

Earl was just 22 years old when he died. A few weeks later, his parents were informed and an obituary was published in the local newspaper, the *Courier-News*. In Margraten, Earl is buried in Plot G, Row 15, Grave 18.

RUSSELL G. FRETZ JR.
Corporal
58th Armored Infantry Battalion

Killed in action near Roermond

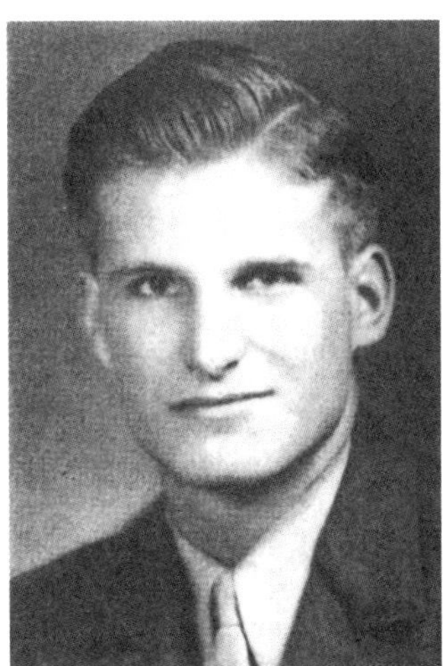

Corporal Russell G. Fretz Jr. from Pennsylvania was born in 1923. During his education at Sellersville-Perkasie High School, he excelled in track, basketball, and football. In 1941, the year he graduated there, Russell was the president of his class.

After graduation, Russell took evening classes at Temple University, Philadelphia, and was employed in the chemical laboratories of the Midvale Steel Company. Meanwhile, Russell was also an active member of his Reformed Church community.

Russell entered the army in April 1943, and in November 1944 he was sent overseas to Europe. Here he fought as a machine gunner in Company C of the 58th Armored Infantry Battalion. This battalion was part of the 8th Armored Division.

On February 27, 1945, Russell's Charlie Company attacked a factory building in Merum, outside the Dutch village of Linne and southwest of Roermond. During the attack, Russell and his ammo carrier PFC Wyman J. French were called forward by their squad leader, Staff Sergeant Burns, to lay down suppressing fire for a platoon that was pinned down by enemy fire. This and what happened next is known to this day thanks to the memories of Sergeant Paul W. Clare, who fought in the same squad at the time. Later, Sergeant Clare shared his memories with his son David – in 'graphic detail,' as David recalls from his youth. Thanks to the stories of his father, David learned that French was killed by a German machine gun nest when he and Russell were setting up their gun. Seeing his buddy killed, Russell picked up the machine gun and charged the enemy position. He was gunned down too and died close to his fallen buddy.

Russell is laid to rest in Margraten, where his final resting place can be found in Plot F, Row 9, Grave 20. Buried next to him is Staff Sergeant Burns, who also died during the attack on the Merum factory and to whom the next story is dedicated. The grave of Wyman J. French is nearby in Plot G, Row 10, Grave 13.

J.W. BURNS
Staff Sergeant
58th Armored Infantry Battalion

Best friend saw him die

Staff Sergeant J.W. 'Jay' Burns was born on April 9, 1923. He grew up with a brother and a sister and lived in Olden, Texas. Before Burns entered the army during the war, he had been a well-known football player in Eastland County.

On the European battlefield, Staff Sergeant Burns was in charge of a machine gun squad in Company C of the 58th Armored Infantry Battalion. This unit was part of the 8th Armored Division, known to the men as the 'Thundering Herd.'

The 8th Armored Division was shipped to England in November 1944. It landed in France in January 1945, and in February the men of the 58th Armored Infantry Battalion were given a short rest in Limburg, the southernmost province of the Netherlands. The battalion arrived in the village of Cadier en Keer on February 3-4 and were quartered there until on February 18 the order came to move out towards Montfort and Roermond, about 25 miles further north. The battalion departed Cadier en Keer the following day.

On February 27, 1945, Burns' Charlie Company was involved in the attack on a factory in Merum, outside Linne and southwest of Roermond. The German defenders resisted fiercely to hold the Allied advance toward the Roer River and not to be pushed back to the western border of their homeland.

During the fighting that took place near the Merum factory, the 21-year-old Burns saw two men of his squad (Wyman French and Russell G. Fretz) gunned down by enemy fire. He decided to run for cover, but was then hit in the back by a burst of German machine gun fire. Burns fell down and died, just a few feet away from the foxhole of his best friend Sergeant Paul Clare. Clare saw the bullets go right through his best friend's body; a traumatic experience he never forgot and which caused mental suffering that would have a big impact on his further life, resulting in a drinking problem and divorce...

Staff Sergeant Burns was buried at the temporary U.S. Military Cemetery in Margraten, where Sergeant Clare visited his grave later in 1945. When it was decided that Margraten would become a permanent American cemetery, Burns' next of kin decided not to repatriate his remains back to the United States but to have him reburied in a permanent grave there. Today, his final resting place in Margraten can be visited in Plot F, Row 9, Grave 19.

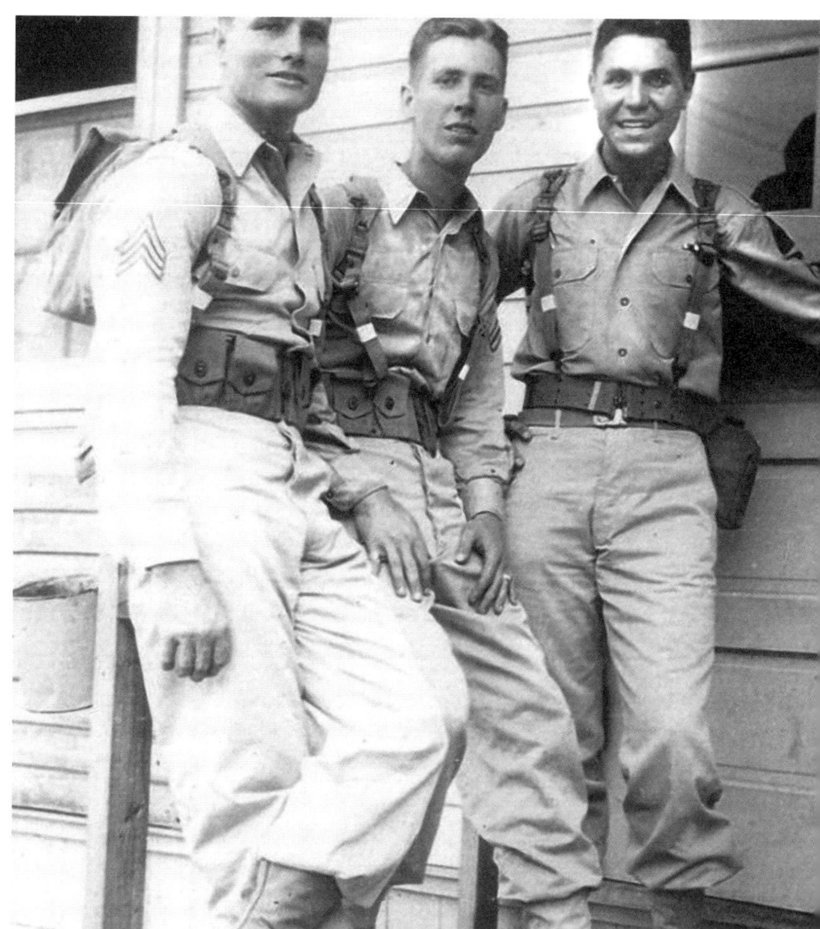

J.W. Burns, on the right, and two fellow soldiers.The soldier in the middle is his friend Paul Clare

LLOYD W. YOUNG

Private First Class

30th Infantry Division

Forced German tanks to withdraw

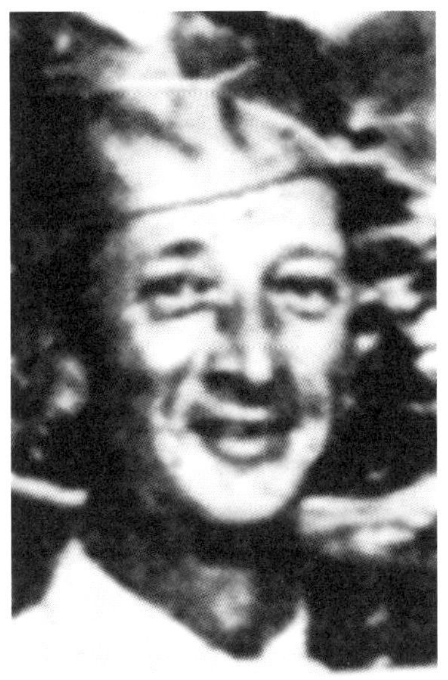

Private First Class Lloyd W. Young from Wolfeboro, New Hampshire was born on March 11, 1908. He was married to his beloved Catherine and had a son with her. In April 1944, Lloyd reported to Fort Devens, Massachusetts, and entered the army. He was then sent to Fort Benning, Georgia, for basic training.

In September 1944, Lloyd left for overseas duty on the Queen Elizabeth. Upon his arrival in Europe, Lloyd was assigned to Company A of the 120th Infantry Regiment. This was one of three regiments of the 30th 'Old Hickory' Infantry Division.

A few months later, on February 27, 1945, Lloyd's company got into a fight with German troops and some tanks near the German village of Kirchherten. Discovering that they could not fire their Bazooka at the enemy tanks from their position in a house, Lloyd and a comrade went outside under intense enemy fire in an attempt to knock out the leading tank. Despite the deadly machine gun fire now being centered on them, they fired two more rounds at the tanks, forcing the tanks to withdraw. While Lloyd was moving back toward the sheltered position in the house, he was instantly killed by the machine gun fire. Therefore, he remained forever 36.

Lloyd was posthumously awarded the Silver Star for his gallant action against the German tanks. In October 1945, the medal was honorably presented to his widow Catherine. Her husband is buried at the Netherlands American Cemetery in Margraten, where he will rest in peace forever in Plot F, Row 8, Grave 17.

CARL W. FIELDS

Private First Class

58th Armored Infantry Battalion

A deadly battle with German machine guns

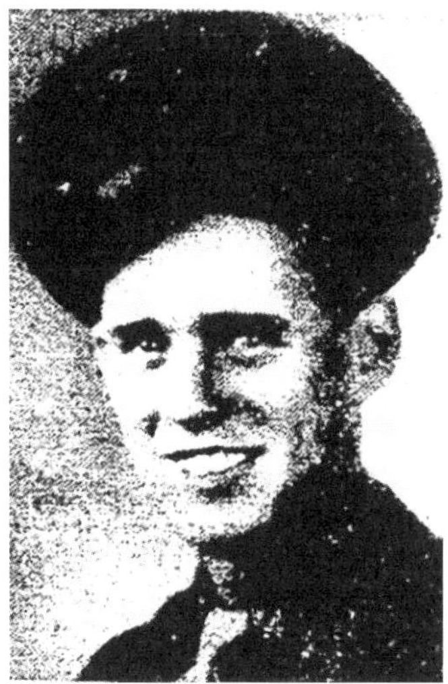

Private First Class Carl W. Fields from Arkansas was born in Amherst, Canada, on June 29, 1922. About a year later, as an infant, he emigrated with his parents to the United States. The family arrived on American soil in Vanceboro, Maine, via the Canadian Pacific Railway.

In November 1942, Carl entered the U.S. Army, receiving his infantry training in Texas and Camp Robinson in Arkansas. In April 1943, Carl was granted U.S. citizenship. Before Carl went overseas to Europe in November 1944, he returned home for a short leave in September.

In Europe, Carl went to fight in the 58th Armored Infantry Battalion, which was part of the 8th Armored Division. On February 26, 1945, his company advanced toward Roermond in the Netherlands. Southwest of this city, however, his platoon was halted at Merum and Linne by strong German opposition. The platoon was pinned down and unable to direct their fire on the enemy positions. Carl, realizing the situation, bravely advanced through the open terrain. Ignoring the intense machine gun and small arms fire, he directed his rifle fire on two positions. He succeeded in forcing the enemy to take cover, which enabled his platoon to continue the advance and eliminate the enemy strong points. During the course of the action, Carl was fatally wounded by machine gun fire. As a result, he died at the age of 22. This presumably was on the following day, as his date of death is listed as February 27, 1945.

A month after his death, 8th Armored Division Headquarters announced that Carl was posthumously awarded the Silver Star because 'his gallant action held casualties to a minimum and was in keeping with the highest traditions of the Armed Forces of the United States.' In Margraten, Carl is buried in Plot H, Row 20, Grave 25.

JIMMIE S. KNIGHT
First Lieutenant
44th Cavalry Reconnaissance Squadron

Wounded officer fought on until he passed out

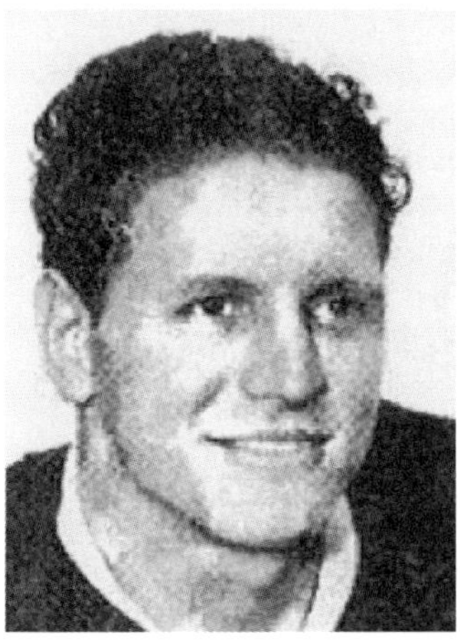

Jimmie S. Knight from Texas was born in 1920. After graduating from La Grange High School, he began studying at The Agricultural and Mechanical College of Texas, where he graduated in 1943. Meanwhile, Jimmie was widely recognized as a talented and successful football player.

Shortly after his graduation, Jimmie was called to active duty. He was sent to Officer's Candidate School at Fort Riley, Kansas, and in October 1944, Jimmie left for Europe. There he served in the 44th Cavalry Reconnaissance Squadron. This mechanized reconnaissance unit's main task was to observe German units. Based on the observations, Jimmie and his fellow scouts tried to estimate how many enemy troops were present in their area of operations and what heavy armament the enemy could have at their disposal to impede the advance of the Allied divisions.

After crossing the Roer River, Jimmie was on a reconnaissance mission in Germany on February 27, 1945, riding in a jeep. As his unit approached the village of Golkrath, they encountered an enemy roadblock and came under heavy enemy fire. Lieutenant D.L. Holder, one of Jimmie's close friends who graduated from A&M college with him and was serving overseas with Jimmie at the time of his death, later wrote a letter to Jimmie's wife Sarah. In it, Holder described that Jimmie started firing the machine gun that was mounted on the jeep until it was empty. While he was reloading the machine gun, Jimmie was shot in the back by a German sniper. Ignoring his mortal wound, he continued loading and firing the machine gun until his men had pulled back to safer positions and he lost his consciousness. He died from his wounds later in the day at the age of 24.

In August 1945, Sarah received the Bronze Star Medal that was posthumously awarded to Jimmie. Besides his widow, Jimmie was also survived by a daughter, Carol Jean, of whose birth Jimmie heard just a few days before his death... Jimmie's final resting place in Margraten is in Plot P, Row 9, Grave 10.

CHARLES H. JEFFERSON
Sergeant
784th Tank Battalion

His unit's first offensive lasted only two days for him

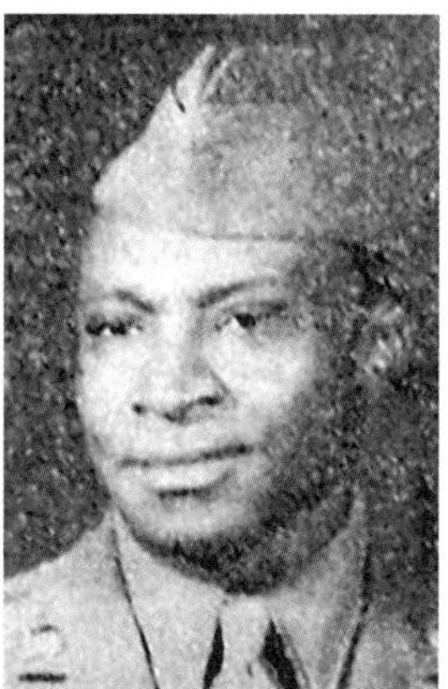

Charles H. Jefferson, who was born on November 16, 1911, was an African American sergeant from Mississippi. His hometown was Poplarville in Pearl River County. There he lived with his wife Roberta. Before entering the army in July 1943, Charles worked as a chauffeur.

After enlisting, Charles eventually served in Company A of the segregated 784th Tank Battalion. This army unit was composed entirely of African Americans, except for the white officers in charge. Charles became a crew member in a Sherman tank.

Charles, still a corporal then, left with his unit for Europe on October 30, 1944. After almost two weeks at sea, they arrived in Liverpool, England and were then sent to Pontypridd in South Wales. It was eventually on New Year's Eve of 1944 that the unit would arrive on the front lines, in Eschweiler, Germany. The battalion was attached to the 104th Infantry Division and supported the division's defensive positions along the Roer River. In early February 1945, the battalion was transferred to the 35th Infantry Division, whereupon it remained in Division Reserve for about three weeks. On February 26, as the 35th Division started its push towards the Rhine River, Charles and his unit took part in the offensive. He had been promoted to the rank of Sergeant just the week before.

A day after the start of the offensive, in the late afternoon of February 27, Charles was severely wounded in the attack on Wassenberg, Germany. A description in the book *The 784th Tank Battalion in World War II* states that Charles' tank was knocked out by enemy fire. It also stated that Charles would have perished inside the burning hulk. However, this is incorrect. His medical records show that he was brought into an aid station with a penetrating head wound, caused by an artillery shell or cannon fire. His condition was severe and therefore, in just a matter of hours, he was rushed to the 110th Clearing Station and then to the 105th Evacuation Hospital. At the time, this military hospital was set up in some buildings belonging to the church by the name 'Heilig Hart van Jezuskerk' in the Dutch city of Sittard.

Charles never regained consciousness. He passed away at 8:10 a.m. on March 1, 1945. He was 33 years old at the time and was buried that same afternoon in Margraten. He was also given his final resting place there, which can be visited in Plot F, Row 8, Grave 16.

TERENCE M. O'BRIEN

First Lieutenant

7th Armored Infantry Battalion

Refused to be removed to safety

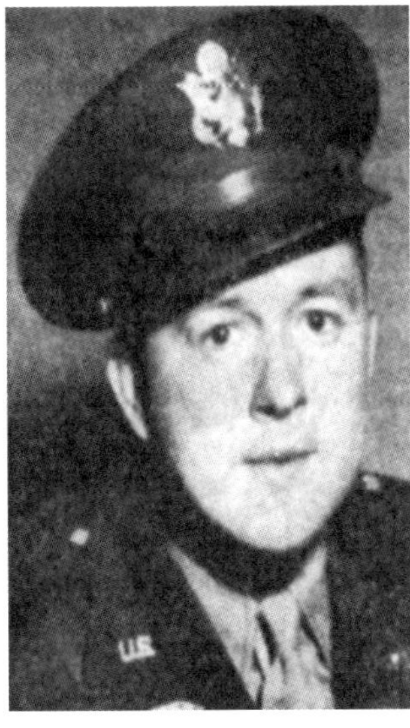

Terence M. O'Brien was born on August 25, 1912. His hometown was Davenport in Iowa. There he lived with his uncle and aunt after the death of both his parents.

When Terence was in his senior year at Davenport High School, he simultaneously participated in a program for the Reserve Officers Training Corps (ROTC). After graduation, Terence attended St. Ambrose College and then the University of Iowa. Before entering the military, Terence was employed as a cost accountant for the U.S. district engineers. He also was the accounting clerk during the construction of the Schick General Hospital in Clinton. Additionally, Terence was well known in Davenport's local dramatic circles as he appeared in many amateur plays.

In August 1942, Terence entered the army. He was first sent to Fort Benjamin Harrison in Indiana. Later, Terence successfully attended Armored Officer Candidate School at Fort Knox, Kentucky, where he was commissioned in February 1943.

Terence went overseas to Europe in November 1944, where he served in the 7th Armored Infantry Battalion of the 8th Armored Division. As a First Lieutenant, Terence was given command of Company C.

On March 3, 1945, Terence led his company during street fighting in the German town of Wachtendonk. Without regard for his own safety, he constantly exposed himself to the enemy fire. While leading his men, he was wounded by machine gun fire, but he refused to be removed to a place of safety and continued to direct and encourage his men. A short time later, the German machine gun opened fire again, instantly killing Terence at the age of 32. Because his gallantry and leadership in the face of the enemy fire were an inspiration to his men, Terence was posthumously awarded the Silver Star. In Margraten, Terence is permanently laid to rest in Plot E, Row 11, Grave 20.

JAMES V. JOHNSTON JR.

Major

84th Infantry Division

One-man army became a legend at the front

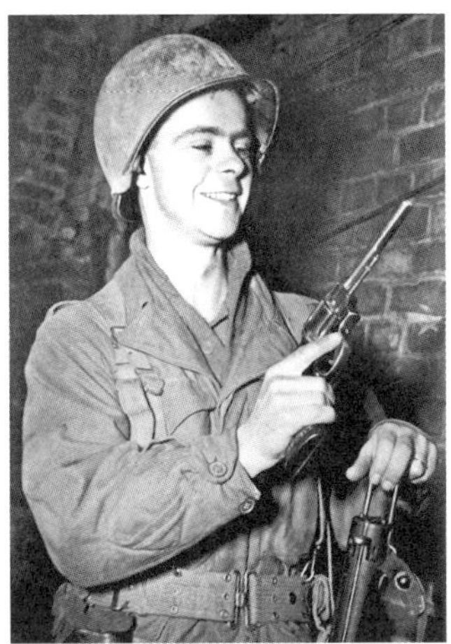

James 'Jimmy' V. Johnston Jr. from Portland, Oregon was a talented tenor saxophonist and played in his own band. His band played for all the local tea dances and at clubs and restaurants to earn money. Besides music, James enjoyed skiing, mountain climbing, and kayaking. In 1939, he graduated from Oregon State College and then entered military service.

James wanted to be a pilot, but it turned out that he had insufficient aptitude for this. Therefore, he ended up in the infantry. James' brother Mitchell became a Navy fighter pilot and served in the Pacific. Three months before James left for Europe, he married his girlfriend 'Mac.'

In 1944, James was given command of Company H of the 334th Infantry Regiment. This regiment was part of the 84th Infantry Division. When the commander of the 2nd Battalion was wounded at some point, James was promoted from Captain to Major and appointed as its new commander.

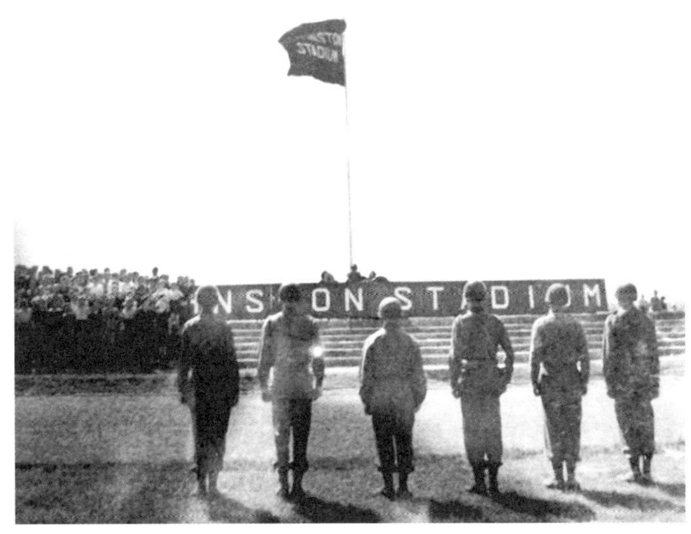

In May 1945, a stadium was named after Major James V. Johnston Jr. to honor him. SOURCE: U.S. Army Signal Corps/Johnston family

James quickly managed to make a great impression on his troops. His fighting spirit and courage were extraordinary, and he acted as a true leader. For example, James led half a dozen so-called 'march fire' assaults, which consisted of firing from the hip on the run when he and his men broke out of cover to attack.

Conducting 'march fire' assaults with firing rifles and submachine guns from the hip was certainly not the only evidence of his courageous leadership. An article in *The Sunday Oregonian*, published on January 21, 1945, sums up more examples of James' apparent fearlessness:

> ***'In his first action near Geilenkirchen, Germany, shortly after he was ordered to take over the outfit, he was ordered to pull a company out of a trap. He crawled 1200 yards across an open field under heavy machine gun and sniper fire. After dark, he guided the whole outfit safely to a reinforced position. Near Gereonsweiler, Germany, he led an attack which jumped off at 6 a.m. By noon he held the objective after killing twenty Germans and capturing 86 prisoners. In the same sector his men were once held up by machine gun fire. Crawling to a tank, Johnston directed the driver to within 50 yards of the enemy position and opened fire with the tank's main 75mm gun, killing seven Germans... During the Mullendorf attack he led the way, running and firing machine pistols. Fifteen minutes after the jump-off he walked down the steps of the erstwhile enemy headquarters with the Nazis' flag under one arm and a cigar in his mouth... His most typical deed came when the battalion was losing equipment to a mine field through which a supply line was running to reach combat fighters. He took a trench knife and cleared a pathway through the field.'***

The above-mentioned account of James personally directing the fire of a tank was also recalled by Cpl. Art Mahler, who served in James' battalion at the time:

> ***'I was a replacement and joined the unit just before Thanksgiving. I was "dug in" alongside the rest of the rifle squad because the company was pinned down by two machine guns with overlapping fields of fire and we could not advance. Artillery was beginning to find us and we had to do something. (...) As I looked out of my shallow hole, I see a guy run up to a tank – it was a Sherman of the British Sherwood Rangers – and climb up on it. The tank commander pops up and the guy points out the machine guns. The tank moves up and takes them both out with the guy and the commander directing fire. The guy that climbed on the tank was Major Johnston! The Major was a great guy. Everybody liked the Major.'***

James' heroic leadership tragically ended on March 4, 1945. While he was again leading his men, he was killed by a German 88mm shell. One source claims that the fatal shell was fired by a gun that was mounted on a Tiger tank, but it has not been possible to verify whether this is true.

Major James V. Johnston Jr., who came to be known as the 'pint-size, one-man army,' made the ultimate sacrifice at the age of 28 and was buried in Margraten. Here visitors can find his final resting place today in Plot P, Row 15, Grave 17.

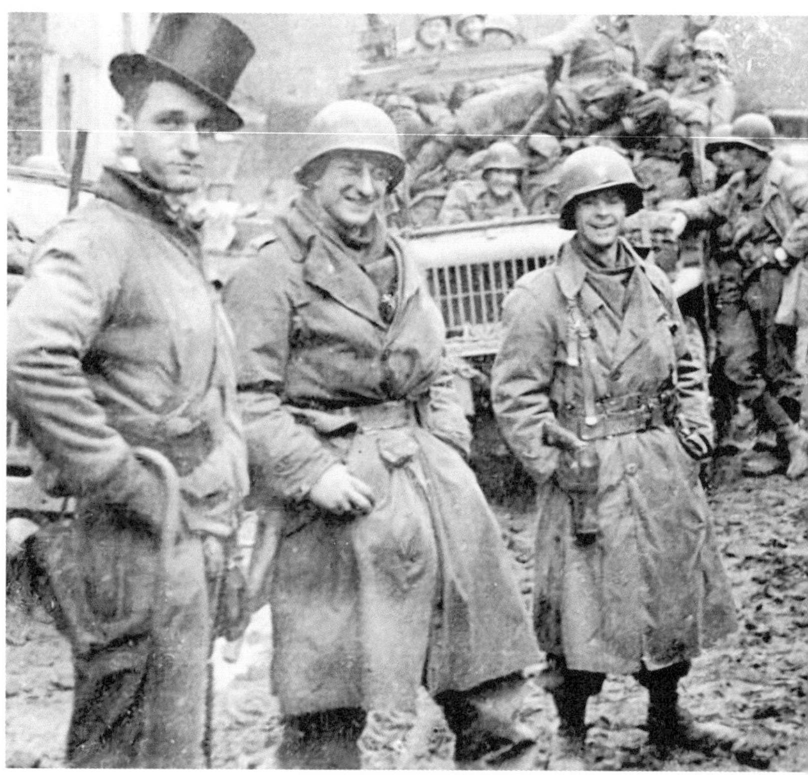

James Johnston, on the right, not far from the front line. SOURCE: Johnston family

ARTHUR J. WHITBECK

Technician Fourth Grade

784th Tank Battalion

'The life of the company'

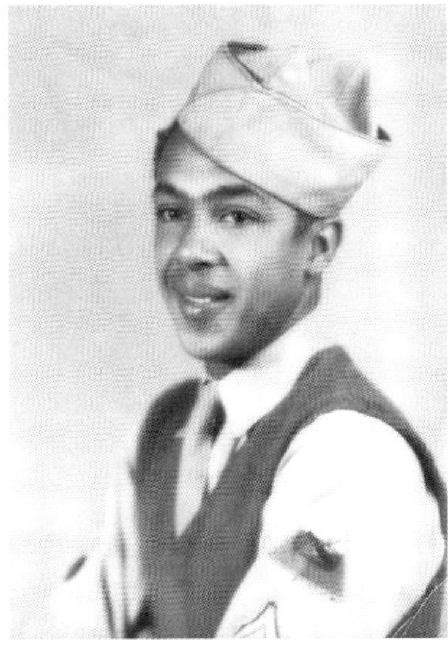

Arthur J. Whitbeck was born in 1923. His hometown was Hudson, New York. Arthur's grandfather nicknamed him 'Snookie,' and he was very athletic. Arthur played basketball, softball, and football, among other sports. In addition to his African American descent, Arthur's family also directly descended from the Dutch colonist Jan Thomas van Witbeck. Around 1660, he had bought land from local Indians (the Mohicans) and settled there with his family.

Just after he graduated from Hudson High School, Arthur entered the army in December 1942. At Camp Claiborne, Louisiana, and Camp Hood, Texas, he was trained as a member of a tank crew, assigned to Company B, 784th Tank Battalion. This segregated army unit consisted entirely of African American soldiers. Only the senior officers in charge were white.

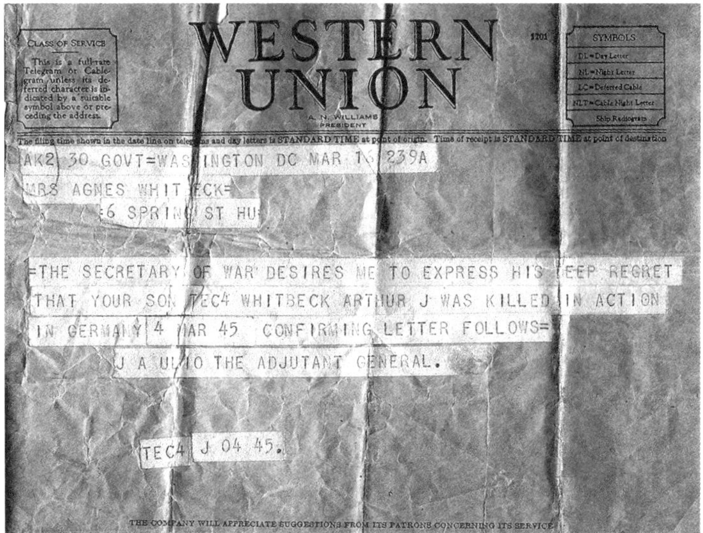

WESTERN UNION

A. N. WILLIAMS
PRESIDENT

CLASS OF SERVICE
This is a full-rate Telegram or Cablegram unless its deferred character is indicated by a suitable symbol above or preceding the address.

1201

SYMBOLS
DL = Day Letter
NL = Night Letter
LC = Deferred Cable
NLT = Cable Night Letter
Ship Radiogram

The filing time shown in the date line on telegrams and day letters is STANDARD TIME at point of origin. Time of receipt is STANDARD TIME at point of destination

AK2 30 GOVT=WASHINGTON DC MAR 16 239A
MRS AGNES WHITBECK=
6 SPRING ST HU

=THE SECRETARY OF WAR DESIRES ME TO EXPRESS HIS DEEP REGRET THAT YOUR SON TEC4 WHITBECK ARTHUR J WAS KILLED IN ACTION IN GERMANY 4 MAR 45 CONFIRMING LETTER FOLLOWS=
J A ULIO THE ADJUTANT GENERAL.

TEC4 J 04 45.

THE COMPANY WILL APPRECIATE SUGGESTIONS FROM ITS PATRONS CONCERNING ITS SERVICE

The telegram that notified Arthur's family of his death. SOURCE: Karen Velasquez/Arie-Jan van Hees

On March 4, 1945, Arthur's Baker Company took part in the battle for the German village of Kamperbruch. There his tank was hit by German anti-tank guns. Arthur and two other crew members – Tec5 Albert S. Harte and Pvt. William H. Hogue – were killed. Arthur was 21 years old at the time and his final resting place in Margraten is in Plot K, Row 14, Grave 1. Tec5 Harte and Pvt. Hogue are buried in respectively Plot E, Row 5, Grave 6 and Plot D, Row 9, Grave 11.

After Arthur's death, his family received a personal letter from 1st Sergeant Evans. He wrote:

> ***'I knew your son Arthur, I was his 1st Sergeant of the Company. Arthur was liked by everyone of the company, and those who knew him. Arthur was a clean cut soldier and held up the morale of the army. We, the men of the company have missed him so much, he was the life of the company. The men of the company send best regards and our prayers. If there is anything we can do don't fail to let us know.'***

At some point before he was killed, Arthur had sent a small piece of paper to his grandmother, asking her to send him the things he and his best friend Austin Anderson had written on it. The shopping list included writing paper, a toothbrush, soap, candy, and 'funny books.' After Arthur's death, it was preserved.

KENNETH R. ROBINSON

First Lieutenant

36th Tank Battalion

'I loved him like a brother'

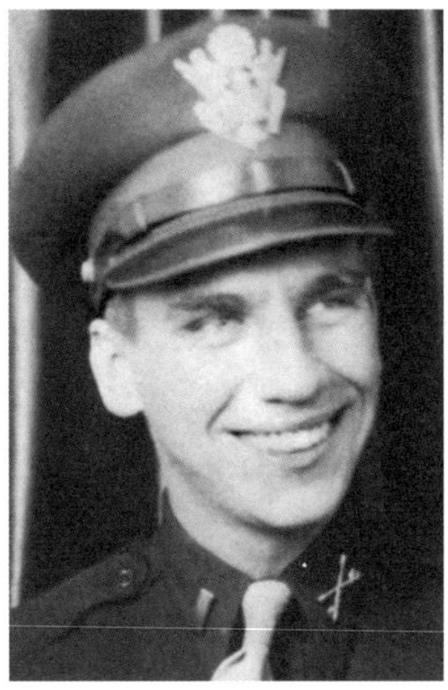

First Lieutenant Kenneth R. Robinson was born in Girard, Erie County, Pennsylvania, in 1922. His boyhood friend Harold Sutch later wrote they 'became good friends very quickly. He was 8 years old and I was 6. At that age, we played croquet and catch with a softball. Other activities were playing cards, dominoes, and reading Tom Swift books.'

After completing high school in 1940, Kenneth entered the military the same year. He graduated from Officer Candidate School at Fort Knox and was eventually assigned to Company D, 36th Tank Battalion. This battalion operated under the command of the 8th Armored Division.

From January 1945, the 36th Tank Battalion in which Kenneth served was one of the few U.S. tank units equipped exclusively with light M24 Chaffee tanks. These tanks had a lower silhouette than the standard M4 Sherman tanks, but were armed with the same 75mm gun. Kenneth was the commander of one such light tank. He also commanded Dog Company's 1st Platoon.

Before going to the front in Germany, Kenneth and his company were stationed in Margraten for a few days in early February 1945. From there the battalion was then sent to Posterholt. There they took over the positions of a British unit. From Posterholt, the tanks of Kenneth's battalion entered Germany on the 27th.

One week later, Kenneth's Company D attacked the German city of Rheinberg on March 5, 1945. Kenneth and the other men of the company reportedly had no idea what awaited them here. The German defenders resisted fiercely, and many light tanks of Company D were knocked out there by German anti-tank guns or Panzerfausts.

During the battle for Rheinberg, Kenneth's tank and Sgt. McRae's tank together knocked out an enemy anti-tank gun and a self-propelled gun. This was reported in an after-action interview with several survivors of the battle. In the same interview it is stated that Kenneth's tank was hit by a German 'Bazooka' – a Panzerfaust or Panzerschreck – shortly after. Kenneth then mounted the back of Sgt. Willard Horine's tank and started firing the .50 caliber machine gun mounted on the turret. When enemy artillery fire was directed on the tanks and an anti-tank gun again opened fire from the east, Sgt. Horine's tank was hit. Kenneth and those that did escape took cover in a nearby ditch. He then told his men that he was going to contact some infantry to help them. Kenneth was unable to complete this self-imposed task, as he was fatally struck by small arms fire. He died instantly and was only 22 years old at the time. His final resting place in Margraten is in Plot M, Row 10, Grave 5.

'I still miss Ken,' Harold Sutch wrote. 'He was a fine person and I loved him like a brother. I'm proud to say "we grew up together".'

CLARENCE E. SMITH

Captain

49th Armored Infantry Battalion

A German shell exploded above his tank

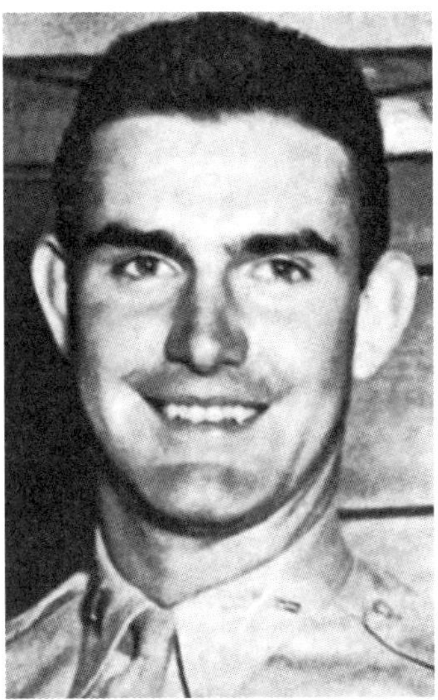

Captain Clarence E. Smith was born on April 18, 1918. His hometown was Fairmont, West Virginia. There he grew up amidst the coal industry. Clarence's father had served as a colonel in the army and was a member of the Bituminous Coal Commission, which was set up by President Roosevelt in the 1930s to regulate U.S. coal prices.

Clarence graduated from his state's university in 1941 and entered the U.S. Army. He served in the 49th Armored Infantry Battalion of the 8th Armored Division. This division entered combat in Europe in January 1945.

On March 5, 1945, Clarence, assigned as commander of Company B, was involved in the attack on the German town of Winterswick, a few miles west of the Rhine. He coordinated the attack from the turret of a tank, but dismounted to lead his men into the town. Clarence was then forced to seek more cover from the flying shrapnel. He lowered himself about waist deep in the turret of his tank and continued to direct the action from this position. While doing so, he was killed by an artillery or mortar shell. According to a tribute written by his father, the enemy guns – reportedly 88s – were aimed for tree bursts and one of the shells exploded above Clarence's tank.

Clarence was 26 years old when the enemy shelling fatally caught him. He was lifted from the turret by some of his men and placed on the ground just behind the tank. Shortly thereafter, advanced elements of the 35th Infantry Division reached the scene, and his body was removed from the battlefield and taken to the U.S. Military Cemetery at Margraten, where he was given his final resting place in Plot G, Row 7, Grave 6. For his courageous leadership, Clarence later received the Silver Star Medal in September 1945.

VICTOR M. ZUCK

Second Lieutenant

36th Tank Battalion

Tank commander would not let himself be stopped

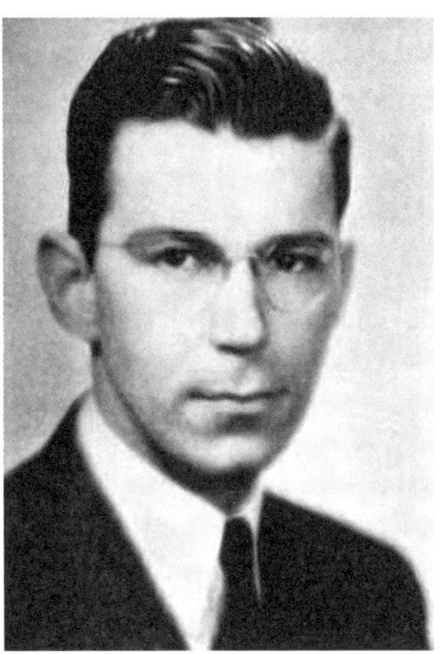

Second Lieutenant Victor M. Zuck was of Polish descent, but emigrated with his family to the United States in 1921. Here they had then settled in Buffalo, Erie County, New York. Victor studied sociology, philosophy, and German at Saint Bonaventure College, graduating in 1941. He also was the editor of *The Laurel*, the periodical student publication.

Not long after his graduation, Victor enlisted into the military. He earned an officer's rank in 1943 and eventually fought as a tank commander in Europe. His unit was Company B, 36th Tank Battalion, which was part of the 8th Armored Division.

During the advance to the Rhine, the tanks of Victor's battalion attacked the German city of Rheinberg on March 5, 1945. During the battle that took place there, Victor displayed inspiring gallantry that was posthumously rewarded with the Silver Star. His citation reads:

> ***'Attacking along a road completely covered by anti-tank weapons, Lieutenant Zuck advanced his tank without regard to personal safety. His gallant assault added greatly to the impetus of the action and enabled his company to penetrate a heavily fortified enemy position. Lieutenant Zuck's tank had overrun the enemy position when it was finally knocked out by anti-tank guns. Lieutenant Zuck was killed. His gallantry and courage in the face of enemy fire were an inspiration to all and were in keeping with the highest traditions of the Military Service of the United States.'***

Victor's body was laid to rest at the American cemetery in Margraten. One can find his final resting place there in Plot F, Row 13, Grave 24.

SAMPSON C. WILLOUGHBY
Technician Fourth Grade
36th Tank Battalion

A jovial smile

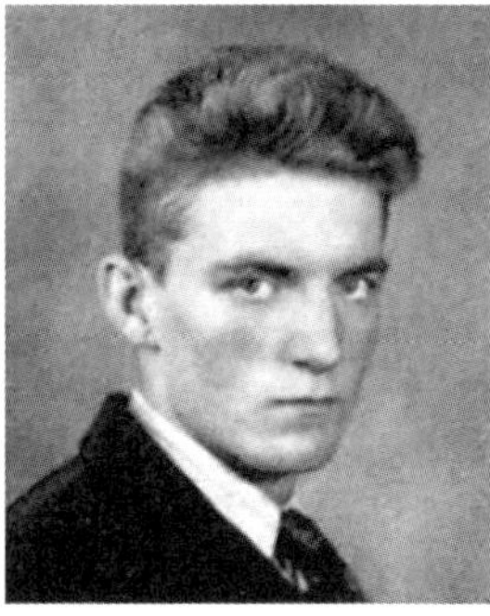

Sampson C. Willoughby was born in Kentucky on March 1, 1924, but later lived in Columbus, Indiana. He grew up in a family with three brothers and four sisters. After four years of high school, he went to work. Sampson was employed by Noblitt-Sparks Industries, but in March 1943 he entered the army. In November 1944, he said goodbye to his fiancée Miss Ellen Henderson and left for Europe.

During his service, Sampson was a tank mechanic in Company D of the 36th Tank Battalion. This tank unit operated under the command of the 8th Armored Division. As a mechanic, Sampson's job was to make sure his company's tanks could keep moving and technical problems were fixed.

On March 5, 1945, Sampson's company moved toward the German town of Kamp-Lintfort. Sampson himself was driving the maintenance tank, which at some point stalled during intense enemy action. Sampson dismounted from his tank under a hail of mortar and machine gun fire to hook a tow cable to his tank. After the vehicle had been started, he again dismounted to uncouple the tow cable. While so doing, he fell victim to German sniper fire. Sampson was fatally wounded and died as a result. He was 21 years old...

For his gallant efforts to get the tank running again, Sampson was later posthumously awarded the Silver Star. In Margraten, he is buried in Plot D, Row 2, Grave 4.

About a month after Sampson was killed, his parents received a letter from Captain John E. McLaughlin. He wrote:

> ***'We wish to extend to you our deepest sympathy in the recent death of your son, Sampson, on 5 March 1945, who was killed in action in Germany. He had been with the company for almost two years and during that time had made many friends who miss him and share in your grief. (...) While repairing a tank in the vicinity of Lintfort, Germany, he was struck by enemy small arms fire which caused his death. He was an excellent tank mechanic and at the time of death was driving the maintenance tank. He was always cooperative and untiring in his efforts. His jovial smile made him a hit with every member of the organization. His sacrifice was part of the effort that will exact the same price from many more of us. He has not ceased to be a comrade, fighting and working with us.'***

ALVIN WELCH
Staff Sergeant
35th Infantry Division

Covered the reorganization of his outfit

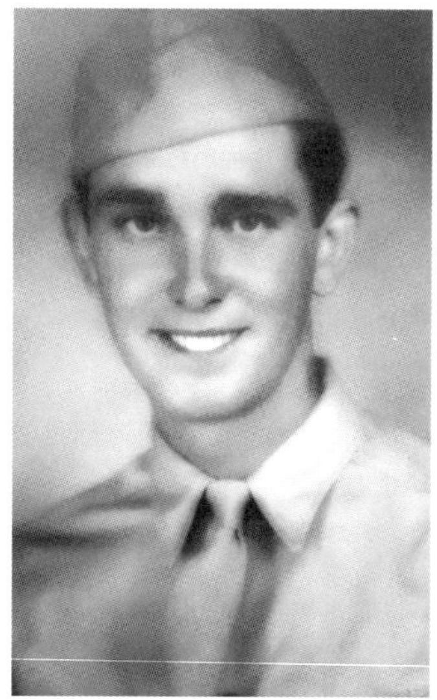

Staff Sergeant Alvin Welch from Tennessee was born on March 31, 1925. He attended school in Wildwood and worked on his father's farm. In April 1944, Alvin reported to Camp Shelby, Mississippi, to enter the army.

Eight months after enlisting, Alvin went overseas to Europe in December 1944. There he was assigned to Company L of the 137th Infantry Regiment. This regiment was part of the 35th Infantry Division, which by then had been involved in combat since the summer.

On March 8, 1945, Alvin and his company attacked the German town of Ossenberg. The unit was pinned down and encountered heavy opposition from the enemy. Alvin then voluntarily covered the reorganization of his squad from an exposed position. His gallant performance attracted the attention of the German soldiers, enabling his squad to resume its advance.

When his squad was advancing again, Alvin left his exposed position to rejoin it. But, while he was making his way back to his comrades, a German sniper killed him. He was nineteen years old...

Alvin's body was buried at the American cemetery in Margraten, where he still lies today. Visitors can pay tribute to him there by going to Plot C, Row 16, Grave 25. For courageously covering his squad in the face of the enemy fire, Alvin was posthumously awarded the Silver Star on April 3, 1945.

BILL G. HARTLEY

Private First Class

35th Infantry Division

Sadly missed

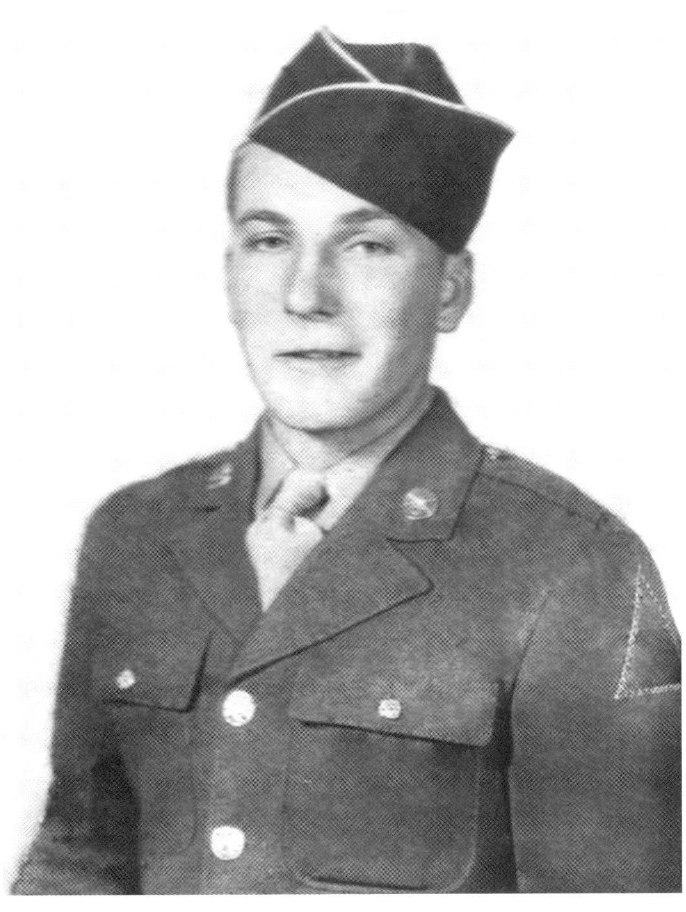

'Hers was, indeed, a sad life,' Kathy McDermott says about Leona Hartley. Leona, who passed away at the age of 93, had outlived five of her six children. Two of them had died in the war, just over a month apart. Bill, 19, rests in Margraten; his older brother by two years, Loren, who went by 'Bud' in the family, in Honolulu. 'I never once saw her smile, but now I know why: she didn't have any smile left,' Kathy says.

Bill and Loren grew up in the city of Vincennes, Indiana. Prior to his enlistment, Bill worked in the mailing department of the *Vincennes Sun-Commercial*, a local newspaper that would run his obituary after he had been killed. 'Music was evidently important to them, as my mom said that whenever she would get together with them, they would all sing together,' Kathy recalls. While Kathy grew up, her mother would remark how much she loved and missed her cousins.

Loren volunteered for the army just ten days after the Japanese attack on Pearl Harbor. Bill was drafted in September 1943. After training for almost a year, he was sent overseas in the late summer of 1944 and was wounded by artillery fire in Fossieux, France, on October 10 while serving with Company L, 137th Infantry Regiment, 35th Infantry Division. After almost three months, he was finally able to return to his unit. Like Alvin Welch, he was killed in Ossenberg, Germany, on March 8, 1945.

On March 23, the family received a telegram notifying them that Bill had gone missing. Within a week, another telegram confirmed his death. Not sure what to make of it, or perhaps it was just idle hope, Leona inquired with the War Department whether her son had indeed been killed. 'If true, we can put some of our hopes on our other son that we have over there,' she wrote. 'But we sure hope this is all a mistake about him.' When she wrote this letter, she did not know that Loren had already been dead for nine days as well, killed on Okinawa.

A grieving Leona wrote the government in 1946, asking how she could bring her boys home. 'What I wanted to know is whether the government is going to return any of the soldier dead. I would not have enough money to have it done. I had to give them up and I think I am entitled to have their bodies back at the least and I think all the mothers would do the same.' The government had to tell her that Loren's body still had not been recovered at that time, but that she would receive information about the repatriation program when it was put in place.

Loren's body was ultimately found, but the family decided to bring neither Bill nor Loren back home, even though the annual in memoriam tributes in the newspaper read that they were 'sadly missed by mother, father, and two sisters.' Kathy thinks that 'perhaps Leona just wanted to hold on to the fantasy that they might walk in her door someday. If she had brought them back home, there would have been funerals and that was probably more than she could bear.' For many years, she would launder and fold the boys' clothes in case they would come back.

They did not. Bill eternally rests in Plot E, Row 11, Grave 19.

HOWARD D. KEPLINGER

Private First Class

35th Infantry Division

A fatal effort to rescue a comrade

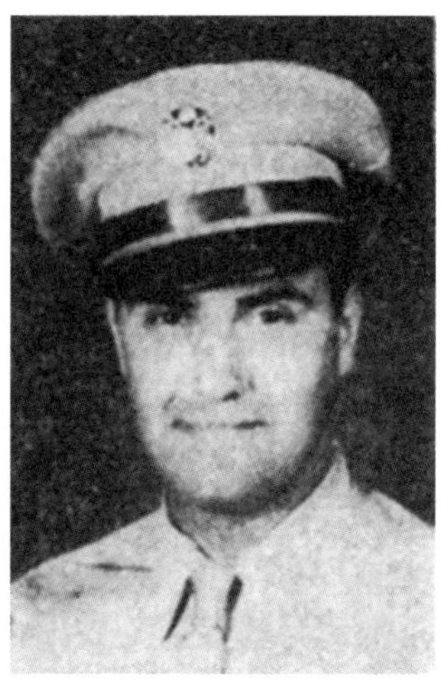

Private First Class Howard D. Keplinger from Hagerstown, Maryland, was born on November 4, 1919. Before entering the army in March 1944, he worked for the M.P. Moller Company as an inspector of Fairchild aircraft. Howard received his military training at Camp Wheeler, Georgia, and eventually served eight months in Europe.

Howard was a member of Company E, 137th Infantry Regiment, 35th Infantry Division. As a rifleman, Howard fought with this division in France, Belgium, and Holland before he lost his life in Germany on March 9, 1945. Over a month later, Howard was posthumously awarded the Silver Star for gallantry in action. His citation describes why he received this medal and how he was killed:

> ***'The President of the United States of America, authorized by Act of Congress July 9, 1918, takes pride in presenting the Silver Star (Posthumously) to Private First Class Howard D. Keplinger (ASN: 33845493), United States Army, for gallantry in action while serving with the 137th Infantry Regiment, 35th Infantry Division, in action near Ossenberg, Germany, on 9 March 1945. Although himself wounded by shell fragments during the course of a sharp enemy counterattack supported by artillery fire and tanks, Private Keplinger, a rifleman, made his way to a wounded comrade some 50 yards distant. As he carried the soldier to cover, Private Keplinger was killed by the near burst of another enemy artillery shell. His gallant self-sacrifice in placing the life of a wounded comrade above any thought of personal safety reflects the highest credit upon Private Keplinger's character as a soldier.'***

Howard was 25 years old when he died on German soil. Besides his parents and wife Evelyn he was survived by three children, two sisters and five brothers. One of his brothers, Rudolph, was wounded in combat on March 12, 1945, while fighting the Japanese army on the Philippines. He died of his wounds on May 24, 1945...

Rudolph is buried at the Manila American Cemetery on the Philippines. Howard was laid to rest in Margraten, where he was given his final resting place in Plot H, Row 6, Grave 27.

HERBERT L. REYNERSON

Staff Sergeant

35th Infantry Division

Shot dead as he dashed to the door of a house

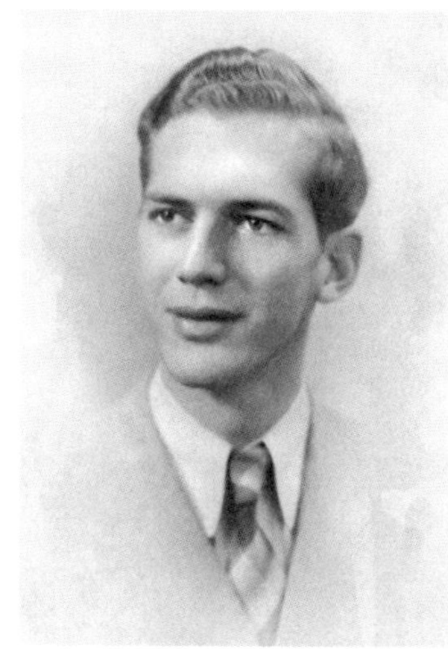

Staff Sergeant Herbert L. Reynerson was born in Arkansas on July 4, 1918. Later he lived in Oklahoma. After high school, he was employed by the Standard Theatre Corporation. In June 1942, Herbert entered the military.

While in active duty, Herbert was hospitalized in April 1944 because he fractured his lumbar vertebrae during judo. He recovered and at some point, went overseas to Europe.

Herbert fought in Company B of the 320th Infantry Regiment, which was part of the 35th Infantry Division. This division arrived in England in May 1944. There the troops were then subjected to further training until they arrived on Omaha Beach in Normandy in July. On July 11, the division was thrown into battle north of Saint-Lô.

On March 9, 1945, Herbert's division was involved in the advance into the German Rhineland. On this day, Herbert led his squad in an assault on a house from which an enemy machine gun was firing. He threw a smoke grenade through a window, but was killed by enemy fire as he dashed to the door of the house. He was 26 years old at the time and was buried at the American Cemetery in Margraten. Today, his final resting place there can be found in Plot D, Row 16, Grave 6.

Despite the fact that Herbert himself did not survive the assault, the smoke from his grenade forced the Germans to leave the house. Outside they promptly surrendered. Therefore, Herbert was later posthumously awarded the Bronze Star Medal for his part in this success. The medal was presented to Herbert's widow Ruth shortly after the war in Europe had ended.

DAVID A. TEALE

Private First Class

87th Infantry Division

A writer grieving the death of his son

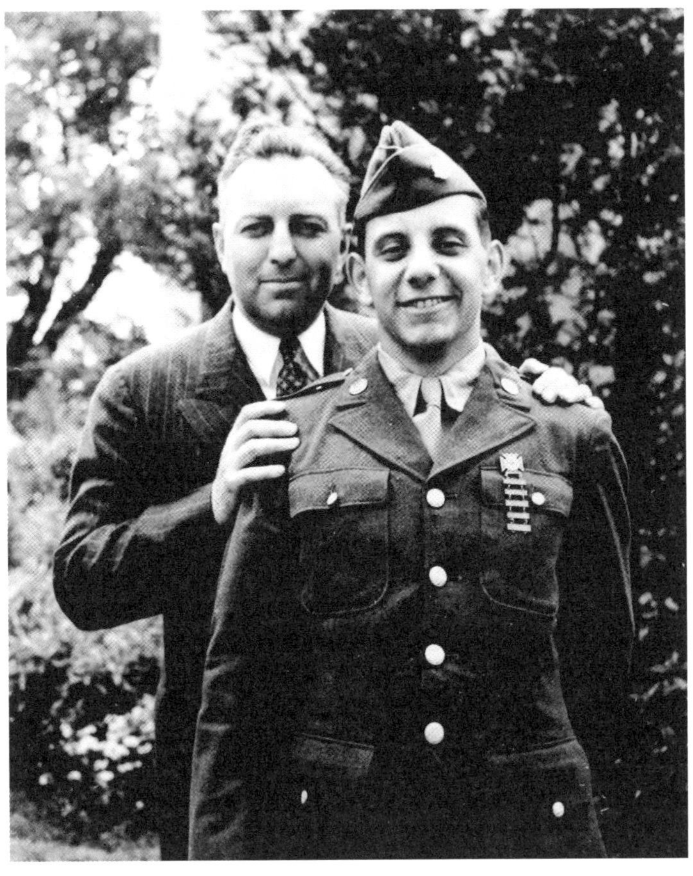

It will come to no surprise that his son David also became infected with the love of nature. For example, David was an active member of the Boy Scouts. His love was also reflected in his work as a volunteer for Camp Dudley, the oldest boys camp in the U.S.

One month before his eighteenth birthday, David enrolled in the Army Specialized Training Program. It was the summer of 1943. When the program was disbanded, he was called to report for active duty. In the fall of 1944, he left for Europe, much to his parents' anxiety. Edwin wrote: 'Here David was overseas, a thing that has hung in the back of our lives like a menacing storm cloud, growing in size and drawing nearer—the thing that threatened had become —as in a dream—a reality.'

David came through the first few months unscathed, serving with the 346th Infantry Regiment, 87th Infantry Division. On March 10, 1945, he wrote: 'So far, I am still healthy. I hope, with the will of God, that I remain that way thru out the war.' However, on March 16, he volunteered to go on a patrol with eleven others. They crossed the Moselle River for a reconnaissance mission southwest of the city of Koblenz, which the division had been ordered to capture. The twelve men gathered valuable information, but they came under fire when trying to make their way back across the river. Eight soldiers were killed, including David.

Everyone deals with the loss of a loved one differently. Even though they lived in New York City, everyone at the Teale home was a lover of all things nature. So, after the death of their son David, Edwin and Nellie turned to nature rather than faith to cope with his death. Or as Edwin would say: 'there are no -isms in heaven.' The grieving parents made several trips across the country in the years after his death. The account of one of these trips, *Wandering Through Winter*, would win Edwin the Pulitzer Prize in 1966.

For Edwin, the love of nature began as a small boy on his grandparents' farm in Indiana, called 'Lone Oak Farm'. Ultimately, he would become a naturalist, photographer, and writer. After earning his master's degree at Columbia University in New York, he began working for *Popular Science* magazine. Meanwhile, he started writing his own books, and he decided to focus entirely on that at the beginning of the war.

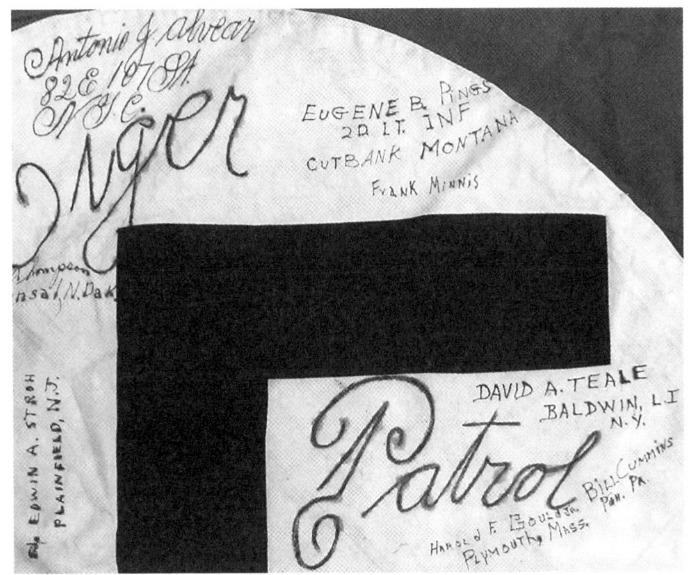

The names on the Nazi flag that David had sent home. SOURCE: Library of the University of Connecticut

David was reported missing and his parents were distraught. The army told them that David was last seen clinging onto the boat. Because he was still alive at the time and his body had not yet been found, the army could not officially declare him dead. His parents tried to reach out to the men whose names were on a Nazi flag that David had sent home a few days before his death for more information. They confirmed what Edwin and Nellie had been dreading to hear. 'All hope gone,' wrote Edwin in his diary.

Yet, it wasn't until 1946 that his body was found. The nineteen-year-old David was then buried in Margraten. He now rests in Plot E, Row 8, Grave 21.

In the 1950s, the parents moved to Connecticut, where they had bought an old farm that they named 'Trail Wood'. They created walking trails on the former farming lands and would remain committed to preserving nature until their deaths. After Edwin's death in 1980 and Nellie's death in 1993, the home became a residence for writers and artists. Edwin's study has remained unchanged. A portrait of David still hangs on the wall today.

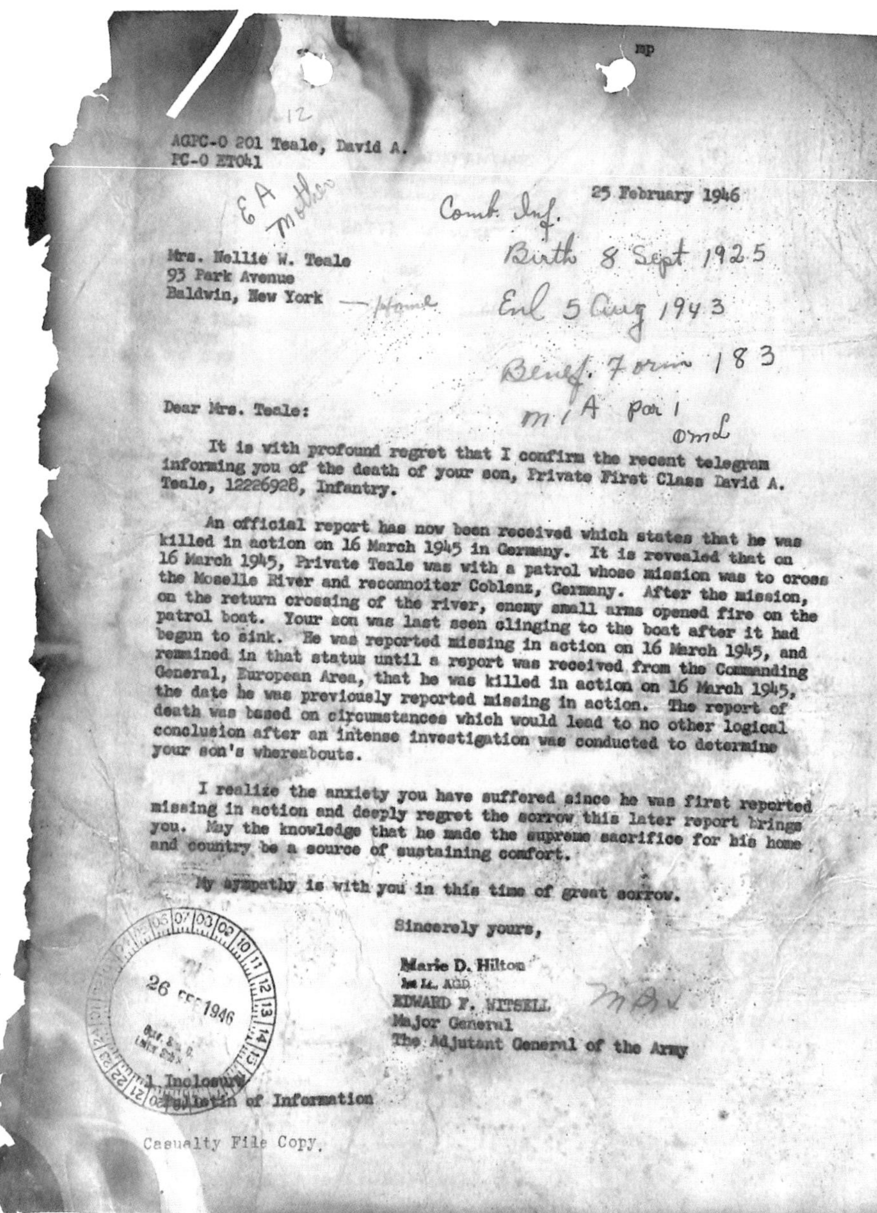

mp

AGPC-O 201 Teale, David A.
PC-O ET041

25 February 1946

Mrs. Nellie W. Teale
93 Park Avenue
Baldwin, New York

Dear Mrs. Teale:

It is with profound regret that I confirm the recent telegram informing you of the death of your son, Private First Class David A. Teale, 12226928, Infantry.

An official report has now been received which states that he was killed in action on 16 March 1945 in Germany. It is revealed that on 16 March 1945, Private Teale was with a patrol whose mission was to cross the Moselle River and reconnoiter Coblenz, Germany. After the mission, on the return crossing of the river, enemy small arms opened fire on the patrol boat. Your son was last seen clinging to the boat after it had begun to sink. He was reported missing in action on 16 March 1945, and remained in that status until a report was received from the Commanding General, European Area, that he was killed in action on 16 March 1945, the date he was previously reported missing in action. The report of death was based on circumstances which would lead to no other logical conclusion after an intense investigation was conducted to determine your son's whereabouts.

I realize the anxiety you have suffered since he was first reported missing in action and deeply regret the sorrow this later report brings you. May the knowledge that he made the supreme sacrifice for his home and country be a source of sustaining comfort.

My sympathy is with you in this time of great sorrow.

Sincerely yours,

Marie D. Hilton
1st Lt. AGD
EDWARD F. WITSELL
Major General
The Adjutant General of the Army

1 Inclosure
Bulletin of Information

Casualty File Copy.

David's parents finally learned in February 1946 what had happened to their son

ELDRIDGE I. HUTTO

Staff Sergeant

65th Infantry Division

Despite injuries, he went on

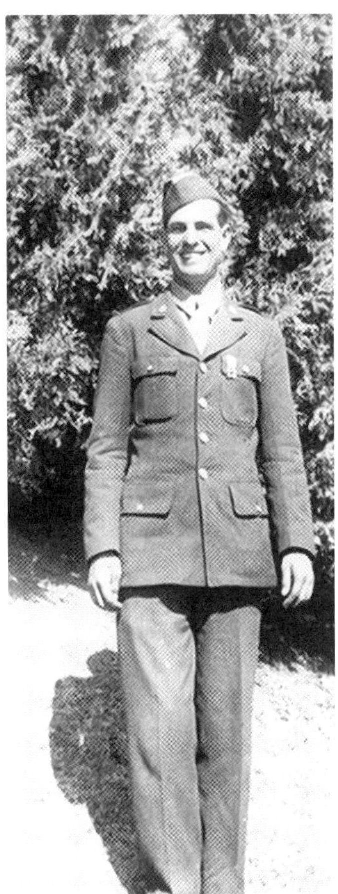

Staff Sergeant Eldridge I. Hutto was born in Georgia on November 2, 1917. He grew up in a large family and married his beloved Jeanette in 1939. By the time Eldridge entered the army in November 1942, he was living with her in Florida.

Eldridge was assigned to the 259th Infantry Regiment of the 65th Infantry Division. This division was called the 'Battle Axe' division by the troops, referring to the battle axe in the shoulder emblem they wore on their uniforms. In January 1945, the division came to Europe, and in March it engaged in combat for the first time.

On March 19, 1945, Eldridge conducted a dangerous reconnaissance patrol near the German town of Saarlautern. His Silver Star citation tells us what happened:

'While reconnoitering a possible route of advance for his squad in Saarlautern, Sergeant Hutto was severely wounded by machine gun fire. Despite his profusely bleeding wound, he completed his reconnaissance, returned to his squad and, in his determination to direct the advance of his men, refused all medical aid. In the advance, Sergeant Hutto was killed by fragments from an 88mm artillery burst, but his men, inspired by the fortitude and outstanding valor of their leader, carried on in his name and gained their objective. Sergeant Hutto's determination in spite of his painful wounds and his devotion to duty reflect the greatest credit upon himself and the military department.'

Eldridge was 27 years old when he made the ultimate sacrifice. The Silver Star Medal, which was posthumously awarded to him a few months after his death, was presented to Eldridge's widow Jeanette by Lieutenant Colonel Ralph L. Joyner. A local Florida newspaper, *The Tampa Tribune*, published an article on this in September 1945. In Margraten, Eldridge rests in Plot H, Row 15, Grave 6.

Eldridge and his mother Gertrude

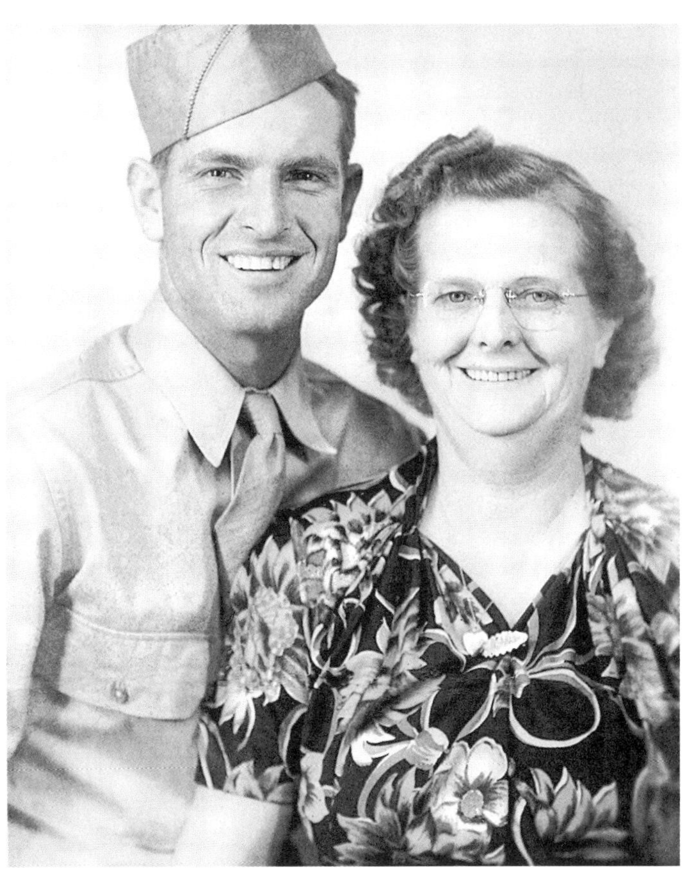

GEORGE J. PETERS
Private
17th Airborne Division

A hero's death

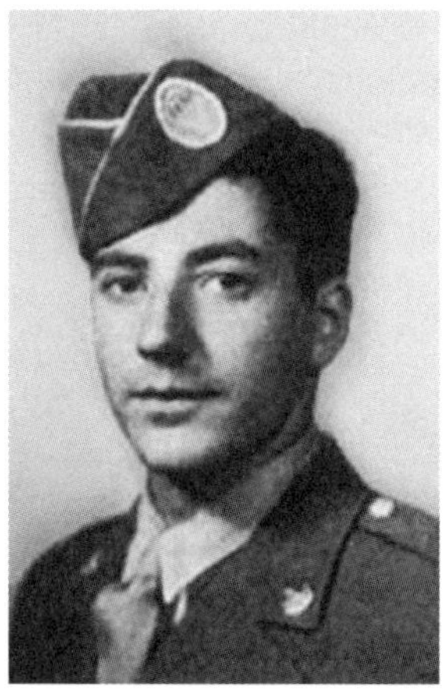

Private George J. Peters from Cranston, Rhode Island, who was born on March 19, 1924, was a paratrooper in the 507th Parachute Infantry Regiment. Initially, this regiment was part of the 82nd Airborne Division, but after returning to England from Normandy in July 1944, it was permanently assigned to the 17th Airborne Division. George served as his platoon's radio operator in Company G.

On March 24, 1945, George participated in Operation Varsity. He made a parachute jump into Germany near Flüren, east of the Rhine. With ten others, he landed in a field about 75 yards from a German machine gun supported by riflemen, and was immediately pinned down by murderous fire.

Technical Sergeant Cleo L. Hohn landed close to George and recalled: 'I was lucky enough to land in a fold of ground that protected me from the gun. Private Peters was halfway between me and the machine gun, trying to wiggle free of his chute harness while ducking the hail of bullets. We were all forced to hug the ground.'

The position of the small unit seemed hopeless with the men struggling to free themselves of their parachutes in a hail of bullets that cut them off from their nearby equipment bundles. But then George stood up and without orders began a one-man charge: armed only with his rifle and grenades, he ran toward the firing machine gun nest. His brave assault immediately drew the enemy fire away from his comrades.

George had run halfway to his objective, pitting rifle fire against that of the machine gun, when he was struck and knocked to the ground by a burst. Heroically, he regained his feet and struggled onward. George made it to within twenty yards of the machine gun before he was once again struck by bullets. By now he was so badly wounded that he was unable to rise again. With gallant devotion to his self-imposed mission, George crawled directly into the fire that had mortally wounded him until he was close enough to hurl hand grenades.

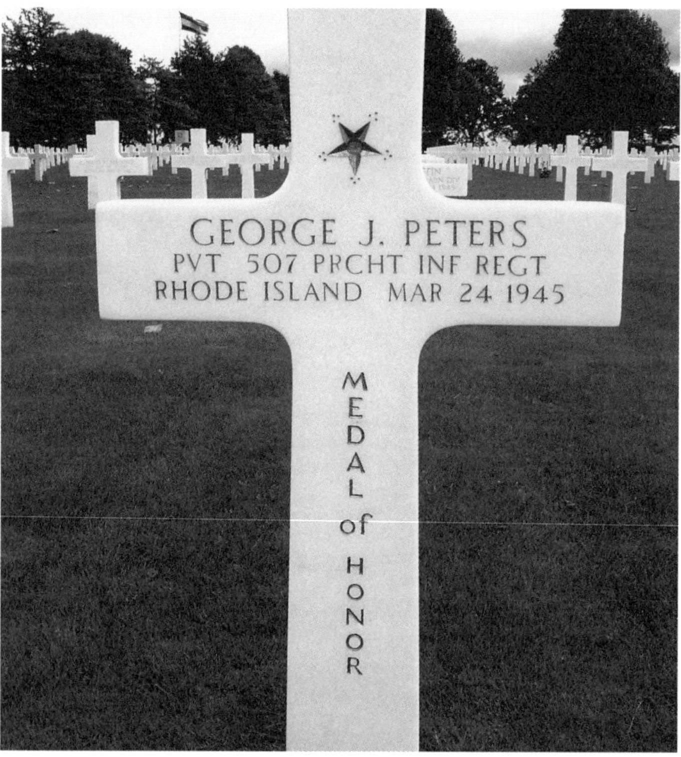

'When his grenades exploded the machine gun stopped firing immediately, and riflemen who had been covering the gun crew ran into the woods,' reported another trooper, PFC Howard A. Thullbery. 'We shot at them and then went over to the enemy nest. The gun was wrecked and two dead Germans were sprawled beside it.'

Meanwhile, George lost consciousness. Thullbery and some other troopers carried him into the woods. 'He died within a few minutes,' Thullbery recalled. George was only 21 years old. Because he had sacrificed his own life to eliminate the crew of the German machine gun that threatened the lives of his buddies as they struggled from their parachute harnesses. George was posthumously awarded the Medal of Honor. George's final resting place in Margraten can be found in Plot G, Row 17, Grave 8.

EDWIN B. BOOTH

Sergeant

17th Airborne Division

A visit to his grave made his family decide to leave him here

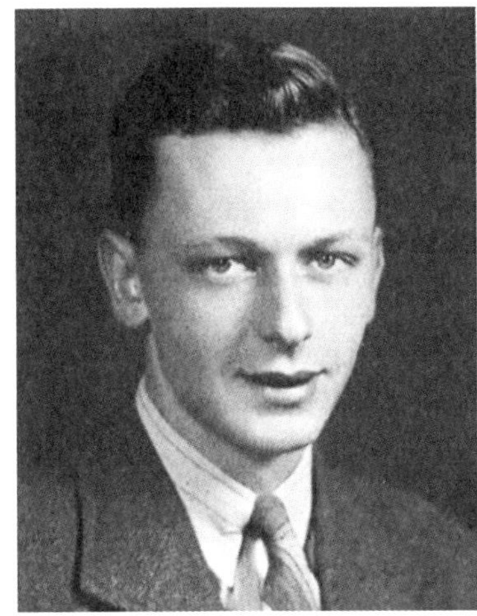

Even before the war ended, the name Margraten appeared more and more often in American newspapers, almost always as the burial place in a soldier's obituary. Immediately after the war, Margraten increasingly became national news as well, in part because of the adoption of graves. However, no article appeals so much to the imagination as the account of a visit to a son's grave by a father seeking an answer to one important question: where should I have my son buried?

That son was nineteen-year-old Sergeant Edwin Bray Booth, named after his father. The Booth family lived in the town of Islington, Massachusetts, just south of the city of Boston. His father was a professor of church history at the city's university. Son Edwin began an education at the prestigious Harvard University, but dropped out after only two years to enlist in the summer of 1943. He too was killed in the airborne landings near Wesel on that 24th of March 1945.

Ever since they knew he was buried in Margraten, the family had a desire to visit the grave, 'going, as it were, to him since he could not come to us,' father Booth described their wish. Through his circle of friends, he knew that many other families had a similar wish, but did not have the opportunity to go. 'I thought to stand at many an American grave in the place of those who could not come.'

In November 1946, a year and a half after their son's death, the time had come. A father, a mother, and two brothers made the crossing. A day after Thanksgiving, they stood in the cemetery. The first sight was overwhelming:

'Row upon row, they lie as they marched. Side by side, they sleep in death or as they had slept in camp, no rank or honor sets one aside from the other. No great room is needed for each. But perfectly spaced, in beautiful order, under clipped grass, before white crosses and stars of David of uniform and appropriate size, each soldier's body lies. They a face a little south of west, looking toward the homes they loved so much and never shall see.'

A Father's Thou

EDITOR'S NOTE: Mr. Booth wrote the following article after visiting his son's grave in the American military cemetery at Margraten, Holland. Like thousands of American families whose relatives were killed in the second World war, he and Mrs. Booth must soon decide whether they want their son's body to be brought back to the United States or allowed to remain in the European soil that Americans liberated. To help themselves make this difficult decision, the Booths made a special trip to Europe this winter, and this is what they found.

By EDWIN P. BOOTH
Professor of Church History, Boston University

PARIS—As to many an American parent whose son is buried in a foreign land, so to me came the longing to visit the cemetery where he lay. He was killed in action when his regiment, the 513th infantry, was parachuted into the German lines at Wesel, on March 24, 1945. The British troops followed in and buried him, with other American dead, on or near the field of battle. One month later his body was transferred to the United States military cemetery at Margraten, Holland.

From that time on I longed to take my family and stand by his grave, going, as it were, to him since he could not come to us. It is my fortune to be a university professor, a work in which time off for travel and study is to be expected. Mindful of friends whose work does not permit this opportunity, I thought to stand at many an American grave in the place of these friends who could not come.

And so we came, my wife and I, and our two sons, his brothers. The cemetery is in the very small village of Margraten, from which it takes its name, but is very near to Maestricht, capital and largest city of the province of Limberg. We came into Maestricht on the evening of Thanksgiving day, 1946, too late to go the few miles out to Margraten.

ON NOV. 29, THEN, one year and a half after he was buried there, we stood for the first time in Margraten cemetery. We rode out from Maestricht to the cemetery entrance on a bus, and then walked up the quarter-mile-long approach.

This approach road is through a farm, and in the field to our right the farmer followed his horses along deep furrows in rich soil. On the opposite side some winter planting was in, and a fresh green growth covered half of the furrowed acres.

My heart was quiet with the expectancy of unbelief for just a moment, and then I caught my first real glimpse of the cemetery itself. A fine white-gray light, it seemed to me, took the place on the crown of the hill of the dark earth plowed and the green growing grain.

Over my consciousness crept the realization, slowly, that this light was formed by thousands of small white crosses in perfect symmetry

Inability To Lead Deflates Bob Taft

By DREW PEARSON

WASHINGTON—Most interesting, though somewhat deflated political figure in the senate today is Robert A. Taft of Ohio together with the question: Will he achieve his long-cherished

▶ **The article that was run in multiple U.S. newspapers from all over the country. SOURCE: *Akron Bacon Journal*/Newspapers.com**

As he stood at his son's grave, he was also struck by how peaceful the place was. He described the sight of a mill, the view of the valley with hard-working farmers and the surrounding villages. It reminded him of home. So, he expressed the hope that the harmony of the fields with the simple wooden crosses and Stars of David and the landscape would never be disturbed. It is 'as nearly perfect as we could wish.'

He did not want to tell other families who were struggling with the question whether to return their loved one's body what they should do, but he did end his report with an ardent plea. Not only was the cemetery an impressive place, one could also always find grateful locals there, weather or no weather. He realized that 'in a real sense, every American grave is getting personal attention.' The Booth family's decision was therefore firm. Edwin is buried in Plot E, Row 1, Grave 11.

ughts On Visiting A U.S. Military Cemeter

upon the hill-top. At the head, as it were, of this field of white, quietly, from a tall white pole, flew the American flag.

WE DID NOT SPEAK to each other much, and each knew only what was in his own mind. But I had come to stand in tribute at the grave of my son, and so had his mother and his brothers.

It was a thing of awe and majesty to see the quiet peaceful field of crosses. Row upon row, they lie as they marched. Side by side, they sleep in death as they had slept in camp, no rank or honor sets one aside from the other.

No great room is needed for each. But perfectly spaced, in beautiful order, under clipped grass, before white crosses and Stars-of-David of uniform and appropriate size, each soldier's body lies. They face a little south of west, looking toward the homes they loved so much and never more shall see.

WE FOLLOWED the broad gravel walks through the plots and came finally to stand by a cross with our own beloved name upon it. To stand in simple dignity and "bear what men must" was all that was left for me to do.

There, by his cross, I looked upon the landscape all around me and saw it to be much like the hills of his home in New England. Far off to the north, high on a hill, a single windmill stood guard as though it would symbolize all Holland. And the valleys, dropping away on three sides, contain the homes and farms and tiny villages of hard working people.

The village of Margraten itself lies still further up the gentle eastern slopes and gives a perfect background for the peace and quiet so much desired.

THIS IS A CATHOLIC section of the land and no Protestant church stands in Margraten, although there is a strong and thoughtful Protestant community in Maestricht.

But the parish priest of Margraten has felt himself, and guided his people into feelings, that here in this vast sorrow there is no room for separation. So I, a Protestant, felt no barrier in the love with which South Limberg's people surround this American cemetery.

Some things must be changed. The chapel must be brought forward where it belongs and kept in better order. But this is easily accomplished. And some things must not be done. Above all else, the natural surroundings must not be disturbed. No park, little cement, no formalism should invade this now so quiet and so beautiful scene. What can better surround these boys in the spring-time than fields of growing grain; and what in autumn than the stacked harvests? It is for spring planting in peace and autumn harvests of plenty that they died. Let us not now disturb them in their resting place.

WE VISITED THE CEMETERY in all kinds of weather. Always there is some person or persons from Maestricht, Margraten, Heerlen or some other nearby town bringing tribute of flowers and prayers to an American grave. In every kind of weather, and on every day, someone stands for Holland's gratitude to America's homes.

I have journeyed, too, with my heart held quiet in reverent honor to other cemeteries to stand by the graves of friends from home. Always it is the same. Careful, considerate, beautiful use of the environment; as the long row of tall trees that line the road at Neuville, and the gentle slope toward the little woodland at Henri-Chapelle, or the very quiet nestled-downness of Foy.

It gradually grew on me that, in a real sense, every American grave is getting personal attention. The superintendents of the cemeteries are men who sense the delicacy and the honor with which their work must be done.

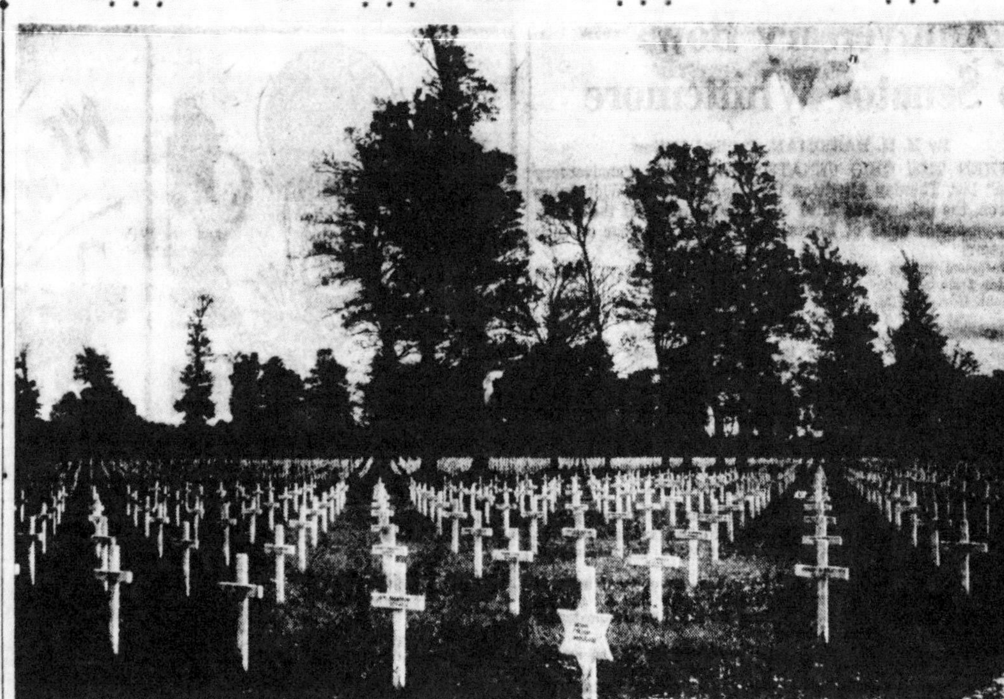

A THING OF AWE AND MAJESTY, THE QUIET, PEACEFUL FIELD OF CROSSES
St. Marie Eglise Cemetery No. 2, Normandy, France

IF MY VOICE COULD BE HEARD in America, I would say to my government that we should do all in our power to keep the simplicity and the naturalness of these surroundings unchanged. White wooden crosses and Stars-of-David are so perfect.

And if I could speak to our homes, those stricken as mine, I would not want to advise them whether or not to bring the body of their soldier home, but I would like to say two things. First, the cemeteries here are beautiful and as nearly perfect as we could wish. Second, the people in the midst of whom our sons lie buried are kindly, thoughtful, appreciative people, conscious that it is an honor to pay tribute to the young warrior dead.

When Monnica, mother of Augustine of Thagaste, lay dyi Italy, far from her Numidian home, it was urged that she shou hurried home for burial in native soil. She answered, "Bury me for nowhere is far from God. Only remember me at the altars o wherever you go." She is right.

New dignity and new contentment have entered into my thou the burial places of the American men here where the common has received them and where the common people cherish the ta honoring them. Nothing will restore what once has been. pilgrimage to Margraten cemetery consoles and strengthens. many thousands look so quiet—let them rest in that quietness!

RUDOLPH R. SIMEK

Corporal

17th Airborne Division

Killed during Operation Varsity

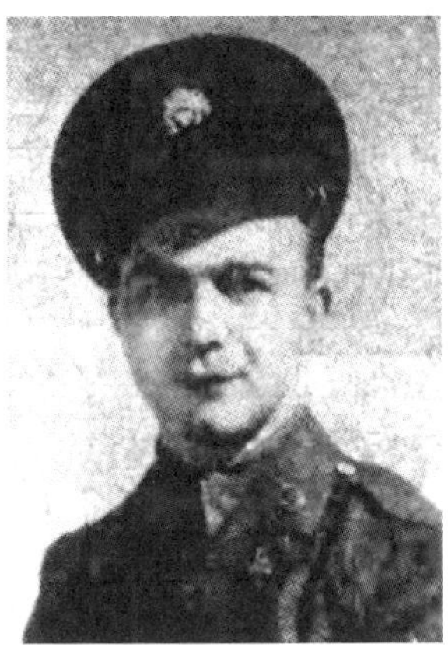

Corporal Rudolph R. Simek was born on July 16, 1917. His hometown was McHenry, a small town in Illinois. He had attended high school for three years and before entering the military, Rudolph worked on the Frank Kaiser farm.

In March 1942, Rudolph reported to Camp Grant to enlist in the army and volunteered for the airborne troops. As a paratrooper, Rudolph served in the Headquarters Company of the 507th Parachute Infantry Regiment. This regiment was initially assigned to the 82nd Airborne Division.

On D-Day, Rudolph and his regiment participated in Operation Overlord, the Allied invasion of Normandy. In July, the 507th PIR returned to England. There it was then permanently assigned to another airborne formation: the 17th Airborne Division.

On March 24, 1945, Rudolph and the 17th Airborne Division were deployed in Operation Varsity, the largest airborne operation in history conducted on a single day and on one location (the airborne component of Operation Market Garden was a larger operation, but the drop zones were split over three distinct areas and spread over several days). This large-scale deployment of airborne troops was planned to support Operation Plunder, the assault of Field Marshal Bernard Montgomery's 21st Army Group across the Rhine near Wesel and Rees.

In the morning of the 24th, the 507th Parachute Infantry Regiment in which the then 27-year-old Rudolph served landed on the east side of the Rhine. Rudolph was dropped near Wesel, where he was killed that same day. This occurred after he was given orders to run across an open field. While Rudolph was crossing the field, he was mortally wounded by enemy machine gun fire. He died a short time later and was buried in Margraten. Today, visitors can find his final resting place there in Plot P, Row 8, Grave 17.

Exactly one year after Rudolph lost his life, Rudolph's brother James and sister Josephine posted a brief tribute in a local newspaper: 'In loving memory of our brother, who gave his life for his country March 24, 1945, in Germany. He will always be remembered by all who loved him dearly. Sister and Brother.'

RALPH L. CHRISTY

Captain

30th Infantry Division

Jeep blown up by a mine

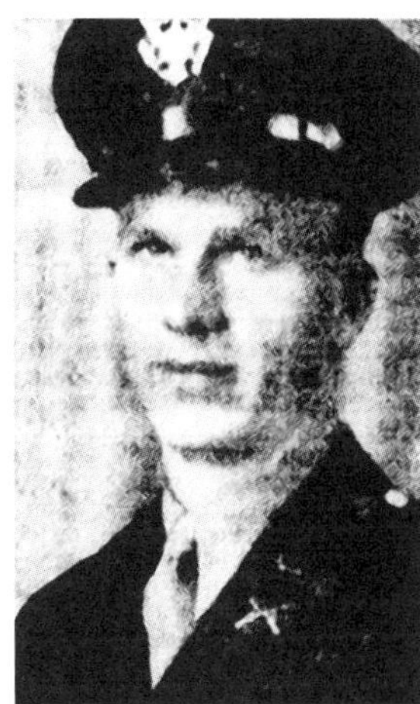

Captain Ralph L. Christy from Tidioute, Pennsylvania, was born in 1921. He graduated from the local high school in 1940 and was employed in his brother's meat market prior to entering the army in February 1941. Ralph attended officer training and was commissioned as a Second Lieutenant in 1943.

Ralph served in the 120th Infantry Regiment of the 30th 'Old Hickory' Infantry Division. Within his regiment, Ralph was the Executive Officer of the 3rd Battalion.

On March 25, 1945, Ralph was driving in a jeep in Germany to direct troops through a break that was made in the German line. Next to Ralph was the driver, George F. Schneider, who later wrote an autobiography in which he described what happened when they approached an advancing column of tanks near Holthausen:

> ***'We had already radioed for tanks to assist us in advancing through the break in the German line. As we traveled down a gently sloping gravel road, we could see the dust from approaching tanks. As we approached the first tank PFC Ralph Storm [who sat in the back of the jeep] said his last words, "Beaucoup dust." The second tank was approaching us and, when it was about 10 feet from us it struck a mine with the outside edge of its left track. The explosion was expended on the roadway. The tank suffered no damage and never slowed down. My first reaction from the explosion 10 feet away was to stop but before I could react, I had progressed to a line in the road where a string of mines has been laid. I hit one with the right rear wheel and was blown over the steering wheel and to the left front. Captain Christy was blown straight forward and landed about 75 feet away. He was killed outright. Storm landed between Captain Christy and the wreckage and had one leg completely blown off [he died the same day]. He had been sitting directly over the blast.'***

Eight months before Captain Ralph Christy was killed, when he was already in Europe, his wife Mary Clinger Christy had given birth to their son Ralph T. Christy in July 1944. Ralph's remains were buried in Margraten, where he is permanently interred in Plot E, Row 19, Grave 16.

Several months after the end of the war in Europe, Mary received the Silver Star Medal that was posthumously awarded to her husband for his gallantry in action from March 23 to March 25, 1945. The citation was published in a local newspaper in November 1945. It reads as follows:

> ***'Although he had been exposed to intense enemy shelling for several days, Captain Christy voluntarily set out on a supply mission and traveled along a heavily shelled route. Due to traffic congested roads, he drove along the shoulders, fully aware of the danger from enemy land mines. However, he elected to continue his mission until his vehicle exploded a mine and he was mortally wounded. Captain Christy's gallant actions will remain a lasting inspiration to all who served with him.'***

HERMAN LEMBERGER

Second Lieutenant

17th Airborne Division

Called back crucial coordinates

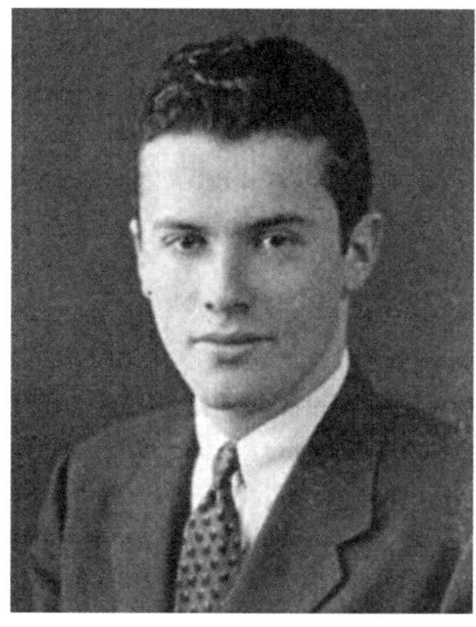

Second Lieutenant Herman Lemberger from The Bronx, New York, was born on November 23, 1917, and was a Jewish officer. Following his graduation from De Witt Clington High School, he studied at the University of Pennsylvania. In 1940, Herman graduated from the Field Artillery Officer Candidate School at Fort Sill, Oklahoma.

Herman served as a Forward Observer in the 681st Glider Field Artillery Battalion of the 17th Airborne Division. On March 24, 1945, he landed in a glider east of the Rhine River during Operation Varsity. The Landing Zone – LZ 'S' – was near the German town of Wesel. Herman was attached to Company G of the 194th Glider Infantry Regiment, for which he coordinated the artillery support.

During the afternoon, Company G was confronted with a German counterattack across a large metal bridge where the Issel Canal came off the Issel River. Herman moved toward the attack and saw enemy tanks approaching. He needed a better view, so he climbed to the top of the canal bank to call back accurate instructions to the artillery batteries. One of the tank crews must have spotted him or his radio. Herman had just managed to send the coordinates when a German tank shell killed him. Thanks to the instructions he had called back, the gunners could rake the enemy formation with salvos of high-explosive shells. As a result, the attack was broken up and the enemy tanks dispersed.

When he lost his life, Herman was 27 years old. He was posthumously awarded the Silver Star. In Margraten, he is permanently laid to rest under a marble Star of David in Plot O, Row 1, Grave 4.

WILLIAM A. STANFIELD JR.
Captain
17th Airborne Division

Gave inspiration and his life

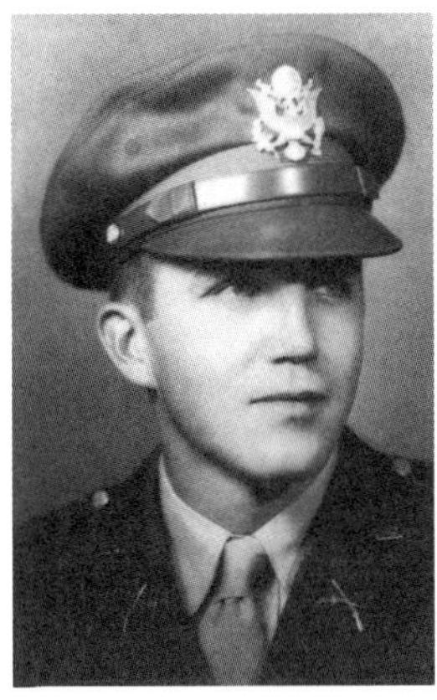

Captain William A. Stanfield Jr. from Tennessee was born in 1917 and lived in Maryville. He was a paratrooper in Company B of the 513th Parachute Infantry Regiment (PIR). This regiment was formed in 1942 and assigned to the 17th Airborne Division in 1944.

On March 24, 1945, William's division was deployed in Operation Varsity, the airborne operation near Wesel and Rees that supported the Rhine crossing assault of Field Marshal Montgomery's 21st Army Group. Varsity would be the last major airborne operation of the war and the first combat jump for the 513th PIR. Despite the fact that two-thirds of the C-46's were either damaged or in flames due to German anti-aircraft fire and the regiment was mis-dropped, it had secured all of its objectives by mid-afternoon.

Two days later, on March 26, 1945, William's company attacked across a German superhighway near Wesel. First Lieutenant Arthur Millman was involved in the same attack and later wrote the following account in a letter to William's father:

> ***'We moved off, and one platoon was pinned down by fire of German weapons. Some tanks came up and I moved my platoon behind the tanks. I took charge of one group behind a tank, and Captain Stanfield took another. We moved off in the face of machine gun, mortar and German Bazooka fire. We crossed the superhighway and then crossed an open field. Captain Stanfield was hit and killed instantly.'***

In the same letter, Millman also described that the men of Company B were proud to have William as their commanding officer:

> ***'The men in that attack will never forget Captain Stanfield. Without regard of his own safety, he calmly led us toward our objective, giving us the needed inspiration to accomplish our mission. Twice we were pinned down but each time Captain Stanfield moved ahead and we followed. (...) He was there when we needed someone or something to lead us. He gave two things, inspiration and his life.'***

When the enemy fire killed him, William was 27 years old. In Margraten, he is permanently interred in Plot G, Row 17, Grave 4.

ALBERT O. HARDENBURGH
Private First Class
58th Armored Infantry Battalion

The second hit was fatal

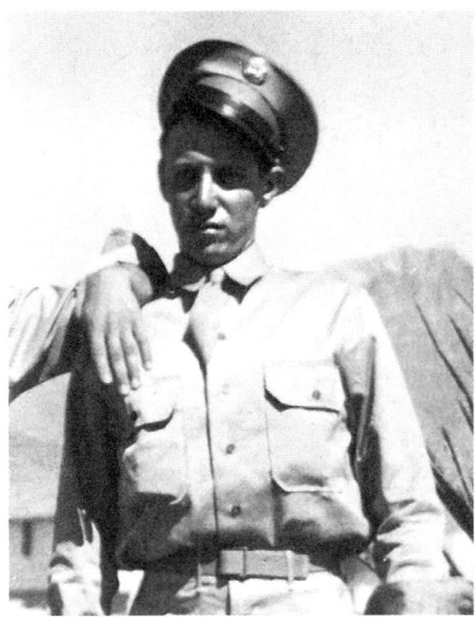

Private First Class Albert O. Hardenburgh from Michigan was born on October 23, 1923. Prior to entering the army in February 1943, he was employed by Morton's Manufacturing in his hometown Muskegon.

Albert was assigned to Company B of the 58th Armored Infantry Battalion, which fought under the command of the 8th Armored Division. This division had arrived in England in November 1944 and had been involved in combat on the European mainland since January 1945.

During combat, the men of Albert's battalion worked closely with the crews of the tanks. For example, the tanks tried to help the vulnerable infantrymen take out enemy machine gun positions. In turn, the foot soldiers did everything they could to warn the tank crews in time for German soldiers with Bazookas and enemy anti-tank guns.

On March 28, 1945, Albert and another man from his battalion rode along on the back deck of a Sherman tank. The driver of this tank was T/5 Lloyd 'Dick' Kemp, who later reported what happened when they were in the German town of Kirchhellen. In 2000 he wrote:

> ***'We were about 200 yards into the open when a German 88mm [gun] fired. The tank rocked and white-hot steel was flying everywhere inside. Fire started almost immediately. Don Elshire [the assistant driver] and I flew out through our hatches. The sandbags on the front were being ripped with machine gun fire as we jumped over the side. I had PFC Hardenburgh by the hand and was trying to pull him off the back deck when another 88 skimmed the back deck killing him.'***

At the moment the hit of the second German shell took his life, Albert was just 21 years old. His final resting place in Margraten is in Plot I, Row 13, Grave 21.

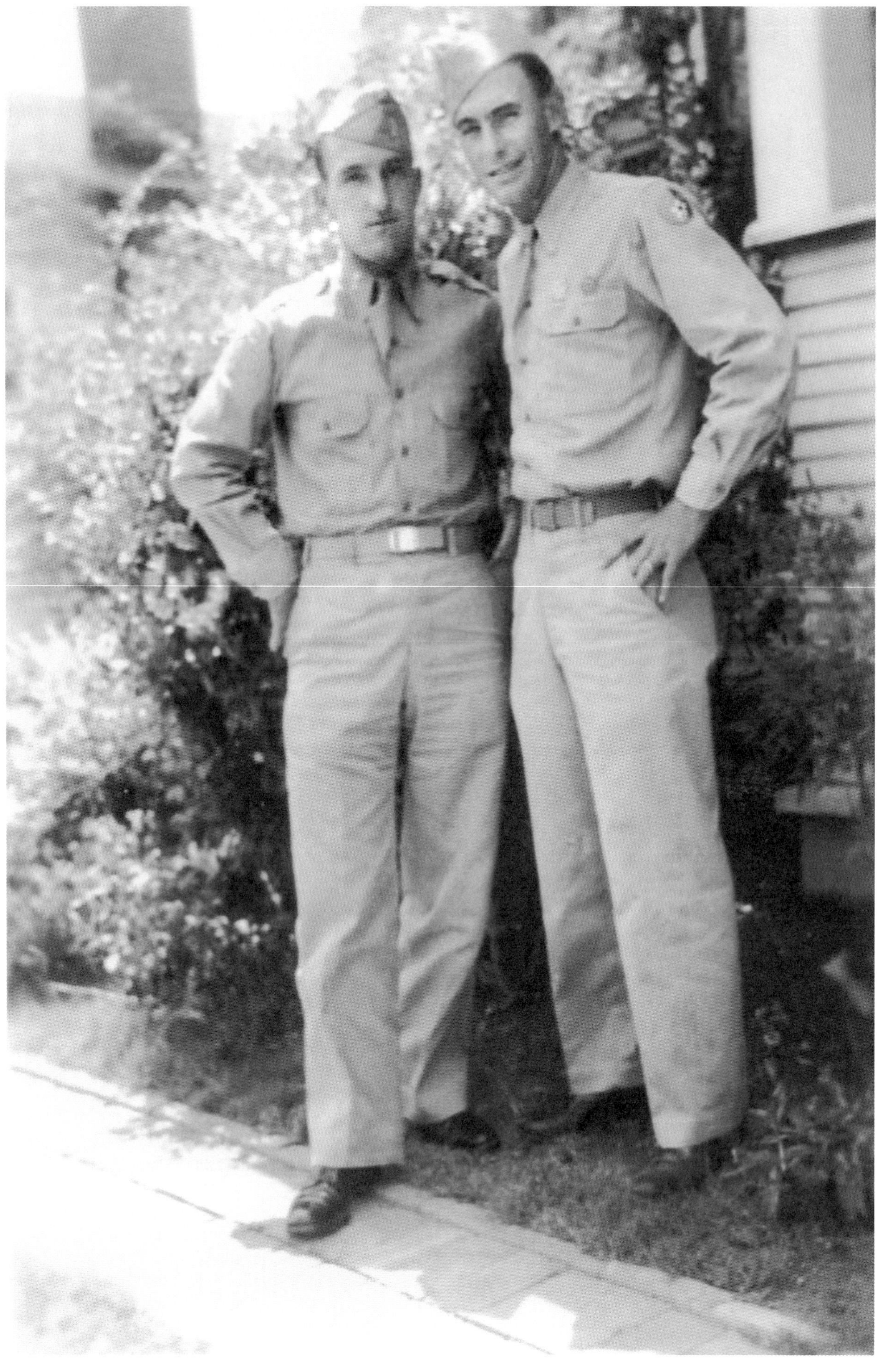

Harold N. Smith, left, and his brother Thomas A. Smith

HAROLD N. SMITH

First Lieutenant

80th Tank Battalion

Not everyone surrendered

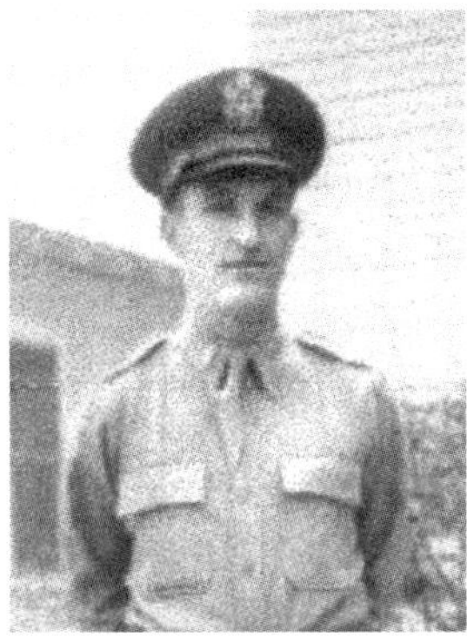

Harold N. Smith from San Antonio, Texas, was born in 1916. His father was a local garage owner. Harold had inherited the genes for engineering from him and went to study at the San Antonio Vocational and Technical High School. His subject area was operating and maintaining all kinds of machinery.

Harold wanted to succeed in life. Therefore, in addition to his job as an accountant with the Alamo Planing Mill, he took evening classes in advanced accounting, business English, and courses that were job related such as, for example, understanding technical drawings.

After the United States entered the war, Harold joined the military. He received officer training at Fort Knox, Kentucky, and was assigned to Company C of the 80th Tank Battalion. While stationed at Camp Polk in Louisiana, Harold was promoted to First Lieutenant.

On November 7, 1944, Harold went overseas. He embarked in New York City and arrived in England on the 19th. In January 1945, his battalion arrived in France. After heading through Luxembourg, Harold's unit stopped at Vilt, a small village in the south of the Netherlands. There, Harold was billeted in the house of the Dutch Duyzings family. Harold became good friends with the family and joined them for dinner each night. They also drank tea together and listened to the wireless radio the soldiers brought. Harold and the other Americans had fun teaching the family's children English and in turn learning Dutch.

Harold was a deeply religious person. He attended the field mass before every battle, and so he did on March 25, 1945, the day before he left the family in Vilt and was sent to the front line in Germany. Harold received both the Holy Communion and the General Absolution. After mass he went to Confession. The following day he left to cross the Rhine.

On March 28, 1945, Harold's tank platoon encountered strong German opposition in the vicinity of Kirchhellen. The tanks advanced and most of the Germans surrendered soon after the first fight. Harold, standing in the turret of his tank, was waiting for them when a German sniper who did not want to surrender killed him. He was only 28 years old. His final resting place in Margraten is in Plot F, Row 17, Grave 10.

EUGENE VILHAUER

Technician Fourth Grade

750th Tank Battalion

Two times shot

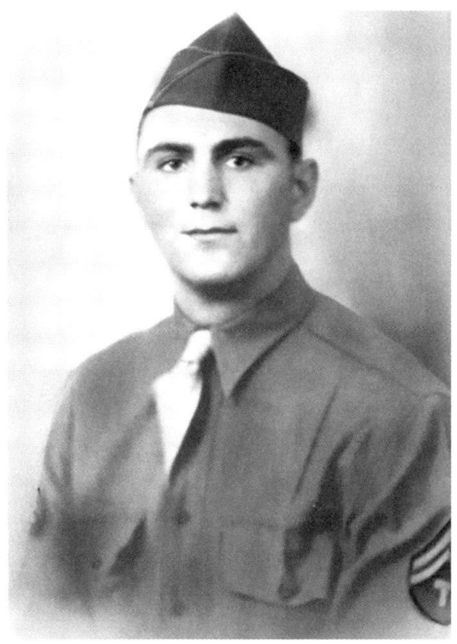

Eugene Vilhauer was born in South Dakota on September 10, 1920. He was the eldest of eleven children. His youngest brother Jake was only two years old when Eugene entered the army in September 1942.

After he had reported for active duty, Eugene was sent to the Armored Force Replacement Training Center for a twelve-week training period. For this he went to Fort Knox in Kentucky. After completing training, Eugene went overseas to Europe in 1944. There he served as a technician in a tank of the 750th Tank Battalion. This tank unit arrived in Normandy on September 25, 1944 and entered combat near Aachen in early November 1944.

Eugene was killed on March 29, 1945, while crossing the Rhine near Friedensdorf and Leipzig. The tank's tracks were shot off by German gunfire. Therefore, all the men of the crew had to abandon the tank immediately. Eugene was the last man to leave the tank because he wanted to make sure that everyone was off safely before he left. While running to take cover, Eugene was shot. He fell to the ground and as his crew tried to get him to safety, he was shot again, this time in the heart. He died instantly and was only 24 years old.

Eugene's remains were buried in Margraten, first in a temporary grave. After the war, when his parents had decided to leave him with his fallen comrades in the Netherlands and not have him repatriated, Eugene was reburied in his permanent grave in 1949. His parents received official notification of this in June of that year. The letter informed them that they could find his final resting place in Margraten in Plot P, Row 5, Grave 2.

WILLIE G. BECKNER
Corporal
80th Tank Battalion

A poem of grieving parents

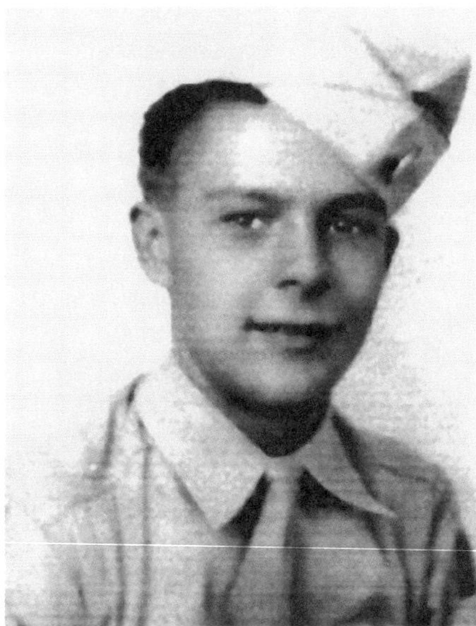

Corporal Willie G. Beckner was born in Roanoke, Virginia, on December 23, 1924. His hometown was Norwood, Ohio, and in March 1943 he entered the army. He reported to Fort Thomas Newport in Kentucky and was then trained to fight in a tank.

After his training, Willie served as gunner in a Sherman tank. His unit was Company A of the 80th Tank Battalion. This tank battalion was part of the 8th Armored Division and arrived in France in January 1945. After stops in the Dutch villages of Vilt and Maasbracht and battles near Linne and Roermond, it crossed the German border. Then, after crossing the Rhine, Company A advanced near Kirchhellen, where Willie's tank was hit by an enemy shell, killing him and another crew member, PFC Willard M. Bean.

More details about how the then 20-year-old Willie lost his life can be found in his IDPF. This includes testimonies and letters from various eyewitnesses. One of them was Lloyd R. Kemp, the driver of the tank. 'The tank was hit in the turret by an 88mm anti-tank projectile,' Kemp recalled. 'It entered the tank on the gunner's side and went out of the tank on the loader's site. The tank burnt for a day and a half. There was absolutely nothing left of Willie G. Beckner or Willard Bean. They were completely cremated.'

Further on in his letter, Kemp wrote the following: 'I was the last to leave the tank and attempted to help them. Corporal Beckner had his head blown completely off. PFC Bean was not dead although the 88mm round had gone through his stomach. He died as I asked him if he needed help.'

It is notable and confusing that Kemp stated that Willie died on March 28, while the official reports and other documentation included in Willie's IDPF state that he was killed in action on March 29, 1945. Another statement included in Willie's IDPF, written by his tank commander Lt. Donald R. Martin, offers no explanation for this discrepancy, but does largely confirm Kemp's description of what had happened to Willie:

> ***'Cpl. Beckner was the gunner in my tank. The tank sustained a direct hit through the turret from an 88mm gun, killing Beckner and the loader and seriously wounding me. The driver and assistant driver were uninjured and climbed out safely. I managed to pull myself out and slid to the ground. At least two more rounds went through or close to the turret as I remember. I can also remember hearing the rounds go off inside the tank as it burned. As far as I know, both bodies were burned up in the tank.'***

Despite the fact that the tank had burned, PFC Bean's remains were recovered as Unknown X-214 in Margraten. He was later buried in the United States at the request of his family. Willie's remains couldn't be recovered and are still missing. Therefore, his name is recorded on the Walls of the Missing in Margraten.

To express their feelings of love and loss, Willie's parents posted a poem in a local newspaper three years after his death on the occasion of Memorial Day.

> ***Every day brings memories,***
> ***every memory brings a tear.***
> ***Deep within our hearts we cherish,***
> ***thoughts of him we love so dear.***

WALTER J. WILL
First Lieutenant
1st Infantry Division

Silenced four machine gun nests

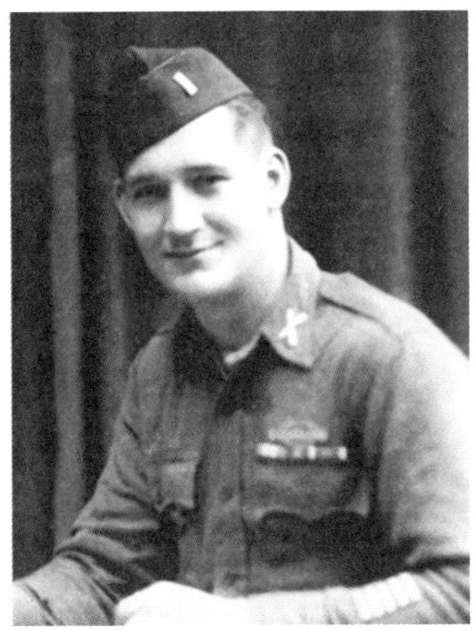

First Lieutenant Walter J. Will was born in Pittsburgh, Pennsylvania, on March 19, 1922. He later moved with his parents to West Winfield, New York. Walter attended West Winfield Central School and enlisted in the army at the age of seventeen in December 1940. After completing training, he was assigned to the 18th Infantry Regiment of the 1st Infantry Division, the 'Big Red One.' With this division, Walter participated in three major invasions: North Africa, Sicily, and Omaha Beach in Normandy.

In Tunisia, Walter was awarded the Silver Star for gallantry in action during Christmas 1942. The citation stated that in the face of German artillery fire, Walter made fifteen trips to men who had been pinned down by enemy fire. During these trips he supplied the men with food and ammunition, and then also removed the wounded.

In November 1944, Walter was awarded a battlefield commission as Second Lieutenant to Company K of the 18th Infantry Regiment. The same month he was slightly wounded, for which he received the Purple Heart. Four months later, Walter was promoted to First Lieutenant on March 26, 1945.

On March 30, 1945, Walter's unit was pinned down by deadly enemy fire from German positions on the edge of Eisern, Germany. Walter courageously exposed himself to the withering hostile fire to rescue two wounded men and then, although painfully wounded himself, made a third trip to carry another soldier to safety from an open area. Ignoring the profuse bleeding of his wound, he gallantly led men of his platoon forward until they were pinned down by murderous flanking fire from two enemy machine guns. Walter fearlessly crawled alone to within 30 feet of the first machine gun and silenced it with rifle grenades. The four Germans in the nest were killed.

After this, Walter continued to crawl through the intense enemy fire to within twenty feet of the second machine gun nest. 'He then got up and charged like a madman,' a witness, Staff Sergeant George H. Johnston, later reported. 'The riflemen and the machine gunners, nine of them, threw up their hands and surrendered.'

Having just captured the second machine gun nest, Walter observed that two more German machine guns were pinning down another platoon. He led a squad on a flanking approach and, rising to his knees in the face of direct fire, coolly and deliberately killed the crew of one machine gun with grenades. 'Then, he got to his feet and rushed the other machine gun nest,' another witness, PFC Leland E. Lloyd, stated. 'On the way he fired a rifle grenade that knocked out the nest and killed the crew.' Walter then returned to his platoon and led it in a fierce charge against the protecting enemy riflemen. 'The enemy riflemen fell back with scattered firing and it was one of those shots that got him,' Lloyd concluded. Walter fell and died. Eleven days earlier he had celebrated his 23rd birthday...

In October 1945, Walter's incredible acts of bravery were posthumously rewarded with the highest and most prestigious U.S. military decoration for valor, the Medal of Honor. That he received this medal is engraved in golden letters on his marble cross in Margraten. Visitors can find it there in Plot D, Row 3, Grave 32.

MAURICE ROSE

Major General

3rd Armored Division

Tank general in the front line

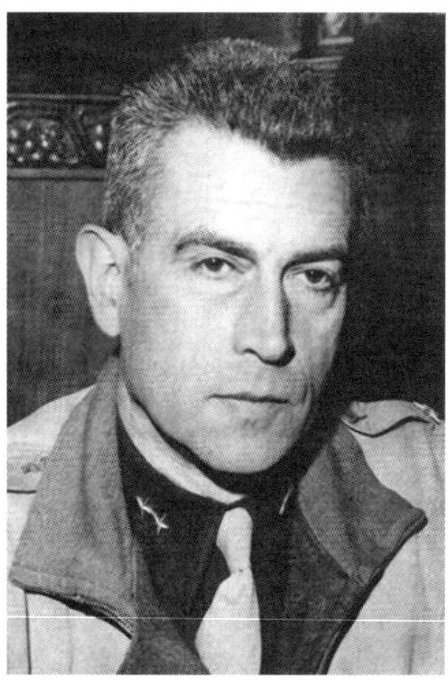

Maurice Rose was born on November 26, 1899, and his hometown was Denver, Colorado. His parents were Jewish, but he himself later converted to Christianity. Maurice joined the army at an early age and fought in Europe during the final year of World War I. In 1918, he was wounded in the Battle of Saint-Mihiel during the American Meuse-Argonne offensive in France.

After the war, he left the army and was briefly employed as a salesman. But the attraction of the military was too strong. Maurice returned in 1920 and was promoted to Captain. From then until the time of his death he served in the army.

During World War II, Maurice became Chief of Staff of the 2nd Armored Division, which participated in the North African campaign. In the desert war there, Anglo-American forces fought against the German Africa Corps, commanded by Erwin Rommel. Although the Germans fought fiercely, it soon became clear that the German army was not strong enough to win this battle.

In 1943, the German opposition in North Africa collapsed, and on May 13 the surrender was signed in Tunisia. Maurice played an important role in this. He was the one who led the negotiations with the Germans, which eventually led to the first massive unconditional surrender of German forces.

After the Allies had gained control of North Africa, Maurice and the 2nd Armored Division were involved in the invasion of Sicily to defeat Italy and bring the Mediterranean under Allied control. In November 1943, the 2nd Armored Division was transferred to England to prepare for the invasion of Normandy. On November 24, 1943, Maurice was given the rank of Brigadier General and was promoted to Commanding Officer of the 2nd Armored Division. In August 1944, after he had led the 2nd Armored Division through the bocage of Normandy, Maurice was given command of another armored unit, the 3rd Armored Division. Simultaneously, he was promoted to Major General.

During the Allied campaign in Europe, Maurice and his tanks were always at the forefront of the battle. Maurice himself personally led his tank units from his jeep.

On March 30, 1945, Maurice was enroute toward the German city of Paderborn to search for Allied troops in enemy territory. He rode in a jeep along with his driver Glenn Shaunce and assistant Robert Bellinger. They were accompanied by a second jeep and a tank in front. Behind them was an armored car and a messenger on a motorcycle.

During the advance, the small convoy suddenly encountered heavy enemy fire. Maurice and his men fled into a ditch, while the accompanying tank suffered a direct hit. When they saw that they were surrounded by German tanks, Maurice and the others jumped back into the jeeps and tried to escape by a detour to the road through a field. When they reached it, several Tiger II-tanks were blocking the road. The driver of the first jeep accelerated and managed to get past the tanks. Maurice's driver Shaunce tried to do the same, but one of the German tanks cut them off. The jeep got stuck between the tank and a tree. The tank hatch opened and the upper body of the German commander appeared. The German immediately began screaming at Maurice, Shaunce, and Bellinger, and aimed his Schmeisser MP 38/40 or small submachine gun at them. It was dark now and the three men got out of their trapped jeep quickly with their hands in the air. Reportedly, Maurice then reached for his pistol holster, presumably to surrender. The German commander opened fire, hitting him with several bullets from his submachine gun. Maurice fell to the ground and died instantly. He was 45 years old.

Why Maurice reached for his pistol and the German soldier pulled his trigger so fast will probably never be known. What is certain is that the Germans did not realize that they had just killed a Major General. They could have seen this by the two stars on his helmet, but the German soldiers just left his body. U.S. troops found Maurice the following day.

▶ Maurice Rose was initially buried in Germany just after his death. SOURCE: *The Knoxville News-Sentinel/* Newspapers.com

The day after he was killed, Maurice was initially buried in Ittenbach. Several months later, his body was transferred to the temporary American cemetery in Margraten. After the U.S. government had decided that Margraten was to become a permanent cemetery, Maurice was permanently reinterred in Plot C, Row 1, Grave 1. He is the highest-ranking soldier buried here. He is also the highest-ranking American soldier killed by enemy fire during the war in Europe.

To honor him, a hospital bearing his name was built in his hometown Denver shortly after the war: General Rose Memorial Hospital, now called the Rose Medical Center. General Dwight D. Eisenhower personally laid the foundation stone.

Maurice is also honored in a special way in Margraten, as the local elementary school was named after him. Pupils and teachers of this school regularly visit his grave and every last Friday before Memorial Day, the school brings flowers to the cemetery to pay tribute to him.

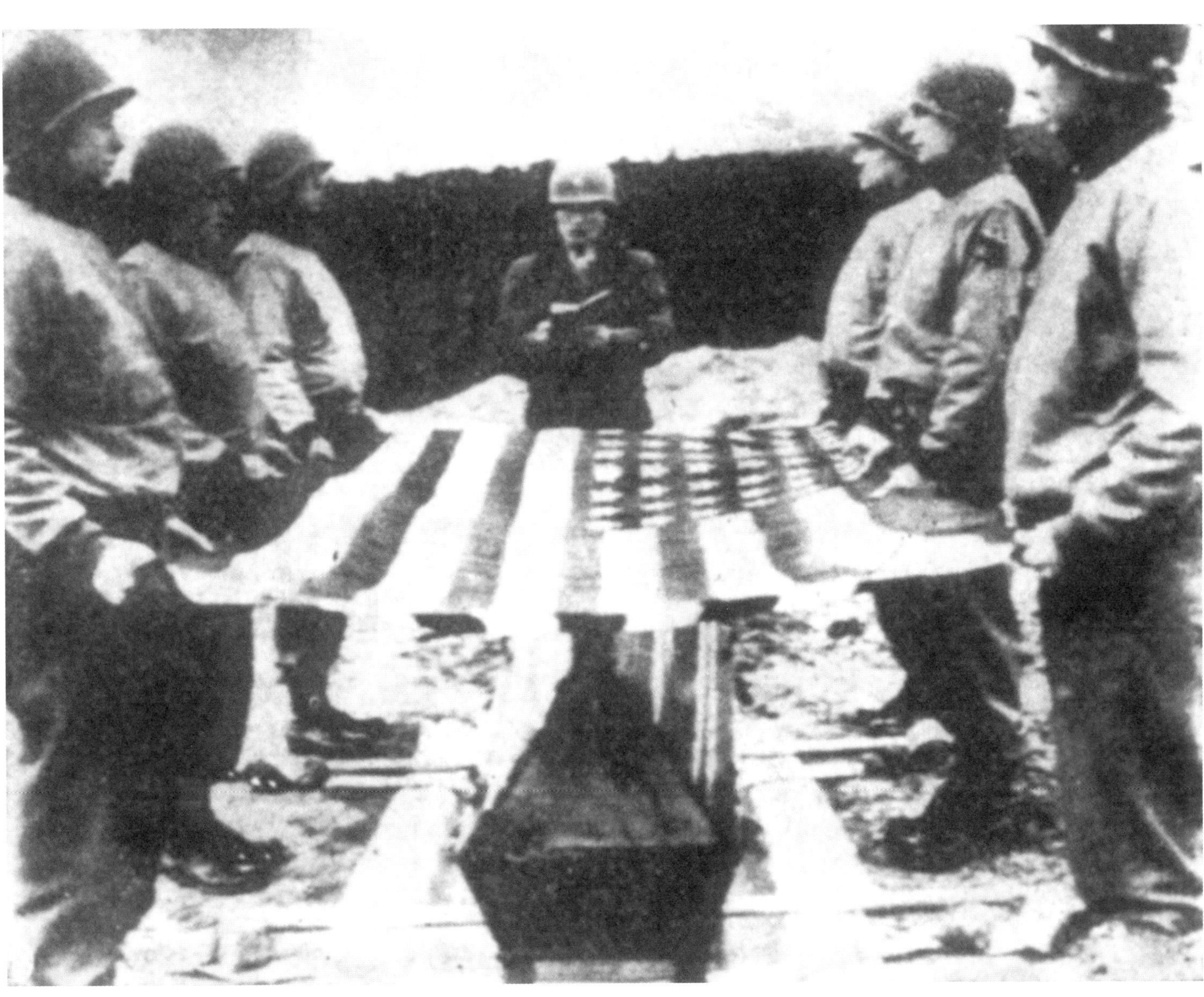

GEORGE PETERSON

Staff Sergeant

1st Infantry Division

Ignored his own wounds

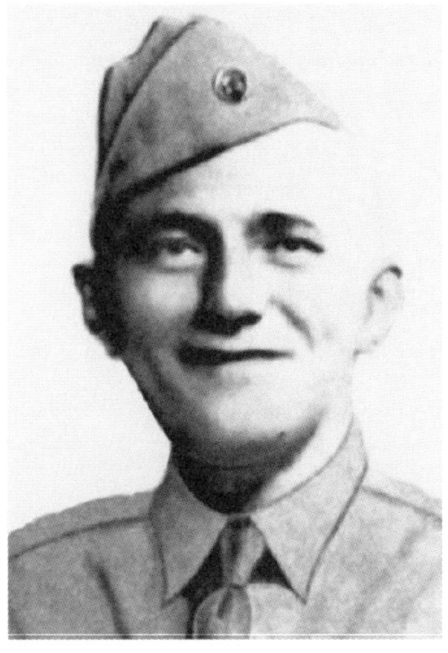

George Peterson from Brooklyn, New York, was born on May 28, 1912, and entered the Regular Army in 1933. He eventually served as a Staff Sergeant in the 18th Infantry Regiment of the 1st Infantry Division. George was a veteran of his division's landings in North Africa, Sicily, and France.

On March 30, 1945, George's platoon of Company K was ordered to make a flanking attack on strong enemy positions near Eisern, Germany. In the face of heavy small arms, machine gun, and mortar fire, George crept and crawled to a position in the lead and motioned for his 2nd Platoon to follow. A mortar shell fell close by and severely wounded him in the legs. 'The men tried to urge him to come back, but he continued forward,' First Sergeant Rufus J. Salyer later reported. 'Two of the machine guns opened up on him, but he crawled steadily toward them until he was close enough to the first machine gun nest to throw a hand grenade. With the two machine guns trained directly on him, he got to his knees and hurled the grenade. It knocked out the gun and the enemy in the nest,' Salyer recalled.

The second machine gun was immediately turned on him, but George calmly and deliberately threw another grenade which also silenced this one and killed the four Germans who occupied the position. George then continued forward but was spotted by an enemy rifleman, who shot him in the arm. Despite being weak from loss of blood and suffering great pain, George crawled toward a third machine gun nest. Near the nest, he raised himself to his knees again and fired a rifle grenade into it, killing three of the enemy machine gun crew and causing the remaining one to flee.

With the first objective now seized, George allowed himself to be treated by an aid man. While being treated he saw one of the men he had dispatched to an outpost position getting seriously wounded by a mortar burst. George wrenched himself from the hands of the aid man and began to crawl forward to get the wounded man. According to another witness, PFC John Molent, George 'got within only a few feet of the man when he was hit himself by a sniper bullet. He died at once, before we reached him in our advance.'

George's life ended at the age of 32. Several months later, he was posthumously awarded the Medal of Honor. The citation concluded with the statement that George 'by his gallant, intrepid actions, unrelenting fighting spirit, and outstanding initiative, silenced three enemy machine guns against great odds and while suffering from severe wounds, enabling his company to advance with minimum casualties.'

The fact that George received the prestigious Medal of Honor is engraved in golden letters on the white cross at his gravesite in Margraten. Visitors can find it in Plot D, Row 21, Grave 10.

LOUIS J. GLAVAN

Sergeant

1st Infantry Division

Two of the family's sons never came home again

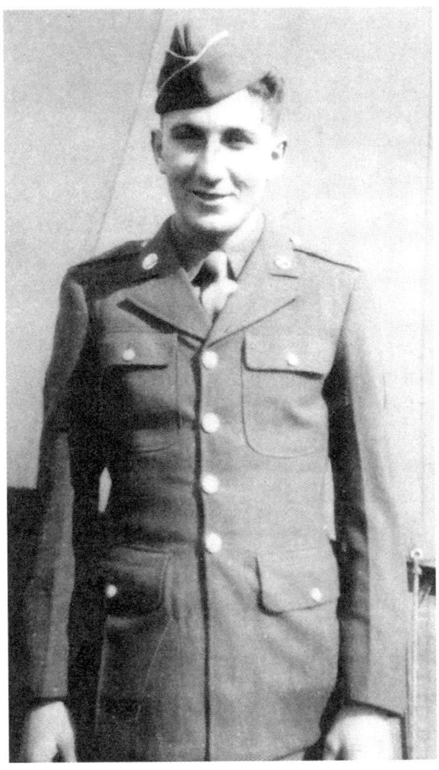

Sergeant Louis J. Glavan was born on January 19, 1922. His hometown was Kinney, a small village located in an iron mining area in northeast Minnesota called the Iron Range. Both Louis' parents, Frank and Mary Glavan, were immigrants from Slovenia.

Louis had six brothers and one sister. On November 25, 1942, he was drafted into the army. 'He was the fourth Glavan brother to join the army,' Louis' nephew Tony Glavan wrote. 'Two more brothers would also join the military by June of 1943 for a total of six brothers in service to their country.'

In late March or early April 1943, Louis was transferred to the Replacement Depot in Shenango, Pennsylvania and soon after was shipped to North Africa, where he became a replacement in the 18th Infantry Regiment of the 1st Infantry Division – the 'Big Red One.' First, he was a runner, but later he became part of a 60mm mortar squad in Company A.

After the Allies had pushed the Germans out of North Africa, Louis took part in the Allied landings on the beaches of Sicily in early July 1943 as part of Operation Husky. In a letter to his oldest brother Frank, Louis wrote the following about his experiences in Sicily: 'There is little to tell of my battle experiences that you wanted to hear about except that for the guy who's first time it was in combat, it was bad. (...) If you think you want to fight, your head isn't where it should be.' Louis was clearly impressed by the grim reality of war.

Nearly a year later, Louis went ashore on Omaha Beach on D-Day. It was his great fortune that the 18th Infantry Regiment was not part of the first assault waves, which had been bloodily decimated by the murderous German machine gun fire and shell bursts.

In another letter to Frank, Louis briefly spoke of the D-Day landings:

> ***'How did you take the news of the invasion? I'll bet the people were kind of puzzled as how to feel. They could not feel glad because of the casualties and yet they couldn't feel sad because it meant the beginning of the end of Hitler. (...) I can tell you that beach was hot. We were fortunate that we landed during a lull and missed getting shelled on the beach by a very few minutes. I was close enough to see the next bunch get it and it wasn't very nice. Well, I guess that completes the letter. Except I'm well and I can't say happy. Unless it's to be alive, and I hope you are the same. Louis.'***

Several months after D-Day, Louis was involved in the bloody Battle of the Hürtgen Forest in November and early December 1944. According to Sergeant John Macik from Pennsylvania, who knew Louis very well, it was here that after a tremendous German artillery barrage had finished, Louis came up to him and was visibly upset. A fellow soldier that Louis shared a foxhole with had suffered a terrible head wound. Sgt. Macik returned to the foxhole with Louis and saw the wounded soldier was covered with blood. The wounded man was sent to an aid station but did not survive...

In February 1945, Louis received a letter from his sister-in-law that told him terrible news: his younger brother Fred, who was a member of the 513th Parachute Infantry Regiment, 17th Airborne Division was killed by a German sniper on January 7, 1945, west of Bastogne. He was just nineteen years old. Sgt. Macik remembered that when Louis read the letter he began to cry (PFC Fred A. Glavan is buried at the American Military Cemetery and Memorial in Hamm, Luxembourg – Plot E, Row 8, Grave 19).

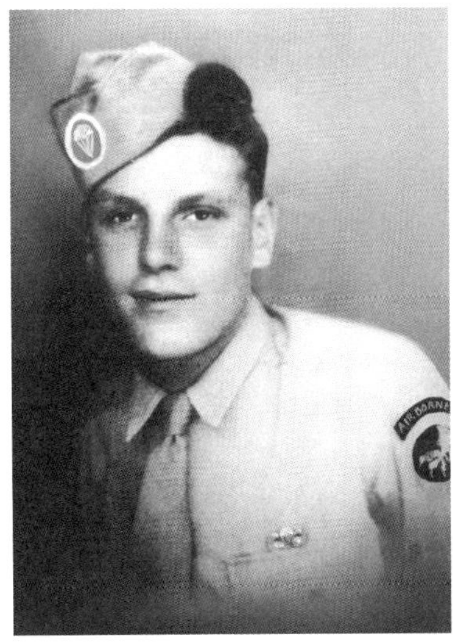

Fred Glavan, Louis' younger brother who was killed on January 7, 1945 and who is buried at the Luxembourg American Cemetery.
SOURCE: Antony Glavan

The news of Fred's death hit Louis just as hard as it did the other brothers. In their letters written home, all the brothers were really worried how their mother was dealing with the news of her son's death and one even wrote he hoped no further tragedy would befall the family, Tony Glavan later learned. But on March 30, 1945, disaster struck again: Louis was killed in action too. According to Tony, who was dedicated to find out what had possibly happened to his uncle, Louis was riding in a jeep as they approached a tiny German hamlet called Rodgen. 'There was a roadblock and I think it may have been a German 20mm anti-aircraft gun, firing horizontally, that killed Louis instantly.' Louis was just 23 years old. His final resting place in Margraten can be found in Plot D, Row 21, Grave 9.

Sometime in late March 1945, the oldest brother Frank had arrived back home in Kinney on an extended medical leave. Frank had contracted a serious skin disease on his feet (sometimes called 'jungle rot') while being stationed in New Guinea. On Saturday April 14, 1945, Frank walked about a kilometer to the post office to get the mail. While there he was handed a telegram announcing the death of Louis. As Frank slowly walked back home, he wondered how he was going to tell his mother. 'He said it was the hardest thing he ever had to do in his life,' Tony wrote. The family was still heartbroken over the death of Fred in January, but then received the news of Louis' death. As their sister Julie told later to Tony, the grief in that tiny house in Kinney was almost unbearable. What made it even more painful was that the date Louis was killed would have been the 20th birthday of Fred. 'March 30 would forever be a terrible date for the family.'

After Fred's and Louis' deaths, the War Department decided to remove the remaining brothers from the front line combat overseas. Frank was home already, but Albin, Ludwig, and John were still fighting overseas.

John and Ludwig were removed from areas of combat in Europe and ultimately sent home. Albin, however, was severely wounded on Ie Shima, a small island a couple of kilometers off the coast of Okinawa. On April 20, 1945 – just five days before he too was to be removed from front line combat – two Japanese soldiers threw explosives under his tank, whereupon he was also shot at while exiting his damaged tank. To everyone's great relief, Albin was eventually reunited with the family as well.

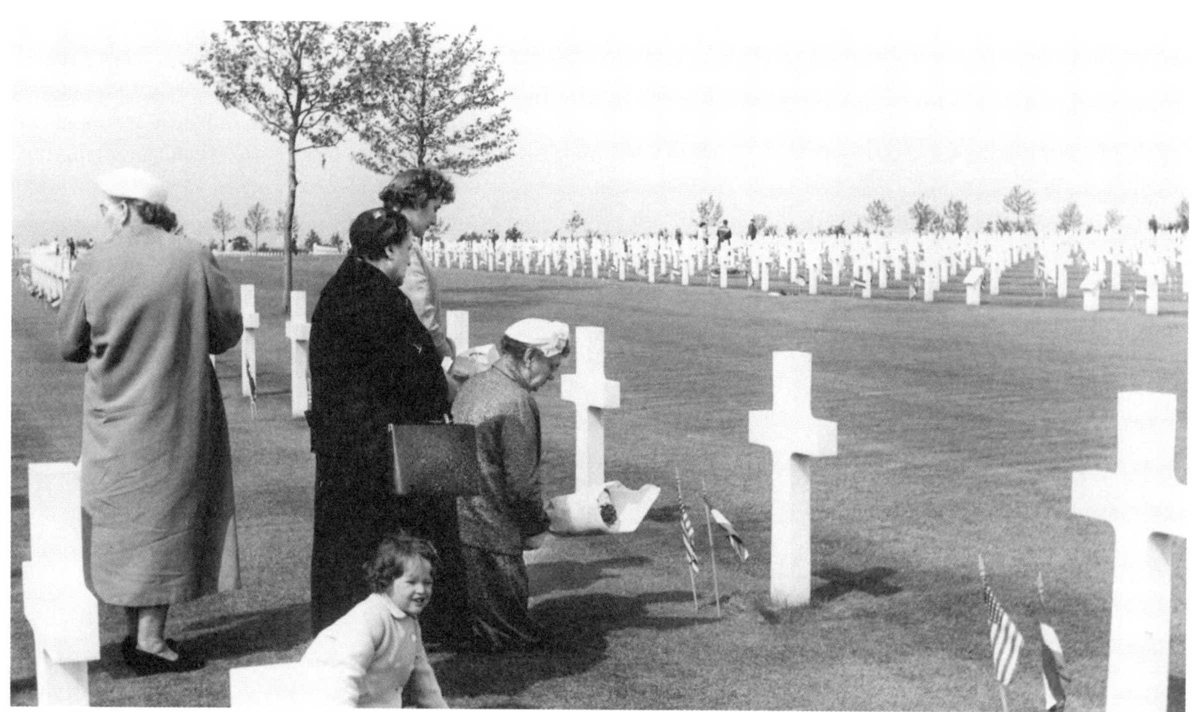

Louis' grave in Margraten after the final reburial of the fallen

MACK L. OLDHAM
Staff Sergeant
58th Armored Infantry Battalion

A fond and loving Daddy

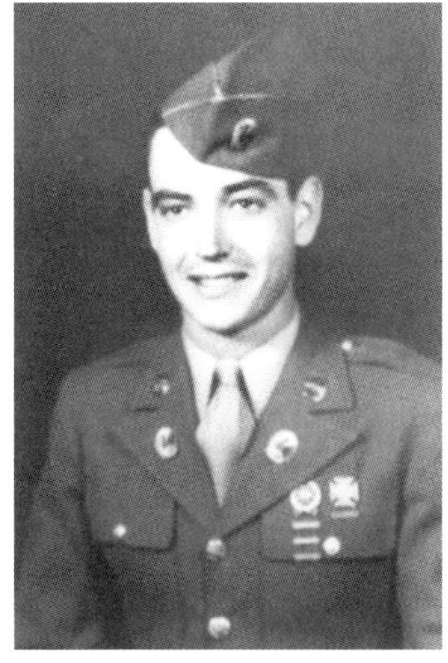

Mack L. Oldham was a Staff Sergeant from Carthage, Missouri. In 1941, he married Kathryn Alice Berry, with whom he had a son named Mack L. Oldham Jr. Prior to entering the service, Mack was employed by the Atlas Powder Company plant. According to a local newspaper, Mack was a well-known Carthage young man and a member of the Dudman church.

Mack entered the army in April 1943. While being stationed at the Armored Force Replacement Training Center at Fort Knox, Kentucky, he showed himself to be an outstanding marksman. Captain Charles W. Clark, his commanding officer at the time, wrote that 'thanks to his mental alertness and conduct during the course of instruction, Pvt. Mack L. Oldham attained a thorough knowledge of the handling of the sub-machine gun, with which he fired a perfect score. Private Oldham's performance justifies our belief that a man who is physically fit and mentally alert cannot help but make a good soldier.'

Following his training, Mack went overseas in October 1944. He was assigned to the 58th Armored Infantry Battalion of the 8th Armored Division and acted as a squad leader in Company A. One of his fellow soldiers at the time, a Sergeant named David P. O'Brien, remembered Mack as the best leader he had since he joined the division himself. 'He was liked by everyone,' O'Brien later wrote to Mack's parents. 'He was repeatedly asked for advice on various subjects and his word was respected because of the foresight and logical mind with which he was possessed.'

In that same letter, O'Brien also explained why he considered Mack a true leader:

> ***'Mack was always the first one in his squad and he would always weigh the situation before he'd lead us out into it. He never once would send a man any place he would not go himself. Men admired him for this because so many times there are so many leaders who rather than risk his own neck would send his men forward. Mack was not this type. That is one of the reasons he was so respected, that was one of the reasons we would gladly go anyplace he desired.'***

Mack was highly religious, and the Bible was his guide. 'Mack was ever a church goer and he lived by the Bible,' O'Brien recalled. 'His character showed it plainly. One could always enter his room and find his Bible lying on his bed or table (...). He knew the Bible almost verbatim.'

That his faith and the Bible played a major role in Mack's life is also reflected in one of the letters he wrote to his parents and sister Rebecca, dated March 11, 1945. He concluded this letter with a Bible quote (Romans 14: 7–9): 'For none of us liveth to himself, and no man dieth to himself. For whether we live, we live unto the Lord; and whether we die, we die unto the Lord: whether we live therefore, or die, we are the Lord's. For to this end Christ both died, and rose, and revived, that he might be Lord both of the dead and living.'

Earlier in this letter, Mack wrote that he was in Germany and that he had finally been able to get a bath – 'my 3rd bath for the year' – and wash his clothes. 'I'm now in Germany, and I must say it is a beautiful country, the best I've seen so far on the continent.' He also wrote he had attended a church service, which he had enjoyed very much. Further on, his tone became suddenly less cheerful as he wrote he had been lonesome for the last few days and missed home. 'I've naturally not forgotten any of you, and it does seem that all the things back there is only a dream.'

Almost three weeks after writing this letter, Mack was killed in action on March 30, 1945. In a letter Mack's mother received from Major Thomas K. Spande, the Division's Chaplain, she could read that Mack's company was fighting with the Ninth U.S. Army and that he was killed in the attack on the enemy stronghold near Bergmannsglück, Germany. 'While advancing with his squad, over a field in order to reach some houses, Mack was hit by rifle fire from an enemy sniper, whose shot was immediately fatal,' Spande wrote.

Sergeant O'Brien also described Mack's death in his letter because he had witnessed it himself and had reported his death. 'It was not easy and I'm not ashamed to say that I cried. Mack was like a brother to me and the squad members were a sad bunch of boys when I broke the news to them.'

Near the end of his letter, O'Brien wrote the following:

> ***'I realize also that Mack has a son, and I say to you and to him that you can certainly be proud of Mack because he was everything an American soldier should be, brave, courageous and sensible. But he had attributes which were above the ordinary good soldier. He had a superior sense of justice and honesty, a superior sense of goodness and care for his men. He was an ideal in our squad and every man respected him for what he was made of.'***

Mack was 25 years old when he met his death. He was buried at the U.S. Military Cemetery in Margraten, where he was later permanently interred in Plot K, Row 13, Grave 12.

Mack's son, who was only three years old when the war took his father's life, later received a letter from one of his father's former teachers. She remembered Mack well and wrote to Mack Jr. that he may rightly be proud to be his son. Furthermore, she told him that his father was 'handsome both in face and action, and his pleasant smile and happy ways made friends for him of all he met.' Then she wrote: 'He was a fond and loving Daddy, and loved you deeply. Cherish his memory always. He was worthy of it.'

SAMUEL O. PILE

Private First Class

8th Infantry Division

Killed by a pillbox

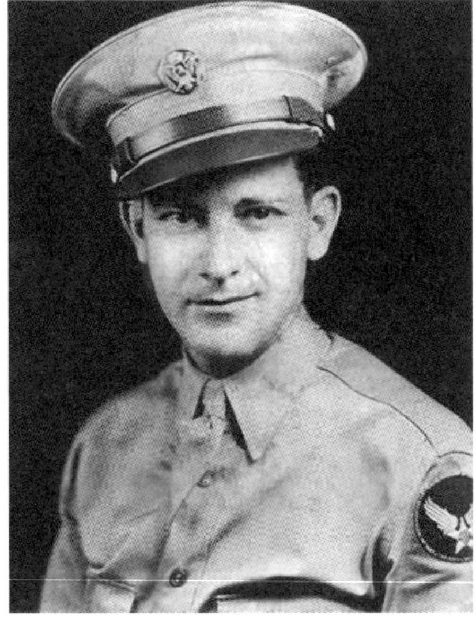

Private First Class Samuel O. Pile was born in 1910 and lived in Irvington, Breckinridge County, Kentucky. On May 9, 1942, he enlisted at Fort Benjamin Harrison in Indiana. Samuel was initially stationed at Lincoln Air Base in Nebraska, but was later transferred to the infantry.

In January 1945, Samuel was sent overseas to Europe. There he was attached to Company B of the 13th Infantry Regiment. This regiment was part of the 8th Infantry Division, which had entered combat in Normandy in July 1944. After advancing through France and across the German border, the 8th Infantry Division moved into the Hürtgen Forest in November 1944. Through this notorious forest, the division had to push forward to the Roer, which the division crossed on February 23, 1945.

After crossing the Roer, the division's advance continued toward the Rhine. It reached this major river near Rodenkirchen, after which Samuel and the 13th Infantry Regiment seized the northern part of the German city of Cologne.

On March 28, 1945, troops of the 8th Infantry Division began to move across the Rhine in the Remagen area. Two days later, Samuel lost his life in combat on March 30, 1945. According to information obtained by his next of kin, he was killed by a German machine gun nest ('pillbox'), about a mile over the river. Samuel was 34 years old. He was given his final resting place in Margraten, where visitors can pay tribute to him in Plot I, Row 2, Grave 10.

EDWARD BRODOWSKI

Staff Sergeant

80th Tank Battalion

A fatal duel with a German tank

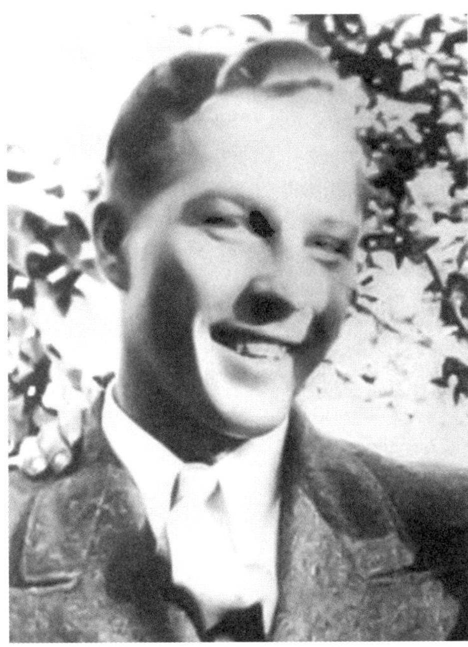

Edward Brodowski was born in Forestport, New York, on September 19, 1919. In 1936, he enlisted into the army's 33rd Infantry, which purpose it was to guard the Panama Canal. Ed was discharged in 1940, but in March 1943, he was called back into the army.

During the last months of the war, Ed commanded a Sherman tank in Company A of the 80th Tank Battalion. This unit was part of the 8th Armored Division, also known as the 'Thundering Herd.'

In February 1945, Ed and the 80th Tank Battalion were involved in heavy fighting near Linne and Roermond in the Netherlands. For meritorious achievement displayed there on February 26, 1945, Ed was awarded the Bronze Star. His citation reads:

> ***'Sgt. Brodowski displayed outstanding courage moving his tank up under intense enemy fire and dismounting to evacuate wounded. He was later assigned the mission of attacking an enemy network of trenches. In carrying out the mission, he exposed himself continually to enemy fire to man the machine gun on his tank. He continued his advance despite the fact his tank was struck once by anti-tank fire. His action enabled the pinned down infantry to resume their advance.'***

On March 30, 1945 – Good Friday – Ed led his tank into Buer-Hassel, a northern suburb of the German city of Gelsenkirchen. As they reached the marketplace there, a camouflaged German Tiger-tank drove out from behind a building. The Tiger fired a round that hit the right track of Ed's tank and disabled it. Ed ordered his crew to leave the tank. While some of his crew escaped, he himself slipped down into the gunner's seat with Corporal Richard McStay as his ammo loader. Ed decided to battle it out with the German Tiger. After he had fired three rounds from his tank gun, his Sherman tank was hit again. This time the 88mm gun of the German tank shot into the turret of Ed's tank, instantly killing him and his loader McStay. Ed was 25 years old.

Several weeks later, Ed's wife Maryanne gave birth to their son Bruce, who thus never knew his father. This had a great impact on him, as he many years later wrote in his book *The Dad I Never Knew: A War Orphan's Search for Inner Healing*, which was published in 2010. In it, Bruce describes how difficult it was for him to grow up without his dad:

> ***'I often wonder what we would have done together. He liked deer hunting as attested by the mounted deer head hanging in his mother's dining room. Ah, those weekends hunting and fishing trips. Just me and Dad. Or maybe we would have thrown a baseball around in the summer; or a football; or played basketball or tennis. Yeah, tennis! I remember his old wooden tennis racket gathering dust in the attic. He would have taught me tennis and we would have played together. Just me and Dad...'***

In 2015, Bruce traveled to Europe with his wife Ellen and visited the exact intersection where Ed was killed in his tank. He then also visited his dad's grave in Margraten, which he found in Plot E, Row 16, Grave 20.

CHESTER D. WILKINS

Captain

41st Tank Battalion

Never got to see his youngest daughter

Chester D. Wilkins was born in Tennessee on May 24, 1918, and grew up in a family that eventually numbered nine children. The family's hometown was Hopkinsville, Kentucky.

When Chester was eighteen years old, he entered military service with the 5th Cavalry at Fort Sam, Texas. In April 1938, Chester married his beloved Iola, with whom he eventually had three children. A few years later, Chester began training at the Officer Candidate School at Fort Knox in 1942. Once he completed officer school, Chester was stationed at several other army camps before going overseas to Europe in September 1944. He arrived in England in October and went to France in December.

In Europe, Chester served as a tank commander in the 41st Tank Battalion. This unit was part of the 11th Armored Division, which came under the command of General Patton's Third Army during the Battle of the Bulge and was then sent to the Ardennes as reinforcements.

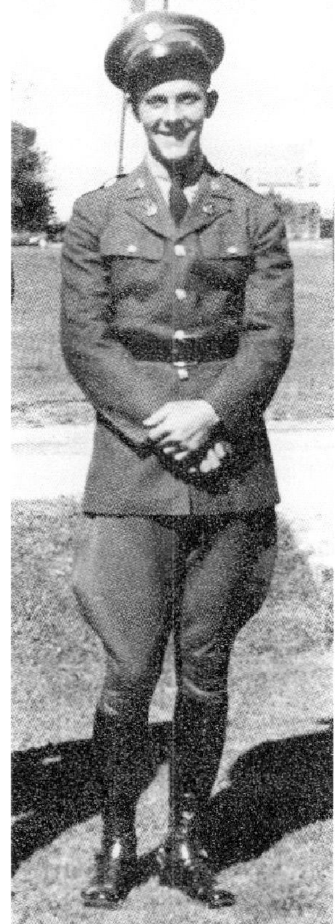

After the Battle of the Bulge, the 41st Tank Battalion fought its way deeper into Germany. On March 29, 1945, the battalion then crossed the Rhine at Oppenheim. By then, Chester was acting as Commanding Officer of the Headquarters Company.

Two days later, on March 31, 1945, the 41st Tank Battalion received heavy fire while advancing toward the manufacturing town of Fulda. The battalion's combat history describes how Chester lost his life in this action:

'The Battalion moved through a heavy wood to the outskirts of Fulda. Here heavy fire was received and from the sound of it one could tell it was from very large guns. No doubt the enemy was going to try tenaciously to hold on to that important manufacturing town.

Further proof of their determination was the fact that all the bridges leading into the city had been blown. Capt. Chester D. Wilkins, Commanding Officer of Headquarters Company, in an effort to ascertain whether or not the conditions of the bridges were true, moved his light tank boldly right down towards the riverbank. An unseen bazooka-man [armed with a Panzerfaust or Panzerschreck] fired at the tank and scored a direct hit. Capt. Wilkins was killed instantly. The news of his death infuriated the rest of the command.'

Chester made the ultimate sacrifice at the age of 26. He was survived by his wife and three young children. The youngest child was only two months old at the time... Chester's final resting place in Margraten is in Plot L, Row 21, Grave 14.

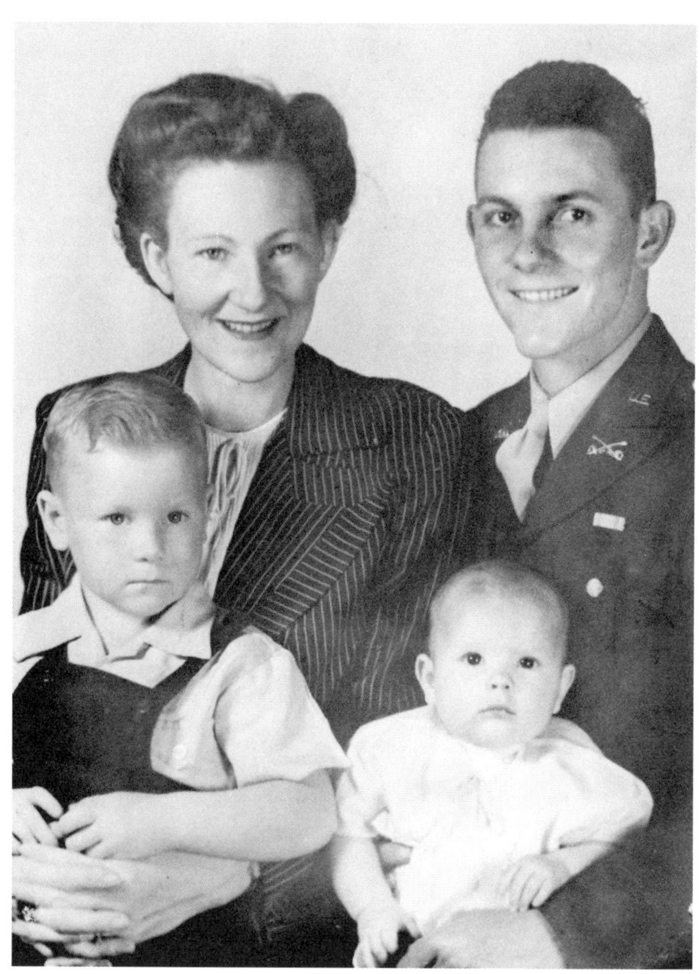

Iola and Chester posing with their first two children.

STEPHEN S. MOSBACHER

Staff Sergeant

8th Armored Division

Jewish serviceman died in his country of birth

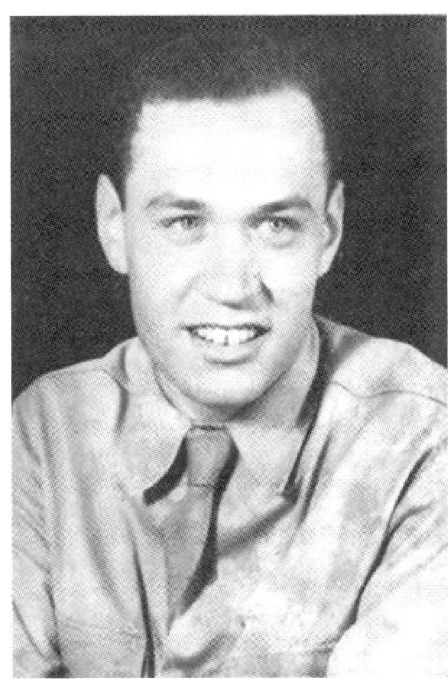

Sigmund Mosbacher was born in the German city of Nürnberg on October 14, 1923, ten years before Hitler became chancellor of Germany. His parents were Jewish, so was he himself. About three years after Sigmund's birth, his mother Anna died. His father Emil therefore later remarried.

Emil, who was a Jewish doctor, was no longer allowed to practice his profession in 1938. Therefore, and because the anti-Semitism of the Nazi regime became increasingly violent, he decided that they had to leave their homeland. Sigmund then emigrated to the United States with his father, stepmother, and stepsister Marianne.

At some point after their arrival in the United States, Sigmund Americanized his name to Stephen. He attended Newtown High School in Queens, New York, and after school he worked in a market next door to the family's apartment. Stephen made excellent grades and earned a scholarship to the University of North Dakota in Fargo, but returned to Toledo, Ohio, where the Mosbacher family had moved in the spring of 1940. He attended the university there and was majoring in chemistry when the Japanese attacked Pearl Harbor on December 7, 1941 and America became involved in World War II.

When Stephen was nineteen years old, he enlisted into the U.S. Army in 1943. He eventually became a Staff Sergeant in the HQ Company of the 8th Armored Division. In September 1944, he was shipped overseas to Europe. Because he could speak German very well, Stephen was frequently tasked with the interrogation of German prisoners of war. He also accompanied his commanding officer as an interpreter.

In the winter of 1944–1945 Stephen – nicknamed 'Moose' – was billeted in Margraten at the home of a Dutch family. In late December 1944, his commanding officer gave him a leave to Paris.

On April 2, 1945, the 8th Armored Division was advancing towards the Elbe River in Germany. However, near Schloss Neuhaus, north of the city of Paderborn, the Americans were confronted with a fierce German counterattack. The resulting fight was rough, but the Americans held the SS troops until they brought up their tanks.

During this counterattack Stephen, Major John R. Elting, and Elting's jeep driver – a recruit named Smith – rescued a soldier who had been left behind when the rest had started retreating. The man was running frantically across a field with several SS troopers at his heels. Elting jumped out of the jeep and began to shoot at the SS men. Stephen and Smith then turned the jeep around and went right down into the advancing Germans to pick up the man. In the face of heavy enemy fire, Stephen pulled the man into the jeep.

In a letter to Stephen's father, Major Elting later wrote what happened next:

> ***'I jumped onto the radiator of the jeep as it came back past me. We shot our way out. Thought again that we had gotten away with it. But, as we went back out of the town, I saw one of our light trucks wrecked alongside the road. A shot from the German tank which was firing down the road had wrecked its front wheels. A wounded man was beside it. We pulled up to try to save him too. It was then that the tank hit us. Having your jeep hit by a high-velocity shell is something you can't describe. It was a glare of white light and a screaming crash. Then we were in the ditch. Smith and I were wounded, Stephen and the rescued soldier were dead. Stephen was still smiling and still had a firm grip on his submachine gun.'***

Because the German tank shell instantly killed him, Stephen remained forever 21. For his gallant efforts to rescue two men of his outfit, he was posthumously awarded the Silver Star in September 1945.

Stephen, who gave his life in the country in which he was born, is permanently laid to rest under a marble Star of David in Margraten, in Plot I, Row 11, Grave 19.

WALTER J. HUCHTHAUSEN
Captain
Headquarters Ninth Army

One of the 'Monuments Men'

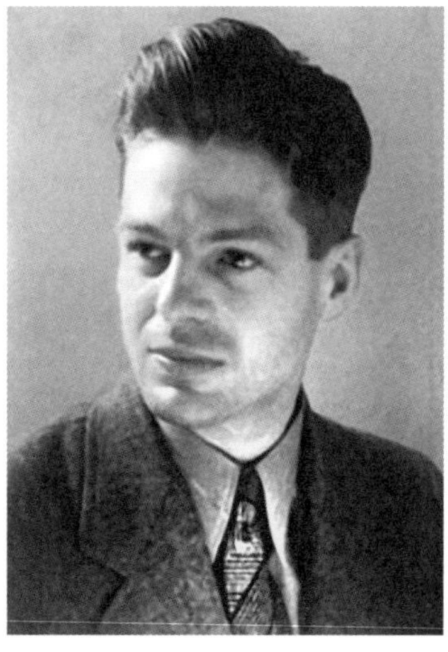

Walter J. Huchthausen was born on December 19, 1904. He was one of five children born to German immigrant Julius Huchthausen and his wife Ida. The family first lived in Oklahoma and Washington before settling in Minnesota in the 1920s.

Walter attended the University of Minnesota, where he earned several awards for academic achievements and architectural drawing. He graduated in 1928. Later he earned a master's degree in architecture from Harvard. He then studied in Germany under a Harvard fellowship.

In 1939, Walter returned to the University of Minnesota to teach architectural design, drawing, and painting. During the next few years, he also designed buildings, created designs for monuments, and painted watercolors. One of the buildings Walter designed was the Mt. Olive Lutheran Church in St. Paul, which was built in 1942.

That same year, Walter enlisted in the U.S. Army Air Forces. After training in Texas, he was deployed to Great Britain. There he was wounded in London during a German V-1 bombing in 1944. After he recovered, Walter was recruited to the so-called 'Monuments, Fine Arts and Archives Commission' (MFAA). In recent years, this group has often been called the 'Monuments Men.' Many of the men and women who became involved in this specialized group had worked as artists, museum curators, or architects before the war. Now their role was to protect Europe's cultural treasures endangered by the war and to collect cultural artifacts and art looted or displaced by the Nazis.

After the Allies had seized the German city of Aachen in October 1944, Walter organized a team there for recovery and restauration efforts across the heavily damaged city. He worked tirelessly to preserve the city's magnificent medieval cathedral, which was (and still is) also the resting place of Charlemagne. He organized the repair of its roof, the bricking up of the choir buttresses, and the covering of broken windows to preserve the interior wall paintings.

Walter also discovered a repository of the area's art in Aachen's Suermondt Museum. He used the building as a base from which to direct operations and as a collection point for altarpieces and other artifacts that were found during the further advance through Germany.

On April 2, 1945, Walter and his assistant Sheldon Keck, an art conservator in civilian life, were traveling north of Essen by jeep to recover an important cultural artifact, reportedly an altarpiece. Finding their chosen route impassable, they tried to detour around, and soon found themselves on an Autobahn heading east. After a while, Keck noticed that there were suddenly no other American vehicles in sight. Finally, they saw American soldiers peering over the highway embankment. They decided to ask directions, but when they stopped to do so, their jeep was raked with German machine gun fire. Walter was hit in the head and died instantly. His body fell onto Keck, which saved Keck's life.

Walter lost his life at the age of 40 and was buried in Margraten. There he is permanently laid to rest in Plot L, Row 1, Grave 15.

David Finley, the Vice Chairman of the 'American Commission for the Protection and Salvage of Artistic and Historic Monuments in War Areas,' to which the MFAA was closely associated, sent a letter of condolence to Walter's family. In it he wrote:

> ***'The American Commission has learned with the deepest regret of the death of your son Captain Walter Huchthausen. Captain Huchthausen was, in the opinion of this Commission, one of the outstanding Monuments Officers in the field, and his work in the Valley of the Loire and at Aachen will remain as a signal contribution to the cultural preservation of Europe. His knowledge of Germany made him uniquely fitted for the work there and his loss is an irreparable one.'***

▶ Generals Eisenhower, Patton, and Bradley examine paintings found in a German salt mine, which was confiscated by the Nazi's to hide stolen art, April 1945. The 'Monuments Men' had been tasked with recovering these treasures. SOURCE: National Archives and Records Administration

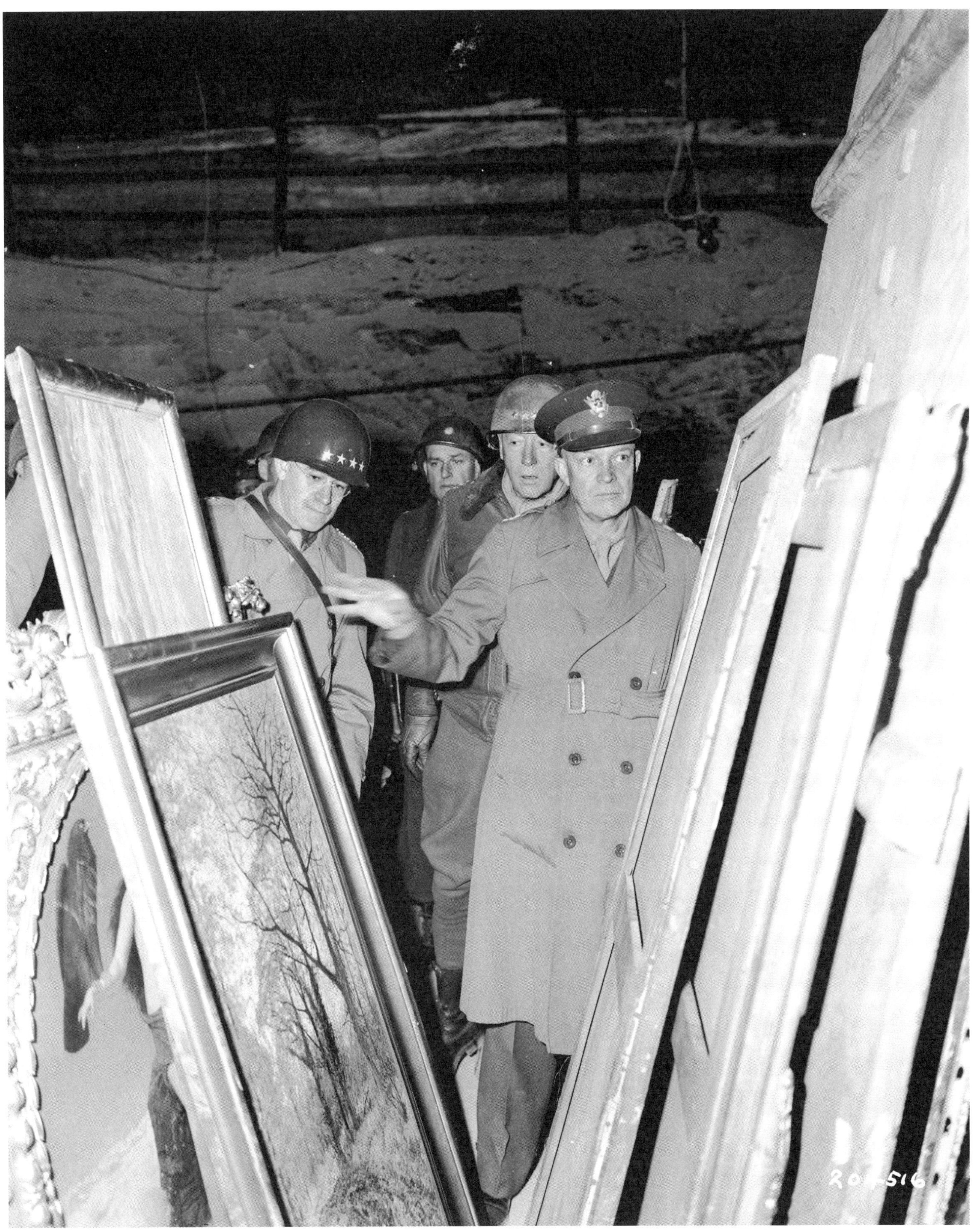

LAWRENCE F. SHEA

Corporal

80th Infantry Division

An ordinary New Yorker

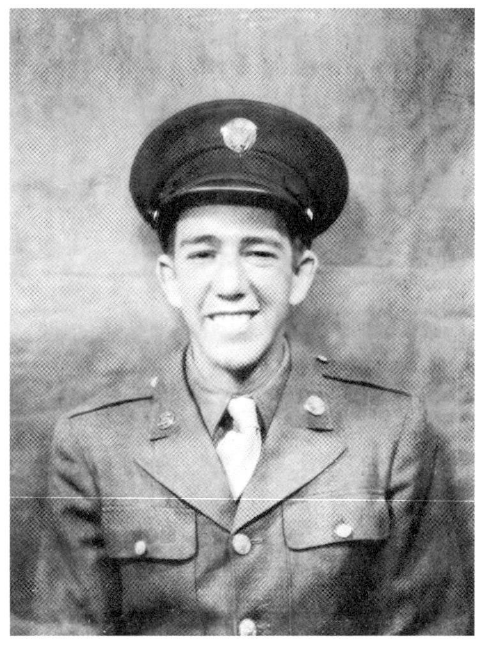

Corporal Lawrence F. Shea from Brooklyn, New York, was born on September 12, 1923. Because his mother died in the 1930s, he, like one of his sisters, partly grew up in an orphanage. Lawrence, who also went by 'Lally' and 'Larry' among family and friends, was an ordinary boy and a sports lover. He liked to play football, basketball, and baseball. He went to the Alexander Hamilton High School.

At the age of seventeen, Lawrence reported to Sea Girt, New Jersey, to work with the Civilian Conservation Corps. This was one of the New Deal programs that President Roosevelt set up during the Great Depression to help unmarried, unemployed men find work. He got out of the corps in January 1942. Later he was employed by Oakite Products, Inc. at the Bush Terminal, New York. According to a newspaper article, published in *The Brooklyn Daily Eagle*, Lawrence also pitched on the company's baseball team.

In January 1943, Lawrence entered military service. He served stateside at Avon Park Army Airfield in Florida, until he was transferred to the infantry in November 1944. Several months later, on March 22, 1945, Lawrence joined the 80th Infantry Division as a replacement in Mainz, Germany. He was attached to Company A of the 318th Infantry Regiment.

A few days after he was deployed in combat for the first time, Lawrence and the other men of Company A moved into positions along the road leading to the German industrial city of Kassel. There, on April 2, 1945, when they were entering the city's outskirts, German infantry and tanks counterattacked. Some of the German tanks the Americans then encountered were large and heavily armored Tiger tanks with 88mm guns that were believed to have been built in the city. While the division repulsed the attacks that day, it suffered a high number of casualties. Lawrence, killed by a shell that was likely fired by one of the tanks, was just one of 26 members of his regiment that were killed that day; about 40 were wounded.

The 21-year-old Lawrence was initially buried in the temporary cemetery in Butzbach. Per his family's wishes, he was permanently laid to rest overseas. His final resting place in Margraten is in Plot D, Row 11, Grave 26. Lawrence's brothers James and Walter, who also served in the Armed Forces, would survive the war.

Lawrence was greatly missed by his family. 'Just a token of love's devotion / That our hearts still long for you,' reads the in memoriam that the family posted in a Brooklyn newspaper in 1953. They found some comfort in prayer and would traditionally offer mass in the St. Francis Xavier Church on the anniversary of his death. But family members said that the mood in the family's house on Brooklyn's President Street had changed. It had become 'the home of aching hearts.'

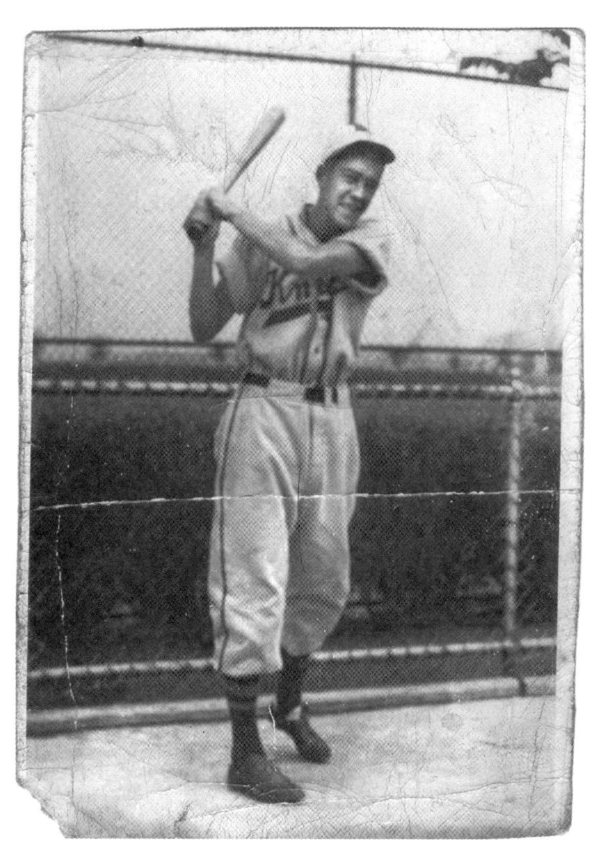

EDWARD L. FORREST
First Lieutenant
712th Tank Battalion

Tank officer had a difficult childhood

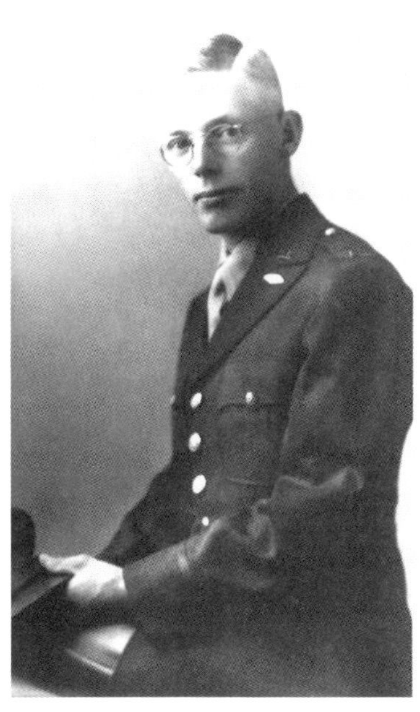

First Lieutenant Edward L. Forrest from Massachusetts was born in 1908. He did not have a pleasant childhood. His father was an alcoholic and was frequently drunk. His mother didn't heal properly from giving birth to their fourth child. An infection had set in where the doctor had torn her during the birth of the baby. The pain became so bad that it affected her mind and she attempted suicide several times in the next few months. After the fifth attempt, Ed's father decided to put her in a sanatorium. However, the night before she was to be taken away, she walked out of the house, threw herself into the cold Housatonic River and died. Ed blamed her death on his father's drinking and he ultimately left him.

At the time, Ed worked at St. Paul's Episcopal Church in Stockbridge after school, doing odd jobs for Rev. Edmund R. Laine. Laine offered Ed a room in the rectory and proceeded to raise him like a son. Ed graduated from the former Williams High School and went to Clark University, where he was the goalie on the soccer team, played tennis, and won a basketball free-throw shooting contest.

After graduation, Ed taught at his former high school, but after a year or two he went to work at the Housatonic National Bank. In April 1942, however, Ed was drafted into the army. Over a year later, he completed Tank Officers' School at Fort Knox, Kentucky. In February 1944, Ed went overseas, whereupon he entered combat in Normandy, France, being assigned to Company A of the 712th Tank Battalion.

During the fighting in Normandy, Ed volunteered to lead a patrol of three tanks into enemy territory without infantry support. After advancing nearly three miles, they turned to withdraw. On the way back, however, they came under fire. Although one of the tanks ran over a mine and Ed's tank was hit in the suspension by an artillery shell, the platoon made it back to friendly lines. On the way, they had knocked out one German tank, disabled another, and ran over three parked German motorcycles.

Toward the end of July, Ed was wounded. When he was standing on the side of one of his platoon's tanks, he was caught in a mortar or artillery barrage. He sought cover against the base of a hedgerow, but a shell exploded near him. Ed was hit by shrapnel and had to be evacuated for treatment. While he was recovering in England, he received a visit from his brother Elmer (named after their father), who was waiting to go into combat with the 30th Infantry Division. 'He said they're gonna leave the shrapnel in until after the war is over because he volunteered to go back to his outfit,' Elmer later recalled. After recovering Ed rejoined his unit in November 1944. A few weeks later, in December, Ed earned the Silver Star. His citation states:

> ***'After crossing the Saar River, all of a platoon's tanks except that of First Lieutenant Forrest became embedded in the marshy soil near the bank. Driving through constant enemy observed fire, First Lieutenant Forrest made four trips to the town to obtain cables and clevises. Working tirelessly, he helped extricate the vehicles and led them into ... [the name of the town is not mentioned in it] where they provided the only tank support for the Infantry for the next three days. He then reconnoitered routes subjected to artillery, mortar and small arms fire to enable his platoon to reach and give urgently needed tank support to another regiment. His gallant actions contributed materially to the success of two infantry regiments in the Saar River operations and were in accordance with high military tradition.'***

A month later, Ed also earned the Bronze Star 'for heroic achievement from 14 to 19 January 1945. When an infantry battalion in the town was in need of more armored support, First Lieutenant Forrest reconnoitered a route and led a tank column over this road to the town. Later he subjected himself to heavy fire of various calibers and directed the tanks in repelling numerous counter-attacks and in destroying or disabling fire tanks and a prime mover.'

Ed's war and life abruptly ended on April 3, 1945. While he was setting up his headquarters in the basement of a three-story house near a small railroad depot in the German town of Heimbolds-hausen, suddenly a large explosion occurred nearby. It was caused by a German fighter plane, a Messerschmitt, which strafed and hit either a train car filled with black powder for use in artillery shells or a gasoline tanker car which was empty but filled with fumes. The resulting explosion was so huge that the house Ed was in collapsed. Ed did not survive this and died at the age of 36. His remains were laid to rest in Margraten, where he still lies. Ed's gravesite here can be found in Plot P, Row 11, Grave 8.

WALTER C. WETZEL

Private First Class

8th Infantry Division

An ultimate act of self-sacrifice

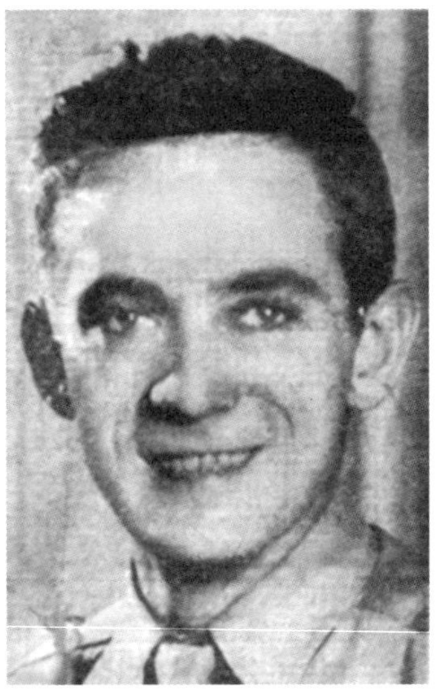

Private First Class Walter C. Wetzel was born in Huntington, West Virginia, on June 7, 1919. In July 1941, he entered the army. By then he was a resident of Roseville, Michigan. Walter completed basic training at Camp Wolters, Texas. He then joined the Anti-Tank Company of the 13th Infantry Regiment, 8th Infantry Division, at Fort Jackson, South Carolina, in October 1941.

In December 1943, Walter went overseas to fight the Nazis. His division entered combat in Normandy in July 1944. About nine months later, Walter sacrificed his own life to save the lives of his comrades. He therefore was posthumously awarded the Medal of Honor.

The citation tells us Walter was acting as a squad leader and was guarding his platoon's command post in a house at Birken, Germany, when during the early morning hours of April 3, 1945, he suddenly spotted enemy troops creeping toward the command post to attack. He fired several shots at the approaching enemy before he ran into the house and alerted the others. Walter then immediately manned a machine gun and began defending the command post against heavy automatic weapons and rifle fire coming from the hostile troops.

Under cover of darkness the German soldiers forced their way close to the building where they hurled grenades. Two of the grenades landed in the room where Walter and the others had taken up firing positions. According to Walter's comrades he shouted to them, 'Watch out for the grenades!', whereupon he threw himself on the grenades and absorbed their explosions. As a result, he suffered wounds from which he died. His unhesitating sacrifice saved his comrades from death or serious injury and made it possible for them to continue the defense of the command post and break the power of a dangerous local counterthrust by the enemy.

Walter was 25 years old when he gave his life so that his comrades might live. His Medal of Honor was presented to his widow Dorothy in February 1946. The fact that Walter received this prestigious award is displayed on his marble cross in Margraten, which can be found in Plot N, Row 18, Grave 10.

Mrs. Dorothy Wetzel receives her husband's Medal of Honor in 1946. SOURCE: *Detroit Free Press*/Newspapers.com

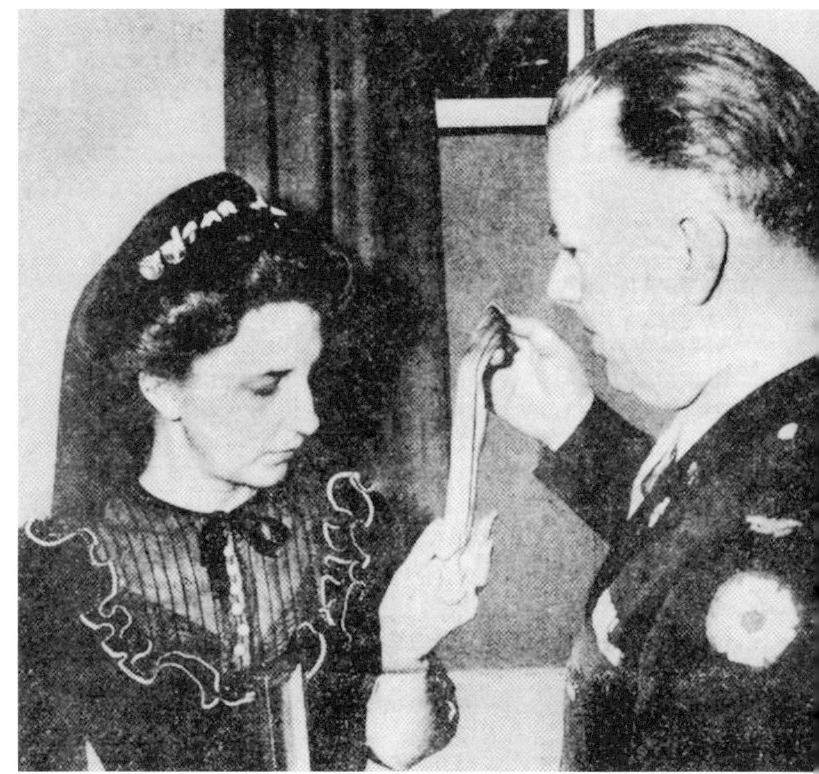

ROBERT J. HUBBARD

Private First Class

58th Armored Infantry Battalion

Covered the withdrawal of his platoon

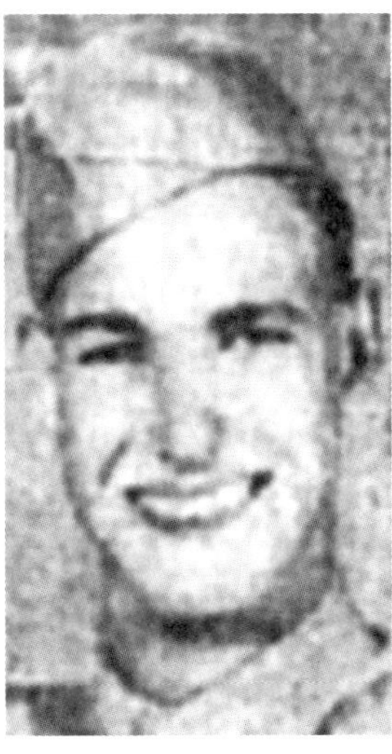

Private First Class Robert J. Hubbard from New York, was born on September 26, 1925. His mother died when he was six years old. He attended Cooperstown High School and, in the meantime, worked at the local A&P store. Just after he finished school, Robert was inducted into the army in March 1944.

Robert was assigned to the infantry and trained at Camp Maxey, Texas, and at Camp Polk, Louisiana. In August 1944, he was given sixteen days of leave and returned home for the last time. Robert then went overseas to Europe in November.

While on the European battlefield, Robert served as a scout in the Headquarters Company of the 58th Armored Infantry Battalion. This battalion was part of the 8th Armored Division and worked closely with the crews of the tank battalions.

On April 3, 1945, Robert and other men of his reconnaissance platoon became pinned down by enemy fire in Germany. He immediately moved to the foremost position with a one-quarter ton truck and opened fire with the machine gun mounted on the vehicle. By doing so, he covered the withdrawal of the platoon.

After exhausting two full boxes of ammunition, Robert dismounted. Remaining at his position, he then opened fire with his carbine, firing two clips at the enemy, enabling the platoon to complete its withdrawal without casualties. While engaged in this mission, Robert was fatally wounded by an enemy sniper. He was only nineteen years old. The army posthumously awarded him with the Silver Star several months later.

Robert, who was too young to vote but old enough to serve his country in a war, found his final resting place at the Netherlands American Cemetery and Memorial in Margraten. Visitors can find his gravesite there by going to Plot N, Row 1, Grave 14.

ROBERT L. MAINS

First Lieutenant

448th Bombardment Group

Shot down by a jet-powered fighter plane

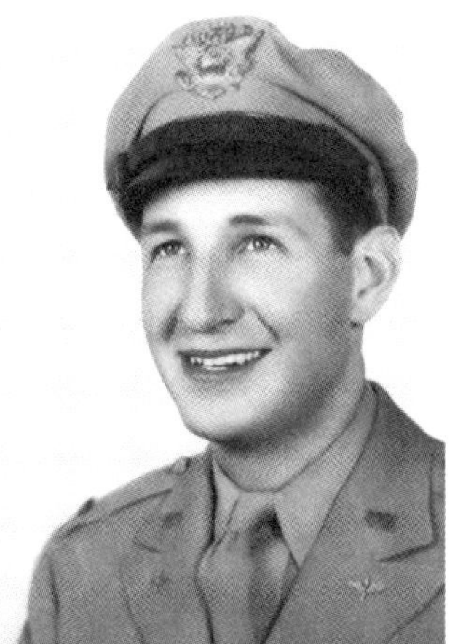

First Lieutenant Robert L. Mains from Rochester, New York, was born on October 9, 1917. He graduated from Monroe High School and then worked for the Will Corporation before enlisting in the U.S. Army Air Forces in April 1942. Robert earned his pilot wings and was then assigned to the 714th Bomb Squadron of the 448th Bombardment Group. He went overseas in August 1944.

On April 4, 1945, Robert piloted a B-24 Liberator bomber that was involved in an aerial attack on enemy airbases located at Parchim, Perleberg, and Wesendorf, Germany. East of Hamburg, the formation was attacked by Messerschmitt Me 262 twin-engine jet fighters. According to several witnesses, Robert's B-24 was hit and broke in two. Given the photographic evidence, it is likely that the damage that resulted in the plane breaking in two was caused by an R4M rocket fired by one of the Me 262s.

The broken-up bomber crashed near the German town of Ludwigslust. Nine crew members, including Robert, were killed. Only Technical Sergeant Charles E. Cupp Jr., the radio operator, survived. He was able to escape from the doomed bomber through its bomb bay and parachuted into Ludwigslust, whereupon he was captured and held as a prisoner of war.

Robert was 27 years old when he lost his life. He was looking forward to going home to his wife Alice and baby daughter Barbara, who was eight months old when Robert died. Her father's remains were not found until many decades after his death. In 2007, a U.S. investigation team traveled to Ludwigslust and found aircraft artifacts correlating to Robert's B-24. When U.S. government teams returned to the crash site in 2014 and 2015, they re-excavated the area and recovered human remains. In 2017, analysts from the Defense POW/MIA Accounting Agency (DPAA) used advanced forensic techniques to examine these collective remains and eventually identified 1st Lt. Robert L. Mains from among them. He was then buried at Calverton National Cemetery, and in March 2018 a rosette was placed next to his name on the Walls of the Missing in Margraten.

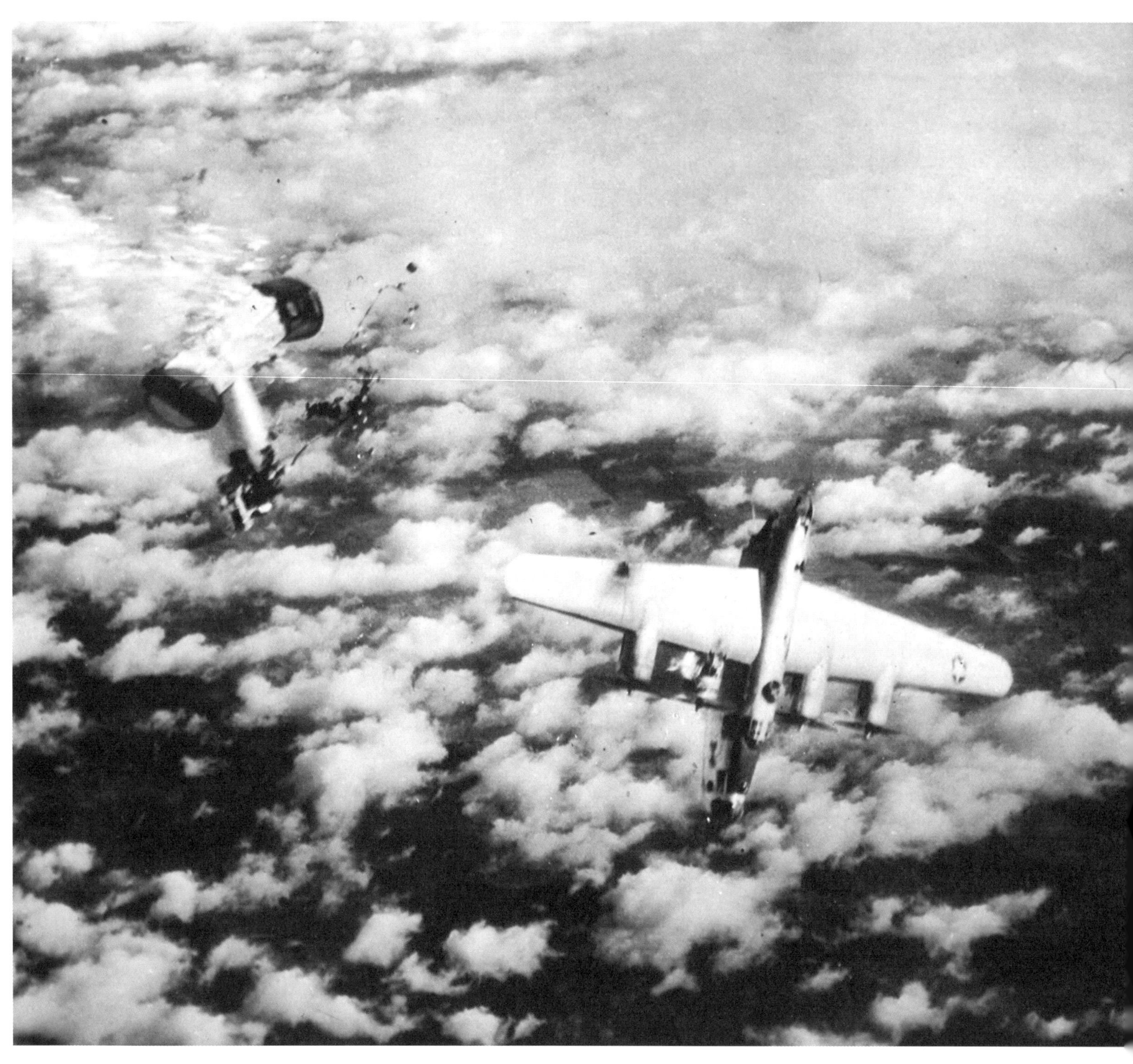

Robert Mains' plane broke in half and crashed.
SOURCE: U.S. Army Air Forces via Arie-Jan van Hees

JOHN W. HULING
First Lieutenant
12th Engineer Combat Battalion

Exposed himself to furious hostile fire

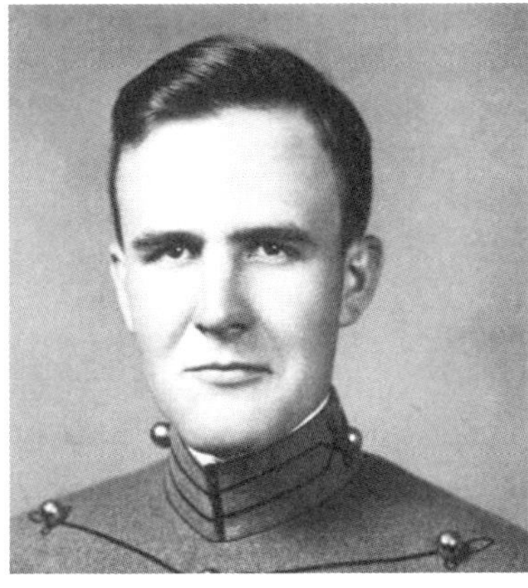

First Lieutenant John W. Huling was born at Fort Banks, Massachusetts, on September 11, 1922. His father was a Colonel and John himself was an intelligent young man. He entered Harvard college at the age of sixteen, where he received an appointment to the prestigious United States Military Academy at West Point, New York, at the end of his junior year. Three years later, John graduated from West Point and was assigned to the Corps of Engineers. He went overseas in December 1944.

After arriving in the European Theater of Operations, John served in the 12th Engineer Combat Battalion of the 8th Infantry Division, which he joined in Germany on the left bank of the Rhine near Cologne. He commanded assault craft during the Rhine crossing and then continued with his unit into the so-called 'Ruhr Pocket' battle. John was involved in this battle as far as Siegen, where he gave his life on April 5, 1945. Several months later, his parents were informed that their son was posthumously awarded the Silver Star. The citation was published in a local newspaper and reads as follows:

> ***'For gallantry in action on April 5, 1945 in the vicinity of Siegen, Germany. When resistance was encountered from strongly defended enemy-held barracks which commanded a view of the entire area, Lieutenant Huling, in the face of intense small arms and machine gun fire, led his men in the attack against the position. Exposing himself to furious hostile fire in an attempt to spot the enemy guns, Lieutenant Huling was killed by enemy machine gun fire. His outstanding leadership, courage and devotion to duty gained for him the respect and admiration of his men and were in the highest traditions of the military service.'***

John was only 22 years old when he died in combat. Initially, he was buried at the American Military Cemetery at Ittenbach, Germany, but later his body was transferred to Margraten. There he is permanently laid to rest in Plot H, Row 5, Grave 5.

WILLIAM J. ELLIS
First Lieutenant
893rd Tank Destroyer Battalion

Armor-piercing tank fire

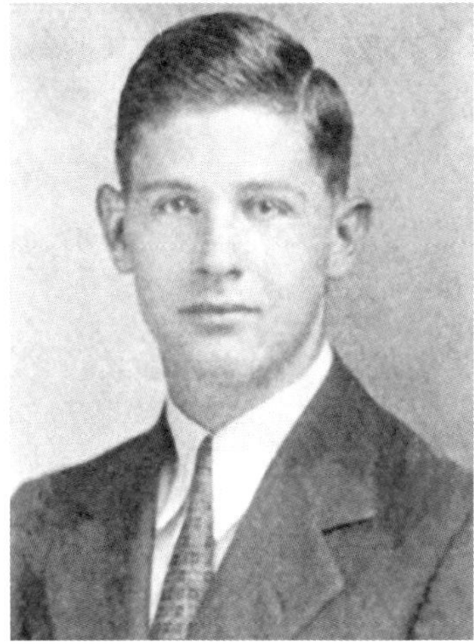

First Lieutenant William J. Ellis was born in Dawson, Pennsylvania, on September 13, 1915. It is not possible to say exactly when, but at some point, the family moved to the town of Sewickley. There, William also attended high school.

During his years at Sewickley High School, William played both basketball and baseball. The school's 1933 yearbook mentions that he was also a member of the Science Club, a group of students who met regularly on Thursdays for scientific lectures and demonstrations.

Before entering the U.S. Army, William was employed by the Pittsburgh Forgings Company. In January 1942, he married his girlfriend Harriet Ford.

In January 1944, William went overseas to Europe with the 893rd Tank Destroyer Battalion. After spending several months in England, this unit arrived in Normandy on July 1, 1944, equipped with M10s. William was the commander of one of these tank destroyers. He was also in charge of his platoon.

In November 1944, William was involved in the fierce fighting near Vossenack, a village located in the German Hürtgen Forest. About five months later, the 893rd Tank Destroyer Battalion was one of the units advancing along the Sieg River after crossing the Rhine. During their advance, which was part of the 'Ruhr Pocket' operation, William was killed near the village of Katzwinkel on April 6, 1945. His death is mentioned in the battalion's Unit History. According to this source, William lost his life when his tank destroyer was hit by armor-piercing fire from a German tank. He was 29 years old.

William is permanently laid to rest at the Netherlands American Cemetery in Margraten. Visitors of this hallowed site can find his final resting place in Plot P, Row 5, Grave 7.

JOHN BEATY

Private First Class

69th Infantry Division

The man of the picture and the ring

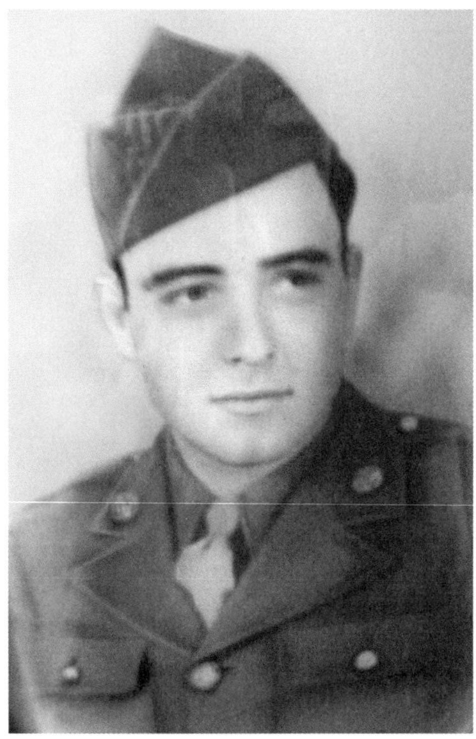

As a child, Danny Hudson of Tennessee regularly visited his grandmother. There, on a wall full of photos, well above all the others hung a gilded photograph of her deceased brother: Private First Class John Beaty. Danny became increasingly curious about who the person was behind the face on the photo, so he began to delve into his story.

John Beaty was born on August 23, 1923. He grew up in the rural west of Tennessee. As with most of his generation, poverty was a constant due to the Great Depression. John was physically strong and worked on the family's farm. With his good 'shooting eye' and rifle he put many a Sunday meal on the table.

In April 1943, John was drafted into the army. Eight months later, he went overseas to Great Britain. There he served as a military policeman, spending most of his time garrisoning in southern England. However, shortly after the Battle of the Bulge, John volunteered as an infantry replacement. He was then attached to the 272nd Infantry Regiment of the 69th Infantry Division.

John was a BAR (Browning Automatic Rifle) gunner with the 1st Squad, 3rd Platoon, Company C, under Staff Sergeant Hrnchar. He fought in Germany and was killed there on April 6, 1945. Nathan Fullmer, a surviving squad member later wrote an account about how John and two other members of the squad lost their lives:

> ***'The next day, April 6, 1945, the 1st Battalion continued its attack, clearing several small towns. Company C attacked Scheinstein. Our Squad moved through woods into a clearing and laid down small arms fire into the woods on the other side of the clearing. Our two BARs got the German's attention. Although the History of the 272nd Infantry describes the enemy opposition as sniper resistance, the sniper shooting at our Squad was using an 88 (mm gun). After three rounds we suffered three dead: Squad Leader S/Sgt John Hrnchar, and both our BAR men, PFC Robert Aseltine, and PFC John Beaty.'***

John was 21 years old when the German 88mm fire fatally caught him. When his body was checked by members of a Graves Registration unit, the ring he still had on his finger was removed from his hand. Like his other personal effects, it was sent to his family. His sister always kept the ring, carefully tucked away in her cedar chest. When her grandson Danny found this ring during one of his many visits to his grandmother, he was deeply moved: it was still burdened with the soil on which he fell and died. The cold marble cross in Margraten of course does not tell visitors how Danny, his grandmother, and other relatives were affected by John's sacrifice during the war. With this in mind, Danny wrote a tribute to John, which he shared on the Internet. He concluded it with a humble request to all who cherish the fallen of World War II:

> ***'When you think of the fallen on VE day, please find a small place for this simple farmer.'***

This simple farmer's final resting place in Margraten can be found in Plot B, Row 8, Grave 32.

SAVAS J. BATSOS

Private

76th Infantry Division

A Greek-born machine gunner

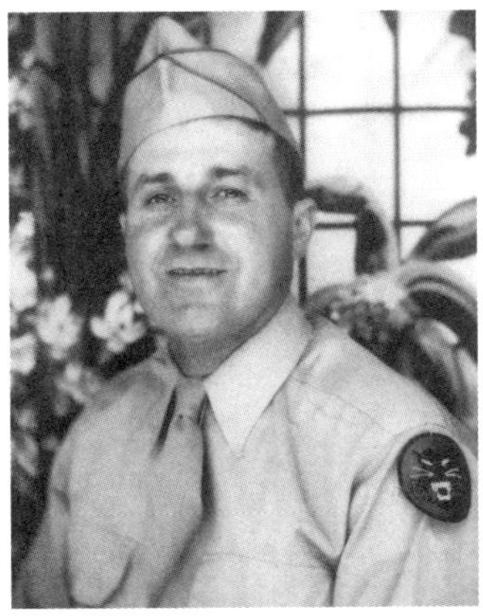

Savas J. Batsos was born in Greece, but had moved to the United States at some point before he entered the U.S. Army in April 1944. At the time of his death, Savas was assigned to Company L of the 417th Infantry Regiment. This was one of the regiments of the 76th Infantry Division. Savas was married and his home was in Fairfield County, Connecticut.

On April 6, 1945, Savas and the other men of Company L were advancing through a wooded area near Oberkaufungen, Germany, when his platoon was suddenly pinned down by the shattering chatter of a German machine gun. The men dropped in their tracks, stunned by the suddenness of the fire. Every man there knew their lives were in serious danger until the machine gun was silenced, but no one could move. Savas looked around at his buddies and saw them hugging the ground as he was doing. He decided to risk his own life to rescue the others and sprang to his feet. He then charged forward while firing his machine gun from his hip. The Germans concentrated all of their fire on him. Bullets splintered trees around him and kicked up the dirt at his feet, but he kept going forward. Savas yelled some encouragements to his buddies, who jumped up and moved forward to follow him. The men reached the German positions and knocked them out.

While the platoon was reorganizing afterwards, word came that another platoon was caught in a similar trap, pinned down, unable to advance or withdraw. Without saying a word, Savas picked up his machine gun again and started moving toward the trapped platoon. Sizing up the situation, he immediately worked himself up to the platoon's front and for the second time stood up in full view of the enemy, charging toward them, firing his machine gun from his hip. Once again men were spurred to action by his display of courage. The platoon moved out quickly and plastered the enemy troops with fire, forcing those who were not killed or captured to retreat.

This second display of extraordinary gallantry was Savas' last assault. He was fatally wounded as he fought toward the enemy with his machine gun spitting death. His by now digitalized Hospital Admission Card states that he suffered multiple wounds, including a bullet in the head, which caused his death. He was 35 years old and for this courageous act he was later posthumously awarded the Silver Star. In Margraten, Savas is buried in Plot I, Row 18, Grave 6.

PHILIP J. ROCCO

Staff Sergeant

68th Tank Battalion

Former boxing champion guided tanks

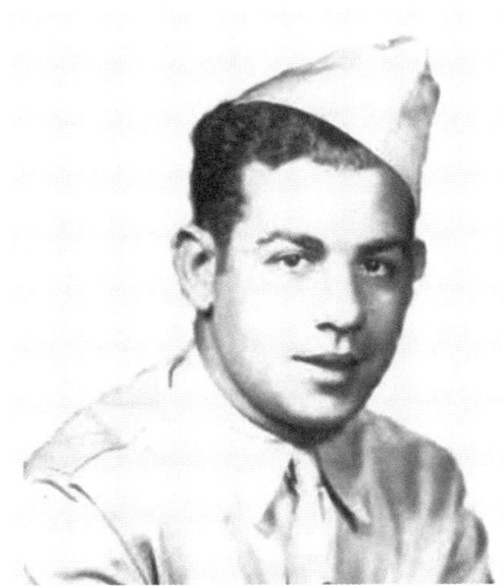

Staff Sergeant Philip J. Racco, registered in the U.S. military records with the last name 'Rocco,' was born in Pennsylvania on June 16, 1915. He moved to Akron, Ohio, where he attended Jennings Junior High School. Philip became a professional boxer and won a local Golden Gloves competition in Akron.

By the time Philip entered the army, he was living in Miami, Florida. Four of his brothers – Joseph, James Jr., Frank, and John – also served in the U.S. armed forces during the war.

After enlisting in the army, Philip was initially stationed at Camp Polk, Louisiana. While being stationed there, he spent some time at home on sick leave after an operation in 1941, after which he returned to his army post. He then at some point went overseas to Europe, where he served in the 68th Tank Battalion. This unit was part of the 6th Armored Division, which fought under the command of General Patton's Third Army.

When the front had moved far into Germany, Philip lost his life near Kefferhausen on April 7, 1945. He was mortally wounded by enemy machine gun fire while acting as point for a column of vehicles, most likely tanks. He was 29 years old. A few months later, the *Akron Beacon Journal* announced that Philip was posthumously awarded the Silver Star for his gallantry in action on the day he was killed. The medal was presented to his father James. Philip's final resting place in Margraten is in Plot O, Row 12, Grave 2.

ROBERT B. MC ALPINE JR.

Private First Class

50th Armored Infantry Battalion

A personal tribute

November 2007. When Mario Nouwen of Susteren, the Netherlands, adopted the grave of Private First Class Robert Bruce Mc Alpine Jr., he only had the information listed on his headstone. He became curious about the story behind the name and began investigating Robert's life and service. Thanks to the Internet and e-mail, he was able to collect answers to his questions: was he married, and did he perhaps have any children? What characterized him? Where did he fight, and how did he lose his life?

With the invaluable help from several others, from the Netherlands, the United States, and Germany, Mario eventually managed to learn a lot about 'his' soldier. He found out, for example, that Robert was born in Morgan Mill, Erath County, Texas, on April 25, 1922, and that he had both a younger sister and brother. His sister, named Maxine, sadly died at the age of four due to meningitis.

Robert worked as a farmer, but during the off-season he also worked as an auto mechanic. He married Stella Stephens and on December 2, 1942, their son James was born. About a year and a half later, Robert was inducted into the army on May 19, 1944. He reported to Camp Wolters, Texas, which was one of the Army's Infantry Replacement Training Centers at the time.

Following his training, Robert was sent overseas to Europe. There, he was attached to Company C of the 50th Armored Infantry Battalion. This unit was assigned to the 6th Armored Division, nicknamed 'Super Sixth.' During the Battle of the Bulge, the 6th Armored Division was ordered to advance to the Belgian Ardennes to relieve the encircled U.S. paratroopers in Bastogne and push back the German forces. It was during the aftermath of the fighting around Bastogne that Robert distinguished himself in the face of the enemy and earned the Silver Star. His citation reads:

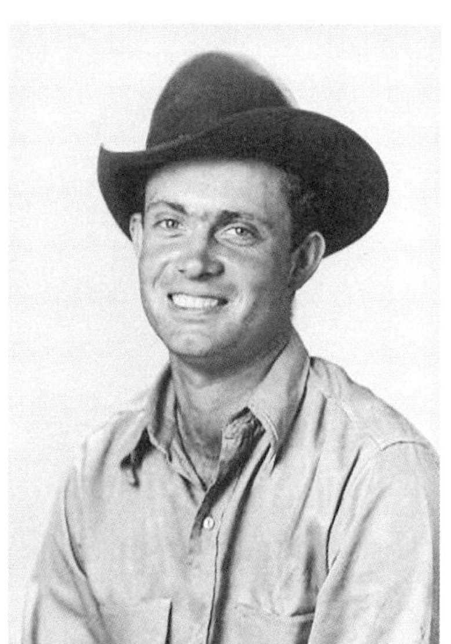

'For gallantry in action in the vicinity of Arloncourt [about three to four miles northeast of Bastogne], Belgium on 15 January 1945. When the lead scout of the platoon was seriously wounded while crossing an exposed ridge, Private First Class Mc Alpine, with complete disregard for his own safety, crossed the ridge under a withering hail of machine gun fire and evacuated the wounded man. His courageous action was instrumental in saving the life of the soldier.'

Robert himself was wounded in February 1945. His digitalized Hospital Admission Card states that he received a wound to his foot and that it was caused by one or more fragments of an artillery shell. He had to recover in a hospital and later, on March 5, 1945, wrote the following about it in a letter to his aunt:

'I will answer your letter I received yesterday, was glad to hear from you all. I have been in the hospital, and when I came back, I had a bunch of mail, and four packages, so you see I have so much mail to answer I may never get caught up with my writing. I got a letter from grannie, the first one I have received, but I am sure she has written more than that. I don't know what is wrong, but I don't get lots of my mail. Stella writes every day, and lots of them I never get. (...) I didn't tell grannie about being hit because she would only worry about it, and I wasn't hurt, just barely nicked me. But she would worry more about me if she knew I was hit once. So don't tell her. I don't know anything to write, so I guess might as well close this time. Tell Dixie I said take care of herself and be careful. Your nephew, Bruce Jr.'

Just over one month after writing this letter and only two and a half weeks short of his 23rd birthday, Robert was killed in action on April 7, 1945. He died near Wachstedt, Germany, and his death was caused by a head injury. According to information Robert's family had obtained at the time, it is assumed that he was fatally shot by a German sniper.

When U.S. Graves Registration personnel was preparing Robert's body for burial, they did not discover his dog tags. However, thanks to one clothing mark containing the last four numbers of his Army Serial Number (38687403) and because they found his paybook, Motor Operator's license, and award paper for the Silver Star in his pockets, they were still able to identify him.

Initially, Robert was buried at the temporary U.S. Military Cemetery at Butzbach, Germany, but in August 1945 he was reburied at Margraten. He was given his final resting place there in 1949, which can be found in Plot P, Row 7, Grave 3.

Mario Nouwen, the current adopter of his grave, is glad that his intensive research has enabled him to discover the identity of his soldier. 'Investigating Robert's life and military service I consider a personal tribute. With this, I aimed to honor the fallen liberators who gave their lives so far from home.'

DWIGHT M. HELFENSTEIN

Private First Class

7th Armored Infantry Battalion

Recognized as an excellent soldier

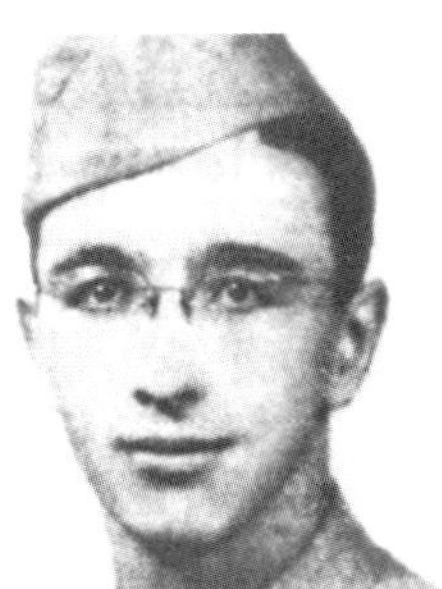

Private First Class Dwight M. Helfenstein was born in Dover, the capital of Delaware, on June 20, 1926. He grew up with three sisters and in 1938 the family moved to Mason City, Iowa, where his father Roy became pastor of a church.

In the spring of 1944, Dwight graduated from Mason City High School. Shortly thereafter, he was called to active duty and entered the army on August 17, 1944. After spending three and a half months training at Camp Hood, Texas, Dwight went overseas to Europe in January 1945. There he was attached to Company C of the 7th Armored Infantry Battalion. This unit was part of the 8th Armored Division.

On April 7, 1945, Dwight was killed in action in Germany. He was eighteen years old. Within a month, his parents received a letter of condolence from Lt. Col. D.L. Hairston of the 8th Armored Division that told them how Dwight met his death:

> ***'It is with deep sympathy that I offer you our heartfelt condolence on behalf of the officers and men of this division, upon the death of your son, PFC Dwight M. Helfenstein, Company C, 7th Armored Infantry Battalion, who was killed in action on April 7, 1945. We have been able to gather the following facts surrounding your son's untimely death. Dwight was a member of an advance squad in the attack upon the city of Belecke, Germany, when the entire division was fighting as a part of the 9th U.S. Army's drive into the vaunted Ruhr. The halftrack on which he was riding was knocked out of action by enemy bazooka [Panzerfaust or Panzerschreck] fire and he was hit by enemy automatic machine pistol fire, causing instant death.'***

Hairston then concluded his letter with some words of consolation:

> ***'Dwight left us a memory of his outstanding courage and devotion to duty. He was recognized as an excellent soldier and well-liked by the officers and men of his company. We will all miss him greatly. There is little more that I can say to console you when you have suffered such a great personal loss.'***

In the same letter, his parents were notified that Dwight was buried at the U.S. Military Cemetery in Margraten. After the war, Dwight was permanently reinterred there in Plot G, Row 21, Grave 14.

WILLY F. JAMES JR.

Private First Class

104th Infantry Division

African American received Medal of Honor 52 years too late

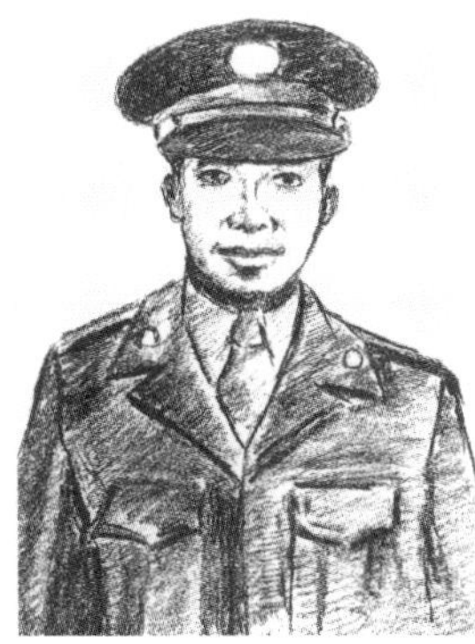

Private First Class Willy F. James Jr. was born in Kansas City, Missouri, on March 18, 1920. He was one of the so-called 'negro infantry volunteers'; although black Americans like Willy were considered not good enough to fight for their country, it was decided in 1944 that the U.S. Army was to be temporarily desegregated due to the mounting casualties among the white troops. African American soldiers serving with supporting units were called upon to volunteer for the infantry. Some 5,000 black soldiers answered this call. More than 2,000 of them were selected and trained in the first months of 1945. In March of that year, the black troops were assigned to existing infantry units. Willy became an infantry scout assigned to Company G of the 413th Infantry Regiment. This regiment formed a part of the 104th 'Timberwolf' Infantry Division.

On April 8, 1945, Willy distinguished himself in the vicinity of Lippoldsberg, Germany. Acting as first scout of the lead squad, he volunteered to go forward to fully reconnoiter a group of enemy-held houses on the edge of the town. After making his way forward approximately 200 yards across open terrain, furious crossfire from enemy snipers and machine guns pinned him down. Lying in an exposed position for more than an hour, Willy intrepidly observed the enemy's positions that were given away by the fire he was daringly drawing upon himself. Then, with utter indifference to his personal safety, in a storm of enemy small arms fire, Willy made his way back to the positions of his platoon. There he gave a detailed report on the enemy disposition, which helped the officers to develop an assault plan.

Sometime later, when his platoon attacked one of the key houses he had observed, Willy voluntarily led a squad toward this objective. He made his way forward and designated targets accurately and continuously as he moved along. While doing so, he saw his platoon leader being shot down by enemy small arms fire (reportedly from a sniper). Willy instantly went to the aid of his wounded platoon leader, First Lieutenant Armand J. Serrabella. However, as he was making his way across the open ground, Willy was hit himself and killed; either by a burst of machine gun fire, an enemy sniper, or by a shell fragment wound in the back – the available sources each indicate a different cause of death. Whatever it was, Willy was 25 years old when he lost his life. Serrabella died at the age of 35.

In September 1945, Willy was posthumously awarded the Distinguished Service Cross for his actions that day. However, during the following decades growing discontent arose within U.S. society over the fact that during World War II not a single African American soldier had received the nation's highest decoration for valor in combat, the Medal of Honor. In 1993, this resulted in a study by Shaw University 'to determine if there was a racial disparity in the way Medal of Honor recipients were selected.' At the end of the study, it was concluded that 'although there is no explicit, official documentation for racial prejudice in the award process for the Medal of Honor (...) the failure of an African American soldier to win a Medal of Honor definitely lay in the racial climate and practice within the Army in World War II.' Following this conclusion, the army reviewed the military action reports of ten African American servicemen who had received awards for their bravery. Nine of them were Distinguished Service Cross recipients. The other soldier had received the Silver Star. As a result of the reassessment, six of the Distinguished Service Crosses and one Silver Star were upgraded to the Medal of Honor.

PFC Willy F. James Jr. was among the seven servicemen who eventually received the medals they deserved. On January 13, 1997, President Bill Clinton presented his Medal of Honor to his widow Valcenie during a solemn ceremony at the White House. For Valcenie, however, it was already too late. At the time of the ceremony, she was suffering from Alzheimer's and therefore did not fully understand what was happening.

Willy's portrait and personal documents were lost during a move. All that remains is a drawing that was based on his widow's memories that she had on her good days. A relative of Valcenie, Margaret Pender, said: 'It's kind of a sad love story. And it's a sad story about someone's life that was almost forgotten. We couldn't find his own family, and then his records were burned, and it's just really sad to me that you could be born and your whole life could go unrecorded, unremembered. And so, this was a good thing, him being honored.'

The fact that Willy has received the Medal of Honor is also displayed on his marble cross in Margraten. People who want to pay tribute to him there can find his final resting place in Plot P, Row 9, Grave 9. First Lieutenant Serrabella rests in Plot H, Row 9, Grave 12.

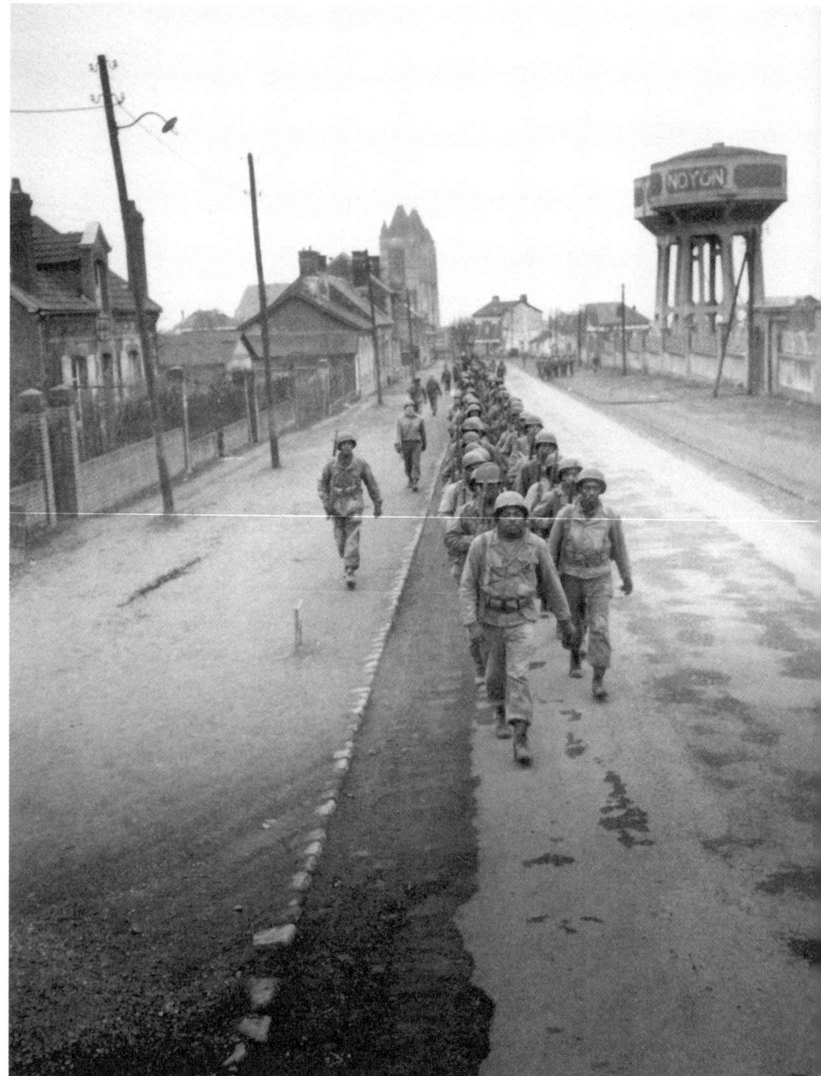

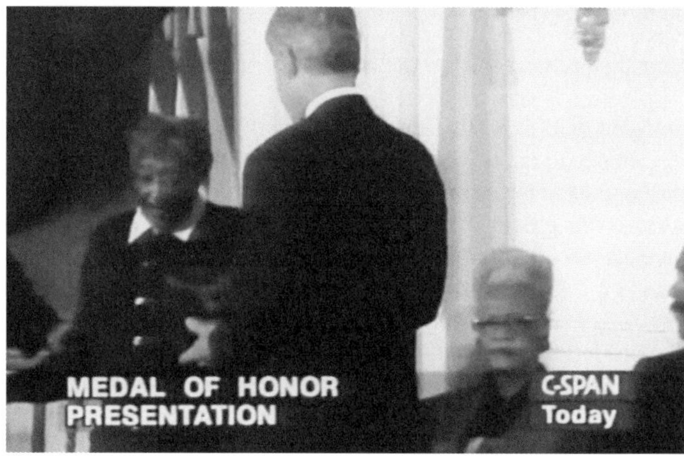

The so-called 'negro infantry volunteers' on their way to training. SOURCE: National Archives and Records Administration

President Clinton presents the Medal of Honor to the widow of Willy F. James Jr., 1997. SOURCE: C-SPAN

ROBERT E. L. PRICE

Private

7th Armored Division

An unexpected encounter

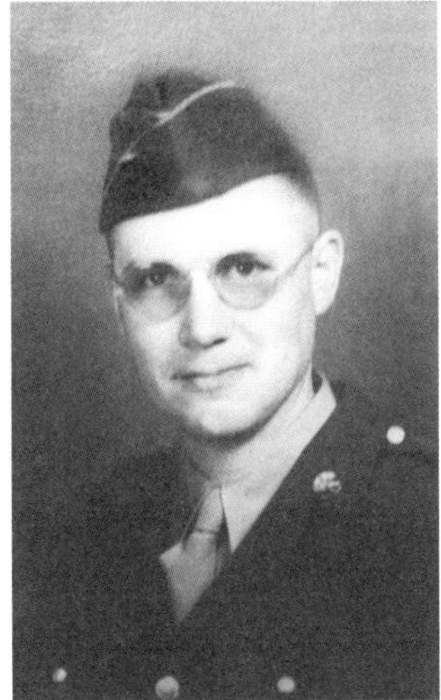

Lina Peters was wandering around the cemetery during *The Faces of Margraten* in 2018 when she stumbled upon an elderly couple. Frans and Cora Stevens were taking turns when photographing each other next to the headstone of Robert E. L. Price. She asked the couple if they liked to have a photo of the two of them together. Lisa did not yet know that these two grave adopters had brought a special item with them. And even less so that they had remarkable stories to share.

Robert had enlisted in August 1944. Before being sent to Europe in January 1945, he came home one last time to spend Christmas with his wife Mary and his son Jim. Private Robert Price joined Company B, 48th Infantry Battalion, 7th Armored Division as a replacement on February 1, 1945. Robert was critically injured in the battle for Schmallenberg, Germany. He died of his wounds on April 8, only 26 years old. His son Jim was just three at the time of his father's death. His daughter Mary was born almost six months later.

After Lisa had taken some photos, Frans started to talk about how the Stevens family had adopted Robert's grave ever since 1945. The family lived in Valkenburg during the war, just across a laundromat that washed the clothes of soldiers that had been killed. It was there that they learned about the nearby cemetery in Margraten. Even though it had been 73 years since his first visit, Frans still vividly remembered the mud and the wooden crosses.

Robert's grave has been passed on within the Stevens family from generation to generation. He became 'part of the family,' Frans said, and Roberts' family has become good friends of the Stevens'. They would frequently exchange letters with his widow Mary, who visited the gravesite in 1950. Robert's children Jim and Mary visited their father's grave together in 1992. When Frans' mother passed away shortly after, the contact was lost until the families reconnected in 2015.

It led to another trip to Margraten by Jim, who brought something special with him: it was his father's Purple Heart that he had found after the death of his mother. The medal was still in the original box, addressed to his mother. He decided to gift it to Frans and Cora, who had taken the medal with them on that day in May 2018. One other special item Jim kept for himself: it was the ring that his father had worn until the day he died and which had been returned to the family, together with a framed photo that Robert had of his wife and son.

But Cora had a story to share as well. She too, like Jim and Mary, was a war orphan. Her dad had been a resistance fighter during the war, but was betrayed near the war's end. He was sent to Germany and never returned home. As a matter of fact, nobody knew where her dad had been buried. So, there was not a place where Cora could go to mourn her father. Therefore, every time she visited Robert's grave, she not only grieved over a soldier who had lost his life, but also over her father who she missed so deeply.

Frans passed away in 2019, but the Stevens family continues to visit Robert's grave in Plot A, Row 9, Grave 26 every month up until this day.

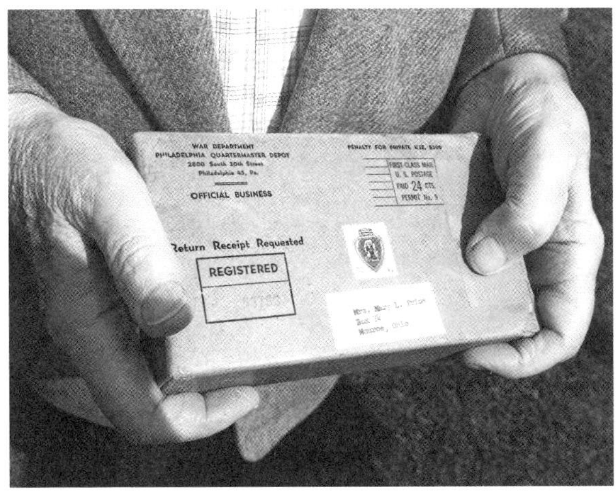

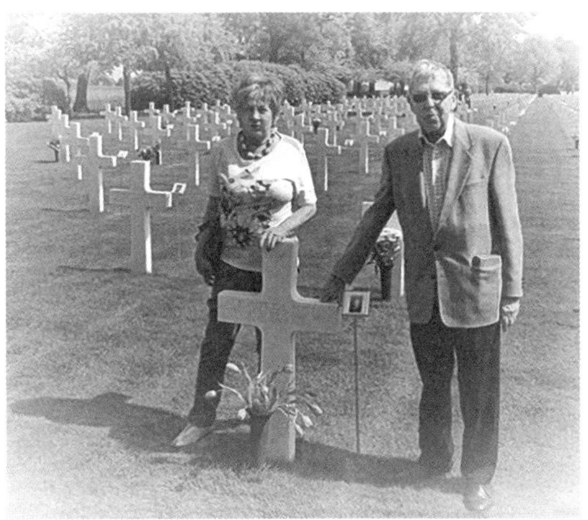

Frans and Cora Stevens brought the Purple Heart awarded to Robert Price with them when visiting his grave during *The Faces of Margraten* of 2018. SOURCE: Lina Peters

ROGER E. WASHBURN

Private First Class

69th Infantry Division

Presumably killed in a rain of shells

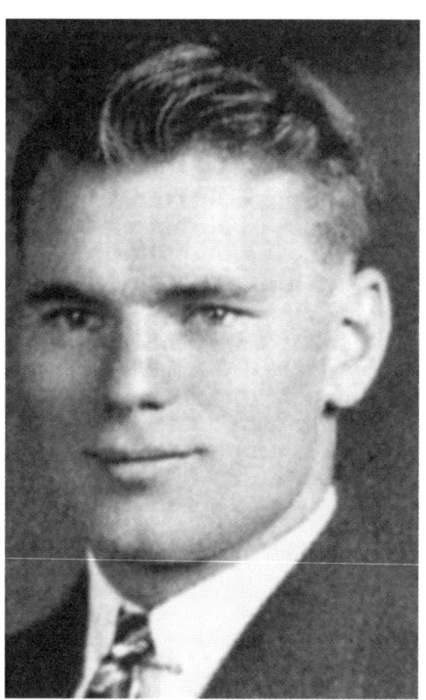

Private First Class Roger E. Washburn from Massachusetts was born in 1923 and entered the army in April 1943. During the last months of the war, he fought as a rifleman in Company L of the 272nd Infantry Regiment. This was one of the regiments of the 69th Infantry Division, which the men themselves called the 'Fighting 69th.'

Roger's division was formed at Camp Shelby, Mississippi, in May 1943, where the new recruits then had to endure eighteen months of demanding training and were drilled by the officers. After this, the troops were transferred to England from New York Harbor in December 1944. There the units were prepared for combat on the European mainland.

In January 1945, the 69th Infantry Division left for France and arrived at Le Havre. In February, the troops were deployed to the front line for the first time. Roger and the other soldiers of the division then relieved the troops of the 99th Infantry Division.

Two months later, Roger was killed near the German towns of Berge and Nieder-Gandern on April 8, 1945. The exact cause of death is not known, but according to the Unit History of the 272nd Infantry Regiment's 3rd Battalion, Roger's company was under constant fire from German Tiger tanks as the men were digging in. Therefore, it can be considered highly plausible that Roger was killed by an enemy shell, possibly fired by one of the German tanks that had retreated to a nearby town. Roger was given his final resting place in Margraten, where he lies in Plot A, Row 7, Grave 23.

MICHAEL J. TOMKO

Corporal

774th Tank Battalion

Skillfully maneuvered his tank

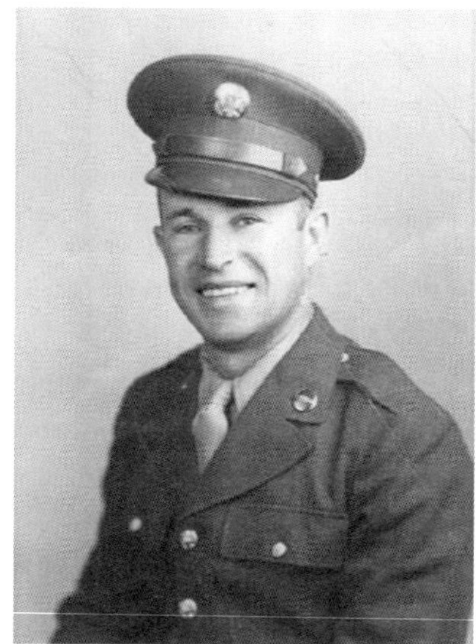

Corporal Michael J. Tomko from Hazleton, Pennsylvania, was born on October 25, 1907. Both his father and mother were immigrants from Slovakia. Michael married his beloved Margaret and entered the U.S. Army in September 1943. He then trained successively at Fort Knox, Kentucky, and Fort George G. Meade, Maryland, before going overseas in May 1944. In Europe, Michael served as a driver of a Sherman tank. His unit was the 774th Tank Battalion.

One month before Germany's unconditional surrender was signed in Reims and Berlin, Michael's tank unit was involved in the so-called 'Ruhr Pocket' battle. During this battle, he lost his life on April 9, 1945. The citation of the Bronze Star he posthumously received provides details of the circumstances of his death:

> ***'Cpl. Michael J. Tomko, while serving with the army of the United States, distinguished himself by heroic achievement in action. On April 9, 1945 in the vicinity of Lichtenberg, Germany, while engaging the enemy in the Ruhr Pocket, the tank he was driving was subjected to direct fire from three enemy tanks. His tank was hit eleven times, instantly killing the gunner sitting next to him and wounding Tomko. Disregarding his wounds, he skillfully maneuvered his tank and reached cover from further fire. After the remaining crew members had cleared the tank safely, Tomko was mortally wounded by enemy artillery fire.'***

Michael was 37 years old when he met his death. He is buried in Margraten, where his gravesite can be found in Plot B, Row 19, Grave 15.

ALONZO L. CLARK

Private First Class

893rd Tank Destroyer Battalion

A deadly encounter with German tanks

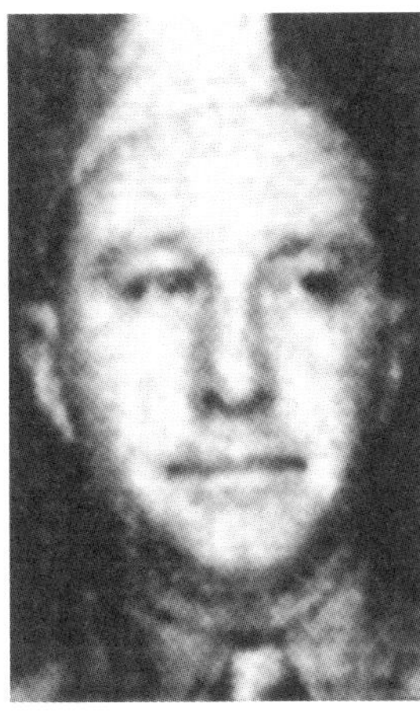

Private First Class Alonzo L. Clark from Wayne County, Indiana was 29 years old when a photograph of him was published in the *Palladium-Item*, a local Richmond newspaper, on August 2, 1942. The related article immediately below his photograph reported he had entered the U.S. Army. His brother Lowell E. Clark was also serving in the army, the article stated.

While in the service, Alonzo was assigned to Company C of the 893rd Tank Destroyer Battalion, which set sail for England in December 1943. On July 1, 1944 – almost one month after D-Day – the Battalion arrived on Omaha Beach in Normandy, equipped with M10s. These were tank destroyers fitted with an open turret and a counterweight to balance the weight of the long-barreled 76mm cannon. As secondary armament, the M10s were equipped with a heavy anti-aircraft machine gun.

The 893rd Tank Destroyer Battalion entered combat just two days upon its arrival in Normandy. The tank destroyer crews then fought their way to Paris, whereupon they became involved in the bloody fighting in the Hürtgen Forest, Germany. Subsequently, the battalion took part in the Allied advance across the Roer and Rhine rivers, after which it supported operations against the so-called 'Ruhr Pocket.'

During the Ruhr Pocket battle, Company C ran into much enemy armor north of Morsbach on April 9, 1945. On that day, Alonzo's tank destroyer, commanded by Sgt. Ullery, opened fire on a German tank. The enemy tank immediately picked up their muzzle flash and fired an armor-piercing round through the driving compartment. The M10 caught fire but instead of climbing out, Alonzo and his fellow crew members decided to battle it out. They stuck to their posts, knocked out two towed guns and a probable enemy tank before more enemy tanks returned the fire. The enemy tanks scored several hits, which caused the tank destroyer's ammunition to explode. Sgt. Ullery and the driver survived, but Alonzo and two others – PFC Cannizzo, the gunner, and PFC Blatnick – did not. Alonzo's remains have never been found since. Therefore, his name is listed on the Walls of the Missing in Margraten. Cannizzo and Blatnick are listed on the Walls of the Missing as well.

CHARLES E. CASPER

Private First Class

84th Infantry Division

Young medic bled to death

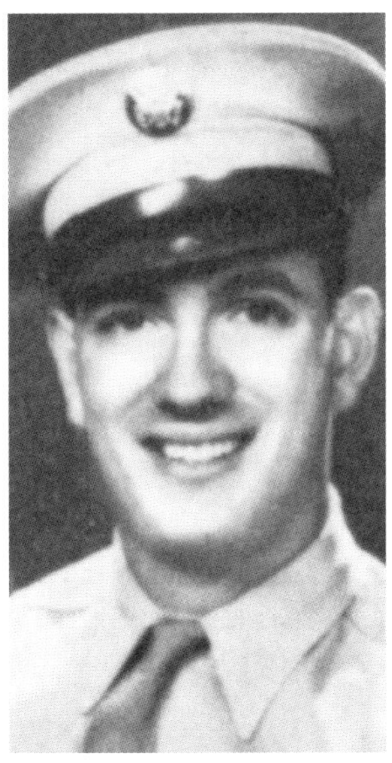

Private First Class Charles E. Casper was born in 1924. His hometown was Mount Lebanon, a suburb of Pittsburgh, Pennsylvania. He graduated from the local high school and was a student at Carnegie Tech before being inducted in March 1943. Charles was then selected for the Army Specialized Training Program (ASTP) at Lafayette College, Pennsylvania. This special program was instituted to meet the army's wartime demands for both junior officers and soldiers with medical and technical skills.

Charles went overseas to Europe to serve as a medic. He was assigned to Company E of the 333rd Infantry Regiment. This regiment formed a part of the 84th Infantry Division, which entered combat near Geilenkirchen, Germany, in November 1944.

In January 1945, Charles earned the Bronze Star Medal for administering medical aid and rescuing two wounded comrades under enemy fire in Belgium. Several months later, only four weeks before Germany surrendered, he made the ultimate sacrifice near the German town of Weetzen on April 9, 1945. A newspaper article, published in *The Pittsburgh Press*, and several other sources provide more details: Charles' arm was severely wounded by an enemy artillery shell. He refused evacuation and put a tourniquet on his arm. Charles then showed others how to provide medical aid to several infantrymen who had sustained injuries when the tank they were riding on was hit by the enemy shelling (two sources suggest that Charles himself was also riding on this tank when it was hit by a German shell). Sadly, the tourniquet could not stop the flow of his blood and Charles died before he could get medical treatment for himself. He was twenty years old.

For his heroic action Charles was posthumously awarded the Distinguished Service Cross. By the time this was announced, he had already been buried in Margraten. Charles was also given his final resting place there, which can be found in Plot F, Row 15, Grave 9.

ERNEST B. SCHLAUD

Sergeant

2nd Infantry Division

'Smiling Ernie'

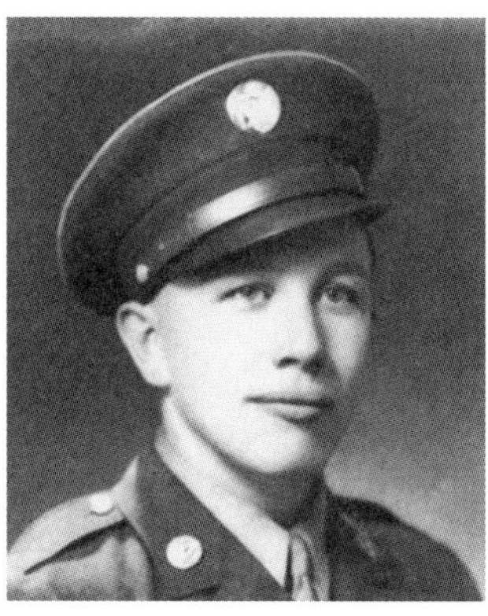

Sergeant Ernest B. Schlaud from Michigan was born in 1918. He grew up in a little rural community called Five Lakes. Ernie, as he was called by his family and friends, worked in an automobile factory before he enlisted.

In April 1941, Ernie heeded the call of his friends and neighbors to leave his job at Fisher Body in Flint for a one-year tour of duty with the army. His friends and family, including his brothers Bill, John, and Tom, were present when he left the Michigan Central depot in Lapeer. Eight months later, Japanese aircraft attacked Pearl Harbor. The United States became involved in the war and Ernie's tour of duty was extended 'for the duration of the emergency.'

Ernie was trained as an artilleryman and stationed in Alaska for two years. The Japanese had invaded Alaska's Aleutian Islands, but had been driven out by U.S. forces. Ernie returned to the States and was reassigned to Europe. There he was sent to the front as an infantry replacement after the Battle of the Bulge. The army assigned him to the 23rd Infantry Regiment of the 2nd Infantry Division, which had entered combat in Normandy shortly after D-Day.

On April 8, 1945, the 2nd Infantry Division captured the German university city of Göttingen. The following day, in the vicinity of Etzenborn, Ernie was mortally wounded during a German artillery barrage. He had volunteered to walk beside a tank and was cut down by shrapnel when a shell hit the tank. He was taken to a field hospital, but succumbed to his injuries there the same day. As a result, Ernie remained forever 26.

Ernie's commanding officer wrote a letter to his parents, in which he told them that Ernie was a favorite with the men in his unit. 'The men called him "Smiling Ernie,"' he wrote. 'He often volunteered for dangerous duty in place of married men.'

Ernie and a number of his buddies were buried in a temporary cemetery in Germany, located near Kassel. In July 1945, his remains were exhumed and moved to Margraten. There he still lies today, in Plot B, Row 9, Grave 14.

GUY A. RINGBLOOM

First Lieutenant

97th Infantry Division

'A leader any man would be proud of'

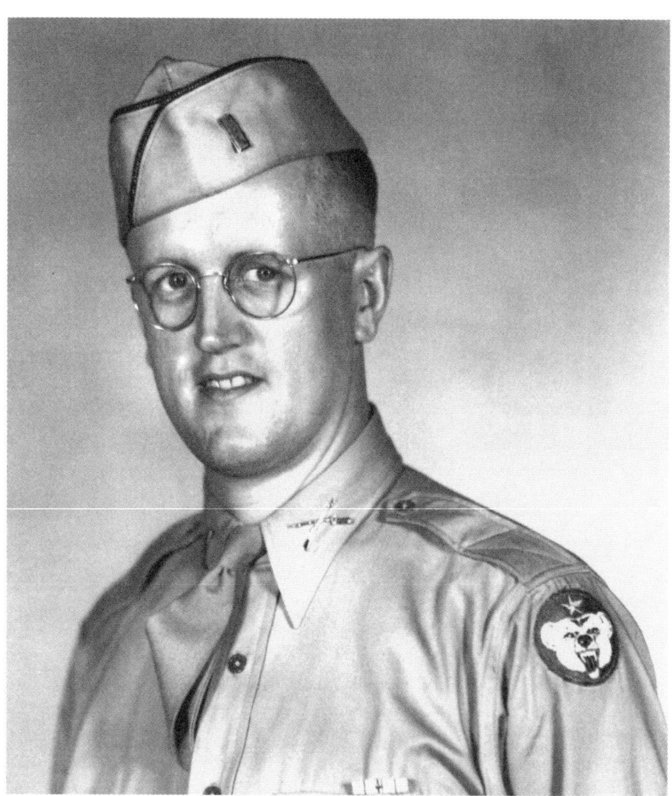

First Lieutenant Guy A. Ringbloom from Minnesota was born on March 21, 1916. He graduated from West High School and was a former student of the University of Minnesota in Minneapolis. While studying there, he was a member of the Alpha Sigma Chapter of the Sigma Chi fraternity. In the fraternity's magazine of December 1935, one of its authors wrote that Guy was 'splashing away in the University pool every day with the swimming squad.'

On January 20, 1942, Guy volunteered for the army at Fort Snelling, Minnesota. After basic training, he graduated from Officer Candidate School at Fort Benning, Georgia, in 1942. He then first served twenty months in the Aleutians before going to the European war theater in command of a rifle platoon in Company F, 387th Infantry Regiment of the 97th Infantry Division, which crossed the German border west of Aachen on March 28, 1945. Nearly two weeks later, on April 9, 1945, Guy lost his life at Allner while he was attempting to rescue a wounded man of his platoon. The citation of the Silver Star that was posthumously awarded to him gives us more details about how he met his death during this gallant action:

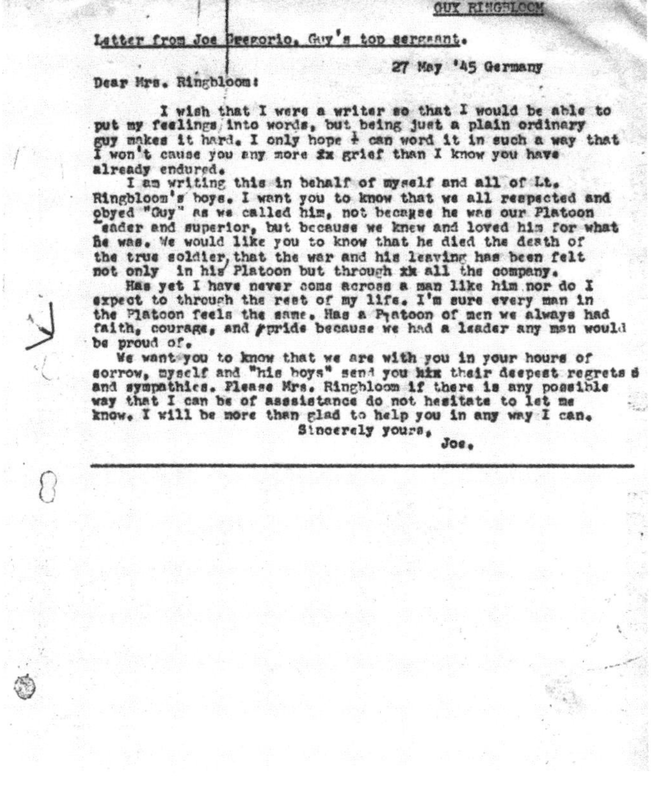

GUY RINGBLOOM

Letter from Joe Gregorio, Guy's top sergeant.

27 May '45 Germany

Dear Mrs. Ringbloom:

I wish that I were a writer so that I would be able to put my feelings into words, but being just a plain ordinary guy makes it hard. I only hope I can word it in such a way that I won't cause you any more xx grief than I know you have already endured.

I am writing this in behalf of myself and all of Lt. Ringbloom's boys. I want you to know that we all respected and obyed "Guy" as we called him, not becayse he was our Platoon leader and superior, but because we knew and loved him for what he was. We would like you to know that he died the death of the true soldier, that the war and his leaving has been felt not only in his Platoon but through xx all the company.

Has yet I have never come across a man like him nor do I expect to through the rest of my life. I'm sure every man in the Platoon feels the same. Has a Platoon of men we always had faith, courage, and /pride because we had a leader any man would be proud of.

We want you to know that we are with you in your hours of sorrow, myself and "his boys" send you him their deepest regrets & and sympathies. Please Mrs. Ringbloom if there is any possible way that I can be of assistance do not hesitate to let me know. I will be more than glad to help you in any way I can.

Sincerely yours,

Joe.

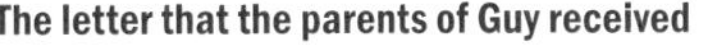

The letter that the parents of Guy received

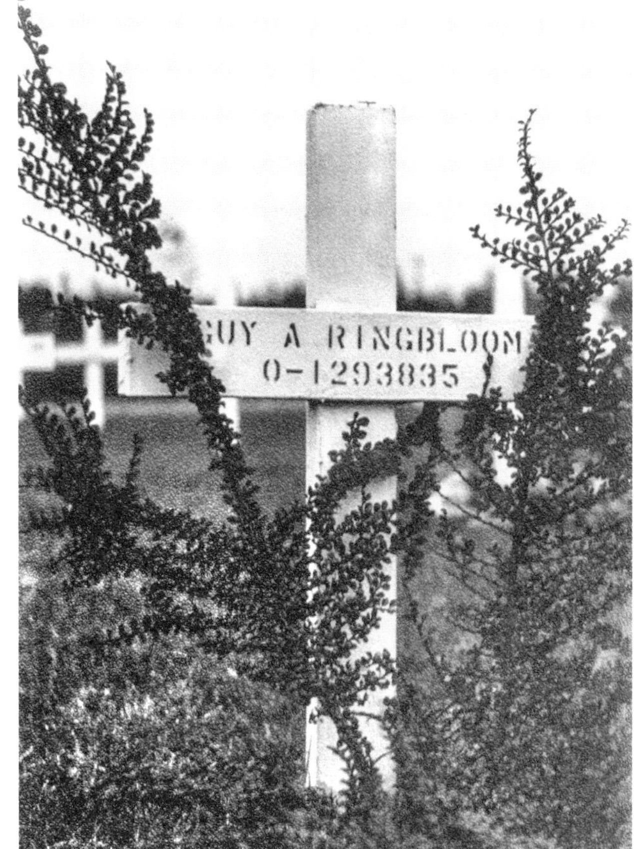

Guy's temporary grave

'A member of Lieutenant Ringbloom's platoon was seriously wounded by enemy machine gun fire and fell in a position completely exposed at close range to the hostile fire. Fully aware of the great danger to his own life, Lieutenant Ringbloom daringly and courageously moved to the wounded man to take him to a place of safety. First Lieutenant Ringbloom was mortally wounded by sniper fire as he assisted the wounded man out of the line of enemy fire. His gallant action reflects high credit upon himself and the Armed Forces.'

Guy died a short time later at the age of 29. He was laid to rest in Margraten, initially in a temporary grave. Over 75 years later, one can find his final resting place here in Plot I, Row 21, Grave 7.

Several weeks after the German capitulation, Guy's mother received a moving letter from Sergeant Joe Gregorio, one of Guy's men. In it, Gregorio wrote that all of Guy's 'boys' respected him and Guy 'died the death of the true soldier.' He then honored Guy even more by writing that 'as a platoon of men we always had faith, courage, and pride because we had a leader any man would be proud of.'

WAYNE C. CLARK
Private First Class
89th Infantry Division

A father of four

Private First Class Wayne C. Clark was born in Mosinee, Wisconsin, on December 16, 1918. He attended Waupaca High School and married Beatrice McCabe in 1940. Together they had four children: David, Sydney, Leah Jeanne, and Arletta Rae. Before he was inducted in the army, Wayne was employed as a truck driver in Clintonville.

Wayne was attached to Company B, 354th Infantry Regiment, 89th Infantry Division and left for overseas duty in Europe on December 26, 1944. In March 1945, Wayne and his division were on the march towards the heart of what was left of Hitler's Third Reich. Like many fellow soldiers he was optimistic. More and more German troops were taken prisoner and the war seemed almost won. The optimistic feeling that the final victory was only a matter of time also echoed in the letter Wayne wrote to his parents on March 23, 1945:

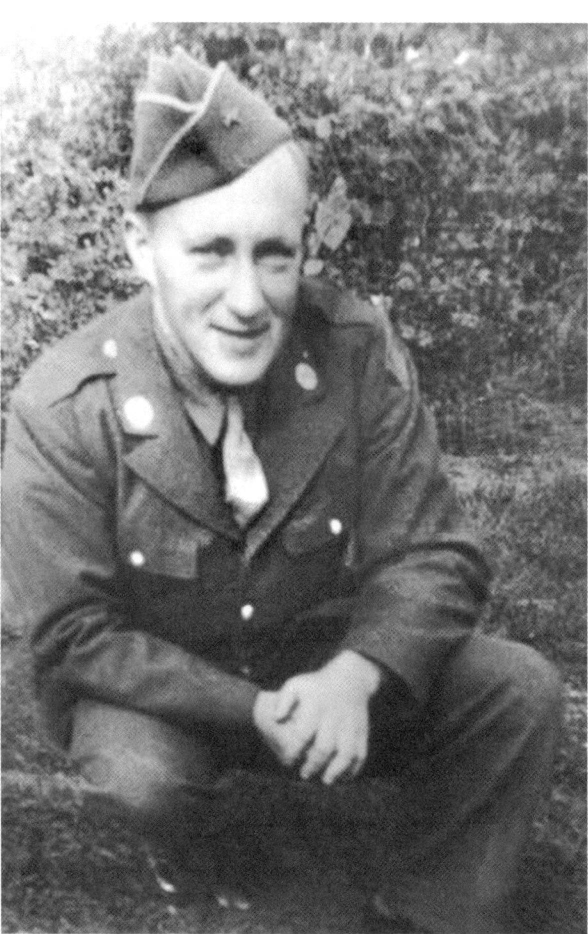

'Dear Mom + Dad:
Just a few lines to let you know that I am feeling fine and hope you are the same. I have got quite a few letters lately which were appreciated very much. As you see by the letter heading I am now in Germany with the 3rd Army and in combat. We sure got those "Heinies" on the run and I personally hope they keep running until they all drown in the sea. (...) I have seen a few good Germans (dead ones) and a lot of prisoners. They sure do know how to surrender and I don't think Hitler taught it to them. Well after all that's what we want to get this war over with. [sic]
Don't worry about me as I am O.K. Don't go working to [sic] hard and run yourself down and get sick again. Take things easy and I'll try and do the same. With all my love I remain your son.
Wayne
I'll Be Seeing You.'

About two and a half weeks after writing this letter, Wayne was killed when he and his unit attacked a machine gun position in Crawinkel, Germany, on April 9, 1945. According to an article by the *Wausau Daily Herald*, he was shot by a German sniper. This statement corresponds to a description in the Unit History of the 354th Infantry Regiment: 'Co. B tried to enter the woods but was held up by automatic fire. During the ensuing firefight Pvt. Wayne Clark, the lead scout, was killed by sniper fire which covered the German's automatic weapons position.'

Wayne was 26 years old. He was given his final resting place at the Netherlands American Cemetery and Memorial in Margraten, where he lies in Plot I, Row 12, Grave 8.

Leah Jeanne was two years old when her mother was informed that her father had been killed in Germany. 'I was so little, I don't remember my father,' she said. 'I have just some vague memories. I remember a Christmas in a trailer house, and I got Boston baked beans. Things like that.'

Shortly after their father's death, Wayne's children also lost their mother. Beatrice gave up the care of the four children after Wayne died, presumably because she was too emotionally affected by the loss of her husband. David went to live with Beatrice's parents; the younger three lived with Wayne's sister, Delia Green, and her husband, Laurence Green.

The loss of their parents had deep and lasting effects on the children's lives and left them in grief that lasted for decades. There was nothing left for them but to try to make the best of their own lives...

ELDON L. CASE

Private First Class

102nd Infantry Division

Killed by an SS officer

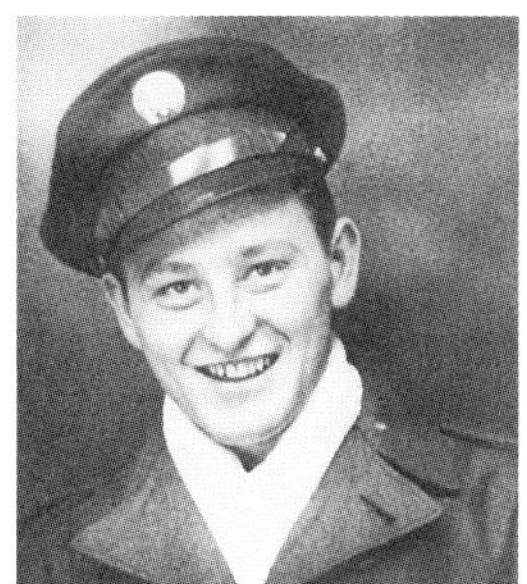

Private First Class Eldon L. Case was born in Good Thunder, Minnesota, on March 8, 1925. When he turned eighteen in 1943 and was registered for a possible future draft, he was still a high school student and resided in Madison Lake, a village in the southern part of the state.

About two weeks short of his nineteenth birthday, Eldon reported to Fort Snelling and entered the army as a draftee. He went through basic training and was assigned to the 102nd Reconnaissance Troop of the 102nd Infantry Division. This division arrived in the European Theater of Operations at Cherbourg, France, in September 1944 and entered combat the following month across the Dutch border with Germany. During the last days of November, the 'Ozark' Division went into the attack toward the river Roer.

About seven months after the division's arrival on the European battlefield, and one month before Germany's capitulation, Eldon was part of a two-jeep patrol that drove into an enemy ambush near Steinbergen, Germany, on April 9, 1945. German machine gun fire suddenly raked the road; bullets hit the front tire and went through the steering wheel of the jeep Eldon was in. Eldon, acting as the jeep's machine gunner, and the other occupants jumped out of the vehicle. Soon after, German SS troops came forward and approached them. Eldon was lying next to Corporal Aarol 'Bud' Irish, who commanded the jeep's crew. Decades after the war's end, Bud described what had happened next in a letter to one of his army pals. He wrote:

> ***'There was an officer in front with a small machine gun. About 25 yards away they spotted us and Eldon Case said, "My God, they're going to get us" or "they're going to get me," I never really knew which. The SS officer emptied his machine gun at us and every bullet went into the ground and into Case. We were so close together I could feel them hit. I either buried my face into the dirt, or my guardian angel pushed it there. They slammed Case over the head with a gun butt and then me.'***

Bud feigned death and survived, which he said he owed to Eldon. In a letter to his own mother, written a few weeks after the tragic event, Bud wrote the following about it: 'I'm also enclosing a picture of Eldon Case who was my machine gunner. I can say that due to him lying so close to me and getting all the bullets, was the reason I'm here today.' Eldon was only twenty years old when the SS officer shot him. He is buried at the Netherlands American Cemetery and Memorial in Margraten, where he lies in Plot G, Row 14, Grave 27.

FRED H. BROWN

Staff Sergeant

76th Infantry Division

Zealous devotion to duty

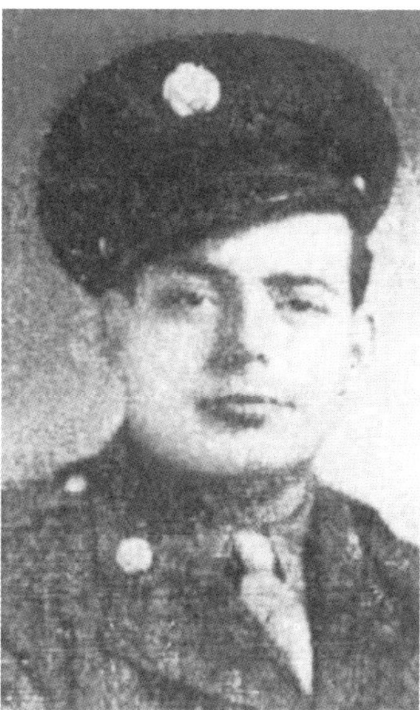

Staff Sergeant Fred H. Brown was born on December 14, 1909, and was a native of Murfreesboro, Rutherford County, Tennessee. Before entering the army in February 1942, he was co-owner of a barber shop.

Fred served overseas from December 1944 until his death, and was a member of Company E, 304th Infantry Regiment, 76th Infantry Division. He was awarded the Silver Star Medal for heroism during the fighting near the German town of Olk on March 1, 1945. When Fred and his squad were attempting to occupy a high ridge beyond the outskirts of this town, they were suddenly pinned down by an intense concentration of German artillery, mortar, Nebelwerfer, and small arms fire. The hostile fire killed his squad leader, whereupon Fred immediately took charge and reorganized the scattered squad. Fred then saw that one of the men had been struck by German shrapnel and was lying wounded in full view of the Germans. Leaving the comparative safety of his foxhole, Fred crawled five yards under fire to the side of the wounded man and began administering first aid. The enemy fire intensified, but Fred refused to leave the side of his wounded comrade until it was possible to carry him back to a safe area from which he could be evacuated to an aid station for medical treatment. Fred's act undoubtedly resulted in the saving of the wounded man's life, the citation said.

The following month, Fred again displayed extraordinary courage, this time at the cost of his life. Several months later, the army honored Fred by posthumously awarding him the Distinguished Service Cross. His citation was published in a local Tennessee newspaper and reads as follows:

> ***'For extraordinary heroism in connection with military operations against enemy forces in Germany. On April 10, 1945, during an advance upon the town of Schwerstadt, Germany, Sergeant Brown's company was pinned down by a withering hail of small arms and machine gun fire emanating from concealed enemy positions. With utter disregard for his own safety, this gallant soldier left cover and fearlessly charged the first machine gun emplacement, firing from the hip as he ran. Although wounded, he continued his gallant***

charge until mortally wounded by a second hostile machine gun. Sergeant Brown's heroic, self-sacrificing actions enabled his company to locate and destroy the two enemy machine gun positions. His dauntless courage and supreme devotion to duty will live on as an inspiration to the men with whom he fought. Staff Sergeant Brown's intrepid actions, personal bravery and zealous devotion to duty at the cost of his life, exemplify the highest traditions of the military forces of the United States and reflect great credit upon himself, the 76th Infantry Division, and the United States Army.'

Fred was 35 years old when he made the ultimate sacrifice in Germany. He was given his final resting place at the U.S. Military Cemetery in Margraten, where visitors can pay tribute to him in Plot K, Row 6, Grave 14.

ELDON W. LEE
Corporal
784th Tank Battalion

A good-natured young man

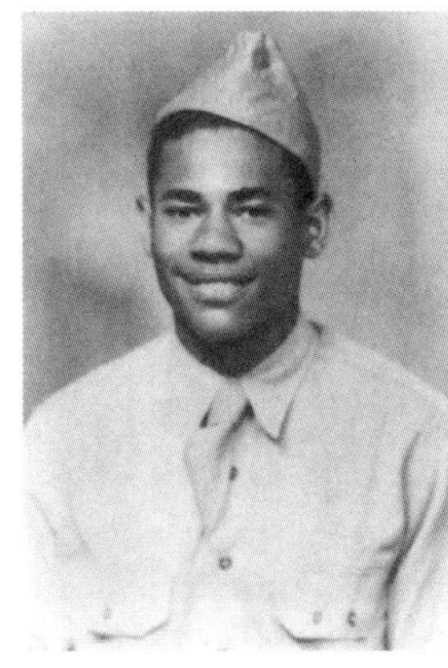

Eldon W. Lee, known to his family and friends as 'Skinny,' was born on June 22, 1924 and was a native of Sabina, a village in Clinton County, Ohio. He attended Sabina High School, where he was a member of the varsity basketball team during the 1941–1942 and 1942–1943 seasons. He graduated from the school in 1943 and in a local newspaper, he was characterized as 'a good-natured young man,' well-liked by his friends in Sabina. Fresh out of high school, Eldon was inducted into the army on August 2, 1943. He reported to Fort Thomas, Kentucky, which was just south of Cincinnati. He also trained at Fort Knox, Kentucky, and Camp Hood, Texas.

Eldon went overseas to the European Theater of Operations during the fall of 1944 and served in Company A, 784th Tank Battalion. On April 10, 1945, less than a month before Germany's unconditional surrender, Eldon's company supported the 134th Infantry Regiment of the 35th Infantry Division in an attack towards the Ruhr River through Bochum, Germany. Eldon was wounded – reportedly when a Panzerfaust struck his tank – and was rushed to the 48th Field Hospital. He succumbed to his wounds on the same day.

Eldon was twenty years old when he met his death so far from home. According to the earlier mentioned newspaper article, he was Clinton County's first reported 'colored casualty' of the war. The same article stated that Eldon had been promoted to the rank of Sergeant just before his death. This is not reflected in the army's records and his marble cross at Margraten in Plot D, Row 17, Grave 26 still reads the rank of Corporal.

Just days after the news of his death broke, teachers and pupils of the Sabina High School gathered in the school's auditorium to remember Eldon. Music was played and prayers said. Both faculty and his former classmates recollected memories of him in the presence of his parents. His father Otis was the school's janitor. In *Sabina Remembered*, Otis is described as a beloved man, 'who not only cleaned the classrooms, but who looked after the students as though they were his own.' Otis, however, 'aged visibly and never fully recovered' from the loss of his son. In December 1946, several black veterans organized a 'colored Legion Post' in the nearby city of Wilmington, which they named after Eldon. At some point, the Eldon Lee Post 649 had about 25 members and also its own post home. However, the post had become inactive by 1951. Therefore, the American Legion decided to cancel its charter.

RUSSELL F. DIEHL

Sergeant

99th Infantry Division

Killed by enemy artillery

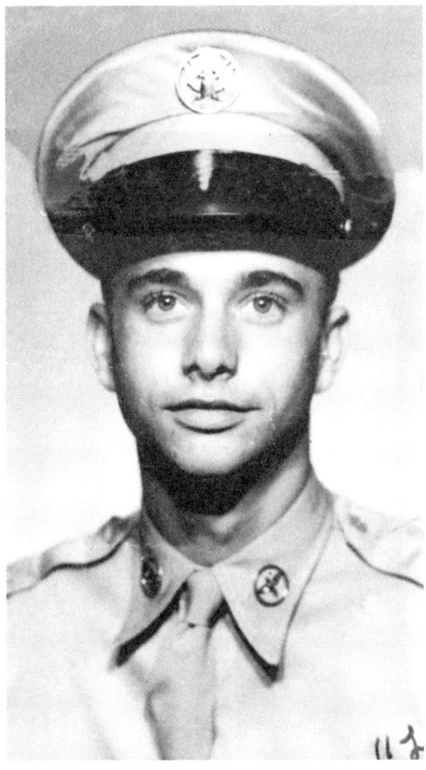

Russell F. Diehl from Fredericktown, a small farming village in central Ohio, was born in 1921. He was one of eight children born to Charles and Cecile Diehl. Charles and one child died several years before the war, so Cecile had to work hard to raise the remaining children.

'Dub,' as Russell was known to his friends and family, was deeply concerned about the war and decided to volunteer for the army in November 1942. His older brother was already serving in the military. He had been part of the famous 'Darby's Rangers' and was seriously injured while fighting behind enemy lines in Tunisia.

After enlisting, Russell became a sergeant in the 394th Infantry Regiment of the 99th Infantry Division. He was first posted near Aubel, Belgium, and was then involved in the Battle of the Bulge, where his battalion was instrumental in protecting the northern flank.

In the spring of 1945, Russell was involved in the Rhineland campaign. He was killed by artillery fire on April 10, 1945 in Oberelspe, Germany, during the battle to capture the German industrial complexes in the so-called 'Ruhr Pocket.' He was 23 at the time of his death and was initially interred in a temporary grave in Ittenbach, Germany. Later, Russell was re-interred at the U.S. Military Cemetery in Margraten on July 11, 1945, where he still lies today. His final resting place there can be found in Plot A, Row 8, Grave 5.

MAURICE E. GOSNEY

Staff Sergeant

71st Infantry Division

Letters to a second mother

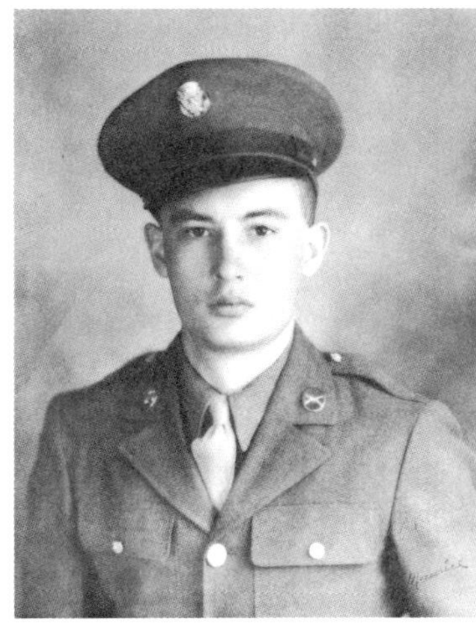

Maurice Gosney was the eldest of four brothers. Their father Leo constructed bridges and highways, which likely explains how the Illinois native met their mother Elva Mason in Nebraska. They married there in 1920. A year later, Maurice was born. After the birth of another son, the family moved to Illinois, where Maurice's two other brothers were born. He was almost five years old when Maurice's father Leo came home one day in 1925 to find three of the brothers home alone. Elva had disappeared. She had only taken her youngest son, who was still a baby and needed breastfeeding, with her. It is said that she was homesick and that she felt that marriage wasn't for her. Maurice never spoke to his biological mother again.

The family fell apart. Because of his work in construction, Leo was often far from home. The three brothers were placed in the Illinois Soldiers' and Sailors' Children's School, originally an orphanage for children of soldiers killed in the Civil War. Leo could send them there because he was a World War I veteran. The boys stayed there for about nine years, until Leo married Alma Donohue in 1934. The two had five more children. Moreover, Dot, who Elva had taken with her, returned to the family.

The brothers considered Alma to be their actual mother, as much as she treated them as her own sons. Without exception, the four brothers, who all served during World War II, addressed her as 'mom' in the letters they sent home.

Maurice mostly wrote about ordinary things. About packages that didn't arrive. About how they had lost track of time at the front line. About how he had seen some of the places his father had been to in World War I. However, he wrote, 'I wouldn't trade the backyard for the whole place over here.' Above all, his letters to his mother were reassuring. 'Here is what you are most likely looking for. I am o.k. and still getting around like I use to.' He said he tried to send her flowers for Easter, but was not sure whether she got them.

On April 6, 1945, Maurice sent his last letter home. It was five days before his death. Maurice was 23 then; two weeks later he would have turned 24. In that letter he wrote, 'In my previous letter I told you to start saving coffee and now by the time you get this one, get a quart of whiskey a week so that I can get a good one and catch up on what I am not getting now.' On April 11, however, he was killed near Sulzfeld, Germany, while trying to get his unit out of a German ambush. A German sniper shot him through the head.

Leo and Alma knew what news they were about to receive when there was a knock at their door. Therefore, they refused to open it. They did not want to know which of the four boys had died. When his brother Max heard of Maurice's death, he immediately wrote to Alma: 'I know his death has hurt you as much as if he were your own son. I am deeply sorry that I cannot be there with you and Dad to cry and help you get over this shock.' The other brothers, unlike Maurice, returned home safely to their new mother. Maurice rests in Plot I, Row 2, Grave 11.

Friday
April 6, 1945

Dear Mom & all.

I got a letter from the War Department to-night and I was kind of surprise to be hearing from Phyllis. because of me not writing to her.

I am still looking for the cake that Phyllis thinks is on the way.

I suppose that when the month of May is over with you will be wishing for School to be starting again kind of quiet like. And how did the squirt & Peggy do this year in school.

We are having a little trouble of keeping track of the days & date of the Week. I guess we need a book keeper for that but can't have any one here.

In my last letter I told you to start saving up on coffee and now by the time you get this one get a quart of whiskey a week so that I can get one a good

The last letter that Maurice sent home. SOURCE: Gosney family

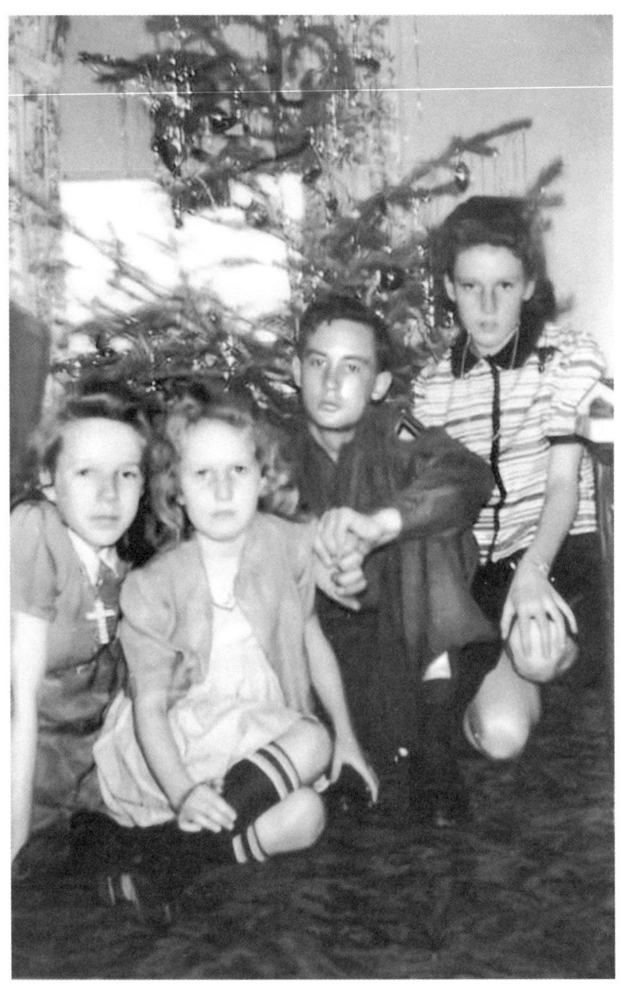

Maurice and, among others, two of his sisters in front of the Christmas tree. His sister Lucretia, second from left, was finally able to visit her brother's grave in September 2022, 77 years after his death. SOURCE: Gosney family

ROBERT W. SHIELDS
First Lieutenant
717th Tank Battalion

'The very best the battalion could give its country'

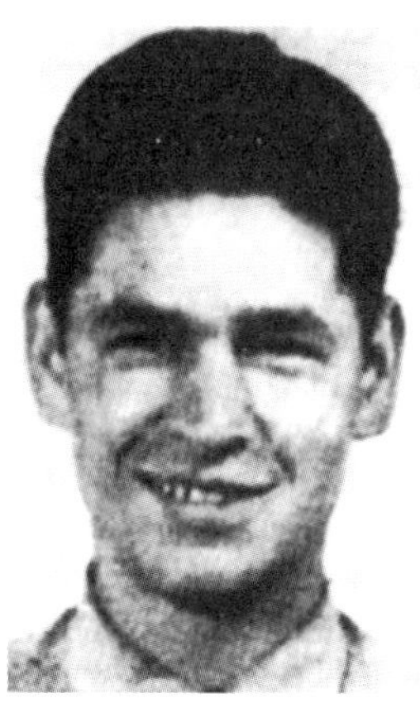

First Lieutenant Robert W. Shields from New York was in command of a platoon of Sherman tanks in Company A, 717th Tank Battalion. This battalion was formed at Camp Chaffee, Arkansas, in September 1943, and after a training period at Fort Knox, Kentucky, it boarded the *S.S. Cristobal* to set sail for the ETO in December 1944.

After arriving in France, the battalion moved toward Limburg, the southernmost province of the Netherlands, where it arrived at the small town of Brunssum on March 7, 1945. According to the Unit History, 'it was there that the Dutch showed how they felt about American soldiers. Before the last tank had been gassed up in the motor park that was once the town square, every man knew where he would sleep that night – in the softest bed, or in the warmest room a brave people had to offer.'

Upon arrival in Brunssum, the 717th Tank Battalion established liaison with the Headquarters of the 79th Infantry Division, to which the battalion was attached. On March 24, 1945, the battalion crossed the Rhine and also fired its first shots in combat. Over two weeks later, Robert was killed on April 11, 1945. He was the battalion's third fatal casualty, losing his life southwest of Essen, Germany when his tank was hit by an 88mm shell. His death was deeply felt within the whole battalion, as was described in the following excerpt from the Unit History:

> ***'From the old Chaffee days, Bob Shields was one of the best liked men in the battalion, and his death hit as hard as the others. He was one of the battalion's best instructors in gunnery. But what put him across – bar or no bar – was the belief that he constantly practiced: the way to treat a man was to treat him like a man. We lost only four men killed in action in the fighting in Germany. But when we lost those four, we lost four of the very best the battalion could give its country.'***

Robert is permanently laid to rest at the U.S. Military Cemetery in Margraten, which was originally designated as a burial site for the Ninth U.S. Army of which his battalion was a part. His final resting place in Margraten is situated in Plot C, Row 1, Grave 19.

WALTER E. SNYDER JR.
Technician Fifth Grade
80th Infantry Division

'I really thought he had been killed'

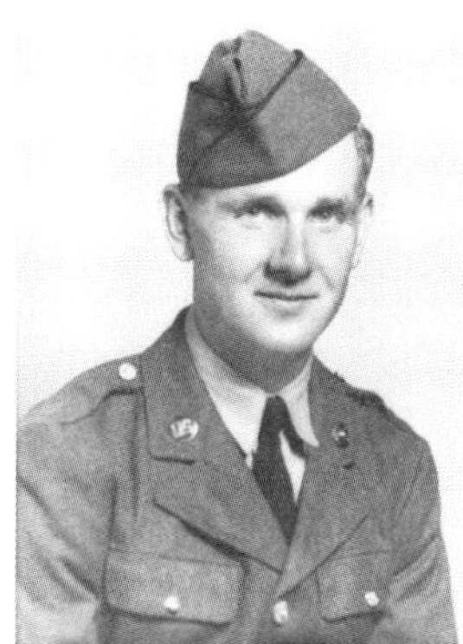

James Drylie had lost two good friends in the war. They had been his foxhole buddies. Sergeant Will M. Boyer was killed in action on March 16, 1945. Walter E. Snyder Jr. took his place, but was hit only days later. For over 60 years, James had thought that Walter had died right next to him. But he had not. Unfortunately, that does not mean that Walter had survived the war.

Walter, born on July 8, 1920, came from the small town of Lykens, Pennsylvania. When the war broke out, it only had about 3,000 inhabitants. His father was a successful jeweler with a store right on Main Street. Moreover, Walter Sr. held several public offices, such as burgess of the town and subsequently was its postmaster. His son, called 'Junior' in the family, graduated in 1938 from the town's high school. He had played in the school band and won the 1937-1938 championship with the school's football team. The family (Walter also had one sister) were members of the St. John's Lutheran Church.

On February 9, 1942, Walter voluntarily enlisted. He was sent to Ft. Eustis, Virginia, to join the Coast Artillery. He spent considerable time with the 605th Coast Artillery Anti-Aircraft Regiment in Charlestown, Boston. Furthermore, he was stationed at Camp Stewart, Georgia. He could make use of his musical skills as he was asked to play the bugle during his time with the Coast Artillery. However, at the end of 1944, Walter was transferred to the infantry. Mid-January 1945, about two weeks before Walter went overseas, he visited home one last time.

James and Walter joined Company A, 318th Infantry Regiment, 80th Infantry Division likely around the same time. James sailed for Europe on the *Queen Elizabeth* on January 31, 1945 and joined the unit as a replacement on February 11. In his memory, Walter had been killed about a month later, on March 19. 'I thought he was hit by shrapnel from a tree burst when we both jumped into our foxhole. I thought he had been killed and our platoon immediately moved away from the area when the artillery was coming in.' James was astounded when he learned in 2007 that Walter had not been killed that day. 'He may have been more lightly wounded than I thought and taken to a hospital without my knowledge of it.' Yet, there was no mention of Walter being wounded in the unit reports either. A puzzled James said that 'during combat there were probably a lot of inaccurate reports issued.' But he also said: 'I cannot explain it.'

What is known for sure, is that Walter was killed on April 11, 1945. The 80th Division closed in on Erfurt from the south that day. There was fighting going on in the city's outskirts and the Germans also launched a counterattack, which the division repulsed. Walter died from a gunshot wound in the chest. James said that he 'would not have been with him on April 11, because I took over driving our ammunition jeep on March 31' after the previous driver had been wounded.

Three days after his death, Walter was buried in the temporary cemetery in Eisenach. On both sides, he was flanked by members of his company who died on the same day. When their remains were transferred to Margraten only two months later, they stayed together. Some were ultimately repatriated to the U.S., but Walter's parents decided that he would remain overseas. And so, he was reburied in Plot B, Row 12, Grave 8 on December 14, 1948.

While James would never be able to visit the gravesite, he appreciated learning what had happened to his buddy and where Walter had been buried after all these years. Even more so, he appreciated seeing a photo of him. 'I did not have a picture of Walter and after more than 64 years I don't remember much about what he looked like.' James himself passed away in 2014.

ALFRED G. CORGAN
Private First Class
101st Airborne Division

Young paratrooper drowned in the Rhine

Private First Class Alfred G. Corgan from Unadilla, New York, was born on June 22, 1925. He was only thirteen years old when his mother died in 1938. At the age of sixteen, Alfred left high school to work as an automobile serviceman. In February 1944, he entered the army. From Camp Upton, Long Island, he was sent to Camp Blanding, Florida, where he was stationed for seventeen weeks and where he was awarded marksmanship badges for rifle sharpshooting, operating machine guns, and expert pistol shooting. Alfred then asked for a transfer to the paratroopers. He passed his examination and was stationed at Fort Benning, Georgia, where he completed jump training. Shortly before Alfred left for Europe, he married Muriel Dorothy Cross.

Alfred was attached to the 506th Parachute Infantry Regiment of the 101st Airborne Division as a replacement shortly after the Battle of the Bulge. This unit was just relieved from fighting in Bastogne, where it suffered heavy losses. Alfred was assigned to Company A and his squad was led by Sergeant Donald Burgett, who later wrote several books about his experiences during the war.

During the night of April 11–12, 1945, Alfred and Burgett were involved in a company strength patrol across the river Rhine to attack the German town of Himmelgeist, just below Düsseldorf. Able Company's objectives were to take enemy prisoners and hold positions there as though this were a major attack into the Ruhr Valley. When the Germans moved their armor and troops against them, the men were to fall back across the river.

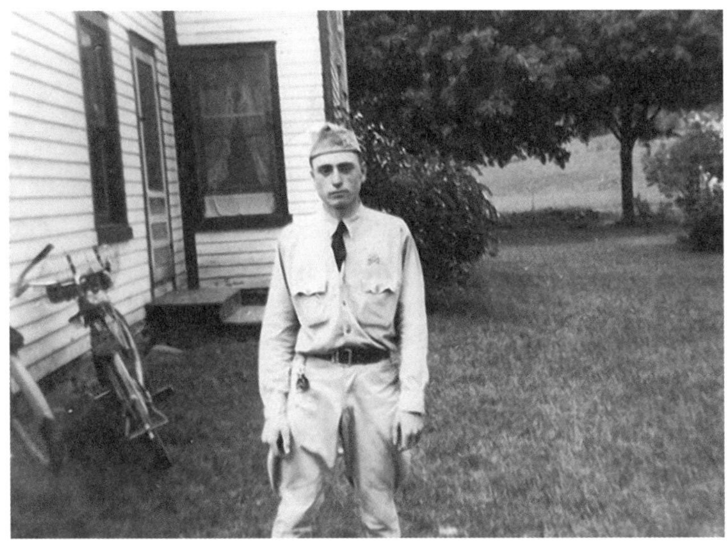

Just after dark, the men crossed the river in a small assault boat. Once across, German artillery started shelling the positions of Sergeant Burgett's squad. The shells exploded violently and at some point, Alfred was severely wounded. In an attempt to stop the bleeding, his arms were bound tight with bandages around the arms and chest.

As shells hit their positions more and more accurately, the order came to retreat. The men boarded their boats again and then moved out toward the friendly side of the river. On returning, they received artillery and tank fire all the way back across the Rhine.

'The German artillery was accurate and followed us all the way back across the Rhine,' Sergeant Burgett later wrote in one of his books. 'I believe it was coming from German tanks that had arrived just as we shoved off. Artillery adjusted by observer would not have been able to follow speeding boats that accurately and keep constant contact with their shells. It had to be coming from tanks that had visual contact with us. The barrage rained around us with fiery explosions, sending among our small craft huge geysers of brightly illuminated water that soaked us all with spray.'

While the men were returning across the river, a shell landed close to Alfred's boat. When it exploded, the boat capsized. Because he was wounded and had his arms bandaged and bound tight to his chest, he was unable to swim. Alfred was caught in the swift current and drowned. Two men dove into the water to look for him, but due to the darkness they couldn't find him...

Alfred was only nineteen years old at the time of his death. His body was found some days later about two miles downstream. He is permanently interred in Margraten, where visitors can pay tribute to him by going to Plot D, Row 10, Grave 5.

PAUL C. ROSENTHAL
Corporal
820th Tank Destroyer Battalion

Knocked out five tanks in one battle

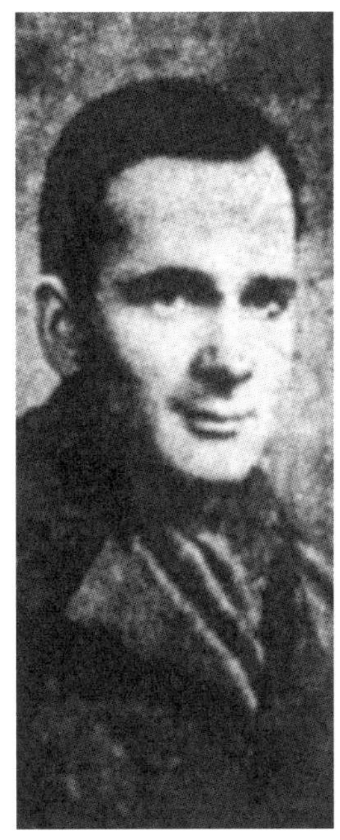

Corporal Paul C. Rosenthal from Michigan was born on June 17, 1918. He was employed by the Clark Equipment Company and entered the army in January 1943. He eventually served as a gunner on an M18 'Hellcat' tank destroyer in Company B, 820th Tank Destroyer Battalion.

On December 16, 1944 – the day Hitler launched his massive armored counterattack through the woods of the Ardennes – the 820th Tank Destroyer Battalion was deployed in the path of the German offensive near Winterspelt, Germany. Paul, acting as gunner of a towed 3-inch gun – the battalion was not yet equipped with the M18s at that time – sighted a column of enemy tanks, an enemy ammunition truck, and enemy infantry troops at an estimated range of 2,000 yards. He put his gun into position and opened fire. Using eighteen armor-piercing and high explosive shells, Paul knocked out five of the enemy tanks and the ammunition truck. A sixth tank withdrew with fire and smoke pouring out of its hull. His gun also accounted for at least 80 enemy casualties. For this action Paul was promoted to Corporal and awarded the Bronze Star.

In March 1945, several weeks after the Battle of the Bulge had ended, Paul's battalion received its M18s. From March 12 to April 2, 1945, the men spent time at Hehlrath, Germany, to train on the brand-new tank destroyers. Then they penetrated deeper into Germany.

On April 11, 1945, while moving through the Ruhr Valley, Paul's platoon was subjected to heavy enemy fire in the vicinity of Leidenhusen, Germany. Paul returned 76mm fire on the strongly dug-in and concealed position of the enemy, until his tank destroyer was set afire from a direct hit by an enemy bazooka. The crew abandoned the vehicle and Paul covered the withdrawal of his buddies with his personal weapon. While doing so, he was struck and killed by enemy machine gun fire. Paul was only 26 years old at the time and for this act of heroism he was later posthumously awarded his second Bronze Star. It was presented to his mother Molly. The moment that she received the medal was captured in a photograph published in two local newspapers. The photograph shows her visibly struggling with mixed emotions of pride and grief. Her brave son is buried in Margraten in Plot J, Row 2, Grave 19.

JOHN D. STINSON
First Lieutenant
18th Tank Battalion

Deadly bazooka fire

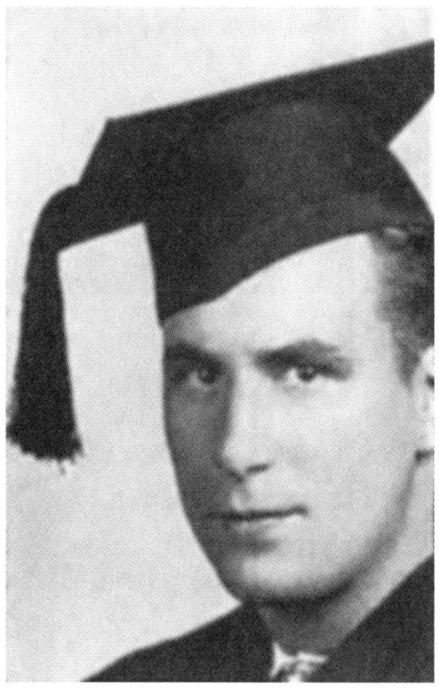

First Lieutenant John D. Stinson from California was born on December 7, 1917. Before entering the army and joining the armored forces, he had graduated from the University of San Francisco in 1939. He had been a well-known football player there.

At some point after enlisting, John was assigned to the Headquarters Company of the 18th Tank Battalion. This battalion was part of the 8th Armored Division, which was shipped to England in November 1944. After some additional training there, it landed in France in January 1945. The same month it was deployed to combat for the first time.

On April 11, 1945, John's tank supported infantry troops in the German town of Unna. He was in charge of the Assault Gun Platoon, which consisted of three modified tanks armed with a powerful 105mm howitzer and a heavy machine gun. These motorized and armored assault guns were used to provide mobile artillery support to advancing troops and tanks.

While John was leading his platoon in Unna, his tank was hit by enemy bazooka fire – the German Panzerfaust and Panzerschreck were called 'bazooka' by the U.S. troops. John himself and two of his crew were killed. He was 27 years old.

For his gallant and inspiring leadership from March 2, 1945 until his death, John was posthumously awarded the Silver Star. This was announced by 8th Armored Division Headquarters on May 5, 1945. In Margraten, John is buried in Plot H, Row 11, Grave 16.

MICHAEL DE FEBIO
Sergeant
643rd Tank Destroyer Battalion

A deadly ambush

Sergeant Michael de Febio was born in Providence, the capital of Rhode Island, on May 13, 1918. He had three sisters, a brother and a half-brother. In February 1941, Michael enlisted. He married his girlfriend Olga in June 1942.

Michael served in the Reconnaissance Company of the 643rd Tank Destroyer Battalion. His job was to proceed ahead of the gun companies searching for the enemy, mines, or blown bridges that made it necessary to find a different route to get to their destination. They also had some equipment that they could use to mend shell or bomb holes in the road so the tank destroyers could reach their destinations too.

On April 12, 1945, less than a month before the war in Europe ended, Michael lost his life during such a reconnaissance mission near Barby, Germany. Ben Savelkoul, who adopted Michael's grave in Margraten, managed to find out more details about Michael's death. Crucial to his research was a letter he received in April 2008. It was written by Lew Reynolds, who was riding on the same M8 'Greyhound' armored car as Michael when they ran into the German ambush that caused Michael's death. 'Mike [Michael] and I raised up out of the turret and caught a spray of machine gun fire just as we approached the Elbe River,' Reynolds wrote. 'Mike caught three bullets and sank back in his seat. He never suffered, never moved.'

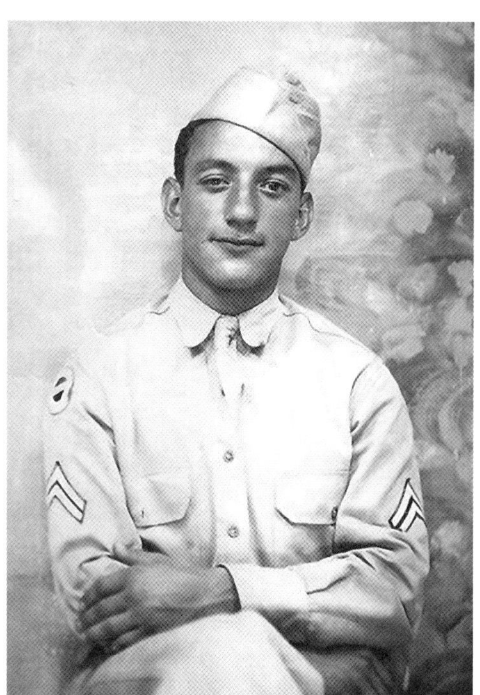

Michael died a month short of his 27th birthday. Several days after his death, he was temporarily buried at the U.S. Military Cemetery in Margraten, where he still lies today. Michael was laid to rest in his permanent grave on January 24, 1949. It can be found in Plot E, Row 2, Grave 7.

CHARLES H. HOUSEHOLDER

Sergeant

34th Tank Battalion

Mortally wounded by sniper fire

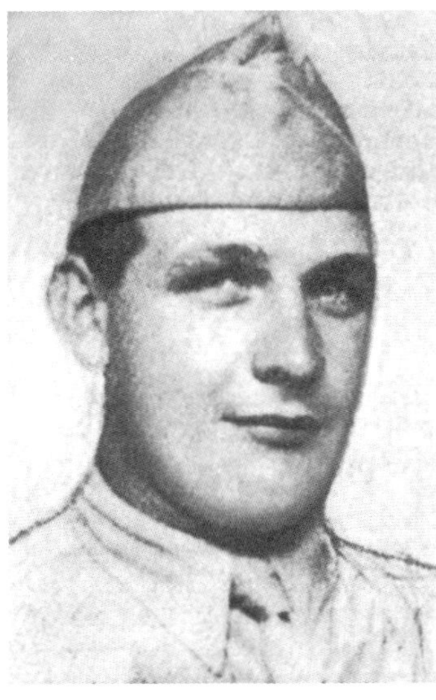

Sergeant Charles H. Householder was born in Huron, New York on June 1, 1919. He entered the army in Syracuse on January 16, 1941 and was assigned to Company C of the 34th Tank Battalion. This unit was an element of the 5th Armored Division.

By the time Charles lost his life, the 5th Armored Division had seen a lot of combat. The division arrived in Normandy at the end of July 1944 and had then fought its way through France, Luxembourg, and across the German border. In November, the division entered the Hürtgen Forest, where it was involved in very heavy fighting. In late December, it was withdrawn from combat duty and placed in reserve until February 1945, when the unit rejoined the Allied advance and spearheaded the drive toward the Rhine.

On April 12, 1945, Charles' Company C attacked the historic German town of Tangermünde, some 80 kilometers west of Berlin. The objective of the attack was to capture a bridge across the Elbe River but as the Americans moved out toward it, they ran into serious enemy resistance. Charles was the commander of the first tank to enter the town. As the Germans fired Panzerfausts at them, Charles' tank and Sgt. Haymaker's tank started blasting the buildings with their tank cannons. Their machine guns poured tracers into basement windows and through doors. Charles himself stood in his turret, firing his tommy gun. While thus being exposed, he was suddenly struck by sniper fire and his tank was disabled by a Panzerfaust. Charles was mortally wounded and died at the age of 25. In Margraten, his final resting place can be found in Plot P, Row 19, Grave 4.

WALTER J. FRYER

Sergeant

741st Tank Battalion

Killed by a Panzerfaust

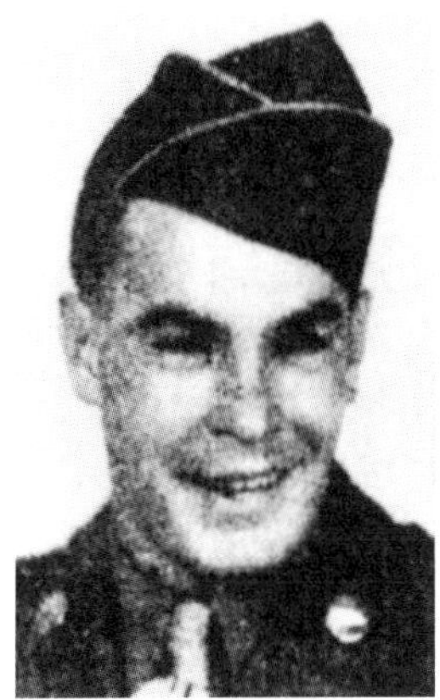

Sergeant Walter J. Fryer was born in Coburn, Pennsylvania on December 23, 1916. Both his mother and father died at a relatively young age. Prior to entering the service, Walter was employed by the Sheffield Dairy Company, and in December 1941 he married his girlfriend Rebecca Steele, who gave birth to a daughter named Linda Florence.

In May 1942, five months after the wedding, Walter entered the army. He was trained at Fort George G. Meade, Maryland, Camp Young in California, and Camp Polk in Louisiana, before heading to England in October 1943, after also having spent some time first at Camp Picket, Virginia.

Once in Europe, Walter served as a tank driver in Company C of the 741st Tank Battalion. According to a local newspaper, the *Altoona Tribune*, he entered combat in Normandy on D-Day, where his unit supported the 1st Infantry Division's amphibious landing on Omaha Beach. For this purpose, Companies B and C were equipped with special 'Duplex Drive' tanks (DD tanks), which could 'swim' ashore from the sea. However, 27 of the 29 launched DD tanks sank within minutes due to the strong winds and choppy sea, which damaged or collapsed their canvas flotation screens. Some tankers drowned, while others were rescued from the water by vessels.

Unfortunately, it cannot be said with certainty what Walter experienced on D-Day. The reason for this is that so far it has not been possible to find out whether he was already in Company C. Most likely he was. Therefore, there is a good chance that he was also in a sinking tank that day, since all the DD tanks of Company C sank and did not make it to the beach. If Walter was indeed in one of the sunken tanks, he must have been one of the lucky ones who were rescued from the water by vessels.

Ten months after D-Day, Walter lost his life in Germany on April 13, 1945 when his tank unit was involved in fierce fighting in the vicinity of Merseburg and Bad Lauchstädt. That day, when his company was conducting a flank assault on a German Flak battery, his tank was hit by a Panzerfaust. The tank's commander, Lt. Joe Dew, was wounded and Walter was killed. He was 28 years old. His daughter Linda was only two years old when her father died.

Walter is buried at the U.S. Military Cemetery in Margraten. His final resting place there is situated in Plot B, Row 2, Grave 9.

ROBERT M. WATTS

Private First Class

101st Airborne Division

Shot out of a boat by 'friendly fire'

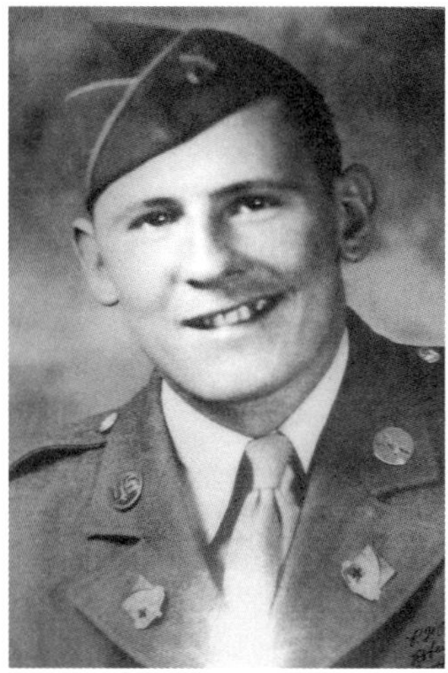

Robert Watts from New Hampshire was born in 1918 and was a paratrooper in the 506th Parachute Infantry Regiment of the 101st Airborne Division. As a soldier in this division, he participated in D-Day and Operation Market Garden in 1944. Robert was attached to the S-2 intelligence section of his regiment, and his task was to acquire information from locals and from members of the resistance.

During the unexpected German winter offensive in the Ardennes that started on December 16, 1944, Robert was sent to this part of Belgium with the 101st Airborne Division to defend the crucial road junction of Bastogne. Immediately upon arrival, the paratroopers began to organize their defenses, digging foxholes in the woods. On the night of December 21–22, 1944, they were completely surrounded by German infantry and tanks. However, the German troops did not succeed in capturing Bastogne, because Robert and the other paratroopers of the 'Screaming Eagles' managed to repel the German attacks every time. Partly because of this, the Germans began to shell the American lines around Bastogne with their artillery more and more intensely. On December 25, 1944, Robert was slightly wounded during one of the many German artillery bombardments.

Three months later, on April 2, 1945, Robert's regiment was transferred to Germany's Ruhr area after a rest period behind the front. Here, the paratroopers were deployed south of Düsseldorf and near the village of Dormagen along the west bank of the Rhine.

On the night of April 12–13, 1945, Robert joined a five-man combat patrol just north of this village led by Major William H. Leach. The small group of soldiers crossed the river Rhine at Himmelgeist in a rubber boat. The patrol went well, but when Robert and the others returned across the river they were seen, and German soldiers opened fire. This alerted the American paratroopers of Easy Company who were manning the guard posts on the west bank.

Since Major Leach had not passed on the fact that he was going on patrol before they set out, the Easy Company men assumed that there were German soldiers in the boat. Therefore, they too opened fire with rifles and machine guns. The tragic result was that Robert and three other men were hit by bullets from their own troops and fell out of the boat. They were either killed instantly or subsequently drowned. Only one paratrooper survived. Robert's body drifted into the river and went missing. Because his body was not recovered, he is still listed as missing in action. That is why Robert's name is engraved in the Walls of the Missing in Margraten. Robert was only 26 years old when he died....

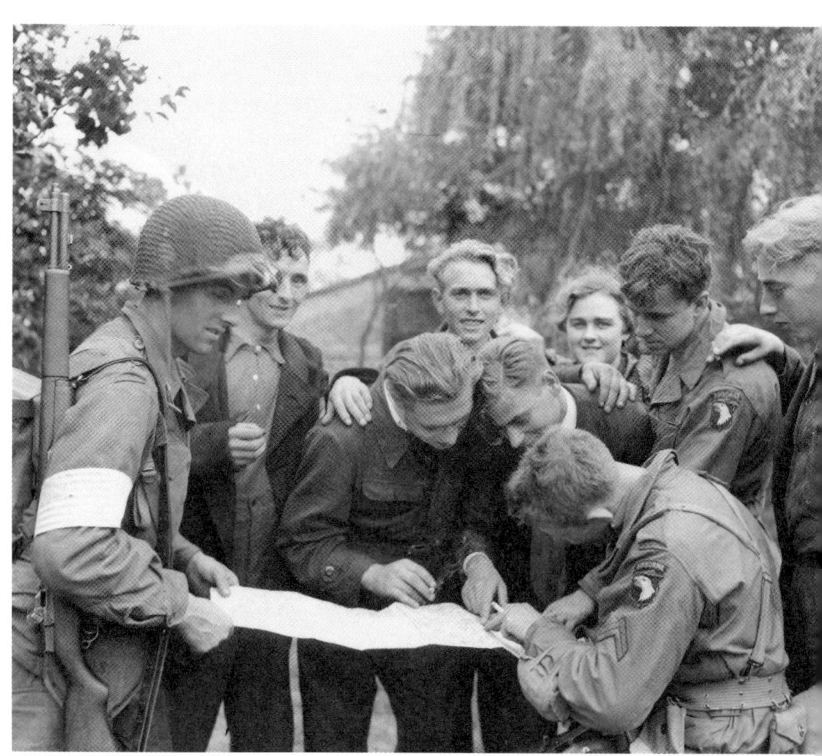

Local civilians offer their help to American paratroopers who have just landed, September 1944. Robert Watts stands far left. SOURCE: U.S. Army via Karel Margry, *After The Battle Magazine* via Arie-Jan van Hees.

KURT FRANZMAN

Sergeant

8th Infantry Division

Unknown X-1159

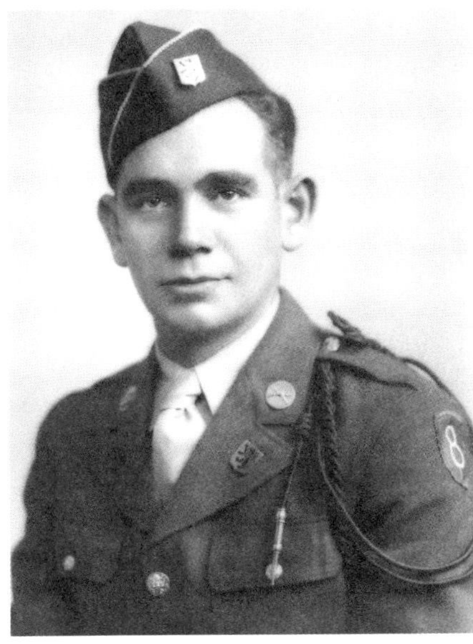

Sergeant Kurt Franzman was born in Kirschweiler, Germany, on January 21, 1911. In 1928, Kurt and his family emigrated to the United States, where he settled in Providence, Rhode Island. Before entering the service, he worked as a salesman in a grocery store.

On May 27, 1942, Kurt was inducted into the U.S. Army. He was assigned to the 28th Infantry Regiment of the 8th Infantry Division. While serving with this unit near Vossenack in the German Hürtgen Forest, he earned the Silver Star in December 1944. This medal was posthumously awarded to him in 1945. The description of his gallantry in action reads as follows:

> *'Sgt. Franzman was communication Sergeant for Co. I when it became necessary to lay wire between the platoons and Company CP in the Hürtgen Forest because the radio did not work due to atmospheric conditions. Sgt. Franzman with one other man went out on the mission. Many times it was necessary to lay the wire over enemy minefields and across open spaces in the forest. While crossing an enemy minefield Sgt. Franzman's companion was seriously wounded by the explosion of a Box mine. Sgt. Franzman immediately rendered first aid to the wounded man and although under the fire of enemy machine guns attracted by the noise of the explosion, he carried him back to the aid station. When he saw that the wounded man was taken care of Sgt. Franzman went back through the enemy fire and finished laying the wire until his mission was completed.'*

Several months later, on April 13, 1945, Kurt and three other men, including Captain Donald L. Keeler, were riding on a tank in the vicinity of Schwelm. According to a statement by Captain Keeler, the tank was hit by German 88mm fire. Keeler and one of the others, PFC Humphreys, were wounded and crawled into a ditch. Upon emerging from the ditch, he saw two badly mutilated dead bodies, one on the tank and the other on the ground. 'I could not identify either of them,' he reported.

Because Kurt's body was so badly mutilated, he initially couldn't be identified by Graves Registration troops. His remains were first buried as 'Unidentified X-13' at the temporary cemetery in Breuna, Germany. Shortly after the end of the war in Europe, the remains were transferred to the U.S. Military Cemetery in Margraten, where they were reburied as 'Unknown X-1159.' Shortly afterwards, it was reported that Unknown X-1159 was identified as Sgt. Kurt Franzman through fingerprints. As a result, it was possible to mark his final resting place in Margraten with a cross that bears his name. Today his gravesite can be found in Plot B, Row 6, Grave 9.

FRANK K. WHEELER

Staff Sergeant

34th Tank Battalion

German sniper took his chance

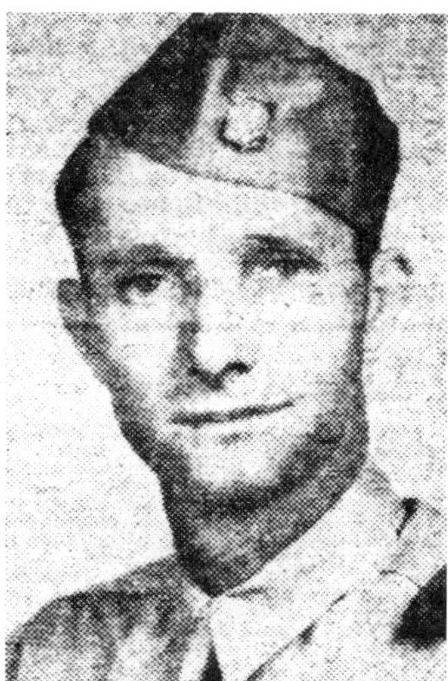

Staff Sergeant Frank K. Wheeler was born in Edmore, North Dakota, on August 29, 1909. In 1940, he moved to Great Falls, Montana, where he was employed by the Great Northern Railway.

In March 1942, Frank enlisted in the army. Before going overseas on February 10, 1944, he trained at Fort Knox, Kentucky, Camp Cooke, California, Pine Camp, New York, and Fort Indiantown Gap in Pennsylvania.

In Europe, Frank served as a tank commander in the 34th Tank Battalion. This unit was part of the 5th Armored Division, which arrived at Utah Beach in July 1944 and saw a lot of combat thereafter, crossing the German border in September. On February 25, 1945, it crossed the Roer River, after which the tanks pushed on toward the Rhine. When this formidable obstacle was also crossed, the advance continued to the Elbe.

Near this river, Frank's platoon was subjected to enemy bazooka, 20mm, and artillery fire on April 13, 1945. About a mile south of Arneburg, Frank's tank was hit. He was injured by a shell fragment and bailed out, but when he looked around, he saw that one of his tank crew was missing. Frank ran back to the burning and smoking tank and then started to climb on it to check if the missing soldier was still inside. While doing so, he was shot and killed by a German sniper. Therefore, Frank remained forever 35. He is laid to rest in Margraten, where anyone who visits the U.S. Military Cemetery can pay tribute to him by visiting Plot H, Row 16, Grave 9.

MARTIN J. WEISS

First Lieutenant

45th Field Artillery Battalion

Directed artillery fire on the enemy

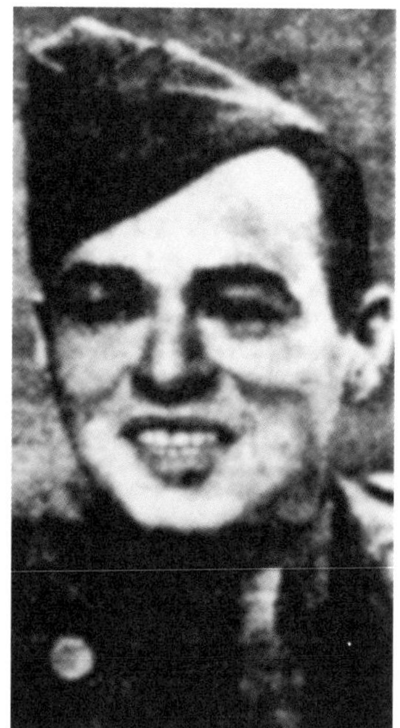

First Lieutenant Martin J. Weiss, a Jewish officer, was born in Philadelphia, Pennsylvania, on May 19, 1916. On January 13, 1941, he went to Conshohocken, Pennsylvania, to enlist in the army. During the war, Martin became a lieutenant in the 45th Field Artillery Battalion, which provided artillery support to the 8th Infantry Division.

On April 9, 1945, Martin's unit was caught by incoming enemy artillery fire in Germany. Martin himself was slightly wounded to one of his legs, but after treatment he could report back to duty.

Four days later, on April 13, 1945, troops of the 8th Infantry Division attacked toward Schwelm. They encountered some artillery and mortar fire and were halted by a tank block consisting of one enemy tank, one self-propelled gun and about 200 German infantrymen. Martin established an observation post far ahead of the friendly infantry and directed artillery fire on the enemy. Unable to see the German armored vehicles, Martin then mounted an American tank to get closer to the tank block. Disregarding enemy machine gun and artillery fire, he led the tank forward until he was killed when the tank was hit by fire from an enemy self-propelled gun. He was 28 years old.

Several months after Martin's death, *The Philadelphia Inquirer* announced he was posthumously awarded the Silver Star for his heroism on the day he was killed. In Margraten, Martin is permanently laid to rest beneath a marble Star of David in Plot K, Row 3, Grave 18.

SHANNON E. ESTILL

First Lieutenant

474th Fighter Group

Pilot never got to see his daughter

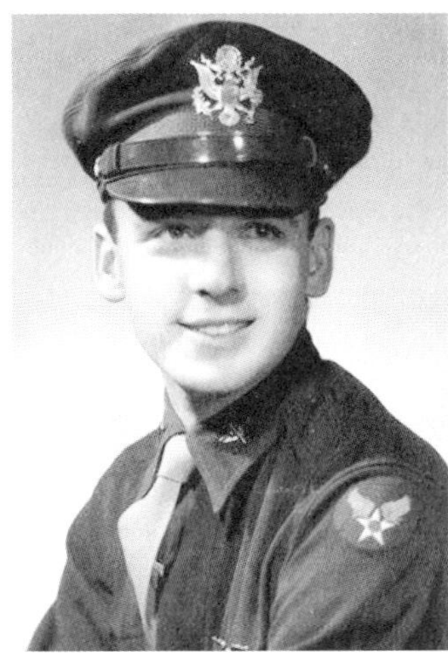

First Lieutenant Shannon E. Estill was born on June 26, 1922, and grew up in Cedar Rapids, Iowa. While attending Franklin High School, Shannon met his future wife Mary, with whom he married before he left for Europe during the war.

Shannon was inducted into active service in February 1943, after which he trained to become a pilot. He was assigned to the 428th Fighter Squadron of the 474th Fighter Group, which was deployed to Europe in 1944. Shannon's squadron flew two-engine P-38 Lightnings that were used as long-range fighters and fighter bombers.

On Easter Sunday 1945, Shannon wrote a letter to Mary, who had just given birth to their daughter Sharon. It reads as follows:

> ***'Dearest Angels, I simply can't express how I feel at our daughter: so happy and glad, yet almost afraid. Afraid that I won't measure up to the shadowy indeterminate standards of parenthood. How I should love to be with you two now. Just can't understand how old Estill happened to land the two cutest gals in the world, but won't argue. Am afraid the Big Chief [God] might check the records and discover that you really don't belong to me at all, but perhaps are angels that have sneaked down from heaven to tease this poor mortal.'***

Shannon never got the chance to see his baby daughter. On April 13, 1945, about three weeks after Sharon was born, Shannon was shot down by enemy anti-aircraft fire while attacking enemy targets in eastern Germany. According to a statement in the Missing Air Crew Report by another pilot, Lt. John J. Bentley, Shannon's P-38 was hit by an 88mm Flak anti-aircraft gun. The plane started to burn and went into a spin, after which it hit the ground and exploded in a field near the village of Elsnig. Shannon had no chance to bail out and was killed. He was only 22 years old. Less than a month later, the war in Europe was over... According to Shannon's crew chief, Henry Ham, Shannon was the only guy in the squadron with a baby and the best man and pilot he ever knew. 'He would have been the best father too,' he later told to Sharon.

Because the location of the crash site was within the Russian-controlled sector of occupied Germany after the war, U.S. military personnel could not recover his remains. But Sharon was determined to find her father's remains. During her lifelong quest for her father, she eventually met Hans-Guenther Ploes, a German researcher. In 2003, Ploes and other members of a search team found the crash site and discovered human remains. They reported the site to the U.S. military and turned the remains over to U.S. Army officials. The Americans took over and a team from the Joint POW/MIA Accounting Command (JPAC) further investigated the site. Another JPAC team completed the excavation of the site in 2005. While doing so, the researchers recovered additional human remains and the wreckage of Shannon's P-38.

In 2006, the Department of Defense POW/Missing Personnel Office (DPMO) announced that the remains found in the field near Elsnig had been identified as being Shannon's. This could be determined through the use of mitochondrial DNA. Shannon's remains were then buried at Arlington National Cemetery on October 10, 2006. Sharon took part in the funeral service, as did Shannon's then 82-year-old brother Wesley.

Seven months after the funeral, Sharon traveled to the Netherlands American Cemetery in Margraten. There she and Hans-Guenther Ploes stood in front of the Walls of the Missing when a small rosette was placed next to her father's name.

Shannon Estill was given his final resting place in Arlington. SOURCE: Gary Koch/ FindAGrave.com

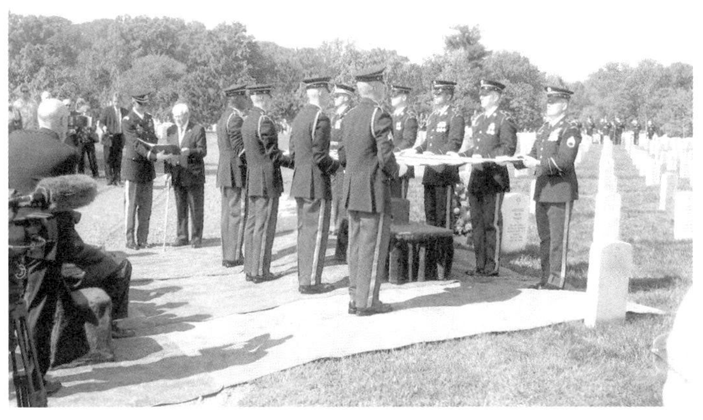

RICHARD S. FLEMING
Second Lieutenant
771st Tank Battalion

Danger could not stop him

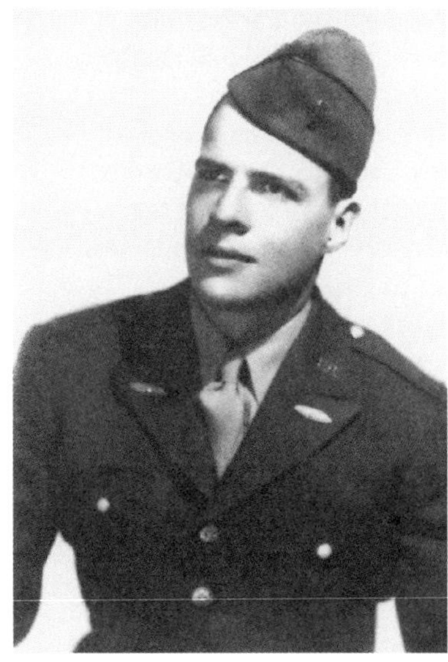

Richard S. Fleming was born in East Orange, New Jersey, on December 11, 1923. At some point the family moved to New Haven, Connecticut, where he was a member of the Trinity on the Green Episcopal Church. Richard graduated from New Haven High School and then entered Yale University in September 1941. He held a Sterling Memorial scholarship, but after his freshman year he withdrew from college to enter the army in September 1942.

After completing basic training, Richard attended Armored Forces Officer Candidate School at Fort Knox, Kentucky, where he was commissioned Second Lieutenant in September 1943. He was then stationed at Camp Polk, Camp Shelby, and Fort Jackson. Finally, he was transferred to Fort George G. Meade. Richard was then sent overseas to Europe, where he was attached to Company A, 771st Tank Battalion and commanded the crew of a tank.

On February 25, 1945, Richard personally turned the tide when the advance of infantry troops that his tank platoon was supporting was temporarily checked by hostile artillery and small arms fire. He conducted a dismounted reconnaissance that enabled him to direct effective fire on an enemy anti-tank gun and armored vehicle. The fire he directed on the enemy allowed the infantry unit to complete its mission.

Two days later, on February 27, 1945, Richard again distinguished himself. When a German anti-tank gun had disabled one tank in his column and constituted a serious threat to the entire column, Richard quickly put his tank into position and destroyed the enemy gun. For his courage in action displayed on these two occasions, he was awarded the Bronze Star Medal.

On April 13, 1945, less than a month before Nazi Germany's unconditional surrender, Richard's tank platoon was ordered to attack a concentration of enemy troops in a wooded area near Offensen, Germany. On the way they came upon a bridge that had been blown up and while waiting for the engineers to repair the bridge for a crossing, an enemy halftrack and some infantry were sighted. Richard then decided not to wait any longer and went into the woods with an infantry patrol. While Richard was conducting this mission, he was killed in action at the age of 21. He posthumously received the Silver Star for his initiative and leadership during this action.

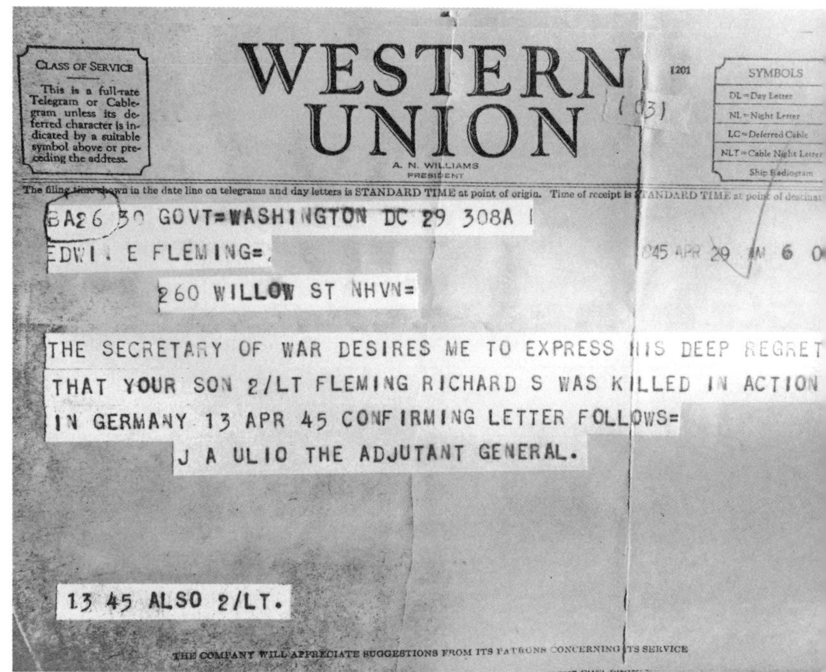

CLASS OF SERVICE
This is a full-rate Telegram or Cablegram unless its deferred character is indicated by a suitable symbol above or preceding the address.

WESTERN UNION
A. N. WILLIAMS PRESIDENT

1201

SYMBOLS
DL=Day Letter
NL=Night Letter
LC=Deferred Cable
NLT=Cable Night Letter
Ship Radiogram

The filing time shown in the date line on telegrams and day letters is STANDARD TIME at point of origin. Time of receipt is STANDARD TIME at point of destination

BA26 30 GOVT=WASHINGTON DC 29 308A
EDWI E FLEMING=
260 WILLOW ST NHVN=

945 APR 29 AM 6 0

THE SECRETARY OF WAR DESIRES ME TO EXPRESS HIS DEEP REGRET THAT YOUR SON 2/LT FLEMING RICHARD S WAS KILLED IN ACTION IN GERMANY 13 APR 45 CONFIRMING LETTER FOLLOWS=
J A ULIO THE ADJUTANT GENERAL.

13 45 ALSO 2/LT.

THE COMPANY WILL APPRECIATE SUGGESTIONS FROM ITS PATRONS CONCERNING ITS SERVICE

The telegram announcing Richard's death to his next of kin. SOURCE: Michael Fleming

Richard's commanding officer, Captain Raymond R. Latvamaki, described the details surrounding his death. In a letter of condolence to Richard's father Edwin, he wrote that Richard was struck and killed by enemy small arms fire after he went into the woods. In his letter, Captain Latvamaki also told Edwin that Richard's death was deeply felt within his outfit. 'Words cannot express the sorrow we feel at your son's death, or our sympathy for you at this difficult time. We, here in the Company counted him as a brother. He was sincerely loved by every man and every officer in the organization,' he wrote. 'Richard, more than anyone else I know, exemplified the things for which we fight. His death has made us more than ever conscious of the things for which we fight, and the obligation we have to him and others like him, to see this war through to a speedy and just end.'

Richard's death was also described by Pat Wolfe, a fellow soldier who remembered Richard as a 'very brave guy, much respected by his men and the officers over him.' Wolfe also wrote that 'the woods up ahead were extremely dense, and it became necessary for the tankers to make a reconnaissance on foot in order to locate an avenue of approach for their tanks. Fleming was a platoon commander, and it was his job to make the reconnaissance, which he did without hesitation, and fully aware of the danger involved. He climbed down from his tank together with two of his men, and all three were cut down almost immediately with automatic weapons fire [machine gun or submachine gun fire]. Fleming and one of the men were killed, and the other was seriously wounded.'

Shortly after he had lost his life, Richard was temporarily buried at the U.S. Military Cemetery in Margraten. The last rites were performed by a Protestant Chaplain, Captain Latvamaki wrote in his letter. After the war, when the field of honor in Margraten became a permanent American cemetery, Richard was given his final resting place there in Plot D, Row 15, Grave 26.

KARL O. HOLLIDAY
Captain
561st Field Artillery Battalion

A German ambush

Karl O. Holliday was born in a farmhouse in rural Wayne County, Iowa, on December 18, 1918. During his youth, he worked on the farm with his parents and siblings. After graduating from high school, Karl attended Drake University in Des Moines. He graduated there with a degree in Commerce and was drafted into the army following the Japanese attack on Pearl Harbor. While he was studying at Drake, Karl was a member of the Alpha Tau Omega social fraternity. He was also an athlete, playing both football and basketball.

Karl completed his basic training at Fort Bragg, North Carolina, and was then assigned to the Field Artillery at Fort Sill, Oklahoma. At Fort Sill he successfully completed Officers Candidate School, whereupon he received his commission. He eventually reached the rank of Captain while serving in the 561st Field Artillery Battalion, which sailed for Europe in January 1944.

While Karl was still stationed at Fort Sill he met his future wife Gloria Patterson, whom he married on January 10, 1943. Eight months later, when Karl was stationed at Camp Robinson in Arkansas, Gloria gave birth to their son Robert ('Bob').

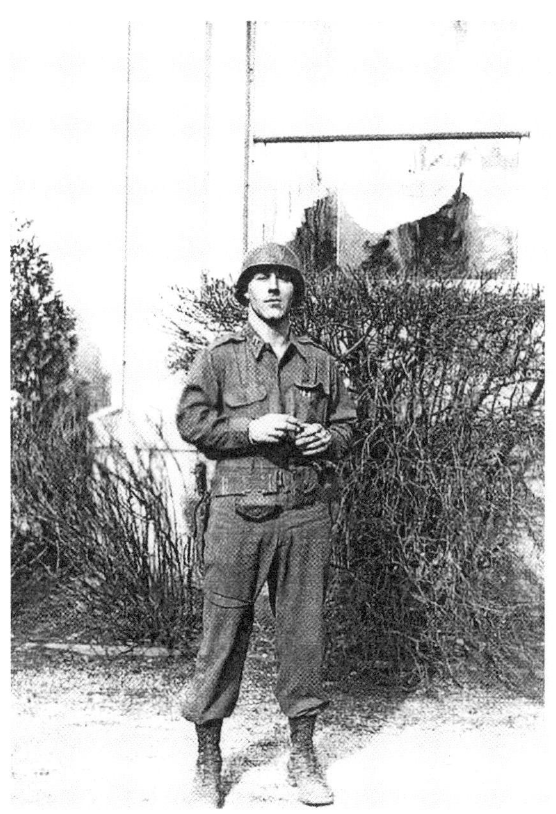

Karl's artillery battalion entered combat in Normandy and consisted of five batteries. Three of these batteries were firing batteries, with each firing battery having four 155mm guns, known as 'Long Toms.' Karl was the battery commander of the Headquarters Battery. His job was to find housing for the men. He was also in charge of the battalion's Fire Direction Center and its communication network. Furthermore, he was to make sure the battery was secure from the enemy. Karl performed these duties well as evidenced by what some veterans of the battalion later said of him to his son Bob: 'He had a sense of humor which could carry the day.' 'He had no fear of the enemy' and 'his leadership and spirit served us well during our most fearful and trying times.'

On April 13, 1945, Karl fell victim to a German ambush. He was a member of an 'advance party' comprised of about fifteen American vehicles. The colonel in charge decided to bypass the American Infantry and to take the group further than was ordered. As the vehicles approached a hill near the village of Klotz, German troops hiding on both sides of the road suddenly opened fire on the column with machine guns and rifles. Karl and the other three men from his jeep jumped into a shallow ditch. He and his first sergeant then stood up. They both carried a Thompson submachine gun and started firing at the enemy. Both were hit and killed by fire from a German 'Burp gun' – a (sub)machine gun. Karl was 26 years old. In Margraten, he is buried in Plot C, Row 7, Grave 17.

ALVIN A. BRODBECK
Private First Class
6th Armored Division

'Mommy, are you going to cry again?'

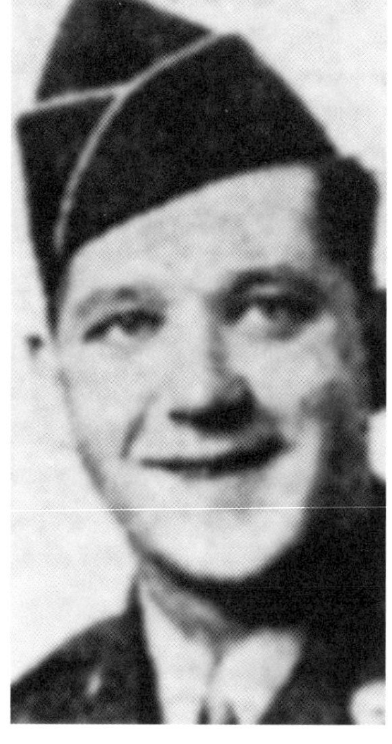

Private First Class Alvin A. Brodbeck from Louisville, Kentucky, was born in 1920. Initially, he had received a deferment from military service because his work as mechanical draftsman was important to the U.S. war effort. Nevertheless, to his own surprise, he was called to arms in July 1944. Alvin was overwhelmed: together with his wife he had just purchased a piece of land where they wanted to build a cottage. He had already begun drawing the design when he received the call for active duty.

It soon turned out that Alvin's call to the army was the result of an error. The administrator of his company had forgotten to submit the usual forms for the periodic renewal of his deferment. There was nothing more to do. Alvin traveled to Camp Hood, Texas, where he received his basic training to become an infantryman. However, after completing his training, Alvin was told that he was being added to the cadet school for officers at the cartographic service in New Jersey, where he would have to draw staff maps. But first he was allowed to return home to his wife Mildred and two-year-old son Butch for a ten-day leave. When these wonderful days at home were over, Alvin boarded the troop train that would take him to New Jersey.

Enroute to the East Coast it turned out that one of the conscripts in Alvin's coupé had the mumps. The whole wagon was shunted in quarantine and had to get sidetracked. However, soon afterwards the wagon was mistakenly linked to an army train with replacements for the front, which took the men to New York. There Alvin and the others were ordered to board the *Queen Mary* and sent to Europe. Upon arrival in France, Alvin was attached to the 44th Infantry Battalion of the 6th Armored Division. With this unit he crossed the German border. On April 13, 1945, Alvin volunteered for a night patrol near Groitzsch. During this action he was killed by a German rifle bullet.

Shortly thereafter, his wife Mildred received the telegram that informed her of her husband's death. 'My world was crushed,' she later said of this.'Our son was almost three years old and I still can see his face and the fearful look in his eyes when he asked me: "Mommy, are you going to cry again?" After the war I had a terrible time seeing families happily reunited all around me while I was struggling alone. But thank God I was able to pick up the pieces and built for myself and my son a good living.'

Alvin was initially buried in a temporary grave in Brenau, Germany, but after the war his remains were moved to Margraten. There he was permanently laid to rest in Plot C, Row 18, Grave 5.

CHRISTINE A. GASVODA
First Lieutenant
817th Medical Air Evacuation Squadron

Flying nurse dies in bad weather

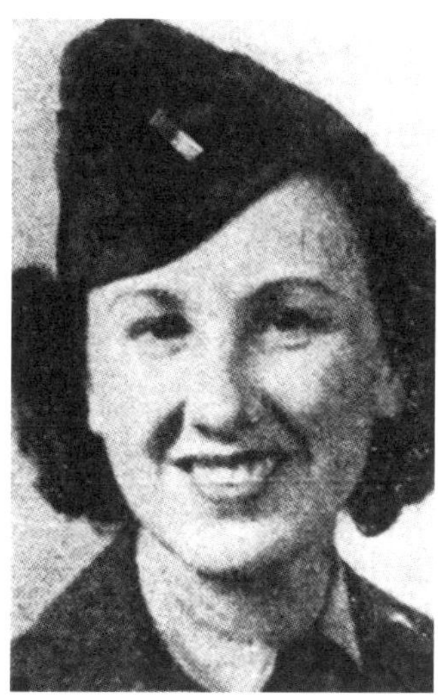

Christine Annette Gasvoda was born in Detroit, Michigan, in 1915. In Chicago, Illinois, she worked as a nurse in a hospital. When war broke out, she enlisted in the United States Army Nurse Corps.
The 817th Medical Air Evacuation Squadron (MAES) – Christine's unit – was activated at Bowman Field, Kentucky, on November 12, 1943. Christine was one of twenty-five 'Flight Nurses' who attended a four-week training course at Bowman Field. The purpose of her training: to stabilize injured patients so they could be airlifted to a hospital where further treatment would follow.

On March 14, 1944, 817 MAES departed from Camp Kilmer, New Jersey, by ship for Scotland. Prior to D-Day, the flight nurses accompanied patients who were transported by air within the United Kingdom or brought back to the United States via the transatlantic route for further specialist treatment.

On June 10, 1944, the first operational evacuation flight took place: wounded were picked up near Sainte-Mère-Église in Normandy and brought back to England for emergency treatment in a British hospital. In October 1944, the unit was placed on the mainland near Orléans, France. Another move to Dreux-Chartres followed shortly thereafter.

On April 13, 1945, fourteen C-47A transport aircraft took off from 'Advanced Landing Ground' A-41 / Dreux-Chartres in France. Their destination was airfield R-16 near Hildesheim in Germany. These aircraft were to carry supplies and bring back wounded to be delivered to a well-equipped hospital as quickly as possible. One of the aircraft was #43-15086 nicknamed 'Hi.' The crew of this unit consisted of five men; Christine Gasvoda was added to accompany the wounded as 'Air Evacuation Nurse.' The cargo consisted of a large number of jerrycans filled with fuel. Prior to this flight, Christine was awarded an Air Medal.' This indicates that she made at least five operational flights to pick up wounded behind the front.

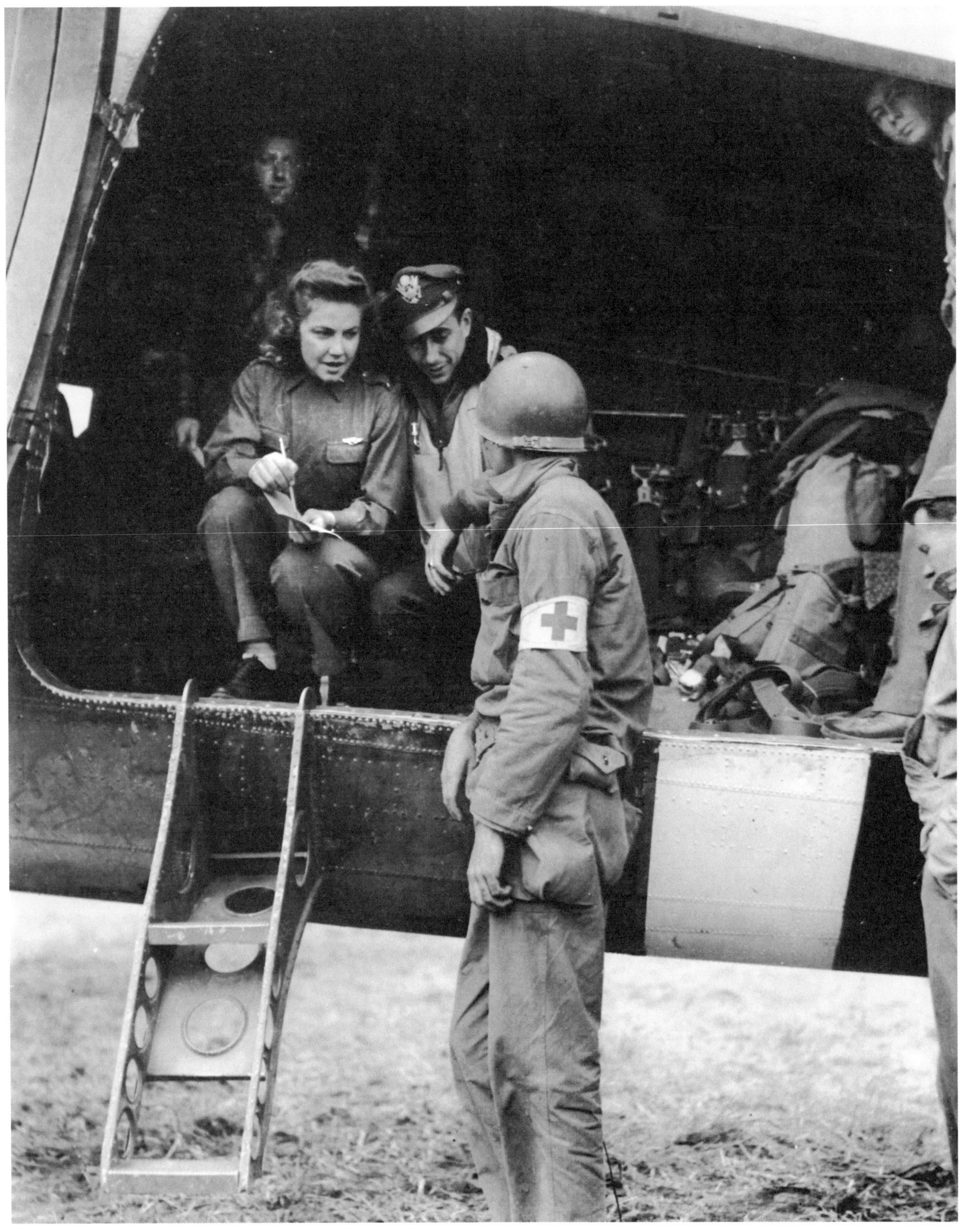

During the flight the weather conditions became worse and the formation was informed by radio to divert to an airfield near Paderborn. Apparently, this radio message did not reach the plane Christine was in. Why, we do not know. Was it a result of a temporary glitch that interfered with the reception of the message?
Did the radio operator not have his headphones on at that moment? We will never know. Thirteen of the fourteen aircraft made a 180-degree turn and landed at Paderborn airport shortly thereafter. Christine's plane did not arrive. A subsequent report indicated that the C-47 was last seen twelve miles northeast of Paderborn in the vicinity of Nieheim. Shortly thereafter, information was received that the aircraft had flown into a hill near Altenbeken in bad weather. All six occupants were killed in the crash.

Christine's final resting place in Margraten is in Plot F, Row 19, Grave 4.

◀ **The crew of an evacuation plane talks to a medic. The nurse in the photo is not Gasvoda. SOURCE: U.S. Army Air Forces via Arie-Jan van Hees**

WILMA R. VINSANT
First Lieutenant
806th Medical Air Evacuation Squadron

One flight too many

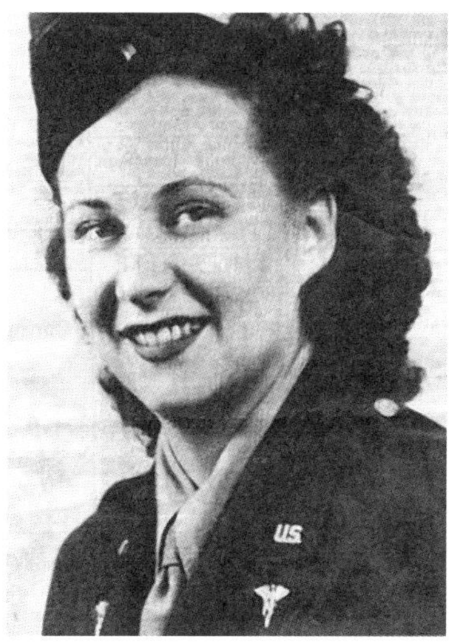

Wilma 'Dolly' Vinsant was born in San Benito, Texas, on February 20, 1917. With her parents, a doctor and a nurse, as role models, she went to John Sealy Hospital in Galveston to study to become a nurse. Buoyed by the daring feats of Amelia Earhart, the first female aviator to fly solo across the Atlantic Ocean, she then went on to train as a stewardess with Braniff Airways.

In September 1942, Dolly volunteered for service in the U.S. Army Nurse Corps. She attended training in air evacuation at Bowman Field, Kentucky, to become a flight nurse, graduating in 1943. Shortly thereafter, she was assigned to the 806th Medical Air Evacuation Squadron.

Dolly was soon sent overseas to Europe. There she was involved in evacuation flights, caring for badly wounded soldiers who were airlifted from the battlefield to hospitals in England and later also Belgium. Occasionally, she provided medical care to the wounded on special flights from Londen to New York.

During the evacuation flights, Dolly and the other flight nurses faced the risk of being shot down by enemy aircraft and anti-aircraft guns. Their planes, usually C-47s, were also used for military purposes such as dropping paratroopers and transporting fuel, weapons, ammunition, and supplies to the front. For this reason, their transport planes were not allowed to carry the protective Red Cross sign.

Overall, the approximately 500 flight nurses evacuated over 1,176,000 wounded and sick servicemen worldwide during the war. Thanks to the excellent care Dolly and the other flight nurses provided, 'only' 46 wounded soldiers succumbed to their injuries during evacuation flights.

On April 14, 1945, Dolly was supposed to be off duty. Although she had already flown 30 sorties and was due to return to the U.S. to train new flight nurses, she volunteered for another mission to replace a colleague. It would be her last flight, because the C-47 crashed near Eschwege, Germany. Still nothing can be said with certainty about the cause of the crash. Most likely the plane was shot down by enemy fire or crashed due to bad weather conditions.

Dolly did not survive the crash and was 28 years old at the time. Three months earlier she had married Walter L. Shea, an air force navigator from New York. Dolly is one of four women buried at the U.S. Military Cemetery in Margraten, where she is permanently laid to rest in Plot B, Row 17, Grave 4.

WALTER STERN

Private First Class

76th Infantry Division

A soldier in the land he had once called home

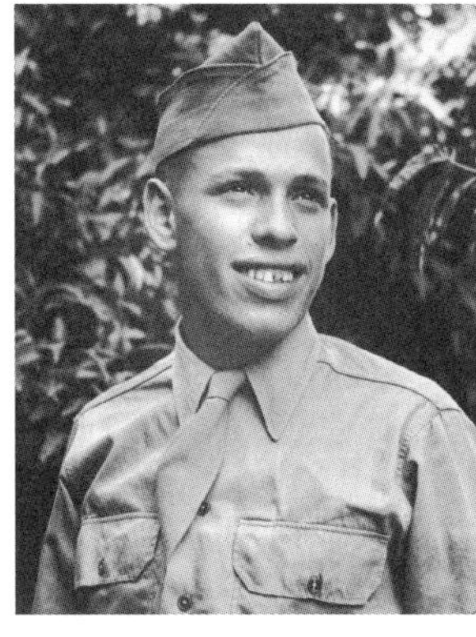

During one of the last times that Walter Stern came home, 'I was standing in the kitchen cooking. Somebody embraced me from the back. I felt he had really now come around and felt that I liked him, and that I was crying and worrying about him and his well-being at Camp Roberts, only meaning the best,' Hedi recollected in her memoires. She had married Walter's father Fritz in 1930. However, Hedi and Fritz did not live happily ever after. Ever since the rise of Hitler, the Jewish couple felt that they could not stay in Germany. So, they took their six children and fled to the United States in 1936. But Walter would still be killed in the land that he had once called home.

Walter was born in Munich, Germany, on January 14, 1926. He was only three when his mother Hedwig passed away in 1929. She died from complications caused by the childbirth of his sister Gertrude. When his father remarried a year later, he not only gained a stepmother, but also two stepsisters and a stepbrother. Moreover, Fritz and Hedi had one daughter, Eva, together in 1931. The combined family of eight lived on the Kepplerstrasse in Munich.

In 1933, Fritz and Hedi visited Palestine and considered moving there. They already had some good friends there. Hedi noted that 'it was such a good feeling to be with other Jewish people all around,' but they ultimately decided not to emigrate there due to the poor conditions of the country at the time.

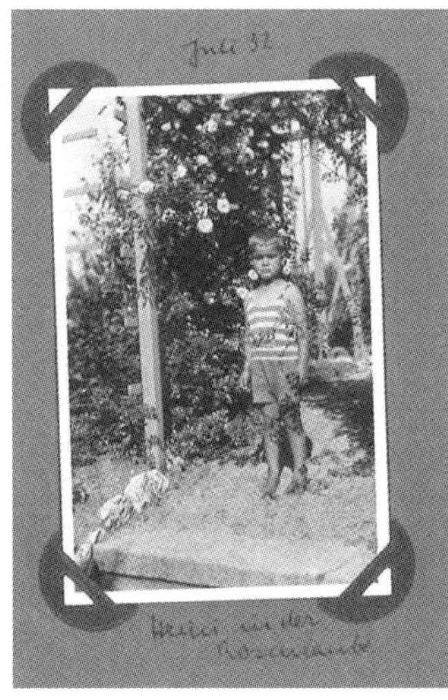

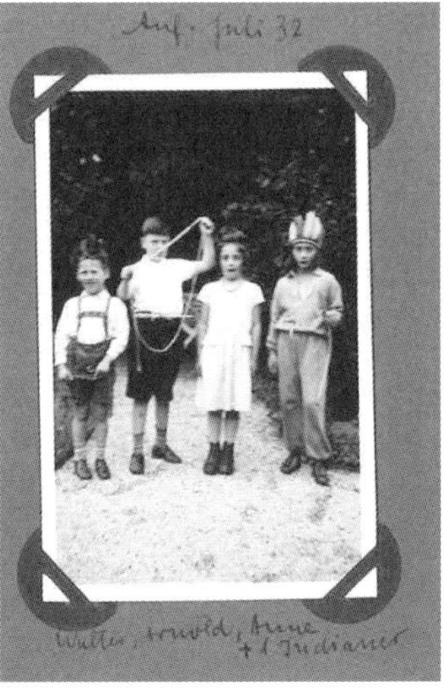

Meanwhile, the situation in Germany was getting worse. 'Gradually the impact of the surrounding enmity did weigh terribly on us.' Walter and his stepsister Marianne were no longer allowed to go to their elementary school and were sent to the Jewish Hebrew School instead. Hedi recalled the sight of banners in the streets of her parents' hometown saying 'Juden raus': Jews out. 'By and by, the whole population got infected by the anti-Semitic current.' Hedi and Fritz felt 'that there was no more air for our children to breathe.' Ultimately, they decided to emigrate to the United States after Karl Landauer, a family friend who had fled to Berkeley, California, because of his political affiliation, had suggested them to move to the 'golden state.' While preparing for their move, they sent their eldest children, including Walter, to a Jewish institute in Switzerland, where they stayed for nearly a year. After various setbacks, they finally sailed out of Hamburg on the *S.S. Washington* on December 29, 1936.

Walter was about to turn eleven when they arrived in New York. The family settled in Pasadena, California. At his Bar Mitzvah, he thanked his parents for bringing him 'out of Germany, where our fellow Jews have to suffer and to work live slaves. I thank God for the resolution of my parents to bring me into the wonderful country of freedom and tolerance.' He concluded his speech by making a promise: 'I will try my best to be a good son, an ambitious student, a loyal Jew, and an intelligent citizen of this country and of the world.'

After four years, Walter and his family moved to Los Angeles. He graduated from high school and enrolled at Stanford University thanks to the Army Specialized Training Reserve Program. However, the program was canceled three to four months after he got in, as the army was in dire need of replacements. And so, Walter was sent to Camp Roberts, Georgia, and to Wisconsin to receive his training. 'It was an awfully hot summer and he had a terribly hard time there with all the infantry practice which they had to perform,' Hedi remembered. Early December 1944, Walter arrived in England. He wrote home that 'a troopship is not a luxury liner.'

In Europe, Walter served with the 304th Infantry Regiment, 76th Infantry Division. After more than eight years, he was back in Germany. 'The majority are glad to see us hear [sic] because they are sick and tired of war. Most of them claim they are not nazis and the real ones went into the interior (ha-ha-ha),' Walter wrote to Fritz and Hedi in March 1945.

In her memoirs, Hedi said that Walter was on a reconnaissance mission in the German state of Thuringia when he was wounded. He sat right next to the jeep driver as he spoke German. When they stopped at a crossroads in the middle of a forest to read the signs, Walter was shot in the head, according to Hedi. He never regained consciousness and died of his wounds at the age of nineteen on April 14, 1945. Walter's death hit the family hard. It was particularly hard on Fritz, who had lost his only son. 'America had won this war, but our family had paid a terrible price and the so-called victory mood was certainly not present in our house.'

They decided to leave Walter in Margraten, where he rests in Plot A, Row 6, Grave 30. Far away from his family in the U.S., but just across the border of Germany: the country where he both had been born and had died.

Page from the family's photo album with photos taken in Germany in 1932. The young Walter wears traditional lederhosen in several pictures.
SOURCE: Deborah Silver

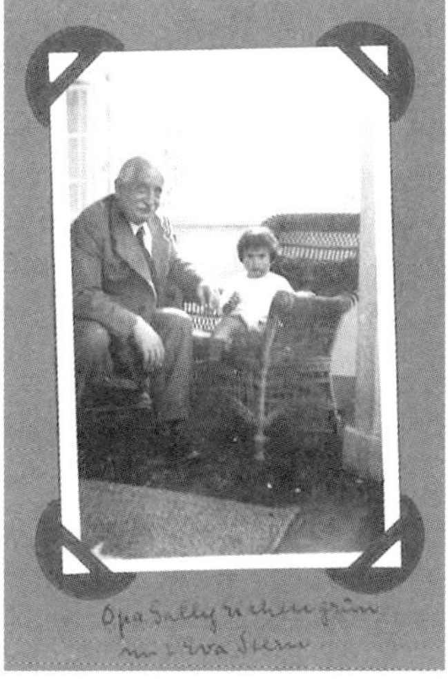

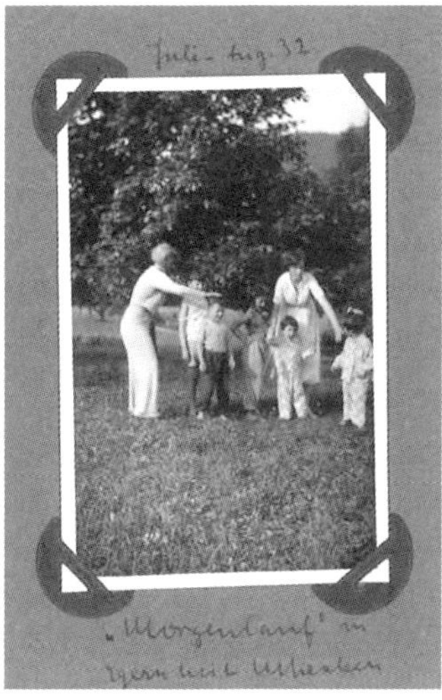

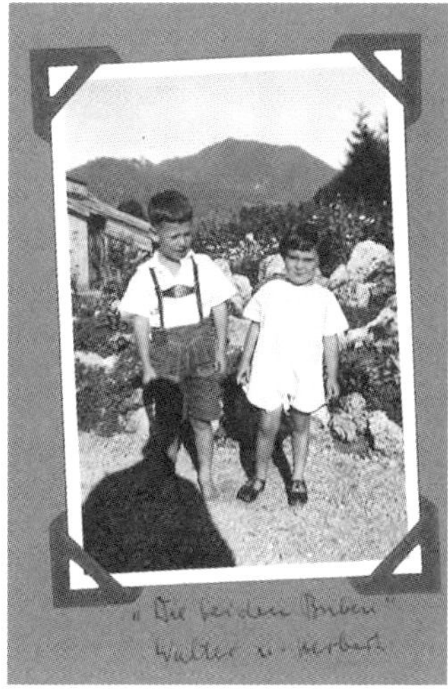

PHILIP T. BIXBY JR.

First Lieutenant

2nd Armored Division

Quiet heroism and aggressive courage

First Lieutenant Philip Taylor Bixby Jr. from Appleton, Wisconsin, was born on September 5, 1916. He was raised on a farm and running it was a tradition he wanted to continue. Therefore, he took a short course 'Farm and Industry' at the University of Wisconsin–Madison. Philip was known to be business-oriented and pragmatic, and his commitment to the family was unwavering. In 1941, he married the love of his life, his high school sweetheart Rosemary Pekarske. Together, they managed a family farm along Prospect Avenue in Appleton until Philip left home to enter the army in January 1942. Following his training, Philip served as a tank commander in the 67th Armored Regiment of the 2nd Armored Division 'Hell on Wheels.'

While Philip was already serving overseas, his father died in March 1943. A few weeks later, his brother Charles Howard Bixby, a Navy pilot, was reported missing in action in the Pacific. He was killed in a plane crash in the Solomon Sea on March 28, 1943 and never returned home...

In January 1945, Philip was back home in the U.S. for a 30-day leave. When this short but pleasant time with his family in Appleton ended, he returned to the European battlefield and rejoined his unit in Germany. There, on April 14, 1945, he made the ultimate sacrifice for his country at the age of 28. According to a book titled *History of the 67th Armored Regiment*, Philip 'was shot and killed by an enemy sniper as he was placing his H Co. platoon in position. Thus ended a career the hallmark of which was quiet heroism and aggressive courage,' the book says of him. 'His loss was keenly felt by all officers and men of the command.'

Besides his widow Rosemary, Philip was survived by his mother Alice, his sister Janet, a brother named John, and two sons. Ronald, his second son, was born in November 1945, several months after Philip's passing...

Philip was given his final resting place at the Netherlands American Cemetery and Memorial in Margraten, where he rests in peace in Plot J, Row 8, Grave 17.

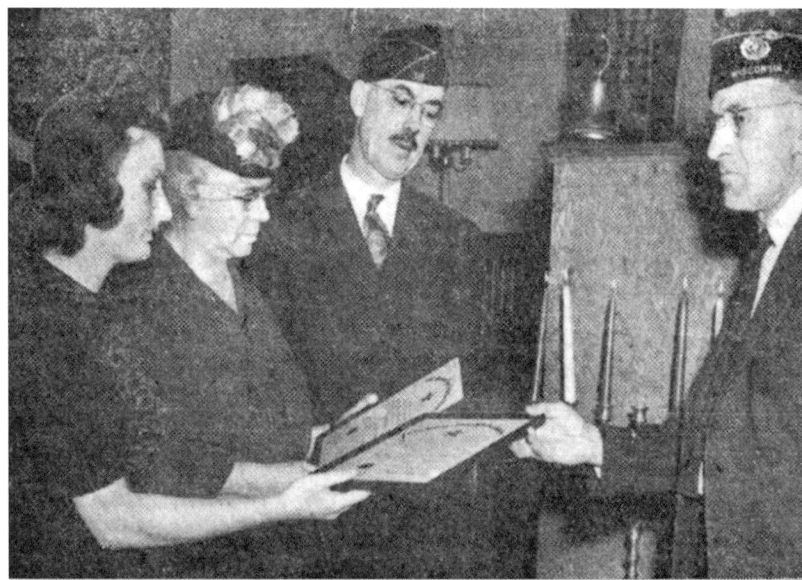

RECEIVE GOLD STAR CERTIFICATES—Oney Johnston post of the American Legi
served Pearl Harbor day last evening with presentation of gold star certificates to r
kin of 70 veterans who died in the service. The above picture shows presentation by th
Dascomb E. Forbush of certificates to Mrs. Phil T. Bixby, Jr., 510 West Eighth stree
Mrs. Phil T. Bixby, Sr., 512 Memorial drive, as Helm C. Hussner, post commander lo
Mrs. Bixby, Sr., lost two sons, Phil T. Bixby, Jr., and Charles Howard Bixby. (Post-C
Photo.)

Presentation of two Gold Star certificates in honor of Philip and Charles Howard Bixby to their mother and Philip's widow, December 1945. SOURCE: terraceviews.org/*The Post-Crescent*

HARRY G. BRICKHOUSE JR.

First Lieutenant

45th Tank Battalion

'A nice tank commander'

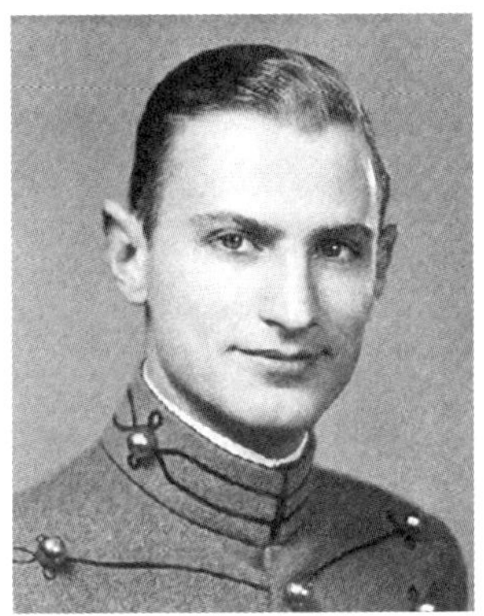

First Lieutenant Harry G. Brickhouse Jr. was born on October 21, 1919. He grew up in Fort Worth and Galveston, Texas, where his father was an executive with Southwest Bell Telephone. Harry attended St. Mary's College in San Antonio, where he participated in the Reserve Officers' Training Corps (ROTC) for four years. He was also on the boxing team and played football.

Less than a month after graduating from St. Mary's with a Bachelor's degree in June 1941, Harry entered the United States Military Academy in West Point, New York. As a cadet he demonstrated leadership potential from the start. He was also generous in contributing what little free time he had toward helping classmates resolve academic or military problems. He was a member of the Corps Squad lacrosse and cross-country teams, and he coached intramural football.

Harry graduated from West Point in 1944, and on the day he graduated he married his girlfriend, Mary McDonald. They were not able to spend time together for long because Harry was deployed to Europe in January 1945. He assumed command of a platoon of Company A, 45th Tank Battalion, 13th Armored Division, which he led into the German town of Hiddinghausen on April 15, 1945. Because Harry was in command, his Sherman tank was the lead tank of the platoon.

Corporal Al Morehouse, Harry's radio operator and gunner, later told what happened to his tank commander there. While moving slowly through the village, Morehouse looked out of the hatch and Harry came up to take a look around from the other hatch. Then a sharp cracking sound caused them to look at each other and ask, 'What was that?' 'That was our last conversation because ten, fifteen seconds later he got shot through the head by a sniper,' Morehouse told decades later during a filmed interview in which he struggled with his emotions. 'Lieutenant Brickhouse was a nice officer, a nice tank commander,' Morehouse also said of him.

Harry was 25 years old when he died. He was survived by his wife Mary and his daughter Mary Anne, who was born three months after his death. In Margraten, Harry is buried in Plot J, Row 8, Grave 6.

HARLAN L. HERRSCHER

Private First Class

8th Armored Division

The recovered dog tags

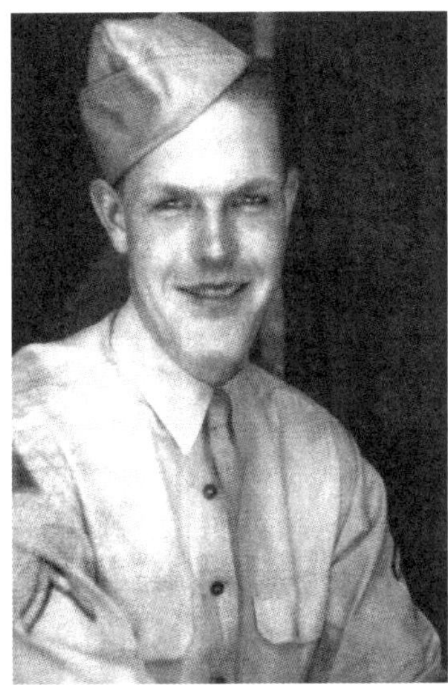

War leaves its traces for a long time, both mentally and physically. Remnants of the battle continue to mark the locations of former battlefields today. Those who look for them are likely to find bullets, shell cases, perhaps a helmet, or other pieces of equipment. With the help of metal detectors sometimes even the remains of missing soldiers have been recovered. Near Margraten, father and son Jorritsma discovered something remarkable as well: the dog tags of Harlan Herrscher. They were immediately set on returning the set of tags to his family. They were found in St. Louis, where Harlan grew up.

Harlan was an only child, but not the only child in the house. He lived with his father and mother, his uncle and aunt, and their three children in a house in south St. Louis. It was a poor neighborhood in the 1930s. One of the children slept on the couch, another in the dining room. For Harlan, the porch had been turned into a bedroom. The two fathers tried to sustain their families by accepting any job they could get. Life in poverty was not easy, but at least the four boys had each other, seeing themselves as actual brothers.

On June 23, 1943, just before his nineteenth birthday, Harlan reported for duty. He was assigned to the 8th Armored Division. After almost two years of service, a German boobytrap killed him. One of his friends found a Luger, a German army pistol that was a popular souvenir among American soldiers. However, they could not phantom that it was a trap. Attached to the weapon was an explosive device that went off when they picked it up. Harlan died on April 15, 1945, at the age of twenty.

The quest to find his family was successful within just one week. With help coming from as far as Australia, the search of the Jorritsma family led them to two surviving brothers. It helped that one of them, Rick, had played for the New York Mets.

After that, things moved quickly. The families exchanged addresses, and the Jorritsma family posted the envelope with the tag as soon as they could. A few days after the first contact, Rick held the slightly rusted dog tag in his hands.

We are talking about the year 2016 here. 71 years after his death, a part of Harlan came home. Harlan himself rests in Plot I, Row 19, Grave 11.

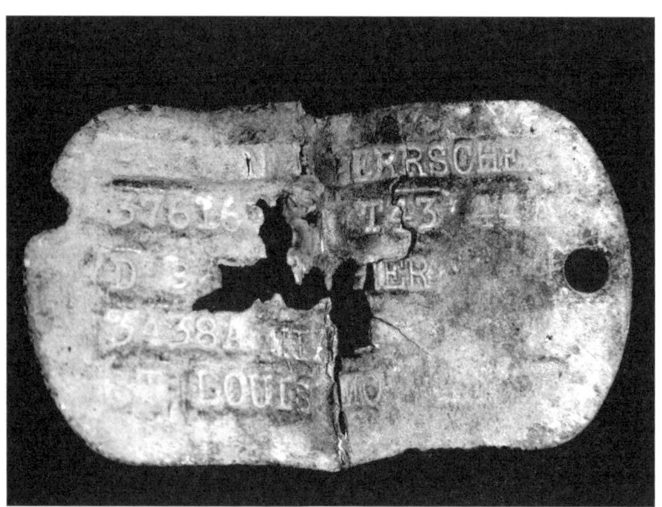

The dog tag of Harlan L. Herrscher.
SOURCE: Peter van Pelt

DONALD L. GILES

Technical Sergeant

35th Infantry Division

Died from lack of medical care

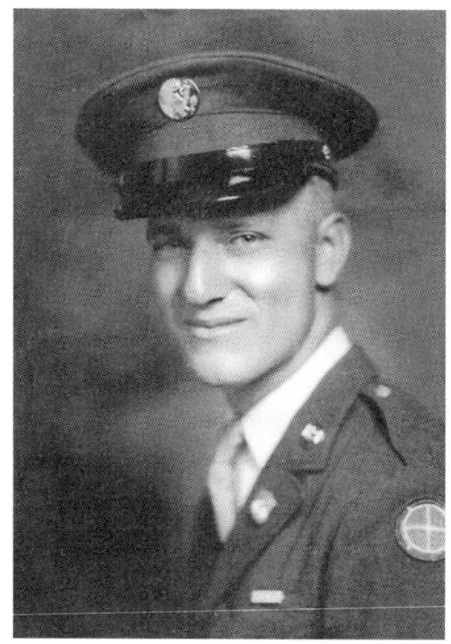

Donald L. Giles from Nebraska was born in 1919. He grew up on his family's farm and in 1936 he graduated from Nebraska City High School with excellent grades. Before entering the army in February 1941, he was a farmer north of Nebraska City. Two months after joining the armed forces, Donald married Eileen Harris in April 1941.

According to a newspaper article, Donald joined the 320th Infantry Regiment of the 35th Infantry Division in March 1942. This division arrived in England in May 1944 and was then transferred to Normandy in July. Several days upon its arrival on the Normandy battlefield, Donald earned the Silver Star, which was awarded to him in October. His citation reads:

> ***'At the outset of an attack against the enemy on the morning of 11 July 1944, Sergeant Giles was struck in the shoulder by a sniper bullet. Despite his wound, he remained at the head of his men, personally destroyed an enemy machine gun nest with automatic rifle fire, and continued to lead his squad for ten hours before allowing himself to be evacuated for first aid. The qualities of leadership, unusual devotion to duty, and tenacity of purpose displayed by Sergeant Giles served as an inspiration to his men, and reflect high credit upon his character as a soldier.'***

After a recovery period behind the front, Donald reported back to his regiment at the end of the month. On November 8, 1944, however, he was wounded for a second time. His by now digitalized Hospital Admission Card states he suffered wounds to his buttock, hip and arm, and that they were caused by enemy artillery fire. It was not until March that he returned to his outfit in Germany.

On April 15, 1945, Donald was shot in the hip and taken prisoner by the Germans. He died the following day from lack of medical care. He was 26 years old and the father of a three-year-old daughter, named Sherry Ann. Donald is buried in Margraten, where his final resting place can be found in Plot E, Row 11, Grave 26.

THOMAS B. KILMER

Technician Fifth Grade

1301st Engineer General Service Regiment

The cab with the telegram

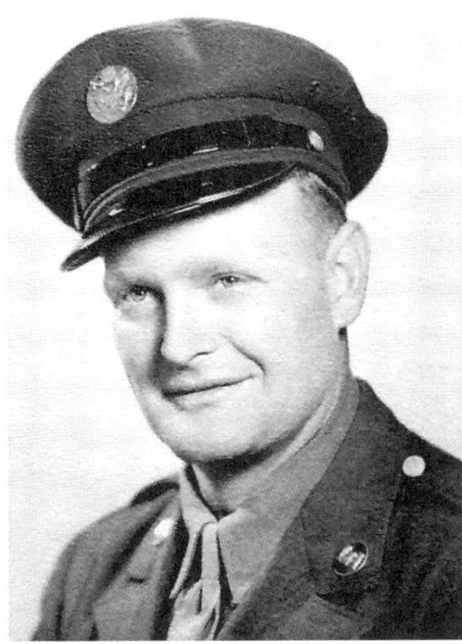

On the early morning of May 1, 1945, a cab turned into the driveway of Harry and Etta Purcell. They were the in-laws of Thomas Kilmer, who lived on a farm in Hood, Texas. His wife Nora and their son Larry moved in with them after Thomas had entered the army in June 1943. On the passenger seat of the cab was a telegram with the dreaded words 'deep sympathy in the loss of ...' Still unsuspecting, the twelve-year-old Larry was waiting for the school bus when the driver asked him if Nora Kilmer lived here. 'Yes, that's my mother. She's up at the house,' he replied. Soon after, he knew it was bad news.

His grandparents' farm was not unknown territory for Larry. After his parents got married at the age of seventeen, they were given a piece of land to farm there. His father's parents had died at an early age. Larry, born in 1932, had therefore never met them. However, he knew his maternal grandparents all the better. After a few years of living as a farmer, Thomas, who went by his middle name Blake, got a job with an oil company. So, he and Nora had to move every few months. Larry continued to live with his grandparents so that he would not have to find a new school and make new friends over and over again. He spent the summers with his parents, wherever they lived at the time.

This came to an end in June 1943. Because his work in the oil industry was important to the war effort, Thomas had been exempted from the service. Larry's father, however, felt that it was unfair to all his friends and family who served. So, he voluntarily enlisted anyway. Thomas served with the 1301st Engineer General Service Regiment until April 16, 1945. He mostly worked with explosives, as he did on that fateful day. Fearing that an unstable bridge near the German city of Jena was going to collapse, the regiment decided to blow it up. However, the bridge collapsed while the men of the unit were still putting the explosives in place. Thomas was one of many who perished. He was 34 years old.

On the bus to school, Larry could think of nothing but the telegram. Initially, he thought one of his uncles might have been killed. However, he knew that this could not be true when the cab driver asked for his mother. Not much later, an aunt came chasing down the school bus. He got in with her in the car. She was crying. 'Larry, your daddy is dead.' He felt numb. All he could say was 'OK.'

At home, his mother sat silently staring in the chair. She handed him the telegram. 'Well, you are the man of the family now.' Larry, still just a child, did not know what to say. But he knew he had to keep going. However, at every important moment in life, he would deeply miss his father, who would never know what had become of his son. His father rests in Plot D, Row 11, Grave 32.

JOHN T. RESLER

First Lieutenant

3rd Armored Division

Utter disregard for his own personal safety

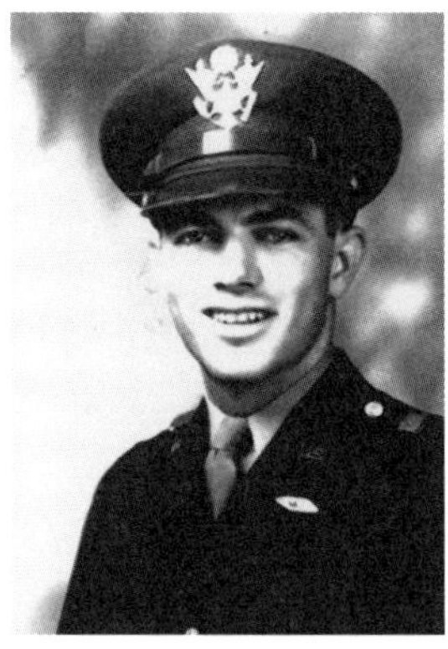

First Lieutenant John T. Resler from Oklahoma was born in 1920. He attended the Oklahoma Military Academy in Claremore and graduated in 1940. He then attended Oklahoma Agricultural and Mechanical College in Stillwater, but while in his senior year, he enlisted into the army in February 1942.

John was a tank commander in the 83rd Armored Reconnaissance Battalion of the 3rd Armored Division, which sailed to England in September 1943 and entered combat in Normandy in July 1944. While in France, John was wounded on August 9, 1944, when the Luftwaffe bombed the general area of the Battalion CP and a bomb landed about ten feet from his tank. He recovered but was wounded again on November 14, 1944, in Germany, this time by a mortar. John was given a leave and returned home in January 1945 to recuperate and spend time with family and friends in Oklahoma. He returned to Europe in February and reported back to his unit in Germany.

On April 17, 1945, three weeks before Nazi Germany surrendered, John gave his life at the age of 24. Several months later, John's parents received a letter from the War Department in which they were told that their son had been awarded the Bronze Star Medal posthumously for his heroic action on the day he was killed. Also included in this letter was the citation by which they learned how John had lost his life. The citation was published in the *Claremore Progress* on August 29, 1945, and reads as follows:

> ***'For heroic achievement in action against the enemy in Germany on 17 April 1945. First Lieutenant Resler, in command of a platoon, took part in the attack on the town of Thurland, Germany, and in the assault one of his tank crew dismounted to procure more ammunition from a nearby ammunition carrier. The man was shot in the arm and fell to the ground. Lt. Resler, with utter disregard for his own personal safety, went to his aid in spite of heavy small arms and bazooka fire. As he reached his side, he was fired upon by several snipers and mortally wounded.'***

At a later date, the decoration was presented to John's parents. He was given his final resting place in Margraten because they decided to let him rest peacefully in Europe among other fallen servicemen. John's permanent gravesite in Margraten can be found in Plot I, Row 14, Grave 6.

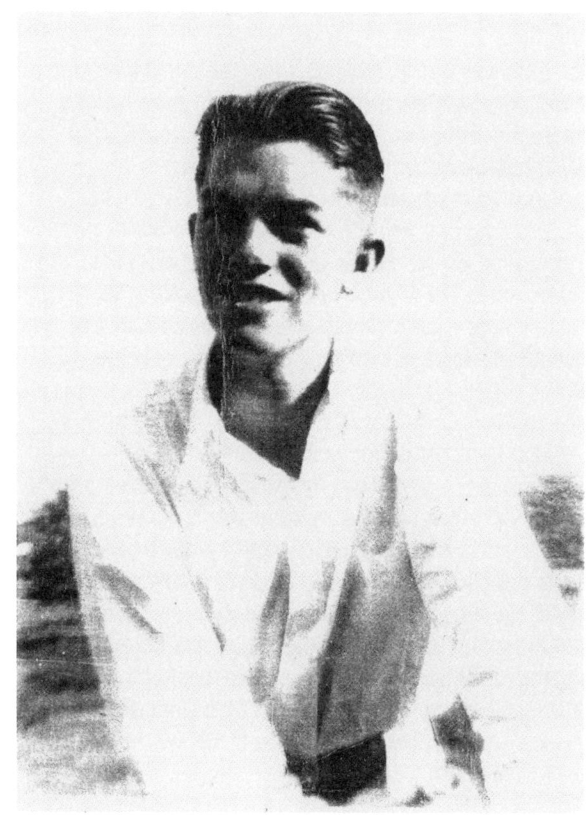

RICHARD E. DAVIS

Corporal

743rd Tank Battalion

One of the final battle casualties of his battalion

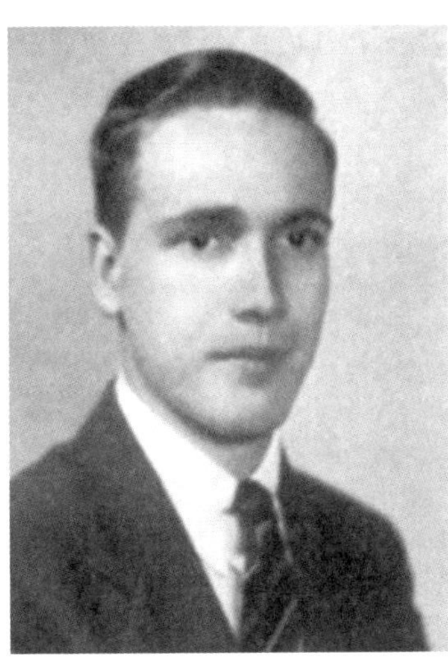

Corporal Richard E. Davis was born in 1923. His hometown was Metuchen, New Jersey, where he graduated from high school in 1940. He married Kathryn McDevitt with whom he had two children.

On September 21, 1943, Richard reported to Newark, New Jersey, to enter the army. He was assigned to Company C, 743rd Tank Battalion and served overseas as gunner in a Sherman tank. This type of tank was usually armed with a 75mm gun fitted in its turret that proved to be not powerful enough to knock out Germany's heavy tanks at long range.

On D-Day, Richard's unit was deployed on Omaha Beach in Normandy. With the available sources, it cannot be determined whether he himself participated in the invasion or not. But given the date of his enlistment, this could well have been the case. Anyway, after the invasion, the 743rd Tank Battalion was involved in the entire campaign in France and Belgium, after which its tanks crossed the Dutch border and – along with the 30th Infantry Division – advanced through the southern part of Limburg. Subsequently, the battalion was engaged in bitter fighting to penetrate the Siegfried Line. In December, the tank companies withdrew into Belgium, where they supported the 30th Infantry Division to repel the German winter offensive in the Ardennes.

Three weeks before the war in Europe ended, the 743rd Tank Battalion had advanced as far as the German city of Magdeburg. There the battalion suffered its final battle casualties. One of them was Richard. He was killed in action on April 17, 1945, when his tank was struck by a Panzerfaust – the German's version of a bazooka on a stick. The armor-piercing rocket penetrated the cast steel directly beside Richard's gunner's seat, killing him at the age of 22. His commander, Lieutenant Bernard Fruhwirth, was alive when he was lifted from the turret but died shortly afterward in a hospital. The third man in the turret, PFC Robert Andrews, the loader, escaped with wounds.

Richard, who was survived by his wife and two children, got his final resting place at the U.S. Military Cemetery in Margraten. He is permanently laid to rest in Plot B, Row 6, Grave 18.

CHARLES O. FRINKS

Private

44th Cavalry Reconnaissance Squadron

A 'Good Time Charlie'

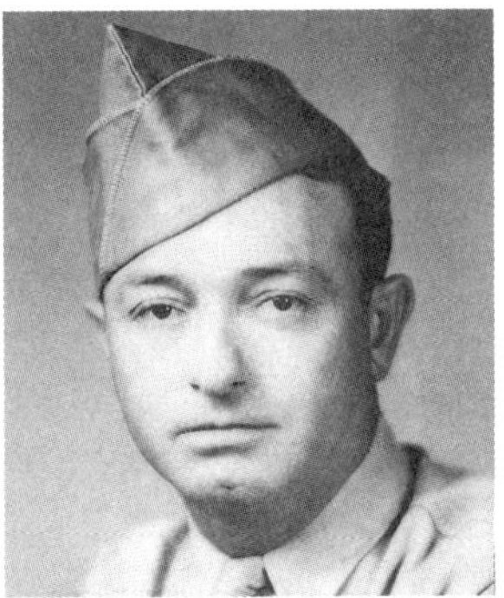

Private Charles O. Frinks from Alexandria, Virginia, was born on October 26, 1905. In 1927, he married Faye Purvis, with whom he had two children, a daughter named Jean and a son named Charles. According to Jean's memories, her father was a 'Good Time Charlie' in every respect, meaning he was a carefree and convivial person given to his frequent pursuit of fun and amusement. He loved to dance, had a pleasing singing voice, and enjoyed fishing and hunting.

Charles worked as a machinist at Fruit Growers Express in Alexandria. The family moved to Lansdowne, Pennsylvania, in 1940, where Charles had taken a job at the U.S. Navy Yard in Philadelphia. They remained there until the U.S. entered the war, at which time Charles enlisted in the Regular Army.

'I doubt that he would have been drafted given his occupation, age and having two children, but he enlisted out of patriotism and his sense of adventure,' his daughter Jean later wrote. Charles entered the military in November 1942, received basic training at Fort Leonard Wood, Missouri, and was subsequently assigned to the 8th Reconnaissance Troop of the 8th Infantry Division. In 1943, this unit was re-designated as the 44th Cavalry Reconnaissance Squadron. In spite of the age difference, Charles was well liked by his fellow soldiers. He was referred to as 'Pop' and was assigned to C Troop, in which he served until he met his death in Salzwedel, Germany, on April 17, 1945.

According to a brief biography of him published by the American World War II Orphans Network, Charles was riding in a jeep enroute to a guard post when he was killed by a sniper's bullet (although his digitized Hospital Admission Card File states his death would have been caused by fragments of an artillery shell). Charles was 39 years old and is permanently interred at the Netherlands American Cemetery and Memorial in Margraten. There, he is laid to rest in Plot E, Row 2, Grave 14.

A week prior to his death, Charles had received injuries on April 10, for which he had been awarded the Purple Heart on April 13, Jean recalled. 'He mailed the medal to my mother and enclosed a note dated April 16th which read: "Hi One and Only! Just a word or two to say I'm OK and still love you. Just a little remembrance or souvenir for my Honey. Please excuse the scribble. Love to all, COF [Charles O. Frinks]. PS – Will meet you again at the spring." He was killed the next day...'

HENRY W. JOHNSON
Captain
2nd Armored Division

Killed by a bazooka shell

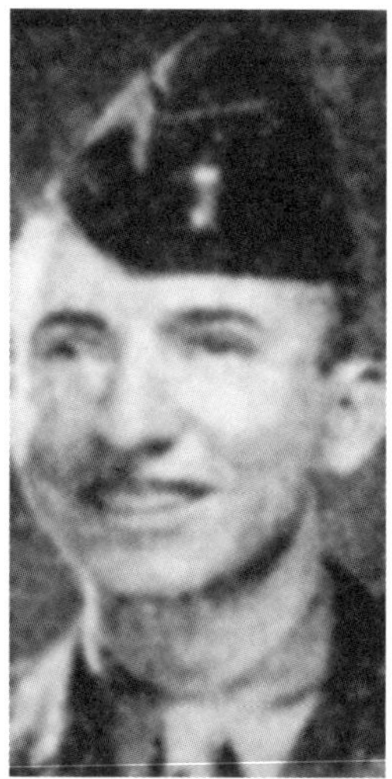

Henry W. Johnson from Alabama was born in 1919. He graduated from the University of Florida in June 1942 and then immediately joined the army. In September 1943, Henry was sent overseas to England, where he was assigned to the 66th Armored Regiment of the 2nd Armored Division 'Hell on Wheels.'

Henry entered combat in France, where his division disembarked on Omaha Beach three days after the initial Normandy landings. He was wounded on October 11, 1944, after which he was sent to a hospital in England. His recovery took three months.

In January 1945, Henry returned to his regiment to be deployed in combat again. The following month, he was promoted to Captain and given command of Company F. By this time Henry was an experienced tank officer who had seen a lot of combat. Thanks to his experience on the European battlefield, Henry also knew that in many cases the Sherman tanks were no match for the heavier German tanks. His opinion regarding the quality of American tanks compared to those of the Germans is included in a report produced in March 1945 for General Eisenhower titled 'United States vs. German Equipment.' Henry's conclusion was very clear:

> ***'In general, it is my opinion that our Sherman tanks rank clumsily with the German Mark III and Mark IV tanks, and their Mark V [Panther] and Mark VI [Tiger] tanks are in a class by themselves, having a better silhouette, better armor, better flotation and maneuverability, far better guns with much better sight reticules, and superior ammunition.'***

During the final weeks of the war in Europe, the 'Hell on Wheels' Division penetrated deeper into Germany. Final victory was within reach for the Allies, but Henry did not live to see it. He was killed in action during an attack on the city of Magdeburg on April 17, 1945. He was 25 years old.

Shortly after the war in Europe ended, Henry's parents received a letter from Captain Luke Bolin, Regimental Protestant chaplain. He had learned details about Henry's death and described them in his letter. He wrote:

> ***'On March 28, this Division crossed the Rhine River and began a rapid push which sealed this Ruhr pocket and took us within sixty miles of Berlin. On April 17, combat command "A", in conjunction with the 30th Infantry Division, began an attack on the city of Magdeburg, Germany. From a hill outside the city, I watched the attack begin and then went back to the medical company [to] support our part of the attack. Before very long some slightly wounded men from "F" Company came in for treatment and they informed me that Captain Johnson had been killed in action. A little later an Infantry Lieutenant whose infantrymen were working with "F" Company, came in and told me how it happened. As they were advancing through the suburbs of the town he was wounded and Captain Johnson got out of his tank to remove him to a safe position. Then, unfortunately, a German bazooka shell [fired by a Panzerfaust or Panzerschreck] hit near them and shrapnel from it killed Captain Johnson. The Infantry Lieutenant had the highest praise for Captain Johnson as an efficient Combat Officer and was very sad that he was killed.'***

Henry's body was transferred to the U.S. Military Cemetery at Margraten and laid to rest after a Protestant chaplain had conducted a funeral service. Henry is still buried there. His final resting place can be found in Plot J, Row 9, Grave 14.

JAMES L. HELMS
First Lieutenant
30th Infantry Division

'Died for the worthy cause of human freedom'

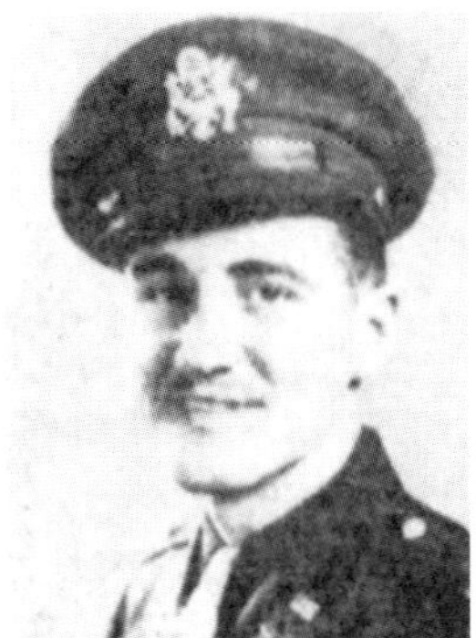

First Lieutenant James L. Helms, who was born in Concord, North Carolina, on March 19, 1922, grew up with four brothers and two sisters. He fell in love with Frances Russell of Hattiesburg, Mississippi, whom he married. When James was killed, he had been in the army for six years. James had first been stationed at the Panama Canal for two years before going to Europe in the spring of 1944.

James joined the 30th 'Old Hickory' Infantry Division and was attached to Item Company of the 119th Infantry Regiment. Along with several other units, the Old Hickory Division liberated much of southern Limburg in September 1944. Troops of the 119th Infantry Regiment liberated the village of Margraten on the 13th. Without being aware of it at the time, the men walked across the fields and through the fruit meadows on which, a few months later, the U.S. Military Cemetery would be created and where many of them would be buried...

One of the Old Hickory men who would be interred there was James. He was killed at the age of 23 during an attack on the German town of Diesdorf on April 17, 1945. How he met his death in combat was revealed to his widow Frances in a letter she received from Colonel R. A. Baker, commanding officer of the 119th Infantry Regiment. In it, he described that James had set up a forward observation post to direct artillery fire in support of a rifle company that was attacking the town.

'He was killed instantly by machine gun fire from a tank,' the colonel wrote. 'He is keenly missed by his comrades here, both officers and enlisted men. Because of his courageous example in making the supreme sacrifice, we are devoting ourselves to the unfinished tasks before us with renewed strength. (...) Lieutenant Helms came to this theater of operations in an hour of international crisis, and had a part in the greatest military struggle in history,' Colonel Baker continued. 'He served his country nobly and well, and acquitted himself with honor as a soldier in the United States Army. In your hours of bereavement, may it be a source of real comfort for you to know that he died for the worthy cause of human freedom, and to help bring this war to an end.'

Colonel Baker also wrote that James was buried in Margraten. James was given his final resting place here as well, situated among the graves of dozens of other men of his regiment. Visitors of the cemetery can pay tribute to him by going to Plot P, Row 14, Grave 6.

LESLIE I. LOVELAND
Technician Fifth Grade
782nd Airborne Ordnance Maintenance Company

Died with mother and brother by his side

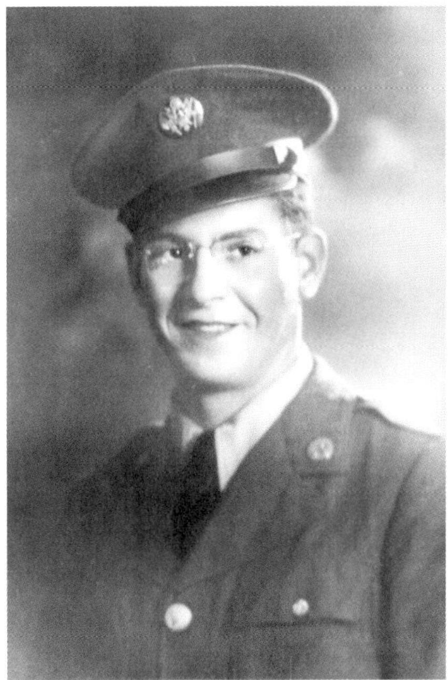

In places they had never heard of, far from their homes, families, and friends, soldiers lost their lives. But Leslie Loveland was not alone in Europe. Like his brother Freeman, Leslie Loveland served in the 82nd Airborne Division; their mother Laura worked for Supreme Commander Dwight D. Eisenhower. So, when Leslie was badly injured and doctors feared for his life, no effort was spared to get Laura and Freeman to him in time.

The Lovelands lived in the rural village of Harrisonville, New Jersey. On their motorcycles, the brothers regularly made Main Street, also the only street in the village, unsafe. It was also there that Leslie met Dorothy Hunt, to whom he got engaged before entering the army.

All four members of the family did their part during the war. Freeman had enlisted even before the U.S. was attacked at Pearl Harbor. A year later, in October 1942, his brother Leslie also voluntarily entered the service. Before that, just like his father, he had worked at the Deepwater DuPont plant, which produced for the war industry. Mother Laura decided she also wanted to contribute to the war effort and signed up for the Women's Auxiliary Corps. That's how almost the entire family ended up in Europe. While overseas, the three family members would meet on several occasions when they were on leave.

Leslie arrived in Europe in December 1943. His unit was assigned to the 82nd Airborne Division, which took him to England, France, the Netherlands, and Belgium, among other places. He sent all the money that he earned in the army to his 'Dot' so they could save for their wedding and a house.

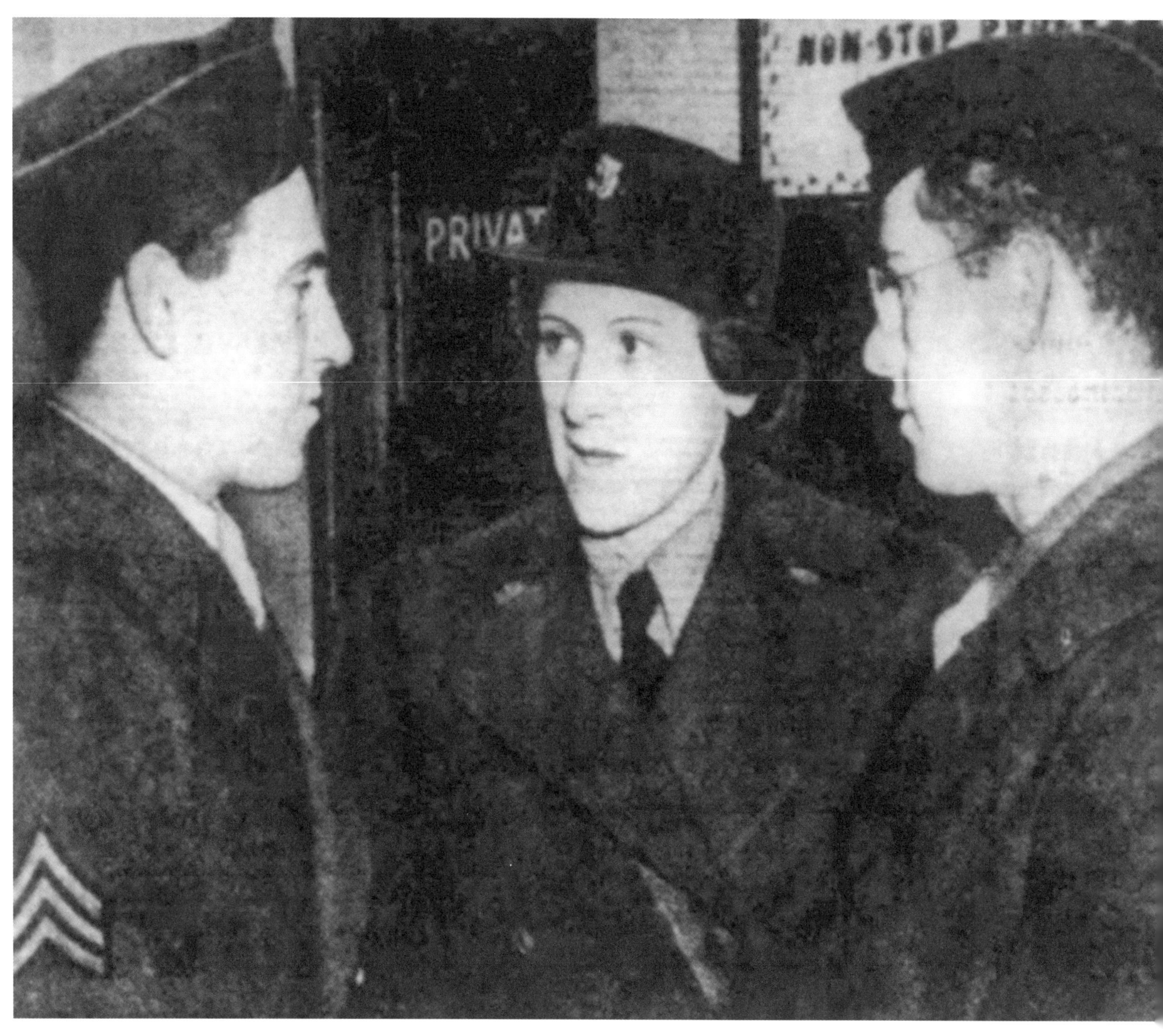
NON-STOP
PRIVAT

On April 18, 1945, Leslie was seriously injured when he tried to defuse a German Panzerfaust. He was transferred to a hospital in Cologne, Germany, where his leg had to be amputated. His injuries were so severe that his brother, who was in Germany as well, and mother were informed. 82nd Airborne Division commander James Gavin sent his personal plane to make sure that not only Freeman, but also Laura could be with Leslie. In their presence, he died two days later. Together they buried him in Margraten. There he rests in Plot G, Row 1, Grave 26.

Speaking to a newspaper later, his mother Laura tried to stay strong. 'Just to have been with my son through his last hours and the consolation of having known exactly what happened to him gives me courage to carry on,' she said. Not long before his death, Laura had received a Bronze Star from Supreme Commander Eisenhower for her work at his headquarters.

His brother Freeman named his own son after Leslie to ensure that his memory would live on.

◀ **A family reunion in Ireland. Leslie stands on the right. SOURCE:** ***The Morning Post*****/Newspapers.com**

KENNETH W. NICKEL
Corporal
741st Tank Battalion

A sunken tank

Corporal Kenneth W. Nickel was born in Union Township, Guthrie County, Iowa, on April 27, 1922. Along with seven siblings, he grew up on the family farm. The family was not very well off financially. Kenneth's father therefore did odd jobs as a painter.

At the age of twenty, with World War II in full swing, Kenneth entered the army at Camp Dodge Herrold, Iowa, in January 1943. He was assigned to Company C of the 741st Tank Battalion and completed training to become a crew member of a Sherman tank.

Kenneth's battalion left for England in October 1943 and on D-Day the unit was deployed to support the 1st Infantry Division's landing on Omaha Beach. For this purpose, companies B and C were equipped with so-called DD or 'Duplex Drive' tanks. These amphibious tanks were modified M4 Shermans with a canvas flotation screen and two propellers powered by the tank's engine. The planners of the invasion had figured out that these tanks should swim ashore just before the landing of the first assault wave of infantry. On the beach, the DD tanks would knock out German machine gun nests and pillboxes that could otherwise decimate the vulnerable infantry troops.

However, the deployment of the 741st's DD tanks became almost a complete failure. The canvas flotation screens proved unable to withstand the high waves in the English Channel. As a result, 27 of the 29 launched DD tanks almost immediately sank upon leaving the Landing Craft Tanks (LCTs).

Kenneth's tank was one of the DD tanks that foundered in the rough seas while trying to 'swim' toward the sandy beach. Like the crew-men of the other sunken tanks, he was caught in a life and death struggle in the waves off Omaha Beach. Kenneth, however, was one of the lucky ones because he did not sink to a watery grave but survived, likely by latching on to one of the many life rafts thrown from the decks of the nearby LCTs.

After the initial Normandy landings, Kenneth rejoined the Allied advance toward Germany. He participated in many battles, including the assault on Germany's Siegfried Line and the Battle of the Bulge in the Ardennes.

When the German offensive in the Ardennes was finally repelled, Kenneth and his battalion pushed deeper into Germany. On April 18, 1945, the 741st Tank Battalion entered the city of Leipzig. While advancing around a street corner there, Kenneth's tank was suddenly struck by a Panzerfaust. The Panzerfaust penetrated the armor, killing Kenneth and the four other members of his crew. Therefore, Kenneth remained forever 22. He got his final resting place at the Netherlands American Cemetery in Margraten, which can be found in Plot N, Row 22, Grave 11.

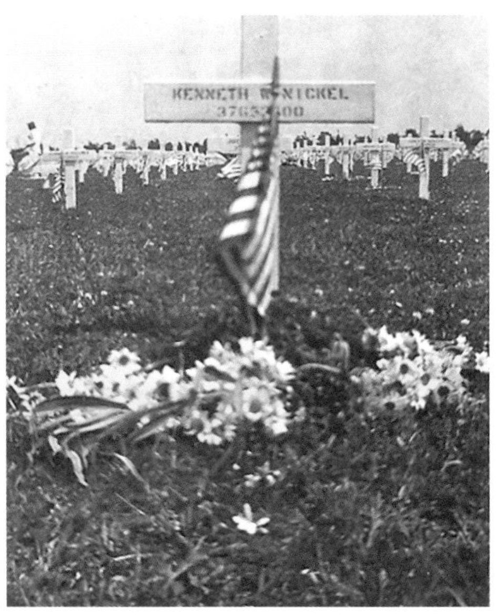

Kenneth Nickel's grave in the temporary American cemetery in Eisenach, Germany. SOURCE: Jochen Reinders

JOSEPH A. BARNSHAW

Private

135th Anti-Aircraft Artillery Gun Battalion

Regret

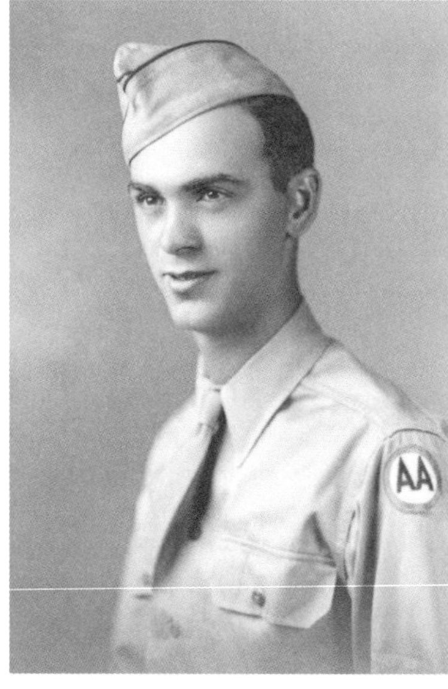

Around 1947, many next of kins had a difficult decision to make about where to permanently bury their loved ones. The parents of Joseph Andrew Barnshaw opted for leaving him overseas. However, they came to terribly regret their decision. They wanted him back home.

Joseph was born in Norristown, Pennsylvania, on April 17, 1920. He was the youngest of the three sons that Mary and Stanley Barnshaw had. Two of them, Joseph and Thomas, would serve during World War II. Before Joseph enlisted on July 17, 1943, he had married Elsie Hofsas. They did not have any children.

In August 1944, Joseph went overseas. At the time of his death, he served with Battery D of the 135th Anti-Aircraft Artillery Gun Battalion. He was killed in Osterberg, Germany, on April 22, 1945, and was buried in Margraten three days later. However, a letter to the army states that while Elsie 'notified his parents of his death, she has since refused to inform them as to where he is buried.' Mary and Stanley asked for any information about his burial place, which they received.

Elsie remarried in 1947 and relinquished her rights as a next of kin to Joseph's father. Before making a decision where to have their son buried, Mary inquired whether his body would be moved to another part of the cemetery or whether it would stay where it was. The army's response must have been satisfactory to them, as Stanley put on the 'Request of the Disposition of Remains' form that he had 'selected option #1 [interment in a permanent overseas cemetery] with the understanding that my son will be permanently buried in the United States Military Cemetery Margraten.'

In April 1949, Mary wrote to the army that they would travel to the Netherlands early August and asked for permission to visit her son's grave, 'which is the main reason for making this trip.' The army agreed, saying 'it is felt that this cemetery, while still incomplete, may be presentable for limited visits by the next of kin.'

A month after their trip, Stanley wrote a short note, saying that 'we have reconsidered our past decision in regards to our son,' without specifying why. The parents asked if Joseph could still be brought back home. The army's response was negative, briefly noting that the cemetery would soon be transferred to the care of the American Battle Monuments Commission and, therefore, that all burials were now considered to be permanent.

The parents then asked their congressman to make a plea on their behalf. Rep. Samuel K. McConnell wrote in November that 'Mrs. Barnshaw is ill and grieving over the fact that they previously consented for her son's remains to be interred in Holland. Is there no way that your regulations in such matters may be relaxed to relieve the above situation[?]' This time, the army offered a lengthier explanation, referring to the fact that all 'permanent burials' in Margraten had been completed by September 9, two days after Joseph's father had sent his initial letter. Therefore, as they explained, it would be impossible to make any changes as 'a grave cannot be exhumed without impairing the appearance of the cemetery as a permanent shrine.' It would have required to move the bodies from other graves to the vacant spot. It was a step the army was not willing to take, 'particularly when such moves involve the writing of new grave location letters to next of kin who have already been given permanent grave locations for the remains of their loved ones.'

Therefore, Joseph still rests in Plot L, Row 18, Grave 17. His brother Thomas returned home safe.

ERNEST C. LACY JR.
Captain
327th Engineer Combat Battalion

A true American soldier

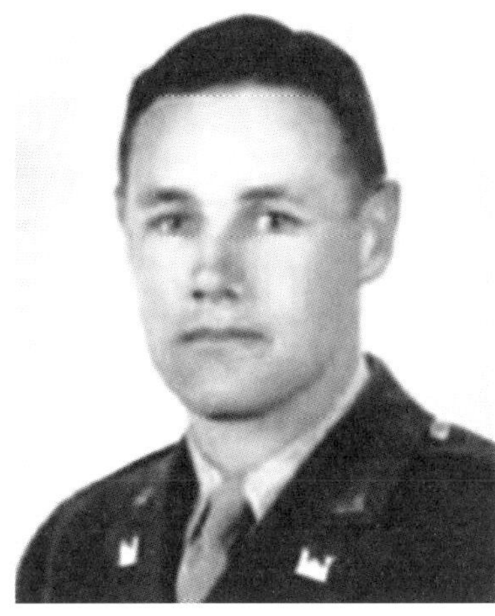

Captain Ernest C. Lacy Jr. was born in Virginia on June 6, 1920. He spent his childhood and boyhood days at Halifax, attending the Halifax High School from which he graduated in June 1936. In September 1936, he entered the Virginia Polytechnic Institute, leaving the school after three years of study to enter the famous United States Military Academy at West Point, New York, in 1939. Buck, as Ernest was known to his family and friends, graduated from West Point in January 1943, and was assigned to the Corps of Engineers. After a brief course at the Engineer Branch School at Fort Belvoir, Virginia, he joined the 327th Engineer Combat Battalion of the 102nd Infantry Division at Camp Maxey, Texas.

Buck's intelligence was unquestionable and while studying at West Point, his leadership was clearly demonstrated. Modesty, straightforwardness, sincerity, and clean thinking were characteristic of him. Buck had to spend little time studying. He learned quickly, and as a result was able to spend a great deal of time working on his favorite hobbies: movie making and pistol practice.

As an army officer, Buck was rapidly promoted to the rank of Captain. He was engaged in combat from October 1944 until his life was instantly ended by enemy small arms fire on April 28, 1945. An excerpt from *The Margraten Boys*, a book written by war historian Peter Schrijvers, provides more details: Buck was cut down by German machine gun fire while he was leading a patrol across the Elbe River in Germany. The purpose of the patrol was to prepare a crossing aimed at establishing contact with the Russians.

Buck was only 24 years old when he met his death, just ten days before the war in Europe finally came to an end. He had been an outstanding officer. This was emphasized by the battalion commander of the 327th Engineer Combat Battalion who wrote a letter of condolence to Buck's father:

> ***'Captain Lacy was a member of my staff, a natural born leader and commanded the respect of all the officers and enlisted men who knew him. His friendliness, sincerity, and loyalty, which distinguished him as a true American soldier, made him one of the best liked officers of my command.'***

Soon after the Allies had secured victory in Europe, it turned out that Buck was the only one from his small village who had not survived the war. His mother sometime later wrote: 'In our little town of 500 inhabitants he was the only one who lost his life. It was sad to see all of his friends coming home knowing I would never see him again.' In Margraten, Buck is buried in Plot D, Row 11, Grave 23.

DOROTHY JANE BURDGE

American Red Cross

An ill-fated pleasure flight in a captured German aircraft

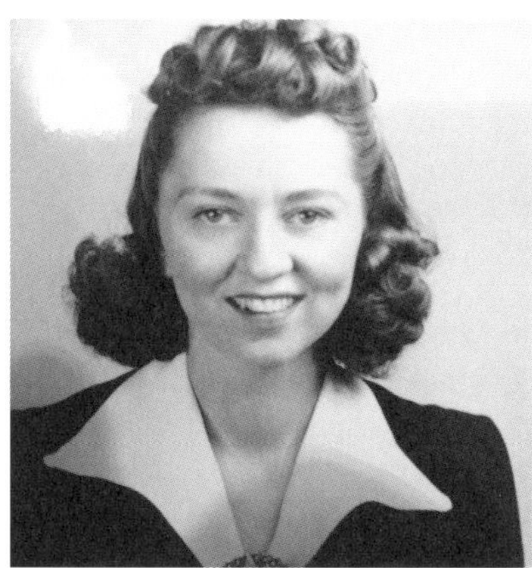

Dorothy Jane Burdge was born in Marion County, Ohio, on August 14, 1915. When she died in 1945, she was 29 years old. Dorothy had two sisters, Edna Lilian (age 32) and Grace (age 27). Dorothy trained as a teacher prior to volunteering with the American Red Cross (ARC). Her sister Grace also volunteered with this organization. After undergoing brief training, the sisters, along with a group of other volunteers, left for Great Britain in September 1943. Here they would be deployed as employees of the so-called Red Cross 'Club Mobiles,' canteen buses that delivered coffee, cigarettes, newspapers, and doughnuts to remote places such as shooting ranges, practice locations, and airfields.

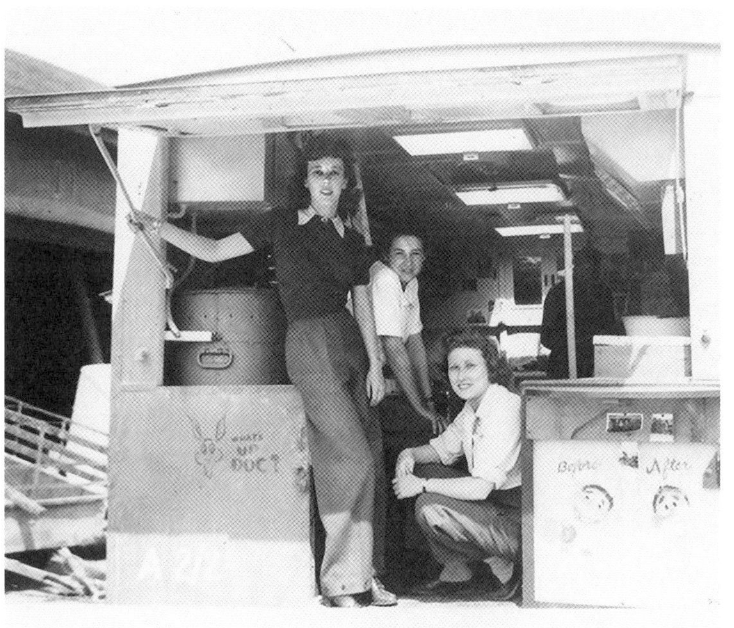

Clubmobiles visited the troops to offer them some relaxation. SOURCE: Arie-Jan van Hees

▶ The plane in which Dorothy Burdge died. SOURCE: Jerry Pinkowski via Arie-Jan van Hees

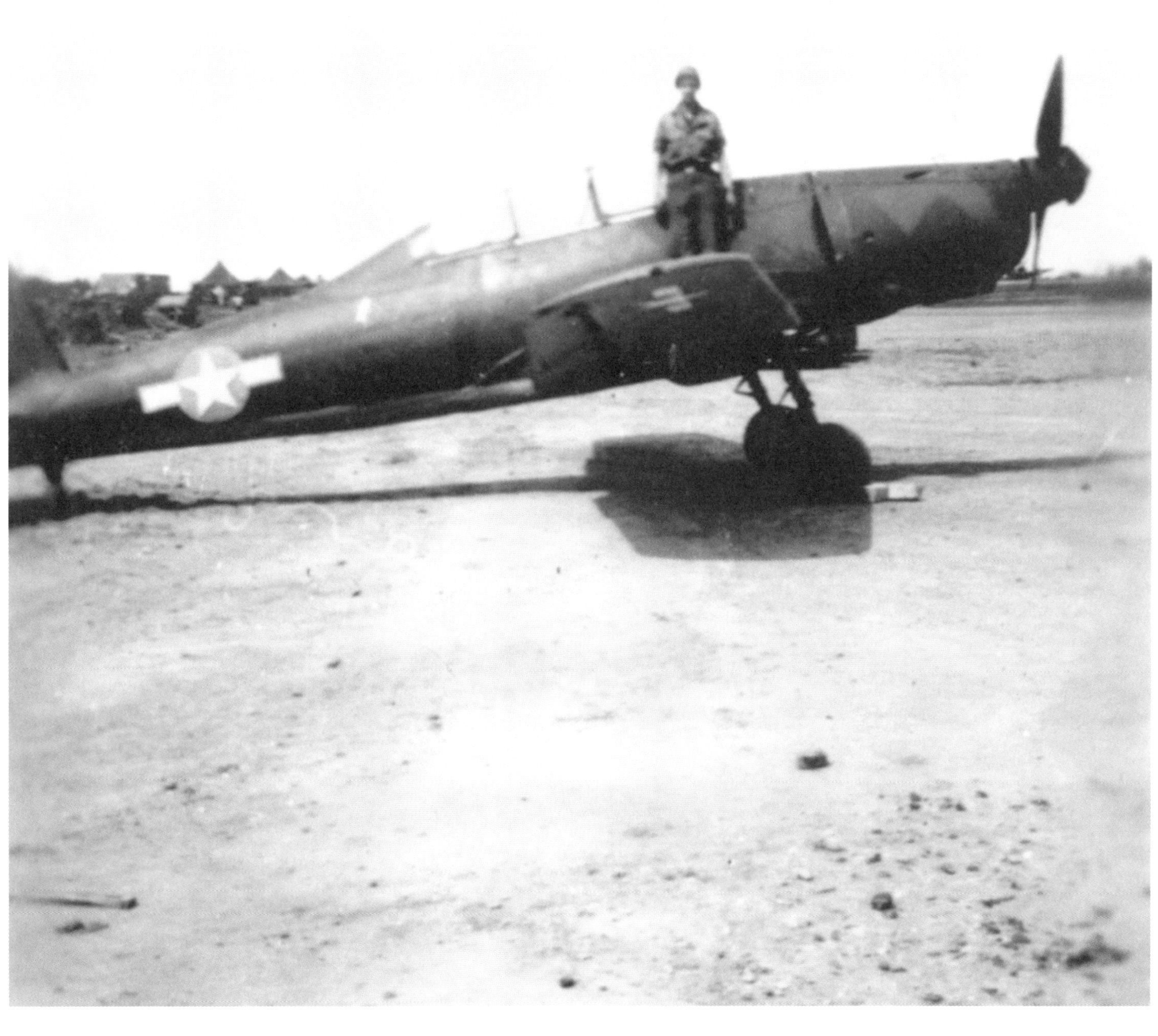

After the invasion of Normandy, the 'Club Mobiles,' in converted GMC trucks, followed the troops and the 'Donut Dollies' worked shortly behind the front lines. Dorothy and Grace Burdge, along with a third girl, were assigned to Club Mobile Group 'F.'

The converted GMC 6x6 truck they drove was nicknamed 'Atlanta.' With the troops advancing, Dorothy came to places we now know from the military history books. On July 16, 1944, her Club Mobile went ashore on Utah Beach. The advance took her through Brittany to Paris and Bastogne, St. Vith, and Vielsalm.

On March 15, 1945, F-Group crossed the German Siegfried Line and ten days later crossed the Moselle River, followed by the crossing of the Rhine at Koblenz. The advance progressed rapidly. By the end of April 1945, the front stabilized and the F-Group stopped in the vicinity of Altenburg, southeast of Leipzig. From here they would supply the troops of the 6th Armored Division with mobile canteen services.

East of Altenburg is the German training airfield Fliegerhorst Leinawald. From 1943 a German flying school was stationed here and several training aircraft of the type Arado 96 were left behind at this airfield. Often usable aircraft were repaired, provided with American identification markings ('Stars and Bars') and then used to provide additional transport services.

On Tuesday, May 1, 1945, the Club Mobile 'Atlanta' of the F-Group was at work at Leinawald airfield. A USAAF Fighter Group pilot, First Lieutenant Branch, had already flown several 'touring' trips with the Arado 96, letting his passengers enjoy the scenery. The American Red Cross girls were eventually invited for a ride in the two-seater aircraft as well. Grace was the first to make a flight, followed by Dorothy.

While attempting to fly under a power line, the pilot hit a tree with a wingtip as he pulled up, causing the plane to crash 200 yards east of the village of Munsa.

Lieutenant Branch and Dorothy Jane Burdge were killed instantly. Dorothy's final resting place is in Plot B, Row 7, Grave 4.

WILLIE F. WILLIAMS

Technical Sergeant

668th Ordnance Ammunition Company

The suitcase with answers

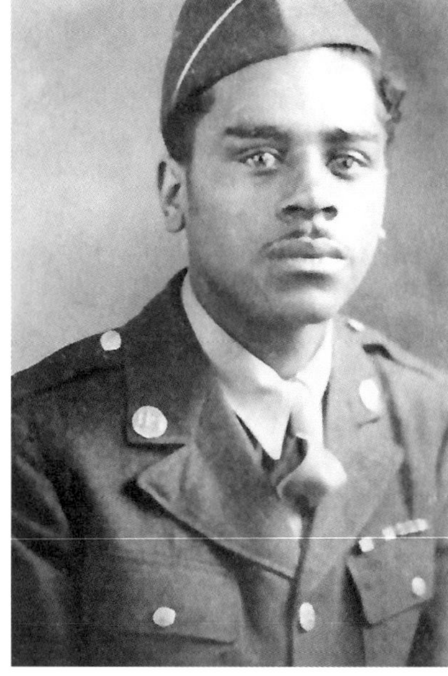

The war led to empty chairs at the table in many American families. For those who returned, it was often difficult to talk about their experiences. But for those who had been left behind, it was often as painful to talk about their lost loved ones. David McGhee, therefore, knew very little about his grandfather Willie Frank Williams. 'My mother didn't know her father. She was an infant. My grandmother never talked about her husband. He was forgotten.' That changed when he inherited a suitcase with Willie's belongings from his grandmother Effie.

Willie was born in Georgia in 1921, but two years later he moved with his parents, three brothers, and sister to Hartford, Connecticut. It was a family of entrepreneurs. His father Thomas ran a barber shop, but died when Willie was seven. Three of his brothers would later open their own businesses; Willie worked as a barber in one of them. However, their lives dramatically changed once again when the war broke out. The four brothers all went into the service.

In late November 1942, Willie's time in the service began, which would eventually last 2.5 years. Willie was assigned to the Ordnance Corps. The notes kept by his wife Effie in the old suitcase show that after receiving basic training at Camp Breckinridge, Kentucky, he specialized in ammunition and explosives in Aberdeen, Maryland. For David, after studying his grandfather's training notes, one thing was clear: they refuted 'the general assumption that Blacks in the military were uneducated and lacked ability for higher level learning.'

Willie arrived in Europe somewhere in 1943. Maps drawn by him show that the war took him to England, Belgium, and Germany, among other places.

In a letter home, he wrote that he himself didn't have it bad, but clearly was worried about Effie and their daughters Gwen and Pattie. 'If I am able when I come home to you, I am going to do everything in my power to make you + the two kids very happy. I know what you have to go through taking care of a house + two children by yourself.' He concludes by saying that he hopes that 'the war will soon end so I can be with you again.' And as a matter of fact, Willie survived the war. However, on June 4, 1945, he and five others were killed when an explosion occurred while unloading a truck. The other brothers returned home safely.

It took David several years to gather the courage to open the suitcase. When he did, he finally had a picture of his grandfather. 'You're looking at him in his uniform, and you're looking at the gloss in his eyes, and you're looking at some resemblance.'

Through the Internet, he then found out that his grandfather was buried in Margraten. A few months later he took the plane. At the home of the adopter of Willie's grave, the Smeets family, he found a picture of his grandfather standing on the mantlepiece. Knowing that his grandfather had not been forgotten was deeply meaningful to David. Together, they visited Willie's grave in Plot N, Row 9, Grave 17.

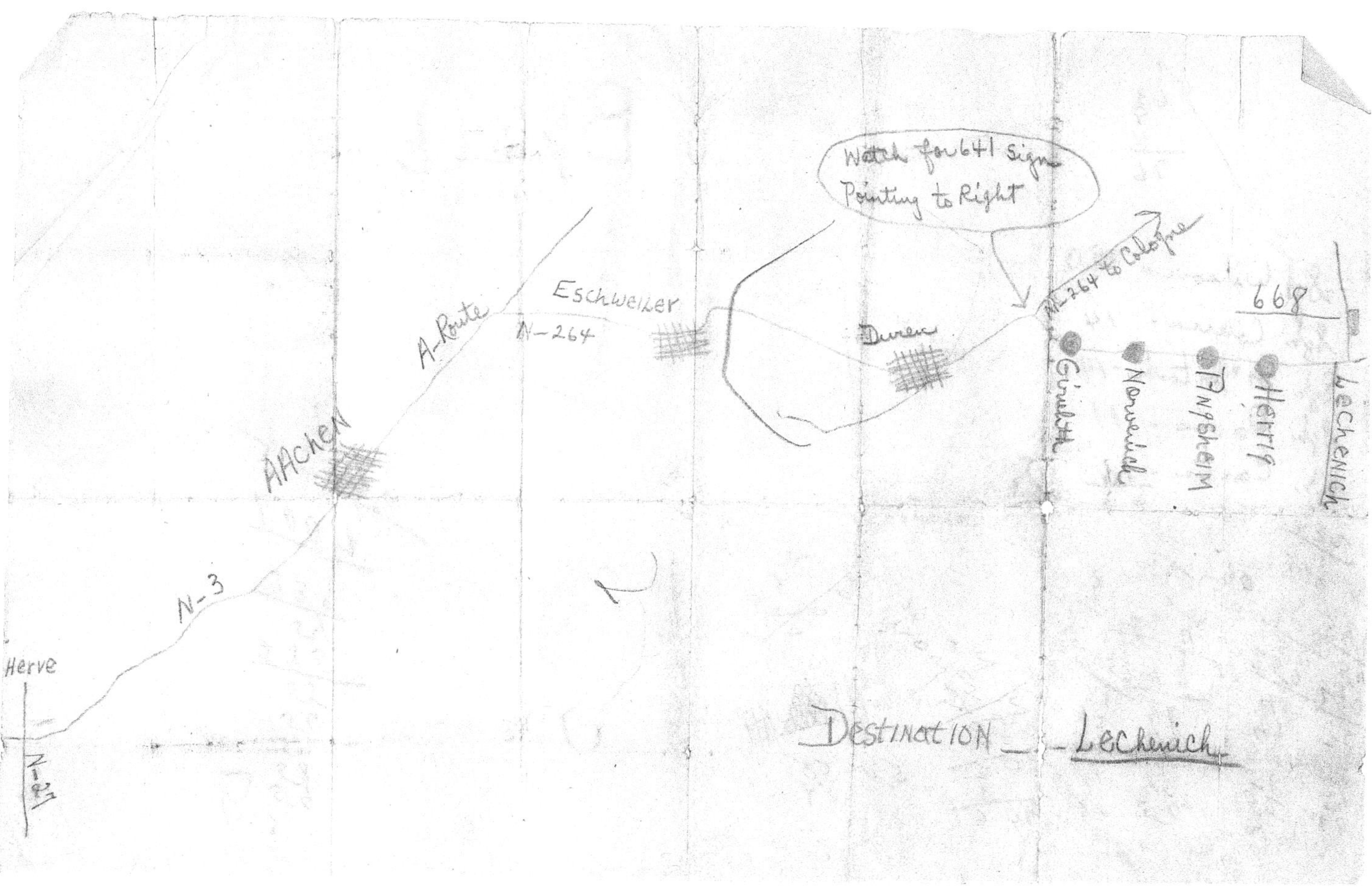

Willie Williams drew maps to document where he and his unit had been. SOURCE: Williams family

MAX CHOTIN
Staff Sergeant
Staging Area 3

'We are forever grateful. Bedankt.'

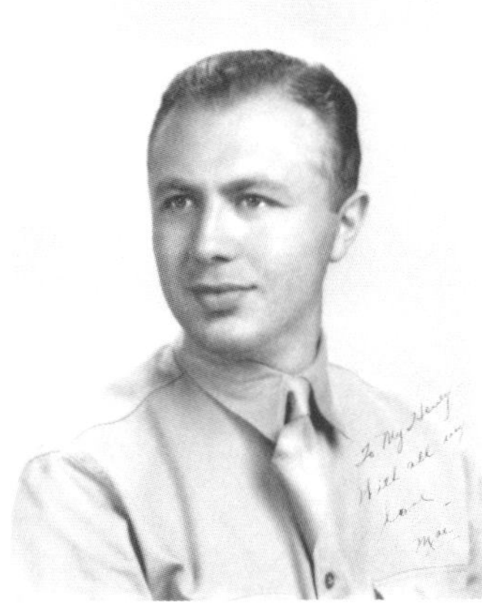

'As a kid it probably would have been better for me if he was buried here. It would have made it more real. It would have made it something I could have dealt with,' said Arthur Chotin about the loss of his father, Staff Sergeant Max Chotin. However, 'now as an adult I am very grateful that he is buried in the military cemetery in the Netherlands. I can't imagine a more appropriate setting for him to be in.' Arthur was, and is, particularly grateful for the Dutch having adopted not only the grave of his father, but also those of the fathers of the other 'Margraten kids.' And so, he asked if he could say a few words at the cemetery during the Memorial Day ceremony of 2015. His words may have been some of the most impressive ever spoken at the site.

Max Chotin was born in Brooklyn, New York City on April 27, 1915, as the son of the Jewish Charles and Rose, who had emigrated from Russia. He lived most of his life in the city. He grew up in Brooklyn, studied at St. John's University, worked as an accountant, and married Sylvia Anderman there in 1943. Their son Arthur was born late 1944.

By then, Max had already been in the service for almost two years, working as a chief clerk at Fort Knox, Kentucky. But casualties had mounted in Europe. So, his unit was sent overseas as replacements in February 1945. Again, he ended up working as a chief clerk, this time for an armored unit stationed at Camp Home Run. It was one out of many tented camps in a staging area nicknamed 'Red Horse' in Le Havre, France.

Max made it through the war, but could not go home as he did not have enough points yet. In October 1945, he hoped to get himself and some of the other men of his unit home by the end of the year. Max was asked to deliver the required paperwork in Belgium immediately. On November 2, he wrote his wife: 'I'm going to stay up all night and do this so that I can maybe get home in time for Christmas or Arthur's birthday.' The next day, he got into a jeep and was on his way to deliver the asked-for documents, but the jeep was hit by a British truck. Max was instantly killed.

When Western Union came to deliver a telegram, his wife Sylvia thought it harbored the news of Max finally coming home. 'When I opened the letter, I started screaming. It was such a shock. It was such a tragedy,' Sylvia said. 'And it's really a shame because he was such a decent person. Wonderful, kind, and generous. Handsome. I used to say: "what did I do in my lifetime to deserve somebody as wonderful as he?"'

During his speech at Margraten, Arthur said that his 'mother, although she never told me this directly, somewhere deep inside (...) held out the hope that one day there would be a knock at the door and she would learn that it had all been a mistake.' He believes that is why she never visited Margraten. Seeing Max's grave in Plot A, Row 7, Grave 8 'would make it real and would destroy that dream.'

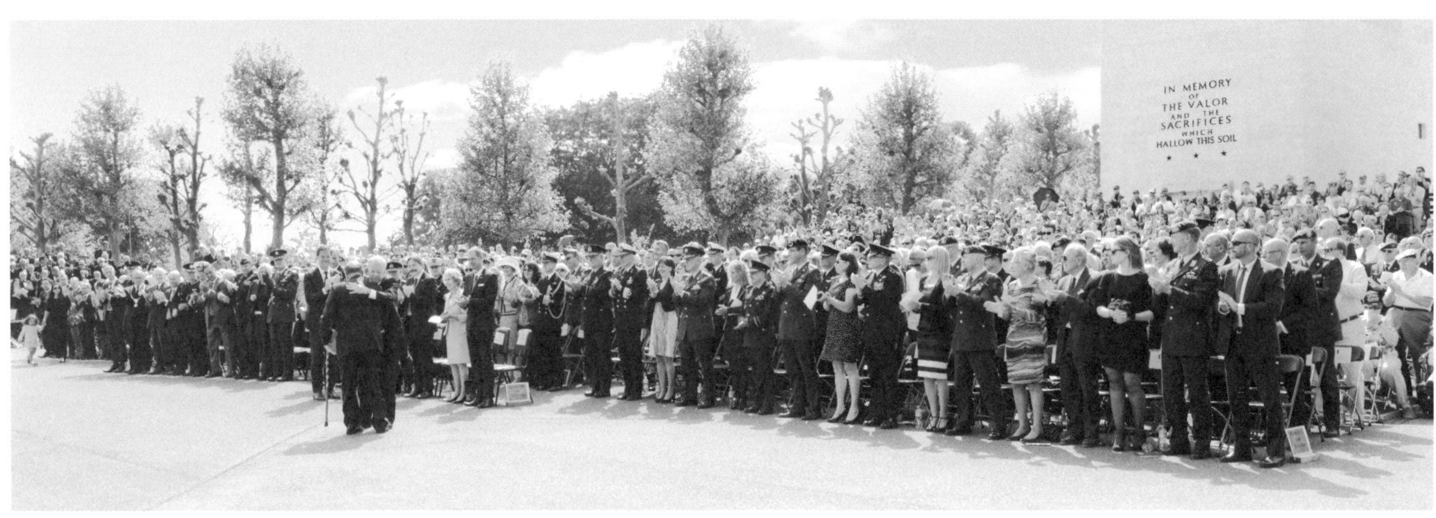

Arthur also spoke of how he missed his father. 'Even though I didn't know him, I think of him almost every day; what he missed and what my mother and I missed. So here I am, 70 years old, more than twice the age of the father I never played catch with, never argued with, never even hugged, and the single thought in my mind today is that I hope he would be proud of me. Oh, the power these dead have over those they left behind.'

However, he and his mother had been comforted by the care of the Dutch people for his father's grave. 'When she met Dutch people traveling in the United States, she made a point of speaking with them and thanking them,' Arthur said of his mother, who mourned Max until the day she died. Arthur wondered, 'what would cause a nation recovering from losses and trauma of their own to adopt the sons and daughters of another nation? And what would keep that commitment alive for all of these years, when the memory of that war has begun to fade?' He proceeded to say that 'it speaks to the character of the Netherlands and its people that every single grave in this cemetery and virtually every single name on that wall has been adopted. It is a unique occurrence in the history of civilization. And it is deserving of recognition, and of thanks.'

And so, on behalf of both his family and the over 50 other sons and daughters in attendance, he said in conclusion: 'by making these dead part of your family, you have become part of our family. You have created a bond between us that will never be broken. So, from this day forward, from now until the end of time, hartelijk bedankt, a heartfelt thank you. May the kindness and compassion you have shown them, and us, be returned to you many times over. We thank you, we salute you, we are forever grateful. Bedankt.'

Touched by his words, the audience rose to its feet in applause, for once breaking the silence at this cemetery in the hills of Limburg. In that moment, they felt and understood that exact friendship between the two nations that Arthur had spoken of.

◄ A touched audience rose to its feet after the speech by Max's son Arthur, Memorial Day 2015. SOURCE: Ralph Sluysmans/Gemeente Eijsden-Margraten

ANITA R. MC KENNEY
Civilian
War Shipping Administration

A civilian in a military cemetery

Anita Randall was born in Oklahoma in 1917. She married Warren H. Mc Kenney and the couple lived in Chicago, Illinois.

Warren Mc Kenney studied at the Harvard School for Boys and attended military training at the Culver Military Academy. He earned a college degree from the University of Michigan, where he majored in Naval Architecture and Marine Mechanical Engineering. As a midshipman, he was then posted to the U.S. Naval Academy at Annapolis, Maryland. During the war years, Warren worked for the U.S. War Shipping Administration and after the liberation of Antwerp in September 1944, Warren was transferred to Antwerp to work for the U.S. Maritime Commission and the War Shipping Administration. His wife Anita accompanied him to Antwerp.

Anita was then offered an administrative job with the War Shipping Administration. This government organization was responsible for all administration regarding cooperation between civilian and military authorities in the field of military maritime transport.

In addition, she is also said to have possessed singing talent and to have performed for American troops in so-called U.S.O. (United Service Organizations) shows. On November 24, 1945, the couple was involved in a traffic accident in Antwerp. Both were injured. With severe head injuries, Anita was transported to St. Elizabeth's Hospital in Antwerp, where the doctor on duty, First Lieutenant Joseph Grassi, was unable to do anything more for her. She died on November 26, 1945, at 8:30 a.m.

Due to his wounds, Warren H. Mc Kenney was unable to attend her burial at the U.S. Military Cemetery at Margraten. After his recovery, he was transferred to Naples, Italy, where he was appointed director of the U.S. Maritime Commission, Mediterranean Area. In the summer of 1948, he remarried.

Anita R. Mc Kenney's final resting place is in Plot N, Row 19, Grave 7.

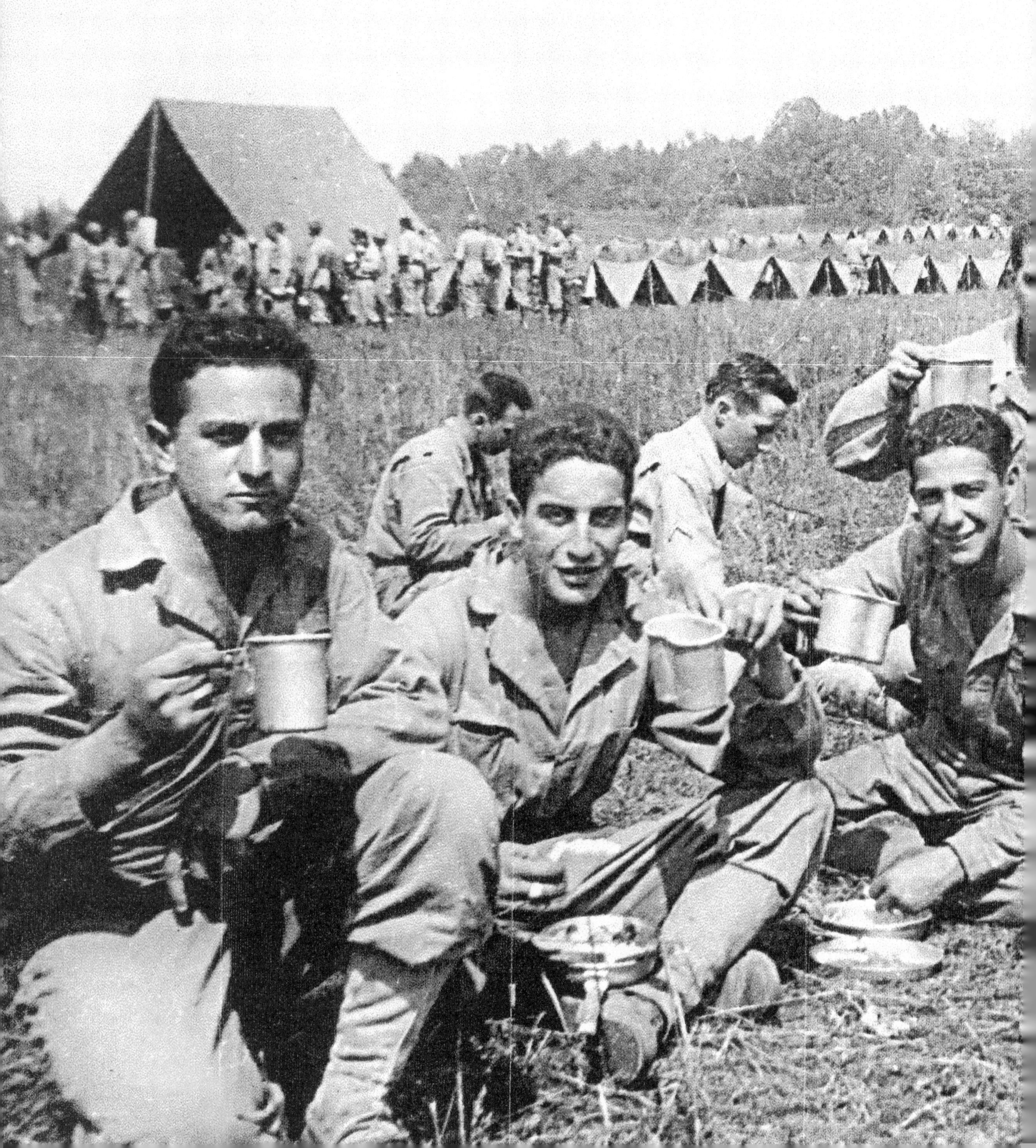

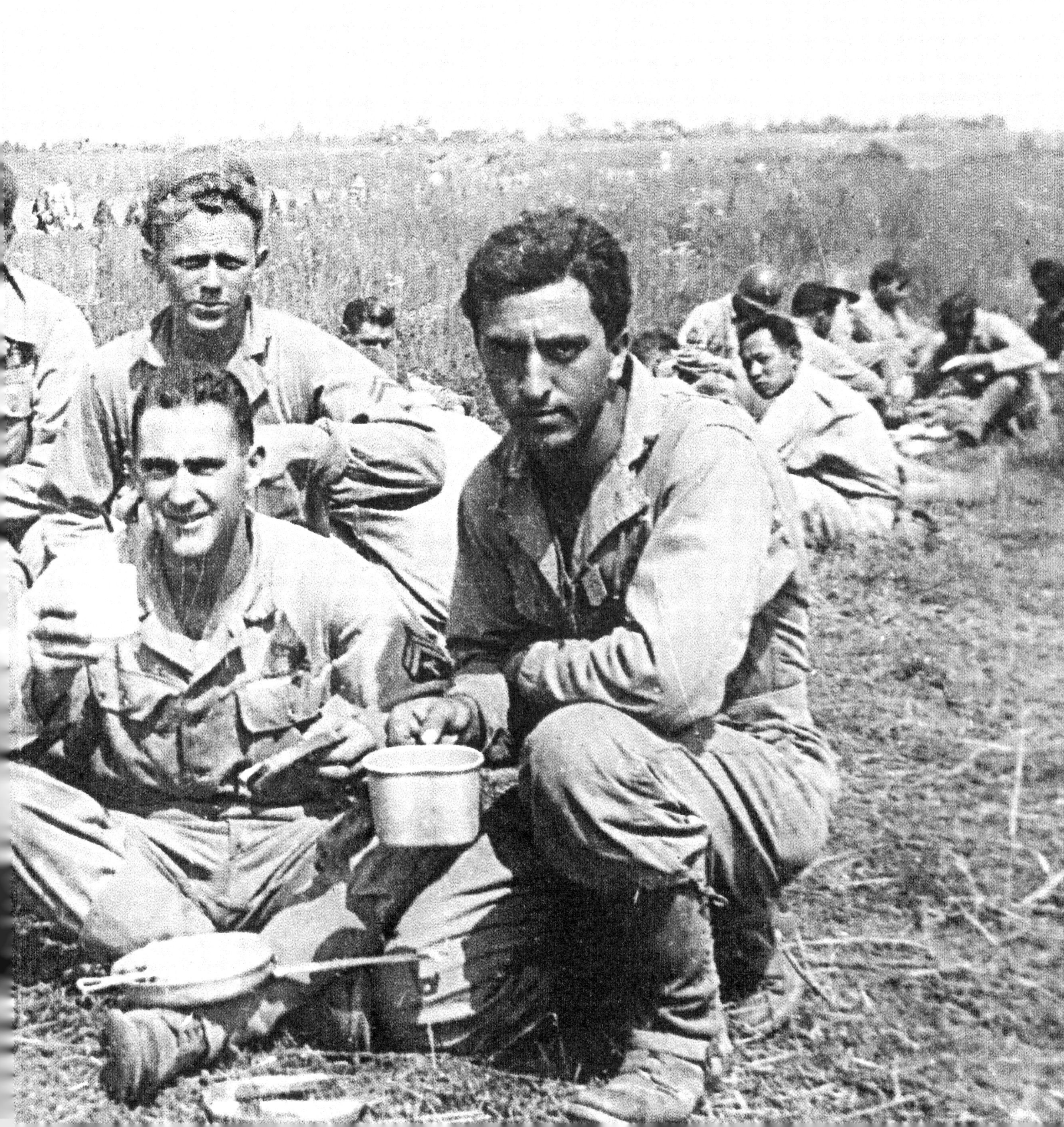

EPILOGUE

SINGING BIRDS

The story of Anita Mc Kenney is the last story that we tell in this book. Both she and Max Chotin were killed in a traffic accident. Like so many who are remembered in Margraten, they simply had bad luck. Indeed, not everyone's story is a heroic one. In addition to those who died in traffic incidents, we know of those who died from an exploding kettle while boiling water, from drowning, or from alcohol poisoning. That is why one will even find the year 1946 inscribed on several headstones. As Arthur Chotin has said, 'just because there was VE Day, [and] just because there was VJ Day, [it] doesn't mean that soldiers didn't die. (...) And I think that that's what people sometimes don't remember.' Indeed, these soldiers had survived the war, but would still not return home. But how they died does not take away from the fact that they had contributed to the liberation of Europe, that we see them as our liberators. They gave us our freedom back.

That freedom has a different meaning for everyone is evident from the messages that visitors of the tribute *The Faces of Margraten* have left over the years. For some, it means something as simple as being able to hear the birds sing, their song not interrupted by the sound of gun and artillery fire. For the young Thijs Mevissen, freedom meant being able 'to go to school.' And for others, their meaning of freedom is closely intertwined with their view of people and society at large. 'We think of freedom as a country in which everyone respects and accepts each other for who they are, so that everyone can live in peace and tranquility.'

Visiting a war cemetery and knowing the stories behind the graves there helps one to think not only about the meaning of freedom, but also about the potential impact of war on ourselves and the role that we can play in this world. For example, a young visitor to *The Faces of Margraten* realized: 'When seeing the pictures, it really hit me that many of these men were of my age.' Others hope that visitors are not just impressed, but will also be inspired to step up themselves. 'It should help and motivate you to pass on the stories of all those killed and the why, how, and what for of it to future generations to ensure together that such a terrible period in our history is prevented and should not be able to happen again.'

Never again. These words might sound hollow. While we were finishing this book, war raged again in Europe after the Russian invasion of Ukraine on February 24, 2022. Simultaneously, there are wars and armed conflicts going on that we might not hear about as often, like in Ethiopia and Yemen. In the face of all these conflicts, we might easily feel overwhelmed. Indeed, as the images from Ukraine of citizens wandering the streets in rubble and trying to flee to a safe space make painstakingly clear, these conflicts are mostly influenced by events beyond our control and our will.

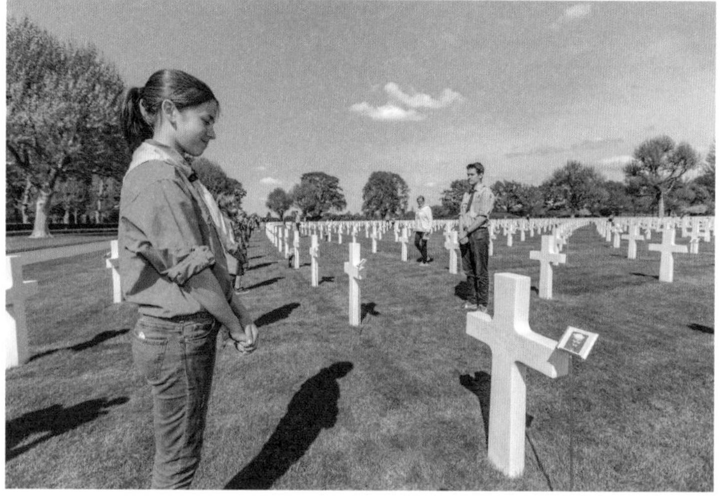

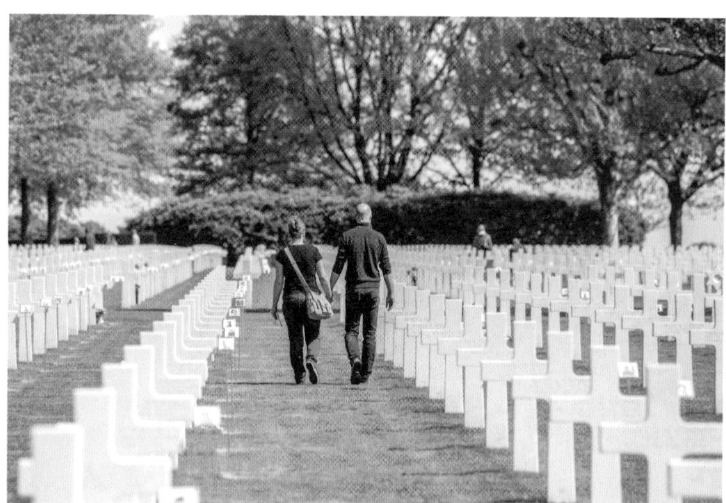

Margraten is a place of both remembrance and reflection

But as the young Thijs, among others, shows: freedom can be something very simple. Freedom is not just about the dichotomy of war and peace. One can live in peace, but that does not necessarily mean that one lives in freedom. And thus, much of it is about how we shape our society and treat those around us. President Franklin Roosevelt underscored that in 1941 when he spoke of the Four Freedoms: freedom of speech, freedom of religion, freedom from fear, and freedom from want. After all, how much freedom does a person who lives in poverty have? Is someone who is seriously ill really free? By thinking of freedom in this way, it means that by simply helping someone, we can do something for that other person's freedom. It might well be the first step on the road to 'never again.'

To make a better world a reality is going to require a commitment of all of us. This reminds us of the words engraved on one of the Walls of the Missing in Margraten, two lines from the famous poem 'In Flanders Fields' by John McCrae:

> ***To you from failing hands we throw***
> ***The torch; be yours to hold it high.***

It is a call made upon us. Now it is our turn.

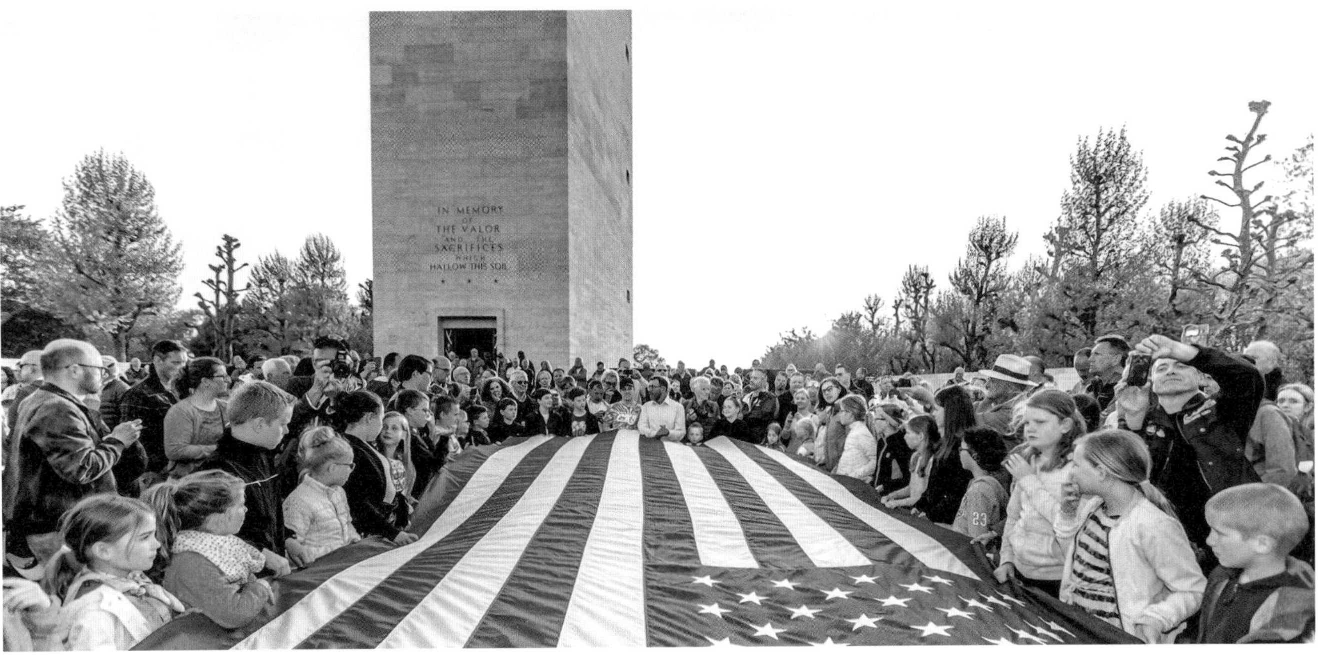

The meaning of freedom is being passed on to younger generations during commemorations

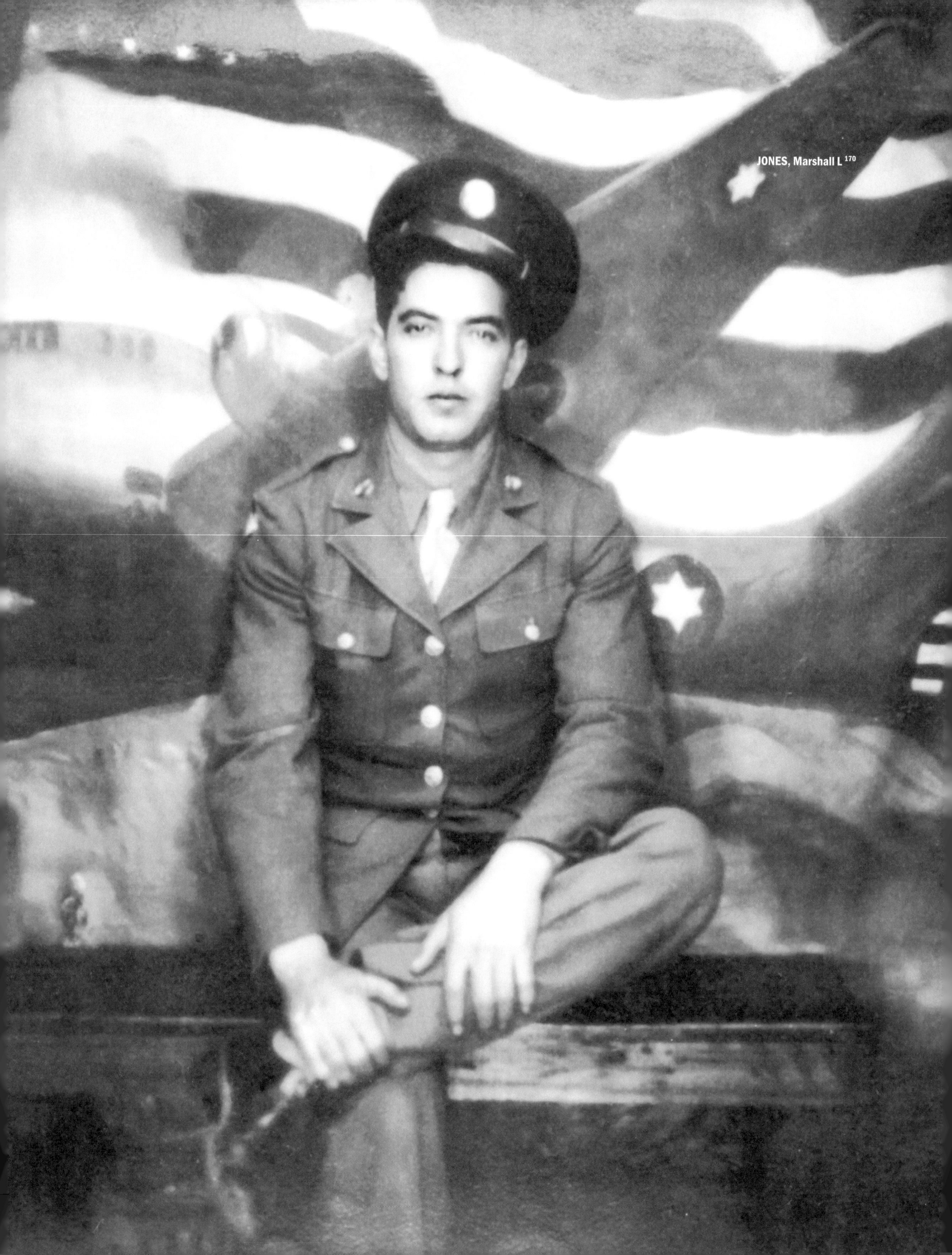

JONES, Marshall L[170]

FOREVER GRATEFUL HONOR ROLL

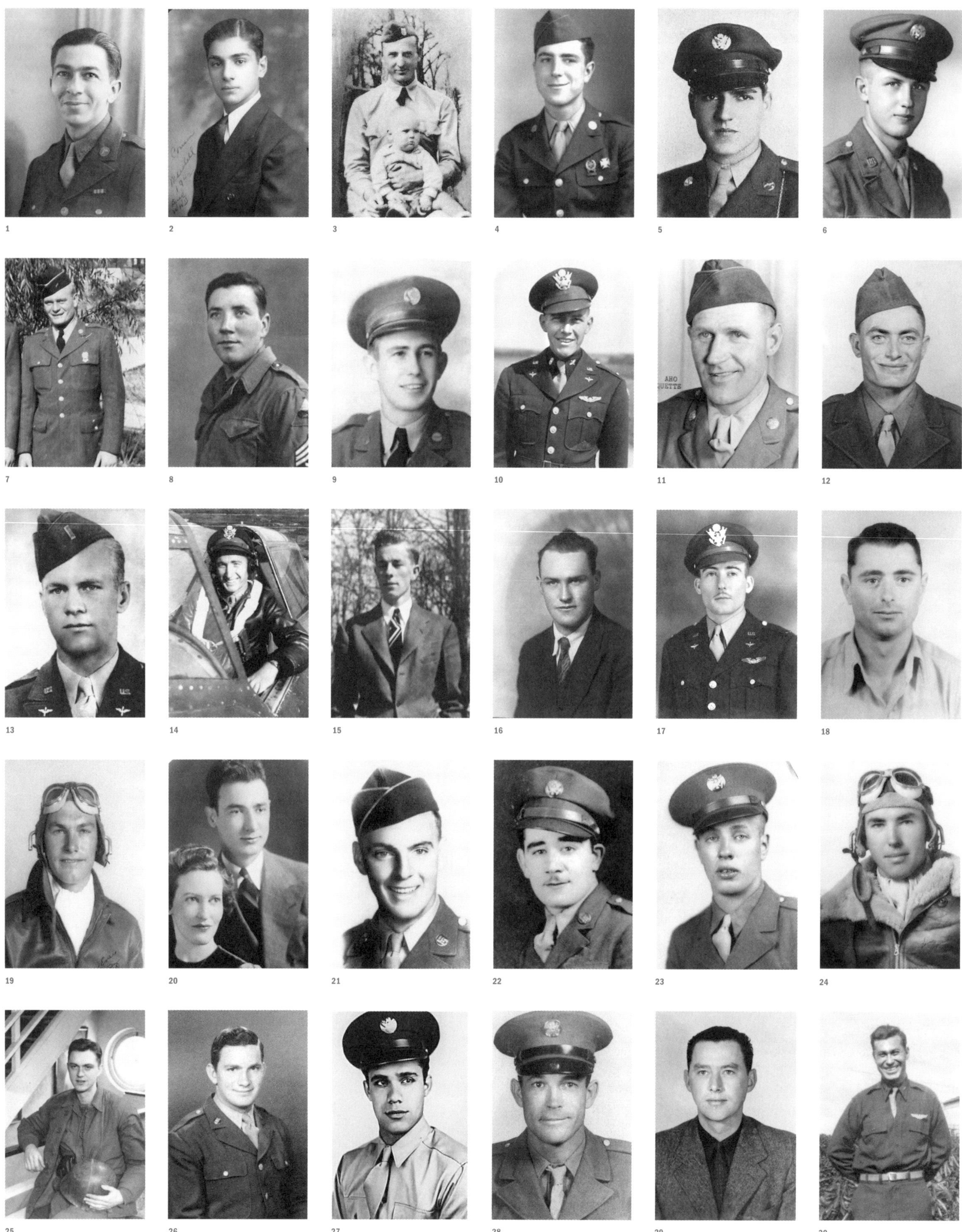

The people of the Netherlands will always remember the about 10,000 Americans who are either buried in or memorialized at the Netherlands American Cemetery and Memorial in Margraten. They have paid the highest price for our freedom. That is why we will continue to speak the names of each and every one. 'So long as they speak your name, you shall never die.'

A

Name	Location
AARON, John D	B-4-32
AASEN, Erling A	D-13-3
ABBATELLO, Joseph	B-9-11
ABBOTT, Thomas J	M-7-12
ABDO, Edward B	K-13-21
ABELE, Joseph R	M-11-14
ABELL, Forrest W	O-1-11
ABERCROMBIE, Alex M	D-18-15
ABERNATHY, Mercer G	Walls of the Missing
ABERNATHY, Raiford	B-15-23
ABRAHAM, Lester L [1]	B-7-29
ABRAHAM, Marshall T [2]	M-16-7
ABRAHAMSON, Philip	D-6-15
ABRAMCZYK, Henry M	K-8-22
ABRAMOWICH, Alex	Walls of the Missing
ABRAMS, Billey	A-10-15
ABRELL, John D	Walls of the Missing
ABRIL, Mike E	C-3-16
ACEY, Henry Jr	A-12-9
ACHESON, Wilbur E	H-1-3
ACKER, Eugene H	B-14-30
ACKER, Joel M Jr	N-18-14
ACKER, Leonard W	L-17-20
ACKERMAN, Albert L Jr [3]	B-8-3
ACKERMAN, Hyman	D-19-7
ACQUISTO, Peter A	B-5-32
ADAIR, John D	Walls of the Missing
ADAIR, William E [4]	G-5-9
ADAMCZYK, Michael S	A-16-22
ADAME, Jose A	A-10-32
ADAMS, Ara J	Walls of the Missing
ADAMS, Arlon L	J-21-22
ADAMS, Charles R E	B-12-14
ADAMS, Chester	Walls of the Missing
ADAMS, Frank L	Walls of the Missing
ADAMS, John W	O-11-2
ADAMS, Johnnie U	Walls of the Missing
ADAMS, Platt Jr [5]	M-5-1
ADAMS, William H [6]	E-3-19
ADAMSON, George J [7]	M-1-9
ADCOCK, O B	N-3-6
ADDICKS, Leroy L [8]	I-16-20
ADDY, Floyd E [9]	N-18-11
ADENSAM, Theodore J	I-11-9
ADKINS, Elwood	B-5-24
ADOLF, Joseph	J-13-12
ADRIAN, Arthur R	B-4-30
AGNA, Reginald A	G-13-23
AGOSTINELLI, Kitan A	M-11-15
AGRESTA, Frank F	A-17-1
AGUERO, Bonifacio	E-11-8
AGUILAR, Francisco E	F-17-15
AHLWARDT, Donald L [10]	Walls of the Missing
AHNER, Claire C	I-9-12
AHO, Augustus	Walls of the Missing
AHO, Edward W [11]	Walls of the Missing
AHO, Eino R	C-5-12
AIBAVICH, Julius W	H-13-10
AIELLO, Michel	Walls of the Missing
AKER, Fred T [12]	L-8-13
AKERS, Joseph	Walls of the Missing
AKIN, J B	C-13-23
AKIN, John H	D-7-19
AKIN, John H	Walls of the Missing
AKIN, Robert E	C-21-3
AKINS, Hugh J	F-3-4
AKOSEVICH, Paul M	N-3-2
ALANIZ, Guadalupe A	Walls of the Missing
ALBER, Barend J Jr	O-7-11
ALBERY, Kenneth E	F-1-24
ALBOSZTA, Edward J	G-5-2
ALBRECHT, David F [13]	C-2-11
ALCO, Dominick J	L-4-1
ALCOCK, Berry H Jr	I-17-9
ALDERMAN, Richard L [14]	Walls of the Missing
ALDERSON, Richard J	I-4-16
ALDOM, David R [15]	C-18-7
ALDRICH, Clifford W	H-8-2
ALDRICH, Louis T [16]	C-18-14
ALDRIDGE, Eugene F [17]	H-9-25
ALDY, Willie D	Walls of the Missing
ALEN, Paul O	N-16-16
ALEXANDER, Alvin R	C-4-29
ALEXANDER, Boyd A	M-14-7
ALEXANDER, Bruce C	Walls of the Missing
ALEXANDER, Cecil R [18]	E-9-9
ALEXANDER, Charles M	F-1-1
ALEXANDER, Charles R	I-18-8
ALEXANDER, George S	Walls of the Missing
ALEXANDER, Harry N [19]	H-18-27
ALEXANDER, Marvin C [20]	A-12-16
ALEXANDER, W B [21]	K-15-14
ALEXANDER, William L	Walls of the Missing
ALFONSO, Jafet	Walls of the Missing
ALGE, George W	H-4-4
ALGEO, Jerre M	H-8-12
ALIO, Salvatore J [22]	C-20-7
ALISON, Denis J	Walls of the Missing
ALLABAUGH, Donald J	F-7-13
ALLAN, Robert G	B-21-18
ALLBERT, Frederick M	G-16-22
ALLDREDGE, Curtis C	Walls of the Missing
ALLEN, Arthur R [23]	L-11-14
ALLEN, Clarence E [24]	Walls of the Missing
ALLEN, Edward L [25]	C-7-4
ALLEN. Elbert Q	Walls of the Missing
ALLEN, George W	A-7-17
ALLEN, Grant E	Walls of the Missing
ALLEN, Harry J	Walls of the Missing
ALLEN, Henry H Jr	Walls of the Missing
ALLEN, Henry L	E-15-5
ALLEN, Ossie J [26]	A-17-5
ALLEN, Robert G	G-2-6
ALLEN, Wilkie M	E-13-2
ALLEN, William G	E-2-1
ALLEN, William H Jr	O-18-1
ALLGEIER, Albert G	H-1-13
ALLIE, James J [27]	E-10-11
ALLIE, Leonard E	A-21-22
ALLISON, A J	D-16-7
ALLISON, Byron M	Walls of the Missing
ALLISON, Francis E	G-4-27
ALLMENDINGER, Ervin	E-2-12
ALLSOP, George W	A-20-7
ALLSTOT, Clarence E	M-9-17
ALMASI, Adolph J	B-15-26
ALMLIE, Harlan C	Walls of the Missing
ALSOP, Harold W	Walls of the Missing
ALSTON, Norman P [28]	L-9-20
ALSTON, Tullos Jr	J-6-13
ALTIG, Orton T	D-14-25
ALTMAN, Arthur T Jr [29]	Walls of the Missing
ALVARADO, Edward M	G-17-5
AMAYA, Anthony L W [30]	Walls of the Missing
AMBALAGI, Armando H	Walls of the Missing

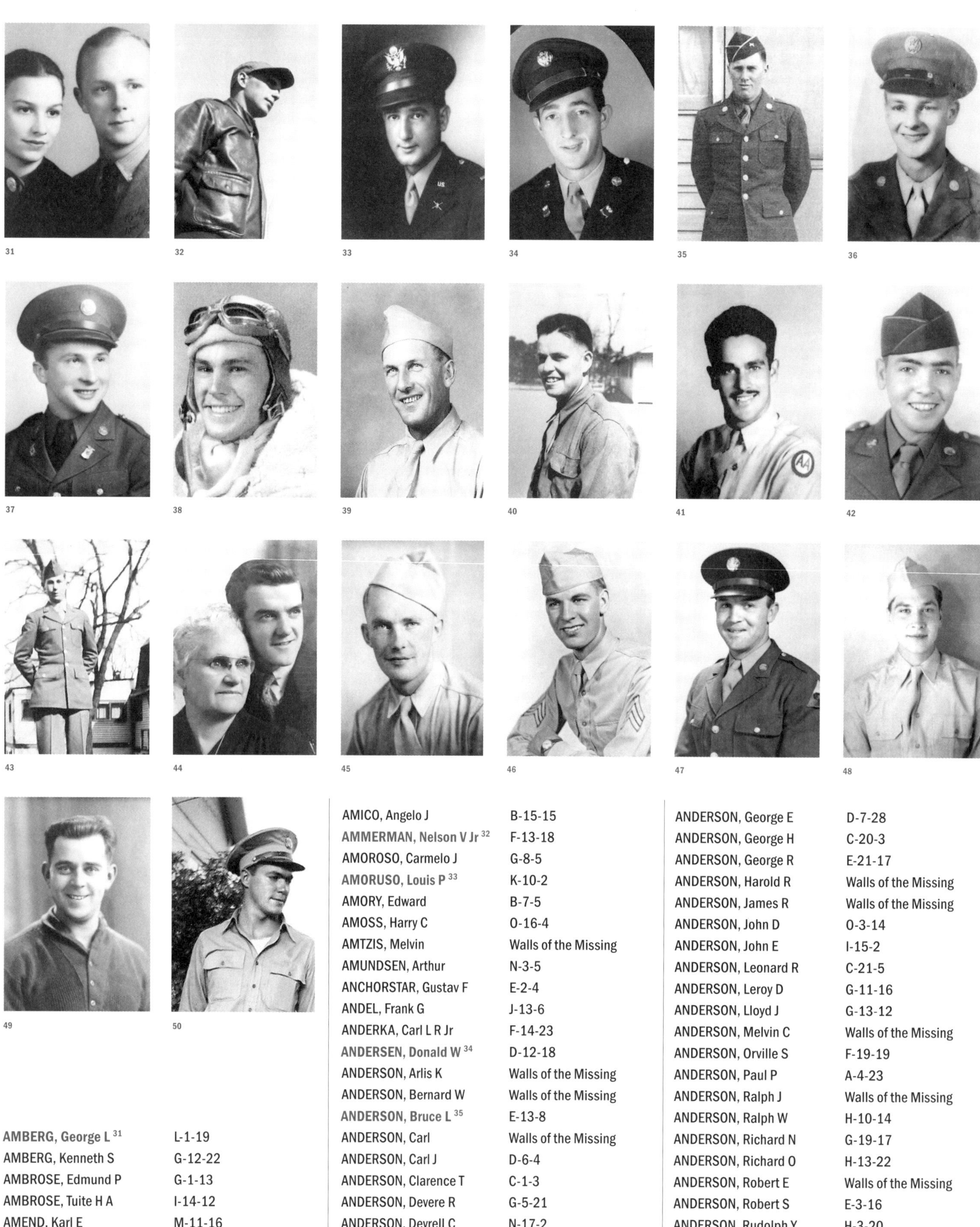

Name	Grave
AMBERG, George L[31]	L-1-19
AMBERG, Kenneth S	G-12-22
AMBROSE, Edmund P	G-1-13
AMBROSE, Tuite H A	I-14-12
AMEND, Karl E	M-11-16
AMERSBACH, Albert M	D-21-28
AMERSON, Leonard C	Walls of the Missing
AMICO, Angelo J	B-15-15
AMMERMAN, Nelson V Jr[32]	F-13-18
AMOROSO, Carmelo J	G-8-5
AMORUSO, Louis P[33]	K-10-2
AMORY, Edward	B-7-5
AMOSS, Harry C	O-16-4
AMTZIS, Melvin	Walls of the Missing
AMUNDSEN, Arthur	N-3-5
ANCHORSTAR, Gustav F	E-2-4
ANDEL, Frank G	J-13-6
ANDERKA, Carl L R Jr	F-14-23
ANDERSEN, Donald W[34]	D-12-18
ANDERSON, Arlis K	Walls of the Missing
ANDERSON, Bernard W	Walls of the Missing
ANDERSON, Bruce L[35]	E-13-8
ANDERSON, Carl	Walls of the Missing
ANDERSON, Carl J	D-6-4
ANDERSON, Clarence T	C-1-3
ANDERSON, Devere R	G-5-21
ANDERSON, Deyrell C	N-17-2
ANDERSON, Edward C	O-3-15
ANDERSON, Ernest L	P-4-11
ANDERSON, George E	D-7-28
ANDERSON, George H	C-20-3
ANDERSON, George R	E-21-17
ANDERSON, Harold R	Walls of the Missing
ANDERSON, James R	Walls of the Missing
ANDERSON, John D	O-3-14
ANDERSON, John E	I-15-2
ANDERSON, Leonard R	C-21-5
ANDERSON, Leroy D	G-11-16
ANDERSON, Lloyd J	G-13-12
ANDERSON, Melvin C	Walls of the Missing
ANDERSON, Orville S	F-19-19
ANDERSON, Paul P	A-4-23
ANDERSON, Ralph J	Walls of the Missing
ANDERSON, Ralph W	H-10-14
ANDERSON, Richard N	G-19-17
ANDERSON, Richard O	H-13-22
ANDERSON, Robert E	Walls of the Missing
ANDERSON, Robert S	E-3-16
ANDERSON, Rudolph Y	H-3-20
ANDERSON, Truman K	C-3-2
ANDERSON, Vernon D	H-16-6

Name	Location
ANDERSON, Walter J	J-1-17
ANDERSON, Walter R	L-16-12
ANDERSON, William M	D-10-12
ANDERSON, William R	I-18-17
ANDRAKO, William	Walls of the Missing
ANDREWS, Arthur C	K-18-8
ANDREWS, Charles	Walls of the Missing
ANDREWS, Clifton N	L-11-20
ANDREWS, Joseph W Jr	Walls of the Missing
ANDREWS, Milford E	M-3-9
ANDREWS, Norman L	Walls of the Missing
ANDRIS, Eugene E	Walls of the Missing
ANDRONIS, Christ J	N-7-6
ANDROSKY, John P	Walls of the Missing
ANGEL, Lee M	B-6-21
ANGELO, Julius T	M-21-1
ANKENBRUCK, James R	A-13-27
ANNIN, Robert E III	M-9-5
ANTHES, Calvin L	A-11-31
ANTOL, Frank	I-6-17
ANTOSZEWSKI, Anthony T	A-19-24
APPERT, Donald A	Walls of the Missing
APPLEBY, Gene J	Walls of the Missing
APPLEMAN, James E	H-18-22
APRILANTE, John R	Walls of the Missing
APRILL, Elwyn D	C-10-10
ARANT, Joseph W	D-12-9
ARCANGELI, Bruno	P-14-1
ARCHAMBEAULT, Francis	Walls of the Missing
ARCHAMBEAULT, James J	P-12-2
ARCHER, Harry V Jr	H-5-23
ARCHER, John S Jr	M-2-2
ARCUNI, Dominic J	I-17-2
ARDEUNE, Vance M	D-11-27
AREL, Rudolph T	C-7-8
ARELLANES, Augustine L	B-15-22
AREMBURG, Raymond H	I-6-13
ARLEDGE, Keith W	G-4-14
ARLEDGE, William H	Walls of the Missing
ARLUCK, Jack	Walls of the Missing
ARMIJO, Antonio B	L-8-1
ARMOUR, Theodore E	P-13-3
ARMSTRONG, Arden C	H-15-21
ARMSTRONG, Claudius J	H-19-21
ARMSTRONG, William B	F-19-22
ARNEBERG, Norman E	M-18-16
ARNKIL, Thor V	Walls of the Missing
ARNOLD, Henry	D-13-31
ARNOLD, James W	B-6-19
ARNOLD, Levi A	C-8-10
ARNOLD, Marvin J	H-15-26
ARNOLD, Robert B	B-14-15
ARPAJIAN, Harry A	D-18-3
ARRIAGA, Reyes M	A-20-24
ARROWSMITH, John W Jr	G-11-5
ARTER, John R	Walls of the Missing
ASBORNSEN, Norman	Walls of the Missing
ASCANIO, Vincent A	Walls of the Missing
ASCHOFF, Harry E	G-12-19
ASERO, Matthew M	Walls of the Missing
ASH, Merlin T	Walls of the Missing
ASHER, Willis E	B-13-13
ASHLEY, Robert W	M-16-13
ASHMAN, Charles A	Walls of the Missing
ASHWORTH, Ralph W	I-10-10
ASHWORTH, Wilson P	L-8-5
ASKREN, William V	Walls of the Missing
ASMUS, George M [36]	J-13-2
ATCHLEY, Alfred A	P-2-1
ATCHLEY, William E T	P-2-2
ATHERTON, Roger L	F-2-22
ATKINS, Donald L	A-11-25
ATKINSON, Edward L	K-13-19
ATKINSON, Gerald V	Walls of the Missing
AUBUT, William G	D-7-8
AUDESSE, Arthur A	G-10-4
AUDETTE, Rene N	A-10-20
AUGER, Morris C	B-8-4
AUGUSTINE, Charles H	Walls of the Missing
AULD, Phillip H	B-20-19
AULENBACH, Aaron A	O-2-1
AULETTE, George J	Walls of the Missing
AURELI, Angelo A	H-21-8
AUSMER, Curley J	J-11-2
AUSTIN, Eugene	A-1-31
AUSTIN, Ralph M	F-15-22
AVERY, Franklin K	E-16-4
AVILA, John L	G-8-14
AVRAAM, Paul	N-3-4
AXLINE, Sherman E	F-2-15
AXTON, William G Jr	Walls of the Missing
AYALA, Matias V	P-14-3
AYERS, Joe B	H-18-8
AZUR, George J	D-21-12

B

Name	Location
BABBAGE, Westmoreland	C-14-12
BABCANEC, Cyril M	O-16-5
BABELAY, Herbert Carson	N-13-12
BABICH, George [37]	Walls of the Missing
BABICH, Michael	L-15-9
BABIEC, Edward J	L-4-3
BACA, Julius V	B-11-27
BACH, Robert A	C-2-26
BACHER, Edward C	J-15-18
BACHMAN, Arthur W	H-13-12
BACHMAN, Harold M	Walls of the Missing
BACK, Troy	C-10-17
BACK, Walter P	Walls of the Missing
BACLE, Peter	P-17-1
BADER, Alvin G	H-5-16
BADER, Joseph P	A-6-17
BADER, Robert E	Walls of the Missing
BADURA, John	Walls of the Missing
BAER, Ernest L	O-16-2
BAER, John M L	G-4-15
BAGBY, Paul D	H-12-21
BAGGETT, Julian F	Walls of the Missing
BAHAM, Joe Jr	E-17-13
BAIL, David E Jr	Walls of the Missing
BAILEY, Bert J Jr	I-21-10
BAILEY, Burnie B [38]	J-5-17
BAILEY, Donald H	F-18-16
BAILEY, Frederick M	I-20-5
BAILEY, John H [39]	D-21-11
BAILEY, Milton R	G-20-2
BAILEY, Shirley E	Walls of the Missing
BAIR, Carl L [40]	C-14-30
BAIRD, Durward D	J-16-3
BAISLY, Edward F [41]	G-18-20
BAJULA, John R	O-11-14
BAKER, Carlton [42]	C-21-31
BAKER, Douglas H	Walls of the Missing
BAKER, Dwight D	C-3-13
BAKER, James A	A-17-27
BAKER, James B [43]	K-3-5
BAKER, Leslie H	A-19-4
BAKER, Lester L	H-21-21
BAKER, Paul W	C-17-6
BAKER, Raymond W [44]	B-3-8
BAKER, Wilfred	H-1-19
BAKER, William E	A-4-31
BALABAN, Robert E	D-15-2
BALDASSAR, John J	L-1-20
BALDRY, Floyd M	M-15-16
BALDWIN, Frederick V	J-19-17
BALDWIN, Ira O [45]	J-16-10
BALDWIN, James D [46]	C-12-7
BALDWIN, Leon E	Walls of the Missing
BALDWIN, Marvin A [47]	B-2-28
BALDWIN, Matthew J	D-11-20
BALDWIN, Roy S Jr	H-8-3
BALDWIN, William H	A-16-12
BALDWIN, William L Jr	Walls of the Missing
BALES, Ross C	Walls of the Missing
BALESTRUCCI, Frank M	J-11-14
BALISTRERI, Jack S	G-9-18
BALK, Byron M	K-11-16
BALL, Edwin C	P-4-16
BALL, Harold J	A-1-6
BALL, Rollin P	Walls of the Missing
BALL, Warren G [48]	L-5-6
BALLARD, Calvin T	H-14-18
BALLONE, Raymond J	J-17-2
BALLOU, Howard W	K-20-1
BALTIER, Jose A	N-19-11
BALTUSNIK, Stanley J	H-12-15
BAMBURY, Joseph W [49]	K-3-2
BAMM, Arthur C Jr [50]	Walls of the Missing
BANDOSZ, William J	G-12-5
BANEVICH, Walter E	C-14-27
BANEY, James L	C-21-9
BANGE, John A	E-11-22
BANICKY, Michael	A-2-5

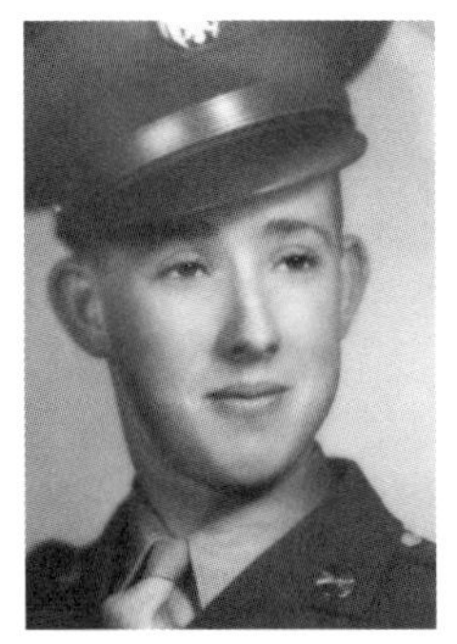
51

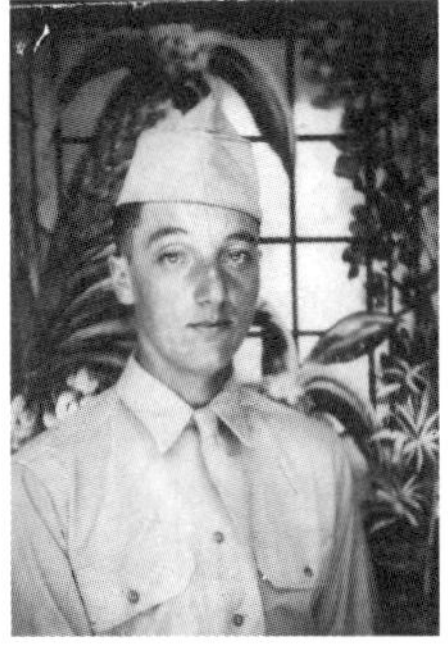
52

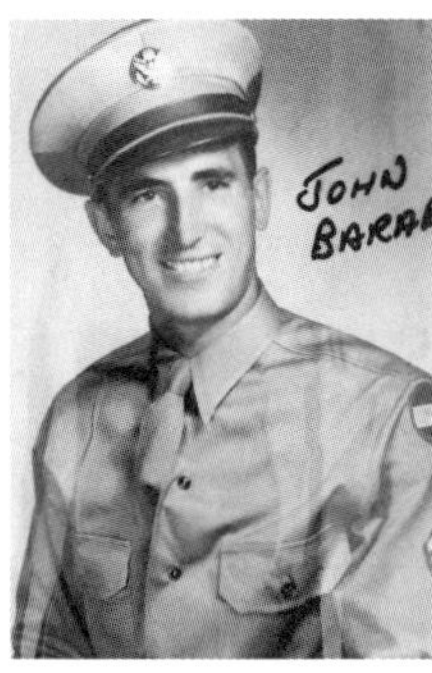

53

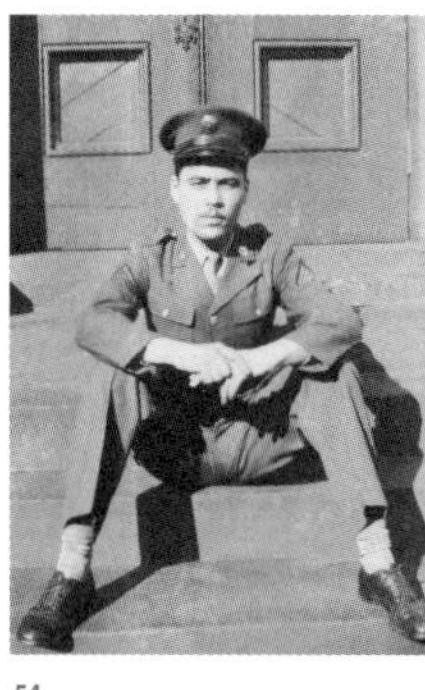
54

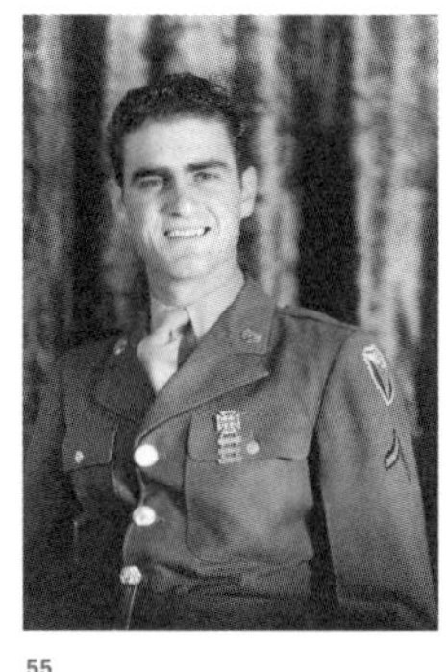
55

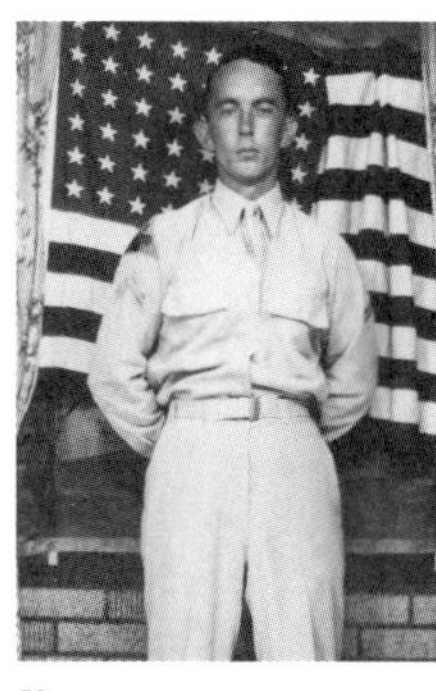
56

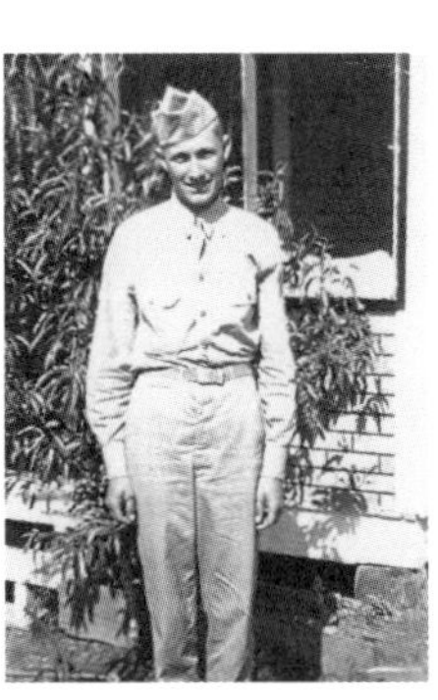
57

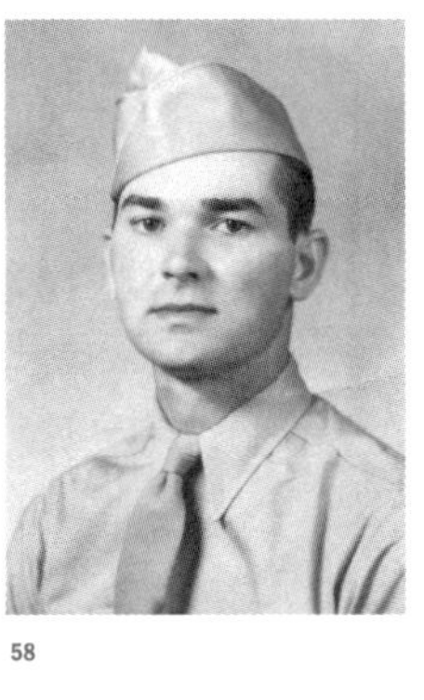
58

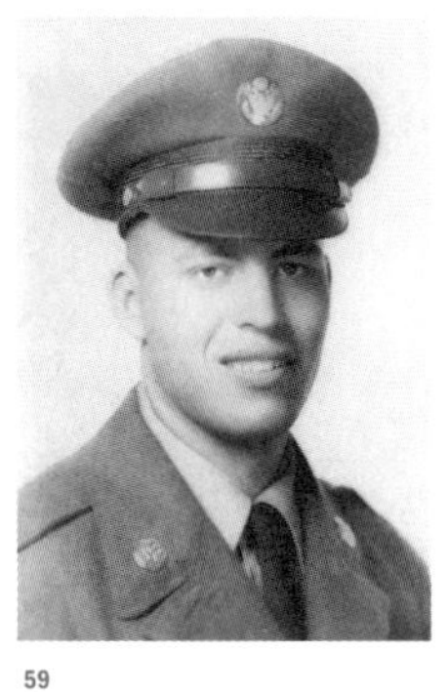
59

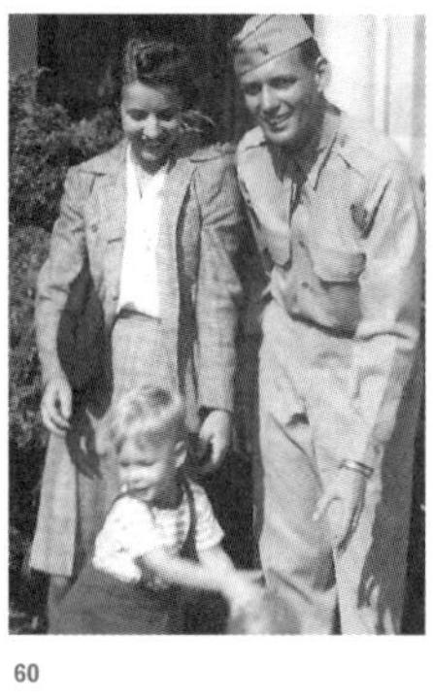
60

BANKS, Cecil [51]	Walls of the Missing
BANKS, Royal E	L-4-7
BANNER, Walter M	C-13-31
BANNICK, Timothy [52]	A-5-13
BANNISTER, Albert J	Walls of the Missing
BANOTAI, Charles G	K-1-20
BARABAS, John J [53]	Walls of the Missing
BARACH, Marvin S	K-4-20
BARAN, Joseph [54]	J-10-3
BARANOWSKI, Joseph W	D-9-17
BARBEE, John H [55]	I-17-11
BARBER, Donald C	I-20-19
BARBER, James W	N-1-13
BARBER, Robert L	F-8-27
BARBERO, Michael P	A-11-22
BARBOUR, Carson M [56]	Walls of the Missing
BARER, David	L-1-14
BARFIELD, Noah W	Walls of the Missing
BARGFREDE, Henry L	B-4-16
BARIANI, John F	K-20-19
BARKER, Cecil	Walls of the Missing
BARKER, Delford W [57]	Walls of the Missing
BARKER, John W	Walls of the Missing
BARKER, Monzel	M-9-4
BARKER, Phillip N	I-14-21
BARKEY, Raymond O	G-2-7
BARKLEY, Haden E	D-14-13
BARKS, Arthur E	Walls of the Missing
BARKSDALE, Harry E [58]	I-18-5
BARLEY, Frederick W	H-5-10

BARLOW, Albert E	I-5-12
BARLOW, Arvill D	E-18-17
BARLOW, Ed L Jr	H-7-2
BARLOW, Ward L	O-5-6
BARNA, John	G-12-16
BARNARD, John R	A-14-4
BARNARD, Norris C Jr	K-19-9
BARNARD, Wilson	C-21-19
BARNES, Clyde W	O-11-7
BARNES, George W	Walls of the Missing
BARNES, Jesse L	Walls of the Missing
BARNES, Leo F	F-10-9
BARNES, Robert C	G-9-20
BARNES, Royal E	G-8-22
BARNES, William C	C-9-1
BARNETT, Charles Lynn	C-10-30
BARNETT, Daniel J	A-9-7
BARNETT, James M	O-16-14
BARNETT, Joseph V	M-21-15
BARNETT, Robert L [59]	Walls of the Missing
BARNEY, Ervin C	L-16-22
BARNHART, John H	J-14-13
BARNHART, Kenneth C	A-15-1
BARNHILL, Wilbur R	Walls of the Missing
BARNITZ, Latrobe M Jr [60]	C-10-18
BARNSHAW, Joseph A	L-18-17
BARNUM, Eugene E Jr	D-12-24
BARNUM, William J	D-12-23
BARR, Ralph	A-5-12
BARRAS, James J	Walls of the Missing

BARRETT, Andrew J	C-18-8
BARRETT, David P Jr	A-7-5
BARRETT, Francis P Jr	B-21-31
BARRETT, George B	C-20-4
BARRETT, Johnie W	G-14-3
BARRICK, Rodney T	B-8-18
BARRIX, James D	H-4-27
BARRON, George E	F-2-6
BARRON, Thomas P	Walls of the Missing
BARROW, Pearl F	Walls of the Missing
BARRY, Charles R	K-20-11
BARRY, John K	D-6-10
BARTALINO, Joseph	G-6-13
BARTELS, Earl E	G-15-9
BARTH, Leo T	I-2-22
BARTHOLOMEW, Harry H	M-12-11
BARTHOLOW, Ralph	Walls of the Missing
BARTLETT, Robert E	Walls of the Missing
BARTLETT, William H Jr	G-7-14
BARTO, John	B-8-13
BARTON, Harold T	Walls of the Missing
BARTON, Junior R	I-18-4
BARTON, Virgil E	I-20-21
BARTROPE, Walter D	M-14-8
BASALYGA, Walter	B-21-15
BASDEN, Clovis C	D-19-14
BASHAM, Millis	D-4-26
BASS, Albert	L-13-16
BASS, Charles W	Walls of the Missing
BASS, Warren G	B-1-23
BASSETT, George S	I-1-3
BASSING, Charles H	Walls of the Missing
BATCHELOR, William J	J-12-5
BATEMAN, Henry F	E-18-19
BATES, Cecil R	Walls of the Missing
BATES, Edgar S	D-11-16
BATES, Homer P	L-8-18
BATES, Joseph C	O-4-9
BATHURST, Verlan E	L-16-8
BATSOS, Savas J	I-18-6
BATTJES, Edwin H	M-11-17
BATTLES, Nathaniel	A-1-26
BAUER, Harold F	J-18-17
BAUER, Raymond J	F-6-18
BAUM, Vern E	F-5-3
BAUM, William J	Walls of the Missing

BAUMAN, Hubert T II	C-6-24
BAUMANN, Harold W	O-10-12
BAUMANN, James S	E-8-19
BAUMANN, Jay W	A-18-13
BAUMGARTEN, Bernard V	Walls of the Missing
BAVOSA, John J	L-7-17
BAXTER, Edward O	H-8-22
BAXTER, Luther	L-7-3
BAYLEY, William G	A-19-1
BAZAN, Robert P	H-14-24
BAZIER, Herbert H	P-13-17
BEACHLER, Alan	O-5-10
BEACHLER, Ray	Walls of the Missing
BEACHT, William F	F-18-10
BEADLES, William H	I-12-21
BEALL, Charles E	B-17-19
BEAMON, William H	K-15-5
BEAN, Donald J	D-13-1
BEARD, Raymond C	D-18-22
BEARDSLEY, Joseph W	C-13-30
BEARDSLEY, Terence G	O-15-1
BEARDSLEY, Theodore A	C-13-29
BEASLEY, Dale D	D-12-29
BEASLEY, Herman E	Walls of the Missing
BEASLEY, Inman	Walls of the Missing
BEASLEY, James H Jr	P-14-15
BEATTIE, Norman J	A-11-24
BEATTY, Dwight E	F-9-27
BEATTY, John P	O-2-6
BEATY, John	B-8-32
BEAUCHAMP, Armand R	G-3-25
BEAUDIN, Abel L	F-21-15
BEAUPREY, Clarence J	E-2-22
BECHLER, Harold J	A-5-30
BECK, Efird D	K-14-6
BECK, Eugene M	Walls of the Missing
BECK, Paul Z	C-9-4
BECK, Sidney S	J-20-1
BECK, Silas P	L-1-4
BECKER, Aaron M	H-16-8
BECKER, Charles P	Walls of the Missing
BECKER, James R	Walls of the Missing
BECKER, John L	Walls of the Missing
BECKNELL, Wallace E	Walls of the Missing
BECKNER, Willie G	Walls of the Missing
BEDARD, Earl G	P-19-7
BEDENFIELD, Ollie L	N-11-11
BEEBE, Frederick G	B-8-7
BEEKEN, Lewis L	K-4-12
BEELE, George F	F-8-3
BEERMAN, Milan C	G-3-9
BEESON, Clarence S	O-5-4
BEESON, William H	I-8-21
BEETHE, Alvin	Walls of the Missing
BEHLER, Curtis F	H-4-24
BEI, Anthony	F-4-6
BEIDEMAN, George W	L-1-18
BEIN, George F	C-5-20
BEINE, George K	A-3-11
BEIREIS, Robert G	H-1-21
BEISEKER, Marvin H Jr	O-9-10
BEKIERSKI, Michael J	K-15-8
BELANGER, Raymond J	A-19-19
BELCHER, George B	K-9-19
BELCHER, Glenn L	I-5-18
BELCHER, Guy E	G-4-19
BELCHER, William A	O-14-11
BELILES, Otis E H	Walls of the Missing
BELL, Arthur E	D-16-11
BELL, Benjamin P Jr	A-15-20
BELL, Carl G	G-9-2
BELL, Donald D	E-16-17
BELL, Frank L	G-11-7
BELL, Henry J	H-20-11
BELL, Ivan G	I-19-2
BELL, James H	L-4-14
BELL, Le Vert W Jr	Walls of the Missing
BELL, Marion L	H-6-2
BELL, Walter E	C-12-9
BELL, William J	N-9-7
BELL, Wilson M	E-12-26
BELLAVIA, Anthony P	Walls of the Missing
BELTCH, Marcus W	N-1-9
BELVEAL, Clyde S	C-12-21
BENDER, Paul R	C-16-28
BENDER, Ralph R	Walls of the Missing
BENDON, Louis A	H-3-15
BENEDETTO, Mario T	C-9-26
BENEDICT, Francis L	Walls of the Missing
BENGSON, Wallace W	L-16-16
BENISH, Jacob E	B-11-23
BENN, Harry C	K-11-3
BENNER, Nevin C	G-11-6
BENNETHUM, Nelson W	B-19-30
BENNETT, John H	E-1-24
BENNETT, Robert L	Walls of the Missing
BENNETT, Robert L	F-17-2
BENNETT, Stanley D	Walls of the Missing
BENNETT, Sydney F	G-9-25
BENNETT, Willie A	A-9-24
BENSE, Wilbert H	D-19-15
BENSON, Dorcey G	L-18-18
BENSON, Edward	K-13-9
BENSUK, John A	K-21-18
BENT, Bertram L	G-2-27
BENTIS, James	D-11-12
BENTON, Robert Tyrie	I-9-3
BENTSON, Rhody M	Walls of the Missing
BERAN, Roman B	Walls of the Missing
BERARDI, Robert M	B-12-28
BERDUCCI, Alphonse A	E-21-21
BERG, George J	A-5-7
BERGEN, James N	B-10-23
BERGER, Arnold	B-10-5
BERGER, Carl J	J-9-21
BERGER, Herbert R	N-16-8
BERGER, Samuel W Jr	E-20-18
BERGERON, Dean	F-19-5
BERGERON, George O	H-5-6
BERGGREN, Kenneth R	B-11-7
BERGMAN, Harold E	Walls of the Missing
BERGMAN, William E	G-4-7
BERGMAYR, Hans	F-5-21
BERGONZI, Frank A	E-4-20
BERGREEN, Carl G	B-16-25
BERGSTEDT, Sten E	C-4-6
BERGSTROM, Carl W	L-10-3
BERGSTROM, Donald E	Walls of the Missing
BERGUM, Arne O	P-4-17
BERKEY, George P	D-21-15
BERNACCHI, Adolph	Walls of the Missing
BERNACKI, Andrew S	I-15-18
BERNAL, Seferino	Walls of the Missing
BERNARD, Charles H Jr	Walls of the Missing
BERNARD, Ernest C	B-6-2
BERNARDINI, Mario J	H-10-26
BERNAT, Joseph F	D-13-2
BERNIER, Camille J	K-10-12
BERREY, Vernon L	O-8-1
BERRY, Donald K	J-18-9
BERRY, Donald L	B-9-1
BERRY, Martin J	I-6-3
BERRY, Melvin C	N-9-8
BERRY, William L	G-12-7
BERTELS, La Verne A	C-14-20
BERTELSON, John E	G-11-15
BERTOGLIO, James S	G-12-18
BERTON, Leno L	A-12-23
BERTONNEAU, George M	A-12-2
BERUBE, Leo G	B-17-25
BEST, James R	H-18-20
BEST, William E	A-18-27
BESTE, Clement O	H-3-10
BESTE, Jack J	G-5-8
BESTIC, Joseph	F-3-12
BESTUL, Luther J	C-14-29
BETHEL, James F	G-20-22
BETHUY, Reginald J	M-2-3
BETTIN, Norman F	C-19-30
BETZ, Francis P	B-9-30
BETZ, Wiliam R	I-7-16
BEUS, Raymon C	Walls of the Missing
BEVERLY, Kenneth W	C-15-21
BEVINS, Raymond G	G-18-25
BEYER, Lynwood W	F-7-1
BICA, Thomas	L-9-13
BICK, John W	C-19-4
BICKLEY, Vernon E	M-13-3
BIDDLE, Cleon B	Walls of the Missing
BIDDLECOMB, Samuel F	L-10-12
BIDNEY, Joseph R	M-9-9
BIDWELL, John E	E-16-22
BIEBER, Arnold	H-17-12
BIEDERMAN, Carl A	E-13-15

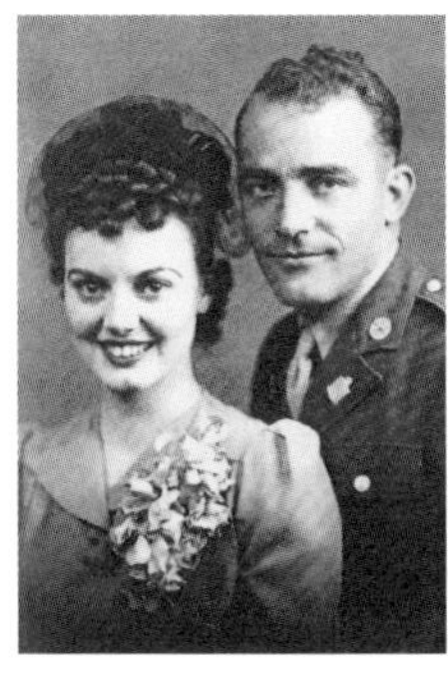

61

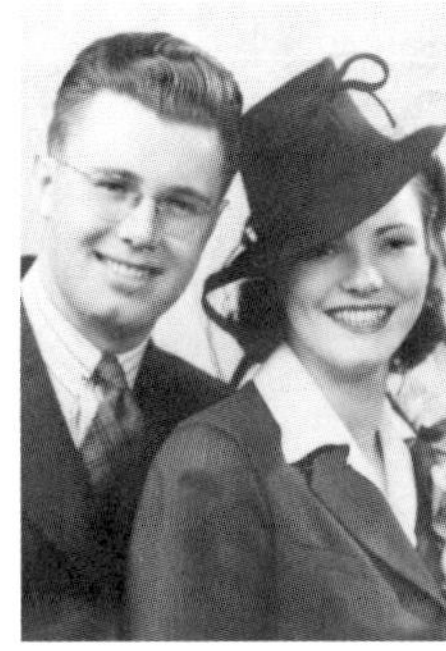

62

Name	Location
BIELASKI, Michael J	C-11-21
BIELAWSKI, Stanley F	B-16-14
BIELER, Mike	E-9-2
BIENKOWSKI, Chester J	Walls of the Missing
BIGGERSTAFF, Harry W	B-1-1
BIGLER, John M	C-12-20
BIGLIN, Joseph H	M-11-8
BILBAO, Roy J	Walls of the Missing
BILLINGS, Earl R	M-9-8
BILLINGSLEY, Floyd T R	B-13-14
BILLITER, Charles M	F-3-2
BILODEAU, Henry F	A-3-12
BILYEU, Gail W	H-13-5
BINDREIFF, Laurence W	E-4-13
BINDRIM, Edward G	J-7-19
BINNIX, John H Jr	H-20-27
BIRD, Ward B	F-15-27
BIRDSEY, Charles B	Walls of the Missing
BIREK, Martin L	Walls of the Missing
BIRKET, Noble L	F-14-12
BISANZ, Edward R	Walls of the Missing
BISBEE, David D	D-17-15
BISH, Dickie O	K-6-12
BISHOP, Dewey K	Walls of the Missing
BISHOP, Edward L	G-11-23
BISHOP, Houston	O-17-15
BISHOP, Robert R	Walls of the Missing
BISHOP, William M	Walls of the Missing
BISLICH, Robert H	F-14-1
BISSAILLON, Edmond A	I-12-20
BISSELL, John R	F-19-10
BISSEN, Henry	C-7-3
BITTERMAN, Frederick D	M-16-9
BIXBY, Philips T Jr	J-8-17
BIXLER, Clarence C	Walls of the Missing
BIZAY, Frank J	H-4-12
BJERTNESS, Theodore O	A-2-26
BJORNSGAARD, Calvin O	B-20-20
BJORNSTAD, Philip R	D-3-16
BLACK, Boyd M	O-11-17
BLACK, Howard T	E-3-6
BLACK, Howard V	F-16-6
BLACK, John K Jr	N-2-3
BLACK, Napoleon	Walls of the Missing
BLACK, Robert C	M-20-3
BLACK, Robert E	G-21-22
BLACKARD, George J	C-7-13
BLACKBURN, Charles E	Walls of the Missing
BLACKETT, Jack B	E-6-2
BLACKWELDER, David E	L-7-21
BLACKWELL, Howard R	P-11-1
BLACKWELL, Thomas B	Walls of the Missing
BLACKWOOD, Joseph R	A-3-5
BLADECKI, Jerome E	G-15-16
BLAHA, Robert L	K-19-13
BLAIDA, Henry	D-7-13
BLAIR, Earl L	D-10-2
BLAIR, Walter A	Walls of the Missing
BLAIR, Walter E	Walls of the Missing
BLAKE, Dewey J	A-21-31
BLAKE, Harold S	I-5-11
BLAKE, James E	E-14-19
BLAKE, John T	O-20-6
BLAKELEY, Eugene S	L-6-16
BLANCHARD, Daniel C	Walls of the Missing
BLANCHARD, Joseph T	C-8-14
BLANCHARD, Robert M	Walls of the Missing
BLANCHARD, Theodore A	Walls of the Missing
BLANCHE, Edwin L	E-5-18
BLAND, Whitney C	O-3-9
BLANKENSHIP, Paul G	Walls of the Missing
BLANTON, Claude T	Walls of the Missing
BLANTON, Hermann R	I-20-15
BLANTON, Raymond C	Walls of the Missing
BLASENAK, Arthur F	Walls of the Missing
BLASSINGAME, Cloyce N	K-21-15
BLASTIC, Clarence J	E-18-13
BLATNICK, Anthony	Walls of the Missing
BLATNIK, Joseph A	Walls of the Missing
BLAY, Earl L	E-18-14
BLAZINA, Lawrence F	L-16-29
BLESSEN, John I	H-18-12
BLESSING, William R	K-20-22
BLEYLE, George V	Walls of the Missing
BLINKS, David A	F-7-15
BLISCERD, John W	F-15-15
BLISS, Stephen A	C-11-3
BLOCK, Lawrence	Walls of the Missing
BLOCK, Robert W	J-19-7
BLODGETT, Fred C	Walls of the Missing
BLOMBAUM, Carl	G-5-26
BLOOD, Cyril W	B-12-29
BLOOD, Lloyd J	Walls of the Missing
BLOOMFIELD, Edward K	A-14-5
BLOOMFIELD, Philip J	A-3-26
BLOORE, Robert B	F-14-18
BLOSE, Jack M	F-18-23
BLOSS, Robert J	B-14-3
BLOSSMAN, Allan M	C-8-6
BLOUNT, Edward H	D-13-15
BLOUNT, Lester	B-1-24
BOAL, Vernon C	F-8-4
BOARDMAN, Donald H	D-18-31
BOATRIGHT, Jasper G	A-2-16
BOCCANFUSO, Joseph	G-6-26
BOCHE, Robert C	B-15-10
BOCHINSKI, Stanley A	P-6-5
BODA, John	G-17-11
BODINE, Louie R	F-6-23
BOEGLIN, Richard W	C-12-23
BOEHM, Michael A	Walls of the Missing
BOEHM, Walter A	E-3-10
BOEHME, Robert G Jr	K-5-14
BOERSEMA, Frank	Walls of the Missing
BOESE, Pete	C-1-2
BOGACZ, Walter L	A-11-6
BOGAN, John E	G-12-2
BOGER, Walter	J-14-21
BOGET, James B	F-18-19
BOGGS, Henry B	D-5-17
BOGUE, Daniel L	Walls of the Missing
BOHANNON, Jackson R	J-9-12
BOHLER, Clinton H	F-3-20
BOHLING, Erwin H [61]	C-16-30
BOHRER, Jack D	Walls of the Missing
BOHY, Edward	L-2-19
BOIES, Herbert D	P-11-3
BOISJOLIE, Ernest N	G-21-5
BOITANO, Charles H Jr	B-18-27
BOKENO, Joseph M	F-11-5
BOLAND, John O	I-14-14
BOLAND, John P	A-11-17
BOLDEN, John D	C-19-28
BOLES, Gerald D	A-4-21
BOLESKI, Donald J	O-4-12
BOLICK, Henry P Jr	Walls of the Missing
BOLIN, Rudolph E	K-9-22
BOLLENBACHER, Joseph L	F-15-6
BOLTE, Rudolph E	E-4-26
BOLZ, William F [62]	H-13-14
BOMAR, George R	G-20-23
BOND, Francis R	E-17-7
BONDIOLI, Joe	I-21-17
BONDS, Howard T	Walls of the Missing
BONDS, Jim D	E-20-12
BONDURANT, Melvin P	L-9-15
BONDY, Edward J	Walls of the Missing
BONEN, Albert J	C-19-29
BONET, Pascal B	N-11-13
BONFANTI, Samuel J	F-1-26
BONHAM, John S	H-2-25
BONILLA, Nicholas L	K-17-16
BONNASSIOLLE, John P	Walls of the Missing
BONNER, James R	J-17-9
BONO, John J	Walls of the Missing
BONSER, Wilbur E	M-11-10

BOOD, Earle C	A-19-31
BOOK, Sterling H Jr	Walls of the Missing
BOOKER, Bruce H	M-14-4
BOOM, William C	H-19-2
BOOTH, Carl H Jr	Walls of the Missing
BOOTH, Dwight K	Walls of the Missing
BOOTH, Edwin Bray	E-1-11
BOOTH, Harry B	C-15-11
BORA, Nicholas P	A-20-30
BORACK, Milton	C-10-27
BORDEN, Paul L Jr	M-9-10
BOREL, Gilbert	Walls of the Missing
BORGENS, Harold E	Walls of the Missing
BORK, Kenneth G	J-19-4
BORNEMANN, Albert L Jr	I-14-16
BORNSTEIN, Harry M	H-20-12
BOROWKA, Manny	N-3-7
BOROWSKI, Joseph E	C-15-6
BORRIES, Raymond A	G-17-25
BORTH, Bruce W	G-4-24
BORTON, Don A	P-16-14
BOSCH, Francis H	Walls of the Missing
BOSMAN, Clement C	B-19-18
BOSNAVITS, Eugene Jr	I-12-7
BOSSERT, Bernard	K-13-6
BOTKINS, Conro R	F-12-13
BOTKOWSKI, George S	N-16-2
BOTSIS, Nick	Walls of the Missing
BOTTS, Le Roy E	E-13-14
BOUCHARD, Charles W	L-4-11
BOUDREAUX, Alcide	I-2-4
BOUFFARD, Edward J	N-5-1
BOUNDAR, William	J-16-8
BOURASSA, Wilfred F	G-17-19
BOURG, Robert W	B-14-26
BOUSKEY, Francis O	E-18-7
BOUTON, Thomas L	H-5-19
BOUTWELL, Harold A	F-17-17
BOUZOUKAS, Dimitrios	C-2-29
BOWEN, Clarence M	B-12-11
BOWEN, Gordon K	Walls of the Missing
BOWER, George H	D-18-27
BOWER, James A	G-10-27
BOWERS, Charles W	H-12-11
BOWERS, William W	H-18-16
BOWMAN, Reed O	I-10-18
BOWMAN, Thomas W	N-7-12
BOWSER, Ray F	I-14-8
BOXMAN, Howard F	P-11-4
BOYD, Arthur S	Walls of the Missing
BOYD, Harry E	G-14-8
BOYD, Harvey J	Walls of the Missing
BOYD, Herald R	Walls of the Missing
BOYD, James R	O-18-2
BOYD, John R	B-19-21
BOYD, John T	B-16-9
BOYD, Raymond C	B-7-19
BOYD, Robert H	F-20-25
BOYER, Vincent P	K-9-6
BOYLAN, Frank C	A-19-17
BOYLE, Bernard J	K-9-10
BOYLE, James J	K-2-13
BOYLE, Robert J	K-19-19
BOYLES, William V	E-16-19
BOYLIN, Henry C Jr	Walls of the Missing
BOYNTON, Hugh	Walls of the Missing
BOYSEN, John H	D-19-19
BOZARTH, Theodore R	N-1-17
BOZICH, Michael	Walls of the Missing
BOZOCHOVIC, Edward J	G-14-20
BRAATZ, Elroy J	F-15-11
BRAATZ, Floyd F	D-19-18
BRACK, Alvia E	D-12-14
BRADFIELD, Earl	I-21-6
BRADFIELD, Harold K	I-5-3
BRADISH, Thomas M	Walls of the Missing
BRADLEY, Frederick P	A-4-22
BRADLEY, Raymond E	A-11-32
BRADSHER, Walter L	Walls of the Missing
BRADY, Glen	M-3-6
BRADY, James E Sr	A-18-6
BRADY, James F	H-18-6
BRADY, Paul P	B-13-31
BRAGDON, Charles F	I-11-16
BRAGG, Paul W	Walls of the Missing
BRAMEL, Bruce M	B-4-22
BRAMLEY, Warren J	J-19-1
BRAMMER, Thomas E	H-6-7
BRAMUCCI, Aldo	C-21-11
BRANAM, Leonard M	Walls of the Missing
BRANCH, James S	O-4-14
BRANDENBURG, Lawrence J	Walls of the Missing
BRANLEY, Michael J	C-21-18
BRANN, Fred	Walls of the Missing
BRANNAN, Aubrey T	A-11-13
BRANNAN, Murvyn V	E-5-2
BRANOM, Buford E	D-10-19
BRANSCUM, William C	L-18-21
BRANSKI, Richard J	N-6-1
BRAUCH, Carlton G	A-15-27
BRAUCHLER, Herbert J	I-6-15
BRAUN, William L	H-14-17
BRAWNER, Lesley	I-18-9
BRAY, George M	Walls of the Missing
BRAYMAN, George H	B-4-9
BREAULT, Arthur R	A-20-4
BREAUX, Lawrence	K-11-11
BREAW, Edwin G	Walls of the Missing
BREDLOW, Glen W	A-13-18
BREEDEN, Donald P	Walls of the Missing
BREEDEN, Earl	Walls of the Missing
BREEZE, Thomas Jr	F-7-18
BREILTGENS, Kurt W	D-17-2
BREININGER, Marshall D	E-13-20
BREMER, Glenn A	J-2-18
BREMMER, Joseph J	C-16-24
BREMNER, Ronald	A-2-20
BREN, Bennie F Jr	B-7-2
BRENDEL, John H	L-6-1
BRENDLINGER, Bert	D-14-27
BRENNAN, John T	J-8-15
BRENNER, Irving S	E-3-4
BRENNER, Joseph L	Walls of the Missing
BRENNING, Walter T	A-17-3
BREUNIG, Wilbur W	Walls of the Missing
BREUNING, Charles R	A-2-2
BREWER, Daniel	G-5-16
BREWER, James K	K-19-10
BREWER, Robert R	Walls of the Missing
BREWER, William M Jr	H-18-23
BREZINA, Paul G	F-1-22
BREZNICKY, Joseph F	K-12-1
BRIAN, Donald C	Walls of the Missing
BRICE, Ray E	O-18-16
BRICKER, Daniel M	C-2-10
BRICKHOUSE, Harry G Jr	J-8-6
BRIDGE, Arlie R Jr	Walls of the Missing
BRIDGES, Clarence D	D-9-2
BRIDGES, Melvin W	D-4-7
BRIDGES, Oakey H	Walls of the Missing
BRIDGES, William M	L-2-14
BRIFNEK, John Jr	K-3-7
BRIGGS, Frank Stewart	I-3-13
BRIGHAM, Robert W	G-1-5
BRIGHT, Notra J	P-22-15
BRIGHTSMAN, Gerald	N-8-1
BRILEY, Berton E	Walls of the Missing
BRINEGAR, Junior R	J-19-13
BRINGLE, Ross E	O-3-17
BRINKLEY, Luther R	J-2-17
BRINKMAN, Donald C	Walls of the Missing
BRISACH, Joseph C	P-20-5
BRISKIN, Solon R	Walls of the Missing
BRITT, Robert F	G-2-24
BRITTAIN, Arthur E	Walls of the Missing
BRITTON, Eugene W	A-15-26
BRITTON, Kermit T	A-2-24
BRITTON, Paul M	M-9-16
BRIZENDINE, Clyde B	I-2-13
BRIZENDINE, Luther M	I-2-14
BROADWAY, Henry Jr	A-11-18
BROCKOVICH, Steve	I-17-14
BRODBECK, Alvin A	C-18-5
BRODELL, Alvin M	D-19-13
BRODERSON, Kenneth E	E-16-8
BRODIE, James J	J-13-4
BRODIE, James W	L-15-16
BRODING, Robert C	C-20-26
BRODMAN, Louis H	B-19-19
BRODOCK, Harold E	E-14-21
BRODOWSKI, Edward	E-16-20
BRODSKY, Milton	C-6-12
BROGDEN, John P	O-8-14
BROHMAN, Howard E Jr	D-10-31

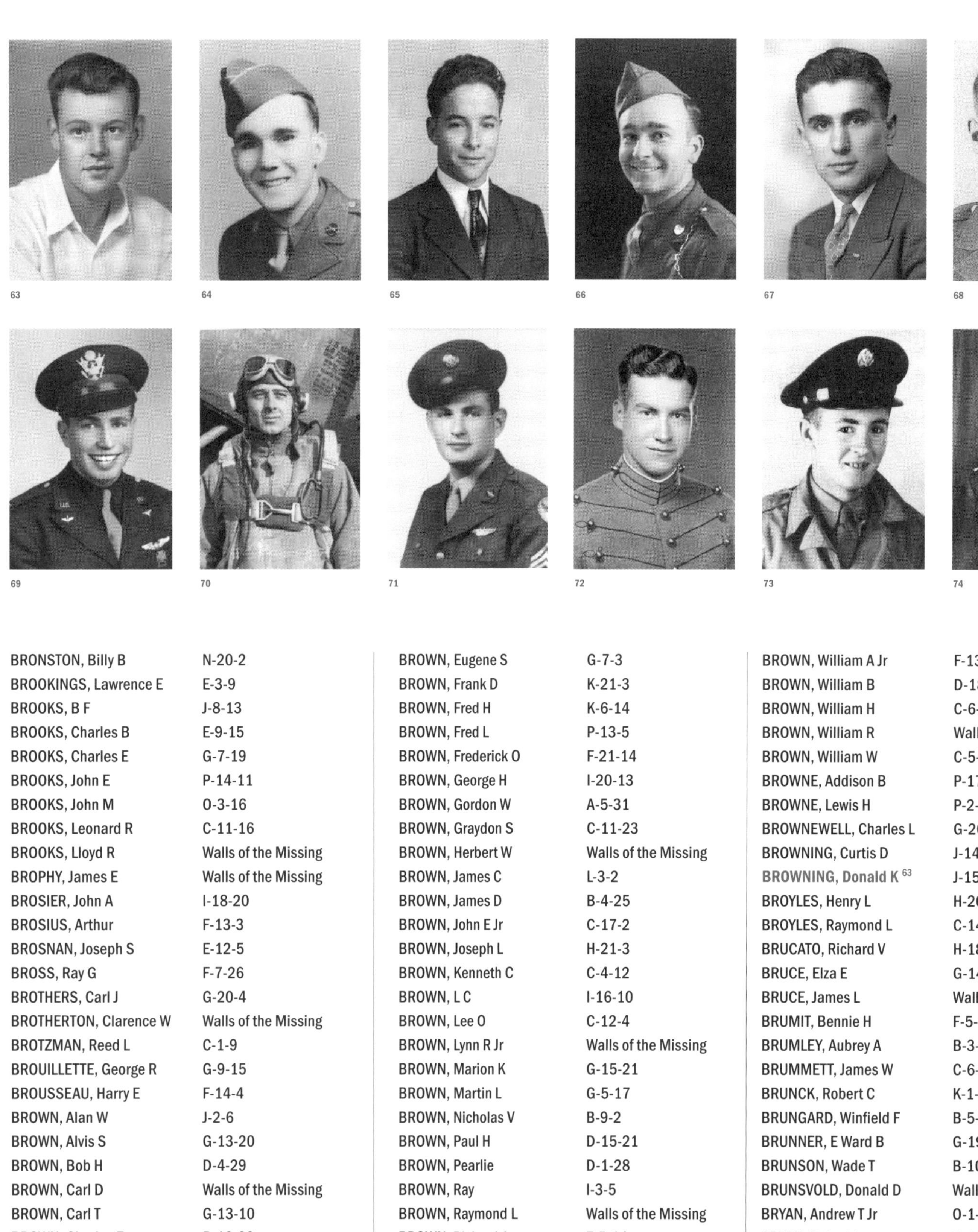

63 64 65 66 67 68

69 70 71 72 73 74

Name	Location
BRONSTON, Billy B	N-20-2
BROOKINGS, Lawrence E	E-3-9
BROOKS, B F	J-8-13
BROOKS, Charles B	E-9-15
BROOKS, Charles E	G-7-19
BROOKS, John E	P-14-11
BROOKS, John M	O-3-16
BROOKS, Leonard R	C-11-16
BROOKS, Lloyd R	Walls of the Missing
BROPHY, James E	Walls of the Missing
BROSIER, John A	I-18-20
BROSIUS, Arthur	F-13-3
BROSNAN, Joseph S	E-12-5
BROSS, Ray G	F-7-26
BROTHERS, Carl J	G-20-4
BROTHERTON, Clarence W	Walls of the Missing
BROTZMAN, Reed L	C-1-9
BROUILLETTE, George R	G-9-15
BROUSSEAU, Harry E	F-14-4
BROWN, Alan W	J-2-6
BROWN, Alvis S	G-13-20
BROWN, Bob H	D-4-29
BROWN, Carl D	Walls of the Missing
BROWN, Carl T	G-13-10
BROWN, Charles E	B-12-22
BROWN, Charles E	Walls of the Missing
BROWN, Charlie D	B-17-31
BROWN, Chester R	K-5-17
BROWN, Cornelis	B-6-24
BROWN, Donald W	I-1-18
BROWN, Donival H	K-20-20
BROWN, Earl T Jr	A-15-23
BROWN, Emmett Hood	G-19-14
BROWN, Eugene S	G-7-3
BROWN, Frank D	K-21-3
BROWN, Fred H	K-6-14
BROWN, Fred L	P-13-5
BROWN, Frederick O	F-21-14
BROWN, George H	I-20-13
BROWN, Gordon W	A-5-31
BROWN, Graydon S	C-11-23
BROWN, Herbert W	Walls of the Missing
BROWN, James C	L-3-2
BROWN, James D	B-4-25
BROWN, John E Jr	C-17-2
BROWN, Joseph L	H-21-3
BROWN, Kenneth C	C-4-12
BROWN, L C	I-16-10
BROWN, Lee O	C-12-4
BROWN, Lynn R Jr	Walls of the Missing
BROWN, Marion K	G-15-21
BROWN, Martin L	G-5-17
BROWN, Nicholas V	B-9-2
BROWN, Paul H	D-15-21
BROWN, Pearlie	D-1-28
BROWN, Ray	I-3-5
BROWN, Raymond L	Walls of the Missing
BROWN, Richard A	E-5-14
BROWN, Richard C	Walls of the Missing
BROWN, Richard J	C-11-12
BROWN, Roy A	C-3-3
BROWN, Russell	H-3-9
BROWN, Samuel Hoy	D-4-8
BROWN, Thomas M	Walls of the Missing
BROWN, Troy	P-15-3
BROWN, Warren E	Walls of the Missing
BROWN, William A Jr	F-13-11
BROWN, William B	D-18-30
BROWN, William H	C-6-27
BROWN, William R	Walls of the Missing
BROWN, William W	C-5-9
BROWNE, Addison B	P-17-5
BROWNE, Lewis H	P-2-6
BROWNEWELL, Charles L	G-20-15
BROWNING, Curtis D	J-14-7
BROWNING, Donald K [63]	J-15-2
BROYLES, Henry L	H-20-16
BROYLES, Raymond L	C-14-15
BRUCATO, Richard V	H-18-5
BRUCE, Elza E	G-14-15
BRUCE, James L	Walls of the Missing
BRUMIT, Bennie H	F-5-4
BRUMLEY, Aubrey A	B-3-31
BRUMMETT, James W	C-6-17
BRUNCK, Robert C	K-1-8
BRUNGARD, Winfield F	B-5-27
BRUNNER, E Ward B	G-19-9
BRUNSON, Wade T	B-10-1
BRUNSVOLD, Donald D	Walls of the Missing
BRYAN, Andrew T Jr	O-1-14
BRYAN, Robert L	B-1-5
BRYAN, William M	P-15-14
BRYAN, William S	N-15-4
BRYAN, William T	H-6-6
BRYANT, Donald	N-9-3
BRYANT, Leahmon E	B-10-16
BRYANT, Lenard L	G-7-22
BRYANT, Oral E	I-5-8
BRYANT, Richard E	J-12-3

Name	Location
BRYCSAK, Stephen	B-16-11
BRYK, John A	Walls of the Missing
BUCCI, Frank P	C-6-26
BUCCIGROSSI, Anthony R	H-19-7
BUCHANAN, Amos R	N-11-14
BUCHANAN, Franklin	H-18-25
BUCHER, Ralph B	H-4-14
BUCHHEIT, Edward L	Walls of the Missing
BUCHHOLZ, Raymond F	C-8-4
BUCK, John	K-12-2
BUCKBERG, Henry	N-1-4
BUCKLAND, Arthur L	J-5-6
BUCKLEY, Fergus P	J-18-14
BUCKLEY, Lawrence M	A-19-8
BUCKLEY, Robert H	J-18-12
BUCKLIN, John F	G-10-6
BUDDES, Anthony G	Walls of the Missing
BUGELER, Walter J	G-3-8
BUGG, Woodrow	H-15-17
BUHL, Vernon	F-21-18
BULGER, Martin P Jr	P-8-9
BULGER, Robert J	P-8-10
BULHACK, Mitchel	Walls of the Missing
BULKLEY, Herbert S	G-8-24
BULLARD, Frank E	Walls of the Missing
BULLARD, Talmadge A	E-1-18
BULPITT, Lorne F	D-1-20
BUMGARNER, Hansel D	F-5-1
BUMPUS, Julian	J-7-9
BUNCH, Robert E L Jr	B-11-28
BUNNER, Vance N	A-11-14
BUNTYN, James W T	O-6-11
BURACKER, Richard S	E-17-3
BURAN, Walter J	J-3-19
BURANICH, Joseph	A-6-31
BURBRIDGE, Michael J	C-1-8
BURCHETT, Grady M	F-10-8
BURD, William G	G-3-11
BURDGE, Dorothy Jane	B-7-4
BURDGE, Myron M	G-2-20
BURDICK, Eugene F	A-7-11
BURDICK, Kenneth J	E-21-6
BURDISS, Cornelius F	G-3-5
BURDULIS, John F	O-11-4
BUREN, Clifford L	Walls of the Missing
BURG, Sol	L-17-9
BURGE, Floyd E	B-12-9
BURGER, Thomas O Jr	I-5-16
BURGERT, Howard R	M-19-6
BURGESON, Lawrence L	P-21-4
BURGESS, Robert L	E-1-9
BURGETT, Marcus C	D-15-31
BURGGRAF, Carl T	O-1-5
BURGHDUFF, Charles L	P-6-12
BURGINS, Hubert B	N-8-6
BURITSCH, William R	B-2-13
BURK, Forrest G	A-4-28
BURKARDT, Robert B	A-19-16
BURKE, Daniel C	F-5-20
BURKE, Joseph R	H-9-18
BURKE, Loras A	D-17-3
BURKE, Vernon C Jr	I-15-13
BURKETT, Leroy D	O-1-7
BURKEY, Albert R	E-15-18
BURKEY, James R	D-18-14
BURKHALTER, Hans	A-8-32
BURKHAMMER, James F	H-17-21
BURKHARDT, Robert H	D-16-15
BURKHART, Donald L	N-18-4
BURKS, Virgil L	L-11-16
BURLEIGH, Lawrence C	Walls of the Missing
BURLINGAME, Harrison J [64]	F-16-13
BURMEISTER, Rueben B	E-17-24
BURNETT, Henry O	Walls of the Missing
BURNETT, John F	F-4-8
BURNETT, Monroe	B-12-15
BURNETTE, Floyd A	A-9-10
BURNETTE, R L [65]	D-6-18
BURNS, Alwin C Jr	L-10-16
BURNS, Cecil H	Walls of the Missing
BURNS, David Y	J-1-14
BURNS, Frank J	I-15-9
BURNS, Fred A	D-20-30
BURNS, J W	F-9-19
BURNS, James E	H-1-11
BURNS, John H	B-19-11
BURNS, Joseph F	J-5-22
BURNS, Loris E	O-18-10
BURNS, Robert W	B-12-17
BURNS, William J	M-9-7
BURR, Thomas J	C-16-12
BURRIS, Charles L	E-11-25
BURRIS, Frank E	D-21-29
BURROUGHS, Joseph T [66]	H-21-11
BURTON, Harlan D	Walls of the Missing
BURTON, James D Jr	Walls of the Missing
BURTON, Jerome E	Walls of the Missing
BURY, Leonard A	C-6-6
BURZANKO, Chester [67]	D-5-7
BUSBY, Harry F	F-1-8
BUSBY, William G [68]	H-9-16
BUSENBARK, Joseph S	Walls of the Missing
BUSEY, Robert W	H-21-26
BUSH, Frank B	I-10-5
BUSH, Gilbert M	M-8-10
BUSHEE, Frederick G	L-7-15
BUSHEY, Benjamin J	M-13-13
BUSHON, Arthur A	C-11-32
BUSK, Alman F	H-6-22
BUSKIRK, Jack L	Walls of the Missing
BUSKIRK, James S	E-17-20
BUSS, Elmer [69]	D-14-29
BUSSARD, Eugene P	M-13-14
BUSSEAR, Max H	G-7-5
BUSSIERE, Arsene H	G-7-26
BUTCHKO, George	I-6-12
BUTLER, Cecil R	E-13-5
BUTLER, Ival E [70]	Walls of the Missing
BUTLER, Wade H Jr	D-1-2
BUTSCH, James A	J-10-13
BUTTERFIELD, Joseph V Jr	K-7-5
BUTTS, Clarence A	A-21-17
BUTZ, Wallace H	L-6-6
BUZZARD, Hampton	Walls of the Missing
BUZZES, Alvorida	Walls of the Missing
BYARD, Robert J	Walls of the Missing
BYERLY, John T	F-19-8
BYERMAN, Harry E	G-5-18
BYERS, Glenn E	Walls of the Missing
BYERS, John F	N-5-3
BYERS, Leon A [71]	P-22-6
BYERS, Oscar G	L-1-3
BYRD, Ernest G	D-1-1
BYRD, Orville Jr	K-7-18
BYRNE, Alfred B	C-8-13
BYRNE, Austin P [72]	Walls of the Missing
BYRNE, William H	H-14-22
BYRNES, Robert L	J-13-10
BYRNES, William J [73]	J-18-7
BYROM, Glenn K	L-3-14

C

Name	Location
CABE, Kenneth R	Walls of the Missing
CABIC, James F	O-3-13
CABRAL, Albert	E-4-11
CACCESE, John J	G-2-1
CADDICK, William E Jr	B-14-21
CAHILL, Edward F	F-19-25
CAHILL, Edward R	P-3-9
CAHILL, John W	J-1-8
CAHILL, Robert J	E-7-2
CAHOW, Robert T	Walls of the Missing
CAIN, James F	L-3-22
CAIN, Morris A Jr	A-19-18
CAIRNEY, Thomas	H-10-15
CAIRO, Raymond A	Walls of the Missing
CALCAGNO, Joseph A	L-17-13
CALDWELL, John E Jr	H-6-5
CALDWELL, John T	Walls of the Missing
CALDWELL, Merlin F	L-5-21
CALDWELL, Perley A	C-8-3
CALEF, Robert C Jr [74]	Walls of the Missing
CALHOUN, Charles B	O-11-16
CALIGURI, Anthony C	G-12-25
CALL, Thomas W	M-14-3
CALLAHAN, Francis E	Walls of the Missing
CALLAWAY, Larkin M	O-17-10
CALLAWAY, Paul J	C-17-23
CALLAWAY, Van D	H-6-12
CALLEA, Joseph A	F-14-6
CALLERY, James J	G-6-12
CAMERON, Gerard Guyot	G-19-15
CAMERON, Kenneth W	Walls of the Missing
CAMP, Seaborn S	D-4-14

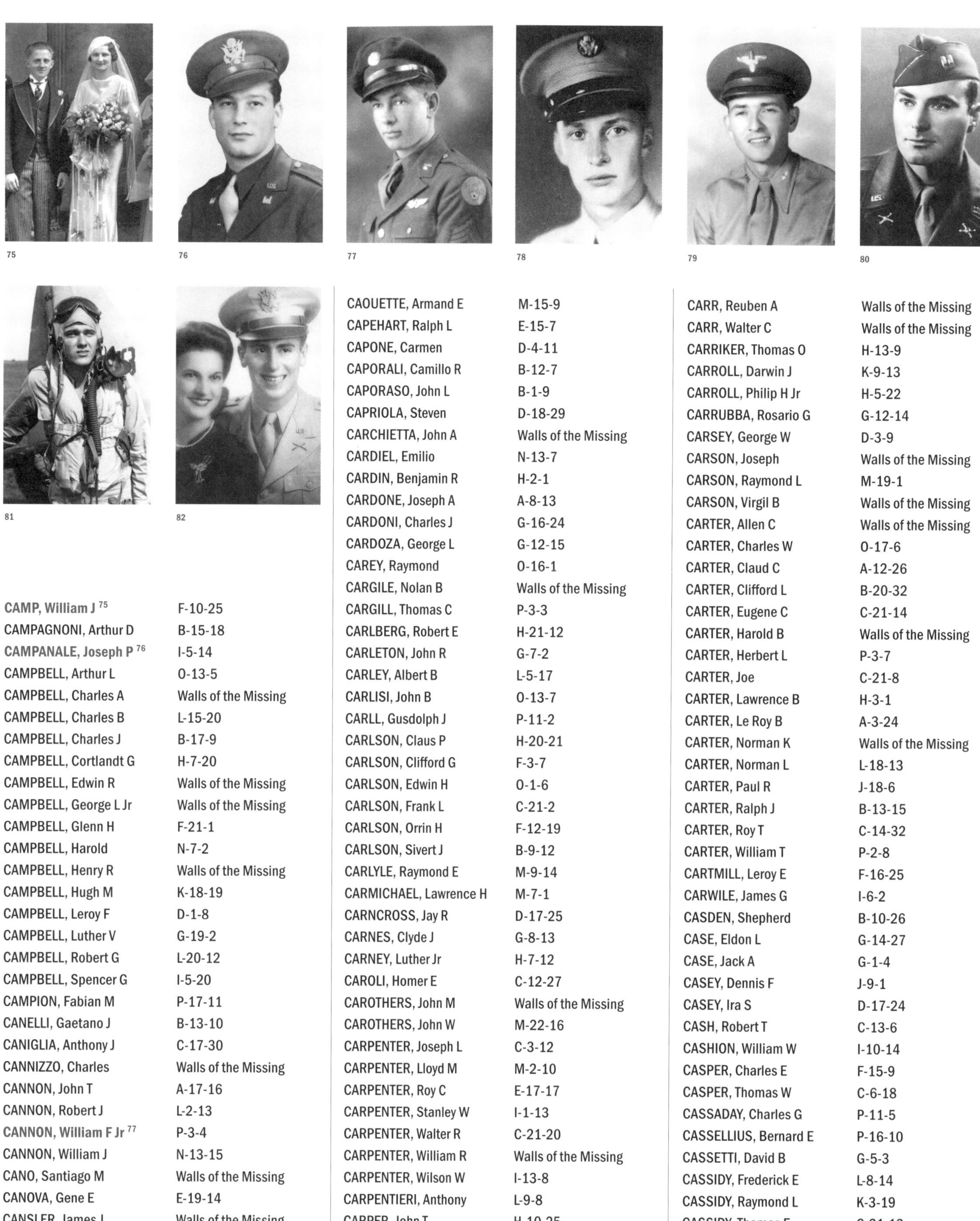

75 76 77 78 79 80

81 82

Name	Location
CAMP, William J [75]	F-10-25
CAMPAGNONI, Arthur D	B-15-18
CAMPANALE, Joseph P [76]	I-5-14
CAMPBELL, Arthur L	O-13-5
CAMPBELL, Charles A	Walls of the Missing
CAMPBELL, Charles B	L-15-20
CAMPBELL, Charles J	B-17-9
CAMPBELL, Cortlandt G	H-7-20
CAMPBELL, Edwin R	Walls of the Missing
CAMPBELL, George L Jr	Walls of the Missing
CAMPBELL, Glenn H	F-21-1
CAMPBELL, Harold	N-7-2
CAMPBELL, Henry R	Walls of the Missing
CAMPBELL, Hugh M	K-18-19
CAMPBELL, Leroy F	D-1-8
CAMPBELL, Luther V	G-19-2
CAMPBELL, Robert G	L-20-12
CAMPBELL, Spencer G	I-5-20
CAMPION, Fabian M	P-17-11
CANELLI, Gaetano J	B-13-10
CANIGLIA, Anthony J	C-17-30
CANNIZZO, Charles	Walls of the Missing
CANNON, John T	A-17-16
CANNON, Robert J	L-2-13
CANNON, William F Jr [77]	P-3-4
CANNON, William J	N-13-15
CANO, Santiago M	Walls of the Missing
CANOVA, Gene E	E-19-14
CANSLER, James J	Walls of the Missing
CANTRELL, Carl E	M-13-1
CANTWELL, Francis J	O-11-6
CANUP, Grady H	Walls of the Missing
CAOUETTE, Armand E	M-15-9
CAPEHART, Ralph L	E-15-7
CAPONE, Carmen	D-4-11
CAPORALI, Camillo R	B-12-7
CAPORASO, John L	B-1-9
CAPRIOLA, Steven	D-18-29
CARCHIETTA, John A	Walls of the Missing
CARDIEL, Emilio	N-13-7
CARDIN, Benjamin R	H-2-1
CARDONE, Joseph A	A-8-13
CARDONI, Charles J	G-16-24
CARDOZA, George L	G-12-15
CAREY, Raymond	O-16-1
CARGILE, Nolan B	Walls of the Missing
CARGILL, Thomas C	P-3-3
CARLBERG, Robert E	H-21-12
CARLETON, John R	G-7-2
CARLEY, Albert B	L-5-17
CARLISI, John B	O-13-7
CARLL, Gusdolph J	P-11-2
CARLSON, Claus P	H-20-21
CARLSON, Clifford G	F-3-7
CARLSON, Edwin H	O-1-6
CARLSON, Frank L	C-21-2
CARLSON, Orrin H	F-12-19
CARLSON, Sivert J	B-9-12
CARLYLE, Raymond E	M-9-14
CARMICHAEL, Lawrence H	M-7-1
CARNCROSS, Jay R	D-17-25
CARNES, Clyde J	G-8-13
CARNEY, Luther Jr	H-7-12
CAROLI, Homer E	C-12-27
CAROTHERS, John M	Walls of the Missing
CAROTHERS, John W	M-22-16
CARPENTER, Joseph L	C-3-12
CARPENTER, Lloyd M	M-2-10
CARPENTER, Roy C	E-17-17
CARPENTER, Stanley W	I-1-13
CARPENTER, Walter R	C-21-20
CARPENTER, William R	Walls of the Missing
CARPENTER, Wilson W	I-13-8
CARPENTIERI, Anthony	L-9-8
CARPER, John T	H-10-25
CARR, Alexander R	Walls of the Missing
CARR, D Ben	I-19-10
CARR, Eugene S	I-13-7
CARR, Reuben A	Walls of the Missing
CARR, Walter C	Walls of the Missing
CARRIKER, Thomas O	H-13-9
CARROLL, Darwin J	K-9-13
CARROLL, Philip H Jr	H-5-22
CARRUBBA, Rosario G	G-12-14
CARSEY, George W	D-3-9
CARSON, Joseph	Walls of the Missing
CARSON, Raymond L	M-19-1
CARSON, Virgil B	Walls of the Missing
CARTER, Allen C	Walls of the Missing
CARTER, Charles W	O-17-6
CARTER, Claud C	A-12-26
CARTER, Clifford L	B-20-32
CARTER, Eugene C	C-21-14
CARTER, Harold B	Walls of the Missing
CARTER, Herbert L	P-3-7
CARTER, Joe	C-21-8
CARTER, Lawrence B	H-3-1
CARTER, Le Roy B	A-3-24
CARTER, Norman K	Walls of the Missing
CARTER, Norman L	L-18-13
CARTER, Paul R	J-18-6
CARTER, Ralph J	B-13-15
CARTER, Roy T	C-14-32
CARTER, William T	P-2-8
CARTMILL, Leroy E	F-16-25
CARWILE, James G	I-6-2
CASDEN, Shepherd	B-10-26
CASE, Eldon L	G-14-27
CASE, Jack A	G-1-4
CASEY, Dennis F	J-9-1
CASEY, Ira S	D-17-24
CASH, Robert T	C-13-6
CASHION, William W	I-10-14
CASPER, Charles E	F-15-9
CASPER, Thomas W	C-6-18
CASSADAY, Charles G	P-11-5
CASSELLIUS, Bernard E	P-16-10
CASSETTI, David B	G-5-3
CASSIDY, Frederick E	L-8-14
CASSIDY, Raymond L	K-3-19
CASSIDY, Thomas E	C-21-13
CASSIDY, William H	Walls of the Missing
CASSITY, Cecil W	Walls of the Missing
CASSON, Edward R	E-8-13

CAST, Virgil A	B-10-2
CASTANEDA, Jose A	L-4-15
CASTIE, Albert C	E-10-21
CASTILLO, Remigio M	Walls of the Missing
CASTLE, Francis E	H-1-22
CASTLE, Robert H	K-17-10
CASTRO, Arthur V	P-16-15
CASTRO, Silvestre P	M-11-3
CATANZARO, John J	D-14-30
CATE, Richard E	Walls of the Missing
CATER, William G	M-8-17
CATES, Anthony W	Walls of the Missing
CATHEY, Sam	P-3-6
CAUGHEY, Isaac K	A-15-29
CAVALIERI, Nando A	Walls of the Missing
CAVENDER, Franklin M	C-2-13
CAVER, Roy E	A-16-5
CAWLEY, Edward R	C-3-14
CECCARINI, Lido	K-11-14
CECIL, Terry J	K-7-3
CEGLIA, Joseph T	L-8-9
CELESTINO, Joseph A	L-9-3
CENAC, Bert L	Walls of the Missing
CENNAMI, Salvatore	G-19-1
CENTEN, Donald R	Walls of the Missing
CERASARO, Victor P	J-8-1
CERAVOLO, Santo	A-18-25
CERVENKA, Cyril S	A-13-22
CESSARINI, Elio	G-2-10
CHADDOCK, Robert G	I-3-3
CHADWICK, William A	B-13-2
CHADWICK, William O Jr	B-8-17
CHAIRES, Simon H	O-6-4
CHAMBERLAIN, Gordon C	C-13-13
CHAMBERLIN, William B	C-8-22
CHAMBERS, Charles T	Walls of the Missing
CHAMBERS, Landon H	I-7-2
CHAMBERS, Roy E	M-1-13
CHAMBERS, William H	B-20-10
CHAMBLISS, Harrell C	A-12-24
CHAMPLIN, John B	Walls of the Missing
CHANCE, Walter E	Walls of the Missing
CHANDLER, Charles E	G-17-6
CHANDLER, George N	K-19-6
CHANEY, Benjamin F	C-16-3
CHANEY, Cleotus C	N-11-12
CHANEY, Clifton A	B-2-15
CHANEY, Harold C	C-1-29
CHANEY, Richard D	K-6-3
CHANEY, Robert E	B-18-21
CHANNELL, John S	Walls of the Missing
CHAPLIN, Emil	C-10-12
CHAPMAN, Carl F Jr	L-3-1
CHAPMAN, Robert J	F-2-21
CHAPPEL, Hubert W	F-8-25
CHAPPELL, Claudius H	F-6-2
CHAPPELL, Cubie C	F-15-25
CHAPPELL, Laurence W	L-7-19
CHAPPELL, Louis C	Walls of the Missing
CHARAIT, Albert A	F-13-20
CHAREST, Robert W	M-17-7
CHARRON, Romeo J	B-19-1
CHASE, Francis R	Walls of the Missing
CHASE, Howard T Jr	D-15-8
CHASSE, Leo F	D-15-17
CHASTAIN, Kenneth R	H-10-8
CHATAM, J C	B-8-2
CHATFIELD, Keith G	D-7-3
CHEADLE, Aaron C	A-6-26
CHEATHAM, Clyde C	H-11-23
CHEATHAM, John W	A-1-17
CHEEK, Earle C	L-21-4
CHEMERES, John P	I-6-5
CHENEY, Russell D	E-11-2
CHENGA, Frank W	K-12-8
CHEPAN, John	D-5-6
CHERAN, George	E-6-10
CHERIVASSI, John J	D-14-6
CHERNANSKY, Michael	H-9-8
CHERNIN, Bernard	Walls of the Missing
CHERRY, Edward G Jr [78]	C-3-18
CHERRY, Lloyd D	J-3-2
CHERRY, Paul	O-16-11
CHERRY, William E	Walls of the Missing
CHESNEY, Lawrence B	N-5-15
CHESTER, Lewis H	J-3-10
CHESTNUTWOOD, Joseph D	D-7-11
CHICKNOWSKI, George R	A-11-16
CHILCOAT, James M [79]	O-5-1
CHILDERS, Jack W	I-18-13
CHILDERS, James C	Walls of the Missing
CHILDERS, Julius L	D-21-4
CHILDRESS, Clyde W	K-15-7
CHILDRESS, Robert L	P-19-17
CHILDS, James A	F-3-1
CHILDS, Robert L	F-20-15
CHIODO, Michael A	Walls of the Missing
CHISHOLM, John A Jr [80]	I-17-13
CHISM, David B	G-8-12
CHLUDZIENSKI, Henry J	B-2-12
CHMELA, Earl F	F-12-14
CHOATE, George R Jr [81]	A-3-4
CHODYNICKY, Edward J	G-17-27
CHOJNACKI, Anthony J	L-4-17
CHOPP, John	H-7-22
CHOQUETTE, Joseph D	K-13-8
CHOTIN, Max	A-7-8
CHOUINARD, Merton L	J-9-4
CHRISMAN, Thomas W	K-13-17
CHRISMON, Henry C Jr	I-7-3
CHRISTAL, Allen	Walls of the Missing
CHRISTENSEN, Holger R	O-1-16
CHRISTENSEN, Willard M	Walls of the Missing
CHRISTIAN, Alonzo H	G-11-21
CHRISTIAN, Warren W	H-11-9
CHRISTIANO, Rocco	O-1-15
CHRISTIANS, Roger W	A-17-30
CHRISTIANSEN, John C	C-11-22
CHRISTOPHER, John W	G-15-5
CHRISTY, John M	N-16-14
CHRISTY, Ralph L	E-19-16
CHURCH, Clarence C	H-17-7
CHURCH, Edward S	G-20-10
CIARLELLI, Robert W	D-20-3
CICCHETTI, John F	Walls of the Missing
CICCONI, Salvatore J	Walls of the Missing
CICHOCKI, Edward J	H-3-3
CICOGNA, Ernest G Jr	B-6-3
CIPRIANO, Arnold W	G-11-17
CIROCCO, Carmen A	L-9-6
CITROCK, Joseph R	M-18-10
CLABAUGH, Paul H	Walls of the Missing
CLAGG, George F	I-6-8
CLARE, Maurice W Jr	A-14-16
CLARK, Albert	N-13-14
CLARK, Alonzo L	Walls of the Missing
CLARK, Andrew F Jr	J-20-21
CLARK, Bertram J [82]	P-12-10
CLARK, Charles H	E-16-3
CLARK, Clifford J	Walls of the Missing
CLARK, Edward J	E-6-11
CLARK, Frederick L	H-13-21
CLARK, Frederick W	B-1-8
CLARK, Howard J	I-21-14
CLARK, Hurlan R	I-4-19
CLARK, Jack L	Walls of the Missing
CLARK, James F Jr	D-17-11
CLARK, James L	D-10-22
CLARK, James L	E-21-16
CLARK, Jesse J	I-16-22
CLARK, John J	Walls of the Missing
CLARK, John J Jr	F-1-21
CLARK, Preston C	H-21-24
CLARK, Robert W	B-20-24
CLARK, Roderick C	Walls of the Missing
CLARK, Stanley V	G-2-15
CLARK, Walter S	B-20-21
CLARK, Wayne C	I-12-8
CLARK, Wilson J	A-14-25
CLARKE, Charles R Jr	K-6-1
CLAUSEN, Robert L	Walls of the Missing
CLAWSON, Harry A	Walls of the Missing
CLAY, Willard L	A-8-16
CLAYPOOL, James G	G-11-18
CLAYTON, Richard F	P-19-11
CLEARY, Thomas H Jr	I-10-12
CLEGG, Delbert E	G-1-19
CLEMENT, Robert L Jr	E-16-24
CLEMONS, Archie D	Walls of the Missing
CLEMONS, Luther H	D-21-25
CLIFFORD, William W	Walls of the Missing
CLIFTON, Mainard D	E-6-27
CLIFTON, Raymond C	Walls of the Missing
CLINARD, Everett L Jr	Walls of the Missing

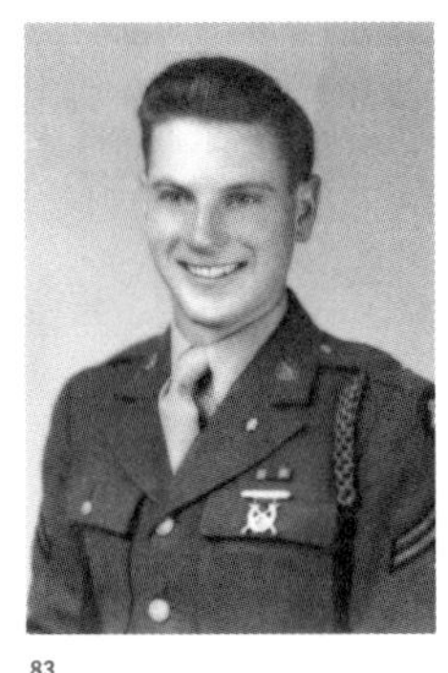
83

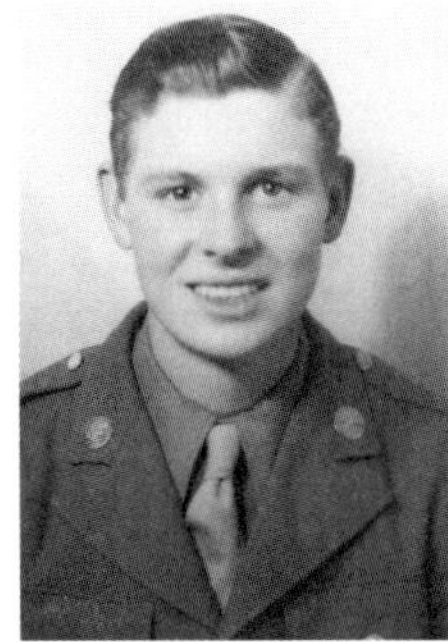
84

CLINE, Edward F	A-8-2
CLINE, Okle O	N-15-8
CLINE, Richard G	C-14-23
CLINGERMAN, Hillery	D-9-5
CLINGMAN, Foy R	L-6-7
CLINTON, Ivan A	Walls of the Missing
CLIPPINGER, Donald K	G-9-9
CLOGSTON, William M	M-19-14
CLOSE, Winder Lane	D-7-16
CLOSEN, Francis E	B-17-32
CLOTHIER, Bill E	J-11-1
CLOUD, Merle M	Walls of the Missing
CLOUGH, Charles W	E-21-8
CLOYD, Wayne	G-15-11
CLUM, Merrell J	D-11-10
COADY, Francis X	B-19-29
COALBURN, James L	M-3-11
COATES, Clarence R	B-21-8
COATES, Howard C	D-13-30
COBB, George F	Walls of the Missing
COBBE, Thomas D	Walls of the Missing
COBBS, Charlie T	L-6-17
COBISKEY, Raymond J	N-2-5
COBLENTZ, Myron P	A-9-12
COBURN, Harold	Walls of the Missing
COBURN, Raymond W Jr	E-16-25
COCCITTI, Cosmo P	Walls of the Missing
COCHRUN, Donald E	L-9-1
CODA, Edmond	G-3-4
CODDINGTON, Robert E	G-5-25
CODY, Paul M	L-15-21
COFFEY, Shelley C	J-2-11
COFFIN, Alfred B	G-18-8
COFFIN, Donald J	D-7-9
COFFIN, Harold E	N-19-13
COFFIN, Roger F [83]	F-2-10
COFFMAN, Stanley	F-9-13
COGGESHALL, Alan W Jr	P-20-6
COGGESHALL, Clifford A	L-10-6
COGSWELL, Fred M Jr	F-17-24
COHEN, Abram R	M-13-8
COHEN, Howard	D-11-24
COHEN, Sam	P-12-4
COKER, Henry B	A-16-32
COLBURN, Finis W	L-15-2
COLBY, Bevan W Jr	M-13-17
COLBY, Loyd A	H-8-23
COLDICOTT, Frederick	L-9-22
COLE, Arthur	Walls of the Missing
COLE, Benjamin D	J-19-19
COLE, James L	C-20-5
COLE, Le Roy M	O-17-14
COLE, Neil	Walls of the Missing
COLE, Robert G	B-15-27
COLE, Robert W	Walls of the Missing
COLE, Thomas B	P-18-16
COLE, Warren F	A-4-19
COLE, William K	B-4-1
COLEBANK, Robert E	A-18-28
COLEMAN, Andrew E Jr	D-5-32
COLEMAN, Donald A	B-7-9
COLEMAN, Idus F	Walls of the Missing
COLEMAN, Joseph G	D-18-4
COLEMAN, Robert L	J-17-3
COLEY, Lester G	L-9-21
COLISHION, Peter L	F-4-5
COLLIER, Garland W	Walls of the Missing
COLLINS, Clarence W	A-2-17
COLLINS, Clark	Walls of the Missing
COLLINS, Floyd S	F-9-24
COLLINS, Harry T	J-3-21
COLLINS, Howard L	J-21-13
COLLINS, James T	O-11-11
COLLINS, Jimmie D III	Walls of the Missing
COLLINS, John M	C-21-22
COLLINS, Leo F	H-11-17
COLLINS, Robert H	A-11-28
COLLINS, Roger W	I-10-4
COLLINS, Wilbur H	A-15-19
COLLINS, William C [84]	F-20-3
COLLINSWORTH, Lacy	Walls of the Missing
COLLIVER, Billie B	C-12-13
COLLURA, Joseph S	J-5-13
COLOE, Philip J	C-14-14
COLON, James A	G-3-7
COLSTON, Ben F	C-20-21
COLSTON, H B	D-6-12
COLTRIN, Walter L	F-3-25
COLTS, George E	C-7-5
COLVIN, Vance R	J-14-6
COMBS, Howard R Jr	I-6-22
COMBS, James G	G-2-21
COMBS, Robert W	Walls of the Missing
COMERFORD, James C	F-10-21
COMMANDER, Louis F	E-18-2
COMMEAN, William L	A-7-24
COMPA, Neil A	L-14-10
COMPTON, Paul D	E-19-25
COMSTOCK, Jack B	D-4-3
COMTOIS, Rene H	D-7-6
CONARD, Hughes J	K-5-15
CONAWAY, Nevin O	D-9-10
CONCATELLI, Frank J	O-9-5
CONDIT, Sherwood W	L-15-4
CONDON, William J	M-21-12
CONGELLI, Joseph P	Walls of the Missing
CONIGLIO, John	P-11-6
CONKLIN, Harry E	F-8-5
CONKLIN, John M	Walls of the Missing
CONKLIN, Richard M	D-7-30
CONKLING, John R	M-19-9
CONLEY, Bernard L	M-18-11
CONLEY, Carl F	E-8-5
CONLEY, Patrick T	I-12-16
CONLEY, Sidney	B-5-29
CONN, Arthur A Jr	N-15-10
CONN, Robert J	D-6-7
CONNARD, Norman L	D-14-16
CONNELL, Daniel R	C-21-26
CONNELL, John D Jr	Walls of the Missing
CONNELLY, John Jr	J-7-13
CONNER, Alfred W	P-17-12
CONNER, Francis J	A-3-9
CONNER, W D	Walls of the Missing
CONNOLLY, Lawrence H	L-7-16
CONNOLLY, Thomas J	A-13-13
CONNOR, Charles E	K-3-16
CONNOR, Floyd T	N-7-1
CONNOR, John P	C-14-25
CONRAD, Alfred H	K-1-7
CONRAD, John F	C-5-19
CONRAD, Ralph L	I-8-2
CONROY, Steve J	M-9-3
CONTES, William A	A-11-15
CONTIOSO, Alfred A	Walls of the Missing
CONTRERAS, Gustavo E	B-19-12
CONVERSE, William	A-8-29
CONWAY, David L	B-2-31
CONWAY, Jack H	H-13-4
COOGAN, William R	I-11-20
COOK, Basil M	Walls of the Missing
COOK, Ernest R	F-16-4
COOK, George T	Walls of the Missing
COOK, Jack	F-21-20
COOK, Lester R	B-14-16
COOK, Robert E	A-7-30
COOK, Robert E	I-20-3
COOK, Roy	A-8-25
COOK, Walter C	C-9-23
COOK, William N	C-14-10
COOKE, Kenneth H	Walls of the Missing
COOKE, Willard R Jr	C-11-26
COOLEY, Ernest C	D-17-14
COOLIDGE, Lloyd F	E-9-19
COOMBS, Kenneth M	Walls of the Missing
COON, Carl W	D-15-29
COON, Segal Q	G-16-15
COONROD, Lyle E	I-2-16
COOPER, David T	C-20-14

COOPER, Robert P	Walls of the Missing
COOPER, Sam A Jr	B-8-10
COOPER, William F	B-3-16
COOTER, Walter E	G-2-16
COOTER, William M	E-13-11
COOTS, Gerald C	H-9-3
COPE, Forrest R	Walls of the Missing
COPELAND, Donald H	C-1-23
COPELAND, James A Jr	O-9-17
COPELAND, William C	I-3-15
COPEN, Edgar L	A-1-21
COPLIN, Guy R	C-11-15
COPPOLA, Charles	Walls of the Missing
CORBETT, Elliott R II	D-8-11
CORBIN, Eugene W	Walls of the Missing
CORBIN, John A	B-19-5
CORCORAN, John P	F-3-13
CORDEIRO, Francisco	A-9-13
CORDES, Thomas H	K-7-15
CORDES, William J Jr	I-9-5
CORGAN, Alfred G	D-10-5
CORKERY, Cornelius V	Walls of the Missing
CORL, Frank J	D-14-17
CORMACK, Douglas C	J-8-2
CORMIER, Lawrence T	A-4-2
CORNELIO, Orester J	E-1-15
CORNELIUS, Marshall Jr	G-3-2
CORNER, James W	E-7-15
CORNIA, Charles O	B-19-23
CORREIRA, Joseph J Jr	B-21-16
CORRIGAN, David W	B-13-21
CORRIGAN, Emmett T	K-12-21
CORSACK, Aleck T	H-10-7
CORSINI, Victor P	Walls of the Missing
CORT, Jack	P-16-12
CORWIN, Leo F	A-13-21
CORWIN, Robert J	L-13-3
COSGROVE, Robert S	I-21-15
COSTA, Joseph S	L-5-18
COSTELLO, John J Jr	Walls of the Missing
COSTLEY, Francis W	N-2-7
COSTLOW, Joseph R	E-5-26
COTTINGHAM, John P	I-19-1
COTTON, Donald J	D-5-19
COTTON, Joseph	C-7-11
COTTONE, Jack P	Walls of the Missing
COTTRELL, Amos K	I-4-13
COTTRELL, Glynn O	H-15-15
COTTS, George W	D-21-14
COUCH, Cecil C	J-13-18
COUDIRA, Richard J	K-14-9
COUGHLIN, Robert P	H-17-9
COULTER, Ellis J	E-6-16
COUNTRYMAN, Arthur W	Walls of the Missing
COUNTS, Arthur H	J-6-9
COURSEY, Edward E	B-14-1
COURSON, Arthur G	B-11-15
COUSINS, James J	O-7-12
COVEL, Orlin E	Walls of the Missing
COVELLO, Frank H	C-17-1
COVENEY, Byron T	K-14-8
COVERT, James W	N-13-13
COVERT, Phil R	A-12-8
COVERT, Wallace A	H-20-4
COVEY, Fred O	N-13-8
COVINGTON, William L	Walls of the Missing
COWAN, William A	A-9-31
COWBURN, Frederick	F-11-8
COX, Clarence W	Walls of the Missing
COX, David J	J-19-14
COX, Glenn E	L-2-18
COX, J T	B-18-16
COX, James B	B-2-24
COX, James L	K-5-10
COX, John J	K-15-13
COX, John W	O-1-17
COXSON, Donald J	M-1-16
COYLE, James A	F-14-15
COYLE, William J	B-10-7
COZART, James N	N-10-1
COZZA, Salvatore E	Walls of the Missing
CRABTREE, William H	B-18-1
CRAFT, Orlin L D	L-13-4
CRAGO, Gordon D	C-21-30
CRAIG, Gavin G Jr	B-16-21
CRAIG, James W	J-17-20
CRAIG, John K	B-5-21
CRAIG, Othel	A-9-2
CRAIG, Parl W	F-11-19
CRAIG, Percy D	E-2-27
CRAIG, Robert E	G-20-6
CRAMER, Clarence	P-3-5
CRAMER, William A Jr	A-14-1
CRANDALL, Lawrence E	H-7-6
CRANDELL, Fay J	F-2-7
CRANDELL, Leonard J	H-16-26
CRANE, Clell C	F-20-8
CRANE, Paul M	Walls of the Missing
CRANE, William L	N-13-16
CRANFILL, M D	H-8-4
CRASANAKIS, Emmanuel	H-1-2
CRATE, George A	F-6-10
CRAWFORD, Bayley K	O-10-7
CRAWFORD, Charles E	Walls of the Missing
CRAWFORD, Charles W	C-21-4
CRAWFORD, Gordon P	Walls of the Missing
CREAMER, Harley D	B-15-28
CREATORE, John M	H-1-12
CREE, Charles R	K-6-20
CREEVY, Edward J	Walls of the Missing
CREGER, Waymon L Jr	N-13-2
CRESWICK, Stanley	Walls of the Missing
CRETE, Laureat W	A-9-30
CREUTZMANN, Harry E	Walls of the Missing
CRIBBS, La Rue F	C-21-7
CRICKENBERGER, Lawrence H Jr	Walls of the Missing
CRILL, Ronald R	E-1-25
CRIMMINS, Timothy E J	Walls of the Missing
CRITES, Arnold L	A-18-31
CRIVELLO, Sebastian B	K-15-16
CROCKETT, Howard W	L-6-22
CROFT, Robert I	Walls of the Missing
CROMARTY, George D	F-14-9
CRONIN, John L	D-18-11
CROOK, Thomas W Jr	Walls of the Missing
CROOKS, Robert L	D-9-18
CROOKSTON, John R	Walls of the Missing
CROSBIE, Lloyd C	C-10-5
CROSBY, Bryce E	G-5-20
CROSBY, Floyd R	Walls of the Missing
CROSBY, Robert G	G-14-4
CROSLYN, Hollis F	P-4-7
CROSS, Mathew S	O-10-4
CROSSWELL, Allen J	I-1-2
CROSSWHITE, Charles C	D-7-24
CROTEAU, Harold E	C-14-31
CROTTY, Gerrald E	F-17-18
CROTTY, John V	E-19-10
CROUSE, John C	O-2-3
CROUSE, Richard	E-17-26
CROW, Napoleon	C-13-21
CROZIER, Lawrence W	L-4-18
CRUCE, Clois N	K-12-10
CRUM, James C	C-2-9
CRUMPLER, Thomas P	Walls of the Missing
CRUMPTON, Elmer R	M-1-15
CRUMPTON, Robert D	E-19-22
CRUZ, Rafael V	A-9-1
CSUHTA, John A	O-10-9
CUDDEBACK, Aaron E	Walls of the Missing
CUFF, Martin J	N-15-15
CULBERHOUSE, Tommie	G-18-16
CULBERTSON, Dean C	A-9-3
CULLEN, Clifford E	O-1-13
CULLENS, Jack	G-4-12
CULLER, Irvin W	Walls of the Missing
CULLER, John D	D-20-10
CULLIGAN, Carl W	A-13-15
CULPEPPER, Joseph	D-15-23
CULVER, George S	O-3-10
CUMMING, James D	Walls of the Missing
CUMMING, Robert F	K-11-5
CUMMINGS, John S	A-1-24
CUNEO, John J	E-4-17
CUNIS, Robert H	C-19-10
CUNNIFF, Peter M	Walls of the Missing
CUNNINGHAM, Frank R	F-21-26
CUNNINGHAM, Jarrett E	H-3-14
CUNNINGHAM, John E	D-16-12
CUOZZO, Michael	Walls of the Missing
CURLETT, Raymond J	O-1-1
CURLEY, George L	G-15-6
CURLEY, John F	B-7-28
CURLEY, Raymond R	B-5-9

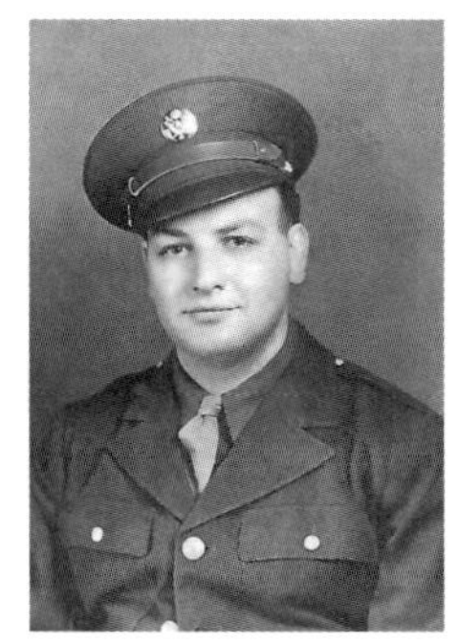
85

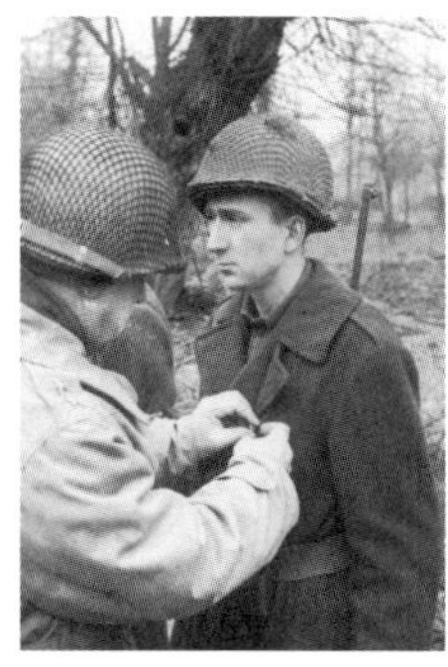
86

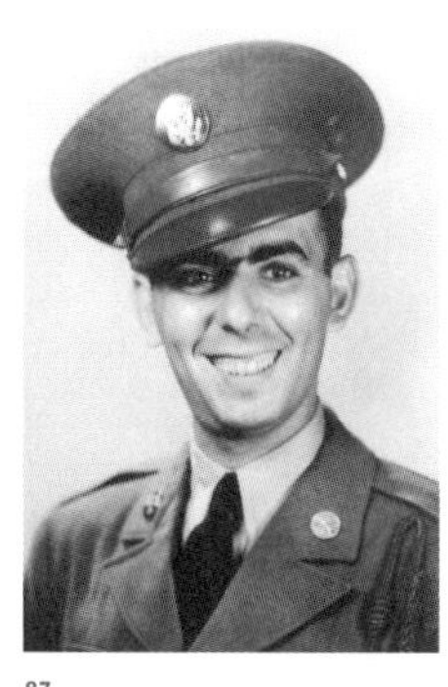
87

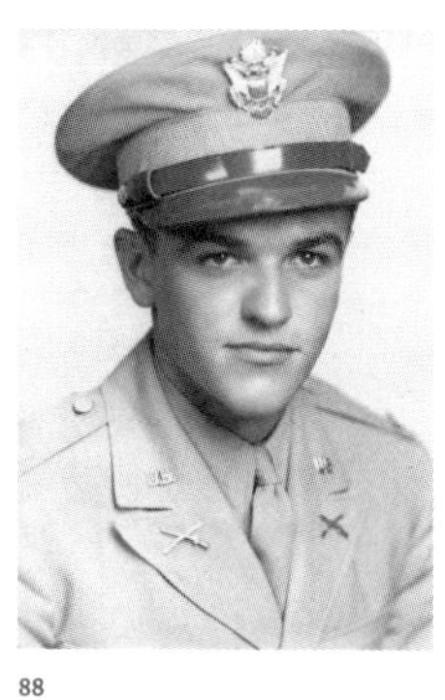
88

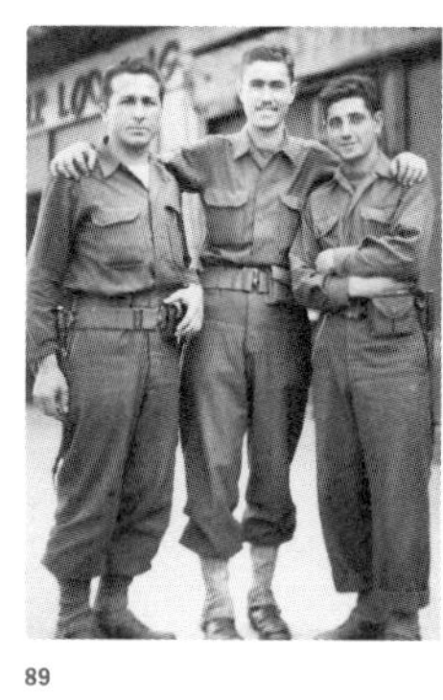
89

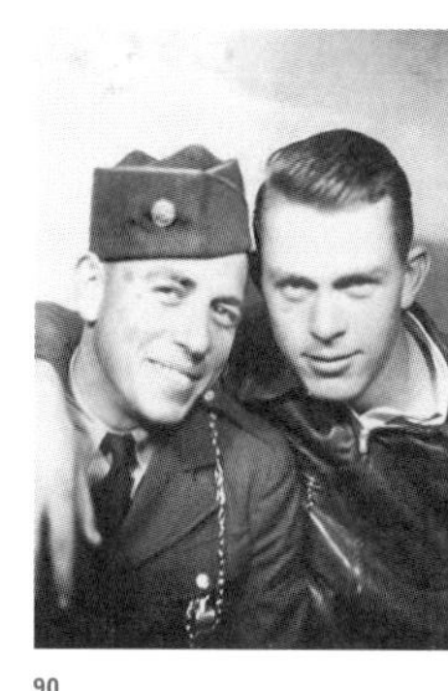
90

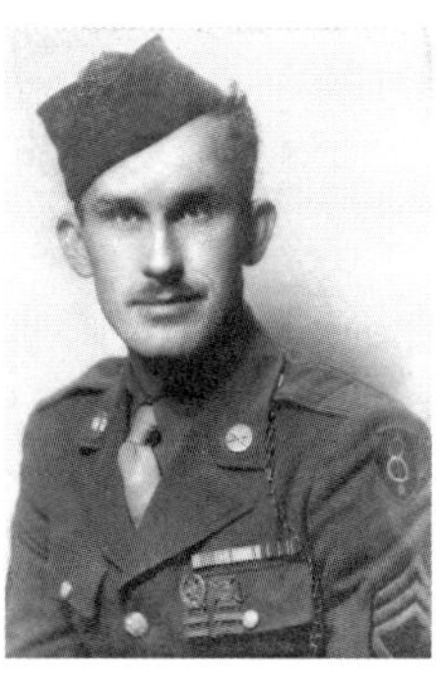
91

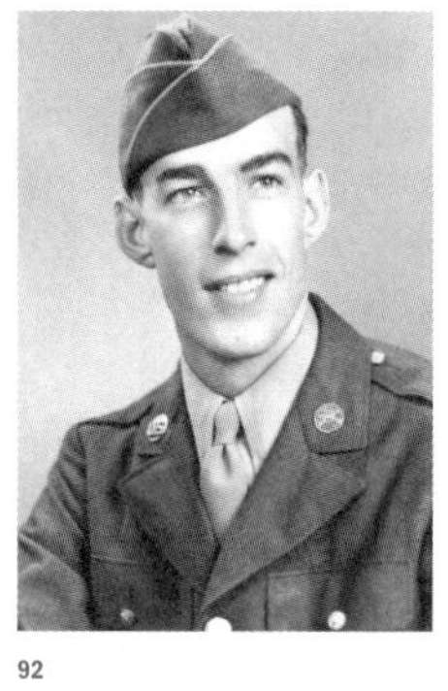
92

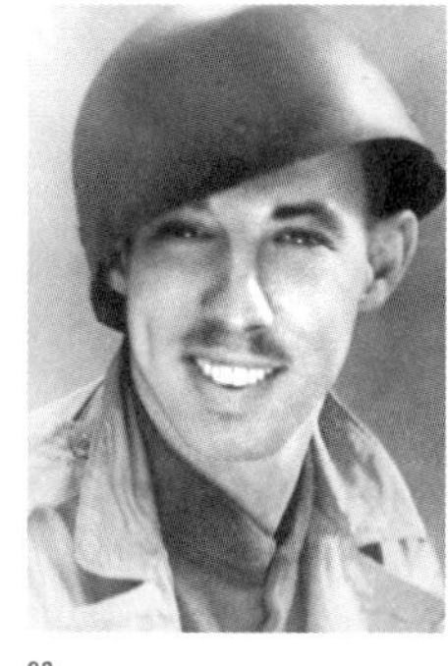
93

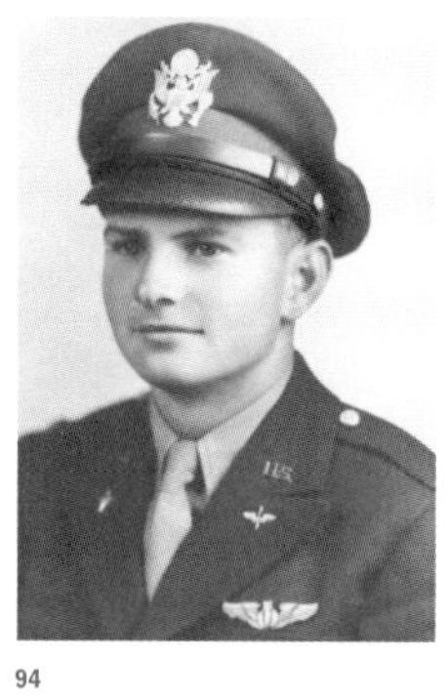
94

CURRAN, Bernard C	D-5-29
CURRAN, Joseph J	Walls of the Missing
CURRIE, Willie Jr	D-12-7
CURRY, Everett M	N-11-9
CURRY, Robert L	A-6-32
CURRY, Thomas R	Walls of the Missing
CURTIS, Charles W	A-8-11
CURTIS, James C	D-7-2
CURTIS, James N Jr	A-9-18
CURTIS, Richard O	I-17-16
CURTIS, Sidney A	P-3-8
CURTISS, Albert B	C-15-19
CUSHENBERRY, Ivan L	Walls of the Missing
CUSHING, Harold G	D-17-9
CUTHBERTSON, James F	B-17-6
CUTHRELL, Orville C	L-1-1
CUTLER, Elisha P Jr	I-20-10
CUTTER, William H Jr	Walls of the Missing
CUTTS, Jerauld I	I-18-7
CYBULSKI, John E	A-9-8
CYCON, Thomas F	N-9-13
CZAPLICKI, Chester A	P-12-8
CZECHOWICZ, Julius P	E-18-1
CZOPAR, John J	A-16-21
CZUHAJEWSKI, Stanley J	F-3-18
CZUJAK, Henry F	C-19-6
CZUKIEWSKI, John S	C-18-4

D

D'ALESIO, Phillip A	A-5-27
D'ALESSANDRO, James A	L-2-6
D'AMICO, Geldino P[85]	O-15-11
D'AOUST, Wallace W	Walls of the Missing
DA ROCHA, Edward R	A-6-27
DA SARO, Louis J	D-19-24
DAHL, Walter A	L-13-20
DAIL, George W Jr[86]	G-9-13
DAILEY, Francis J Jr	A-15-6
DAILY, Paul M	M-17-11
DAILY, Richard L	D-19-32
DAINOTTO, James V[87]	J-8-18
DALBY, Robert M	H-12-6
DALE, Daniel W	H-21-14
DALE, William R[88]	B-15-11
DALEY, Walter A	B-13-27
DALOE, Alfred W[89]	D-9-20
DALTON, Dean H	B-10-11
DALTON, William R	E-13-18
DALY, Lilbern D	Walls of the Missing
DALY, William J	Walls of the Missing
DAMAN, Charles H	Walls of the Missing
DAMASKE, Robert W	A-18-29
DAMATO, Neil J	Walls of the Missing
DAMICO, August G	M-8-14
DANAJOVITS, Carl F	C-15-23
DANFORD, Ross C	H-1-1
DANIEL, Ralph A	K-1-14
DANIELCZYK, Sigmund J	C-15-22
DANIELS, Ell G	G-14-10
DANIELS, Harry	Walls of the Missing
DANIELS, Herman W Jr	E-21-5
DANIELSON, William C	H-8-10
DARBEE, Harold C	A-11-9
DARCY, George J	H-19-16
DARLING, Eugene R	C-21-28
DASSO, Carl H	O-9-3
DASSO, Eugene E	O-9-2
DAUER, Paul F	L-16-3
DAUGHERTY, Fred H	J-14-17
DAVENPORT, Doyel C Jr	H-5-12
DAVENPORT, Foster R	J-7-22
DAVENPORT, Herbert C	L-5-5
DAVENPORT, William G	Walls of the Missing
DAVES, Richard C	Walls of the Missing
DAVEY, James R	J-9-10
DAVIDIAN, Charlie	Walls of the Missing
DAVIDSON, Burton S	Walls of the Missing
DAVIDSON, Charles K	A-4-12
DAVIDSON, William G	L-11-1
DAVIES, Hugh W	P-11-9
DAVIES, Jerald M	G-18-1
DAVIES, Leonardo F	K-1-1
DAVIS, Byron C	M-5-3
DAVIS, Charles E	E-17-18
DAVIS, Charles J	F-1-3
DAVIS, Dale A	F-4-1
DAVIS, Dayton L	G-14-2
DAVIS, Donald B	A-2-31
DAVIS, Douglas L	E-12-1
DAVIS, Earl J	M-2-17
DAVIS, Everette A	N-20-15
DAVIS, George W	D-21-2
DAVIS, Harold N	I-2-6
DAVIS, Jack T	A-7-21
DAVIS, Jackson[90]	H-9-6
DAVIS, James D	L-3-20
DAVIS, James H	H-19-13
DAVIS, James K	F-15-2
DAVIS, Loran W	C-8-16
DAVIS, Louis S	C-21-29
DAVIS, Maynard M	F-6-25
DAVIS, Murray	D-13-10
DAVIS, Phillip F	B-4-21
DAVIS, Richard E	B-6-18
DAVIS, Robert C	J-1-16
DAVIS, Robert D	C-4-9
DAVIS, Robert E	N-18-6
DAVIS, Roy C	C-15-2

Name	Location
DAVIS, Roy F	F-14-19
DAVIS, Thomas C	K-15-3
DAVIS, Thomas E Jr	C-7-1
DAVIS, William F	G-4-5
DAVISON, Ronald L	G-4-21
DAVOREN, John F	Walls of the Missing
DAWIDOWICZ, Milton	Walls of the Missing
DAWKINS, Edgar J	F-7-10
DAWSON, Daniel W	B-13-25
DAWSON, Jennings B	O-13-4
DAY, Clifford C Sr [91]	F-18-21
DAY, Irving L	F-16-2
DAYTON, Lloyd L	M-16-11
DAYTON, William G	B-2-26
DAYWALT, Harry A Jr	B-4-14
DE BELLIS, Demetrio M	D-1-24
DE BENEDETTO, Frederick S	J-8-3
DE BOER, Quentin A	H-19-4
DE COOK, Bernard J [92]	F-17-27
DE CRESCENZO, Emingil	A-14-21
DE CUMBER, Philip Jr	K-17-6
DE FEBIO, Michael	E-2-7
DE FISHER, Abraham J	H-2-12
DE GRAFFENREID, Fayette R	D-21-20
DE GRASSE, Harold A	N-11-17
DE HARTOG, Hendrik Th	L-21-2
DE JARNETTE, Joe A	Walls of the Missing
DE JEAN, Garrigues A	I-9-18
DE KEYREL, Henry R	Walls of the Missing
DE LANEY, Emmett C	K-3-6
DE LASSUS, Joseph F	I-8-15
DE LEEUW, Wayne R	J-18-21
DE LEON, Trene	K-18-9
DE LUCA, Charles J	F-5-13
DE LUCA, Frank P	E-1-14
DE MAND, Francis W	I-13-11
DE MARCO, Alfio	J-14-11
DE MARCO, Ding A	J-18-18
DE MARCO, Michael J	K-17-21
DE MASTERS, Earl N	Walls of the Missing
DE PINTO, Natoli C	C-17-28
DE PUE, John N	P-17-15
DE RAMO, Henry J	Walls of the Missing
DE ROCHE, Robert L	D-13-25
DE SHAZER, Arnold W	M-12-7
DE SHONG, Irving	J-20-7
DE SIMONE, Frank W	E-8-20
DE TORIS, James	I-18-3
DE VALK, Robert G	I-3-21
DE VAULT, Warren G H	Walls of the Missing
DE VILLEZ, Theodore J	D-10-24
DE VOGE, Eugene J	Walls of the Missing
DE WITT, Marvin J	N-16-11
DE YOUNG, Robert G	C-2-27
DEABLER, Richard T	F-3-26
DEAKYNE, Duane D	D-13-8
DEAL, Kenneth A	O-11-10
DEAN, Jim H	Walls of the Missing
DEAN, John C	J-10-17
DEANE, King J	N-13-10
DEARBORN, Gayle W	O-18-6
DEATS, Laurence E Jr	C-4-3
DEBICH, George	C-21-15
DECK, Leon H	C-3-6
DECKER, Frank	H-10-13
DECKER, Harvey F	C-19-2
DEDE, Robert R	D-8-2
DEEDE, George W	M-2-9
DEERING, Robert P	D-10-11
DEHNERT, Henry J	L-2-2
DEIBLER, Clifford V	F-12-5
DEINES, Herman	B-3-15
DEITMAN, Thomas G	Walls of the Missing
DEL CONTE, Albert J	G-11-8
DEL PERO, Otto D	E-13-7
DEL TORTO, Joseph V	K-16-8
DELANEY, William F	Walls of the Missing
DELAVAN, Robert E	J-3-1
DELIA, Carmine	I-9-15
DELLA ROCCA, Don	N-3-8
DELLAGE, Donald L	F-20-6
DELLAPENTA, William J	G-3-19
DELMONACO, Frank A	C-11-30
DELMONICO, Dominick	C-11-29
DELP, Allen	N-7-7
DELUCA, Victor J	A-4-6
DELWO, Howard F	C-4-14
DEMEROLIS, Mario W	N-17-5
DEMPFLE, Francis N	Walls of the Missing
DEMPSEY, Bernard F	E-21-3
DENCH, Francis J	O-13-15
DENMAN, George W	Walls of the Missing
DENMEAD, Donald R	Walls of the Missing
DENNEY, Cecil H	C-1-16
DENNING, Norman E	I-15-3
DENNIS, Garland E	I-4-2
DENNIS, Jack K	Walls of the Missing
DENT, Harry L	A-4-20
DENT, Richard C	A-17-4
DENTON, Johnie W	E-6-19
DERFLINGER, James M	Walls of the Missing
DERHAMMER, Robert T	K-15-12
DERRICK, Johnathan A	K-1-10
DERRICK, Pete E	Walls of the Missing
DERRINGER, Emmet H E [93]	N-1-8
DERSHIMER, Harold W	M-20-6
DESERNIO, James	M-16-2
DESPOT, Thomas A	K-17-9
DETLEFSEN, Heinz W	H-6-11
DETLEFSEN, John	H-12-16
DETTLOFF, Leonard J	Walls of the Missing
DEUBNER, Victor A	L-5-22
DEVERTS, Gilbert L	F-9-25
DEVINE, Samuel A Jr	C-21-12
DEVOY, Charles E	E-18-24
DEW, John H	D-13-4
DEW, Robert G	Walls of the Missing
DEWBERRY, Curtis	A-1-1
DEWBERRY, John P	Walls of the Missing
DEWEESE, Charley R Jr	I-21-8
DEWEY, Charles F	C-8-28
DEZARN, Thurman	B-16-1
DHONAU, Charles M Jr [94]	I-9-13
DI BAGIO, Michael	P-1-6
DI CESARE, Attilio R	A-10-12
DI COSMO, Salvador J	Walls of the Missing
DI FAZIO, Joseph J	B-13-29
DI IORIO, Libaerato A	Walls of the Missing
DI MASCOLA, Michael G	N-1-3
DI RENNO, Fortunato R	F-15-17
DI TRAPANI, John E	O-3-11
DIAS, George V	Walls of the Missing
DICK, Andrew Jr	P-3-11
DICK, James O Jr	H-21-16
DICK, Walter W	M-9-11
DICKERSON, Edwin F	C-3-8
DICKERSON, James A	E-4-3
DICKERSON, Kenneth G	P-13-13
DICKERSON, Ordell	G-11-12
DICKEY, Charles Jr	M-11-13
DICKEY, Vollie B	Walls of the Missing
DICKSON, George E	F-21-23
DICKSON, Marvin E	Walls of the Missing
DIECEDUE, Manuel	O-11-9
DIECKMANN, Norman T	G-14-11
DIEDERICH, Raymond J	Walls of the Missing
DIEFFENBACH, Rudolph A	A-8-20
DIEHL, David R	I-19-6
DIEHL, Russell F	A-8-5
DIEL, James L	L-15-8
DIEM, Veryl W	A-5-16
DIENES, Tony E	K-8-20
DIETEL, William Jr	P-22-11
DIETZ, Calvin G	B-6-17
DIETZEN, Anton R	E-21-7
DIETZSCH, Maroy C	H-19-12
DIFALCO, Guy L	A-14-19
DIGGS, Graham W Jr	Walls of the Missing
DIGMAN, Clarence A	C-10-7
DIKOON, Walter	F-4-10
DILL, Charles	E-12-10
DILLARD, George O	K-10-10
DILSAVER, Jewell I	I-3-12
DIMITRE, John J	B-6-5
DIMMOCK, Charles A	F-8-20
DININO, Francis P	G-19-4
DIONNE, Raymond J	Walls of the Missing
DIORIO, Anthony	F-9-7
DIPPEL, Albert F	L-17-7
DIPPEL, Joseph H	Walls of the Missing
DIRAGO, Jimmie E Jr	Walls of the Missing
DISBRO, Warren	G-17-1
DISHER, John W	C-18-1
DITTMER, Arthur H	E-14-14

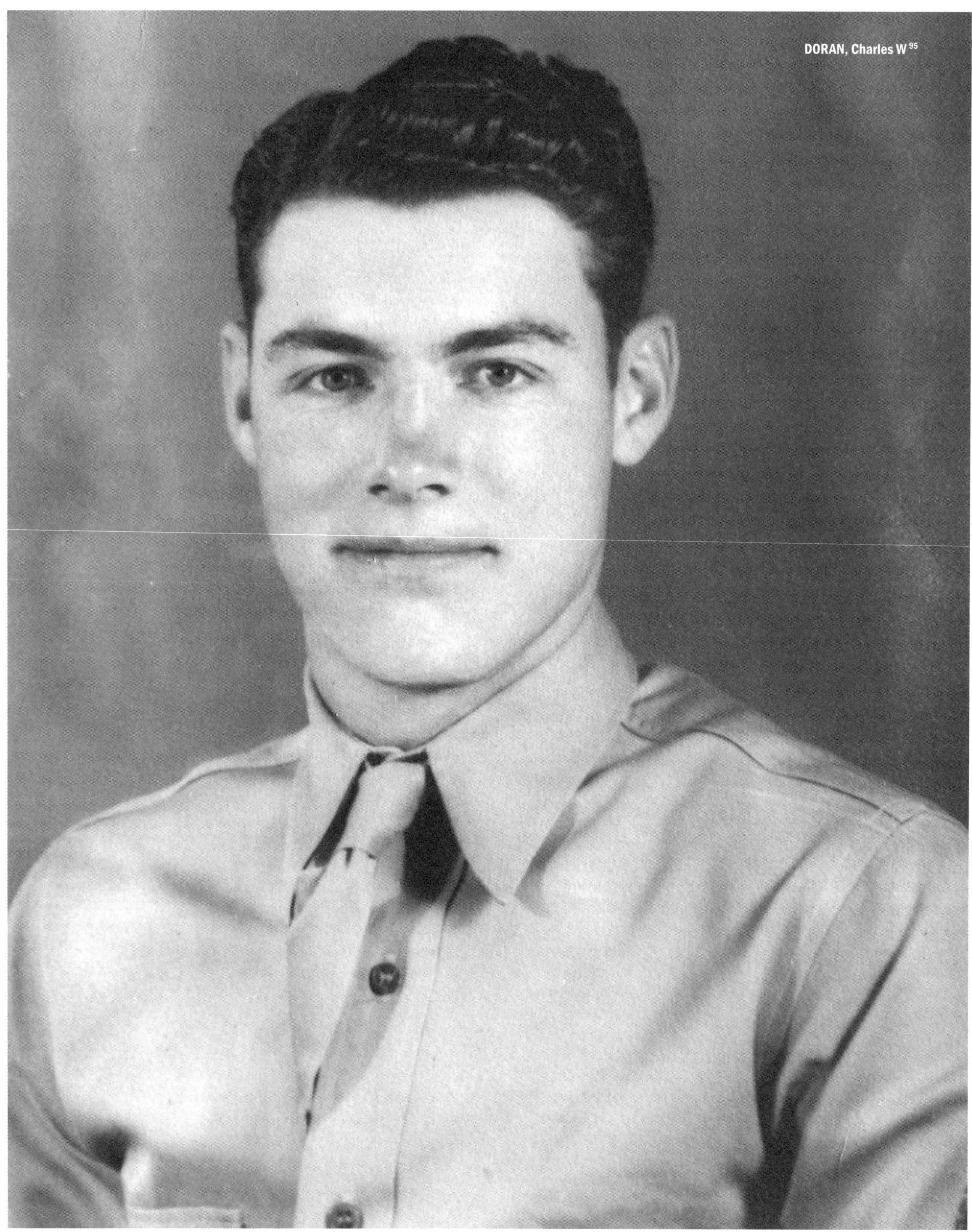

DORAN, Charles W[95]

Name	Location
DIXON, Burton O	P-20-12
DIXON, Clarence J	G-13-4
DIXON, Wilford N	P-8-5
DLUGOSZ, Edward W	C-6-4
DLUGOSZ, Leo G	C-6-3
DOBBINS, Maurice H	Walls of the Missing
DOBOSKI, Ernest	H-2-10
DOBROWOLSKI, Harry	B-10-21
DODD, James E	Walls of the Missing
DODGE, Howard R	D-12-13
DODGE, William H	Walls of the Missing
DODSON, Homie A	D-17-16
DODSON, James M	Walls of the Missing
DOGOSTINO, John J	B-21-21
DOHERTY, John S	Walls of the Missing
DOHERTY, Joseph J	C-2-5
DOKE, Earl J	B-11-32
DOLAN, Charles Jr	B-3-32
DOLAN, Russel E	D-6-27
DOLAN, William P	E-14-7
DOLECEK, Victor D	Walls of the Missing
DOLLENMEYER, William M	A-9-15
DOLLINGER, Louis F	B-12-30
DOLS, Gilbert M	E-21-12
DOMINGUEZ, Louis	G-21-21
DOMINIC, Ralph J	A-16-18
DOMINICK, Samuel V	G-20-12
DOMINY, Reed H	Walls of the Missing
DONAHOE, Ralph	M-5-16
DONALDSON, Edward C	O-6-10
DONALDSON, John B	C-7-9
DONALDSON, Melvin E	O-17-5
DONALDSON, Robert I	C-19-24
DONLIN, John M	K-21-7
DONLIN, Robert P	K-21-6
DONNELLY, Daniel L	D-6-5
DONNELLY, James E	I-8-8
DONOHO, Larry M	G-2-5
DONOHUE, John P	C-5-10
DONOHUE, Joseph A Jr	P-18-9
DONOHUE, Richard C	K-7-4
DONOVAN, John D	H-6-26
DONOVAN, William	H-15-9
DONVITO, Nicholas W	L-6-19
DOOLEY, James Jr	H-7-26
DOPIERALA, Marion	E-11-18
DORAN, Charles W [95]	D-16-19
DORAN, Harold J	P-3-13
DORAN, Robert E	B-5-19
DORE, Joseph A	I-11-18
DORMAN, Daniel F	G-1-6
DORMAN, Kent	D-13-28
DORR, Earle L Jr	Walls of the Missing
DORR, Michael W	L-17-3
DORRIS, Archie U	Walls of the Missing
DORSEY, Carl G	Walls of the Missing
DORSEY, Joseph H	E-7-9
DORULLA, John W	D-21-13
DOTSON, Carl	B-20-9
DOTSON, Glenn	Walls of the Missing
DOTTERWEICH, Joseph J	Walls of the Missing
DOTY, Amos E	L-3-9
DOTY, Claude E	C-19-13
DOTY, George B	J-12-11
DOTY, Harold B	G-13-27
DOTY, Wesley R	D-7-27
DOUGHERTY, Aloysius F	J-6-17
DOUGHERTY, James R Jr	O-16-15
DOUGHERTY, John L	I-7-13
DOUGHERTY, William G	Walls of the Missing
DOUGLAS, Charlie	G-18-21
DOUGLAS, Oscar A Jr	D-15-1
DOUGLAS, Paul E	E-14-8
DOUGLAS, Walter	K-11-1
DOUGLASS, Donald R	I-8-19
DOUGLASS, Frederick A	E-2-24
DOVER, Roland V Jr	Walls of the Missing
DOVICA, Frank V	P-11-7
DOW, William E	Walls of the Missing
DOWD, Raymond H	H-3-5
DOWDA, Thomas B	M-22-2
DOWNEY, Earl R Jr	M-13-15
DOWNING, Francis W	B-10-8
DOWNING, Herbert L	C-4-2
DOWNS, Francis L	F-1-7
DOWSLEY, James F	E-16-13
DOYLE, Francis J	I-11-3
DOYLE, Joseph A	O-4-6
DOZIER, Allan M	M-7-14
DOZIER, Nicholas M	F-10-15
DRABECKI, Anthony T	Walls of the Missing
DRAGWA, Charles	D-9-27
DRAKE, Euel T	K-17-4
DRAKE, Walter E	A-20-12
DREES, Edward A	D-21-16
DREES, Oscar C	B-12-19
DREICHLER, Kenneth J	F-12-22
DREIER, Robert F	D-16-17
DRENK, Stanley H	J-9-2
DRIESEN, Daniel	B-8-16
DRISCOLL, Francis X	D-8-3
DRISKEL, Regis H	B-18-8
DRIVER, Sherman H	I-4-3
DRIVER, William F	B-4-24
DROBNER, Martin S	P-3-10
DRYDEN, Earl	D-10-17
DRYDEN, Philip C	H-8-14
DU BEAU, William F	I-19-19
DU BOSE, Dieudonne B	B-16-30
DU LANEY, James W	C-12-10
DU PREY, John W	H-16-17
DUBIEL, Karol S	Walls of the Missing
DUCA, Joseph F	D-9-12
DUDA, Joseph F	G-1-25
DUDEK, Jerome W	A-11-3
DUDLEY, Harold C	I-20-18
DUDLEY, John D	N-6-9
DUDLEY, Joseph L	K-10-7
DUFAULT, Leon J	H-16-2
DUFF, Raymond A	Walls of the Missing
DUFFEY, Elmer E	B-5-15
DUFFIELD, Stanley D	Walls of the Missing
DUFFY, Joseph M	G-5-7
DUGGAN, Eugene T	Walls of the Missing
DUKEMAN, William H Jr	G-2-11
DUKES, Harold C	G-17-23
DULIK, Stephen J	A-14-24
DULIN, Charles L	Walls of the Missing
DULZ, Rudolph M	P-3-12
DUMAS, George E	L-10-15
DUMM, James J Jr	H-2-5
DUNBAR, Harry G Jr	N-19-12
DUNBAR, Samuel J	O-13-9
DUNCAN, George F Jr	B-12-10
DUNCAN, Glenn F	Walls of the Missing
DUNCAN, Jack W	A-4-25
DUNCAN, John A	C-3-20
DUNCAN, Loys	E-12-4
DUNDON, Lewis J	K-5-1
DUNFORD, John P	E-14-12
DUNGAN, Allen B	F-12-11
DUNIGAN, Louis P	G-5-5
DUNKLE, Clyde W	E-4-18
DUNN, Aaron	L-17-12
DUNN, Clarence H	Walls of the Missing
DUNN, Robert P	B-14-6
DUNN, William F	O-2-11
DUPEE, Harry C	E-21-25
DUPLANTIS, Marshall H	L-19-16
DUPLESSIS, Henry E	Walls of the Missing
DURAND, Viateur C	I-17-22
DURANT, Harry W	Walls of the Missing
DURBIN, Anthony G	K-17-20
DURBOROW, John B	P-6-14
DURBOROW, Paul J	P-6-13
DURETT, Harold E	I-20-20
DURHAM, Julius G	F-8-7
DURHAM, Richard L	C-13-10
DURHAM, Robert S Jr	E-19-17
DURKEE, Lawrence L	G-1-8
DURNELL, Richard E	J-3-13
DURNEY, Gerard J	F-11-14
DUSENBURY, James V	F-20-7
DUSICK, Paul G	B-7-6
DUST, Floyd W	B-13-12
DWELLEY, William J	Walls of the Missing
DWYER, Warren J	M-20-17
DYE, Columbus J	C-8-2
DYE, Everett D	A-4-4
DYE, Filbert F	Walls of the Missing
DYER, Charles T	H-3-23
DYL, Benjamin W	H-9-2
DYMEK, Anthony J	J-6-15
DYNAN, Thomas W Jr	O-4-7

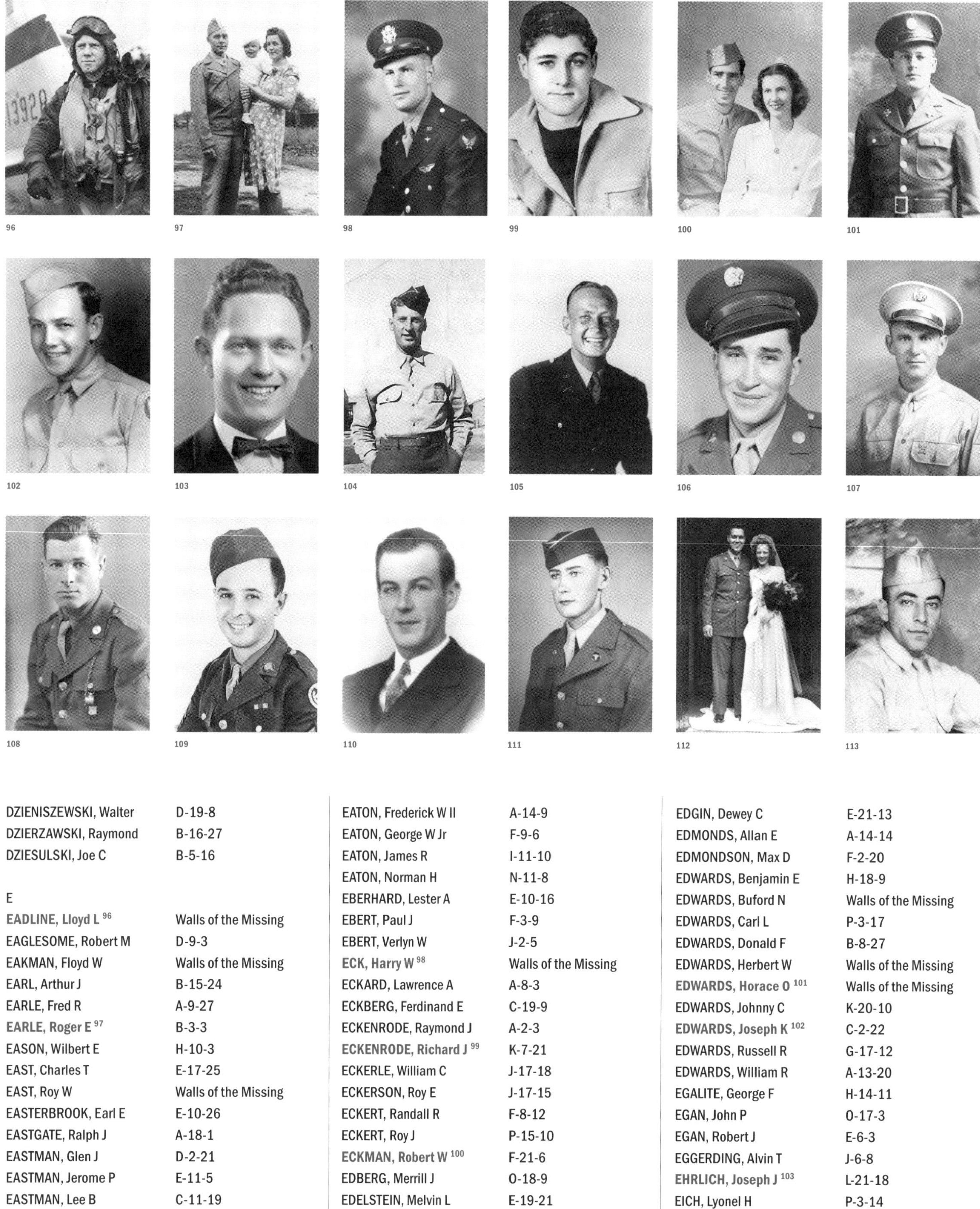

96 97 98 99 100 101

102 103 104 105 106 107

108 109 110 111 112 113

DZIENISZEWSKI, Walter	D-19-8
DZIERZAWSKI, Raymond	B-16-27
DZIESULSKI, Joe C	B-5-16

E

EADLINE, Lloyd L [96]	Walls of the Missing
EAGLESOME, Robert M	D-9-3
EAKMAN, Floyd W	Walls of the Missing
EARL, Arthur J	B-15-24
EARLE, Fred R	A-9-27
EARLE, Roger E [97]	B-3-3
EASON, Wilbert E	H-10-3
EAST, Charles T	E-17-25
EAST, Roy W	Walls of the Missing
EASTERBROOK, Earl E	E-10-26
EASTGATE, Ralph J	A-18-1
EASTMAN, Glen J	D-2-21
EASTMAN, Jerome P	E-11-5
EASTMAN, Lee B	C-11-19
EASTMAN, Norman E	D-7-10
EASTON, Rockwell R	B-13-11
EATON, Frederick W II	A-14-9
EATON, George W Jr	F-9-6
EATON, James R	I-11-10
EATON, Norman H	N-11-8
EBERHARD, Lester A	E-10-16
EBERT, Paul J	F-3-9
EBERT, Verlyn W	J-2-5
ECK, Harry W [98]	Walls of the Missing
ECKARD, Lawrence A	A-8-3
ECKBERG, Ferdinand E	C-19-9
ECKENRODE, Raymond J	A-2-3
ECKENRODE, Richard J [99]	K-7-21
ECKERLE, William C	J-17-18
ECKERSON, Roy E	J-17-15
ECKERT, Randall R	F-8-12
ECKERT, Roy J	P-15-10
ECKMAN, Robert W [100]	F-21-6
EDBERG, Merrill J	O-18-9
EDELSTEIN, Melvin L	E-19-21
EDGERLY, Everett E	D-17-19
EDGERTON, Henry Y Jr	H-6-13
EDGIN, Dewey C	E-21-13
EDMONDS, Allan E	A-14-14
EDMONDSON, Max D	F-2-20
EDWARDS, Benjamin E	H-18-9
EDWARDS, Buford N	Walls of the Missing
EDWARDS, Carl L	P-3-17
EDWARDS, Donald F	B-8-27
EDWARDS, Herbert W	Walls of the Missing
EDWARDS, Horace O [101]	Walls of the Missing
EDWARDS, Johnny C	K-20-10
EDWARDS, Joseph K [102]	C-2-22
EDWARDS, Russell R	G-17-12
EDWARDS, William R	A-13-20
EGALITE, George F	H-14-11
EGAN, John P	O-17-3
EGAN, Robert J	E-6-3
EGGERDING, Alvin T	J-6-8
EHRLICH, Joseph J [103]	L-21-18
EICH, Lyonel H	P-3-14
EICHHORN, Edison	Walls of the Missing
EILMAN, Richard H	H-14-19

Name	Location
EISENHUTH, Charles W [104]	K-20-21
ELAM, John D	E-2-15
ELDER, Richard	J-19-11
ELDER, Willard R	D-1-15
ELIAS, Thomas	I-5-6
ELINSKI, John	E-12-23
ELKE, Walter E	H-14-12
ELKINS, Hugh C	D-17-27
ELL, James R	D-6-22
ELL, John W	D-16-31
ELLEDGE, Ralph J	F-7-12
ELLENBURG, Harold C	B-3-9
ELLENBURG, James T	Walls of the Missing
ELLERBUSCH, Clarence L	C-13-16
ELLERBUSCH, Herbert W	Walls of the Missing
ELLINGER, Jerome H	I-16-21
ELLIOTT, Charles F	Walls of the Missing
ELLIOTT, Charles M	H-10-5
ELLIOTT, Dorral B	M-9-13
ELLIOTT, Eugene L	K-7-14
ELLIOTT, Glen D	D-3-24
ELLIOTT, John Glide	A-16-2
ELLIOTT, Walter M	C-13-9
ELLIS, Duane E	E-1-2
ELLIS, Grover W Jr	O-15-14
ELLIS, Henry E	C-17-24
ELLIS, Jack H	K-13-4
ELLIS, William J	P-5-7
ELLISON, Charles A	E-11-27
ELLISON, Oscar V	J-7-15
ELOE, Robert N	J-8-7
ELSEA, Palmore	D-11-28
EMERICK, Ulysses S	P-16-6
EMERSON, Donald R	B-15-21
EMERSON, James F	M-8-5
EMERY, Charles T	A-8-1
EMERY, James R	C-18-18
EMERY, William K	K-4-3
EMMERT, Ralph O	D-15-12
EMOND, Ludger R	E-7-12
EMORY, John R	P-3-16
ENCINIAS, Fidel A	I-19-15
ENGELBRETSON, Donald E	C-13-20
ENGELHARDT, Herman A	J-10-9
ENGELHART, George L	H-1-6
ENGEMAN, Ernest F	Walls of the Missing
ENGLE, Leon J	G-19-22
ENGLE, Robert M	G-10-25
ENGLEHARDT, Albert J	K-18-20
ENGLES, Allen R	C-12-1
ENMAN, Warren A	E-1-1
ENSLEY, Joseph W	A-15-18
ENTLER, Paul L	C-18-9
ENTREKIN, Jesse P	K-9-5
EPPERSON, Arnold B	P-3-15
EPPIG, Gerald L	A-13-5
EPPS, William E	D-3-28
EPRIGHT, Wilbur E	C-15-32
EPTING, Harry E	G-15-10
ERDMAN, Roland H	Walls of the Missing
ERDMAN, Theodore W	K-21-1
ERICKSON, Bernard G	Walls of the Missing
ERICKSON, Carl D	I-8-9
ERICKSON, Glenn V W	K-9-1
ERICKSON, Hilmar G	B-19-2
ERICKSON, Malcolm J	Walls of the Missing
ERICKSON, Ralph L	J-12-14
ERICKSON, Toivo W	D-20-1
ERIKSSON, Axel I	H-4-6
ERLINGS, Lawrence W	Walls of the Missing
ERNEST, Robert B	A-9-29
ERNST, Austin A	G-20-20
ERNST, Michel D	I-6-4
ERNST, Thomas C	M-9-1
ERVIN, Buford	H-16-3
ERVIN, Roy C	D-3-20
ERWIN, Robert E	K-2-12
ESCALERA, Joe J	M-20-8
ESCOBEDO, Eusebio Z	N-3-9
ESER, Boyd F Sr	H-5-18
ESKELIN, Thurston E [105]	E-7-8
ESPE, Arthur H	C-4-22
ESPINO, Richard	C-16-15
ESPOSITO, Gennaro J	G-8-16
ESPOSITO, Michael C	D-14-2
ESQUEDA, Antonio C	E-8-1
ESQUIBEL, Daniel Jr	E-21-2
ESQUIBEL, Joe S [106]	E-21-1
ESSARY, Dewey	Walls of the Missing
ESTERLY, Joseph J	C-19-12
ESTES, Norman B	F-16-17
ESTILL, James D	A-15-13
ESTILL, Shannon E	Walls of the Missing
ESTLE, Dale R	B-5-17
ESTLINBAUM, Fred E	H-5-2
ESTRADA, Louis H	G-11-27
ETHERIDGE, Mart T	Walls of the Missing
ETHRIDGE, Henry S	Walls of the Missing
ETTER, Charles E	F-9-21
ETZEL, Edward Jr	P-19-12
ETZIN, Roy B	Walls of the Missing
ETZLER, Vernon L	O-6-7
EUSE, Frank Jr	C-14-4
EVANCHO, George	N-7-14
EVANCHO, Peter	N-7-13
EVANCHUCK, Paul	J-13-3
EVANOVICH, Joseph	J-17-19
EVANS, Albert C	G-17-20
EVANS, Charles H Jr	K-19-18
EVANS, Charlie	N-14-15
EVANS, Dewey L	B-19-7
EVANS, Forrest R	N-5-4
EVANS, George H	B-8-15
EVANS, Grover C	B-20-18
EVANS, Lloyd W	K-7-17
EVANS, Lyle W	N-2-1
EVANS, Ralph R Sr	B-10-13
EVANS, Randolph L	M-1-11
EVANS, Raymond L	C-4-18
EVANS, Robert L	Walls of the Missing
EVANS, Robert T	C-13-7
EVANS, Roy W	H-2-18
EVANUK, Walter [107]	N-16-12
EVELAND, Berthal D	Walls of the Missing
EVERETT, Arthur L	J-3-11
EVERHART, Robert C	D-7-20
EWAN, Avory L	Walls of the Missing
EWART, William H	Walls of the Missing
EXLINE, Robert R Jr	N-14-9
EYE, Harold F	D-12-6
EYLENS, John T Jr	E-15-26
EZERNACK, Herman	I-13-2

F

Name	Location
FAAS, John E	B-10-3
FABER, Jean D	P-6-9
FAGER, Peter J	Walls of the Missing
FAHED, Edward A	N-7-4
FAHNERT, Clarence C	D-17-31
FAIGLEY, Lester L	A-13-24
FAIN, Raymond L	E-17-16
FAIRCHILD, Ulmer	E-18-18
FAJANS, Walter T Jr	Walls of the Missing
FAKLIS, Peter J	E-3-20
FALAT, Walter L	C-16-10
FALBO, Arthur	N-16-17
FALCO, Philip F	O-1-10
FALEDAS, James T	D-3-26
FALK, James E	A-9-6
FALLIN, Thomas J	C-2-3
FALLON, James F	E-20-24
FALLS, Max E	K-4-9
FAMULARO, Nicholas A	J-11-9
FANELLO, Joseph J [108]	J-19-8
FANNING, Glen B	D-6-2
FANNING, James W	D-6-1
FANNING, Joseph G	Walls of the Missing
FARGHER, Harold H	P-20-7
FARINELLA, Frank [109]	G-17-16
FARISS, Jack P	Walls of the Missing
FARKAS, John J	C-10-15
FARLEY, John A	M-8-2
FARLEY, William R	J-16-20
FARMER, Edward J	Walls of the Missing
FARMER, John A [110]	M-14-1
FARNER, Ivan P	H-18-17
FARNI, Robert F [111]	H-2-16
FARNON, George Jr	B-8-29
FARR, Floyd T Jr	C-2-17
FARRELL, James H	B-20-2
FARRELL, Peter J	L-20-10
FARRELL, Vincent J	F-16-21
FARRINGTON, Parker Jr [112]	G-17-2
FARRIS, Fred C [113]	A-5-9

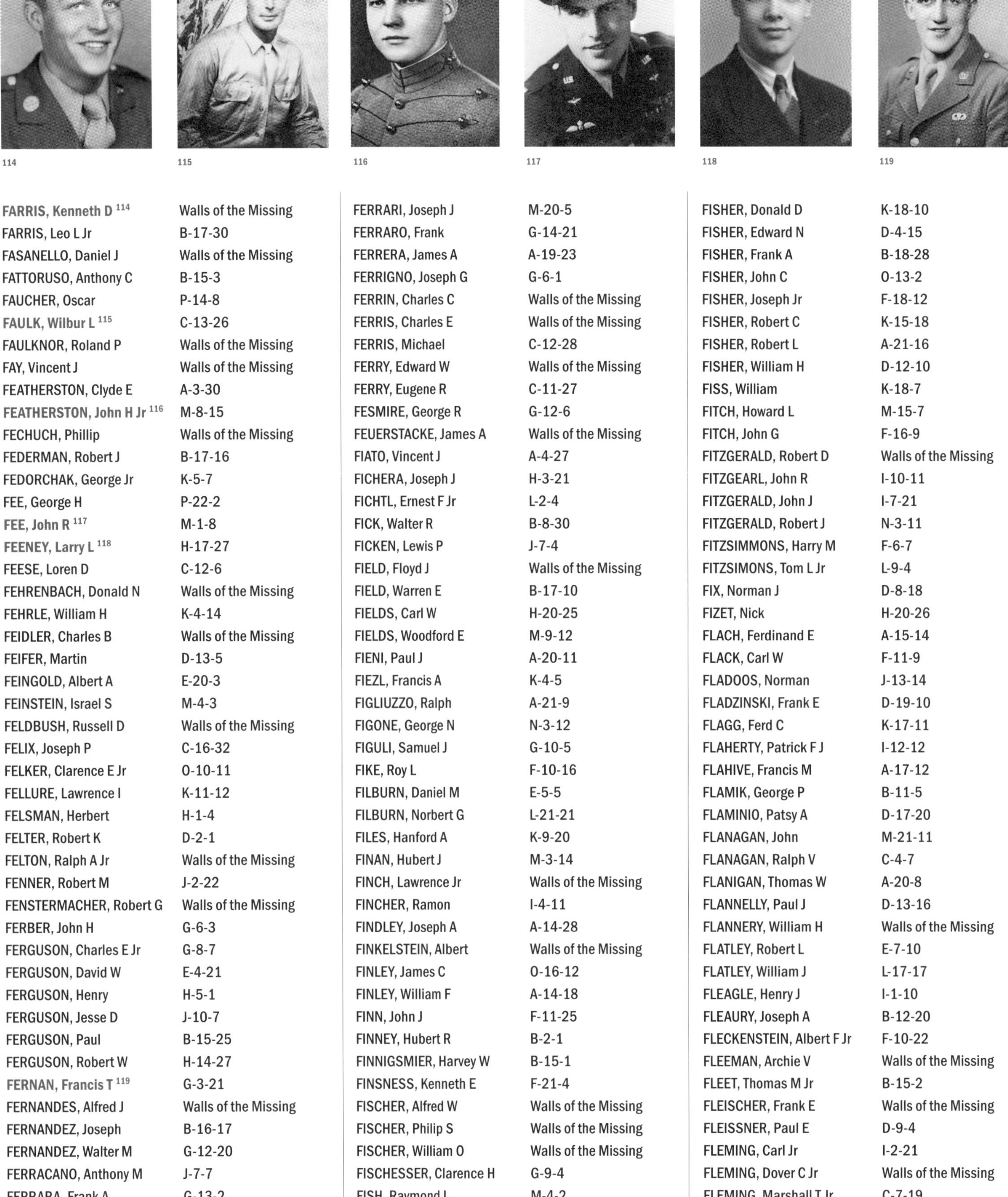

114 115 116 117 118 119

Name	Location
FARRIS, Kenneth D [114]	Walls of the Missing
FARRIS, Leo L Jr	B-17-30
FASANELLO, Daniel J	Walls of the Missing
FATTORUSO, Anthony C	B-15-3
FAUCHER, Oscar	P-14-8
FAULK, Wilbur L [115]	C-13-26
FAULKNOR, Roland P	Walls of the Missing
FAY, Vincent J	Walls of the Missing
FEATHERSTON, Clyde E	A-3-30
FEATHERSTON, John H Jr [116]	M-8-15
FECHUCH, Phillip	Walls of the Missing
FEDERMAN, Robert J	B-17-16
FEDORCHAK, George Jr	K-5-7
FEE, George H	P-22-2
FEE, John R [117]	M-1-8
FEENEY, Larry L [118]	H-17-27
FEESE, Loren D	C-12-6
FEHRENBACH, Donald N	Walls of the Missing
FEHRLE, William H	K-4-14
FEIDLER, Charles B	Walls of the Missing
FEIFER, Martin	D-13-5
FEINGOLD, Albert A	E-20-3
FEINSTEIN, Israel S	M-4-3
FELDBUSH, Russell D	Walls of the Missing
FELIX, Joseph P	C-16-32
FELKER, Clarence E Jr	O-10-11
FELLURE, Lawrence I	K-11-12
FELSMAN, Herbert	H-1-4
FELTER, Robert K	D-2-1
FELTON, Ralph A Jr	Walls of the Missing
FENNER, Robert M	J-2-22
FENSTERMACHER, Robert G	Walls of the Missing
FERBER, John H	G-6-3
FERGUSON, Charles E Jr	G-8-7
FERGUSON, David W	E-4-21
FERGUSON, Henry	H-5-1
FERGUSON, Jesse D	J-10-7
FERGUSON, Paul	B-15-25
FERGUSON, Robert W	H-14-27
FERNAN, Francis T [119]	G-3-21
FERNANDES, Alfred J	Walls of the Missing
FERNANDEZ, Joseph	B-16-17
FERNANDEZ, Walter M	G-12-20
FERRACANO, Anthony M	J-7-7
FERRARA, Frank A	G-13-2
FERRARA, Vincent J	Walls of the Missing

Name	Location
FERRARI, Joseph J	M-20-5
FERRARO, Frank	G-14-21
FERRERA, James A	A-19-23
FERRIGNO, Joseph G	G-6-1
FERRIN, Charles C	Walls of the Missing
FERRIS, Charles E	Walls of the Missing
FERRIS, Michael	C-12-28
FERRY, Edward W	Walls of the Missing
FERRY, Eugene R	C-11-27
FESMIRE, George R	G-12-6
FEUERSTACKE, James A	Walls of the Missing
FIATO, Vincent J	A-4-27
FICHERA, Joseph J	H-3-21
FICHTL, Ernest F Jr	L-2-4
FICK, Walter R	B-8-30
FICKEN, Lewis P	J-7-4
FIELD, Floyd J	Walls of the Missing
FIELD, Warren E	B-17-10
FIELDS, Carl W	H-20-25
FIELDS, Woodford E	M-9-12
FIENI, Paul J	A-20-11
FIEZL, Francis A	K-4-5
FIGLIUZZO, Ralph	A-21-9
FIGONE, George N	N-3-12
FIGULI, Samuel J	G-10-5
FIKE, Roy L	F-10-16
FILBURN, Daniel M	E-5-5
FILBURN, Norbert G	L-21-21
FILES, Hanford A	K-9-20
FINAN, Hubert J	M-3-14
FINCH, Lawrence Jr	Walls of the Missing
FINCHER, Ramon	I-4-11
FINDLEY, Joseph A	A-14-28
FINKELSTEIN, Albert	Walls of the Missing
FINLEY, James C	O-16-12
FINLEY, William F	A-14-18
FINN, John J	F-11-25
FINNEY, Hubert R	B-2-1
FINNIGSMIER, Harvey W	B-15-1
FINSNESS, Kenneth E	F-21-4
FISCHER, Alfred W	Walls of the Missing
FISCHER, Philip S	Walls of the Missing
FISCHER, William O	Walls of the Missing
FISCHESSER, Clarence H	G-9-4
FISH, Raymond L	M-4-2
FISHER, Androclus R	P-4-4

Name	Location
FISHER, Donald D	K-18-10
FISHER, Edward N	D-4-15
FISHER, Frank A	B-18-28
FISHER, John C	O-13-2
FISHER, Joseph Jr	F-18-12
FISHER, Robert C	K-15-18
FISHER, Robert L	A-21-16
FISHER, William H	D-12-10
FISS, William	K-18-7
FITCH, Howard L	M-15-7
FITCH, John G	F-16-9
FITZGERALD, Robert D	Walls of the Missing
FITZGEARL, John R	I-10-11
FITZGERALD, John J	I-7-21
FITZGERALD, Robert J	N-3-11
FITZSIMMONS, Harry M	F-6-7
FITZSIMONS, Tom L Jr	L-9-4
FIX, Norman J	D-8-18
FIZET, Nick	H-20-26
FLACH, Ferdinand E	A-15-14
FLACK, Carl W	F-11-9
FLADOOS, Norman	J-13-14
FLADZINSKI, Frank E	D-19-10
FLAGG, Ferd C	K-17-11
FLAHERTY, Patrick F J	I-12-12
FLAHIVE, Francis M	A-17-12
FLAMIK, George P	B-11-5
FLAMINIO, Patsy A	D-17-20
FLANAGAN, John	M-21-11
FLANAGAN, Ralph V	C-4-7
FLANIGAN, Thomas W	A-20-8
FLANNELLY, Paul J	D-13-16
FLANNERY, William H	Walls of the Missing
FLATLEY, Robert L	E-7-10
FLATLEY, William J	L-17-17
FLEAGLE, Henry J	I-1-10
FLEAURY, Joseph A	B-12-20
FLECKENSTEIN, Albert F Jr	F-10-22
FLEEMAN, Archie V	Walls of the Missing
FLEET, Thomas M Jr	B-15-2
FLEISCHER, Frank E	Walls of the Missing
FLEISSNER, Paul E	D-9-4
FLEMING, Carl Jr	I-2-21
FLEMING, Dover C Jr	Walls of the Missing
FLEMING, Marshall T Jr	C-7-19
FLEMING, Richard S	D-15-26

FLEMING, Samuel	Walls of the Missing
FLETCHER, Marion E	M-5-4
FLETCHER, Milton L	C-1-32
FLETCHER, Robert L	H-10-1
FLETCHER, Walter A	F-18-5
FLEURY, Alphonse	D-10-28
FLING, Roy T	Walls of the Missing
FLINT, Dewitt C	C-20-8
FLODBERG, Frederice T	J-20-3
FLORENTINO, Charles E	M-21-13
FLORES, Manuel R	I-7-6
FLOWER, Jacob J	N-6-6
FLOWERS, Arthur W	I-18-19
FLOWERS, Joe	I-18-22
FLOYD , Lewis F	Walls of the Missing
FLUTY, Fred	G-15-14
FLYNN, Clarence J	D-3-13
FLYNN, Edmund A	D-8-19
FLYNT, Charles A	A-1-4
FOCHT, Norman T	G-7-25
FOCHT, William J	J-12-2
FOER, Bernard W	I-9-6
FOGEL, Frederick W Jr	B-14-28
FOHR, Milton E	J-5-20
FOLEY, Frank J	O-10-5
FOLEY, Frank T	E-6-13
FOLEY, James E	L-17-18
FOLEY, Joseph E	B-20-7
FOLEY, William E	G-15-22
FOLEY, William T	H-12-4
FOLLENDER, Seymour B	O-4-8
FOLSOM, Robert H	A-15-30
FOLTZ, David E	A-15-2
FOLTZ, Kenneth L	J-20-9
FOLTZ, Nicholas A	F-14-14
FONTEYN, Albert L	O-7-8
FORBES, Duncan Jr	B-21-20
FORBREGD, George W	J-19-12
FORCE, Robert R	I-15-10
FORD, George H	O-16-13
FORD, George Jr	N-16-1
FORD, Grady	H-9-26
FORD, John A	G-13-16
FORD, John J	B-18-4
FORD, John T IV	F-6-15
FORD, Joseph M	G-14-25
FORD, Robert L	L-8-4
FORD, Roy L	K-20-15
FORD, Walter A Jr	F-5-14
FORD, William E	C-18-2
FOREIN, Donald W	F-2-2
FOREMAN, Earnest C	D-2-11
FOREMAN, Harry W Jr	Walls of the Missing
FORJAN, Warren A	H-8-15
FORMOSA, Silvio G Jr	E-21-4
FORREST, Edward L	P-11-8
FORRESTER, Edward	C-6-25
FORTENER, Robert F	K-6-19
FORTIER, Robert J	K-20-3
FORTIN, Charles A	M-22-9
FOSSETT, Elwood F	C-2-18
FOSTER, Frank M	Walls of the Missing
FOSTER, George A	A-17-13
FOSTER, James B Jr	N-8-2
FOSTER, John T	G-19-16
FOSTER, Luther D	G-16-7
FOSTER, Robert G	Walls of the Missing
FOSTER, Thomas J	M-18-8
FOSTER, Todd S	N-20-14
FOUBERT, Charles A	Walls of the Missing
FOUNTAIN, James E	I-17-5
FOURAKER, Jesse E	B-12-2
FOURNIER, Albert G	K-18-21
FOUST, Corbet	G-19-6
FOUST, Marion	A-20-22
FOUTZ, Stanley	Walls of the Missing
FOWLER, Bryan P	A-19-15
FOWLER, Paul F	O-20-14
FOWLER, Van	O-19-5
FOWLKES, Alpheus E Jr	M-11-2
FOWLKES, Paschal D	C-17-20
FOX, Eugene	F-13-25
FOX, John E	G-6-10
FOX, Joseph P	E-20-21
FOX, Keith B	N-16-15
FOX, Wayne C	N-2-14
FOX, Woodrow W	A-20-14
FRAIOLI, Domenico	C-21-32
FRAME, Slaten O	C-7-25
FRANCEK, Stanley S	B-16-16
FRANCIS, Irving V Jr	K-21-4
FRANCIS, Pott	K-4-1
FRANCIS, Robert F	Walls of the Missing
FRANCIS, Thomas R	Walls of the Missing
FRANK, William	F-7-22
FRANKE, Ellick	Walls of the Missing
FRANKEL, Arthur B	Walls of the Missing
FRANKLIN, Edward G	D-16-23
FRANKLIN, Marthal N	Walls of the Missing
FRANKLIN, Sherman	M-15-17
FRANKLIN, Thomas A	N-16-7
FRANKOVITZ, John	H-2-7
FRANKS, Adolph A	E-21-18
FRANTZ, Gerald R	Walls of the Missing
FRANTZ, Leo H	F-18-8
FRANZBLAU, Maurice J	E-19-2
FRANZEN, Arthur W	C-17-29
FRANZIN, Wesley S	A-19-30
FRANZMAN, Kurt	B-6-9
FRASER, Gordon S	Walls of the Missing
FRASER, Harry L	I-10-21
FRASER, Raymond H	M-3-12
FRAZIER, Isac W	A-18-12
FRAZIER, Lloyd W	Walls of the Missing
FRAZIER, Robert M	D-8-22
FREDA, Anthony R	M-5-2
FREDERICK, Clifford W	D-5-30
FREDERICK, George W	C-18-10
FREDERICKSEN, Harold K	Walls of the Missing
FREDRICKS, Lewis J	Walls of the Missing
FREEBORN, Franklin W	A-3-7
FREED, Warren D	I-9-8
FREEMAN, Charles S	Walls of the Missing
FREEMAN, Don A	Walls of the Missing
FRENCH, Bernard J	Walls of the Missing
FRENCH, Julius E	G-10-26
FRENCH, Robert F	F-17-1
FRENCH, Wyman J	G-10-13
FRESCHAUF, Charles W	Walls of the Missing
FRETWELL, Thomas E Jr	Walls of the Missing
FRETZ, Russell G Jr	F-9-20
FREYERMUTH, Harry Frank	H-14-15
FRICK, Robert E	E-4-1
FRIDUSS, Jarvis H	Walls of the Missing
FRIEDMAN, Harry H	N-20-6
FRIEDMAN, Morris S	O-20-12
FRIEND, William E Jr	Walls of the Missing
FRIES, Roy T	Walls of the Missing
FRIESEMA, John J	M-4-1
FRINKS, Charles O	E-2-14
FRISBY, Orven E	K-17-17
FRISON, Henry Jr	N-20-4
FRISONE, Domenic	J-6-19
FRISONE, John J	J-6-18
FRISTIK, Henry E	D-4-31
FRITZ, Edwin A	E-2-25
FRITZ, Elwood E	K-17-14
FRITZINGER, Raymond W	Walls of the Missing
FROBISH, Eldon C	Walls of the Missing
FROLICK, Edwin J	P-7-9
FRUEHWIRTH, William J	G-21-4
FRUZEN, Edward B	A-18-15
FRY, Bobby W	B-2-17
FRY, Edward Jr	M-9-2
FRY, Leo W	P-21-3
FRY, Woodrow	C-20-12
FRYE, Floyd L	Walls of the Missing
FRYE, Warren H	A-4-30
FRYER, Walter J	B-2-9
FUERST, Michael J	H-5-14
FULARA, Edward F	E-15-9
FULARA, John J	E-15-8
FULKERSON, Douglas M	N-19-17
FULL, Henry H	K-20-17
FULLER, Edwin W	I-1-21
FULLER, Herman R	P-7-7
FULLER, James A	D-9-24
FULLER, Paul Jr	F-9-16
FULLERTON, Thomas F	A-5-17
FULMER, Floyd A	Walls of the Missing
FUNKHOUSER, Stanley P	H-4-2
FUQUA, Allen A	E-20-10
FUQUA, George E	A-20-10
FURR, Arnet L	Walls of the Missing

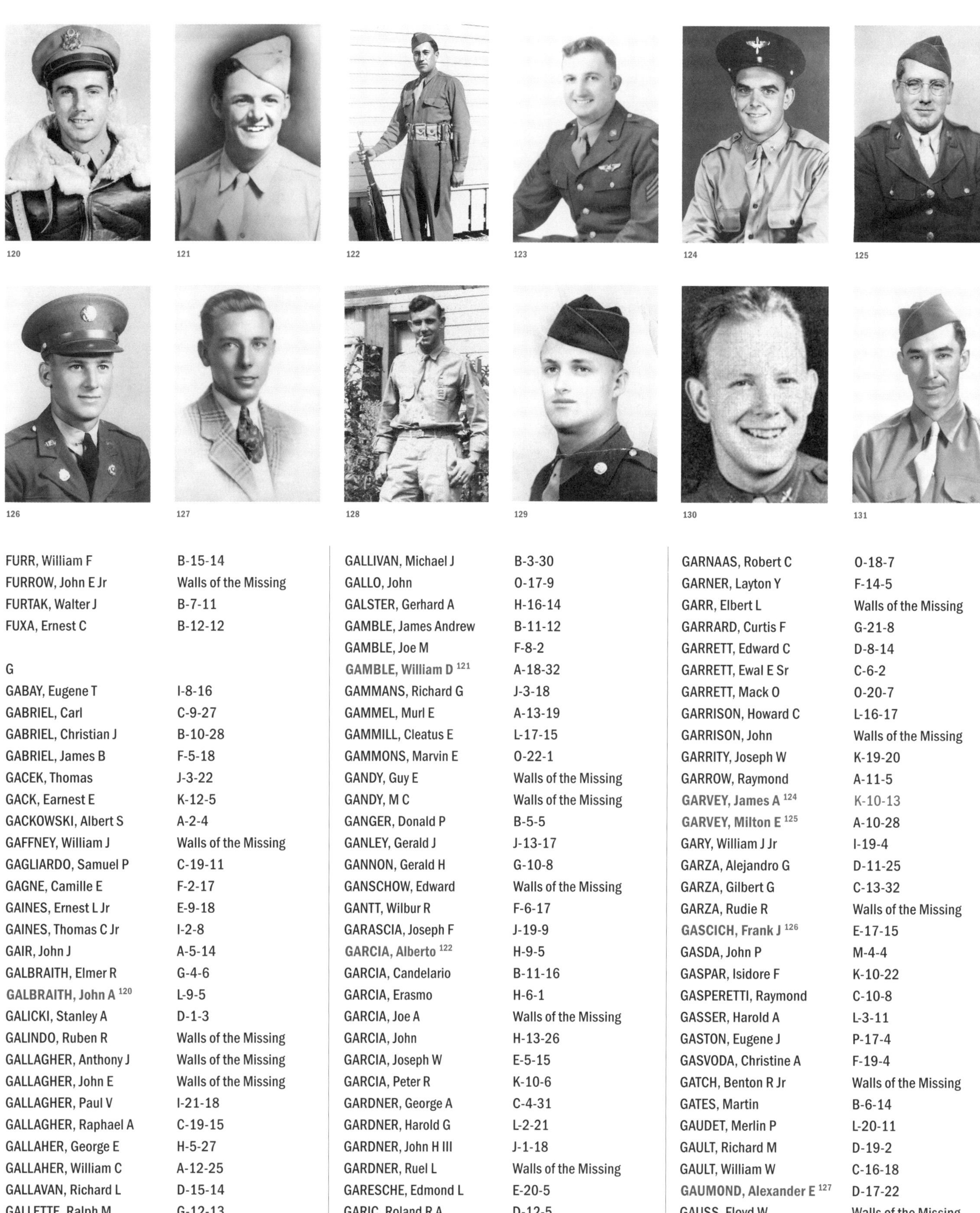

120 121 122 123 124 125

126 127 128 129 130 131

Name	Location
FURR, William F	B-15-14
FURROW, John E Jr	Walls of the Missing
FURTAK, Walter J	B-7-11
FUXA, Ernest C	B-12-12
G	
GABAY, Eugene T	I-8-16
GABRIEL, Carl	C-9-27
GABRIEL, Christian J	B-10-28
GABRIEL, James B	F-5-18
GACEK, Thomas	J-3-22
GACK, Earnest E	K-12-5
GACKOWSKI, Albert S	A-2-4
GAFFNEY, William J	Walls of the Missing
GAGLIARDO, Samuel P	C-19-11
GAGNE, Camille E	F-2-17
GAINES, Ernest L Jr	E-9-18
GAINES, Thomas C Jr	I-2-8
GAIR, John J	A-5-14
GALBRAITH, Elmer R	G-4-6
GALBRAITH, John A [120]	L-9-5
GALICKI, Stanley A	D-1-3
GALINDO, Ruben R	Walls of the Missing
GALLAGHER, Anthony J	Walls of the Missing
GALLAGHER, John E	Walls of the Missing
GALLAGHER, Paul V	I-21-18
GALLAGHER, Raphael A	C-19-15
GALLAHER, George E	H-5-27
GALLAHER, William C	A-12-25
GALLAVAN, Richard L	D-15-14
GALLETTE, Ralph M	G-12-13
GALLION, Frank D	Walls of the Missing
GALLION, John L Jr	D-6-24
GALLIPEAU, Eugene H	O-20-9
GALLIVAN, Michael J	B-3-30
GALLO, John	O-17-9
GALSTER, Gerhard A	H-16-14
GAMBLE, James Andrew	B-11-12
GAMBLE, Joe M	F-8-2
GAMBLE, William D [121]	A-18-32
GAMMANS, Richard G	J-3-18
GAMMEL, Murl E	A-13-19
GAMMILL, Cleatus E	L-17-15
GAMMONS, Marvin E	O-22-1
GANDY, Guy E	Walls of the Missing
GANDY, M C	Walls of the Missing
GANGER, Donald P	B-5-5
GANLEY, Gerald J	J-13-17
GANNON, Gerald H	G-10-8
GANSCHOW, Edward	Walls of the Missing
GANTT, Wilbur R	F-6-17
GARASCIA, Joseph F	J-19-9
GARCIA, Alberto [122]	H-9-5
GARCIA, Candelario	B-11-16
GARCIA, Erasmo	H-6-1
GARCIA, Joe A	Walls of the Missing
GARCIA, John	H-13-26
GARCIA, Joseph W	E-5-15
GARCIA, Peter R	K-10-6
GARDNER, George A	C-4-31
GARDNER, Harold G	L-2-21
GARDNER, John H III	J-1-18
GARDNER, Ruel L	Walls of the Missing
GARESCHE, Edmond L	E-20-5
GARIC, Roland R A	D-12-5
GARLAND, Ernest P	Walls of the Missing
GARLINGTON, Creswell Jr	A-12-7
GARMAN, Paul J [123]	P-21-15
GARNAAS, Robert C	O-18-7
GARNER, Layton Y	F-14-5
GARR, Elbert L	Walls of the Missing
GARRARD, Curtis F	G-21-8
GARRETT, Edward C	D-8-14
GARRETT, Ewal E Sr	C-6-2
GARRETT, Mack O	O-20-7
GARRISON, Howard C	L-16-17
GARRISON, John	Walls of the Missing
GARRITY, Joseph W	K-19-20
GARROW, Raymond	A-11-5
GARVEY, James A [124]	K-10-13
GARVEY, Milton E [125]	A-10-28
GARY, William J Jr	I-19-4
GARZA, Alejandro G	D-11-25
GARZA, Gilbert G	C-13-32
GARZA, Rudie R	Walls of the Missing
GASCICH, Frank J [126]	E-17-15
GASDA, John P	M-4-4
GASPAR, Isidore F	K-10-22
GASPERETTI, Raymond	C-10-8
GASSER, Harold A	L-3-11
GASTON, Eugene J	P-17-4
GASVODA, Christine A	F-19-4
GATCH, Benton R Jr	Walls of the Missing
GATES, Martin	B-6-14
GAUDET, Merlin P	L-20-11
GAULT, Richard M	D-19-2
GAULT, William W	C-16-18
GAUMOND, Alexander E [127]	D-17-22
GAUSS, Floyd W	Walls of the Missing
GAUSS, George	I-3-10
GAUTHIER, Leo A	I-14-4
GAUTIER, George J	K-2-4

GAVAGHAN, James J	H-17-3
GAVANDULA, John J [128]	F-7-6
GAWTHROP, William R Jr	B-9-31
GAXIOLA, Gus J	Walls of the Missing
GAYDOSH, Charles J	D-16-30
GAYLOR, George W Jr	Walls of the Missing
GAZIA, Tony S	Walls of the Missing
GEBO, Lyle M	L-18-22
GEE, Niles G	I-16-6
GEE, Robert E [129]	L-21-20
GEER, Gilbert T	A-1-11
GEER, Joseph W Jr	H-20-22
GEERING, Dennis J	H-4-17
GEERLINGS, Lambert J	Walls of the Missing
GEIGER, Alvin O Jr	M-18-14
GEIGER, Donald J	A-16-10
GEIGER, Orville M	I-11-4
GEMBORSKI, John J	M-4-6
GENGLER, Ralph T	B-9-28
GENNARO, Salvador	N-18-13
GENOVA, Albert J	I-18-21
GENTILE, Benjamin J	J-21-3
GENTRY, Marion E	J-14-9
GENTZEL, Richard H	Walls of the Missing
GEORGE, Earl	D-12-21
GEORGE, Harold C	H-17-23
GEORGE, James J	F-5-22
GEORGE, John P	J-7-8
GEORGE, Lloyd A	L-12-20
GEPHART, Raymond D	C-16-4
GERACI, Joseph P	D-11-8
GERCEVICH, Walter C	C-19-25
GERDES, Woodrow F	Walls of the Missing
GERE, James S	D-4-10
GERIOK, Michael	Walls of the Missing
GERKE, Wright E	O-6-6
GERKING, Carl E	E-9-25
GERLACH, Frank J	K-13-1
GERMAIN, Fred H	H-6-14
GERMAINE, Walden J	F-16-15
GEROMINI, Everett H	A-20-17
GERSTENMAIER, George A	C-4-13
GERVAIS, William A Jr	Walls of the Missing
GESSERT, Charles E	Walls of the Missing
GESSICK, John M	O-7-6
GETHIN, William G	I-5-5
GETTINGS, Lawrence J	I-10-17
GETZ, Eugene W	D-5-16
GEWEHR, Ralph P	Walls of the Missing
GHERE, Bobby G	C-3-17
GHISOLFI, Harold A	F-11-3
GIACOMO, Joseph S	G-21-16
GIANDOMENICO, Dominic V	B-20-27
GIANDONATO, John N	A-19-32
GIANNOBULE, Frank W	G-16-10
GIBBIE, Cecil J	C-7-27
GIBBONS, John J	G-16-6
GIBBS, Fred A	E-5-27
GIBSON, Bryce C Jr	L-19-5
GIBSON, James L	A-8-10
GIBSON, Raymond D	O-19-17
GIBSON, Robert L	B-2-14
GIEDRIS, Raymond J	D-17-5
GIEL, Jacob F	Walls of the Missing
GIENGER, Theodore H	K-1-11
GIFFEY, Donald J	P-21-9
GIL, Emmanuel J	L-8-2
GILBERT, Luther H	N-9-4
GILBERT, Richard L	H-14-21
GILBERT, Robert N	L-5-13
GILBERT, William T Jr	F-21-2
GILBERTSON, Willard G	Walls of the Missing
GILBREATH, Ray	Walls of the Missing
GILCHRIST, Kenneth M	F-11-12
GILCHRIST, Vincent J	I-19-21
GILCHRIST, William L	H-6-19
GILCREAST, William L	B-19-31
GILES, Donald L	E-11-26
GILES, Harold	F-11-22
GILES, Harold R	Walls of the Missing
GILES, Lavelle E	Walls of the Missing
GILES, William R	Walls of the Missing
GILIA, Andrew P	I-4-10
GILL, Donald D	Walls of the Missing
GILLESPIE, Glenn H	N-2-15
GILLETTE, Henry A	D-12-20
GILLIES, John N	O-17-7
GILLILAN, George M	A-10-2
GILLINGS, Norman P	F-9-17
GILLIS, Angus A	P-21-6
GILLIS, James H	P-17-8
GILMORE, Glen E	F-14-3
GILMORE, Howard D	D-16-16
GILROY, James S	M-14-2
GILROY, Robert F	K-15-17
GINGRICH, Albert H	Walls of the Missing
GINSBERG, Morris	E-4-25
GIOFFE, Frank A	Walls of the Missing
GIOVANNINI, George D	Walls of the Missing
GIRARD, Bernard W	A-7-12
GIRAUD, Wilbur R	H-19-18
GIRVIN, Robert P	E-2-26
GISEWITE, Clarence E	A-14-15
GIUSTI, Louis J	F-8-8
GIVENS, Jacob W	Walls of the Missing
GJERDE, Carroll J	Walls of the Missing
GLADDING, Edward T	I-1-17
GLADFELTER, Kenneth E	D-4-2
GLAMAN, Robert F	A-8-23
GLANZER, Robert	A-9-21
GLASER, Lester P	M-4-7
GLASGOW, William H	G-15-7
GLASS, William H	H-15-11
GLASSEN, Joseph A	C-3-32
GLASSMAN, Kenneth E	Walls of the Missing
GLATT, William E	J-8-10
GLAVAN, Louis J	D-21-9
GLAWE, Jack W	F-7-16
GLAZE, Gerald D	Walls of the Missing
GLEDHILL, Alfred E	A-13-12
GLEMBOSKI, Stanley W	Walls of the Missing
GLIARMIS, Richard D	M-13-7
GLOGAU, Donald M	B-13-4
GLOOZMAN, Melvin J	E-15-27
GLOVER, Faris M	G-10-16
GLOVER, James H	D-17-12
GLOWACKI, Walter S	J-11-3
GNIDA, Thaddeus	B-12-23
GOBER, John H	B-12-5
GODDARD, Howard W	E-19-6
GODDARD, Maurice C	K-21-11
GODFREY, Robert A	H-20-1
GODMAN, Melvin W	D-4-18
GODWIN, Peter F	K-11-21
GOERS, Leo W	Walls of the Missing
GOETZ, Ernest E	A-3-16
GOETZ, John W	Walls of the Missing
GOETZ, Robert P	E-1-13
GOFF, Donald R	D-4-1
GOFF, Homer W	P-11-10
GOGAL, Thomas P	J-12-4
GOIN, Dallas J	G-11-22
GOINS, Claud R	M-8-11
GOINS, Everette	F-13-14
GOLBSKI, James	Walls of the Missing
GOLD, Leon C	B-19-4
GOLDBERG, Abraham	A-8-19
GOLDBERG, Irving	K-6-8
GOLDBERG, Martin	Walls of the Missing
GOLDEN, Jack E	B-9-22
GOLDEN, Mark L	G-20-17
GOLDEN, William J	Walls of the Missing
GOLDFARB, Kenneth S	J-9-6
GOLDIE, William	H-13-2
GOLDSTEIN, Aaron	Walls of the Missing
GOLDSTEIN, Harry	Walls of the Missing
GOLLADAY, William D	I-12-10
GOMEZ, Arthur G	L-4-5
GOMEZ, Austin	L-9-19
GOMEZ, Juan A	A-18-22
GONDELA, Thadeus S	F-1-9
GONDER, Joseph R [130]	Walls of the Missing
GONNEVILLE, Roland A	L-8-22
GONSOWSKI, Aloysius	Walls of the Missing
GONZALES, Alejandro	A-20-19
GONZALES, Eugenio	A-18-16
GONZALES, Ysidro Jr [131]	A-21-19
GONZALEZ, Emiliano G	E-8-15
GOO, William L Y	Walls of the Missing
GOOD, Floyd L	B-6-29
GOOD, Max E	P-15-15
GOOD, Orville S	H-9-20
GOOD, Walter P	H-17-25
GOODALL, Edward M	O-8-11

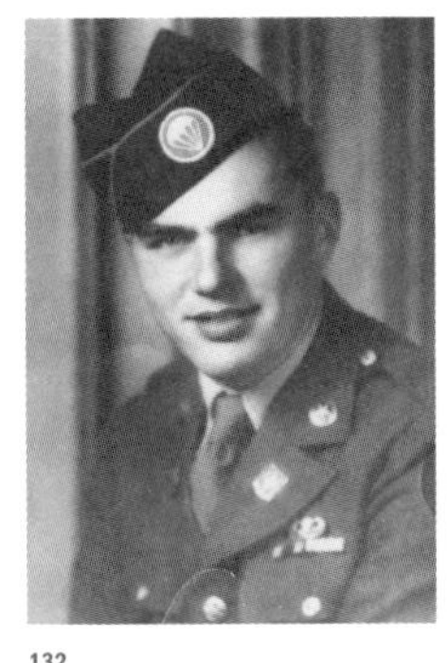
132

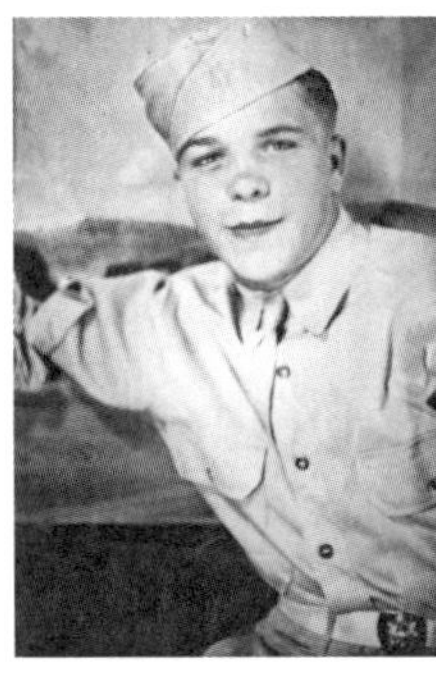
133

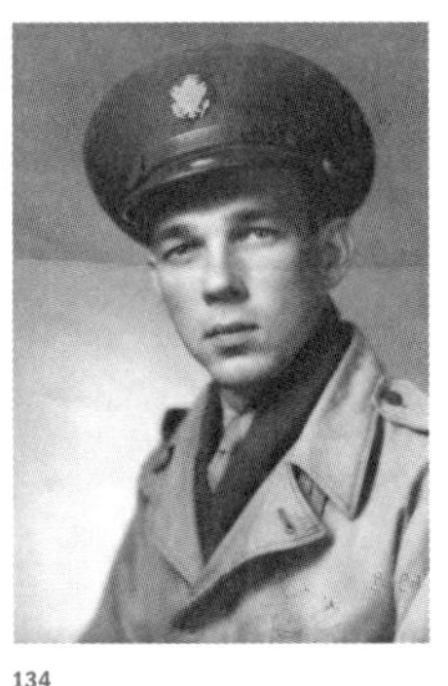
134

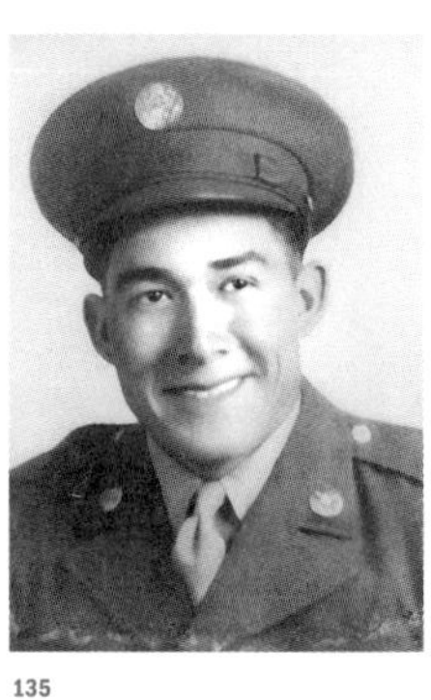
135

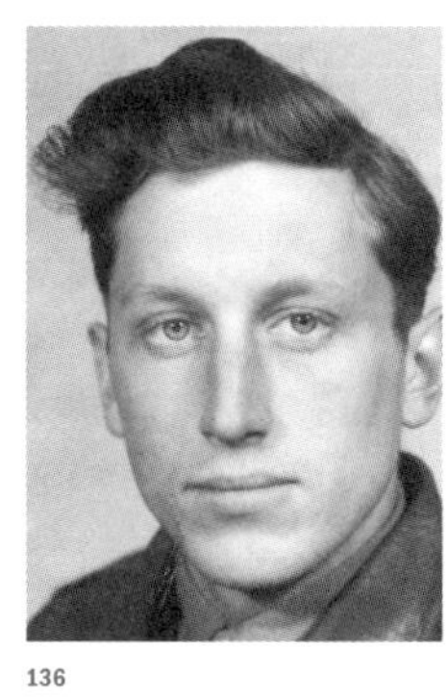
136

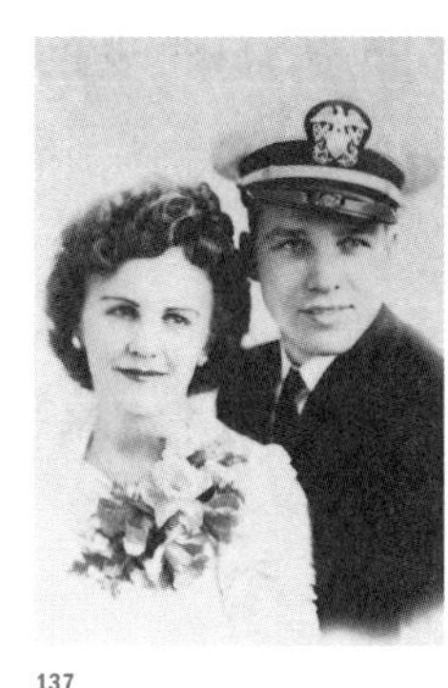
137

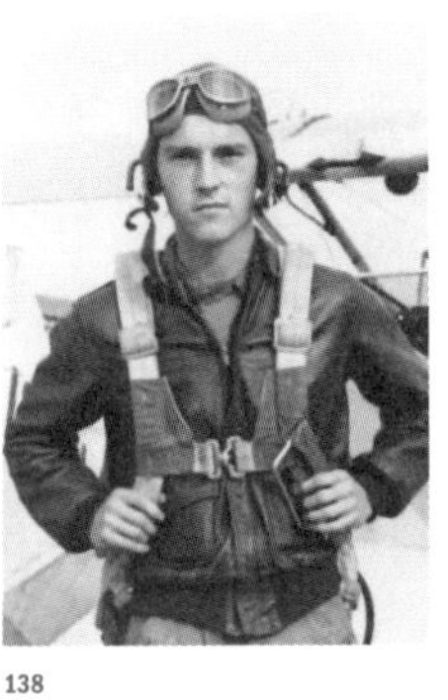
138

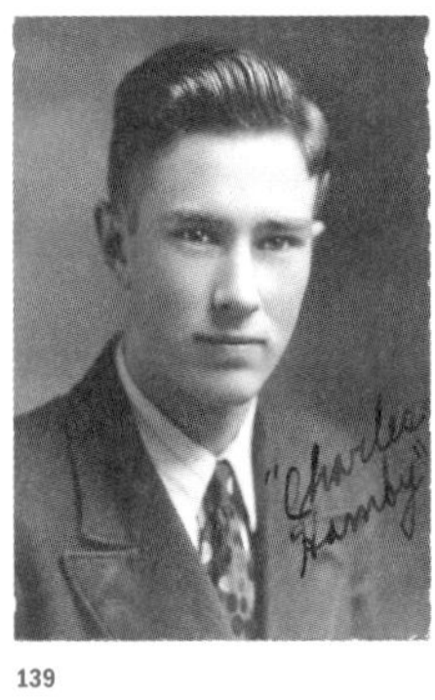

139

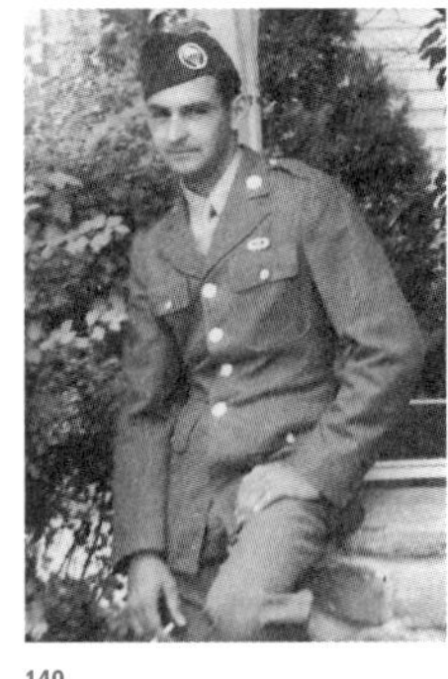
140

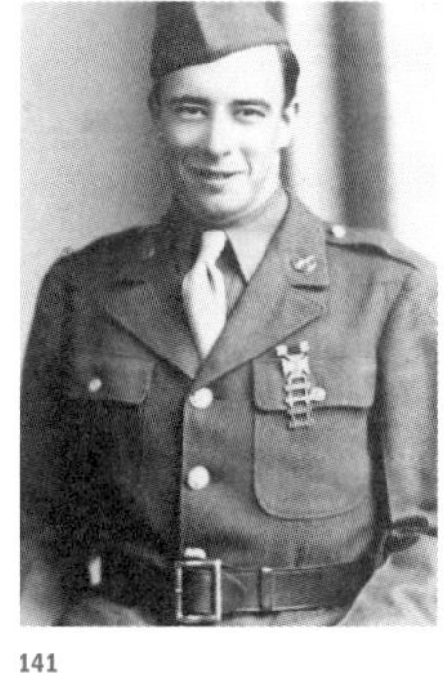
141

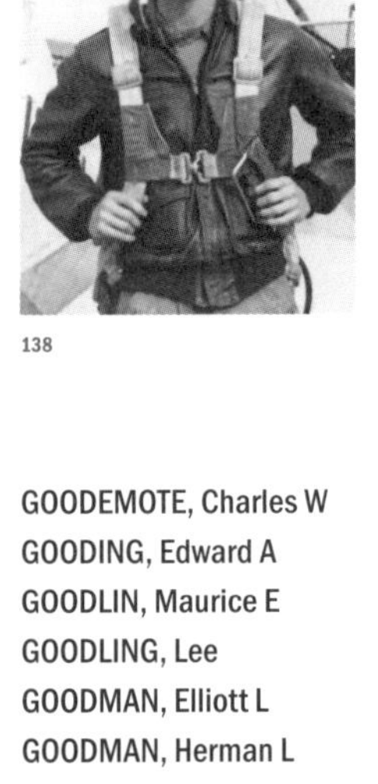

GOODEMOTE, Charles W	N-2-4
GOODING, Edward A	P-14-17
GOODLIN, Maurice E	C-10-20
GOODLING, Lee	C-20-18
GOODMAN, Elliott L	P-16-1
GOODMAN, Herman L	N-5-14
GOODMAN, Irving S	B-3-10
GOODMAN, Luther	G-9-22
GOODMAN, Rathel R	I-19-18
GOODMAN, Sanford	P-16-2
GOODMAN, Vernon W	F-3-23
GOODMANSON, Merlyn C	G-20-7
GOODRICH, William M	C-5-32
GOODWIN, Apolis N Jr	B-21-23
GOODWIN, Wayne R	Walls of the Missing
GOODWYN, William S II	J-1-9
GOODYKOONTZ, Homer A	L-7-4
GOOLSBY, Jack	I-4-14
GOOLSBY, Louie D	I-3-11
GORDEN, Kenneth L	A-16-30
GORDEY, Vincient H	M-16-8
GORDON, Barney	M-15-4
GORDON, Edward F	M-19-11
GORDON, John M Jr	A-17-23
GORDON, Norman H	A-5-11
GORDON, Robert	Walls of the Missing
GORDON, William H	Walls of the Missing
GORDONI, Don M	Walls of the Missing
GORHAM, Roy S	D-1-19
GORIS, George E Jr	Walls of the Missing
GORKA, Walter T	Walls of the Missing
GORMAN, John F	M-21-14
GORMLEY, Raymond J	M-18-1

GORN, Lion A	Walls of the Missing
GORSKI, Walter F	A-21-20
GORTON, Ernest	P-15-7
GOSNEY, Maurice E	I-2-11
GOSS, Paul L	G-8-19
GOSSAGE, Robert V	Walls of the Missing
GOTSES, Nicholas C	N-9-16
GOTT, Edwin J	Walls of the Missing
GOTTHARDT, Robert J	K-12-4
GOTTORF, Edward H	P-15-4
GOUGEON, Roland H	M-15-2
GOUGH, Robert F	I-3-7
GOULD, Frank E	D-15-19
GOULD, Harris A	F-12-8
GOULDIN, Robert A	D-15-30
GOUSHAKJIAN, Steven	G-6-24
GOVANUS, Robert E	B-9-32
GOVERN, Stanley M	J-9-20
GOWER, William J	B-13-6
GRABER, Louis	C-17-15
GRABOWSKI, Leonard E	F-16-3
GRACIE, Archibald R	B-11-31
GRADZIEL, John T	D-15-13
GRAEF, Robert S	I-21-12
GRAF, David V	Walls of the Missing
GRAF, Rudolph J	C-17-32
GRAFFUNDER, Carl H	P-11-11
GRAGE, Glen E	C-4-11
GRAHAL, Steve S	E-10-3
GRAHAM, Francis R	Walls of the Missing
GRAHAM, Harold Q	K-17-3
GRAHAM, Kenneth N	A-20-15
GRAHAM, Leroy	I-18-12

GRAHAM, Owen L	A-6-18
GRAHAM, Robert F	I-18-1
GRAHAM, Thomas L	D-14-20
GRAINGER, Fred	F-2-1
GRAMBO, Frederick C	H-5-13
GRAME, Robert E	H-4-8
GRANAT, John R	I-11-2
GRANDBOUCHE, Leroy D	O-10-6
GRANIER, William P	I-16-14
GRANT, Henry H	A-17-10
GRANT, Nelson	F-20-5
GRANT, Otis L	A-11-19
GRANTHAM, Edward O	F-16-22
GRASSHOFF, Lee F Jr	I-18-2
GRASSMICK, David H	I-13-18
GRASSO, Frank	Walls of the Missing
GRAUBART, Adolf	I-7-12
GRAUVOGL, Laverne H	A-7-6
GRAVEL, Donald A	Walls of the Missing
GRAVES, Hudie E	O-10-1
GRAVES, Joe P	C-9-20
GRAY, Charles W	P-17-13
GRAY, Dwight M	O-6-3
GRAY, Edward F	B-16-7
GRAY, Glenn R	A-2-30
GRAY, Lloyd G	E-10-18
GRAY, Melvin A	L-9-14
GRAY, Roy G	Walls of the Missing
GRAY, Thomas	F-1-16
GRAY, William J Jr	Walls of the Missing
GRAYSON, Sylvester	D-13-17
GRCICH, Joseph W	L-5-15
GREATHOUSE, Harold A	O-14-16
GREBLE, William E	J-11-7
GRECO, Randolph R	E-19-15
GREEK, George H	F-20-2
GREEN, Aubrey L	K-19-8
GREEN, Daniel H	Walls of the Missing
GREEN, Dennis J	E-10-10
GREEN, Harry	J-15-9
GREEN, John E	P-11-12
GREEN, Lonnie Jr	J-21-10
GREEN, William	L-15-11
GREEN, William E	Walls of the Missing
GREENBACK, Frederick L [132]	G-15-15
GREENBERG, Benjamin	L-2-12

Name	Location
GREENBERG, Bertram	C-14-19
GREENE, Alonzo H	D-3-27
GREENE, Austin G	J-3-7
GREENE, James P Jr	C-14-28
GREENE, Kenneth E	F-17-9
GREENE, Rex E Jr	D-19-6
GREENMAN, William J	P-16-9
GREENUP, Charles E	F-19-20
GREENWELL, Joseph C	Walls of the Missing
GREER, Carl E Jr	Walls of the Missing
GREER, Julius F Jr	Walls of the Missing
GREGG, Barney W	B-20-26
GREGORY, Alfred C Jr	F-7-17
GREGORY, Arthur L	J-10-4
GREGORY, Jesse L	Walls of the Missing
GREGORY, Matthews	Walls of the Missing
GREGORY, Ralph E Jr	Walls of the Missing
GREGORY, Robert N	H-18-21
GREINER, George E	G-4-25
GREINER, Joseph G Jr	E-7-24
GRELLE, Frank J	K-21-19
GRENIER, David A	E-16-11
GRENO, Paul J	Walls of the Missing
GRESCAK, George	P-13-1
GRESKO, John P	J-17-6
GREYNO, Peter	A-15-22
GRIBBEN, Thomas A	A-15-11
GRICE, Delbert W	F-13-1
GRIEBE, Floyd G	F-19-11
GRIER, Julius D	Walls of the Missing
GRIER, Warren W Jr	I-20-9
GRIESI, Patsy J	E-1-20
GRIFFIN, Calvin B	I-2-2
GRIFFIN, Clifford G	I-16-12
GRIFFIN, Donald G	H-9-17
GRIFFIN, Henry A	I-17-7
GRIFFIN, James T	H-9-7
GRIFFIN, John V	H-15-12
GRIFFIN, John W	D-5-14
GRIFFIN, Joseph F	Walls of the Missing
GRIFFIN, Samuel	L-2-11
GRIFFITH, George P	Walls of the Missing
GRIFFITH, Mark G Jr	H-19-17
GRIGAITIS, Edward G [133]	Walls of the Missing
GRIGGS, William D	F-7-14
GRILES, Joseph D	E-17-4
GRILL, Mark R	N-16-13
GRIMES, Clarke P	I-6-6
GRIMES, George G	Walls of the Missing
GRIMES, Lawrence A	E-9-22
GRIMES, Wilbur E	E-9-21
GRIMSEHL, Georg H C	H-21-22
GRINDSTAFF, Earl T	Walls of the Missing
GRISSOM, Jeff C	J-6-20
GRISSOM, Lawrence D	A-10-17
GRISWEL, Wilson	D-2-28
GROCEMAN, William E Jr	O-13-16
GRODY, William H	Walls of the Missing
GROFF, Benjamin F	P-11-13
GROSE, Arnold F	I-21-13
GROSSKLAGS, Ralph A	D-20-27
GROVES, Kenneth E	K-12-15
GROW, Raymond L	C-18-32
GRUBB, Joel N Jr	B-11-2
GRUBB, William T	K-4-18
GRUBBS, David Edgar	C-14-5
GRUBBS, Raymond E	P-6-17
GRUCA, Walter P	M-4-5
GRUMMER, Raymond H	M-11-1
GRUNERT, Warren P	M-2-16
GRUNTMEIR, Herman E	H-13-11
GRUSS, Edward W	E-13-25
GRZELOK, Zigmund J	E-16-26
GUDAITIS, Benjamin [134]	M-9-15
GUDYKA, Peter	Walls of the Missing
GUENTHER, William G	D-21-3
GUENZIG, Bernard A	Walls of the Missing
GUERRERO, Gilberto	L-21-9
GUEST, William M	O-10-8
GUIDO, Carmelo B	Walls of the Missing
GUIDO, Robert S	A-15-15
GUIDORIZZI, John J	J-21-4
GUILBAULT, Charles L	F-17-19
GUILTNER, Harry C	G-5-14
GUIMOND, Alfred O	G-20-25
GUIOU, Stanley C	Walls of the Missing
GUISE, Harmen E	A-10-4
GULBRANDSON, Neal I	E-12-12
GULLAGE, Edmund	P-13-9
GUM, Robert A	M-12-10
GUMM, Elmer	N-6-8
GUNDERSON, Loran A	Walls of the Missing
GUNDERSON, Raymond	J-6-4
GUNN, William R	F-6-1
GUNNOE, Joseph H	Walls of the Missing
GUNSON, Robert F	I-21-5
GUNVALSON, Ervin W	A-14-32
GURLEY, James E	Walls of the Missing
GURNEY, Herbert	I-21-22
GUSE, William G	Walls of the Missing
GUTHMANN, Richard F	K-7-1
GUTHRIE, George L	D-1-32
GUTIERREZ, Henry [135]	G-18-13
GUTIERREZ, Luis	N-6-15
GUTKUHN, Herbert	C-8-27
GUTMANN, Ernest	F-5-2
GUYER, Albert J	L-17-6
GUZIK, Chester M	G-19-5
GUZIK, Frank J	L-10-7
GWIN, Edward P	P-20-8
GWIN, Grady H	Walls of the Missing

H

Name	Location
HAAS, Samuel D	A-14-6
HABOIAN, Casper	Walls of the Missing
HACKENBERG, Theodore H	F-18-3
HACKER, William E	Walls of the Missing
HACKNEY, Claude J Jr	H-12-10
HADAWAY, J C	L-12-21
HADDEN, Donald R	Walls of the Missing
HADDOX, James R	Walls of the Missing
HADFIELD, Lynn W	Walls of the Missing
HAEFT, Richard E	A-11-8
HAEHER, Frank J	M-20-9
HAGAN, Lloyd D	N-6-5
HAGAN, William C	A-19-22
HAGEN, David L	D-20-5
HAGER, Clarence W Jr	Walls of the Missing
HAGER, William H	I-9-17
HAGETTER, Edward K	J-9-9
HAGGART, John M Jr	C-13-15
HAGGERTY, Fred J Jr	P-6-16
HAGLUND, Guy L [136]	D-2-22
HAHL, Frank H	A-6-19
HAJDUK, Stanley F	C-7-31
HAJEK, Charles J Jr	F-2-14
HAKAMAA, John	I-12-3
HALBROOK, Le Roy F	Walls of the Missing
HALE, Luther D	F-17-21
HALE, Roland E	O-10-2
HALE, Thomas	F-5-25
HALEY, Donald J	A-11-7
HALL, Boggs C	G-10-1
HALL, Cecil D	B-18-15
HALL, Charles P	D-16-27
HALL, Felix C	Walls of the Missing
HALL, Garland R	I-19-14
HALL, Howard	E-14-22
HALL, Joseph J	P-19-3
HALL, Lewis W	A-21-10
HALL, Loren R	F-5-10
HALL, Robert J	C-12-19
HALL, Russell E	J-10-10
HALL, Victor J	M-4-9
HALL, William L	F-13-27
HALL, Willie N	E-13-27
HALLDEN, Robert H	M-17-15
HALLETT, Marvin C [137]	L-21-6
HALLOCK, Edward R	Walls of the Missing
HALSTEAD, Earl B	G-17-9
HALTER, Joseph J	K-11-4
HALTERMAN, Claude A Jr	Walls of the Missing
HALVORSON, Robert L	O-11-1
HAMANN, William M	I-13-13
HAMBLIN, Herschel O [138]	Walls of the Missing
HAMBY, Charles L [139]	I-7-1
HAMEL, Romeo J [140]	K-9-21
HAMER, George W	H-15-1
HAMES, Hubert Jr	A-2-6
HAMILL, Robert W	L-19-2
HAMILTON, Calvin	N-7-16
HAMILTON, Gerald E	N-20-16
HAMILTON, Marion B	I-15-14
HAMILTON, Paul E [141]	D-15-15

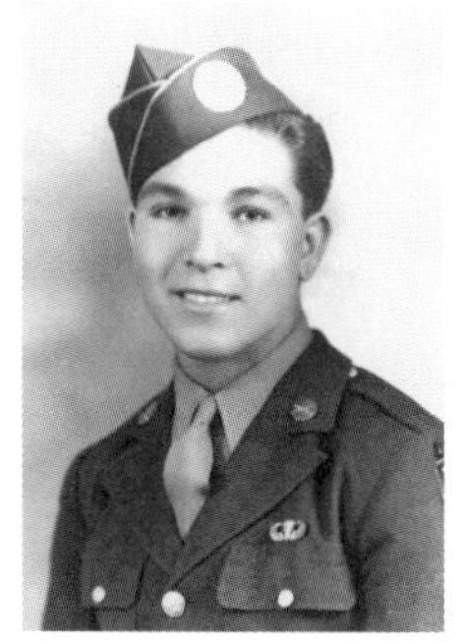
142

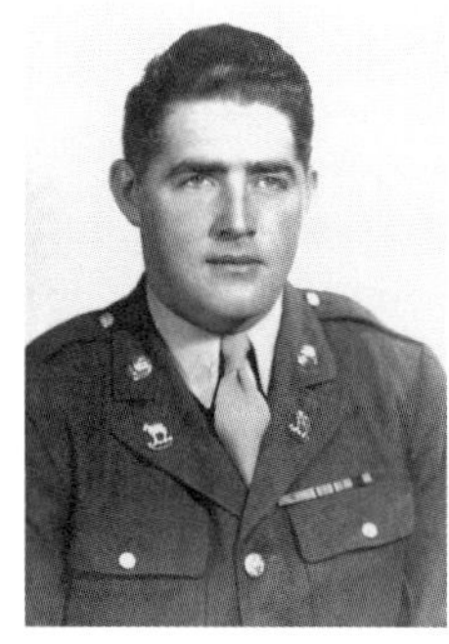
143

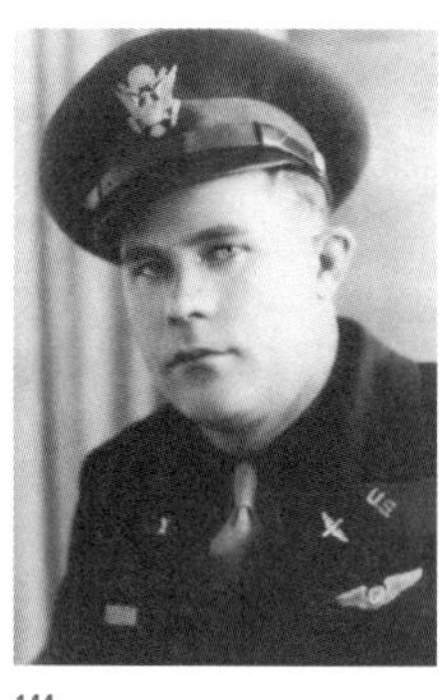
144

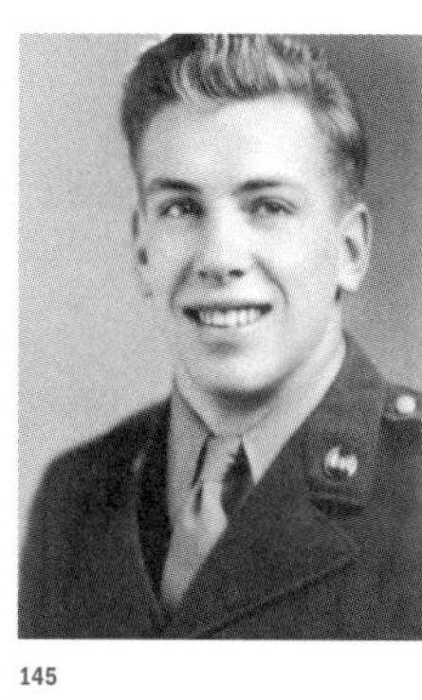
145

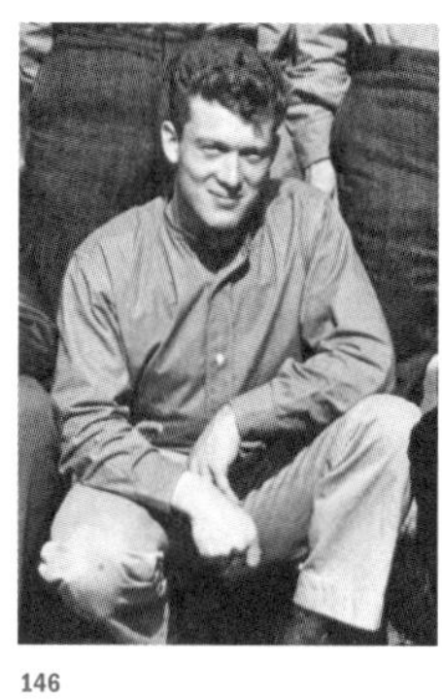
146

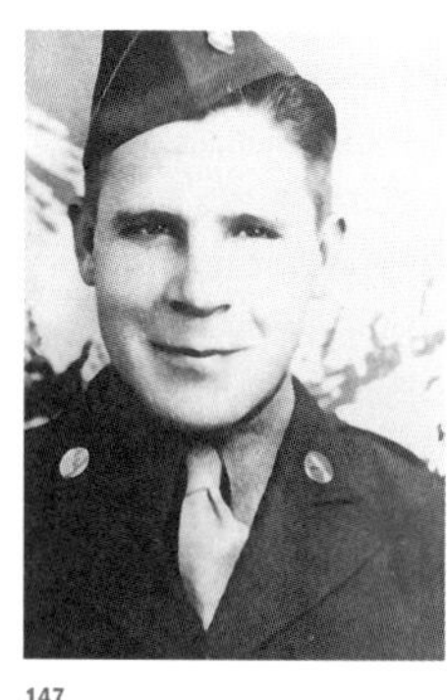
147

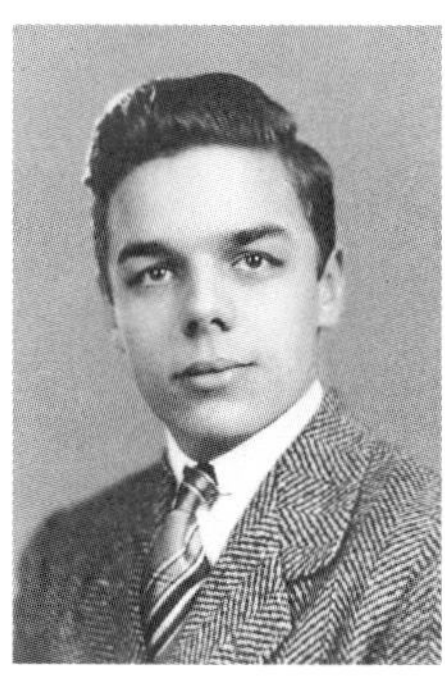
148

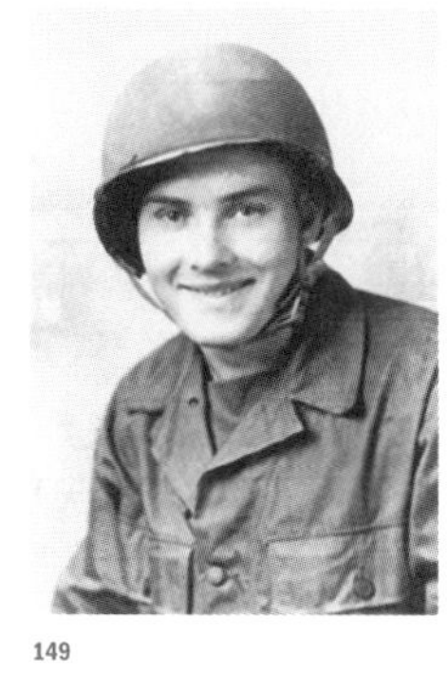
149

HAMILTON, Richard W	D-10-23
HAMILTON, Robert L Sr	I-4-22
HAMILTON, Thurman C	Walls of the Missing
HAMILTON, Vernon L	Walls of the Missing
HAMLIN, Dayton D	L-6-3
HAMLIN, Gilbert S	H-16-23
HAMLIN, Glenn E	G-2-9
HAMM, Robert E	Walls of the Missing
HAMMEL, Harold L	N-16-3
HAMMERSCHMIDT, Martin M	J-16-9
HAMMOND, James M Jr	P-20-3
HAMMOND, Wesley H	A-16-19
HAMMONDS, Victor R Jr	H-15-3
HAMPTON, John F	F-16-12
HAMPTON, Neil H	K-17-13
HAMRE, Edward B	H-14-3
HAMRICK, Victor L	Walls of the Missing
HAMSHER, Howard L	C-8-18
HANCIN, Stephen E	K-20-12
HANCOCK, Asa T	M-12-12
HANCOCK, Tip	E-10-6
HANCY, Eldred E	Walls of the Missing
HAND, Richard F	F-6-11
HANDEL, John A	C-2-6
HANDLEY, Olin I	D-11-14
HANDORF, Edward	Walls of the Missing
HANES, Clarence E [142]	M-4-11
HANEY, Edsel E	Walls of the Missing
HANEY, Joseph C	D-15-9
HANLEY, Edward F	B-4-31
HANLEY, Harold V	J-8-8
HANLEY, William C [143]	A-12-5
HANNABURY, Edward J	H-18-26
HANNAMAN, James D	O-13-8
HANNER, Francis J [144]	H-4-26
HANNYE, William R	I-4-8
HANRAHAN, Thomas A Jr	A-9-17
HANSEN, Charles L	C-10-32
HANSEN, Henry E	E-9-8
HANSEN, James M	K-1-5
HANSEN, Knut E	C-17-9
HANSEN, Leslie H	P-1-8
HANSEN, Niels A	B-9-13
HANSEN, Theodore R	Walls of the Missing
HANSON, Bertill W	G-20-19
HANSON, Elwood J	J-12-13
HANSON, Ervin O	O-16-6
HANSON, Leo E	H-9-24
HANSON, Robert J [145]	I-11-12
HANSON, Russell A	D-3-21
HARALDSEN, Harald	B-3-7
HARBOUR, Marvin L	Walls of the Missing
HARDEN, Eugene	H-9-4
HARDEN, Ira I	Walls of the Missing
HARDENBURGH, Albert O	I-13-21
HARDERS, Marvin G Jr	A-19-14
HARDING, Julius T	E-10-2
HARDWAY, Golden F	M-5-11
HARDY, Leopold	M-6-13
HARDY, Michael H	Walls of the Missing
HARDY, Robert W	Walls of the Missing
HARDY, Robert W	Walls of the Missing
HARGIS, Jack A [146]	N-7-9
HARGUS, John W	H-20-13
HARIG, John T	D-11-7
HARINGA, Edward H	E-2-5
HARKEY, Carrol E	Walls of the Missing
HARLEN, Charles Jr	Walls of the Missing
HARLEY, Joseph M Jr	I-16-11
HARLOW, Harley E	M-20-7
HARMAN, Marvin A	B-21-14
HARMON, David	A-14-10
HARMON, Donald P	G-20-9
HARMON, Donald T	Walls of the Missing
HARMON, Joseph	A-3-8
HARPER, Corbin A	B-12-13
HARPER, Walter B [147]	D-16-4
HARPER, William A Jr	L-20-5
HARPER, Woodrow W	Walls of the Missing
HARRINGER, John J Jr	Walls of the Missing
HARRINGTON, Oscar H	D-15-18
HARRINGTON, Patrick J	C-14-13
HARRIS, Arthur W	O-10-3
HARRIS, Carlton O	J-18-4
HARRIS, Dewey W	Walls of the Missing
HARRIS, Earl B	J-20-16
HARRIS, Earl F	E-5-12
HARRIS, Elwood R	J-18-5
HARRIS, Erskin P	L-8-6
HARRIS, Frank C	J-21-6
HARRIS, George W	B-13-19
HARRIS, Henry N	P-4-13
HARRIS, Hugh	F-17-13
HARRIS, John H	Walls of the Missing
HARRIS, John M	O-13-6
HARRIS, Kenneth L	I-13-1
HARRIS, Preston	Walls of the Missing
HARRIS, Robert J	Walls of the Missing
HARRIS, Rodney W	G-13-22
HARRIS, Walter L	A-13-26
HARRIS, William J	C-4-20
HARRISON, Cloy T	Walls of the Missing
HARRISON, James C	C-20-29
HARRISON, John W	A-20-27
HARRISON, William J	Walls of the Missing
HARSIN, Harold E	N-14-7
HART, Carl J [148]	P-2-16
HART, Carroll A	D-8-24
HART, David L	P-1-14
HART, Eddie	E-2-2
HART, Elbert E	L-5-2
HART, Eugene E	F-3-6
HART, Gerald L	P-12-6
HART, Leonard W	B-3-17
HART, Lyman B	A-16-29
HART, Robert S	Walls of the Missing
HART, Theodore W	G-9-8
HART, Thomas J	M-4-8
HARTE, Albert S	E-5-6
HARTE, Frank W	K-2-21
HARTENSTEIN, Robert E	E-3-18
HARTIS, Thomas B	A-7-13
HARTLEY, Bill G	E-11-19
HARTMAN, John H	D-8-21

Name	Location
HARTMANN, Thomas E Jr	C-11-20
HARTMANN, Vincent F	B-16-3
HARTWELL, Arthur M	I-6-1
HARTWICK, Walter J	D-21-22
HARTZELL, Richard L	G-6-15
HARVEY, Charles E	G-6-22
HARVEY, Herbert H	Walls of the Missing
HARVEY, James J	F-6-21
HARVEY, Robert R	F-11-17
HARVEY, Thomas D	N-15-3
HARVEY, Willie	P-11-14
HARVISON, William C	Walls of the Missing
HARWOOD, Craig J	J-4-12
HASCALL, John S	H-8-9
HASFURTHER, Lloyd G	M-5-6
HASKELL, James A	F-6-19
HASKELL, Leroy	Walls of the Missing
HASKINS, Luther	Walls of the Missing
HASLOUER, Elvin G	B-13-20
HASPER, Donald T	H-10-20
HASS, Julius S	G-10-3
HASSELBUSCH, Robert A	F-17-7
HASSELL, Cecil M	B-9-29
HASSMAN, Morton	O-7-9
HASTIE, Thomas A	B-8-24
HASTINGS, Kenneth S	F-8-26
HASTINGS, Winthrope N	G-20-14
HASTON, Clarence E Jr	H-13-25
HATFIELD, Dale W	C-6-9
HATHAWAY, Alevin A	Walls of the Missing
HATHORNE, Clyde	N-6-13
HAUER, Carl L	C-6-22
HAUGEN, Rolf E	O-6-9
HAUGHEY, Francis J	P-11-15
HAUGHTON, Earl F	A-1-3
HAUGHTON, Henry S	P-11-16
HAULMAN, Floyd W Sr	E-9-23
HAURY, Marvin R [149]	Walls of the Missing
HAUSENFLUCK, Luther A	G-20-1
HAUSER, Andrew L	A-17-11
HAVEN, Donald L	I-17-17
HAVERLY, John Jr	H-17-20
HAVILAND, Barry	C-13-2
HAVRAN, George	K-8-13
HAWKE, Robert A	A-19-28
HAWKINS, Grover H	D-20-20
HAWKINS, Joseph A	H-15-27
HAWKINS, Monell R	K-20-8
HAWKINS, Siegel L	I-5-22
HAWKINS, William R	C-4-1
HAWLEY, Palmer F	G-21-20
HAWLEY, Warren L	P-11-17
HAWLEY, William S	G-21-7
HAWS, Robert S	O-16-3
HAWVERMALE, Arnold F	F-17-6
HAYES, Bert C	L-18-11
HAYES, Beverly A	J-21-17
HAYES, Davison	Walls of the Missing
HAYES, Frank W	F-6-14
HAYES, Leroy J	K-19-16
HAYES, Roland O	H-3-27
HAYES, Tommy	F-5-24
HAYES, William T	E-1-4
HAYMAKER, Leonard B	E-7-23
HAYNES, Benjamin L Jr	Walls of the Missing
HAYNES, Harry Jr	D-8-8
HAYNES, Lawrence D	E-3-12
HAYNES, Le Roy L	N-3-13
HAYNES, Robert A	J-5-16
HAYS, David S	D-2-7
HAYS, Harold M	J-5-21
HAZEN, Fred P	K-4-21
HEAD, Marvel A	F-19-1
HEAGY, Melvin M	B-19-3
HEALEY, Malcolm O	Walls of the Missing
HEALION, Arthur J	Walls of the Missing
HEALY, Michael J Jr	N-12-1
HEAPS, Clyde	P-1-17
HEATH, Mark A	L-17-22
HEATHERLEY, Robert V	K-1-3
HEATHMAN, Jimmie R	J-17-11
HEATON, William M	B-4-23
HEAVNER, Gerald A	Walls of the Missing
HEBDA, John J	D-12-25
HEBERT, Kenneth C	Walls of the Missing
HEBERT, Lawrence R	M-15-14
HEBLE, Edward J	H-5-9
HECKATHORN, Louis J	P-9-8
HEDLAND, David A	L-14-8
HEDMAN, Arthur L	Walls of the Missing
HEDTKE, William D	Walls of the Missing
HEEDE, Tony	F-20-16
HEESE, Walter B	D-14-5
HEGNES, James H	A-16-24
HEIBERG, Lowell M	A-6-15
HEIBERGER, Harry W	E-4-27
HEIBY, Charles R	G-18-10
HEIDELMARK, Frederick	F-6-12
HEIDEN, Norman H	G-5-6
HEIDORN, Edgar M	B-20-13
HEIM, Warren E	P-8-14
HEINE, Richard O	L-7-7
HEINZMAN, Oscar F	N-7-3
HEISER, William H Jr	N-1-10
HEKIMIAN, George H	Walls of the Missing
HELBING, Richard H	O-14-10
HELD, Abraham	I-8-20
HELDER, Julius M	C-11-17
HELDERMAN, Max A	K-3-10
HELFENSTEIN, Dwight M	G-21-14
HELINE, Carl W	J-2-16
HELLER, Herman	D-13-24
HELLER, Samuel F	D-20-25
HELLERUD, John H	K-15-9
HELLWEGE, Ira E	B-14-7
HELM, Christopher	P-4-1
HELM, Robert F	N-15-7
HELMS, Gerald R	Walls of the Missing
HELMS, James L	P-14-6
HELPS, Ronald W	F-11-20
HELTON, Edwin M	Walls of the Missing
HELVEY, Wesley V	I-12-14
HEMMINGSON, Theodore L	J-13-16
HEMSTREET, John S	G-17-21
HENDEE, James W	H-2-6
HENDERSON, Gordon W	Walls of the Missing
HENDERSON, Kenneth L	C-8-11
HENDERSON, Preston R	O-4-5
HENDERSON, William H	Walls of the Missing
HENDRICKS, Harold	N-12-2
HENDRICKS, Leslie M	A-7-20
HENDRICKS, Robert L	K-6-22
HENDRICKSON, Harold H	B-1-7
HENDRICKSON, Milton C	P-5-1
HENDRY, Iverson W	B-14-27
HENE, Julius A	F-17-25
HENEY, Philip J Jr	G-9-5
HENKE, Charles J	K-15-19
HENKE, Phillip O	K-3-14
HENKELMAN, Leonard J	C-20-15
HENLIN, Leonard R	B-21-26
HENNINGS, William V	J-12-16
HENRY, James M	D-1-12
HENRY, Justus D Jr	Walls of the Missing
HENRY, Robert P	C-19-5
HENRY, Stanford W	Walls of the Missing
HENSCHLER, Edward V	F-4-7
HENSHAW, Vernon C	B-18-23
HENSLEY, Claude	B-8-8
HENSLEY, George B	Walls of the Missing
HENSLEY, Wayne	O-6-8
HENSON, Arthur S	G-15-27
HENTSCHEL, James	G-11-1
HENWOOD, John E	N-13-17
HEPLER, Donald B	Walls of the Missing
HERB, John W	Walls of the Missing
HERBEL, Franklin A	B-4-8
HERBERT, Harvey H	P-7-1
HERBERT, Lloyd H	Walls of the Missing
HERBST, Harold C	K-4-7
HERCKER, Joseph H	B-17-15
HERGENHAN, Wiliam N	P-7-13
HERIN, Ralph D	C-16-20
HERLETT, James R	D-2-19
HERLING, Richard C	C-7-29
HERMAN, Jacob T Jr	F-4-22
HERMANCE, Alan E	Walls of the Missing
HERMANN, Jerome R	K-5-19
HERNANDEZ, Arthur	A-4-17
HERNANDEZ, Elias M	I-12-13
HERNANDEZ, Emilio H	M-4-14
HERNANDEZ, Joaquin	M-15-15
HERNANDEZ, Valente P	I-13-9
HERNDON, J P	O-21-1

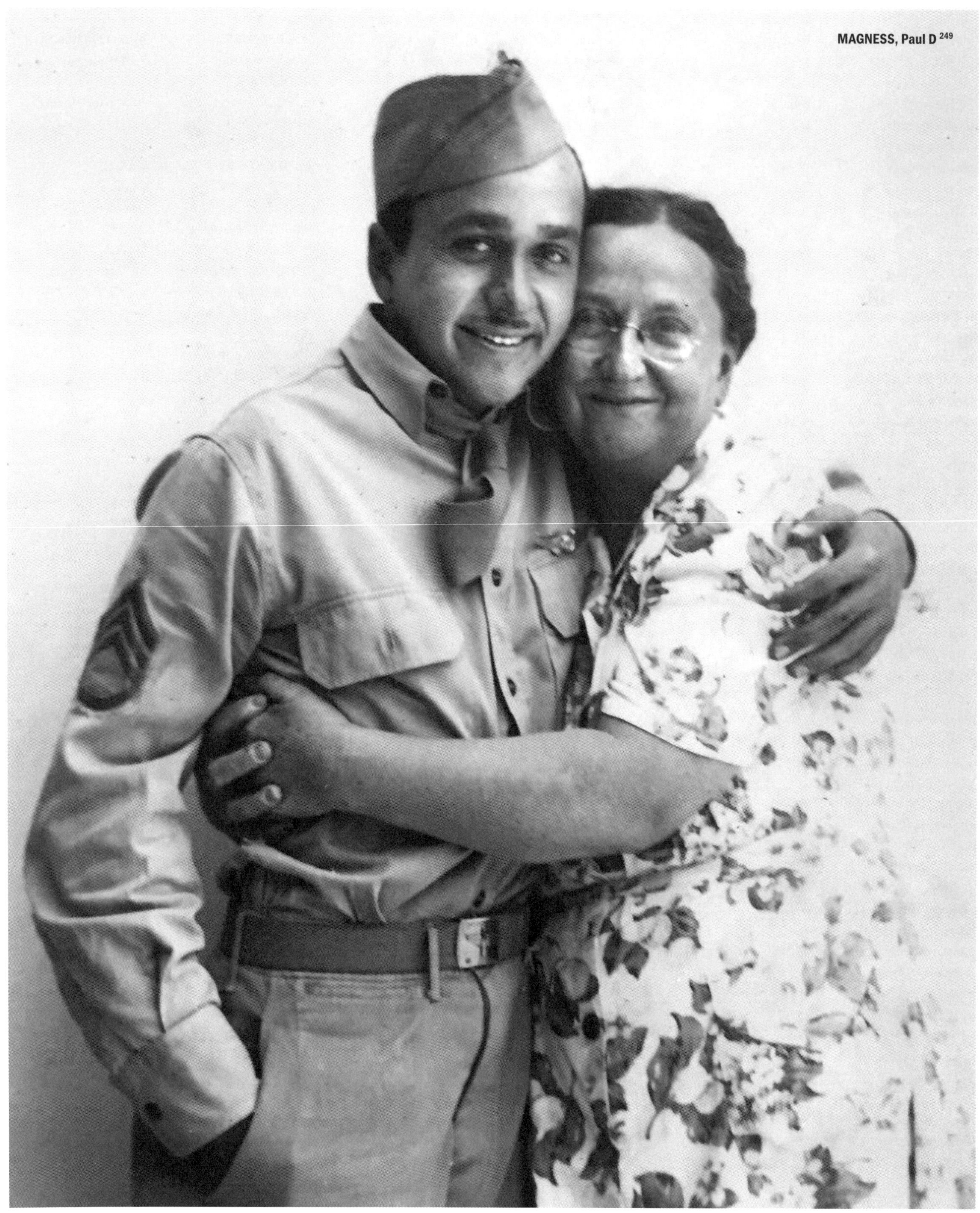

MAGNESS, Paul D [249]

Name	Location
HERR, Sam	J-11-16
HERRELL, George W	J-17-22
HERRERA, Edward	C-15-17
HERRON, William A	E-19-8
HERRSCHER, Harlan L	I-19-11
HERSH, Austin J	K-16-14
HERSHISER, Alden J	Walls of the Missing
HERTEL, Joseph J	D-20-29
HERTIG, David M	N-6-12
HERTZ, Julius	O-8-3
HERTZENBERG, John C	L-11-6
HESS, Donald W	Walls of the Missing
HESS, Everett L	N-11-2
HESS, Harold	M-6-16
HESS, Raymond E	B-10-4
HESS, Robert C Jr	A-2-11
HESSLER, Robcrt M	J-7-12
HESTER, Paul R	B-21-22
HETHERINGTON, Malvern W	Walls of the Missing
HETRICK, Everett L	G-1-9
HEURICH, William H	Walls of the Missing
HEUSTON, Mark N	D-7-26
HEWEL, Joseph V	P-9-16
HEWITT, John R	D-1-14
HEWITT, Richard D	A-18-4
HEYM, Walter E	K-3-4
HIBBARD, Howard J	B-8-6
HIBBS, Leo R	F-17-16
HICKERSON, James O	M-21-3
HICKEY, Albert C	Walls of the Missing
HICKEY, John G	E-12-16
HICKLIN, Raymond W	O-9-13
HICKS, Floyd W	G-11-13
HICKS, Gordon D	J-8-16
HICKS, Howard B	E-8-12
HICKS, James B	H-3-13
HICKS, James B	H-8-16
HICKS, Robert C	D-4-16
HIDDLESTON, Ford O	M-4-12
HIDLAY, Fred F Jr	H-4-20
HIFFMAN, Melvin G	H-19-19
HIGGINBOTHAM, J P	J-14-2
HIGGINS, Charles A Jr	N-7-17
HIGGINS, David P	Walls of the Missing
HIGGINS, Edwin P	H-12-18
HIGGINS, George E	P-16-16
HIGGINS, William D	B-18-6
HIGLEY, Lester R	H-11-14
HILDEBRAND, Preston	A-10-26
HILDITCH, Hugh F	G-3-26
HILDRETH, Delbert J	M-14-10
HILGER, James W	Walls of the Missing
HILKEY, Joseph R	G-8-20
HILL, Barley E	N-18-17
HILL, Carl Mc Donald	J-17-1
HILL, Charles D	Walls of the Missing
HILL, Eugene V	Walls of the Missing
HILL, Ford R	F-9-14
HILL, Harris C	C-8-9
HILL, Irvin B	A-10-7
HILL, Jack W	A-13-16
HILL, John C Jr	K-20-7
HILL, Joseph F	K-1-2
HILL, Joseph R	Walls of the Missing
HILL, Julian D	Walls of the Missing
HILL, Leo	I-1-12
HILL, Lloyd J	N-12-3
HILL, Oscar	A-6-3
HILL, Paul D	M-6-8
HILL, Robert A	A-2-28
HILL, Robert F	H-2-23
HILL, Roy A	K-1-4
HILL, Roy A	L-10-21
HILL, Roy A	D-11-18
HILL, Warren L	P-18-2
HILLARD, Charles P	H-13-15
HILLER, Arthur C	Walls of the Missing
HILLMAN, Fernald J	F-6-24
HILLSTROM, Rudolph E	J-21-8
HILLWEG, Charles U	Walls of the Missing
HILLYARD, Owen T	Walls of the Missing
HILSCHER, Louis M	Walls of the Missing
HILTEBEITEL, Noble	H-17-10
HILTUNEN, Ray J	K-6-16
HILTY, Kenneth F	G-11-2
HINCHEE, Harry L	F-7-25
HINCHEY, John L	Walls of the Missing
HINES, Eugene T	Walls of the Missing
HINES, Rodney D	H-4-1
HINES, Stephen A	H-14-13
HINES, Walker	Walls of the Missing
HINKLE, Kerman L	I-7-11
HINMAN, Bruce F	O-19-1
HINRICHS, Christian E	H-7-21
HINSON, Francis L	G-10-18
HIRNER, Paul J	D-4-25
HIRO, Edwin W	Walls of the Missing
HITCHLER, Arthur J Jr	B-9-27
HITES, Bennett D Jr	G-7-21
HITTMAN, Norman A	L-1-16
HITZFIELD, Robert N	M-17-12
HOBBS, John D	I-7-19
HOBGOOD, Charles P Jr	K-3-17
HOBSON, John J	A-10-9
HOBSON, Robert L	C-2-16
HOCH, Ervin G	A-19-7
HOCKERT, Edward D	Walls of the Missing
HODDER, John T	J-4-19
HODGE, Herman L	E-11-7
HODGES, Arlin H	C-9-15
HODGES, Fred D	Walls of the Missing
HODGES, James S Jr	E-17-2
HODGES, Thomas A	Walls of the Missing
HODGINS, Charles S	B-17-1
HODNETT, Francis J	B-18-7
HODSON, Lee A	H-10-18
HOEDING, Eugene L	N-1-16
HOEFELMEYER, Edwin H	B-16-32
HOEHN, Herbert H	A-21-23
HOFBAUER, William W	J-13-22
HOFFER, John I	C-18-20
HOFFER, Marion E	N-17-9
HOFFER, William F	Walls of the Missing
HOFFMAN, Adrian W	D-10-32
HOFFMAN, Donald M	L-11-9
HOFFMAN, Elmer E Jr	O-18-11
HOFFMAN, Elwood M	B-11-11
HOFFMAN, Glenn W	N-10-2
HOFFMAN, Henry	Walls of the Missing
HOFFMAN, John C	D-2-5
HOFFMAN, Thomas R	E-14-1
HOFFMAN, Warren F	Walls of the Missing
HOFFMANN, Edwln R	K-16-16
HOFLIN, Russell G	K-16-5
HOGAN, Hugh F	Walls of the Missing
HOGAN, John E	Walls of the Missing
HOGAN, Raymond A	K-3-15
HOGANSON, Harvey G	P-9-11
HOGUE, William L	D-9-11
HOHMANN, Kenneth T	J-18-20
HOHN, Charles J	E-21-10
HOJNACKI, Stanley	K-8-2
HOLBACH, Lawrence C	E-12-24
HOLBERT, Paul M	H-5-21
HOLBROOK, J P	Walls of the Missing
HOLCOMBE, Ralph W	H-16-4
HOLDER, Samuel A	I-21-20
HOLLAND, Clifford W	G-17-15
HOLLAND, John H	D-3-18
HOLLAND, Paul F	B-11-20
HOLLEY, Howard R	A-21-13
HOLLIDAY, Daniel D Jr	A-6-29
HOLLIDAY, Frank W	H-9-22
HOLLIDAY, Karl O	C-7-17
HOLLIS, Terrell L	O-19-11
HOLLIS, William T	I-7-9
HOLLON, Leighton	E-12-20
HOLLOWAY, Ernest J	O-17-13
HOLLOWAY, Joe F	A-21-11
HOLLY, John S	N-8-7
HOLMAN, Cornell C	F-18-1
HOLMES, Howard W	Walls of the Missing
HOLMES, Roscoe S	A-6-7
HOLMES, William P	Walls of the Missing
HOLSTEIN, Donald	H-16-19
HOLSTEIN, Richard H	F-5-19
HOLT, Alvis J	B-20-23
HOLT, Arthur R	H-7-13
HOLT, Lindell F	H-19-26
HOLT, Vanoy	B-19-20
HOLTZ, Harold A	I-8-3
HOLTZER, Martin	B-21-4
HOLTZMAN, Lawrence W	E-19-3
HOLY, Edward C	F-7-9

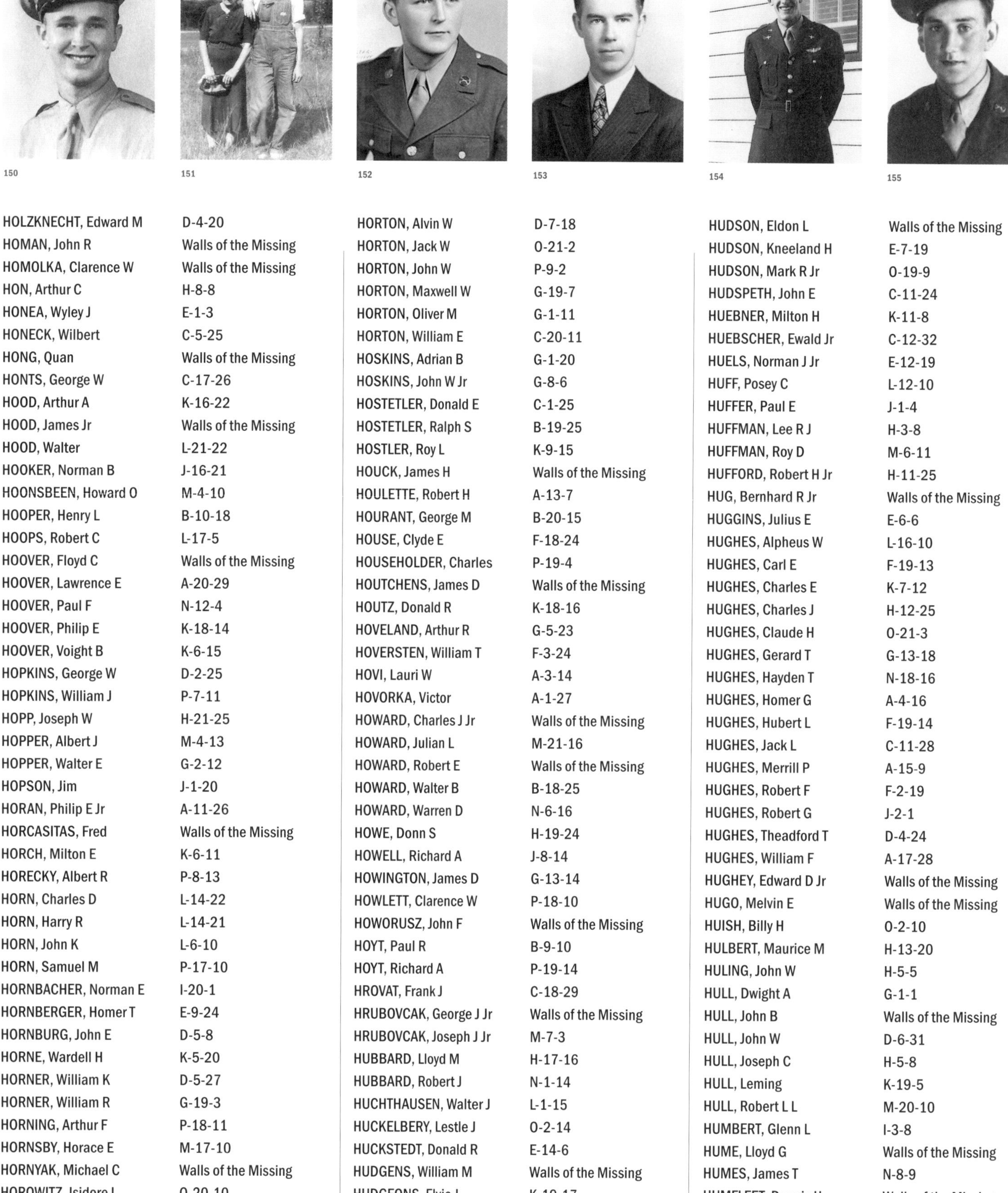

150 151 152 153 154 155

HOLZKNECHT, Edward M	D-4-20
HOMAN, John R	Walls of the Missing
HOMOLKA, Clarence W	Walls of the Missing
HON, Arthur C	H-8-8
HONEA, Wyley J	E-1-3
HONECK, Wilbert	C-5-25
HONG, Quan	Walls of the Missing
HONTS, George W	C-17-26
HOOD, Arthur A	K-16-22
HOOD, James Jr	Walls of the Missing
HOOD, Walter	L-21-22
HOOKER, Norman B	J-16-21
HOONSBEEN, Howard O	M-4-10
HOOPER, Henry L	B-10-18
HOOPS, Robert C	L-17-5
HOOVER, Floyd C	Walls of the Missing
HOOVER, Lawrence E	A-20-29
HOOVER, Paul F	N-12-4
HOOVER, Philip E	K-18-14
HOOVER, Voight B	K-6-15
HOPKINS, George W	D-2-25
HOPKINS, William J	P-7-11
HOPP, Joseph W	H-21-25
HOPPER, Albert J	M-4-13
HOPPER, Walter E	G-2-12
HOPSON, Jim	J-1-20
HORAN, Philip E Jr	A-11-26
HORCASITAS, Fred	Walls of the Missing
HORCH, Milton E	K-6-11
HORECKY, Albert R	P-8-13
HORN, Charles D	L-14-22
HORN, Harry R	L-14-21
HORN, John K	L-6-10
HORN, Samuel M	P-17-10
HORNBACHER, Norman E	I-20-1
HORNBERGER, Homer T	E-9-24
HORNBURG, John E	D-5-8
HORNE, Wardell H	K-5-20
HORNER, William K	D-5-27
HORNER, William R	G-19-3
HORNING, Arthur F	P-18-11
HORNSBY, Horace E	M-17-10
HORNYAK, Michael C	Walls of the Missing
HOROWITZ, Isidore I	O-20-10
HORSFALL, Robert R	E-7-6
HORTON, Allen D	M-22-12
HORTON, Alvin W	D-7-18
HORTON, Jack W	O-21-2
HORTON, John W	P-9-2
HORTON, Maxwell W	G-19-7
HORTON, Oliver M	G-1-11
HORTON, William E	C-20-11
HOSKINS, Adrian B	G-1-20
HOSKINS, John W Jr	G-8-6
HOSTETLER, Donald E	C-1-25
HOSTETLER, Ralph S	B-19-25
HOSTLER, Roy L	K-9-15
HOUCK, James H	Walls of the Missing
HOULETTE, Robert H	A-13-7
HOURANT, George M	B-20-15
HOUSE, Clyde E	F-18-24
HOUSEHOLDER, Charles	P-19-4
HOUTCHENS, James D	Walls of the Missing
HOUTZ, Donald R	K-18-16
HOVELAND, Arthur R	G-5-23
HOVERSTEN, William T	F-3-24
HOVI, Lauri W	A-3-14
HOVORKA, Victor	A-1-27
HOWARD, Charles J Jr	Walls of the Missing
HOWARD, Julian L	M-21-16
HOWARD, Robert E	Walls of the Missing
HOWARD, Walter B	B-18-25
HOWARD, Warren D	N-6-16
HOWE, Donn S	H-19-24
HOWELL, Richard A	J-8-14
HOWINGTON, James D	G-13-14
HOWLETT, Clarence W	P-18-10
HOWORUSZ, John F	Walls of the Missing
HOYT, Paul R	B-9-10
HOYT, Richard A	P-19-14
HROVAT, Frank J	C-18-29
HRUBOVCAK, George J Jr	Walls of the Missing
HRUBOVCAK, Joseph J Jr	M-7-3
HUBBARD, Lloyd M	H-17-16
HUBBARD, Robert J	N-1-14
HUCHTHAUSEN, Walter J	L-1-15
HUCKELBERY, Lestle J	O-2-14
HUCKSTEDT, Donald R	E-14-6
HUDGENS, William M	Walls of the Missing
HUDGEONS, Elvie J	K-19-17
HUDSON, Charles N	D-3-19
HUDSON, Donald J	D-6-16
HUDSON, Eldon L	Walls of the Missing
HUDSON, Kneeland H	E-7-19
HUDSON, Mark R Jr	O-19-9
HUDSPETH, John E	C-11-24
HUEBNER, Milton H	K-11-8
HUEBSCHER, Ewald Jr	C-12-32
HUELS, Norman J Jr	E-12-19
HUFF, Posey C	L-12-10
HUFFER, Paul E	J-1-4
HUFFMAN, Lee R J	H-3-8
HUFFMAN, Roy D	M-6-11
HUFFORD, Robert H Jr	H-11-25
HUG, Bernhard R Jr	Walls of the Missing
HUGGINS, Julius E	E-6-6
HUGHES, Alpheus W	L-16-10
HUGHES, Carl E	F-19-13
HUGHES, Charles E	K-7-12
HUGHES, Charles J	H-12-25
HUGHES, Claude H	O-21-3
HUGHES, Gerard T	G-13-18
HUGHES, Hayden T	N-18-16
HUGHES, Homer G	A-4-16
HUGHES, Hubert L	F-19-14
HUGHES, Jack L	C-11-28
HUGHES, Merrill P	A-15-9
HUGHES, Robert F	F-2-19
HUGHES, Robert G	J-2-1
HUGHES, Theadford T	D-4-24
HUGHES, William F	A-17-28
HUGHEY, Edward D Jr	Walls of the Missing
HUGO, Melvin E	Walls of the Missing
HUISH, Billy H	O-2-10
HULBERT, Maurice M	H-13-20
HULING, John W	H-5-5
HULL, Dwight A	G-1-1
HULL, John B	Walls of the Missing
HULL, John W	D-6-31
HULL, Joseph C	H-5-8
HULL, Leming	K-19-5
HULL, Robert L L	M-20-10
HUMBERT, Glenn L	I-3-8
HUME, Lloyd G	Walls of the Missing
HUMES, James T	N-8-9
HUMFLEET, Dennis H	Walls of the Missing
HUMMEL, Calvin W	D-4-19
HUMMEL, Daniel J	E-5-21

HUMMEL, Harry F	Walls of the Missing
HUMMEL, William J	F-11-7
HUMMER, William M	C-15-4
HUMPHREY, Joseph W	M-7-7
HUMPHREY, Paul T	H-6-20
HUMPHREY, Ross W	D-10-1
HUMPHREYS, Fred C	Walls of the Missing
HUNNEFELD, Vincent	Walls of the Missing
HUNNEL, Thomas J	C-10-22
HUNSBERGER, Henry A	N-2-9
HUNT, Arthur B Jr	E-6-18
HUNT, Arthur L	C-10-3
HUNT, George A	N-20-3
HUNT, John C	J-7-10
HUNT, Max L	C-11-4
HUNT, William H	I-19-22
HUNTER, Ashby	Walls of the Missing
HUNTER, Clyde M	J-12-7
HUNTER, Donald E	C-6-10
HUNTER, Fred L	J-1-2
HUNTER, George	B-7-31
HUNTER, Jack B	P-7-2
HUNTER, James K	D-21-7
HUNTER, John F	G-7-13
HUNTER, John P	N-18-7
HUNTER, Kenneth G	N-10-7
HUNTER, Robert W	Walls of the Missing
HUNTER, Thaddeus W Jr	J-1-5
HUNTER, Willard O	Walls of the Missing
HUNTER, William F	N-2-11
HUNTING, Raymond D Jr	F-2-13
HUNTSBERGER, Mortimer C	H-14-23
HUNTWORK, Ralph C	D-6-13
HUPMAN, Byron E Jr	B-16-24
HUPP, Gale W	I-8-5
HURD, John W	Walls of the Missing
HURD, Raymond	Walls of the Missing
HURLBERT, Earl R	P-9-7
HURLBURT, Don M	Walls of the Missing
HURLBURT, Richard C	Walls of the Missing
HURLEY, Charles A	C-9-21
HURLEY, David W	Walls of the Missing
HURRIZZISSTEIZZII, L	O-6-1
HURT, Jewel H	P-12-12
HURTIG, Werner J	F-18-25
HUSBAND, Wilfred M	O-21-4
HUSELTINE, George A E	C-7-2
HUSKINS, Howard	A-14-22
HUSSMAN, Peter R	H-15-10
HUSTED, Bernard J	D-20-7
HUSVAR, Floyd L Jr	P-2-3
HUTCHENS, Raymond	I-12-18
HUTCHINS, John E	Walls of the Missing
HUTCHISON, Earl R	E-10-13
HUTSON, Cecil E	O-15-8
HUTTO, Eldridge I	H-15-6
HUTTON, Robert F	A-17-21
HUTTON, Russell H	B-4-12

HYATT, John L	I-13-12
HYDE, Paul H Jr	Walls of the Missing
HYDE, William H	F-12-25
HYDOCK, Paul	Walls of the Missing
HYLAND, Edward J	J-3-14
HYLKA, Bernard V	J-4-15
HYLTON, William H	Walls of the Missing
HYNOSKI, Benjamin S	C-15-26
HYRY, Reino J	D-5-12
HYVONEN, Edward E	B-21-25

I

IACONIS, Frank	Walls of the Missing
IBACH, Andrew K	K-5-21
IBE, Raymond A	Walls of the Missing
IDEC, Joseph P	C-1-17
IDELER, Martin	C-7-10
IDLET, Phillip D	Walls of the Missing
IGO, Robert B	Walls of the Missing
IMM, Paul R	B-1-22
IMRIE, Donn H	A-19-27
INGLE, Edward L	E-12-11
INGLE, William L	B-9-9
INGLEFIELD, William D	A-3-19
INGRAHAM, Robert F	P-22-17
INGRAM, Gerald H	B-15-31
INGRAM, Lester	F-9-10
INGRAM, Richard M	Walls of the Missing
INGWERSON, Lowell J [150]	A-19-2
INTIHAR, Edward M	D-16-32
IORGOV, George W	B-1-3
IOVACCHINI, James V P	B-6-15
IRVEN, Sidney W	B-5-23
IRVIN, Kenneth [151]	L-2-15
IRVINE, John S Jr	Walls of the Missing
IRVING, Jesse T Jr	P-19-15
IRWIN, Charles B	P-9-4
IRWIN, John S	P-12-7
IRWIN, William R	H-19-8
ISAACS, Jesse D	G-18-5
ISABELLE, Benjamin F	C-17-25
ISBELL, Albert E Jr	F-11-24
ISBELL, Clinton A Jr	Walls of the Missing
ISBELL, Howard V	B-16-22
ISBELL, John E	G-18-27
ISEMAN, George C	P-9-15
ISENBERG, Bernard	N-11-3
ISGETT, Harry E	C-19-1
ISLIP, Charles A	K-14-3
ISON, James	Walls of the Missing
IVAN, Paul	M-6-5
IZBICKI, Walter F [152]	A-10-29
IZYDORCZAK, Henry	A-14-11

J

JABLONSKI, Walter J	A-16-9
JACKMAN, Lon E Jr	J-9-18
JACKSON, Carl M	I-19-17
JACKSON, Doyle K	A-5-5
JACKSON, Garfield	C-8-17
JACKSON, George W [153]	B-21-24
JACKSON, Hugh M	I-20-22
JACKSON, John R	F-15-23
JACKSON, Kenneth D	E-6-15
JACKSON, Lloyd H	K-4-16
JACKSON, Willard A	A-11-12
JACKSON, William F	C-7-7
JACOBIUS, Herman L	M-3-8
JACOBS, Fredrick W	Walls of the Missing
JACOBS, Roger A	G-10-15
JACOBS, Ronald H	F-19-6
JACOBSEN, Edwin S [154]	Walls of the Missing
JACOBSON, Donald J	L-19-20
JACOBSON, L D	F-14-7
JACOBUS, Louis S	N-9-15
JACQUART, Francis L	L-5-19
JAEGER, George	A-14-27
JAEGER, William C	Walls of the Missing
JAEGER, William C	O-21-5
JAEGLE, Adolph L	D-9-14
JAMES, Charles Jr	C-18-16
JAMES, Cletus R	B-11-21
JAMES, Ellis E	G-17-10
JAMES, George L	M-5-5
JAMES, Jackson J	B-1-31
JAMES, John	Walls of the Missing
JAMES, John W	K-1-22
JAMES, Willy F Jr	P-9-9
JAMIESON, Donald P	K-11-2
JAMISON, Leonard O	C-16-2
JAMISON, Walter	M-4-16
JAMRAZ, Stanley	K-14-12
JANICKI, John A	E-1-19
JANIS, Robert L	J-19-15
JANOS, John Jr	K-15-10
JANTAC, Anthony V	B-13-18
JARABEK, John	K-21-14
JAROSZ, Walter A [155]	N-15-6
JARRARD, Walter W	E-10-15
JARRATT, James L	C-10-21
JASINEK, Donald L	Walls of the Missing
JASKOLSKI, Frank J	C-3-19
JASO, Selestino B	H-1-9
JASURA, Peter Jr	E-14-26
JATROS, George	F-4-24
JAZWINSKI, Gilbert R	D-2-8
JEFFERS, Oliver	Walls of the Missing
JEFFERSON, Charles H	F-8-16
JEHLEN, John A	I-15-5
JENKINS, Elmore L	N-12-5
JENKINS, Frank H	H-16-1
JENKINS, Robert U K	P-6-3
JENKINS, Samuel T	G-7-15
JENKINS, Thomas O	D-20-26
JENKINS, Willard	Walls of the Missing
JENNINGS, Theodore E I	Walls of the Missing

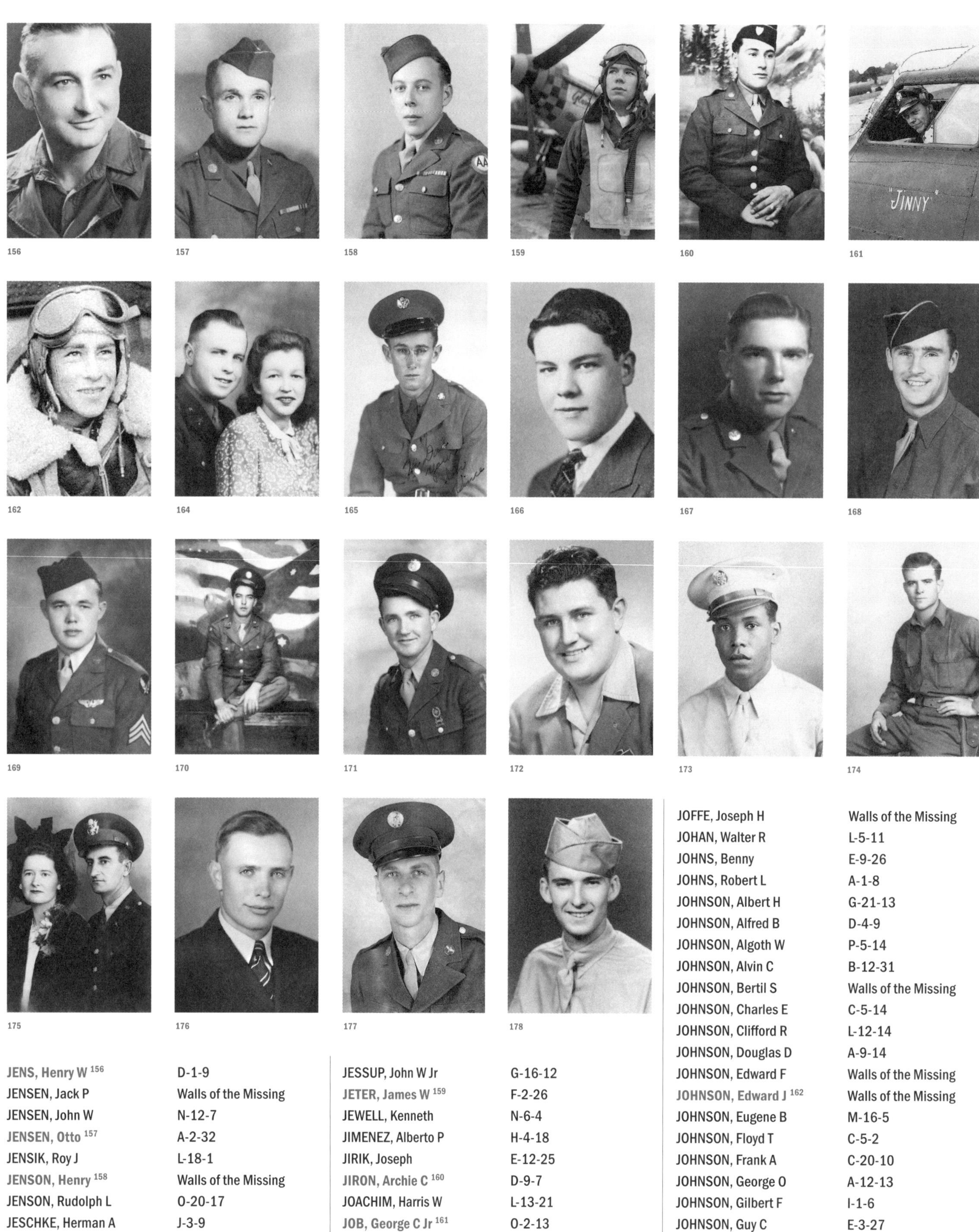

156 157 158 159 160 161 162 164 165 166 167 168 169 170 171 172 173 174 175 176 177 178

JENS, Henry W [156]	D-1-9
JENSEN, Jack P	Walls of the Missing
JENSEN, John W	N-12-7
JENSEN, Otto [157]	A-2-32
JENSIK, Roy J	L-18-1
JENSON, Henry [158]	Walls of the Missing
JENSON, Rudolph L	O-20-17
JESCHKE, Herman A	J-3-9
JESKE, Arnold O	C-10-25
JESKE, John H	D-19-26
JESSUP, John W Jr	G-16-12
JETER, James W [159]	F-2-26
JEWELL, Kenneth	N-6-4
JIMENEZ, Alberto P	H-4-18
JIRIK, Joseph	E-12-25
JIRON, Archie C [160]	D-9-7
JOACHIM, Harris W	L-13-21
JOB, George C Jr [161]	O-2-13
JOBE, Robert G	K-5-22
JODRIE, Kenneth F	O-21-6
JOFFE, Joseph H	Walls of the Missing
JOHAN, Walter R	L-5-11
JOHNS, Benny	E-9-26
JOHNS, Robert L	A-1-8
JOHNSON, Albert H	G-21-13
JOHNSON, Alfred B	D-4-9
JOHNSON, Algoth W	P-5-14
JOHNSON, Alvin C	B-12-31
JOHNSON, Bertil S	Walls of the Missing
JOHNSON, Charles E	C-5-14
JOHNSON, Clifford R	L-12-14
JOHNSON, Douglas D	A-9-14
JOHNSON, Edward F	Walls of the Missing
JOHNSON, Edward J [162]	Walls of the Missing
JOHNSON, Eugene B	M-16-5
JOHNSON, Floyd T	C-5-2
JOHNSON, Frank A	C-20-10
JOHNSON, George O	A-12-13
JOHNSON, Gilbert F	I-1-6
JOHNSON, Guy C	E-3-27
JOHNSON, Harold L	K-16-17
JOHNSON, Harry E	B-1-28

JOHNSON, Henry W	J-9-14
JOHNSON, Holmes	K-9-9
JOHNSON, Hugh D	N-12-6
JOHNSON, Iver O	F-13-10
JOHNSON, James D	C-18-3
JOHNSON, John C	F-13-23
JOHNSON, Kenneth E	Walls of the Missing
JOHNSON, Kenneth L	Walls of the Missing
JOHNSON, Kurt R	H-12-17
JOHNSON, Leonard A	H-20-17
JOHNSON, Leonard M	F-15-4
JOHNSON, Lewis F	Walls of the Missing
JOHNSON, Nathan Jr	Walls of the Missing
JOHNSON, Ray M	F-3-15
JOHNSON, Raymond E [164]	M-6-10
JOHNSON, Richard H	Walls of the Missing
JOHNSON, Robert E	H-2-22
JOHNSON, Robert L	Walls of the Missing
JOHNSON, Robert O	Walls of the Missing
JOHNSON, Sidney A	Walls of the Missing
JOHNSON, Silas A	A-2-23
JOHNSON, Stanley W	D-1-17
JOHNSON, Thurman A	L-18-4
JOHNSON, Vince P [165]	P-6-2
JOHNSON, Wallace C	F-5-15
JOHNSON, William R	J-9-11
JOHNSTON, Arthur B	C-20-20
JOHNSTON, George R [166]	G-1-18
JOHNSTON, Guy V [167]	C-12-22
JOHNSTON, James A	L-14-5
JOHNSTON, James V Jr	P-15-17
JOHNSTON, John A	A-18-3
JOHNSTON, William J	I-9-16
JOHNSTON, William P	H-12-9
JOINER, Glenn A	G-11-4
JOKINEN, Reino E	E-7-3
JOLLEY, Ben F [168]	D-9-26
JOLLIMORE, John C	H-2-26
JONAS, Melvin P	L-4-8
JONATHAN, Harold	M-6-17
JONES, Charlie M	D-14-4
JONES, David E	G-19-8
JONES, Edgar C	G-20-27
JONES, Edward H	Walls of the Missing
JONES, Edward R B	K-12-14
JONES, Eugene H	Walls of the Missing
JONES, Everett H	G-18-15
JONES, Everette R	H-15-20
JONES, Francis L	A-7-10
JONES, Frank J	C-9-13
JONES, George E	B-11-22
JONES, Harry P	F-1-12
JONES, Henry A	H-2-14
JONES, Hugh	E-9-5
JONES, James C	P-1-10
JONES, James E	H-6-21
JONES, James H	E-13-12
JONES, James P [169]	I-18-14
JONES, Jearld H	Walls of the Missing
JONES, John E	B-6-20
JONES, Joseph A	O-21-7
JONES, Joseph J	A-17-9
JONES, Kenneth C	J-12-22
JONES, Lloyd R	I-6-10
JONES, Lyle S	Walls of the Missing
JONES, Marshall F	H-12-12
JONES, Marshall L [170]	P-7-4
JONES, Milton C	G-5-22
JONES, Murray A	D-19-22
JONES, Nelson B	C-8-30
JONES, Orville D	D-2-9
JONES, Owen L	H-11-24
JONES, Paul D [171]	H-16-27
JONES, Pink D	I-3-17
JONES, Raymond W	B-10-27
JONES, Robert K [172]	C-6-21
JONES, Robert W	E-10-24
JONES, Roy W	D-19-30
JONES, Samuel Q	P-5-11
JONES, Theodore [173]	M-4-15
JONES, Thomas B Jr	Walls of the Missing
JONES, Trevor	N-3-14
JONES, Walter R Jr	M-6-9
JONES, Walter W	L-8-20
JONES, Wendell P	I-19-12
JONES, Wilbert G	H-17-17
JONES, William H Jr	I-3-1
JONES, William R	J-3-12
JONSON, James J	J-6-3
JOOS, Albert L	F-8-11
JORDAN, Alfred R	E-11-4
JORDAN, Floyd A	G-21-18
JORDAN, Harold W	Walls of the Missing
JORDAN, Houston V	O-15-3
JORDAN, J L [174]	E-17-12
JORDAN, John W Jr	Walls of the Missing
JORDAN, Walter R	J-18-8
JORDAN, William A	J-17-12
JORDAN, William E	C-2-4
JORDAN, William K Jr	E-10-27
JORGE, Joaquin H	N-13-9
JORGENSEN, Frederick E	G-14-18
JORGENSEN, Winther	D-14-22
JOSCELYN, Earl F	J-21-15
JOSEPH, Ford E	M-20-16
JOSEY, James F [175]	E-8-27
JOSH, Myron G	Walls of the Missing
JOSLIN, John W Jr	Walls of the Missing
JOURNEY, Orville B	A-15-24
JOYCE, Barney R	H-13-8
JOYCE, William P	O-7-10
JOYSLIN, Paul C	P-9-1
JOZOVICH, Nicholas J	N-12-8
JUDAY, Charles G	Walls of the Missing
JUDD, Cale E	K-6-10
JUDD, Charles R Jr	Walls of the Missing
JUDD, Emanuel	K-20-4
JUDD, Stephen P	B-11-26
JUDKINS, James A	I-9-10
JUDSON, Maynard E	F-6-27
JUHAS, Michael	C-8-8
JULIAN, William M Jr	P-2-17
JUNEK, Jack R	G-17-26
JUPINA, Joseph P	A-12-32
JURAK, William	Walls of the Missing
JURKIC, Joseph J	A-1-13
JUSSILA, Hedvig M	H-20-5
JUSTIN, Lawrence M	M-2-4
JUSTUS, Raymond D	H-19-22
JUTRZONKA, Leo V	J-11-8

K

KACERAUKAS, Alfred F	O-8-13
KACHADOORIAN, Jake	Walls of the Missing
KACHINSKAS, Albert J	I-11-13
KACPURA, Joseph A	A-16-13
KACUCEWICZ, Stanley	E-4-12
KADLUBOWSKI, Melvin W	E-11-16
KAER, Robert L	G-6-11
KAFKA, John V	Walls of the Missing
KAHLER, George J	B-9-20
KAHN, Herbert	J-5-4
KAISER, Leo W	Walls of the Missing
KAJUT, Norman F	G-16-26
KALANDER, Victor I	N-12-9
KALAS, Charles	C-8-29
KALAUSICH, John	Walls of the Missing
KALE, James L	A-10-1
KALINEJKO, Stanley J	P-19-10
KALIVODA, Joseph M	C-5-21
KALLEMEYN, Lester	I-12-4
KAMINSKI, Stanley W	C-2-20
KAMMARCAL, Harold H [176]	H-20-2
KAMMERER, Clayton C	M-22-5
KAMPEN, Percy R	K-8-4
KAMPES, Milford T	H-19-5
KANABLE, Richard E	N-11-7
KANDCER, Bernard H	I-17-19
KANDEFER, Frank J	N-12-10
KANE, Freddie E	I-11-15
KANE, John D	L-10-9
KANE, William H [177]	H-15-7
KANTGIAS, Nicholas	L-7-9
KAPACIEWICZ, George J	N-9-9
KAPLAN, Benjamin	Walls of the Missing
KAPLAN, Victor F	G-19-26
KAPPEL, William J	K-18-22
KAPR, Joseph V	Walls of the Missing
KAPUSTA, George R	O-8-4
KARASO, Joseph J	Walls of the Missing
KARBA, Joseph	G-11-25
KARGER, Harold E	A-2-13
KARHULA, John [178]	Walls of the Missing
KARICH, Louis N	Walls of the Missing

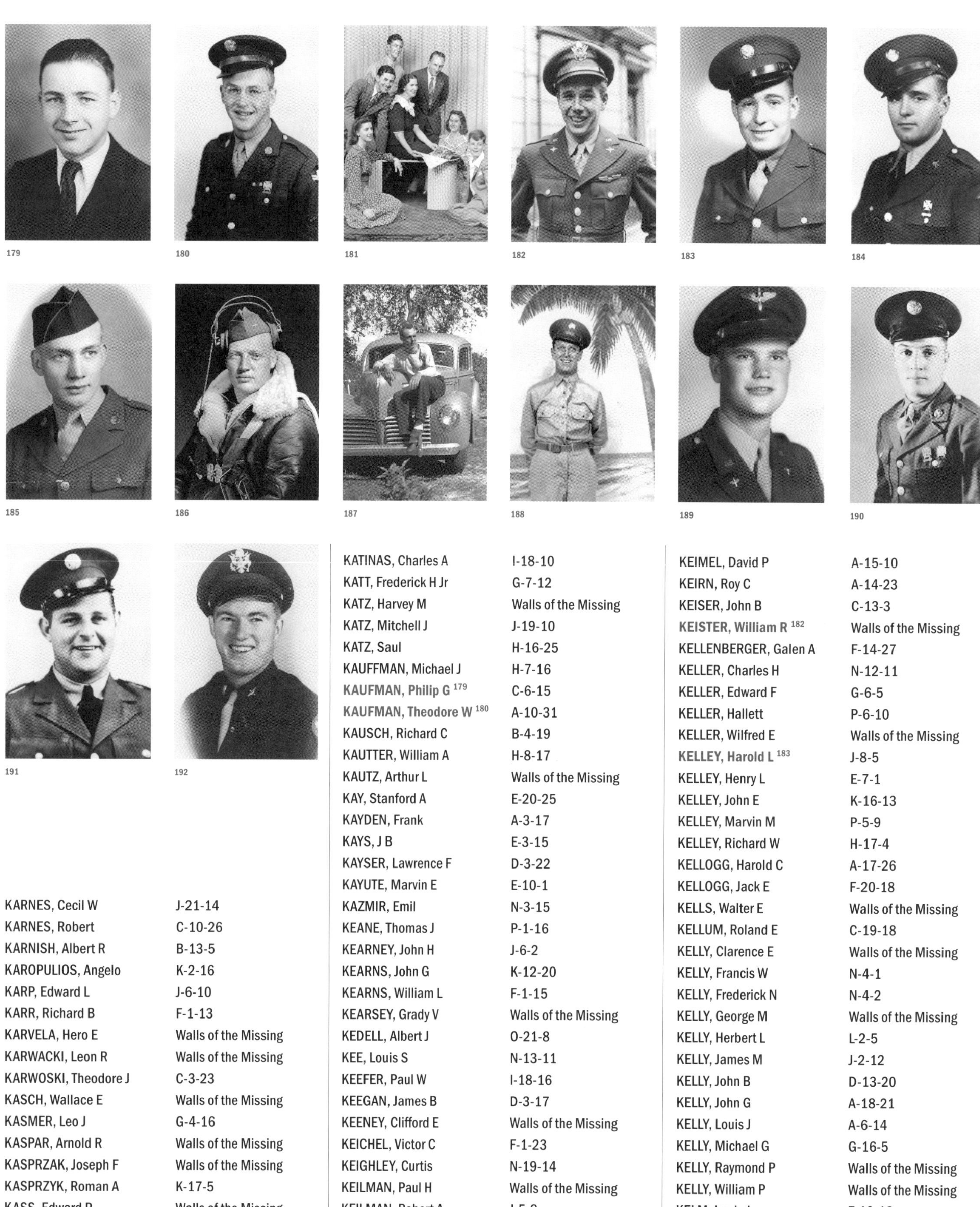

179 180 181 182 183 184

185 186 187 188 189 190

191 192

KARNES, Cecil W	J-21-14
KARNES, Robert	C-10-26
KARNISH, Albert R	B-13-5
KAROPULIOS, Angelo	K-2-16
KARP, Edward L	J-6-10
KARR, Richard B	F-1-13
KARVELA, Hero E	Walls of the Missing
KARWACKI, Leon R	Walls of the Missing
KARWOSKI, Theodore J	C-3-23
KASCH, Wallace E	Walls of the Missing
KASMER, Leo J	G-4-16
KASPAR, Arnold R	Walls of the Missing
KASPRZAK, Joseph F	Walls of the Missing
KASPRZYK, Roman A	K-17-5
KASS, Edward P	Walls of the Missing
KAST, Willard W	E-18-9
KASTAN, Charles P	G-15-12
KATIN, Cornelius B	J-18-19
KATINAS, Charles A	I-18-10
KATT, Frederick H Jr	G-7-12
KATZ, Harvey M	Walls of the Missing
KATZ, Mitchell J	J-19-10
KATZ, Saul	H-16-25
KAUFFMAN, Michael J	H-7-16
KAUFMAN, Philip G [179]	C-6-15
KAUFMAN, Theodore W [180]	A-10-31
KAUSCH, Richard C	B-4-19
KAUTTER, William A	H-8-17
KAUTZ, Arthur L	Walls of the Missing
KAY, Stanford A	E-20-25
KAYDEN, Frank	A-3-17
KAYS, J B	E-3-15
KAYSER, Lawrence F	D-3-22
KAYUTE, Marvin E	E-10-1
KAZMIR, Emil	N-3-15
KEANE, Thomas J	P-1-16
KEARNEY, John H	J-6-2
KEARNS, John G	K-12-20
KEARNS, William L	F-1-15
KEARSEY, Grady V	Walls of the Missing
KEDELL, Albert J	O-21-8
KEE, Louis S	N-13-11
KEEFER, Paul W	I-18-16
KEEGAN, James B	D-3-17
KEENEY, Clifford E	Walls of the Missing
KEICHEL, Victor C	F-1-23
KEIGHLEY, Curtis	N-19-14
KEILMAN, Paul H	Walls of the Missing
KEILMAN, Robert A	J-5-8
KEIM, Othniel A [181]	O-7-15
KEIM, Robert E	E-19-7
KEIME, Maurice E	O-8-17
KEIMEL, David P	A-15-10
KEIRN, Roy C	A-14-23
KEISER, John B	C-13-3
KEISTER, William R [182]	Walls of the Missing
KELLENBERGER, Galen A	F-14-27
KELLER, Charles H	N-12-11
KELLER, Edward F	G-6-5
KELLER, Hallett	P-6-10
KELLER, Wilfred E	Walls of the Missing
KELLEY, Harold L [183]	J-8-5
KELLEY, Henry L	E-7-1
KELLEY, John E	K-16-13
KELLEY, Marvin M	P-5-9
KELLEY, Richard W	H-17-4
KELLOGG, Harold C	A-17-26
KELLOGG, Jack E	F-20-18
KELLS, Walter E	Walls of the Missing
KELLUM, Roland E	C-19-18
KELLY, Clarence E	Walls of the Missing
KELLY, Francis W	N-4-1
KELLY, Frederick N	N-4-2
KELLY, George M	Walls of the Missing
KELLY, Herbert L	L-2-5
KELLY, James M	J-2-12
KELLY, John B	D-13-20
KELLY, John G	A-18-21
KELLY, Louis J	A-6-14
KELLY, Michael G	G-16-5
KELLY, Raymond P	Walls of the Missing
KELLY, William P	Walls of the Missing
KELM, Louis J	F-19-18
KEMMET, Robert J	L-10-10
KEMOCK, Walter [184]	D-20-16
KEMP, Edward K	O-21-9

Name	Location
KEMP, Leroy E	J-15-20
KEMPF, Theodore	G-8-11
KENDALL, Joseph W	Walls of the Missing
KENDALL, William H	D-3-5
KENDERDINE, Guy R	J-14-4
KENDRICK, Dan F	G-11-9
KENDZIORA, Thomas A	P-17-14
KENEALY, Joseph M	L-12-19
KENNEDY, Amos R	Walls of the Missing
KENNEDY, Bernard J	F-5-26
KENNEDY, H T	B-20-17
KENNEDY, James G	D-21-5
KENNEDY, Michael G	Walls of the Missing
KENNEDY, Robert E	B-16-18
KENNEMER, James C [185]	Walls of the Missing
KENNER, Everett L [186]	B-17-20
KENNER, Harold D	Walls of the Missing
KENNEY, Francis J	A-2-9
KENT, Robert W	F-5-16
KEOHAN, Francis R	E-14-25
KEOWN, Philip Jr	D-9-23
KEPLINGER, Howard D	H-6-27
KERBY, George I	C-2-25
KERCHMAR, Rudolph	A-14-12
KERLEY, Herman L	Walls of the Missing
KERN, Herbert R	Walls of the Missing
KERNAN, Thomas M	B-2-3
KERR, Alfred M	L-5-7
KERR, Edward J	M-5-12
KERR, Ivan H	J-7-16
KERR, James W	I-2-17
KERR, John	Walls of the Missing
KERR, Maurice J	H-16-7
KERR, Richard L	I-13-22
KERRICK, Lewis M	Walls of the Missing
KERRIGAN, George F	Walls of the Missing
KERSHAL, Andrew F	F-8-15
KERSHNER, Robert L	A-3-23
KESSLER, James W	F-9-26
KESSLER, Walter	I-16-2
KESTER, Robert	K-9-3
KETCHERSID, Vernis E	K-17-8
KETCHUM, Archie T	Walls of the Missing
KETTENDORF, Robert F	C-17-18
KEYES, Ernest A	H-9-11
KEYES, Orin F	J-10-21
KIBBEE, Forrest H	Walls of the Missing
KIBURZ, Arthur F	L-10-8
KIEFER, Harold E	B-15-16
KIEHN, Donald R	I-14-17
KIELBLOCK, Albert L	D-11-6
KIGGINS, Russell J	O-21-10
KIGGINS, Wayne D	M-4-17
KIGHT, Gerald W	Walls of the Missing
KILBURN, Orille K	M-3-17
KILBY, James L	L-13-14
KILBY, Lehmon	K-21-12
KILCOIN, John R	O-8-8
KILEY, John W	E-6-26
KILGORE, James M	H-1-20
KILGORE, Raymond H	Walls of the Missing
KILLION, Arthur R	C-16-26
KILLOUGH, Charles T	Walls of the Missing
KILMER, Thomas B	D-11-32
KIM, Kenneth H	G-17-17
KIMBALL, Claude O	D-14-1
KIMBALL, Harry Wales	M-8-9
KIMBALL, John R	I-15-4
KIMBEL, Roy T	C-19-19
KIMBROUGH, William B	D-18-8
KIMSEY, Melvin	K-17-2
KINDIG, Karl K	A-16-17
KINDLE, Delbert D	A-18-2
KING, Carl E	H-18-4
KING, Carl E	G-21-10
KING, Dorsey A	K-2-2
KING, Edward T [187]	A-11-10
KING, Fred E	B-1-14
KING, George F	F-13-9
KING, Harold T	B-2-2
KING, Harry L	A-12-31
KING, James A	C-18-28
KING, John	J-7-11
KING, John D	O-21-11
KING, Kenneth J	E-8-24
KING, Leslie D	A-11-29
KING, Robert D Jr	D-14-23
KING, Willie W	F-2-9
KINGERY, Morris H	B-1-21
KINGSLEY, Noel D	M-11-4
KINGSTON, John A	M-3-15
KINNAMAN, Arlen Z	F-4-20
KINNEY, George A [188]	Walls of the Missing
KINNEY, James W	I-15-1
KINNEY, Joseph A	B-5-14
KINSTLER, Roy A	B-16-2
KINT, John D	A-6-8
KIPLER, Kenneth R	H-7-10
KIRBY, Francis J Jr	G-7-1
KIRCHEVAL, William J	B-18-17
KIRCHUE, James S	A-11-1
KIRDZIK, Joseph J	D-16-29
KIRKCALDY, Mitchell G	I-13-20
KIRKENDALL, Cecil W	C-4-21
KIRKLAND, Paul H	I-12-15
KIRKLAND, William J	K-17-19
KIRKMAN, Ralph E	I-17-4
KIRKPATRICK, Roy D	J-18-3
KIRLIN, William H Jr	M-2-8
KISAMORE, Leo R	Walls of the Missing
KISER, Walter G	D-7-25
KISSACK, James L	F-10-5
KISZKA, Casimer	F-12-17
KITCHELL, James R	H-16-13
KITCHO, John	C-12-11
KITTREDGE, David R	Walls of the Missing
KIZER, Charles L	Walls of the Missing
KIZIS, Justin	J-5-10
KJAR, Ferdinand M [189]	B-2-32
KJELLAND, Leonard B [190]	D-16-25
KLAMSER, Leonard F	C-15-14
KLASE, Paul B	B-15-12
KLAVERNGA, George W	O-15-10
KLEBOFSKI, Raymond V	C-19-26
KLEESE, Lloyd	Walls of the Missing
KLEIN, John W	C-3-9
KLEIN, Robert J	A-17-6
KLEIN, Sherman S	F-17-3
KLEIN, Vern F	E-15-15
KLEINE, Frank R	O-7-14
KLEINTJES, Bertrand	E-11-13
KLEMKE, Reinhold H	F-11-27
KLEMM, August	H-21-6
KLEMM, Roy R	H-21-7
KLEMOLA, Robert B	A-1-7
KLEMP, Arthur E	O-21-12
KLEMP, George H	C-20-25
KLIMA, Norman J	G-12-23
KLINE, Glen O	P-5-13
KLINE, Jose L	G-8-4
KLINE, Robert L	C-6-32
KLIPPEL, John	M-19-16
KLOCEK, Bruno J	G-16-9
KLOCKOWSKI, John J	C-4-28
KLOE, Toke V	G-16-18
KLOSE, Kenneth A	Walls of the Missing
KLOSKIE, Joseph A	O-1-3
KLOSTERMAN, William J Jr	H-21-23
KLUM, Philip H	Walls of the Missing
KLUMB, William J	E-12-22
KNACK, Joseph R	G-16-23
KNAPIK, Boles S	Walls of the Missing
KNAPP, Kenneth L	G-12-12
KNAPPE, William L Jr	N-12-12
KNAUER, Darrell L [191]	J-10-16
KNEALE, John P	C-20-27
KNECHT, Charles H	Walls of the Missing
KNECHTGES, Harlan J J	B-6-31
KNEPPER, Elah E	D-2-6
KNIERIM, Gussie L Jr	E-2-6
KNIGHT, Ancil W	A-7-22
KNIGHT, Dan	E-6-12
KNIGHT, Donzel C	H-7-11
KNIGHT, Edgar F	F-6-9
KNIGHT, Jimmie S	P-9-10
KNIGHT, Robert M	H-4-9
KNOBLE, Arthur R	B-19-6
KNOTT, Richard A	F-20-13
KNOWLES, William A [192]	Walls of the Missing
KNOX, Arthur D	D-5-2
KNOX, Edward R	F-13-6
KNOX, James L	J-4-7
KNOX, William O	D-8-1
KNUDSEN, Frank	A-1-23

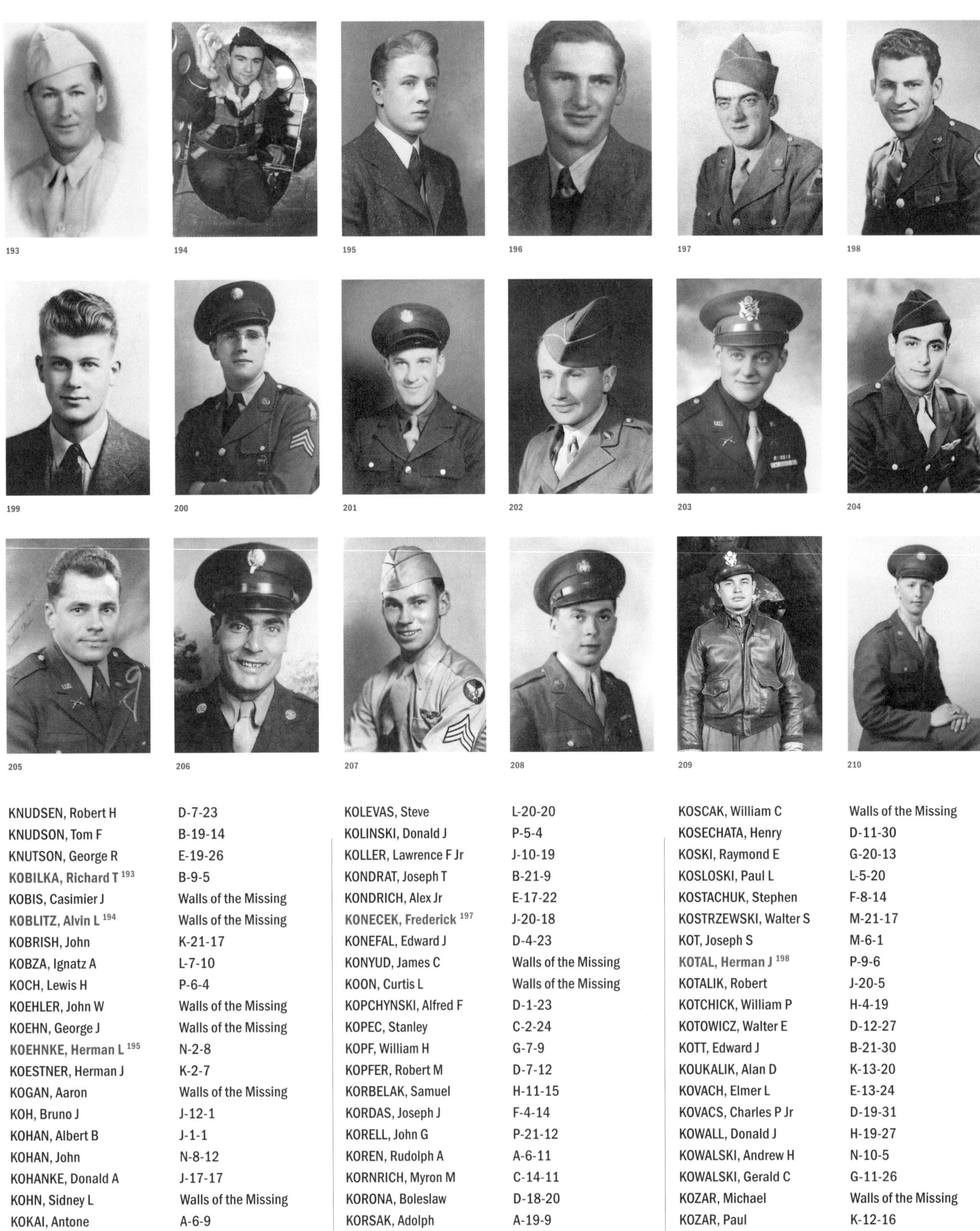

193 194 195 196 197 198

199 200 201 202 203 204

205 206 207 208 209 210

KNUDSEN, Robert H	D-7-23	KOLEVAS, Steve	L-20-20	KOSCAK, William C	Walls of the Missing
KNUDSON, Tom F	B-19-14	KOLINSKI, Donald J	P-5-4	KOSECHATA, Henry	D-11-30
KNUTSON, George R	E-19-26	KOLLER, Lawrence F Jr	J-10-19	KOSKI, Raymond E	G-20-13
KOBILKA, Richard T [193]	B-9-5	KONDRAT, Joseph T	B-21-9	KOSLOSKI, Paul L	L-5-20
KOBIS, Casimier J	Walls of the Missing	KONDRICH, Alex Jr	E-17-22	KOSTACHUK, Stephen	F-8-14
KOBLITZ, Alvin L [194]	Walls of the Missing	**KONECEK, Frederick** [197]	J-20-18	KOSTRZEWSKI, Walter S	M-21-17
KOBRISH, John	K-21-17	KONEFAL, Edward J	D-4-23	KOT, Joseph S	M-6-1
KOBZA, Ignatz A	L-7-10	KONYUD, James C	Walls of the Missing	**KOTAL, Herman J** [198]	P-9-6
KOCH, Lewis H	P-6-4	KOON, Curtis L	Walls of the Missing	KOTALIK, Robert	J-20-5
KOEHLER, John W	Walls of the Missing	KOPCHYNSKI, Alfred F	D-1-23	KOTCHICK, William P	H-4-19
KOEHN, George J	Walls of the Missing	KOPEC, Stanley	C-2-24	KOTOWICZ, Walter E	D-12-27
KOEHNKE, Herman L [195]	N-2-8	KOPF, William H	G-7-9	KOTT, Edward J	B-21-30
KOESTNER, Herman J	K-2-7	KOPFER, Robert M	D-7-12	KOUKALIK, Alan D	K-13-20
KOGAN, Aaron	Walls of the Missing	KORBELAK, Samuel	H-11-15	KOVACH, Elmer L	E-13-24
KOH, Bruno J	J-12-1	KORDAS, Joseph J	F-4-14	KOVACS, Charles P Jr	D-19-31
KOHAN, Albert B	J-1-1	KORELL, John G	P-21-12	KOWALL, Donald J	H-19-27
KOHAN, John	N-8-12	KOREN, Rudolph A	A-6-11	KOWALSKI, Andrew H	N-10-5
KOHANKE, Donald A	J-17-17	KORNRICH, Myron M	C-14-11	KOWALSKI, Gerald C	G-11-26
KOHN, Sidney L	Walls of the Missing	KORONA, Boleslaw	D-18-20	KOZAR, Michael	Walls of the Missing
KOKAI, Antone	A-6-9	KORSAK, Adolph	A-19-9	KOZAR, Paul	K-12-16
KOKI, Andrew [196]	N-12-13	KOS, George A	B-7-32	KOZELKA, James	E-13-19
KOKOTOVICH, Saul	Walls of the Missing	KOSAK, Stanley E	I-9-4	KOZEN, Joseph E	I-6-11

Name	Location
KOZIOL, Floyd D	L-11-3
KOZLOWSKI, Frederick	E-1-10
KOZMENSKI, William J	A-17-25
KRAEMER, Daniel J	O-21-13
KRAIMER, Harold J	G-3-22
KRAINOVICH, Nicholas	L-15-22
KRAJACIC, Frank G	K-7-11
KRAMAREWICZ, Charles	I-14-18
KRAMER, Carl M	A-7-29
KRAMER, Robert P	C-10-28
KRAPF, Howard G	Walls of the Missing
KRAPF, Norman C	G-19-18
KRAUS, Eugene J	I-8-11
KRAUSE, Charles B	H-6-9
KRAUSE, Leonard F	C-19-32
KRAUSS, Harold F Jr	A-1-30
KRAWIEC, Andrew P	F-17-20
KREAMER, John C II	O-2-17
KRECZMER, Alexander F	C-13-18
KREFT, Rodney H C [199]	A-8-9
KREITNER, Robert W	D-14-10
KRELL, Floyd C	D-4-32
KREMER, Jack R	I-20-17
KRESSLEY, Elwood R	J-4-17
KRIBBS, Elden M	G-2-2
KRIDELBAUGH, Glen E	I-5-21
KRIEBEL, Howard M	D-17-8
KRIZNAR, Frank C	D-6-21
KROGULSKI, Anthony M	G-7-23
KROHN, Ervin L	A-3-1
KROLIKOWSKI, Leonard J	I-15-6
KROLL, Stanley A [200]	Walls of the Missing
KRUER, Edward J	Walls of the Missing
KRZYZAK, Henry R	M-22-13
KUBAS, Joseph B	E-20-14
KUBINSKI, Henry	H-6-18
KUBSCH, Clarence J	C-8-31
KUCHINSKAS, Joseph G	G-1-14
KUDEL, Carl A	A-19-12
KUEMMERLE, Christy R	A-11-23
KUFFNER, John	G-8-1
KUHN, Gail C [201]	N-17-10
KUHN, George J	E-14-15
KUHN, Kermit D	K-12-9
KUKAY, Joseph F	E-13-10
KULCHAR, Louis [202]	K-14-14
KULESA, John E	C-15-27
KULICK, Thomas E	F-8-22
KULIK, Joseph F	Walls of the Missing
KULLMANN, Leonard G	A-6-1
KULP, Merlin F	C-14-6
KUNST, William J Jr	B-5-11
KUNZ, Louis R	J-14-18
KUNZE, Albert H [203]	B-15-4
KUPRIS, Felix F	N-17-14
KURGAN, Stanley Jr	E-11-12
KURNAFIL, Stephen	Walls of the Missing
KUROWSKI, Harry B	F-8-13
KURPIS, Frank	G-17-13
KURTZ, Albert L III	K-21-8
KURTZ, Raymond C	Walls of the Missing
KURTZMAN, Lester	E-19-27
KUSTERKO, Walter W	Walls of the Missing
KUTCH, Andy M	B-4-5
KUTZ, Paul W	Walls of the Missing
KUZIAN, Charles J	C-3-27
KUZMA, Frank J	F-18-17
KUZMINSKY, Abe M	G-15-25
KUZUPAS, Charles	J-6-1

L

Name	Location
LA BADIE, Burton M	H-16-21
LA BUD, Edward J	D-13-12
LA BUTZKE, Ruben A	H-9-14
LA COUR, John M	G-4-1
LA COURT, Efrain F	K-16-4
LA DUCA, Anthony C Jr	G-13-9
LA FOREST, Edmund J	E-13-23
LA FRANCE, Charles J	L-14-17
LA FROMBOISE, Kenneth	L-6-5
LA GIER, Kenneth H	A-18-18
LA MEDICA, Michael T	L-7-22
LA POINTE, Marcel J	B-1-11
LA QUADRA, Angelo C	F-16-10
LA RIVIERE, John E	Walls of the Missing
LA SARGE, Joseph L Sr [204]	Walls of the Missing
LA VELLE, Francis J	J-16-7
LAB, Ralph L	Walls of the Missing
LABATE, Peter J	F-15-24
LABOZETTA, Peter P	J-20-11
LABUZ, Edward A	Walls of the Missing
LACEK, Anthony J	C-12-31
LACHUT, Sigismund	J-13-7
LACI, Joseph	P-8-12
LACKEY, David E	Walls of the Missing
LACKO, Joseph	G-8-17
LACNY, Stanley W	Walls of the Missing
LACOLA, Joseph J	L-4-20
LACY, Carl E	G-16-19
LACY, Ernest C Jr	D-11-23
LADEMAN, Marvin J	Walls of the Missing
LADGINSKI, Paul M [205]	O-9-16
LADNER, Carman S	Walls of the Missing
LAFFERTY, Hugh J	B-18-3
LAFLEUR, Armand W	H-12-24
LAGASSA, Lloyd K	Walls of the Missing
LAGOMARSINO, Joseph	A-10-19
LAIGAIE, Charles F Jr	G-10-10
LAINE, George M [206]	A-21-32
LAING, Richard B [207]	Walls of the Missing
LAINO, Louis A	E-6-25
LAIRD, Francis C	P-2-7
LAIRD, Wesley W	Walls of the Missing
LAJKOWICZ, Joseph F	Walls of the Missing
LAKE, Allan L	Walls of the Missing
LAKE, Herbert [208]	L-10-20
LAKE, Robert W	B-4-2
LAKIN, William T	O-19-2
LALIBERTE, Joseph H A	C-2-7
LALLAS, Charles G	F-10-17
LALLY, John R	A-13-8
LAMB, Billy J	J-4-10
LAMB, Jack D	C-10-11
LAMB, Reed J	Walls of the Missing
LAMBERT, Frederick E	C-5-7
LAMBERT, Harold N	E-10-7
LAMBERT, Joseph T	L-19-1
LAMBERT, Robert E	F-3-8
LAMBERT, Theron E	E-20-11
LAMBERT, William D	D-2-32
LAMBRECHT, Alexander J	Walls of the Missing
LAMBRECHT, Harold W Jr	G-2-23
LAMBRECHT, Leonard R	A-2-15
LAMER, Kenneth E	Walls of the Missing
LAMMERS, Robert K [209]	Walls of the Missing
LAMONT, Erwin E	N-6-7
LAMONT, Hugh W	G-18-7
LAMONTAGNE, Leo J	N-8-11
LAMOREAUX, Al	L-3-15
LAMPART, David C	N-19-9
LAMPLOT, Vernon E	F-21-7
LAMPMAN, Paul A Jr	Walls of the Missing
LANAHAN, Lawrence P [210]	Walls of the Missing
LANCE, Harry E Jr	Walls of the Missing
LAND, John L	B-3-4
LANDERS, Walter L Jr	Walls of the Missing
LANDIS, Sidney R	A-13-1
LANDRICH, William V	L-21-19
LANDRY, Gedeon J	I-14-7
LANE, Elwin A	M-9-6
LANE, Frank	J-4-9
LANE, Jerome R	H-3-2
LANE, Joseph F	J-20-8
LANE, Loring	K-5-11
LANE, Louis M	L-21-15
LANE, Rufus E	Walls of the Missing
LANG, Ethan A Jr	G-16-25
LANG, Merle L	H-6-25
LANG, Robert J	M-15-11
LANGAGER, Leonard I	D-15-16
LANGEVIN, Alfred T	Walls of the Missing
LANGFORD, Rayburn L	E-3-8
LANGFORD, William H	Walls of the Missing
LANGJAHR, Charles	L-1-13
LANGLINAIS, Euel J	K-16-2
LANGONE, Dominic J Jr	H-1-16
LANGSTON, Everett V	Walls of the Missing
LANIDES, Thomas N	E-11-24
LANIER, Phillip H	E-16-6
LANIOUS, Horace P	F-9-2
LANNUTTI, Carmen T	B-4-11
LANPHEAR, Byron E	N-20-17
LANSDALE, Gilbert	M-5-13
LANTZ, Donald H	B-7-8

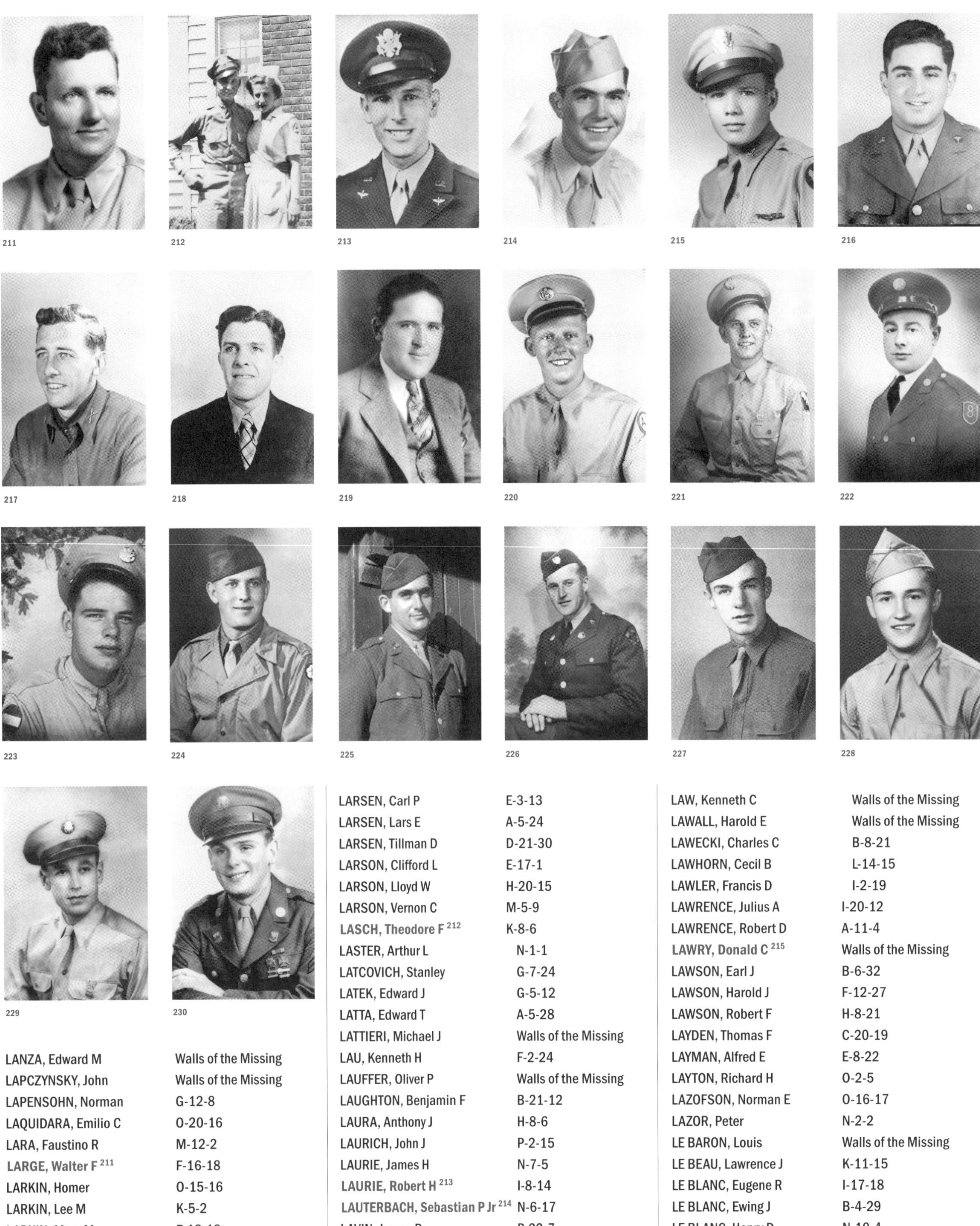

211 212 213 214 215 216 217 218 219 220 221 222 223 224 225 226 227 228 229 230

LANZA, Edward M Walls of the Missing
LAPCZYNSKY, John Walls of the Missing
LAPENSOHN, Norman G-12-8
LAQUIDARA, Emilio C O-20-16
LARA, Faustino R M-12-2
LARGE, Walter F [211] F-16-18
LARKIN, Homer O-15-16
LARKIN, Lee M K-5-2
LARKIN, Marx M F-18-18
LARRIVEE, Edward R E-14-24
LARSEN, Carl P E-3-13
LARSEN, Lars E A-5-24
LARSEN, Tillman D D-21-30
LARSON, Clifford L E-17-1
LARSON, Lloyd W H-20-15
LARSON, Vernon C M-5-9
LASCH, Theodore F [212] K-8-6
LASTER, Arthur L N-1-1
LATCOVICH, Stanley G-7-24
LATEK, Edward J G-5-12
LATTA, Edward T A-5-28
LATTIERI, Michael J Walls of the Missing
LAU, Kenneth H F-2-24
LAUFFER, Oliver P Walls of the Missing
LAUGHTON, Benjamin F B-21-12
LAURA, Anthony J H-8-6
LAURICH, John J P-2-15
LAURIE, James H N-7-5
LAURIE, Robert H [213] I-8-14
LAUTERBACH, Sebastian P Jr [214] N-6-17
LAVIN, James R P-22-7
LAW, George J Jr P-13-8
LAW, Kenneth C Walls of the Missing
LAWALL, Harold E Walls of the Missing
LAWECKI, Charles C B-8-21
LAWHORN, Cecil B L-14-15
LAWLER, Francis D I-2-19
LAWRENCE, Julius A I-20-12
LAWRENCE, Robert D A-11-4
LAWRY, Donald C [215] Walls of the Missing
LAWSON, Earl J B-6-32
LAWSON, Harold J F-12-27
LAWSON, Robert F H-8-21
LAYDEN, Thomas F C-20-19
LAYMAN, Alfred E E-8-22
LAYTON, Richard H O-2-5
LAZOFSON, Norman E O-16-17
LAZOR, Peter N-2-2
LE BARON, Louis Walls of the Missing
LE BEAU, Lawrence J K-11-15
LE BLANC, Eugene R I-17-18
LE BLANC, Ewing J B-4-29
LE BLANC, Henry D N-10-4
LE BLANC , Joseph E L-19-10

LE BRUN, Paul L	Walls of the Missing
LE CURSI, Nicholas A [216]	I-21-4
LE FEVRE, Charles H	N-12-14
LE FEVRE, Louis M	L-7-18
LE FURJAH, Keith E	A-2-8
LE GAL, Charles R	O-19-7
LE GALL, Bertram T	M-1-1
LE HOTY, Jerold J	L-10-13
LE MAY, Robert J	L-9-11
LE ROY, Edward B [217]	L-2-16
LE VAN, Joseph M	J-11-18
LE VARIO, Dolores	H-4-13
LEABO, Herschel W [218]	B-14-22
LEACH, Clarence H	Walls of the Missing
LEAFTY, Junior E	P-15-1
LEAHY, James P	Walls of the Missing
LEARY, Frederick D	G-14-17
LEATHERS, Harlan R	H-7-27
LEATHERWOOD, Hilliard C Jr	J-18-1
LEATHERWOOD, James H	L-19-13
LEBESON, David R	E-11-6
LEBOW, Stanley M	M-5-14
LEDOUX, Elphie E	B-13-24
LEE, Burton L	J-12-20
LEE, Eldon W	D-17-26
LEE, Eugene F	G-5-27
LEE, Floyd E	O-10-10
LEE, Harlan R	G-10-7
LEE, Harry E	Walls of the Missing
LEE, Hewitt D	I-2-20
LEE, Leon	O-16-10
LEE, Marshall F	H-18-2
LEE, Richard D	P-13-14
LEE, Robert E	N-17-16
LEE, Tollie C	I-4-1
LEE, Warren A	P-21-11
LEE, William H Jr	A-13-30
LEE, Wilson L	K-16-1
LEECH, Irvin H	B-7-7
LEEDY, Norman E	D-19-27
LEFFELMAN, Ralph J	L-1-7
LEFFLER, Loyal E [219]	N-11-15
LEGER, John C	G-13-26
LEGG, Raymond F	E-13-22
LEGGETT, William J [220]	P-22-4
LEGGION, James H	J-21-16
LEGLER, Leory C	Walls of the Missing
LEHMAN, Edward J	P-8-16
LEHMAN, George E	F-20-27
LEHMAN, Jay E	M-11-9
LEHMAN, Walter R [221]	Walls of the Missing
LEHMANN, Monroe J	I-5-17
LEHR, Leo R	A-11-20
LEHRMANN, Louis A Jr	Walls of the Missing
LEIBENSPERGER, Russell F	D-1-22
LEIBENSPERGER, Stewart J	D-1-21
LEICHLITER, Wayne	Walls of the Missing
LEIDECKER, Theodore W	Walls of the Missing

LEIGHTY, John L	F-6-5
LEINER, Fred	A-8-24
LEIST, Leroy E	Walls of the Missing
LEISTER, Harry S	H-11-2
LEISURE, Max F	J-13-13
LEKANIDIS, Costas	F-3-27
LELAND, Allen	E-11-14
LEMBCKE, Donald F	M-13-11
LEMBERGER, Herman	O-1-4
LEMIEUX, Arthur L	Walls of the Missing
LEMIEUX, Joseph P C	I-20-16
LEMLEY, Marcus J	I-10-16
LEMMON, George F	C-8-7
LEMPKA, Daniel B	M-17-5
LENAGHAN, Robert W	L-7-6
LENDER, Dale A	L-20-19
LENNO, Donald C	K-3-13
LENNON, John T	E-18-10
LENTI, Neal M	H-9-13
LENTZ, Gilbert E	E-1-17
LEOGRANDE, Dominic G	Walls of the Missing
LEONARD, Alex E	P-21-7
LEONARD, Maurice J	J-20-20
LEONARDO, Joseph Jr	G-16-13
LEONE, Vito	I-9-21
LEOPOLD, George O	E-2-18
LERARIS, Michael	L-20-22
LERMA, William	D-7-29
LESSARD, Lawrence	J-15-13
LETERSKY, William H	B-2-22
LETTERA, Alfred P	B-13-28
LEVASSEUR, Louis P	J-14-15
LEVE, Franklin	M-5-15
LEVER, Robert T	M-6-6
LEVESQUE, George R	J-5-12
LEVEY, Paul D	Walls of the Missing
LEVINE, Israel	E-17-11
LEVINSON, Moses	J-11-4
LEVITAN, Henry T	B-20-6
LEVORSON, Mark C	E-12-3
LEVY, Bertram R	F-21-13
LEVY, Henry I	M-21-4
LEVY, Rubin	E-4-9
LEWANDOWSKI, Alex F	L-16-5
LEWIS, Arthur E	E-1-5
LEWIS, Billy G	O-7-1
LEWIS, Charles H	F-7-4
LEWIS, Cyrus A	C-11-13
LEWIS, Earl B	M-6-15
LEWIS, Herbert J	Walls of the Missing
LEWIS, Howard E	Walls of the Missing
LEWIS, Ivan C	Walls of the Missing
LEWIS, Jack K	Walls of the Missing
LEWIS, James J	Walls of the Missing
LEWIS, John E	M-3-16
LEWIS, Joseph W	Walls of the Missing
LEWIS, Lemuel J Jr	G-15-2
LEWIS, Mars	C-7-15

LEWIS, Raymond A	A-19-3
LEWIS, Raymond J Jr	I-9-7
LEWIS, Roy B	F-3-3
LEWIS, Sidney F	G-20-5
LEWIS, Troy I	H-13-18
LEWIS, William F	Walls of the Missing
LEWTER, Wilto A	M-16-6
LEYS, Fred	D-15-10
LIBBEE, Dick L	B-5-12
LICATO, Angelo J	Walls of the Missing
LICHTEN, Leo	E-7-13
LIEDL, William G	P-12-16
LIGAARD, Herburne W	E-15-1
LIGGETT, Hunter	K-19-12
LIGHT, Robert C	Walls of the Missing
LIGUORI, Edward J	J-4-11
LILL, Dean T	C-4-26
LILLEY, John A	B-19-9
LILLIG, Thomas J	E-17-21
LIMA, John [222]	J-20-10
LINCICOME, Clark F	E-10-23
LINCOLN, Glen A [223]	Walls of the Missing
LINDAMAN, Wallace C	K-7-19
LINDAU, Edward W	Walls of the Missing
LINDBERG, Evert	N-6-2
LINDEMANN, Harry J	B-3-28
LINDER, Charles O Jr	E-4-8
LINDER, Eugene J	G-18-4
LINDER, Gerard P [224]	G-18-3
LINDHEIM, Donald R [225]	J-4-4
LINDSAY, Bernard E	J-18-11
LINDSAY, Kenneth L [226]	C-3-7
LINDSEY, Nathan F	Walls of the Missing
LINDSEY, Robert J	M-19-2
LINDSEY, Wendling T	P-15-12
LINEAR, Oscar L	E-18-3
LING, Clarence K	Walls of the Missing
LINGO, Arthur M	Walls of the Missing
LINK, Donald R [227]	J-13-11
LINK, Jack E	O-6-15
LINK, William H	C-15-24
LINKENHOKER, Roy L	H-11-26
LINKLETTER, George B	L-3-3
LINN, Francis J	E-10-9
LINTEMAN, Grant K	B-15-29
LINVILL, Harry J	Walls of the Missing
LIOTTA, Aldo	A-6-10
LIOTTI, Carmine G	J-21-11
LIPPITT, Fred A Jr	H-5-4
LIRA, Andrew [228]	J-17-16
LISTER, John J	A-9-16
LISTER, Walter W	A-12-20
LISTVAN, Adam	L-7-2
LITTLE, Ernest W	F-10-6
LITTLE, Kenneth A [229]	C-15-20
LITTLE, Robert M	J-1-3
LITTLE, Roy H [230]	Walls of the Missing
LITTLETON, George	H-7-7

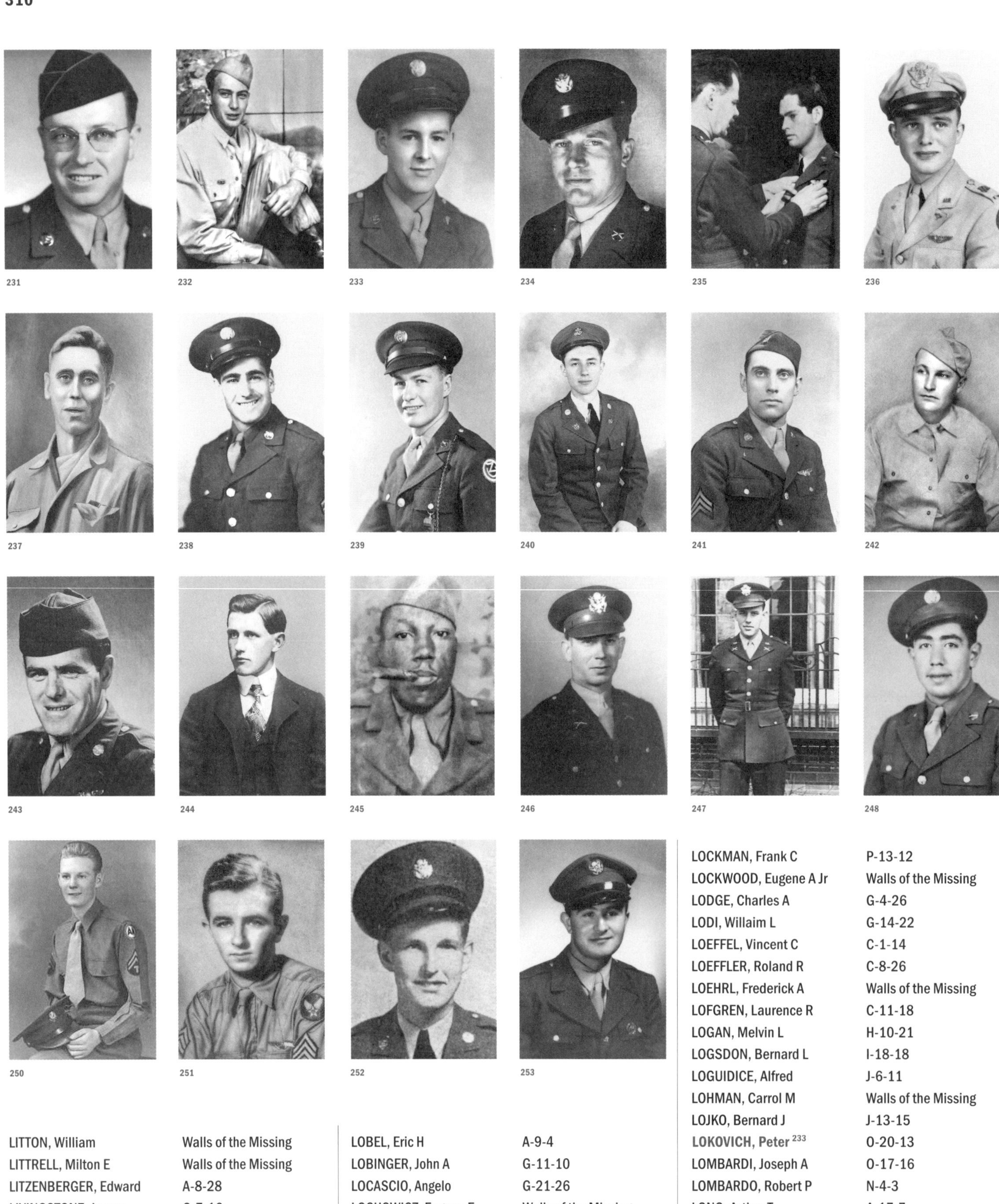

LITTON, William	Walls of the Missing
LITTRELL, Milton E	Walls of the Missing
LITZENBERGER, Edward	A-8-28
LIVINGSTONE, James	C-7-16
LIVSEY, Joe T Jr[231]	H-10-12
LLOYD, Donald R	C-5-13
LLOYD, Robert V	Walls of the Missing
LO CARRO, Anthony L	D-8-28
LOAN, Blake C	I-11-11
LOBEL, Eric H	A-9-4
LOBINGER, John A	G-11-10
LOCASCIO, Angelo	G-21-26
LOCHOWICZ, Eugene E	Walls of the Missing
LOCHRIDGE, Harold D[232]	A-4-18
LOCKE, James A	J-14-10
LOCKE, Stanley N	F-21-5
LOCKEY, Robert B	I-4-5
LOCKHART, Eugene E	Walls of the Missing
LOCKMAN, Frank C	P-13-12
LOCKWOOD, Eugene A Jr	Walls of the Missing
LODGE, Charles A	G-4-26
LODI, Willaim L	G-14-22
LOEFFEL, Vincent C	C-1-14
LOEFFLER, Roland R	C-8-26
LOEHRL, Frederick A	Walls of the Missing
LOFGREN, Laurence R	C-11-18
LOGAN, Melvin L	H-10-21
LOGSDON, Bernard L	I-18-18
LOGUIDICE, Alfred	J-6-11
LOHMAN, Carrol M	Walls of the Missing
LOJKO, Bernard J	J-13-15
LOKOVICH, Peter[233]	O-20-13
LOMBARDI, Joseph A	O-17-16
LOMBARDO, Robert P	N-4-3
LONG, Arthur T	A-17-7
LONG, Clifford E	D-9-30
LONG, Clyde W	M-6-4
LONG, Ellis F	N-4-4
LONG, Lewie B	E-19-12
LONG, Robert L	H-11-27

LONG, Sherman M	B-2-19
LONG, William I[234]	G-8-2
LONGBERG, Floyd E	A-17-32
LONGENBERGER, Curtis R	F-2-11
LONGER, William J	F-11-4
LONGLEY, Eugene L	C-12-15
LONGTON, Gordon T	K-16-11
LOOK, Lester S Jr	B-17-29
LOOK, Robert E	D-11-11
LOOMIS, Cliff D Jr	L-6-11
LOOMIS, Everett W	C-16-27
LOPEZ, Anselmo C	A-11-11
LOPEZ, Richard L	J-5-1
LOPEZ, Victor A[235]	Walls of the Missing
LORD, Bernard H Jr	B-8-11
LORD, Emory L	H-9-27
LORD, John	H-15-22
LORD, Truman R	Walls of the Missing
LORE, Charles R	E-13-17
LORENTZEN, John A	E-5-4
LORIA, Philip	E-8-11
LORING, Allan W	E-9-17
LOSACCO, Michael A	C-5-8
LOTERBAUGH, James G	Walls of the Missing
LOTT, Edgar G	Walls of the Missing
LOTZE, Harold E	C-11-2
LOUCKS, Glenn W	M-7-15
LOUGHMAN, Alan D	B-21-19
LOUGHRAN, Edwin J	Walls of the Missing
LOVE, Earl F	C-3-1
LOVEDAY, Dudley J	A-20-32
LOVELADY, George M	P-5-15
LOVELAND, Leslie I	G-1-26
LOVELY, John B	B-21-1
LOVETT, Dozier S Jr	E-3-5
LOVETT, Jim J	J-8-21
LOVETT, William C	J-8-22
LOWE, Calvin	C-15-10
LOWE, Floyd	E-12-27
LOWE, Laverne F	C-16-9
LOWE, Robert E[236]	A-11-2
LOWELL, Linton L[237]	A-1-14
LOWEN, Victor A	P-5-12
LOWER, Stanley E	J-10-15
LOWERY, Homer D	G-18-11
LOWMAN, Lealin R	B-6-6
LOWNEY, John B	B-18-13
LOWREY, Jewell W	Walls of the Missing
LOWREY, William H C	H-16-20
LOWRY, Richard J	D-14-15
LOYD, Vernon E	N-14-13
LOZICH, Nick	A-17-18
LOZOWSKI, Stanley J	J-2-21
LUBLINSKY, Stanley	Walls of the Missing
LUCAS, Benjamin W	B-13-1
LUCAS, Joseph A[238]	Walls of the Missing
LUCAS, Joseph Sr	O-6-12
LUCAS, Martin L	E-7-18
LUCAS, Vernon	G-18-23
LUCE, Arthur W	Walls of the Missing
LUCERO, Arturo	N-4-5
LUCERO, Gregorio	N-4-6
LUCERO, Steven A	P-6-1
LUCHT, Arno A	D-16-13
LUCKETT, Thomas B	Walls of the Missing
LUDINGTON, Kenneth E	B-8-22
LUDVIKSO, Magnus R	G-3-14
LUDWIGSEN, Peter K	Walls of the Missing
LUICK, Ferdinand W	Walls of the Missing
LUITZ, Erich	K-3-12
LUKACENA, Nicholas	M-17-6
LUKACH, George Jr	B-17-24
LUKACS, James S	D-3-29
LUKASWSKI, Harry[239]	J-12-10
LUKOWITZ, Stanley Jr	Walls of the Missing
LUKOWSKI, Walter F Jr	H-1-10
LUKSCO, William E	E-8-25
LUM, Jerry M	M-16-10
LUND, Gerhard R	D-14-9
LUND, Kenneth A[240]	L-18-10
LUNDELL, Malte	F-8-23
LUNDINE, Homer W[241]	B-19-17
LUNDQUIST, Chester H	H-14-6
LUNDSTROM, John V	A-8-30
LUNDY, William V Jr	C-19-3
LUNETTA, Salvatore J	Walls of the Missing
LUNIEWICZ, Theodore E	Walls of the Missing
LUPOI, John J	G-9-24
LUPTON, Walter R	K-9-18
LUSK, Jack K	L-19-11
LUSK, Robert A Jr	B-18-32
LUSTER, Sam	Walls of the Missing
LUTHI, Adolph	F-9-1
LUTHJE, Henry	K-2-15
LUTKEHAUS, Edward L	Walls of the Missing
LUTKER, Paul V[242]	L-21-1
LUTZ, Gustav T	P-5-17
LUTZ, Herbert	F-12-16
LUTZ, Wilbur L	C-9-10
LYBARGER, Herbert W	J-5-3
LYBRAND, Lawrence E	L-5-4
LYFORD, George E	Walls of the Missing
LYLES, Clarence A	M-18-7
LYMAN, Edward F	Walls of the Missing
LYNAM, John R	B-1-18
LYNCH, John	E-20-20
LYNCH, John E	K-8-8
LYNCH, Leo T Jr	Walls of the Missing
LYNCH, Robert J[243]	B-13-16
LYNCH, William P	C-18-11
LYNDSEY, Joseph M	N-6-14
LYNHAM, Ernest H	H-10-2
LYNN, William F	L-15-3
LYNN, William G Jr	B-5-10
LYONS, Donald E	Walls of the Missing
LYONS, Gerald[244]	L-21-17
LYONS, Lester J	C-15-28
LYONS, William J	C-5-17
LYSKAWA, Sylvester A	G-19-25

M

MAANUM, Raymond L	B-1-25
MABIE, Leslie W	G-6-16
MAC DONALD, Andrew V	C-7-6
MAC DOUGALL, Ralph H	P-22-3
MAC ELWEE, Roy S Jr	F-18-9
MAC GREGOR, Wilburt A	Walls of the Missing
MAC INTOSH, Irving J	O-21-14
MAC KAY, Norman C	H-3-16
MAC KENZIE, John D	K-21-13
MAC LELLAN, Arthur N	C-4-19
MAC LENNAN, Gordon G	A-10-27
MAC LENNAN, Walter E	F-14-24
MAC QUEEN, John C	M-12-5
MAC WILLIAM, Paul A	N-2-13
MACHEN, Thomas S	K-10-5
MACHLOWSKI, Henry	N-12-15
MACHO, Edward F	A-1-22
MACIAG, Valentine J	J-19-16
MACK, Willmore[245]	H-21-1
MACKENZIE, Robert	A-7-28
MACKINDER, Gerald R	G-8-27
MACNAB, William G	O-21-15
MACULLEY, Richard O	O-15-5
MADDEN, Norman W	A-6-25
MADDOX, Jewel C	Walls of the Missing
MADDOX, Ted E	E-11-17
MADELEY, Claude L[246]	N-4-9
MADETZKE, Kenneth H	H-13-23
MADORY, Carl Jr[247]	I-16-13
MADRYGA, Michael	I-17-15
MADSEN, Louis F	K-13-3
MAES, Arthur	E-11-3
MAFFIA, Victor E	Walls of the Missing
MAFFITT, Carl R	E-20-4
MAGALETTA, Fred	P-9-3
MAGANA, Joe C[248]	J-11-12
MAGEE, Edward J	K-17-7
MAGEE, Eugene P	B-16-12
MAGEE, Walter R	N-12-16
MAGIERSKI, Raymond J	H-17-8
MAGLIONE, Everett R	G-10-17
MAGNER, Francis J	Walls of the Missing
MAGNESS, Paul D[249]	Walls of the Missing
MAHAN, Robert H	A-18-11
MAHONEY, Albin A	O-12-8
MAHONEY, Edward T	G-6-25
MAHONEY, Frank J Jr[250]	C-9-9
MAHONEY, Jean A[251]	Walls of the Missing
MAHULA, John J	C-16-22
MAIER, Ronald F[252]	N-3-10
MAINARD, Verman A	D-5-9
MAINS, Robert L	Walls of the Missing
MAISTERMAN, Nathan[253]	A-13-10

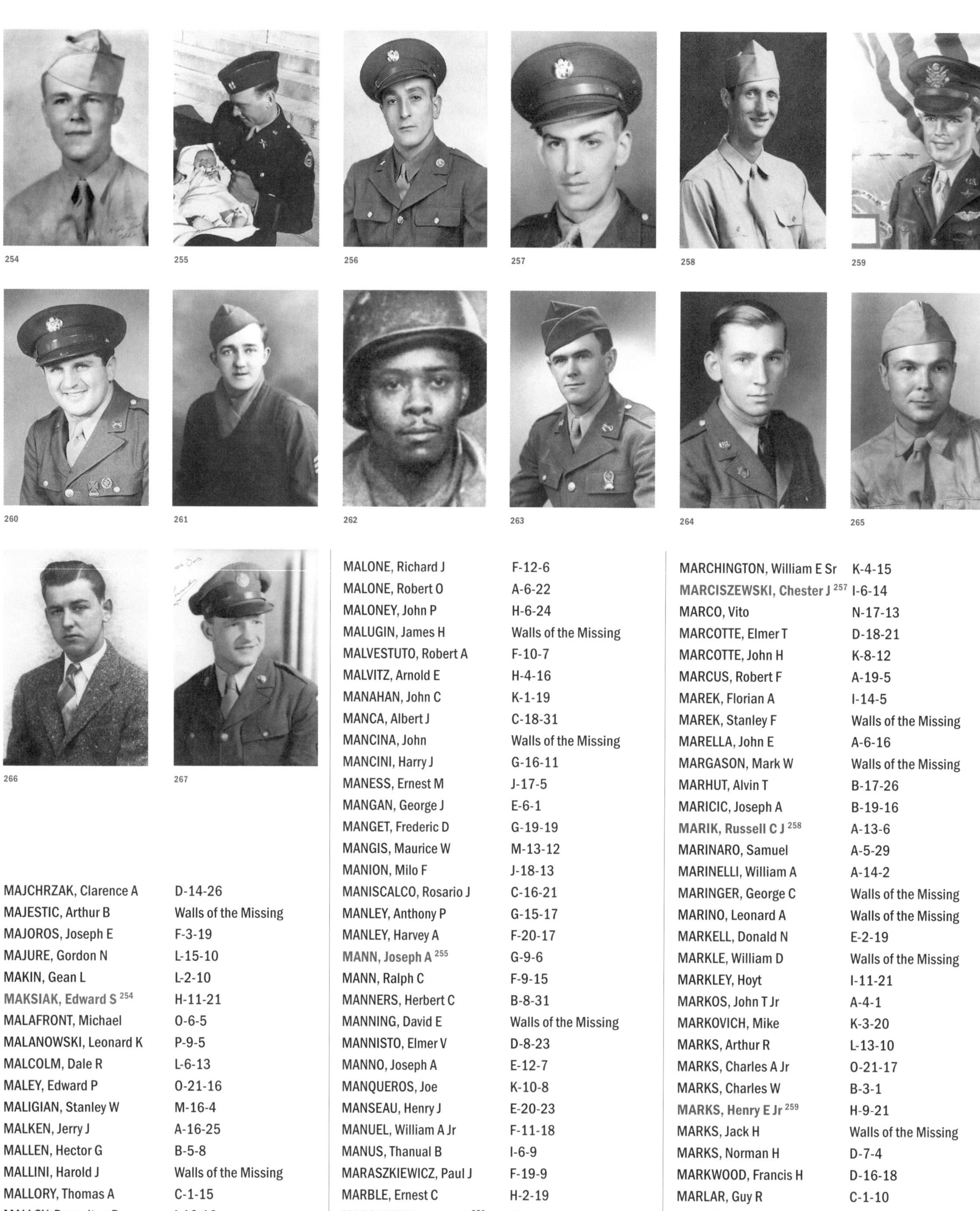

254 255 256 257 258 259

260 261 262 263 264 265

266 267

Name	Location
MAJCHRZAK, Clarence A	D-14-26
MAJESTIC, Arthur B	Walls of the Missing
MAJOROS, Joseph E	F-3-19
MAJURE, Gordon N	L-15-10
MAKIN, Gean L	L-2-10
MAKSIAK, Edward S [254]	H-11-21
MALAFRONT, Michael	O-6-5
MALANOWSKI, Leonard K	P-9-5
MALCOLM, Dale R	L-6-13
MALEY, Edward P	O-21-16
MALIGIAN, Stanley W	M-16-4
MALKEN, Jerry J	A-16-25
MALLEN, Hector G	B-5-8
MALLINI, Harold J	Walls of the Missing
MALLORY, Thomas A	C-1-15
MALLOY, Deovelton R	I-16-16
MALLOY, John E	K-15-4
MALONE, Elbert	E-17-27
MALONE, James W	H-3-11
MALONE, Richard J	F-12-6
MALONE, Robert O	A-6-22
MALONEY, John P	H-6-24
MALUGIN, James H	Walls of the Missing
MALVESTUTO, Robert A	F-10-7
MALVITZ, Arnold E	H-4-16
MANAHAN, John C	K-1-19
MANCA, Albert J	C-18-31
MANCINA, John	Walls of the Missing
MANCINI, Harry J	G-16-11
MANESS, Ernest M	J-17-5
MANGAN, George J	E-6-1
MANGET, Frederic D	G-19-19
MANGIS, Maurice W	M-13-12
MANION, Milo F	J-18-13
MANISCALCO, Rosario J	C-16-21
MANLEY, Anthony P	G-15-17
MANLEY, Harvey A	F-20-17
MANN, Joseph A [255]	G-9-6
MANN, Ralph C	F-9-15
MANNERS, Herbert C	B-8-31
MANNING, David E	Walls of the Missing
MANNISTO, Elmer V	D-8-23
MANNO, Joseph A	E-12-7
MANQUEROS, Joe	K-10-8
MANSEAU, Henry J	E-20-23
MANUEL, William A Jr	F-11-18
MANUS, Thanual B	I-6-9
MARASZKIEWICZ, Paul J	F-19-9
MARBLE, Ernest C	H-2-19
MARCALETTI, Angelo P [256]	N-1-11
MARCEAU, Leo P	C-13-12
MARCHESI, Joseph A	Walls of the Missing
MARCHETTI, Leroy P	Walls of the Missing
MARCHINGTON, William E Sr	K-4-15
MARCISZEWSKI, Chester J [257]	I-6-14
MARCO, Vito	N-17-13
MARCOTTE, Elmer T	D-18-21
MARCOTTE, John H	K-8-12
MARCUS, Robert F	A-19-5
MAREK, Florian A	I-14-5
MAREK, Stanley F	Walls of the Missing
MARELLA, John E	A-6-16
MARGASON, Mark W	Walls of the Missing
MARHUT, Alvin T	B-17-26
MARICIC, Joseph A	B-19-16
MARIK, Russell C J [258]	A-13-6
MARINARO, Samuel	A-5-29
MARINELLI, William A	A-14-2
MARINGER, George C	Walls of the Missing
MARINO, Leonard A	Walls of the Missing
MARKELL, Donald N	E-2-19
MARKLE, William D	Walls of the Missing
MARKLEY, Hoyt	I-11-21
MARKOS, John T Jr	A-4-1
MARKOVICH, Mike	K-3-20
MARKS, Arthur R	L-13-10
MARKS, Charles A Jr	O-21-17
MARKS, Charles W	B-3-1
MARKS, Henry E Jr [259]	H-9-21
MARKS, Jack H	Walls of the Missing
MARKS, Norman H	D-7-4
MARKWOOD, Francis H	D-16-18
MARLAR, Guy R	C-1-10
MARLER, Carl F	O-8-12
MARLOW, Murray [260]	G-21-17
MARLOWE, Joe H	P-21-14
MAROHN, Raymond A	G-20-24

Name	Location
MARQUEZ, Henry E	Walls of the Missing
MARRIOTT, Myles T	N-20-8
MARS, Hymen H	P-2-4
MARSH, Joseph M	Walls of the Missing
MARSH, William H Jr	N-15-11
MARSH, William R	I-3-14
MARSHALL, Albert W	C-8-20
MARSHALL, Charles E	E-19-23
MARSHALL, Colan M	P-4-5
MARSHALL, Darold E	O-3-1
MARSHALL, Durward	I-10-20
MARSHALL, Lemon T	C-14-3
MARSHALL, Murry G	E-10-22
MARSHALL, Thomas M	A-10-18
MARSHALL, Woodrow W	D-12-19
MARSHOK, Edward T	P-6-7
MARSIGLIANO, Frank	Walls of the Missing
MARTEL, Wilfred E	B-10-9
MARTELL, Eugene	B-13-22
MARTIN, Albert E	Walls of the Missing
MARTIN, Albert Jr	P-5-16
MARTIN, Arthur E	L-19-15
MARTIN, Charles A	D-8-7
MARTIN, Chester	K-21-2
MARTIN, Donald	M-15-1
MARTIN, Douglas A	Walls of the Missing
MARTIN, Earl A	D-17-17
MARTIN, Ernest E	Walls of the Missing
MARTIN, Forrest K	O-11-8
MARTIN, Francis B	C-15-13
MARTIN, Frank J	Walls of the Missing
MARTIN, Fred M	L-6-12
MARTIN, Harold J	I-10-15
MARTIN, Hiram K	H-14-10
MARTIN, James C Sr	K-17-18
MARTIN, John J Jr [261]	L-14-20
MARTIN, Johnnie F	N-18-8
MARTIN, Manuel R	C-5-3
MARTIN, Marion F	L-15-13
MARTIN, Orville D	H-1-17
MARTIN, Paul I	A-6-5
MARTIN, Richard G	H-11-19
MARTIN, Robert F	Walls of the Missing
MARTIN, Tom [262]	H-15-2
MARTIN, Torrence V	L-17-8
MARTIN, Wayne F [263]	D-18-26
MARTIN, William J	B-15-19
MARTIN, William J	J-16-5
MARTINEZ, Alfred S	Walls of the Missing
MARTINEZ, Carlos V	C-18-26
MARTINEZ, Charles	H-8-27
MARTINEZ, Luis G	B-6-4
MARTINEZ, Mose	F-21-3
MARTINEZ, Roy J	Walls of the Missing
MARTINI, Thomas P	I-11-22
MARTINO, Joseph A	M-15-10
MARTINSON, Robert George	L-13-1
MARTIRE, Silvio	Walls of the Missing
MARTNER, Lewis P	N-1-6
MARUCAS, Nickolas A	O-18-14
MARUSO, Stanley J	Walls of the Missing
MARX, Donald L	J-3-5
MARX, Harry A	E-20-16
MARX, Kenneth A	F-7-11
MARZ, Raymond R	P-7-10
MARZAILL, Bernard E	F-12-23
MASLIN, Robert L	C-13-28
MASNICA, John J	F-20-20
MASON, George H	I-8-12
MASON, Jack L	O-9-6
MASON, Kenneth E	B-14-2
MASON, Ray H	P-6-8
MASON, Richard E	B-17-22
MASON, Robert L [264]	D-6-30
MASON, Stephen C	Walls of the Missing
MASON, Woodrow H	Walls of the Missing
MASS, Charles	Walls of the Missing
MASSA, Attilio	Walls of the Missing
MASSANELLI, Sonny V	K-16-20
MASSAR, Baptist J	Walls of the Missing
MASSEY, Alfred J	I-1-5
MASSEY, Donald W	F-21-25
MAST, John W	J-15-14
MASTERMAN, Edward W	Walls of the Missing
MASTERS, Russell E	Walls of the Missing
MASTROMONACO, Thomas	E-10-8
MATALIK, George E	I-16-18
MATEY, John	A-4-5
MATH, Frank W	K-6-21
MATHER, Alexander M	D-11-1
MATHERS, Joseph W Jr	N-5-16
MATHEW, Bernard B	P-12-13
MATHEWS, Clyde A	D-11-13
MATHIS, Harry C	M-2-7
MATHIS, Rhude M Jr	Walls of the Missing
MATHIS, Wiliiam K	P-12-9
MATHISEN, Ralph J	F-12-3
MATHISON, Paul L	P-2-13
MATRAS, Joseph A Jr	B-13-9
MATSON, Robert P Jr	F-1-17
MATTAROCHIA, John	M-16-15
MATTERN, Lester A [265]	E-17-19
MATTES, Robert L [266]	B-5-25
MATTHEWS, Clyde L	K-8-3
MATTHEWS, Gilbert E	E-14-11
MATTHEWS, Leslie C	Walls of the Missing
MATTHEWS, Paul C	L-9-12
MATTHEWS, Rudolph S	Walls of the Missing
MATTHEWS, Wiliam G	C-7-20
MATTIS, Le Roy W	H-21-15
MATTISON, Gordon P	A-21-26
MATTOX, Harold E	H-5-24
MATUS, Rudolph W	Walls of the Missing
MATUSCIN, Rudolph J	A-10-25
MATY, Michael A	Walls of the Missing
MATYOLA, Peter	G-9-21
MATZ, Harold D	N-22-1
MAUCK, James M	Walls of the Missing
MAURIN, John F	Walls of the Missing
MAURYCY, Conroy J	A-2-10
MAVIS, Howard H [267]	A-16-8
MAXSON, William H	P-13-7
MAXWELL, Harry J	H-12-5
MAXWELL, Virgil W	H-2-2
MAXWELL, Wallace G	Walls of the Missing
MAY, Andrew G	G-2-26
MAY, Donald G	Walls of the Missing
MAY, Frank J	J-5-18
MAY, Howard Jr	D-10-29
MAY, John E	Walls of the Missing
MAY, Lewis	G-8-9
MAY, Raymond G	J-20-4
MAYALL, James S Jr	Walls of the Missing
MAYBERRY, Paul R	F-11-16
MAYBURY, Leslie E	Walls of the Missing
MAYER, Walter M	Walls of the Missing
MAYERS, Raymond T	E-16-27
MAYES, Norris E	F-9-5
MAYFIELD, Andrew L	N-10-3
MAYFIELD, William M	Walls of the Missing
MAYHEW, Arthur E	D-4-4
MAYKO, Andrew	B-20-25
MAYNARD, Claiborne R	J-9-15
MAYO, Oliver E	D-14-28
MAZIARZ, John J	D-18-1
MAZUR, Irving	Walls of the Missing
MAZUR, Michael F	Walls of the Missing
MAZZAFERRI, Vincent F	H-12-13
MAZZIE, Patrick J	C-3-31
MC ADAMS, Willaim B	Walls of the Missing
MC ADOO, Jesse J	J-15-19
MC ALLISTER, Omer U Jr	O-12-16
MC ALPIN, Virgil R	J-5-5
MC ALPINE, Robert B	P-7-3
MC ANALLY, Bernard M	F-9-23
MC ARTHUR, Donald A	Walls of the Missing
MC BANE, Vance R Jr	H-19-1
MC BEE, Robert W	F-15-5
MC BRIEN, Thomas A	B-19-13
MC BURNEY, Robert W	A-13-25
MC CABE, Clyde L	P-1-12
MC CABE, Harry Lemuel	G-12-1
MC CABE, Joseph P	O-14-8
MC CAFFREY, Philip J	D-20-22
MC CALL, Cleo	P-18-4
MC CALL, Frederic C	F-19-17
MC CALL, John F Jr	B-11-1
MC CANN, Edward B	F-4-21
MC CANN, Kenneth L	D-18-7
MC CANN, Morton L	H-18-14
MC CARSON, Roy M	H-19-23
MC CARTER, Edward C	Walls of the Missing
MC CARTHY, Francis J	Walls of the Missing
MC CARTHY, John C	J-4-1

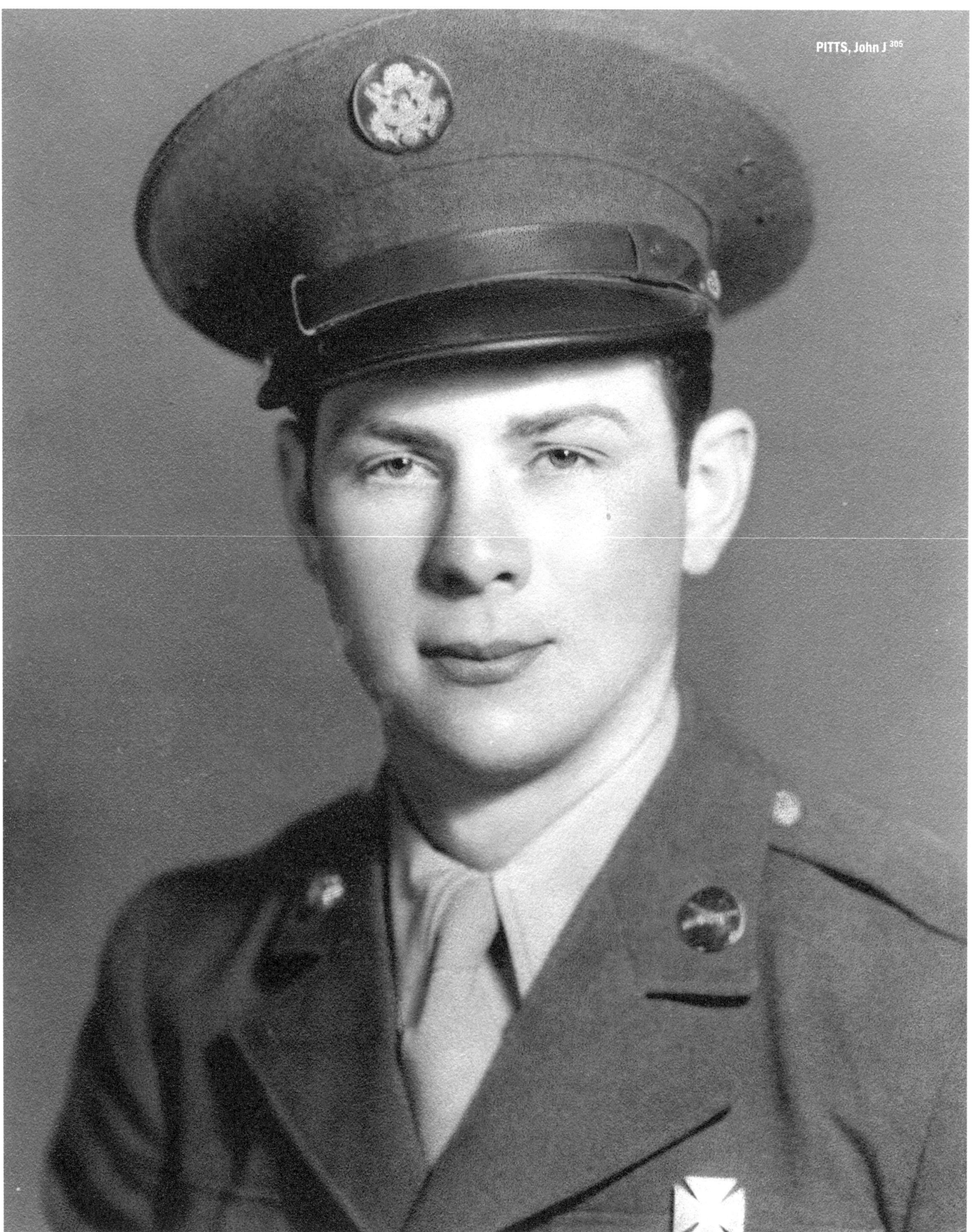

PITTS, John J[305]

MC CARTHY, John J	P-7-16
MC CARTHY, Robert F	D-14-11
MC CARTHY, Timothy J	L-20-9
MC CARTNEY, Robert A	P-16-11
MC CASLIN, Robert J	H-1-5
MC CAULEY, Clarence	J-4-20
MC CLAIN, Francis H	E-7-20
MC CLAIN, William M J	G-21-19
MC CLELLAN, William B	O-7-13
MC CLELLAND, Ewing R	J-3-8
MC CLENEGHAN, Sam A	J-2-13
MC CLOSKY, Adam	Walls of the Missing
MC CLOUD, Thomas J	D-8-6
MC CLOY, Jim T	C-1-31
MC CLURE, James S	A-9-9
MC CLURE, John C	O-13-12
MC CLURE, Warren H	Walls of the Missing
MC CLURKIN, Joseph K	Walls of the Missing
MC COLLUM, Clarence E	G-8-25
MC COLLUM, Ross A	N-22-2
MC COLLUM, Ross M	Walls of the Missing
MC COLLUM, Samuel D	Walls of the Missing
MC COLLUM, William	N-10-6
MC COMB, James D	D-1-7
MC CONNAHA, Wendell K	C-1-11
MC CONNELL, Donald W	L-5-8
MC CONNELL, Peter S	C-2-19
MC COOL, Jack D	A-10-5
MC CORD, Gerald D	H-16-11
MC CORMICK, Hugh R	Walls of the Missing
MC CORMICK, Ray J	D-2-12
MC CORMICK, Roy H	G-12-27
MC CORMICK, William M	D-2-10
MC COY, Dennis J	H-10-19
MC COY, Houston G	H-17-14
MC COY, Larry D	Walls of the Missing
MC COY, Lawrence Jr	G-15-13
MC COY, Richard J	L-14-16
MC CRADY, Aubra N	E-5-24
MC CRAW, John H	K-14-16
MC CRAY, Elvin L	N-8-17
MC CRAY, William W	Walls of the Missing
MC CREARY, Raymond E	L-15-18
MC CREERY, Donald L	N-17-12
MC CROSKY, William N	Walls of the Missing
MC CUE, Robert F	D-9-6
MC CUEN, Theodore J	C-14-8
MC CULLICK, Harry W	K-6-9
MC CULLOUGH, Charles	H-20-18
MC CULLOUGH, Pearl R	O-15-13
MC CULLY, Marion M	H-10-6
MC CULLY, William C	P-2-9
MC CUNE, Robert N	Walls of the Missing
MC CUTCHEN, Doyle C	J-3-20
MC DADE, Paul I	J-5-2
MC DANIEL, John C	B-16-28
MC DANNEL, Wesley H	N-22-3
MC DERMOTT, Joseph E	A-3-25
MC DERMOTT, Richard Z	D-18-9
MC DERMOTT, Rodney J	L-1-17
MC DONALD, Kenneth C	C-16-5
MC DONALD, Ralph L	Walls of the Missing
MC DONALD, Russell J	Walls of the Missing
MC DONALD, Thomas C	E-18-6
MC DONALD, William	E-3-7
MC DONALD, William A	L-8-17
MC DONELL, Alexander A Jr	Walls of the Missing
MC DONELL, Kenneth J	F-6-6
MC DONNELL, Bernard	P-10-13
MC DONNELL, John E	M-15-6
MC DONOUGH, John E	F-14-25
MC DOWELL, Ira P	L-6-18
MC DOWELL, James A	F-19-21
MC DOWELL, Roy L	K-13-2
MC ELROY, Goodwin W	M-13-9
MC ELROY, Walter E	H-1-24
MC ELROY, William J	L-20-16
MC ERLANE, Paul E	Walls of the Missing
MC FADDEN, De Lee	A-16-27
MC FADDEN, Patrick M	L-2-3
MC FADDEN, William S	E-8-6
MC FADDIN, Robert E	Walls of the Missing
MC FARLAND, Martin J	F-7-7
MC FARLAND, Richard R	Walls of the Missing
MC FARLAND, William P	H-18-1
MC FATHER, Adrian E	E-9-20
MC GARRY, John J	A-21-12
MC GEE, Gerald	N-17-8
MC GEE, John E	Walls of the Missing
MC GEE, Leonard J	L-20-18
MC GEE, Willard R	J-9-3
MC GHEE, William E	D-18-25
MC GILL, Clement F	H-17-13
MC GILL, Donald A	C-10-19
MC GILL, Elliton N	I-5-9
MC GILLIVRAY, Frank W	J-10-2
MC GILLIVRAY, Harold A	Walls of the Missing
MC GILVRAY, Kenneth E	J-3-6
MC GINLEY, William J	E-21-24
MC GINNIS, William R	D-10-18
MC GINTY, William D	G-19-27
MC GLASSON, Edward T	H-6-16
MC GLINCHEY, Paul C	I-3-9
MC GLYNN, John G	Walls of the Missing
MC GOLDRICK, James C	H-9-23
MC GOWAN, Frank B	L-1-21
MC GRATH, Patrick J	K-9-2
MC GREGOR, John R	N-9-2
MC GREW, Joseph L Jr	A-9-23
MC GUINESS, George V	Walls of the Missing
MC GUIRE, Denis J	I-20-14
MC GUIRE, Joseph P	K-8-19
MC GUIRE, Robert E	Walls of the Missing
MC GUIRE, William O	Walls of the Missing
MC GUIRE, Willis R	L-15-19
MC HENRY, Jack A	J-13-8
MC HENRY, Ralph C	N-4-10
MC HUGH, Edward M	Walls of the Missing
MC HUGH, John P	G-1-17
MC HUGH, John T	K-19-22
MC ILVEEN, Clarence S	Walls of the Missing
MC INERNEY, William T	C-1-7
MC INNIS, Hugh L	H-18-18
MC INTYRE, Arzie	K-21-9
MC INTYRE, John T	F-4-27
MC INTYRE, Neil W	I-15-17
MC INTYRE, Roemer Jr	C-21-1
MC KAIN, Lloyd J	E-4-10
MC KAY, Donald R	D-14-18
MC KEE, Arnold	Walls of the Missing
MC KEE, John J	H-4-25
MC KEE, Merwin	I-1-20
MC KEE, Robert D	Walls of the Missing
MC KEE, William C III	Walls of the Missing
MC KEE, William J Jr	Walls of the Missing
MC KELVIN, Lloyd H	A-15-32
MC KELVY, Edward A Jr	E-21-11
MC KENDRICK, Arnold S	C-19-7
MC KENDRY, Norman J	G-6-23
MC KENNA, William A Jr	B-16-29
MC KENNEY, Anita R	N-19-7
MC KENZIE, Harry T	B-13-26
MC KEON, Matthew L	Walls of the Missing
MC KEOWN, Francis J	A-3-3
MC KEOWN, Thomas F	P-14-5
MC KIE, Marvin B	Walls of the Missing
MC KINLEY, Albert L	A-18-20
MC KINLEY, David S	G-11-3
MC KINNEY, Daniel L	I-16-1
MC KINNIE, Thomas H Jr	A-13-28
MC KNIGHT, Lee R	A-15-25
MC LAIN, Neil J	E-3-24
MC LAREN, William J	L-12-18
MC LAUGHLIN, Barrett T	H-4-21
MC LAUGHLIN, Donald C	E-9-16
MC LAUGHLIN, Holland	I-9-20
MC LAUGHLIN, John T	C-5-31
MC LEAN, Aloysious J	Walls of the Missing
MC LEAN, Harry L	A-21-14
MC LEAN, William J	P-15-9
MC LEMORE, Paul L	Walls of the Missing
MC LENDON, Jay D Jr	L-11-4
MC LEOD, Rufus J	J-1-21
MC LINDEN, Charles J	L-20-15
MC LOUD, Emmett L Jr	C-17-10
MC MAHON, Richard P	D-10-13
MC MAHON, Thomas H	D-7-7
MC MANIMAN, Thomas E	H-21-10
MC MANN, George F Jr	N-22-4
MC MANUS, Frederick W	H-3-4
MC MENAMIN, John F Jr	J-7-5
MC MILLAN, Charles H	C-7-24
MC MILLAN, James A	G-14-5
MC NABB, Thomas G	N-14-1

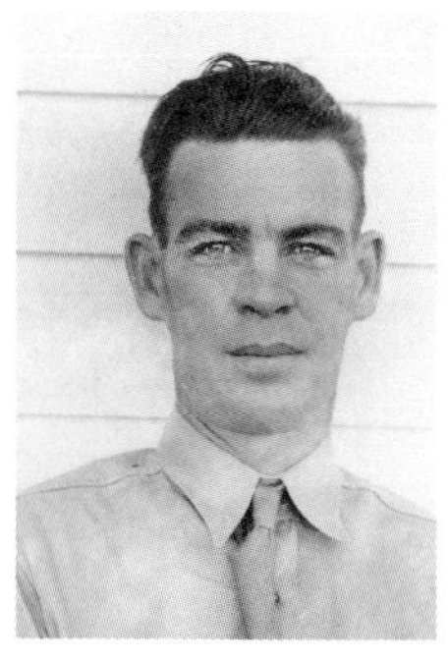
268

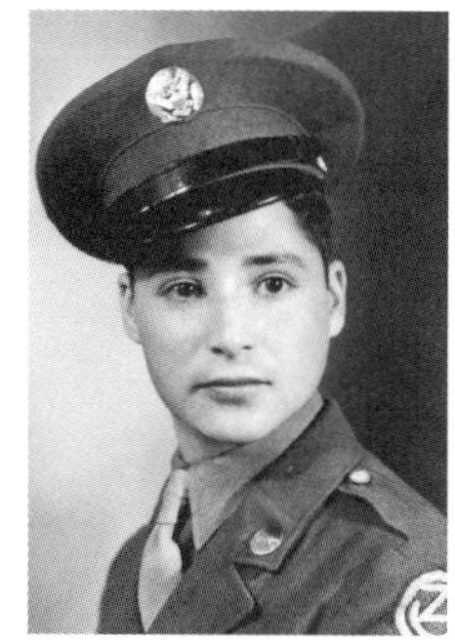
269

MC NAMARA, Owen J F-12-10
MC NAMARA, Robert J Walls of the Missing
MC NAMEE, Raymond T E-6-8
MC NATT, Wylie Jr L-7-13
MC NEAL, David D D-17-32
MC NEELEY, Cicero J Walls of the Missing
MC NEIL, James S B-13-8
MC NEILL, Hugh E-5-23
MC NEILL, Lionel L J-19-5
MC NIVICK, Stanley V D-10-8
MC NUTT, Maurice M P-19-13
MC NUTT, Robert L Jr Walls of the Missing
MC PEEK, Russell E E-20-19
MC PETERS, David E D-5-15
MC PHEE, Jay B A-3-27
MC QUADE, Edwin J H-12-19
MC SHAFFERY, Joseph F G-10-2
MC TAGGART, Donald H-5-26
MC TAMNEY, James H D-16-5
MC VAY, Noel W Walls of the Missing
MC VAY, Sam E D-19-29
MC VICKER, Donald T M-10-15
MC WHIRTER, Oscar F M-1-2
MC WHORTER, Jerry C-3-28
MC WILLIAMS, Frank X M-1-7
MC WILLIAMS, James W L-12-22
MEAD, Lynn H Jr G-8-21
MEADE, Russell O K-21-22
MEADE, William J Walls of the Missing
MEADOR, John H P-7-5
MEADOWS, Frank H M-10-3
MEADOWS, William D A-3-32
MEAKER, Merril A M-16-1
MECK, John W B-9-7
MECKLEY, John K D-15-32
MEDDLEY, Harold J B-9-23
MEDEIROS, Frank J-16-13
MEDFORD, William E B-14-29
MEDLEY, Clarence E P-8-1
MEDRANO, Jose J-21-18
MEECH, Richard A Walls of the Missing

MEEHAN, Thomas A L-4-6
MEEKIN, Clarence E Walls of the Missing
MEEKS, Thurman Walls of the Missing
MEETING, Robert L E-6-5
MEGGINSON, Oscar H P-18-8
MEIER, Roy C Walls of the Missing
MEIGS, Gates T M-8-4
MELEGH, Julius Z D-8-12
MELI, Joseph A Jr Walls of the Missing
MELLERS, Paul E H-18-10
MELLON, James B Jr L-20-21
MELNIK, John R I-4-21
MELOMO, Salvatore J Walls of the Missing
MELQUIST, John H B-18-19
MELTON, Emmett M Jr Walls of the Missing
MELTON, Frederick D D-10-6
MELTON, John F B-7-27
MELTON, Prentis H-3-7
MELVIN, George R F-4-25
MELVIN, Norman E K-20-13
MELZER, Louis E B-8-23
MENDEZ, Trino A-4-14
MERCER, Garry D Walls of the Missing
MEREDITH, Edward D J-16-17
MERIT, Thomas E Walls of the Missing
MERKEL, Anthony W A-20-18
MERKOSKY, John P Walls of the Missing
MERKOVICH, Frank S Walls of the Missing
MERLINO, Alfred J G-9-1
MERRELL, Cecil R G-21-15
MERRILL, Leon H B-4-6
MERRILL, Manley J J-20-15
MERRITT, Thomas J G-3-10
MERSHON, George L I-21-11
MERVYN, Richard C G-10-23
MERVYN, Robert D G-10-22
MERWEDE, Albert K G-4-10
MESCHIEVITZ, Theodore Walls of the Missing
MESSAMORE, Jess A H-21-5
MESSING, Harry P-20-9
MESTJIAN, Robert A A-20-23
METROZ, Lee M H-12-20
METZ, Richard T C-21-23
MEYER, Cyril J B-2-4
MEYER, Henry H D-12-15
MEYER, James W D-11-3
MEYER, Joseph H O-5-8
MEYER, Joseph L D-16-24
MEYER, Melvin H H-11-6
MEYER, Paul D K-18-6
MEYER, Rudolph H A-10-30
MEYER, Sidney B G-14-9
MEYER, Victor W Walls of the Missing
MEYERS, James J Walls of the Missing
MEYERS, Melvin A-17-15
MEYRICK, David L H-11-10
MEYRING, Herbert A Walls of the Missing
MEZZETTI, Peter A E-14-13

MIADLE, Joseph J L-20-17
MICEK, John M Walls of the Missing
MICHAEL, Maurice O E-13-6
MICHALAK, Marion L-14-2
MICHAUD, Aurele J K-12-17
MICHAUD, Raymond J Walls of the Missing
MICHEL, Joseph I-6-20
MICHELS, Carroll A M-19-3
MICHON, Stanislaus J D-9-29
MIDDLEKAUFF, Raymond Walls of the Missing
MIDKIFF, Frank L K-14-15
MIDKIFF, Howard A K-13-16
MIDZINSKI, Stanley J L-10-14
MIELOSZYK, Frank E I-21-1
MIER, Phillip J D-19-5
MIEZIS, Charles A D-20-28
MIGLIORE, Thomas N P-8-8
MIHALIC, Steve J E-16-16
MIKLICH, Ivan J F-9-11
MIKLICH, Louis F F-9-12
MIKOLAJCZAK, Joseph A Jr I-15-22
MILBURY, Norman W B-21-7
MILCHAK, Elmer A E-3-1
MILDE, Robert C E-1-22
MILES, Vincent P L-5-14
MILES, William G F-15-14
MILESKI, Henry E G-5-10
MILEWSKI, Casimer A-20-21
MILISZEWSKI, Eugene J I-4-18
MILLAN, Carlos Walls of the Missing
MILLAN, William W Jr Walls of the Missing
MILLAR, Samuel C D-20-14
MILLARD, Donald L B-16-26
MILLER, Albert F Jr Walls of the Missing
MILLER, Alvin S P-18-1
MILLER, Andrew B-3-6
MILLER, Archie H J-10-5
MILLER, Arthur A-20-2
MILLER, Athel J Walls of the Missing
MILLER, Ben L B-20-12
MILLER, Carl H I-19-8
MILLER, Cecil F A-3-28
MILLER, Charles N-4-8
MILLER, Charles C Walls of the Missing
MILLER, David H Walls of the Missing
MILLER, Doyle C O-13-11
MILLER, Edward L B-9-3
MILLER, Frederic W D-10-3
MILLER, Galen E Jr M-5-17
MILLER, George Walls of the Missing
MILLER, Gordon F A-18-8
MILLER, Harold A B-18-20
MILLER, Harry L Walls of the Missing
MILLER, Harvey L Jr D-2-2
MILLER, Herman H Jr Walls of the Missing
MILLER, Howard J D-2-20
MILLER, Jack C-10-29
MILLER, Jerome W F-12-21

Name	Location
MILLER, Jesse R Jr	B-6-1
MILLER, John E	C-18-22
MILLER, John R	Walls of the Missing
MILLER, Joseph A	G-3-24
MILLER, Joseph H	A-10-10
MILLER, Judson C	E-5-25
MILLER, Kenneth E	Walls of the Missing
MILLER, Kenneth R	E-12-14
MILLER, Kent F	Walls of the Missing
MILLER, Lawrence	E-14-17
MILLER, Le Moyne	Walls of the Missing
MILLER, Lee S Jr	Walls of the Missing
MILLER, Leo M	M-12-14
MILLER, Martin F	K-3-11
MILLER, Maynard M	K-5-6
MILLER, Philip T	L-13-15
MILLER, Raymond L	P-16-8
MILLER, Richard C	Walls of the Missing
MILLER, Robert	D-13-27
MILLER, Robert A	Walls of the Missing
MILLER, Robert B	H-16-12
MILLER, Robert F	C-13-11
MILLER, Robert V	E-10-25
MILLER, Roy	B-16-13
MILLER, Roy C	G-8-10
MILLER, Verl E	H-6-4
MILLER, W D	J-21-9
MILLER, Warren R	G-21-25
MILLER, William B	H-14-4
MILLER, William H	Walls of the Missing
MILLER, William M	E-12-6
MILLER, Wilton D	H-7-15
MILLER, Winfred E	J-21-12
MILLHOUSEN, George R	Walls of the Missing
MILLIGAN, Joe W	F-21-9
MILLIGAN, Philip L	H-20-23
MILLIMAN, Robert A	H-15-13
MILLIMAN, Robert G	C-5-27
MILLING, Bennie L	Walls of the Missing
MILLNER, Jack E	A-18-23
MILLS, Ben F	N-7-11
MILLS, Clifford M	Walls of the Missing
MILLS, Fredrick S	A-15-28
MILLS, Harold E	A-21-24
MILLS, Joseph C	B-5-4
MILLS, Raymond K Jr	K-2-17
MILLS, William C	K-10-1
MILLSAP, Eugene B	D-1-18
MILLSTONE, Seymour	N-15-12
MILNE, Britton J [268]	M-15-13
MILNER, Thomas G	N-4-7
MILONAS, John C	L-13-5
MIMS, Reuben P	P-1-9
MINER, Wilbur C	E-2-8
MINETTI, Anito	B-3-21
MINGINO, Bernard G	D-8-30
MINGONET, Aime M	Walls of the Missing
MINTON, Daymon J	G-11-14
MINTON, Willie	C-6-31
MIRABAL, Vincenti J	B-8-19
MIRABELLA, Paul	J-15-1
MISCEVICH, Joseph	L-13-8
MISCHIK, Joseph M	L-14-19
MISCHISSIN, Nicholas	F-11-13
MISHAGA, Frank	O-18-8
MISQUEZ, Albert	A-12-12
MISSEY, Everett J	Walls of the Missing
MISURACA, Valentino A	F-16-16
MITCHELL, Anthony B	O-8-6
MITCHELL, Donald L	C-9-16
MITCHELL, Fred F	E-20-7
MITCHELL, Harold A	N-19-2
MITCHELL, John C	E-15-14
MITCHELL, Robert G	Walls of the Missing
MITCHELL, Robert Mazyck	K-9-7
MITCHELL, Vernie L	F-5-8
MITCHELL, William E	C-16-31
MITTS, Robert	F-13-22
MIXER, John J	B-18-29
MIXON, James C	Walls of the Missing
MIZERAK, Joseph W	G-1-12
MIZIANTY, Frederick M	L-3-17
MIZZELL, Charles A	A-21-2
MLYNSKI, Konstanty F	H-2-3
MOAK, Hudson J	C-5-15
MOAN, Charles S	N-14-4
MOCCO, Clyde F	L-9-9
MOCIO, Edward	B-21-13
MOCK, Donald E	Walls of the Missing
MOCK, James D	A-5-22
MOCKLER, Robert E	A-2-12
MODA, Anthony J	F-21-22
MODLIN, Richard E	N-22-5
MODZEL, Walter A	G-4-9
MOEN, Richard S	L-3-4
MOFFETT, Walter S	F-6-13
MOGUSH, Paul T	Walls of the Missing
MOHLER, Norman S	C-12-16
MOHR, Leonard F	L-16-18
MOHS, Peter M	A-18-9
MOLES, Frank P	C-5-5
MOLLER, Russell A	C-18-24
MOLNAR, George	G-20-21
MOLNAR, Robert S	Walls of the Missing
MOLONEY, Edwin J	B-4-13
MONAHAN, Christopher	H-8-20
MONAHAN, Edward J	H-17-22
MONFORD, Joseph M	M-6-7
MONGES, Frank L	J-13-5
MONIZ, Daniel	Walls of the Missing
MONK, Wesley J	O-17-17
MONNES, Fred	Walls of the Missing
MONSON, Charles F	I-7-17
MONSON, Douglas	Walls of the Missing
MONTANA, Roland A	K-9-8
MONTELEON, Joseph J	I-4-6
MONTERIO, Francis T	N-16-4
MONTGOMERY, Ellis E	I-15-11
MONTGOMERY, James W	M-17-3
MONTGOMERY, Warren A	H-20-7
MONTGOMERY, William F	H-1-7
MONTICONE, Julius J	I-9-11
MONTOYA, Ben [269]	A-7-2
MONZA, Vincent J	D-6-32
MONZINGO, Garland W	C-10-16
MONZINGO, Jake S	N-2-12
MOODY, Eleazar L	Walls of the Missing
MOODY, Harold E	G-9-16
MOODY, Jacob G	B-20-1
MOON, Calvin J	J-7-1
MOON, Charles E	A-5-15
MOON, Ivan R	M-20-15
MOONEY, John L Jr	A-17-20
MOONEY, Thomas C	P-14-10
MOORE, Bill F	G-9-27
MOORE, Charles E	N-9-12
MOORE, Charles P	Walls of the Missing
MOORE, Clarence C	P-4-2
MOORE, Claude T	C-9-2
MOORE, Daniel M	D-5-28
MOORE, Frank	P-10-11
MOORE, Gardner H	H-18-24
MOORE, George H	J-11-21
MOORE, Herbert E	A-17-2
MOORE, Hubert A	E-4-16
MOORE, Hughlan L	G-13-25
MOORE, J D	Walls of the Missing
MOORE, James H	J-10-8
MOORE, John W	I-1-8
MOORE, Kenneth H	Walls of the Missing
MOORE, Lamoine C	Walls of the Missing
MOORE, Lawrence R	Walls of the Missing
MOORE, Lucas E	C-9-19
MOORE, Mervin S	D-20-19
MOORE, Owen W	A-9-25
MOORE, Phillip M	I-15-12
MOORE, Raymond A	C-10-6
MOORE, Robert E	K-17-12
MOORE, Robert P	A-13-4
MOORE, Robert V	A-15-31
MOORE, Roy R	A-11-21
MOORE, Russell G	G-12-3
MOORE, Thomas J	P-18-15
MOORE, Vincent	B-8-5
MOORE, Walter J Jr	C-20-28
MOORE, Wayne H	E-18-20
MOORMAN, Floyd F	P-22-1
MORALES, Jesus E	B-17-7
MORAN, Francis V	F-8-19
MORAN, Henry E	B-11-18
MORAN, Jakie P	I-4-7
MORAN, James R	A-13-32
MORAN, Paul J	C-3-29
MORAN, Robert B	O-12-14

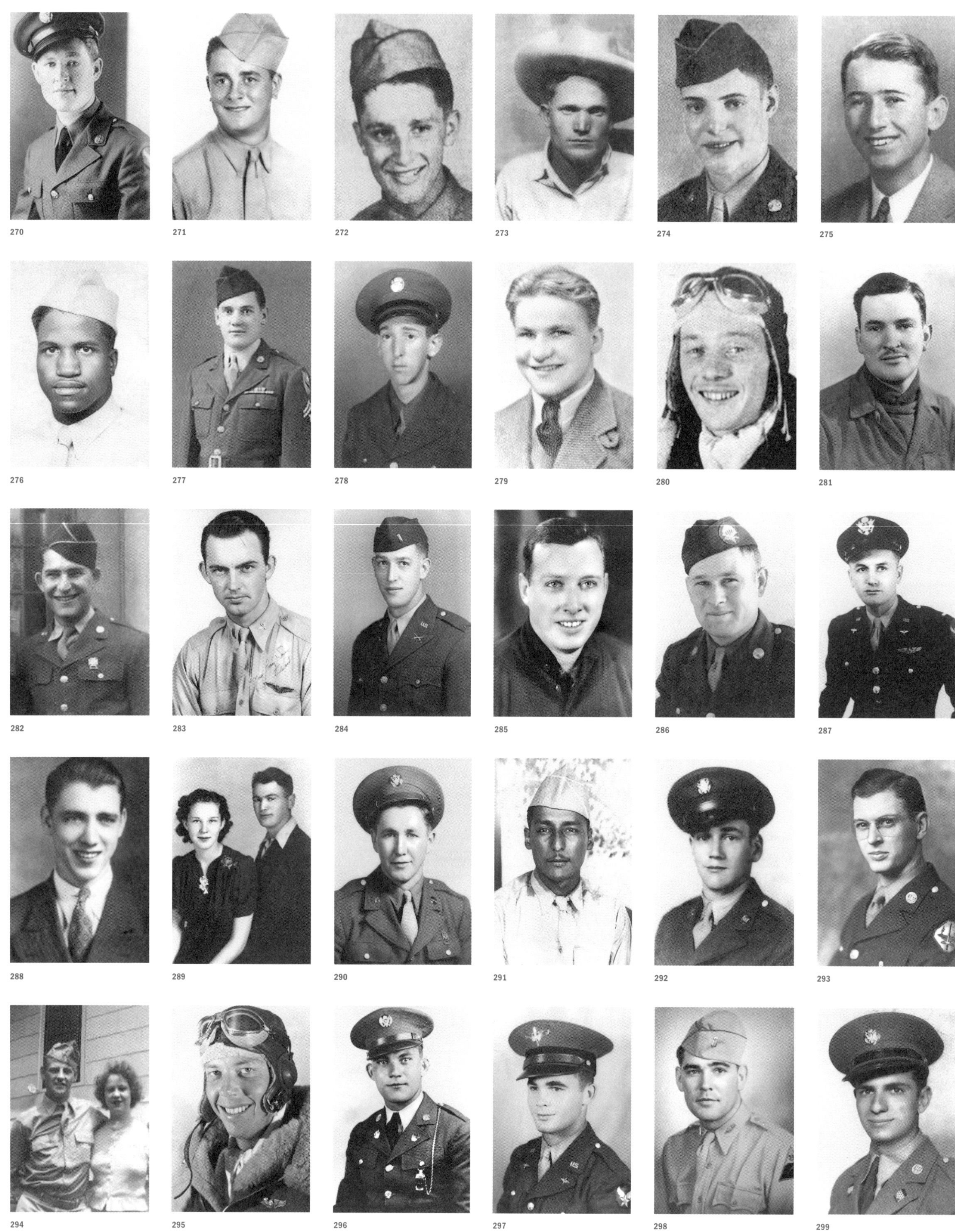

270 271 272 273 274 275

276 277 278 279 280 281

282 283 284 285 286 287

288 289 290 291 292 293

294 295 296 297 298 299

MORANG, William W M-10-1
MORAVEC, Adolf D-8-26
MORBY, Roy S [270] K-4-6
MORELAND, Dale J E-7-21
MORELLI, Philip J J-15-6
MORENO, Basil H L-8-12
MORENO, Emilio Jr C-9-3
MORETTI, Albert A [271] A-21-6
MORGAN, Aston H III [272] D-16-10
MORGAN, Earl G-15-18
MORGAN, General L Sr [273] M-1-4
MORGAN, Richard G-16-16
MORGAN, Robert A A-12-22
MORGART, John R [274] B-10-25
MORIARTY, John C [275] C-12-17
MORIARTY, John D B-10-29
MORNEAU, Francis J N-22-6
MORNEWECK, Robert E E-20-17
MORRIS, Arthur J L-9-17
MORRIS, Christopher A G-2-19
MORRIS, Daniel T M-10-11
MORRIS, Deris L B-3-11
MORRIS, Eugene A A-4-24
MORRIS, Haskell L D-2-29
MORRIS, Henry E D-3-31
MORRIS, John J O-4-15
MORRIS, John V G-5-1
MORRIS, Julius W [276] J-18-10
MORRIS, Richard E B-5-1
MORRIS, Robert F L-4-2
MORRIS, Robert H C-11-31
MORRIS, Robert L G-14-23
MORRIS, T B M-13-2
MORRIS, William T [277] D-2-23
MORRIS, Zack T B-17-12
MORRISON, Doris K-15-11
MORRISON, George W P-12-11
MORRISON, Hugh R B-11-14
MORRISON, Richard P Walls of the Missing
MORRONE, Alfonso F-11-6
MORROW, Cletus E N-22-7
MORROW, Kendall L Walls of the Missing
MORSE, James E B-3-18
MORSE, Melvin R A-4-3
MORSE, Robert W Jr [278] E-21-14
MORSE, Russell C C-17-19
MORSE, Verne V C-1-26
MORSTADT, Frederick F B-7-22
MORTON, Bernard L E-16-14
MORTON, Leroy E Walls of the Missing
MORTON, Marion M P-1-15
MORTON, Odison J I-14-19
MORTON, Ralph W Jr E-15-20
MOSBACHER, Stephen S I-11-19
MOSEBACH, George F F-3-17
MOSELEY, William H H-14-14
MOSHER, Elza [279] F-1-27
MOSHER, Harvey R L-3-13
MOSHIER, Robert L Walls of the Missing
MOSKALUK, Wasil O-18-3
MOSLEY, Henry H Walls of the Missing
MOSS, Carroll E [280] M-22-15
MOSS, Joe E E-18-23
MOSS, John D-9-32
MOTE, Kingston H K-11-17
MOTT, Harold R Walls of the Missing
MOTTERN, Robert L Walls of the Missing
MOTTS, Ross E C-20-30
MOUNCE, Arthur S A-11-30
MOURER, Ralph L Walls of the Missing
MOUTON, Jerome E D-18-2
MOUTON, John [281] K-4-2
MOUTOUX, James W C-7-26
MOVSESSIAN, Souren D O-14-17
MOWERS, Charles H O-7-16
MOWRER, Richard G A-1-25
MOYER, Henry K [282] A-21-30
MOYER, Philip J C-10-13
MOZEK, Egan, J L-18-16
MROWINSKI, Aldred R C-4-5
MUDAR, Walter E-14-23
MUELLER, Edward T [283] Walls of the Missing
MUELLER, John J K-12-22
MUIRHEAD, William J E-11-23
MULANAX, K C B-1-26
MULDER, John T [284] Walls of the Missing
MULDOWNEY, John W E-5-10
MULHALL, Vincent J [285] A-20-28
MULL, Charles A Walls of the Missing
MULLANE, Martin J F-5-5
MULLEN, Clarence L A-12-14
MULLEN, Fred L G-15-8
MULLEN, John P H-13-17
MULLEN, John T D-21-19
MULLEN, Paul N [286] H-3-12
MULLER, Bernard D I-21-16
MULLIGAN, Joseph G Walls of the Missing
MULLINNEX, Harold H P-16-13
MULLINS, Daniel I B-3-25
MULLINS, Richard M [287] Walls of the Missing
MULLINS, Robert A G-2-3
MULLOY, Martin J D-18-19
MUNCY, James A [288] J-11-19
MUNDEE, Albert R Jr F-21-24
MUNGER, Lyle [289] C-17-16
MUNJOY, Richard P K-14-20
MUNN, David L [290] G-6-17
MUNNINGS, George H Jr O-11-12
MUNSON, Robert B Jr M-1-3
MURCHISON, Ivan E C-17-22
MURDOCK, Davis D Walls of the Missing
MURNAN, Merlin P O-15-7
MURO, Lawrence M [291] C-12-14
MURPHY, Charles T G-9-12
MURPHY, Edward C Jr [292] M-19-17
MURPHY, Edward H O-19-10
MURPHY, Francis J C-16-19
MURPHY, Jerry M M-14-5
MURPHY, John J F-9-22
MURPHY, John J P-9-12
MURPHY, John S Walls of the Missing
MURPHY, John T G-1-2
MURPHY, Joseph L I-15-7
MURPHY, Leonard Walls of the Missing
MURPHY, Patrick F E-18-22
MURPHY, William C N-22-8
MURPHY, William D A-13-23
MURRAY, Donald C [293] A-16-26
MURRAY, James [294] P-7-15
MURRAY, Kenneth G [295] Walls of the Missing
MURRAY, Lawrence J A-9-5
MURRAY, Patrick F M-15-8
MURRAY, Robert I Walls of the Missing
MURRAY, Vernard R Walls of the Missing
MURRY, George B Walls of the Missing
MURY, Vern E M-14-14
MUSA, James H M-17-13
MUSCENTE, Anthony P-12-14
MUSOLFF, Leroy O [296] C-10-4
MUSSO, Baptist Jr B-6-26
MUSTOE, Albert E [297] D-16-20
MUSZYNSKI, Walter J F-19-26
MUYSKENS, Edward S B-13-23
MYERS, Carroll C Jr P-10-1
MYERS, Cletis P C-17-3
MYERS, Conwell [298] L-13-9
MYERS, Everette L P-2-14
MYERS, George W Walls of the Missing
MYERS, Hugh M D-10-7
MYERS, John P G-7-10
MYERS, Joseph F Walls of the Missing
MYERS, Norman G I-14-10
MYERS, Patrick B-5-22
MYERS, Paul H G-16-3
MYERS, William H Jr F-9-3
MYERS, William R M-2-11
MYKIETYN, Genio K-19-21
MYRAND, Harry J-7-20

N

NACARATO, Patrick [299] M-14-12
NADEL, Rudolph F-18-22
NADER, Francis J P-21-13
NADLER, Paul J N-19-16
NAFZ, Harry C E-21-9
NAGY, Andrew R M-8-1
NAGY, Joseph E-14-10
NAIL, Archie N G-10-9
NAILS, James H P-20-11
NALL, John B Walls of the Missing
NANKO, John Jr F-6-3
NANNERY, Edward J F-19-23
NAPIER, Vernon J-2-4
NARAMORE, Maurice J A-13-11

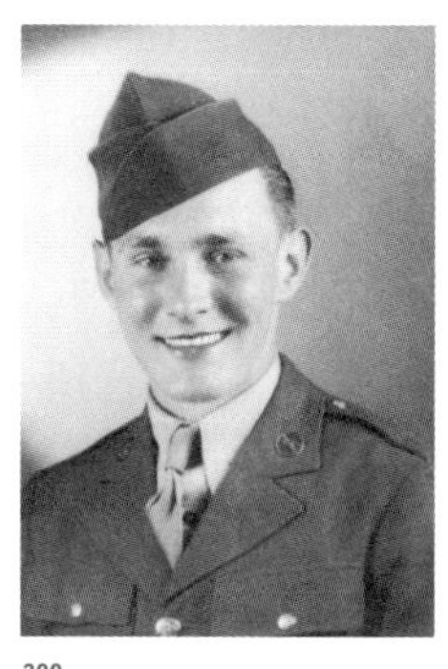
300

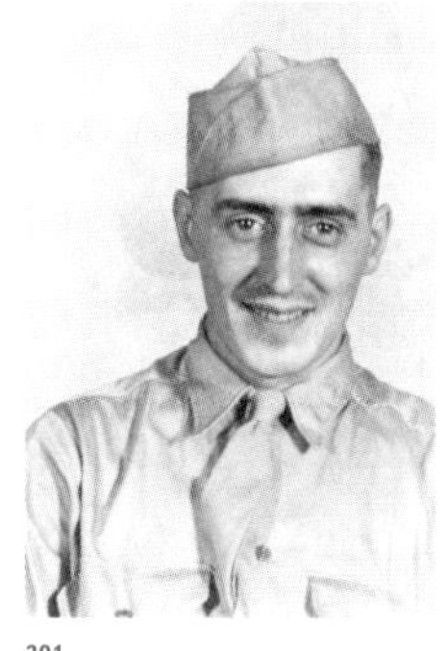
301

NARDONE, Armundo A	D-4-12
NAREWSKI, John F	K-14-4
NASH, John L	B-19-10
NASH, Joseph	O-14-4
NASH, Joseph A	I-10-22
NASH, Phillip E	A-19-10
NASH, Thomas V	O-9-7
NASH, Travis E	F-21-19
NASO, Michael	I-4-4
NASON, Charles M	J-2-9
NASON, Donald E	I-19-20
NATE, William H	L-12-2
NATHAN, Eric	G-4-23
NATHAN, Ralph M	N-22-9
NATION, Herbert	O-10-13
NAUMAN, Daniel D	Walls of the Missing
NAUMAN, Russell E	C-19-16
NAVAS, Frank	Walls of the Missing
NAWRACAJ, Jerome C	M-5-7
NAWROCKI, Edwin S	G-19-11
NAZZARETT, Daniel B	B-1-29
NEAL, Henry	O-6-17
NEAL, Latham W	A-1-9
NEAL, Maurice J	C-8-24
NEARHOOD, Alvin H	A-6-13
NEDZA, Joseph	F-17-26
NEEDHAM, Harrel R	L-19-7
NEEDHAM, Robert A	B-9-18
NEELY, Windell D	Walls of the Missing
NEFF, Charles W	K-2-20
NEFF, Don P	Walls of the Missing
NEGA, Theodore J	D-10-26
NEGRI, Adolph J	P-7-8
NEILL, Thomas	Walls of the Missing
NEILSEN, Warren F	I-12-6
NEIMAN, Thomas J	N-18-2
NEITSCH, Billy B	L-7-1
NELSON, Albert C	N-6-11
NELSON, Auther O	Walls of the Missing
NELSON, Duane E	F-16-26
NELSON, Everett H	L-8-7
NELSON, John W	Walls of the Missing
NELSON, Joseph P	Walls of the Missing
NELSON, Laverne W	M-18-15
NELSON, Nels K	I-3-19
NELSON, Ole K	N-22-10
NELSON, Percy C	L-10-17
NELSON, Robert R	O-3-2
NELSON, Robert W Jr	A-12-4
NELSON, Thomas M	K-3-1
NELSON, William J	A-14-31
NEMETH, James	O-20-3
NEMITZ, Lewellyn H	Walls of the Missing
NEMKOWICH, Stephan	K-15-15
NESSEL, Charles L	E-16-21
NESTER, Orby M	L-11-7
NETT, Herman J	B-20-3
NETTLESHIP, Chester E	F-20-23
NEUENDORF, Arthur L	P-17-2
NEUHALFEN, Duane H	E-13-3
NEUKAM, Daniel A	I-5-7
NEUMANN, Leo J	G-21-11
NEUMULLER, Carl	N-16-6
NEVAREZ, Joe P	N-13-3
NEW, Robert E	G-7-17
NEWBERRY, Lester S	E-16-18
NEWCOMB, Charles H Jr	F-20-22
NEWCOMB, Raymond D	P-10-15
NEWELL, Freeman W	C-11-25
NEWHOOK, Ernest R	M-22-8
NEWKIRK, Kenneth W	K-19-4
NEWMAN, Burrel F	I-20-8
NEWMAN, Edwin K	D-7-14
NEWMAN, Freeman M	P-13-2
NEWMAN, James G	Walls of the Missing
NEWMAN, Louis G	G-1-3
NEWMAN, Warren B	L-18-2
NEWSOM, Grover C Jr	F-15-19
NEWSOM, Walter W	Walls of the Missing
NEWSOME, Linwood T	D-8-4
NEWSOME, Robert S	J-17-13
NEWTON, Claude A	B-20-5
NEWTON, Raymond E	H-18-13
NEY, Paul J	I-12-5
NEYLAND, John D	Walls of the Missing
NICHOL, James E	L-4-19
NICHOLAS, James	Walls of the Missing
NICHOLAS, Sam A	L-11-11
NICHOLLS, Will H	M-1-12
NICHOLS, Andrew R	Walls of the Missing
NICHOLS, Charles B	L-6-8
NICHOLS, Dean D	O-13-10
NICHOLS, Elton L	P-20-2
NICHOLS, Glenn E	B-6-8
NICHOLS, James O	Walls of the Missing
NICHOLS, Richard S	Walls of the Missing
NICHOLSON, Earl H	F-14-26
NICHOLSON, Harry E	C-5-30
NICHOLSON, John D	P-2-12
NICHOLSON, Joseph E	L-9-18
NICKEL, Kenneth W	N-22-11
NICKLAS, Laverne J	F-4-18
NICKSON, Dock W	E-6-23
NICKSON, Joe G	A-20-16
NICOSIA, Carl A	A-10-6
NIEDZWIECKI, William	M-3-3
NIELSEN, Albert W	O-14-1
NIELSEN, Carl E	M-14-16
NIELSEN, Niels R	L-16-19
NIEMANN, Louis W	E-19-11
NIEMCZURA, John Jr	F-2-5
NIEMEIER, Francis J	A-17-17
NIEMI, Ralph E	B-9-17
NIGHTINGALE, Vernon A	E-13-21
NILAND, William J	D-4-17
NILE, Jack D	P-14-14
NIMTZ, Earl J	E-19-20
NIPPERT, Clifton W	E-14-18
NIRO, Pasquale Jr	J-14-5
NISBET, Richard H	Walls of the Missing
NISSI, George M	A-7-19
NIX, James S	H-11-22
NIXON, Lloyd A	P-9-13
NIXON, William J	C-14-16
NOAK, Theodore A	E-19-19
NOBLE, Keith R	P-20-15
NOBLE, Robert E	D-8-25
NOEHRE, Ernest J	E-10-20
NOEL, Roy G	D-3-1
NOFSINGER, John R Jr	F-10-11
NOGAS, Walter M	B-6-10
NOLLI, Augustine D	F-6-20
NOONAN, Frederick D	C-15-3
NORBY, Harold D	L-21-11
NORD, Don E	P-4-8
NORDAN, William	B-6-7
NORRELL, James M	H-12-3
NORRIS, Althon B	D-3-14
NORRIS, John T	C-6-8
NORTH, Robert E	E-3-14
NORTHEY, Harry L	Walls of the Missing
NORTON, Daniel E	G-14-12
NORTON, Edward R	Walls of the Missing
NORTON, James A Jr	P-16-5
NORTON, Louden H Jr	C-6-14
NORTON, Robert C	E-20-15
NOTTINGHAM, Claude D	B-16-31
NOVICK, Edwin S	I-6-21
NOVICKIE, Victor L	K-20-6
NOVOTNY, Herbert M	P-22-8
NOWAK, Henry T	B-17-23
NOWAKOWSKI, Edward R	J-20-2
NOWAKOWSKI, Joseph E	K-20-14
NOWELL, Douglas	A-18-26
NOWICKI, Walter S	L-12-3
NOXON, Donald E	Walls of the Missing
NOYALLIS, Vincent J	A-21-25
NUNES, Joseph L	Walls of the Missing
NUNLIST, John C	F-2-23
NUNN, Chester R	G-21-3

Name	Location
NUNN, William	L-11-21
NURNBERG, George W	O-18-4
NURSALL, Laurence H	Walls of the Missing
NURSE, Robert E	F-18-27
NUSE, Edgar D	L-17-4
NUSS, Dale H	J-4-2
NUSSBAUM, Charles D	G-8-3
NYE, Frederick M	D-1-27

O

Name	Location
O'BRIEN, James	M-8-3
O'BRIEN, John W	K-18-4
O'BRIEN, Terence M	E-11-20
O'CONNELL, Charles	A-18-10
O'CONNELL, James E	M-19-7
O'CONNELL, Martin W	G-7-18
O'CONNELL, Raymond B	Walls of the Missing
O'CONNOR, Gerard F	M-2-13
O'CONNOR, Michael J	C-11-9
O'CONNOR, Richard J	H-10-11
O'CONNOR, William T II	C-12-3
O'DANIEL, John W Jr	A-21-1
O'DEA, Clifford J	F-19-15
O'DONNELL, Jeremiah J	C-8-15
O'DOWD, John	L-18-6
O'GRADY, Michael D	E-13-16
O'HARA, Michael P	D-16-21
O'HARA, Robert B	B-14-23
O'HORO, Robert	O-2-4
O'KANE, John L	O-9-14
O'KEEFE, Daniel J	Walls of the Missing
O'LAUGHLIN, James F	M-2-14
O'LEARY, Arthur P Jr	H-13-6
O'LEARY, Charles J	G-10-24
O'LEARY, Frank	C-6-7
O'LEARY, Leo R	I-14-1
O'NEAL, Clyde L	J-6-7
O'NEAL, George W	I-8-1
O'NEAL, John E Jr	M-12-4
O'NEIL, Bernard W	B-7-21
O'NEIL, Charles L	Walls of the Missing
O'NEIL, Jeremiah H	M-15-12
O'SHAUGHNESSY, Jeremiah J	I-7-4
O'SULLIVAN, John D	E-16-12
O'TOOLE, Edward L	Walls of the Missing
O'TOOLE, Francis J	K-3-9
O'TOOLE, Robert J	N-14-6
OAKLEY, Vernon L	L-11-5
OBEDNIKOVICH, Jordon S	L-12-7
OCHLAN, Charles	K-15-2
OCHOA, Alejo C	K-18-12
ODELL, Enos H	I-17-20
ODELL, Irvin S	B-11-19
ODOM, Howard N	N-18-3
ODUM, Jerry L	C-15-15
OELRICHS, Vernon J H	D-9-22
OESCH, Harold E	M-3-5
OESTREICHER, Seymour	D-7-15
OFCHINICK, Richard P	A-4-9
OFER, John H	E-15-24
OGDEN, Edward L	H-14-7
OGILVIE, Donald J	M-18-5
OGLENSKY, David	Walls of the Missing
OJA, Andrew A Jr	C-4-24
OKESON, Kenneth N	L-14-1
OLBERG, Frank J	N-14-14
OLDHAM, Mack L	K-13-12
OLDING, Thomas R	C-19-20
OLENDER, Walter V	L-15-12
OLIVER, Charles H	Walls of the Missing
OLIVER, Lynn M	H-17-15
OLIVIERI, Anthony	F-2-25
OLLINGER, Richard J	A-5-3
OLSEN, Arthur E	K-20-5
OLSEN, Richard O	A-9-19
OLSON, Alvin	D-13-32
OLSON, Bertram E	B-17-8
OLSON, Elmer R	M-22-10
OLSON, John E Jr	N-22-12
OLSON, John W	B-11-24
OLSON, Leo G	D-2-18
OLSON, Leonard R	Walls of the Missing
OLSON, Marvin C	J-15-10
OLSON, Melvin J	G-1-23
OLSON, Rayder C	K-2-1
OLSON, Rudolph	F-5-7
OLSZEWSKI, Henry W	H-7-4
ONIE, Milton S	I-7-14
ONLEY, Marvin A	E-2-13
ONORATO, Joseph B	Walls of the Missing
ONTIVEROZ, Gustavo R	E-21-27
OPACICH, Robert S	L-10-4
OPFER, Carl G	Walls of the Missing
OPITZ, Max J	A-21-5
OPOLKO, Nicholas	D-9-19
OPP, Austin L	D-19-17
ORECCHIO, Frank C	F-7-8
ORENDORFF, John E	F-10-14
ORLOWSKI, Frank J	B-17-5
ORPHAN, James J	P-20-13
ORRIS, Verle S	A-4-32
ORSAT, Albert A	L-18-15
ORSBURN, Elwyn R	G-15-1
ORSHAN, Seymour	Walls of the Missing
ORSINI, Joseph J	P-17-16
ORTIZ, Abelardo L Jr	L-12-8
OSBORN, Jack E	K-8-9
OSBORN, Mark A	H-16-10
OSBORN, Marvin R	P-10-12
OSBORNE, William J	Walls of the Missing
OSBURN, Harvey H	P-13-10
OSIER, Frederick E	C-11-6
OST, Henry C	D-17-7
OSTDICK, Robert C	G-6-6
OSTROW, Arnold W	K-5-18
OSWALD, Randolph E	Walls of the Missing
OSWALT, Ralph V	F-13-17
OTENBAKER, George E	I-13-5
OTT, Robert A	K-16-6
OTTERSBACH, Granville	O-12-12
OUELLET, Joyce L	N-22-13
OURADA, Edward R	K-18-1
OUSELEY, William J	L-12-13
OUTHOUSE, Earl C	E-6-9
OUTLAW, William L	O-6-14
OVERDORF, Herbert W	Walls of the Missing
OVERTON, Robert G	E-3-21
OWEN, Allen C	I-2-7
OWEN, Burl M	J-9-17
OWEN, Donald E	O-1-8
OWEN, Harold M	B-2-30
OWEN, Owen Jr [300]	A-4-11
OWEN, Richard C	A-10-22
OWEN, Woodrow	I-4-12
OWENS, Cecil D	C-3-25
OWENS, Claude C	L-12-9
OWENS, David N	Walls of the Missing
OWENS, George W Jr	Walls of the Missing
OWENS, John M	E-15-25
OWENS, R E	E-7-5
OWENS, Wayne C	N-6-3
OXFORD, Earl	O-11-3
OXLEY, Fred C	E-1-6
OZBUN, Harold C	L-20-13

P

Name	Location
PACE, William H	B-10-22
PACECCA, Antonio S	A-3-21
PACHECO, David D	H-20-8
PACHICO, John	B-7-3
PACI, Adrian L	J-16-14
PACK, Elva	E-2-17
PACK, Jessie O	H-14-20
PACKARD, Harold J	O-14-5
PADILLA, Serafin	M-8-12
PAGE, Bernice E	H-19-3
PAGE, Francis P	C-1-6
PAGE, James P	D-8-10
PAGE, Loren E	J-5-11
PAGE, Alvin W	D-12-28
PAHLOW, Donald A	B-2-5
PAIZ, David	F-20-26
PALADINI, Edward E	Walls of the Missing
PALENSKE, Eugene R V	J-17-10
PALMBLAD, John	B-1-30
PALMENTO, Jerry C [301]	G-6-19
PALMER, Barry F	G-8-18
PALMER, Frank M	I-2-18
PALMER, Harry Jr	M-16-14
PALMER, Jackson Jr	N-22-14
PALMER, Joseph F	N-14-8
PALMER, King R Jr	F-2-3
PALMER, Lloyd L Jr	G-21-6
PALMER, Stefan C	G-16-8

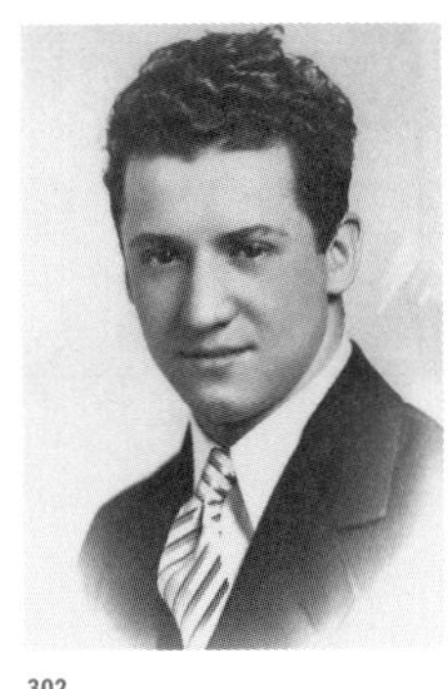
302

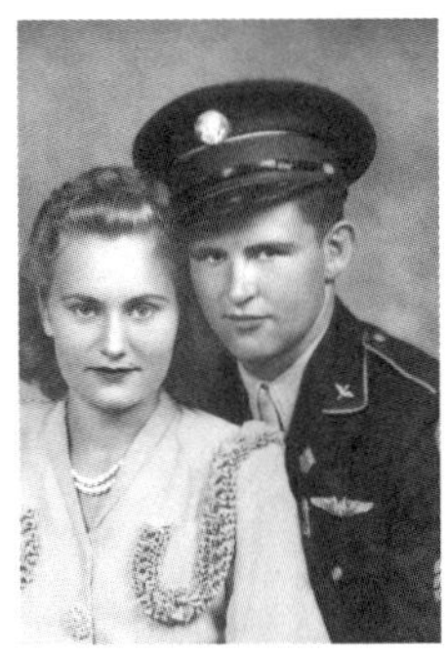
303

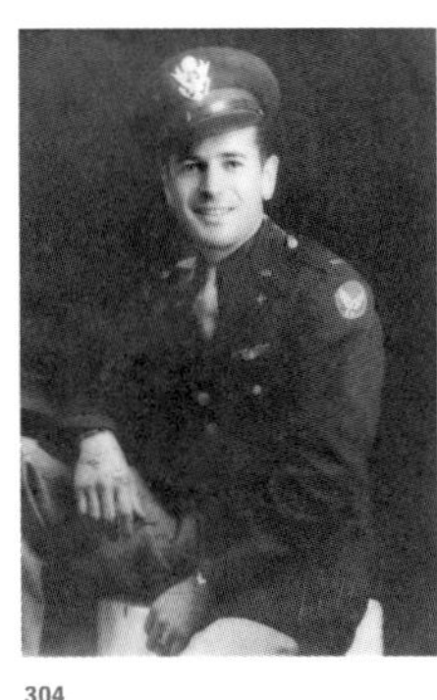
304

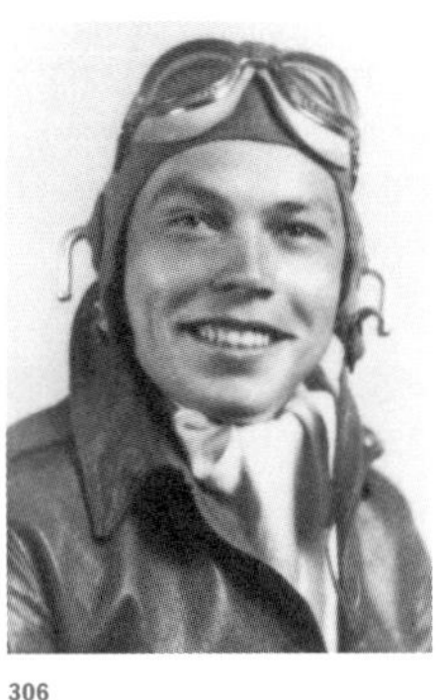
306

PALMER, Warren M	C-16-7
PALMER, Wendell O	Walls of the Missing
PALMERIN, Raymond T	D-10-20
PALTRIDGE, Donald L	P-7-12
PANEK, Louis R	Walls of the Missing
PANEK, Walter P	A-2-19
PANEPINTO, Salvatore	Walls of the Missing
PANKAN, Joseph A	A-9-11
PANTAGES, Nick G	Walls of the Missing
PAOLI, Albert J	Walls of the Missing
PAOLI, Silvio R	N-20-1
PAOLINO, Vincent C	Walls of the Missing
PAPADOPULOS, Michael	Walls of the Missing
PAPE, William H	O-9-9
PARADIS, Lucien R	Walls of the Missing
PARADISE, Alan H	G-21-1
PARADISO, Anthony J	B-4-10
PARADY, Harold D	F-13-4
PARENTI, Carl A	C-15-7
PARHAMOVICH, Paul L	E-18-5
PARIS, Peter J 302	Walls of the Missing
PARIS, Walter C	G-1-21
PARISI, Marion A	F-4-16
PARK, James K	Walls of the Missing
PARK, Robert P	P-4-10
PARK, William N Jr	A-20-25
PARKER, Buril L	C-12-24
PARKER, Emerson	P-2-5
PARKER, Harry B	L-2-22
PARKER, James E	B-6-28
PARKER, James H	H-20-9
PARKER, Odis	Walls of the Missing
PARKER, Oliver J	M-10-6
PARKER, Robert B	C-16-11
PARKER, Rowdy W	J-14-8
PARKER, Vaughn	N-13-5
PARKER, Virgil J	E-8-2
PARKER, Walter E	K-10-21
PARKER, Willard M	H-8-1
PARKER, William H	B-2-7
PARKINS, Walter C	Walls of the Missing
PARKINSON, Roy F	B-19-28
PARKINSON, Thomas H	E-17-10
PARR, Horace J	K-21-5
PARR, William J	E-1-16
PARRA, Ricardo M	L-11-8
PARRA, Roy P	G-17-7
PARRISH, John F	E-13-4
PARROTT, Darrell V	Walls of the Missing
PARSON, Lawrence	E-5-1
PARSONS, Marlow W	A-20-3
PARSONS, Richard H	Walls of the Missing
PARTIN, Lester S	C-6-20
PARTRIDGE, Albert	N-8-4
PASCHIS, Leo R	F-7-19
PASCHKE, Theodore J	N-4-12
PASQUE, William F	I-3-6
PASSANANDO, Ronald E	M-5-8
PASSAVANT, Frank A	Walls of the Missing
PASSOW, Haroldean	D-5-10
PASTRAS, Peter A	M-10-9
PASTULA, Leo M	O-4-4
PASVANIS, George A	Walls of the Missing
PASZKOWSKI, John J	F-21-21
PATE, Dexter B	M-10-10
PATE, Francis A	F-8-18
PATE, Herbert L	I-12-22
PATRICIAN, George	P-10-9
PATRICK, William M	B-14-9
PATSEL, Robert L	G-13-13
PATTEN, Ory S	Walls of the Missing
PATTERSON, Edward L	L-17-10
PATTON, Clifford E	J-8-9
PATTON, Earl S	E-4-4
PATTY, Morris R	F-17-5
PAUL, Carl S	L-14-6
PAUL, George E	E-14-16
PAUL, Norbert W	C-6-28
PAULETT, Deward M	K-11-10
PAULEY, Carl H	L-18-3
PAULEY, James C	Walls of the Missing
PAULSEN, James M III	H-2-21
PAUMER, Louis J	M-7-16
PAVELKO, Joseph J	M-10-14
PAWLIK, James B	Walls of the Missing
PAXTON, Harry M	C-13-27
PAXTON, Lyle	Walls of the Missing
PAYNE, Ardell W	H-12-27
PAYNE, Donald F	E-5-8
PAYNE, Duane W	Walls of the Missing
PAYSON, Burnett M	G-15-23
PAYTON, Josephine B	E-17-5
PEACOCK, James W Jr	Walls of the Missing
PEACOCK, Tryphon D	H-11-3
PEARCE, Dixon F Jr	Walls of the Missing
PEARCE, James W	B-9-24
PEARCE, Wallace E	B-7-26
PEARSON, Alfred	C-19-21
PEARSON, Carl R	B-2-29
PEARSON, James P	A-1-15
PEASE, Carl E	Walls of the Missing
PEASE, Stephen R E	D-9-9
PECK, Carl W	Walls of the Missing
PECK, Herman E	G-4-11
PECK, James C	F-16-20
PECK, Robert F	H-11-7
PECK, Robert J	P-14-7
PECKHAM, Frank B	J-16-18
PECOLAR, Paul J	K-8-11
PECSENYE, Joseph J	E-2-21
PEDERSEN, Perry G	Walls of the Missing
PEDERSON, Adolph N	C-1-13
PEE, William F	A-12-21
PEEL, James R	K-8-21
PEEVY, Charley R	N-22-15
PEFFER, Stanley B	G-1-24
PEGRAM, William G	A-9-32
PEGUES, Robert A	C-14-7
PEIFER, William W	H-9-19
PEIRCE, David	B-7-1
PEIRCE, Henry T	F-18-7
PELC, Joe A	F-14-20
PELCZAR, Henry J	C-11-8
PELLEGRINO, Amrico W	P-1-2
PELLEGRINO, Mario	J-13-19
PELLEGRINO, Nick V	P-1-1
PELLINI, Aldo L	Walls of the Missing
PELTZ, William	K-14-2
PELUSO, Andrew J	G-18-22
PELUSO, Joseph	L-1-6
PELUSO, Vincenzo	O-4-1
PEMBERTON, Leo C	J-4-8
PENDA, Robert P	C-12-26
PENINGER, Robert L	G-5-13
PENISTEN, John H	Walls of the Missing
PENMAN, Fred R	P-20-14
PENNING, Irwin H	K-10-9
PENNINGTON, James L	I-9-9
PENNINGTON, Jess	G-7-8
PENNINGTON, Jessie L	G-2-22
PENNY, William T	A-7-25
PENSABENE, Philip A	G-15-24
PENSINGER, Leander F	I-5-4
PEPLINSKI, Theodore	P-16-17
PEPLOW, Raymond W	D-9-21
PEPPER, Charles J	D-4-28
PEPPLE, Rueben	H-7-3
PERDUE, John P	F-3-11

PEREIR, Augusto	N-22-16
PEREZ, Martin G	I-6-16
PERHONITCH, John	G-15-19
PERKEY, W N Jr	E-17-6
PERKINS, William H	H-7-24
PERKINS, William M	A-8-6
PERLA, Anthony L	J-9-13
PERMAN, Alvin J	F-20-1
PERMAR, Everett E	Walls of the Missing
PERRETTA, Felix A	M-11-7
PERRINE, Ralph C	F-10-1
PERRON, Norman	B-13-32
PERRY, Anthony N	O-12-3
PERRY, Clell E	Walls of the Missing
PERRY, Darwin H	E-20-27
PERRY, J I	Walls of the Missing
PERRY, James H	G-3-17
PERRY, Kenneth G	E-17-9
PERRY, Rodney S	H-19-20
PERSHING, Maurice D	O-13-13
PERUSEK, Frank M	O-18-15
PESSIN, Lewis	F-7-5
PEST, David	Walls of the Missing
PETE, Walter	Walls of the Missing
PETERMAN, Harold E	F-4-13
PETERNELL, Paul	Walls of the Missing
PETERS, Belvin J	A-10-24
PETERS, Charles S	M-1-6
PETERS, Ernest	D-17-6
PETERS, George J	G-17-8
PETERSEN, Henry F	G-20-3
PETERSEN, Kenneth L	H-6-3
PETERSON, Carl E	J-8-11
PETERSON, Clair E	O-15-12
PETERSON, Dale J	O-12-11
PETERSON, Donald V	F-13-8
PETERSON, George	D-21-10
PETERSON, Kenneth L	F-18-15
PETERSON, Lloyd M	M-20-12
PETERSON, Marvin R	I-2-3
PETERSON, Maurice E	B-1-12
PETERSON, Robert G	B-3-29
PETERSON, Roland E	N-3-17
PETERSON, Roy M	Walls of the Missing
PETOSKEY, Henry S	A-7-32
PETRASEK, August F Jr	J-9-16
PETREKOVICH, Frederick J	K-21-10
PETRICKA, George J	C-14-17
PETRIE, Carlton E	E-16-10
PETRIE, Robert E	I-8-6
PETRIE, Thomas D	J-16-22
PETROTTA, Joseph P	D-21-26
PETROW, George J	N-2-6
PETRUZZELLO, Arthur	K-10-11
PETRYCKI, William S	L-21-10
PETRYNA, George	I-2-15
PETTEYS, Alvin H	K-19-3
PETTIGREW, Carl E	I-2-9

PETTUS, Jewell L	B-6-30
PETTY, Ralph O	F-6-22
PETULA, George	L-14-12
PETZOLDT, Albert W	D-1-16
PFAHLER, Ervin J	B-7-20
PFAU, William R	I-11-1
PFEIFER, Ambrose R [303]	Walls of the Missing
PFEIFFER, Clifford	D-17-23
PFLUGH, Arthur W	Walls of the Missing
PFOHL, Christian T	C-19-17
PHALEN, Glenn O	L-18-9
PHELPS, Charles P	A-14-20
PHELPS, Franklin E	N-7-8
PHELPS, Lawrence W	H-15-4
PHIFER, James H	J-3-4
PHILBRICK, Earl R	Walls of the Missing
PHILIPPS, James A	B-16-23
PHILLIPS, Carl H	N-5-10
PHILLIPS, Dorman E	L-8-16
PHILLIPS, George W	P-8-4
PHILLIPS, Hymen	Walls of the Missing
PHILLIPS, John S	H-8-7
PHILLIPS, Moorehead	M-17-8
PHILLIPS, Robert B	G-16-17
PHILLIPS, Roger W	B-16-19
PHILLIPS, Toby B Jr	Walls of the Missing
PHILLIPS, Wendell G	Walls of the Missing
PHILLIPS, Winfred	M-8-16
PHILLIPSON, Burton M	E-5-16
PIANI, John T	O-17-1
PIASECKI, Eugene C	D-1-31
PIATKOWSKI, Chester L	Walls of the Missing
PICKARD, Charles B	B-14-18
PICKELL, Kenneth R	Walls of the Missing
PICKELL, Willis E	L-7-12
PICKERING, Ernest Arthur	E-13-26
PICKERING, Kelton P	H-21-2
PICKETT, Arthur C	A-15-16
PICKETT, Stephen G	C-5-29
PICKLESIMER, Gordon B	A-2-1
PIEGZIK, John A J	H-8-25
PIEL, Derrell C	P-9-14
PIELAK, Stanley F	P-13-4
PIENDEL, Henry M	N-17-4
PIERCE, Hugh S	E-4-6
PIERCEFIELD, Alvin L	E-8-17
PIERSON, George R	H-18-11
PIERSON, Warren W	H-2-9
PIESZCHALA, Peter R	P-15-11
PIKE, Charles B	C-12-18
PIKULA, Adam	D-5-11
PILCH, Stanley Jr	Walls of the Missing
PILE, Samuel O	I-2-10
PILTZECKER, Charles H	H-13-7
PINDER, George H	E-20-8
PINDROCH, John	E-5-3
PINGS, Eugene B	N-5-6
PINHEIRO, Daniel D	G-16-14

PINKUS, Robert F	D-12-22
PINNEY, Kenneth J	F-4-15
PINSON, Harry A	F-18-13
PINTO, John G	E-4-24
PIPER, George B	A-1-18
PIPER, Thoburn E	J-2-14
PIPHER, George F [304]	Walls of the Missing
PIPPITT, Donald D	H-4-3
PIRTLE, James H	G-6-20
PISCHKE, Robert L	B-3-27
PITCHEL, Stanley T	F-19-12
PITT, Milo S	J-12-17
PITTMAN, Ralph	Walls of the Missing
PITTS, Cherry C	Walls of the Missing
PITTS, John J [305]	F-6-4
PITTS, John L Jr	L-19-19
PITTS, Marc F	H-11-13
PLAGIANOS, Leon M	Walls of the Missing
PLAINE, Alton J	E-3-3
PLANSTER, John J	K-2-3
PLANTE, Irenee R	Walls of the Missing
PLASSON, Victor P	Walls of the Missing
PLATECK, Stephen	G-6-21
PLATT, Gerald E Jr	C-1-24
PLAUNT, Grover E	K-9-11
PLEASANT, A C	D-5-4
PLESKAC, James E	E-10-19
PLESKUNAS, John S	O-8-2
PLUMMER, Earl K	N-1-15
PLUMMER, William H	O-1-12
PODOLSKY, Irving	C-16-1
POE, Curtis C [306]	Walls of the Missing
POFF, Henry W	N-2-16
POGUE, William A	P-15-6
POIRIER, Raymond W	J-10-14
POKRASKY, Anthony J	H-13-13
POLEY, Albert J	Walls of the Missing
POLLARD, George A	D-5-24
POLLOCK, Frank E	C-14-26
POLLOCK, Raymond R	C-8-21
POLTON, Charles M	G-19-23
POMPILIO, Gennaro	H-7-19
POMPONIO, Charles R	I-1-15
PONCE, Baltazar L	H-20-6
PONCIROLI, Albert	F-8-21
POND, William M	N-15-9
POOL, Richard I	N-7-10
POOL, Woodrow W	E-2-20
POOLE, Paul L	C-17-5
POPE, Janney L	H-4-15
POPESEN, John S	C-1-28
POPHAL, Norman A	A-2-25
POPLAR, Joseph P	C-7-18
POPULORUM, William C	G-3-27
PORTER, Hollis G	J-6-16
PORTER, Jack Jr	O-12-17
PORTER, Jerald G	M-10-17
PORTER, Richard E	Walls of the Missing

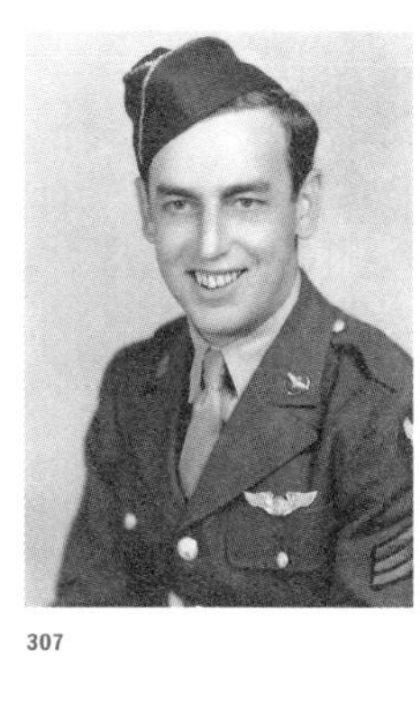
307

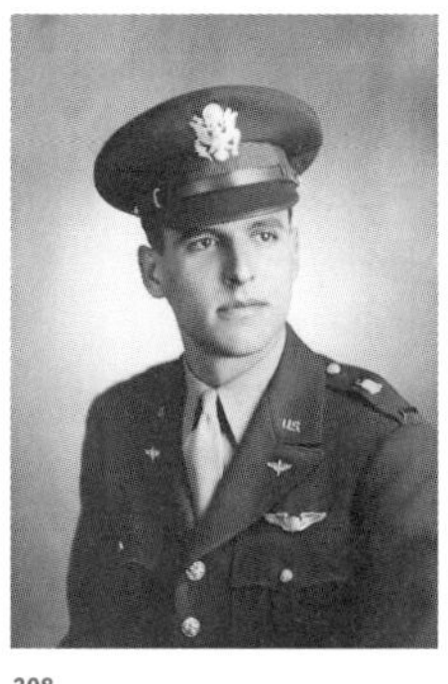
308

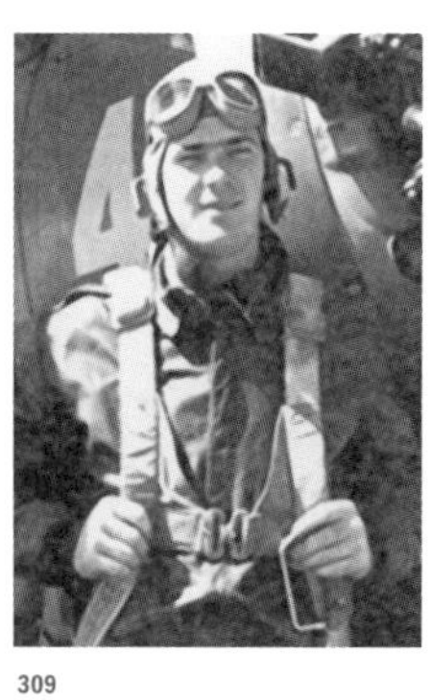
309

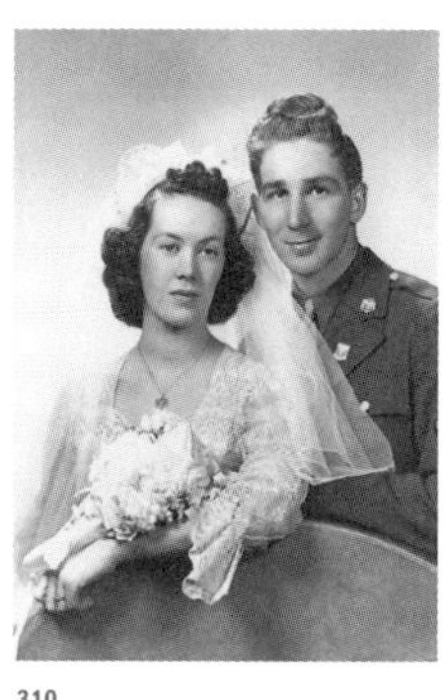
310

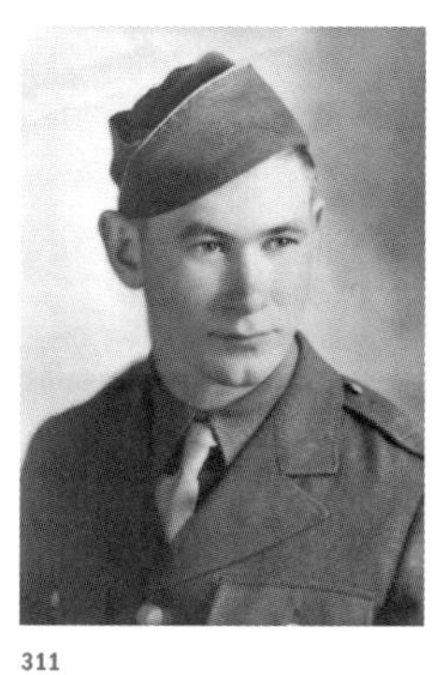
311

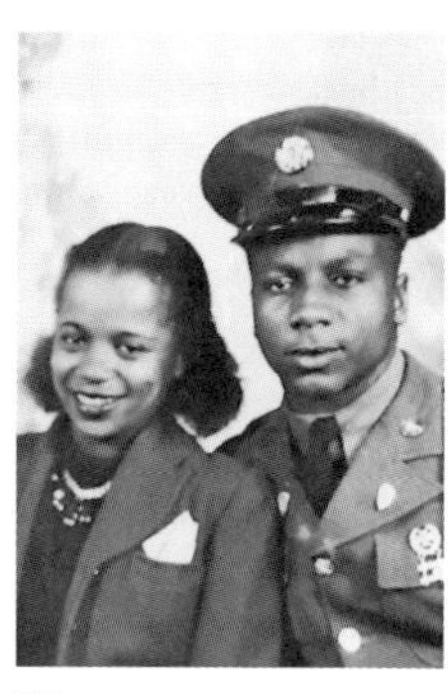
312

PORTER, Roy O	N-22-17
PORTER, Stanley F	L-8-3
PORTIS, John	N-5-17
PORZ, Robert O	P-17-3
POSADA, Frank G	J-7-14
POSEY, Gerald D	E-1-7
POSNER, Solomon	I-11-6
POSSEMATO, John J	H-21-9
POSTLEWAIT, Rhae K [307]	Walls of the Missing
POTOPA, Walter J	J-12-9
POTTENGER, James O	E-15-2
POTTER, Clyde M	K-6-7
POTTER, Eldon M	E-9-13
POTTER, Robert G	C-9-31
POTTER, Wilbur J	K-7-13
POTTS, Benjamin T	Walls of the Missing
POTTS, Herbert	O-10-14
POTTS, William D	H-18-3
POTUCEK, Emil V	O-12-5
POULOS, Steve S	Walls of the Missing
POULSEN, Alexander	D-12-30
POULSON, Glenn W	N-21-1
POURNEY, Leslie F	A-16-11
POWELL, Bruce M	P-10-16
POWELL, Cecil C	B-15-7
POWELL, Charles L	L-16-2
POWELL, Charlie B	F-4-12
POWELL, David T	B-21-11
POWELL, Raleigh C Jr	H-17-18
POWER, Clifton H	C-2-2
POWER, Ellsworth C	Walls of the Missing
POWER, Herbert E	J-15-11
POWER, Merle S	C-10-14
POWERS, Frank E	O-8-7
POWERS, Robert F	O-15-17
POWERS, William B Jr	N-18-12
POWLEDGE, Robert B	Walls of the Missing
POYTHRESS, Whitney F [308]	Walls of the Missing
PRAHL, Elmer C	O-19-3
PRANGL, Louis S	H-16-24
PRATHER, Bondy E	J-21-2
PRATHER, John T	Walls of the Missing
PRATT, Donald G	B-3-14
PRATT, Walter S	H-3-17
PREDER, Rolland G	B-19-8
PRELUTZKY, George	H-12-22
PRENOSIL, Charles H	B-19-32
PRESCOTT, William R	E-9-6
PRESNELL, James B	A-10-3
PRESSEL, David F	Walls of the Missing
PRESSENTIN, Robert H	I-3-22
PRESTON, Strother J	D-16-22
PRESTON, Wesley L	C-16-16
PRESTON, William H	F-2-16
PRIBBLE, Robert W	I-14-20
PRICE, Charles F	B-21-10
PRICE, Edward E Jr	Walls of the Missing
PRICE, George B	Walls of the Missing
PRICE, Leo V	J-5-7
PRICE, Lewis E	Walls of the Missing
PRICE, Maryld D	G-4-22
PRICE, Ralph E	C-16-6
PRICE, Robert E L	A-9-26
PRICE, Russell L Jr	J-8-4
PRICE, Thomas G	I-16-7
PRIDDY, Henry W	O-12-7
PRIEBE, Vernon M B	G-6-18
PRIEGEL, Lewis W	Walls of the Missing
PRINCE, Albert S	Walls of the Missing
PRINE, Park M	B-14-10
PRINGLE, Paul E	N-4-11
PRINGLE, Ralph K	K-21-16
PRITCHARD, Charles F	A-15-4
PRITCHARD, Robert L	D-8-15
PRITCHARD, Willis C	Walls of the Missing
PROBY, Clyde V	L-17-1
PROCTOR, Robert D	M-19-10
PROGAR, Frank L	F-8-9
PROHOROFF, Alex	K-10-17
PROIETTI, Louis	H-14-5
PROKOP, Nicholas J	C-14-18
PROPST, Charles E	Walls of the Missing
PROSNICK, Leonard	H-8-5
PROSSER, Parker E	F-8-10
PROUDFIT, Richard D	M-1-17
PROUTY, James W	E-3-23
PROZZO, Patsy A	E-20-22
PRUETT, Henry E	Walls of the Missing
PRUITT, Boyce L	A-2-27
PRUITT, George H	L-4-4
PRUITT, John R	Walls of the Missing
PRUITT, Raymond A	C-17-7
PRZYBOROWSKI, Edward T	F-3-16
PSZCZOLKOWSKI, Edward	N-20-13
PUCKETT, Grant E	C-6-29
PUETZ, Harold W	C-7-28
PUGLIA, Nicholas D	E-8-4
PUHALLA, Steve J	G-7-11
PUHALSKI, Henry J	M-21-2
PULLIAM, Gilford D	P-17-6
PULLIAM, Ralph C	F-4-2
PULVER, Albert G Jr	E-12-8
PUNTENEY, Charles E	B-6-11
PURDIE, John B	E-7-27
PURDY, Benjamin M	Walls of the Missing
PURDY, Harry M	Walls of the Missing
PURDY, James F Jr	Walls of the Missing
PURDY, Robert F [309]	Walls of the Missing
PURE, Leonard	I-15-8
PURINTON, Albert H	J-11-5
PUSA, Henry W	L-12-17
PUSKAR, Steve T	N-17-15
PUSTELNIK, William H	L-9-7
PUTNAM, Robert A	O-6-13
PUZZUOLI, Herman	M-7-4
PYLE, George T	L-4-16
PYTEL, John J	I-21-2
PYTEL, Ludvick L	I-21-3

Q

QUALLS, Archie	D-13-29
QUARANTA, Robert J	Walls of the Missing
QUARLES, Loyd C	M-18-3
QUEBMAN, Robert B Sr	D-9-25
QUEENER, William A	H-3-25
QUEER, Harry E	I-1-16
QUERQUES, Leonard	D-20-2
QUICK, Chester G	K-6-13
QUICK, John H	C-5-11
QUICK, Richard H	Walls of the Missing
QUIGLEY, Clyde S	D-13-9
QUILLIAM, Kenneth B	H-2-20
QUINLAN, John M	K-16-3

QUINN, Donald F	E-16-5
QUINN, Frank	P-13-15
QUINN, Joseph W	J-4-6
QUINN, Roland H	D-13-6
QUINN, William F	A-5-1
QUINONEZ, Florencio E	N-18-9
QUINTANA, Julian	C-7-30
QUINTO, John V	H-12-26
QUIRING, Otto A	A-8-7

R

RABAGO, Fernando H	L-12-11
RABEL, Wilbur D	O-11-15
RABELL, Milton K	E-14-2
RACHOFSKY, Robert C	Walls of the Missing
RACZNIAK, Louis E	C-7-21
RADANOVICH, John W	Walls of the Missing
RADEBAUGH, Bernard J	C-16-17
RADEL, Walter J	G-5-15
RADICH, Bogan	I-20-11
RADICH, Srecko F	L-20-8
RADMANN, James B [310]	C-7-32
RADUL, Trian	O-16-8
RAETHER, Theodore H	L-4-13
RAFFERTY, William J	O-12-15
RAFFETY, Louis E	A-4-15
RAGAN, William H	J-14-1
RAGON, Bailey J	F-13-12
RAHN, Herman W	I-16-15
RAIDER, Raymond R	O-1-9
RAINES, Loyd J	K-7-10
RAKOFF, Leo	Walls of the Missing
RAKOWSKI, Steve V	J-21-20
RALEIGH, Herman E Jr	I-10-9
RALSTON, Bryce A	L-2-17
RAMER, John T	D-8-20
RAMIREZ, Charles	H-7-1
RAMSDELL, Robert K	E-19-1
RAMSEY, Frank R	Walls of the Missing
RAMSEY, Jackson T	F-4-11
RAMSEY, Ronald H	K-3-3
RAMSTETTER, Walter E	B-8-1
RANDALL, Francis A	E-19-24
RANDALL, Jack H	Walls of the Missing
RANDALL, Rudy	P-8-6
RANDEL, Charles R	J-1-13
RANDEL, Lawrence W	E-2-9
RANDEL, Leonard E	H-10-24
RANDOLPH, Raymond M	E-19-9
RANGEL, Fernando B	P-22-13
RANGEL, Joe M	D-10-27
RANGER, Donald G	L-11-13
RANKIN, Harold O	C-16-8
RANKIN, Warren M	Walls of the Missing
RANKO, Charles William	H-17-5
RANO, Carl R	Walls of the Missing
RANSOM, William V	J-1-15
RAPKO, Michael	B-11-10
RAPOSKY, Albert H	C-9-30
RAPP, Charles G	A-20-26
RAPP, Edward B	M-7-13
RAPPS, Oliver J	Walls of the Missing
RASCH, Abraham J	Walls of the Missing
RASKE, Harold	F-10-18
RASMUSSEN, Howard W	F-18-20
RATCHFORD, Robert H	N-2-10
RATERMANN, Joseph A	C-12-5
RATHGEBER, William A	Walls of the Missing
RATKELIS, Thomas S	I-16-4
RATLIFF, George R	C-16-23
RATTS, Dean M	P-13-11
RAVASIO, Bernard A	H-10-23
RAVASIO, Michael A Jr	Walls of the Missing
RAVENOR, Thomas J	I-12-2
RAWLINGS, James W	D-10-15
RAWSON, James L	I-3-18
RAY, Luther B	N-9-6
RAYBURN, Wayne H	Walls of the Missing
REA, Thomas L	L-3-16
REAB, Lyle W [311]	Walls of the Missing
READ, Thomas	D-2-17
REAVES, Dudley W	C-13-19
REAVES, Vaughn	Walls of the Missing
REBARSKY, Andrew Jr	E-16-15
RECTOR, Bengie M	E-5-11
RECTOR, Edward C	A-6-6
REDDING, Henry L [312]	L-21-16
REDDINGTON, John V Jr	B-2-23
REDFERN, Lloyd H	N-18-1
REED, Charles B	A-17-8
REED, George R Jr	I-17-10
REED, Gerald C	K-13-14
REED, James M	Walls of the Missing
REED, Lester L	K-13-18
REED, Merlin H	Walls of the Missing
REED, Norbert G	F-13-15
REED, Walter S	L-14-11
REEDER, Merrill E	I-18-15
REEKS, Reginald T	D-8-29
REEL, Leander	J-3-17
REESE, Frank M	D-17-1
REESE, Halmyth C	A-14-26
REESE, Vincent J	M-21-6
REESE, Whitney J	N-21-2
REESE, William R	Walls of the Missing
REEVE, Virgil E	C-6-30
REEVES, Harry E	K-19-15
REEVES, Joseph E	N-1-12
REEVES, Noah C	Walls of the Missing
REEVES, Robert L	H-1-8
REGAN, Robert C	Walls of the Missing
REGAN, Robert M	D-1-29
REGEN, Chester A	G-7-7
REIBER, Edwin T	B-20-8
REICH, Charles F	M-7-10
REICHENBACH, Arno K	F-14-11
REICHENBACH, Theodore	N-21-3
REICHERT, Paul F	P-19-5
REICHOLD, Walter H	B-20-4
REID, Alvah D	J-6-14
REID, Howard D Jr	M-2-1
REID, James W	M-16-12
REID, Joseph S	K-19-14
REIDY, Charles E	M-7-9
REILEY, Glenn V	H-16-15
REILLER, Kenneth P	K-19-11
REIN, John J	B-11-9
REINEHR, Edward A	Walls of the Missing
REINERIO, Alexander J	D-10-9
REINHARDT, John A	F-13-7
REINHART, Wendall D	Walls of the Missing
REINWAND, Charles V	C-15-9
REISER, Alois P	L-3-6
REISHUS, Alton H	K-1-18
REITER, Clarence A	F-16-7
REITZ, William	A-12-15
REKAS, Joseph A	Walls of the Missing
REMCUS, Jack T	I-13-19
REMISZEWSKI, Frank	H-10-10
REMPEL, Calvin A	C-14-22
REMUS, Franklin G	B-15-5
RENAUD, William G	Walls of the Missing
RENCH, Duane F	K-5-9
RENDA, George J	Walls of the Missing
RENDER, Harold J	B-7-17
RENDINA, Joseph M	F-19-7
RENDLER, Carl Jr	B-4-28
RENDON, Luis M	L-10-19
RENNER, Marvin	D-10-4
RENO, Charley N	J-19-20
RENSINK, Henry A	Walls of the Missing
RENTFROW, Robert R	I-9-1
RENTZ, Bennett J	P-15-13
RENYER, Lester J	A-12-28
REPA, Alois F	B-19-24
REPINE, Alex J	D-2-31
REPKO, George J	L-11-19
RESLER, John T	I-14-6
RESSANI, Mario L	D-6-3
RESWEBER, Ellis J	H-9-10
RETAN, George O	A-4-8
RETONE, Anthony Jr	Walls of the Missing
REUFF, Oscar L	H-4-22
REUTER, Walter H Jr	Walls of the Missing
REVILOCK, Steven	I-12-1
REW, Howard A	I-16-19
REWERTS, Herman R	J-20-13
REYERSON, James H	G-7-4
REYES, Joseph	E-11-10
REYES, Miguel A	Walls of the Missing
REYNERSON, Herbert L	D-16-6
REYNOLDS, Elvis	C-11-1
REYNOLDS, Layman R	D-5-21
REYNOLDS, Oris L	B-11-17

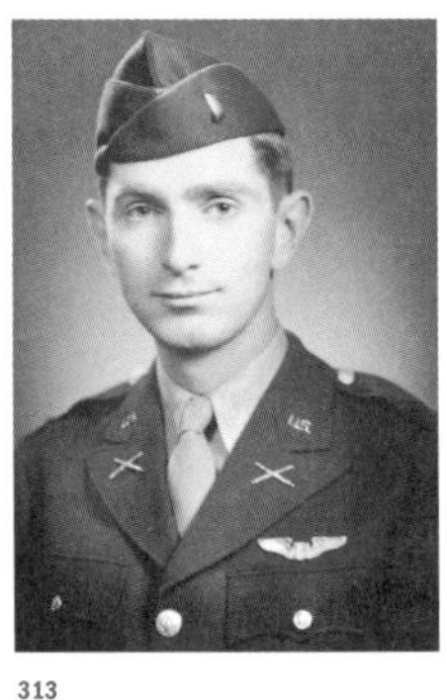
313

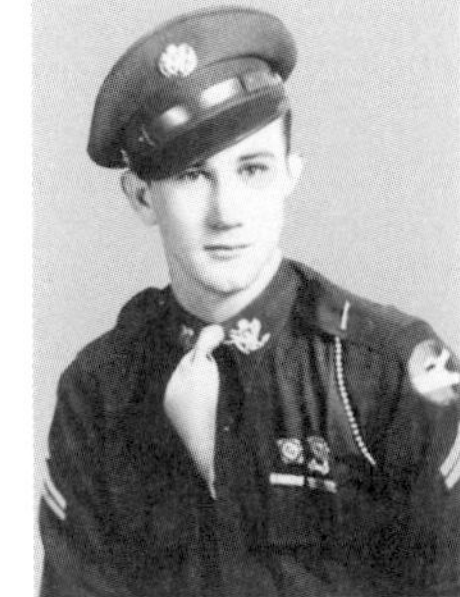
314

REYNOLDS, Roy M	C-9-6
RHATIGAN, Robert H	E-18-27
RHOADARMER, Floyd W	M-14-11
RHODES, Carney C Jr	Walls of the Missing
RHODES, Edward B	D-20-31
RHODES, Gene B	F-17-12
RHODES, Marshall D	E-14-4
RHODES, William H	A-20-13
RIBET, Joseph J	L-20-2
RICCIARDI, Ignatius J	A-19-6
RICCIO, Samuel H	N-10-17
RICE, Bernard	Walls of the Missing
RICE, Bernard S	B-1-19
RICE, Donald B	K-4-17
RICE, Donald S	H-14-25
RICE, Everett J	O-19-8
RICE, Stanley	J-16-19
RICE, William O	C-8-25
RICH, Floyd P	A-5-19
RICH, Frank	L-3-7
RICH, Mack	H-15-14
RICH, Otto A	K-14-5
RICHARD, Armand R	Walls of the Missing
RICHARD, Wallace	B-5-7
RICHARDS, Alfred J	G-11-20
RICHARDS, Herman V	D-8-27
RICHARDS, Ira T Jr	E-3-17
RICHARDS, Louis L	Walls of the Missing
RICHARDSON, Allen E	D-6-8
RICHARDSON, Charles B	G-13-11
RICHARDSON, David L J	E-4-19
RICHARDSON, Donald E	O-11-5
RICHARDSON, Earl H	Walls of the Missing
RICHARDSON, Harold M	I-8-22
RICHARDSON, Jackson C	A-3-10
RICHARDSON, John A	Walls of the Missing
RICHARDSON, John P	Walls of the Missing
RICHARDSON, Merle L	M-21-5
RICHARDSON, Orley C	F-5-27
RICHARDSON, Ralph	M-15-5
RICHARDSON, Richard E	L-3-10
RICHARDSON, Thomas L	Walls of the Missing
RICHARDSON, Vernon L	D-1-6
RICHEY, Charles V	N-21-4
RICHMOND, Herman D Sr	G-11-19

RICKARD, Patrick J	F-18-26
RICKENBAKER, Tourie B	D-7-5
RICKETTS, John W	A-12-11
RIDDEL, Jacques E	M-22-7
RIDDELL, John F	N-21-5
RIDDLEHOOVER, Joyce C	Walls of the Missing
RIDENOUR, Donald W	C-3-24
RIDENOUR, Edward E	C-1-30
RIDEOUT, James A	P-15-16
RIDEOUT, Robert M	G-13-6
RIDER, Dale G	D-12-8
RIDER, James J	E-6-22
RIEGER, Elroy F	F-14-10
RIEGER, Warren C	G-10-19
RIELAG, Lester E	A-10-16
RIEVE, Fred K	L-16-15
RIFE, John R	C-11-10
RIGAPOULOS, John	K-1-9
RIGG, Donald G	Walls of the Missing
RIGGALL, Frederick F	L-7-11
RIGGINS, Francis L	O-17-11
RIGGS, Edwin L	I-7-18
RIGGS, James W	L-20-7
RIGGS, Richard V	K-6-4
RIGGS, Wenzel C	D-11-4
RIGHTMIRE, Roy E Jr	J-17-14
RIGSBY, Louis H	J-10-18
RILEY, Charles W	Walls of the Missing
RILEY, George H Jr	O-4-17
RILEY, Harley H Jr	Walls of the Missing
RILEY, James W	D-14-32
RILEY, Robert D	F-15-16
RIMMER, James D	B-11-13
RIND, Robert R	C-7-14
RINFRETTE, Hugh F	D-8-32
RING, Leonard S	B-16-20
RINGBLOOM, Guy A	I-21-7
RINGHEIM, Earl N	Walls of the Missing
RINKA, Clarence L	D-15-7
RINKER, Carl J	L-6-14
RIPPEN, Donald D	A-9-20
RISER, William C	Walls of the Missing
RISH, Wendel E	Walls of the Missing
RISO, Peter J	C-9-28
RIST, Harold E	A-3-18
RITCHIE, Robert G	Walls of the Missing
RITCHIE, William H	Walls of the Missing
RITCHIE, William H	J-10-6
RITTER, Edward W L	J-10-11
RITTER, Marvin B	Walls of the Missing
RIVERA, Herbert	Walls of the Missing
RIVERS, Clifton W	K-13-5
RIVERS, James C	H-11-18
ROACH, Agnew	F-16-24
ROACH, Harry P	B-10-24
ROACH, Henry V	G-21-24
ROAN, Francis S	I-14-9
ROAT, Earl L	D-20-32

ROBACZYNSKI, John S	B-3-22
ROBBINS, Edward J	Walls of the Missing
ROBERSON, Bernard L	I-19-16
ROBERTS, Albert R	B-20-14
ROBERTS, Alexander G	B-4-27
ROBERTS, Basil	B-2-10
ROBERTS, Benjamin G	P-12-5
ROBERTS, Charles B	Walls of the Missing
ROBERTS, Earl T	E-1-12
ROBERTS, George E	Walls of the Missing
ROBERTS, Gerald W	K-11-20
ROBERTS, James E	K-1-12
ROBERTS, James V	L-13-13
ROBERTS, John J	Walls of the Missing
ROBERTS, John O	L-16-13
ROBERTS, Merlin	O-20-4
ROBERTS, Raymond C	M-12-9
ROBERTS, William R	Walls of the Missing
ROBERTSON, Curtis E	J-13-21
ROBERTSON, Ezell M	J-19-6
ROBERTSON, James C	A-7-4
ROBERTSON, John Jr	F-21-27
ROBERTSON, John M II	B-18-12
ROBERTSON, Melvin J	K-10-19
ROBESON, Ralph G	Walls of the Missing
ROBILLARD, Frank C	G-16-21
ROBINSON, Frank M	Walls of the Missing
ROBINSON, Frederick A	Walls of the Missing
ROBINSON, Frederick B	F-11-26
ROBINSON, George F	B-8-20
ROBINSON, George J	Walls of the Missing
ROBINSON, Harold T Jr	H-8-24
ROBINSON, James K	D-5-18
ROBINSON, James W	Walls of the Missing
ROBINSON, Kenneth R	M-10-5
ROBINSON, Mc Calvin J	Walls of the Missing
ROBINSON, Pervey S	G-4-4
ROBINSON, Richard E	D-9-31
ROBINSON, Robert	B-13-7
ROBINSON, Russell K Jr	I-2-12
ROBINSON, Thomas D	D-13-13
ROBKEN, Harold F	Walls of the Missing
ROBLES, Julian C	B-19-26
ROBLING, John A	K-6-18
ROBY, George T	Walls of the Missing
ROCCHIO, Charles A	E-6-24
ROCCO, Philip J	O-12-2
ROCHA, Miguel	G-19-24
ROCHEFORT, William H	I-10-7
ROCHELLE, Kenneth	M-10-12
ROCK, Lawrence J	Walls of the Missing
ROCKFORD, Sonnie J	F-1-5
ROCKWELL, Tom R	F-20-11
ROCQUE, Francis L	M-5-10
RODDY, Travis A	E-6-4
RODE, Raf F Jr	H-2-15
RODEK, Alex M	Walls of the Missing
RODENHIZER, Duke H	A-12-3

RODGERS, Harry C I-19-5
RODGERS, Laymon I-21-21
RODGERS, Martin G P-13-6
RODGERS, Walter W E-2-11
RODOLA, Joseph Jr C-4-32
RODRIGUES, Edward P K-15-6
RODRIGUES, Rudolfo M-17-4
RODRIGUEZ, Ebdon J Jr B-12-27
RODRIGUEZ, Herminio Jr N-21-6
RODRIGUEZ, John B C-4-15
RODRIGUEZ, Louis O A-18-17
RODRIGUEZ, Mariano T J-11-6
RODRIGUEZ, Tony H-17-11
RODRUAN, Robert D E-7-22
ROE, Edgar Allan I-15-19
ROEHRICH, Carl F B-13-30
ROESER, Harry G-12-21
ROGAN, Charles J F-1-10
ROGAN, Thomas A H-14-2
ROGER, Weston F-2-27
ROGERS, Charles H F-2-12
ROGERS, Clare K C-6-19
ROGERS, Donald E N-20-9
ROGERS, Gerald O J-20-17
ROGERS, Harry J D-6-20
ROGERS, Hilliard C A-16-7
ROGERS, Howard H C-9-12
ROGERS, John R E-11-9
ROGERS, Julian H Walls of the Missing
ROGERS, Robert M J-10-20
ROGUES, Ernest B-4-26
ROGUSKI, Leonard J K-8-5
ROHNER, Ronald R D-6-6
ROHR, Norbert P A-6-24
ROHRBACH, Walter N-10-10
ROHWEDDER, John C Jr C-13-14
ROJOWSKI, Frank G-12-26
ROKITA, John S A-8-26
ROLAND, John W F-15-7
ROLFE, George W F-14-8
ROLLAND, William E Jr N-14-17
ROLLET, Lee H E-20-26
ROLLINS, B D F-15-13
ROLLINS, Howell R J-15-4
ROLLINS, Kenneth G O-15-9
ROLPH, Robert C D-9-8
ROMA, Angelo G-12-4
ROMAN, Eugene C G-2-18
ROMAN, Joseph A A-10-13
ROMAN, Leo J H-1-26
ROMANIELLO, George M F-21-16
ROMERO, Wallace R Sr C-3-15
ROMIG, Charles E D-16-8
ROMKEMA, John R C-1-22
ROMNESS, Vernon R I-12-19
RONK, Herbert B G-8-15
RONKETTE, George S I-3-4
ROONEY, Francis E A-6-2

ROONEY, George W Walls of the Missing
ROOR, Dirk M-19-13
ROOS, Charles G D-5-26
ROOT, William A II C-13-17
ROPER, Elbert P G-21-23
ROPIAK, George V Walls of the Missing
ROPP, John D H-2-24
ROPPLE, William T Jr D-18-18
RORER, Frank H Walls of the Missing
ROSAK, Albert H-21-4
ROSATI, Dominic A I-9-22
ROSE, Charles D B-18-24
ROSE, Charley T H-15-16
ROSE, Edward A K-20-2
ROSE, Jake L-8-15
ROSE, John L F-15-1
ROSE, Maurice C-1-1
ROSE, Olin W A-12-1
ROSE, Philip M O-14-9
ROSE, Shirley I-9-19
ROSEBERRY, Joseph E[313] N-10-16
ROSEN, Arthur S E-15-10
ROSENBERG, Donald N D-5-1
ROSENKRANTZ, David Walls of the Missing
ROSENTHAL, John B J-8-19
ROSENTHAL, Paul C J-2-19
ROSETTA, Charles A D-5-3
ROSFELD, David V L-7-20
ROSICK, William S O-18-17
ROSKOWICK, Thomas L P-8-11
ROSS, Charles F Walls of the Missing
ROSS, Clark E B-1-13
ROSS, Denver G E-7-25
ROSS, Edward F M-19-12
ROSS, Eric G K-18-2
ROSS, Eugene G I-5-1
ROSS, George W Jr I-16-8
ROSS, Joseph H G-17-24
ROSS, Kenneth S H-1-18
ROSS, Madison H Walls of the Missing
ROSS, Novie N O-9-11
ROSS, Robert F A-20-31
ROSSELET, John U N-17-3
ROSSETTI, Joseph F A-6-23
ROSSI, Alfred P E-3-26
ROSSI, Rocco J H-4-7
ROSSITER, Joel H E-14-3
ROSSON, Melvin V Walls of the Missing
ROSTAD, Dale R D-19-9
ROTARIUS, Joseph A Walls of the Missing
ROTH, David M H-7-25
ROTH, Frank E Jr L-10-18
ROTH, John L O-14-15
ROTH, Joseph B E-9-27
ROTH, Paul E C-14-1
ROTH, Virgil H M-21-10
ROTH, Wesley F H-18-7
ROTHE, Alex G-9-10

ROTHFUSS, Lewis W N-11-16
ROTHROCK, John B P-3-1
ROTHSTEIN, Sylvester A H-2-11
ROUNSEVILLE, Arthur G C-12-12
ROUPA, Eduardo F D-3-15
ROUSE, John H C-3-5
ROUTHIER, Austin W Walls of the Missing
ROWE, Albert O H-11-8
ROWE, Harrison A K-16-10
ROWE, Robert B F-19-3
ROWELL, James M C-1-4
ROWLAND, Sims A C-9-11
ROWLAND, Thomas H Jr F-10-19
ROWLEY, Fitch H J-20-12
ROWLEY, Paul H D-21-21
ROWSE, Robert M N-14-3
ROY, Anthony J Walls of the Missing
ROY, Sanford G Walls of the Missing
ROYAL, Howard O B-11-6
ROYALL, Dayton C D-4-13
ROYALL, William M D-15-3
ROYSE, Everett G N-14-16
ROZAK, Alex J N-15-5
ROZNIATA, Chester E P-12-17
ROZWALKA, Leonard S O-3-4
RUANE, James F H-21-18
RUBENSTEIN, Isidore L-1-11
RUBENSTEIN, Murry E-1-21
RUBLE, Charles G Walls of the Missing
RUBLEWSKY, Henry A Walls of the Missing
RUCH, Kenneth R O-20-11
RUCINSKI, Joseph P-14-16
RUCKER, George O-19-15
RUCKER, Richard W Walls of the Missing
RUCKMAN, Jeff D F-15-8
RUDD, Carl D[314] I-5-19
RUDES, Marx C L-20-1
RUDIN, George C F-1-19
RUDISAIL, Charles A N-8-15
RUDNITSKY, Bud E P-20-10
RUDYNSKI, Albert F H-10-27
RUFENER, John I-9-2
RUFKAHR, Omar H D-7-31
RUGGLES, Richard C N-21-7
RUHL, Raymond P E-8-3
RUIZ, Arthur F L-19-9
RUIZ, Ray S J-20-6
RULLO, Umberto J G-9-3
RUMBLE, Francis L P-21-8
RUMOLO, Carmen J-16-16
RUOTOLO, Frank J-6-21
RUPE, Robert J B-4-15
RUSH, Foy A Walls of the Missing
RUSH, Frederick A H-12-23
RUSH, Orville A A-13-9
RUSHMORE, George W B-9-6
RUSHTON, Richard H I-4-20
RUSSELL, Edward E A-18-30

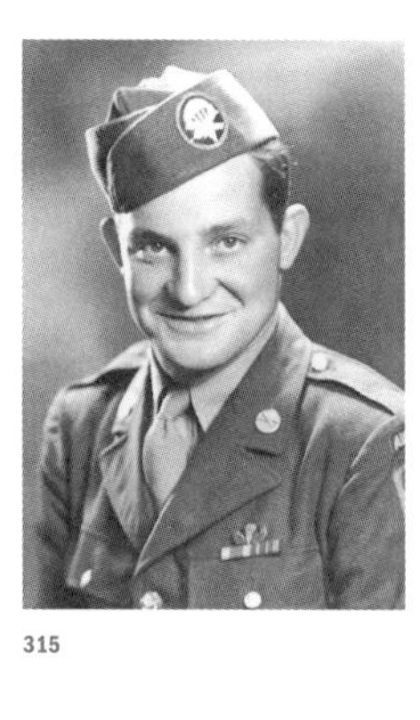
315

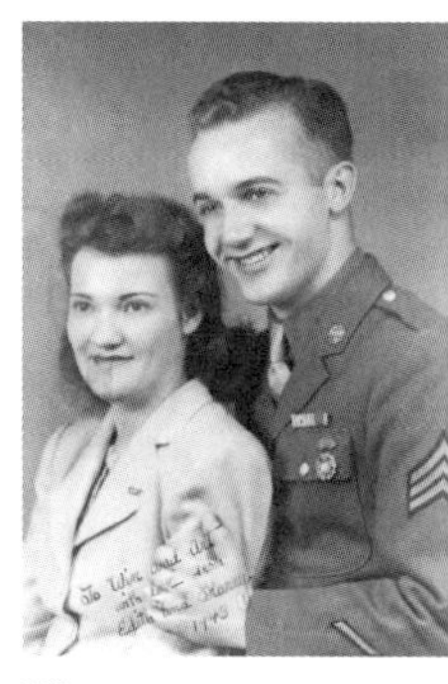
316

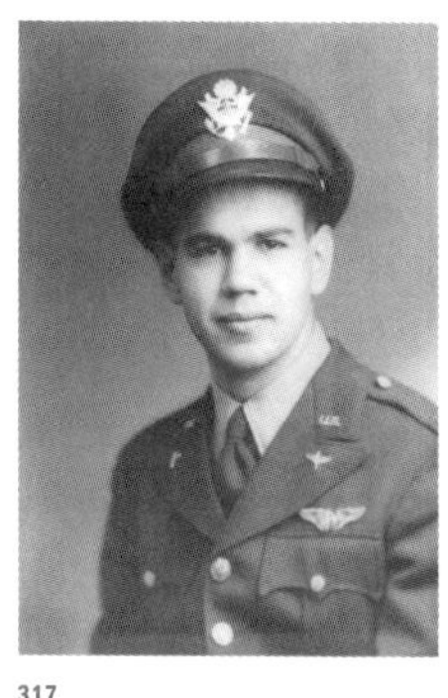
317

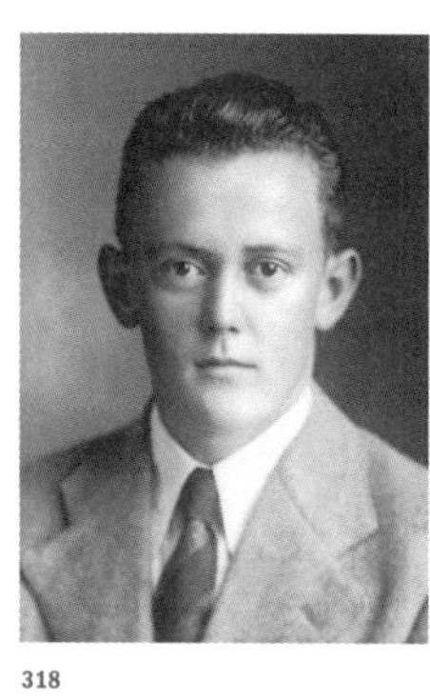
318

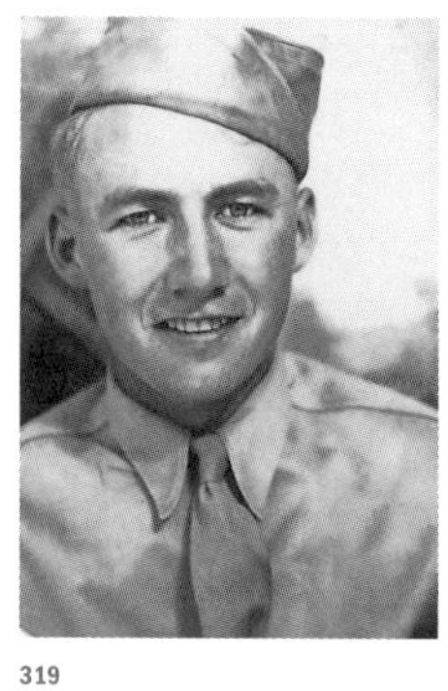
319

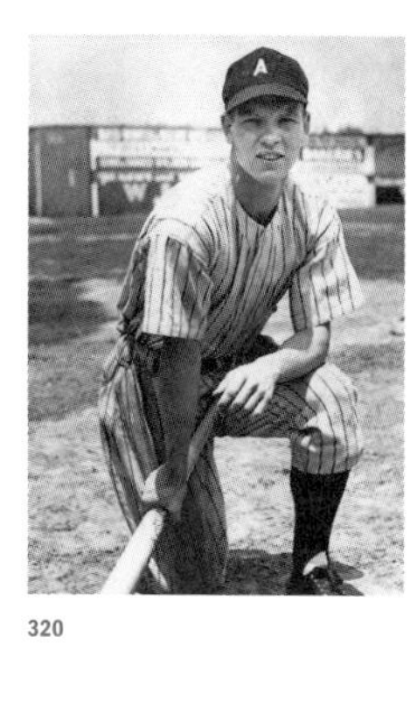
320

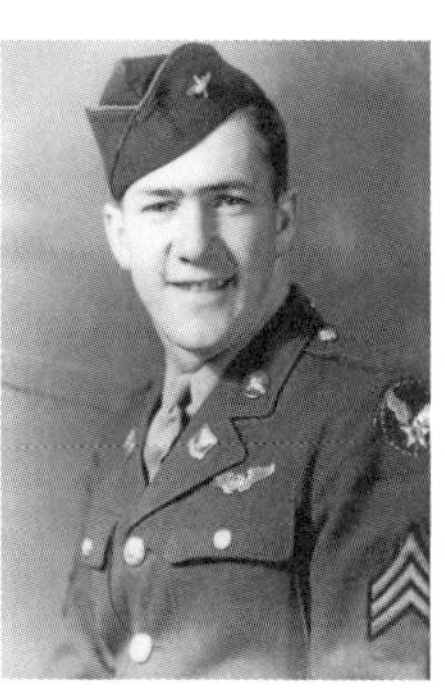
321

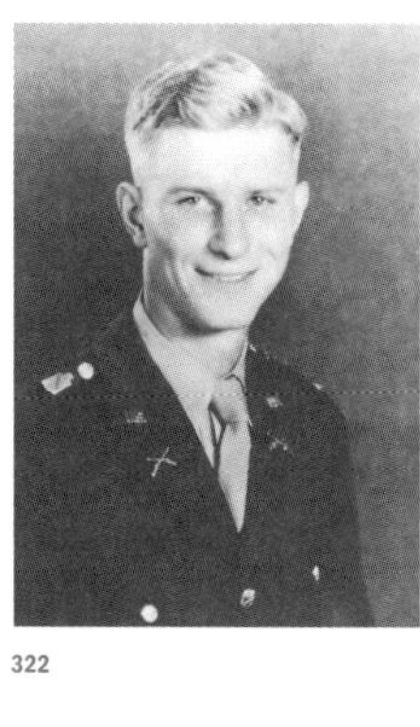
322

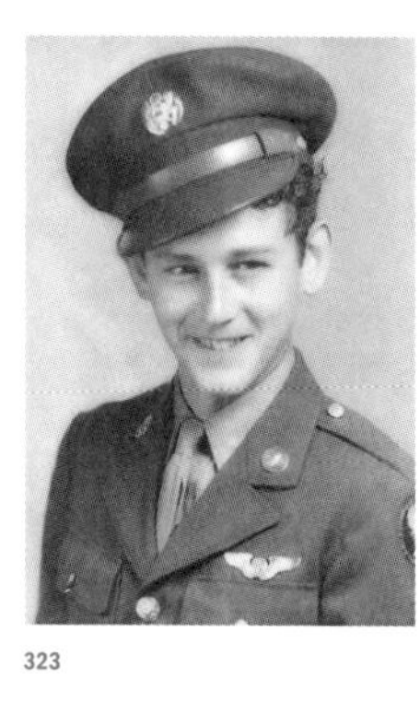
323

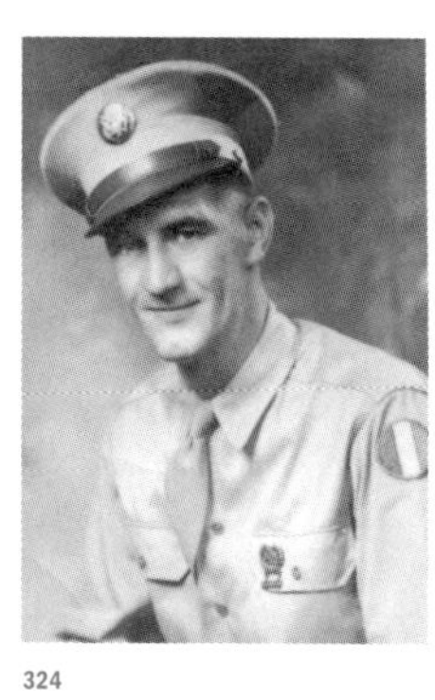
324

RUSSELL, Eldo A	Walls of the Missing
RUSSELL, Gordon R Jr	J-9-7
RUSSELL, Jack R	P-22-10
RUSSELL, Raymond D	E-10-12
RUSSELL, Wayne E	G-12-17
RUSSELL, William A	G-4-13
RUSSO, Cosmo M	G-16-1
RUSSO, Daniel H	M-2-12
RUSTAD, Vernon R	B-5-2
RUTH, Raymond J	Walls of the Missing
RUTHERFORD, John H	B-21-3
RUTIGLIANO, Dominick	O-12-1
RUTJES, Donald A [315]	P-1-13
RUTKOWSKI, Victor S	Walls of the Missing
RUTLEDGE, James C	C-4-25
RUTLEDGE, Robert L	D-7-21
RUTTER, John R	A-6-28
RUYBAL, Cresencio	D-1-10
RUZICKA, Victor H	B-9-19
RUZZO, Walter L	O-7-7
RYAN, Edward J	M-18-9
RYAN, Edward P	B-8-26
RYAN, George J	L-14-4
RYAN, James L Jr	O-7-17
RYAN, John F	L-21-8
RYAN, Joseph A	L-19-17
RYAN, Richard I	C-5-18
RYAN, Thomas	D-18-6
RYBCINSKI, Joseph E	E-11-15
RYBIN, Eldon	C-20-13
RYBOLT, Donald L	Walls of the Missing
RYCHTER, Andrew	A-2-14
RYCKMAN, Robert E	H-2-27
RYMER, Andrew M	L-17-2
RYZINSKI, Theodore J	G-15-20
RZASA, Joseph F	E-11-1
RZEPPA, Robert L	Walls of the Missing

S

SAAKE, Harry A Jr [316]	C-18-13
SAARENPAA, George O	H-9-15
SAATHOFF, Roy E	A-20-20
SABELLA, Charles T	D-15-11
SABIN, Rex	J-2-3
SABO, Steve	H-1-23
SACHEWICZ, William P	O-15-4
SACKVILLE, George E	M-19-8
SADLER, Ralph H	P-10-17
SAFKO, Michael J Jr	B-3-5
SAGELY, Daniel E	B-1-32
SAGER, Herbert O	H-21-17
SAGER, Robert W [317]	Walls of the Missing
SAHLBERG, Raymond E	Walls of the Missing
SALAJCZYK, Jesse G	K-12-12
SALAMONE, Sylvester	H-8-18
SALAZAR, Albert M	Walls of the Missing
SALAZAR, Santiago C	H-20-14
SALEK, Peter S	B-2-18
SALL, Henry	P-20-1
SALLEE, Robert B	O-3-5
SALLES, Gilbert	D-13-14
SALTZER, James P	J-11-22
SALZBRUNN, Kenneth L	O-16-7
SAM, Paul	P-19-1
SAMBANIS, George	O-20-1
SAMPLE, Arthur M	L-14-13
SAMPLE, James W	Walls of the Missing
SAMPSEL, George F	O-14-12
SANCHEZ, Mike P	A-21-4
SANDBERG, Richard R	Walls of the Missing
SANDERS, Ewell W	F-17-22
SANDERS, John J	Walls of the Missing
SANDERS, Lewis L Jr	Walls of the Missing
SANDERS, Marvin E	K-12-6
SANDERS, Robert A [318]	G-12-24
SANDHAGEN, Paul R	O-14-6
SANDISON, James T	B-2-11
SANDNESS, Ervin A	E-21-20
SANDOR, Frank A	D-6-28
SANDOVAL, William L	Walls of the Missing
SANDS, Harlie W	M-8-7
SANDS, John G	P-21-1
SANDS, Willie M	O-12-4
SANDY, Stanley H	A-6-20
SANFORD, Frederick K	Walls of the Missing
SANG, Frederick B	A-20-1
SANSUM, Harry R	N-21-8
SANTELLO, John F Jr	B-1-6
SANTILLAN, Paul J	Walls of the Missing
SANTOMIERY, Anthony J	I-16-3
SANTORA, Peter	Walls of the Missing
SANTOS, William V	A-5-2
SAPONARO, Rocco D	H-1-15
SAPP, Walter L	C-6-13
SARGEANT, Philip E	L-2-9
SARGENT, Kermit E [319]	Walls of the Missing
SARIYAN, Ohannes	A-14-8
SARKA, Charles	F-2-4
SARNIKOWSKI, Frank	K-18-18
SAROCKAS, Charles Jr	Walls of the Missing
SARUBBI, Arthur J	J-13-20
SARVER, William A [320]	K-8-17
SARZILLO, Salvatore A	H-2-4
SASAOKA, Itsumu	Walls of the Missing
SASSEN, Marvin L	N-1-5
SASSON, Edward	I-2-5
SATCHELL, George W	D-13-18
SATOSK, Harold E	N-10-11
SATTERFIELD, Audalee	J-16-15
SAUER, Allen C	E-3-22

SAUER, John R	Walls of the Missing
SAUNDERS, Charles R	L-8-10
SAUNDERS, James H	P-16-4
SAUNDERS, John C	J-15-22
SAUNDERS, Stewart R	M-11-11
SAUNDERSON, George M	Walls of the Missing
SAUR, Robert V	H-5-11
SAVAGE, Donald E [321]	I-7-5
SAVALLI, Michael R	B-16-6
SAVILLE, Harry L Jr [322]	D-21-1
SAVITZ, Ellis B	L-3-18
SAWATZKY, Martin W	O-4-11
SAWYER, Elmo	B-6-23
SAWYER, Phillip F	N-8-13
SAWYERS, Louie L	L-19-18
SAXON, James A	L-19-4
SAXONIS, Nicholas	P-17-17
SAYDACK, Ervin L	F-16-8
SAYER, Joseph	P-21-2
SAYERS, James L	N-5-8
SAYLOR, Russell E	L-14-3
SCAFIDE, Salvatore C	H-7-8
SCALF, Andrew J	C-15-30
SCALLY, Marvin E	K-7-16
SCANLON, Thomas J	Walls of the Missing
SCARBROUGH, John D	Walls of the Missing
SCARLETT, Leo S	Walls of the Missing
SCAVELLO, Sebastian	Walls of the Missing
SCHADEGG, Louis G	K-1-6
SCHAEFFER, Homer H	F-10-10
SCHAEFFLER, Albert C	B-17-17
SCHAFER, Harlan E	D-4-27
SCHAFER, Roscoe E	F-12-12
SCHAFF, Grant C	Walls of the Missing
SCHANE, Charles E	Walls of the Missing
SCHANKE, E Wilkie	A-3-20
SCHANTZ, John D	D-14-12
SCHAPER, Ellenwood R	K-2-18
SCHAPKA, Robert C	Walls of the Missing
SCHARFF, George	N-10-14
SCHATZ, Laverne E	D-13-21
SCHAUBE, Charles H	I-19-3
SCHEAR, Robert L	Walls of the Missing
SCHEIBELEIN, Edward M	F-1-18
SCHEIER, August E	H-20-10
SCHENCK, Harold S	E-9-4
SCHENKEL, Emil H	B-12-32
SCHENKENBERGER, Jacob	G-13-8
SCHERER, Fred M	Walls of the Missing
SCHERPE, William A	D-13-22
SCHERZ, Edwin C	D-15-6
SCHEUBER, Harold B	Walls of the Missing
SCHEXNAYDER, Joseph L	Walls of the Missing
SCHIFFERNS, Walter B	Walls of the Missing
SCHILLER, George	I-4-9
SCHILLER, Robert D	P-1-5
SCHILTZ, Nicholas C	B-7-16
SCHIMMER, Alfred J	B-11-29
SCHINASI, Seymour B	C-15-31
SCHINDLER, Robert D	F-9-4
SCHIPPANG, Alvin T	Walls of the Missing
SCHLAUD, Ernest B	B-9-14
SCHLOBOHM, Leland R [323]	Walls of the Missing
SCHLOENDORN, John G	Walls of the Missing
SCHLORMAN, Louis J	H-6-17
SCHLUETER, Harold F	N-21-9
SCHLUETER, Roy H	B-5-31
SCHMAL, Fred G	Walls of the Missing
SCHMALENBACH, Paul J	Walls of the Missing
SCHMEISER, Frederick	F-18-2
SCHMIDT, Arthur P	H-16-5
SCHMIDT, Berl O	B-14-11
SCHMIDT, Donald A	I-3-16
SCHMIDT, Eugene F	G-18-2
SCHMIDT, Ivan E	J-1-22
SCHMIDT, Leo	Walls of the Missing
SCHMIDT, Thomas	J-12-15
SCHMIDTKE, Louis F	B-3-24
SCHMITT, Benedict G	D-15-5
SCHMITT, Martin	A-7-3
SCHMITT, Richard J	D-20-24
SCHMITZ, Howard W	Walls of the Missing
SCHMITZ, Raymond G	K-18-17
SCHMITZ, Robert R	G-1-22
SCHMITZ, William V [324]	G-8-26
SCHMOLLER, William	K-13-7
SCHMOLLINGER, Charles L	P-5-5
SCHNABEL, Lester E	E-12-9
SCHNAGL, Frank J	L-11-22
SCHNEBLY, Dexter C	J-21-5
SCHNEIDER, Albert	F-5-12
SCHNEIDER, Alfred F	D-18-32
SCHNEIDER, Arthur	I-1-7
SCHNEIDER, Arthur A	L-15-14
SCHNEIDER, Carroll R	Walls of the Missing
SCHNEIDER, Elmer E	O-5-3
SCHNEIDER, George	B-12-25
SCHNEIDER, Paul H JR	E-2-23
SCHNEIDEWIND, Raymond	H-21-13
SCHNELL, Albert E	D-19-16
SCHNIER, Manfred W	A-1-29
SCHNUELLE, Vernon R	Walls of the Missing
SCHOENGRUND, Gerhardt	C-13-24
SCHOENTHALER, Reinhold A	B-10-30
SCHOEPF, Charles J	F-17-11
SCHOEPP, Jacob A	G-17-22
SCHOLL, Harlan B	A-14-7
SCHOLTZ, Frank W	A-10-8
SCHOONAERT, Raymond C	N-1-7
SCHOONMAKER, George B	N-4-14
SCHRADER, Harold L	Walls of the Missing
SCHRAFF, Frederick E Jr	G-8-23
SCHRECK, Joseph L	M-7-11
SCHREIER, Edward W	Walls of the Missing
SCHRODER, John F	D-12-17
SCHROEDER, Harold R	Walls of the Missing
SCHROEDER, Merl L	Walls of the Missing
SCHROLL, Lawrence E	O-1-2
SCHROYER, George S	Walls of the Missing
SCHUBERT, Elmer R	I-2-1
SCHUBERT, George Jr	F-19-27
SCHUCHARD, Lewis A	G-18-24
SCHUETZLE, Palmer F	F-1-14
SCHULKE, John J	C-8-12
SCHULTE, Donald E	M-3-2
SCHULTE, Herbert F	L-11-15
SCHULTE, Norman E	Walls of the Missing
SCHULTZ, Chester J	M-12-8
SCHULTZ, Edwin W Jr	C-3-30
SCHULTZ, George J	B-18-5
SCHULTZ, Harvey W	F-1-2
SCHULTZ, William W	F-13-13
SCHULZ, James E	P-18-5
SCHUSTER, Francis W	O-16-9
SCHUTT, Edward J	K-9-16
SCHUTT, Merle S	Walls of the Missing
SCHUTTE, Ralph E	N-14-5
SCHUVIE, Adolph G	J-18-2
SCHUYLER, Robert E	Walls of the Missing
SCHUYLER, Steven B	E-8-23
SCHWARTZ, David	O-5-17
SCHWARTZ, Emmet W	Walls of the Missing
SCHWARTZ, Paul	Walls of the Missing
SCHWARTZ, Robert	H-2-17
SCHWARZ, Edward V	F-16-11
SCHWEITZER, Carl F	D-16-26
SCHWENSEN, Richard L	B-6-16
SCHWEYER, Leonard W	N-4-15
SCHWINDT, Henry	D-17-21
SCIARRINO, Joseph A	O-20-15
SCIFO, Salvatore A	H-21-19
SCIRTO, Joseph J	C-17-4
SCOBEY, Wilfley Jr	B-13-17
SCOBY, Lyle J	O-9-4
SCOFIELD, Robert D	E-16-23
SCOTT, Austin B	Walls of the Missing
SCOTT, Bert E	A-8-8
SCOTT, Daniel J	D-14-21
SCOTT, David D	M-18-4
SCOTT, Frank J	B-10-6
SCOTT, George E	B-10-31
SCOTT, Howard M	G-1-7
SCOTT, James C	Walls of the Missing
SCOTT, James D Sr	O-5-16
SCOTT, James W	I-14-13
SCOTT, Paul J	O-4-3
SCOTT, Paul R	J-16-1
SCOTT, Robert D	D-8-17
SCOTT, Robert M	K-9-17
SCOTT, Wallace K	K-4-13
SCOTT, Weaver N	A-6-4
SCOURBYS, Constantine	Walls of the Missing
SCRIVANI, Lawrence J	Walls of the Missing
SCRUGGS, Wiley T	E-15-11

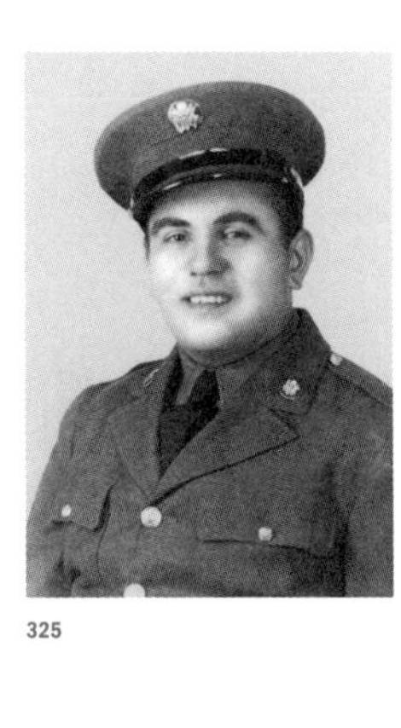
325

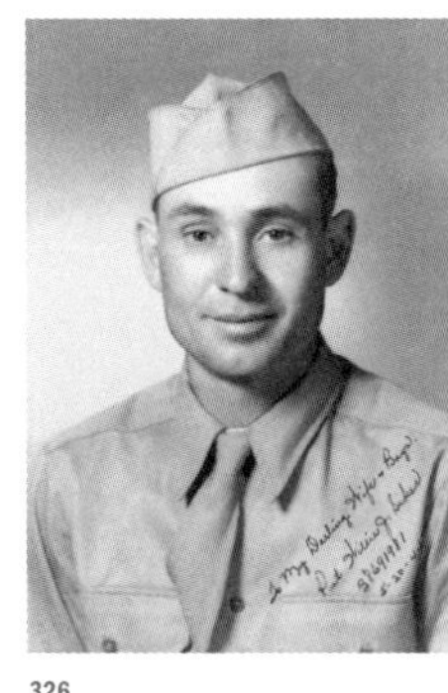
326

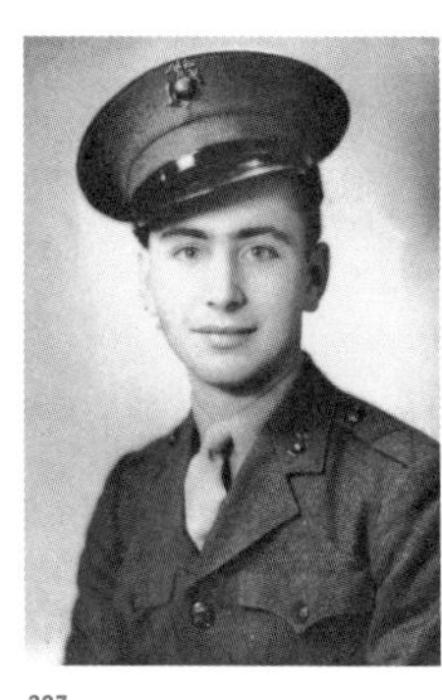
327

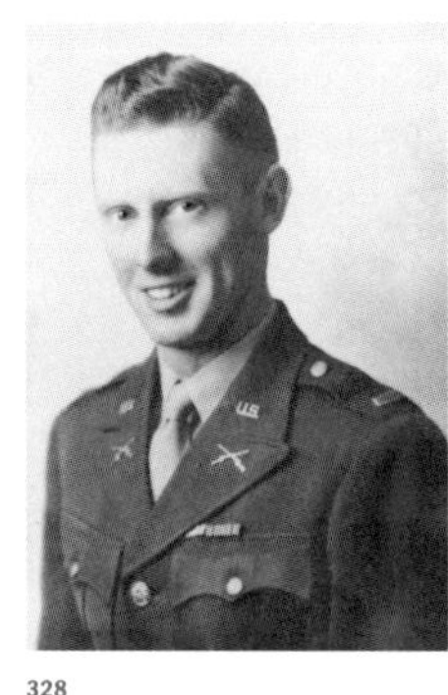
328

SCRUPSKI, Peter	K-13-11
SCULLEY, Charles W	E-4-2
SCULLY, John E	B-10-10
SCURLOCK, Walter B	A-5-25
SEABROOKE, Ernest R	I-14-15
SEAMAN, Alvin F	K-13-15
SEAMAN, Owen M	Walls of the Missing
SEAMAN, Robert H	Walls of the Missing
SEARS, Wyley V	G-8-8
SEAVER, Vernon R	N-9-1
SECAUR, Lee W	E-19-5
SECHRIST, Theodore D	L-11-12
SECON, Robert	K-4-11
SEDERQUIST, Donald L	Walls of the Missing
SEDLACEK, Edward E Jr	H-4-10
SEE, Philip J	B-18-31
SEEFELDT, Edward S	H-2-8
SEEGER, Robert W	Walls of the Missing
SEEL, Elsworth L	D-2-26
SEELEY, Aldrich A	Walls of the Missing
SEELY, Eugene W	I-11-17
SEEMON, Bernard	N-12-17
SEENEY, Albert T	A-14-29
SEESE, Robert L	E-20-6
SEGER, Eugene W	Walls of the Missing
SEGER, Robert R	B-9-25
SEGRAVES, Nelson T	H-15-19
SEIBEL, Thomas J	H-16-18
SEIBERT, Adolph J	A-8-12
SEIDENSTRICKER, James	A-7-1
SEIDL, Sylvan H	F-11-2
SEIFERT, Raymond W	B-19-27
SEIFERT, Robert B	Walls of the Missing
SEIFRIED, Philip	B-7-24
SEIGLER, James C	Walls of the Missing
SEITZ, John H	D-10-25
SEITZINGER, Jack M	F-4-23
SELF, Leroy L Jr	Walls of the Missing
SELFRIDGE, William	C-20-32
SELL, Edward W	D-19-25
SELL, Raymond H	Walls of the Missing
SELLERS, Charles L	E-4-15
SELMES, Charles R	L-10-11
SELMON, Dwight C	B-12-24
SELSER, Joseph K	N-17-11

SEMANEK, Paul E	F-12-18
SEMRAD, Marion F	Walls of the Missing
SEMSEY, John J [325]	I-14-2
SENDLOCK, Edward W	G-15-3
SENDZICK, William A	Walls of the Missing
SENGER, Joseph	L-14-18
SENIOR, William G	E-14-20
SENK, John J	Walls of the Missing
SERING, Joe	P-16-7
SERPICO, Frank R	Walls of the Missing
SERRABELLA, Armand J	H-9-12
SERRATA, Matias Jr	A-12-10
SERSHA, John P	Walls of the Missing
SESSA, Frank A	Walls of the Missing
SESSER, William H	K-5-13
SESSMER, Oscar L	M-1-14
SESTITO, Rinaldo L	N-13-1
SETTLE, William D	B-14-12
SETTLER, Harrison	A-1-2
SEUBERLI, Richard E	A-16-15
SEVERINE, Donald G	Walls of the Missing
SEVERINO, Frank J	D-10-30
SEVIER, Jerry A	G-2-8
SEVIGNY, Normand P	M-10-4
SEWA, Charles L	O-9-8
SEXSON, Luther D	C-11-14
SEXTON, Haskell G	D-1-30
SEYFRIED, Francis J	Walls of the Missing
SEYMOUR, Clifford C	K-12-18
SGRIGNUOLI, Carmen J	O-5-11
SHACKLEY, Charles A Jr	Walls of the Missing
SHAEFFER, Roy M	L-3-8
SHAFER, Robert T	Walls of the Missing
SHAFFER, Donald E	Walls of the Missing
SHAFFER, Raymond G	C-4-27
SHAMBURG, Kenneth F	E-7-26
SHANK, Corwin P Jr	J-4-18
SHANK, Harold I	F-19-16
SHANK, Lloyd C Jr	K-4-22
SHANK, Lyle J	N-10-12
SHANKLES, Leslie E	Walls of the Missing
SHANKS, Andrew B	I-17-8
SHANN, Paul	Walls of the Missing
SHANNON, Truman A	Walls of the Missing
SHAPIRO, Joseph	M-2-6

SHAPLEY, Joseph R	H-6-23
SHARKEY, Bernard E	J-1-7
SHARP, Dabney W	Walls of the Missing
SHARP, John E	D-21-18
SHAUGHNESSY, James T	C-2-23
SHAUVER, Melvin Jr	J-2-15
SHAUVIN, Eugene P	Walls of the Missing
SHAW, Howard A	B-4-4
SHAW, Robert W	Walls of the Missing
SHAW, Teddy G	Walls of the Missing
SHAWVER, Lee E	M-11-5
SHEA, Edward T	F-3-14
SHEA, Frank L	E-19-13
SHEA, Lawrence F	D-11-26
SHEAHAN, Maurice E Jr	G-18-17
SHEARER, Martin G	Walls of the Missing
SHEBECK, Daniel A	H-11-1
SHEEHAN, Arthur E Jr	O-5-14
SHEEHAN, Joseph J	K-9-14
SHEEHAN, William V	G-9-26
SHEELY, Howard T	D-21-32
SHEETS, Glen H	Walls of the Missing
SHEFFER, Howard F	Walls of the Missing
SHELDEN, Harold R	L-10-5
SHELDON, Melvin S	Walls of the Missing
SHELDON, Robert M	I-20-4
SHELDON, Stanley W	Walls of the Missing
SHELTON, Junior J	Walls of the Missing
SHENK, Martin H	N-4-13
SHENKEL, Carson E	F-13-21
SHEPARD, James W	Walls of the Missing
SHEPHERD, Ancil U	Walls of the Missing
SHEPHERD, Marshall M	Walls of the Missing
SHEPPARD, John J	P-18-14
SHERASKI, Richard	E-4-5
SHERE, Fred C Jr	I-8-17
SHERET, Leslie E	N-3-16
SHERIDAN, Morbey A	A-16-4
SHERMAN, Albert	O-17-2
SHERMAN, Elmer E	D-19-3
SHERMAN, Harry F	A-8-31
SHERMAN, Jefferson Jr	F-6-16
SHERMAN, Lavern W	E-6-7
SHERRILL, Halsted	E-5-13
SHERRY, Horace L	B-1-20
SHERRY, John M	J-17-4
SHERWOOD, Robert Z	F-4-9
SHIELDS, Edward F Jr	D-12-3
SHIELDS, Kennedy J	Walls of the Missing
SHIELDS, Robah C Jr	H-14-16
SHIELDS, Robert W	C-1-19
SHIELDS, Thomas S	E-18-8
SHIELDS, William F	D-16-3
SHIFFER, James L	Walls of the Missing
SHILLEY, Frank S	M-10-2
SHIMEK, John	F-10-26
SHIMEK, Joseph M	H-13-24
SHIMOSKIE, Joseph Sr	D-12-4

Name	Location
SHINHOLSTER, Johnnie	Walls of the Missing
SHIPE, Cletis P	Walls of the Missing
SHIPP, Robert Jr	Walls of the Missing
SHIRE, Donald O	F-13-5
SHIRILLA, George J	K-20-16
SHIRLEY, Ralph C	P-19-16
SHOCKCOR, William T	L-19-14
SHOEMAKER, Eugene L	E-13-1
SHOEMAKER, Gilbert G	Walls of the Missing
SHOFF, William H	C-3-11
SHORES, Edwin E	B-3-12
SHORT, Emerson D	Walls of the Missing
SHORT, Harry L	Walls of the Missing
SHORT, Lee A	J-13-1
SHORTESS, Frank E Jr	E-16-7
SHORTRIDGE, Francis W	M-11-6
SHOTWELL, Gordon S	C-11-11
SHOUGH, James A	K-9-4
SHOUP, Clyde M	K-15-22
SHOVER, Russell A	A-3-6
SHROKA, Harold W	B-10-15
SHROUT, Clarence L	G-2-25
SHUFELBERGER, Lloyd R	A-4-10
SHULL, Alfred M	E-18-16
SHULTS, Charles C	D-20-23
SHULTZ, Norman D	L-6-4
SHUMSKI, Anthony J	D-4-6
SHUPE, Richard W	Walls of the Missing
SHURLEY, Harold E	B-19-22
SHURTLEFF, Dwight K	Walls of the Missing
SHURTZ, Guy F	E-20-13
SHUTE, Herbert C	G-6-2
SHUTTLEWORTH, Walter	C-18-21
SICILIANO, John J	Walls of the Missing
SIDDON, Desmond A	B-15-8
SIECKMAN, Donald D	B-1-16
SIEFFERT, Regis C	M-2-15
SIEGLE, Conrad B	P-12-15
SIEGWARTH, George J	B-7-15
SIEMON, Wayne E	C-2-15
SIERENS, Ernest J	Walls of the Missing
SIERGIEJ, Stanley V	J-17-7
SIERKS, Frederick V	J-10-1
SIERZEGA, Andrew S	C-19-31
SIES, Walter M	K-16-12
SIEVERS, Robert L	Walls of the Missing
SIGLE, Charles E	C-1-18
SIGLIN, George E	B-4-18
SIGLIN, James H	H-8-13
SIGMON, Rufus	F-20-19
SIGNORELLI, Benjamin	J-12-12
SIKES, Willie J [326]	D-15-4
SIKKENGA, Albert L Jr	I-10-13
SIKORSKI, Alfred	Walls of the Missing
SIKUT, Walter S	J-5-9
SILBERMAN, Bert	K-3-8
SILCOX, Herbert J	O-14-3
SILKOWSKI, Bernard P	E-7-16
SILLO, Albert A	O-17-8
SILVER, Sidney S	C-20-6
SILVERSTEIN, Harry P	Walls of the Missing
SILVERSTON, Robert L	H-10-4
SIMCO, Joseph G	D-3-2
SIMCOX, John W	E-15-12
SIMECHAK, John J	L-18-14
SIMEK, Rudolph R	P-8-17
SIMMONS, Charles B	N-10-9
SIMMONS, Colonel C	D-10-21
SIMMONS, Gordon E	C-7-12
SIMMONS, William C	M-22-1
SIMMONS, William D III	Walls of the Missing
SIMMS, Milton	K-16-7
SIMON, Anton C	K-5-5
SIMON, John M Jr	G-1-10
SIMON, John W	Walls of the Missing
SIMON, William L	Walls of the Missing
SIMONE, Attilio, J	L-21-5
SIMONEAU, Cleo E	B-12-6
SIMONS, Earle E	C-4-17
SIMONS, Robert W	M-22-11
SIMONSON, Paul F	Walls of the Missing
SIMONSON, Willis P	I-12-11
SIMPKINS, Jesse H	N-19-10
SIMPSON, Earl R	G-16-4
SIMPSON, Frederick J	N-15-16
SIMPSON, Joseph Robinson	N-11-6
SIMPSON, Maynard F	M-1-10
SIMPSON, Willard O	Walls of the Missing
SIMS, Jack	A-5-6
SINCLAIR, Kirk L Jr	A-9-22
SINGLETON, Charles A	L-15-17
SIPE, Daniel A Jr	Walls of the Missing
SIPES, Edwin H	N-21-11
SIPSEY, William B	E-12-17
SIQUEIROS, Carlos	P-1-3
SIRACUSANO, Clement J	C-18-6
SIROIS, Romeo A	Walls of the Missing
SISK, Jesse R	L-20-14
SITZMAN, August G Jr	K-19-7
SIZEMORE, Richard L	P-4-14
SJOERDSMA, Theodore	M-20-11
SKAFF, Irving W	P-12-3
SKAGGS, Robert L	N-21-12
SKAGGS, Wallace	H-13-19
SKALSKI, Chester F	I-15-20
SKEATS, Kenneth J	M-16-16
SKELLY, Thomas M	O-5-2
SKHAL, Melvin O	M-6-14
SKIBA, Merchie J	A-1-5
SKIDMORE, Eric S	E-1-8
SKIEN, Leif	G-18-19
SKINNER, Edward P	Walls of the Missing
SKINNER, Johnnie M	N-16-10
SKOLFIELD, Emery R	D-6-11
SKOLNICK, Philip M	E-5-9
SKUBE, Steve G	O-2-9
SLACK, Charles M	E-21-23
SLADE, David H	I-19-7
SLAGER, Eldon A	Walls of the Missing
SLATER, John T Jr	Walls of the Missing
SLAUGHTER, Chester C	L-18-20
SLAVEN, John E	I-17-12
SLAWECKI, Roman W	C-5-1
SLAY, William F	D-15-25
SLAYSMAN, James J	G-3-20
SLEDZIK, Anthony S	H-11-5
SLEETER, Robert J	A-17-31
SLEETH, Victor Jr	A-8-17
SLENKER, Kenneth E	Walls of the Missing
SLEPIN, Jerome	B-5-18
SLIFF, Lawrence J	Walls of the Missing
SLIGHT, Samuel E	C-6-23
SLIVKOFF, George	Walls of the Missing
SLOAN, Billy B	E-1-23
SLOMA, John E	B-1-10
SLONINE, Fredrick C	G-19-12
SLOSAR, Paul P	D-14-19
SLOSSON, Wyman C	Walls of the Missing
SLOTA, Louis	C-7-22
SLOTNICK, Max	Walls of the Missing
SLOVACEK, John C	D-1-11
SMALL, Asha P	O-14-2
SMALL, Austin J	A-4-26
SMALLEY, Walter G	C-19-22
SMALLEY, Win R	Walls of the Missing
SMALLING, William H	G-13-3
SMART, Ozal R	D-11-29
SMART, Raymond E Jr	N-21-13
SMELLA, John	A-7-26
SMERGALSKI, Edwin S	D-19-21
SMETANA, Emil	M-17-16
SMILEY, Richard C	G-14-14
SMILEY, Walter N	Walls of the Missing
SMISEK, Milton C [327]	D-21-24
SMITH, Alan F	G-16-20
SMITH, Albert C	L-15-15
SMITH, Allen E [328]	J-19-2
SMITH, Benjamin E	P-10-8
SMITH, Benjamin L	E-12-18
SMITH, Bow	M-10-8
SMITH, Brian T	Walls of the Missing
SMITH, Cecil B	B-11-25
SMITH, Charles E	O-10-15
SMITH, Charles E	L-5-3
SMITH, Charley F	G-6-14
SMITH, Clarence E	G-7-6
SMITH, Clyde J	N-10-8
SMITH, Darvin A	O-14-7
SMITH, Don	A-16-28
SMITH, Douglas H	Walls of the Missing
SMITH, Doyne E	B-21-27
SMITH, Edward G	E-7-7
SMITH, Edward J	O-2-8
SMITH, Edward M	C-20-17

329

330

SMITH, Edwin R	P-1-7
SMITH, Elbert R	A-3-31
SMITH, Elmer J Jr	K-4-19
SMITH, Frank W Jr	K-10-18
SMITH, Garnet L	N-11-1
SMITH, George A	C-13-1
SMITH, George F	A-16-14
SMITH, George W	C-3-22
SMITH, Glen W	Walls of the Missing
SMITH, Halcott L	H-19-10
SMITH, Harold N	F-17-10
SMITH, Harold S	Walls of the Missing
SMITH, Harris E	B-8-28
SMITH, Harry R	B-6-27
SMITH, Harry W	D-21-8
SMITH, Henry E	C-9-24
SMITH, Herbert R	C-18-19
SMITH, Herbert W	G-3-1
SMITH, Hilton A	Walls of the Missing
SMITH, Howard	F-6-8
SMITH, Howard A	M-19-4
SMITH, J Wesley O	C-13-4
SMITH, Jack E	M-10-16
SMITH, James A	A-19-13
SMITH, James B	C-20-23
SMITH, Jesse A	F-12-9
SMITH John H	D-11-17
SMITH, Joseph M	F-1-4
SMITH, Joseph R Jr	Walls of the Missing
SMITH, Kenneth D	L-16-1
SMITH, Lester	F-13-16
SMITH, Levert L Jr	F-17-23
SMITH, Lewis J	D-11-2
SMITH, Lloyd R	H-19-11
SMITH, Lorentz B	F-15-3
SMITH, Louis A	A-17-24
SMITH, Mart	F-13-26
SMITH, Milton E	Walls of the Missing
SMITH, Miner R	F-13-19
SMITH, Neal H	C-2-30
SMITH, Norman J	B-5-6
SMITH, Oaks H	Walls of the Missing
SMITH, Odell	C-21-17
SMITH, Oscar	F-10-2
SMITH, Otis	J-12-21

SMITH, Otto A	C-5-23
SMITH, Parker L	F-17-14
SMITH, Paul C	E-14-9
SMITH, Paul E	Walls of the Missing
SMITH, Phillip	B-20-29
SMITH, Rafe H	H-8-11
SMITH, Ralph D	A-19-21
SMITH, Ralph F	Walls of the Missing
SMITH, Ray V	P-14-4
SMITH, Richard C	D-11-22
SMITH, Richard E	B-3-20
SMITH, Robert J	K-12-3
SMITH, Robert L	K-7-8
SMITH, Robert O	M-18-12
SMITH, Robert W	J-4-5
SMITH, Robert W	E-3-11
SMITH, Roland G L	Walls of the Missing
SMITH, Teddy A	Walls of the Missing
SMITH, Theodore H	N-20-5
SMITH, Walter M	L-13-19
SMITH, Warren E	N-21-14
SMITH, Wayne R	K-2-14
SMITH, Wesley E Jr	B-20-11
SMITH, William	Walls of the Missing
SMITH, William D	O-14-14
SMITH, William F	A-7-18
SMITH, William I Jr	C-4-30
SMITH, William W	Walls of the Missing
SMITHHART, James D	Walls of the Missing
SMITS, Henry J	A-13-17
SMITTLE, Floyd D	Walls of the Missing
SMOAK, Clarence	O-19-14
SMOLLEN, Edward	L-19-12
SMORADO, Mike J	L-6-2
SNEAD, Jeff	C-18-27
SNEDDON, Thomas G Jr	P-10-4
SNELL, Jack D	Walls of the Missing
SNIDER, Charles T	C-9-17
SNIDER, Jack O	N-15-2
SNIDER, Paul F	F-11-15
SNODGRASS, Wilford L	J-2-10
SNOICH, Peter S	F-11-23
SNOVER, Mahlon E	Walls of the Missing
SNOWDAY, John D	H-15-23
SNYDER, Jack L	G-10-21
SNYDER, John	J-21-1
SNYDER, John R	E-18-4
SNYDER, John W Jr	C-9-25
SNYDER, Paul P	D-11-5
SNYDER, Walter E Jr	B-12-8
SNYDER, William H Jr	N-19-3
SOBASKI, John R Jr	F-4-17
SOBEK, Matthew	A-15-5
SOBOTIK, Stanley A	P-2-11
SOESBE, James A	Walls of the Missing
SOFFEN, Lester	Walls of the Missing
SOFFER, Lewis R	B-1-2
SOGGE, Wilmer D	A-18-19

SOILEAU, Vetile	P-1-4
SOJKA, Donald B	Walls of the Missing
SOKOL, Alexander R	K-11-13
SOKOLOFSKY, Philip	J-19-18
SOLDATIS, Frank J Jr	L-17-19
SOLIS, Ernest E	L-3-12
SOLIS, Gonzalo [329]	E-15-19
SOLLAZZO, Angelo J	L-5-9
SOLOMON, Arthur A	F-4-26
SOLOMON, Melvin J	C-8-23
SOMERS, Howard L	N-1-2
SOMERS, Raymond H	Walls of the Missing
SOMERS, Victor J	F-20-24
SOMMERLAD, Nelson E	I-10-2
SOMMERS, Paul A	B-20-16
SONDAG, Willis	O-22-2
SONSINI, Frank P	K-8-16
SORBINO, Joseph G	N-18-5
SORENSEN, Alan L	P-14-2
SORENSON, William A	H-18-19
SORROW, William O	L-4-10
SOTO, Carlos	C-14-9
SOUDERS, Eddie B	I-1-11
SOUDERS, George C	L-6-20
SOUTHERN, George F	D-9-15
SOUTHWORTH, Jesse W	Walls of the Missing
SOUZA, Albert	J-4-16
SOUZA, John A Jr	K-2-5
SOVAK, Julius J	L-16-11
SOVERNS, Charles F	P-7-14
SOVIN, Frank	A-5-21
SOWARD, James E	Walls of the Missing
SOWRY, James D	Walls of the Missing
SPADARO, Rocco A	H-3-6
SPAID, Eugene R	I-1-1
SPAIN, William A Jr	G-13-17
SPANGENBERG, Milton C	D-5-31
SPANGLER, Lester F	E-8-8
SPARKS, Harold E	Walls of the Missing
SPARKS, Joseph A	I-7-7
SPARKS, William C	Walls of the Missing
SPATARELLA, Enrico J	Walls of the Missing
SPAVEN, George N Jr	D-12-12
SPAYD, Warren P	A-15-12
SPEAS, Vestal K [330]	I-3-2
SPECK, Raymond L	M-18-2
SPECTOR, Sidney M	Walls of the Missing
SPEDDING, Edward W	Walls of the Missing
SPELLMAN, Thomas L	G-5-19
SPENCER, Earl J	I-21-9
SPENCER, James	K-10-14
SPENCER, James E	A-12-18
SPENGER, Arthur C	B-16-5
SPERLAZZO, Samuel C	C-4-4
SPERRY, Richard H	A-5-18
SPEVACEK, George F	F-18-6
SPICER, Harold E	H-5-20
SPIEGLE, Charles	C-11-7

SPIEKERMAN, Ramon C	J-1-19
SPILMAN, James J	H-3-19
SPINKS, Kenneth U	C-20-9
SPIVAK, Harry B	A-17-14
SPIVAK, Saul	Walls of the Missing
SPIVEY, Rex W	P-15-2
SPLEEN, Frank P	A-13-14
SPOONER, John W	N-9-14
SPOONER, Joseph H	A-21-28
SPOR, Howard C	H-2-13
SPRAGUE, Edgar P Jr	L-16-21
SPRAGUER, Harold J	B-7-13
SPRIGGS, Harry L	B-9-26
SPRIGGS, John H	Walls of the Missing
SPRINGFIELD, Berkeley	Walls of the Missing
SPRINGSTEEN, Gordon L	F-21-11
SPROUDT, Frank L	B-14-5
SPROULE, Peter S W	C-16-14
SPURGIASZ, Jan	Walls of the Missing
SPURLOCK, Arthur E	J-4-21
SPURLOCK, Carey W	D-12-2
SPURRIER, Chester L	K-14-18
SPURRIER, James H	K-14-17
SQUIBB, Clark M	A-12-30
SRIGLEY, John E	B-12-4
SROUBEK, Pravdomil	I-7-8
ST ARMAND, Robert R	Walls of the Missing
ST CLAIR, James	H-21-27
ST JOHN, Glen W	H-10-22
ST JOHNS, Horace F	C-12-2
ST LOUIS, Roger J	K-6-17
STABILE, Vincent M	E-20-1
STABILE, William F	Walls of the Missing
STACKHOUSE, Charles E	D-21-27
STACKPOLE, Claude	G-18-6
STACY, John J	P-7-17
STACY, Joseph G	D-13-7
STADY, Kenneth C	B-7-14
STAGGS, Walter R	C-19-8
STAHL, Richard A	D-16-1
STAHLMAN, Leroy M	Walls of the Missing
STAIFF, Roy K	Walls of the Missing
STAKE, Richard G	J-21-19
STALL, William G	N-21-15
STALLINGS, Roland C	Walls of the Missing
STALLMAN, George E	Walls of the Missing
STAMBUK, Jerome C	E-15-4
STAMIROWSKI, Theodore R	O-12-6
STAMMER, Ralph L	K-1-21
STAMPER, Arnold E	F-5-11
STAMPFER, Sigmund F	D-13-26
STANBERY, Howard R	Walls of the Missing
STANCHFIELD, Milton A	D-4-30
STANDFIELD, Cecil E	D-3-25
STANDIFIRD, Frank H	Walls of the Missing
STANDIFIRD, Gyll C	Walls of the Missing
STANFIELD, Amos L	G-18-12
STANFIELD, William A	G-17-4
STANFORD, David S	Walls of the Missing
STANFORD, Donald	N-20-7
STANFORD, James A	D-18-5
STANFORD, Merwyn F Jr	J-16-6
STANFORD, Thomas N	F-5-23
STANGOHR, Bruce C	E-13-9
STANISLAW, Joseph J Jr	O-7-3
STANLEY, Martin E	K-12-19
STANLEY, William J	E-8-18
STANTIAL, Frederic W	D-7-22
STANTON, Clifford A Jr	M-13-10
STANTON, John J	O-4-16
STAPLES, Kenneth T	E-5-22
STAPLETON, Francis E	F-7-24
STAPLETON, Vernon	D-15-28
STARCHER, Charles A	D-6-14
STARINA, Charles W	C-9-7
STARK, George E	D-11-31
STARKEL, Ervin G	Walls of the Missing
STARKEY, Robert R	N-21-16
STARLING, Leo F	G-4-18
STARNS, William H	B-18-18
STARON, Chester H	C-20-16
STARR, Wilfred L	N-7-15
STASZEWSKI, Dominic	N-8-3
STATEN, George E	C-20-31
STAUB, Alexander J	H-7-14
STAUB, Fred L	Walls of the Missing
STAUDER, Donald O	J-12-19
STAUDT, William G Jr	L-12-4
STAVRU, James N	J-15-7
STAWICKI, Alexander	L-7-14
STEADHAM, Roy J	Walls of the Missing
STEARNS, Frank L	M-7-8
STEARNS, Robert A	C-1-12
STEARS, John K	H-15-18
STECKMYER, Gerald T	F-19-24
STEDMAN, Ben H	Walls of the Missing
STEELE, Claudie L	L-12-5
STEELE, James L	E-5-7
STEELE, Nathaniel Jr	H-4-5
STEELE, Robert Breckinridge Jr	C-14-24
STEELE, Thomas Jr	A-15-17
STEELSMITH, Henry A	A-1-20
STEFFAN, Leonard J	I-8-13
STEHLIN, William F	Walls of the Missing
STEHNACH, Harry R	Walls of the Missing
STEICHEN, Daniel J	K-10-20
STEIKA, Charles W	C-2-12
STEINBRUCK, Theodore	I-15-21
STEINER, Cecil S	J-15-15
STEINER, Walter H Jr	J-15-16
STEINKE, William W	Walls of the Missing
STEINMANN, Bill H	P-8-7
STEINMETZER, Walter D	C-17-8
STEINSIEK, Henry F	A-14-30
STELDT, Robert C	M-21-7
STENCEL, Stanley E	L-12-1
STENSTROM, Fred H	B-21-5
STEPHANY, Alexander	D-8-9
STEPHENS, Elbert L	I-8-10
STEPHENS, John H Jr	L-13-17
STEPHENS, John L	A-14-3
STEPHENS, Richard J	B-14-14
STEPHENS, Rufus B	Walls of the Missing
STEPHENSON, Charles B	F-21-12
STEPHENSON, James Sterling	F-1-20
STEPMAN, Alfred C	Walls of the Missing
STERN, Arthur	H-7-18
STERN, Carl	C-20-2
STERN, Walter	A-6-30
STETZ, Andrew J	A-2-29
STEUDLE, William J	N-4-16
STEVENS, Donald E	M-6-2
STEVENS, Earl A	D-3-4
STEVENS, Hirschall M	Walls of the Missing
STEVENS, James D	D-10-10
STEVENS, James F	L-1-2
STEVENS, Leonard D	G-17-14
STEVENS, Percy G	J-3-3
STEVENS, Sumner W	Walls of the Missing
STEVENS, William K	E-9-1
STEVENSON, Charles W	A-3-15
STEVENSON, Louis C	C-10-2
STEVENSON, Robert W	B-17-14
STEWART, Alan B	A-15-8
STEWART, Albert C	J-15-21
STEWART, Angus D	Walls of the Missing
STEWART, Carl D	D-20-17
STEWART, Clay H	E-12-13
STEWART, Edward F	F-18-14
STEWART, Joe L	D-14-7
STEWART, Robert C	M-18-17
STINE, Robert O	Walls of the Missing
STING, Herbert A Jr	P-12-1
STINNETTE, Murrell F	C-9-14
STINSON, James E	K-16-18
STINSON, John D	H-11-16
STINSON, Paul G	K-1-15
STIPE, Carl W	A-21-7
STIRLING, James E	J-16-12
STOBAK, Eugene	L-11-10
STOCKER, John T	G-4-17
STOE, Robert J	M-12-17
STOFER, Joseph F	I-5-13
STOFFEL, Glenn C	Walls of the Missing
STOFFREGEN, Henry P	E-3-2
STOISITS, William G	D-5-22
STOJEK, Edward J	C-21-16
STOKES, George J	Walls of the Missing
STOKES, Harry L	Walls of the Missing
STOLTZ, Jackie W	Walls of the Missing
STONE, Fred S	H-7-23
STONE, Haney	O-18-13
STONE, Harry	F-14-16
STONE, Joseph J	K-10-15

331

332

STONE, Joseph V	E-8-14
STONE, Raymond E	G-9-11
STONE, Robert G	I-18-11
STONE, Ryal G	F-3-22
STONE, Todd G	F-20-4
STONEBERG, Edward R	P-14-12
STONEMAN, Charles M	O-19-6
STONESIFER, Clarence	Walls of the Missing
STONICH, Paul W	Walls of the Missing
STOPKA, John	B-11-4
STORCH, Lawrence A	N-19-4
STORCH, Werner	I-13-4
STORINO, William	K-17-15
STORM, Ralph C	D-17-10
STOTLER, Paul R	N-18-15
STOUT, Ora F	E-8-7
STOUT, William G	B-21-28
STOVALL, Herbert E	J-14-19
STOVALL, William H Jr	A-12-19
STOVER, James E	K-15-1
STOWERS, William G	K-14-19
STOWITS, Duane E	Walls of the Missing
STOYLE, Gerald T Jr	C-15-12
STRACK, Francis W	K-12-7
STRAESSER, David R	O-11-13
STRAIN, Samuel D	D-12-16
STRAND, Lawrence R	Walls of the Missing
STRANEY, Calvin E	N-21-17
STRANSEL, Daniel J	O-12-10
STRASTER, Fenn T	F-10-13
STRATHERN, George A [331]	F-9-8
STRAUSS, Martin M	Walls of the Missing
STRAWN, James H	A-19-11
STRAYER, Robert M	H-15-24
STREET, Clyde M	Walls of the Missing
STREET, Richard E	Walls of the Missing
STREETER, Henry W	P-13-16
STRICKLAND, Jennis M	D-17-13
STRICKLAND, Robert F	P-14-9
STRIKER, Lynn A	F-1-6
STRITE, Kenneth I	B-8-12
STROBEL, Victor E	D-15-24
STROHMEIER, William F	B-18-14
STROJNY, Adolphe P	J-21-21
STRONG, James W	Walls of the Missing
STRONG, Robert H	J-16-2
STROUD, James E	E-7-14
STROUD, John D	P-18-7
STROUP, Richard C	C-14-2
STRUBLE, John E	G-3-6
STRUTH, Henry J	Walls of the Missing
STRYKER, Frank P	D-5-23
STRYKER, James Baume	A-5-26
STUCK, Robert E	A-11-27
STUCKEY, Albert E	C-21-10
STUCKEY, Joseph L	D-5-13
STUMP, Charles C	G-14-19
STURDEVANT, Warren M	Walls of the Missing
STURM, Jack	E-5-17
STURM, Robert P	G-13-1
STUTSMAN, Robert E	B-3-13
STYPE, Charles H	C-17-31
SUDBURY, Robert E	Walls of the Missing
SUGGS, Roosevelt	N-16-9
SUHREN, Arthur J Jr	J-7-21
SULLIVAN, Francis A	O-22-3
SULLIVAN, George S	C-8-1
SULLIVAN, Henry J	D-6-29
SULLIVAN, John A	Walls of the Missing
SULLIVAN, John C	C-9-29
SULLIVAN, John J	O-22-5
SULLIVAN, John J	G-3-15
SULLIVAN, Joseph F	B-11-8
SULLIVAN, Joseph W	Walls of the Missing
SULLIVAN, Maxwell W Jr	P-22-9
SULLIVAN, Robert A	O-19-16
SULLIVAN, Robert F [332]	L-20-6
SULLIVAN, William J	A-7-31
SUMMER, Joseph T	C-21-27
SUMMERS, Charles D	Walls of the Missing
SUMMERS, Charles L	B-2-16
SUMMERS, Charles T Jr	J-11-10
SUMMERS, Harold L	F-14-17
SUMMY, Bennie	Walls of the Missing
SUNBERG, John L	Walls of the Missing
SUNDBERG, Alex E	K-18-3
SUNDE, Harland V	O-9-12
SUNGAILA, Joseph M	K-1-13
SUNSET, Randolph G	C-19-27
SUOZZO, Mario	Walls of the Missing
SUPERNAVAGE, Edward J	C-20-1
SUPPES, Jacob	I-7-20
SURIK, Frank A	J-2-2
SURRENCY, George A	G-5-24
SUSHKO, Peter	D-20-13
SUSKIND, Saul	M-22-6
SUTHERLAND, Harlett B	E-11-11
SUTTER, John T	L-6-9
SUTTLE, Claud E	F-20-9
SUTTON, John C	L-19-21
SUTTON, Karl E	J-2-7
SUTTON, Myron P	E-18-15
SUTTON, William E	L-17-16
SVENDSEN, James J	C-10-31
SWAB, Mike Jr	I-5-15
SWAN, Harold D	E-2-10
SWAN, Thomas F	G-9-19
SWANK, Robert D	H-12-7
SWANSON, Arthur W	Walls of the Missing
SWANSON, Carl G	D-19-1
SWANSON, Floyd C	C-21-21
SWANSON, Francis L	A-4-13
SWANSON, Maurice L	H-20-3
SWANSON, Sidney D	L-18-5
SWANSON, Stanley D	Walls of the Missing
SWARTLEY, Clarence E	C-17-13
SWARTZ, William C	H-19-6
SWEARINGEN, John P	M-12-1
SWEAT, Ellis J	Walls of the Missing
SWEENEY, Bernard J Jr	Walls of the Missing
SWEENEY, Harry O	B-12-3
SWEENEY, Martin W	C-2-8
SWEET, Bernard	C-15-18
SWEEZY, Edward J	H-6-10
SWICEGOOD, Calvin H	A-14-13
SWICK, Jessie F	A-1-32
SWIDER, Walter E	H-16-22
SWIDERSKI, Zygmunt J	N-19-8
SWIFT, Dempster	O-9-15
SWIGER, Carl V	K-8-1
SWILLEY, Doyle E	G-20-8
SWILLEY, Earl C	O-13-1
SWINFORD, Robert R	Walls of the Missing
SWINGLE, Lester R	A-5-4
SWITZ, John J	B-6-12
SWITZER, Delmar E	K-14-7
SWOGER, Leonard	B-17-13
SYER, Charles A	N-15-13
SYKES, Byron T	L-13-6
SYKORA, Roy J	Walls of the Missing
SYLVESTER, Thomas	C-6-11
SYMANK, John H Jr	H-6-15
SYMONDS, Ralph D	Walls of the Missing
SYMONS, Thomas W III	K-7-7
SYNOWSKI, George T	J-5-15
SZABANOWSKI, Anthnoy	Walls of the Missing
SZAKACS, Lewis	J-15-17
SZAPKA, Walter E	H-14-9
SZAYBEL, Stephen A	J-5-14
SZCZEPANEK, Edward J	G-7-20
SZWAK, Raymond A	D-19-4

T

TABER, Kenneth A	D-3-10
TACELT, Joseph Jr	D-2-24
TACKETT, Charles P	J-12-8
TAFF, Jack L	E-16-2
TAFT, James M	L-13-12
TAGGART, Lyle A	L-7-8
TAGLIABOSKI, John W	J-20-22
TALBERT, Clyde	F-10-23
TALIAFERRO, Jack C	G-14-13

TALIAFERRO, William G I-13-6
TALIFERRO, Lenwood M-17-1
TAMANDLI, Frank F G-7-16
TAMBASCIA, Edward Walls of the Missing
TANKSLEY, Carl V D-21-31
TANSEY, Raymond E Walls of the Missing
TANSKI, Thaddeus L J-14-16
TAPPE, Robert W D-1-4
TAPPEN, Earl O F-14-13
TAPSCOTT, Joseph R L-1-22
TARDIER, JACK E-2-3
TARKOWSKI, Alex F P-14-13
TARNOWSKI, Raymond A E-8-16
TARPEY, Timothy N Walls of the Missing
TARTAGLIA, Mauro M F-10-27
TARTAMELLA, Thomas J J-15-3
TASCHNER, Daniel J D-9-16
TATE, James W Jr G-14-6
TATE, Robert C N-17-17
TATE, Robert J M-12-15
TATEM, Lester H F-9-18
TATUM, Frank W N-13-4
TAVAREZ, Jesus A Walls of the Missing
TAVIS, Melvin J A-5-23
TAYLOR, Allan W P-16-3
TAYLOR, Caswell O-17-4
TAYLOR, Charles L Jr A-3-2
TAYLOR, Clyde S A-5-32
TAYLOR, Elmo J-20-14
TAYLOR, Elvie G E-9-14
TAYLOR, Frank R H-3-22
TAYLOR, George L F-16-14
TAYLOR, Harold F F-3-10
TAYLOR, Harold F D-18-10
TAYLOR, Herman D L-16-7
TAYLOR, Jack C A-7-16
TAYLOR, James B D-12-31
TAYLOR, James I D-6-17
TAYLOR, Merrill E E-15-13
TAYLOR, Raymond H E-13-13
TAYLOR, Robert C Jr D-11-9
TAYLOR, Robert L L-13-2
TAYLOR, Royce D D-21-6
TAYLOR, Victor H M-12-16
TAYLOR, Victor V Jr A-17-29
TAYLOR, William A K-1-16
TEACHEY, Ira B Jr L-14-9
TEAFF, William F Walls of the Missing
TEALE, David A E-8-21
TEETER, Claude E Jr F-10-3
TEICHMANN, James S Jr J-7-6
TEIGEN, Richard A B-14-25
TEIXEIRA, Joseph M Jr Walls of the Missing
TEMPLETON, Donald J Walls of the Missing
TENAGLIA, Nicholas A Walls of the Missing
TENBERG, Robert L B-18-11
TENNANT, Philip E E-18-26
TENNISON, Raymond C C-19-23

TEPLITZ, Leo Walls of the Missing
TER HAAR, Jay A P-21-17
TEREBIENIEC, John P J-18-16
TERNETTI, Albert J B-1-15
TERRANO, Mario J Walls of the Missing
TERRELL, Thomas L F-10-20
TERRIO, Robert L B-15-17
TERRY, De Witt S G-3-3
TERRY, John B Jr B-17-28
TERRY, Walter E D-14-14
TERRY, William J Walls of the Missing
TESTON, Welton P E-15-21
TETI, Albert I-3-20
TEYNOR, Francis M C-18-23
THALL, Mark M Walls of the Missing
THALMAN, Norman E Walls of the Missing
THAMES, Jack M Walls of the Missing
THARP, Freeland M C-15-16
THATCHER, Jack E F-10-4
THEADO, Robert J C-6-5
THEDE, Ivan W B-5-30
THEER, William M F-21-17
THELLEFSEN, Merrill A B-8-14
THERIAULT, Joseph J Walls of the Missing
THERIAULT, Sylvio J C-15-25
THERIOT, Raymond F Sr Walls of the Missing
THISTLETHWAITE, William T O-14-13
THOMAS, Charles L C-1-5
THOMAS, Clifton O D-20-8
THOMAS, Dalton M A-7-7
THOMAS, Dock G Jr I-12-17
THOMAS, Gordon H I-14-11
THOMAS, Gregory N-19-15
THOMAS, Herbert H Walls of the Missing
THOMAS, James C B-14-8
THOMAS, James L K-7-6
THOMAS, John R M-17-9
THOMAS, John W B-16-8
THOMAS, Joseph V L O-22-6
THOMAS, Marcum E J-9-8
THOMAS, Marvin E K-6-2
THOMAS, Morris L Walls of the Missing
THOMAS, Patrick V C-12-29
THOMAS, Paul E E-18-11
THOMAS, Rayford C F-11-10
THOMAS, Richard H G-5-11
THOMAS, Robert L D-2-3
THOMAS, Verne Jr A-1-10
THOMAS, Walter E L-15-7
THOMPSON, Basil P D-3-30
THOMPSON, Byron W G-19-10
THOMPSON, Clifford J I-1-9
THOMPSON, David L-8-11
THOMPSON, E B F-5-6
THOMPSON, Harry E Jr Walls of the Missing
THOMPSON, Harry M Walls of the Missing
THOMPSON, J D C-10-1
THOMPSON, Jesse W D-1-5

THOMPSON, John E Jr Walls of the Missing
THOMPSON, Joseph L B-17-27
THOMPSON, Leonard A B-13-3
THOMPSON, Lloyd Walls of the Missing
THOMPSON, Lloyd G N-17-7
THOMPSON, Ralph R H-12-1
THOMPSON, Reed P-18-12
THOMPSON, Robert J H-12-2
THOMPSON, Stacy W Jr M-19-5
THOMPSON, Sylvester J M-19-15
THOMPSON, Tommy M H-20-24
THOMPSON, Walter W Walls of the Missing
THOMPSON, William B D-20-9
THOMPSON, William C Jr E-20-2
THOMPSON, William G A-7-27
THOMPSON, William L C-10-9
THOMSON, Kenneth B G-4-8
THORN, Estes D M-8-8
THORNBURG, Forrest P D-4-21
THORNE, Thomas P D-1-26
THORNTON, Charles V I-8-7
THRASHER, Jack W I-20-6
THURMAN, Afton J C-3-10
THURSTON, Max W Walls of the Missing
TICHY, Edwin R M-14-13
TICKNOR, Charles G M-14-9
TIDWELL, James T F-10-12
TIGHE, Edward F Jr L-21-13
TILLEY, Ralph J B-7-25
TILTON, Barney M N-5-5
TIMKO, John J Walls of the Missing
TIMMERMAN, Edison C H-5-25
TINKLEPAUGH, Arthur J D-11-19
TINTERA, William J Jr L-20-4
TIPPET, Paul S Walls of the Missing
TIPPETT, William L F-21-8
TIPTON, Charles R B-10-17
TIPTON, Dorsey E B-18-2
TIPTON, Strawder H I-8-4
TIRONE, Michael J F-12-26
TISDALE, Sanford F Walls of the Missing
TISINGER, Ben F E-9-7
TITTLE, Warren J K-2-8
TITUS, David L-12-15
TJOMSLAND, Earl E B-18-22
TKALEC, Anthony J E-4-14
TOBIAS, Stephen A Jr G-9-14
TOBIN, Patrick D Jr Walls of the Missing
TODD, Charles N F-15-18
TODD, Clarence J H-13-16
TODESCO, Felix A D-6-9
TOM, Bernard B G-1-15
TOM, Chin T O-7-2
TOMASELLO, Joseph J Walls of the Missing
TOMASIEWICZ, Chester E N-15-1
TOMASZAWSKI, George J Jr P-17-9
TOMAZATIS, Dominic F F-7-2
TOMKO, Michael J B-19-15

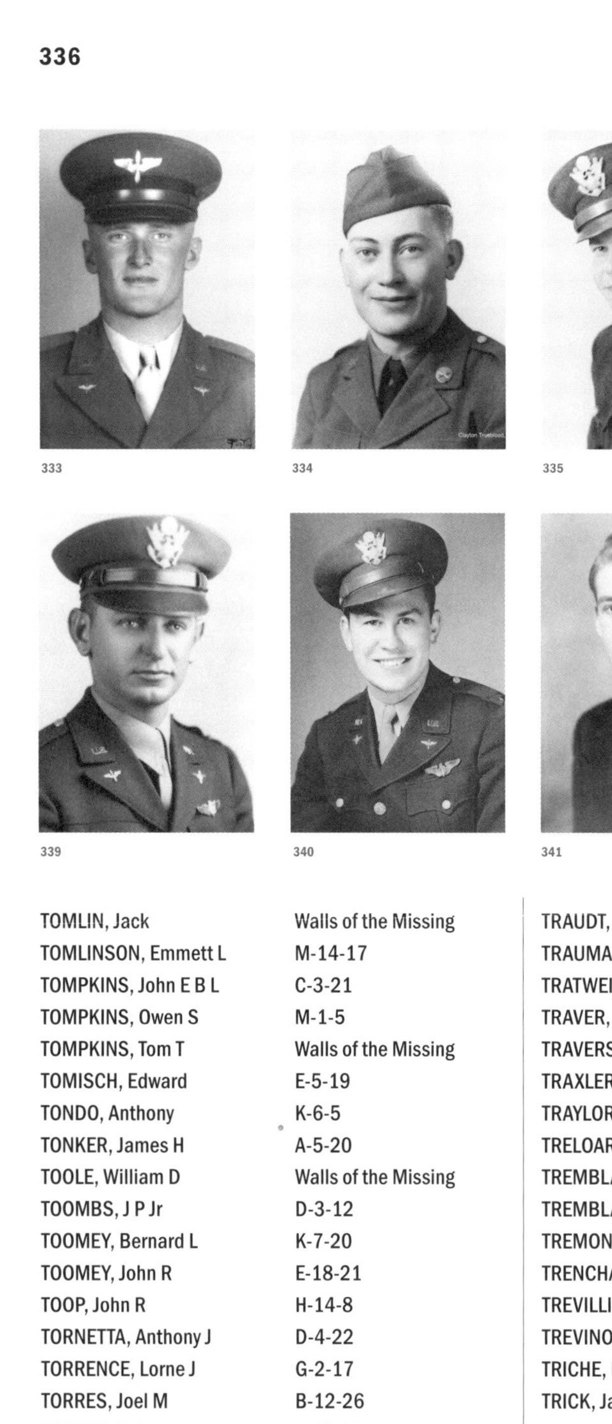

333

334

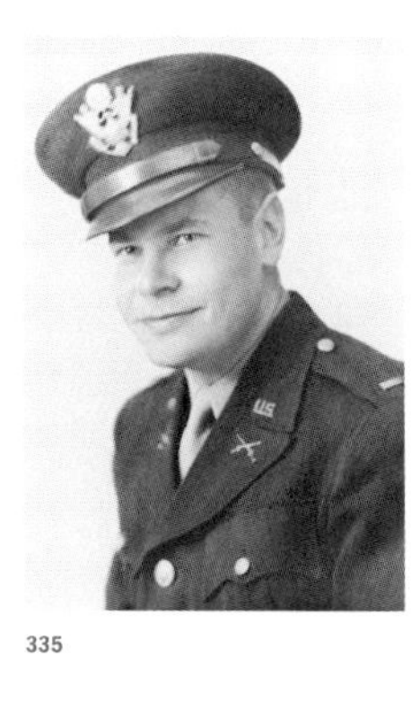

335

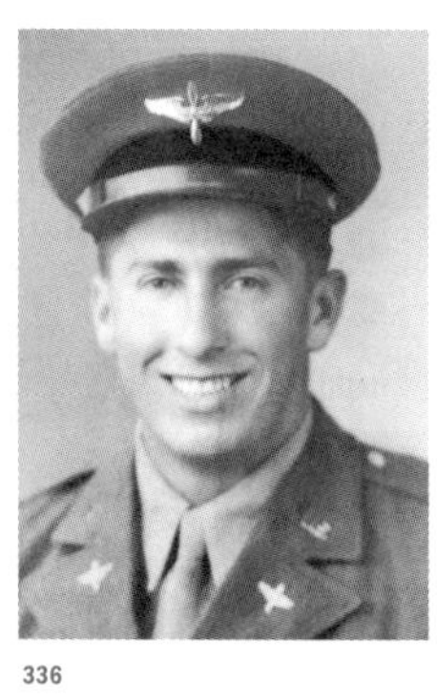

336

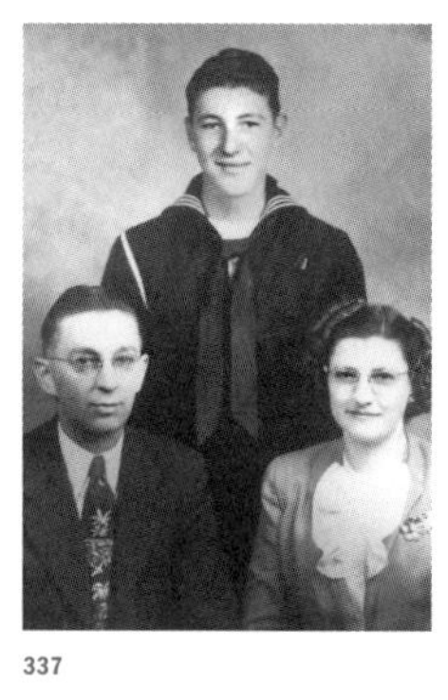

337

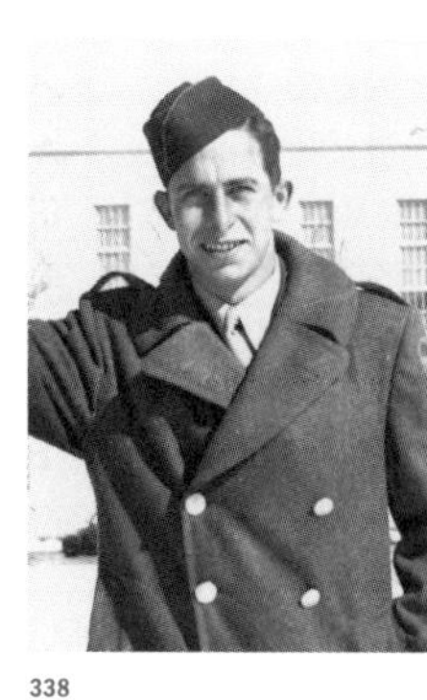

338

339

340

341

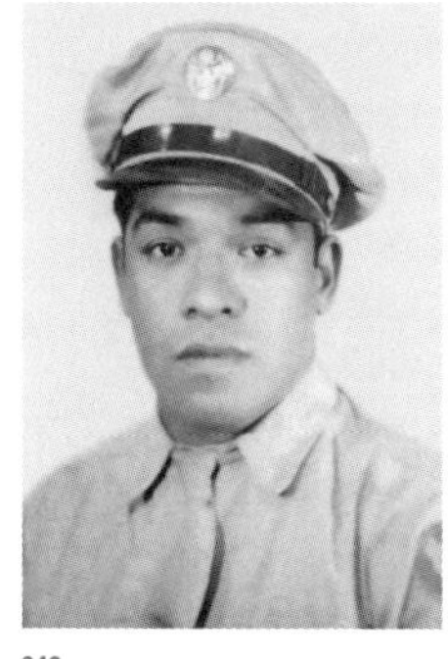

342

TOMLIN, Jack	Walls of the Missing
TOMLINSON, Emmett L	M-14-17
TOMPKINS, John E B L	C-3-21
TOMPKINS, Owen S	M-1-5
TOMPKINS, Tom T	Walls of the Missing
TOMISCH, Edward	E-5-19
TONDO, Anthony	K-6-5
TONKER, James H	A-5-20
TOOLE, William D	Walls of the Missing
TOOMBS, J P Jr	D-3-12
TOOMEY, Bernard L	K-7-20
TOOMEY, John R	E-18-21
TOOP, John R	H-14-8
TORNETTA, Anthony J	D-4-22
TORRENCE, Lorne J	G-2-17
TORRES, Joel M	B-12-26
TORRES, Robert	F-12-15
TORREY, Arthur M	C-9-32
TOSI, Julian	Walls of the Missing
TOTTEN, Franklin Parker	O-8-9
TOURGEE, William M	C-18-25
TOURTELLOTT, Theodore F	M-22-17
TOVEY, George A	P-3-2
TOWERS, Frederic J	I-4-15
TOWLE, Arthur R	C-17-27
TOWLE, John C [333]	J-14-14
TOWLE, John R	Walls of the Missing
TOWNE, Hollis L	A-15-21
TOWNSEND, Barney L	O-22-7
TOWNSEND, Raymond H Jr	Walls of the Missing
TOWNSEND, Talbot	D-20-6
TRACY, Henry A	B-4-3
TRANBARGER, Darrell M	K-13-13
TRAPANI, Eugene	G-6-27
TRAUDT, Walter	Walls of the Missing
TRAUMAN, John F	Walls of the Missing
TRATWEIN, John R	N-17-6
TRAVER, Morris S Jr	A-19-20
TRAVERSO, Elio	Walls of the Missing
TRAXLER, Chester E	B-2-25
TRAYLOR, Charles M	I-5-10
TRELOAR, Burdette L	D-1-13
TREMBLAY, Henry J	M-20-4
TREMBLAY, Henry S	B-14-20
TREMONTI, Brom	A-16-20
TRENCHARD, William H	J-12-6
TREVILLIAN, Robert P	D-15-27
TREVINO, Jesus	G-6-8
TRICHE, Lloyd J	Walls of the Missing
TRICK, James I	Walls of the Missing
TRILLING, Frank H	Walls of the Missing
TRIPP, Enoch L	L-14-7
TRIPP, John R	B-14-13
TRIVETT, Walter L	P-18-6
TRLICA, George H	H-18-15
TROHA, Andrew W	L-8-19
TROLIO, Arthur B	I-1-19
TRONTEL, Joseph J	F-12-24
TROTTER, David H	Walls of the Missing
TROTTER, Lester S	D-11-15
TROUT, John L	P-8-2
TROUTT, Vernon M	O-5-7
TROUVILLE, Rudolph L	K-18-15
TROWBRIDGE, James F	O-18-12
TROXLER, Joseph	C-13-8
TRUDEAU, Frank V	G-2-4
TRUDEAU, Raymond J	K-12-13
TRUE, Joseph N	E-20-9
TRUE, Robert G	Walls of the Missing
TRUEBLOOD, Clayton E [334]	F-20-10
TRUETT, Jim R	N-14-2
TRUJILLO, Ignacio	A-10-21
TRUMP, Paul W	Walls of the Missing
TRUPIA, Salvatore A	Walls of the Missing
TRYBULOWSKI, Edward	P-1-11
TRYON, Edgar L	M-14-6
TSCHURWALD, Lloyd A	K-4-10
TUCHOLSKI, Walter R J	Walls of the Missing
TUCK George E	L-13-18
TUCK, Moses H	B-3-19
TUCKER, John R	Walls of the Missing
TUCKER, Kemble	F-12-2
TUCKER, Terrell H	J-14-12
TUCKER, Trenton T	O-10-16
TULAI, Stephen	G-10-12
TULBURE, Arthur J	C-2-1
TUMAS, Edward P	B-9-16
TUNE, Elmer E	N-4-17
TURCSAK, John	C-15-5
TURKINGTON, Calvin G	K-8-10
TURNBOUGH, Willard A	H-1-14
TURNER, Dennis R Jr	H-17-24
TURNER, George A Jr	J-18-22
TURNER, Harry	O-22-9
TURNER, Herbert S	O-20-5
TURNER, James W	Walls of the Missing
TURNER, John S	E-8-26
TURNER, Leroy	A-21-27
TURNER, Marion A	A-20-9
TURNER, Merlin F	Walls of the Missing
TURNER, Ralph B	D-3-6
TURNER, Raymond	Walls of the Missing
TURNER, Robert C	A-19-25
TURNER, Robert W	Walls of the Missing
TURNER, William D	J-11-13
TURNOWCHYK, Joseph S	B-20-31
TURSI, Nick	H-20-19
TUSCHINSKI, William J	I-20-7
TUSING, Cletus W	Walls of the Missing
TUSKAN, James R	K-14-10
TUTTLE, Winburn R Sr	E-11-21
TWEEDY, Paul E	N-14-12
TWETEN, Ernest A	Walls of the Missing

Name	Location
TWETTEN, Norman E [335]	K-7-9
TYLER, Charles L	O-6-2
TYMSTRA, Justin C	M-18-13
TYNER, Herman W	N-15-14
TYRELL, Clarence E	L-1-9

U

Name	Location
UHLER, Emil [336]	M-11-12
UHLER, Raymond R [337]	H-13-3
ULENBURG, Howard J	M-2-5
ULFENG, Milton J	I-10-8
ULLMANN, Ralph G	L-19-8
ULLRICH, Raymond A	A-21-18
ULMER, Charles E III	K-5-12
ULRICH, Gordon F	O-13-3
ULRICK, Ervin	K-6-6
ULTIMO, Augustus P Jr	K-11-19
UMBRICHT, William F	L-5-1
UMSTEAD, Sam P [338]	K-4-8
UNDERWOOD, Henry L	K-11-18
UNDERWOOD, Virgil L	M-14-15
UPHAM, Raymond F	B-18-9
Unknown Soldier	A-1-16
Unknown Soldier	A-1-28
Unknown Soldier	A-3-22
Unknown Soldier	A-3-29
Unknown Soldier	B-1-27
Unknown Soldier	B-9-4
Unknown Soldier	C-2-21
Unknown Soldier	C-4-23
Unknown Soldier	C-5-28
Unknown Soldier	C-10-23
Unknown Soldier	C-13-5
Unknown Soldier	C-13-22
Unknown Soldier	C-14-21
Unknown Soldier	C-17-17
Unknown Soldier	C-19-14
Unknown Soldier	C-21-6
Unknown Soldier	C-21-25
Unknown Soldier	D-2-27
Unknown Soldier	D-3-7
Unknown Soldier	D-4-5
Unknown Soldier	D-5-5
Unknown Soldier	D-6-19
Unknown Soldier	D-8-16
Unknown Soldier	D-11-21
Unknown Soldier	D-14-24
Unknown Soldier	D-16-2
Unknown Soldier	D-17-29
Unknown Soldier	D-18-17
Unknown Soldier	D-20-4
Unknown Soldier	E-19-18
Unknown Soldier	E-21-15
Unknown Soldier	E-21-22
Unknown Soldier	F-5-9
Unknown Soldier	F-15-26
Unknown Soldier	F-16-27
Unknown Soldier	G-1-27
Unknown Soldier	G-2-13
Unknown Soldier	G-7-27
Unknown Soldier	G-12-10
Unknown Soldier	G-13-15
Unknown Soldier	G-13-19
Unknown Soldier	G-14-26
Unknown Soldier	G-16-27
Unknown Soldier	G-21-12
Unknown Soldier	H-1-27
Unknown Soldier	H-3-26
Unknown Soldier	H-5-17
Unknown Soldier	H-8-26
Unknown Soldier	H-11-4
Unknown Soldier	H-14-26
Unknown Soldier	H-17-26
Unknown Soldier	I-1-22
Unknown Soldier	I-7-22
Unknown Soldier	I-14-22
Unknown Soldier	J-1-11
Unknown Soldier	J-14-3
Unknown Soldier	J-14-22
Unknown Soldier	J-15-22
Unknown Soldier	K-2-11
Unknown Soldier	K-3-22
Unknown Soldier	K-14-13
Unknown Soldier	K-14-22
Unknown Soldier	M-3-1
Unknown Soldier	M-3-4
Unknown Soldier	M-3-7
Unknown Soldier	M-3-10
Unknown Soldier	M-3-13
Unknown Soldier	M-6-12
Unknown Soldier	M-7-2
Unknown Soldier	M-7-6
Unknown Soldier	M-7-17
Unknown Soldier	M-22-4
Unknown Soldier	N-3-1
Unknown Soldier	N-3-3
Unknown Soldier	N-5-9
Unknown Soldier	N-5-12
Unknown Soldier	N-8-5
Unknown Soldier	N-8-10
Unknown Soldier	N-8-16
Unknown Soldier	N-21-10
Unknown Soldier	O-3-3
Unknown Soldier	O-3-8
Unknown Soldier	O-3-12
Unknown Soldier	O-4-2
Unknown Soldier	O-4-10
Unknown Soldier	O-4-13
Unknown Soldier	O-5-5
Unknown Soldier	O-5-9
Unknown Soldier	O-5-12
Unknown Soldier	O-5-15
Unknown Soldier	O-6-16
Unknown Soldier	O-8-5
Unknown Soldier	O-8-15
Unknown Soldier	O-22-4
Unknown Soldier	O-22-8
Unknown Soldier	O-22-12
Unknown Soldier	O-22-16
Unknown Soldier	P-4-3
Unknown Soldier	P-4-12
Unknown Soldier	P-4-15
Unknown Soldier	P-5-10
Unknown Soldier	P-7-6
Unknown Soldier	P-22-5
Unknown Soldier	P-22-14
Unknown Soldier	P-22-16
UPLINGER, Charles J	F-2-8
UPSHAW, Charles C	Walls of the Missing
UPSHAW, Kenneth C	H-21-20
UPTON, Bennie S	L-10-2
UPTON, Robert C	D-9-28
URDIA, John	Walls of the Missing
URICHER, William	B-5-13
URMAN, Harry [339]	Walls of the Missing
URSO, Jack	B-2-8
URY, Arthur E	L-19-3
UTECHT, Willis A	N-23-1/ Walls of the Missing
UTLEY, Walter A [340]	Walls of the Missing
UTTER, Paul [341]	E-21-19
UTTERBACK, David R	E-4-7

V

Name	Location
VACHOUT, John J	Walls of the Missing
VAIL, John J	Walls of the Missing
VALADEZ, Paul	A-16-6
VALDEZ, Isabel G Sr [342]	E-15-17
VALENTA, Irvin E	Walls of the Missing
VALENTE, Louis J	B-21-29
VALENTI, Joseph N	I-17-6
VALENTIK, Robert P	Walls of the Missing
VALENZUELA, George R	J-21-7
VALNEY, Harold G	K-11-7
VALOUSKY, Jospeh A	G-9-23
VAN AALTEN, Sylvan	K-20-18
VAN ALSTINE, Nathan G	L-18-7
VAN ANNE, Louis E	K-2-10
VAN AUKEN, Arthur H	C-17-12
VAN BLAIR, Howard B	C-5-16
VAN CLEEF, Arthur A	Walls of the Missing
VAN DE WALL, Alvin L	A-13-3
VAN DE WEGHE, Charles	P-10-2
VAN DER STEEN, Bernard J	B-2-21
VAN DEVENTER, Stuart D	Walls of the Missing
VAN DYK, William H	G-18-18
VAN ERDEWYK, Leo J	Walls of the Missing
VAN ETTEN, James R	Walls of the Missing
VAN EYCK, Willard H	E-5-20
VAN GIESEN, George T	A-9-28
VAN HANDEL, Nicholas	K-12-11
VAN HOOSER, Ray	D-5-20
VAN HYNING, Oren G	J-4-13
VAN KEUREN, Gilbert F	D-18-23

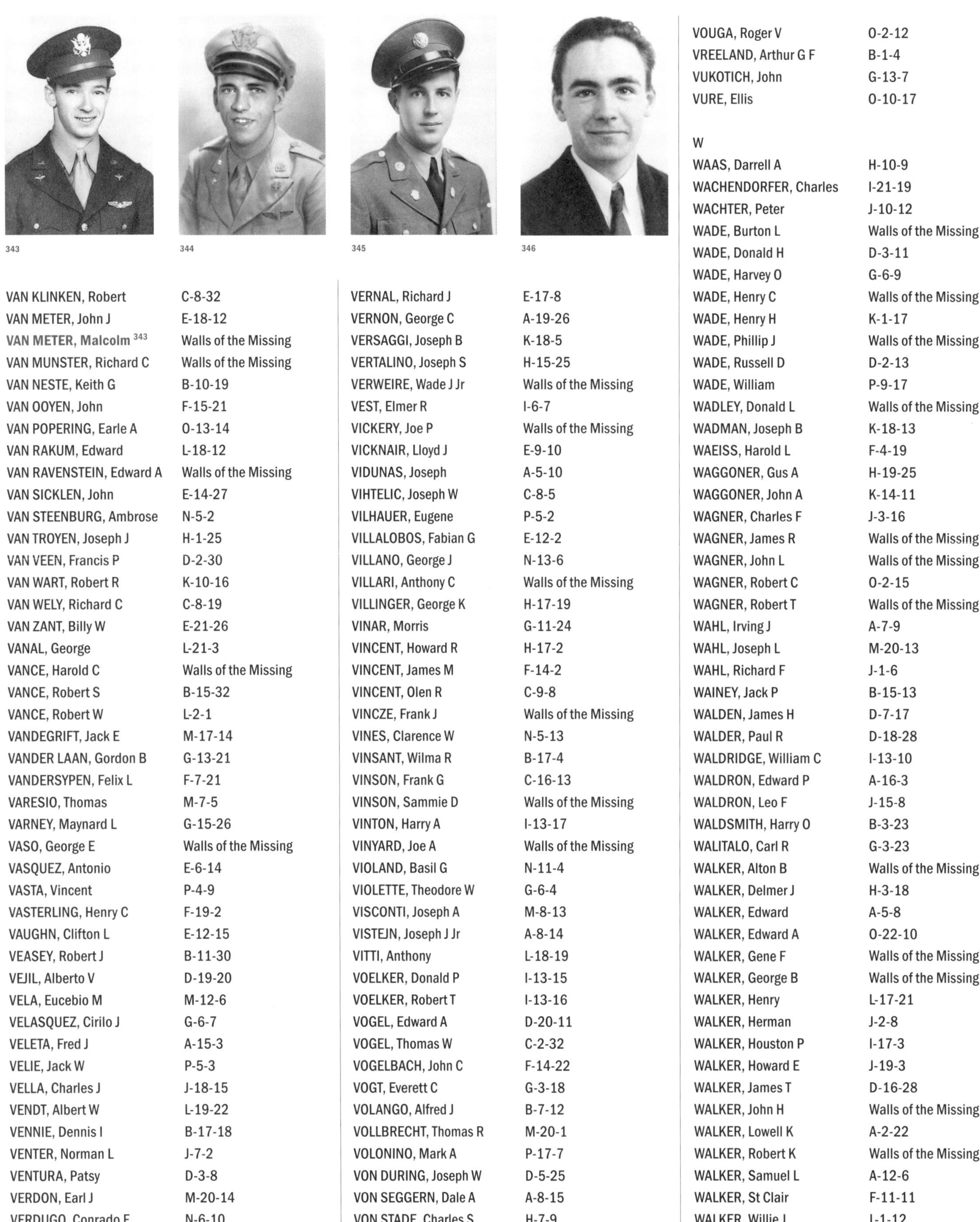

343 344 345 346

Name	Location
VAN KLINKEN, Robert	C-8-32
VAN METER, John J	E-18-12
VAN METER, Malcolm [343]	Walls of the Missing
VAN MUNSTER, Richard C	Walls of the Missing
VAN NESTE, Keith G	B-10-19
VAN OOYEN, John	F-15-21
VAN POPERING, Earle A	O-13-14
VAN RAKUM, Edward	L-18-12
VAN RAVENSTEIN, Edward A	Walls of the Missing
VAN SICKLEN, John	E-14-27
VAN STEENBURG, Ambrose	N-5-2
VAN TROYEN, Joseph J	H-1-25
VAN VEEN, Francis P	D-2-30
VAN WART, Robert R	K-10-16
VAN WELY, Richard C	C-8-19
VAN ZANT, Billy W	E-21-26
VANAL, George	L-21-3
VANCE, Harold C	Walls of the Missing
VANCE, Robert S	B-15-32
VANCE, Robert W	L-2-1
VANDEGRIFT, Jack E	M-17-14
VANDER LAAN, Gordon B	G-13-21
VANDERSYPEN, Felix L	F-7-21
VARESIO, Thomas	M-7-5
VARNEY, Maynard L	G-15-26
VASO, George E	Walls of the Missing
VASQUEZ, Antonio	E-6-14
VASTA, Vincent	P-4-9
VASTERLING, Henry C	F-19-2
VAUGHN, Clifton L	E-12-15
VEASEY, Robert J	B-11-30
VEJIL, Alberto V	D-19-20
VELA, Eucebio M	M-12-6
VELASQUEZ, Cirilo J	G-6-7
VELETA, Fred J	A-15-3
VELIE, Jack W	P-5-3
VELLA, Charles J	J-18-15
VENDT, Albert W	L-19-22
VENNIE, Dennis I	B-17-18
VENTER, Norman L	J-7-2
VENTURA, Patsy	D-3-8
VERDON, Earl J	M-20-14
VERDUGO, Conrado F	N-6-10
VERETTE, Joseph V	A-2-21
VERLINDE, Julius V	E-10-4
VERMIE, Layton P	Walls of the Missing

Name	Location
VERNAL, Richard J	E-17-8
VERNON, George C	A-19-26
VERSAGGI, Joseph B	K-18-5
VERTALINO, Joseph S	H-15-25
VERWEIRE, Wade J Jr	Walls of the Missing
VEST, Elmer R	I-6-7
VICKERY, Joe P	Walls of the Missing
VICKNAIR, Lloyd J	E-9-10
VIDUNAS, Joseph	A-5-10
VIHTELIC, Joseph W	C-8-5
VILHAUER, Eugene	P-5-2
VILLALOBOS, Fabian G	E-12-2
VILLANO, George J	N-13-6
VILLARI, Anthony C	Walls of the Missing
VILLINGER, George K	H-17-19
VINAR, Morris	G-11-24
VINCENT, Howard R	H-17-2
VINCENT, James M	F-14-2
VINCENT, Olen R	C-9-8
VINCZE, Frank J	Walls of the Missing
VINES, Clarence W	N-5-13
VINSANT, Wilma R	B-17-4
VINSON, Frank G	C-16-13
VINSON, Sammie D	Walls of the Missing
VINTON, Harry A	I-13-17
VINYARD, Joe A	Walls of the Missing
VIOLAND, Basil G	N-11-4
VIOLETTE, Theodore W	G-6-4
VISCONTI, Joseph A	M-8-13
VISTEJN, Joseph J Jr	A-8-14
VITTI, Anthony	L-18-19
VOELKER, Donald P	I-13-15
VOELKER, Robert T	I-13-16
VOGEL, Edward A	D-20-11
VOGEL, Thomas W	C-2-32
VOGELBACH, John C	F-14-22
VOGT, Everett C	G-3-18
VOLANGO, Alfred J	B-7-12
VOLLBRECHT, Thomas R	M-20-1
VOLONINO, Mark A	P-17-7
VON DURING, Joseph W	D-5-25
VON SEGGERN, Dale A	A-8-15
VON STADE, Charles S	H-7-9
VONDEYLEN, Henry	C-5-6
VOOST, Raymond E	B-14-17
VORIS, Kenneth E	D-21-23

Name	Location
VOUGA, Roger V	O-2-12
VREELAND, Arthur G F	B-1-4
VUKOTICH, John	G-13-7
VURE, Ellis	O-10-17

W

Name	Location
WAAS, Darrell A	H-10-9
WACHENDORFER, Charles	I-21-19
WACHTER, Peter	J-10-12
WADE, Burton L	Walls of the Missing
WADE, Donald H	D-3-11
WADE, Harvey O	G-6-9
WADE, Henry C	Walls of the Missing
WADE, Henry H	K-1-17
WADE, Phillip J	Walls of the Missing
WADE, Russell D	D-2-13
WADE, William	P-9-17
WADLEY, Donald L	Walls of the Missing
WADMAN, Joseph B	K-18-13
WAEISS, Harold L	F-4-19
WAGGONER, Gus A	H-19-25
WAGGONER, John A	K-14-11
WAGNER, Charles F	J-3-16
WAGNER, James R	Walls of the Missing
WAGNER, John L	Walls of the Missing
WAGNER, Robert C	O-2-15
WAGNER, Robert T	Walls of the Missing
WAHL, Irving J	A-7-9
WAHL, Joseph L	M-20-13
WAHL, Richard F	J-1-6
WAINEY, Jack P	B-15-13
WALDEN, James H	D-7-17
WALDER, Paul R	D-18-28
WALDRIDGE, William C	I-13-10
WALDRON, Edward P	A-16-3
WALDRON, Leo F	J-15-8
WALDSMITH, Harry O	B-3-23
WALITALO, Carl R	G-3-23
WALKER, Alton B	Walls of the Missing
WALKER, Delmer J	H-3-18
WALKER, Edward	A-5-8
WALKER, Edward A	O-22-10
WALKER, Gene F	Walls of the Missing
WALKER, George B	Walls of the Missing
WALKER, Henry	L-17-21
WALKER, Herman	J-2-8
WALKER, Houston P	I-17-3
WALKER, Howard E	J-19-3
WALKER, James T	D-16-28
WALKER, John H	Walls of the Missing
WALKER, Lowell K	A-2-22
WALKER, Robert K	Walls of the Missing
WALKER, Samuel L	A-12-6
WALKER, St Clair	F-11-11
WALKER, Willie J	L-1-12
WALKO, John A	Walls of the Missing
WALL, Charles D	Walls of the Missing
WALL, Norman D	Walls of the Missing

WALLA, Mitchell A F-17-4
WALLACE, Leon W L-15-1
WALLENBERG, Frank E-7-17
WALLER, David G L-9-16
WALLERSTEIN, Edward M-16-3
WALLWORK, Albert G-14-16
WALLY, Walter S I-1-4
WALSER, Aubrey C E-17-14
WALSH, Albert F O-2-16
WALSH, James E Walls of the Missing
WALSH, Mac Murtry L-4-9
WALSH, Richard L E-2-16
WALSH, Robert P-20-16
WALSH, Robert R C-1-21
WALSH, William J G-12-9
WALTER, Arthur B F-1-11
WALTER, Cebert G N-19-1
WALTER, Harry G N-19-6
WALTERS, Eugene A N-19-5
WALTERS, Frank L A-18-7
WALTERS, Garner Jr E-15-23
WALTERS, James H G-4-20
WALTERS, John C G-17-3
WALTERS, Thomas L H-3-24
WALTERS, Verdon L E-3-25
WALTON, Harrison B Jr J-13-9
WALTON, Jimmie D K-4-4
WALTZ, Marion Walls of the Missing
WAMBACH, James A G-3-13
WAMPLER, Roy M F-21-10
WANAMAKER, Paul D-6-23
WANDACHOWICZ, Joseph J-14-20
WANDER, Roy G A-12-29
WANG, Alfred A B-21-17
WARBLE, Lawrence L N-9-10
WARD, Benjamin F Walls of the Missing
WARD, Corney M D-19-28
WARD, Daniel B K-3-21
WARD, Edward S B-4-17
WARD, Howard J B-7-18
WARD, Ivie A Jr A-3-13
WARD, Joseph H H-15-5
WARD, Robert E B-15-30
WARD, Trynca C B-15-6
WARD, Walter J N-14-11
WARDALE, William H L-3-21
WARDEN, Alexander F-18-11
WARDENBURG, Palmer J L-17-14
WARDLE, Gayle T O-22-11
WARDNER, Fred G D-13-11
WARDWELL, Theodore M C-20-24
WAREHAM, Orson K-9-12
WARENYI, William J C-3-4
WARGO, John G D-18-13
WARLICK, Clyde F D-19-12
WARMUTH, Arnold P Jr [344] O-20-2
WARNE, Gideon W Walls of the Missing
WARNER, George H B-10-12
WARNER, Glenn A B-16-15
WARNER, John E M-13-4
WARNER, Leonard V G-11-11
WARNER, Richard R B-17-2
WARNER, Walter C Jr A-13-29
WARNICK, Herschell A J-11-20
WARPEHA, Frank J L-1-8
WARREN, Charles W C-9-18
WARREN, Fulton O-17-12
WARREN, Kenneth E A-18-14
WARREN, Marion C D-18-24
WARREN, Robert J Walls of the Missing
WARREN, Samuel E-15-16
WARTERS, Charley L-10-22
WARTZENLUFT, Albert L B-6-13
WARWICK, Leroy W Walls of the Missing
WASHBURN, Roger E A-7-23
WASHINGTON, Howard B L-4-12
WASHKO, Robert F-4-3
WASILEWSKI, Emil T Walls of the Missing
WASSERSTEIN, Hyman Walls of the Missing
WASSIL, Larry S Walls of the Missing
WATERLAND, Everett H L-8-8
WATERS, Chester W B-14-31
WATERS, Herman L I-19-13
WATERS, James D C-13-25
WATERS, Phanor B H-10-16
WATERS, Vernon E D-12-26
WATERS, Wendell O C-18-12
WATKINS, A J Jr A-18-24
WATKINS, James M L-3-19
WATKINS, Leroy L-6-21
WATSON, Armer M A-19-29
WATSON, Glen E P-10-10
WATSON, Hale L A-4-7
WATSON, Hector M Walls of the Missing
WATSON, Howard R Walls of the Missing
WATSON, James G C-17-11
WATSON, James M O-8-16
WATSON, James R J-10-22
WATSON, Joe N Walls of the Missing
WATSON, John T I-16-5
WATSON, Leamon W K-17-22
WATSON, Ralph L O-19-13
WATT, William T L-16-14
WATTLES, Fred M Jr Walls of the Missing
WATTS, Gilbert I-15-15
WATTS, John R F-13-2
WATTS, Robert D E-19-4
WATTS, Robert M Walls of the Missing
WATTS, Woodard C P-21-10
WAUNEKA, Milton Walls of the Missing
WAY, Frank W K-11-6
WAY, Harlen W P-8-15
WAY, Henry G Walls of the Missing
WAY, John R Walls of the Missing
WAY, Merlin W B-15-9
WAY, Stanley A H-20-20
WAYE, Richard A B-9-21
WAYENBERG, William D [345] G-10-14
WAYT, Fred Walls of the Missing
WEAKLAND, Clifford D A-21-8
WEATHERSPOON, Vern D Walls of the Missing
WEATHERWAX, Dale W F-4-4
WEAVER, Dennis B Walls of the Missing
WEAVER, Donald C F-3-5
WEAVER, Emerson V Walls of the Missing
WEAVER, Ernest E [346] Walls of the Missing
WEAVER, Louis W G-13-5
WEAVER, Richard C Walls of the Missing
WEAVER, William W A-12-27
WEBB, Donald H F-9-9
WEBB, Eldon L-8-21
WEBB, John C B-5-20
WEBB, Marshal C P-21-5
WEBB, William C C-4-10
WEBBER, Horace G P-6-6
WEBBINK, Paul H A-20-6
WEBER, Alvin L L-21-7
WEBER, John R F-7-20
WEBER, Norman L Walls of the Missing
WEBER, William F N-5-7
WEBSTER, James D L-9-2
WEBSTER, Leroy B C-18-30
WEBSTER, Lynn W H-4-23
WEDDELL, Cyril D E-16-9
WEDGE, Anthony F D-10-14
WEED, David E C-18-17
WEEDEN, Russell G-4-2
WEEKLY, Paul E Jr B-10-14
WEEKS, Julian J C-5-24
WEGERT, Arthur F F-11-1
WEGIEL, Walter F L-5-10
WEINBAUM, David O-22-13
WEINER, Herman F-15-12
WEINGART, Fred A-10-14
WEINGLASS, Ben D-13-23
WEIR, Andrew A-21-21
WEIR, Frank A G-21-9
WEIR, William R Jr J-1-10
WEIRICK, Gregory F G-3-16
WEIS, Donald H G-9-17
WEISER, Robert M C-17-21
WEISS, Alvin S Walls of the Missing
WEISS, Armin D-13-19
WEISS, Charles O-2-7
WEISS, Frank P D-2-15
WEISS, George D-16-14
WEISS, Martin J K-3-18
WEISSGERBER, Clarence L L-2-7
WEISZHAAR, John Jr E-12-21
WEITOCK, Arthur J F-2-18
WELCH, Alvin C-16-25
WELCH, Charles E O-22-14
WELCH, Dallas B N-16-5
WELCH, Johnie J D-6-26

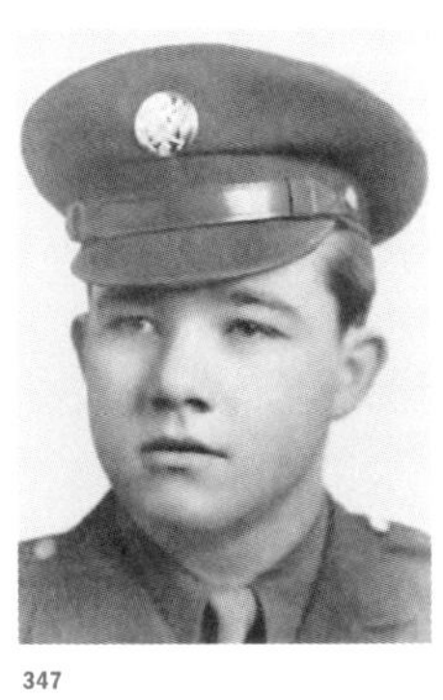
347

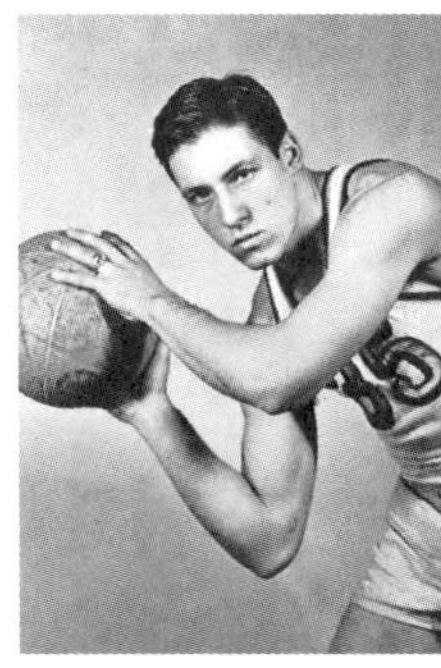
348

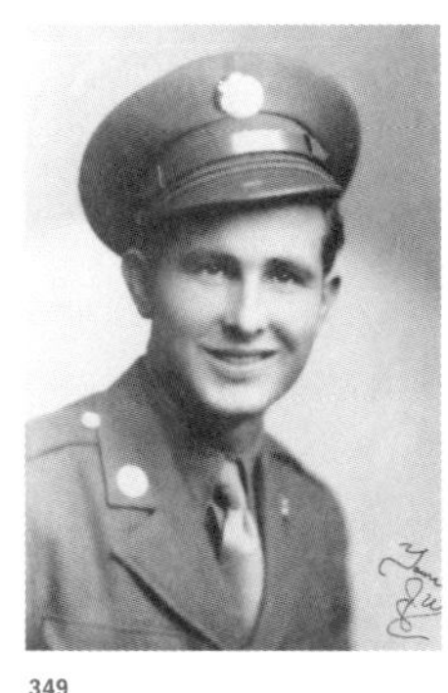
349

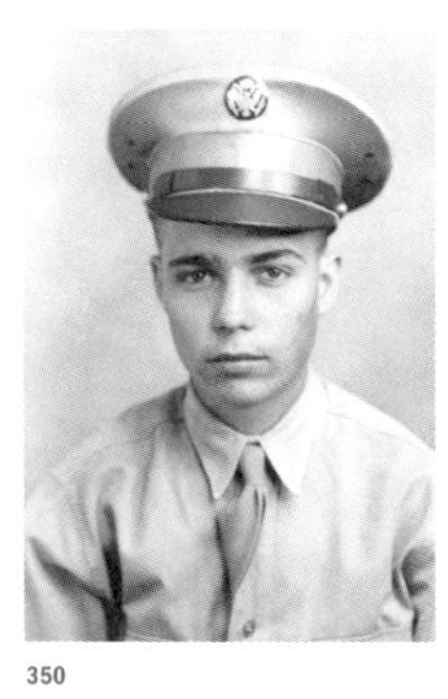
350

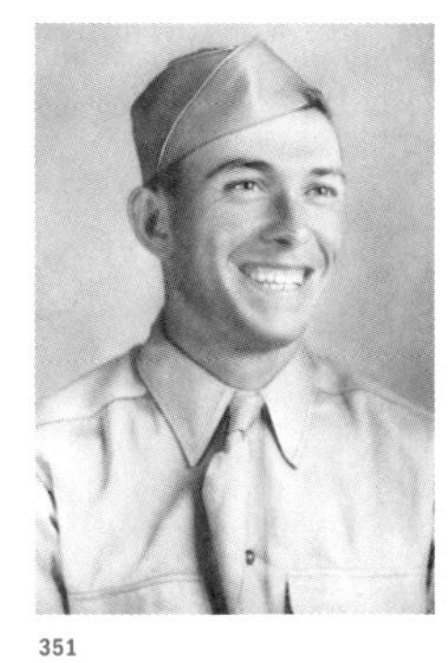
351

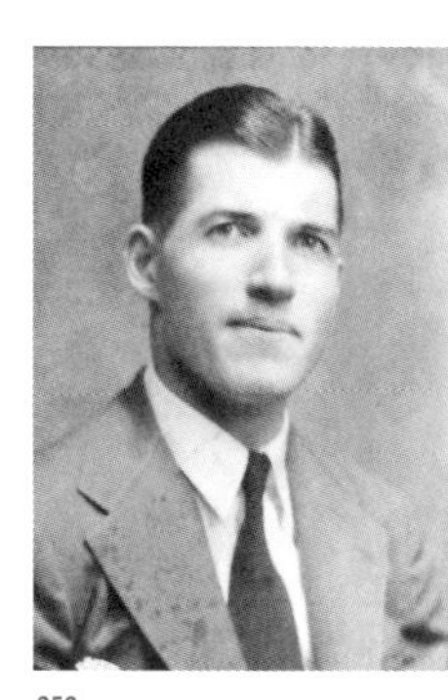
352

Name	Location
WELCH, Patrick G	Walls of the Missing
WELCHEL, Henry L	Walls of the Missing
WELDE, Charles D	F-1-25
WELDON, Russell R Jr	L-12-6
WELLINGTON, Ivan R Jr	F-8-24
WELLINGTON, Roger R	G-10-20
WELLS, Frank	B-3-26
WELLS, John R	D-7-1
WELLS, Redmond D Jr	B-7-30
WELLS, Richard F	J-6-6
WELLS, Virgil W	Walls of the Missing
WELLS, William E	L-19-6
WELSH, James G	M-22-14
WELSH, William R	I-9-14
WELT, Carroll O Jr	Walls of the Missing
WELTER, Vernon T	O-15-15
WEMPE, John R	J-9-22
WENDRZYCKI, Joseph J	L-7-5
WENDT, Oren K	I-12-9
WENDT, Wilson A [347]	J-5-19
WENGER, John L	Walls of the Missing
WENRICH, Ernest A	D-9-1
WENTZELL, Clarence L	Walls of the Missing
WERBLANSKY, Stephen	G-14-24
WERGES, Raymond W	E-14-5
WERNER, Richard W	H-19-9
WERNER, William A	G-18-14
WERNICKI, Edward A	P-10-5
WERNING, Kenneth R	K-10-4
WERTH, Paul D	Walls of the Missing
WERTZ, Edward R	C-10-24
WERTZ, Henry C	N-8-14
WERY, Julius J	C-2-14
WESCOTT, Charles L	F-20-21
WESEMAN, William E	B-12-21
WESOLOWSKI, Edward V	H-9-1
WESP, Robert E	Walls of the Missing
WESS, Robert A	I-19-9
WESSMAN, Helge E	F-17-8
WEST, Benjamin H	Walls of the Missing
WEST, Charles R	O-9-1
WEST, Clarence E	Walls of the Missing
WEST, Miroslav	F-10-24
WEST, Theodore A	Walls of the Missing
WEST, W D Jr	Walls of the Missing
WESTBY, Arthur H	F-12-4
WESTER, Russell W	B-8-9
WESTFALL, Richard R	B-2-27
WESTLUND, Clarence R	Walls of the Missing
WESTLUND, Vernon W	H-4-11
WESTPHAL, William F J	Walls of the Missing
WESTVOLD, Alfred E	I-4-17
WETHERELL, Albert S	I-8-18
WETZEL, Jack R	B-9-8
WETZEL, Lowell L [348]	L-13-11
WETZEL, Walter C	N-18-10
WEXELMAN, Norman R	H-10-17
WHALEN, Edmund D	E-6-21
WHALEN, Edward E	B-6-22
WHALEN, James W	G-20-11
WHALEN, John H	L-5-16
WHALEY, Joseph R	K-15-21
WHALEY, Robert G	K-7-22
WHATLEY, Burrell O	C-2-28
WHATLEY, George A	J-6-5
WHEAT, Warner R	P-10-6
WHEELER, Bill J	Walls of the Missing
WHEELER, Charles E	K-16-9
WHEELER, Frank K	H-16-9
WHEELER, Hubert J	O-15-6
WHEELER, Ralph E	J-17-8
WHEELER, Ralph H	D-8-5
WHEELER, Raymond L	L-16-4
WHEELER, Stewart F	C-15-29
WHEELES, Reuben E	B-10-32
WHELAN, Larry P	M-8-6
WHIGHAM, Clifford L	H-11-12
WHIPPLE, Milo O	Walls of the Missing
WHISENHUNT, Charles E	L-12-12
WHISNER, Clyde H	A-15-7
WHITBECK, Arthur J	K-14-1
WHITE, Arthur E	Walls of the Missing
WHITE, Conwell H	A-16-23
WHITE, Earl	P-6-11
WHITE, Floyd C Sr	Walls of the Missing
WHITE, George A	D-6-25
WHITE, Gordon	M-6-3
WHITE, Harold E	I-10-1
WHITE, Harold G	A-14-17
WHITE, Harold H	I-11-8
WHITE, Harold I	B-6-25
WHITE, Harvey N	A-13-2
WHITE, Henry V	K-10-3
WHITE, Jack W	O-3-6
WHITE, James A	E-8-9
WHITE, James W [349]	M-12-3
WHITE, Jean A Jr	C-12-8
WHITE, John G	P-10-3
WHITE, John L	L-15-6
WHITE, Leland O	P-15-5
WHITE, Orvel C	A-21-3
WHITE, Owen G	M-13-5
WHITE, Robert T	C-5-4
WHITE, Robert W	M-15-3
WHITE, Rupert E	F-20-12
WHITE, Theodore	B-11-3
WHITE, Thomas F	Walls of the Missing
WHITE, Torrance P	L-16-6
WHITE, William E	Walls of the Missing
WHITE, William O Jr	H-6-8
WHITEHAIR, Lawrence T	G-3-12
WHITELOCK, Perry	D-7-32
WHITENACK, Theodore W	K-18-11
WHITESELL, Virgil B	K-11-9
WHITESIDE, Major R	B-12-18
WHITFIELD, Glynn W	C-6-1
WHITFORD, Edward A	F-16-1
WHITING, Robert K	O-12-9
WHITLEY, Eugene	G-20-18
WHITLEY, Richard J	O-2-2
WHITLEY, Robert H Jr	Walls of the Missing
WHITLOW, Mc Ginnis [350]	B-14-24
WHITMAN, Duane	Walls of the Missing
WHITMAN, Nathaniel	I-7-15
WHITMORE, Howard E	J-4-14
WHITNEY, George A	Walls of the Missing
WHITNEY, Howard A	O-12-13
WHITNEY, Wilbur H	L-20-3
WHITTEMORE, Mack C	D-19-11
WHITTINGTON, Herman W	F-7-27
WHITTLE, James	J-8-12
WHOLGEMUTH, Albert G	K-8-15
WIACEK, Edward J	C-9-5
WIARD, William R	E-17-23
WIBERG, Byron A Jr	B-17-21
WIBLITZHOUSER, Kenneth F Sr	G-2-14
WICE, Benjamin F	B-8-25
WICHNIEWICZ, Joseph	L-2-20

WICKENS, Bill	O-22-15
WICKLES, Gerard J	E-10-17
WICKLINE, James E	I-17-21
WICKS, Wayne W	D-3-3
WIDENER, Lorance E	A-18-5
WIDIGER, Theran L	J-19-21
WIDNER, Wayne E	B-17-3
WEICHMAN, Martin W	B-21-32
WIEGERT, Arthur J	K-5-4
WIENEKE, Olin L	Walls of the Missing
WIENING, Paul G	Walls of the Missing
WIENKE, Harold H	A-7-14
WIERCISZEWSKI, Edward	L-17-11
WIERK, Joseph	G-19-20
WIESER, Jerry H	Walls of the Missing
WIGGINS, Frank H	D-8-31
WIGSTONE, Robert B	P-6-15
WIKOFF, Verle L Jr	H-12-8
WILBANKS, James N	C-9-22
WILBERN, Philip M	P-10-7
WILBERT, Leroy M	H-19-15
WILCOX, Ivan H	K-16-19
WILDER, Charles P	Walls of the Missing
WILDER, Harry W	Walls of the Missing
WILDER, Henry C	J-8-20
WILDMAN, Walter G	Walls of the Missing
WILE, Ralph W	C-4-8
WILEY, Dewie E	K-7-2
WILEY, Joseph W	J-9-19
WILEY, Thomas P Jr	I-20-2
WILHELM, Donovan R	N-10-15
WILHELM, Melvin F	Walls of the Missing
WILHOIT, Ernest [351]	Walls of the Missing
WILK, Lester C	M-20-2
WILKE, Berthold F	A-8-4
WILKERSON, George W	O-16-16
WILKIE, John M	B-5-3
WILKIE, Robert D	Walls of the Missing
WILKINS, Chester D	L-21-14
WILKINS, Joseph A	I-10-3
WILKINS, Robert R	K-16-21
WILKINSON, Oscar H	O-8-10
WILL, Walter J	D-3-32
WILLEMS, Bernard	A-6-21
WILLERT, Edwin F	Walls of the Missing
WILLETT, Ralph A	L-4-21
WILLIAMS, Alvis F	C-15-8
WILLIAMS, Blair W	C-6-16
WILLIAMS, Carl	F-15-10
WILLIAMS, Casper S Jr	H-11-11
WILLIAMS, Clifton M	K-19-1
WILLIAMS, Dois J	Walls of the Missing
WILLIAMS, Donald P	A-1-12
WILLIAMS, Edward	B-18-26
WILLIAMS, George F	K-20-9
WILLIAMS, George R	F-16-19
WILLIAMS, Glen E	D-2-16
WILLIAMS, Harold O	A-10-11

WILLIAMS, Harold T	G-5-4
WILLIAMS, Harry J	Walls of the Missing
WILLIAMS, Issac E	J-6-12
WILLIAMS, Jack C	D-21-17
WILLIAMS, James A	O-20-8
WILLIAMS, James M Jr	B-4-7
WILLIAMS, James O	L-13-22
WILLIAMS, Jewell T	A-21-29
WILLIAMS, Joe B	P-20-4
WILLIAMS, John C	E-16-1
WILLIAMS, Joseph C	B-16-4
WILLIAMS, Lyle A	C-4-16
WILLIAMS, Melvin D	H-8-19
WILLIAMS, Myron E	Walls of the Missing
WILLIAMS, Noah W	K-11-22
WILLIAMS, Norman N	I-16-17
WILLIAMS, Raymond W	A-17-19
WILLIAMS, Richard F	K-19-2
WILLIAMS, Richard W	L-11-2
WILLIAMS, Robert P [352]	I-11-7
WILLIAMS, Rosevelt	I-1-14
WILLIAMS, Sherrill R	M-13-16
WILLIAMS, Taffy J	D-1-25
WILLIAMS, William C	M-12-13
WILLIAMS, William D	Walls of the Missing
WILLIAMS, William S Jr	E-15-22
WILLIAMS, Willie F	N-9-17
WILLIAMSON, Austin D	D-17-28
WILLIAMSON, Carl D	Walls of the Missing
WILLIAMSON, Clyde J	Walls of the Missing
WILLIAMSON, Edwin M	E-4-22
WILLIAMSON, W T	L-4-22
WILLIS, Charles W Jr	K-8-7
WILLIS, James R	C-20-22
WILLIS, Willett R	D-18-16
WILLIS, William L	M-16-17
WILLOUGHBY, Richard E	J-1-12
WILLOUGHBY, Sampson C	D-2-4
WILLOWS, Wilba M	N-11-5
WILLS, C D	C-11-5
WILLSON, Louis H	P-2-10
WILLSON, Victor J Jr	Walls of the Missing
WILLUMSEN, Merle R	E-10-14
WILMOT, Donald C	K-14-21
WILMOTH, Arnold H	Walls of the Missing
WILSON, Alonzo H	Walls of the Missing
WILSON, Arthur E	N-17-1
WILSON, Calvin H	C-21-24
WILSON, Carl F	K-13-22
WILSON, Charles B	L-11-18
WILSON, David C	L-6-15
WILSON, Douglas M	H-12-14
WILSON, Gene	Walls of the Missing
WILSON, George R	A-16-1
WILSON, Gerald A	L-11-17
WILSON, James E	Walls of the Missing
WILSON, James O	Walls of the Missing
WILSON, Marvin E	C-5-22

WILSON, Paul B	A-16-31
WILSON, Ray Y	O-13-17
WILSON, Rex S	K-8-14
WILSON, Robert H	B-21-6
WILSON, Robert L	L-9-10
WILSON, William D	F-12-20
WILTSHIRE, Theo M	B-5-26
WINDMAYER, Frederick C	Walls of the Missing
WINDRUM, Morell F	F-12-7
WINEGAR, Ralph E	D-8-13
WINGARD, Jacob H	A-4-29
WINGARD, Kenneth E	F-14-21
WINGATE, Harry W	Walls of the Missing
WINGENROTH, Wayne	B-9-15
WINGFIELD, Kenneth R	A-17-22
WINIARSKI, Joseph E	N-10-13
WINIGER, Bernard A	O-18-5
WINKLER, Raymond W	K-5-16
WINKLER, Richard S	E-8-10
WINNIE, Bruce C	D-20-15
WINSCH, Carl Jr	Walls of the Missing
WINTER, Raymond K Jr	Walls of the Missing
WINTERS, Clinton Jr	G-12-11
WINTON, Merbell C	O-5-13
WINZEY, Patrick M	B-7-10
WIRAK, Elmer	B-7-23
WISDOM, John W	G-19-13
WISE, James E	D-19-23
WISE, Jessie	O-15-2
WISE, Solomon I	Walls of the Missing
WISEMAN, Richard E	G-17-18
WISER, Dallas W	C-3-26
WISLER, Lyman J	F-12-1
WISNIEWSKI, Paul J	Walls of the Missing
WISNIEWSKI, Raymond P	J-7-18
WISSEN, Edgar D	E-4-23
WITALISZ, Casimir J	C-7-23
WITHEROW, Leonard E	F-5-17
WITHEY, Carlous G	H-16-16
WITKOWSKI, Edward H	D-12-1
WITTENBERG, Melvin E	Walls of the Missing
WITTENDORF, Walter	Walls of the Missing
WITTENMYER, Ralph W	B-10-20
WITTS, Glenn W	N-5-11
WITTSTOCK, Robert A	N-14-10
WLASAK, George J	D-15-22
WLODINGER, Arthur	H-14-1
WOHL, David P Jr	Walls of the Missing
WOHLAUER, Wolf H	D-10-16
WOJNAR, Joseph F	P-15-8
WOJNIAK, Frank J	B-14-19
WOJNOWSKI, Eugene L	N-20-10
WOJTACH, Emil R	I-10-19
WOJTANEK, Maryan W	L-2-8
WOJTKUN, Stanley C	A-16-16
WOLD, Archie M	P-4-6
WOLD, Robert G	Walls of the Missing
WOLF, Earl L Sr	J-4-3

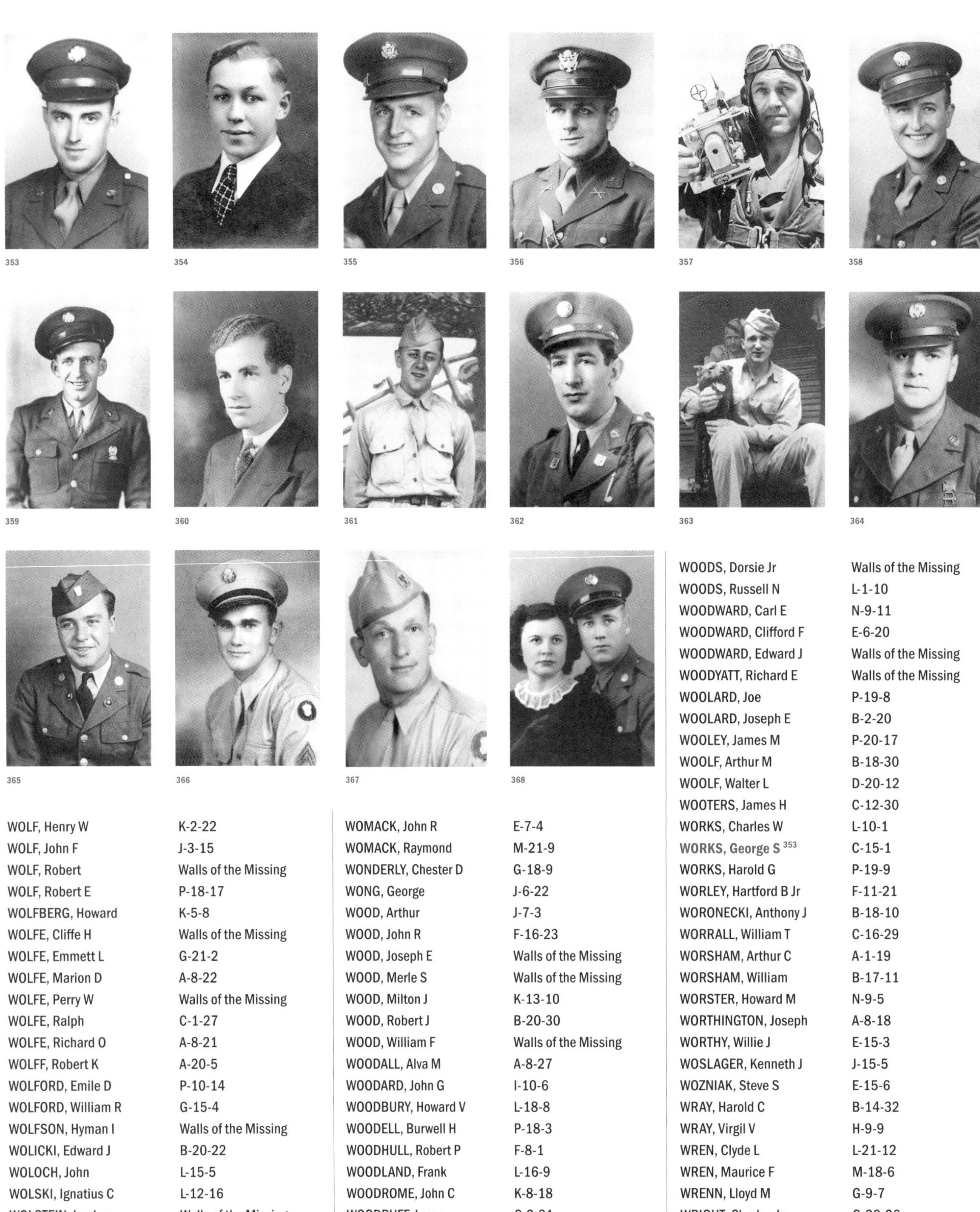
353 354 355 356 357 358
359 360 361 362 363 364
365 366 367 368

WOLF, Henry W	K-2-22
WOLF, John F	J-3-15
WOLF, Robert	Walls of the Missing
WOLF, Robert E	P-18-17
WOLFBERG, Howard	K-5-8
WOLFE, Cliffe H	Walls of the Missing
WOLFE, Emmett L	G-21-2
WOLFE, Marion D	A-8-22
WOLFE, Perry W	Walls of the Missing
WOLFE, Ralph	C-1-27
WOLFE, Richard O	A-8-21
WOLFF, Robert K	A-20-5
WOLFORD, Emile D	P-10-14
WOLFORD, William R	G-15-4
WOLFSON, Hyman I	Walls of the Missing
WOLICKI, Edward J	B-20-22
WOLOCH, John	L-15-5
WOLSKI, Ignatius C	L-12-16
WOLSTEIN, Isadore	Walls of the Missing
WOLSTEIN, William H	K-2-6
WOLZ, Fred C	Walls of the Missing
WOMACK, Jessie M	K-15-20
WOMACK, John R	E-7-4
WOMACK, Raymond	M-21-9
WONDERLY, Chester D	G-18-9
WONG, George	J-6-22
WOOD, Arthur	J-7-3
WOOD, John R	F-16-23
WOOD, Joseph E	Walls of the Missing
WOOD, Merle S	Walls of the Missing
WOOD, Milton J	K-13-10
WOOD, Robert J	B-20-30
WOOD, William F	Walls of the Missing
WOODALL, Alva M	A-8-27
WOODARD, John G	I-10-6
WOODBURY, Howard V	L-18-8
WOODELL, Burwell H	P-18-3
WOODHULL, Robert P	F-8-1
WOODLAND, Frank	L-16-9
WOODROME, John C	K-8-18
WOODRUFF, Leroy	C-2-31
WOODRUFF, Rufus J T	I-13-3
WOODS, Arthur H	Walls of the Missing
WOODS, Carl H	B-12-1
WOODS, Dorsie Jr	Walls of the Missing
WOODS, Russell N	L-1-10
WOODWARD, Carl E	N-9-11
WOODWARD, Clifford F	E-6-20
WOODWARD, Edward J	Walls of the Missing
WOODYATT, Richard E	Walls of the Missing
WOOLARD, Joe	P-19-8
WOOLARD, Joseph E	B-2-20
WOOLEY, James M	P-20-17
WOOLF, Arthur M	B-18-30
WOOLF, Walter L	D-20-12
WOOTERS, James H	C-12-30
WORKS, Charles W	L-10-1
WORKS, George S [353]	C-15-1
WORKS, Harold G	P-19-9
WORLEY, Hartford B Jr	F-11-21
WORONECKI, Anthony J	B-18-10
WORRALL, William T	C-16-29
WORSHAM, Arthur C	A-1-19
WORSHAM, William	B-17-11
WORSTER, Howard M	N-9-5
WORTHINGTON, Joseph	A-8-18
WORTHY, Willie J	E-15-3
WOSLAGER, Kenneth J	J-15-5
WOZNIAK, Steve S	E-15-6
WRAY, Harold C	B-14-32
WRAY, Virgil V	H-9-9
WREN, Clyde L	L-21-12
WREN, Maurice F	M-18-6
WRENN, Lloyd M	G-9-7
WRIGHT, Charles Jr	G-20-26
WRIGHT, Eugene E	I-7-10
WRIGHT, Gordon K	M-17-2
WRIGHT, James W	A-13-31

Name	Location
WRIGHT, Jesse W	G-21-27
WRIGHT, John W	J-12-18
WRIGHT, Kenneth H	B-12-16
WRIGHT, Leon W	F-7-23
WRIGHT, Marcell W	E-1-26
WRIGHT, Raymond W	Walls of the Missing
WRIGHT, Richard D	H-7-5
WRIGHT, Richard J	D-12-32
WRIGHT, Robert E	F-18-4
WRIGHT, Roy B	A-7-15
WRIGHT, Russell E	H-13-1
WRIGHT, Wesley	I-17-1
WRIGHT, Willard J	B-1-17
WRIGHT, William G	N-20-12
WROBEL, Glen R	M-22-3
WROBLEWSKI, Stanley V	G-10-11
WRONKOWSKI, Albert	H-15-8
WULFEKUHLE, Edwin C	Walls of the Missing
WUNDERLICH, Edward L	I-6-19
WUNDERLIN, Carl F	D-2-14
WURST, Paul J	Walls of the Missing
WURZ, Wallace W	D-14-8
WYATT, George A	N-11-10
WYATT, Jesse L	Walls of the Missing
WYATT, Troy H	N-8-8
WYNNE, George	M-10-7
WYNNE, James S	D-20-21
WYNNE, John K	D-16-9
WYNNE, Robert V	
Y	B-2-6
YADLOSKY, Walter	C-12-25
YAEGER, William C	J-7-17
YAKOS, Frank [354]	H-11-20
YANCY, Daniel A	D-17-30
YANKOSKY, Francis	B-14-4
YARBOROUGH, Thomas W	O-3-7
YARBROUGH, Jack E	B-4-20
YARBROUGH, John F	K-21-21
YARBROUGH, William E	H-19-14
YARMER, Norman S	I-5-2
YARNELL, Robert H	Walls of the Missing
YATES, Chester R	C-5-26
YATES, Ira D	A-2-7
YATES, James B	D-20-18
YATES, Josepth H	K-17-1
YATES, Therle E	E-9-3
YBARRA, Joe R	Walls of the Missing
YEAGER, Mercer A	A-21-15
YEAGER, Robert H [355]	I-15-16
YEAKEL, Robert L	D-18-12
YEAROUT, James M	G-14-7
YEARY, Hubert	Walls of the Missing
YEOMANS, Prentice E	A-12-17
YETSOOK, Fred	L-3-5
YETTER, Albert H	J-2-20
YEUELL, Robert V [356]	E-9-11
YOAKUM, Earl D	K-16-15
YOCOM, Dewey M	M-13-6
YODER, Russel J	N-20-11
YODIS, Anthony J	P-5-6
YONAK, Leo E	H-5-15
YONCE, Eugene J	B-5-28
YOO, Mike E	L-14-14
YORIO, William R	J-17-21
YORK, Marion A	D-9-13
YORKO, William J	G-1-16
YORRA, Marshall S	Walls of the Missing
YOST, Harlen L [357]	Walls of the Missing
YOUELL, Thomas B Jr [358]	F-6-26
YOUNG, Carl E	J-11-11
YOUNG, Earnest G	J-16-11
YOUNG, Edward L III	F-15-20
YOUNG, George D	D-17-18
YOUNG, Gerald E	G-16-2
YOUNG, Ira S [359]	I-6-18
YOUNG, James P [360]	Walls of the Missing
YOUNG, John A	L-1-5
YOUNG, John R	D-3-23
YOUNG, Leverett L	J-19-22
YOUNG, Lloyd W	F-8-17
YOUNG, Milburn H	G-4-3
YOUNG, Robert E	Walls of the Missing
YOUNG, Robert K	G-13-24
YOUNG, Sidney S	G-20-16
YOUNG, Victor A	E-9-12
YOUNG, Walter	K-2-9
YOUNGBLOOD, Clifford D	P-18-13
YOUNGBLOOD, Eugene P	G-19-21
YOUNGS, Robert B	G-18-26
YOUNKIN, Lawrence H	G-14-1
YOUNKIN, Louis E	N-15-17
YUCUS, Charles J	B-15-20
YURKO, Joseph J [361]	E-1-27
YURMAN, Meyer [362]	E-6-17
Z	
ZACCARIA, James A Jr	A-10-23
ZACCARO, James D	C-18-15
ZACCHI, John [363]	O-7-5
ZACCHI, Pete	O-7-4
ZACK, Matthew A	M-21-8
ZADNIK, Anthony F [364]	Walls of the Missing
ZAHABA, Chester P	H-5-3
ZAHER, John A Jr	Walls of the Missing
ZAHN, Fred D	J-11-17
ZAKAIB, Louis A	P-5-8
ZAKARIAN, Antrony J	I-16-9
ZAKE, Henry W	Walls of the Missing
ZAKRZEWSKI, Charles	H-17-1
ZAPATKA, Frederick J	Walls of the Missing
ZASKE, Carl F Jr	J-16-4
ZASLOV, Dave	Walls of the Missing
ZAWALICH, Walter S	A-2-18
ZDONEK, Chester R [365]	F-16-5
ZDUNKEWICZ, Steve A	D-17-4
ZEGZUTOR, Victor	J-4-22
ZEIDENFELD, Alvin X	O-22-17
ZEIGLER, Paul L	D-12-11
ZEIGLER, Richard H	Walls of the Missing
ZELEK, Rudolph J	I-13-14
ZELLER, William	M-10-13
ZENISHEK, William G [366]	F-3-21
ZENZ, George R	Walls of the Missing
ZEPEDA, Ramon R	F-7-3
ZEPEDA, Vicente	O-19-12
ZERBE, Ralph J	D-14-31
ZETTNER, Bernard A	A-6-12
ZHANEL, Joe T	J-11-15
ZIEGELE, Walter J	I-14-3
ZIEGMAN, Myron J	F-8-6
ZIELINSKI, Donald F	E-10-5
ZIESEMER, Robert E	C-1-20
ZIETZ, Erwin H	J-20-19
ZIGICH, Mike	D-14-3
ZILINEK, William Jr	F-20-14
ZILINSKY, Joseph R	P-8-3
ZIMBER, Leonard F [367]	E-7-11
ZIMMER, Erwin C	Walls of the Missing
ZIMMERMAN, Alton L	K-2-19
ZIMMERMAN, Forrest	I-11-5
ZIMMERMAN, Glenn F	Walls of the Missing
ZIMMERMAN, Griffin M	B-3-2
ZIMMERMAN, Seymour	Walls of the Missing
ZIMMERMAN, William E	Walls of the Missing
ZIMMERMANN, Russell J [368]	P-19-6
ZINGALE, Louis T	L-13-7
ZINIEL, Joseph M	L-5-12
ZINK, Charles E	I-11-14
ZINN, Francis L	C-17-14
ZINN, Thomas F	H-7-17
ZIRN, Richard H	Walls of the Missing
ZITO, John	Walls of the Missing
ZMUDZINSKI, Henry P	H-13-27
ZOCCHI, John V	H-5-7
ZOELLNER, William H	B-16-10
ZOFF, Vernon L	P-22-12
ZOLYNSKI, Chester	Walls of the Missing
ZORADI, Stephen M	M-17-17
ZORGER, William E	E-18-25
ZOUVELOS, George	H-17-6
ZUCCARELLA, Rocco M	K-5-3
ZUCK, Victor M	F-13-24
ZUEST, Harry W	K-21-20
ZUG, Donald E	B-21-2
ZUIDEMA, John A	P-19-2
ZULICK, Nicholas	D-15-20
ZUMPF, Frderick W	B-20-28
ZUNAMON, Jacob	N-2-17
ZUPEN, Paul	O-19-4
ZWEIER, George J	P-21-16
ZWICKY, Alfred O	J-9-5

LEST WE FORGET...

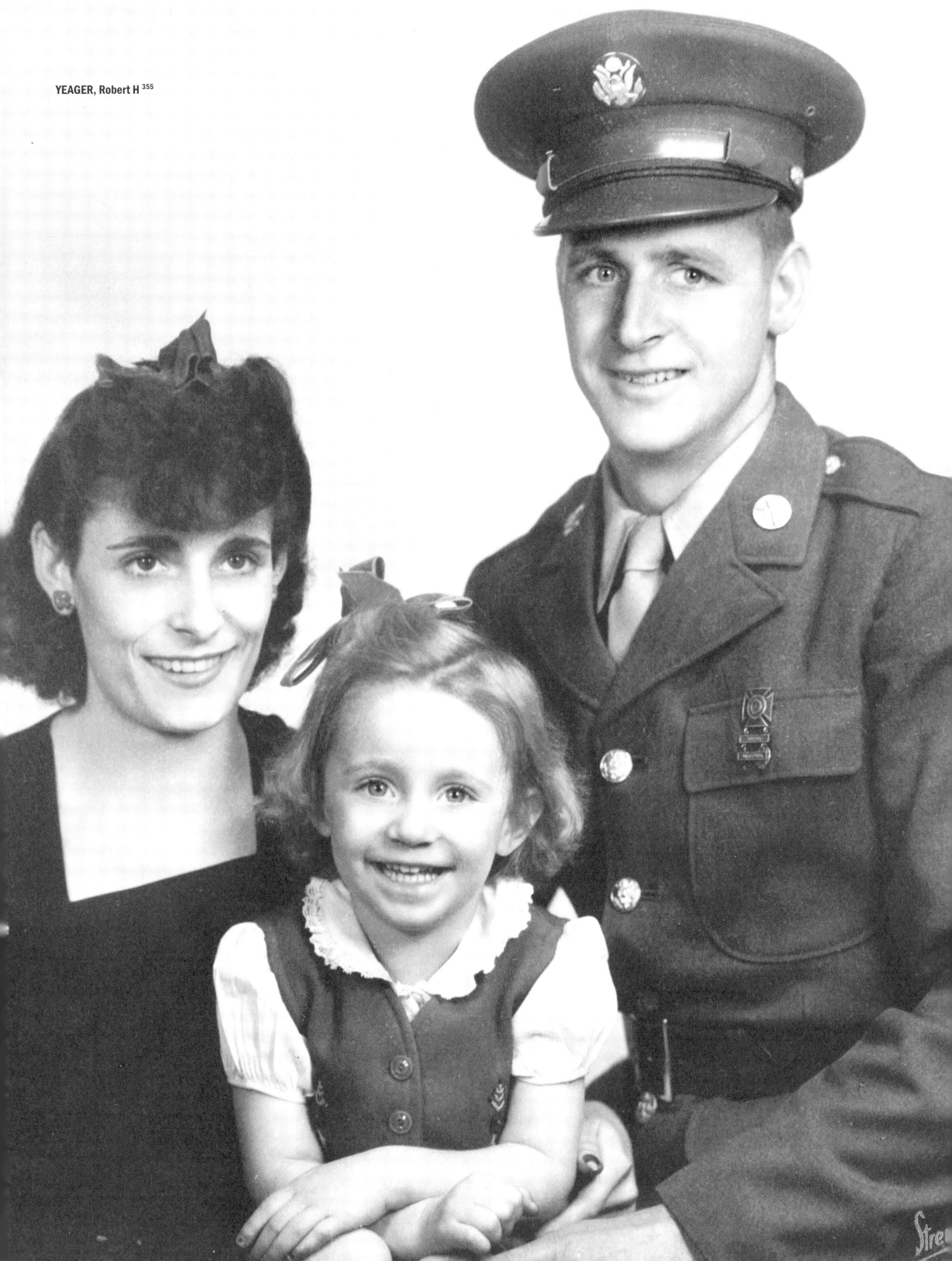

YEAGER, Robert H [355]

GLOSSARY

A

A-20 'Havoc' / 'Boston'
Medium twin-engine bomber. Crew: three men.

After-Action Report
Retrospective analysis and description of combat operations.

Airborne Division
Paratroopers and glider troops. About 9,000 men.

Armored Division
Tank division; about 200 tanks and 12–15,000 men.

Artillery
Heavy military weapons to launch munitions (for example shells) far beyond the range and power of infantry firearms. The term usually refers to large-caliber guns such as cannons, howitzers, and heavy mortars.

B

B-17 'Flying Fortress'
Heavy four-engine bomber. Crew: nine or ten men.

B-24 'Liberator'
Heavy four-engine bomber. Crew: nine or ten men.

B-26 'Marauder'
Medium twin-engine bomber. Crew: six men.

Bailey Bridge
British bridging equipment. Could be assembled as a kind of 'kit.'

Bazooka
American rocket launcher. Was fired from the shoulder to, for example, knock out enemy armored vehicles such as tanks.

Bombardment Group
Bombing unit with 50 to 60 bombers.

Bomb Squadron
Bombing unit with twelve to fifteen bombers. A Bomb Squadron was part of a Bombardment Group.

Bronze Star
American military award for either heroic achievement, heroic service, meritorious achievement, or meritorious service in a combat zone.

Bunker/Pillbox
Concrete combat position, often well-camouflaged.

C

C-47 'Skytrain'
Twin-engine transport aircraft. Derived from the Douglas DC-3.

Company
Group of about 120–150 men (three or four platoons).

Corps of Engineers
Army component responsible for engineering, military construction and civil works like building bridges.

D

Distinguished Service Cross
Second highest U.S. Army decoration for soldiers who display extraordinary heroism in combat with an armed enemy force.

Died of Wounds (DOW)
Soldier who died of his injuries.

Died Non-Battle (DNB)
Soldier who was not killed by an act of combat, but in, for example, a (traffic) accident.

Defense POW/MIA Accounting Agency (DPAA)
Agency within the U.S. Department of Defense whose mission it is to recover American military personnel listed as prisoners of war (POW) or missing in action (MIA). It was formed in 2015, as the result of a merger of the Joint POW/MIA Accounting Command (JPAC), the Defense Prisoner of War/Missing Personnel Office (DPMO), and parts of the United States Air Force's Life Sciences Equipment Laboratory.

Drop Zone (DZ)
Area where paratroopers land.

E

Eagle Squadron (RAF)
Unit of American pilots who volunteered before the United States entered World War II to fly for the British Royal Air Force (1940–1942).

Enlisted Men
A member of the armed forces who ranks below a commissioned officer or warrant officer.
Not to be confused with the term Enlistment. Enlistment could be on call (drafted) or voluntary.

European Theater of Operations (ETO)
Term used by the U.S. Army to designate the land and sea areas in Europe to be invaded or defended by the British-American armed forces.

F

Fighter Group
Group of 50 to 75 fighter aircraft.

Fighter Squadron
Group of twelve to fifteen fighter aircraft. A Fighter Squadron was part of a Fighter Group.

Field Artillery
Mobile artillery (cannons or howitzers) used to support armies in the field.

Finding of Death (FOD)
If it was considered unlikely that a missing soldier would still be found alive, the soldier was declared dead at least one year after going missing. That date is also held as the date of death, but may differ from the actual date of death.

Flak (88)
Abbreviation of German 'Flugzeug Abwehr Kanone' (anti-aircraft gun) with a caliber of 88mm.

Flight nurse
Nurse specialized in providing medical care to patients while they are air transported to a medical facility behind the front lines.

Focke-Wulf 190
German single-engine fighter (deployed from November 1941).

Foxhole
Type of defensive fighting position: a hole dug in the ground for one or two men, about five feet deep.

Friendly fire
Fratricide. Accidentally coming under gunfire from own or friendly troops.

G

Mechanized gun/Self-propelled gun
Cannon on a tank chassis or on another tracked vehicle.

Glider
The American CG-4A 'Waco' military glider could carry twelve men or a jeep, a light gun, or a howitzer.

Graves Registration Company
Military unit responsible for collecting fallen soldiers and establishing military cemeteries.

H

Halftrack
Semi-tracked military vehicle (wheels on the front, tracks on the rear).

I

Individual Deceased Personnel File (IDPF)
Archive folder in which all available information about a fallen/missing soldier is collected.

Infantry Division
Military organization of about 15,000 men which engages in ground combat on foot.

J

Jeep
Small and highly mobile four-wheel vehicle. Particularly versatile.

K

Killed in Action (KIA)
Casualty classification. Killed due to hostile action.

L

Landing Zone (LZ)
Area where gliders land.

M

M4 'Sherman'
Medium American tank.

M8 'Greyhound'
Six-wheeled reconnaissance vehicle armed with a light cannon and two machine guns.

M10 'Wolverine'
Tank destroyer based on a Sherman tank chassis and armed with a 76mm gun in an open turret.

M18 'Hellcat'
Fast and maneuverable tank destroyer with a 76mm cannon in an open turret.

M24 'Chaffee'
American light tank armed with a 75mm cannon.

M36 'Jackson'
Successor of the M10 'Wolverine.' Equipped with a 90mm cannon.

Machine gun
Automatic weapon that fires linked cartridge belts.

Machine pistol
Individual 'personal' weapon. Magazine with 20–30 bullets. Also known as submachine gun.

Medal of Honor
The United States' highest and most prestigious military decoration that may be awarded to recognize American soldiers, sailors, marines, airmen, guardians, and coast guardsmen who have distinguished themselves by acts of valor. The medal is normally awarded by the President of the United States, but as it is presented 'in the name of the United States Congress,' it is often referred to (erroneously) as the 'Congressional Medal of Honor.'

Medic
Soldier who is trained to provide medical aid to wounded soldiers on the battlefield.

Messerschmitt Bf 109
Most-produced German fighter aircraft (from 1937).

Messerschmitt Me 262
German twin-engine jet fighter (deployed from late 1944).

Mine Field
An area in which explosive mines have been invisibly buried.

Missing in Action (MIA)
Casualty classification for a soldier who went missing without it being possible to establish that he had died.

Missing Air Crew Report (MACR)
Report in which all details of an aircraft downed or missing over enemy territory are noted.

Morning Report
Diary in which every basic unit of the U.S. Army noted all personnel changes (promotions/awarded decorations/transfers/deaths). It was produced every morning.

Mortar
Man-portable, muzzle-loaded weapon, consisting of a long tube fixed to a base plate with a lightweight bipod. They launch explosive shells/bombs in high-arching ballistic trajectories. Mortar team: two to four men.

O

Official Military Personnel File (OMPF)
Archive folder containing all the info on every individual soldier who ever enlisted.

Officer
Leader of a military unit or a specialist such as pilot, bomb aimer, navigator.

Ordnance Corps
Sustainment branch of the U.S. Army. Component that deals with armaments and ammunition.

P

P-38 'Lightning'
Twin-engine fighter / fighter-bomber. It had a distinctive double tail.

P-47 'Thunderbolt'
Long-range fighter and fighter-bomber.

P-51 'Mustang'
Most built American long-range fighter aircraft.

Panther tank (Mark V)
Heavy German tank with a 75mm cannon.

Panzerfaust
Light portable German anti-tank weapon. Shoulder fired.

Panzerschreck
Portable German anti-tank rocket launcher. Similar to the American Bazooka.

Patrol
Group of usually eight to ten men sent out (into enemy territory) for the purpose of combat, reconnaissance, or a combination of both.

Prisoner of War (POW)
A person who is held captive by a belligerent power.

Purple Heart
Award given to those wounded or killed while serving with the U.S. military. The addition 'Oak Leaf Cluster' means that the soldier has been wounded more than once.

Q

Quartermaster Corps
U.S. Army unit that performed support duties. Among other things, they were responsible for truck transportation, management of warehouses, laundries, bakeries, supply of fuel, etc. Also responsible for the collection and burial of casualties and the establishment of military cemeteries.

R

Replacement
Soldier who is added to a unit as a replacement for a wounded/fallen soldier.

S

Segregation
Separation of white and non-white American troops.

SHAEF
Supreme Headquarters Allied Expeditionary Force. HQ of the Allied Expeditionary Force in northwest Europe.

Signal Corps
Army component primarily responsible for communications facilities.

Silver Star
The Silver Star Medal (SSM) is the United States Armed Forces' third-highest military decoration for valor in combat. It is awarded primarily to members of the U.S. Armed Forces for gallantry in action against an enemy of the U.S.

Small arms
Term used to designate firearms carried and operated by individual infantrymen, for example: rifles, pistols, carbines, submachine guns, and light machine guns.

Sniper
Marksman who engages targets from concealed positions or from a long distance. Snipers are often armed with rifles equipped with a scope.

STALAG
Abbreviation of the German Stamm Lager: German prisoner of war camp.

T

Tank
Armored (tracked) vehicle with a cannon in a rotating closed turret.

Tank battalion
Unit consisting of about 80 tanks and 720 men.

Tank Destroyer battalion
Tank destroyer unit equipped with 36 Tank destroyers and 644 men.

Tank destroyer
Agile tracked vehicle specially equipped with a fast-firing anti-tank gun in a open turret.

Tiger tank (Mark VI)
Heavy German tank with an 88mm cannon.

U

USAAF
U.S. Army Air Forces.

U.S. Army
U.S. (ground) army.

W

Westwall/Siegfried Line
German defense line that ran from Kleve (on the Dutch border) to the Swiss border. This line of 630 km included bunkers and dragon's teeth.

U.S. ARMY STRUCTURE

UNIT	SIZE	LED BY
Squad	Usually nine to twelve soldiers: Private Private First Class	Corporal Sergeant
Platoon	Three squads	Staff Sergeant Second Lieutenant First Lieutenant
Company	Three or four platoons	First Lieutenant Captain
Battalion	Three or four companies	Major Lieutenant Colonel
Regiment	Three or four battalions	Colonel
Division	Three or four regiments	Brigadier General Major General
Army Corps	Multiple divisions	Major General
Army	Multiple army corps	Lieutenant General
Army Group	Multiple armies	General General of the Army

This above structure is applicable to infantry and airborne divisions. American infantry divisions were usually 15,000 to 20,000 men strong (including the attached engineers, artillery, medical, and other support personnel). The airborne divisions were about half this size.

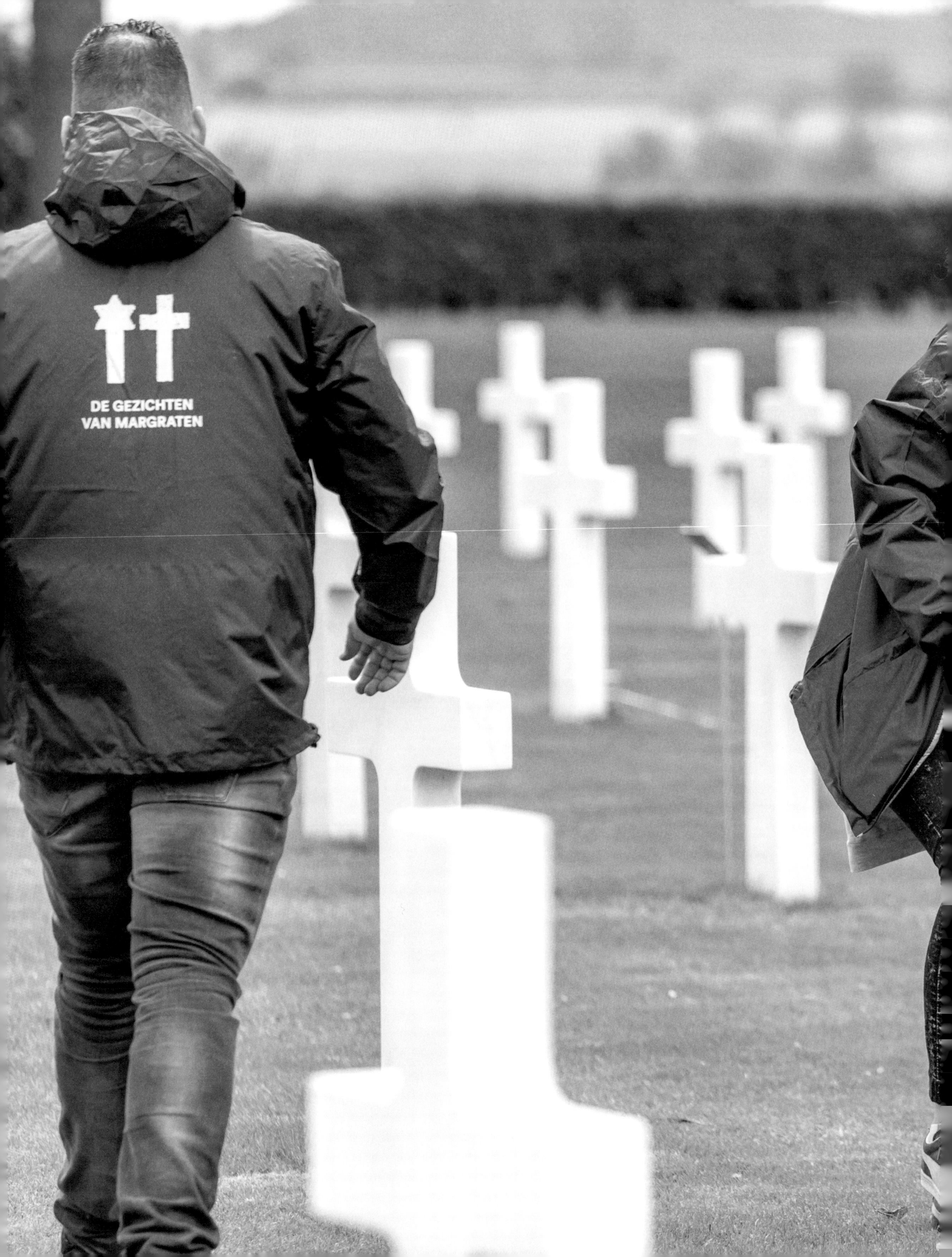
DE GEZICHTEN
VAN MARGRATEN

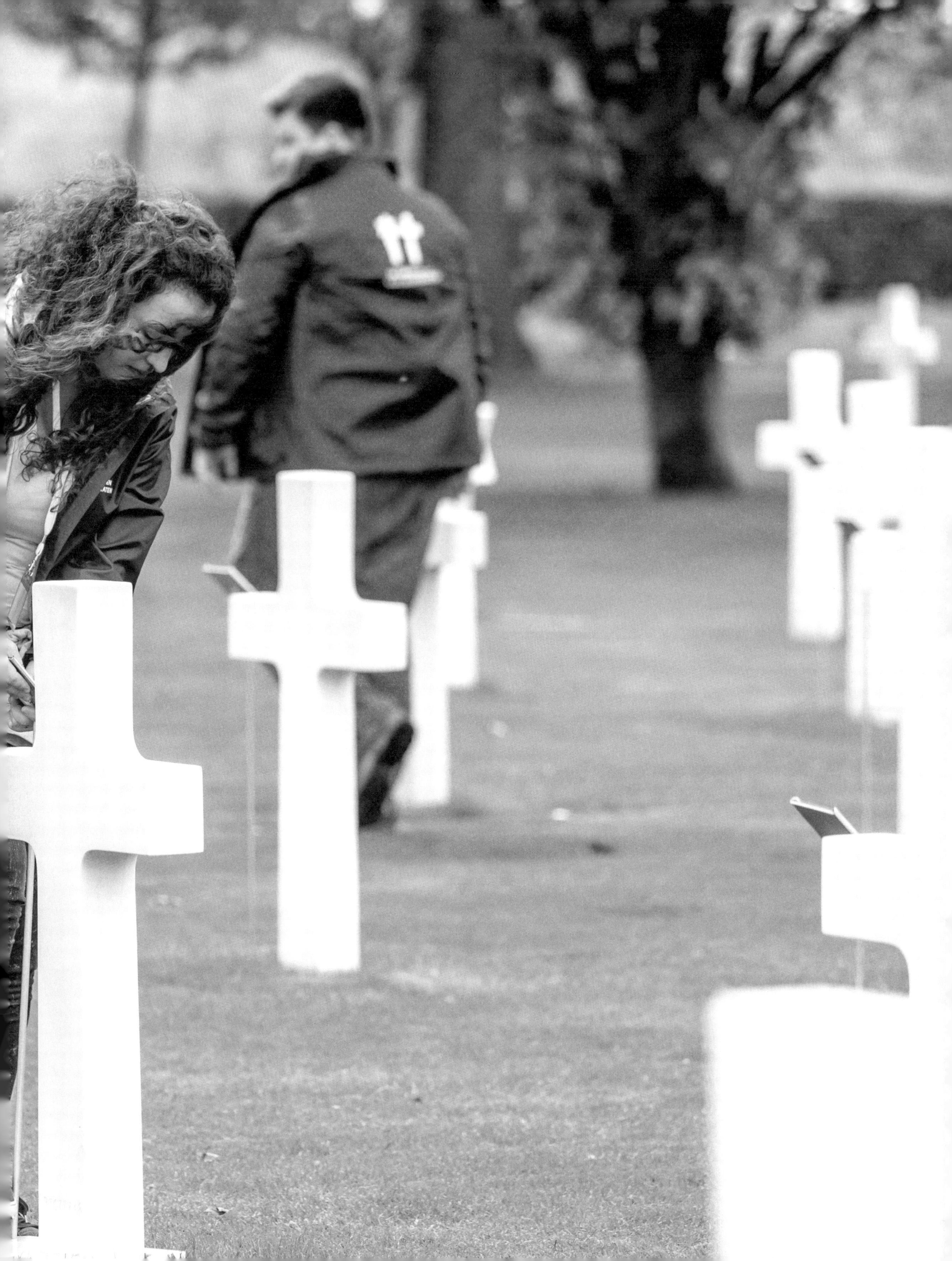

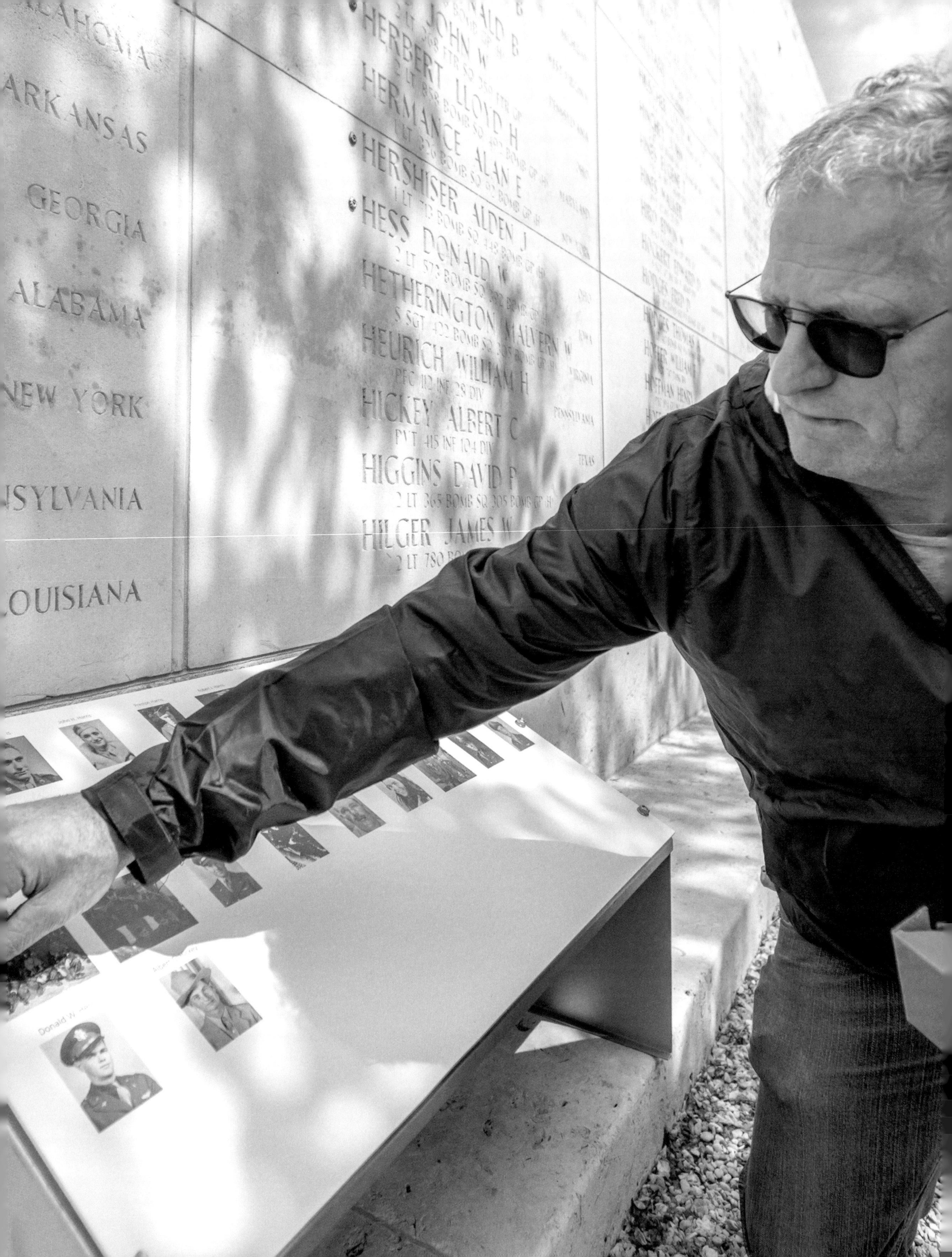
ARKANSAS
GEORGIA
ALABAMA
NEW YORK
HERMANCE ALAN E
HERSHISER ALDEN J
HESS DONALD W
HETHERINGTON MALVERN W
HEURICH WILLIAM H
PFC 112 INF 28 DIV
HICKEY ALBERT C
PVT 415 INF 104 DIV
HIGGINS DAVID P
2 LT 365 BOMB SQ 305 BOMB GP H
HILGER JAMES W

ACKNOWLEDGEMENTS

Finding more information about the soldiers in this book was not always an easy task so many years after their deaths. In addition, having an idea for a book is one thing, making it become a reality is another. We are, therefore, extremely grateful to the following people for their valuable contribution to this book:

Eveliene Smeets, Frida Hemmes, Rudi Videc, Timo Videc, Roger Long, Willem Kiggen, Maurice Heemels, Paul Cober, Tom Peeters, Mark LaPointe, Joshua Hall, Aaron Elson, Geoff Gentilini, Phil Rosenkrantz, Patricia Higbee, Bruce Brodowski, Wiel Goertzen, Mike Etzel, David J. Clare, Dan Diehl, John Heuvelman, Hub Schetters, Ben Savelkoul, Louis Hensgens, Bert Caris, Marcel Kleijkers, Wim Slangen, Jochen Reinders, Rene Francotte, Stephen Rice, Dennis Patriarca, Richard Smeets, Mike Ellis, Evert Vos, Egon Kopatz, Maarten Vossen, Richard van Kessel, Anthony Glavan, Don Schmitz, Louise Dice, Albert Schaart, Ton Hermes, Frans Roebroeks, Foundation for Adopting Graves at the American Cemetery in Margraten, The Citadel Memorial Europe Foundation, Mission Belle Foundation B-17G Memorial, Café Pelt Heerlen, 18 September Foundation Eindhoven, Jeroen Geerts, Dagblad De Limburger, Myra Miller and her team of Footsteps Researchers, Ronald Stassen, Willemijn Doelman, Mariska Sipers-Schijns, Tim Sloots, Harald E.L. Prins, Charles Lundy, Larry Kilmer, Jean-Pierre Geusens, Vilhauer family, Dr. Ian Spurgeon, DPAA, Ruud Huijts, Mario Nouwen, Pierre Erens, Bart van der Sterren, Stories Behind the Stars, Stichting MIA, Michael Fleming, Nancy Young, Caren Austen, Monique Lemmens, Chris Harris, Lisa Abernethy Edwards, Susan Fleury Fortin, Eric Gadet, Yuri Beckers, Robert Meij, Ryan Liskey, Karen Corbett, War Museum Eyewitness Beek, Kristin Wright, David McGhee, Kathy McDermott, Deborah Silver, Brian Papesh, Gail Phelps, Dymphie Weusten, Adrian Caldwell, Scott Rayl, Karen Velasquez, Tim Hendriks, Frans Ammerlaan, Sue Brueggemeier, Verl Dasher, Peter Grimm, Kristi Miller, Tanner Crunelle, and Peter van Kaathoven. Also, a thank you to Winnie Urban, Annelies van der Meij, and all others at Amsterdam University Press/ Walburg Pers.

Furthermore, we owe a big thank you to the current and former volunteers of the *Fields of Honor Foundation.* These volunteers have, without exaggeration, put many of thousands of hours of their time into their research over the past fifteen years. The list is undoubtedly not exhaustive, but this book and projects such as the *Fields of Honor – Database* and *The Faces of Margraten* have owed much to the following people who have dedicated their time to the foundation for long periods of time:

Michel Beckers, An van den Broeck, Mireille Brons, Cor van den Burg, Justine Camps, Ria Cholly, Erwin Derhaag, Danny Dohmen, Annemie Dols, Raf Dyckmans, Jac Engels, Astrid van Erp, Han van Florop, Corrina Halters, Jasper van Haren, Arie-Jan van Hees, Armand Hendriks, Dennis Hermsen, Terry Hirsch, Debbie Holloman, Danny van der Groen, André Koch, Nico Leers, Twan van Leeuwen, Wendy Lensink, Nick Lieten, Susan Linton, Guy Maes, Hannah Majewski, Carla Mans, Kathy McDermott, Leo Minne, Ralph Peeters, Frans Rabuda, Ron Raaijmakers, Niek Schoonbrood, Peter Schouteten, Tjarco Schuurman, Bert-Jan Sengers, Yannick Severeyns, Gerda Smeets, Willem Smeets, Luc van der Sterren, Andy Swinnen, Anja Thijssen, Ed Tiebax, Tom Verheijden, Jori Videc, Jean Vijgen, Hannah Vleugels, Sophie Vleugels, Sebastiaan Vonk, Maarten Vossen, Hans Wijnands, Berry Wolf, Herman Wolters, and Roger Zoontjes.

In addition, we would like to thank everyone who has provided information for the database over the past few years. Every bit of information and every picture are pieces of the puzzle. Together we keep the memory alive.

We are also indebted to several organizations and individuals who have helped us in recent years to organize the actual *The Faces of Margraten* tribute at the cemetery. They too deserve to be mentioned here. A word of thanks to:

American Battle Monuments Commission, U.S. Embassy The Hague, Municipality of Eijsden-Margraten, Province of Limburg, vfonds, Prins Bernhard Cultuurfonds Limburg, Elisabeth Strouven Fonds, Kanunnik Salden Nieuwenhof, Aanmoedigingsfonds van de Koninklijke Facultatieve, Rabobank Zuid-Limburg Oost, Stichting Laudio, Studio Buttons, Est.21, Robin van Hontem Graphic Design, Chriske Margraten, Klomp Bizzprint, Van der Lee Staalbouw, Visit Zuid-Limburg, Embassy of the Kingdom of the Netherlands in Washington D.C., Hout Video, Jean-Pierre Geusens, Ger Hindriks, Ellen Beck, Dieudonné Akkermans, Keith Stadler, and Mieke Kirkels.

Also, a word of thanks to the maintenance staff of the Netherlands American Cemetery and Memorial. Firstly, for their valuable support on the days when the faces can be seen at the cemetery. But most of all for the work they do day after day, in every weather condition, to ensure that the cemetery continues to be a dignified place. We all owe them a debt of gratitude.

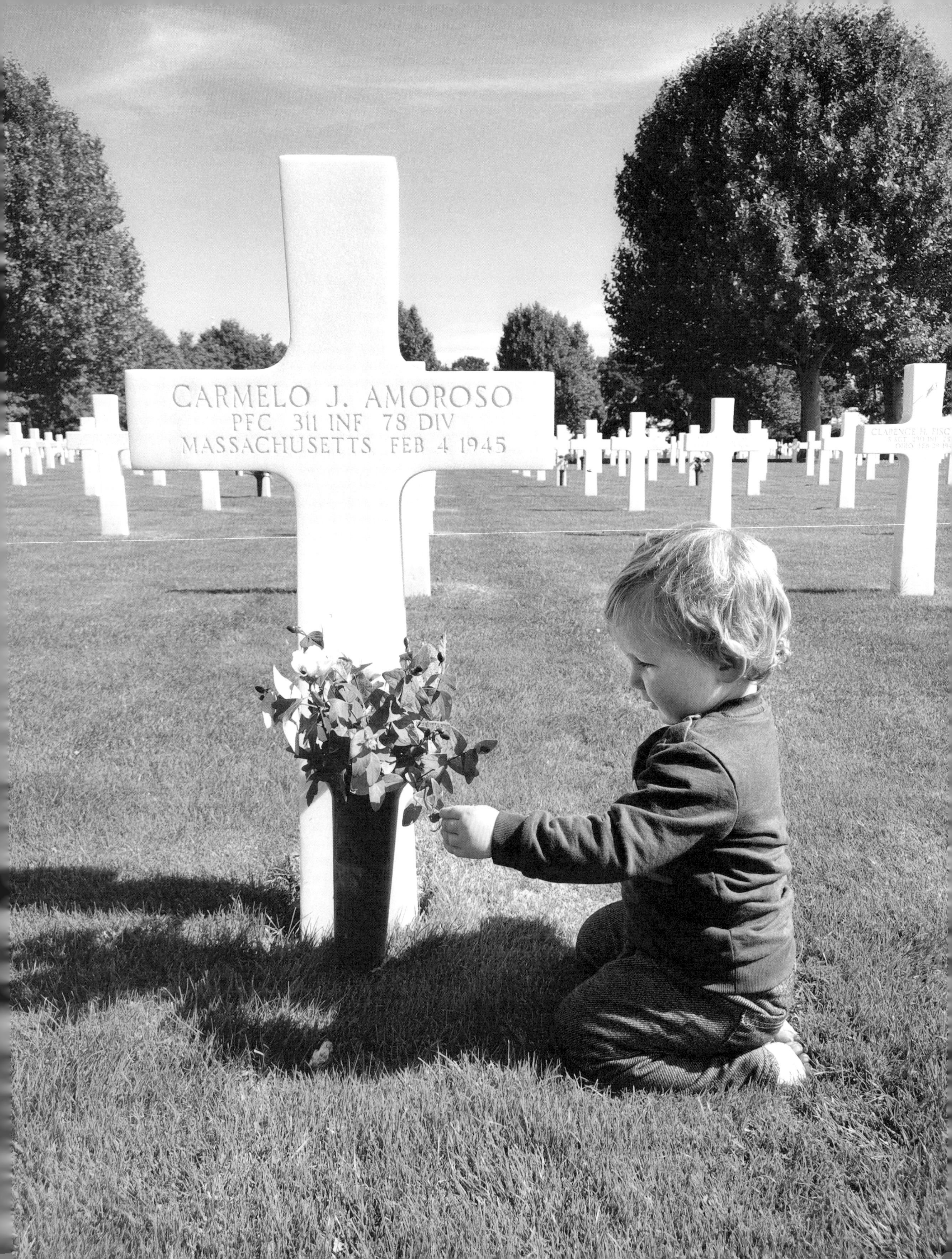
CARMELO J. AMOROSO
PFC 311 INF 78 DIV
MASSACHUSETTS FEB 4 1945

THEY REMEMBER

Our vision for this book was for it to truly be a monument in print. This also meant that it also was a more expensive book to make than the average book that you can find at the bookstore. Therefore, we are most grateful for everyone who has pre-ordered a copy, helping us to finance this book and make it become a reality. So lastly, we would like to acknowledge and thank the more than 300 individuals and organizations who have helped us to ensure that the memory to men and women buried and memorialized in Margraten will be kept alive:

104th Timberwolf Infantry Division
1st Lt. Thomas Paxton Sherwood Archives
8th Armored Division Association
Alayne J. Hammer
Allison Kouns
Alvis W. Tinsley
American Legion Margraten Post NL01
André Koch
Annette Puglia Herskowitz
Anthony S. LoPresti
April Mecham
Arie-Jan van Hees, American Cemetery Tours
Arjan van Hassel
Arjan van Prooijen
Art Mouton, in memory of S/Sgt. Jerome Mouton
Audra Rose-Kight, granddaughter of Major General Maurice Rose
American WWII Orphans Network (AWON)
B-26 Marauder Historical Society
Barbara McNamara, niece of Pvt. Raymond P. Kelly
Bernard Evans
Best Defense Foundation
Beverly Hobbs, in memory of Roland Hale
Bill and Brenda Prescott
Bill Leibnitz
Bob Mallett, in memory of Capt. Ralph Gregory
Bob Pipes
Brewster, MN American Legion
Brian Helms
Brittany Aldom
Brothers in Arms Press
Bryan Riebe
Caro and Hanno Weitering
Carol Jackson
Carol Nash
Carol Pollard
Charles Bestul, nephew of Sgt. Luther J. Bestul
Charles Lundy
Charlotte Herben Branch
Chayne Dessaso
Chris and Chantal Dessaso
Chris Harris
Christian Mewissen
Christy Nixon
Clifford Carlson
Clint Whitwer
Coen Mehlkop
Corrine Samuel
CW5 (Ret) Virgil Martin
Cynthia Glavan Ruppe
Dana Walker
Daniel Diehl
Debora Baud
Derk Kamphuis
Diana Diels
Dick van den Berg, in memory of Ossie J. Allen
Dineke Niemeijer
Dirk Schouten
Donald Baasch
Donna Marsh Peery
Donna Schurman, niece of Lt. James Robert Lavin
Dorothée van Hooff
Dorothy Jongens
Dymphie Weusten
Eastport/Annapolis Legacy of Honor
Edward Whitmarsh
Edwin Ernes
Elias Tieleman
Elly Vogely
Embassy of the Kingdom of the Netherlands in Washington DC
Ernest Keith Gunter
Eva Smith
Eveliene Smeets
Evelyn Vannuys-Smeets
Familie Ettema
Familie Hellebrekers
Familie Meij
Fanny Hubart-Salmon
Flores Hopman
Frida en Rudi Videc
George Pindroh
Gerald and Doris Richardson
Geraldine Conway Morenski
Gerard de Kort
Gerry Hurlbert
Gilles van de Wouw
Glenn Kempff
Glenn Matuszewski
Gough family
Greg and Jill Brooks
Guus Peters
H. den Toom
Hanssen Family
Hein Jansen, Lancaster EE167
Heleen Bakker
Henry and Emily Kenealy
Henry Anderson
Henry Prenger
Herman Thomas
Hotel Creusen Epen
Hudson Louie
Imelda en Peter Schroijen
Irene Reijnen-de Lang
Isaac Steinlicht, Sons of the American Legion Squadron NL01 2021 Sergeant at Arms
Ivor van Hese
Jack H. McCall, Jr.
James Heiberg
James Light
James R. Hersom
James Robinson
Jan M.S. Baggerman
Jan S. Post
Jane Loy Ries
Jasper Kuipers
Jef en Ed Weerts
Jeffrey Lavin, nephew of James R. Lavin
Jen Gerber
Jenny Tresidder
Jim Jacobus
Jim Kinney
Joan McIntyre, niece of Kenneth B. Thomson
Joëll Franssen
Johan Heijkers
John Cox
John Heuvelman, Mission Belle Foundation
John Highgill
John Nofsinger
Jori Videc
Jos Ruigrok
Joshua Steinlicht, American Legion Margraten Post NL01 2021-2022 Commander
Jürgen Mingels, “Old Hickory”
Kandice Steinlicht, American Legion Margraten Post NL01
Karel de Goey
Karl Thompson
Karyn Marie Miller
Kathleen Rehman
Kathy McDermott
Kathy Price, daughter of Lt. Bill Sarver
Kathy V. Dukeman Hight
Kees Vonk
Kelly Tierney, daughter of John M. Tierney – Vietnam Veteran SP4 US Army
Kev and Debs O’Brien
Kevin Wilson, Director 381st Bomb Group Memorial Association
Kristen Harris, in memory of Ernest L. Baer
Kristin Wright
Kurt Anchorstar
Kurt Kooyer, MD
Larry Charles Chambers
Larry Kilmer, son of Tec 5 Thomas B. Kilmer
Larry Köster
LaRue F. Cribbs
Laura M. Phillips
Lauren Crimmins Caserio
Laurie Callery McAnespie
Leon Geelen
Lester Zentner
Lily Debie
Linda M. Griffith, MD
Linda Perrone
Linda Vander Naald
Lindsay Nichols
Lisa Edwards
Lisa Gogal
Lola Whittaker Family
Loretta Beckerink
Louis Kunz
Lt. Col. Glen D. Owen, USAF (Ret)
Lt. Floyd Addy – James Michael McShane
Luc Pennings
Lucy en Jos Dols-Andries
Maj. Bob Loomis, US Army (Ret)
Maj. M. M. Watson
Manon Kouters
Marc en Sonja Geijselaers-Biermans
Marc Salverda
Margit and Lyle Bakke
Marianne Glavan Nanti
Marianne Mihalyo, Co-Founder Iwo Jima/ World War II Museum
Marie-José and Berto Bleijlevens
Marie-Therese Zweers-Rasing
Mariëtte Amkreutz-Stevens
Marijke for Vickie
Marilyn Jensen, 35th Division Association
Mario van Duinen
Mario W.N. Piets
Marit Hoogendijk
Mark and Linda Chernek, “Music 4 Vets Nederland”
Mark A. Dietzen
Mark K. Mulder
Mark LaPointe, in memory of Sgt. William G. Aubut
Mark Venner
Mary Herheim, in memory of George S. Works
Mary Reed, the niece of John P. Dunford
MaryEllen Meier
Maurice Heemels
Medidact
Michael Bishop

Michael Malone, Best Defense Foundation
Michelle Cahill, niece of T/Sgt. John "Jack" Cahill
Miss Carol Baldessari, niece of S/Sgt. Earl Bradfield
Monique en Jos Krick
Monuments Men and Women Foundation for the Preservation of Art
Moon Brothers American Legion Post 275, Independence, KY
Mr. and Mrs. Stephen R. Snow
Mr. Kim Carmean
Mr.John Vitale and Miss Mari Vitale
Museum De Bewogen Jaren 1939-1950, Hooge Mierde
Nancy E. Meyer, AWON
Nehemia Halawane
Neil Moriarty
Nelly Lucas-VanDenMeiracker
Nick Daffern
Nico van Buggenum
Norm Lager
O. van Warmerdam
Omaha Central High School
Oscar L. Harrington, son of S/Sgt. Oscar L. Harrington
Pascal Prickartz
Pascalle Essers
Pat Griffith, daughter of Patrick Mazzie and niece of Joseph Glassen
Patricia Ann Haight, sister of Pvt. Raymond P. Kelly
Patricia Smith Carnes
Paul E. Carter
Paul Vrancken
Peggy Linrud
Peter Robbertsen
Rachel Nilwik
Raphael Morris
Ray Lynch, American Legion Post 10
Raymond Penders
Reed Carpenter
Relia van Dijk-van der Aa
Ria Cholly-Besseling
Ria van Sonnen-Kost
Richard F. Frye
Richard Nagle
Richard Smeets
Rob Pijnenburg
Rob Ramakers
Robert and Michelle Nunn
Robert Anderson Jr.
Robert Birch
Robert Fisher
Robert Fry, cousin of Charley Rose
Robert Schortemeyer
Roberta Brooks
Roel Harryvan, Consul of the Netherlands
Roel Smeets
Ron Swiader
Ronald Busschers
Russ Tyson
S.C. Haverhoek
Sandra Coldicott Britton
Scott and Kim Singer
Sean Kille
Second Schweinfurt Memorial Association
Sheila Dodge
Sheree Dowdle
Silvano Theunissen, in memory of the men of the 26th Infantry Division
SMSgt. John W. Collins
Stacie BeBout
Steven Smith, The Citadel Memorial Europe
Stories Behind the Stars
Susan Fleury Fortin
Susan Kerr Appler
Susan Linton, SSMA/306BG
Susan P. Harris
Susanne Egan
Sylvia Goins, daughter of an Old Hickory veteran
The Bloody Hundred
The Children of M.J. 'Dolly' Cooper
The family of Sgt. William G. Aubut
The family of Norman Beattie
The family of Walter Bogacz
The family of Vern Bolduc
The family of William L. Braun
The family of Pfc Raymond L. Cassidy
The family of Vernon Goodman
The family of Herbert Lake
The family of Paul N. Mullen
The family of Thomas A. Rogan
The family of James W. Sweaney
The Cell Family
The Lindsey family
The Olson Family
The Porter Family
The Sarver family
The Schmitz Family
Thomas Englehart, US Army (Ret)
Thomas Rose
Tina Rempel for Ray Rempel, in memory of beloved older brother Calvin Ainley Rempel
Tony Benjamin
Tony Glavan
Toon De Wildt and Thormin Family
Truus van Thoor
Verl and Sue Dasher
Wanda Stump, in memory of Leander Reel
Warren Davis, in memory of Maj Richard T. Deabler
West York Police Department
Wilfred Kerckhoffs
Willem Korver
William Francis Beacht, Sr.
Wilma en Richard Syen
Wilma Theunissen-Hölscher
WWII Museum Pieces of the Past
Yannick Troupin
Yuri Beckers, 9th Infantry Division In WWII

SOURCES

Websites

www.fieldsofhonor-database.com
www.1limburg.nl
www.506infantry.org
www.517prct.org/bios/woodhull.htm
www.5ad.org
www.69th-infantry-division.com
www.76thdivision.com
www.7tharmddiv.org
www.8th-armored.org
www.9thinfantrydivision.net
www.aad.archives.com
www.abmc.gov
www.adoptiegraven-margraten.nl
www.akkersvanmargraten.nl
www.ambc.org
www.ambceducation.org
www.americanairmuseum.com
www.ancestry.com
www.archive.org/PathsOfArmor
www.arlingtoncemetery.net
www.armydivs.com
www.artilleryocsalumni.com
www.awon.org
www.b24.net
www.band-of-brothers.nl/artikel/vet_uni_460_Woodhull.htm
www.basher82.nl/Data/margraten/woodhull.htm
www.bensavelkoul.nl
www.berkshireeagle.com
www.bezoekditverhaal.nl
www.bndestem.nl
www.books.stonebooks.com
www.boston.com
www.bostonglobe.com
www.canonvanoirschot.nl
www.carol_fus.tripod.com
www.carol_fus.tripod.com/army_hero_search_corgan.html
www.cbn.com
www.cgsc.contentdm.oclc.org
www.cinecrowd.nl
www.coulthart.com
www.cpp.edu/~rosenkrantz
www.d-ekker.nl
www.defense.gov
www.degezichtenvanmargraten.nl
www.dekollenberg.nl
www.digicom.bpl.lib.me.us
www.digital.olivesoftware.com
www.dpaa.mil
www.erenow.net
www.etvma.org
www.eyewitnesstohistory.com
www.fallennotforgotten.nl
www.fayettecountyhistory.org
www.findagrave.com
www.fold3.com
www.fortblissbugle.com
www.gelsenkirchener-geschichten.de
www.gerlachus.nl
www.hazy.home.xs4all.nl
www.hctgs.org
www.henkbaron.nl
www.heroesforever.nl
www.heroesforever.nl/Corgan.htm
www.historiek.net
www.history.santacruzpl.org
www.historynet.com/now-is-when-you-pray.htm
www.historyofwar.org
www.historyonthefox.wordpress.com
www.home.planet.nl/~slang075/Wim-Slangen/Breeden-Henlin.html
www.homeofheroes.com
www.honorstates.org
www.internationalbcc.co.uk
www.krijnen.com
www.l1.nl
www.lebomag.com/the-cost-of-freedom/
www.lib.uconn.edu
www.liberationroute.nl
www.limburger.nl
www.louishensgens.com
www.margratenmemorial.nl
www.markantzuidlimburg.nl
www.mtu.edu
www.nationalmuseum.af.mil
www.newspaperarchive.com
www.newspapers.com
www.nos.nl
www.npr.org
www.oisterwijk-marketgarden.com
www.oldhickory30th.com
www.oorlogsdodennijmegen.nl
www.oralhistoryaudiobooks.blogspot.com
www.questmasters.us
www.scribd.com/Vetrans-Story
www.shawlocal.com
www.stltoday.com
www.tankdestroyer.net
www.text-message.blogs.archives.gov/2013/12/12/walter-j-huchthausen-a-monuments-man-killed-in-action/
www.thecitadelmemorialeurope.wordpress.com
www.tracesofwar.com
www.unithistories.com
www.users.skynet.be/mart.janssen
www.uwgoldstarhonorroll.org
www.valor.militarytimes.com
www.veteransofthebattleofthebulge.org
www.volkskrant.nl
www.warcemeteries.nl
www.wikiofbrothers.wikia.com
www.wikipedia.com
www.witnesstowar.org
www.wo2go.nl
www.wowt.com
www.wvculture.org
www.ww2gravestone.com
www.ww2insouthlimburg.nl
www.ww2marketgarden.com
www.wwiimemorial.com
www.zuidlimburgbevrijd.nl

Books

'717th Tank Battalion Record.' (1946)
Ambrose, S., *Van D-Day tot Berlijn*. Boekerij (2007)
Ambrose, S., *Band of Brothers*. Boekerij (2010)
Ambrose, S., *D-Day: 6 juni 1944*. Boekerij (2011)
Balkoski, J., *Our Tortured Souls: The 29th Infantry Division in the Rhineland, November – December 1944.* Stackpole Books (2013)
Bando, M., *101st Airborne: The Screaming Eagles in World War II*. Voyageur Press (2011)
Beevor, A, *D-Day: The Battle for Normandy*. Penguin Books (2014)
Beevor, A., *Ardennes 1944: Hitler's Last Gamble*. Penguin Random House U.K. (2015)
Bielakowski, A., *Ethnic and Racial Minorities in the U.S. Military: An Encyclopedia*. ABC-CLIO (2013)
Binkoski, J., & Plaut, A., *The 115th Infantry Regiment in World War II*. Arcole Publishing (2019)
Bishhop, S. D., & Hey, J. A., Losses of the US 8th and 9th Air Forces, Volumes 1 to 5. Bishop Book Productions.
Black, R., *The Battalion: The Dramatic Story of the 2nd Ranger Battalion in World War II*. Stackpole Books (2013)
Bowman, M., *So Near and Yet So Far: Air War Market Garden*. Pen & Sword Books Limited (2013)
Briggs, E., *Joe Dew: A Glorious Life*. Createspace Independent Publishing Platform (2018)
Brodowski, B., *The Dad I Never Knew: A War Orphan's Search for Inner Healing* (2010)
Brotherton, M., *Scherpschutter van Band of Brothers. De Tweede Wereldoorlog door de ogen van Shifty Powers*. Boekerij (2012)
Burgett, D., *Beyond the Rhine: A Screaming Eagle in Germany* (2001)
Burgett, D., *Seven Roads to Hell: A Screaming Eagle in Bastogne* (2001)
Burgett, D., *The Road to Arnhem: A Screaming Eagle in Holland*. Drb Enterprise Inc. (2014)
Burris, T., *Strike and Hold: A Memoir of the 82nd Airborne in World War II*. Pontomac Books. (2001)
Caddick-Adams, P., *Sand and Steel: A New History of D-Day*. Cornerstone (2019)
Cahill, M., *Dear Mom: A Family Finds Its Past in World War II Letters Home*. Pleasant Street Publishers (2015)
Caine, P. D., *Eagles of the RAF: The WW2 Eagle Squadrons*. Washington D.C.: National Defense University Press (1991)
Cambell, J. D. & Leinbaugh, H. P., *The Men of Company K: The Autobiography of a World War II Rifle Company*. Bantam Books (1987)
Clark, L., *De Slag om Arnhem. De complete geschiedenis van Operatie Market Garden*. September 1944. Deltas (2013)
'Combat History of the 119th Infantry Regiment.' (1946)
Cook, D., & Evans, W., *Kampfgruppe Peiper: De race naar de Maas*. Just Publishers (2015)
Crost, L., *Honor by Fire: Japanese Americans at War in Europe and the Pacific*. (1994)
Dodd, E. H., *Of Nature, Time, and Teale: A Biographical Sketch of Edwin Way Teale*. Dodd, Mead & Company (1960)
Edsel, R., *The Greatest Treasure Hunt in History: The Story of the Monuments Men*. (2019)
Elson, A., *The Armored Fist. The 712th Tank Battalion in the Second World War*. Fonthill Media (2013)
Fenelon, J., *Four Hours of Fury: The Untold Story of World War II's Largest Airborne Invasion and The Final Push into Nazi Germany*. Simon & Schuster (2019)
Forty, S., & Marroitt, L., *Het Ardennenoffensief december 1944 – januari 1945*. Rebo International (2018)
Forty, S., & Timmermans, T., *Operation Market Garden*. Rebo International (2018)
Frank, M.E.V., *The Forgotten POW: Second Lieutenant Reba Z. Whittle*. U.S. Army War College, Carlise Barracks PA (1990)
Freeman, R. A., *Mighty Eighth War Diary*. Couldson: Jane's Publishing Co Ltd. (1981)
Freeman, R. A., *The Mighty Eighth*. London: Cassell (2000)
Freeman, R. A., *The Mighty Eighth War Manual*. London: Cassell (2001)
Gardner, I., *Deliver Us from Darkness: The Untold Story of Third Battalion 506th Parachute Infantry Regiment During Market Garden*. Bloomsbury (2013)
Green, M., & Brown, J.D., *M4 Sherman at War*. Zenith Press, (2007)
Hageman, R., & Dewelde, N., *De oorlog in Limburg*. BezetBevrijd (2018)
Hendriks, J., & Koenen, H., *D-Day in Zuid-Limburg*. De Limburger (1994)
Hess, W., *America's Top Eighth Air Force Aces in Their Own Words*. MBI (2001)
Hillery, V., & Hurley, E., *Paths of Armor: The Fifth Armored Division in World War II*. Eumenes Publishing (2016)
History of the 84th Infantry Division. Tumer Publishing (1997)
Holt, T., & Holt, V., *Major and Mrs. Holt's Battlefield Guide to Operation Market Garden*. Pen & Sword Books Limited (2013)
Imerman, B., *Soldiers of the Freedom Rock: Stories of Guthrie County Iowa's Combat Veterans*. Createspace Independent Publishing Platform (2015)
Johnson, D., *Fast Tanks and Heavy Bombers: Innovation in the U.S. Army, 1917–1945*. Cornell University Press (1998)
Jordan Sr., K., *Yesterday's Heroes: 433 men of World War II Awarded the Medal of Honor 1941–1945*. Schiffer Publishing Ltd. (1996)
Jordan, G., *History of the 811th Tank Destroyer Battalion*. (1971)
Kaplan, P., *Two-Man Air Force: Don Gentile & John Godfrey World War Two Flying Aces*. Pen & Sword Aviation (2016)
Kershaw, A., *De Invasie: De onvergetelijke geschiedenis van de helden van D-Day*. Balans (2019)
Kirkels, M., *Van Alabama naar Margraten*. Self-published (2014)
Kirkels, M., & Purnot, J., *Van boerenakker tot soldatenkerkhof. Ooggetuigenverhalen over de aanleg van de Amerikaanse begraafplaats in Margraten*. Heinen (2010)
Knopp, G., *De Bevrijding: Het einde van de oorlog in Europa*. Uitgeverij Verba (2011)
Kone, E., *Yale Men Who Died in the Second World War: A Memorial Volume of Biographical Sketches*. Yale University Press (1951)
Klören, H., *Een 'onregelmatig dagboek' uit de oorlogstijd*. Land van Herle (2004)
Korpershoek, H., *Robert van Klinken – Private Soldier*. Heemkundekring De Drijehornick (2019)
Korthals Altes, A., & In 't Veld, N., *Slag in de schaduw*. Peel/Maas 1944–45. (1981)
Koskimaki, G., *Hell's Highway: A Chronicle of the 101st Airborne Division in the Holland Campaign, September-November 1944*. Casemate Publishers (2013)
Langone, L., *The Star in the Window: Select Stories of World War II Veterans*. iUniverse Inc Bloomington (2011)
Lewis, B., *Four Men Went to War*. Leo Cooper (1987)
Lüdeke, A., *Weapons of World War II*. Parragon (2007)
Lundy, C. R., *Finding Finy*. Self-published (2015)
MacDonald, C., *United States Army in WWII – Europe – The Siegfried Line Campaign*. Createspace Independent Publishing Platform (2015)
Margry, K., *Market Garden Then & Now*. After the Battle Magazine (2002)

Miscellaneous

Mayo, L., *The Ordnance Department of Beachhead and Battlefront*. Createspace Independent Publishing Platform (2015)

McGaugh, S., *Honor Before Glory: The Epic World War II Story of the Japanese American GIs*. Da Capo Press (2016)

McLachlan, I., *Night of the Intruders: The Slaughter of Homeward Bound USAAF Mission 311*. Pen & Sword Books Ltd (2010)

McManus, J., *September Hope: The American Side of a Bridge Too Far*. Penguin Putnam Inc. (2013)

McManus, J., *The Americans at D-Day: The American Experience at the Normandy Invasion*. Forge (2004)

Megellas, J., *All the Way to Berlin: A Paratrooper at War in Europe*. Presidio Press (2003)

Miller, D., *Masters of the Air. De Amerikaanse bommenwerperpiloten die tijdens de Tweede Wereldoorlog tegen nazi-Duitsland vochten*. Karakter Uitgevers B.V. (2017)

Miller, E., *A Dark and Bloody Ground: The Hürtgen Forest and the Roer River Dams, 1944–1945*. Texas A&M University Press (1995)

Mitcham Jr., S., *Panzer Commanders of the Western Front: German Tank Generals in World War II*. Stackpole Books (2008)

Murphy, T., *Ambassadors in Arms: The Story of Hawaii's 100th Battalion*. University of Hawaii Press (1954)

Neillands, R., *The Battle for the Rhine*. The Overlook Press (2005)

Nicholas, L., *The Rape of Europe: The Fate of Europe's Treasures in the Third Reich and the Second World War*. Random House USA Inc. (1995)

Nordyke, P., *All American, All the Way: A Combat History of the 82nd Airborne Division in World War II: From Market Garden to Berlin*. Voyageur Press (2010)

Nordyke, P., *For Stars of Valor: The Combat History of the 505th Parachute Infantry Regiment in World War II*. Voyageur Press (2010)

Nordyke, P., *More Than Courage: Sicily, Naples-Foggia, Anzio, Rhineland, Ardennes-Alsace, Central Europe: The Combat History of the 504th Parachute Infantry Regiment in World War II*. Voyageur Press (2018)

Ouweneel-Van Dam, B., *Mission Belle, het verhaal van een B-17G en zijn bemanning*. Stichting West-Alblasserwaard (2017)

Prime, C., *Omaha Beach: Tuesday 6th June 1944*. Orep Editions (2016)

Rosenkrantz, P., *Letters from Uncle Dave: The 73-year Journey to Find a Missing-In-Action World War II Paratrooper*. Self-published (2020)

Ryan, C., *The Last Battle*. Simon & Schuster (1966)

Ryan, C., *De langste dag*. Uitgeverij Lannoo (2019)

Saunders, T., *Battleground Market Garden: Nijmegen. US 82nd Airborne & Guards Armoured Division*. Pen & Sword Books Ltd. (2011)

Saunders, T., *Hell's Highway. 101st Airborne & Guards Armoured Division*. Pen & Sword Books Limited (2011)

Schrijvers, P., *Bastogne. De grootste slag om de Ardennen*. Manteau (2014)

Schrijvers, P., *The Margraten Boys*. Palgrave Macmillan Ltd. (2012)

Steidl, F., *Lost Battalions: Going for Broke in the Vosges, Autumn 1944*. Presidio Press (2001)

Swanston, A., & Swanston, M., *Atlas van de Tweede Wereldoorlog. De belangrijkste veldslagen en operaties in kaart gebracht*. Librero B.V. (2017)

Timmermans, F., *Finding Leo Lichten*. Ministry of Foreign Affairs of the Netherlands (2014)

'Tribute to American Boys Killed in World War II.' Congressional Record. United States Senate (1954)

Van den Dungen, E., *De Slag om Overloon en de bevrijding van Venray*. Oorlogsmuseum Overloon (2014)

Van Lunteren, F., *The Battle of the Bridges: The 504th Parachute Infantry Regiment in Operation Market Garden*. Casemate Publishers (2017)

Wijers, H., *The Battle of the Bulge, Volume Two: Hell at Bütgenbach/Seize the Bridges*. Stackpole Books (2012)

Wilson, J., *The 784th Tank Battalion in World War II: History of an African American Armored Unit in Europe*. McFarland & Co Inc. (2015)

Winters, R., *Voorbij de Band of Brothers. De Memoires van majoor Dick Winters*. Boekerij (2010)

Wright, S., *The Last Drop: Operation Varsity, March 24–25, 1945*. Stackpole Books (2008)

Wukovits, J., *Soldiers of a Different Cloth: Notre Dame Chaplains in World War II*. University of Notre Dame Press (2018)

Zaloga, S., *Siegfried Line 1944–1945: Battles on the German Frontier*. Bloomsbury (2007)

In addition, we frequently consulted After-Action Reports, Unit Histories, Individual Deceased Personnel Files, Official Military Personnel Files, and Morning Reports that have been acquired via the Internet and the National Archives and Records Administration in St. Louis and College Park, United States.

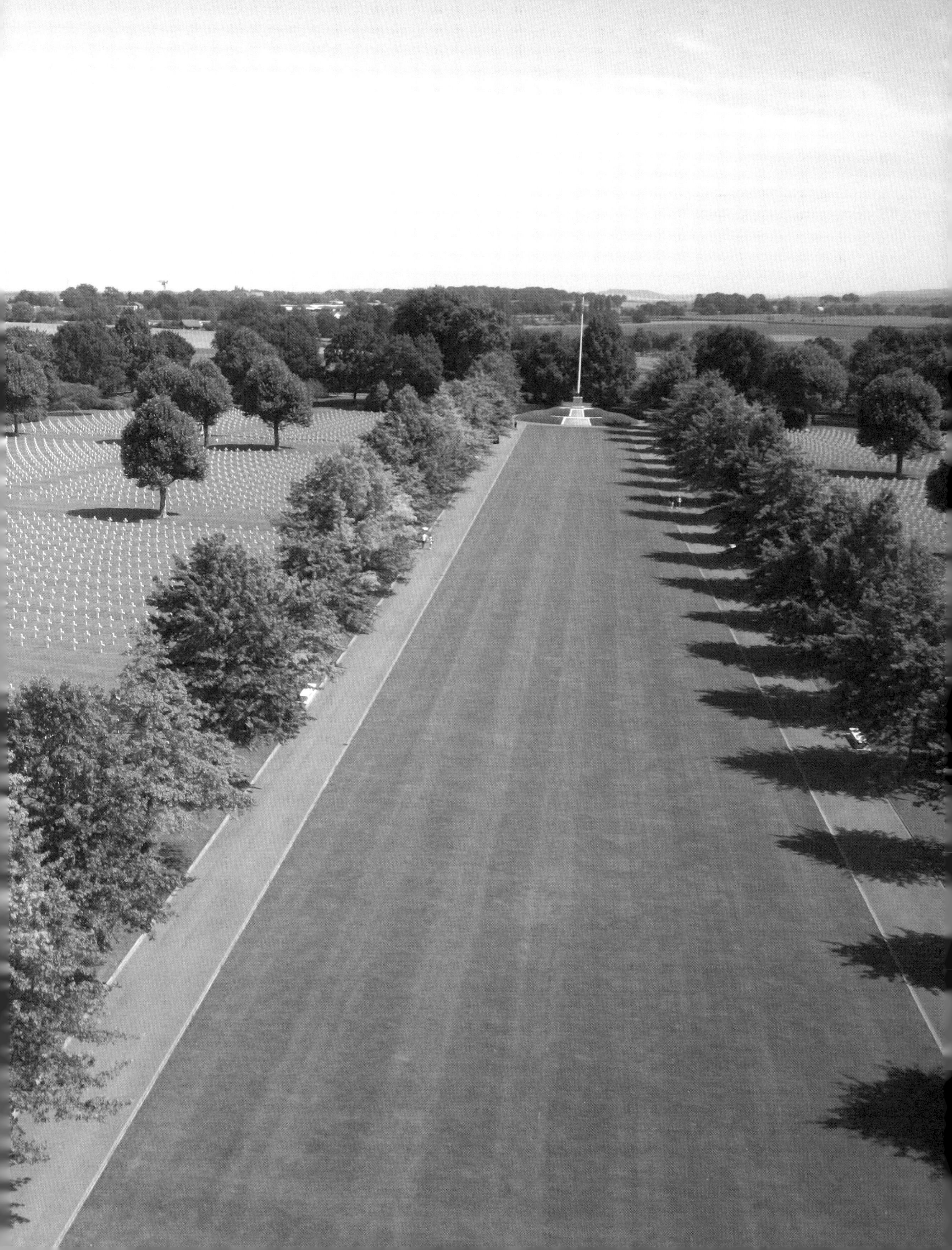

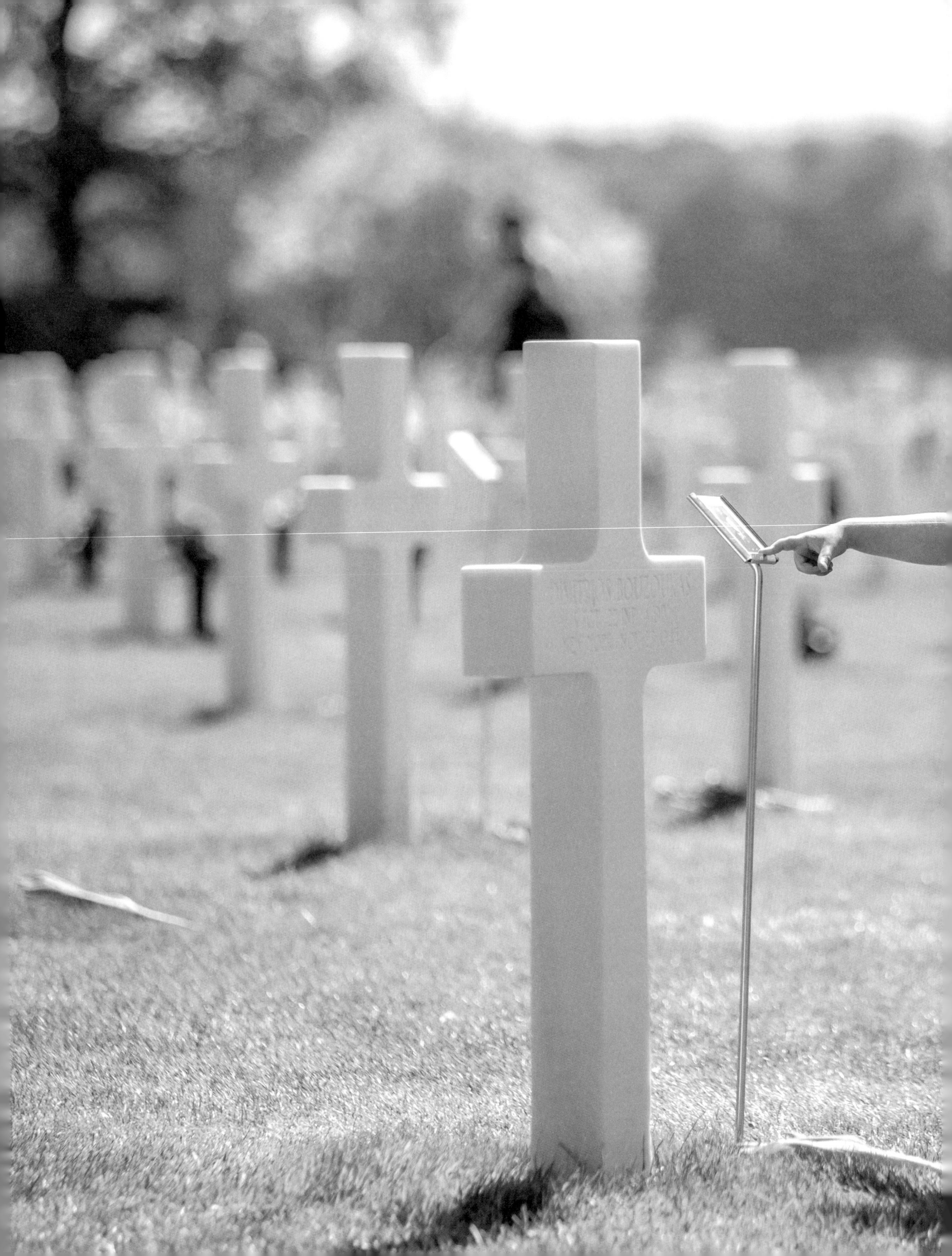

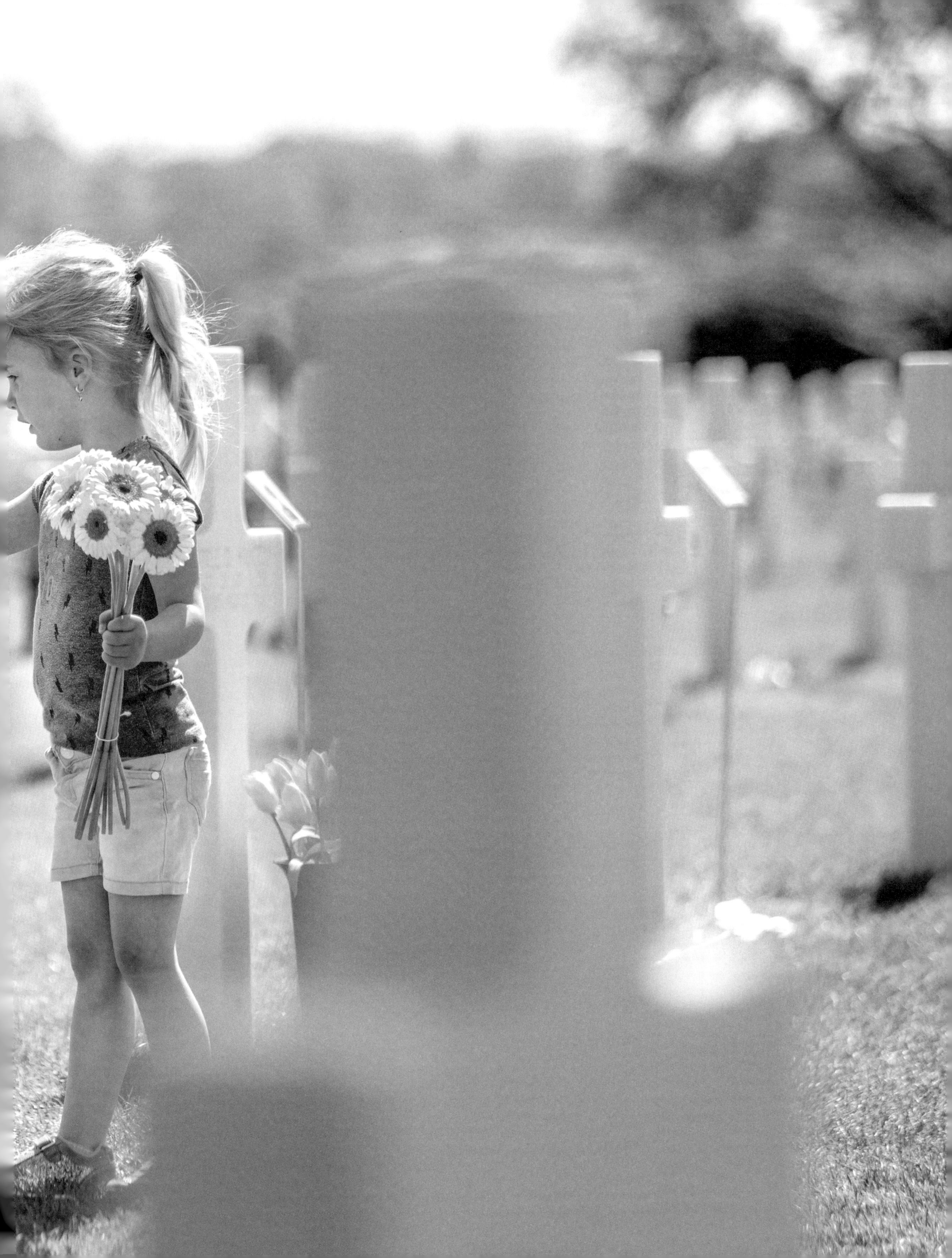

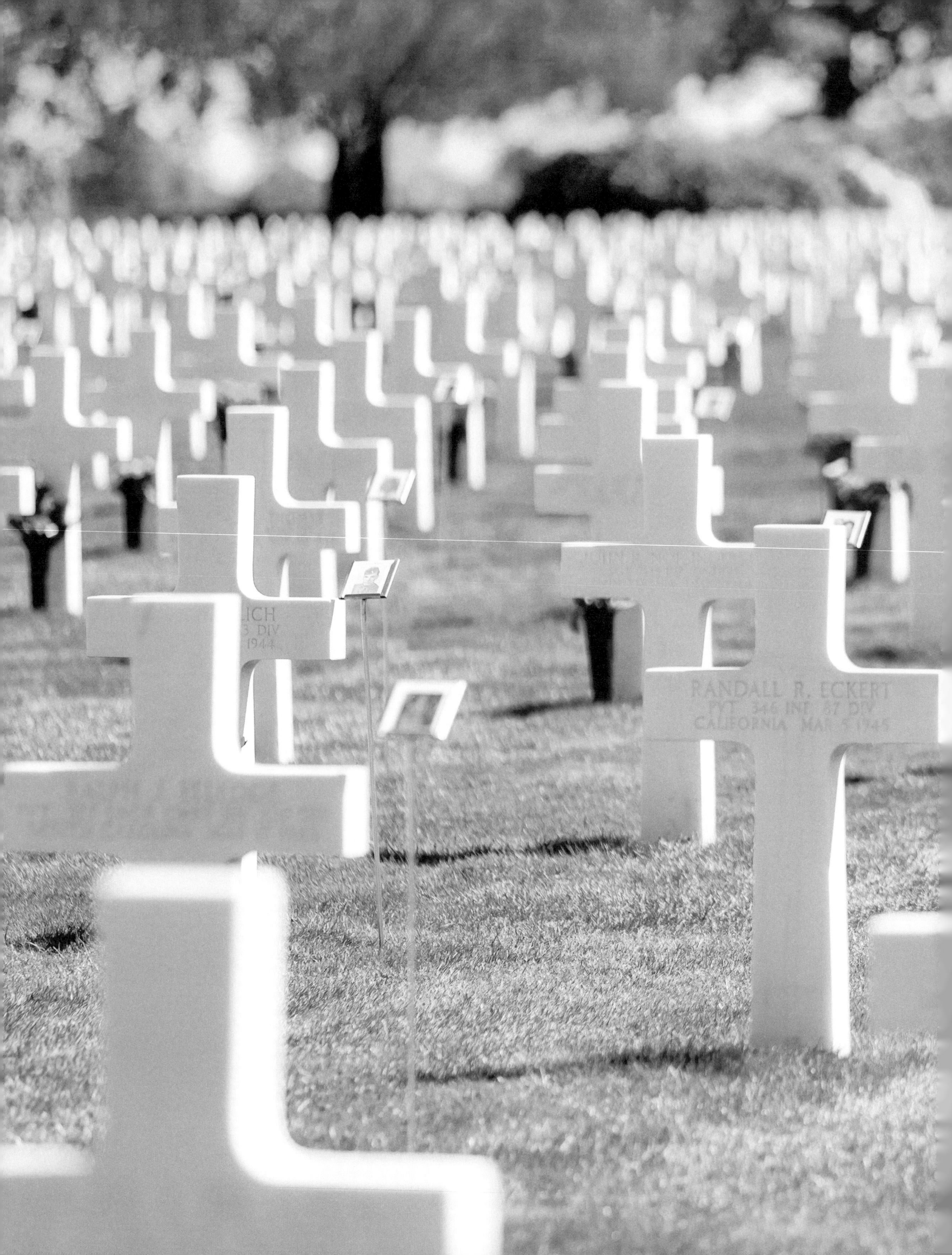
RANDALL R. ECKERT
PVT 346 INF 87 DIV
CALIFORNIA MAR 5 1945

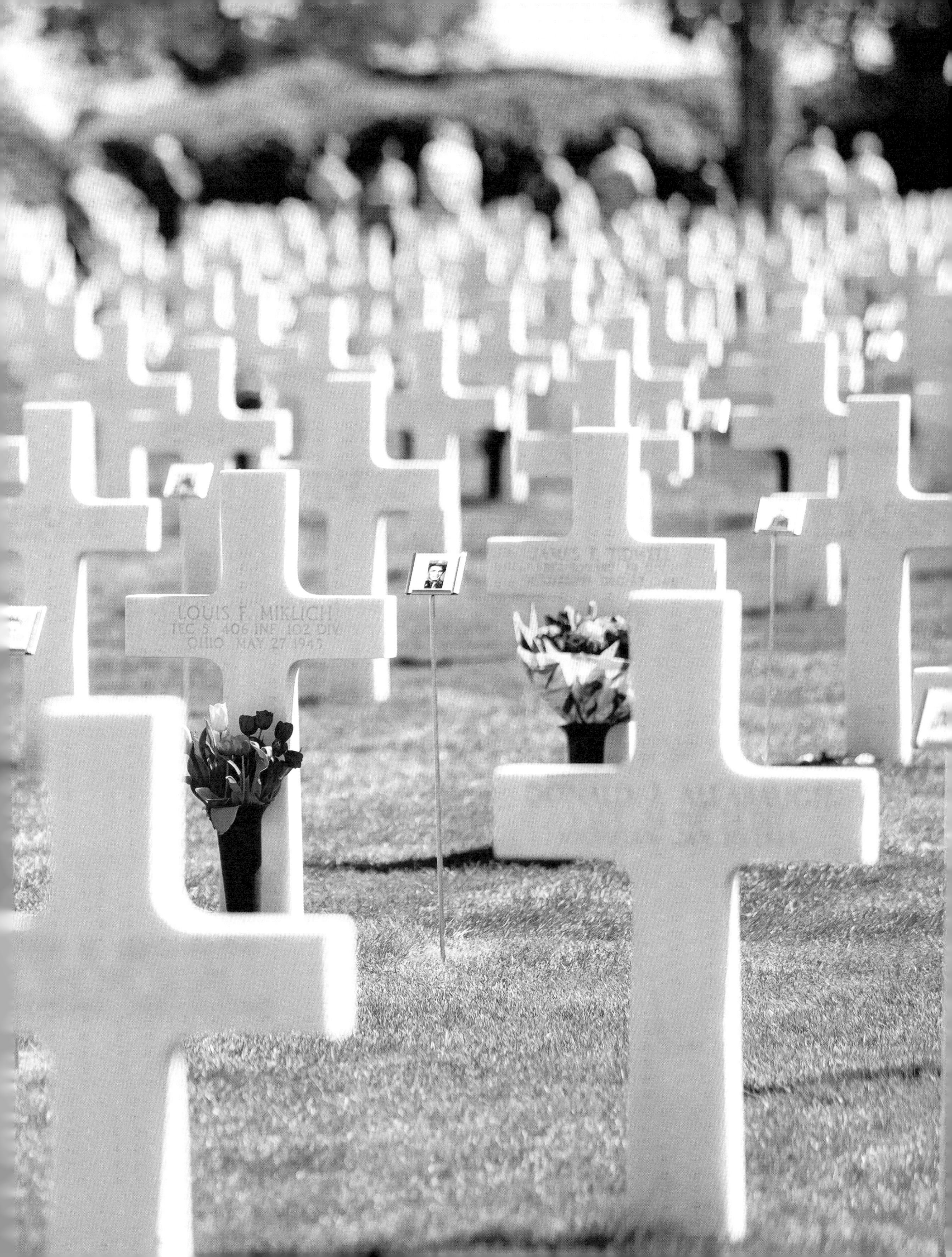
LOUIS F. MIKLICH
TEC 5 406 INF 102 DIV
OHIO MAY 27 1945

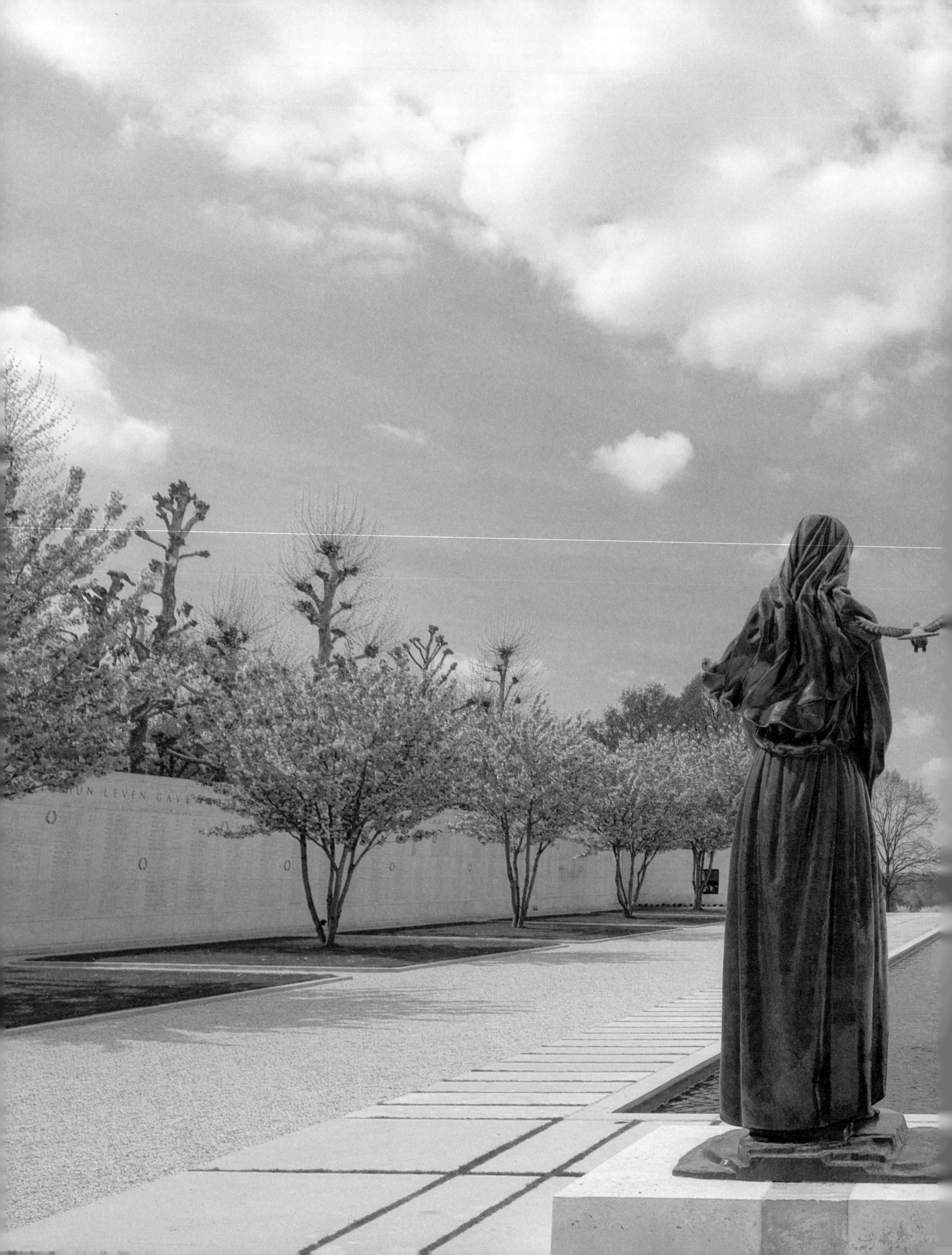
LEVEN

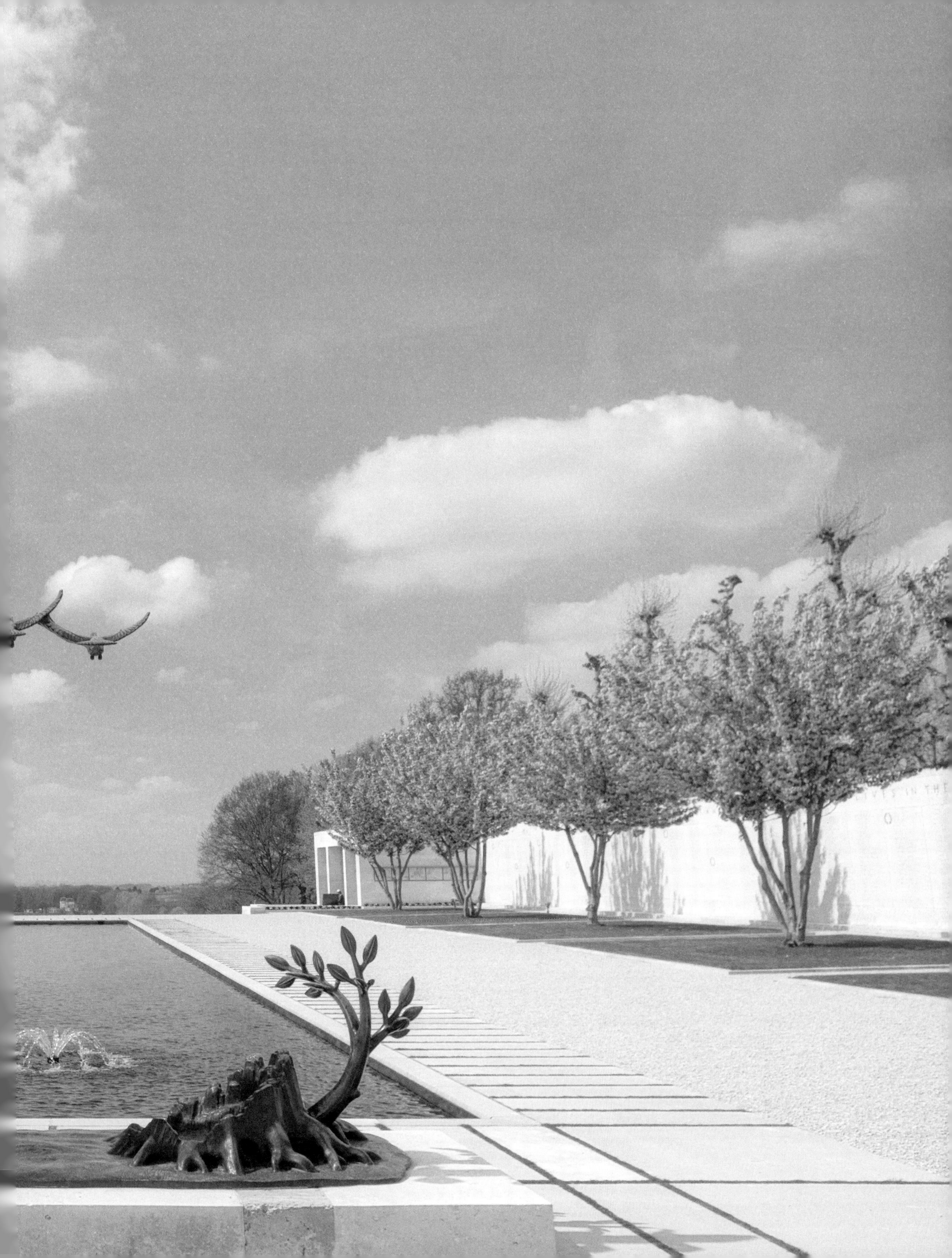

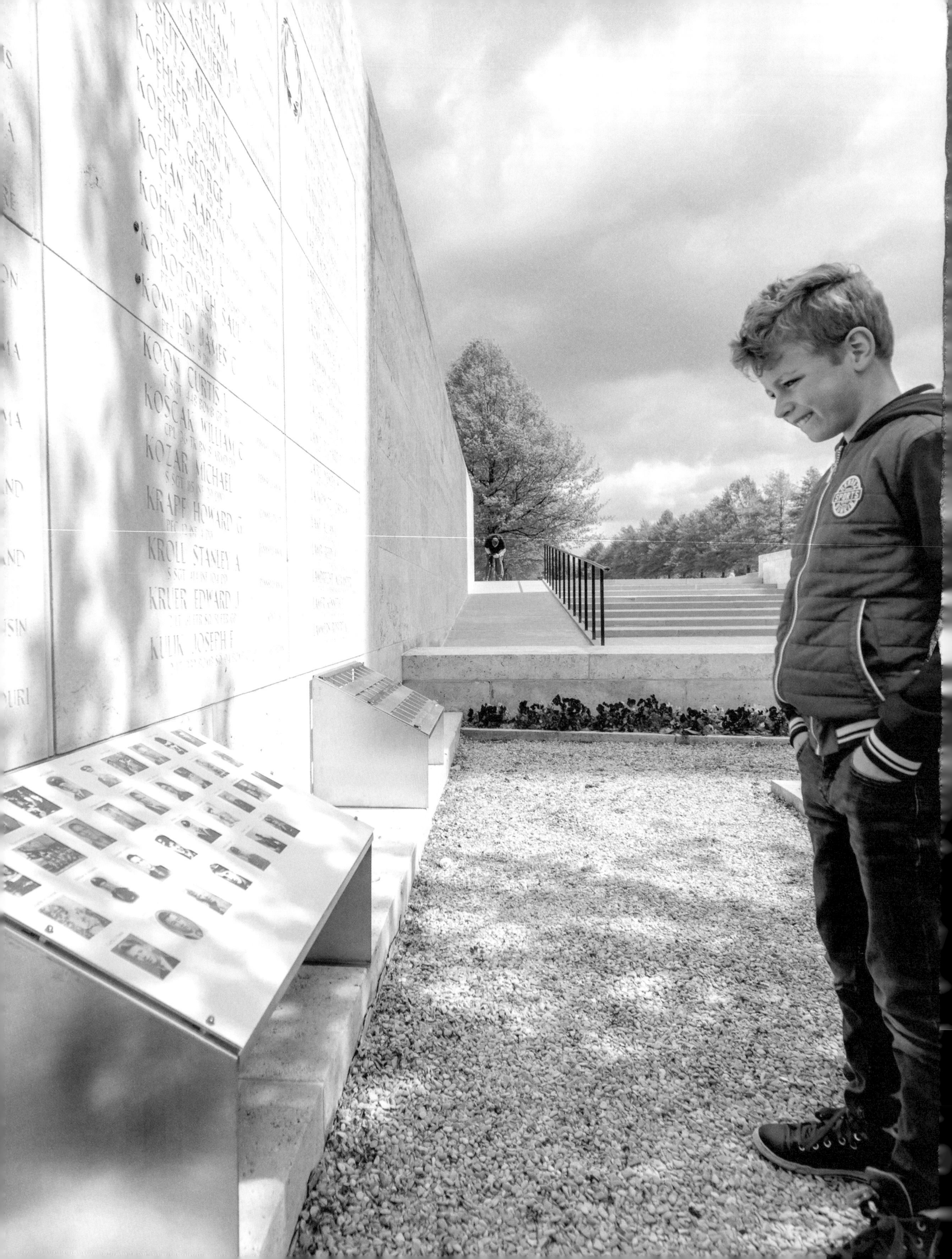

KOON CURTIS L
KOSCAK WILLIAM C
KOZAR MICHAEL
KRAPF HOWARD G
KROLL STANLEY A
KRUER EDWARD J
KULIK JOSEPH F